Collins
gem

School
Dictionary

D0264174

Published by Collins
An imprint of HarperCollins Publishers
Westerhill Road
Bishopbriggs
Glasgow G64 2QT

Fifth Edition 2016

10 9 8 7 6 5 4

© HarperCollins Publishers 2016

ISBN 978-0-00-814646-7

Collins® is a registered trademark of
HarperCollins Publishers Limited

collins.co.uk/dictionaries

Typeset by Davidson Publishing
Solutions, Glasgow

Printed in Italy by Grafica Veneta S.p.A.

Entered words that we have reason to
believe constitute trademarks have
been designated as such. However,
neither the presence nor absence of
such designation should be regarded
as affecting the legal status of any
trademark.

The contents of this publication
are believed correct at the time of
printing. Nevertheless, the Publisher
can accept no responsibility for
errors or omissions, changes in the
detail given or for any expense or loss
thereby caused.

HarperCollins does not warrant that
any website mentioned in this title
will be provided uninterrupted, that
any website will be error free, that
defects will be corrected, or that the
website or the server that makes it
available are free of viruses or bugs.
For full terms and conditions please
refer to the site terms provided on
the website.

A catalogue record for this book is
available from the British Library.

If you would like to comment on any
aspect of this book, please contact us
at the given address or online.
E-mail: dictionaries@harpercollins.co.uk

Acknowledgements

We would like to thank those authors
and publishers who kindly gave
permission for copyright material
to be used in the Collins Corpus. We
would also like to thank Times
Newspapers Ltd for providing
valuable data.

Contents

Editorial Staff

Editors
Ian Brookes
Mary O'Neill

For the publisher
Gerry Breslin
Sarah Woods

Computing support
Claire Dimeo
Agnieszka Urbanowicz

Teacher Consultants: Amanda Alexander and Rachel Gee
of Lex Education, Ben Fitzgerald, Eilidh Whatley-Marshall;
Australian Editor: W. A. Krebs; *New Zealand Editor:* Elizabeth
Gordon; *South African Editor:* Geoffrey Hughes

Using this Dictionary

Entry words are printed in large bold type:

> **abbey**

All entry words, including abbreviations, prefixes, and suffixes, are listed in alphabetical order:

> **able**
> **-able**
> **ably**

Other ways to spell the word are shown:

> **adrenalin** or **adrenaline**

Word classes, also called **parts of speech**, are shown in italics:

> **athlete** *noun*

When a word can be used in more than one word class, the change of word class is shown after a triangle:

> **blight** *noun* **1** something that
> damages or spoils other things ...
> ▷ *verb* **3** When something is
> blighted ...

Word classes may be combined if the meaning of the word is the same for each word class:

> **alone** *adjective, adverb* not with
> other people or things

Pronunciations are given for difficult words:

> **archaic** [ar-**kay**-ik] *adjective*
> very old or old-fashioned

Irregular or confusing forms of verbs, nouns, adjectives, and adverbs are shown after the main entry word to give help with spelling:

> **go** goes, going, went, gone
> **mushy** mushier, mushiest

Meanings are shown in separate categories:

> **electric** *adjective* **1** powered or
> produced by electricity **2** exciting
> or tense

Related words are shown in the same paragraph as the main entry word:

> **abrupt** *adjective* **1** sudden and quick:
> *His career came to an abrupt end* **2** not
> friendly or polite > **abruptly** *adverb*
> > **abruptness** *noun*

Register labels in brackets show the style of the word and when it should be used:

> **ad** *noun* (informal) an advertisement

Word tips give more information on how the word is used or spelt:

> **WORD TIP**
> There is an *n* before the *m* in *environment*

Curriculum Subject Labels

Curriculum subject labels show when an entry word is core vocabulary for a curriculum subject.

A dictionary entry may also have a label if the word is important for exams or using the library.

Here is a list of the subject labels used in the dictionary.

ART	Art
COMPUTING	Computing
D&T	Design and Technology
DRAMA	Drama
ENGLISH	English
EXAM TERM	Word used in exam questions
GEOGRAPHY	Geography
HISTORY	History
LIBRARY	Library skills
MATHS	Maths
MUSIC	Music
PE	Physical Education
PSHE	Personal, Social and Health Education
RE	Religious Education
SCIENCE	Science

a

a *or* **an** *adjective* The indefinite article 'a', or 'an' if the next sound is a vowel, is used when you are talking about one of something: *an apple; There was a car parked behind the hedge*

aback *adverb* If you are taken aback, you are very surprised

abalone [ab-a-**lone**-ee] *noun* a shellfish which can be eaten

abandon *verb* **1** If you abandon someone or something, you leave them or give them up for good ▷ *noun* **2** If you do something with abandon, you do it in an uncontrolled way: *He began to laugh with abandon* > **abandoned** *adjective* > **abandonment** *noun*

abate *verb* If something abates, it becomes less: *His anger abated*

abattoir [ab-a-twahr] *noun* a place where animals are killed for meat

abbey *noun* a church with buildings attached to it in which monks or nuns live

abbot *noun* the monk or priest in charge of all the monks in a monastery

abbreviate *verb* To abbreviate something is to make it shorter

abbreviation *noun* a short form of a word or phrase. An example is 'W', which is short for 'West'

abdicate *verb* If a king or queen abdicates, he or she gives up being a king or queen > **abdication** *noun*

abdomen *noun* the front part of your body below your chest, containing your stomach and intestines > **abdominal** *adjective*

abduct *verb* To abduct someone is to take them away by force > **abduction** *noun*

aberration *noun* something that is not normal or usual

abet abets, abetting, abetted *verb* If you abet someone, you help them to do something: *You've aided and abetted criminals to evade justice*

abhor abhors, abhorring, abhorred *verb (formal)* If you abhor something, you hate it > **abhorrence** *noun* > **abhorrent** *adjective*

abide abides, abiding, abided *verb* **1** If you can't abide something, you dislike it very much **2** If you abide by a decision or law, you act in agreement with it

abiding *adjective* lasting for ever: *an abiding interest in history*

ability abilities *noun* [PSHE] the intelligence or skill needed to do something: *the ability to get on with others*

abject *adjective* very bad: *abject failure* > **abjectly** *adverb*

ablaze *adjective* on fire

able abler, ablest *adjective* [PSHE] **1** If you are able to do something, you can do it **2** Someone who is able is very clever or talented

-able *suffix* **1** forming adjectives which have the meaning 'capable of' an action: *enjoyable; breakable* **2** forming adjectives with the meaning 'able to' or 'causing': *comfortable; miserable*

ably [ay-blee] *adverb* skilfully and successfully: *He is ably supported by the cast*

abnormal *adjective* not normal or usual > **abnormally** *adverb*

abnormality abnormalities *noun*

something that is not normal or usual

aboard *preposition, adverb* on a ship or plane

abode *noun (old-fashioned)* Your abode is your home

abolish *verb* To abolish something is to do away with it: *the campaign to abolish hunting* ▷ **abolition** *noun*

abominable *adjective* very unpleasant or shocking ▷ **abominably** *adverb*

Aborigine [ab-or-**rij**-in-ee] *noun* someone descended from the people who lived in Australia before Europeans arrived ▷ **Aboriginal** *adjective*

abort *verb* 1 If a plan or activity is aborted, it is stopped before it is finished 2 If a pregnant woman aborts, the pregnancy ends too soon and the baby dies

abortion *noun* If a woman has an abortion, the pregnancy is ended deliberately before the foetus can live independently

abortive *adjective* unsuccessful: *an abortive bank raid*

abound *verb* If things abound, there are very large numbers of them

about *preposition, adverb* 1 of or concerning 2 approximately and not exactly ▷ *adverb* 3 in different directions: *There were some bottles scattered about* ▷ *adjective* 4 present or in a place: *Is Jane about?* ▷ *phrase* 5 If you are **about to** do something, you are just going to do it

above *preposition, adverb* 1 directly over or higher than something: *above the clouds* 2 greater than a level or amount: *The temperature didn't rise above freezing point*

above board *adjective* completely open and legal: *They assured me it was above board and properly licensed*

abrasion *noun* 1 an area where your skin has been broken 2 GEOGRAPHY erosion caused by the small stones, etc. carried by a river or glacier scraping against a surface

abrasive *adjective* 1 An abrasive substance is rough and can be used to clean hard surfaces 2 Someone who is abrasive is unpleasant and rude

abreast *adjective* 1 side by side: *youths riding their motorbikes four abreast* 2 If you keep abreast of a subject, you know all the most recent facts about it

abroad *adverb* GEOGRAPHY in a foreign country

abrupt *adjective* 1 sudden and quick: *His career came to an abrupt end* 2 not friendly or polite ▷ **abruptly** *adverb* ▷ **abruptness** *noun*

abscess [ab-**sess**] *noun* a painful swelling filled with pus

abseiling *noun* Abseiling is the sport of going down a cliff or a tall building by sliding down ropes

absent *adjective* Something that is absent is not present in a place or situation ▷ **absence** *noun*

absentee *noun* someone who is not present when they should be

absolute *adjective* 1 total and complete: *absolute honesty* 2 having total power: *the absolute ruler* ▷ **absolutely** *adverb*

absolve *verb* To absolve someone of something is to state they are not to blame for it

absorb *verb* SCIENCE If something absorbs liquid or gas, it soaks it up

absorbent *adjective* Absorbent materials soak up liquid easily

absorption *noun* 1 the soaking up of a liquid 2 great interest in something: *my father's absorption in his business affairs*

abstain verb **1** If you abstain from something, you do not do it or have it: *The patients had to abstain from alcohol* **2** If you abstain in a vote, you do not vote > **abstainer** noun > **abstention** noun

abstinence noun Abstinence is deliberately not doing something you enjoy

abstract [ab-strakt] adjective **1** An abstract idea is based on thoughts and ideas rather than physical objects or events, for example 'bravery' **2** ART Abstract art is a style of art which uses shapes rather than images of people or objects **3** Abstract nouns refer to qualities or ideas rather than physical objects, for example 'happiness' or 'a question' > **abstraction** noun

absurd adjective ridiculous and stupid > **absurdly** adverb > **absurdity** noun

abundance noun Something that exists in abundance exists in large numbers: *an abundance of wildlife*

abundant adjective present in large quantities > **abundantly** adverb

abuse [ab-yoose] noun **1** cruel treatment of someone: *child abuse* **2** rude and unkind remarks directed towards someone **3** the wrong use of something: *an abuse of power; alcohol abuse*

abuse [ab-yooze] verb **1** If you abuse someone, you speak insultingly to them **2** To abuse someone also means to treat them cruelly **3** If you abuse something, you use it wrongly or for a bad purpose > **abuser** noun

abusive adjective rude and unkind > **abusively** adverb > **abusiveness** noun

abysmal [ab-biz-ml] adjective very bad indeed: *an abysmal performance*

> **abysmally** adverb

abyss noun a very deep hole

acacia [a-kay-sha] noun a type of thorny shrub with small yellow or white flowers

academic adjective **1** Academic work is work done in a school, college, or university ▷ noun **2** someone who teaches or does research in a college or university > **academically** adverb

academy academies noun **1** a school or college, usually one that specializes in one particular subject: *the Royal Academy of Dramatic Art* **2** an organization of scientists, artists, writers, or musicians

accelerate verb To accelerate is to go faster

acceleration noun the rate at which the speed of something is increasing

accelerator noun the pedal in a vehicle which you press to make it go faster

accent noun **1** a way of pronouncing a language: *She had an Australian accent* **2** a mark placed above or below a letter in some languages, which affects the way the letter is pronounced **3** ENGLISH stress placed on a particular word, syllable, or note: *In Icelandic the accent usually falls on the first syllable of a word* **4** an emphasis on something: *The accent is on action and special effects*

accentuate verb To accentuate a feature of something is to make it more noticeable

accept verb **1** If you accept something, you say yes to it or take it from someone **2** If you accept a situation, you realize that it cannot be changed: *He accepts criticism as part of his job* **3** If you accept a

A

statement or story, you believe it is true: *The board accepted his explanation* **4** If a group accepts you, they treat you as one of the group > **acceptance** noun

acceptable adjective good enough to be accepted > **acceptably** adverb

access noun **1** the right or opportunity to enter a place or to use something ▷ *verb* **2** If you access information from a computer, you get it

accessible adjective **1** easily reached or seen: *The village was accessible by foot only* **2** easily understood or used: *guidebooks which present information in a clear and accessible style* > **accessibility** noun

accession noun A ruler's accession is the time when he or she becomes the ruler of a country

accessory accessories noun **1** an extra part **2** someone who helps another person commit a crime

accident noun **1** an unexpected event in which people are injured or killed **2** Something that happens by accident happens by chance

accidental adjective happening by chance > **accidentally** adverb

accolade noun (formal) great praise or an award given to someone

accommodate verb **1** If you accommodate someone, you provide them with a place to sleep, live, or work **2** If a place can accommodate a number of things or people, it has enough room for them

accommodating adjective willing to help and to adjust to new situations

accommodation noun a place provided for someone to sleep, live, or work in

accompaniment noun **1** The

accompaniment to a song is the music played to go with it **2** An accompaniment to something is another thing that comes with it: *Melon is a good accompaniment to cold meats*

accompany accompanies, accompanying, accompanied verb **1** If you accompany someone, you go with them **2** If one thing accompanies another, the two things exist at the same time: *severe pain accompanied by fever* **3** If you accompany a singer or musician, you play an instrument while they sing or play the main tune

accomplice noun a person who helps someone else to commit a crime

accomplish verb If you accomplish something, you succeed in doing it

accomplished adjective very talented at something: *an accomplished cook*

accomplishment noun Someone's accomplishments are the skills they have gained

accord verb **1** If you accord someone or something a particular treatment, you treat them in that way: *He was accorded a proper respect for his status* ▷ noun **2** agreement ▷ *phrase* **3** if you do something **of your own accord**, you do it willingly and not because you are forced to do it

accordance phrase If you act **in accordance with** a rule or belief, you act in the way the rule or belief says you should

accordingly adverb in a way that is appropriate for the circumstances: *The street had changed its character, and the shops changed accordingly*

according to preposition **1** If something is true according to a particular person, that person says that it is true **2** If something is done according to a principle or plan, that principle or plan is used as the basis for it

accordion noun a musical instrument like an expanding box. It is played by squeezing the two sides together while pressing the keys on it

accost verb If someone accosts you, especially someone you do not know, they come up and speak to you: *She says she is accosted when she goes shopping*

account noun **1** a written or spoken report of something **2** If you have a bank account, you can leave money in the bank and take it out when you need it **3** (in plural) Accounts are records of money spent and received by a person or business ▷ phrase **4** If you **take something into account**, you include it in your planning **5 On account of** means because of ▷ verb **6** To account for something is to explain it: *This might account for her strange behaviour* **7** If something accounts for a particular amount of something, it is that amount: *The brain accounts for three per cent of body weight*

accountable adjective If you are accountable for something, you are responsible for it and have to explain your actions: *The committee is answerable to Parliament* > **accountability** noun

accountancy noun the job of keeping or inspecting financial accounts

accountant noun a person whose job is to keep or inspect financial accounts

accounting noun the keeping and checking of financial accounts

accrue accrues, accruing, accrued verb If money or interest accrues, it increases gradually

accumulate verb If you accumulate things or they accumulate, they collect over a period of time

accurate adjective (SCIENCE) completely correct or precise > **accurately** adverb > **accuracy** noun

accuse verb If you accuse someone of doing something wrong, you say they have done it > **accusation** noun > **accuser** noun

accustom verb If you accustom yourself to something new or different, you get used to it

accustomed adjective used to something

ace noun **1** In a pack of cards, a card with a single symbol on it ▷ adjective **2** (informal) good or skilful: *an ace squash player*

acerbic [as-**ser**-bik] adjective (formal) Acerbic remarks are harsh and bitter

ache verb **1** If you ache, you feel a continuous dull pain in a part of your body **2** If you are aching for something, you want it very much ▷ noun **3** a continuous dull pain

achieve verb (PSHE) If you achieve something, you successfully do it or cause it to happen

achievement noun (PSHE) something which you succeed in doing, especially after a lot of effort

acid noun **1** An acid is a substance with a pH value of less than 7. There are many different acids; some are used in chemical processes and others in household substances ▷ adjective **2** Acid tastes are sharp or sour **3** Acid comments are unkind and critical ▷ phrase **4** Something that is an **acid test** is used as a way of testing whether something is

true or not, or whether it is of good quality or not **3** *adverb*
> **acidic** *adjective* > **acidity** *noun*

acid rain *noun* GEOGRAPHY rain polluted by acid in the atmosphere which has come from factories

acknowledge *verb* **1** If you acknowledge a fact or situation, you agree or admit it is true **2** If you acknowledge someone, you show that you have seen and recognized them **3** If you acknowledge a message, you tell the person who sent it that you have received it
> **acknowledgment** or
> **acknowledgement** *noun*

acne [ak-nee] *noun* lumpy spots that cover someone's face

acoustic [a-koo-stik] *adjective* **1** relating to sound or hearing **2** An acoustic guitar is not made louder with an electric amplifier

acoustics *plural noun* The acoustics of a room are its structural features which are responsible for how clearly you can hear sounds made in it

acquaintance *noun* someone you know slightly but not well

acquire *verb* If you acquire something, you obtain it

acquisition *noun* something you have obtained

acquit acquits, acquitting, acquitted *verb* **1** If someone is acquitted of a crime, they have been tried in a court and found not guilty **2** If you acquit yourself well on a particular occasion, you behave or perform well > **acquittal** *noun*

acre *noun* a unit for measuring areas of land. One acre is equal to 4840 square yards or about 4047 square metres

acrid *adjective* sharp and bitter: *the acrid smell of burning plastic*

acrimony [ak-rim-on-ee] *noun* (formal) bitterness and anger
> **acrimonious** *adjective*

acrobat *noun* an entertainer who performs gymnastic tricks
> **acrobatic** *adjective* > **acrobatics** *plural noun*

acronym *noun* a word made up of the initial letters of a phrase. An example of an acronym is 'BAFTA', which stands for 'British Academy of Film and Television Arts'

across *preposition, adverb* **1** going from one side of something to the other **2** on the other side of a road or river

acrylic [a-kril-ik] *noun* **1** Acrylic is a type of man-made cloth **2** ART Acrylics, or acrylic paints, are thick artists' paints which can be used like oil paints or thinned down with water

act *verb* **1** If you act, you do something: *It would be irresponsible not to act swiftly* **2** If you act in a particular way, you behave in that way **3** If a person or thing acts as something else, it has the function or does the job of that thing: *She was able to act as an interpreter* **4** If you act in a play or film, you play a part ▷ *noun* **5** a single thing someone does: *It was an act of disloyalty to the King* **6** An Act of Parliament is a law passed by the government **7** In a play, ballet, or opera, an act is one of the main parts it is divided into

acting *noun* the profession of performing in plays or films

action *noun* **1** the process of doing something **2** something that is done **3** a physical movement **4** In law, an action is a legal proceeding: *a libel action*

activate *verb* To activate something is to make it start working

active *adjective* **1** PE full of energy **2** busy and hardworking **3** In grammar, a verb in the active voice is one where the subject does the action, rather than having it done to them > **actively** *adverb*

activist *noun* a person who tries to bring about political and social change

activity activities *noun* **1** Activity is a situation in which a lot of things are happening at the same time **2** PE something you do for pleasure: *sport and leisure activities*

actor *noun* a man or woman whose profession is acting

actress *noun* a woman whose profession is acting

actual *adjective* real, rather than imaginary or guessed at: *That is the official figure: the actual figure is much higher* > **actually** *adverb*

acumen *noun* the ability to make good decisions quickly: *business acumen*

acupuncture *noun* the treatment of illness or pain by sticking small needles into special places in a person's body

acute *adjective* **1** severe or intense: *an acute shortage of accommodation* **2** very intelligent: *an acute mind* **3** MATHS An acute angle is less than 90° **4** In French and some other languages, an acute accent is a line sloping upwards from left to right placed over a vowel to indicate a change in pronunciation, as in the word *café*

ad *noun* (*informal*) an advertisement

AD You use 'AD' in dates to indicate the number of years after the birth of Jesus Christ

adage [ad-dij] *noun* a saying that expresses some general truth about life

adamant *adjective* If you are adamant, you are determined not to change your mind > **adamantly** *adverb*

adapt *verb* **1** If you adapt to a new situation, you change so you can deal with it successfully **2** If you adapt something, you change it so it is suitable for a new purpose or situation **3** SCIENCE If a plant or animal adapts, it gradually changes over generations to become better suited to its environment > **adaptable** *adjective* > **adaptation** *noun*

adaptor or **adapter** *noun* a type of electric plug which can be used to connect two or more plugs to one socket

add *verb* **1** If you add something to a number of things, you put it with the things **2** If you add numbers together or add them up, you work out the total

addict *noun* PSHE someone who cannot stop doing something, especially something harmful > **addicted** *adjective* > **addiction** *noun*

addictive *adjective* If something is addictive, people cannot stop once they have started to do it.

addition *noun* **1** something that has been added to something else **2** MATHS the process of adding numbers together

additional *adjective* extra or more: *They made the decision to take on additional staff* > **additionally** *adverb*

additive *noun* something added to something else, usually in order to improve it

address addresses, addressing, addressed *noun* **1** the number of the house where you live, together with the name of the street and the town or village **2** a speech given to a group of people ▷ *verb* **3** If a letter is addressed to you, it has your name and address written on it **4** If you address a problem or task, you start to deal with it

adept *adjective* very skilful at doing something: *She is adept at motivating others*

adequate *adjective* enough in amount or good enough for a purpose: *an adequate diet*
> **adequately** *adverb* > **adequacy** *noun*

adhere *verb* **1** If one thing adheres to another, it sticks firmly to it **2** If you adhere to a rule or agreement, you do what it says **3** If you adhere to an opinion or belief, you firmly hold that opinion or belief > **adherence** *noun*

adherent *noun* An adherent of a belief is someone who holds that belief

adhesive *noun* **1** any substance used to stick two things together, for example glue ▷ *adjective* **2** Adhesive substances are sticky and able to stick to things

adjacent [ad-**jay**-sent] *adjective* (*formal*) **1** If two things are adjacent, they are next to each other: *a hotel adjacent to the beach* **2** MATHS Adjacent angles share one side and have the same point opposite to their bases

adjective *noun* ENGLISH a word that adds to the description given by a noun. For example, in 'They live in a large white Georgian house', 'large', 'white', and 'Georgian' are all adjectives > **adjectival** *adjective*

adjoining *adjective* If two rooms are next to each other and are connected, they are adjoining

adjourn *verb* **1** If a meeting or trial is adjourned, it stops for a time: *The case was adjourned until September* **2** If people adjourn to another place, they go there together after a meeting: *We adjourned to the lounge* > **adjournment** *noun*

adjust *verb* **1** If you adjust something, you change its position or alter it in some other way **2** If you adjust to a new situation, you get used to it > **adjustment** *noun* > **adjustable** *adjective*

administer *verb* **1** To administer an organization is to be responsible for managing it **2** To administer the law or administer justice is to put it into practice and apply it **3** If medicine is administered to someone, it is given to them

administration *noun*
1 Administration is the work of organizing and supervising an organization **2** Administration is also the process of administering something: *the administration of criminal justice* **3** The administration is the group of people that manages an organization or a country
> **administrative** *adjective*
> **administrator** *noun*

admirable *adjective* very good and deserving to be admired
> **admirably** *adverb*

admiral *noun* the commander of a navy

admiration *noun* a feeling of great liking and respect

admire *verb* If you admire someone or something, you respect and approve of them > **admirer** *noun*
> **admiring** *adjective* > **admiringly** *adverb*

admission *noun* **1** If you are allowed admission to a place, you are allowed to go in **2** If you make an admission of something, you agree, often reluctantly, it is true: *It was an admission of guilt*

admit admits, admitting, admitted *verb* **1** If you admit something, you agree, often reluctantly, it is true **2** To admit someone or something to a place or organization is to allow them to enter it **3** If you are admitted to hospital, you are taken there to stay until you are better

admittedly *adverb* People use 'admittedly' to show that what they are saying contrasts with something they have already said or are about to say, and weakens their argument: *My studies, admittedly only from books, taught me much*

adolescent *noun* SCIENCE A young person who is no longer a child but who is not yet an adult > **adolescence** *noun*

adopt *verb* **1** If you adopt a child that is not your own, you take him or her into your family as your son or daughter **2** (*formal*) If you adopt a particular attitude, you start to have it > **adoption** *noun*

adorable *adjective* sweet and attractive

adore *verb* If you adore someone, you feel deep love and admiration for them > **adoration** *noun*

adorn *verb* To adorn something is to decorate it: *The cathedral is adorned with statues* > **adornment** *noun*

adrenalin or **adrenaline** [a-**dren**-al-in] *noun* Adrenalin is a hormone which is produced by your body when you are angry, nervous, or excited. Adrenalin makes your heart beat faster, and gives you more energy

adrift *adjective, adverb* If a boat is adrift or goes adrift, it floats on the water without being controlled

adulation [ad-yoo-**lay**-shn] *noun* great admiration and praise for someone > **adulatory** *adjective*

adult *noun* a mature and fully developed person or animal

adulthood *noun* the time during someone's life when they are an adult

advance *verb* **1** To advance is to move forward **2** To advance a cause or interest is to help it to be successful **3** If you advance someone a sum of money, you lend it to them ▷ *noun* **4** Advance in something is progress in it: *scientific advance* **5** a sum of money lent to someone ▷ *adjective* **6** happening before an event: *The event received little advance publicity* ▷ *phrase* **7** If you do something **in advance**, you do it before something else happens: *We booked the room well in advance*

advantage *noun* **1** a benefit or something that puts you in a better position ▷ *phrase* **2** If you **take advantage of** someone, you treat them unfairly for your own benefit **3** If you **take advantage of** something, you make use of it

advantageous *adjective* likely to benefit you in some way: *an advantageous marriage*

advent *noun* **1** The advent of something is its start or its coming into existence: *The advent of the submarine changed naval warfare* **2** Advent is the season just before Christmas in the Christian calendar

adventure *noun* a series of events that are unusual and exciting

adventurer *noun* someone who enjoys doing dangerous and exciting things

adventurous *adjective* willing to take risks and do new and exciting things > **adventurously** adverb

adverb noun ENGLISH a word that adds information about a verb or a following adjective or other adverb, for example, 'slowly', 'now', and 'here', which say how, when, or where something is done
> **adverbial** adjective

adversary adversaries [ad-ver-sar-ee] noun someone who is your enemy or who opposes what you are doing

adverse adjective not helpful to you or opposite to what you want or need: adverse weather conditions
> **adversely** adverb

adversity adversities noun a time of danger or difficulty

advert noun (informal) an advertisement

advertise verb ENGLISH **1** If you advertise something, you tell people about it in a newspaper or poster, or on TV **2** To advertise is to make an announcement in a newspaper or poster, or on TV
> **advertiser** noun > **advertising** noun

advertisement [ad-**ver**-tiss-ment] noun ENGLISH an announcement about something in a newspaper or poster, or on TV

advice noun a suggestion from someone about what you should do

> **WORD TIP**
> The noun advice is spelt with a c and the verb advise is spelt with an s

advisable adjective sensible and likely to achieve the result you want: It is advisable to buy the visa before travelling > **advisably** adverb > **advisability** noun

advise verb **1** If you advise someone to do something, you tell them you think they should do it **2** (formal) If

you advise someone of something, you inform them of it > **advisory** adjective

> **WORD TIP**
> The verb advise is spelt with an s and the noun advice is spelt with a c

adviser noun a person whose job is to give advice

advocate verb **1** If you advocate a course of action or plan, you support it publicly ▷ noun **2** An advocate of something is someone who supports it publicly **3** (formal) a lawyer who represents clients in court > **advocacy** noun

aerial [**air**-ee-al] adjective **1** Aerial means happening in the air: aerial combat ▷ noun **2** a piece of wire for receiving television or radio signals

aerobics noun a type of fast physical exercise, which increases the oxygen in your blood and strengthens your heart and lungs
> **aerobic** adjective

aerodynamic adjective having a streamlined shape that moves easily through the air

aeroplane noun a vehicle with wings and engines that enable it to fly

aerosol noun SCIENCE a small metal container in which liquid is kept under pressure so that it can be forced out as a spray

aerospace adjective involved in making and designing aeroplanes and spacecraft

aesthetic or **esthetic** [eess-**thet**-ik] adjective D&T (formal) relating to the appreciation of beauty or art > **aesthetically** adverb > **aesthetics** noun

afar noun (literary) From afar means from a long way away

affable adjective pleasant and easy

to talk to > **affably** adverb
> **affability** noun

affair noun **1** an event or series of events: The funeral was a sad affair **2** To have an affair is to have a secret romantic relationship, especially when one of the people involved is married **3** (in plural) Your affairs are your private and personal life: Why had he meddled in her affairs?

affect verb **1** If something affects you, it influences you in some way **2** (formal) If you affect a particular way of behaving, you behave in that way: He affected an Italian accent

> **WORD TIP**
> Do not confuse the spelling of the verb affect with the noun effect. Something that affects you has an effect on you

affectation noun An affectation is behaviour that is not genuine but is put on to impress people

affection noun **1** a feeling of love and fondness for someone **2** (in plural) Your affections are feelings of love you have for someone

affectionate adjective full of fondness for someone: an affectionate embrace
> **affectionately** adverb

affiliate verb If a group affiliates itself to another, larger group, it forms a close association with it: organizations affiliated to the ANC
> **affiliation** noun

affinity noun affinities a close similarity or understanding between two things or people: There are affinities between the two poets

affirm verb If you affirm an idea or belief, you clearly indicate your support for it: We affirm our commitment to broadcast quality programmes > **affirmation** noun

affirmative adjective An affirmative

word or gesture is one that means yes

afflict verb If illness or pain afflicts someone, they suffer from it: She was afflicted by depression
> **affliction** noun

affluent adjective having a lot of money and possessions
> **affluence** noun

afford verb **1** If you can afford to do something, you have enough money or time to do it **2** If you cannot afford something to happen, it would be harmful or embarrassing for you if it happened: We cannot afford to be complacent

affordable adjective If something is affordable, most people have enough money to buy it: the availability of affordable housing

affray noun (formal) a noisy and violent fight

affront verb **1** If you are affronted by something, you are insulted and angered by it ▷ noun **2** something that is an insult: Our prisons are an affront to civilized society

afield adverb Far afield means a long way away: competitors from as far afield as Russia and China

afloat adverb, adjective **1** floating on water **2** successful and making enough money: Companies are struggling hard to stay afloat

afoot adjective, adverb happening or being planned, especially secretly: Plans are afoot to build a new museum

afraid adjective **1** If you are afraid, you are very frightened **2** If you are afraid something might happen, you are worried it might happen

afresh adverb again and in a new way: The couple moved abroad to start life afresh

Africa noun Africa is the second largest continent. It is almost

A

surrounded by sea, with the Atlantic on its west side, the Mediterranean to the north, and the Indian Ocean and the Red Sea to the east

African adjective **1** belonging or relating to Africa ▷ noun **2** someone, especially a Black person, who comes from Africa

African-American noun an American whose ancestors came from Africa

Afrikaans [af-rik-**ahns**] noun a language spoken in South Africa, similar to Dutch

Afrikaner noun a white South African with Dutch ancestors

aft adverb, adjective towards the back of a ship or boat

after preposition, adverb **1** later than a particular time, date, or event **2** behind and following someone or something: They ran after her

afterlife noun The afterlife is a life some people believe begins when you die

aftermath noun The aftermath of a disaster is the situation that comes after it

afternoon noun the part of the day between noon and about six o'clock

aftershave noun a pleasant-smelling liquid men put on their faces after shaving

afterthought noun something you do or say as an addition to something else you have already done or said

afterwards adverb after an event or time

again adverb **1** happening one more time: He looked forward to becoming a father again **2** returning to the same state or place as before: there and back again

against preposition **1** touching and leaning on: He leaned against the wall

2 in opposition to: the Test match against England **3** in preparation for or in case of something: precautions against fire **4** in comparison with: The pound is now at its lowest rate against the dollar

age ages, ageing or aging, aged noun **1** The age of something or someone is the number of years they have lived or existed **2** Age is the quality of being old: a wine capable of improving with age **3** a particular period in history: the Iron Age **4** (in plural, informal) Ages means a very long time: He's been talking for ages ▷ verb **5** To age is to grow old or to appear older

aged adjective **1** [rhymes with **raged**] having a particular age: people aged 16 to 24 **2** [**ay**-jid] very old: an aged invalid

agency agencies noun an organization or business which provides certain services: a detective agency

agenda noun a list of items to be discussed at a meeting

agent noun **1** someone who arranges work or business for other people, especially actors or singers **2** someone who works for their country's secret service

aggravate verb **1** To aggravate a bad situation is to make it worse **2** (informal) If someone or something aggravates you, they make you annoyed ▷ aggravating adjective ▷ aggravation noun

WORD TIP
Some people think that using aggravate to mean 'annoy' is wrong

aggregate noun a total that is made up of several smaller amounts

aggression noun violent and hostile behaviour

aggressive *adjective* full of hostility and violence > **aggressively** *adverb* > **aggressiveness** *noun*

aggressor *noun* a person or country that starts a fight or a war

aggrieved *adjective* upset and angry about the way you have been treated

aghast [a-**gast**] *adjective* shocked and horrified

agile *adjective* [PE] able to move quickly and easily: *He is as agile as a cat* > **agilely** *adverb* > **agility** *noun*

agitate *verb* **1** If you agitate for something, you campaign energetically to get it **2** If something agitates you, it worries you > **agitation** *noun* > **agitator** *noun*

agnostic *noun* someone who believes we cannot know definitely whether God exists or not > **agnosticism** *noun*

ago *adverb* in the past: *She bought her flat three years ago*

agog *adjective* excited and eager to know more about an event or situation: *She was agog to hear his news*

agonizing or **agonising** *adjective* extremely painful, either physically or mentally: *an agonizing decision*

agony *noun* very great physical or mental pain

agrarian [ag-**rare**-ee-an] *adjective* (*formal*) relating to farming and agriculture: *agrarian economies*

agree agrees, agreeing, agreed *verb* **1** If you agree with someone, you have the same opinion as them **2** If you agree to do something, you say you will do it **3** If two stories or totals agree, they are the same **4** Food that doesn't agree with you makes you ill

agreeable *adjective* **1** pleasant or enjoyable **2** If you are agreeable to

something, you are willing to allow it or to do it: *She was agreeable to the project* > **agreeably** *adverb*

agreement *noun* **1** a decision that has been reached by two or more people **2** Two people who are in agreement have the same opinion about something

agriculture *noun* [HISTORY] Agriculture is farming > **agricultural** *adjective*

aground *adverb* If a boat runs aground, it becomes stuck in a shallow stretch of water

ahead *adverb* **1** in front: *He looked ahead* **2** more advanced than someone or something else: *We are five years ahead of the competition* **3** in the future: *I haven't had time to think far ahead*

aid *noun* **1** Aid is money, equipment, or services provided for people in need: *food and medical aid* **2** something that makes a task easier: *teaching aids* ▷ *verb* **3** (*formal*) If you aid a person or an organization, you help or support them

aide *noun* an assistant to an important person, especially in the government or the army: *the Prime Minister's closest aides*

AIDS *noun* a disease which destroys the body's natural system of immunity to diseases. AIDS is an abbreviation for 'acquired immune deficiency syndrome'

ailing *adjective* **1** sick or ill, and not getting better **2** getting into difficulties, especially with money: *an ailing company*

ailment *noun* a minor illness

aim *verb* **1** If you aim an object or weapon at someone or something, you point it at them **2** If you aim to do something, you are planning or hoping to do it ▷ *noun* **3** Your aim is what you intend to achieve **4** If you take aim, you point an object or weapon at someone or something

aimless *adjective* having no clear purpose or plan > **aimlessly** *adverb* > **aimlessness** *noun*

air *noun* **1** Air is the mixture of oxygen and other gases which we breathe and which forms the earth's atmosphere **2** An air someone or something has is the impression they give: *an air of defiance* **3** 'Air' is used to refer to travel in aircraft: *I have to travel by air a great deal* ▷ *verb* **4** If you air your opinions, you talk about them to other people

airborne *adjective* in the air and flying

air-conditioning *noun* a system of providing cool, clean air in buildings > **air-conditioned** *adjective*

aircraft *noun* any vehicle which can fly

airfield *noun* an open area of ground with runways where small aircraft take off and land

air force *noun* the part of a country's armed services that fights using aircraft

airlift *noun* an operation to move people or goods by air, especially in an emergency

airline *noun* a company which provides air travel

airliner *noun* a large passenger plane

airman airmen *noun* a man who serves in his country's air force

airport *noun* a place where people go to catch planes

air raid *noun* an attack by enemy aircraft, in which bombs are dropped

airship *noun* a large, light aircraft, consisting of a rigid balloon filled with gas and powered by an engine, with a passenger compartment underneath

airstrip *noun* a stretch of land that has been cleared for aircraft to take off and land

airtight *adjective* not letting air in or out

airy airier, airiest *adjective* full of fresh air and light > **airily** *adverb*

aisle [rhymes with **mile**] *noun* a long narrow gap that people can walk along between rows of seats or shelves

ajar *adjective* A door or window that is ajar is slightly open

akin *adjective* (formal) similar: *The taste is akin to veal*

alacrity *noun* (formal) eager willingness: *He seized this offer with alacrity*

alarm *noun* **1** a feeling of fear and worry: *The cat sprang back in alarm* **2** an automatic device used to warn people of something: *a car alarm* ▷ *verb* **3** If something alarms you, it makes you worried and anxious > **alarming** *adjective*

alas *adverb* unfortunately or regrettably: *But, alas, it would not be true*

albatross *noun* a large white sea bird

albeit [awl-**bee**-it] *conjunction* (formal) although: *He was making progress, albeit slowly*

albino albinos *noun* a person or animal with very white skin, white hair, and pink eyes

album *noun* **1** a recording with a number of songs on it **2** a book in which you keep a collection of things such as photographs or stamps

alchemy [al-kem-ee] *noun* a medieval science that attempted to change ordinary metals into gold > noun **alchemist**

alcohol noun Alcohol is any drink that can make people drunk; also the colourless flammable liquid found in these drinks, produced by fermenting sugar

alcoholic adjective **1** An alcoholic drink contains alcohol > noun **2** someone who is addicted to alcohol > **alcoholism** noun

alcove noun an area of a room which is set back slightly from the main part

ale noun a type of beer

alert adjective **1** paying full attention to what is happening: *The criminal was spotted by an alert member of the public* > noun **2** a situation in which people prepare themselves for danger: *The troops were on a war alert* > verb **3** If you alert someone to a problem or danger, you warn them of it. > **alertness** noun

A level noun an advanced exam taken by students in many British schools and colleges, usually following GCSEs

algae [al-jee] plural noun plants that grow in water or on damp surfaces

algebra noun a branch of mathematics in which symbols and letters are used instead of numbers to express relationships between quantities > **algebraic** adjective

Algerian adjective **1** belonging or relating to Algeria > noun **2** someone who comes from Algeria

alias aliases [ay-lee-ass] noun a false name: *Leonard Nimoy, alias Mr Spock*

alibi alibis [al-li-bye] noun An alibi is evidence proving you were somewhere else when a crime was committed

alien [ay-lee-an] adjective **1** not normal to you: *a totally alien culture* > noun **2** someone who is not a citizen of the country in which he or she lives **3** In science fiction, an alien is a creature from outer space

alienate verb If you alienate someone, you do something that makes them stop being sympathetic to you: *The Council's approach alienated many local residents* > **alienation** noun

alight adjective **1** Something that is alight is burning > verb **2** If a bird or insect alights somewhere, it lands there **3** (formal) When passengers alight from a vehicle, they get out of it at the end of a journey

align [a-line] verb **1** If you align yourself with a particular group, you support them **2** If you align things, you place them in a straight line > **alignment** noun

alike adjective **1** Things that are alike are similar in some way > adverb **2** If people or things are treated alike, they are treated in a similar way

alimony [al-li-mon-ee] noun money someone has to pay regularly to their wife or husband after they are divorced

alive adjective **1** living **2** lively and active

all adjective, pronoun, adverb **1** used when referring to the whole of something: *Why did he have to say all that?*; *She managed to control it all* > adverb **2** 'All' is also used when saying the two sides in a game or contest have the same score: *The final score was six points all*

Allah proper noun the Muslim name for God

allay verb To allay someone's fears or doubts is to stop them feeling afraid or doubtful

allege [a-lej] verb If you allege that something is true, you say it is true

A

but do not provide any proof: *It is alleged that she died as a result of neglect* ▷ **allegation** *noun* ▷ **alleged** *adjective*

allegiance [al-lee-jenss] *noun* loyal support for a person or organization

allegory allegories [**al**-li-gor-ee] *noun* a piece of writing or art in which the characters and events are symbols for something else ▷ **allegorical** *adjective*

allergy allergies [**al**-er-jee] *noun* a sensitivity someone has to something, so that they become ill when they eat it or touch it: *an allergy to cows' milk* ▷ **allergic** *adjective*

alleviate *verb* To alleviate pain or a problem is to make it less severe: *measures to alleviate poverty* ▷ **alleviation** *noun*

alley *noun* a narrow passage between buildings

alliance *noun* a group of people, organizations, or countries working together for similar aims

alligator *noun* a large animal, similar to a crocodile

alliteration *noun* ENGLISH (*literary*) the use of several words together which all begin with the same sound, for example 'around the rugged rock the ragged rascal ran' ▷ **alliterative** *adjective*

allocate *verb* If you allocate something, you decide it should be given to a person or place, or used for a particular purpose: *funds allocated for nursery education* ▷ **allocation** *noun*

allot allots, allotting, allotted *verb* If something is allotted to you, it is given to you as your share: *Space was allotted for visitors' cars*

allotment *noun* a piece of land which people can rent to grow

vegetables on ▷ **a** share of something

allow *verb* **1** If you allow something, you say it is all right or let it happen **2** If you allow a period of time or an amount of something, you set it aside for a particular purpose: *Allow four hours for the paint to dry* ▷ **allowable** *adjective*

allowance *noun* **1** money given regularly to someone for a particular purpose: *a petrol allowance* ▷ *phrase* **2** If you **make allowances** for something, you take it into account: *The school made allowances for Muslim cultural customs*

alloy *noun* a mixture of two or more metals

all right or **alright** *adjective* **1** If something is all right, it is acceptable **2** If someone is all right, they are safe and not harmed **3** You say 'all right' to agree to something

allude *verb* If you allude to something, you refer to it in an indirect way

> **WORD TIP**
> Do not confuse *allude* with *elude*: *She alluded to the report in the newspaper*; *I knew his face but his name eluded me*

allure *noun* The allure of something is an exciting quality that makes it attractive: *the allure of foreign travel* ▷ **alluring** *adjective*

allusion *noun* ENGLISH an indirect reference to or comment about something: *English literature is full of classical allusions*

ally allies, allying, allied *noun* **1** a person or country that helps and supports another ▷ *verb* **2** If you ally yourself with someone, you agree to help and support each other

almighty *adjective* **1** very great or

serious: *I've just had an almighty row with the chairman* ▷ *proper noun* **2** The Almighty is another name for God

almond *noun* a pale brown oval nut

almost *adverb* very nearly: *Prices have almost doubled*

aloft *adverb* up in the air or in a high position: *He held aloft the trophy*

alone *adjective, adverb* not with other people or things: *He just wanted to be alone*

along *preposition* **1** moving, happening, or existing continuously from one end to the other of something, or at various points beside it: *Put rivets along the top edge* ▷ *adverb* **2** moving forward: *We marched along, singing as we went* **3** with someone: *Why could she not take her along?* ▷ *phrase* **4 All along** means from the beginning of a period of time right up to now: *You've known that all along*

alongside *preposition* **1** next to something: *They had a house in the park alongside the river* ▷ *preposition* **2** If you work alongside other people, you are working in the same place and cooperating with them: *He was thrilled to work alongside Robert De Niro*

aloof *adjective* distant from someone or something

aloud *adverb* When you read or speak aloud, you speak loudly enough for other people to hear you

alphabet *noun* LIBRARY a set of letters in a fixed order that is used in writing a language ▷ **alphabetical** *adjective* ▷ **alphabetically** *adverb*

alpine *adjective* existing in or relating to high mountains: *alpine flowers*

already *adverb* having happened before the present time or earlier than expected: *She has already gone to bed*

alright another spelling for **all right**

> **WORD TIP**
> Some people think that *all right* is the only correct spelling and that *alright* is wrong

also *adverb* in addition to something that has just been mentioned

altar *noun* a holy table in a church or temple

alter *verb* If something alters or if you alter it, it changes ▷ **alteration** *noun*

> **WORD TIP**
> Do not confuse the spellings of *alter* and *altar*: *His tone altered suddenly; The priest stood at the altar*

altercation *noun* (formal) a noisy disagreement

alternate *verb* [ol-tern-ate] **1** If one thing alternates with another, the two things regularly occur one after the other ▷ *adjective* [ol-**tern**-at] **2** If something happens on alternate days, it happens on the first day but not the second, and happens again on the third day but not the fourth, and so on **3** MATHS Alternate angles are two angles on opposite sides of a line that crosses two other lines ▷ **alternately** *adverb* ▷ **alternation** *noun*

alternative *noun* **1** something you can do or have instead of something else: *alternatives to prison such as community service* ▷ *adjective* **2** Alternative plans or actions can happen or be done instead of what is already happening or being done ▷ **alternatively** *adverb*

although *conjunction* in spite of the fact that: *He wasn't well-known in America, although he did make a film there*

altitude *noun* GEOGRAPHY The altitude of something is its height above sea level: *The mountain range reaches an altitude of 1330 metres*

altogether *adverb* **1** entirely: *She wasn't altogether sorry to be leaving* **2** in total; used of amounts: *I get paid £1000 a month altogether*

aluminium *noun* SCIENCE Aluminium is a light silvery-white metallic element. It is used to make aircraft and other equipment, usually in the form of aluminium alloys.

always *adverb* all the time or for ever: *She's always moaning*

am the first person singular, present tense of **be**

a.m. used to specify times between 12 midnight and 12 noon, eg *I get up at 6 a.m.* It is an abbreviation for the Latin phrase 'ante meridiem', which means 'before noon'

amalgamate *verb* If two organizations amalgamate, they join together to form one new organization > **amalgamation** *noun*

amass *verb* If you amass something such as money or information, you collect large quantities of it: *He amassed a huge fortune*

amateur *noun* someone who does something as a hobby rather than as a job

amateurish *adjective* not skilfully made or done > **amateurishly** *adverb*

amaze *verb* If something amazes you, it surprises you very much

amazement *noun* complete surprise

amazing *adjective* very surprising or remarkable > **amazingly** *adverb*

ambassador *noun* a person sent to a foreign country as the representative of his or her own government

amber *noun* **1** a hard, yellowish-brown substance used for making jewellery ▷ *noun, adjective* **2** orange-coloured

ambience *noun* (formal) The ambience of a place is its atmosphere

ambient *adjective* **1** surrounding: *low ambient temperatures* **2** creating a relaxing atmosphere: *ambient music*

ambiguous *adjective* A word or phrase that is ambiguous has more than one meaning > **ambiguously** *adverb* > **ambiguity** *noun*

ambition *noun* **1** If you have an ambition to achieve something, you want very much to achieve it: *His ambition is to be an actor* **2** a great desire for success, power, and wealth: *He's talented and full of ambition*

ambitious *adjective* **1** Someone who is ambitious has a strong desire for success, power, and wealth **2** An ambitious plan is a large one and requires a lot of work: *an ambitious rebuilding schedule*

ambivalent *adjective* having or showing two conflicting attitudes or emotions > **ambivalence** *noun*

amble *verb* If you amble, you walk slowly and in a relaxed manner

ambulance *noun* a vehicle for taking sick and injured people to hospital

ambush *verb* **1** To ambush someone is to attack them after hiding and lying in wait for them ▷ *noun* **2** an attack on someone after hiding and lying in wait for them

amenable [am-**mee**-na-bl] *adjective* willing to listen to suggestions, or to cooperate with someone: *Both brothers were amenable to the arrangement* > **amenably** *adverb*

> **amenability** noun

amend verb To amend something that has been written or said is to alter it slightly: *Our constitution had to be amended* > **amendment** noun

amenity amenities [am-**mee**-nit-ee] noun GEOGRAPHY Amenities are things that are available for the public to use, such as sports facilities or shopping centres

America noun America refers to the United States, or to the whole of North, South, and Central America

American adjective **1** belonging or relating to the United States, or to the whole of North, South, and Central America ▷ noun **2** someone who comes from the United States

amiable adjective pleasant and friendly: *The hotel staff were very amiable* > **amiably** adverb > **amiability** noun

amicable adjective fairly friendly: *an amicable divorce* > **amicably** adverb

amid or **amidst** preposition (formal) surrounded by: *She enjoys cooking amid her friends*

amiss adjective If something is amiss, there is something wrong

ammonia noun Ammonia is a colourless, strong-smelling gas or alkaline liquid. It is used in household cleaning materials, explosives, and fertilizers. It has the chemical formula NH_3

ammunition noun anything that can be fired from a gun or other weapon, for example bullets and shells

amnesia noun loss of memory

amnesty amnesties noun an official pardon for political or other prisoners

amok [am-**muk**] phrase If a person or animal **runs amok**, they behave in a violent and uncontrolled way

among or **amongst** preposition **1** surrounded by: *The bike lay among piles of chains and pedals* **2** in company of: *He was among friends* **3** between more than two: *The money will be divided among seven charities*

WORD TIP

If there are more than two things, you should use *among*. If there are only two things you should use *between*. The form *amongst* is a bit old-fashioned and *among* is more often used

amoral adjective Someone who is amoral has no moral standards by which to live

WORD TIP

Do not confuse *amoral* and *immoral*. You use *amoral* to talk about people with no moral standards, but *immoral* for people who are aware of moral standards but go against them

amorous adjective passionately affectionate: *an amorous relationship* > **amorously** adverb > **amorousness** noun

amount MATHS noun **1** An amount of something is how much there is of it ▷ verb **2** If something amounts to a particular total, all the parts of it add up to that total: *Her vocabulary amounted to only 50 words*

amp noun An amp is the same as an amplifier

amphetamine noun a drug that increases people's energy and makes them excited. It can have dangerous and unpleasant side effects

amphibian noun SCIENCE a creature that lives partly on land and partly in water, for example a frog or a newt

amphibious adjective An

amphibious animal, such as a frog, lives partly on land and partly in the water

amphitheatre noun [HISTORY] An amphitheatre is a large, semicircular open area with sloping sides covered with rows of seats. Amphitheatres were built originally by the Greeks and Romans for theatrical performances

ample adjective If there is an ample amount of something, there is more than enough of it > **amply** adverb

amplifier noun a piece of equipment which causes sounds or electrical signals to become louder

amplify amplifies, amplifying, amplified verb If you amplify a sound, you make it louder > **amplification** noun

amputate verb To amputate an arm or a leg is to cut it off as a surgical operation > **amputation** noun

amuse verb **1** If something amuses you, you think it is funny **2** If you amuse yourself, you find things to do which stop you from being bored > **amused** adjective > **amusing** adjective

amusement noun **1** Amusement is the state of thinking something is funny **2** Amusement is also the pleasure you get from being entertained or from doing something interesting **3** Amusements are ways of passing the time pleasantly

an adjective 'An' is used instead of 'a' in front of words that begin with a vowel sound

-an suffix '-an' comes at the end of nouns and adjectives which show where or what someone or something comes from or belongs to: American; Victorian; Christian

anachronism [an-**ak**-kron-izm]

noun something that belongs or seems to belong to another time > **anachronistic** adjective

anaemia [a-**nee**-mee-a] noun a medical condition resulting from too few red cells in a person's blood. People with anaemia look pale and feel very tired > **anaemic** adjective

anaesthetic [an-niss-**thet**-ik] noun a substance that stops you feeling pain. A general anaesthetic stops you from feeling pain in the whole of your body by putting you to sleep, and a local anaesthetic makes just one part of your body go numb

anaesthetist noun a doctor who is specially trained to give anaesthetics

anagram noun a word or phrase formed by changing the order of the letters of another word or phrase. For example, 'triangle' is an anagram of 'integral'

anal [**ay**-nl] adjective relating to the anus

analogy analogies [an-**al**-o-jee] noun a comparison showing that two things are similar in some ways > **analogous** adjective

analyse verb [EXAM TERM] To analyse something is to break it down into parts, or investigate it carefully, so that you can describe its main aspects, or find out what it consists of

analysis analyses noun the process of investigating something in order to understand it or find out what it consists of: a full analysis of the problem

analyst noun a person whose job is to analyse things to find out about them

analytic or **analytical** adjective using logical reasoning: Planning in detail requires an acute analytical mind

> **analytically** adverb

anarchy [an-nar-kee] noun a situation where nobody obeys laws or rules

anatomy anatomies noun **1** the study of the structure of the human body or of the bodies of animals **2** An animal's anatomy is the structure of its body > **anatomical** adjective > **anatomically** adverb

ANC noun one of the main political parties in South Africa. ANC is an abbreviation for 'African National Congress'

ancestor noun Your ancestors are the members of your family who lived many years ago and from whom you are descended > **ancestral** adjective

ancestry ancestries noun Your ancestry consists of the people from whom you are descended: *a French citizen of Greek ancestry*

anchor noun **1** a heavy, hooked object at the end of a chain, dropped from a boat into the water to keep the boat in one place ▷ **verb 2** To anchor a boat or another object is to stop it from moving by dropping an anchor or attaching it to something solid

anchorage noun a place where a boat can safely anchor

anchovy anchovies noun a type of small edible fish with a very strong salty taste

ancient [ayn-shent] adjective **1** existing or happening in the distant past: *ancient Greece* **2** very old or having a very long history: *an ancient monastery*

ancillary [an-**sil**-lar-ee] adjective The ancillary workers in an institution are the people such as cooks and cleaners, whose work supports the main work of the institution

and conjunction You use 'and' to link two or more words or phrases together

androgynous [an-**droj**-in-uss] adjective (formal) having both male and female characteristics

android noun In science fiction, a robot that looks like a human being

anecdote noun a short, entertaining story about a person or event > **anecdotal** adjective

anew adverb If you do something anew, you do it again: *They left their life in Britain to start anew in France*

angel noun Angels are spiritual beings some people believe live in heaven and act as messengers for God > **angelic** adjective

anger noun **1** the strong feeling you get when you feel someone has behaved in an unfair or cruel way ▷ verb **2** If something angers you, it makes you feel angry

angina [an-**jy**-na] noun a brief but very severe heart pain, caused by lack of blood supply to the heart. It is also known as 'angina pectoris'

angle noun **1** [MATHS] the distance between two lines at the point where they join together. Angles are measured in degrees **2** the direction from which you look at something: *He had painted the vase from all angles* **3** An angle on something is a particular way of considering it: *the same story from a German angle*

angler noun someone who fishes with a fishing rod as a hobby > **angling** noun

Anglican noun, adjective (a member of) one of the churches belonging to the Anglican Communion, a group of Protestant churches which includes the Church of England

Anglo-Saxon noun **1** The Anglo-Saxons were a race of people who settled in England from the fifth century AD and were the dominant people until the Norman invasion in 1066. They were composed of three West Germanic tribes, the Angles, Saxons, and Jutes **2** Anglo-Saxon is another name for **Old English**

Angolan [ang-**goh**-ln] *adjective* **1** belonging or relating to Angola ▷ *noun* **2** someone who comes from Angola

angry angrier, angriest *adjective* very cross or annoyed > **angrily** *adverb*

anguish *noun* extreme suffering > **anguished** *adjective*

angular *adjective* Angular things have straight lines and sharp points: *He has an angular face and pointed chin*

animal *noun* any living being except a plant, or any mammal except a human being

animate *verb* To animate something is to make it lively and interesting

animated *adjective* lively and interesting: *an animated conversation* > **animatedly** *adverb*

animation *noun* **1** a method of film-making in which a series of drawings are photographed. When the film is projected, the characters in the drawings appear to move **2** Someone who has animation shows liveliness in the way they speak and act: *The crowd showed no sign of animation* > **animator** *noun*

animosity animosities *noun* a feeling of strong dislike and anger towards someone

ankle *noun* the joint which connects your foot to your leg

annex or **annexe** *noun* **1** an extra building which is joined to a larger main building **2** an extra part added to a document ▷ *verb* **3** If one

country annexes another, it seizes the other country and takes control of it > **annexation** *noun*

annihilate [an-**nye**-ill-ate] *verb* If something is annihilated, it is completely destroyed > **annihilation** *noun*

anniversary anniversaries *noun* a date which is remembered because something special happened on that date in a previous year

announce *verb* If you announce something, you tell people about it publicly or officially: *The team was announced on Friday morning*

announcement *noun* a statement giving information about something

announcer *noun* someone who introduces programmes on radio and television

annoy *verb* If someone or something annoys you, they irritate you and make you fairly angry > **annoyed** *adjective*

annoyance *noun* **1** a feeling of irritation **2** something that causes irritation

annual *adjective* **1** happening or done once a year: *their annual conference* **2** happening or calculated over a period of one year: *the United States' annual budget for national defence* ▷ *noun* **3** a book or magazine published once a year **4** a plant that grows, flowers, and dies within one year > **annually** *adverb*

annuity annuities *noun* a fixed sum of money paid to someone every year from an investment or insurance policy

annul annuls, annulling, annulled *verb* If a marriage or contract is annulled, it is declared invalid, so that legally it is considered never to have existed > **annulment** *noun*

anoint *verb* To anoint someone is to put oil on them as part of a ceremony > **anointment** *noun*

anomaly anomalies [an-**nom**-al-ee] *noun* Something is an anomaly if it is unusual or different from normal > **anomalous** *adjective*

anon. an abbreviation for **anonymous**

anonymous *adjective* If something is anonymous, nobody knows who is responsible for it: *The police received an anonymous phone call* > **anonymously** *adverb* > **anonymity** *noun*

anorak *noun* a warm waterproof jacket, usually with a hood

anorexia *noun* a psychological illness in which the person refuses to eat because they are frightened of becoming fat > **anorexic** *adjective*

another *adjective, pronoun* Another thing or person is an additional thing or person

answer *verb* **1** If you answer someone, you reply to them using words or actions or in writing ▷ *noun* **2** the reply you give when you answer someone **3** a solution to a problem

answerable *adjective* If you are answerable to someone for something, you are responsible for it: *He must be made answerable for these terrible crimes*

answering machine *noun* a machine which records telephone calls while you are out

ant *noun* Ants are small insects that live in large groups

-ant *suffix* '-ant' is used to form adjectives: *important*

antagonism *noun* hatred or hostility

antagonist *noun* an enemy or opponent

antagonistic *adjective* Someone who is antagonistic towards you shows hate or hostility > **antagonistically** *adverb*

antagonize or **antagonise** *verb* If someone is antagonized, they are made to feel anger and hostility

Antarctic *noun* The Antarctic is the region south of the Antarctic Circle

Antarctic Circle *noun* The Antarctic Circle is an imaginary circle around the southern part of the world

ante- *prefix* 'Ante-' means 'before'. For example, *antenatal* means 'before birth'

antelope *noun* an animal which looks like a deer

antenatal *adjective* concerned with the care of pregnant women and their unborn children: *an antenatal clinic*

antenna antennae or antennas *noun* **1** The antennae of insects and certain other animals are the two long, thin parts attached to their heads which they use to feel with. The plural is 'antennae' **2** In Australian, New Zealand, and American English, an antenna is a radio or television aerial. The plural is 'antennas'

anthem *noun* a hymn written for a special occasion

anthology anthologies *noun* LIBRARY a collection of writings by various authors published in one book

anthropology *noun* the study of human beings and their society and culture > **anthropological** *adjective* > **anthropologist** *noun*

anti- *prefix* 'Anti-' means opposed to or opposite to something: *antiwar marches*

antibiotic *noun* a drug or chemical

used in medicine to kill bacteria and cure infections

antibody antibodies noun a substance produced in the blood which can kill the harmful bacteria that cause disease

anticipate verb If you anticipate an event, you are expecting it and are prepared for it: She had anticipated his visit > **anticipation** noun

anticlimax noun something that disappoints you because it is not as exciting as expected, or because it occurs after something that was very exciting

anticlockwise adjective, adverb moving in the opposite direction to the hands of a clock

antics plural noun funny or silly ways of behaving

antidote noun a chemical substance that acts against the effect of a poison

antipathy noun a strong feeling of dislike or hostility towards something or someone

antiquarian adjective relating to or involving old and rare objects: antiquarian books

antiquated adjective very old-fashioned: an antiquated method of teaching

antique [an-**teek**] noun **1** an object from the past that is collected because of its value or beauty ▷ adjective **2** from or concerning the past: antique furniture

antiquity antiquities noun **1** Antiquity is the distant past, especially the time of the ancient Egyptians, Greeks, and Romans **2** Antiquities are interesting works of art and buildings from the distant past

anti-Semitism noun hatred of Jewish people > **anti-Semitic**

adjective > **anti-Semite** noun

antiseptic adjective Something that is antiseptic kills germs

antisocial adjective **1** An antisocial person is unwilling to meet and be friendly with other people **2** Antisocial behaviour is annoying or upsetting to other people: Smoking in public is antisocial

antithesis antitheses [an-**tith**-iss-iss] noun (formal) The antithesis of something is its exact opposite: Work is the antithesis of leisure

anus noun the hole between the buttocks

anvil noun a heavy iron block on which hot metal is beaten into shape

anxiety anxieties noun nervousness or worry

anxious adjective **1** If you are anxious, you are nervous or worried **2** If you are anxious to do something or anxious that something should happen, you very much want to do it or want it to happen: She was anxious to have children > **anxiously** adverb

any adjective, pronoun **1** one, some, or several: Do you have any paperclips I could borrow? **2** even the smallest amount or even one: He was unable to tolerate any dairy products **3** whatever or whichever, no matter what or which: Any type of cooking oil will do

anybody pronoun any person

anyhow adverb **1** in any case **2** in a careless way: They were all shoved in anyhow

anyone pronoun any person

anything pronoun any object, event, situation, or action

anyway adverb in any case

anywhere adverb in, at, or to any place

Anzac noun **1** In World War I, an Anzac was a soldier in the Australia and New Zealand Army Corps **2** an Australian or New Zealand soldier

aorta [ay-**or**-ta] noun the main artery in the body, which carries blood away from the heart

apart adverb, adjective **1** When something is apart from something else, there is a space or a distance between them: *The couple separated and lived apart for four years; The gliders landed about seventy metres apart* ▷ adverb **2** If you take something apart, you separate it into pieces

apartheid [ap-**par**-tide] noun In South Africa apartheid was the government policy and laws which kept people of different races apart. It was abolished in 1994

apartment noun a set of rooms for living in, usually on one floor of a building

apathetic adjective not interested in anything

apathy [**ap**-path-ee] noun a state of mind in which you do not care about anything

ape noun **1** Apes are animals with a very short tail or no tail. They are closely related to man. Apes include chimpanzees, gorillas, and gibbons ▷ verb **2** If you ape someone's speech or behaviour, you imitate it

aphid noun a small insect that feeds by sucking the juices from plants

apiece adverb If people have a particular number of things apiece, they have that number each

aplomb [uh-**plom**] noun If you do something with aplomb, you do it with great confidence

apocalypse [uh-**pok**-ka-lips] noun The Apocalypse is the end of the world > **apocalyptic** adjective

apocryphal adjective A story that is apocryphal is generally believed not to have really happened

apolitical [ay-poll-**it**-i-kl] adjective not interested in politics

apologetic adjective showing or saying you are sorry > **apologetically** adverb

apologize or **apologise** verb When you apologize to someone, you say you are sorry for something you have said or done

apology apologies noun something you say or write to tell someone you are sorry

apostle noun The Apostles are the twelve followers who were chosen by Christ

apostrophe [ap-**poss**-troff-ee] noun (ENGLISH) a punctuation mark that is used to show that one or more letters have been missed out of a word. An example is 'he's' for 'he is'. Apostrophes are also used with -s at the end of a noun to show that what follows belongs to or relates to the noun, for example *my brother's books*

app noun (COMPUTING) a computer program designed to do a particular thing, especially one that you can download to a mobile electronic device

appal appals, appalling, appalled verb If something appals you, it shocks you because it is very bad

appalling adjective so bad as to be shocking: *She escaped with appalling injuries*

apparatus noun (SCIENCE) The apparatus for a particular task is the equipment used for it

apparent adjective **1** seeming real rather than actually being real: *an apparent hit and run accident*

2 obvious: It was apparent that he had lost interest ▷ **apparently** adverb

apparition noun something you think you see but that is not really there: a ghostly apparition on the windscreen

appeal verb **1** If you appeal for something, you make an urgent request for it: The police appealed for witnesses to come forward **2** If you appeal to someone in authority against a decision, you formally ask them to change it **3** If something appeals to you, you find it attractive or interesting ▷ noun **4** a formal or serious request: an appeal for peace **5** The appeal of something is the quality it has which people find attractive or interesting: the rugged appeal of the Rockies ▷ **appealing** adjective

appear verb **1** When something which you could not see appears, it moves (or you move) so that you can see it **2** When something new appears, it begins to exist **3** When an actor or actress appears in a film or show, they take part in it **4** If something appears to be a certain way, it seems or looks that way: He appeared to be searching for something

appearance noun **1** The appearance of someone in a place is their arrival there, especially when it is unexpected **2** The appearance of something new is the time when it begins to exist: the appearance of computer technology **3** Someone's or something's appearance is the way they look to other people: His gaunt appearance had sparked fears for his health

appease verb If you try to appease someone, you try to calm them down when they are angry, for example by giving them what they want > **appeasement** noun

appendage noun a less important part attached to a main part

appendicitis [app-end-i-**site**-uss] noun a painful illness in which a person's appendix becomes infected

appendix appendices or appendixes noun **1** a small closed tube forming part of your digestive system **2** An appendix to a book is extra information placed after the end of the main text

> **WORD TIP**
> The plural of the part of the body is *appendixes*. The plural of the extra section in a book is *appendices*

appetite noun **1** Your appetite is your desire to eat **2** If you have an appetite for something, you have a strong desire for it and enjoyment of it: She had lost her appetite for air travel

appetizing or **appetising** adjective Food that is appetizing looks and smells good, and makes you want to eat it

applaud verb **1** When a group of people applaud, they clap their hands in approval or praise **2** When an action or attitude is applauded, people praise it

applause noun DRAMA Applause is clapping by a group of people

apple noun a round fruit with smooth skin and firm white flesh

appliance noun any machine in your home you use to do a job like cleaning or cooking: kitchen appliances

applicable adjective Something that is applicable to a situation is relevant to it: The rules are applicable to everyone

applicant noun someone who is applying for something: We had problems recruiting applicants for the post

application noun 1 a formal request for something, usually in writing 2 The application of a rule, system, or skill is the use of it in a particular situation

apply applies, applying, applied verb 1 If you apply for something, you formally ask for it, usually by sending an email or writing a letter 2 If you apply a rule or skill, you use it in a situation: He applied his mind to the problem 3 If something applies to a person or a situation, it is relevant to that person or situation: The legislation applies only to people living in England and Wales 4 If you apply something to a surface, you put it on: She applied lipstick to her mouth

appoint verb 1 If you appoint someone to a job or position, you formally choose them for it 2 If you appoint a time or place for something to happen, you decide when or where it will happen > **appointed** adjective

appointment noun 1 an arrangement you have with someone to meet them 2 The appointment of a person to do a particular job is the choosing of that person to do it 3 a job or a position of responsibility: He applied for an appointment in Russia

apposite [app-o-zit] adjective well suited for a particular purpose: He went before Cameron could think of anything apposite to say

appraise verb If you appraise something, you think about it carefully and form an opinion about it > **appraisal** noun

appreciable [a-pree-shuh-bl] adjective large enough to be noticed: an appreciable difference > **appreciably** adverb

appreciate verb 1 If you appreciate something, you like it because you recognize its good qualities: He appreciates fine wines 2 If you appreciate a situation or problem, you understand it and know what it involves 3 If you appreciate something someone has done for you, you are grateful to them for it: I really appreciate you coming to visit me 4 If something appreciates over a period of time, its value increases: The property appreciated by 50% in two years > **appreciation** noun

appreciative adjective 1 understanding and enthusiastic: They were a very appreciative audience 2 thankful and grateful: I am particularly appreciative of the help my family and friends have given me > **appreciatively** adverb

apprehend verb (formal) 1 When the police apprehend someone, they arrest them and take them into custody 2 If you apprehend something, you understand it fully: They were unable to apprehend his hidden meaning

apprehensive adjective afraid something bad may happen: I was very apprehensive about the birth > **apprehensively** adverb > **apprehension** noun

apprentice noun a person who works for a period of time with a skilled craftsman in order to learn a skill or trade > **apprenticeship** noun

approach verb 1 To approach something is to come near or nearer to it 2 When a future event approaches, it gradually gets nearer: As winter approached, tents were set up to accommodate refugees 3 If you approach someone about something, you ask them about it 4 If you approach a situation or

problem in a particular way, you think about it or deal with it in that way ▷ noun **5** The approach of something is the process of it coming closer: *the approach of spring* **6** An approach to a situation or problem is a way of thinking about it or dealing with it **7** a road or path that leads to a place
> **approaching** *adjective*

appropriate *adjective* [a-**proh**-pri-it] **1** suitable or acceptable for a particular situation: *He didn't think jeans were appropriate for a vice-president* ▷ *verb* [a-**proh**-pri-ate] **2** (*formal*) If you appropriate something which does not belong to you, you take it without permission
> **appropriately** *adverb*
> **appropriation** *noun*

approval *noun* PSHE **1** Approval is agreement given to a plan or request: *The plan will require approval from the local authority* **2** Approval is also admiration: *She looked at James with approval*

approve *verb* PSHE **1** If you approve of something or someone, you think that thing or person is acceptable or good **2** If someone in a position of authority approves a plan or idea, they formally agree to it
> **approved** *adjective* > **approving** *adjective*

approximate *adjective* MATHS almost exact: *What was the approximate distance between the cars?*
> **approximately** *adverb*

apricot *noun* a small, soft, yellowish-orange fruit

April *noun* the fourth month of the year. April has 30 days

apron *noun* a piece of clothing worn over the front of normal clothing to protect it

apt *adjective* **1** suitable or relevant: *a very apt description* **2** having a particular tendency: *They are apt to jump to the wrong conclusions*

aptitude *noun* Someone's aptitude for something is their ability to learn it quickly and to do it well: *I have a natural aptitude for painting*

aquarium *noun* aquaria or aquariums *noun* a glass tank filled with water in which fish are kept

Aquarius *noun* Aquarius is the eleventh sign of the zodiac, represented by a person carrying water. People born between January 20th and February 18th are born under this sign

aquatic *adjective* **1** An aquatic animal or plant lives or grows in water **2** involving water: *aquatic sports*

Arab *noun* a member of a group of people who used to live in Arabia but who now live throughout the Middle East and North Africa

Arabic *noun* a language spoken by many people in the Middle East and North Africa

arable *adjective* Arable land is used for growing crops

arbiter *noun* the person who decides about something

arbitrary *adjective* An arbitrary decision or action is one that is not based on a plan or system
> **arbitrarily** *adverb*

arc *noun* **1** a smoothly curving line **2** in geometry, a section of the circumference of a circle

> **WORD TIP**
> Do not confuse the spellings of *arc* and *ark*

arcade *noun* a covered passage with shops or market stalls along one or both sides

arcane *adjective* mysterious and

difficult to understand

arch noun **1** a structure that has a curved top supported on either side by a pillar or wall **2** the curved part of bone at the top of the foot ▷ verb **3** When something arches, it forms a curved line or shape ▷ adjective **4** most important: my arch enemy

archaeology or **archeology** [ar-kee-ol-loj-ee] noun the study of the past by digging up and examining the remains of buildings, tools, and other things
> **archaeological** adjective
> **archaeologist** noun

archaic [ar-kay-ik] adjective very old or old-fashioned

archbishop noun a bishop of the highest rank in a Christian Church

archeology another spelling of **archaeology**

archer noun someone who shoots with a bow and arrow

archery noun a sport in which people shoot at a target with a bow and arrow

archipelago archipelagos [ar-kip-pel-lag-oh] noun a group of small islands

architect [ar-kit-tekt] noun ART a person who designs buildings

architecture noun ART the art or practice of designing buildings
> **architectural** adjective

archive [ar-kive] noun Archives are collections of documents and records about the history of a family or some other group of people

arctic noun **1** The Arctic is the region north of the Arctic Circle ▷ adjective **2** Arctic means very cold indeed: arctic conditions

Arctic Circle noun The Arctic Circle is an imaginary circle around the northern part of the world

ardent adjective full of enthusiasm

and passion > **ardently** adverb

ardour noun a strong and passionate feeling of love or enthusiasm

arduous [ard-yoo-uss] adjective tiring and needing a lot of effort: the arduous task of rebuilding the country

are noun the plural form of the present tense of **be**

area noun **1** a particular part of a place, country, or the world: a built-up area of the city **2** The area of a piece of ground or a surface is the amount of space it covers, measured in square metres or square feet **3** MATHS The area of a geometric object is the amount of space enclosed within its lines

arena noun **1** a place where sports and other public events take place **2** A particular arena is the centre of attention or activity in a particular situation: the political arena

Argentinian [ar-jen-tin-ee-an] adjective **1** belonging or relating to Argentina ▷ noun **2** someone who comes from Argentina

arguable adjective An arguable idea or point is not necessarily true or correct and should be questioned
> **arguably** adverb

argue argues, arguing, argued verb **1** If you argue with someone about something, you disagree with them about it, sometimes in an angry way **2** If you argue that something is the case, you give reasons why you think it is so: She argued that her client had been wrongly accused

argument noun **1** a disagreement between two people which causes a quarrel **2** a point or a set of reasons you use to try to convince people about something

argumentative adjective An argumentative person is always disagreeing with other people

aria [**ah**-ree-a] noun a song sung by one of the leading singers in an opera

arid adjective Arid land is very dry because it has very little rain

Aries [**air**-reez] noun Aries is the first sign of the zodiac, represented by a ram. People born between March 21st and April 19th are born under this sign

arise arises, arising, arose, arisen verb **1** When something such as an opportunity or problem arises, it begins to exist **2** (formal) To arise also means to stand up from a sitting, kneeling, or lying position

aristocracy aristocracies noun a class of people who have a high social rank and special titles

aristocrat noun someone whose family has a high social rank, and who has a title > **aristocratic** adjective

arithmetic noun the part of mathematics which is to do with the addition, subtraction, multiplication, and division of numbers > **arithmetical** adjective > **arithmetically** adverb

ark noun In the Bible, the ark was the boat built by Noah for his family and the animals during the Flood

> **WORD TIP**
> Do not confuse the spellings of arc and ark

arm noun **1** Your arms are the part of your body between your shoulder and your wrist **2** The arms of a chair are the parts on which you rest your arms **3** An arm of an organization is a section of it: the political arm of the armed forces **4** (in plural) Arms are weapons used in a war > verb **5** To arm someone is to provide them with weapons

armada [ar-**mah**-da] noun An armada is a large fleet of warships. In 1588, the Spanish Armada was sent against England by Philip II of Spain, but was defeated in the Channel by the English and destroyed

Armageddon noun In Christianity, Armageddon is the final battle between good and evil at the end of the world

armament noun Armaments are the weapons and military equipment that belong to a country

armchair noun a comfortable chair with a support on each side for your arms

armed adjective A person who is armed is carrying a weapon or weapons

armistice [ar-**miss**-tiss] noun an agreement in a war to stop fighting in order to discuss peace

armour noun In the past, armour was metal clothing worn for protection in battle

armoured adjective covered with thick steel for protection from gunfire and other missiles: an armoured car

armoury armouries noun a place where weapons are stored

armpit noun the area under your arm where your arm joins your shoulder

army armies noun a large group of soldiers organized into divisions for fighting on land

aroma noun a strong, pleasant smell > **aromatic** adjective

aromatherapy noun a type of therapy that involves massaging the body with special fragrant oils

around preposition **1** placed at various points in a place or area: There are many seats around the building **2** from place to place inside an area: *We walked around the showroom* **3** at approximately the time or place mentioned: *The attacks began around noon* ▷ *adverb* **4** here and there: *His papers were scattered around*

arouse *verb* If something arouses a feeling in you, it causes you to begin to have this feeling: *His death still arouses very painful feelings* > **arousal** *noun*

arrange *verb* **1** If you arrange to do something, you make plans for it **2** If you arrange something for someone, you make it possible for them to have it or do it: *The bank has arranged a loan for her* **3** If you arrange objects, you set them out in a particular position: *He started to arrange the books in piles* > **arrangement** *noun*

array *noun* An array of different things is a large number of them displayed together

arrears *plural noun* **1** Arrears are amounts of money you owe: *mortgage arrears* ▷ *phrase* **2** If you are paid in arrears, you are paid at the end of the period for which the payment is due

arrest *verb* **1** If the police arrest someone, they take them into custody to decide whether to charge them with an offence ▷ *noun* **2** An arrest is the act of taking a person into custody > **arresting** *adjective*

arrival *noun* **1** the act or time of arriving: *The arrival of the train was delayed* **2** something or someone that has arrived: *The tourist authority reported record arrivals over Christmas*

arrive *verb* **1** When you arrive at a place, you reach it at the end of your journey **2** When a letter or a piece of

news arrives, it is brought to you: *A letter arrived at her lawyer's office* **3** When you arrive at an idea or decision you reach it **4** When a moment, event, or new thing arrives, it begins to happen: *The Easter holidays arrived*

arrogant *adjective* Someone who is arrogant behaves as if they are better than other people > **arrogantly** *adverb* > **arrogance** *noun*

arrow *noun* a long, thin weapon with a sharp point at one end, shot from a bow

arsenal *noun* a place where weapons and ammunition are stored or produced

arsenic *noun* Arsenic is a strongly poisonous element used in insecticides and weedkillers. Arsenic's atomic number is 33 and its symbol is As

arson *noun* the crime of deliberately setting fire to something, especially a building

art *noun* **1** Art is the creation of objects such as paintings and sculptures, which are thought to be beautiful or which express a particular idea; also used to refer to the objects themselves **2** An activity is called an art when it requires special skill or ability: *the art of diplomacy* **3** (*in plural*) The arts are literature, music, painting, and sculpture, considered together

artefact [ar-tif-fact] *noun* any object made by people

artery arteries *noun* **1** Your arteries are the tubes that carry blood from your heart to the rest of your body **2** a main road or major section of any system of communication or transport

artful *adjective* clever and skilful,

often in a cunning way ▷ **artfully** adverb

arthritis noun a condition in which the joints in someone's body become swollen and painful ▷ **arthritic** adjective

artichoke noun **1** the round green partly edible flower head of a thistle-like plant; the flower head is made up of clusters of leaves that have a soft fleshy part that is eaten as a vegetable **2** A Jerusalem artichoke is a small yellowish-white vegetable that grows underground and looks like a potato

article noun **1** a piece of writing in a newspaper or magazine **2** a particular item: an article of clothing **3** In English grammar, 'a' and 'the' are sometimes called articles: 'a' (or 'an') is the indefinite article; 'the' is the definite article

articulate adjective **1** If you are articulate, you are able to express yourself well in words ▷ verb **2** When you articulate your ideas or feelings, you express in words what you think or feel: She could not articulate her grief **3** When you articulate a sound or word, you speak it clearly ▷ **articulation** noun

artificial adjective **1** created by people rather than occurring naturally: artificial colouring **2** pretending to have attitudes and feelings which other people realize are not real: an artificial smile ▷ **artificially** adverb

artillery noun **1** Artillery consists of large, powerful guns such as cannons **2** The artillery is the branch of an army which uses large, powerful guns

artist noun **1** a person who draws or paints or produces other works of art **2** a person who is very skilled at a particular activity

artistic adjective **1** able to create good paintings, sculpture, or other works of art **2** concerning or involving art or artists ▷ **artistically** adverb

artistry noun Artistry is the creative skill of an artist, writer, actor, or musician: a supreme demonstration of his artistry as a cellist

arty artier, artiest adjective (informal) interested in painting, sculpture, and other works of art

as conjunction **1** at the same time that: She waved at fans as she arrived for the concert **2** in the way that: They had talked as only the best of friends can **3** because: As I won't be back tonight, don't bother to cook a meal **4** You use the structure as ... as when you are comparing things that are similar: It was as big as four football pitches ▷ preposition **5** You use 'as' when you are saying what role someone or something has: She worked as a waitress ▷ phrase **6** You use as if or as though when you are giving a possible explanation for something: He looked at me as if I were mad

asbestos noun a grey heat-resistant material used in the past to make fireproof articles

ascend [ass-end] verb (formal) To ascend is to move or lead upwards: We finally ascended to the brow of a steep hill

ascendancy noun (formal) If one group has ascendancy over another, it has more power or influence over the other

ascendant adjective **1** rising or moving upwards ▷ phrase **2** Someone or something in the ascendant is increasing in power or popularity

ascent noun an upward journey, for example up a mountain

ascertain [ass-er-**tain**] verb (formal) If you ascertain that something is the case, you find out it is the case: *He had ascertained that she had given up smoking*

ascribe verb **1** If you ascribe an event or state of affairs to a particular cause, you think that it is the cause of it: *His stomach pains were ascribed to his intake of pork* **2** If you ascribe a quality to someone, you think they have it

ash noun **1** the grey or black powdery remains of anything that has been burnt **2** a tree with grey bark and hard tough wood used for timber

ashamed adjective **1** feeling embarrassed or guilty **2** If you are ashamed of someone, you feel embarrassed to be connected with them

ashore adverb on land or onto the land

ashtray noun a small dish for ash from cigarettes and cigars

Asia noun Asia is the largest continent. It has Europe on its western side, with the Arctic to the north, the Pacific to the east, and the Indian Ocean to the south. Asia includes several island groups, including Japan, Indonesia, and the Philippines

Asian adjective **1** belonging or relating to Asia ▷ noun **2** someone who comes from India, Pakistan, Bangladesh, or from some other part of Asia

aside adverb **1** If you move something aside, you move it to one side ▷ noun **2** a comment made away from the main conversation or dialogue that all those talking are not meant to hear

ask verb **1** If you ask someone a question, you put a question to them for them to answer **2** If you ask someone to do something or give you something, you want them to do it or to give it to you **3** If you ask someone's permission or forgiveness, you try to obtain it **4** If you ask someone somewhere, you invite them there: *Not everybody had been asked to the wedding*

askew adjective not straight

asleep adjective sleeping

asparagus noun a vegetable that has long shoots which are cooked and eaten

aspect noun **1** An aspect of something is one of its features: *Exam results illustrate only one aspect of a school's success* **2** The aspect of a building is the direction it faces: *The southern aspect of the cottage faces over fields*

asphalt noun a black substance used to make road surfaces and playgrounds

aspiration noun Someone's aspirations are their desires and ambitions

aspire verb If you aspire to something, you have an ambition to achieve it: *He aspired to work in music journalism* > **aspiring** adjective

aspirin noun **1** a white drug used to relieve pain, fever, and colds **2** a tablet of this drug

ass noun a donkey

assailant noun someone who attacks another person

assassin noun someone who has murdered a political or religious leader

assassinate verb To assassinate a political or religious leader is to murder him or her > **assassination** noun

assault noun 1 a violent attack on someone ▷ verb 2 To assault someone is to attack them violently

assemble verb 1 To assemble is to gather together 2 If you assemble something, you fit the parts of it together

assembly assemblies noun 1 a group of people who have gathered together for a meeting 2 The assembly of an object is the fitting together of its parts: *DIY assembly of units*

assent [as-**sent**] noun 1 If you give your assent to something, you agree to it ▷ verb 2 If you assent to something, you agree to it

assert verb 1 If you assert a fact or belief, you state it firmly and forcefully 2 If you assert yourself, you speak and behave in a confident and direct way, so that people pay attention to you

assertion noun a statement or claim

assertive adjective If you are assertive, you speak and behave in a confident and direct way, so that people pay attention to you
> **assertively** adverb
> **assertiveness** noun

assess EXAM TERM If you assess something, you consider it carefully and make a judgment about it
> **assessment** noun

assessor noun someone whose job is to assess the value of something

asset noun 1 a person or thing considered useful: *He will be a great asset to the club* 2 (in plural) The assets of a person or company are all the things they own that could be sold to raise money

assign verb 1 To assign something to someone is to give it to them officially or to make them

responsible for it 2 If someone is assigned to do something, they are officially told to do it

assignment noun a job someone is given to do

assimilate verb 1 If you assimilate ideas or experiences, you learn and understand them 2 When people are assimilated into a group, they become part of it > **assimilation** noun

assist verb To assist someone is to help them do something
> **assistance** noun

assistant noun someone whose job is to help another person in their work

associate verb 1 If you associate one thing with another, you connect the two things in your mind 2 If you associate with a group of people, you spend a lot of time with them ▷ noun 3 Your associates are the people you work with or spend a lot of time with

association noun 1 an organization for people who have similar interests, jobs, or aims 2 Your association with a person or group is the connection or involvement you have with them 3 An association between two things is a link you make in your mind between them: *The place contained associations for her*

assorted adjective Assorted things are different in size and colour: *assorted swimsuits*

assortment noun a group of similar things that are different sizes and colours: *an amazing assortment of old toys*

assume verb 1 If you assume that something is true, you accept it is true even though you have not thought about it: *I assumed that he* _would turn up_ **2** To assume responsibility for something is to put yourself in charge of it

assumption noun **1** a belief that something is true, without thinking about it **2** Assumption of power or responsibility is the taking of it

assurance noun **1** something said which is intended to make people less worried: _She was emphatic in her assurances that she wanted to stay_ **2** Assurance is a feeling of confidence: _He handled the car with ease and assurance_ **3** Life assurance is a type of insurance that pays money to your dependants when you die

assure verb If you assure someone that something is true, you tell them it is true

asterisk noun the symbol (*) used in printing and writing

astern adverb, adjective (Nautical) backwards or at the back

asteroid noun one of the large number of very small planets that move around the sun between the orbits of Jupiter and Mars

asthma [ass-ma] noun a disease of the chest which causes wheezing and difficulty in breathing
> **asthmatic** adjective

astonish verb If something astonishes you, it surprises you very much > **astonished** adjective
> **astonishing** adjective
> **astonishingly** adverb
> **astonishment** noun

astound verb If something astounds you, it shocks and amazes you
> **astounded** adjective
> **astounding** adjective

astray phrase **1** To lead someone astray is to influence them to do something wrong **2** If something goes astray, it gets lost: _The money had gone astray_

astride preposition with one leg on either side of something: _He is pictured astride his new motorbike_

astringent [ass-**trin**-jent] noun a liquid that makes skin less greasy and stops bleeding

astrology noun the study of the sun, moon, and stars in order to predict the future > **astrological** adjective
> **astrologer** noun

astronaut noun a person who operates a spacecraft

astronomical adjective **1** involved with or relating to astronomy **2** extremely large in amount: _astronomical legal costs_
> **astronomically** adverb

astronomy noun the scientific study of stars and planets
> **astronomer** noun

astute adjective clever and quick at understanding situations and behaviour: _an astute diplomat_

asunder adverb (literary) If something is torn asunder, it is violently torn apart

asylum [ass-**eye**-lum] noun **1** (old-fashioned) a hospital for psychiatric patients **2** Political asylum is protection given by a government to someone who has fled from their own country for political reasons

asymmetrical [ay-sim-**met**-ri-kl] or **asymmetric** adjective unbalanced or with one half not exactly the same as the other half
> **asymmetry** noun

at preposition **1** used to say where someone or something is: _Bert met us at the airport_ **2** used to mention the direction something is going in: _He threw his plate at the wall_ **3** used to say when something happens: _The game starts at 3 o'clock_ **4** used to mention the rate or price of

A

something: *The shares were priced at fifty pence*

atheist [ayth-ee-ist] *noun* someone who believes there is no God
> **atheistic** *adjective* > **atheism** *noun*

athlete *noun* PE someone who is good at sport and takes part in sporting events

athletic *adjective* **1** strong, healthy, and good at sports **2** involving athletes or athletics: *I lost two years of my athletic career because of injury*

athletics *plural noun* Sporting events such as running, jumping, and throwing are called athletics

Atlantic *noun* The Atlantic is the ocean separating North and South America from Europe and Africa

atlas atlases *noun* GEOGRAPHY a book of maps

atmosphere *noun* **1** SCIENCE GEOGRAPHY the air and other gases that surround a planet; also the air in a particular place: *a musty atmosphere* **2** the general mood of a place: *a relaxed atmosphere* **3** ENGLISH the mood created by the writer of a novel or play
> **atmospheric** *adjective*

atom *noun* the smallest part of an element that can take part in a chemical reaction

atomic *adjective* relating to atoms or to the power released by splitting atoms: *atomic energy*

atomic bomb *noun* an extremely powerful bomb which explodes because of the energy that comes from splitting atoms

atone *verb* (formal) If you atone for something wrong you have done, you say you are sorry and try to make up for it > **atonement** *noun*

atrocious *adjective* extremely bad
> **atrociously** *adverb*

atrocity atrocities *noun* an extremely cruel and shocking act

attach *verb* If you attach something to something else, you join or fasten the two things together

attached *adjective* If you are attached to someone, you are very fond of them

attachment *noun* **1** Attachment to someone is a feeling of love and affection for them **2** Attachment to a cause or ideal is a strong belief in it and support for it **3** a piece of equipment attached to a tool or machine to do a particular job **4** an extra document attached to or included with another document **5** a file that is attached to an e-mail

attack *verb* **1** To attack someone is to use violence against them so as to hurt or kill them **2** If you attack someone or their ideas, you criticize them strongly: *He attacked the government's economic policies* **3** If a disease or chemical attacks something, it damages or destroys it: *fungal diseases that attack crops* **4** In a game such as football or hockey, to attack is to get the ball into a position from which a goal can be scored ▷ *noun* **5** An attack is a violent physical assault against someone **6** An attack on someone or on their ideas is strong criticism of them **7** An attack of an illness is a short time in which you suffer badly with it > **attacker** *noun*

attain *verb* (formal) If you attain something, you manage to achieve it: *He eventually attained the rank of major* > **attainable** *adjective*
> **attainment** *noun*

attempt *verb* **1** If you attempt to do something, you try to do it or achieve it, but may not succeed: *They attempted to escape* ▷ *noun* **2** an act of trying to do something: *He made no attempt to go for the ball*

attend verb **1** If you attend an event, you are present at it **2** To attend school, church, or hospital is to go there regularly **3** If you attend to something, you deal with it: *We have business to attend to first*
> **attendance** noun

attendant noun someone whose job it is to serve people in a place such as a garage or cloakroom

attention noun Attention is the thought or care you give to something: *The woman needed medical attention*

attentive adjective paying close attention to something: *an attentive audience* > **attentively** adverb
> **attentiveness** noun

attest verb (formal) To attest something is to show or declare it is true > **attestation** noun

attic noun a room at the top of a house immediately below the roof

attire noun (formal) Attire is clothing: *We will be wearing traditional wedding attire*

attitude noun Your attitude to someone or something is the way you think about them and behave towards them

attorney [at-**turn**-ee] noun In America, an attorney is the same as a lawyer

attract verb **1** If something attracts people, it interests them and makes them want to go to it: *The trials have attracted many leading riders* **2** If someone attracts you, you like and admire them: *He was attracted to her outgoing personality* **3** If something attracts support or publicity, it gets it **4** [SCIENCE] If something attracts objects to it, it has a force that pulls them towards it

attraction noun **1** Attraction is a feeling of liking someone or something very much **2** something people visit for interest or pleasure: *The temple is a major tourist attraction* **3** a quality that attracts someone or something: *the attraction of moving to seaside resorts* **4** [SCIENCE] In physics, attraction is a force that pulls two objects towards each other

attractive adjective **1** interesting and possibly advantageous: *an attractive proposition* **2** pleasant to look at or be with: *an attractive woman; an attractive personality*
> **attractively** adverb
> **attractiveness** noun

attribute verb [a-**trib**-yoot] **1** If you attribute something to a person or thing, you believe it was caused or created by that person or thing: *Water pollution was attributed to the use of fertilizers; a painting attributed to Raphael* ▷ noun [a-**trib**-yoot] **2** a quality or feature someone or something has > **attribution** noun
> **attributable** adjective

attrition noun **1** Attrition is the constant wearing down of an enemy **2** [GEOGRAPHY] the process by which rocks gradually become smaller and smoother as they rub against one another in moving water

attuned adjective accustomed or well adjusted to something: *His eyes quickly became attuned to the dark*

aubergine [**oh**-ber-jeen] noun a dark purple, pear-shaped fruit that is eaten as a vegetable. It is also called an **eggplant**

auburn adjective Auburn hair is reddish brown

auction noun **1 a** a public sale in which goods are sold to the person who offers the highest price ▷ verb **2** To auction something is to sell it in an auction

auctioneer noun the person in charge of an auction

audacious adjective very daring: an audacious escape from jail
> **audaciously** adverb > **audacity** noun

audible adjective loud enough to be heard: She spoke in a barely audible whisper > **audibly** adverb
> **audibility** noun

audience noun **1** the group of people who are watching or listening to a performance **2** a private or formal meeting with an important person: an audience with the Queen

audio adjective used in recording and reproducing sound: audio equipment

audit verb **1** To audit a set of financial accounts is to examine them officially to check they are correct ▷ noun **2** an official examination of an organization's accounts
> **auditor** noun

audition noun a short performance given by an actor or musician, so that a director can decide whether they are suitable for a part in a play or film or for a place in an orchestra

auditorium auditoriums or auditoria noun the part of a theatre where the audience sits

augment verb (formal) To augment something is to add something to it

August noun the eighth month of the year. August has 31 days

aunt noun Your aunt is the sister of your mother or father, or the wife of one of your parents' siblings

au pair [oh **pair**] noun a young foreign girl who lives with a family to help with the children and housework and sometimes to learn the language

aura noun an atmosphere that surrounds a person or thing: She has a great aura of calmness

aural [rhymes with **floral**] adjective relating to or done through the sense of hearing: an aural comprehension test

auspices [**aw**-spiss-eez] plural noun (formal) If you do something under the auspices of a person or organization, you do it with their support: military intervention under the auspices of the United Nations

auspicious adjective (formal) favourable and seeming to promise success: It was an auspicious start to the month

austere adjective plain and simple, and without luxury: an austere grey office block > **austerity** noun

Australasia [ost-ral-**lay**-sha] noun Australasia consists of Australia, New Zealand, and neighbouring islands in the Pacific
> **Australasian** adjective

Australia noun Australia is the smallest continent and the largest island in the world, situated between the Indian Ocean and the Pacific

Austrian adjective **1** belonging or relating to Austria ▷ noun
2 someone who comes from Austria

authentic adjective real and genuine
> **authentically** adverb
> **authenticity** noun

author noun [ENGLISH] The author of a book is the person who wrote it

authoritarian adjective believing in strict obedience: thirty years of authoritarian government
> **authoritarianism** noun

authoritative adjective **1** having authority: his deep, authoritative voice **2** accepted as being reliable and accurate: an authoritative biography of the President > **authoritatively** adverb

authority authorities noun
1 Authority is the power to control people: *the authority of the state*
2 GEOGRAPHY In Britain, an authority is a local government department: *local health authorities*
3 Someone who is an authority on something knows a lot about it: *the world's leading authority on fashion*
4 (in plural) The authorities are the people who have the power to make decisions

authorize or **authorise** verb To authorize something is to give official permission for it to happen
> **authorization** noun

autobiography autobiographies noun Someone's autobiography is an account of their life which they have written themselves
> **autobiographical** adjective

autograph noun the signature of a famous person

automatic adjective **1** An automatic machine is programmed to perform tasks without needing a person to operate it: *The plane was flying on automatic pilot* **2** Automatic actions or reactions take place without involving conscious thought
3 A process or punishment that is automatic always happens as a direct result of something: *The penalty for murder is an automatic life sentence* > **automatically** adverb

automobile noun In American English, an automobile is a car

autonomous [aw-**ton**-nom-uss] adjective An autonomous country governs itself rather than being controlled by anyone else
> **autonomy** noun

autopsy autopsies noun a medical examination of a dead body to discover the cause of death

autumn noun the season between summer and winter > **autumnal** adjective

auxiliary auxiliaries noun **1** a person employed to help other members of staff: *nursing auxiliaries* ▷ adjective
2 Auxiliary equipment is used when necessary in addition to the main equipment: *Auxiliary fuel tanks were stored in the bomb bay*

avail phrase If something you do is **of no avail** or **to no avail**, it is not successful or helpful

available adjective **1** Something that is available can be obtained: *Artichokes are available in supermarkets* **2** Someone who is available is ready for work or free for people to talk to: *She will no longer be available at weekends* > **availability** noun

avalanche [av-a-lahnsh] noun a huge mass of snow and ice that falls down a mountain side

avant-garde [av-vong-**gard**] adjective extremely modern or experimental, especially in art, literature, or music

avarice noun (formal) greed for money and possessions
> **avaricious** adjective

avenge verb If you avenge something harmful someone has done to you or your family, you punish or harm the other person in return: *He was prepared to avenge the death of his friend* > **avenger** noun

avenue noun a street, especially one with trees along it

average noun **1** MATHS a result obtained by adding several amounts together and then dividing the total by the number of different amounts: *Six pupils were examined in a total of 39 subjects, an average of 6.5 subjects per*

A

pupil ▷ *adjective* **2** Average means standard or normal: *the average American teenager* ▷ *verb* **3** To average a number is to produce that number as an average over a period of time: *Monthly sales averaged more than 110,000* ▷ *phrase* **4** You say **on average** when mentioning what usually happens in a situation: *Men are, on average, taller than women*

averse *adjective* unwilling to do something: *He was averse to taking painkillers*

aversion *noun* If you have an aversion to someone or something, you dislike them very much

avert *verb* **1** If you avert an unpleasant event, you prevent it from happening **2** If you avert your eyes from something, you turn your eyes away from it

aviary aviaries *noun* a large cage or group of cages in which birds are kept

aviation *noun* the science of flying aircraft

aviator *noun* (*old-fashioned*) a pilot of an aircraft

avid *adjective* eager and enthusiastic for something ▷ **avidly** *adverb*

avocado avocados *noun* a pear-shaped fruit, with dark green skin, soft greenish yellow flesh, and a large stone

avoid *verb* **1** If you avoid doing something, you make a deliberate effort not to do it **2** If you avoid someone, you keep away from them ▷ **avoidable** *adjective* ▷ **avoidance** *noun*

avowed *adjective* **1** (*formal*) If you are an avowed supporter or opponent of something, you have declared that you support it or oppose it **2** An avowed belief or aim is one you hold very strongly

avuncular *adjective* friendly and helpful in manner towards younger people, rather like an uncle

await *verb* **1** If you await something, you expect it **2** If something awaits you, it will happen to you in the future

awake awakes, awaking, awoke, awoken *adjective* **1** Someone who is awake is not sleeping ▷ *verb* **2** When you awake, you wake up **3** If you are awoken by something, it wakes you up

awaken *verb* If something awakens an emotion or interest in you, you start to feel this emotion or interest

award *noun* **1** a prize or certificate for doing something well **2** a sum of money an organization gives to students for training or study ▷ *verb* **3** If you award someone something, you give it to them formally or officially

aware *adjective* **1** If you are aware of something, you realize it is there **2** If you are aware of something, you know about it > **awareness** *noun*

awash *adjective, adverb* covered with water: *After the downpour the road was awash*

away *adverb* **1** moving from a place: *I saw them walk away* **2** at a distance from a place: *Our nearest vet is 12 kilometres away* **3** in its proper place: *He put his wallet away* **4** not at home, school, or work: *She had been away from home for years*

awe *noun* (*formal*) a feeling of great respect mixed with amazement and sometimes slight fear

awesome *adjective* **1** Something that is awesome is very impressive and frightening **2** (*informal*) Awesome also means excellent or outstanding

awful *adjective* **1** very unpleasant or

very bad **2** (*informal*) very great:
It took an awful lot of courage
> **awfully** *adverb*

awkward *adjective* **1** clumsy and
uncomfortable: *an awkward gesture*
2 embarrassed or nervous: *He was a
shy, awkward young man* **3** difficult to
deal with: *My lawyer is in an awkward
situation*

awning *noun* a large roof of canvas
or plastic attached to a building or
vehicle

awry [a-**rye**] *adjective* wrong or not
as planned: *Why had their plans gone
so badly awry?*

axe axes, axing, axed *noun* **1** a tool
with a handle and a sharp blade,
used for chopping wood ▷ *verb*
2 To axe something is to end it

axiom *noun* a statement or saying
that is generally accepted to be true
> **axiomatic** *adjective*

axis axes [**ak**-siss] *noun* MATHS **1** an
imaginary line through the centre of
something, around which it moves
2 one of the two sides of a graph

axle *noun* the long bar that connects
a pair of wheels on a vehicle

azure [az-**yoor**] *adjective* (*literary*)
bright blue

b

babble *verb* When someone babbles,
they talk in a confused or excited way

baboon *noun* an African monkey
with a pointed face, large teeth, and
a long tail

baby babies *noun* a child in the first
year or two of its life > **babyhood**
noun > **babyish** *adjective*

bach [**batch**] *noun* **1** In New Zealand,
a small holiday cottage ▷ *verb*
2 (*informal*) In Australian and New
Zealand English, to bach is to live
and keep a house on your own,
especially when you are not used to
it

bachelor *noun* a man who has never
been married

back *adverb* **1** When people or things
move back, they move in the
opposite direction from the one
they are facing **2** When people or
things go back to a place or
situation, they return to it: *She went
back to sleep* **3** If you get something
back, it is returned to you **4** If you do
something back to someone, you do
to them what they have done to
you: *I smiled back at them* **5** Back also
means in the past: *It happened back
in the early eighties* ▷ *noun* **6** the rear
part of your body **7** the part of
something that is behind the front
▷ *adjective* **8** The back parts of
something are the ones near the
rear: *an animal's back legs* ▷ *verb* **9** If a
building backs onto something, its
back faces in that direction **10** When
a car backs, it moves backwards
11 To back a person or organization
means to support or finance that
person or organization > **back
down** *verb* If you back down on a
demand or claim, you withdraw and
give up > **back out** *verb* If you back
out of a promise or commitment,
you decide not to do what you had
promised to do > **back up** *verb* **1** If
you back up a claim or story, you
produce evidence to show that it is
true **2** If you back someone up, you
help and support them

b

backbone noun **1** the column of linked bones along the middle of a person's or animal's back **2** strength of character

backdate verb If an arrangement is backdated, it is valid from a date earlier than the one on which it is completed or signed

backdrop noun the background to a situation or event: *The visit occurred against the backdrop of the political crisis*

backer noun The backers of a project are the people who give it financial help

backfire verb **1** If a plan backfires, it fails **2** When a car backfires, there is a small but noisy explosion in its exhaust pipe

background noun **1** the circumstances which help to explain an event or caused it to happen **2** the kind of home you come from and your education and experience: *a rich background* **3** If sounds are in the background, they are there but no one really pays any attention to them: *She could hear voices in the background*

backing noun support or help: *The project got government backing*

backlash noun a hostile reaction to a new development or a new policy

backlog noun a number of things which have not yet been done, but which need to be done

backpack noun a large bag that hikers or campers carry on their backs

backside noun (informal) the part of your body that you sit on

backward adjective **1** Backward means directed behind you: *without a backward glance* **2** A backward country or society is one that does not have modern industries or technology > **backwardness** noun

backwards adverb **1** Backwards means behind you: *Lucille looked backwards* **2** If you do something backwards, you do the opposite of the usual way: *He instructed them to count backwards*

bacon noun meat from the back or sides of a pig, which has been salted or smoked

bacteria plural noun SCIENCE Bacteria are very tiny organisms which live in air, water, soil, plants, and the bodies of animals. Some bacteria provide food for plants, others cause diseases such as typhoid > **bacterial** adjective

bad worse, worst adjective **1** Anything harmful or upsetting can be described as bad: *I have some bad news; Is the pain bad?* **2** insufficient or of poor quality: *bad roads* **3** evil or immoral in character or behaviour: *a bad person* **4** lacking skill in something: *I was bad at sports* **5** Bad language consists of swearwords **6** If you have a bad temper, you become angry easily > **badness** noun

bade a form of the past tense of **bid**

badge noun a piece of plastic or metal with a design or message on it that you can pin to your clothes

badger noun **1** a wild animal that has a white head with two black stripes on it > verb **2** If you badger someone, you keep asking them questions or pestering them to do something

badly adverb in an inferior or unimpressive way

badminton noun PE Badminton is a game in which two or more players use rackets to hit a shuttlecock over a high net. It was first played at Badminton House in Gloucestershire

baffle verb If something baffles you, you cannot understand or explain it: *The symptoms baffled the doctors* ▷ **baffled** adjective ▷ **baffling** adjective

bag noun **1** a container for carrying things in **2** (in plural, informal) Bags of something is a lot of it: *bags of fun*

baggage noun the suitcases and bags that you take on a journey

baggy baggier, baggiest adjective Baggy clothing hangs loosely

bagpipes plural noun [MUSIC] a musical instrument played by squeezing air out of a leather bag through pipes, on which a tune is played

bail noun **1** Bail is a sum of money paid to a court to allow an accused person to go free until the time of the trial: *He was released on bail* ▷ verb **2** If you bail water from a boat, you scoop it out ▷ **bail out** or **bale out** verb To bail out of an aircraft means to jump out of it with a parachute

bailiff noun **1** a law officer who makes sure that the decisions of a court are obeyed **2** a person employed to look after land or property for the owner

bait noun **1** a small amount of food placed on a hook or in a trap, to attract a fish or wild animal so that it gets caught **2** something used to tempt a person to do something ▷ verb **3** If you bait a hook or trap, you put some food on it to catch a fish or wild animal

bake verb **1** To bake food means to cook it in an oven without using liquid or fat **2** To bake earth or clay means to heat it until it becomes hard

baker noun a person who makes and sells bread and cakes

bakery bakeries noun a building where bread and cakes are baked and sold

bakkie [buck-ee] noun In South African English, a bakkie is a small truck

balance verb **1** When someone or something balances, they remain steady and do not fall over ▷ noun **2** Balance is the state of being upright and steady **3** Balance is also a situation in which all the parts involved have a stable relationship with each other: *the chemical balance of the brain* **4** The balance in someone's bank account is the amount of money in it

balanced adjective A balanced account or report presents information in a fair and objective way

balcony balconies noun **1** a platform on the outside of a building with a wall or railing round it **2** an area of upstairs seats in a theatre or cinema

bald adjective **1** A bald person has little or no hair on their head **2** A bald statement or question is made in the simplest way without any attempt to be polite ▷ **baldly** adverb ▷ **baldness** noun

bale noun **1** a large bundle of something, such as paper or hay, tied tightly ▷ verb **2** If you bale water from a boat, you remove it using a container; also spelt **bail** ▷ **bale out** or **bail out** verb To bale out of an aircraft means to jump out of it with a parachute

balk or **baulk** verb If you balk at something, you object to it and may refuse to do it: *He balked at the cost*

ball noun **1** a round object, especially one used in games such as cricket and soccer **2** The ball of your foot or thumb is the rounded part where your toes join your foot or your thumb joins your hand **3** a large formal social event at which people dance

ballad noun **1** (ENGLISH) A long song or poem which tells a story **2** a slow, romantic pop song

ballast noun any heavy material placed in a ship to make it more stable

ballerina noun a woman ballet dancer

ballet [bal-lay] noun Ballet is a type of artistic dancing based on precise steps

balloon noun **1** a small bag made of thin rubber that you blow into until it becomes larger and rounder **2** a large, strong bag filled with gas or hot air, which travels through the air carrying passengers in a compartment underneath

ballot noun **1** a secret vote in which people select a candidate in an election, or express their opinion about something ▷ verb **2** When a group of people are balloted, they are asked questions to find out what they think about a particular problem or question

ballpoint noun a pen with a small metal ball at the end which transfers the ink onto the paper

ballroom noun a very large room used for dancing or formal balls

balmy balmier, balmiest adjective mild and pleasant: balmy summer evenings

balustrade noun a railing or wall on a balcony or staircase

bamboo noun Bamboo is a tall tropical plant with hard, hollow stems used for making furniture. It is a species of giant grass The young shoots can be eaten

ban bans, banning, banned verb **1** If

something is banned, or if you are banned from doing it or using it, you are not allowed to do it or use it ▷ noun **2** If there is a ban on something, it is not allowed

banal [ba-nahl] adjective very ordinary and not at all interesting: He made some banal remark
> **banality** noun

banana noun a long curved fruit with a yellow skin

band noun **1** a group of musicians who play jazz or pop music together, or a group who play brass instruments together **2** a group of people who share a common purpose: a band of rebels **3** a narrow strip of something used to hold things together or worn as a decoration: an elastic band; a headband > **band together** verb When people band together, they join together for a particular purpose

bandage noun **1** a strip of cloth wrapped round a wound to protect it ▷ verb **2** If you bandage a wound, you tie a bandage round it

bandit noun (old-fashioned) a member of an armed gang who rob travellers

bandwagon phrase To **jump on the bandwagon** means to become involved in something because it is fashionable or likely to be successful

bandwidth noun The bandwidth of a telecommunications signal is the range of frequencies used to transmit it

bandy bandies, bandying, bandied verb If a name is bandied about, many people mention it about

bane noun (literary) Someone or something that is the bane of a person or organization causes a lot of trouble for them: the bane of my life

bang verb 1 If you bang something, you hit it or put it somewhere violently, so that it makes a loud noise: *He banged down the receiver* 2 If you bang a part of your body against something, you accidentally bump it ▷ noun 3 a sudden, short, loud noise 4 a hard or painful bump against something

Bangladeshi [bang-glad-**desh**-ee] adjective 1 belonging or relating to Bangladesh ▷ noun 2 someone who comes from Bangladesh

bangle noun an ornamental band worn round someone's wrist or ankle

banish verb 1 To banish someone means to send them into exile 2 To banish something means to get rid of it: *It will be a long time before cancer is banished* ▷ **banishment** noun

banjo banjos or banjoes noun a musical instrument, like a small guitar with a round body

bank noun 1 a business that looks after people's money 2 A bank of something is a store of it kept ready for use: *a blood bank* 3 the raised ground along the edge of a river or lake 4 the sloping side of an area of raised ground ▷ verb 5 When you bank money, you pay it into a bank 6 If you bank on something happening, you expect it and rely on it ▷ **banker** noun ▷ **banking** noun

bank holiday noun a public holiday, when banks are officially closed

banknote noun a piece of paper money

bankrupt adjective 1 People or organizations that go bankrupt do not have enough money to pay their debts ▷ noun 2 someone who has been declared bankrupt ▷ verb 3 To bankrupt someone means to make them bankrupt: *Restoring the house*

nearly bankrupted them ▷ **bankruptcy** noun

banner noun a long strip of cloth with a message or slogan on it

banquet noun a grand formal dinner, often followed by speeches

banter noun Banter is friendly joking and teasing

baptism noun [RE] a ceremony in which someone is baptized

Baptist noun a member of a Protestant church who believe that people should be baptized when they are adults rather than when they are babies

baptize or **baptise** verb When someone is baptized water is sprinkled on them, or they are immersed in water, as a sign that they have become a Christian

bar bars, barring, barred noun 1 a counter or room where alcoholic drinks are served 2 a long, straight piece of metal 3 a piece of something made in a rectangular shape: *a bar of soap* 4 The bars in a piece of music are the many short parts of equal length that the piece is divided into 5 [GEOGRAPHY] In meteorology, a bar is a unit of pressure, equivalent to 100,000 newtons per square metre ▷ verb 6 If you bar a door, you place something across it to stop it being opened 7 If you bar someone's way, you stop them going somewhere by standing in front of them

barb noun a sharp curved point on the end of an arrow or fish-hook

barbarian noun a member of a wild or uncivilized people

barbaric adjective cruel or brutal: *Ban the barbaric sport of fox hunting* ▷ **barbarity** noun

barbecue barbecues, barbecuing, barbecued noun 1 a grill with a charcoal fire on which you cook food, usually outdoors; also an outdoor party where you eat food cooked on a barbecue ▷ *verb* **2** When food is barbecued, it is cooked over a charcoal grill

barbed *adjective* A barbed remark is one that seems straightforward but is really unkind or spiteful

barbed wire *noun* Barbed wire is strong wire with sharp points sticking out of it, used to make fences

barber *noun* a man who cuts men's hair

bar code *noun* a small pattern of numbers and lines on something you buy in a shop, which can be electronically scanned at a checkout to give the price

bard *noun* (*literary*) A bard is a poet. Some people call Shakespeare the Bard

bare barer, barest *adjective* **1** If a part of your body is bare, it is not covered by any clothing **2** If something is bare, it has nothing on top of it or inside it: *bare floorboards; a small bare office* **3** When trees are bare, they have no leaves on them **4** The bare minimum or bare essentials means the very least that is needed: *They were fed the bare minimum* ▷ *verb* **5** If you bare something, you uncover or show it

barefoot *adjective, adverb* not wearing anything on your feet

barely *adverb* only just: *The girl was barely sixteen*

bargain *noun* **1** an agreement in which two people or groups discuss and agree what each will do, pay, or receive in a matter which involves them both **2** something which is sold at a low price and which is good value ▷ *verb* **3** When people bargain

with each other, they discuss and agree terms about what each will do, pay, or receive in a matter which involves both ▷ **bargain for** *verb* If you had not bargained for or on something, you were not prepared for it

barge *noun* **1** a boat with a flat bottom used for carrying heavy loads, especially on canals ▷ *verb* **2** (*informal*) If you barge into a place, you push into it in a rough or rude way

bark *verb* **1** When a dog barks, it makes a short, loud noise, once or several times ▷ *noun* **2** the short, loud noise that a dog makes **3** the tough material that covers the outside of a tree

barley *noun* a cereal that is grown for food and is also used for making beer and whisky

barmy barmier, barmiest *adjective* (*informal*) mad or very foolish

barn *noun* a large farm building used for storing crops or animal food

barometer *noun* an instrument that measures air pressure and shows when the weather is changing

baron *noun* a member of the lowest rank of the nobility > **baronial** *adjective*

baroness *noun* a woman who has the rank of baron, or who is the wife of a baron

barracks *plural noun* a building where soldiers live

barrage *noun* **1** A barrage of questions or complaints is a lot of them all coming at the same time **2** A barrage is continuous artillery fire over a wide area, to prevent the enemy from moving

barrel *noun* **1a** a wooden container with rounded sides and flat ends

2 The barrel of a gun is the long tube through which the bullet is fired

barren adjective **1** Barren land has soil of such poor quality that plants cannot grow on it **2** A barren woman or female animal is not able to have babies ▷ **barrenness** noun

barricade noun **1** a temporary barrier put up to stop people getting past ▷ verb **2** If you barricade yourself inside a room or building, you put something heavy against the door to stop people getting in

barrier noun **1** a fence or wall that prevents people or animals getting from one area to another **2** If something is a barrier, it prevents two people or groups from agreeing or communicating, or prevents something from being achieved: Cost is a major barrier to using the law

barrister noun a lawyer who is qualified to represent people in the higher courts

barrow noun **1** the same as a **wheelbarrow 2** a large cart from which fruit or other goods are sold in the street

barter verb **1** If you barter goods, you exchange them for other goods, rather than selling them for money ▷ noun **2** Barter is the activity of exchanging goods

base noun **1** the lowest part of something, which often supports the rest **2** A place which part of an army, navy, or air force works from **3** SCIENCE In chemistry, a base is any compound that reacts with an acid to form a salt **4** MATHS In mathematics, a base is a system of counting and expressing numbers. The decimal system uses base 10, and the binary system uses base 2 **5** MATHS The base of a triangle is the side that is horizontal **6** MATHS

The base of a trapezoid is either of the parallel sides ▷ verb **7** To base something on something else means to use the second thing as a foundation or starting point of the first: The opera is based on a work by Pushkin **8** If you are based somewhere, you live there or work from there

baseball noun Baseball is a team game played with a bat and a ball, similar to rounders

basement noun a floor of a building built completely or partly below the ground

bases plural noun **1** [bay-seez] the plural of **basis 2** [bay-siz] the plural of **base**

bash (informal) verb **1** If you bash someone or bash into them, you hit them hard ▷ noun **2** A bash is a hard blow ▷ phrase **3** If you **have a bash** at something, you try to do it

bashful adjective shy and easily embarrassed

basic adjective **1** The basic aspects of something are the most necessary ones: the basic necessities of life **2** Something that is basic has only the necessary features without any extras or luxuries: The accommodation is pretty basic ▷ **basically** adverb

basics plural noun The basics of something are the things you need to know or understand: the basics of map-reading

basilica noun an oblong church with a rounded end called an apse

basin noun **1** a round wide container which is open at the top **2** The basin of a river is a bowl of land from which water runs into the river

basis noun **1** The basis of something is the essential main principle from which it can be developed: The same colour theme is used as the basis for several patterns **2** The basis for a belief is the facts that support it: *There is no basis for this assumption*

bask verb If you bask in the sun, you sit or lie in it, enjoying its warmth

basket noun a container made of thin strips of cane woven together

basketball noun Basketball is a game in which two teams try to score goals by throwing a large ball through one of two circular nets suspended high up at each end of the court

bass [rhymes with **lace**] noun MUSIC **1** A bass is a man who sings the lowest part in four-part harmony **2** A bass is also a musical instrument that provides the rhythm and lowest part in the harmonies. A bass may be either a large guitar or a very large member of the violin family: see **double bass**

bass [rhymes with **gas**] noun a type of edible sea fish

bastion noun (literary) something that protects a system or way of life: *The country is the last bastion of communism*

bat bats, batting, batted noun **1** a specially shaped piece of wood with a handle, used for hitting the ball in a game such as cricket or table tennis **2** a small flying animal, active at night, that looks like a mouse with wings **3** In certain sports, when someone is batting, it is their turn to try to hit the ball and score runs

batch noun a group of things of the same kind produced or dealt with together

bated phrase With bated breath means very anxiously

bath noun a long container that you fill with water and sit in to wash yourself

bathe verb **1** When you bathe, you swim or play in open water **2** When you bathe a wound, you wash it gently **3** (literary) If a place is bathed in light, a lot of light reaches it: *The room was bathed in spring sunshine* > **bather** noun > **bathing** noun

bathroom noun a room with a bath or shower, a washbasin, and often a toilet in it

baton noun **1** a light, thin stick that a conductor uses to direct an orchestra or choir **2** In athletics, the baton is a short stick passed from one runner to another in a relay race **3** A baton is also a short stick used by policemen in some countries as a weapon, lighter than a truncheon

batsman batsmen noun In cricket, the batsman is the person who is batting

battalion noun an army unit consisting of three or more companies

batten noun a strip of wood that is fixed to something to strengthen it or hold it firm > **batten down** verb If you batten something down, you make it secure by fixing battens across it

batter verb **1** To batter someone or something means to hit them many times: *The waves kept battering the life raft* ▷ noun **2** Batter is a mixture of flour, eggs, and milk, used to make pancakes, or to coat food before frying it > **battering** noun

battery batteries noun **1** a device, containing two or more cells, for storing and producing electricity, for example in a torch or a car **2** a large group of things or people ▷ adjective **3** A battery hen is one of a large number of hens kept in small cages for the mass production of eggs

battle noun **1** HISTORY A fight between armed forces or a struggle between two people or groups within society: *the battle between town and country* **2** A battle for something difficult is a determined attempt to obtain or achieve it: *the battle for equality*

battlefield noun a place where a battle is or has been fought

battleship noun a large, heavily armoured warship

batty battier, battiest adjective (informal) crazy or eccentric

bauble noun a pretty but cheap ornament or piece of jewellery

baulk another spelling of **balk**

bawl verb **1** (informal) To bawl at someone means to shout at them loudly and harshly **2** When a child is bawling, it is crying very loudly and angrily

bay noun **1** a part of a coastline where the land curves inwards **2** a space or area used for a particular purpose: *a loading bay* **3** Bay is a kind of tree similar to the laurel, with leaves used for flavouring in cooking ▷ phrase **4** If you **keep something at bay**, you prevent it from reaching you: *Eating oranges keeps colds at bay* ▷ verb **5** When a hound or wolf bays, it makes a deep howling noise

bayonet noun a sharp blade that can be fixed to the end of a rifle and used for stabbing

bazaar noun **1** an area with many small shops and stalls, especially in Eastern countries **2** a sale to raise money for charity

BC BC means 'before Christ'. You use 'BC' in dates to indicate the number of years before the birth of Jesus Christ: *in 49 BC*

be am, is, are; being; was, were; been auxiliary verb **1** 'Be' is used with a present participle to form the continuous tense: *Crimes of violence are increasing* **2** 'Be' is also used to say that something will happen: *We are going to America next month* **3** 'Be' is used to form the passive voice: *The walls were being repaired* ▷ verb **4** 'Be' is used to give more information about the subject of a sentence: *Her name is Melanie*

beach noun an area of sand or pebbles beside the sea

beacon noun In the past, a beacon was a light or fire on a hill, which acted as a signal or warning

bead noun **1** Beads are small pieces of coloured glass or wood with a hole through the middle, strung together to make necklaces **2** Beads of liquid are drops of it

beady beadier, beadiest adjective Beady eyes are small and bright like beads

beagle noun A beagle is a short-haired dog with long ears and short legs. Beagles are kept as pets or used for hunting hares

beak noun A bird's beak is the hard part of its mouth that sticks out

beam noun **1** a broad smile **2** A beam of light is a band of light that shines from something such as a torch **3** a long, thick bar of wood or metal, especially one that supports a roof ▷ verb **4** If you beam, you smile because you are happy

bean noun Beans are the seeds or pods of a climbing plant, which are eaten as a vegetable; also used of some other seeds, for example the seeds from which coffee is made

bear bears, bearing, bore, borne noun **1** a large, strong wild animal with thick fur and sharp claws ▷ verb **2** (formal) To bear something means to carry it or support its weight: *The ice wasn't thick enough to bear their weight* **3** If something bears a mark or typical feature, it has it: *The room bore all the signs of a violent struggle* **4** If you bear something difficult, you accept it and are able to deal with it: *He bore his last illness with courage* **5** If you can't bear someone or something, you dislike them very much **6** (*formal*) When a plant or tree bears flowers, fruit, or leaves, it produces them > **bearable** *adjective* > **bear out** *verb* To bear someone out or to bear out their story or report means to support what they are saying: *These claims are not borne out by the evidence*

beard *noun* the hair that grows on the lower part of a man's face > **bearded** *adjective*

bearer *noun* The bearer of something is the person who carries or presents it: *the bearer of bad news*

bearing *noun* **1** If something has a bearing on a situation, it is relevant to it **2** the way in which a person moves or stands

beast *noun* **1** (*old-fashioned*) a large wild animal **2** (*informal*) If you call someone a beast, you mean that they are cruel or spiteful

beastly beastlier, beastliest *adjective* (*old-fashioned, informal*) cruel or spiteful

beat beats, beating, beat, beaten *verb* **1** To beat someone or something means to hit them hard and repeatedly: *He threatened to beat her* **2** If you beat someone in a race or game, you defeat them or do better than them **3** When a bird or insect beats its wings, it moves them up and down **4** When your heart is beating, it is pumping blood with a regular rhythm **5** If you beat eggs or butter, you mix them

vigorously using a fork or a whisk > *noun* **6** The beat of your heart is its regular pumping action **7** MUSIC The beat of a piece of music is its main rhythm **8** A police officer's beat is the area which he or she patrols > **beat up** *verb* To beat someone up means to hit or kick them repeatedly > **beater** *noun* > **beating** *noun*

beaut (*informal*) *noun* **1** In Australian and New Zealand English, a beaut is an outstanding person or thing > *adjective* **2** In Australian and New Zealand English, beaut means good or excellent: *a beaut house*

beautiful *adjective* very attractive or pleasing: *a beautiful girl; beautiful music* > **beautifully** *adverb*

beauty beauties *noun* **1** Beauty is the quality of being beautiful **2** (*old-fashioned*) a very attractive woman **3** The beauty of an idea or plan is what makes it attractive or worthwhile: *The beauty of the fund is its simplicity*

beaver *noun* an animal with a big, flat tail and webbed hind feet. Beavers build dams

because *conjunction* **1** 'Because' is used with a clause that gives the reason for something: *I went home because I was tired* > *phrase* **2** Because of is used with a noun that gives the reason for something: *He quit playing because of a knee injury*

beck *phrase* If you are at someone's beck and call, you are always available to do what they ask

beckon *verb* **1** If you beckon to someone, you signal with your hand that you want them to come to you **2** If you say that something beckons, you mean that you find it very attractive: *A career in journalism beckons*

become becomes, becoming, became, become verb To become something means to start feeling or being that thing: I became very angry; He became an actor

bed noun 1 a piece of furniture that you lie on when you sleep 2 A bed in a garden is an area of ground in which plants are grown 3 The bed of a sea or river is the ground at the bottom of it

bedding noun Bedding is sheets, blankets, and other covers that are used on beds

bedlam noun You can refer to a noisy and disorderly place or situation as bedlam: The delay caused bedlam at the station

bedraggled adjective A bedraggled person or animal is in a messy or untidy state

bedridden adjective Someone who is bedridden is too ill or disabled to get out of bed

bedrock noun 1 Bedrock is the solid rock under the soil 2 The bedrock of something is the foundation and principles on which it is based: His life was built on the bedrock of integrity

bedroom noun a room used for sleeping in

bedspread noun a cover put over a bed, on top of the sheets and blankets

bee noun a winged insect that makes honey and lives in large groups

beech noun a tree with a smooth grey trunk and shiny leaves

beef noun Beef is the meat of a cow, bull, or ox

beefy beefier, beefiest adjective (informal) A beefy person is strong and muscular

beehive noun a container in which bees live and make their honey

beeline phrase (informal) If you make a beeline for a place, you go there quickly and directly as possible

been the past participle of be

beer noun an alcoholic drink made from malt and flavoured with hops

beetle noun a flying insect that has hard wings which cover its body when it is not flying

beetroot noun A beetroot is the round, dark red root of a type of beet. It is cooked and eaten, especially cold as a salad vegetable or preserved in vinegar

befall befalls, befalling, befell, befallen verb (old-fashioned) If something befalls you, it happens to you: A similar fate befell my cousin

before adverb, preposition, conjunction 1 'Before' is used to refer to a previous time: Apply the ointment before going to bed ▷ adverb 2 If you have done something before, you have done it on a previous occasion: Never before had he seen such poverty ▷ preposition 3 (formal) Before also means in front of: They stopped before a large white villa

beforehand adverb before: It had been agreed beforehand that they would spend the night there

befriend verb If you befriend someone, you act in a friendly and helpful way and so become friends with them

beg begs, begging, begged verb 1 When people beg, they ask for food or money, because they are very poor 2 If you beg someone to do something, you ask them very anxiously to do it

beggar noun someone who lives by asking people for money or food

begin begins, beginning, began, begun verb If you begin to do something, you start doing it. When something begins, it starts

beginner noun someone who has just started learning to do something and cannot do it very well yet

beginning noun The beginning of something is the first part of it or the time when it starts: They had now reached the beginning of the

begrudge verb If you begrudge someone something, you are angry or envious because they have it: No one could begrudge him the glory

behalf phrase To do something on **behalf of** someone or something means to do it for their benefit or as their representative

behave verb 1 If you behave in a particular way, you behave in that way: They were behaving like animals 2 To behave yourself means to act correctly or properly

behaviour noun Your behaviour is the way in which you behave

behead verb To behead someone means to cut their head off

behind preposition 1 at the back of: He was seated behind the desk 2 responsible for or causing: He was the driving force behind the move 3 supporting someone: The whole country was behind him ▷ adverb 4 If you stay behind, you remain after other people have gone 5 If you leave something behind, you do not take it with you

behold beholds, beholding, beheld (literary) verb 1 To behold something means to notice it or look at it ▷ interjection 2 You say 'behold' when you want someone to look at something ▷ **beholder** noun

beige [bayj] noun, adjective pale creamy-brown

being 1 Being is the present participle of **be** ▷ noun 2 Being is the

state or fact of existing: The party came into being in 1923 3 a living creature, either real or imaginary: alien beings from a distant galaxy

belated adjective (formal) A belated action happens later than it should have done: a belated birthday present ▷ **belatedly** adverb

belch verb 1 If you belch, you make a sudden noise in your throat because air has risen up from your stomach 2 If something belches smoke or fire, it sends it out in large amounts: Smoke belched from the steelworks ▷ noun 3 the noise you make when you belch

beleaguered adjective 1 struggling against difficulties or criticism: the beleaguered meat industry 2 besieged by an enemy: the beleaguered garrison

Belgian adjective 1 belonging or relating to Belgium ▷ noun 2 someone who comes from Belgium

belief noun 1 a feeling of certainty that something exists or is true 2 one of the principles of a religion or moral system

believable adjective possible or likely to be the case

believe verb 1 If you believe that something is true, you accept that it is true 2 If you believe someone, you accept that they are telling the truth 3 If you believe in things such as God and miracles, you accept that they exist or happen 4 If you believe in something such as a plan or system, you are in favour of it: They really believe in education ▷ **believer** noun

belittle verb If you belittle someone or something, you make them seem unimportant: He belittled my opinions

bell noun 1 a cup-shaped metal object with a piece inside that swings and hits the sides, producing a ringing sound **2** an electrical device that rings or buzzes in order to attract attention

belligerent adjective aggressive and keen to start a fight or an argument
> **belligerently** adverb
> **belligerence** noun

bellow verb **1** When an animal such as a bull bellows, it makes a loud, deep roaring noise **2** If someone bellows, they shout in a loud, deep voice

belly bellies noun **1** Your belly is your stomach or the front of your body below your chest **2** An animal's belly is the underneath part of its body

belong verb **1** If something belongs to you, it is yours and you own it **2** To belong to a group means to be a member of it **3** If something belongs in a particular place, that is where it should be: *It did not belong in the music room*

belongings plural noun Your belongings are the things that you own

beloved [bil-**luv**-id] adjective A beloved person or thing is one that you feel great affection for

below preposition, adverb **1** If something is below a line or the surface of something else, it is lower down: *six inches below soil level* **2** Below also means at or to a lower point, level, or rate: *The temperature fell below the legal minimum*

belt noun **1** a strip of leather or cloth that you fasten round your waist to hold your trousers or skirt up **2** In a machine, a belt is a circular strip of rubber that drives moving parts or carries objects along **3** a specific area of a country: *Poland's industrial belt* ▷ verb **4** (informal) To belt someone means to hit them very hard

bemused adjective If you are bemused, you are puzzled or confused

bench noun **1** a long seat that two or more people can sit on **2** a long, narrow table for working at, for example in a laboratory

bend bends, bending, bent verb **1** When you bend something, you use force to make it curved or angular **2** When you bend, you move your head and shoulders forwards and downwards ▷ noun **3** a curved part of something

beneath preposition, adjective, adverb **1** an old-fashioned word for **underneath** ▷ preposition **2** If someone thinks something is beneath them, they think that it is too unimportant for them to bother with it

benefactor noun a person who helps to support a person or institution by giving money

beneficial adjective Something that is beneficial is good for people: *the beneficial effects of exercise*
> **beneficially** adverb

beneficiary beneficiaries noun A beneficiary of something is someone who receives money or other benefits from it

benefit noun **1** The benefits of something are the advantages that it brings to people: *the benefits of relaxation* **2** Benefit is money given by the government to people who are unemployed or ill ▷ verb **3** If you benefit from something or something benefits you, it helps you

> **WORD TIP**
> *Benefit* is spelt with two es, not two is

benevolent adjective kind and helpful > **benevolence** noun
> **benevolently** adverb

benign [be-**nine**] *adjective*
1 Someone who is benign is kind and gentle **2** A benign tumour is one that will not cause death or serious illness > **benignly** *adverb*

bent 1 Bent is the past participle and past tense of **bend** ▷ *phrase* **2** If you are **bent on** doing something, you are determined to do it

bequeath *verb (formal)* If someone bequeaths money or property to you, they give it to you in their will, so that it is yours after they have died

bequest *noun (formal)* money or property that has been left to someone in a will

berate *verb (formal)* If you berate someone, you scold them angrily: *He berated them for getting caught*

bereaved *adjective (formal)* You say that someone is bereaved when a close relative of theirs has recently died > **bereavement** *noun*

bereft *adjective (literary)* If you are bereft of something, you no longer have it: *The government seems bereft of ideas*

beret [ber-**ray**] *noun* a circular flat hat with no brim

berry berries *noun* Berries are small, round fruits that grow on bushes or trees

berserk *phrase* If someone **goes berserk**, they lose control of themselves and become very violent

berth *noun* **1** a space in a harbour where a ship stays when it is being loaded or unloaded **2** In a boat or caravan, a berth is a bed

beset *adjective (formal)* If you are beset by difficulties or doubts, you have a lot of them

beside *preposition* If one thing is beside something else, they are next to each other

besiege *verb* **1** When soldiers besiege a place, they surround it and wait for the people inside to surrender **2** If you are besieged by people, many people want something from you and continually bother you

best *adjective, adverb* **1** the superlative of **good** and **well** ▷ *adverb* **2** The thing that you like best is the thing that you prefer to everything else ▷ *noun* **3** the thing most preferred

best man *noun* The best man at a wedding is the man who acts as the bridegroom's attendant

bestow *verb (formal)* If you bestow something on someone, you give it to them

bet bets, betting, bet *verb* **1** If you bet on the result of an event, you will win money if something happens and lose money if it does not ▷ *noun* **2** the act of betting on something, or the amount of money that you agree to risk ▷ *phrase* **3** *(informal)* You say **I bet** to indicate that you are sure that something is or will be so: *I bet the answer is no* > **betting** *noun*

betray *verb* **1** If you betray someone who trusts you, you do something which harms them, such as helping their enemies **2** If you betray your feelings or thoughts, you show them without intending to > **betrayal** *noun* **betrayer** *noun*

better *adjective, adverb* **1** the comparative of **good** and **well** ▷ *adverb* **2** If you like one thing better than another, you like it more than the other thing ▷ *adjective* **3** If you are better after an illness, you are no longer ill

between *preposition, adverb* **1** If something is between two other things, it is situated or happens in the space or time that separates them: *flights between Europe and Asia* **2** A relationship or difference between two people or things involves only those two

beverage noun (formal) a drink

bevy bevies noun a group of people: *a bevy of lawyers*

beware verb If you tell someone to beware of something, you are warning them that it might be dangerous or harmful

bewilder verb If something bewilders you, it is too confusing or difficult for you to understand
> **bewildered** adjective
> **bewildering** adjective
> **bewilderment** noun

bewitch verb **1** To bewitch someone means to cast a spell on them **2** If something bewitches you, you are so attracted to it that you cannot pay attention to anything else
> **bewitched** adjective
> **bewitching** adjective

beyond preposition **1** If something is beyond a certain place, it is on the other side of it: *Beyond the hills was the Sahara* **2** If something continues beyond a particular point, it continues further than that point: *an education beyond the age of 16* **3** If someone or something is beyond understanding or help, they cannot be understood or helped

bias noun Someone who shows bias favours one person or thing unfairly

biased or **biassed** adjective favouring one person or thing unfairly: *biased attitudes*

bib noun a piece of cloth or plastic which is worn under the chin of very young children when they are eating, to keep their clothes clean

Bible noun RE The Bible is the sacred book of the Christian religion

> **biblical** adjective

bicentenary bicentenaries noun The bicentenary of an event is its two-hundredth anniversary

biceps noun PE the large muscle in your upper arms

bicker verb When people bicker, they argue or quarrel about unimportant things

bicycle noun a two-wheeled vehicle which you ride by pushing two pedals with your feet

bid bids, bidding, bade, bidden, bid noun **1** an attempt to obtain or do something: *He made a bid for freedom* **2** an offer to buy something for a certain sum of money ▷ verb **3** If you bid for something, you offer to pay a certain sum of money for it **4** (old-fashioned) If you bid someone a greeting or a farewell, you say it to them

bide bides, biding, bided phrase If you **bide your time**, you wait for a good opportunity before doing something

big bigger, biggest adjective **1** of a large size **2** of great importance
> **biggish** adjective > **bigness** noun

bigot noun someone who has strong and unreasonable opinions which they refuse to change > **bigoted** adjective > **bigotry** noun

bike noun (informal) a bicycle or motorcycle

bikini bikinis noun a small two-piece swimming costume worn by women

bilateral adjective A bilateral agreement is one made between two groups or countries

bile noun Bile is a bitter yellow liquid produced by the liver which helps the digestion of fat. In the Middle Ages, it was believed to cause anger

bilge noun the lowest part of a ship, where dirty water collects

bilingual *adjective* involving or using two languages: *bilingual street signs*

bill *noun* **1** a written statement of how much is owed for goods or services **2** a formal statement of a proposed new law that is discussed and then voted on in Parliament **3** a notice or a poster **4** A bird's bill is its beak

billboard *noun* a large board on which advertisements are displayed

billiards *noun* Billiards is a game played on a large table, with a long, leather-tipped stick called a cue is used to strike one of three balls. The aim is to hit a second ball with the first so that either the third ball is also hit or one of the balls goes into one of the six pockets at the edges of the table

billion *noun* a thousand million. Formerly, a billion was a million million > **billionth** *adjective*

billow *verb* **1** When things made of cloth billow, they swell out and flap slowly in the wind **2** When smoke or cloud billows, it spreads upwards and outwards > *noun* **3** a large wave

bin *noun* a container, especially one that you put rubbish in

binary [by-nar-ee] *adjective* COMPUTING The binary system expresses numbers using only two digits, o and 1

bind binds, binding, bound *verb* **1** If you bind something, you tie rope or string round it so that it is held firmly **2** If something binds you to a course of action, it makes you act in that way: *He was bound by that decision*

binding *adjective* **1** If a promise or agreement is binding, it must be obeyed > *noun* **2** The binding of a book is its cover

binge *noun* (*informal*) a wild bout of drinking or eating too much

bingo *noun* Bingo is a game in which players aim to match the numbers that someone calls out with the numbers on the card that they have been given

binoculars *plural noun* Binoculars are an instrument with lenses for both eyes, which you look through in order to see objects far away

biochemistry *noun* Biochemistry is the study of the chemistry of living things > **biochemical** *adjective* > **biochemist** *noun*

biodegradable *adjective* If something is biodegradable, it can be broken down into its natural elements by the action of bacteria: *biodegradable cleaning products*

biodiversity *noun* the existence of a wide variety of plant and animal species in a particular area

biography biographies *noun* A biography is an account of someone's life, written by someone else. Compare **autobiography** > **biographer** *noun* > **biographical** *adjective*

biology *noun* Biology is the study of living things > **biological** *adjective* > **biologically** *adverb* > **biologist** *noun*

bionic *adjective* having a part of the body that works electronically

biopsy biopsies *noun* an examination under a microscope of tissue from a living body to find out the cause of a disease

birch *noun* a tall deciduous tree with thin branches and thin bark

bird *noun* an animal with two legs, two wings, and feathers

birth *noun* **1** The birth of a baby is when it comes out of its mother's womb at the beginning of its life **2** The birth of something is its beginning: *the birth of modern art*

birthday noun Your birthday is the anniversary of the date on which you were born

biscuit noun a small flat cake made of baked dough

bisexual adjective attracted to both men and women

bishop noun **1** a high-ranking clergyman in some Christian Churches **2** In chess, a bishop is a piece that is moved diagonally across the board

bison noun A bison is a large hairy animal, related to cattle, with a large head and shoulders. Bison used to be very common on the prairies in North America, but they are now almost extinct

bistro bistros [**bee**-stroh] noun a small informal restaurant

bit 1 Bit is the past tense of **bite** ▷ noun **2** A bit of something is a small amount of it: *a bit of coal* ▷ phrase **3** A bit means slightly or to a small extent: *That's a bit tricky*

bitch noun a female dog

bite bites, biting, bit, bitten verb **1** To bite something or someone is to cut it or cut through it with the teeth ▷ noun **2** a small amount that you bite off something with your teeth **3** the injury you get when an animal or insect bites you

bitter adjective **1** If someone is bitter, they feel angry and resentful **2** A bitter disappointment or experience makes people feel angry or unhappy for a long time afterwards **3** In a bitter argument or war, people argue or fight fiercely and angrily: *a bitter power struggle* **4** A bitter wind is an extremely cold wind **5** Something that tastes bitter has a sharp, unpleasant taste > **bitterly** adverb > **bitterness** noun

bizarre [biz-**zahr**] adjective very strange or eccentric

black noun, adjective **1** Black is the darkest possible colour, like tar or soot **2** Someone who is Black is a member of a dark-skinned race **3** Black coffee or tea has no milk or cream added to it **4** Black humour involves jokes about death or suffering > **blackness** noun > **black out** verb If you black out, you lose consciousness

> **WORD TIP**
> When you are writing about a person or people, *Black* should start with a capital letter

blackberry blackberries noun Blackberries are small dark fruits that grow on prickly bushes called brambles

blackboard noun a dark-coloured board in a classroom, which teachers write on using chalk

black box noun A black box is an electronic device in an aircraft which collects and stores information during flights. This information can be used to provide evidence if an accident occurs

blackcurrant noun Blackcurrants are very small dark purple fruits that grow in bunches on bushes

blacken verb To blacken something means to make it black: *The smoke from the chimney blackened the roof*

blacklist noun **1** a list of people or organizations who are thought to be untrustworthy or disloyal ▷ verb **2** When someone is blacklisted, they are put on a blacklist

blackmail verb **1** If someone blackmails another person, they threaten to reveal an unpleasant secret about them unless that person gives them money or does something for them ▷ noun

2 Blackmail is the action of blackmailing people > **blackmailer** noun

black market noun If something is bought or sold on the black market, it is bought or sold illegally

blackout noun If you have a blackout, you lose consciousness for a short time

blacksmith noun a person whose job is making things out of iron, such as horseshoes

bladder noun the part of your body where urine is held until it leaves your body

blade noun **1** The blade of a weapon or cutting tool is the sharp part of it **2** The blades of a propeller are the thin, flat parts that turn round **3** A blade of grass is a single piece of it

blame verb **1** If someone blames you for something bad that has happened, they believe you have caused it > noun **2** The blame for something bad that happens is the responsibility for letting it happen

blameless adjective Someone who is blameless has not done anything wrong

blanch verb If you blanch, you suddenly become very pale

bland adjective tasteless, dull, or boring: a bland diet; bland pop music > **blandly** adverb

blank adjective **1** Something that is blank has nothing on it: a blank sheet of paper **2** If you look blank, your face shows no feeling or interest > noun **3** If your mind is a blank, you cannot think of anything or remember anything

blanket noun **1** a large rectangle of thick cloth that is put on a bed to keep people warm **2** A blanket of something such as snow is a thick covering of it

blare verb To blare means to make a loud, unpleasant noise: The radio blared pop music

blasphemy noun Blasphemy is speech or behaviour that shows disrespect for God or religion > **blasphemous** adjective

blast verb **1** When people blast a hole in something they make a hole with an explosion > noun **2** a big explosion, especially one caused by a bomb **3** a sudden strong rush of wind or air

blatant adjective If you describe something you think is bad as blatant, you mean that rather than hide it, those responsible actually seem to be making it obvious: a blatant disregard for the law

blaze noun **1** a large, hot fire **2** A blaze of light or colour is a great or strong amount of it: a blaze of red **3** A blaze of publicity or attention is a lot of it > verb **4** If something blazes it burns or shines brightly

blazer noun a kind of jacket, often in the colours of a school or sports team

bleach verb **1** To bleach material or hair means to make it white, usually by using a chemical > noun **2** Bleach is a chemical that is used to make material white or to clean thoroughly and kill germs

bleak adjective **1** If a situation is bleak, it is bad and seems unlikely to improve **2** If a place is bleak, it is cold, bare, and exposed to the wind

bleat verb **1** When sheep or goats bleat, they make a high-pitched cry > noun **2** the high-pitched cry that a sheep or goat makes

bleed bleeds, bleeding, bled verb When you bleed, you lose blood as a result of an injury

bleep noun a short high-pitched

sound made by an electrical device such as an alarm

blemish noun a mark that spoils the appearance of something

blend verb **1** When you blend substances, you mix them together to form a single substance **2** When colours or sounds blend, they combine in a pleasing way ▷ noun **3** A blend of things is a mixture of them, especially one that is pleasing **4** a word formed by joining together the beginning and the end of two other words; for example, 'brunch' is a blend of 'breakfast' and 'lunch'

blender noun a machine used for mixing liquids and foods at high speed

bless blesses, blessing, blessed or blest verb When a priest blesses people or things, he or she asks for God's protection for them

blessed [blest] adjective If someone is blessed with a particular quality or skill, they have it: He was blessed with a sense of humour ▷ **blessedly** adverb

blessing noun **1** something good that you are thankful for: Good health is the greatest blessing ▷ phrase **2** If something is done with someone's blessing, they approve of it and support it

blew the past tense of **blow**

blight noun **1** something that damages or spoils other things: the blight of the recession ▷ verb **2** When something is blighted, it is seriously harmed: His life had been blighted by sickness

blind adjective **1** Someone who is blind cannot see **2** If someone is blind to a particular fact, they do not understand it ▷ verb **3** If something blinds you, you become unable to see, either for a short time or permanently ▷ noun **4** a roll of cloth or paper that you pull down over a window to keep out the light ▷ **blindly** adverb ▷ **blindness** noun

blindfold noun **1** a strip of cloth tied over someone's eyes so that they cannot see ▷ verb **2** To blindfold someone means to cover their eyes with a strip of cloth

blinding adjective A blinding light is so bright that it hurts your eyes: There was a blinding flash

blindingly adverb (informal) If something is blindingly obvious, it is very obvious indeed

bling (informal) noun **1** jewellery that looks expensive in a vulgar way ▷ adjective **2** flashy; expensive-looking in a vulgar way

blink verb When you blink, you close your eyes rapidly for a moment. Blinking is an involuntary action that keeps the eyes moist

blinkers plural noun Blinkers are two pieces of leather placed at the side of a horse's eyes so that it can only see straight ahead

bliss noun Bliss is a state of complete happiness ▷ **blissful** adjective ▷ **blissfully** adverb

blister noun **1** a small bubble on your skin containing watery liquid, caused by a burn or rubbing ▷ verb **2** If someone's skin blisters, blisters appear on it as result of burning or rubbing

blistering adjective **1** Blistering heat is very hot **2** A blistering remark expresses great anger or criticism

blitz noun HISTORY **1** a bombing attack by enemy aircraft on a city **2** a sudden intensive attack or concerted effort

blizzard noun a heavy snowstorm with strong winds

bloated adjective Something that is

bloated is much larger than normal, often because there is a lot of liquid or gas inside it

blob noun a small amount of a thick or sticky substance

bloc noun A group of countries or political parties with similar aims acting together is often called a bloc: *the world's largest trading bloc*

block noun **1** A block of flats or offices is a large building containing flats or offices **2** In a town, a block is an area of land with streets on all its sides: *He lives a few blocks down* **3** A block of something is a large rectangular piece of it ▷ verb **4** To block a road or channel means to put something across it so that nothing can get through **5** If something blocks your view, it is in the way and prevents you from seeing what you want to see **6** If someone blocks something, they prevent it from happening: *The council blocked his plans*

blockade noun **1** an action that prevents goods from reaching a place ▷ verb **2** When a place is blockaded, supplies are prevented from reaching it

blockage noun When there is a blockage in a pipe or tunnel, something is clogging it

blog noun (informal) short for weblog: a person's online diary that he or she puts on the internet so that other people can read it

blogger noun (informal) a person who keeps a blog

bloke noun (informal) a man

blonde or **blond** adjective **1** Blonde hair is pale yellow in colour. The spelling 'blond' is used when referring to men ▷ noun **2** A blonde, or blond, is a person with light-coloured hair

blood noun **1** Blood is the red liquid that is pumped by the heart round the bodies of human beings and other mammals ▷ phrase **2** If something cruel is done **in cold blood**, it is done deliberately and without showing any emotion

bloodless adjective **1** If someone's face or skin is bloodless, it is very pale **2** In a bloodless coup or revolution, nobody is killed

blood pressure noun Your blood pressure is a measure of the force with which your blood is being pumped round your body

bloodshed noun When there is bloodshed, people are killed or wounded

bloodshot adjective If a person's eyes are bloodshot, the white parts have become red

bloodstream noun the flow of blood through your body

bloodthirsty adjective Someone who is bloodthirsty enjoys using or watching violence

blood transfusion noun a process in which blood is injected into the body of someone who has lost a lot of blood

blood vessel noun Blood vessels are the narrow tubes in your body through which your blood flows

bloody bloodier, bloodiest adjective, adverb **1** Bloody is a common swearword, used to express anger or annoyance ▷ adjective **2** A bloody event is one in which a lot of people are killed: *a bloody revolution* **3** Bloody also means covered with blood: *a bloody gash on his head*

bloom noun **1** a flower on a plant ▷ verb **2** When a plant blooms, it produces flowers **3** When something like a feeling blooms, it grows:

Romance can bloom where you least expect it

blossom noun **1** Blossom is the growth of flowers that appears on a tree before the fruit ▷ verb **2** When a tree blossoms, it produces blossom

blot blots, blotting, blotted noun **1** a drop of ink that has been spilled on a surface **2** A blot on someone's reputation is a mistake or piece of bad behaviour that spoils their reputation > **blot out** verb To blot something out means to be in front of it and prevent it from being seen: *The smoke blotted out the sky*

blouse noun a light shirt, worn by a girl or a woman

blow blows, blowing, blew, blown verb **1** When the wind blows, the air moves **2** If something blows or is blown somewhere, the wind moves it there **3** If you blow a whistle or horn, you make a sound by blowing into it ▷ noun **4** If you receive a blow, someone or something hits you **5** something that makes you very disappointed or unhappy: *Marc's death was a terrible blow* > **blow up** verb **1** To blow something up means to destroy it with an explosion **2** To blow up a balloon or a tyre means to fill it with air

blubber noun The blubber of animals such as whales and seals is the layer of fat that protects them from the cold

bludgeon verb To bludgeon someone means to hit them several times with a heavy object

blue bluer, bluest; blues adjective, noun **1** Blue is the colour of the sky on a clear, sunny day ▷ phrase **2** If something happens **out of the blue**, it happens suddenly and unexpectedly > **bluish** or > **blueish** adjective

blue-collar adjective Blue-collar workers do physical work as opposed to office work

blueprint noun a plan of how something is expected to work: *the blueprint for successful living*

blues noun The blues is a type of music which is similar to jazz, but is always slow and sad

bluff noun **1** an attempt to make someone wrongly believe that you are in a strong position ▷ verb **2** If you are bluffing, you are trying to make someone believe that you are in a position of strength

blunder verb **1** If you blunder, you make a silly mistake ▷ noun **2** a silly mistake

blunt adjective **1** A blunt object has a rounded point or edge, rather than a sharp one **2** If you are blunt, you say exactly what you think, without trying to be polite

blur blurs, blurring, blurred noun **1** a shape or area which you cannot see clearly because it has no distinct outline or because it is moving very fast ▷ verb **2** To blur the differences between things means to make them no longer clear: *The dreams blurred confusingly with her memories* > **blurred** adjective

blush verb **1** If you blush, your face becomes red, because you are embarrassed or ashamed ▷ noun **2** the red colour on someone's face when they are embarrassed or ashamed

bluster verb **1** When someone blusters, they behave aggressively because they are angry or frightened ▷ noun **2** Bluster is aggressive behaviour by someone who is angry or frightened

blustery adjective Blustery weather is rough and windy

boa noun 1 A boa, or a boa constrictor, is a large snake that kills its prey by coiling round it and crushing it 2 a woman's long thin scarf of feathers or fur

boar noun a male wild pig, or a male domestic pig used for breeding

board noun 1 a long, flat piece of wood 2 the group of people who control a company or organization 3 Board is the meals provided when you stay somewhere: The price includes full board ▷ verb 4 If you board a ship or aircraft, you get on it or in it ▷ phrase 5 If you are on board a ship or aircraft, you are on it or in it

boarder noun a pupil who lives at school during term

boarding school noun a school where the pupils live during the term

boardroom noun a room where the board of a company meets

boast verb 1 If you boast about your possessions or achievements, you talk about them proudly ▷ noun 2 something that you say which shows that you are proud of what you own or have done

boastful adjective tending to brag about things

boat noun a small vehicle for travelling across water

bob bobs, bobbing, bobbed verb 1 When something bobs, it moves up and down ▷ noun 2 a woman's hair style in which her hair is cut level with her chin

bode phrase (literary) If something bodes ill, or bodes well, it makes you think that something bad, or good, will happen

bodice noun the upper part of a dress

bodily adjective 1 relating to the body: bodily contact ▷ adverb 2 involving the whole of someone's body: He was carried bodily up the steps

body bodies noun 1 Your body is either all your physical parts, or just the main part not including your head, arms, and legs 2 a person's dead body 3 the main part of a car or aircraft, not including the engine 4 A body of people is also an organized group

bodyguard noun a person employed to protect someone

bodywork noun the outer part of a motor vehicle

bog noun an area of land which is always wet and spongy

boggle verb If your mind boggles at something, you find it difficult to imagine or understand

bogus adjective not genuine: a bogus doctor

bohemian [boh-**hee**-mee-an] adjective Someone who is bohemian does not behave in the same way as most other people in society, and is usually involved in the arts

boil verb 1 When a hot liquid boils, bubbles appear in it and it starts to give off steam 2 When you boil a kettle, you heat it until the water in it boils 3 When you boil food, you cook it in boiling water ▷ noun 4 a red swelling on your skin

boiler noun a piece of equipment which burns fuel to provide hot water

boiling adjective (informal) very hot

boisterous adjective Someone who is boisterous is noisy and lively

bold adjective 1 confident and not shy or embarrassed: He was not bold enough to ask them 2 not afraid of risk or danger 3 clear and noticeable: bold colours ▷ boldly adverb ▷ boldness noun

bolster verb To bolster something means to support it or make it stronger: *She relied on others to bolster her self-esteem*

bolt noun 1a a metal bar that you slide across a door or window in order to fasten it 2 a metal object which screws into a nut and is used to fasten things together ▷ verb 3 If you bolt a door or window, you fasten it using a bolt. If you bolt things together, you fasten them together using a bolt 4 To bolt means to escape or run away 5 To bolt food means to eat it very quickly

bomb noun 1 a container filled with material that explodes when it hits something or is set off by a timer ▷ verb 2 When a place is bombed, it is attacked with bombs

bombard verb 1 To bombard a place means to attack it with heavy gunfire or bombs 2 If you are bombarded with something you are made to face a great deal of it: *I was bombarded with criticism* > **bombardment** noun

bomber noun an aircraft that drops bombs

bombshell noun a sudden piece of shocking or upsetting news

bona fide [boh-na **fie**-dee] adjective genuine: *We are happy to donate to bona fide charities*

bond noun 1 a close relationship between people 2 (*literary*) Bonds are chains or ropes used to tie a prisoner up 3 a certificate which records that you have lent money to a business and that it will repay you the loan with interest 4 SCIENCE In chemistry, a bond is the means by which atoms or groups of atoms are combined in molecules 5 Bonds are also feelings or obligations that force you to behave in a particular way: *the social bonds of community*

▷ verb 6 When two things bond or are bonded, they become closely linked or attached

bondage noun Bondage is the condition of being someone's slave

bone noun Bones are the hard parts that form the framework of a person's or animal's body > **boneless** adjective

bonfire noun a large fire made outdoors, often to burn rubbish

bonnet noun 1 the metal cover over a car's engine 2 a baby's or woman's hat tied under the chin

bonus noun 1 an amount of money added to your usual pay 2 Something that is a bonus is a good thing that you get in addition to something else: *The view from the hotel was an added bonus*

bony bonier, boniest adjective Bony people or animals are thin, with very little flesh covering their bones

boo noun 1 a shout of disapproval ▷ verb 2 When people boo, they shout 'boo' to show their disapproval

book noun 1 a number of pages held together inside a cover ▷ verb 2 When you book something such as a room, you arrange to have it or use it at a particular time

bookcase noun a piece of furniture with shelves for books

booking noun an arrangement to book something such as a hotel room

booklet noun a small book with a paper cover

bookmaker noun a person who makes a living by taking people's bets and paying them when they win

bookmark noun a piece of card which you put between the pages of a book to mark your place

boom noun 1 a rapid increase in something: *the baby boom* 2 a loud deep echoing sound ▷ verb 3 When something booms, it increases rapidly: *Sales are booming* 4 To boom means to make a loud deep echoing sound

boomerang noun a curved wooden missile that can be thrown so that it returns to the thrower, originally used as a weapon by Australian Aborigines

boon noun Something that is a boon makes life better or easier: *Credit cards have been a boon to shoppers*

boost verb 1 To boost something means to cause it to improve or increase: *The campaign had boosted sales* ▷ noun 2 an improvement or increase: *a boost to the economy* > **booster** noun

boot noun 1 Boots are strong shoes that come up over your ankle and sometimes your calf 2 the covered space in a car, usually at the back, for carrying things in ▷ verb 3 (*informal*) If you boot something, you kick it ▷ phrase 4 To boot means also or in addition: *The story was compelling and well written to boot*

booth noun 1 a small partly enclosed area: *a telephone booth* 2 a stall where you can buy goods

booty noun Booty is valuable things taken from a place, especially by soldiers after a battle

booze (*informal*) noun 1 Booze is alcoholic drink ▷ verb 2 When people booze, they drink alcohol > **boozer** noun > **boozy** adjective

border noun 1 the dividing line between two places or things 2 a strip or band round the edge of something: *plain tiles with a bright border* 3 a long flower bed in a garden ▷ verb 4 To border

something means to form a boundary along the side of it: *Tall poplar trees bordered the fields*

borderline adjective only just acceptable as a member of a class or group: *a borderline case*

bore verb 1 If something bores you, you find it dull and not at all interesting 2 If you bore a hole in something, you make it using a tool such as a drill ▷ noun 3 someone or something that bores you

bored adjective If you are bored, you are impatient because you do not find something interesting or because you have nothing to do

boredom noun a lack of interest

boring adjective dull and lacking interest

born verb 1 When a baby is born, it comes out of its mother's womb at the beginning of its life ▷ adjective 2 You use 'born' to mean that someone has a particular quality from birth: *He was a born pessimist*

borne the past participle of **bear**

borough [*bur-ah*] noun a town, or a district within a large town, that has its own council

borrow verb If you borrow something that belongs to someone else, they let you have it for a period of time > **borrower** noun

> **WORD TIP**
>
> Do not confuse *borrow* and *lend*. If you *borrow* something, you get it from another person for a while; if you *lend* something, someone else gets it from you for a while

Bosnian adjective 1 belonging or relating to Bosnia ▷ noun 2 someone who comes from Bosnia

bosom noun 1 A woman's bosom is her chest ▷ adjective 2 A bosom friend is a very close friend

boss bosses, bossing, bossed noun
1 Someone's boss is the person in charge of the place where they work
▷ verb **2** If someone bosses you around, they keep telling you what to do

bossy bossier, bossiest adjective
A bossy person enjoys telling other people what to do > **bossiness** noun

botany noun Botany is the scientific study of plants > **botanic** or
> **botanical** adjective > **botanist** noun

botch verb (informal) If you botch something, you do it badly or clumsily

both adjective, pronoun 'Both' is used when saying something about two things or people

bother verb **1** If you do not bother to do something, you do not do it because it takes too much effort or it seems unnecessary **2** If something bothers you, you are worried or concerned about it. If you do not bother about it, you are not concerned about it: She is not bothered about money **3** If you bother someone, you interrupt them when they are busy ▷ noun **4** Bother is trouble, fuss, or difficulty
> **bothersome** adjective

bottle noun **1** a glass or plastic container for keeping liquids in
▷ verb **2** To bottle something means to store it in bottles > **bottle up** verb
If you bottle up strong feelings, you do not let yourself think about them

bottleneck noun a narrow section of road where traffic has to slow down or stop

bottom noun **1** The bottom of something is its lowest part **2** Your bottom is your buttocks ▷ adjective **3** The bottom thing in a series of things is the lowest one

> **bottomless** adjective

bought the past tense and past participle of **buy**

> **WORD TIP**
> Do not confuse bought and brought. Bought comes from buy and brought comes from bring

boulder noun a large rounded rock

boulevard [boo-le-vard] noun a wide street in a city, usually with trees along each side

bounce verb **1** When an object bounces, it springs back from something after hitting it **2** To bounce also means to move up and down: Her long black hair bounced as she walked **3** If a cheque bounces, the bank refuses to accept it because there is not enough money in the account

bouncy bouncier, bounciest adjective **1** Someone who is bouncy is lively and enthusiastic
2 Something that is bouncy is capable of bouncing or being bounced on: a bouncy ball; a bouncy castle

bound adjective **1** If you say that something is bound to happen, you mean that it is certain to happen **2** If a person or a vehicle is bound for a place, they are going there **3** If someone is bound by an agreement or regulation, they must obey it ▷ noun **4** a large leap **5** (in plural) Bounds are limits which restrict or control something: Their enthusiasm knew no bounds ▷ phrase **6** If a place is out of bounds, you are forbidden to go there ▷ verb **7** When animals or people bound, they move quickly with large leaps: He bounded up the stairway **8** Bound is also the past tense and past participle of **bind**

boundary boundaries noun something that indicates the

farthest limit of anything: *the city boundary*; *the boundaries of taste*

boundless *adjective* without end or limit: *her boundless energy*

bountiful *adjective* (literary) freely available in large amounts: *a bountiful harvest*

bounty *noun* **1** (literary) Bounty is a generous supply: *autumn's bounty of fruits* **2** Someone's bounty is their generosity in giving a lot of something

bouquet [boo-**kay**] *noun* an attractively arranged bunch of flowers

bourgeois [boor-jhwah] *adjective* typical of fairly rich middle-class people

bourgeoisie [boor-jhwah-**zee**] *noun* the fairly rich middle-class people in a society

bout *noun* **1** If you have a bout of something such as an illness, you have it for a short time: *a bout of flu* **2** If you have a bout of doing something, you do it enthusiastically for a short time **3** a boxing or wrestling match

boutique [boo-**teek**] *noun* a small shop that sells fashionable clothes

bovine *adjective* (technical) relating to cattle

bow [rhymes with **now**] *verb* **1** When you bow, you bend your body or lower your head as a sign of respect or greeting **2** If you bow to something, you give in to it: *He bowed to public pressure* ▷ *noun* **3** the movement you make when you bow **4** the front part of a ship

bow [rhymes with **low**] *noun* **1** a knot with two loops and two loose ends **2** a long thin piece of wood with horsehair stretched along it, which you use to play a violin **3** a long flexible piece of wood used for shooting arrows

bowel [rhymes with **towel**] *noun* Your bowels are the tubes leading from your stomach, through which waste passes before it leaves your body

bowl [rhymes with **mole**] *noun* **1** A bowl is a round container with a wide uncovered top, used for holding liquid or for serving food **2** A bowl is also the hollow, rounded part of something: *a toilet bowl*; *the bowl of his pipe* PE A bowl is a large heavy ball used in the game of bowls or in bowling ▷ *verb* **4** PE In cricket, to bowl means to throw the ball towards the batsman; if a batsman is bowled, or bowled out, his wicket is knocked over by the ball and he is out ▷ **bowler** *noun*

bowling *noun* Bowling is a game in which you roll a heavy ball down a narrow track towards a group of wooden objects called pins and try to knock them down

bowls *noun* Bowls is a game in which the players try to roll large wooden balls as near as possible to a small ball

bow tie [rhymes with **low**] *noun* a man's tie in the form of a bow, often worn at formal occasions

box *noun* **1** a container with a firm base and sides and usually a lid **2** On a form, a box is a rectangular space which you have to fill in **3** In a theatre, a box is a small separate area where a few people can watch the performance together ▷ *verb* **4** To box means to fight someone according to the rules of boxing

boxer *noun* **1** a person who boxes **2** a type of medium-sized, smooth-haired dog with a flat face

boxing *noun* Boxing is a sport in which two people fight using their fists, wearing padded gloves

box office noun the place where tickets are sold in a theatre or cinema

boy noun a male child > **boyhood** noun > **boyish** adjective

boycott verb **1** If you boycott an organization or event, you refuse to have anything to do with it ▷ noun **2** the boycotting of an organization or event: *a boycott of the elections*

boyfriend noun Someone's boyfriend is the man or boy with whom they are having a romantic relationship

bra noun a piece of underwear worn by a woman to support her breasts

braaivleis [bry-flayss] or **braai** braais noun In South African English, a braaivleis is a picnic where meat is cooked on an open fire

brace verb **1** When you brace yourself, you stiffen your body to steady yourself: *The ship lurched and he braced himself* **2** If you brace yourself for something unpleasant, you prepare yourself to deal with it: *The police are braced for violent reprisals* ▷ noun **3** an object fastened to something to straighten or support it: *a neck brace* **4** (in plural) Braces are a pair of straps worn over the shoulders and fastened to the trousers to hold them up

bracelet noun a chain or band worn around someone's wrist as an ornament

bracing adjective Something that is bracing makes you feel fit and full of energy: *the bracing sea air*

bracken noun Bracken is a plant like a large fern that grows on hills and in woods

bracket noun **1** Brackets are a pair of written marks, ( ) or [ ], placed round a word or sentence that is not part of the main text, or to show that the items inside the brackets belong together **2** a range between two limits, for example of ages or prices: *the four-figure price bracket* **3** a piece of metal or wood fastened to a wall to support something such as a shelf

brag brags, bragging, bragged verb When someone brags, they boast about their achievements: *Both leaders bragged they could win by a landslide*

braid noun **1** Braid is a strip of decorated cloth used to decorate clothes or curtains **2** a length of hair which has been plaited and tied ▷ verb **3** To braid hair or thread means to plait it

Braille noun Braille is a system of printing for blind people in which letters are represented by raised dots that can be felt with the fingers. It was invented by the French inventor Louis Braille in the 19th century

brain noun **1** Your brain is the mass of nerve tissue inside your head that controls your body and enables you to think and feel; also used to refer to your mind and to the way that you think: *I admired his legal brain* **2** (in plural) If you say that someone has brains, you mean that they are very intelligent

brainchild noun (informal) Someone's brainchild is something that they have invented or created

brainwash verb If people are brainwashed into believing something, they accept it without question because they are told it repeatedly > **brainwashing** noun

brainwave noun (informal) a clever idea you think of suddenly

brainy brainier, brainiest adjective (informal) clever

braise verb To braise food means to fry it for a short time, then cook it slowly in a little liquid

brake noun **1** a device for making a vehicle stop or slow down ▷ verb **2** When a driver brakes, he or she makes a vehicle stop or slow down by using its brakes

> **WORD TIP**
> Do not confuse the spellings of brake and break, or braking and breaking

bran noun Bran is the ground husks that are left over after flour has been made from wheat grains

branch noun **1** The branches of a tree are the parts that grow out from its trunk **2** A branch of an organization is one of a number of its offices or shops **3** A branch of a subject is one of its areas of study or activity: *specialists in certain branches of medicine* ▷ verb **4** A road that branches off from another road splits off from it to lead in a different direction > **branch out** verb To branch out means to take up an additional pursuit

brand noun **1** A brand of something is a particular kind or make of it: *a popular brand of chocolate* ▷ verb **2** When an animal is branded, a mark is burned on its skin to show who owns it

brandish verb (literary) If you brandish something, you wave it vigorously: *He brandished his sword over his head*

brand-new adjective completely new

brandy noun brandies A strong alcoholic drink, usually made from wine

brash adjective If someone is brash, they are overconfident or rather rude

brass noun, adjective **1** Brass is a yellow-coloured metal made from copper and zinc **2** In an orchestra, the brass section consists of the brass wind instruments such as trumpets and trombones

brat noun (informal) A badly behaved child may be referred to as a brat

bravado [bra-**vah**-doh] noun Bravado is a display of courage intended to impress other people

brave adjective **1** A brave person is willing to do dangerous things and does not show any fear ▷ verb **2** If you brave an unpleasant or dangerous situation, you face up to it in order to do something: *His fans braved the rain to hear him sing* > **bravely** adverb

bravery noun the quality of being courageous

brawl noun **1** a rough fight ▷ verb **2** When people brawl, they take part in a rough fight

brawn noun Brawn is physical strength > **brawny** adjective

brazen adjective When someone's behaviour is brazen, they do not care if other people think they are behaving wrongly > **brazenly** adverb

Brazilian adjective **1** belonging or relating to Brazil ▷ noun **2** someone who comes from Brazil

breach verb **1** (formal) If you breach an agreement or law, you break it **2** To breach a barrier means to make a gap in it: *The river breached its banks* ▷ noun **3** A breach of an agreement or law is an action that breaks it: *a breach of contract* **4** a gap or break

bread noun a food made from flour and water, usually raised with yeast, and baked

breadth noun The breadth of

something is the distance between its two sides

breadwinner noun the person who earns the money in a family

break breaks, breaking, broke, broken verb **1** When an object breaks, it is damaged and separates into pieces **2** If you break a rule or promise you fail to keep it **3** When a boy's voice breaks, it becomes permanently deeper **4** When a wave breaks, it falls and becomes foam ▷ noun **5** a short period during which you rest or do something different > **breakable** adjective > **break down** verb **1** When a machine or a vehicle breaks down, it stops working **2** When a discussion or relationship breaks down, it ends because of problems or disagreements > **break up** verb If something breaks up, it ends: The marriage broke up after a year

> **WORD TIP**
> Do not confuse the spellings of break and brake, or breaking and braking

breakaway adjective A breakaway group is one that has separated from a larger group

breakdown noun **1** The breakdown of something such as a system is its failure: a breakdown in communications **2** is the same as a nervous breakdown **3** If a driver has a breakdown, their car stops working **4** A breakdown of something complex is a summary of its important points: He demanded a breakdown of the costs

breaker noun Breakers are big sea waves

breakfast noun the first meal of the day

break-in noun the illegal entering of a building, especially by a burglar

breakneck adjective (informal) Someone or something that is travelling at breakneck speed is travelling dangerously fast

breakthrough noun a sudden important development: a medical breakthrough

breakwater noun a wall extending into the sea which protects a coast from the force of the waves

bream noun an edible fish

breast noun **1** A woman's breasts are the two soft, fleshy parts on her chest, which secrete milk after she has had a baby **2** (literary or old-fashioned) The human breast is the upper front part of the body, sometimes regarded as the place where emotions are felt: His breast was red with blood

breath noun **1** Your breath is the air you take into your lungs and let out again when you breathe ▷ phrase **2** If you are out of breath, you are breathing with difficulty after doing something energetic **3** If you say something under your breath, you say it in a very quiet voice

breathe verb When you breathe, you take air into your lungs and let out again

breathless adjective If you are breathless, you are breathing fast or with difficulty > **breathlessly** adverb > **breathlessness** noun

breathtaking adjective If you say that something is breathtaking, you mean that it is very beautiful or exciting

bred the past tense and past participle of **breed**

breeches [brit-chiz] plural noun Breeches are trousers reaching to just below the knee, nowadays worn especially for riding

breed breeds, breeding, bred noun

1 A breed of a species of domestic animal is a particular type of it ▷ *verb* **2** Someone who breeds animals or plants keeps them in order to produce more animals or plants with particular qualities **3** When animals breed, they mate and produce offspring

breeze *noun* a gentle wind

brevity *noun* (*formal*) Brevity means shortness: *the brevity of his report*

brew *verb* **1** If you brew tea or coffee, you make it in a pot by pouring hot water over it **2** To brew beer means to make it, by boiling and fermenting malt **3** If an unpleasant situation is brewing, it is about to happen: *Another scandal is brewing* > **brewer** *noun*

brewery *noun* breweries *noun* a place where beer is made, or a company that makes it

bribe *noun* **1** a gift or money given to an official to persuade them to make a favourable decision ▷ *verb* **2** To bribe someone means to give them a bribe > **bribery** *noun*

bric-a-brac *noun* Bric-a-brac consists of small ornaments or pieces of furniture of no great value

brick *noun* Bricks are rectangular blocks of baked clay used in building

bricklayer *noun* a person whose job is to build with bricks

bride *noun* a woman who is getting married or who has just got married > **bridal** *adjective*

bridegroom *noun* a man who is getting married or who has just got married

bridesmaid *noun* a woman who helps and accompanies a bride on her wedding day

bridge *noun* **1** a structure built over a river, road, or railway so that vehicles and people can cross **2** the platform from which a ship is steered and controlled **3** the hard ridge at the top of your nose **4** Bridge is a card game for four players based on whist

bridle *noun* a set of straps round a horse's head and mouth, which the rider uses to control the horse

brief *adjective* **1** Something that is brief lasts only a short time ▷ *verb* **2** [D G T] When you brief someone on a task, you give them all the necessary instructions and information about it > **briefly** *adverb*

briefcase *noun* a small flat case for carrying papers

briefing *noun* a meeting at which information and instructions are given

brigade *noun* an army unit consisting of three battalions

brigadier [brig-ad-**ear**] *noun* an army officer of the rank immediately above colonel

bright *adjective* **1** strong and startling: *a bright light* **2** clever: *my brightest student* **3** cheerful: *a bright smile* > **brightly** *adverb* > **brightness** *noun*

brighten *verb* **1** If something brightens, it becomes brighter: *The weather had brightened* **2** If someone brightens, they suddenly look happier > **brighten up** *verb* To brighten something up means to make it more attractive and cheerful

brilliant *adjective* **1** A brilliant light or colour is extremely bright **2** A brilliant person is extremely clever **3** A brilliant career is extremely successful > **brilliantly** *adverb* > **brilliance** *noun*

brim *noun* **1** the wide part of a hat is the part that sticks outwards at the bottom ▷ **phrase 2** If a container is filled **to the brim**, it is filled right to the top

brine noun Brine is salt water

bring brings, bringing, brought verb **1** If you bring something or someone with you when you go to a place, you take them with you: *You can bring a friend to the party* **2** To bring something to a particular state means to cause it to be like that: *Bring the vegetables to the boil* ▷ **bring about** verb To bring something about means to cause it to happen: *We must try to bring about a better world* ▷ **bring off** verb If you bring off something difficult, you succeed in doing it ▷ **bring out** verb **1** To succeed in bringing out a new product means to produce it and offer it for sale **2** If something brings out a particular kind of behaviour, it causes it to occur: *Sunny days seem to bring out the best in us* ▷ **bring up** verb **1** To bring up children means to look after them while they grow up **2** If you bring up a subject, you introduce it into the conversation: *She brought up the subject at dinner*

brink noun If you are on the brink of something, you are just about to do it or experience it

brisk adjective **1** A brisk action is done quickly and energetically: *A brisk walk restores your energy* **2** If someone's manner is brisk, it shows that they want to get things done quickly and efficiently ▷ **briskly** adverb ▷ **briskness** noun

bristle noun **1** Bristles are strong animal hairs used to make brushes ▷ **verb 2** If the hairs on an animal's body bristle, they rise up, because it is frightened ▷ **bristly** adjective

British adjective belonging or relating to the United Kingdom of Great Britain and Northern Ireland

Briton noun someone who comes from the United Kingdom of Great Britain and Northern Ireland

brittle adjective An object that is brittle is hard but breaks easily

broach verb When you broach a subject, you introduce it into a discussion

broad adjective **1** wide: *a broad smile* **2** having many different aspects or concerning many different people: *A broad range of issues was discussed* **3** general rather than detailed: *the broad concerns of the movement* **4** If someone has a broad accent, the way that they speak makes it very clear where they come from: *She spoke in a broad Irish accent*

broadband noun Broadband is a digital system used on the internet and in other forms of telecommunication which can process and transfer information input from various sources, such as from telephones, computers, or televisions

broadcast broadcasts, broadcasting, broadcast noun **1** a programme or announcement on radio or television ▷ **verb 2** To broadcast something means to send it out by radio waves, so that it can be seen on television or heard on radio ▷ **broadcaster** noun ▷ **broadcasting** noun

broaden verb **1** When something broadens, it becomes wider: *His smile broadened* **2** To broaden something means to cause it to involve more things or concern more people: *We must broaden the scope of this job*

broadly adverb true to a large extent or in most cases: *There are broadly two schools of thought on this*

broadsheet noun a newspaper with large pages and long news stories

brocade noun Brocade is a heavy, expensive material, often made of silk, with a raised pattern

broccoli noun Broccoli is a green vegetable, similar to cauliflower

brochure [broh-sher] noun a booklet which gives information about a product or service

broke 1 the past tense of **break** ▷ adjective 2 (informal) If you are broke, you have no money

broken 1 the past participle of **break** ▷ adjective 2 in pieces 3 not kept

broker noun a person whose job is to buy and sell shares for other people

bronchitis noun Bronchitis is an illness in which the two tubes which connect your windpipe to your lungs become infected, making you cough

bronze noun Bronze is a yellowish-brown metal which is a mixture of copper and tin; also the yellowish-brown colour of this metal

brooch [rhymes with **coach**] noun a piece of jewellery with a pin at the back for attaching to clothes

brood noun 1 a family of baby birds ▷ verb 2 If you brood about something, you keep thinking about it in a serious or unhappy way

brook noun a stream

broom noun 1 a long-handled brush 2 Broom is a shrub with yellow flowers

broth noun Broth is soup, usually with vegetables in it

brother noun Your brother is a boy or man who has the same parents as you > **brotherly** adjective

brotherhood noun 1 Brotherhood is the affection and loyalty that brothers or close male friends feel for each other 2 a group of men with common interests or beliefs

brother-in-law brothers-in-law noun Someone's brother-in-law is the brother of their husband or wife, or their sibling's husband

brought the past tense and past participle of **bring**

> **WORD TIP**
> Do not confuse *brought* and *bought*. *Brought* comes from *bring* and *bought* comes from *buy*

brow noun 1 Your brow is your forehead 2 Your brows are your eyebrows 3 The brow of a hill is the top of it

brown adjective, noun Brown is the colour of earth or wood

browse verb 1 If you browse through a book, you look through it in a casual way 2 If you browse in a shop, you look at the things in it for interest rather than because you want to buy something

browser noun a piece of computer software that lets you look at websites on the World Wide Web

bruise noun 1 a purple mark that appears on your skin after something has hit it ▷ verb 2 If something bruises you, it hits you so that a bruise appears on your skin

brumby brumbies noun In Australia and New Zealand, a wild horse

brunette noun a girl or woman with dark brown hair

brunt phrase If you **bear the brunt** of something unpleasant, you are the person who suffers most: *Women bear the brunt of crime*

brush noun 1 an object with bristles which you use for cleaning things, painting, or tidying your hair ▷ verb 2 If you brush something, you clean it or tidy it with a brush 3 To brush against something means to touch it while passing it: *Her lips brushed his cheek* ▷ **brush up** *verb* If you brush up on a subject, you improve your knowledge of it: *They need to brush up their French*

brusque [**broosk**] *adjective* Someone who is brusque deals with people quickly and without considering their feelings ▷ **brusquely** *adverb* ▷ **brusqueness** *noun*

brussels sprout *noun* Brussels sprouts are vegetables that look like tiny cabbages

brutal *adjective* Brutal behaviour is cruel and violent: *the victim of a brutal murder* ▷ **brutally** *adverb* ▷ **brutality** *noun*

brute *noun* **1** a rough and insensitive man ▷ *adjective* **2** Brute force is strength alone, without any skill: *You have to use brute force to open the gates* ▷ **brutish** *adjective*

bubble *noun* **1** a ball of air in a liquid **2** a hollow, delicate ball of soapy liquid ▷ *verb* **3** When a liquid bubbles, bubbles form in it **4** If you are bubbling with something like excitement, you are full of it ▷ **bubbly** *adjective*

bucket *noun* a deep round container with an open top and a handle

buckle *noun* **1** a fastening on the end of a belt or strap ▷ *verb* **2** If you buckle a belt or strap, you fasten it **3** If something buckles, it becomes bent because of severe heat or pressure

bud buds, budding, budded *noun* **1** a small, tight swelling on a tree or plant, which develops into a flower or a cluster of leaves ▷ *verb* **2** When a tree or plant buds, new buds appear on it

Buddha *proper noun* RE The Buddha is the title of Gautama Siddhartha, a religious teacher living in the 6th century BC in India and founder of Buddhism. Buddha means 'the enlightened one'

Buddhism *noun* RE an Eastern religion which teaches that the way to end suffering is by overcoming your desires. It was founded in the 6th century BC by the Buddha (a title meaning 'the enlightened one'), Gautama Siddhartha, a nobleman and religious teacher of northern India ▷ **Buddhist** *noun*, *adjective*

budding *adjective* just beginning to develop: *a budding artist*

budge *verb* If something will not budge, you cannot move it

budgerigar *noun* A budgerigar is a small brightly coloured pet bird. Budgerigars originated in Australia

budget *noun* **1** a plan showing how much money will be available and how it will be spent ▷ *verb* **2** If you budget for something, you plan your money carefully, so that you are able to afford it ▷ **budgetary** *adjective*

budgie *noun* (*informal*) a budgerigar

buff *adjective* **1** a pale brown colour ▷ *noun* **2** (*informal*) someone who knows a lot about a subject: *a film buff*

buffalo buffaloes *noun* a wild animal like a large cow with long curved horns

buffer *noun* **1** Buffers on a train or at the end of a railway line are metal discs on springs that reduce shock when they are hit **2** something that prevents something else from being harmed: *keep savings as a buffer against unexpected cash needs*

buffet [**boof**-ay] *noun* **1** a café at a station **2** a meal at which people serve themselves

buffet [buff-it] *verb* If the wind or sea buffets a place or person, it strikes them violently and repeatedly

bug bugs, bugging, bugged *noun* **1** an insect, especially one that causes damage **2** a small error in a computer program which means that the program will not work properly **3** (*informal*) a virus or minor infection: *a stomach bug* ▷ *verb* **4** If a place is bugged, tiny microphones are hidden there to pick up what people are saying

bugle *noun* MUSIC a brass musical instrument that looks like a small trumpet ▷ **bugler** *noun*

build builds, building, built *verb* **1** To build something such as a house means to make it from its parts **2** To build something such as an organization means to develop it gradually ▷ *noun* **3** Your build is the shape and size of your body ▷ **builder** *noun*

building *noun* a structure with walls and a roof

building society *noun* a business in which some people invest their money, while others borrow from it to buy a house

bulb *noun* **1** the glass part of an electric lamp **2** an onion-shaped root that grows into a flower or plant

Bulgarian *adjective* belonging or relating to Bulgaria ▷ *noun* **2** someone who comes from Bulgaria **3** the main language spoken in Bulgaria

bulge *verb* **1** If something bulges, it swells out from a surface ▷ *noun* **2** a lump in a normally flat surface

bulk *noun* **1** a large mass of something: *The book is more impressive for its bulk than its content* **2** The bulk of something is most of it: *the bulk of the world's great poetry* ▷ *noun* **3** To buy something in bulk means to buy it in large quantities

bulky bulkier, bulkiest *adjective* large and heavy: *a bulky package*

bull *noun* the male of some species of animals, including the cow family, elephants, and whales

bulldog *noun* a squat dog with a broad head and muscular body

bulldozer *noun* a powerful tractor with a broad blade in front, which is used for moving earth or knocking things down

bullet *noun* a small piece of metal fired from a gun

bulletin *noun* **1** a short news report on radio or television **2** a leaflet or small newspaper regularly produced by a group or organization

bullion *noun* Bullion is gold or silver in the form of bars

bully bullies, bullying, bullied *noun* **1** someone who uses their strength or power to hurt or frighten other people ▷ *verb* **2** If you bully someone, you frighten or hurt them deliberately **3** If someone bullies you into doing something, they make you do it by using force or threats

bump *verb* **1** If you bump or bump into something, you knock it with a jolt ▷ *noun* **2** a soft or dull noise made by something knocking into something else **3** a raised, uneven part of a surface ▷ **bumpy** *adjective* ▷ **bump off** *verb* (*informal*) To bump off someone means to kill them

bumper *noun* **1** Bumpers are bars on the front and back of a vehicle which protect it if there is a collision ▷ *adjective* **2** A bumper crop or harvest is larger than usual

bun *noun* a small, round cake

bunch noun **1** a group of people **2** a number of flowers held or tied together **3** a group of things **4** a group of bananas or grapes growing on the same stem ▷ verb **5** When people bunch together or bunch up, they stay very close to each other

bundle noun **1** a number of things tied together or wrapped up in a cloth ▷ verb **2** If you bundle someone or something somewhere, you push them there quickly and roughly

bung noun **1** a stopper used to close a hole in something such as a barrel ▷ verb **2** (informal) If you bung something somewhere, you put it there quickly and carelessly

bungalow noun a one-storey house

bungle verb To bungle something means to fail to do it properly

bunk noun a bed fixed to a wall in a ship or caravan

bunker noun **1** On a golf course, a bunker is a large hole filled with sand **2** A coal bunker is a storage place for coal **3** an underground shelter with strong walls to protect it from bombing

bunting noun Bunting is strips of small coloured flags displayed on streets and buildings on special occasions

buoy [boy] noun a floating object anchored to the bottom of the sea, marking a channel or warning of danger

buoyant adjective **1** able to float **2** lively and cheerful: She was in a buoyant mood ▷ **buoyancy** noun

burden noun **1** a heavy load **2** If something is a burden to you, it causes you a lot of worry or hard work ▷ **burdensome** adjective

bureau bureaux [byoo-roh] noun **1** an office that provides a service: an employment bureau **2** a writing desk with shelves and drawers

bureaucracy noun Bureaucracy is the complex system of rules and procedures which operates in government departments > **bureaucratic** adjective

bureaucrat noun a person who works in a government department, especially one who follows rules and procedures strictly

burgeoning adjective growing or developing rapidly: a burgeoning political crisis

burglar noun a thief who breaks into a building > **burglary** noun

burgle verb If your house is burgled, someone breaks into it and steals things

burial noun [RE] a ceremony held when a dead person is buried

burly burlier, burliest adjective A burly man has a broad body and strong muscles

burn burns, burning, burned or burnt verb **1** If something is burning, it is on fire **2** To burn something means to destroy it with fire **3** If you burn yourself or are burned, you are injured by fire or by something hot ▷ noun **4** an injury caused by fire or by something hot

> **WORD TIP**
> You can write either burned or burnt as the past form of burn

burrow noun **1** a tunnel or hole in the ground dug by a small animal ▷ verb **2** When an animal burrows, it digs a burrow

bursary bursaries noun a sum of money given to someone to help fund their education

burst bursts, bursting, burst verb **1** When something bursts, it splits open because of pressure from inside it **2** If you burst into a room, you enter it suddenly **3** To burst means to happen or come suddenly and with force: *The aircraft burst into flames* **4** (*informal*) If you are bursting with something, you find it difficult to keep it to yourself: *We were bursting with joy* ▷ noun **5** A burst of something is a short period of it: *He had a sudden burst of energy*

bury buries, burying, buried *verb*
1 When a dead person is buried, their body is put into a grave and covered with earth **2** To bury something means to put it in a hole in the ground and cover it up **3** If something is buried under something, it is covered by it: *My bag was buried under a pile of old newspapers*

bus noun a large motor vehicle that carries passengers

bush noun **1** a thick plant with many stems branching out from ground level **2** In Australia and South Africa, an area of land in its natural state outside of city areas is called the bush In New Zealand, the bush is land covered with rain forest

bushman bushmen *noun*
1 In Australia and New Zealand, someone who lives or travels in the bush **2** In New Zealand a bushman is also someone whose job it is to clear the bush for farming

Bushman Bushmen *noun* A Bushman is a member of a group of people in southern Africa who live by hunting and gathering food

bushranger noun In Australia and New Zealand in the past, an outlaw living in the bush

bushy bushier, bushiest *adjective* Bushy hair or fur grows very thickly: *bushy eyebrows*

business noun **1** Business is work relating to the buying and selling of

goods and services **2** an organization which produces or sells goods or provides a service **3** You can refer to any event, situation, or activity as a business: *This whole business has upset me*
▷ **businessman** noun
▷ **businesswoman** noun

businesslike adjective dealing with things in an efficient way

busker noun someone who plays music or sings for money in public places

bust busts, busting, bust or busted noun **1** a statue of someone's head and shoulders: *a bust of Beethoven* **2** A woman's bust is her chest and her breasts ▷ verb **3** (*informal*) If you bust something, you break it ▷ adjective **4** (*informal*) If a business goes bust, it becomes bankrupt and closes down

bustle verb **1** When people bustle, they move in a busy, hurried way ▷ noun **2** Bustle is busy, noisy activity

busy busier, busiest; busies, busying, busied *adjective* **1** If you are busy, you are in the middle of doing something **2** A busy place is full of people doing things or moving about: *a busy seaside resort* ▷ verb **3** If you busy yourself with something, you occupy yourself by doing it
▷ **busily** adverb

but conjunction **1** used to introduce an idea that is opposite to what has gone before: *I don't miss teaching but I miss the pupils* **2** used when apologizing: *I'm sorry, but I can't come tonight* **3** except: *We can't do anything but wait*

butcher noun a shopkeeper who sells meat

butler noun the chief male servant in a rich household

butt noun **1** The butt of a weapon is the thick end of its handle **2** If you are the butt of teasing, you are the target of it ▷ verb **3** If you butt something, you ram it with your head > **butt in** verb If you butt in, you join in a private conversation or activity without being asked to

butter noun **1** Butter is a soft fatty food made from cream, which is spread on bread and used in cooking ▷ verb **2** To butter bread means to spread butter on it

butterfly butterflies noun a type of insect with large colourful wings

buttocks plural noun Your buttocks are the part of your body that you sit on

button noun **1** Buttons are small, hard objects sewn on to clothing, and used to fasten two surfaces together **2** a small object on a piece of equipment that you press to make it work ▷ verb **3** If you button a piece of clothing, you fasten it using its buttons

buxom adjective A buxom woman is large, healthy, and attractive

buy buys, buying, bought verb If you buy something, you obtain it by paying money for it > **buyer** noun

buzz verb **1** If something buzzes, it makes a humming sound, like a bee ▷ noun **2** the sound something makes when it buzzes

buzzer noun a device that makes a buzzing sound, to attract attention

by preposition **1** used to indicate who or what has done something: The statement was issued by his solicitor **2** used to indicate how something is done: He frightened her by hiding behind the door **3** located next to: I sat by her bed **4** before a particular time: It should be ready by next spring ▷ preposition, adverb **5** going past:

We drove by his house

by-election noun an election held to choose a new member of parliament after the previous member has resigned or died

bygone adjective (literary) happening or existing a long time ago: the ceremonies of a bygone era

bypass noun a main road which takes traffic round a town rather than through it

bystander noun someone who is not included or involved in something but is there to see it happen

byte noun COMPUTING a unit of storage in a computer

C

cab noun **1** a taxi **2** In a lorry, bus, or train, the cab is where the driver sits

cabaret [kab-bar-ray] noun a show consisting of dancing, singing, or comedy acts

cabbage noun a large green or reddish purple leafy vegetable

cabin noun **1** a room in a ship where a passenger sleeps **2** a small house, usually in the country and often made of wood **3** the area where the passengers or the crew sit in a plane

cabinet noun **1** a small cupboard **2** The cabinet in a government is a group of ministers who advise the leader and decide policies

cable noun **1** a strong, thick rope or chain **2** a bundle of wires with a rubber covering, which carries electricity **3** a message sent abroad by using electrical signals sent along a wire

cable car noun a vehicle pulled by a moving cable, for taking people up and down mountains

cable television noun a television service people can receive from underground wires which carry the signals

cache [kash] noun a store of things hidden away: a cache of guns

cachet [kash-shay] noun (formal) Cachet is the status and respect something has: the cachet of shopping at Harrods

cackle verb **1** If you cackle, you laugh harshly ▷ noun **2** a harsh laugh

cacophony [kak-koff-fon-nee] noun (formal) a loud, unpleasant noise: a cacophony of barking dogs

cactus cacti or cactuses noun a thick, fleshy plant that grows in deserts and is usually covered in spikes

cad noun (old-fashioned) a man who treats people unfairly

caddie or **caddy** noun **1** a person who carries golf clubs for a golf player **2** A tea caddy is a box for keeping tea in

cadence [kay-denss] noun The cadence of someone's voice is the way it goes up and down as they speak

cadet noun a young person being trained in the armed forces or police

caesarean [siz-air-ee-an], **caesarian** or **cesarean** noun A caesarean or caesarean section is an operation in which a baby is lifted out of a woman's womb through a cut in her abdomen

café [kaf-fay] noun **1** a place where you can buy light meals and drinks **2** In South African English, a café is a

corner shop or grocer's shop

cafeteria [kaf-fit-ee-ree-ya] noun a restaurant where you serve yourself

caffeine [kaf-feen] noun Caffeine is a chemical in coffee and tea which makes you more active

cage noun a box made of wire or bars in which birds or animals are kept > **caged** adjective

cagey cagier, cagiest [kay-jee] adjective (informal) cautious and not open: They're very cagey when they talk to me

cahoots phrase (informal) If you are **in cahoots** with someone, you are working closely with them on a secret plan

cajole verb If you cajole someone into doing something, you persuade them to do it by saying nice things to them

cake noun **1** a sweet food made by baking flour, eggs, fat, and sugar **2** a block of a hard substance such as soap ▷ verb **3** If something cakes or is caked, it forms or becomes covered with a solid layer: caked with mud

calamity calamities noun an event that causes disaster or distress > **calamitous** adjective

calcium [kal-see-um] noun SCIENCE Calcium is a soft white element found in bones and teeth. Its atomic number is 20 and its symbol is Ca

calculate verb MATHS If you calculate something, you work it out, usually by doing some arithmetic > **calculation** noun

calculating adjective carefully planning situations to get what you want: Toby was always a calculating type

calculator noun a small electronic machine used for doing mathematical calculations

calculus noun Calculus is a branch of mathematics concerned with amounts that can change and rates of change

calendar noun **1** a chart showing the date of each day in a particular year **2** a system of dividing time into fixed periods of days, months, and years: *the Jewish calendar*

calf calves noun **1** a young cow, bull, elephant, whale, or seal **2** the thick part at the back of your leg below your knee

calibre [kal-lib-ber] noun **1** the ability or intelligence someone has: *a player of her calibre* **2** The calibre of a gun is the width of the inside of the barrel of the gun

call verb **1** If someone or something is called a particular name, that is their name: *a man called Jeffrey* **2** If you call people or situations something, you use words to describe your opinion of them: *They called me crazy* **3** If you call someone, you telephone them **4** If you call or call out something, you say it loudly: *He called out his daughter's name* **5** If you call on someone, you pay them a short visit: *Don't hesitate to call on me* ▷ noun **6** If you get a call from someone, they telephone you or pay you a visit **7** a cry or shout: *a call for help* **8** a demand for something: *The call for art teachers was small* > **call off** verb If you call something off, you cancel it > **call up** verb If someone is called up, they are ordered to join the army, navy, or air force

call centre noun an office in which most staff are employed to answer telephone calls on behalf of a particular company or organization

calling noun **1** a profession or career **2** If you have a calling to a particular job, you have a strong feeling that you should do it

callous adjective cruel and not concerned with other people's feelings > **callously** adverb > **callousness** noun

calm adjective **1** Someone who is calm is quiet and does not show any worry or excitement **2** If the weather or the sea is calm, it is still because there is no strong wind ▷ noun **3** Calm is a state of quietness and peacefulness: *He liked the calm of the evening* ▷ verb **4** To calm someone means to make them less upset or excited > **calmly** adverb > **calmness** noun

calorie noun a unit of measurement for the energy food and drink gives you: *Chocolate cake is high in calories* > **calorific** adjective

calves the plural of **calf**

calypso calypsos [kal-lip-soh] noun a type of song from the West Indies, accompanied by a rhythmic beat, about something happening at the time

camaraderie [kam-mer-rah-der-ree] noun Camaraderie is a feeling of trust and friendship between a group of people

camel noun a large mammal with either one or two humps on its back. Camels live in hot desert areas and are sometimes used for carrying things

cameo cameos noun **1** a small but important part in a play or film played by a well-known actor or actress **2** a brooch with a raised stone design on a flat stone of another colour

camera noun a piece of equipment used for taking photographs or for filming

camouflage [kam-mof-flahj] noun

1 Camouflage is a way of avoiding being seen by having the same colour or appearance as the surroundings. To camouflage something is to hide it by giving it the same colour or appearance as its surroundings

camp noun **1 a** a place where people live in tents or stay in tents on holiday **2** a collection of buildings for a particular group of people such as soldiers or prisoners **3** a group of people who support a particular idea or belief: *the pro-government camp* ▷ verb **4** If you camp, you stay in a tent > **camper** noun > **camping** noun

campaign [kam-**pane**] noun **1** a set of actions aiming to achieve a particular result: *a campaign to educate people* ▷ verb **2** To campaign means to carry out a campaign: *He has campaigned against smoking* > **campaigner** noun

campus campuses noun the area of land and the buildings that make up a university or college

can could verb **1** If you can do something, it is possible for you to do it or you are allowed to do it: *You can go to the cinema* **2** Also, you have the ability to do it: *I can speak Italian*

can cans, canning, canned noun **1 a** metal container, often a sealed one with food or drink inside ▷ verb **2** To can food or drink is to seal it in cans

Canadian adjective **1** belonging or relating to Canada ▷ noun **2** someone who comes from Canada

canal noun a long, narrow man-made stretch of water

canary canaries noun a small yellow bird

cancel cancels, cancelling, cancelled verb **1** If you cancel something that has been arranged, you stop it from happening **2** If you cancel a cheque or an agreement, you make sure that it is no longer valid > **cancellation** noun

cancer noun **1** a serious disease in which abnormal cells in a part of the body increase rapidly, causing growths **2** Cancer is also the fourth sign of the zodiac, represented by a crab. People born between June 21st and July 22nd are born under this sign > **cancerous** adjective

candelabra or **candelabrum** noun an ornamental holder for a number of candles

candid adjective honest and frank > **candidly** adverb > **candour** noun

candidate noun **1** a person who is being considered for a job **2** a person taking an examination > **candidacy** noun

candied adjective covered or cooked in sugar: *candied fruit*

candle noun a stick of hard wax with a wick through the middle. The lighted wick gives a flame that provides light

candy candies noun In America, candy is sweets

cane noun **1** Cane is the long, hollow stems of a plant such as bamboo **2** Cane is also strips of cane used for weaving things such as baskets **3** a long narrow stick, often one used to beat people as a punishment ▷ verb **4** To cane someone means to beat them with a cane as a punishment

canine [**kay**-nine] adjective relating to dogs

canister noun a container with a lid, used for storing foods such as sugar or tea

cannabis noun Cannabis is a drug made from the hemp plant, which some people smoke

canned adjective **1** Canned food is

kept in cans **2** Canned music or laughter on a television or radio show is recorded beforehand

cannibal noun a person who eats other human beings; also used of animals that eat animals of their own type > **cannibalism** noun

cannon noun **1** A cannon is a large gun, usually on wheels, used in battles to fire heavy metal balls ▷ verb **2** To cannon into people or things means to collide into them with force

cannot verb Cannot is the same as can not: She cannot come home yet

canny cannier, canniest adjective clever and cautious: canny business people > **cannily** adverb

canoe [ka-noo] noun a small, narrow boat that you row using a paddle > **canoeing** noun > **canoeist** noun

canon noun **1** a member of the clergy in a cathedral **2** a basic rule or principle: the canons of political economy **3** In literature, a canon is all the writings by a particular author which are known to be genuine

canopy canopies noun a cover for something, used for shelter or decoration: a frilly canopy over the bed

cantankerous adjective Cantankerous people are quarrelsome and bad-tempered

canteen noun **1** the part of a workplace where the workers can go to eat **2** A canteen of cutlery is a set of cutlery in a box

canter verb When a horse canters, it moves at a speed between a gallop and a trot

canvas noun **1** Canvas is strong, heavy cloth used for making things such as sails and tents **2** a piece of canvas on which an artist does a painting

canvass verb **1** If you canvass people or a place, you go round trying to persuade people to vote for a particular candidate or party in an election **2** If you canvass opinion, you find out what people think about a particular subject by asking them

canyon noun a narrow river valley with steep sides

cap caps, capping, capped noun **1** a soft, flat hat, often with a peak at the front **2** the top of a bottle **3** Caps are small explosives used in toy guns ▷ verb **4** To cap something is to cover it with something **5** If you cap a story or a joke that someone has just told, you tell a better one

capable adjective **1** able to do something: a man capable of extreme violence **2** skilful or talented: She was a very capable woman > **capably** adverb > **capability** noun

capacity capacities [kap-**pas**-sit-tee] noun **1** the maximum amount that something can hold or produce: a seating capacity of eleven thousand **2** a person's power or ability to do something: his capacity for consuming hamburgers **3** someone's position or role: in his capacity as councillor

cape noun **1** a short cloak with no sleeves **2** a large piece of land sticking out into the sea: the Cape of Good Hope

caper noun **1** Capers are the flower buds of a spiky Mediterranean shrub, which are pickled and used to flavour food **2** a light-hearted practical joke: Jack would have nothing to do with such capers

capital noun **1** The capital of a country is the city where the government meets **2** Capital is the amount of money or property owned or used by a business

3 Capital is also a sum of money that you save or invest in order to gain interest **4** A capital or capital letter is a larger letter used at the beginning of a sentence or a name

capitalism noun Capitalism is an economic and political system where businesses and industries are not owned and run by the government, but by individuals who can make a profit from them ▷ **capitalist** adjective, noun

capitalize or **capitalise** verb If you capitalize on a situation, you use it to get an advantage

capital punishment noun Capital punishment is legally killing someone as a punishment for a crime they have committed

capitulate verb To capitulate is to give in and stop fighting or resisting: *The Finns capitulated in March 1940* ▷ **capitulation** noun

cappuccino cappuccinos [kap-poot-**sheen**-oh] noun coffee made with frothy milk

capricious [kap-**prish**-uss] adjective often changing unexpectedly: *the capricious English weather*

Capricorn noun Capricorn is the tenth sign of the zodiac, represented by a goat. People born between December 22nd and January 19th are born under this sign

capsize verb If a boat capsizes, it turns upside down

capsule noun **1** a small container with medicine inside which you swallow **2** the part of a spacecraft in which astronauts travel

captain noun **1** the officer in charge of a ship or aeroplane **2** an army officer of the rank immediately above lieutenant **3** a navy officer of the rank immediately above

commander **4** the leader of a sports team: *captain of the cricket team* ▷ verb **5** If you captain a group of people, you are their leader

caption noun a title printed underneath a picture or photograph

captivate verb To captivate someone is to fascinate or attract them so that they cannot take their attention away: *I was captivated by her* ▷ **captivating** adjective

captive noun **1** a person who has been captured and kept prisoner ▷ adjective **2** imprisoned or enclosed: *a captive bird* ▷ **captivity** noun

captor noun someone who has captured a person or animal

capture verb **1** To capture someone is to take them prisoner **2** To capture a quality or mood means to succeed in representing or describing it: *capturing the mood of the riots* ▷ noun **3** The capture of someone or something is the action of taking them prisoner: *the fifth anniversary of his capture*

car noun **1** a four-wheeled road vehicle with room for a small number of people **2** a railway carriage used for a particular purpose: *the buffet car*

caramel noun **1** a chewy sweet made from sugar, butter, and milk **2** Caramel is burnt sugar used for colouring or flavouring food

carat noun **1** A carat is a unit for measuring the weight of diamonds and other precious stones, equal to 0.2 grams **2** A carat is also a unit for measuring the purity of gold. The purest gold is 24 carats

caravan noun **1** a vehicle pulled by a car in which people live or spend their holidays **2** a group of people and animals travelling together, usually across a desert

carbohydrate noun $\boxed{\text{D G T}}$ Carbohydrate is a substance that gives you energy. It is found in foods like sugar and bread

carbon noun $\boxed{\text{SCIENCE}}$ Carbon is a chemical element that is pure in diamonds and also found in coal. All living things contain carbon. Its atomic number is 6 and its symbol is C

carbonated adjective Carbonated drinks contain bubbles of carbon dioxide that make them fizzy

carbon dioxide noun $\boxed{\text{SCIENCE}}$ Carbon dioxide is a colourless, odourless gas that humans and animals breathe out. It is used in industry, for example in making fizzy drinks and in fire extinguishers

carcass or **carcase** noun the body of a dead animal

card noun **1** a piece of stiff paper or plastic with writing on it or a message on it: *a birthday card* **2** Cards can mean playing cards: *a poor set of cards with which to play* **3** When you play cards, you play any game using playing cards **4** Card is thick, stiff paper

cardboard noun Cardboard is thick, stiff paper

cardiac adjective (Medicine) relating to the heart: *cardiac disease*

cardigan noun a knitted jacket that fastens up the front

cardinal noun **1** a high-ranking member of the Roman Catholic clergy who chooses and advises the Pope ▷ adjective **2** extremely important: *a cardinal principle of law*

care verb **1** If you care about something, you are concerned about it and interested in it **2** If you care about someone, you feel affection towards them **3** If you care for someone, you look after them ▷ noun **4** Care is concern or worry **5** Care of someone or something is treatment for them or looking after them: *the care of the elderly* **6** If you do something with care, you do it with close attention

career noun **1** the series of jobs that someone has in life, usually in the same occupation: *a career in insurance* ▷ verb **2** To career somewhere is to move very quickly, often out of control: *His car careered off the road*

carefree adjective having no worries or responsibilities

careful adjective **1** acting sensibly and with care: *Be careful what you say to him* **2** complete and well done: *It needs very careful planning* > **carefully** adverb

careless adjective **1** done badly without enough attention: *careless driving* **2** relaxed and unconcerned: *careless laughter* > **carelessly** adverb > **carelessness** noun

caress verb **1** If you caress someone, you stroke them gently and affectionately ▷ noun **2** a gentle, affectionate stroke

caretaker noun **1** a person who looks after a large building such as a school ▷ adjective **2** having an important position for a short time until a new person is appointed: *O'Leary was named caretaker manager*

cargo noun cargoes noun the goods carried on a ship or plane

caricature noun **1** a drawing or description of someone that exaggerates striking parts of their appearance or personality ▷ verb **2** To caricature someone is to give a caricature of them

carnage [kahr-nij] noun Carnage is the violent killing of large numbers of people

carnival noun a public festival with music, processions, and dancing

carnivore noun an animal that eats meat > **carnivorous** adjective

carol noun a religious song sung at Christmas time

carousel [kar-ros-**sel**] noun a merry-go-round

carp noun **1** a large edible freshwater fish ▷ verb **2** To carp means to complain about unimportant things

carpenter noun a person who makes and repairs wooden structures > **carpentry** noun

carpet noun **1** a thick covering for a floor, usually made of a material like wool ▷ verb **2** To carpet a floor means to cover it with a carpet

carriage noun **1** one of the separate sections of a passenger train **2** an old-fashioned vehicle for carrying passengers, usually pulled by horses **3** a machine part that moves and supports another part: *a typewriter carriage* **4** Someone's carriage is the way they hold their head and body when they move

carriageway noun one of the sides of a road where traffic travels along in one direction only

carrier noun **1** a vehicle that is used for carrying things: *a troop carrier* **2** A carrier of a germ or disease is a person or animal that can pass it on to others

carrier bag noun a bag made of plastic or paper, which is used for carrying shopping

carrot noun a long, thin orange root vegetable

carry carries, carrying, carried verb **1** To carry something is to hold it and take it somewhere **2** When a vehicle carries people, they travel in it **3** A person or animal that carries a germ can pass it on to other people or animals: *I still carry the disease* **4** If a sound carries, it can be heard far away: *Jake's voice carried over the cheering* **5** In a meeting, if a proposal is carried, it is accepted by a majority of the people there > **carry away** verb If you are carried away, you are so excited by something that you do not behave sensibly > **carry on** verb To carry on doing something means to continue doing it > **carry out** verb To carry something out means to do it and complete it: *The conversion was carried out by a local builder*

cart noun a vehicle with wheels, used to carry goods and often pulled by horses or cattle

cartilage noun Cartilage is a strong, flexible substance found around the joints and in the nose and ears

carton noun a cardboard or plastic container

cartoon noun **1** a drawing or a series of drawings which are funny or make a point **2** a film in which the characters and scenes are drawn > **cartoonist** noun

cartridge noun **1** a tube containing a bullet and an explosive substance, used in guns **2** a plastic container full of ink that you put in a printer or pen

carve verb **1** To carve an object means to cut it out of a substance such as stone or wood **2** To carve meat means to cut slices from it

carving noun a carved object

cascade noun **1** a waterfall or group of waterfalls ▷ verb **2** To cascade means to flow downwards quickly: *Gallons of water cascaded from the attic*

case noun **1** a particular situation, event, or example: *a clear case of mistaken identity* **2** a container for something, or a suitcase: *a camera case* **3** Doctors sometimes refer to a patient as a case **4** Police detectives refer to a crime they are investigating as a case **5** In an argument, the case for an idea is the reasons used to support it **6** In law, a case is a trial or other inquiry **7** In grammar, the case of a noun or pronoun is the form of it which shows its relationship with other words in a sentence: *the accusative case* ▷ *phrase* **8** You say **in case** to explain something that you do because a particular thing might happen: *I didn't want to shout in case I startled you* **9** You say **in that case** to show that you are assuming something said before is true: *In that case we won't do it*

cash cashes, cashing, cashed *noun* **1** Cash is money in notes and coins rather than cheques ▷ *verb* **2** If you cash a cheque, you take it to a bank and exchange it for money

cashew [kash-oo] *noun* a curved, edible nut

cash flow *noun* Cash flow is the money that a business makes and spends

cashier *noun* the person that customers pay in a shop or get money from in a bank

cashmere *noun* Cashmere is very soft, fine wool from goats

cash register *noun* a machine in a shop which records sales, and where the money is kept

casing *noun* a protective covering for something

casino casinos [kass-ee-noh] *noun* a place where people go to play gambling games

cask *noun* a wooden barrel

casket *noun* a small box for jewellery or other valuables

casserole *noun* a dish made by cooking a mixture of meat and vegetables slowly in an oven; also used to refer to the pot a casserole is cooked in

cassette *noun* a small flat container with magnetic tape inside, which is used for recording and playing back sounds

cassowary cassowaries *noun* a large bird found in Australia with black feathers and a brightly coloured neck. Cassowaries cannot fly

cast casts, casting, cast *noun* **1** all the people who act in a play or film **2** an object made by pouring liquid into a mould and leaving it to harden: *the casts of classical sculptures* **3** a stiff plaster covering put on broken bones to keep them still so that they heal properly ▷ *verb* **4** To cast actors is to choose them for roles in a play or film **5** When people cast their votes in an election, they vote **6** To cast something is to throw it **7** If you cast your eyes somewhere, you look there: *I cast my eyes down briefly* **8** To cast an object is to make it by pouring liquid into a mould and leaving it to harden: *An image of him has been cast in bronze* > **cast off** *verb* If you cast off, you untie the rope fastening a boat to a harbour or shore

caste *noun* **1** one of the four classes into which Hindu society is divided **2** Caste is a system of social classes decided according to family, wealth, and position

castigate *verb (formal)* To castigate someone is to criticize them severely

castle *noun* **1** HISTORY a large building with walls or ditches round it to protect it from attack **2** In chess, a castle is the same as a rook

castor or **caster** noun a small wheel fitted to furniture so that it can be moved easily

casual adjective **1** happening by chance without planning: *a casual remark* **2** careless or without interest: *a casual glance over his shoulder* **3** Casual clothes are suitable for informal occasions **4** Casual work is not regular or permanent > **casually** adverb > **casualness** noun

casualty casualties noun a person killed or injured in an accident or war: *Many of the casualties were office workers*

cat noun **1 a** a small furry animal with whiskers, a tail, and sharp claws, often kept as a pet **b** any of the family of mammals that includes lions and tigers

catalogue catalogues, cataloguing, catalogued noun **1** a book containing pictures and descriptions of goods that you can buy in a shop or through the post **2** LIBRARY a list of things such as the objects in a museum or the books in a library ▷ verb **3** To catalogue a collection of things means to list them in a catalogue

catalyst [kat-a-list] noun **1** something that causes a change to happen: *the catalyst which provoked civil war* **2** SCIENCE a substance that speeds up a chemical reaction without changing itself

catamaran noun a sailing boat with two hulls connected to each other

catapult noun **1 a** Y-shaped object with a piece of elastic tied between the two ends, used for shooting small stones ▷ verb **2** To catapult something is to throw it violently

through the air **3** If someone is catapulted into a situation, they find themselves unexpectedly in that situation: *Tony has been catapulted to the limelight*

cataract noun **1** an area of the lens of someone's eye that has become white instead of clear, so that they cannot see properly **2** a large waterfall

catastrophe [kat-**tass**-trif-fee] noun a terrible disaster > **catastrophic** adjective

catch catches, catching, caught verb **1** If you catch a ball moving in the air, you grasp hold of it when it comes near you **2** To catch an animal means to trap it: *I caught ten fish* **3** When the police catch criminals, they find them and arrest them **4** If you catch someone doing something they should not be doing, you discover them doing it: *He caught me playing the church organ* **5** If you catch a bus or train, you get on it and travel somewhere **6** If you catch a cold or a disease, you become infected with it **7** If something catches on an object, it sticks to it or gets trapped: *The white fibres caught on the mesh* ▷ noun **8** a device that fastens something **9** a problem or hidden complication in something > **catch on** verb **1** If you catch on to something, you understand it **2** If something catches on, it becomes popular: *This drink has never really caught on in New Zealand* > **catch out** verb To catch someone out is to trick them or trap them > **catch up** verb **1** To catch up with someone in front of you is to reach the place where they are by moving slightly faster than them **2** To catch up with someone is also to reach the same

level or standard as them

catching *adjective* tending to spread very quickly: *Measles is catching*

catchy catchier, catchiest *adjective* attractive and easily remembered: *a catchy little tune*

categorical *adjective* absolutely certain and direct: *a categorical denial* ▷ **categorically** *adverb*

categorize or **categorise** *verb* To categorize things is to arrange them in different categories

category categories *noun* a set of things with a particular characteristic in common: *Occupations can be divided into four categories*

cater *verb* To cater for people is to provide them with what they need, especially food

caterer *noun* a person or business that provides food for parties and groups

caterpillar *noun* the larva of a butterfly or moth. It looks like a small coloured worm and feeds on plants

catharsis catharses [kath-**ar**-siss] *noun (formal)* Catharsis is the release of strong emotions and feelings by expressing them through drama or literature

cathedral *noun* HISTORY an important church with a bishop in charge of it

cattle *plural noun* Cattle are cows and bulls kept by farmers

catty cattier, cattiest *adjective* unpleasant and spiteful ▷ **cattiness** *noun*

catwalk *noun* a narrow pathway that people walk along, for example over a stage

Caucasian [kaw-**kayz**-yn] *noun* a person belonging to the race of people with fair or light-brown skin

caught the past tense and past participle of **catch**

cauldron *noun* a large, round, metal cooking pot, especially one that sits over a fire

cauliflower *noun* a large, round, white vegetable surrounded by green leaves

cause *noun* **1** The cause of something is the thing that makes it happen: *the most common cause of back pain* **2** an aim or principle which a group of people are working for: *dedication to the cause of peace* **3** If you have cause for something, you have a reason for it: *They gave us no cause to believe that* ▷ *verb* **4** To cause something is to make it happen: *This can cause delays* ▷ **causal** *adjective*

causeway *noun* a raised path or road across water or marshland

caustic *adjective* **1** A caustic chemical can destroy substances: *caustic liquids such as acids* **2** bitter or sarcastic: *your caustic sense of humour*

caution *noun* **1** Caution is great care which you take to avoid danger: *You will need to proceed with caution* **2** a warning: *Sutton was let off with a caution* ▷ *verb* **3** If someone cautions you, they warn you, usually not to do something again: *A man has been cautioned by police* ▷ **cautionary** *adjective*

cautious *adjective* acting very carefully to avoid danger: *a cautious approach* ▷ **cautiously** *adverb*

cavalcade *noun* a procession of people on horses or in cars or carriages

cavalier [kav-val-**eer**] *adjective* arrogant and behaving without sensitivity: *a cavalier attitude to women*

cavalry *noun* The cavalry is the part of an army that uses armoured vehicles or horses

cave noun **1** a large hole in rock, that is underground or in the side of a cliff ▷ verb **2** If a roof caves in, it collapses inwards

caveman cavemen noun Cavemen were people who lived in caves in prehistoric times

cavern noun a large cave

cavernous adjective large, deep, and hollow: a cavernous warehouse

caviar [kav-vee-ar] noun Caviar is the tiny salted eggs of a fish called the sturgeon

cavity cavities noun a small hole in something: There were dark cavities in his back teeth

cavort verb When people cavort, they jump around excitedly

cc an abbreviation for 'cubic centimetres'

CD an abbreviation for 'compact disc'

CD-ROM CD-ROM is a method of storing video, sound, or text on a compact disc which can be played on a computer using a laser. CD-ROM is an abbreviation for 'Compact Disc Read-Only Memory'

cease verb **1** If something ceases, it stops happening **2** If you cease to do something, or cease doing it, you stop doing it

ceaseless adjective going on without stopping: the ceaseless movement of the streets
> **ceaselessly** adverb

cedar noun a large evergreen tree with wide branches and needle-shaped leaves

cede [seed] verb To cede something is to give it up to someone else: Haiti was ceded to France in 1697

ceiling noun the top inside surface of a room

celebrate verb **1** If you celebrate or celebrate something, you do something special and enjoyable because of it: a party to celebrate the end of the exams **2** RE When a priest celebrates Mass, he performs the ceremonies of the Mass

celebrated adjective famous: the celebrated Italian mountaineer

celebration noun an event in honour of a special occasion
> **celebratory** adjective

celebrity celebrities noun a famous person

celery noun Celery is a vegetable with long, pale green stalks

celestial [sil-lest-yal] adjective (formal) concerning the sky or heaven: The telescope is pointed at a celestial object

celibate [sel-lib-bit] adjective Someone who is celibate does not marry > **celibacy** noun

cell noun **1** SCIENCE In biology, a cell is the smallest part of an animal or plant that can exist by itself. Each cell contains a nucleus **2** a small room where a prisoner is kept in a prison or police station **3** a small group of people set up to work together as part of a larger organization **4** D G T a device that converts chemical energy to electricity

cellar noun a room underneath a building, often used to store wine

cello cellos [chel-loh] noun MUSIC a large musical stringed instrument which you play sitting down, holding the instrument upright with your knees > **cellist** noun

cellphone noun a small portable telephone

cellular adjective Cellular means relating to the cells of animals or plants

celluloid [sel-yul-loyd] noun

Celluloid is a type of plastic which was once used to make photographic film

Celsius [**sel**-see-yuss] noun Celsius is a scale for measuring temperature in which water freezes at 0 degrees (0°C) and boils at 100 degrees (100°C). It is named after Anders Celsius (1701–1744), who invented it. Celsius is the same as 'Centigrade'

Celtic [**kel**-tik] adjective A Celtic language is one of a group of languages that includes Gaelic and Welsh

cement noun **1** Cement is a fine powder made from limestone and clay, which is mixed with sand and water to make concrete ▷ verb **2** To cement things is to stick them together with cement or cover them with cement **3** Something that cements a relationship makes it stronger: to cement relations between them

cemetery cemeteries noun an area of land where dead people are buried

cenotaph [sen-not-ahf] noun a monument built in memory of dead people, especially soldiers buried elsewhere

censor noun **1** a person officially appointed to examine books or films and to ban parts that are considered unsuitable ▷ verb **2** If someone censors a book or film, they cut or ban parts of it that are considered unsuitable for the public
> **censorship** noun

censure [sen-sher] noun **1** Censure is strong disapproval of something ▷ verb **2** To censure someone is to criticize them severely

census censuses noun an official survey of the population of a country

cent noun a unit of currency. In the USA, a cent is worth one hundredth of a dollar; in Europe, it is worth one hundredth of a euro

centenary centenaries [sen-**teen**-er-ee] noun the hundredth anniversary of something

centimetre noun (MATHS) a unit of length equal to ten millimetres or one hundredth of a metre

central adjective **1** in or near the centre of an object or area: central ceiling lights **2** main or most important: the central idea of this work > **centrally** adverb
> **centrality** noun

Central America noun Central America is another name for the Isthmus of Panama, the area of land joining North America to South America

central heating noun Central heating is a system of heating a building in which water or air is heated in a tank and travels through pipes and radiators round the building

centralize or **centralise** verb To centralize a system is to bring the organization of it under the control of one central group
> **centralization** noun

centre noun **1** the middle of an object or area **2** a building where people go for activities, meetings, or help: a health centre **3** Someone or something that is the centre of attention attracts a lot of attention ▷ verb **4** To centre something is to move it so that it is balanced or at the centre of something else **5** If something centres on or around a particular thing, that thing is the main subject of attention: The discussion centred on his request

centrifugal [sen-trif-**yoo**-gl]

C

adjective [SCIENCE] In physics, centrifugal force is the force that makes rotating objects move outwards

centurion noun an ancient Roman officer in charge of a hundred soldiers

century centuries noun 1 a period of one hundred years 2 In cricket, a century is one hundred runs scored by a batsman

ceramic [sir-ram-mik] noun 1 Ceramic is a hard material made by baking clay to a very high temperature 2 Ceramics is the art of making objects out of clay

cereal noun 1 a food made from grain, often eaten with milk for breakfast 2 a plant that produces edible grain, such as wheat or oats

cerebral [ser-reb-ral] adjective (formal) relating to the brain: a cerebral haemorrhage

cerebral palsy noun Cerebral palsy is an illness caused by damage to a baby's brain, which makes its muscles and limbs very weak

ceremonial adjective relating to a ceremony: ceremonial dress
> **ceremonially** adverb

ceremony ceremonies noun 1 a set of formal actions performed at a special occasion or important public event: his recent coronation ceremony 2 Ceremony is very formal and polite behaviour: He hung up without ceremony

certain adjective 1 definite or reliable: He is certain to be in Italy 2 having no doubt in your mind 3 You use 'certain' to refer to a specific person or thing: certain aspects of the job 4 You use 'certain' to suggest that a quality is noticeable but not obvious: There's a certain resemblance to Joe

certainly adverb 1 without doubt: My boss was certainly interested 2 of course: 'Will you be there?' — 'Certainly'

certainty certainties noun 1 Certainty is the state of being certain 2 something that is known without doubt: There are no certainties and no guarantees

certificate noun a document stating particular facts, for example of someone's birth or death: a marriage certificate

certify certifies, certifying, certified verb 1 To certify something means to declare formally that it is true: certifying the cause of death 2 To certify someone means to declare officially that they are insane

cervical [ser-vik-kl] adjective (technical) relating to the cervix

cervix cervixes or cervices noun (technical) The cervix is the entrance to the womb

cessation noun (formal) The cessation of something is the stopping of it: a swift cessation of hostilities

cf. cf. means 'compare'. It is written after something in a text to mention something else which the reader should compare with what has just been written

CFC noun CFCs are manufactured chemicals that are used in aerosol sprays. They damage the ozone layer. CFC is an abbreviation for 'chlorofluorocarbon'

chaff noun Chaff is the outer parts of grain separated from the seeds by beating

chagrin [shag-rin] noun (formal) Chagrin is a feeling of annoyance or disappointment

chain noun 1 a number of metal rings connected together in a line: a bicycle chain 2 a number of things in

chain *noun* **1** a series or connected to each other: *a chain of shops* ▷ *verb* **3** If you chain one thing to another, you fasten them together with a chain: *They had chained themselves to railings*

chair *noun* **1** a seat with a back and four legs for one person **2** the person in charge of a meeting who decides when each person may speak ▷ *verb* **3** The person who chairs a meeting is in charge of it

chairman chairmen *noun* **1** the person in charge of a meeting who decides when each person may speak **2** the head of a company or committee > **chairperson** *noun* > **chairwoman** *noun* > **chairmanship** *noun*

chalet [**shall**-lay] *noun* a wooden house with a sloping roof, especially in a mountain area or a holiday camp

chalice [**chal**-liss] *noun* RE a gold or silver cup used in churches to hold the Communion wine

chalk *noun* **1** ART Chalk is a soft white rock. Small sticks of chalk are used for writing or drawing on a blackboard ▷ *verb* **2** To chalk up a result is to achieve it: *He chalked up his first win* > **chalky** *adjective*

challenge *noun* **1** something that is new and exciting and requires a lot of effort: *It's a new challenge at the right time in my career* **2** a suggestion from someone to compete with them **3** A challenge to something is a questioning of whether it is correct or true: *a challenge to authority* ▷ *verb* **4** If someone challenges you, they suggest that you compete with them in some way **5** If you challenge something, you question whether it is correct or true > **challenger** *noun* > **challenging** *adjective*

chamber *noun* **1** a large room, especially one used for formal meetings: *the Council Chamber* **2** a group of people chosen to decide laws or administrative matters **3** a hollow place or compartment inside something, especially inside an animal's body or inside a gun: *the chambers of the heart*

chameleon [kam-**mee**-lee-on] *noun* a lizard which is able to change the colour of its skin to match the colour of its surroundings

champagne [sham-**pain**] *noun* Champagne is a sparkling white wine made in France

champion *noun* **1** a person who wins a competition **2** someone who supports or defends a cause or principle: *a champion of women's causes* ▷ *verb* **3** Someone who champions a cause or principle supports or defends it

championship *noun* a competition to find the champion of a sport

chance *noun* **1** The chance of something happening is how possible or likely it is: *There's a chance of rain later* **2** an opportunity to do something: *Your chance to be a TV star!* **3** a possibility that something dangerous or unpleasant may happen: *Don't take chances, he's armed* **4** Chance is also the way things happen unexpectedly without being planned: *I only found out by chance* ▷ *verb* **5** If you chance something, you try it although you are taking a risk

chancellor *noun* **1** the head of government in some European countries **2** In Britain, the Chancellor is the Chancellor of the Exchequer **3** the honorary head of a university

Chancellor of the Exchequer
noun In Britain, the minister responsible for finance and taxes

chandelier [shan-del-**leer**] noun an ornamental light fitting which hangs from the ceiling

change noun 1 a difference or alteration in something: *Steven soon noticed a change in Penny's attitude* 2 a replacement of something with something else: *a change of clothes* 3 Change is money you get back when you have paid more than the actual price of something ▷ verb 4 When something changes or when you change it, it becomes different: *It changed my life* 5 If you change something, you exchange it for something else 6 When you change, you put on different clothes 7 To change money means to exchange it for smaller coins of the same total value, or to exchange it for foreign currency

changeable adjective likely to change all the time

changeover noun a change from one system or activity to another: *the changeover between day and night*

channel channels, channelling, channelled noun 1 a wavelength used to receive programmes broadcast by a television or radio station; also the station itself: *I was watching another channel* 2 a passage along which water flows or along which something is carried 3 The Channel or the English Channel is the stretch of sea between England and France 4 a method of achieving something: *We have tried to do things through the right channels* ▷ verb 5 To channel something such as money or energy means to direct it in a particular way: *Their efforts are being channelled into worthy causes*

chant noun 1 a group of words repeated over and over again: *a rousing chant* 2 a religious song sung on only a few notes ▷ verb 3 If people chant a group of words, they repeat them over and over again: *Crowds chanted his name*

chaos [**kay**-oss] noun Chaos is a state of complete disorder and confusion ▷ **chaotic** adjective

chap chaps, chapping, chapped noun 1 (informal) a man ▷ verb 2 If your skin chaps, it becomes dry and cracked, usually as a result of cold or wind

chapel noun 1 a section of a church or cathedral with its own altar 2 a type of small church

chaperone [**shap**-per-rone] or **chaperon** noun an older woman who accompanies a young unmarried woman on social occasions, or any person who accompanies a group of younger people

chaplain noun a member of the Christian clergy who regularly works in a hospital, school, or prison > **chaplaincy** noun

chapter noun 1 one of the parts into which a book is divided 2 a particular period in someone's life or in history

char chars, charring, charred verb If something chars, it gets partly burned and goes black > **charred** adjective

character noun 1 all the qualities which combine to form the personality or atmosphere of a person or place 2 A person or place that has character has an interesting, attractive, or admirable quality: *an inn of great character and simplicity* 3 ENGLISH The characters in a film, play, or book are the people in it 4 a person: *an odd character* 5 a letter, number, or other written symbol

characteristic noun **1** a quality that is typical of a particular person or thing: *Silence is the characteristic of the place* **2** SCIENCE a feature that is typical of a particular living thing ▷ adjective **3** Characteristic means typical of a particular person or thing: *Two things are very characteristically of his driving* > **characteristically** adverb

characterize or **characterise** verb A quality that characterizes something is typical of it: *a condition characterized by muscle stiffness*

charade [shar-**rahd**] noun a ridiculous and unnecessary activity or pretence

charcoal noun SCIENCE Charcoal is a black form of carbon made by burning wood without air, used as a fuel and also for drawing

charge verb **1** If someone charges you money, they ask you to pay it for something you have bought or received: *The company charged £150 on each loan* **2** To charge someone means to accuse them formally of having committed a crime **3** To charge a battery means to pass an electrical current through it to make it store electricity **4** To charge somewhere means to rush forward, often to attack someone: *The rhino charged at her* ▷ noun **5** the price that you have to pay for something **6** a formal accusation that a person is guilty of a crime and has to go to court **7** To have charge or be in charge of someone or something means to be responsible for them and be in control of them **8** an explosive put in a gun or other weapon **9** An electrical charge is the amount of electricity that something carries

charger noun a device for charging or recharging batteries

chariot noun a two-wheeled open vehicle pulled by horses

charisma [kar-**riz**-ma] noun Charisma is a special ability to attract or influence people by your personality > **charismatic** adjective

charity charities noun **1** an organization that raises money to help people who are ill, poor, or disabled **2** Charity is money or other help given to poor, disabled, or ill people: *to help raise money for charity* **3** Charity is also a kind, sympathetic attitude towards people > **charitable** adjective

charlatan [**shar**-lat-tn] noun someone who pretends to have skill or knowledge that they do not really have

charm noun **1** Charm is an attractive and pleasing quality that some people and things have: *a man of great personal charm* **2** a small ornament worn on a bracelet **3** a magical spell or an object that is supposed to bring good luck ▷ verb **4** If you charm someone, you use your charm to please them

charmer noun someone who uses their charm to influence people

charming adjective very pleasant and attractive: *a rather charming man* > **charmingly** adverb

chart noun **1** a diagram or table showing information: *He noted the score on his chart* **2** a map of the sea or stars ▷ verb **3** If you chart something, you observe and record it carefully

charter noun **1** a document stating the rights or aims of a group or organization, often written by the government: *the new charter for commuters* ▷ verb **2** To charter transport such as a plane or boat is to hire it for private use > **chartered** adjective

chase verb **1** If you chase someone or something, you run after them in order to catch them **2** If you chase someone, you force them to go somewhere else ▷ noun **3** The activity of chasing or hunting someone or something: *a high-speed car chase*

chasm [kazm] noun **1** A deep crack in the earth's surface **2** A very large difference between two ideas or groups of people: *the chasm between rich and poor in America*

chassis [shas-ee] noun The frame on which a vehicle is built

chaste [chayst] adjective (old-fashioned) pure and well-behaved > **chastity** noun

chastise verb (formal) If someone chastises you, they criticize you or punish you for something that you have done

chat chats, chatting, chatted noun **1** a friendly conversation with someone, usually about things that are not very important ▷ verb **2** When people chat, they talk to each other in a friendly way ▷ **chat up** verb (informal) If you chat up someone, you talk to them in a friendly way, because you are attracted to them

chateau chateaux [shat-toe] noun a large country house or castle in France

chatroom noun an internet site where users have group discussions using e-mail

chatter verb **1** When people chatter, they talk very fast **2** If your teeth are chattering, they are knocking together and making a clicking noise because you are cold ▷ noun **3** Chatter is a lot of fast unimportant talk

chatty chattier, chattiest adjective talkative and friendly

chauffeur [show-fur] noun a person whose job is to drive another person's car

chauvinist noun **1** a person who thinks their country is always right **2** A male chauvinist is a man who believes that men are superior to women > **chauvinistic** adjective > **chauvinism** noun

cheap adjective **1** costing very little money **2** inexpensive but of poor quality **3** A cheap joke or cheap remark is unfair and unkind > **cheaply** adverb

cheat verb **1** If someone cheats, they do wrong or unfair things to win or get something that they want **2** If you are cheated of or out of something, you do not get what you are entitled to ▷ noun **3** a person who cheats

check verb **1** To check something is to examine it in order to make sure that everything is all right **2** To check the growth or spread of something is to make it stop: *a policy to check fast population growth* ▷ noun **3** an inspection to make sure that everything is all right **4** Checks are different coloured squares which form a pattern ▷ phrase **5** If you keep something **in check**, you keep it under control: *She kept her emotions in check* ▷ adjective **6** Check or checked means marked with a pattern of squares: *check design* > **check in** verb When you check in at a hotel or airport, you arrive and sign your name or show your ticket > **check out** verb If you check something out, you inspect it and find out whether everything about it is right

checkout noun a counter in a

supermarket where the customers pay for their goods

checkpoint noun a place where traffic has to stop in order to be checked

checkup noun an examination by a doctor to see if you are healthy

cheek noun **1** Your cheeks are the sides of your face below your eyes **2** Cheek is speech or behaviour that is rude or disrespectful: *an expression of sheer cheek*

cheeky cheekier, cheekiest *adjective* rather rude and disrespectful

cheer verb When people cheer, they shout with approval or in order to show approval for a person or team ▷ noun **2** a shout of approval or support > **cheer up** verb When you cheer up, you feel more cheerful

cheerful adjective **1** happy and in good spirits: *I had never seen her so cheerful* **2** bright and pleasant-looking: *a cheerful and charming place* > **cheerfully** adverb > **cheerfulness** noun

cheery cheerier, cheeriest adjective happy and cheerful: *He gave me a cheery nod*

cheese noun a hard or creamy food made from milk

cheesecake noun a dessert made of biscuit covered with cream cheese

cheetah noun a wild animal like a large cat with black spots

chef noun a head cook in a restaurant or hotel

chemical noun SCIENCE **1** Chemicals are substances manufactured by chemistry ▷ adjective **2** involved in chemistry or using chemicals: *chemical weapons* > **chemically** adverb

chemist noun **1** a person who is qualified to make up drugs and

medicines prescribed by a doctor **2** a shop where medicines and cosmetics are sold **3** a scientist who does research in chemistry

chemistry noun Chemistry is the scientific study of substances and the ways in which they change when they are combined with other substances

chemotherapy [keem-oh-**ther**-a-pee] noun Chemotherapy is a way of treating diseases such as cancer by using chemicals

cheque noun a printed form on which you write an amount of money that you have to pay. You sign the cheque and your bank pays the money from your account

chequered [**chek**-kerd] adjective **1** covered with a pattern of squares **2** A chequered career is a varied career that has both good and bad parts

cherish verb **1** If you cherish something, you care deeply about it and want to keep it or look after it lovingly **2** If you cherish a memory or hope, you have it in your mind and care deeply about it: *I cherish the good memories I have of him*

cherry cherries noun **1** a small, juicy fruit with a red or black skin and a hard stone in the centre **2** a tree that produces cherries

chess noun Chess is a board game for two people in which each player has 16 pieces and tries to move his or her pieces so that the other player's king cannot escape

chest noun **1** the front part of your body between your shoulders and your waist **2** a large wooden box with a hinged lid

chestnut noun **1** Chestnuts are reddish-brown nuts that grow inside a prickly green outer covering

2 a tree that produces these nuts ▷ *adjective* **3** Something that is chestnut is reddish-brown

chest of drawers *noun* a piece of furniture with drawers in it, used for storing clothes

chew *verb* When you chew something, you use your teeth to break it up in your mouth before swallowing it ▷ **chewy** *adjective*

chewing gum *noun* Chewing gum is a kind of sweet that you chew for a long time, but which you do not swallow

chic [sheek] *adjective* elegant and fashionable: *a chic restaurant*

chick *noun* a young bird

chicken *noun* a bird kept on a farm for its eggs and meat; also the meat of this bird: *roast chicken* ▷ **chicken out** (*informal*) If you chicken out of something, you do not do it because you are afraid

chickenpox *noun* Chickenpox is an illness which produces a fever and blister-like spots on the skin

chicory *noun* Chicory is a plant with bitter leaves that are used in salads

chide chides, chiding, chided *verb* (*old-fashioned*) To chide someone is to tell them off

chief *noun* **1** the leader of a group or organization ▷ *adjective* **2** most important: *the chief source of oil* ▷ **chiefly** *adverb*

chieftain *noun* the leader of a tribe or clan

chiffon [shif-fon] *noun* Chiffon is a very thin lightweight cloth made of silk or nylon

chihuahua [chi-wah-wah] *noun* a breed of very small dog with short hair and pointed ears

child children *noun* **1** a young person who is not yet an adult **2** Someone's child is their son or daughter

childbirth *noun* Childbirth is the act of giving birth to a child

childhood *noun* Someone's childhood is the time when they are a child

childish *adjective* immature and foolish: *I don't have time for childish arguments* ▷ **childishly** *adverb* ▷ **childishness** *noun*

childless *adjective* having no children

childlike *adjective* like a child in appearance or behaviour: *childlike enthusiasm*

Chilean *adjective* **1** belonging or relating to Chile ▷ *noun* **2** someone who comes from Chile

chill *verb* **1** To chill something is to make it cold: *The cheesecake is chilling* **2** If something chills you, it makes you feel worried or frightened: *The thought chilled her* ▷ *noun* **3** a feverish cold **4** a feeling of cold: *the chill of the night air*

chilli chillies *noun* the red or green seed pod of a type of pepper which has a very hot, spicy taste

chilly chillier, chilliest *adjective* **1** rather cold: *the chilly November breeze* **2** unfriendly and without enthusiasm: *a chilly reception*

chime *verb* When a bell chimes, it makes a clear ringing sound

chimney *noun* a vertical pipe or other hollow structure above a fireplace or furnace through which smoke from a fire escapes

chimpanzee *noun* a small ape with dark fur that lives in forests in Africa

chin *noun* the part of your face below your mouth

china *noun* **1** China is items like cups, saucers, and plates made from very fine clay **2** (*informal*) In South African English, a china is a friend

Chinese *adjective* belonging or

relating to China ▷ **noun 2** someone who comes from China **3** Chinese refers to any of a group of related languages and dialects spoken by Chinese people

chink noun **1** a small, narrow opening: *a chink in the roof* **2** a short, light, ringing sound, like one made by glasses touching each other

chip chips, chipping, chipped noun **1** Chips are thin strips of fried potato **2** In electronics, a chip is a tiny piece of silicon inside a computer which is used to form electronic circuits **3** a small piece broken off an object, or the mark made when a piece breaks off **4** In some gambling games, chips are counters used to represent money ▷ verb **5** If you chip an object, you break a small piece off it

chirp verb When a bird chirps, it makes a short, high-pitched sound

chisel chisels, chiselling, chiselled noun **1** a tool with a long metal blade and a sharp edge at the end which is used for cutting and shaping wood, stone, or metal ▷ verb **2** To chisel wood, stone, or metal is to cut or shape it using a chisel

chivalry [shiv-val-ree] noun Chivalry is polite and helpful behaviour, especially by men towards women > **chivalrous** adjective

chive noun Chives are grasslike hollow leaves that have a mild onion flavour

chlorine [klaw-reen] noun SCIENCE Chlorine is a chemical element which is a poisonous greenish-yellow gas with a strong, unpleasant smell. It is used to disinfect water and to make bleach. Its atomic number is 17 and its symbol is Cl

chlorophyll [klor-rof-fil] noun

SCIENCE Chlorophyll is a green substance in plants which enables them to use the energy from sunlight in order to grow

chocolate noun **1** Chocolate is a sweet food made from cacao seeds **2** a sweet made of chocolate ▷ adjective **3** dark brown

choice noun **1** a range of different things that are available to choose from: *a wider choice of treatments* **2** something that you choose: *You've made a good choice* **3** Choice is the power or right to choose: *I had no choice*

choir [kwire] noun MUSIC a group of singers, for example in a church

choke verb **1** If you choke, you stop being able to breathe properly, usually because something is blocking your windpipe: *the diner who choked on a fish bone* **2** If things choke a place, they fill it so much that it is blocked or clogged up: *The canal was choked with old tyres*

cholera [kol-ler-ra] noun Cholera is a serious disease causing severe diarrhoea and vomiting. It is caused by infected food or water

cholesterol [kol-less-ter-rol] noun Cholesterol is a substance found in all animal fats, tissues, and blood

chook noun (informal) In Australian and New Zealand English, a chicken

choose chooses, choosing, chose, chosen verb To choose something is to decide to have it or do it: *He chose to live in Kenya*

choosy choosier, choosiest adjective fussy and difficult to satisfy: *You can't be too choosy about jobs*

chop chops, chopping, chopped verb **1** To chop something is to cut it with quick, heavy strokes using an axe or a knife ▷ noun **2** a small piece of lamb or pork containing a bone, usually cut from the ribs

chopper noun (informal) a helicopter

choppy choppier, choppiest adjective Choppy water has a lot of waves because it is windy

choral adjective relating to singing by a choir: choral music

chore noun an uninteresting job that has to be done: the chore of cleaning

choreography [kor-ree-**og**-raf-fee] noun Choreography is the art of composing dance steps and movements > **choreographer** noun

chorus choruses, chorusing, chorused MUSIC noun **1** a large group of singers; also a piece of music for a large group of singers **2** a part of a song which is repeated after each verse > verb **3** If people chorus something, they all say or sing it at the same time

Christ proper noun Christ is the name for Jesus. Christians believe that Jesus is the son of God

christen verb When a baby is christened, it is named by a member of the clergy in a religious ceremony

Christian noun RE **1** a person who believes in Jesus Christ and his teachings > adjective **2** relating to Christ and his teachings: the Christian faith **3** good, kind, and considerate > **Christianity** noun

Christmas noun RE The Christian festival celebrating the birth of Christ, falling on December 25th

chrome [krome] noun Chrome is metal plated with chromium, a hard grey metal

chromosome [krome] noun SCIENCE In biology, a chromosome is one of a number of rod-shaped parts in the nucleus of a cell which contains genes that determine the characteristics of an animal or plant

chronic [kron-nik] adjective lasting a very long time or never stopping: a chronic illness > **chronically** adverb

chronicle noun **1** a record of a series of events described in the order in which they happened > verb **2** To chronicle a series of events is to record or describe them in the order in which they happened

chronological [kron-nol-**loj**-i-kl] adjective HISTORY arranged in the order in which things happened: Tell me the whole story in chronological order > **chronologically** adverb

chronology [kron-**nol**-loj-jee] noun HISTORY The chronology of events is the order in which they happened

chubby chubbier, chubbiest adjective plump and round: his chubby cheeks

chuck verb (informal) To chuck something is to throw it casually

chuckle verb When you chuckle, you laugh quietly

chug chugs, chugging, chugged verb When a machine or engine chugs, it makes a continuous dull thudding sound

chum noun (informal) a friend

chunk noun a thick piece of something

chunky chunkier, chunkiest adjective Someone who is chunky is broad and heavy but usually short

church noun **1** a building where Christians go for religious services and worship **2** In the Christian religion, a church is one of the groups with their own particular beliefs, customs, and clergy: the Catholic Church

Church of England noun The Church of England is the Anglican church in England, where it is the state church, with the King or Queen as its head

churchyard noun an area of land

around a church, often used as a graveyard

churn noun a container used for making milk or cream into butter

chute [shoot] noun a steep slope or channel used to slide things down: a rubbish chute

chutney noun Chutney is a strong-tasting thick sauce made from fruit, vinegar, and spices

cider noun Cider is an alcoholic drink made from apples

cigar noun a roll of dried tobacco leaves which people smoke

cigarette noun a thin roll of tobacco covered in thin paper which people smoke

cinema noun 1 a place where people go to watch films 2 Cinema is the business of making films

cinnamon noun Cinnamon is a sweet spice which comes from the bark of an Asian tree

circa [sir-ka] preposition (formal) about or approximately; used especially before dates: portrait of a lady, circa 1840

circle noun 1 MATHS a completely regular round shape. Every point on its edge is the same distance from the centre 2 a group of people with the same interest or profession: a character well known in yachting circles 3 an area of seats on an upper floor of a theatre ▷ verb 4 To circle is to move round and round as though going round the edge of a circle: A police helicopter circled above

circuit [sir-kit] noun 1 any closed line or path, often circular, for example a racing track; also the distance round this path: three circuits of the 26-lap race remaining 2 SCIENCE An electrical circuit is a complete route around which an electric current can flow. A **closed circuit** is a

complete electrical circuit around which current can flow; a **parallel circuit** is a closed circuit in which the current divides into two or more paths before coming back together to complete the circuit; a **series circuit** is an electrical circuit in which the elements are connected one after the other so that the same current flows through them all

circular adjective 1 in the shape of a circle 2 A circular argument or theory is not valid because it uses a statement to prove a conclusion and the conclusion to prove the statement ▷ noun 3 a letter or advert sent to a lot of people at the same time > **circularity** noun

circulate verb 1 SCIENCE When something circulates or when you circulate it, it moves easily around an area: an open position where the air can circulate freely 2 When you circulate something among people, you pass it round or tell it to all the people: We circulate a regular newsletter

circulation noun 1 The circulation of something is the act of circulating it or the action of it circulating: traffic circulation 2 The circulation of a newspaper or magazine is the number of copies that are sold of each issue 3 SCIENCE Your circulation is the movement of blood through your body

circumference noun MATHS The circumference of a circle is its outer line or edge; also the length of this line

circumstance noun 1 The circumstances of a situation or event are the conditions that affect what happens: He did well in the circumstances 2 Someone's circumstances are their position and conditions in life: Her circumstances had changed

circus circuses *noun* a show given by a travelling group of entertainers such as clowns, acrobats, and specially trained animals

cistern *noun* a tank in which water is stored, for example one in the roof of a house or above a toilet

citadel *noun* a fortress in or near a city

cite *verb* **1** (formal) If you cite something, you quote it or refer to it: *He cited a letter written by Newall* **2** If someone is cited in a legal action, they are officially called to appear in court

citizen *noun* HISTORY The citizens of a country or city are the people who live in it or belong to it: *American citizens*

citizenship *noun* the status of being a citizen, with all the rights and duties that go with it: *I'm applying for Australian citizenship*

citrus fruit *noun* Citrus fruits are juicy, sharp-tasting fruits such as oranges, lemons, and grapefruit

city cities *noun* a large town where many people live and work

civic *adjective* relating to a city or citizens: *the Civic Centre*

civil *adjective* **1** relating to the citizens of a country: *civil rights* **2** relating to people or things that are not connected with the armed forces: *the history of civil aviation* **3** polite > **civilly** *adverb* > **civility** *noun*

civil engineering *noun* Civil engineering is the design and construction of roads, bridges, and public buildings

civilian *noun* a person who is not in the armed forces

civilization or **civilisation** *noun* HISTORY **1** a society which has a

highly developed organization and culture: *the tale of a lost civilization* **2** Civilization is an advanced state of social organization and culture

civilized or **civilised** *adjective* **1** A civilized society is one with a developed social organization and way of life **2** A civilized person is polite and reasonable

civil servant *noun* a person who works in the civil service

civil service *noun* The civil service is the government departments responsible for the administration of a country

civil war *noun* a war between groups of people who live in the same country

clad *adjective* (literary) Someone who is clad in particular clothes is wearing them

claim *verb* **1** If you claim that something is the case, you say that it is the case: *He claims to have lived in the same house all his life* **2** If you claim something, you ask for it because it belongs to you or you have a right to it: *Cartier claimed the land for the King of France* > *noun* **3** a statement that something is the case, or that you have a right to something: *She will make a claim for damages*

claimant *noun* someone who is making a claim, especially for money

clairvoyant *adjective* **1** able to know about things that will happen in the future > *noun* **2** a person who is, or claims to be, clairvoyant

clam *noun* a kind of shellfish

clamber *verb* If you clamber somewhere, you climb there with difficulty

clammy clammier, clammiest *adjective* unpleasantly damp and sticky: *clammy hands*

clamour verb **1** If people clamour for something, they demand it noisily or angrily: *We clamoured for an explanation* ▷ noun **2** Clamour is noisy or angry shouts or demands by a lot of people

clamp noun **1** an object with movable parts that are used to hold two things firmly together ▷ verb **2** To clamp things together is to fasten them or hold them firmly with a clamp ▷ **clamp down on** verb To clamp down on something is to become stricter in controlling it: *The Queen has clamped down on all expenditure*

clan noun a group of families related to each other by being descended from the same ancestor

clandestine adjective secret and hidden: *a clandestine meeting with friends*

clap claps, clapping, clapped verb **1** When you clap, you hit your hands together loudly to show your appreciation **2** If you clap someone on the back or shoulder, you hit them in a friendly way **3** If you clap something somewhere, you put it there quickly and firmly: *I clapped a hand over her mouth* ▷ noun **4** A sound made by clapping your hands **5** A clap of thunder is a sudden loud noise of thunder

claret noun a type of red wine, especially one from the Bordeaux region of France

clarify clarifies, clarifying, clarified verb EXAM TERM To clarify something is to make it clear and easier to understand: *Discussion will clarify your thoughts* ▷ **clarification** noun

clarinet noun MUSIC a woodwind instrument with a straight tube and a single reed in its mouthpiece

clarity noun The clarity of something is its clearness

clash verb **1** If people clash with each other, they fight or argue **2** Ideas or styles that clash are so different that they do not go together **3** If two events clash, they happen at the same time so you cannot go to both **4** When metal objects clash, they hit each other with a loud noise ▷ noun **5** a fight or argument **6** A clash of ideas, styles, or events is a situation in which they do not go together **7** a loud noise made by metal objects when they hit each other

clasp verb **1** To clasp something means to hold it tightly or fasten it: *He clasped his hands* ▷ noun **2** a fastening such as a hook or catch

class noun **1** A class of people or things is a group of them of a particular type or quality: *the old class of politicians* **2** a group of pupils or students taught together, or a lesson that they have together **3** Someone who has class is elegant in appearance or behaviour **4** SCIENCE A class is a major division of living organisms that is smaller than a phylum and larger than an order ▷ verb **5** To class something means to arrange it in a particular group or to consider it as belonging to a particular group: *They are officially classed as visitors*

classic adjective **1** typical and therefore a good model or example of something: *a classic case of misuse* **2** of very high quality: *one of the classic films of all time* **3** simple in style and form: *the classic dinner suit* ▷ noun **4** something of the highest quality: *one of the great classics of rock music* **5** Classics is the study of Latin and Greek, and the literature of ancient Greece and Rome

classical *adjective* **1** traditional in style, form, and content: *classical ballet* **2** Classical music is serious music considered to be of lasting value **3** characteristic of the style of ancient Greece and Rome: *Classical friezes decorate the walls*
> **classically** *adverb*

classified *adjective* officially declared secret by the government: *access to classified information*

classify classifies, classifying, classified *verb* [LIBRARY] To classify things is to arrange them into groups with similar characteristics: *We can classify the differences into three groups* > **classification** *noun*

classroom *noun* a room in a school where pupils have lessons

classy classier, classiest *adjective* (*informal*) stylish and elegant

clatter *verb* **1** When things clatter, they hit each other with a loud rattling noise > *noun* **2** a loud rattling noise made by hard things hitting each other

clause *noun* **1** a section of a legal document **2** [ENGLISH] In grammar, a clause is a group of words with a subject and a verb, which may be a complete sentence or one of the parts of a sentence

claustrophobia [klos-trof-**foe**-bee-ya] *noun* Claustrophobia is a fear of being in enclosed spaces
> **claustrophobic** *adjective*

claw *noun* **1** An animal's claws are hard, curved nails at the end of its feet **2** The claws of a crab or lobster are the two jointed parts, used for grasping things > *verb* **3** If an animal claws something, it digs its claws into it

clay *noun* Clay is a type of earth that is soft and sticky when wet and hard

when baked dry. It is used to make pottery and china

clean *adjective* **1** free from dirt or marks **2** free from germs or infection **3** If humour is clean it is not rude and does not involve bad language **4** A clean movement is skilful and accurate **5** Clean also means free from fault or error: *a clean driving licence* > *verb* **6** To clean something is to remove dirt from it
> **cleanly** *adverb* > **cleaner** *noun*

cleanliness [**klen**-lin-ness] *noun* Cleanliness is the practice of keeping yourself and your surroundings clean

cleanse [klenz] *verb* To cleanse something is to make it completely free from dirt

clear *adjective* **1** easy to understand, see, or hear: *He made it clear he did not want to talk* **2** easy to see through: *a clear liquid* **3** free from obstructions or unwanted things: *clear of debris* > *verb* **4** To clear an area is to remove unwanted things from it **5** If you clear a fence or other obstacle, you jump over it without touching it **6** When fog or mist clears, it disappears **7** If someone is cleared of a crime, they are proved to be not guilty > **clearly** *adverb*
> **clear out** *verb* **1** If you clear out a room or cupboard, you tidy it and throw away unwanted things **2** (*informal*) To clear out means to leave: *You can clear out right now!*
> **clear up** *verb* **1** If you clear up, you tidy a place and put things away **2** When a problem or misunderstanding is cleared up, it is solved or settled

clearance *noun* **1** Clearance is the removal of old buildings in an area **2** If someone is given clearance to do something, they get official permission to do it

clearing noun an area of bare ground in a forest

cleaver noun a knife with a large square blade, used especially by butchers

cleft noun a narrow opening in a rock

clench verb 1 When you clench your fist, you curl your fingers up tightly 2 When you clench your teeth, you squeeze them together tightly

clergy plural noun The clergy are the ministers of the Christian Church

clergyman clergymen noun a male member of the clergy

clerical adjective 1 relating to work done in an office: clerical jobs with the City Council 2 relating to the clergy

clerk [klahrk] noun a person who keeps records or accounts in an office, bank, or law court

clever adjective 1 intelligent and quick to understand things 2 very effective or skilful: a clever plan > **cleverly** adverb > **cleverness** noun

cliché [klee-shay] noun ENGLISH an idea or phrase which is no longer effective because it has been used so much

click verb 1 When something clicks or when you click it, it makes a short snapping sound 2 When you click on an area of a computer screen, you point the cursor at it and press one of the buttons on the mouse in order to make something happen > noun 3 a sound of something clicking: I heard the click of a bolt

client noun someone who pays a professional person or company for a service

clientele [klee-on-**tell**] plural noun The clientele of a place are its customers

cliff noun a steep, high rock face by the sea

climactic adjective (formal) bringing a climax: Her death is the climactic point of the film

climate noun 1 GEOGRAPHY The climate of a place is the typical weather conditions there: The climate was dry in the summer 2 the general attitude and opinion of people at a particular time: the American political climate > **climatic** adjective

climax noun ENGLISH The climax of a process, story, or piece of music is the most exciting moment in it, usually near the end

climb verb 1 To climb is to move upwards 2 If you climb somewhere, you move there with difficulty: She climbed out of the driving seat > noun 3 a movement upwards: this long climb up the slope; the rapid climb in murders > **climber** noun

clinch verb If you clinch an argument, you settle it in a definite way: Peter clinched a deal

cling clings, clinging, clung verb To cling to something is to hold onto it or stay closely attached to it: still clinging to his old-fashioned values

clinic noun a building where people go for medical treatment

clinical adjective 1 relating to the medical treatment of patients: clinical tests 2 Clinical behaviour or thought is logical and unemotional: the cold, clinical attitudes of his colleagues > **clinically** adverb

clip clips, clipping, clipped noun 1 a small metal or plastic object used for holding things together 2 a short piece of a film shown by itself > verb 3 If you clip things together, you fasten them with clips 4 If you clip something, you cut bits from it to shape it: clipped hedges

clipping noun an article cut from a newspaper or magazine

clique [rhymes with **seek**] noun a small group of people who stick together and do not mix with other people

cloak noun **1** a wide, loose coat without sleeves ▷ verb **2** To cloak something is to cover or hide it: *a land permanently cloaked in mist*

cloakroom noun a room for coats or a room with toilets and washbasins in a public building

clock noun **1** a device that measures and shows the time ▷ phrase **2** If you work **round the clock**, you work all day and night

clockwise adjective, adverb in the same direction as the hands on a clock

clockwork noun **1** Toys that work by clockwork move when they are wound up with a key ▷ phrase **2** If something happens **like clockwork**, it happens with no problems or delays

clog clogs, clogging, clogged verb **1** To clog something is to block it: *pavements clogged up with people* ▷ noun **2** Clogs are heavy wooden shoes

clone [SCIENCE] noun **1** In biology, a clone is an animal or plant that has been produced artificially from the cells of another animal or plant and is therefore identical to it ▷ verb **2** To clone an animal or plant is to produce it as a clone

close verb [**kloze**] noun **1** To close something is to shut it **2** To close a road or entrance is to block it so that no-one can go in or out **3** If a shop closes at a certain time, then it does not do business after that time ▷ adjective, adverb [**kloass**] **4** near to something: *a restaurant close to their home* ▷ adjective [**kloass**] **5** People who are close to each other other are very friendly and know each other well **6** You say the weather is close when it is uncomfortably warm and there is not enough air ▷ **closely** adverb > **closeness** [kloass] **close down** verb If a business closes down, all work stops there permanently

closet noun **1** a cupboard ▷ verb **2** If you are closeted somewhere, you shut yourself away alone or in private with another person ▷ adjective **3** Closet beliefs or habits are kept private and secret: *a closet romantic*

close-up noun a detailed close view of something, especially a photograph taken close to the subject

closure [klohz-yur] noun **1** The closure of a business is the permanent shutting of it **2** The closure of a road is the blocking of it so it cannot be used

clot clots, clotting, clotted noun **1** a lump, especially one that forms when blood thickens ▷ verb **2** When a substance such as blood clots, it thickens and forms a lump

cloth noun **1** Cloth is fabric made by a process such as weaving **2** a piece of material used for wiping or protecting things

clothe clothes, clothing, clothed verb To clothe someone is to give them clothes to wear

clothes plural noun the things people wear on their bodies

clothing noun the clothes people wear

cloud noun **1** a mass of water vapour, smoke, or dust that forms in the air and is seen floating in the sky ▷ verb **2** If something clouds or is clouded, it becomes cloudy or difficult to see through: *The sky clouded over* **3** Something that clouds an issue makes it more confusing

cloud computing noun
COMPUTING Cloud computing is a system where a person's files and programs are stored on the Internet so that the person can use them at any time from any place

cloudy cloudier, cloudiest adjective **1** full of clouds: *the cloudy sky* **2** difficult to see through: *a glass of cloudy liquid*

clout (informal) noun **1** Someone who has clout has influence **2** A clout is a hit: *a clout on the head* ▷ verb **3** If you clout someone, you hit them

clove noun **1** Cloves are small, strong-smelling dried flower buds from a tropical tree, used as a spice in cooking **2** A clove of garlic is one of the separate sections of the bulb

clover noun Clover is a small plant with leaves made up of three similar parts

clown noun **1** a circus performer who wears funny clothes and make-up and does silly things to make people laugh ▷ verb **2** If you clown, you do silly things to make people laugh

cloying adjective unpleasantly sickly, sweet, or sentimental: *something less cloying than whipped cream*

club clubs, clubbing, clubbed noun **1** an organization of people with a particular interest, who meet regularly; also the place where they meet **2** a thick, heavy stick used as a weapon **3** a stick with a shaped head that a golf player uses to hit the ball **4** Clubs is one of the four suits in a pack of playing cards. It is marked by a black symbol in the shape of a clover leaf ▷ verb **5** To club someone is to hit them hard with a heavy

object ▷ **club together** verb If people club together, they all join together to give money to buy something

clue noun something that helps to solve a problem or mystery

clump noun **1** a small group of things close together ▷ verb **2** If you clump about, you walk with heavy footsteps

clumsiness noun awkwardness in the way someone or something moves

clumsy clumsier, clumsiest adjective **1** moving awkwardly and carelessly **2** said or done without thought or tact: *his clumsy attempts to catch her out* ▷ **clumsily** adverb

cluster noun **1** A cluster of things is a group of them together: *a cluster of huts at the foot of the mountains* ▷ verb **2** If people cluster together, they stay together in a close group

clutch verb **1** If you clutch something, you hold it tightly or seize it ▷ noun **2** (in plural) If you are in someone's clutches, they have power or control over you

clutter noun **1** Clutter is an untidy mess ▷ verb **2** Things that clutter a place fill it and make it untidy

cm an abbreviation for 'centimetres'

co- prefix 'Co-' means 'together': *Paula is now co-writing a book with Pierre*

coach noun **1** a long motor vehicle used for taking passengers on long journeys **2** a section of a train that carries passengers **3** a four-wheeled vehicle with a roof pulled by horses, which people used to travel in **4** a person who coaches a sport or a subject ▷ verb **5** If someone coaches you, they teach you and help you to get better at a sport or a subject

coal noun **1** Coal is a hard black rock obtained from under the earth and burned as a fuel **2** Coals are burning pieces of coal

coalition noun a temporary alliance, especially between different political parties forming a government

coarse adjective **1** Something that is coarse is rough in texture, often consisting of large particles: *a coarse blanket* **2** Someone who is coarse talks or behaves in a rude or rather offensive way > **coarsely** adverb > **coarseness** noun

coast noun **1** the edge of the land where it meets the sea ▷ verb **2** A vehicle that is coasting is moving without engine power > **coastal** adjective

coastguard noun an official who watches the sea near a coast to get help for sailors when they need it, and to prevent smuggling

coastline noun the outline of a coast, especially its appearance as seen from the sea or air

coat noun **1 a** piece of clothing with sleeves which you wear over your other clothes **2** An animal's coat is the fur or hair on its body **3** A coat of paint or varnish is a layer of it ▷ verb **4** To coat something means to cover it with a thin layer of something: *walnuts coated with chocolate*

coating noun a layer of something

coax verb If you coax someone to do something, you gently persuade them to do it

cobalt noun Cobalt is a hard silvery-white metallic element which is used in alloys and for producing a blue dye. Its atomic number is 27 and its symbol is Co

cobble noun Cobbles or cobblestones are stones with a rounded surface that were used in the past for making roads

cobbler noun a person who makes or mends shoes

cobra [koh-bra] noun a type of large poisonous snake from Africa and Asia

cobweb noun the very thin net that a spider spins for catching insects

cocaine noun Cocaine is an addictive drug

cock noun an adult male chicken; also used of any male bird

cockatoo cockatoos noun a type of parrot with a crest, found in Australia and New Guinea

Cockney noun a person born in the East End of London

cockpit noun The place in a small plane where the pilot sits

cockroach noun a large dark-coloured insect often found in dirty rooms

cocktail noun an alcoholic drink made from several ingredients

cocky cockier, cockiest; cockies (informal) adjective **1** cheeky or too self-confident ▷ noun **2** in Australian English, a cockatoo **3** in Australian and New Zealand English, a farmer, especially one whose farm is small > **cockiness** noun

cocoa noun Cocoa is a brown powder made from the seeds of a tropical tree and used for making chocolate; also a hot drink made from this powder

coconut noun a very large nut with white flesh, milky juice, and a hard hairy shell

cocoon noun a silky covering over the larvae of moths and some other insects

cod noun a large edible fish

code noun **1** a system of replacing the letters or words in a message with other letters or words, so that nobody can understand the message unless they know the system **2** a group of numbers and letters which is used to identify something: *the telephone code for Melbourne* > **coded** adjective

coffee noun Coffee is a substance made from by roasting and grinding the beans of a tropical shrub; also a hot drink made from this substance

coffin noun a box in which a dead body is buried or cremated

cog noun a wheel with teeth which turns another wheel or part of a machine

cognac [**kon**-yak] noun Cognac is a kind of brandy

coherent adjective **1** If something such as a theory is coherent, its parts fit together well and do not contradict each other **2** If someone is coherent, what they are saying makes sense and is not jumbled or confused > **coherence** noun

cohesive adjective If something is cohesive, its parts fit together well: *The team must work as a cohesive unit* > **cohesion** noun

coil noun **1** a length of rope or wire wound into a series of loops; also one of the loops ▷ verb **2** If something coils, it turns into a series of loops

coin noun **1** a small metal disc which is used as money ▷ verb **2** If you coin a word or a phrase, you invent it

coinage noun The coinage of a country is the coins that are used there

coincide verb **1** If two events coincide, they happen at about the same time **2** When two people's ideas or opinions coincide, they agree: *What she said coincided exactly with his own thinking*

coincidence noun **1** what happens when two similar things occur at the same time by chance: *I had*

moved to London, and by coincidence, Helen had too **2** the fact that two things are surprisingly the same > **coincidental** adjective > **coincidentally** adverb

coke noun Coke is a grey fuel produced from coal

colander [**kol**-an-der] noun a bowl-shaped container with holes in it, used for washing or draining food

cold adjective **1** having a low temperature **2** Someone who is cold does not show much affection ▷ noun **3** You can refer to cold weather as the cold: *She was complaining about the cold* **4** a minor illness in which you sneeze and may have a sore throat > **coldly** adverb > **coldness** noun

cold-blooded adjective **1** Someone who is cold-blooded does not show any pity: *two cold-blooded killers* **2** A cold-blooded animal has a body temperature that changes according to the surrounding temperature

cold war noun Cold war is a state of extreme unfriendliness between countries not actually at war

coleslaw noun Coleslaw is a salad of chopped cabbage and other vegetables in mayonnaise

colic noun Colic is pain in a baby's stomach

collaborate verb When people collaborate, they work together to produce something: *The two bands have collaborated in the past* > **collaboration** noun > **collaborator** noun

collage [**kol**-lahj] noun [ART] a picture made by sticking pieces of paper or cloth onto a surface

collapse verb **1** If something such as a building collapses, it falls down suddenly. If a person collapses, they fall down suddenly because they are ill **2** If something such as a system or a business collapses, it suddenly stops working: *50,000 small firms collapsed last year* ▷ *noun* **3** The collapse of something is what happens when it stops working: *the collapse of his marriage*

collapsible *adjective* A collapsible object can be folded flat when it is not in use: *a collapsible ironing board*

collar *noun* **1** The collar of a shirt or coat is the part round the neck which is usually folded over **2** a leather band round the neck of a dog or cat

collateral *noun* Collateral is money or property which is used as a guarantee that someone will repay a loan, and which the lender can take if the loan is not repaid

colleague *noun* A person's colleagues are the people he or she works with

collect *verb* **1** To collect things is to gather them together for a special purpose or as a hobby: *collecting money for charity* **2** If you collect someone or something from a place, you call there and take them away: *We had to collect her from school* **3** When things collect in a place, they gather there over a period of time: *Food collects in holes in the teeth* ▷ **collector** *noun*

collected *adjective* calm and self-controlled

collection *noun* **1** ⟨ART⟩ a group of things acquired over a period of time: *a collection of paintings* **2** Collection is the collecting of something: *tax collection* **3** the organized collecting of money, for example for charity, or the sum of money collected

collective *adjective* **1** involving every member of a group of people: *The wine growers took a collective decision* ▷ *noun* **2** a group of people who share the responsibility both for running something and for doing the work ▷ **collectively** *adverb*

college *noun* **1** a place where students study after they have left school **2** a name given to some secondary schools **3** one of the institutions into which some universities are divided **4** In New Zealand English, a college can also refer to a teacher training college

collide *verb* If a moving object collides with something, it hits it

collie *noun* a dog that is used for rounding up sheep

colliery collieries *noun* a coal mine

collision *noun* A collision occurs when a moving object hits something

colloquial [kol-**loh**-kwee-al] *adjective* Colloquial words and phrases are informal and used especially in conversation ▷ **colloquially** *adverb* ▷ **colloquialism** *noun*

cologne [kol-**lone**] *noun* Cologne is a kind of weak perfume

colon *noun* **1** the punctuation mark (:) **2** part of your intestine

colonel [**kur**-nl] *noun* an army officer with a fairly high rank

colonial *adjective* **1** relating to a colony **2** In Australia, colonial is used to relate to the period of Australian history before the Federation in 1901

colonize or **colonise** *verb* ⟨HISTORY⟩ **1** When people colonize a place, they go to live there and take control of it: *the Europeans who colonized North America* **2** When a lot of animals colonize a place, they go there and make it their home: *Toads are colonizing the whole place* > **colonization** *noun* > **colonist** *noun*

colony colonies *noun* HISTORY **1** a country controlled by a more powerful country **2** a group of people who settle in a country controlled by their homeland

colossal *adjective* very large indeed

colour *noun* **1** ART The appearance something has as a result of reflecting light **2** a substance used to give colour **3** Someone's colour is the normal colour of their skin **4** Colour is also a quality that makes something interesting or exciting: *bringing more culture and colour to the city* > *verb* **5** If you colour something, you give it a colour **6** If something colours your opinion, it affects the way you think about something > **coloured** *adjective* > **colourless** *adjective* > **colouring** *noun*

colourful *adjective* **1** full of colour **2** interesting or exciting > **colourfully** *adverb*

colt *noun* a young male horse

column *noun* **1** a tall solid upright cylinder, especially one supporting a part of a building **2** a group of people moving in a long line

columnist *noun* a journalist who writes a regular article in a newspaper or magazine

coma *noun* Someone who is in a coma is in a state of deep unconsciousness

comb *noun* **1** a flat object with pointed teeth used for tidying your hair > *verb* **2** When you comb your hair, you tidy it with a comb **3** If you comb a place, you search it thoroughly to try to find someone or something

combat *noun* **1** Combat is fighting: *his first experience of combat* > *verb* **2** To combat something means to try to stop it happening or developing: *a way to combat crime*

combination *noun* **1a** a mixture of things: *a combination of charm and skill* **2** a series of letters or numbers used to open a special lock

combine *verb* **1** To combine things is to cause them to exist together: *to combine a career with being a mother* **2** To combine things also means to join them together to make a single thing: *Combine all the ingredients* **3** If something combines two qualities or features, it has both: *a film that combines great charm and scintillating performances*

combustion *noun* SCIENCE Combustion is the act of burning something or the process of burning

come comes, coming, came, come *verb* **1** To come to a place is to move there or arrive there **2** To come to a place also means to reach as far as that place: *The sea water came up to his waist* **3** 'Come' is used to say that someone or something reaches a particular state: *They came to power in 1997; We had come to a decision* **4** When a particular time or event comes, it happens: *The peak of his career came early in 1990* **5** If you come from a place, you were born there or it is your home > *phrase* **6** A time or event to come is a future time or event: *The public will thank them in years to come* > **come about** *verb* The way something comes about is the way it happens: *The discussion came about because of the proposed changes* > **come across** *verb* If you come across something, you find it by chance > **come off** *verb* If something comes off, it succeeds:

His rescue plan had come off > **come on** *verb* If something is coming on, it is making progress: *Let's go and see how the grapes are coming on* > **come round** *verb* **1** To come round means to recover consciousness **2** To come round to an idea or situation means to eventually accept it **3** When a regular event comes round, it happens: *Beginning of term came round too quickly* > **come to** *verb* To come to means to recover consciousness > **come up** *verb* If something comes up in a conversation or meeting, it is mentioned or discussed > **come up with** *verb* If you come up with an idea, you suggest it

comeback *noun* To make a comeback means to be popular or successful again

comedian *noun* an entertainer whose job is to make people laugh

comedienne [kom-mee-dee-**en**] *noun* a female comedian

comedy comedies *noun* a light-hearted play or film with a happy ending

comet *noun* an object that travels around the sun leaving a bright trail behind it

comfort *noun* **1** Comfort is the state of being physically relaxed: *He settled back in comfort* **2** Comfort is also a feeling of relief from worries or unhappiness: *The thought is a great comfort to me* **3** (*in plural*) Comforts are things which make your life easier and more pleasant: *all the comforts of home* ▷ *verb* **4** To comfort someone is to make them less worried or unhappy

comfortable *adjective* **1** If you are comfortable, you are physically relaxed **2** Something that is comfortable makes you feel relaxed:

a comfortable bed **3** If you feel comfortable in a particular situation, you are not afraid or embarrassed > **comfortably** *adverb*

comic *adjective* **1** funny: *a comic monologue* ▷ *noun* **2** someone who tells jokes **3** a magazine that contains stories told in pictures

comical *adjective* funny: *a comical sight*

comma *noun* ENGLISH the punctuation mark (,)

command *verb* **1** To command someone to do something is to order them to do it **2** If you command something such as respect, you receive it because of your personal qualities **3** An officer who commands part of an army or navy is in charge of it ▷ *noun* **4** an order to do something **5** Your command of something is your knowledge of it and your ability to use this knowledge: *a good command of English*

commandant [kom-man-dant] *noun* an army officer in charge of a place or group of people

commander *noun* an officer in charge of a military operation or organization

commandment *noun* RE The commandments are ten rules of behaviour that, according to the Old Testament, people should obey

commando commandos *noun* Commandos are soldiers who have been specially trained to carry out raids

commemorate *verb* **1** An object that commemorates a person or an event is intended to remind people of that person or event **2** If you commemorate an event, you do something special to show that you remember it > **commemorative**

adjective ▷ **commemoration** noun

commence verb (formal) To
commence is to begin
▷ **commencement** noun

commend verb To commend
someone or something is to praise
them: *He has been commended for his
work* ▷ **commendation** noun
▷ **commendable** adjective

comment verb **1** If you comment on
something, you make a remark
about it ▷ noun **2** a remark about
something: *She received many
comments about her appearance*

commentary commentaries noun
a description of an event which is
broadcast on radio or television
while the event is happening

commentator noun someone
who gives a radio or television
commentary

commerce noun Commerce is the
buying and selling of goods

commercial adjective **1** relating to
commerce **2** Commercial activities
involve producing goods on a large
scale in order to make money: *the
commercial fishing world* ▷ noun **3** an
advertisement on television or radio
▷ **commercially** adverb

commission verb **1** If someone
commissions a piece of work, they
formally ask someone to do it: *a
study commissioned by the government*
▷ noun **2** a piece of work that has
been commissioned **3** Commission
is money paid to a salesperson each
time a sale is made **4** an official
body appointed to investigate or
control something

commit commits, committing,
committed verb **1** To commit a crime
or sin is to do it **2** If you commit
yourself, you state an opinion or
state that you will do something **3** If
someone is committed to hospital

or prison, they are officially sent
there ▷ **committal** noun

commitment noun **1** RE
Commitment is a strong belief in an
idea or system **2** something that
regularly takes up some of your
time: *business commitments*

committed adjective A committed
person has strong beliefs: *a
committed feminist*

committee noun a group of people
who make decisions on behalf of a
larger group

commodity commodities noun
(formal) Commodities are things
that are sold

common adjective **1** Something that
is common exists in large numbers
or happens often: *a common
complaint* **2** If something is common
to two or more people, they all have
it or use it: *I realized we had a common
interest* **3** 'Common' is used to
indicate that something is of the
ordinary kind and not special **4** If
you describe someone as common,
you mean they do not have good
taste or good manners **5** an
area of grassy land where everyone
can go ▷ phrase **6** If two things or
people have something **in
common**, they both have it
▷ **commonly** adverb

commoner noun someone who is
not a member of the nobility

commonplace adjective Something
that is commonplace happens
often: *Foreign holidays have become
commonplace*

common sense noun Your
common sense is your natural
ability to behave sensibly and make
good judgments

commotion noun A commotion is a
lot of noise and excitement

communal adjective shared by a

group of people: *a communal canteen*

commune [kom-yoon] *noun* a group of people who live together and share everything

communicate *verb* **1** If you communicate with someone, you keep in touch with them **2** If you communicate information or a feeling to someone, you make them aware of it

communication *noun* **1** PSHE Communication is the process by which people or animals exchange information **2** (*in plural*) Communications are the systems by which people communicate or broadcast information, especially using electricity or radio waves **3** (*formal*) a letter or telephone call

communicative *adjective* Someone who is communicative is willing to talk to people

communion *noun* **1** Communion is the sharing of thoughts and feelings **2** RE In Christianity, Communion is a religious service in which people share bread and wine in remembrance of the death and resurrection of Jesus Christ

communism *noun* Communism is the doctrine that the state should own the means of production and that there should be no private property > **communist** *adjective, noun*

community communities *noun* all the people living in a particular area; also used to refer to particular groups within a society: *the heart of the local community; the Asian community*

commute *verb* People who commute travel a long distance to work every day > **commuter** *noun*

compact *adjective* taking up very little space: *a compact microwave*

compact disc *noun* a music or video recording in the form of a plastic disc which is played using a laser on a special machine, and gives good quality sound or pictures

companion *noun* someone you travel or spend time with > **companionship** *noun*

company companies *noun* **1** a business that sells goods or provides a service: *the record company* **2** a group of actors, opera singers, or dancers: *the Royal Shakespeare Company* **3** If you have company, you have a friend or visitor with you: *I enjoyed her company*

comparable [kom-pra-bl] *adjective* If two things are comparable, they are similar in size or quality: *The skill is comparable to playing the violin* > **comparably** *adverb*

comparative *adjective* **1** You add comparative to indicate that something is true only when compared with what is normal: *eight years of comparative calm* > *noun* **2** ENGLISH In grammar, the comparative is the form of an adjective which indicates that the person or thing described has more of a particular quality than someone or something else. For example, 'quicker', 'better', and 'easier' are all comparatives > **comparatively** *adverb*

compare *verb* **1** EXAM TERM When you compare things, you look at them together and see in what ways they are different or similar **2** If you compare one thing to another, you say it is like the other thing: *His voice is often compared to Frank Sinatra's*

comparison *noun* ENGLISH When you make a comparison, you consider two things together and

see in what ways they are different
or similar

compartment noun 1 a section of a
railway carriage 2 one of the
separate parts of an object: *a special
compartment inside your vehicle*

compass noun 1 an instrument with
a magnetic needle for finding
directions 2 (*in plural*) Compasses
are a hinged instrument for drawing
circles

compassion noun pity and
sympathy for someone who is
suffering

compassionate adjective feeling or
showing sympathy and pity for
others > **compassionately** adverb

compatible adjective If people or
things are compatible, they can live
or work together successfully
> **compatibility** noun

compatriot noun Your compatriots
are people from your own country

compel compels, compelling,
compelled verb To compel someone
to do something is to force them to
do it

compelling adjective 1 If a story or
event is compelling, it is extremely
interesting: *a compelling novel* 2 A
compelling argument or reason
makes you believe that something
is true or should be done: *compelling
new evidence*

compensate verb 1 To compensate
someone is to give them money to
replace something lost or damaged
2 If one thing compensates for
another, it cancels out its bad
effects: *The trip more than
compensated for the hardship*
> **compensatory** adjective

compensation noun something
that makes up for loss or damage

compere [kom-pare] noun 1 the
person who introduces the guests

or performers in a show ▷ verb 2 To
compere a show is to introduce the
guests or performers

compete verb 1 When people or
firms compete, each tries to prove
that they or their products are the
best 2 If you compete in a contest or
game, you take part in it

competent adjective Someone who
is competent at something can do it
satisfactorily: *a very competent
engineer* > **competently** adverb
> **competence** noun

competition noun 1 When there is
competition between people or
groups, they are all trying to get
something that not everyone can
have: *There's a lot of competition for
places* 2 an event in which people
take part to find who is best at
something 3 When there is
competition between firms, each
firm is trying to get people to buy its
own goods

competitive adjective 1 A
competitive situation is one in
which people or firms are
competing with each other: *a
crowded and competitive market*
2 A competitive person is eager to
be more successful than others
3 Goods sold at competitive prices
are cheaper than other goods of the
same kind > **competitively** adverb

competitor noun a person or firm
that is competing to become the
most successful

compilation noun A compilation is
a book, recording, or programme
consisting of several items that were
originally produced separately: *this
compilation of his solo work*

compile verb When someone
compiles a book or report, they
make it by putting together
several items

complacent *adjective* If someone is complacent, they are unconcerned about a serious situation and do nothing about it ▷ **complacently** *adverb* ▷ **complacency** *noun*

complain *verb* 1 If you complain, you say that you are not satisfied with something 2 If you complain of pain or illness, you say that you have it

complaint *noun* If you make a complaint, you complain about something

complement *verb* 1 If one thing complements another, the two things go well together: *The tiled floor complements the pine furniture* ▷ *noun* 2 If one thing is a complement to another, it goes well with it 3 In grammar, a complement is a word or phrase that gives information about the subject or object of a sentence. For example, in the sentence 'Rover is a dog', 'is a dog' is a complement ▷ **complementary** *adjective*

> **WORD TIP**
> Do not confuse the spellings of complement and compliment: *The rice should complement the curry nicely; I must compliment you on your garden*

complete *adjective* 1 to the greatest degree possible: *a complete mess* 2 If something is complete, none of it is missing: *a complete set of tools* 3 When a task is complete, it is finished: *The planning stage is now complete* ▷ *verb* 4 If you complete something, you finish it 5 If you complete a form, you fill it in ▷ **completely** *adverb* ▷ **completion** *noun*

complex *adjective* 1 Something that is complex has many different parts: *a very complex problem* ▷ *noun* 2 A complex is a group of buildings, roads, or other things connected with each other in some way: *a hotel and restaurant complex* 3 If someone has a complex, they have an emotional problem because of a past experience: *an inferiority complex* ▷ **complexity** *noun*

complexion *noun* the quality of the skin on your face: *a healthy glowing complexion*

complicate *verb* To complicate something is to make it more difficult to understand or deal with

complicated *adjective* Something that is complicated has so many parts or aspects that it is difficult to understand or deal with

complication *noun* something that makes a situation more difficult to deal with: *One possible complication was that it was late in the year*

compliment *noun* 1 If you pay someone a compliment, you tell them you admire something about them ▷ *verb* 2 If you compliment someone, you pay them a compliment

> **WORD TIP**
> Do not confuse the spellings of compliment and complement: *I must compliment you on your garden; The rice should complement the curry nicely*

complimentary *adjective* 1 If you are complimentary about something, you express admiration for it 2 A complimentary seat, ticket, or publication is given to you free

comply complies, complying, complied *verb* If you comply with an order or rule, you obey it ▷ **compliance** *noun*

component *noun* DGT The components of something are the parts it is made of

compose verb 1 If something is composed of particular things or people, it is made up of them 2 To compose a piece of music, letter, or speech means to write it 3 If you compose yourself, you become calm after being excited or upset

composed adjective calm and in control of your feelings

composer noun someone who writes music

composition noun 1 The composition of something is the things it consists of: *the composition of the ozone layer* 2 MUSIC The composition of a poem or piece of music is the writing of it 3 MUSIC a piece of music or writing

compost noun Compost is a mixture of decaying plants and manure added to soil to help plants grow

composure noun Someone's composure is their ability to stay calm: *Jarvis was able to recover his composure*

compound noun 1 an enclosed area of land with buildings used for a particular purpose: *the prison compound* 2 SCIENCE In chemistry, a compound is a substance consisting of two or more different substances or chemical elements ▷ verb 3 To compound something is to put together different parts to make a whole 4 To compound a problem is to make it worse by adding to it: *Water shortages were compounded by taps left running*

comprehend verb (formal) To comprehend something is to understand or appreciate it: *He did not fully comprehend what was puzzling me* > **comprehension** noun

comprehensible adjective able to be understood

comprehensive adjective 1 Something that is comprehensive includes everything necessary or relevant: *a comprehensive guide* ▷ noun 2 a school where children of all abilities are taught together > **comprehensively** adverb

compress verb To compress something is to squeeze it or shorten it so that it takes up less space: *compressed air* > **compression** noun

comprise verb (formal) What something comprises is what it consists of: *The district then comprised 66 villages*

compromise noun 1 an agreement in which people accept less than they originally wanted: *In the end they reached a compromise* ▷ verb 2 When people compromise, they agree to accept less than they originally wanted > **compromising** adjective

compulsion noun a very strong desire to do something

compulsive adjective 1 You use 'compulsive' to describe someone who cannot stop doing something: *a compulsive letter writer* 2 If you find something such as a book or television programme compulsive, you cannot stop reading or watching it

compulsory adjective If something is compulsory, you have to do it: *School attendance is compulsory*

computer noun an electronic machine that can quickly make calculations or store and find information

computerize or **computerise** verb When a system or process is computerized, the work is done by computers

computing noun Computing is the

use of computers and the writing of programs for them

comrade noun A soldier's comrades are his fellow soldiers, especially in battle ▷ **comradeship** noun

con cons, conning, conned (informal) verb **1** If someone cons you, they trick you into doing or believing something ▷ noun **2** a trick in which someone deceives you into doing or believing something

concave adjective A concave surface curves inwards, rather than being level or bulging outwards

conceal verb To conceal something is to hide it: He had concealed his gun ▷ **concealment** noun

concede [kon-**seed**] verb **1** If you concede something, you admit that it is true: I conceded that he was entitled to his views **2** When someone concedes defeat, they accept that they have lost something such as a contest or an election

conceit noun Conceit is someone's excessive pride in their appearance or abilities

conceited adjective Someone who is conceited is too proud of their appearance or abilities

conceivable adjective If something is conceivable, you can believe that it could exist or be true: It's conceivable that you also met her ▷ **conceivably** adverb

conceive verb **1** If you can conceive of something, you can imagine it or believe it: Could you conceive of doing such a thing yourself? **2** If you conceive something such as a plan, you think of it and work out how it could be done **3** When a woman conceives, she becomes pregnant

concentrate verb **1** If you concentrate on something, you give it all your attention **2** When

something is concentrated in one place, it is all there rather than in several places: They are mostly concentrated in the urban areas ▷ **concentration** noun

concentrated adjective A concentrated liquid has been made stronger by having water removed from it: concentrated apple juice

concentration camp noun a prison camp, especially one set up by the Nazis during World War Two

concept noun an abstract or general idea: the concept of tolerance ▷ **conceptual** adjective ▷ **conceptually** adverb

conception noun **1** Your conception of something is the idea you have of it **2** Conception is the process by which a woman becomes pregnant

concern noun **1** Concern is a feeling of worry about something or someone: public concern about violence **2** If something is your concern, it is your responsibility **3** a business: a large manufacturing concern ▷ verb **4** If something concerns you or if you are concerned about it, it worries you **5** You say that something concerns you if it affects or involves you: My business does not concern you ▷ phrase **6** If something is of concern to you, it is important to you ▷ **concerned** adjective

concerning preposition You use 'concerning' to show what something is about: documents concerning arms sales to Iraq

concert noun a public performance by musicians

concerted adjective A concerted action is done by several people together: concerted action to cut interest rates

concerto concertos or concerti [kon-**cher**-toe] noun MUSIC a piece of music for a solo instrument and an orchestra

concession noun If you make a concession, you agree to let someone have or do something: *Her one concession was to let me come into the building*

concise adjective giving all the necessary information using as few words as necessary: *a concise guide* > **concisely** adverb

conclude verb 1 If you conclude something, you decide that it is so because of the other things that you know: *An inquiry concluded that this was untrue* 2 When you conclude something, you finish it: *At that point I intend to conclude the interview* > **concluding** adjective

conclusion noun 1 a decision made after thinking carefully about something 2 the finish or ending of something

conclusive adjective Facts that are conclusive show that something is certainly true > **conclusively** adverb

concoct verb 1 If you concoct an excuse or explanation, you invent one 2 If you concoct something, you make it by mixing several things together > **concoction** noun

concourse noun a wide hall in a building where people walk about or gather together

concrete noun 1 Concrete is a solid building material made by mixing cement, sand, and water ▷ adjective 2 definite, rather than general or vague: *I don't really have any concrete plans* 3 real and physical, rather than abstract: *concrete evidence*

concur concurs, concurring, concurred verb (formal) To concur is to agree: *She concurred with me*

concurrent adjective If things are concurrent, they happen at the same time > **concurrently** adverb

concussed adjective confused or unconscious because of a blow to the head > **concussion** noun

condemn verb 1 If you condemn something, you say it is bad and unacceptable: *Teachers condemned the new plans* 2 If someone is condemned to a punishment, they are given it: *She was condemned to death* 3 If you are condemned to something unpleasant, you must suffer it: *Many women are condemned to poverty* 4 When a building is condemned, it is going to be pulled down because it is unsafe > **condemnation** noun

condensation noun SCIENCE Condensation is a coating of tiny drops formed on a surface by steam or vapour

condense verb 1 If you condense a piece of writing or a speech, you shorten it 2 SCIENCE When a gas or vapour condenses, it changes into a liquid

condescending adjective If you are condescending, you behave in a way that shows that you think you are superior to other people

condition noun 1 the state someone or something is in 2 (*in plural*) The conditions in which something is done are the location and other factors likely to affect it: *The very difficult conditions continued to affect our performance* 3 a requirement that must be met for something else to be possible: *He had to report to the police each week as a condition of bail* 4 You can refer to an illness or other medical problem as a condition: *a heart condition* ▷ phrase 5 If you are out of condition, you are unfit

▷ *verb* **6** If someone is conditioned to behave or think in a certain way, they do it as a result of their upbringing or training

conditional *adjective* If one thing is conditional on another, it can only happen if the other thing happens: *You feel his love is conditional on you pleasing him*

condolence *noun* Condolence is sympathy expressed for a bereaved person

condominium *noun* In Canadian, Australian, and New Zealand English, an apartment block in which each apartment is owned by the person who lives in it

condone *verb* If you condone someone's bad behaviour, you accept it and do not try to stop it: *We cannot condone violence*

conducive [kon-**joo**-siv] *adjective* If something is conducive to something else, it makes it likely to happen: *a situation that is conducive to relaxation*

conduct *verb* **1** To conduct an activity or task is to carry it out: *He seemed to be conducting a conversation* **2** (*formal*) The way you conduct yourself is the way you behave **3** MUSIC When someone conducts an orchestra or choir, they stand in front of it and direct it **4** SCIENCE If something conducts heat or electricity, heat or electricity can pass through it ▷ *noun* **5** If you take part in the conduct of an activity or task, you help to carry it out **6** Your conduct is the way you behave

conductor *noun* **1** MUSIC someone who conducts an orchestra or choir **2** someone who moves round a bus or train selling tickets **3** SCIENCE a substance that conducts heat or electricity

cone *noun* **1** a regular three-dimensional shape with a circular base and a point at the top **2** A fir cone or pine cone is the fruit of a fir or pine tree

confectionery *noun* Confectionery is sweets

confederation *noun* an organization formed for business or political purposes

confer confers, conferring, conferred *verb* When people confer, they discuss something in order to make a decision

conference *noun* a meeting at which formal discussions take place

confess *verb* If you confess to something, you admit it: *Your son has confessed to his crimes*

confession *noun* **1** If you make a confession, you admit you have done something wrong **2** Confession is the act of confessing something, especially a religious act in which people confess their sins to a priest

confessional *noun* RE a small room in some churches where people confess their sins to a priest

confetti *noun* Confetti is small pieces of coloured paper thrown over the bride and groom at a wedding

confidant [kon-fid-dant] *noun* (*formal*) a person you discuss your private problems with

confide *verb* If you confide in or to someone, you tell them a secret: *Marian confided in me that she was very worried*

confidence *noun* **1** If you have confidence in someone, you feel you can trust them **2** Someone who has confidence is sure of their own abilities or qualities **3** a secret you tell someone

confident *adjective* **1** If you are confident about something, you are sure it will happen the way you want it to **2** People who are confident are sure of their own abilities or qualities > **confidently** *adverb*

confidential *adjective* Confidential information is meant to be kept secret > **confidentially** *adverb* > **confidentiality** *noun*

confine *verb* **1** If something is confined to one place, person, or thing, it exists only in that place or affects only that person or thing **2** If you confine yourself to doing or saying something, it is the only thing you do or say: *They confined themselves to discussing the weather* **3** If you are confined to a place, you cannot leave it: *She was confined to bed for two days* ▷ *plural noun* **4** The confines of a place are its boundaries: *outside the confines of the prison* > **confinement** *noun*

confined *adjective* A confined space is small and enclosed by walls

confirm *verb* **1** To confirm something is to say or show that it is true: *Police confirmed that they had received a call* **2** If you confirm an arrangement or appointment, you say it is definite **3** RE When someone is confirmed, they are formally accepted as a member of a Christian Church > **confirmation** *noun*

confirmed *adjective* You use 'confirmed' to describe someone who has a belief or way of life that is unlikely to change: *a confirmed bachelor*

confiscate *verb* To confiscate something is to take it away from someone as a punishment

conflict *noun* [kon-flikt] **1** Conflict is disagreement and argument: *conflict between workers and management* **2** HISTORY a war or battle **3** When there is a conflict of ideas or interests, people have different ideas or interests which cannot all be satisfied ▷ *verb* [kon-flikt] **4** When ideas or interests conflict, they are different and cannot all be satisfied

conform *verb* **1** If you conform, you behave the way people expect you to **2** If something conforms to a law or to someone's wishes, it is what is required or wanted > **conformist** *noun, adjective*

confront *verb* **1** If you are confronted with a problem or task, you have to deal with it **2** If you confront someone, you meet them face to face like an enemy **3** If you confront someone with evidence or a fact, you present it to them in order to accuse them of something

confrontation *noun* a serious dispute or fight: *a confrontation between police and fans*

confuse *verb* **1** If you confuse two things, you mix them up and think one of them is the other: *You are confusing facts with opinion* **2** To confuse someone means to make them uncertain about what is happening or what to do **3** To confuse a situation means to make it more complicated

confused *adjective* **1** uncertain about what is happening or what to do **2** in an untidy mess

confusing *adjective* puzzling or bewildering

confusion *noun* **1** a bewildering state **2** an untidy mess

congenial [kon-jeen-yal] *adjective* If something is congenial, it is pleasant and suits you: *We wanted to talk in congenial surroundings*

congenital adjective (Medicine) If someone has a congenital disease or disability, they have had it from birth but did not inherit it

congested adjective 1 When a road is congested, it is so full of traffic that normal movement is impossible 2 If your nose is congested, it is blocked and you cannot breathe properly
> **congestion** noun

conglomerate noun a large business organization consisting of several companies

congratulate verb If you congratulate someone, you express pleasure at something good that has happened to them, or praise them for something they have achieved > **congratulation** noun
> **congratulatory** adjective

congregate verb When people congregate, they gather together somewhere

congregation noun the congregation are the people attending a service in a church

congress noun a large meeting held to discuss ideas or policies: a medical congress

conical adjective shaped like a cone

conifer noun any type of evergreen tree that produces cones
> **coniferous** adjective

conjecture noun Conjecture is guesswork about something: There was no evidence, only conjecture

conjunction noun 1 ENGLISH In grammar, a conjunction is a word that links two other words or two clauses, for example 'and', 'but', 'while', and 'that' ▷ phrase 2 If two or more things are done **in conjunction**, they are done together

connect verb 1 To connect two things is to join them together 2 If you connect something with something else, you think of them as being linked: High blood pressure is closely connected to heart disease

connection or **connexion** noun 1 a link or relationship between things 2 SCIENCE the point where two wires or pipes are joined together: a loose connection 3 (in plural) Someone's connections are the people they know: He had powerful connections in the army

connective noun ENGLISH a word or short phrase that connects clauses, phrases, or words

connoisseur [kon-nis-**sir**] noun someone who knows a lot about the arts, or about food or drink: a great connoisseur of champagne

connotation noun ENGLISH The connotations of a word or name are what it makes you think of: the word grey has connotations of dullness

conquer verb 1 To conquer people is to take control of their country by force 2 If you conquer something difficult or dangerous, you succeed in controlling it: Conquer your fear!
> **conqueror** noun

conquest noun 1 Conquest is the conquering of a country or group of people 2 Conquests are lands captured by conquest

conscience noun the part of your mind that tells you what is right and wrong

conscientious [kon-shee-**en**-shus] adjective Someone who is conscientious is very careful to do their work properly
> **conscientiously** adverb

conscious adjective 1 If you are conscious of something, you are aware of it: She was not conscious of the time 2 A conscious action or effort is done deliberately: *I made a conscious decision not to hide* **3** Someone who is conscious is awake, rather than asleep or unconscious: *Still conscious, she was taken to hospital* > **consciously** *adverb* > **consciousness** *noun*

consecrated *adjective* A consecrated building or place is one that has been officially declared to be holy

consecutive *adjective* Consecutive events or periods of time happen one after the other: *eight consecutive games*

consensus *noun* Consensus is general agreement among a group of people: *The consensus was that it could be good*

consent *noun* **1** Consent is permission to do something: *Thomas reluctantly gave his consent to my writing this book* **2** Consent is also agreement between two or more people: *By common consent it was the best game of these championships* > *verb* **3** If you consent to something, you agree to it or allow it

consequence *noun* **1** The consequences of something are its results or effects: *the dire consequences of major war* **2** (*formal*) If something is of consequence, it is important

consequent *adjective* Consequent describes something as being the result of something else: *an earthquake in 1980 and its consequent damage* > **consequently** *adverb*

conservation *noun* Conservation is the preservation of the environment > **conservationist** *noun, adjective*

conservative *noun* **1** in Britain, a member or supporter of the Conservative Party, a political party that believes that the government

should interfere as little as possible in the running of the economy > *adjective* **2** In Britain, Conservative views and policies are those of the Conservative Party **3** Someone who is conservative is not willing to accept changes or new ideas **4** A conservative estimate or guess is a cautious or moderate one > **conservatively** *adverb* > **conservatism** *noun*

conservatory conservatories *noun* a room with glass walls and a glass roof attached to a house

conserve *verb* If you conserve a supply of something, you make it last: *the only way to conserve energy*

consider *verb* **1** If you consider something to be the case, you think or judge it to be so: *The manager does not consider him an ideal team member* **2** EXAM TERM To consider something is to think about it carefully: *If an offer were made, we would consider it* **3** If you consider someone's needs or feelings, you take account of them

considerable *adjective* A considerable amount of something is a lot of it: *a considerable sum of money* > **considerably** *adverb*

considerate *adjective* Someone who is considerate pays attention to other people's needs and feelings

consideration *noun* **1** Consideration is careful thought about something: *a decision demanding careful consideration* **2** If you show consideration for someone, you take account of their needs and feelings **3** something that has to be taken into account: *Money was also a consideration*

considered *adjective* A considered opinion or judgment is arrived at by careful thought

considering conjunction, preposition You say 'considering' to indicate that you are taking something into account: *I know that must sound callous, considering that I was married to the man for seventeen years*

consign verb (formal) To consign something to a particular place is to send or put it there

consignment noun A consignment of goods is a load of them being delivered somewhere

consist verb What something consists of is its different parts or members: *The brain consists of millions of nerve cells*

consistency consistencies noun **1** Consistency is the quality of being consistent **2** The consistency of a substance is how thick or smooth it is: *the consistency of single cream*

consistent adjective **1** If you are consistent, you keep doing something the same way: *one of our most consistent performers* **2** If something such as a statement or argument is consistent, there are no contradictions in it > **consistently** adverb

console verb [con-**sole**] **1** To console someone who is unhappy is to make them more cheerful ▷ noun [con-sole] **2** A panel with switches or knobs for operating a machine > **consolation** noun

consolidate verb To consolidate something you have gained or achieved is to make it more secure > **consolidation** noun

consonant noun (ENGLISH) A sound such as 'p' or 'm' which you make by stopping the air flowing freely through your mouth

consort verb [con-**sort**] **1** (formal) If you consort with someone, you spend a lot of time with them

▷ noun [con-sort] **2** The wife or husband of the king or queen

consortium consortia or consortiums noun A group of businesses working together

conspicuous adjective If something is conspicuous, people can see or notice it very easily > **conspicuously** adverb

conspiracy conspiracies noun When there is a conspiracy, a group of people plan something illegal, often for a political purpose

conspirator noun someone involved in a conspiracy

conspire verb **1** When people conspire, they plan together to do something illegal, often for a political purpose **2** (literary) When events conspire towards a particular result, they seem to work together to cause it: *Circumstances conspired to doom the business*

constable noun a police officer of the lowest rank

constabulary constabularies noun a police force

constant adjective **1** Something that is constant happens all the time or is always there: *a city under constant attack* **2** If an amount or level is constant, it stays the same **3** People who are constant stay loyal to a person or idea > **constantly** adverb > **constancy** noun

constellation noun a group of stars

consternation noun Consternation is anxiety or dismay: *There was some consternation when it began raining*

constituency constituencies noun a town or area represented by an MP

constituent noun **1** An MP's constituents are the voters who live in his or her constituency **2** The constituents of something are its parts: *the major constituents of bone*

constitute *verb* If a group of things constitute something, they are what it consists of: *Jewellery constitutes 80 per cent of the stock*

constitution *noun* **1** (HISTORY) The constitution of a country is the system of laws which formally states people's rights and duties **2** Your constitution is your health: *a very strong constitution*
> **constitutional** *adjective*
> **constitutionally** *adverb*

constrained *adjective* If a person feels constrained to do something, they feel that they should do that

constraint *noun* something that limits someone's freedom of action: *constraints on trade union power*

construct *verb* To construct something is to build or make it

construction *noun* **1** The construction of something is the building or making of it: *the construction of the harbour* **2** something built or made: *a shoddy modern construction built of concrete*

constructive *adjective* Constructive criticisms and comments are helpful
> **constructively** *adverb*

consul *noun* an official who lives in a foreign city and who looks after people there who are citizens of his or her own country > **consular** *adjective*

consulate *noun* the place where a consul works

consult *verb* **1** If you consult someone, you ask for their opinion or advice **2** When people consult each other, they exchange ideas and opinions **3** If you consult a book or map, you look at it for information

consultancy *noun* an organization whose members give expert advice on a subject

consultant *noun* **1** an experienced doctor who specializes in one type of medicine **2** someone who gives expert advice: *a management consultant*

consultation *noun* **1** a meeting held to discuss something **2** Consultation is discussion or the seeking of advice: *There has to be much better consultation with the public* > **consultative** *adjective*

consume *verb* **1** (formal) If you consume something, you eat or drink it **2** To consume fuel or energy is to use it up

consumer *noun* someone who buys things or uses services: *two new magazines for teenage consumers*

consumerism *noun* Consumerism is the belief that a country will have a strong economy if its people buy a lot of goods and spend a lot of money

consuming *adjective* A consuming passion or interest is more important to you than anything else

consummate *verb* [kons-yum-mate] **1** To consummate something is to make it complete ▷ *adjective* [kon-sum-mit] **2** You use 'consummate' to describe someone who is very good at something: *a consummate politician*
> **consummation** *noun*

consumption *noun* The consumption of fuel or food is the using of it, or the amount used

contact *noun* **1** If you are in contact with someone, you regularly talk to them or write to them **2** When things are in contact, they are touching each other **3** someone you know in a place or organization from whom you can get help or information ▷ *verb* **4** If you contact someone, you telephone them or write to them

contagious adjective A contagious disease can be caught by touching people or things infected with it

contain verb **1** If a substance contains something, that thing is a part of it: *Alcohol contains sugar* **2** The things a box or room contains are the things inside it **3** (formal) To contain something also means to stop it increasing or spreading: *efforts to contain the disease*
> **containment** noun

container noun **1** something such as a box or room that you keep things in **2** a large sealed metal box for transporting things

contaminate verb If something is contaminated by dirt, chemicals, or radiation, it is made impure and harmful: *foods contaminated with lead*
> **contamination** noun

contemplate verb **1** To contemplate is to think carefully about something for a long time **2** If you contemplate doing something, you consider doing it: *I never contemplated marrying Charles* **3** If you contemplate something, you look at it for a long time: *He contemplated his drawings*
> **contemplation** noun
> **contemplative** adjective

contemporary contemporaries adjective **1** produced or happening now: *contemporary literature* **2** produced or happening at the time you are talking about: *contemporary descriptions of Lizzie Borden* ▷ noun **3** Someone's contemporaries are other people living or active at the same time as them: *Shakespeare and his contemporaries*

contempt noun If you treat

someone or something with contempt, you show no respect for them at all

contemptible adjective not worthy of any respect: *this contemptible piece of nonsense*

contemptuous adjective showing contempt ▷ **contemptuously** adverb

contend verb **1** To contend with a difficulty is to deal with it: *They had to contend with injuries* **2** (formal) If you contend that something is true, you say firmly that it is true **3** When people contend for something, they compete for it
> **contender** noun

content noun [con-tent] **1** (in plural) The contents of something are the things inside it ▷ adjective [con-tent] **2** happy and satisfied with your life **3** willing to do or have something: *He would be content to telephone her* ▷ verb [con-tent] **4** If you content yourself with doing something, you do it and do not try to do anything else: *He contented himself with an early morning lecture*

contented adjective happy and satisfied with your life
> **contentedly** adverb
> **contentment** noun

contention noun (formal)
1 Someone's contention is the idea or opinion they are expressing: *It is our contention that the 1980s mark a turning point in planning*
2 Contention is disagreement and argument about something: *What had brought about all this contention?*

contest noun [con-test] **1** a competition or game: *a boxing contest* **2** a struggle for power: *a presidential contest* ▷ verb [con-test] **3** If you contest a statement or decision, you object to it formally

contestant noun someone taking part in a competition

context noun 1 The context of something consists of matters related to it which help to explain it: *English history is treated in a European context* 2 ENGLISH The context of a word or sentence consists of the words or sentences before and after it

continent noun 1 a very large area of land, such as Africa or Asia 2 The Continent is the mainland of Europe > **continental** adjective

contingency contingencies [kon-**tin**-jen-see] noun something that might happen in the future: *I need to examine all possible contingencies*

contingent noun 1 a group of people representing a country or organization: *a strong South African contingent* 2 a group of police or soldiers

continual adjective 1 happening all the time without stopping: *continual headaches* 2 happening again and again: *the continual snide remarks* > **continually** adverb

continuation noun 1 The continuation of something is the continuing of it: *the continuation of the human race* 2 Something that is a continuation of an event follows it and seems like a part of it: *a meeting which was a continuation of a conference*

continue continues, continuing, continued verb 1 If you continue to do something, you keep doing it 2 If something continues, it does not stop 3 You also say something continues when it starts again after stopping: *She continued after a pause*

continuous adjective 1 Continuous means happening or existing

without stopping 2 MATHS A continuous line or surface has no gaps or holes in it. A continuous set of data has an unlimited amount of numbers or items in it > **continuously** adverb > **continuity** noun

contorted adjective twisted into an unnatural, unattractive shape

contour noun 1 The contours of something are its general shape 2 GEOGRAPHY On a map, a contour is a line joining points of equal height

contraception noun Contraception is methods of preventing pregnancy

contraceptive noun a device or pill for preventing pregnancy

contract noun [**con**-trakt] 1 a written legal agreement about the sale of something or work done for money ▷ verb [con-**trakt**] 2 When something contracts, it gets smaller or shorter 3 (formal) If you contract an illness, you get it: *Her husband contracted a virus* > **contractual** adjective

contractor noun a person or company who does work for other people or companies: *a building contractor*

contradict verb If you contradict someone, you say that what they have just said is not true, and that something else is > **contradiction** noun > **contradictory** adjective

contraption noun a strange-looking machine or piece of equipment

contrary adjective 1 Contrary ideas or opinions are opposed to each other and cannot be held by the same person ▷ phrase 2 You say on the contrary when you are contradicting what someone has just said

contrast noun [**con**-trast] 1 a great

difference between things: *the real contrast between the two poems* **2** If one thing is a contrast to another, it is very different from it: *I couldn't imagine a greater contrast to Maxwell* ▷ *verb* [con-**trast**] [EXAM TERM] If you contrast things, you describe or emphasize the differences between them: *The painter contrasted his image of rural America with striking representations of New York* **4** If one thing contrasts with another, it is very different from it: *The interview completely contrasted with the one she gave after Tokyo*

contravene *verb (formal)* If you contravene a law or rule, you do something that it forbids

contribute *verb* **1** If you contribute to something, you do things to help it succeed: *The elderly have much to contribute to the community* **2** If you contribute money, you give it to help to pay for something **3** If something contributes to an event or situation, it is one of its causes: *The dry summer has contributed to perfect conditions* ▷ **contribution** *noun* ▷ **contributor** *noun* ▷ **contributory** *adjective*

contrive *verb (formal)* If you contrive to do something difficult, you succeed in doing it: *Anthony contrived to escape with a few companions*

contrived *adjective* Something that is contrived is unnatural: *a contrived compliment*

control controls, controlling, controlled *noun* **1** Control of a country or organization is the power to make the important decisions about how it is run **2** Your control over something is your ability to make it work the way you want it to **3** The controls on a machine are knobs or other devices

used to work it ▷ *verb* **4** To control a country or organization means to have the power to make decisions about how it is run **5** To control something such as a machine or system means to make it work the way you want it to **6** [PSHE] If you control yourself, you make yourself behave calmly when you are angry or upset ▷ *phrase* **7** If something is **out of control**, nobody has any power over it ▷ **controller** *noun*

controversial *adjective* Something that is controversial causes a lot of discussion and argument, because many people disapprove of it

controversy controversies [kon-triv-ver-see or kon-**trov**-ver-see] *noun* discussion and argument because many people disapprove of something

conundrum *noun (formal)* a puzzling problem

convection *noun* Convection is the process by which heat travels through gases and liquids

convene *verb* **1** *(formal)* To convene a meeting is to arrange for it to take place **2** When people convene, they come together for a meeting

convenience *noun* **1** The convenience of something is the fact that it is easy to use or that it makes something easy to do **2** something useful

convenient *adjective* If something is convenient, it is easy to use or it makes something easy to do ▷ **conveniently** *adverb*

convent *noun* a building where nuns live, or a school run by nuns

convention *noun* **1** an accepted way of behaving or doing something **2** a large meeting of an organization or political group: *the Democratic Convention*

conventional adjective 1 You say that people are conventional when there is nothing unusual about their way of life 2 Conventional methods are the ones that are usually used > **conventionally** adverb

converge verb To converge is to meet or join at a particular place

conversation noun If you have a conversation with someone, you spend time talking to them > **conversational** adjective > **conversationalist** noun

converse verb [con-**verse**] 1 (formal) When people converse, they talk to each other ▷ noun [**con**-verse] 2 The converse of something is its opposite: Don't you think that the converse might also be possible? > **conversely** adverb

convert verb [con-**vert**] 1 To convert one thing into another is to change it so that it becomes the other thing 2 (MATHS) If you convert a unit or measurement, you express it in terms of another unit or scale of measurement. For example, you can convert inches to centimetres by multiplying by 2.54 3 If someone converts you, they persuade you to change your religious or political beliefs ▷ noun [**con**-vert] 4 someone who has changed their religious or political beliefs > **conversion** noun > **convertible** adjective

convey verb 1 To convey information or ideas is to cause them to be known or understood 2 (formal) To convey someone or something to a place is to transport them there

conveyor belt noun A moving strip used in factories for moving objects along

convict verb [kon-**vikt**] 1 To convict someone of a crime is to find them guilty ▷ noun [**kon**-vikt] 2 someone serving a prison sentence

conviction noun 1 a strong belief or opinion 2 The conviction of someone is what happens when they are found guilty in a court of law

convince verb To convince someone of something is to persuade them that it is true

convincing adjective 'Convincing' is used to describe things or people that can make you believe something is true: a convincing argument > **convincingly** adverb

convoluted [kon-vol-**oo**-tid] adjective Something that is convoluted has many twists and bends: the convoluted patterns of these designs

convoy noun a group of vehicles or ships travelling together

convulsion noun If someone has convulsions, their muscles move violently and uncontrollably

coo verb When pigeons and doves coo, they make a soft flutelike sound

cook verb 1 To cook food is to prepare it for eating by heating it ▷ noun 2 someone who prepares and cooks food, often as their job

cooker noun a device for cooking food

cookery noun Cookery is the activity of preparing and cooking food

cookie noun 1 a sweet biscuit 2 a small file placed on a user's computer by a website, containing information about the user's preferences that will be used on any future visits he or she may make to the site

cool adjective 1 Something cool has a low temperature but is not cold 2 If you are cool in a difficult situation, you stay calm and unemotional

▷ verb **3** When something cools or when you cool it, it becomes less warm > **coolly** adverb > **coolness** noun

coop noun a cage for chickens or rabbits

cooperate [koh-op-er-rate] verb **1** When people cooperate, they work or act together **2** To cooperate also means to do what someone asks > **cooperation** noun

cooperative [koh-op-er-ut-tiv] noun **1** a business or organization run by the people who work for it, and who share its benefits or profits ▷ adjective **2** A cooperative activity is done by people working together **3** Someone who is cooperative does what you ask them to

coordinate coordinates, coordinating, coordinated [koh-**or**-din-ate] verb **1** To coordinate an activity is to organize the people or things involved in it: to coordinate the campaign ▷ noun **2** (in plural) MATHS Coordinates are a pair of numbers or letters which tell you how far along and up or down a point is on a grid > **coordination** noun > **coordinator** noun

cop noun (slang) a police officer

cope verb If you cope with a problem or task, you deal with it successfully

copious adjective (formal) existing or produced in large quantities: I wrote copious notes for the solicitor

copper noun **1** SCIENCE Copper is a reddish-brown metallic element. Its atomic number is 29 and its symbol is Cu **2** Coppers are brown metal coins of low value **3** (informal) A copper is also a policeman

copy copies, copying, copied noun **1** something made to look like something else **2** A copy of a book, newspaper, or record is one of many

identical ones produced at the same time ▷ verb **3** If you copy what someone does, you do the same thing **4** If you copy something, you make a copy of it > **copier** noun

copyright noun LIBRARY If someone has the copyright on a piece of writing or music, it cannot be copied or performed without their permission

coral noun Coral is a hard substance that forms in the sea from the skeletons of tiny animals called corals

cord noun **1** Cord is strong, thick string **2** Electrical wire covered in rubber or plastic is also called cord

cordial adjective **1** warm and friendly: a cordial greeting ▷ noun **2** a sweet drink made from fruit juice

cordon noun **1** a line or ring of police or soldiers preventing people entering or leaving a place ▷ verb **2** If police or soldiers cordon off an area, they stop people entering or leaving by forming themselves into a line or ring

corduroy noun Corduroy is a thick cloth with parallel raised lines on the outside

core noun **1** the hard central part of a fruit such as an apple **2** the most central part of an object or place: the earth's core **3** the most important part of something: the core of Asia's problems

cork noun **1** Cork is the very light, spongelike bark of a Mediterranean tree **2** a piece of cork pushed into the end of a bottle to close it

corkscrew noun a device for pulling corks out of bottles

corn noun **1** Corn refers to crops such as wheat and barley and is their seeds **2** a small painful area of hard skin on your foot

cornea [kor-nee-a] noun the transparent skin that covers the outside of your eyeball

corner noun **1** a place where two sides or edges of something meet: *a small corner of one shelf; a street corner* ▷ verb **2** To corner a person or animal is to get them into a place they cannot escape from

cornflour noun Cornflour is a fine white flour made from maize and used in cooking to thicken sauces

cornice noun a decorative strip of plaster, wood, or stone along the top edge of a wall

corny cornier, corniest adjective very obvious or sentimental and not at all original: *corny old love songs*

coronary coronaries noun (Medicine) If someone has a coronary, blood cannot reach their heart because of a blood clot

coronation noun the ceremony at which a king or queen is crowned

coroner noun an official who investigates the deaths of people who have died in a violent or unusual way

corporal noun an officer of low rank in the army or air force

corporal punishment noun Corporal punishment is the punishing of people by beating them

corporate adjective (formal) belonging to or done by all members of a group together: *a corporate decision*

corporation noun **1** a large business **2** a group of people responsible for running a city

corps [rhymes with *more*] noun **1** a part of an army with special duties: *the Engineering Corps* **2** a small group of people who do a special job: *the world press corps*

corpse noun a dead body

correct adjective **1** If something is correct, there are no mistakes in it **2** The correct thing in a particular situation is the right one: *Each has the correct number of coins* **3** Correct behaviour is considered to be socially acceptable ▷ verb **4** If you correct something which is wrong, you make it right ▷ **correctly** adverb ▷ **corrective** adjective, noun

correction noun the act of making something right

correlate verb If two things correlate or are correlated, they are closely connected or strongly influence each other: *Obesity correlates with increased risk of stroke and diabetes* ▷ **correlation** noun

correspond verb **1** If one thing corresponds to another, it has a similar purpose, function, or status **2** MATHS If numbers or amounts correspond, they are the same **3** When people correspond, they write to each other

correspondence noun **1** Correspondence is the writing of letters; also the letters written **2** If there is a correspondence between two things, they are closely related or very similar

correspondent noun a newspaper, television, or radio reporter

corresponding adjective **1** You use 'corresponding' to describe a change that results from a change in something else: *the rise in interest rates and corresponding fall in house values* **2** You also use 'corresponding' to describe something which has a similar purpose or st something else: *Alf corresponding Weste star* ▷ **correspond**

corridor noun a pa building or train

corrode verb [SCIENCE] When metal corrodes, it is gradually destroyed by a chemical or rust ▷ **corrosion** noun ▷ **corrosive** adjective

corrugated adjective Corrugated metal or cardboard is made in parallel folds to make it stronger

corrupt adjective **1** Corrupt people act dishonestly or illegally in return for money or power: corrupt ministers ▷ verb **2** To corrupt someone means to make them dishonest **3** To corrupt someone also means to make them immoral ▷ **corruptible** adjective

corruption noun Corruption is dishonesty and illegal behaviour by people in positions of power

corset noun Corsets are stiff underwear worn by some women round their hips and waist to make them look slimmer

cosmetic noun **1** Cosmetics are substances such as lipstick and face powder which improve a person's appearance ▷ adjective **2** Cosmetic changes improve the appearance of something without changing its basic nature

cosmic adjective belonging or relating to the universe

cosmopolitan adjective A cosmopolitan place is full of people from many countries

cosmos noun The cosmos is the universe

cost costs, costing, cost noun **1** The cost of something is the amount of money needed to buy it, do it, or make it **2** The cost of achieving something is the loss or injury in achieving it: the total cost in human misery ▷ verb **3** You use 'cost' to talk about the amount of money you have to pay for things: The air fares were going to cost a lot **4** If a mistake

costs you something, you lose that thing because of the mistake: a reckless gamble that could cost him his job

costly costlier, costliest adjective expensive: a costly piece of furniture

costume noun [DRAMA] **1** A set of clothes worn by an actor **2** Costume is the clothing worn in a particular place or during a particular period: eighteenth-century costume

cosy cosier, cosiest; cosies adjective **1** warm and comfortable: her cosy new flat **2** Cosy activities are pleasant and friendly: a cosy chat ▷ noun **3** A soft cover put over a teapot to keep the tea warm ▷ **cosily** adverb ▷ **cosiness** noun

cot noun a small bed for a baby, with bars or panels round it to stop the baby falling out

cottage noun a small house in the country

cottage cheese noun Cottage cheese is a type of soft white lumpy cheese

cotton noun **1** Cotton is cloth made from the soft fibres of the cotton plant **2** Cotton is also thread used for sewing

cotton wool noun Cotton wool is soft fluffy cotton, often used for dressing wounds

couch noun **1** a long, soft piece of furniture which more than one person can sit on ▷ verb **2** If a statement is couched in a particular type of language, it is expressed in that language: a comment couched in impertinent terms

cough [koff] verb **1** When you cough, you force air out of your throat with a sudden harsh noise ▷ noun **2** an illness that makes you cough a lot; also the noise you make when you cough

could verb **1** You use 'could' to say that you were able or allowed to do something: *He could hear voices; She could come and go as she wanted* **2** You also use 'could' to say that something might happen or might be the case: *It could rain* **3** You use 'could' when you are asking for something politely: *Could you tell me the name of that film?*

council noun **1** a group of people elected to look after the affairs of a town, district, or county **2** Some other groups have Council as part of their name: *the World Gold Council*

councillor noun an elected member of a local council

counsel counsels, counselling, counselled noun **1** (*formal*) To give someone counsel is to give them advice **2** To counsel people is to give them advice about their problems > **counselling** noun > **counsellor** noun

count verb **1** To count is to say all the numbers in order up to a particular number **2** If you count all the things in a group, you add them up to see how many there are **3** What counts in a situation is whatever is most important **4** To count as something means to be regarded as that thing: *I'm not sure whether this counts as harassment* **5** If you can count on someone or something, you can rely on them > verb **6** a number reached by counting **7** (*formal*) If something is wrong on a particular count, it is wrong in that respect **8** a European nobleman

countdown noun the counting aloud of numbers in reverse order before something happens, especially before a spacecraft is launched

countenance (*formal*) noun

1 Someone's countenance is their face > verb **2** To countenance something means to allow or accept it: *I will not countenance behaviour of this sort*

counter noun **1 a** a long, flat surface over which goods are sold in a shop **2 a** small, flat, round object used in board games > verb **3** If you counter something that is being done, you take action to make it less effective: *I countered that argument with a reference to our sales report*

counteract verb To counteract something is to reduce its effect by producing an opposite effect

counterfeit [kown-ter-fit] adjective **1** Something counterfeit is not genuine but has been made to look genuine to deceive people: *counterfeit money* > verb **2** To counterfeit something is to make a counterfeit version of it

counterpart noun The counterpart of a person or thing is another person or thing with a similar function in a different place: *Unlike his British counterpart, the French mayor is an important personality*

counterterrorism noun Counterterrorism is action to prevent terrorist attacks or destroy terrorist groups

countess noun the wife of a count or earl, or a woman with the same rank as a count or earl

counting preposition You say 'counting' when including something in a calculation: *nearly 4000 of us, not counting women and children*

countless adjective too many to count: *There had been countless demonstrations*

country countries noun GEOGRAPHY **1** one of the political areas the world is divided into **2** The country is land away from towns and cities **3** 'Country' is used to refer to an area with particular features or associations: *the heart of wine country*

countryman countrymen *noun* Your countrymen are people from your own country

countryside *noun* The countryside is land away from towns and cities

county counties *noun* GEOGRAPHY a region with its own local government

coup [rhymes with **you**] or **coup d'état** [koo day-**tah**] *noun* HISTORY When there is a coup, a group of people seize power in a country

couple *noun* **1** Two people who are married or are involved in a romantic relationship **2** A couple of things or people means two of them: *a couple of weeks ago* ▷ *verb* **3** If one thing is coupled with another, the two things are done or dealt with together: *Its stores offer high quality coupled with low prices*

coupon *noun* **1** a piece of printed paper which, when you hand it in, entitles you to pay less than usual for something **2** a form you fill in to ask for information or to enter a competition

courage *noun* Courage is the quality shown by people who do things knowing they are dangerous or difficult > **courageous** *adjective* > **courageously** *adverb*

courgette [koor-**jet**] *noun* a type of small marrow with dark green skin. Courgettes are also called **zucchini**

courier [**koo**-ree-er] *noun* **1** someone employed by a travel company to look after people on holiday **2** someone employed to deliver special letters quickly

course *noun* **1** a series of lessons or lectures **2** a series of medical treatments: *a course of injections* **3** one of the parts of a meal **4** A course or a course of action is one of the things you can do in a situation **5** a piece of land where a sport such as golf is played **6** the route a ship or aircraft takes **7** If something happens in the course of a period of time, it happens during that period: *Ten people died in the course of the day* ▷ *phrase* **8** If you say **of course**, you are showing that something is totally expected or that you are sure about something: *Of course she wouldn't do that*

court *noun* **1** a place where legal matters are decided by a judge and jury or a magistrate. The judge and jury or magistrate can also be referred to as the court **2** a place where a game such as tennis or badminton is played **3** the place where a king or queen lives and carries out ceremonial duties ▷ *verb* **4** (*old-fashioned*) If a man and woman are courting, they are spending a lot of time together because they intend to get married

courteous [**kur**-tee-yuss] *adjective* Courteous behaviour is polite and considerate

courtesy *noun* Courtesy is polite, considerate behaviour

courtier *noun* Courtiers were noblemen and noblewomen at the court of a king or queen

courtship *noun* (*formal*) Courtship is the activity of courting or the period of time during which a man and a woman are courting

courtyard *noun* a flat area of ground surrounded by buildings or walls

cousin *noun* Your cousin is the child

of your uncle or aunt

cove noun a small bay

covenant [kuv-vi-nant] noun a formal written agreement or promise

cover verb 1 If you cover something, you put something else over it to protect it or hide it 2 If something covers something else, it forms a layer over it: *Tears covered his face* 3 If you cover a particular distance, you travel that distance: *He travelled 52 kilometres in 210 laps* ▷ noun 4 something that goes over an object to protect it or keep it warm 5 The cover of a book or magazine is its outside 6 Insurance cover is a guarantee that money will be paid if something is lost or harmed 7 In the open, cover consists of trees, rocks, or other places where you can shelter or hide > **cover up** verb If you cover up something you do not want people to know about, you hide it from them: *He lied to cover up his crime* > **cover-up** noun

coverage noun The coverage of something in the news is the reporting of it

covering noun a layer of something which protects or conceals something else: *A morning blizzard left a covering of snow*

covert [koh-vert] adjective (formal) Covert activities are secret, rather than open > **covertly** adverb

covet [kuv-vit] verb (formal) If you covet something, you want it very much

cow noun a large animal kept on farms for its milk

coward noun someone who is easily frightened and who avoids dangerous or difficult situations > **cowardice** noun

cowardly adjective easily scared

cowboy noun a man employed to look after cattle in America

cower verb When someone cowers, they crouch or move backwards because they are afraid

coy adjective If someone is coy, they pretend to be shy and modest > **coyly** adverb

coyote [koy-ote-ee] noun a North American animal like a small wolf

crab noun a sea creature with four pairs of legs, two pincers, and a flat, round body covered by a shell

crack verb 1 If something cracks, it becomes damaged, with lines appearing on its surface 2 If you crack a joke, you tell it 3 If you crack a problem or code, you solve it ▷ noun 4 one of the lines appearing on something when it cracks 5 a narrow gap ▷ adjective 6 A crack soldier or sportsman is highly trained and skilful

cracker noun 1 a thin, crisp biscuit that is often eaten with cheese 2 a paper-covered tube that pulls apart with a bang and usually has a toy and paper hat inside

crackle verb 1 If something crackles, it makes a rapid series of short, harsh noises ▷ noun 2 a short, harsh noise

cradle noun 1 a box-shaped bed for a baby ▷ verb 2 If you cradle something in your arms or hands, you hold it there carefully

craft noun 1 an activity such as weaving, carving, or pottery 2 a skilful occupation: *the writer's craft* 3 a boat, plane, or spacecraft

craftsman craftsmen noun a man who makes things skilfully with his hands > **craftsmanship** noun > **craftswoman** noun

crafty craftier, craftiest adjective Someone who is crafty gets what they want by tricking people in a clever way

craggy craggier, craggiest adjective A craggy mountain or cliff is steep and rocky

cram crams, cramming, crammed verb If you cram things or things into a place, you put more in than there is room for

cramp noun Cramp or cramps is a pain caused by a muscle contracting

cramped adjective If a room or building is cramped, it is not big enough for the things or things in it

cranberry cranberries noun Cranberries are sour-tasting red berries, often made into a sauce

crane noun 1 a machine that moves heavy things by lifting them in the air 2 a large bird with a long neck and long legs ▷ verb 3 If you crane your neck, you extend your head in a particular direction to see or hear something better

crank noun 1 (informal) someone with strange ideas who behaves in an odd way 2 a device you turn to make something move: The adjustment is made by turning the crank ▷ verb 3 If you crank something, you make it move by turning a handle

cranny crannies noun a very narrow opening in a wall or rock: nooks and crannies

crash noun 1 an accident in which a moving vehicle hits something violently 2 a sudden loud noise: the crash of the waves on the rocks 3 the sudden failure of a business or financial institution ▷ verb 4 When a vehicle crashes, it hits something and is badly damaged

crate noun a large box used for transporting or storing things

crater noun GEOGRAPHY a wide hole in the ground caused by something hitting it or by an explosion

crave verb If you crave something, you want it very much: I crave her approval ▷ **craving** noun

crawl verb 1 When you crawl, you move forward on your hands and knees 2 When a vehicle crawls, it moves very slowly 3 (informal) If a place is crawling with people or things, it is full of them: The place is crawling with tourists ▷ **crawler** noun

crayfish crayfishes or crayfish noun a small shellfish like a lobster

crayon noun a coloured pencil or a stick of coloured wax

craze noun something that is very popular for a short time

crazy crazier, craziest adjective (informal) 1 very strange or foolish: The guy is crazy; a crazy idea 2 If you are crazy about something, you are very keen on it: I was crazy about dancing ▷ **crazily** adverb ▷ **craziness** noun

creak verb 1 If something creaks, it makes a harsh sound when it moves or when you stand on it ▷ noun 2 a harsh squeaking noise ▷ **creaky** adjective

cream noun 1 Cream is a thick, yellowish-white liquid taken from the top of milk 2 Cream is also a substance people can rub on their skin ▷ adjective 3 yellowish-white ▷ **creamy** adjective

crease noun 1 an irregular line that appears on cloth or paper when it is crumpled 2 a straight line on something that has been pressed or folded neatly ▷ verb 3 To crease something is to make lines appear on it ▷ **creased** adjective

create verb 1 To create something is to cause it to happen or exist: This is absolutely vital but creates a problem

2 When someone creates a new product or process, they invent it > **creator** noun > **creation** noun

creative adjective **1** Creative people are able to invent and develop original ideas **2** Creative activities involve the inventing and developing of original ideas: creative writing > **creatively** adverb > **creativity** noun

creature noun any living thing that moves about

credence noun (formal) If something gives credence to a theory or story, it makes it easier to believe

credentials plural noun Your credentials are your past achievements or other things in your background that make you qualified for something

credible adjective If someone or something is credible, you can believe or trust them > **credibility** noun

credit noun **1** If you are allowed credit, you can take something and pay for it later: to buy goods on credit **2** If you get the credit for something, people praise you for it **3** If you say someone is a credit to their family or school, you mean that their family or school should be proud of them **4** (in plural) The list of people who helped make a film, recording, or television programme is called the credits > phrase **5** If someone or their bank account is **in credit**, their account has money in it > verb **6** If you are credited with an achievement, people believe that you were responsible for it

creditable adjective satisfactory or fairly good: a creditable performance

credit card noun a plastic card that allows someone to buy goods on credit

creditor noun Your creditors are the people you owe money to

creed noun **1** a religion **2** any set of beliefs: the feminist creed

creek noun a narrow inlet where the sea comes a long way into the land

creep creeps, creeping, crept verb To creep is to move quietly and slowly

creepy creepier, creepiest adjective (informal) strange and frightening: a creepy feeling

cremate verb When someone is cremated, their dead body is burned during a funeral service > **cremation** noun

crematorium crematoriums or crematoria noun a building in which the bodies of dead people are burned

crepe [krayp] noun **1** Crepe is a thin ridged material made from cotton, silk, or wool **2** Crepe is also a type of rubber with a rough surface

crescendo crescendos [krish-en-doe] noun MUSIC When there is a crescendo in a piece of music, the music gets louder

crescent noun a curved shape that is wider in its middle than at the ends, which are pointed

crest noun **1** The crest of a hill or wave is its highest part **2** a tuft of feathers on top of a bird's head **3** a small picture or design that is the emblem of a noble family, a town, or an organization > **crested** adjective

crevice noun a narrow crack or gap in rock

crew noun **1** The crew of a ship, aeroplane, or spacecraft are the people who operate it **2** people with special technical skills who work together: the camera crew

crib cribs, cribbing, cribbed verb **1** (informal) If you crib, you copy what someone else has written and

pretend it is your own work ▷ noun
2 (old-fashioned) a baby's cot

cricket noun **1** Cricket is an outdoor game played by two teams who take turns at scoring runs by hitting a ball with a bat **2** a small jumping insect that produces sounds by rubbing its wings together
> **cricketer** noun

crime noun an action for which you can be punished by law: *a serious crime*

criminal noun **1** someone who has committed a crime ▷ adjective **2** involving or related to crime: *criminal activities* > **criminally** adverb

criminology noun the scientific study of crime and criminals
> **criminologist** noun

crimson noun, adjective dark purplish-red

cringe verb If you cringe, you back away from someone or something because you are afraid or embarrassed

cripple verb **1** To cripple someone is to injure them severely **2** To cripple a company or country is to prevent it from working > **crippled** adjective > **crippling** adjective

crisis crises [kry-seez in the plural] noun a serious or dangerous situation

crisp adjective **1** Something that is crisp is pleasantly fresh and firm: *crisp lettuce leaves* **2** If the air or the weather is crisp, it is pleasantly fresh, cold, and dry: *crisp wintry days* ▷ noun **3** Crisps are thin slices of potato fried until they are hard and crunchy

crispy crispier, crispiest adjective Crispy food is pleasantly hard and crunchy: *a crispy salad*

criterion criteria [kry-**teer**-ee-on]

noun a standard by which you judge or decide something

critic noun **1** someone who writes reviews of books, films, plays, or musical performances **2** A critic of a person or system is someone who criticizes them publicly: *the government's critics*

critical adjective **1** A critical time is one which is very important in determining what happens in the future: *critical months in the history of the world* **2** A critical situation is a very serious one: *Rock music is in a critical state* **3** If an ill or injured person is critical, they are in danger of dying **4** If you are critical of something or someone, you express severe judgments or opinions about them **5** If you are critical, you examine and judge something carefully: *a critical look at the way he led his life* > **critically** adverb

criticism noun **1** When there is criticism of someone or something, people express disapproval of them **2** If you make a criticism, you point out a fault you think someone or something has

criticize or **criticise** verb If you criticize someone or something, you say what you think is wrong with them

croak verb **1** When animals and birds croak, they make harsh, low sounds ▷ noun **2** a harsh, low sound

Croatian [kroh-shay] adjective **1** belonging or relating to Croatia ▷ noun **2** someone who comes from Croatia **3** Croatian is the form of Serbo-Croat spoken in Croatia

crochet [kroh-shay] noun Crochet is a way of making clothes and other things out of thread using a needle with a small hook at the end

crockery noun Crockery is plates,

cups, and saucers

crocodile noun a large, scaly, meat-eating reptile which lives in tropical rivers

croissant [**krwah**-son] noun a light, crescent-shaped roll eaten at breakfast

crony cronies noun (old-fashioned) Your cronies are the friends you spend a lot of time with

crook noun **1** (informal) a criminal **2** The crook of your arm or leg is the soft inside part where you bend your elbow or knee ▷ adjective **3** In Australian English, crook means ill

crooked [**kroo**-kid] adjective **1** bent or twisted **2** Someone who is crooked is dishonest

croon verb To croon is to sing or hum quietly and gently: *He crooned a love song*

crop crops, cropping, cropped noun **1** Crops are plants such as wheat and potatoes that are grown for food **2** the plants collected at harvest time: *You should have two crops in the year* ▷ verb **3** To crop someone's hair is to cut it very short > **crop up** verb (informal) If something crops up, it happens unexpectedly

croquet [**kroh**-kay] noun Croquet is a game in which the players use long-handled mallets to hit balls through metal arches pushed into a lawn

cross verb **1** If you cross something such as a room or a road, you go to the other side of it **2** Lines or roads that cross meet and go across each other **3** If a thought crosses your mind, you think of it **4** If you cross your arms, legs, or fingers, you put one on top of the other ▷ noun **5** a vertical bar or line crossed by a shorter horizontal bar or line; also

used to describe any object shaped like this **6** RE The Cross is the cross-shaped structure on which Jesus Christ was crucified. A cross is also any symbol representing Christ's Cross **7** a written mark shaped like an X: *Mark the wrong answers with a cross* **8** Something that is a cross between two things is neither one thing nor the other, but a mixture of both ▷ adjective **9** Someone who is cross is rather angry > **crossly** adverb > **cross out** verb If you cross out words on a page, you draw a line through them because they are wrong or because you do not want people to read them

crossbow noun a weapon consisting of a small bow fixed at the end of a piece of wood

cross-country noun **1** Cross-country is the sport of running across open countryside, rather than on roads or on a track ▷ adverb, adjective **2** across open countryside

crossfire noun Crossfire is gunfire crossing the same place from opposite directions

crossing noun **1** a place where you can cross a road safely **2** a journey by ship to a place on the other side of the sea

cross-legged adjective If you are sitting cross-legged, you are sitting on the floor with your knees pointing outwards and your feet tucked under them

cross section noun A cross section of a group of people is a representative sample of them

crossword noun a puzzle in which you work out the answers to clues and write them in the white squares of a pattern of black and white squares

crotch noun the part of your body between the tops of your legs

crouch verb If you are crouching, you are leaning forward with your legs bent under you

crow noun **1** a large black bird which makes a loud, harsh noise ▷ verb **2** When a cock crows, it utters a loud squawking sound

crowbar noun a heavy iron bar used as a lever or for forcing things open

crowd noun **1** a large group of people gathered together ▷ verb **2** When people crowd somewhere, they gather there close together or in large numbers

crowded adjective A crowded place is full of people

crown noun **1** a circular ornament worn on a royal person's head **2** The crown of something such as your head is the top part of it ▷ verb **3** When a king or queen is crowned, a crown is put on their head during their coronation ceremony **4** When something crowns an event, it is the final part of it: The news crowned a dreadful week

crucial [kroo-shl] adjective If something is crucial, it is very important in determining how something else will be in the future

crucifix noun RE a cross with a figure representing Jesus Christ being crucified on it

crucify verb crucifies, crucifying, crucified verb RE To crucify someone is to tie or nail them to a large wooden cross and leave there to die > **crucifixion** noun

crude adjective **1** rough and simple: a crude weapon; a crude method of entry **2** A crude person speaks or behaves in a rude and offensive way: You can be quite crude at times > **crudely** adverb > **crudity** noun

cruel adjective Cruel people deliberately cause pain or distress to other people or to animals > **cruelly** adverb

cruelty noun cruel behaviour

cruise noun **1** a holiday in which you travel on a ship and visit places ▷ verb **2** When a vehicle cruises, it moves at a constant moderate speed

cruiser noun **1** a motor boat with a cabin you can sleep in **2** a large, fast warship

crumb noun Crumbs are very small pieces of bread or cake

crumble verb When something crumbles, it breaks into small pieces

crumbly crumblier, crumbliest adjective Something crumbly easily breaks into small pieces

crumple verb To crumple paper or cloth is to squash it so that it is full of creases and folds

crunch verb If you crunch something, you crush it noisily, for example between your teeth or under your feet

crunchy crunchier, crunchiest adjective Crunchy food is hard or crisp and makes a noise when you eat it

crusade noun a long and determined attempt to achieve something: the crusade for human rights > **crusader** noun

crush verb **1** To crush something is to destroy its shape by squeezing it **2** To crush a substance is to turn it into liquid or powder by squeezing or grinding it **3** To crush an army or political organization is to defeat it completely ▷ noun **4** a dense crowd of people

crust noun **1** the hard outside part of a loaf **2** a hard layer on top of something: The snow had a fine crust on it

crusty crustier, crustiest *adjective*
1 Something that is crusty has a hard outside layer **2** Crusty people are impatient and irritable

crutch *noun* a support like a long stick which you lean on to help you walk when you have an injured foot or leg

crux cruxes *noun* the most important or difficult part of a problem or argument

cry cries, crying, cried *verb* **1** When you cry, tears appear in your eyes **2** To cry something is to shout it or say it loudly: *'See you soon!' they cried* ▷ *noun* **3** If you have a cry, you cry for a period of time **4** a shout or other loud sound made with your voice **5** a loud sound made by some birds: *the cry of a seagull* ▷ **cry off** *verb* (*informal*) If you cry off, you change your mind and decide not to do something ▷ **cry out for** *verb* (*informal*) If something is crying out for something else, it needs it very much

crypt *noun* an underground room beneath a church, usually used as a burial place

cryptic *adjective* A cryptic remark or message has a hidden meaning

crystal *noun* **1** a piece of a mineral that has formed naturally into a regular shape **2** Crystal is a type of transparent rock, used in jewellery **3** Crystal is also a kind of very high quality glass ▷ **crystalline** *adjective*

crystallize or **crystallise** *verb* **1** If a substance crystallizes, it turns into crystals **2** If an idea crystallizes, it becomes clear in your mind

cub *noun* **1** Some young wild animals are called cubs: *a lion cub* **2** The Cubs is an organization for young boys before they join the Scouts

Cuban [**kyoo**-ban] *adjective*

1 belonging or relating to Cuba ▷ *noun* **2** someone who comes from Cuba

cube [MATHS] *noun* **1** a three-dimensional shape with six equally-sized square surfaces **2** If you multiply a number by itself twice, you get its cube ▷ *verb* **3** To cube a number is to multiply it by itself twice

cubic *adjective* [MATHS] used in measurements of volume: *cubic centimetres*

cubicle *noun* a small enclosed area in a place such as a sports centre, where you can dress and undress

cuckoo cuckoos *noun* a grey bird with a two-note call that lays its eggs in other birds' nests

cucumber *noun* a long, thin, green-skinned fruit eaten raw in salads

cuddle *verb* **1** If you cuddle someone, you hold them affectionately in your arms ▷ *noun* **2** If you give someone a cuddle, you hold them affectionately in your arms

cuddly cuddlier, cuddliest *adjective* Cuddly people, animals, or toys are soft or pleasing in some way so that you want to cuddle them

cue *noun* **1** something said or done by a performer that is a signal for another performer to begin: *Chris never misses a cue* **2** a long stick used to hit the balls in snooker and billiards

cuff *noun* the end part of a sleeve

cuisine [kwiz-**een**] *noun* The cuisine of a region is the style of cooking that is typical of it

cul-de-sac [**kul**-des-sak] *noun* a road that does not lead to any other roads because one end is blocked off

culinary *adjective* (*formal*) connected with the kitchen or cooking

cull verb **1** If you cull things, you gather them from different places or sources: *information culled from movies* ▷ noun **2** When there is a cull, weaker animals are killed to reduce the numbers in a group

culminate verb To culminate in something is to finally develop into it: *a campaign that culminated in a stunning success* > **culmination** noun

culprit noun someone who has done something harmful or wrong

cult noun **1** A cult is a religious group with special rituals, usually connected with the worship of a particular person **2** 'Cult' is used to refer to any situation in which someone or something is very popular with a large group of people: *the American sports car cult*

cultivate verb **1** To cultivate land is to grow crops on it **2** If you cultivate a feeling or attitude, you try to develop it in yourself or other people > **cultivation** noun

culture noun **1** Culture refers to the arts and to people's appreciation of them: *He was a man of culture* **2** The culture of a particular society is its ideas, customs, and art: *Japanese culture* **3** In science, a culture is a group of bacteria or cells grown in a laboratory > **cultured** adjective > **cultural** adjective

cumulative adjective Something that is cumulative keeps being added to

cunning adjective **1** Someone who is cunning uses clever and deceitful methods to get what they want ▷ noun **2** Cunning is the ability to get what you want using clever and deceitful methods > **cunningly** adverb

cup cups, cupping, cupped noun **1** a small, round container with a handle, which you drink out of **2** a large metal container with two handles, given as a prize ▷ verb **3** If you cup your hands, you put them together to make a shape like a cup

cupboard noun a piece of furniture with doors and shelves

curable adjective If a disease or illness is curable, it can be cured

curate noun a clergyman who helps a vicar or a priest

curator noun the person in a museum or art gallery in charge of its contents

curb verb **1** To curb something is to keep it within limits: *policies designed to curb inflation* ▷ noun **2** If a curb is placed on something, it is kept within limits: *the curb on spending*

cure verb **1** To cure an illness is to end it **2** To cure a sick or injured person is to make them well **3** If something cures you of a habit or attitude, it stops you having it **4** To cure food, tobacco, or animal skin is to treat it in order to preserve it ▷ noun **5** A cure for an illness is something that cures it

curfew noun If there is a curfew, people must stay indoors between particular times at night

curiosity curiosities noun **1** Curiosity is the desire to know about something or about many things **2** something unusual and interesting

curious adjective **1** Someone who is curious wants to know more about something **2** Something that is curious is unusual and hard to explain > **curiously** adverb

curl noun **1** Curls are lengths of hair shaped in tight curves and circles **2** a curved or spiral shape: *the curls of morning fog* ▷ verb **3** If something curls, it moves in a curve or spiral > **curly** adjective

curler *noun* Curlers are plastic or metal tubes that women roll their hair round to make it curly

currency currencies *noun* **1** A country's currency is its coins and banknotes, or its monetary system generally: *foreign currency; a strong economy and a weak currency* **2** If something such as an idea has currency, it is used a lot at a particular time

current *noun* **1** GEOGRAPHY A strong continuous movement of the water in a river or in the sea **2** GEOGRAPHY An air current is a flowing movement in the air **3** SCIENCE An electric current is a flow of electricity through a wire or circuit ▷ *adjective* **4** Something that is current is happening, being done, or being used now > **currently** *adverb*

current affairs *plural noun* Current affairs are political and social events discussed in newspapers and on television and radio

curriculum curriculums *or* curricula [kur-**rik**-yoo-lum] *noun* the different courses taught at a school or university

curriculum vitae curricula vitae [**vee**-tie] *noun* Someone's curriculum vitae is a written account of their personal details, education, and work experience which they send when they apply for a job

curry curries, currying, curried *noun* **1** Curry is an Indian dish made with hot spices ▷ *phrase* **2** To **curry favour** with someone means to try to please them by flattering them or doing things to help them

curse *verb* **1** To curse is to swear because you are angry **2** If you curse someone or something, you say

angry things about them using rude words ▷ *noun* **3** what you say when you curse **4** something supernatural that is supposed to cause unpleasant things to happen to someone **5** a thing or person that causes a lot of distress: *the curse of recession* > **cursed** *adjective*

cursor *noun* an arrow or box on a computer monitor which indicates where the next letter or symbol is

cursory *adjective* When you give something a cursory glance or examination, you look at it briefly without paying attention to detail

curt *adjective* If someone is curt, they speak in a brief and rather rude way > **curtly** *adverb*

curtail *verb* (formal) To curtail something is to reduce or restrict it: *Injury curtailed his career*

curtain *noun* **1** a hanging piece of material which can be pulled across a window for privacy or to keep out the light **2** DRAMA a large piece of material which hangs in front of the stage in a theatre until a performance begins

curve *noun* **1** a smooth, gradually bending line ▷ *verb* **2** When something curves, it moves in a curve or has the shape of a curve: *The track curved away below him; His mouth curved slightly* > **curved** *adjective* > **curvy** *adjective*

cushion *noun* **1** a soft object put on a seat to make it more comfortable ▷ *verb* **2** To cushion something is to reduce its effect: *We might have helped to cushion the shock for her*

custard *noun* Custard is a sweet yellow sauce made from milk and eggs or milk and a powder

custodian *noun* the person in charge of a collection in an art gallery or a museum

custody noun **1** To have custody of a child means to have the legal right to keep it and look after it: *She won custody of her younger son* ▷ *phrase* **2** Someone who is **in custody** is being kept in prison until they can be tried in a court > **custodial** *adjective*

custom noun **1** a traditional activity: *an ancient Chinese custom* **2** something usually done at a particular time or in particular circumstances by a person or by the people in a society: *It was also my custom to do Christmas shows* **3** Customs is the place at a border, airport, or harbour where you have to declare any goods you are bringing into a country **4** (*formal*) If a shop or business has your custom, you buy things or go there regularly: *Banks are desperate to get your custom*

customary *adjective* usual: *his customary modesty; her customary greeting* > **customarily** *adverb*

custom-built or **custom-made** *adjective* Something that is custom-built or custom-made is made to someone's special requirements

customer noun **1** A shop's or firm's customers are the people who buy its goods **2** (*informal*) You can use 'customer' to refer to someone when describing what they are like to deal with: *a tough customer*

cut cuts, cutting, cut *verb* **1** If you cut something, you use a knife, scissors, or some other sharp tool to mark it or remove parts of it **2** If you cut yourself, you injure yourself on a sharp object **3** If you cut the amount of something, you reduce it: *Some costs could be cut* **4** When writing is cut, parts of it are not printed or broadcast **5** To cut from one scene

or shot to another in a film is to go instantly to the other scene or shot ▷ noun **6** a mark or injury made with a knife or other sharp tool **7** a reduction: *another cut in interest rates* **8** a part in something written that is not printed or broadcast **9** a large piece of meat ready for cooking ▷ *adjective* **10** Well cut clothes have been well designed and made: *this beautifully cut coat* > **cut back** *verb* To cut back or cut back on spending means to reduce it > **cutback** *noun* > **cut down** *verb* If you cut down on an activity, you do it less often: *cutting down on smoking* > **cut off** *verb* **1** To cut someone or something off means to separate them from things they are normally connected with: *The President had cut himself off from the people* **2** If a supply of something is cut off, you no longer get it: *The water had been cut off* **3** If your telephone or telephone call is cut off, it is disconnected > **cut out** *verb* **1** If you cut out something you are doing, you stop doing it: *Cut out drinking* **2** If an engine cuts out, it suddenly stops working

cute *adjective* pretty or attractive

cutlery noun Cutlery is knives, forks, and spoons

cutlet noun a small piece of meat which you fry or grill

cutting noun **1** something cut from a newspaper or magazine **2** a part cut from a plant and used to grow a new plant ▷ *adjective* **3** A cutting remark is unkind and likely to hurt someone

CV an abbreviation for **curriculum vitae**

cyanide [**sigh**-an-nide] noun Cyanide is an extremely poisonous chemical

cyberspace noun all of the data

stored in a large computer or network, seen as a place

cycle verb **1** When you cycle, you ride a bicycle ▷ noun **2** a bicycle or a motorcycle **3** a series of events which is repeated again and again in the same order: *the cycle of births and deaths* **4** SCIENCE a single complete series of movements or events in an electrical, electronic, mechanical, or organic process **5** a series of songs or poems intended to be performed or read together

cyclical or **cyclic** adjective happening over and over again in cycles: *a clear cyclical pattern*

cyclist noun someone who rides a bicycle

cyclone noun a violent tropical storm

cylinder noun **1** MATHS a regular three-dimensional shape with two equally-sized flat circular ends joined by a curved surface **2** the part in a motor engine in which the piston moves backwards and forwards ▷ **cylindrical** adjective

cynic [sin-nik] noun a cynical person

cynical adjective believing that people always behave selfishly or dishonestly ▷ **cynically** adverb ▷ **cynicism** noun

cypress noun a type of evergreen tree with small dark green leaves and round cones

cyst [sist] noun a growth containing liquid that can form under your skin or inside your body

czar another spelling of **tsar**

Czech [chek] adjective **1** belonging or relating to the Czech Republic ▷ noun **2** someone who comes from the Czech Republic **3** Czech is the language spoken in the Czech Republic

d

dab dabs, dabbing, dabbed verb **1** If you dab something, you touch it with quick light strokes: *He dabbed some disinfectant onto the gash* ▷ noun **2** a small amount of something that is put on a surface: *a dab of perfume*

dabble verb If you dabble in something, you work or play at it without being seriously involved in it: *All his life he dabbled in poetry*

dad or **daddy** daddies noun (informal) Your dad or your daddy is your father

daffodil noun A daffodil is an early spring flowering plant, with a yellow trumpet-shaped flower grown from a bulb

daft adjective stupid and not sensible

dagger noun a weapon like a short knife

daily adjective **1** occurring every day: *our daily visit to the gym* **2** of or relating to a single day or to one day at a time: *the average daily wage*

dainty daintier, daintiest adjective very delicate and pretty ▷ **daintily** adverb

dairy dairies noun **1** a shop or company that supplies milk and milk products **2** in New Zealand, a small shop selling groceries, often outside usual opening hours ▷ adjective **3** Dairy products are foods made from milk, such as butter, cheese, cream, and yogurt **4** A dairy farm is one which keeps cattle to produce milk

dais [day-is] noun a raised platform, normally at one end of a hall and used by a speaker

daisy daisies noun a small wild flower with a yellow centre and small white petals

dale noun a valley

dam noun a barrier built across a river to hold back water

damage verb 1 To damage something means to harm or spoil it ▷ noun 2 Damage to something is injury or harm done to it 3 Damages is the money awarded by a court to compensate someone for loss or harm > **damaging** adjective

dame noun the title given to a woman who has been awarded the OBE or one of the other British orders of chivalry

damn [dam] verb 1 To damn something or someone means to curse or condemn them ▷ interjection 2 'Damn' is a swearword > **damned** adjective

damnation [dam-nay-shun] noun Damnation is eternal punishment in Hell after death

damp adjective 1 slightly wet ▷ noun 2 Damp is slight wetness, especially in the air or in the walls of a building > **dampness** noun

dampen verb 1 If you dampen something, you make it slightly wet 2 To dampen something also means to reduce its liveliness or strength: The whole episode has rather dampened my enthusiasm

damper phrase (informal) To **put a damper on** something means to stop it being enjoyable

dance verb 1 To dance means to move your feet and body rhythmically in time to music ▷ noun 2 a series of rhythmic movements or steps in time to

music 3 a social event where people dance with each other > **dancer** noun > **dancing** noun

dandelion noun a wild plant with yellow flowers which form a ball of fluffy seeds

dandruff noun Dandruff is small, loose scales of dead skin in someone's hair

dandy dandies noun (old-fashioned) a man who always dresses in very smart clothes

Dane noun someone who comes from Denmark

danger noun 1 Danger is the possibility that someone may be harmed or killed 2 something or someone that can hurt or harm you

dangerous adjective able to or likely to cause hurt or harm > **dangerously** adverb

dangle verb When something dangles or when you dangle it, it swings or hangs loosely

Danish adjective 1 belonging or relating to Denmark ▷ noun 2 Danish is the main language spoken in Denmark

dank adjective A dank place is unpleasantly damp and chilly

dapper adjective slim and neatly dressed

dappled adjective marked with patches of a different or darker shade

dare verb 1 To dare someone means to challenge them to do something in order to prove their courage 2 To dare to do something means to have the courage to do it ▷ noun 3 a challenge to do something dangerous

daredevil noun a person who enjoys doing dangerous things

daring adjective 1 bold and willing to take risks ▷ noun 2 the courage required to do things which are dangerous

dark *adjective* **1** If it is dark, there is not enough light to see properly **2** Dark colours or surfaces reflect little light and so look deep-coloured or dull **3** 'Dark' is also used to describe thoughts or ideas which are sinister or unpleasant ▷ *noun* **4** The dark is the lack of light in a place ▷ **darkly** *adverb* ▷ **darkness** *noun*

darken *verb* If something darkens, or if you darken it, it becomes darker than it was

darkroom *noun* a room from which daylight is shut out so that photographic film can be developed

darling *noun* **1** Someone who is lovable or a favourite may be called a darling ▷ *adjective* **2** much admired or loved: *his darling daughter*

darn *verb* **1** To darn a hole in a garment means to mend it with crossing stitches ▷ *noun* **2** a part of a garment that has been darned

dart *noun* **1** a small pointed arrow **2** Darts is a game in which the players throw darts at a round board divided into numbered sections ▷ *verb* **3** To dart about means to move quickly and suddenly from one place to another

dash *verb* **1** To dash somewhere means to rush there **2** If something is dashed against something else, it strikes it or is thrown violently against it **3** If hopes or ambitions are dashed, they are ruined or frustrated ▷ *noun* **4** a sudden movement or rush **5** a small quantity of something **6** the punctuation mark (—) which shows a change of subject, or which may be used instead of brackets

dashboard *noun* the instrument panel in a motor vehicle

dashing *adjective* A dashing man is stylish and confident: *He was a dashing figure in his younger days*

data *noun* **1** information, usually in the form of facts or statistics **2** COMPUTING any information put into a computer and which the computer works on or processes

database *noun* COMPUTING a collection of information stored in a computer

date *noun* **1** a particular day or year that can be named **2** If you have a date, you have an appointment to meet someone; also used to refer to the person you are meeting **3** a small dark-brown sticky fruit with a stone inside, which grows on palm trees ▷ *verb* **4** If you are dating someone, you have a romantic relationship with them **5** If you date something, you find out the time when it began or was made **6** If something dates from a particular time, that is when it happened or was made ▷ *phrase* **7** If something is **out of date**, it is old-fashioned or no longer valid

dated *adjective* no longer fashionable

datum the singular form of **data**

daub *verb* If you daub something such as mud or paint on a surface, you smear it there

daughter *noun* Someone's daughter is their female child

daughter-in-law daughters-in-law *noun* Someone's daughter-in-law is the wife of their grown-up child

daunt *verb* If something daunts you, you feel worried about whether you can succeed in doing it: *He was not the type of man to be daunted by adversity* ▷ **daunting** *adjective*

dawn noun 1 the time in the morning when light first appears in the sky 2 the beginning of something: *the dawn of the radio age* ▷ verb 3 If day is dawning, morning light is beginning to appear 4 If an idea or fact dawns on you, you realize it

day noun 1 one of the seven 24-hour periods of time in a week, measured from one midnight to the next 2 Day is the period of light between sunrise and sunset 3 You can refer to a particular day or days meaning a particular period in history: *in Gladstone's day*

daybreak noun Daybreak is the time in the morning when light first appears in the sky

daydream noun 1 a series of pleasant thoughts about things that you would like to happen ▷ verb 2 When you daydream, you drift off into a daydream

daylight noun 1 Daylight is the period during the day when it is light 2 Daylight is also the light from the sun

day-to-day adjective happening every day as part of ordinary routine life

day trip noun a journey for pleasure to a place and back again on the same day

daze phrase If you are **in a daze**, you are confused and bewildered

dazed adjective If you are dazed, you are stunned and unable to think clearly

dazzle verb 1 If someone or something dazzles you, you are very impressed by their brilliance 2 If a bright light dazzles you, it blinds you for a moment ▷ **dazzling** adjective

deacon noun 1 In the Church of England or Roman Catholic Church, a deacon is a member of the clergy below the rank of priest 2 In some other churches, a deacon is a church official appointed to help the minister ▷ **deaconess** noun

dead adjective 1 no longer living or supporting life 2 no longer used or no longer functioning: *a dead language* 3 If part of your body goes dead, it loses sensation and feels numb ▷ noun 5 the middle part of night or winter, when it is most quiet and at its darkest or coldest

dead end noun a street that is closed off at one end

deadline noun a time or date before which something must be completed

deadlock noun a situation in which neither side in a dispute is willing to give in

deadly deadlier, deadliest adjective 1 likely or able to cause death ▷ adverb, adjective 2 'Deadly' is used to emphasize how serious or unpleasant a situation is: *He is deadly serious about his comeback*

deadpan adjective, adverb showing no emotion or expression

deaf adjective 1 partially or totally unable to hear 2 refusing to listen or pay attention to something: *He was deaf to all pleas for financial help* ▷ **deafness** noun

deafening adjective If a noise is deafening, it is so loud that you cannot hear anything else

deal deals, dealing, dealt noun 1 an agreement or arrangement, especially in business ▷ verb 2 If you deal with something, you do what is necessary to sort it out: *He must learn to deal with stress* 3 If you deal in a particular type of goods, you buy and sell those goods 4 If you deal someone or something a blow, you hurt or harm them: *Competition from abroad dealt a heavy blow to the industry*

dealer noun a person or firm whose business involves buying or selling things

dealings plural noun Your dealings with people are the relations you have with them or the business you do with them

dean noun **1** In a university or college, a dean is a person responsible for administration or for the welfare of students **2** In the Church of England, a dean is a clergyman who is responsible for administration

dear noun **1** 'Dear' is used as a sign of affection: *What's the matter, dear?* ▷ adjective **2** much loved: *my dear son* **3** Something that is dear is expensive **4** You use 'dear' at the beginning of a letter before the name of the person you are writing to ▷ **dearly** adverb

dearth [**derth**] noun a shortage of something

death noun Death is the end of the life of a person or animal

debacle [day-**bah**-kl] noun (formal) a sudden disastrous failure

debatable adjective not absolutely certain: *The justness of these wars is debatable*

debate noun **1** Debate is argument or discussion: *There is much debate as to what causes depression* **2** a formal discussion in which opposing views are expressed ▷ verb **3** When people debate something, they discuss it in a fairly formal manner **4** If you are debating whether or not to do something, you are considering it: *He was debating whether or not he should tell her*

debilitating adjective (formal) If

something is debilitating, it makes you very weak: *a debilitating illness*

debit verb **1** to take money from a person's bank account ▷ noun **2** a record of the money that has been taken out of a person's bank account

debrief verb When someone is debriefed, they are asked to give a report on a task they have just completed ▷ **debriefing** noun

debris [**day**-bree] noun Debris is fragments or rubble left after something has been destroyed

debt [**det**] noun **1** a sum of money that is owed to one person by another **2** Debt is the state of owing money

debtor noun a person who owes money

debut [**day**-byoo] noun a performer's first public appearance

debutante [**deb**-yoo-tant] noun (old-fashioned) a girl from the upper classes who has started going to social events

decade noun a period of ten years

decadence noun Decadence is a decline in standards of morality and behaviour ▷ **decadent** adjective

decapitate verb To decapitate someone means to cut off their head

decathlon [de-**cath**-lon] noun a sports contest in which athletes compete in ten different events

decay verb **1** When things decay, they rot or go bad ▷ noun **2** Decay is the process of decaying

deceased (formal) adjective **1** A deceased person is someone who has recently died ▷ noun **2** The deceased is someone who has recently died

deceit noun Deceit is behaviour that is intended to mislead people into

believing something that is not true
> **deceitful** adjective

deceive verb If you deceive someone, you make them believe something that is not true

December noun December is the twelfth and last month of the year. It has 31 days

decency noun **1** Decency is behaviour that is respectable and follows accepted moral standards **2** Decency is also behaviour which shows kindness and respect towards people: *No one had the decency to tell me to my face*

decent adjective **1** of an acceptable standard or quality: *He gets a decent pension* **2** Decent people are honest and respectable: *a decent man*
> **decently** adverb

decentralize or **decentralise** verb To decentralize an organization means to reorganize it so that power is transferred from one main administrative centre to smaller local units > **decentralization** noun

deception noun **1** something that is intended to trick or deceive someone **2** Deception is the act of deceiving someone

deceptive adjective likely to make people believe something that is not true > **deceptively** adverb

decibel noun SCIENCE a unit of the intensity of sound

decide verb If you decide to do something, you choose to do it

deciduous adjective Deciduous trees lose their leaves in the autumn every year

decimal adjective MATHS **1** The decimal system expresses numbers using all the digits from 0 to 9 ▷ noun **2** a fraction in which a dot called a decimal point is followed by numbers representing tenths,

hundredths, and thousandths. For example, 0.5 represents ⁵⁄₁₀ (or ½); 0.05 represents ⁵⁄₁₀₀ (or ¹⁄₂₀)

decimate verb To decimate a group of people or animals means to kill or destroy a large number of them

decipher verb If you decipher a piece of writing or a message, you work out its meaning

decision noun a choice or judgment that is made about something: *The editor's decision is final*

decisive [dis-**sigh**-siv] adjective **1** having great influence on the result of something: *It was the decisive moment of the race* **2** A decisive person is able to make decisions firmly and quickly > **decisively** adverb > **decisiveness** noun

deck noun **1** a floor or platform built into a ship, or one of the two floors on a bus **2** a pack of cards

declaration noun a firm, forceful statement, often an official announcement: *a declaration of war*

declare verb **1** If you declare something, you state it forcefully or officially **2** If you declare goods or earnings, you state what you have bought or earned, in order to pay tax or duty

decline verb **1** If something declines, it becomes smaller or weaker **2** If you decline something, you politely refuse to accept it or do it ▷ noun **3** a gradual weakening or decrease: *a decline in the birth rate*

decode verb If you decode a coded message, you convert it into ordinary language > **decoder** noun

decommission verb When something such as a nuclear reactor or large machine is decommissioned, it is taken to pieces or removed from service because it is no longer going to be used

decompose verb If something decomposes, it decays through chemical or bacterial action
> **decomposition** noun

decor [**day**-kor] noun The decor of a room or house is the style in which it is decorated and furnished

decorate verb **1** If you decorate something, you make it more attractive by adding some ornament or colour to it **2** If you decorate a room or building, you paint or wallpaper it

decoration noun **1** Decorations are features added to something to make it more attractive **2** The decoration in a building or room is the style of the furniture and wallpaper

decorative adjective intended to look attractive

decorator noun a person whose job is painting and putting up wallpaper in rooms and buildings

decorum [dik-**ore**-um] noun (formal) Decorum is polite and correct behaviour

decoy noun a person or object that is used to lead someone or something into danger

decrease verb **1** If something decreases or if you decrease it, it becomes less in quantity or size ▷ noun **2** a lessening in the amount of something; also the amount by which something becomes less
> **decreasing** adjective

decree decrees, decreeing, decreed verb **1** If someone decrees something, they state formally that it will happen ▷ noun **2** an official decision or order, usually of governments or rulers

dedicate verb If you dedicate

yourself to something, you devote your time and energy to it
> **dedication** noun

deduce verb If you deduce something, you work it out from other facts that you know are true

deduct verb To deduct an amount from a total amount means to subtract it from the total

deduction noun **1** an amount which is taken away from a total **2** a conclusion that you have reached because of other things that you know are true

deed noun **1** something that is done **2** a legal document, especially concerning the ownership of land or buildings

deem verb (formal) If you deem something to be true, you judge or consider it to be true: His ideas were deemed unacceptable

deep adjective **1** situated or extending a long way down from the top surface of something, or a long way inwards: a deep hole **2** great or intense: deep suspicion **3** low in pitch: a deep voice **4** strong and fairly dark in colour: The wine was deep ruby in colour > **deeply** adverb

deepen verb If something deepens or is deepened, it becomes deeper or more intense

deer deer noun a large, hoofed mammal that lives wild in parts of Britain

deface verb If you deface a wall or notice, you spoil it by writing or drawing on it: She spitefully defaced her sister's poster

default verb **1** If someone defaults on something they have legally agreed to do, they fail to do it: He defaulted on repayment of the loan ▷ phrase **2** If something happens

by default, it happens because something else which might have prevented it has failed to happen

defeat verb 1 If you defeat someone or something, you win a victory over them, or cause them to fail ▷ noun 2 the state of being beaten or of failing or an occasion on which someone is beaten or fails to achieve something: *He was gracious in defeat*

defect noun 1 a fault or flaw in something ▷ verb 2 If someone defects, they leave their own country or organization and join an opposing one > **defection** noun

defective adjective imperfect or faulty: *defective eyesight*

defence noun 1 Defence is action that is taken to protect someone or something from attack 2 any arguments used in support of something that has been criticized or questioned 3 the case presented, in a court of law, by a lawyer for the person on trial; also the person on trial and his or her lawyers 4 [HISTORY] A country's defences are its military resources, such as its armed forces and weapons

defend verb 1 To defend someone or something means to protect them from harm or danger 2 If you defend a person or their ideas and beliefs, you argue in support of them 3 To defend someone in court means to represent them and argue their case for them 4 In a game such as football or hockey, to defend means to try to prevent goals being scored by your opponents

defendant noun a person who has been accused of a crime in a court of law

defender noun 1 a person who protects someone or something

from harm or danger 2 a person who argues in support of something 3 a person who tries to stop goals being scored in certain sports

defensible adjective able to be defended against criticism or attack

defensive adjective 1 intended or designed for protection: *defensive weapons* 2 Someone who is defensive feels unsure and threatened by other people's opinions and attitudes: *Don't get defensive, I was only joking about your cooking* > **defensively** adverb > **defensiveness** noun

defer defers, deferring, deferred verb 1 If you defer something, you delay or postpone it until a future time 2 If you defer to someone, you agree with them or do what they want because you respect them

deference [def-er-enss] noun Deference is polite and respectful behaviour > **deferential** adjective > **deferentially** adverb

defiance noun Defiance is behaviour which shows that you are not willing to obey or behave in the expected way: *a gesture of defiance* > **defiant** adjective > **defiantly** adverb

deficiency deficiencies noun a lack of something: *vitamin deficiency*

deficient adjective lacking in something

deficit [def-iss-it] noun the amount by which money received by an organization is less than money spent

define verb [EXAM TERM] If you define something, you say clearly what it is or what it means: *Culture can be defined in hundreds of ways*

definite adjective 1 firm and unlikely to be changed: *The answer is a definite 'yes'* 2 certain or true rather than

guessed or imagined: *definite proof*
> **definitely** adverb

definition noun a statement explaining the meaning of a word or idea

definitive adjective **1** final and unable to be questioned or altered: *a definitive answer* **2** most complete, or the best of its kind: *a definitive history of science fiction*
> **definitively** adverb

deflate verb **1** If you deflate something such as a tyre or balloon, you let out all the air or gas in it **2** If you deflate someone, you make them seem less important

deflect verb To deflect something means to turn it aside or make it change direction > **deflection** noun

deforestation noun GEOGRAPHY Deforestation is the cutting down of all the trees in an area

deformed adjective disfigured or abnormally shaped

defraud verb If someone defrauds you, they cheat you out of something that should be yours

defrost verb **1** If you defrost a freezer or refrigerator, you remove the ice from it **2** If you defrost frozen food, you let it thaw out

deft adjective Someone who is deft is quick and skilful in their movements
> **deftly** adverb

defunct adjective no longer existing or functioning

defuse verb **1** To defuse a dangerous or tense situation means to make it less dangerous or tense **2** To defuse a bomb means to remove its fuse or detonator so that it cannot explode

defy defies, defying, defied verb **1** If you defy a person or a law, you openly refuse to obey **2** (*formal*) If you defy someone to do something that you think is impossible, you

challenge them to do it

degenerate verb [de-**jen**-er-ate] **1** If something degenerates, it becomes worse: *The election campaign degenerated into farce* ▷ adjective [de-**jen**-e-rit] **2** having low standards of morality ▷ noun [de-**jen**-e-rit] **3** someone whose standards of morality are so low that people find their behaviour shocking or disgusting
> **degeneration** noun

degradation noun Degradation is a state of poverty and misery

degrade verb If something degrades people, it humiliates them and makes them feel that they are not respected > **degrading** adjective

degree noun **1** an amount of a feeling or quality: *a degree of pain* **2** a unit of measurement of temperature; often written as ° after a number: *20°C* **3** MATHS a unit of measurement of angles in mathematics, and of latitude and longitude: *The yacht was 20° off course* **4** a course of study at a university or college; also the qualification awarded after passing the course

dehydrate verb **1** If something is dehydrated, water is removed or lost from it **2** If someone is dehydrated, they are weak or ill because they have lost too much water from their body
> **dehydrated** adjective
> **dehydration** noun

deity deities noun a god or goddess

deja vu [**day**-ja **voo**] noun Deja vu is the feeling that you have already experienced in the past exactly the same sequence of events as is happening now

dejected adjective miserable and unhappy > **dejectedly** adverb
> **dejection** noun

delay *verb* **1** If you delay doing something, you put it off until a later time **2** If something delays you, it hinders you or slows you down ▷ *noun* **3** Delay is time during which something is delayed

delectable *adjective* very pleasing or delightful

delegate *noun* **1** a person appointed to vote or to make decisions on behalf of a group of people ▷ *verb* **2** If you delegate duties, you give them to someone who can then act on your behalf

delegation *noun* **1** a group of people chosen to represent a larger group of people **2** Delegation is the giving of duties, responsibilities, or power to someone who can then act on your behalf

delete *verb* COMPUTING To delete something means to cross it out or remove it: *He had deleted the computer file by mistake.* ▷ **deletion** *noun*

deliberate *adjective* [di-**lib**-er-it] **1** done on purpose or planned in advance: *It was a deliberate insult* **2** careful and not hurried in speech and action: *She was very deliberate in her movements* ▷ *verb* [di-**lib**-er-ayt] **3** If you deliberate about something, you think about it seriously and carefully ▷ **deliberately** *adverb*

deliberation *noun* Deliberation is careful consideration of a subject

delicacy delicacies *noun* **1** Delicacy is grace and attractiveness **2** Something said or done with delicacy is said or done tactfully so that nobody is offended **3** Delicacies are rare or expensive foods that are considered especially nice to eat

delicate *adjective* **1** fine, graceful, or subtle in character: *a delicate fragrance* **2** fragile and needing to be

handled carefully: *delicate antique lace* **3** precise or sensitive, and able to notice very small changes: *a delicate instrument* ▷ **delicately** *adverb*

delicatessen *noun* a shop selling unusual or imported foods

delicious *adjective* very pleasing, especially to taste ▷ **deliciously** *adverb*

delight *noun* **1** Delight is great pleasure or joy ▷ *verb* **2** If something delights you or if you are delighted by it, it gives you a lot of pleasure . ▷ **delighted** *adjective*

delightful *adjective* very pleasant and attractive ▷ **delightfully** *adverb*

delinquent *noun* a young person who commits minor crimes ▷ **delinquency** *noun*

delirious *adjective* **1** unable to speak or act in a rational way because of illness or fever **2** wildly excited and happy ▷ **deliriously** *adverb*

deliver *verb* **1** If you deliver something to someone, you take it to them and give them it **2** To deliver a lecture or speech means to give it

delivery deliveries *noun* **1** Delivery or a delivery is the bringing of letters or goods to a person or firm **2** Someone's delivery is the way in which they give a speech

delta *noun* a low, flat area at the mouth of a river where the river has split into several branches to enter the sea

delude *verb* To delude people means to deceive them into believing something that is not true

deluge *noun* **1** a sudden, heavy downpour of rain ▷ *verb* **2** To be deluged with things means to be overwhelmed by a great number of them

delusion *noun* a mistaken or

misleading belief or idea

delve verb If you delve into something, you seek out more information about it

demand verb 1 If you demand something, you ask for it forcefully and urgently 2 If a job or situation demands a particular quality, it needs it: *This situation demands hard work* ▷ noun 3 A forceful request for something 4 If there is a demand for something, a lot of people want to buy it or have it

demean verb If you demean yourself, you do something which makes people have less respect for you > **demeaning** adjective

demeanour noun Your demeanour is the way you behave and the impression that this creates

demented adjective Someone who is demented behaves in a wild or violent way

dementia [dee-**men**-sha] noun (Medicine) Dementia is a serious illness of the mind

demise [dee-**myz**] noun (formal) Someone's demise is their death

demo demos noun (informal) a demonstration

democracy democracies noun Democracy is a system of government in which the people choose their leaders by voting for them in elections

democrat noun a person who believes in democracy, personal freedom, and equality

democratic adjective having representatives elected by the people > **democratically** adverb

demolish verb To demolish a building means to pull it down or break it up > **demolition** noun

demon noun 1 an evil spirit or devil ▷ adjective 2 skilful, keen, and

energetic: *a demon squash player* > **demonic** adjective

demonstrate verb EXAM TERM To demonstrate a fact or theory means to prove or show it to be true 2 If you demonstrate something to somebody, you show and explain it by using or doing the thing itself: *She demonstrated how to apply the make-up* 3 If people demonstrate, they take part in a march or rally to show their opposition or support for something

demonstration noun 1 a talk or explanation to show how to do or use something 2 Demonstration is proof that something exists or is true 3 a public march or rally in support of or opposition to something > **demonstrator** noun

demote verb A person who is demoted is put in a lower rank or position, often as a punishment > **demotion** noun

demure adjective Someone who is demure is quiet, shy, and behaves very modestly > **demurely** adverb

den noun 1 the home of some wild animals such as lions or foxes 2 a secret place where people meet

denial noun 1 A denial of something is a statement that it is untrue: *He published a firm denial of the report* 2 The denial of a request or something to which you have a right is the refusal of it: *the denial of human rights*

denigrate verb (formal) To denigrate someone or something means to criticize them in order to damage their reputation

denim noun 1 Denim is strong cotton cloth, used for making clothes 2 (in plural) Denims are jeans made from denim

denomination noun 1 a particular

group which has slightly different religious beliefs from other groups within the same faith **2** a unit in a system of weights, values, or measures: *a high-denomination note*

denominator noun MATHS In maths, the denominator is the bottom part of a fraction

denote verb If one thing denotes another, it is a sign of it or it represents it: *Formerly, a tan denoted wealth*

denounce verb **1** If you denounce someone or something, you express very strong disapproval of them: *He publicly denounced government nuclear policy* **2** If you denounce someone, you give information against them: *He was denounced as a dangerous agitator*

dense adjective **1** thickly crowded or packed together: *the dense crowd* **2** difficult to see through: *dense black smoke* > **densely** adverb

density densities noun the degree to which something is filled or occupied: *a very high population density*

dent verb **1** To dent something means to damage it by hitting it and making a hollow in its surface ▷ noun **2** a hollow in the surface of something

dental adjective relating to the teeth

dentist noun a person who is qualified to treat people's teeth

dentistry noun Dentistry is the branch of medicine concerned with disorders of the teeth

dentures plural noun Dentures are false teeth

denunciation noun A denunciation of someone or something is severe public criticism of them

deny denies, denying, denied verb **1** If you deny something that has

been said, you state that it is untrue **2** If you deny that something is the case, you refuse to believe it: *He denied the existence of God* **3** If you deny someone something, you refuse to give it to them: *They were denied permission to attend*

deodorant noun a substance or spray used to hide the smell of perspiration

depart verb When you depart, you leave > **departure** noun

department noun one of the sections into which an organization is divided: *the marketing department* > **departmental** adjective

depend verb **1** If you depend on someone or something, you trust them and rely on them **2** If one thing depends on another, it is influenced by it: *Success depends on the quality of the workforce*

dependable adjective reliable and trustworthy

dependant noun PSHE someone who relies on another person for financial support

dependence noun Dependence is a constant need that someone has for something or someone in order to survive or operate properly: *He was flattered by her dependence on him*

dependency dependencies noun **1** PSHE Dependency is relying on someone or something to give you what you need: *drug dependency* **2** a country or area controlled by another country

dependent adjective reliant on someone or something

depict verb To depict someone or something means to represent them in painting or sculpture

deplete verb To deplete something means to reduce greatly the amount of it available > **depletion** noun

deplorable adjective shocking or regrettable: deplorable conditions

deplore verb If you deplore something, you condemn it because you feel it is wrong

deploy verb To deploy troops or resources means to organize or position them so that they can be used effectively > **deployment** noun

deport verb If a government deports someone, it sends them out of the country because they have committed a crime or because they do not have the right to be there > **deportation** noun

depose verb If someone is deposed, they are removed from a position of power

deposit verb 1 If you deposit something, you put it or leave it somewhere 2 If you deposit money or valuables, you put them somewhere for safekeeping 3 GEOGRAPHY If something is deposited on a surface, a layer of it is left there as a result of chemical or geological action ▷ noun 4 a sum of money given in part payment for goods or services

depot [**dep**-oh] noun a place where large supplies of materials or equipment may be stored

depraved adjective morally bad

depress verb 1 If something depresses you, it makes you feel sad and gloomy 2 If wages or prices are depressed, their value falls > **depressive** adjective

depressed adjective 1 unhappy and gloomy 2 A place that is depressed has little economic activity and therefore low incomes and high unemployment: depressed industrial areas

depression noun 1 a state of mind in which someone feels unhappy and has no energy or enthusiasm 2 a time of industrial and economic decline 3 GEOGRAPHY In meteorology, a depression is a mass of air that has low pressure and often causes rain 4 GEOGRAPHY A depression in the surface of something is a part which is lower than the rest

deprive verb If you deprive someone of something, you take it away or prevent them from having it > **deprived** adjective > **deprivation** noun

depth noun 1 The depth of something is the measurement or distance between its top and bottom, or between its front and back 2 The depth of something such as emotion is its intensity: the depth of her hostility

deputy deputies noun Someone's deputy is a person appointed to act in their place

deranged adjective mad, or behaving in a wild and uncontrolled way

derby derbies [**dar**-bee] noun A local derby is a sporting event between two teams from the same area

derelict adjective abandoned and falling into ruins

deride verb To deride someone or something means to mock or jeer at them with contempt

derision noun Derision is an attitude of contempt or scorn towards something or someone

derivative noun 1 something which has developed from an earlier source ▷ adjective 2 not original, but based on or copied from something else: The record was not deliberately derivative

derive verb 1 (formal) If you derive

something from someone or something, you get it from them: *He derived so much joy from music* **2** If something derives from something else, it develops from it

derogatory *adjective* critical and scornful: *He made derogatory remarks about them*

descend *verb* **1** To descend means to move downwards **2** If you descend on people or on a place, you arrive unexpectedly

descendant *noun* A person's descendants are the people in later generations who are related to them

descent *noun* **1** a movement or slope from a higher to a lower position or level **2** Your descent is your family's origins

describe *verb* To describe someone or something means to give an account of them or a picture of them in words

description *noun* an account or picture of something in words > **descriptive** *adjective*

desert [dez-ert] *noun* GEOGRAPHY a region of land with very little plant life, usually because of low rainfall

desert [dez-zert] *verb* To desert a person means to leave or abandon them: *His clients had deserted him* > **desertion** *noun*

deserter *noun* someone who leaves the armed forces without permission

deserve *verb* If you deserve something, you are entitled to it or earn it because of your qualities, achievements, or actions: *He deserved a rest*

deserving *adjective* worthy of being helped, rewarded, or praised: *a deserving charity*

design D&T *verb* **1** To design

something means to plan it, especially by preparing a detailed sketch or drawings from which it can be built or made ▷ *noun* **2** a drawing or plan from which something can be built or made **3** The design of something is its shape and style > **designer** *noun*

designate [dez-ig-nate] *verb* **1** To designate someone or something means to formally label or name them: *The room was designated a no smoking area* **2** If you designate someone to do something, you appoint them to do it: *He designated his son as his successor*

designation *noun* a name or title

designing *adjective* crafty and cunning

desirable *adjective* worth having or doing: *a desirable job* > **desirability** *noun*

desire *verb* **1** If you desire something, you want it very much ▷ *noun* **2** a strong feeling of wanting something

desist *verb* (*formal*) To desist from doing something means to stop doing it

desk *noun* **1** a piece of furniture designed for working at or writing on **2** a counter or table in a public building behind which a receptionist sits

desktop *adjective* of a convenient size to be used on a desk or table: *a desktop computer*

desolate *adjective* **1** deserted and bleak: *a desolate mountainous region* **2** lonely, very sad, and without hope: *He was desolate without her* > **desolation** *noun*

despair *noun* **1** Despair is a total loss of hope **2** If you despair, you lose hope: *He despaired of finishing it* > **despairing** *adjective*

despatch another spelling of **dispatch**

desperate *adjective* 1 If you are desperate, you are so worried or frightened that you will try anything to improve your situation: *a desperate attempt to save their marriage* 2 A desperate person is violent and dangerous 3 A desperate situation is extremely dangerous or serious
> **desperately** *adverb*
> **desperation** *noun*

despicable *adjective* deserving contempt

despise *verb* If you despise someone or something, you dislike them very much

despite *preposition* in spite of: *He fell asleep despite all the coffee he'd drunk*

despondent *adjective* dejected and unhappy > **despondency** *noun*

dessert [diz-**ert**] *noun* a sweet food served after the main course of a meal

destination *noun* a place to which someone or something is going or is being sent

destined *adjective* meant or intended to happen: *I was destined for fame and fortune*

destiny *destinies noun* 1 Your destiny is all the things that happen to you in your life, especially when they are considered to be outside human control 2 Destiny is the force which some people believe controls everyone's life

destitute *adjective* without money or possessions, and therefore in great need > **destitution** *noun*

destroy *verb* 1 To destroy something means to damage it so much that it is completely ruined 2 To destroy something means to put an end to it: *The holiday destroyed their friendship*

destruction *noun* Destruction is the act of destroying something or the state of being destroyed

destructive *adjective* causing or able to cause harm, damage, or injury > **destructiveness** *noun*

desultory [dez-ul-tree] *adjective* passing from one thing to another in a fitful or random way: *A desultory, embarrassed chatter began again* > **desultorily** *adverb*

detach *verb* To detach something means to remove it: *The hood can be detached* > **detachable** *adjective*

detached *adjective* 1 separate or standing apart: *a detached house* 2 having no real interest or emotional involvement in something: *He observed me with a detached curiosity*

detachment *noun* 1 Detachment is the feeling of not being personally involved with something: *A stranger can view your problems with detachment* 2 a small group of soldiers sent to do a special job

detail *noun* 1 an individual fact or feature of something: *We discussed every detail of the performance* 2 Detail is all the small features that make up the whole of something: *Look at the detail* > **detailed** *adjective*

detain *verb* 1 To detain someone means to force them to stay: *She was being detained for interrogation* 2 If you detain someone, you delay them: *I mustn't detain you*

detect *verb* 1 If you detect something, you notice it: *I detected a glimmer of interest in his eyes* 2 To detect something means to find it: *Cancer can be detected by X-rays* > **detectable** *adjective*

detection *noun* 1 Detection is the act of noticing, discovering, or sensing something 2 Detection is also the work of investigating crime

detective noun a person, usually a police officer, whose job is to investigate crimes

detector noun an instrument which is used to detect the presence of something: *a metal detector*

detention noun The detention of someone is their arrest or imprisonment

deter deters, deterring, deterred verb To deter someone means to discourage or prevent them from doing something by creating a feeling of fear or doubt: *99 per cent of burglars are deterred by the sight of an alarm box*

detergent noun a chemical substance used for washing or cleaning things

deteriorate verb If something deteriorates, it gets worse: *My father's health has deteriorated lately* > **deterioration** noun

determination noun Determination is great firmness, after you have made up your mind to do something: *They shared a determination to win the war*

determine verb 1 If something determines a situation or result, it causes it or controls it: *The track surface determines his tactics in a race* 2 To determine something means to decide or settle it firmly: *The date has still to be determined* 3 To determine something means to find out or calculate the facts about it: *He bit the coin to determine whether it was genuine*

determined adjective firmly decided: *She was determined not to repeat her error* > **determinedly** adverb

deterrent noun something that prevents you from doing something

by making you afraid of what will happen if you do it: *Capital punishment was no deterrent to domestic murders* > **deterrence** noun

detest verb If you detest someone or something, you strongly dislike them

detonate verb To detonate a bomb or mine means to cause it to explode > **detonator** noun

detour noun an alternative, less direct route

detract verb To detract from something means to make it seem less good or valuable

detriment noun Detriment is disadvantage or harm: *a detriment to their health* > **detrimental** adjective

deuce [joos] noun In tennis, deuce is the score of forty all

devalue verb To devalue something means to lower its status, importance, or worth > **devaluation** noun

devastate verb To devastate an area or place means to damage it severely or destroy it > **devastation** noun

devastated adjective very shocked or upset: *The family are devastated by the news*

develop verb 1 When something develops or is developed, it grows or becomes more advanced: *The sneezing developed into a full blown cold* 2 To develop an area of land means to build on it 3 To develop an illness or a fault means to become affected by it

developer noun a person or company that builds on land

development noun 1 Development is gradual growth or progress 2 The development of land or water is the process of making it more useful or profitable by the expansion of industry or housing: *the development of the old docks* **3** a new stage in a series of events: *developments in technology* > **developmental** *adjective*

deviant *adjective* **1** Deviant behaviour is unacceptable or different from what people consider as normal ▷ *noun* **2** someone whose behaviour or beliefs are different from what people consider to be acceptable > **deviance** *noun*

deviate *verb* To deviate means to differ or depart from what is usual or acceptable > **deviation** *noun*

device *noun* **1** a machine or tool that is used for a particular purpose: *a device to warn you when the batteries need changing* **2** a plan or scheme: *a device to pressurize him into selling*

devil *noun* **1** In Christianity and Judaism, the Devil is the spirit of evil and enemy of God **2** an evil spirit

devious *adjective* insincere and dishonest > **deviousness** *noun*

devise *verb* To devise something means to work it out: *Besides diets, he devised punishing exercise routines*

devoid *adjective* lacking in a particular thing or quality: *His glance was devoid of expression*

devolution *noun* Devolution is the transfer of power from a central government or organization to local government departments or smaller organizations

devote *verb* If you devote yourself to something, you give all your time, energy, or money to it: *She has devoted herself to women's causes*

devoted *adjective* very loving and loyal

devotee *noun* a fanatical or enthusiastic follower of something

devotion *noun* Devotion to someone or something is great love or affection for them > **devotional** *adjective*

devour *verb* If you devour something, you eat it hungrily or greedily

devout *adjective* deeply and sincerely religious: *a devout Buddhist* > **devoutly** *adverb*

dew *noun* Dew is drops of moisture that form on the ground and other cool surfaces at night

dexterity *noun* Dexterity is skill or agility in using your hands or mind: *He had learned to use the crutches with dexterity* > **dexterous** *adjective*

diabetes [dy-a-**bee**-tiss] *noun* Diabetes is a disease in which someone has too much sugar in their blood, because they do not produce enough insulin to absorb it > **diabetic** *noun, adjective*

diabolical *adjective* **1** (*informal*) dreadful and very annoying: *The pain was diabolical* **2** extremely wicked and cruel

diagnose *verb* To diagnose an illness or problem means to identify exactly what is wrong

diagnosis *noun* the identification of what is wrong with someone who is ill > **diagnostic** *adjective*

diagonal *adjective* in a slanting direction > **diagonally** *adverb*

diagram *noun* a drawing that shows or explains something

dial dials, dialling, dialled *noun* **1** the face of a clock or meter, with divisions marked on it so that a time or measurement can be recorded and read **2** a part of a device, such as a radio, used to control or tune it ▷ *verb* **3** To dial a telephone number means to press the number keys to select the required number

dialect *noun* a form of a language spoken in a particular geographical area

d

dialogue noun **1** ENGLISH In a novel, play, or film, dialogue is conversation **2** Dialogue is communication or discussion between people or groups of people: *The union sought dialogue with the council*

dialysis noun Dialysis is a treatment used for some kidney diseases, in which blood is filtered by a special machine to remove waste products

diameter noun MATHS The diameter of a circle is the length of a straight line drawn across it through its centre

diamond noun **1** A diamond is a precious stone made of pure carbon. Diamonds are the hardest known substance in the world and are used for cutting substances and for making jewellery **2** MATHS A diamond is also a shape with four straight sides of equal length forming two opposite angles less than 90° and two opposite angles greater than 90° **3** Diamonds is one of the four suits in a pack of playing cards. It is marked by a red diamond-shaped symbol **4** The diamond is the area between the four bases in the game of baseball ▷ *adjective* **5** A diamond anniversary is the 60th anniversary of an event: *a diamond wedding*

diaphragm [dy-a-fram] noun SCIENCE In mammals, the diaphragm is the muscular wall that separates the lungs from the stomach

diarrhoea [dye-a-**ree**-a] noun Diarrhoea is a condition in which the faeces are more liquid and frequent than usual

diary diaries noun a book which has a separate space or page for each day of the year on which to keep a

record of appointments > **diarist** noun

dice noun **1** a small cube which has each side marked with dots representing the numbers one to six ▷ *verb* **2** To dice food means to cut it into small cubes > **diced** *adjective*

dictate verb **1** If you dictate something, you say or read it aloud for someone else to write down **2** To dictate something means to command or state what must happen: *What we wear is largely dictated by our daily routine* > **dictation** noun

dictator noun HISTORY A dictator is a ruler who has complete power in a country, especially one who has taken power by force > **dictatorial** *adjective*

diction noun Someone's diction is the clarity with which they speak or sing

dictionary dictionaries noun LIBRARY a book in which words are listed alphabetically and explained, or equivalent words are given in another language

didgeridoo noun an Australian musical wind instrument made in the shape of a long wooden tube

die dies, dying, died verb **1** When people, animals, or plants die, they stop living **2** When something dies, dies away, or dies down, it gradually fades away: *The footsteps died away* ▷ *noun* **3** a dice > **die out** verb When something dies out, it ceases to exist

diesel [**dee**-zel] noun **1** a heavy fuel used in trains, buses, lorries, and some cars **2** a vehicle with a diesel engine

diet noun D G T Someone's diet is the usual food that they eat: *a vegetarian diet* **2** a special restricted selection of foods that someone eats to improve their health or regulate their weight > **dietary** adjective > **dieter** noun

dietician or **dietitian** noun a person trained to advise people about healthy eating

differ verb **1** If two or more things differ, they are unlike each other **2** If people differ, they have opposing views or disagree about something

difference noun **1** The difference between things is the way in which they are unlike each other **2** The difference between two numbers is the amount by which one is less than another **3** A difference in someone or something is a significant change in them: *You wouldn't believe the difference in her*

different adjective **1** unlike something else **2** unusual and out of the ordinary **3** distinct and separate, although of the same kind: *The lunch supports a different charity each year* > **differently** adverb

differentiate verb **1** To differentiate between things means to recognize or show how one is unlike the other **2** Something that differentiates one thing from another makes it distinct and unlike the other > **differentiation** noun

difficult adjective **1** not easy to do, understand, or solve: *a very difficult decision to make* **2** hard to deal with, especially because of being unreasonable or unpredictable: *a difficult child*

difficulty noun difficulties **1** a problem: *The central difficulty is his drinking* **2** Difficulty is the fact or quality of being difficult

diffident adjective timid and lacking in self-confidence > **diffidently** adverb > **diffidence** noun

diffuse verb [dif-**yooz**] SCIENCE **1** If something diffuses, it spreads out or scatters in all directions **2** If particles of a gas, liquid, or solid diffuse, they mix together, especially by moving from an area where they are very concentrated to one where there are fewer of them ▷ adjective [dif-**yoos**] **3** spread out over a wide area > **diffusion** noun

dig digs, digging, dug verb **1** If you dig, you break up soil or sand, especially with a spade or garden fork **2** To dig something into an object means to push, thrust, or poke it in ▷ noun **3** a prod or jab, especially in the ribs **4** (informal) A dig at someone is a spiteful or unpleasant remark intended to hurt or embarrass them **5** (in plural) Digs are lodgings in someone else's house

digest verb SCIENCE **1** To digest food means to break it down in the gut so that it can be easily absorbed and used by the body **2** If you digest information or a fact, you understand it and take it in > **digestible** adjective

digestion noun SCIENCE **1** Digestion is the process of digesting food **2** Your digestion is your ability to digest food: *Camomile tea aids poor digestion* > **digestive** adjective

digger noun In Australian English, digger is a friendly name to call a man

digit [**dij**-it] noun **1** (formal) Your digits are your fingers or toes **2** MATHS a written symbol for any of the numbers from 0 to 9

digital adjective displaying information, especially time, by numbers, rather than by a pointer moving round a dial: *a digital watch* > **digitally** adverb

dignified *adjective* full of dignity

dignitary dignitaries *noun* a person who holds a high official position

dignity *noun* Dignity is behaviour which is serious, calm, and controlled: *She conducted herself with dignity*

dilapidated *adjective* falling to pieces and generally in a bad condition: *a dilapidated castle*

dilemma *noun* a situation in which a choice has to be made between alternatives that are equally difficult or unpleasant

diligent *adjective* hard-working, and showing care and perseverance
> **diligently** *adverb* > **diligence** *noun*

dill *noun* Dill is a herb with yellow flowers and a strong sweet smell

dilute *verb* To dilute a liquid means to add water or another liquid to it to make it less concentrated
> **dilution** *noun*

dim dimmer, dimmest; dims, dimming, dimmed *adjective* **1** badly lit and lacking in brightness **2** very vague and unclear in your mind: *dim recollections* **3** (*informal*) stupid or mentally dull: *He is rather dim* ▷ *verb* **4** If lights dim or are dimmed, they become less bright > **dimly** *adverb* > **dimness** *noun*

dimension *noun* **1** A dimension of a situation is an aspect or factor that influences the way you understand it: *This process had a domestic and a foreign dimension* **2** You can talk about the size or extent of something as its dimensions: *It was an explosion of major dimensions* **3** [ART] The dimensions of something are also its measurements, for example its length, breadth, height, or diameter

diminish *verb* If something

diminishes or if you diminish it, it becomes reduced in size or importance

diminutive *adjective* very small

din *noun* a loud and unpleasant noise

dinar [**dee**-nar] *noun* a unit of currency in several countries in southern Europe, North Africa and the Middle East

dine *verb* (*formal*) To dine means to eat dinner in the evening: *We dined together in the hotel*

diner *noun* **1** a person who is having dinner in a restaurant **2** a small restaurant or railway restaurant car

dinghy dinghies [**ding**-ee] *noun* a small boat which is rowed, sailed, or powered by outboard motor

dingo dingoes *noun* an Australian wild dog

dingy dingier, dingiest [**din**-jee] *adjective* dusty, dark, and rather depressing: *a dingy bedsit*

dinkum *adjective* (*informal*) In Australian and New Zealand English, dinkum means genuine or right: *a fair dinkum offer*

dinner *noun* **1** the main meal of the day, eaten either in the evening or at lunchtime **2** a formal social occasion in the evening, at which a meal is served

dinosaur [**dy**-no-sor] *noun* a large reptile which lived in prehistoric times

dint *phrase* By dint of means by means of: *He succeeds by dint of hard work*

diocese *noun* a district controlled by a bishop > **diocesan** *adjective*

dip dips, dipping, dipped *verb* **1** If you dip something into a liquid, you lower it or plunge it quickly into the liquid **2** If something dips, it slopes downwards or goes below a certain

level: *The sun dipped below the horizon*
3 To dip also means to make a quick, slight downward movement: *She dipped her fingers into the cool water*
▷ *noun* **4** a rich creamy mixture which you scoop up with biscuits or raw vegetables and eat: *an avocado dip* **5** (*informal*) a swim

diploma *noun* a certificate awarded to a student who has successfully completed a course of study

diplomacy *noun* **1** Diplomacy is the managing of relationships between countries **2** Diplomacy is also skill in dealing with people without offending or upsetting them
> **diplomatic** *adjective*
> **diplomatically** *adverb*

diplomat *noun* an official who negotiates and deals with another country on behalf of his or her own country

dire *adjective* disastrous, urgent, or terrible: *people in dire need*

direct *adjective* **1** moving or aimed in a straight line or by the shortest route: *the direct route* **2** straightforward, and without delay or evasion: *his direct manner* **3** without anyone or anything intervening: *Schools can take direct control of their own funding* **4** exact: *the direct opposite* ▷ *verb* **5** To direct something means to guide and control it **6** To direct people or things means to send them, tell them, or show them the way **7** To direct a film, a play, or a television programme means to organize the way it is made and performed

direction *noun* **1** the general line that someone or something is moving or pointing in **2** Direction is the controlling and guiding of something: *He was chopping vegetables under the chef's direction* **3** (*in plural*) Directions are instructions that tell you how to do something or how to get somewhere

directive *noun* an instruction that must be obeyed: *a directive banning cigarette advertising*

directly *adverb* in a straight line or immediately: *He looked directly at Rose*

director *noun* **1** a member of the board of a company or institution **2** DRAMA the person responsible for the making and performance of a programme, play, or film
> **directorial** *adjective*

directorate *noun* a board of directors of a company or organization

directory directories *noun* **1** a book which gives lists of facts, such as names and addresses, and is usually arranged in alphabetical order **2** COMPUTING another name for **folder**

dirt *noun* **1** Dirt is any unclean substance, such as dust, mud, or stains **2** Dirt is also earth or soil

dirty dirtier, dirtiest *adjective* **1** marked or covered with dirt **2** unfair, unscrupulous, or dishonest: *She accused her opponents of running a dirty campaign*

disability disabilities *noun* a physical or mental condition or illness that restricts someone's way of life

disable *verb* If something disables someone, it injures or harms them physically or mentally and severely affects their life > **disablement** *noun*

disabled *adjective* lacking one or more physical powers, such as the ability to walk or to coordinate one's movements

disadvantage noun an unfavourable or harmful circumstance > **disadvantaged** adjective

disaffected adjective If someone is disaffected with an idea or organization, they no longer believe in it or support it: disaffected voters

disagree disagrees, disagreeing, disagreed verb **1** If you disagree with someone, you have a different view or opinion from theirs **2** If you disagree with an action or proposal, you disapprove of it and believe it is wrong: He detested her and disagreed with her policies **3** If food or drink disagrees with you, it makes you feel unwell

disagreeable adjective unpleasant or unhelpful and unfriendly: a disagreeable odour

disagreement noun **1** a dispute about something **2** an objection to something

disappear verb **1** If something or someone disappears, they go out of sight or become lost **2** To disappear also means to stop existing or happening: The pain has disappeared > **disappearance** noun

disappoint verb If someone or something disappoints you, it fails to live up to what you expected of it

disappointed adjective sad because something has not happened

disappointment noun **1** a feeling of being disappointed **2** something that disappoints you

disapproval noun the belief that something is wrong or inappropriate

disapprove verb To disapprove of something or someone means to believe they are wrong or bad: Everyone disapproved of their marrying so young > **disapproving** adjective

disarm verb **1** To disarm means to get rid of weapons **2** If someone disarms you, they overcome your anger or doubt by charming or soothing you: Mahoney was almost disarmed by the frankness > **disarming** adjective

disarmament noun Disarmament is the reducing or getting rid of military forces and weapons

disarray noun Disarray is a state of disorder and confusion: Our army was in disarray and practically weaponless

disaster noun **1** an event or accident that causes great distress or destruction **2** a complete failure > **disastrous** adjective > **disastrously** adverb

disband verb When a group of people disbands, it officially ceases to exist

disc or **disk** noun **1** a flat round object: a tax disc; a compact disc **2** one of the thin circular pieces of cartilage which separate the bones in your spine

discard verb To discard something means to get rid of it, because you no longer need it or find it useful

discern [dis-**ern**] verb (formal) To discern something means to notice or understand it clearly: The film had no plot that I could discern

discernible adjective able to be seen or recognized: no discernible talent

discerning adjective having good taste and judgment > **discernment** noun

discharge verb **1** If something discharges or is discharged, it is given or sent out: Oil discharged into the world's oceans **2** To discharge someone from hospital means to allow them to leave **3** If someone is discharged from a job, they are dismissed from it ▷ noun **4** a substance that is released from the inside of something: *a thick nasal discharge* **5** a dismissal or release from a job or an institution

disciple [dis-sigh-pl] *noun* RE a follower of someone or something, especially one of the twelve men who were followers and helpers of Christ

discipline *noun* **1** PSHE Discipline is making people obey rules and punishing them when they break them **2** PSHE Discipline is the ability to behave and work in a controlled way ▷ *verb* PSHE **3** If you discipline yourself, you train yourself to behave and work in an ordered way **4** To discipline someone means to punish them
> **disciplinary** *adjective*
> **disciplined** *adjective*

disc jockey *noun* someone who introduces and plays music on the radio or at a night club

disclose *verb* To disclose something means to make it known or allow it to be seen > **disclosure** *noun*

disco *discos noun* a party or a club where people go to dance to pop music

discomfort *noun* **1** Discomfort is distress or slight pain **2** Discomfort is also a feeling of worry or embarrassment **3** Discomforts are things that make you uncomfortable

disconcert *verb* If something disconcerts you, it makes you feel uneasy or embarrassed
> **disconcerting** *adjective*

disconnect *verb* **1** To disconnect something means to detach it from something else **2** If someone disconnects your fuel supply or telephone, they cut you off

discontent *noun* Discontent is a feeling of dissatisfaction with conditions or with life in general: *He was aware of the discontent this policy had caused* > **discontented** *adjective*

discontinue *discontinues, discontinuing, discontinued verb* To discontinue something means to stop doing it

discord *noun* Discord is unpleasantness or quarrelling between people

discount *noun* **1** a reduction in the price of something ▷ *verb* **2** If you discount something, you reject it or ignore it: *I haven't discounted her connection with the kidnapping case*

discourage *verb* To discourage someone means to take away their enthusiasm to do something
> **discouraging** *adjective*
> **discouragement** *noun*

discourse *(formal) noun* **1** a formal talk or piece of writing intended to teach or explain something **2** Discourse is serious conversation between people on a particular subject

discover *verb* When you discover something, you find it or find out about it > **discovery** *noun*
> **discoverer** *noun*

discredit *verb* **1** To discredit someone means to damage their reputation **2** To discredit an idea means to cause it to be doubted or not believed

discreet *adjective* If you are discreet, you avoid causing embarrassment when dealing with secret or private matters > **discreetly** *adverb*

discrepancy *discrepancies noun* a difference between two things which ought to be the same: *discrepancies in his police interviews*

discrete *adjective* **1** *(formal)* separate

and distinct: *two discrete sets of nerves* **2** MATHS A discrete line or set of data is made up of a limited number of separate points or items

discretion noun **1** Discretion is the quality of behaving with care and tact so as to avoid embarrassment or distress to other people: *You can count on my discretion* **2** Discretion is also freedom and authority to make decisions and take action according to your own judgment: *Class teachers have very limited discretion in decision-making* > **discretionary** adjective

discriminate verb **1** To discriminate between things means to recognize and understand the differences between them **2** To discriminate against a person or group means to treat them unfairly, usually because of their gender, race, or colour **3** To discriminate in favour of a person or group means to treat them more favourably than others > **discrimination** noun > **discriminatory** adjective

discus discuses noun a disc-shaped object with a heavy middle, thrown by athletes

discuss verb **1** When people discuss something, they talk about it in detail **2** EXAM TERM To discuss a question is to look at the points or arguments of both sides and try to reach your own opinion

discussion noun PSHE a conversation or piece of writing in which a subject is considered in detail

disdain noun Disdain is a feeling of superiority over or contempt for someone or something: *The candidates shared an equal disdain for the press* > **disdainful** adjective

disease noun HISTORY SCIENCE an

unhealthy condition in people, animals, or plants > **diseased** adjective

disembark verb To disembark means to land or unload from a ship, aircraft, or bus

disembodied adjective **1** separate from or existing without a body: *a disembodied skull* **2** seeming not to be attached to or come from anyone: *disembodied voices*

disenchanted adjective disappointed with something, and no longer believing that it is good or worthwhile: *She is very disenchanted with the marriage* > **disenchantment** noun

disfigure verb To disfigure something means to spoil its appearance: *Graffiti or posters disfigured every wall*

disgrace noun **1** Disgrace is a state in which people disapprove of someone **2** If something is a disgrace, it is unacceptable: *The overcrowded prisons were a disgrace* **3** If someone is a disgrace to a group of people, their behaviour makes the group feel ashamed: *You're a disgrace to the school* ▷ verb **4** If you disgrace yourself or disgrace someone else, you cause yourself or them to be strongly disapproved of by other people

disgraceful adjective If something is disgraceful, people disapprove of it strongly and think that those who are responsible for it should be ashamed > **disgracefully** adverb

disgruntled adjective discontented or in a bad mood

disguise verb **1** To disguise something means to change its appearance so that people do not recognize it **2** To disguise a feeling means to hide it: *I tried to disguise my* _relief_ ▷ noun **3** something you wear or something you do to alter your appearance so that you cannot be recognized by other people

disgust noun **1** Disgust is a strong feeling of dislike or disapproval ▷ verb **2** To disgust someone means to make them feel a strong sense of dislike or disapproval > **disgusted** _adjective_

disgusting _adjective_ very unpleasant and offensive

dish noun **1** a shallow container for cooking or serving food **2** food of a particular kind or food cooked in a particular way: _two fish dishes to choose from_

dishearten verb If you dishearten someone, you take away their hope and confidence in something

dishevelled [dish-**ev**-ld] _adjective_ If someone looks dishevelled, their clothes or hair look untidy

dishonest _adjective_ not truthful or able to be trusted > **dishonestly** _adverb_

dishonesty noun Dishonesty is behaviour which is meant to deceive people, either by not telling the truth or by cheating

disillusion verb If something or someone disillusions you, you discover that you were mistaken about something you valued, and so you feel disappointed with it > **disillusionment** noun

disillusioned _adjective_ If you are disillusioned with something, you are disappointed because it is not as good as you had expected

disinfectant noun a chemical substance that kills germs

disintegrate verb **1** If something disintegrates, it becomes weakened and is not effective: _My confidence disintegrated_ **2** If an object

disintegrates, it breaks into many pieces and so is destroyed > **disintegration** noun

disinterest noun **1** Disinterest is a lack of interest **2** Disinterest is also a lack of personal involvement in a situation

disinterested _adjective_ If someone is disinterested, they are not going to gain or lose from the situation they are involved in, and so can act in a way that is fair to both sides: _a disinterested judge_

disjointed _adjective_ If thought or speech is disjointed, it jumps from subject to subject and so is difficult to follow

disk noun **1** [COMPUTING] In a computer, the disk is the part where information is stored: _The program takes up 2.5 megabytes of disk space_ **2** another spelling of **disc**

dislike verb **1** If you dislike something or someone, you think they are unpleasant and do not like them ▷ noun **2** Dislike is a feeling that you have when you do not like someone or something

dislocate verb To dislocate your bone or joint means to put it out of place

dislodge verb To dislodge something means to move it or force it out of place

dismal [**diz**-mal] _adjective_ rather gloomy and depressing: _dismal weather_ > **dismally** _adverb_

dismantle verb To dismantle something means to take it apart

dismay noun **1** Dismay is a feeling of fear and worry ▷ verb **2** If someone or something dismays you, it fills you with alarm and worry

dismember verb (formal) To dismember a person or animal means to cut or tear their body into pieces

dismiss verb **1** If you dismiss something, you decide to ignore it because it is not important enough for you to think about **2** To dismiss an employee means to ask that person to leave their job **3** If someone in authority dismisses you, they tell you to leave
> **dismissal** noun

dismissive adjective If you are dismissive of something or someone, you show that you think they are of little importance or value: a dismissive gesture

disobey verb To disobey a person or an order means to deliberately refuse to do what you are told

disorder noun **1** Disorder is a state of untidiness **2** Disorder is also a lack of organization: The men fled in disorder **3** a disease: a stomach disorder

disorganized or **disorganised** adjective If something is disorganized, it is confused and badly prepared or badly arranged
> **disorganization** noun

disown verb To disown someone or something means to refuse to admit any connection with them

disparaging adjective critical and scornful: disparaging remarks

disparate adjective (formal) Things that are disparate are utterly different from one another
> **disparity** noun

dispatch or **despatch** verb **1** To dispatch someone or something to a particular place means to send them there for a special reason: The president dispatched him on a fact-finding visit ▷ noun **2** an official written message, often sent to an army or government headquarters

dispel dispels, dispelling, dispelled verb To dispel fears or beliefs means

to drive them away or to destroy them: The myths are being dispelled

dispensary dispensaries noun a place where medicines are prepared and given out

dispense verb **1** (formal) To dispense something means to give it out: They dispense advice **2** To dispense medicines means to prepare them and give them out **3** To dispense with something means to do without it or to do away with it: We'll dispense with formalities

dispenser noun a machine or container from which you can get things: a cash dispenser

disperse verb **1** When something disperses, it scatters over a wide area **2** When people disperse or when someone disperses them, they move apart and go in different directions > **dispersion** noun

dispirited adjective depressed and having no enthusiasm for anything

dispiriting adjective Something dispiriting makes you depressed: a dispiriting defeat

displace verb **1** If one thing displaces another, it forces the thing out of its usual place and occupies that place itself **2** If people are displaced, they are forced to leave their home or country

displacement noun **1** Displacement is the removal of something from its usual or correct place or position **2** [SCIENCE] In physics, displacement is the weight or volume of liquid displaced by an object submerged or floating in it

display verb **1** If you display something, you show it or make it visible to people **2** If you display something such as an emotion, you behave in a way that shows you feel it ▷ noun **3** [ART] an arrangement of things designed to attract people's attention

displease verb If someone or something displeases you, they make you annoyed, dissatisfied, or offended > **displeasure** noun

disposable adjective designed to be thrown away after use: disposable nappies

disposal noun Disposal is the act of getting rid of something that is no longer wanted or needed

dispose verb 1 To dispose of something means to get rid of it 2 If you are not disposed to do something, you are not willing to do it

disprove verb If someone disproves an idea, belief, or theory, they show that it is not true

dispute noun 1 an argument ▷ verb 2 To dispute a fact or theory means to question the truth of it

disqualify disqualifies, disqualifying, disqualified verb If someone is disqualified from a competition or activity, they are officially stopped from taking part in it: He was disqualified from driving for 18 months > **disqualification** noun

disquiet noun Disquiet is worry or anxiety > **disquieting** adjective

disregard verb 1 To disregard something means to pay little or no attention to it ▷ noun 2 Disregard is a lack of attention or respect for something: He exhibited a flagrant disregard of the law

disrepair phrase If something is in **disrepair** or **in a state of disrepair**, it is broken or in poor condition

disrespect noun Disrespect is contempt or lack of respect: his disrespect for authority > **disrespectful** adjective

disrupt verb To disrupt something such as an event or system means to break it up or throw it into confusion: Strikes disrupted air traffic in Italy > **disruption** noun > **disruptive** adjective

dissatisfied adjective not pleased or not contented > **dissatisfaction** noun

dissect verb To dissect a plant or a dead body means to cut it up so that it can be scientifically examined > **dissection** noun

dissent noun 1 Dissent is strong difference of opinion: political dissent ▷ verb 2 When people dissent, they express a difference of opinion about something > **dissenting** adjective

dissertation noun a long essay, especially for a university degree

disservice noun To do someone a disservice means to do something that harms them

dissident noun someone who disagrees with and criticizes the government of their country

dissimilar adjective If things are dissimilar, they are unlike each other

dissipate verb 1 (formal) When something dissipates or is dissipated, it completely disappears: The cloud seemed to dissipate there 2 If someone dissipates time, money, or effort, they waste it

dissipated adjective Someone who is dissipated shows signs of indulging too much in things such as food and drink

dissolve verb 1 [SCIENCE] If you dissolve something or if it dissolves in a liquid, it becomes mixed with and absorbed in the liquid 2 To dissolve an organization or institution means to officially end it

dissuade [dis-**wade**] verb To dissuade someone from doing something or from believing something means to persuade them not to do it or not to believe it

distance noun 1 The distance between two points is how far it is between them 2 Distance is the fact of being far away in space or time ▷ verb 3 If you distance yourself from someone or something or are distanced from them, you become less involved with them

distant adjective 1 far away in space or time 2 A distant relative is one who is not closely related to you 3 Someone who is distant is cold and unfriendly ▷ **distantly** adverb

distaste noun Distaste is a dislike of something which you find offensive

distasteful adjective If you find something distasteful, you think it is unpleasant or offensive

distil distils, distilling, distilled verb SCIENCE When a liquid is distilled, it is heated until it evaporates and then cooled to enable purified liquid to be collected ▷ **distillation** noun

distillery distilleries noun a place where whisky or other strong alcoholic drink is made, using a process of distillation

distinct adjective 1 If one thing is distinct from another, it is recognizably different from it: A word may have two quite distinct meanings 2 If something is distinct, you can hear, smell, or see it clearly and plainly: There was a distinct buzzing noise 3 If something such as a fact, idea, or intention is distinct, it is clear and definite: She had a distinct feeling that someone was watching them ▷ **distinctly** adverb

distinction noun 1 a difference

between two things: a distinction between the body and the soul 2 Distinction is a quality of excellence and superiority: a man of distinction 3 a special honour or claim: It had the distinction of being the largest square in Europe

distinctive adjective Something that is distinctive has a special quality which makes it recognizable: a distinctive voice ▷ **distinctively** adverb

distinguish verb 1 To distinguish between things means to recognize the difference between them: I've learned to distinguish business and friendship 2 To distinguish something means to make it out by seeing, hearing, or tasting it: I heard shouting but was unable to distinguish the words 3 If you distinguish yourself, you do something that makes people think highly of you ▷ **distinguishable** adjective ▷ **distinguishing** adjective

distinguished adjective 1 dignified in appearance or behaviour 2 having a very high reputation: He was a distinguished professor

distort verb 1 If you distort a statement or an argument, you represent it in an untrue or misleading way 2 If something is distorted, it is changed so that it seems strange or unclear: His voice was distorted 3 If an object is distorted, it is twisted or pulled out of shape ▷ **distorted** adjective ▷ **distortion** noun

distract verb If something distracts you, your attention is taken away from what you are doing ▷ **distracted** adjective ▷ **distractedly** adverb ▷ **distracting** adjective

distraction noun 1 something that

takes people's attention away from something **2** an activity that is intended to amuse or relax someone

distraught adjective so upset and worried that you cannot think clearly: *He was distraught over the death of his mother*

distress noun **1** Distress is great suffering caused by pain or sorrow **2** Distress is also the state of needing help because of difficulties or danger ▷ verb **3** To distress someone means to make them feel alarmed or unhappy: *Her death had profoundly distressed me*

distressing adjective very worrying or upsetting

distribute verb **1** To distribute something such as leaflets means to hand them out or deliver them: *They publish and distribute brochures* **2** If things are distributed, they are spread throughout an area or space: *Distribute the cheese evenly on top of the quiche* **3** To distribute something means to divide it and share it out among a number of people

distribution noun **1** Distribution is the delivering of something to various people or organizations: *the distribution of vicious leaflets* **2** Distribution is the sharing out of something to various people: *distribution of power*

distributor noun a company that supplies goods to other businesses who then sell them to the public

district noun an area of a town or country: *a residential district*

distrust verb **1** If you distrust someone, you are suspicious of them because you are not sure whether they are honest ▷ noun **2** Distrust is suspicion > **distrustful** adjective

disturb verb **1** If you disturb someone, you break their peace or privacy **2** If something disturbs you, it makes you feel upset or worried **3** If something is disturbed, it is moved out of position or meddled with > **disturbing** adjective

disturbance noun **1** Disturbance is the state of being disturbed **2** a violent or unruly incident in public

disuse noun Something that has fallen into disuse is neglected or no longer used > **disused** adjective

ditch noun a channel at the side of a road or field, to drain away excess water

dither verb To dither means to be unsure and hesitant

ditto 'Ditto' means 'the same'. In written lists, 'ditto' is represented by a mark (") to avoid repetition

ditty ditties noun (old-fashioned) a short simple song or poem

diva noun a great or leading female singer, especially in opera

dive dives, diving, dived verb **1** To dive means to jump into water with your arms held straight above your head, usually head first **2** If you go diving, you go down under the surface of the sea or a lake using special breathing equipment **3** If an aircraft or bird dives, it flies in a steep downward path, or drops sharply > **diver** noun > **diving** noun

diverge verb **1** If opinions or facts diverge, they differ: *Theory and practice sometimes diverged* **2** If two things such as roads or paths which have been going in the same direction diverge, they separate and go off in different directions > **divergence** noun > **divergent** adjective

diverse adjective **1** If a group of things is diverse, it is made up of different kinds of things: *a diverse range of goods and services* **2** People, ideas, or objects that are diverse are very different from each other > **diversity** *noun*

diversify diversifies, diversifying, diversified *verb* To diversify means to increase the variety of something: *Has the company diversified into new areas?* > **diversification** *noun*

diversion *noun* **1 a** special route arranged for traffic when the usual route is closed **2** something that takes your attention away from what you should be concentrating on: *A break for tea created a welcome diversion* **3** a pleasant or amusing activity

divert *verb* To divert something means to change the course or direction it is following > **diverting** *adjective*

divide *verb* **1** When something divides or is divided, it is split up and separated into two or more parts **2** If something divides two areas, it forms a barrier between them **3** If people divide over something, or if something divides them, it causes strong disagreement between them **4** MATHS In mathematics, when you divide, you calculate how many times one number contains another ▷ *noun* **5** a separation: *the class divide*

dividend *noun* a portion of a company's profits that is paid to shareholders

divine *adjective* **1** having the qualities of a god or goddess ▷ *verb* **2** To divine something means to discover it by guessing > **divinely** *adverb*

divinity divinities *noun* **1** Divinity is the study of religion **2** Divinity is the state of being a god **3** a god or goddess

division *noun* **1** Division is the separation of something into two or more distinct parts **2** MATHS Division is also the process of dividing one number by another **3** a difference of opinion that causes separation between groups of people: *There were divisions in the Party on economic policy* **4** any one of the parts or groups into which something is split: *the Research Division* > **divisional** *adjective*

divisive *adjective* causing hostility between people so that they split into different groups: *Inflation is economically and socially divisive*

divorce *noun* **1** Divorce is the formal and legal ending of a marriage ▷ *verb* **2** When a married couple divorce, their marriage is legally ended > **divorced** *adjective* > **divorcee** *noun*

divulge *verb* To divulge information means to reveal it

DIY *noun* DIY is the activity of making or repairing things yourself. DIY is an abbreviation for 'do-it-yourself'

dizzy dizzier, dizziest *adjective* having or causing a whirling sensation > **dizziness** *noun*

DNA *noun* SCIENCE DNA is deoxyribonucleic acid, a substance found in the cells of all living things. It determines the structure of every cell and is responsible for characteristics being passed on from parents to their children

do does, doing, did, done; dos *verb* **1** Do is an auxiliary verb, which is used to form questions, negatives, and to give emphasis to the main verb of a sentence **2** If someone does a task or activity, they perform it and finish it: *He just didn't want to do any work* **3** If you ask what people do, you want to know what their job is: *What will you do when you leave school?* **4** If you do well at something, you are successful. If you do badly, you are unsuccessful **5** If something will do, it is adequate but not the most suitable option: *Home-made stock is best, but cubes will do* ▷ noun **6** (*informal*) a party or other social event ▷ **do away with** verb To go away with something means to get rid of it ▷ **do up** verb **1** To do something up means to fasten it **2** To do up something old means to repair and decorate it

docile adjective quiet, calm, and easily controlled

dock noun **1** an enclosed area in a harbour where ships go to be loaded, unloaded, or repaired **2** In a court of law, the dock is the place where the accused person stands or sits ▷ verb **3** When a ship docks, it is brought into dock at the end of its voyage **4** To dock someone's wages means to deduct an amount from the sum they would normally receive **5** To dock an animal's tail means to cut part of it off ▷ **docker** noun

doctor noun **1** a person who is qualified in medicine and treats people who are ill **2** A doctor of an academic subject is someone who has been awarded the highest academic degree: *She is a doctor of philosophy* ▷ verb **3** To doctor something means to alter it in order to deceive people: *Stamps can be doctored*

doctorate noun the highest university degree > **doctoral** adjective

doctrine noun a set of beliefs or principles held by a group > **doctrinal** adjective

document noun **1** HISTORY a piece of paper which provides an official record of something **2** COMPUTING a piece of text or graphics stored in a computer as a file that can be amended or altered by document processing software ▷ verb **3** HISTORY If you document something, you make a detailed record of it > **documentation** noun

documentary documentaries noun **1** a radio or television programme, or a film, which gives information on real events ▷ adjective **2** Documentary evidence is made up of written or official records

dodge verb **1** If you dodge or dodge something, you move suddenly to avoid being seen, hit, or caught **2** If you dodge something such as an issue or accusation, you avoid dealing with it

dodgy dodgier, dodgiest adjective (*informal*) dangerous, risky, or unreliable: *He has a dodgy heart*

dodo dodos noun SCIENCE A dodo was a large, flightless bird that lived in Mauritius and became extinct in the late seventeenth century

doe noun a female deer, rabbit, or hare

does the third person singular of the present tense of **do**

dog dogs, dogging, dogged noun **1** a four-legged, meat-eating animal, kept as a pet, or to guard property or go hunting ▷ verb **2** If you dog someone, you follow them very closely and never leave them

dogged [**dog**-ged] adjective showing determination to continue with something, even if it is very difficult: *dogged persistence* > **doggedly** adverb

dogma noun a belief or system of beliefs held by a religious or political group

dogmatic adjective Someone who is dogmatic about something is convinced that they are right about it > **dogmatism** noun

doldrums phrase (informal) If you are **in the doldrums**, you are depressed or bored

dole verb If you dole something out, you give a certain amount of it to each individual in a group

doll noun a child's toy which looks like a baby or person

dollar noun the main unit of currency in New Zealand, the USA, Canada, and some other countries. A dollar is worth 100 cents

dollop noun an amount of food, served casually in a lump

dolphin noun a mammal which lives in the sea and looks like a large fish with a long snout

domain noun 1 a particular area of activity or interest: the domain of science 2 an area over which someone has control or influence: This reservation was the largest of the Apache domains

dome noun a round roof > **domed** adjective

domestic adjective 1 happening or existing within one particular country: domestic and foreign politics 2 involving or concerned with the home and family: routine domestic tasks

domesticated adjective If a wild animal or plant has been domesticated, it has been controlled or cultivated

domesticity noun (formal) Domesticity is life at home with your family

dominance noun 1 Dominance is power or control 2 If something has dominance over other similar

things, it is more powerful or important than they are: the dominance of the United States in the film business > **dominant** adjective

dominate verb 1 If something or someone dominates a situation or event, they are the most powerful or important thing in it and have control over it: The civil service dominated public affairs 2 If a person or country dominates other people or places, they have power or control over them 3 If something dominates an area, it towers over it: The valley was dominated by high surrounding cliffs > **dominating** adjective > **domination** noun

domineering adjective Someone who is domineering tries to control other people: a domineering mother

dominion noun Dominion is control or authority that a person or a country has over other people

domino dominoes noun Dominoes are small rectangular blocks marked with two groups of spots on one side, used for playing the game called dominoes

don dons, donning, donned noun 1 a lecturer at Oxford or Cambridge university ▷ verb 2 (literary) If you don clothing, you put it on

donate verb To donate something to a charity or organization means to give it as a gift > **donation** noun

done the past participle of **do**

donkey noun an animal like a horse, but smaller and with longer ears

donor noun 1 someone who gives some of their blood while they are alive or an organ after their death to be used to help someone who is ill: a kidney donor 2 someone who gives something such as money to a charity or other organization

doom noun Doom is a terrible fate or

event in the future which you can do nothing to prevent

doomed adjective If someone or something is doomed to an unpleasant or unhappy experience, they are certain to suffer it: *doomed to failure*

doomsday noun Doomsday is the end of the world

door noun a swinging or sliding panel for opening or closing the entrance to something; also the entrance itself

doorway noun an opening in a wall for a door

dope noun **1** (*informal*) Dope is an illegal drug ▷ verb **2** If someone dopes you, they put a drug into your food or drink

dormant adjective Something that is dormant is not active, growing, or being used: *The buds will remain dormant until spring*

dormitory dormitories noun a large bedroom where several people sleep

dosage noun the amount of a medicine or a drug that should be taken

dose noun a measured amount of a medicine or a drug

dossier [**doss**-ee-ay] noun a collection of papers with information on a particular subject or person

dot dots, dotting, dotted noun **1** a very small, round mark ▷ verb **2** If things dot an area, they are scattered all over it: *Fishing villages dot the coastline* ▷ phrase **3** If you arrive somewhere on the dot, you arrive there at exactly the right time

dotcom noun a company that does most of its business on the internet

dote If you dote on someone, you love them very much > **doting** adjective

double adjective **1** twice the usual size: *a double whisky* **2** consisting of two parts: *a double album* ▷ verb **3** If something doubles, it becomes twice as large **4** To double as something means to have a second job or use as well as the main one: *Their home doubles as an office* ▷ noun **5** Your double is someone who looks exactly like you **6** Doubles is a game of tennis or badminton which two people play against two other people > **doubly** adverb

double bass noun a musical instrument like a large violin, which you play standing up

double-decker adjective **1** having two tiers or layers ▷ noun **2** a bus with two floors

double glazing noun Double glazing is a second layer of glass fitted to windows to keep the building quieter or warmer

doubt noun **1** Doubt is a feeling of uncertainty about whether something is true or possible ▷ verb **2** If you doubt something, you think that it is probably not true or possible

doubtful adjective unlikely or uncertain

dough [rhymes with **go**] noun **1** Dough is a mixture of flour and water and sometimes other ingredients, used to make bread, pastry, or biscuits **2** (*informal*) Dough is money

doughnut noun a ring or ball of sweet dough cooked in hot fat

dour [rhymes with **poor**] adjective severe and unfriendly: *a dour portrait of his personality*

douse or **dowse** verb If you douse a fire, you stop it burning by throwing water over it

dove noun a bird like a small pigeon

dovetail verb If two things dovetail together, they fit together closely or neatly

dowdy dowdier, dowdiest adjective wearing dull and unfashionable clothes

down preposition, adverb **1** Down means towards the ground, towards a lower level, or in a lower place **2** If you go down a road or river, you go along it ▷ adverb **3** If you put something down, you place it on a surface **4** If an amount of something goes down, it decreases ▷ adjective **5** If you feel down, you feel depressed ▷ verb **6** If you down a drink, you drink it quickly ▷ noun **7** Down is the small, soft feathers on young birds

downcast adjective **1** feeling sad and dejected **2** If your eyes are downcast, they are looking towards the ground

downfall noun **1** The downfall of a successful or powerful person or institution is their failure **2** Something that is someone's downfall is the thing that causes their failure: *His pride may be his downfall*

downgrade verb If you downgrade something, you give it less importance or make it less valuable

downhill adverb **1** moving down a slope **2** becoming worse: *The press has gone downhill in the last 10 years*

download COMPUTING verb **1** If you download data you transfer it from the memory of one computer to that of another, especially over the internet ▷ noun **2** a piece of data transferred in this way

downpour noun A heavy fall of rain

downright adjective, adverb You use 'downright' to emphasize that something is extremely unpleasant or bad: *Staff are often discourteous and sometimes downright rude*

downstairs adverb **1** going down a staircase towards the ground floor ▷ adjective, adverb **2** on a lower floor or on the ground floor

downstream adjective, adverb Something that is downstream or moving downstream is nearer or moving nearer to the mouth of a river from a point further up

down-to-earth adjective sensible and practical: *a down-to-earth approach*

downtrodden adjective People who are downtrodden are treated badly by those with power and do not have the ability to fight back

downturn noun a decline in the economy or in the success of a company or industry

down under (informal) noun **1** Australia or New Zealand ▷ adverb **2** in or to Australia or New Zealand

downwards or **downward** adverb, adjective **1** If you move or look downwards, you move or look towards the ground or towards a lower level: *His eyes travelled downwards; She slipped on the downward slope* **2** If an amount or rate moves downwards, it decreases

downwind adverb If something moves downwind, it moves in the same direction as the wind: *Sparks drifted downwind*

dowry dowries noun A woman's dowry is money or property which her father gives to the man she marries

doze verb **1** When you doze, you sleep lightly for a short period ▷ noun **2** a short, light sleep

dozen noun A dozen things are twelve of them

Dr 1 [dock-ter] 'Dr' is short for 'Doctor' and is used before the name of someone with the highest form of academic degree or who practises medicine **2** 'Dr' is short for 'drive' in addresses

drab drabber, drabbest *adjective* dull and unattractive ▷ **drabness** *noun*

draft *noun* **1** an early rough version of a document or speech ▷ *verb* **2** When you draft a document or speech, you write the first rough version of it **3** To draft people somewhere means to move them there so that they can do a specific job: *Various different presenters were drafted in* **4** In Australian and New Zealand English, to draft cattle or sheep is to select some from a herd or flock

drag drags, dragging, dragged *verb* **1** If you drag a heavy object somewhere, you pull it slowly and with difficulty **2** If you drag someone somewhere, you make them go although they may be unwilling **3** If things drag behind you, they trail along the ground as you move along **4** If an event or a period of time drags, it is boring and seems to last a long time ▷ *noun* **5** Drag is the resistance to the motion of a body passing through air or a fluid

dragon *noun* In stories and legends, a dragon is a fierce animal like a large lizard with wings and claws that breathes fire

drain *verb* **1** If you drain something, you cause liquid to flow out of it **2** If you drain a glass, you drink all its contents **3** If liquid drains somewhere, it flows there **4** If something drains strength or resources, it gradually uses them up: *The prolonged boardroom battle drained him of energy and money* ▷ *noun* **5** a pipe or channel that carries water or sewage away from a place **6** a metal grid in a road, through which rainwater flows

drainage *noun* **1** Drainage is the system of pipes, drains, or ditches used to drain water or other liquid away from a place **2** Drainage is also the process of draining water away, or the way in which a place drains: *To grow these well, all you need is good drainage*

drama *noun* **1** a serious play for the theatre, television, or radio **2** Drama is plays and the theatre in general: *Japanese drama* **3** You can refer to the exciting events or aspects of a situation as drama: *the drama of real life*

dramatic *adjective* A dramatic change or event happens suddenly and is very noticeable: *a dramatic departure from tradition* ▷ **dramatically** *adverb*

dramatist *noun* DRAMA a person who writes plays

drape *verb* If you drape a piece of cloth, you arrange it so that it hangs down or covers something in loose folds

drastic *adjective* A drastic course of action is very severe and is usually taken urgently: *It's time for drastic action* ▷ **drastically** *adverb*

draught [draft] *noun* **1** a current of cold air **2** an amount of liquid that you swallow **3** Draughts is a game for two people played on a chessboard with round pieces ▷ *adjective* **4** Draught beer is served straight from barrels rather than in bottles

draughtsman draughtsmen *noun* a person who prepares detailed drawings or plans

d

draughty draughtier, draughtiest
adjective A place that is draughty has
currents of cold air blowing through it

draw draws, drawing, drew, drawn
verb 1 When you draw, you use a pen
or crayon to make a picture or
diagram 2 To draw near means to
move closer. To draw away or draw
back means to move away 3 If you
draw something in a particular
direction, you pull it there smoothly
and gently: *He drew his feet under the
chair* 4 If you draw a deep breath,
you breathe in deeply 5 If you draw
the curtains, you pull them so that
they cover or uncover the window
6 If something such as water or
energy is drawn from a source, it is
taken from it 7 If you draw a
conclusion, you arrive at it from the
facts you know 8 If you draw a
distinction or a comparison
between two things, you point out
that it exists ▷ *noun* 9 the result of a
game or competition in which
nobody wins ▷ **draw up** *verb* To
draw up a plan, document, or list
means to prepare it and write it out

drawback *noun* a feature that
makes something less acceptable or
desirable: *Shortcuts usually have a
drawback*

drawer *noun* a sliding box-shaped
part of a piece of furniture used for
storing things

drawing *noun* 1 a picture made with
a pencil, pen, or crayon 2 Drawing is
the skill or work of making drawings

drawing room *noun* (old-fashioned)
a room in a house where people
relax or entertain guests

drawl *verb* If someone drawls, they
speak slowly with long vowel
sounds

drawn Drawn is the past participle
of **draw**

dread *verb* 1 If you dread something,
you feel very worried and frightened
about it: *He was dreading the journey*
▷ *noun* 2 Dread is a feeling of great
fear or anxiety ▷ **dreaded** *adjective*

dreadful *adjective* very bad or
unpleasant ▷ **dreadfully** *adverb*

dream dreams, dreaming, dreamed
or dreamt *noun* 1 a series of events
that you experience in your mind
while asleep 2 a situation or event
which you often think about
because you would very much like it
to happen: *his dream of winning the
lottery* ▷ *verb* 3 When you dream,
you see events in your mind while
you are asleep 4 When you dream
about something happening, you
often think about it because you
would very much like it to happen
5 If someone dreams up a plan or
idea, they invent it 6 If you say you
would not dream of doing
something, you are emphasizing
that you would not do it: *I wouldn't
dream of giving the plot away*
▷ *adjective* 7 too good to be true: *a
dream holiday* ▷ **dreamer** *noun*

Dreamtime *noun* In Australian
Aboriginal legends, Dreamtime is
the time when the world was being
made and the first people were
created

dreamy dreamier, dreamiest
adjective Someone with a dreamy
expression looks as if they are
thinking about something very
pleasant

dreary drearier, dreariest *adjective*
dull or boring

dregs *plural noun* The dregs of a
liquid are the last drops left at the
bottom of a container, and any
sediment left with it

drenched *adjective* soaking wet

dress *noun* 1 a piece of clothing for

women or girls made up of a skirt and top attached **2** Dress is any clothing worn by men or women ▷ **verb 3** When you dress, you put clothes on **4** If you dress for a special occasion, you put on formal clothes **5** To dress a wound means to clean it up and treat it

dresser *noun* a piece of kitchen or dining room furniture with cupboards or drawers in the lower part and open shelves in the top part

dressing gown *noun* an item of clothing shaped like a coat and put on over nightwear

dressing room *noun* a room used for getting changed and putting on make-up, especially a backstage room at a theatre

dress rehearsal *noun* the last rehearsal of a show or play, using costumes, scenery, and lighting

dribble *verb* **1** When liquid dribbles down a surface, it trickles down it in drops or a thin stream **2** If a person or animal dribbles, saliva trickles from their mouth **3** In sport, to dribble a ball means to move it along by repeatedly tapping it with your foot or a stick ▷ *noun* **4** a small quantity of liquid flowing in a thin stream or drops

drift *verb* **1** When something drifts, it is carried along by the wind or by water **2** When people drift somewhere, they wander or move there gradually **3** When people drift in life, they move without any aims from place to place or from one activity to another **4** If you drift off to sleep, you gradually fall asleep ▷ *noun* **5** A snow drift is a pile of snow heaped up by the wind **6** The drift of an argument or speech is its main point > **drifter** *noun*

drill *noun* **1** D G T a tool for making holes: *an electric drill* **2** Drill is a routine exercise or routine training: *lifeboat drill* ▷ *verb* **3** D G T To drill into something means to make a hole in it using a drill **4** If you drill people, you teach them to do something by repetition

drink drinks, drinking, drank, drunk *verb* **1** When you drink, you take liquid into your mouth and swallow it **2** To drink also means to drink alcohol: *He drinks little and eats carefully* ▷ *noun* **3** an amount of liquid suitable for drinking **4** an alcoholic drink > **drinker** *noun*

drip drips, dripping, dripped *verb* **1** When liquid drips, it falls in small drops **2** When an object drips, drops of liquid fall from it ▷ *noun* **3** a drop of liquid falling from something **4** a device for allowing liquid food or medicine to enter the bloodstream of a person who is ill

drive drives, driving, drove, driven *verb* **1** To drive a vehicle means to operate and control its movements **2** If something or someone drives you to do something, they force you to do it: *The illness of his daughter drove him to religion* **3** If you drive a post or nail into something, you force it in by hitting it with a hammer **4** If something drives a machine, it supplies the power that makes it work ▷ *noun* **5** a journey in a vehicle **6** a private road that leads from a public road to a person's house **7** Drive is energy and determination > **driver** *noun* > **driving** *noun*

drive-in *noun* a restaurant, cinema, or other commercial place that is specially designed for customers to use while staying in their cars

drivel *noun* Drivel is nonsense: *He is*

still writing mindless drivel

drizzle noun Drizzle is light rain

drone verb 1 If something drones, it makes a low, continuous humming noise 2 If someone drones on, they keep talking or reading aloud in a boring way ▷ noun 3 a low, continuous humming sound

drool verb If someone drools, saliva dribbles from their mouth without them being able to stop it

droop verb If something droops, it hangs or sags downwards with no strength or firmness

drop drops, dropping, dropped verb 1 If you drop something, you let it fall 2 If something drops, it falls straight down 3 If a level or amount drops, it becomes less 4 If your voice drops, or if you drop your voice, you speak more quietly 5 If you drop something that you are doing or dealing with, you stop doing it or dealing with it: *She dropped the subject and never mentioned it again* 6 If you drop a hint, you give someone a hint in a casual way 7 If you drop something or someone somewhere, you deposit or leave them there ▷ noun 8 A drop of liquid is a very small quantity of it that forms or falls in a round shape 9 a decrease: *a huge drop in income* 10 the distance between the top and bottom of something tall, such as a cliff or building: *It is a sheer drop to the foot of the cliff*

droplet noun a small drop

droppings plural noun Droppings are the faeces of birds and small animals

drought [rhymes with **shout**] noun (GEOGRAPHY) a long period during which there is no rain

drove 1 Drove is the past tense of **drive** ▷ verb 2 To drove cattle or sheep is to drive them over a long distance

drown verb 1 When someone drowns or is drowned, they die because they have been under water and cannot breathe 2 If a noise drowns a sound, it is louder than the sound and makes it impossible to hear it

drowsy drowsier, drowsiest adjective sleepy

drudgery noun Drudgery is hard boring work

drug drugs, drugging, drugged noun 1 a chemical given to people to treat disease 2 Drugs are chemical substances that some people smoke, swallow, inhale, or inject because of their stimulating effects ▷ verb 3 To drug a person or animal means to give them a drug to make them unconscious 4 To drug food or drink means to add a drug to it in order to make someone unconscious > **drugged** adjective

drum drums, drumming, drummed noun 1 a musical instrument consisting of a skin stretched tightly over a round frame 2 an object or container shaped like a drum: *an oil drum* 3 (informal) In Australian English, the drum is information or advice: *The manager gave me the drum* ▷ verb 4 If someone is drumming on a surface, he is hitting it regularly, making a continuous beating sound 5 If you drum something into someone, you keep saying it to them until they understand it or remember it > **drummer** noun

drunk 1 Drunk is the past participle of **drink** ▷ adjective 2 If someone is drunk, they have drunk so much alcohol that they cannot speak clearly or behave sensibly ▷ noun 3 a person who is drunk, or who often

gets drunk ▷ **drunken** adjective
▷ **drunkenly** adverb ▷ **drunkenness**
noun

dry drier or dryer, driest or dryest;
dries, drying, dried adjective
1 Something that is dry contains or
uses no water or liquid **2** Dry bread
or toast is eaten without a topping
3 Dry sherry or wine does not taste
sweet **4** Dry also means plain and
sometimes boring: *the dry facts*
5 Dry humour is subtle and sarcastic
▷ verb **6** When you dry something,
or when it dries, liquid is removed
from it ▷ **dry up** verb **1** If something
dries up, it becomes completely dry
2 (*informal*) If you dry up, you forget
what you were going to say, or find
that you have nothing left to say
▷ **dryness** noun ▷ **drily** adverb

dryer or **drier** noun a device for
removing moisture from something
by heating or by hot air: *a hair dryer*

dual adjective having two parts,
functions, or aspects: *a dual-purpose
trimmer*

dub dubs, dubbing, dubbed verb **1** If
something is dubbed a particular
name, it is given that name: *Smiling
has been dubbed 'nature's secret weapon'*
2 If a film is dubbed, the voices on
the soundtrack are not those of the
actors, but those of other actors
speaking in a different language

dubious [dyoo-bee-uss] adjective
1 not entirely honest, safe, or
reliable: *dubious sales techniques*
2 doubtful: *I felt dubious about the
entire proposition* ▷ **dubiously** adverb

duchess noun a woman who has the
same rank as a duke, or who is a
duke's wife or widow

duck ducks, ducking, ducked noun
1 a bird that lives in water and has
webbed feet and a large flat bill
▷ verb **2** When you duck, you move your

head quickly downwards in order to
avoid being hit by something **3** If
you duck a duty or responsibility,
you avoid it **4** To duck someone
means to push them briefly under
water

duckling noun a young duck

duct noun **1** a pipe or channel
through which liquid or gas is sent
2 a bodily passage through which
liquid such as tears can pass

dud noun something which does not
function properly

due adjective **1** expected to happen or
arrive: *The baby is due at Christmas*
2 If you give something due
consideration, you give it the
consideration it needs ▷ phrase
3 Due to means caused by:
Headaches can be due to stress
▷ adverb **4** Due means exactly in a
particular direction: *About a mile due
west lay the ocean* ▷ noun **5** (*in plural*)
Dues are sums of money that you
pay regularly to an organization you
belong to

duel noun **1** a fight arranged
between two people using deadly
weapons, to settle a quarrel **2** Any
contest or conflict between two
people can be referred to as a duel

duet noun MUSIC a piece of music
sung or played by two people

dug Dug is the past tense and past
participle of **dig**

dugong noun an animal like a whale
that lives in warm seas

dugout noun **1** a canoe made by
hollowing out a log **2** (*Military*) a
shelter dug in the ground for
protection

duke noun a nobleman with a rank
just below that of a prince

dull adjective **1** not at all interesting
in any way **2** slow to learn or
understand **3** not bright, sharp, or

clear **4** A dull day or dull sky is very cloudy **5** Dull feelings are weak and not intense: *He should have been angry but felt only dull resentment* ▷ *verb* **6** If something dulls or is dulled, it becomes less bright, sharp, or clear > **dully** *adverb* > **dullness** *noun*

duly *adverb* **1** (*formal*) If something is duly done, it is done in the correct way: *I wish to record my support for the duly elected council* **2** If something duly happens, it is something that you expected to happen: *Two chicks duly emerged from their eggs*

dumb *adjective* **1** unable to speak: *She was dumb with rage* **2** (*informal*) slow to understand or stupid

dumbfounded *adjective* speechless with amazement: *She was too dumbfounded to answer*

dummy dummies *noun* **1** a rubber teat which a baby sucks or bites on **2** an imitation or model of something which is used for display ▷ *adjective* **3** imitation or substitute

dump *verb* **1** When unwanted waste is dumped, it is left somewhere **2** If you dump something, you throw it down or put it down somewhere in a careless way ▷ *noun* **3** [GEOGRAPHY] a place where rubbish is left **4** a storage place, especially used by the military for storing supplies **5** (*informal*) You refer to a place as a dump when it is unattractive and unpleasant to live in

dumpling *noun* a small lump of dough that is cooked and eaten with meat and vegetables

dunce *noun* a person who cannot learn what someone is trying to teach them

dune *noun* A dune or sand dune is a hill of sand near the sea or in the desert

dung *noun* Dung is the faeces from large animals, sometimes called manure

dungeon [dun-jen] *noun* an underground prison

dunk *verb* To dunk something means to dip it briefly into a liquid: *He dunked a single tea bag into two cups*

duo duos *noun* **1** a pair of musical performers; also a piece of music written for two players **2** Any two people doing something together can be referred to as a duo

dupe *verb* **1** If someone dupes you, they trick you ▷ *noun* **2** someone who has been tricked

duplicate *verb* [dyoop-lik-ayt] **1** To duplicate something means to make an exact copy of it ▷ *noun* [dyoop-lik-it] **2** something that is identical to something else ▷ *adjective* [dyoop-lik-it] **3** identical to or an exact copy of: *a duplicate key* > **duplication** *noun*

durable *adjective* strong and lasting for a long time > **durability** *noun*

duration *noun* The duration of something is the length of time during which it happens or exists

duress [dyoo-ress] *noun* If you do something under duress, you are forced to do it, and you do it very unwillingly

during *preposition* happening throughout a particular time or at a particular point in time: *The mussels will open naturally during cooking*

dusk *noun* Dusk is the time just before nightfall when it is not completely dark

dust *noun* **1** Dust is dry fine powdery material such as particles of earth, dirt, or pollen ▷ *verb* **2** When you dust furniture or other objects, you remove dust from them using a duster **3** If you dust a surface with powder, you cover it lightly with the powder

dustbin noun a large container for rubbish

duster noun a cloth used for removing dust from furniture and other objects

dusty dustier, dustiest adjective covered with dust

Dutch adjective **1** belonging or relating to Holland ▷ noun **2** Dutch is the main language spoken in Holland

dutiful adjective doing everything you are expected to do > **dutifully** adverb

duty duties noun **1** something you ought to do or feel you should do, because it is your responsibility: We have a duty as adults to listen to children **2** a task which you do as part of your job **3** Duty is tax paid to the government on some goods, especially imports

duty-free adjective Duty-free goods are sold at airports or on planes or ships at a cheaper price than usual because they are not taxed: duty-free vodka

duvet [doo-vay] noun a cotton quilt filled with feathers or other material; used on a bed in place of sheets and blankets

DVD noun an abbreviation for 'digital video or digital versatile disc': a type of compact disc that can store large amounts of video and sound information

dwarf verb **1** If one thing dwarfs another, it is so much bigger that it makes it look very small ▷ adjective **2** smaller than average ▷ noun **3** a person who is much smaller than average size

dwell dwells, dwelling, dwelled or dwelt verb **1** (literary) To dwell

somewhere means to live there **2** If you dwell on something or dwell upon it, you think or write about it a lot

dwelling noun (formal) Someone's dwelling is the house or other place where they live

dwindle verb If something dwindles, it becomes smaller or weaker

dye dyes, dyeing, dyed verb **1** To dye something means to change its colour by applying coloured liquid to it ▷ noun **2** a colouring substance which is used to change the colour of something such as cloth or hair

dying adjective **1** likely to die soon **2** (informal) If you are **dying for something**, you want it very much

dyke or **dike** noun a thick wall that prevents water flooding onto land from a river or from the sea

dynamic adjective **1** A dynamic person is full of energy, ambition, and new ideas **2** relating to energy or forces which produce motion

dynamics plural noun **1** SCIENCE In physics, dynamics is the study of the forces that change or produce the motion of bodies or particles **2** The dynamics of a society or a situation are the forces that cause it to change **3** MUSIC Dynamics is the various degrees of loudness needed in the performance of a piece of music, or the symbols used to indicate this in written music

dynamite noun SCIENCE Dynamite is an explosive made of nitroglycerine

dynamo dynamos noun SCIENCE a device that converts mechanical energy into electricity

dynasty dynasties noun HISTORY a series of rulers of a country all belonging to the same family

dysentery [diss-en-tree] noun an

d

infection of the bowel which causes fever, stomach pain, and severe diarrhoea

dyslexia [dis-**lek**-see-a] *noun* Dyslexia is difficulty with reading caused by a slight disorder of the brain > **dyslexic** *adjective, noun*

e

each *adjective, pronoun* **1** every one taken separately: *Each time she went out, she would buy a plant* > *phrase* **2** If people do something to **each other**, each person does it to the other or others: *She and Chris smiled at each other*

eager *adjective* wanting very much to do or have something > **eagerly** *adverb* > **eagerness** *noun*

eagle *noun* a large bird of prey

ear *noun* **1** the parts of your body on either side of your head with which you hear sounds **2** An ear of corn or wheat is the top part of the stalk which contains seeds

earl *noun* a British nobleman

early earlier, earliest *adjective* **1** before the arranged or expected time: *He wasn't late for our meeting, I was early* **2** near the beginning of a day, evening, or other period of time: *the early 1970s* ▷ *adverb* **3** before the arranged or expected time: *I arrived early*

earmark *verb* If you earmark something for a special purpose, you keep it for that purpose

earn *verb* **1** If you earn money, you get it in return for work that you do **2** If you earn something such as praise, you receive it because you deserve it > **earner** *noun*

earnest *adjective* **1** sincere in what you say or do: *I answered with an earnest smile* ▷ *phrase* **2** If something begins **in earnest**, it happens to a greater or more serious extent than before: *The battle began in earnest* > **earnestly** *adverb*

earnings *plural noun* Your earnings are money that you earn

earphones *plural noun* small speakers which you wear on your ears to listen to a radio or mp3 player

earring *noun* Earrings are pieces of jewellery that you wear on your ear lobes

earshot *phrase* If you are **within earshot** of something, you can hear it

earth *noun* **1** The earth is the planet on which we live **2** Earth is the dry land on the surface of the earth, especially the soil in which things grow **3** a hole in the ground where a fox lives **4** The earth in a piece of electrical equipment is the wire through which electricity can pass into the ground and so make the equipment safe for use

earthenware *noun* pottery made of baked clay

earthly earlier, earliest *adjective* concerned with life on earth rather than heaven or life after death

earthquake *noun* SCIENCE GEOGRAPHY a shaking of the ground caused by movement of the earth's crust

earthy earthier, earthiest *adjective* **1** looking or smelling like earth **2** Someone who is earthy is open and direct, often in a crude way: *earthy language*

ease noun **1** lack of difficulty, worry, or hardship: *He had sailed through life with relative ease* ▷ verb **2** When something eases, or when you ease it, it becomes less severe or less intense: *to ease the pain* **3** If you ease something somewhere, you move it there slowly and carefully: *He eased himself into his chair*

easel noun ART an upright frame which supports a picture that someone is painting

easily adverb **1** without difficulty **2** without a doubt: *The song is easily one of their finest*

east noun **1** East is the direction in which you look to see the sun rise **2** The east of a place is the part which is towards the east when you are in the centre: *the east of Africa* **3** The East is the countries in the south and east of Asia ▷ adjective, adverb **4** East means in or towards the east: *The entrance faces east* ▷ adjective **5** An east wind blows from the east

Easter noun RE A Christian religious festival celebrating the resurrection of Christ

easterly adjective **1** Easterly means to or towards the east **2** An easterly wind blows from the east

eastern adjective in or from the east: *a remote eastern corner of the country*

eastward or **eastwards** adverb **1** Eastward or eastwards means towards the east: *The city expanded eastward.* ▷ adjective **2** The eastward part of something is the east part

easy easier, easiest adjective **1** able to be done without difficulty: *It's easy to fall* **2** comfortable and without any worries: *an easy life*

eat eats, eating, ate, eaten verb **1** To eat means to chew and swallow food **2** When you eat, you have a meal: *We like to eat early* ▷ **eat away** verb If something is eaten away, it is slowly destroyed: *The sea had eaten away at the headland*

eaves plural noun The eaves of a roof are the lower edges which jut out over the walls

eavesdrop eavesdrops, eavesdropping, eavesdropped verb If you eavesdrop, you listen secretly to what other people are saying

ebb verb **1** When the sea or the tide ebbs, it flows back **2** If a person's feeling or strength ebbs, it gets weaker: *The strength ebbed from his body*

ebony noun **1** a hard, dark-coloured wood, used for making furniture ▷ noun, adjective **2** very deep black

ebullient adjective (formal) lively and full of enthusiasm > **ebullience** noun

EC noun The EC is an old name for the European Union. EC is an abbreviation for 'European Community'

eccentric [ik-**sen**-trik] adjective **1** having habits or opinions which other people think are odd or peculiar ▷ noun **2** someone who is eccentric > **eccentricity** noun > **eccentrically** adverb

ecclesiastical [ik-leez-ee-**ass**-ti-kl] adjective of or relating to the Christian church

echelon [**esh**-el-on] noun **1** An echelon is a level of power or responsibility in an organization; also used of the group of people at that level **2** An echelon is also a military formation in the shape of an arrowhead

echidna echidnas or echidnae [ik-**kid**-na] noun a small, spiny mammal that lays eggs and has a long snout and claws, found in Australia

echo echoes, echoing, echoed noun **1** a sound which is caused by sound waves reflecting off a surface **2** a repetition, imitation, or reminder of something: *Echoes of the past are everywhere* ▷ verb **3** If a sound echoes, it is reflected off a surface so that you can hear it again after the original sound has stopped

eclipse noun An eclipse occurs when one planet passes in front of another and hides it from view for a short time

ecology noun the relationship between living things and their environment; also used of the study of this relationship > **ecological** adjective > **ecologically** adverb > **ecologist** noun

economic adjective **1** [HISTORY] concerning the management of the money, industry, and trade of a country **2** concerning making a profit: *economic to produce*

economical adjective **1** [HISTORY] another word for **economic** **2** Something that is economical is cheap to use or operate **3** Someone who is economical spends money carefully and sensibly > **economically** adverb

economics noun Economics is the study of the production and distribution of goods, services, and wealth in a society and the organization of its money, industry, and trade

economist noun a person who studies or writes about economics

economy economies noun **1** [HISTORY] The economy of a country is the system it uses to organize and manage its money,

industry, and trade; also used of the wealth that a country gets from business and industry **2** Economy is the careful use of things to save money, time, or energy: *Max dished up deftly, with an economy of movement*

ecosystem noun (technical) the relationship between plants and animals and their environment

ecstasy ecstasies noun Ecstasy is a feeling of extreme happiness > **ecstatic** adjective > **ecstatically** adverb

eczema [ek-sim-ma or ek-**see**-ma] noun a skin disease that causes the surface of the skin to become rough and itchy

edge noun **1** The edge of something is a border or line where it ends or meets something else **2** The edge of a blade is its thin, sharp side **3** If you have the edge over someone, you have an advantage over them ▷ verb **4** If you edge something, you make a border for it: *The veil was edged with matching lace* **5** If you edge somewhere, you move there very gradually: *The ferry edged its way out into the river*

edgy edgier, edgiest adjective anxious and irritable

edible adjective safe and pleasant to eat

edifice [ed-if-iss] noun (formal) a large and impressive building

edit verb **1** If you edit a piece of writing, you correct it so that it is fit for publishing **2** To edit a film or television programme means to select different parts of it and arrange them in a particular order **3** Someone who edits a newspaper or magazine is in charge of it

edition noun **1** [ENGLISH] An edition of a book, magazine, or newspaper is a particular version of it printed at one time; also the total number of copies printed at one time **2** An edition of a television or radio programme is a single programme that is one of a series: *tonight's edition of Panorama*

editor *noun* **1** a person who is responsible for the content of a newspaper or magazine **2** LIBRARY a person who checks books and makes corrections to them before they are published **3** a person who selects different parts of a television programme or a film and arranges them in a particular order
> **editorship** *noun*

editorial *adjective* **1** involved in preparing a newspaper, book, or magazine for publication **2** involving the contents and the opinions of a newspaper or magazine: *an editorial comment* ▷ *noun* **3** an article in a newspaper or magazine which gives the opinions of the editor or publisher on a particular topic > **editorially** *adverb*

educate *verb* To educate someone means to teach them so that they gain knowledge about something

educated *adjective* having a high standard of learning and culture

education *noun* the process of gaining knowledge and understanding through learning or the system of teaching people
> **educational** *adjective*
> **educationally** *adverb*

eel *noun* a long, thin, snakelike fish

eerie *adjective* eerier, eeriest *adjective* strange and frightening: *an eerie silence*
> **eerily** *adverb*

effect *noun* **1** a direct result of someone or something on another person or thing: *the effect of divorce on children* **2** An effect that someone

or something has is the overall impression or result that they have: *The effect of the decor was cosy and antique* ▷ *phrase* **3** If something **takes effect** at a particular time, it starts to happen or starts to produce results at that time: *The law will take effect next year*

> **WORD TIP**
> Do not confuse the spelling of the noun *effect* with the verb *affect*. Something that *affects* you has an *effect* on you

effective *adjective* **1** working well and producing the intended results **2** coming into operation or beginning officially: *The agreement has become effective immediately*
> **effectively** *adverb*

effeminate *adjective* A man who is effeminate behaves, looks, or sounds like a woman

efficient *adjective* capable of doing something well without wasting time or energy > **efficiently** *adverb*
> **efficiency** *noun*

effigy effigies [ef-fij-ee] *noun* a statue or model of a person

effluent [ef-loo-ent] *noun* Effluent is liquid waste that comes out of factories or sewage works

effort *noun* **1** PSHE Effort is the physical or mental energy needed to do something **2** an attempt or struggle to do something: *I went to keep-fit classes in an effort to fight the flab*

effortless *adjective* done easily
> **effortlessly** *adverb*

eg or **e.g.** Eg means 'for example', and is abbreviated from the Latin expression 'exempli gratia'

egalitarian *adjective* favouring equality for all people: *an egalitarian country*

egg *noun* **1** an oval or rounded object

laid by female birds, reptiles, fishes, and insects. A baby creature develops inside the egg until it is ready to be born **2** a hen's egg used as food **3** In a female animal, an egg is a cell produced in its body which can develop into a baby if it is fertilized ▷ **egg on** verb If you egg someone on, you encourage them to do something foolish or daring

eggplant noun a dark purple pear-shaped fruit eaten as a vegetable. It is also called **aubergine**

ego egos [ee-goh] noun Your ego is your opinion of what you are worth: It'll do her good and boost her ego

egocentric adjective only thinking of yourself

egoism or **egotism** noun Egoism is behaviour and attitudes which show that you believe that you are more important than other people ▷ **egoist** or ▷ **egotist** noun ▷ **egoistic**, ▷ **egotistic** or ▷ **egotistical** adjective

Egyptian [ij-**jip**-shn] adjective **1** belonging or relating to Egypt ▷ noun **2** An Egyptian is someone who comes from Egypt

eight **1** the number 8 **2** In rowing, an eight is the crew of a narrow racing boat, consisting of eight rowers ▷ **eighth** adjective

eighteen the number 18 ▷ **eighteenth** adjective

eighty eighties the number 80 ▷ **eightieth** adjective

either adjective, pronoun, conjunction **1** one or the other of two possible alternatives: You can spell it either way; Either of these schemes would cost billions of pounds; Either take it or leave it ▷ adjective **2** both one and the other: on either side of the head

eject verb If you eject something or someone, you forcefully push or send them out: He was ejected from the club ▷ **ejection** noun

elaborate adjective [e-**la**-bor-it] **1** having many different parts: an elaborate system of drains **2** carefully planned, detailed, and exact: elaborate plans **3** highly decorated and complicated: elaborate designs ▷ verb [e-**la**-bor-ate] **4** If you elaborate on something, you add more information or detail about it ▷ **elaborately** adverb ▷ **elaboration** noun

elapse verb When time elapses, it passes by: Eleven years elapsed before you got this job

elastic adjective **1** able to stretch easily ▷ noun **2** Elastic is rubber material which stretches and returns to its original shape ▷ **elasticity** noun

elation noun Elation is a feeling of great happiness ▷ **elated** adjective

elbow noun **1** Your elbow is the joint between the upper part of your arm and your forearm ▷ verb **2** If you elbow someone aside, you push them away with your elbow

elder adjective **1** Your elder brother or sister is older than you ▷ noun **2** a senior member of a group who has influence or authority **3** a bush or small tree with dark purple berries

elderly adjective **1** Elderly is a polite way to describe an old person ▷ noun **2** The elderly are old people: Priority is given to services for the elderly

elect verb **1** If you elect someone, you choose them to fill a position, by voting: He's just been elected president **2** (formal) If you elect to do something, you choose to do it: I have elected to stay ▷ adjective **3** (formal) voted into a position, but not yet carrying out the duties of the position: *the vice-president elect*

election noun the selection of one or more people for an official position by voting > **electoral** *adjective*

electorate noun all the people who have the right to vote in an election

electric adjective **1** powered or produced by electricity **2** very tense or exciting: *The atmosphere is electric*

electrical adjective using or producing electricity: *electrical goods* > **electrically** adverb

electrician noun a person whose job is to install and repair electrical equipment

electricity noun Electricity is a form of energy used for heating and lighting, and to provide power for machines

electrified adjective connected to a supply of electricity

electrifying adjective Something that is electrifying makes you feel very excited

electrocute verb If someone is electrocuted, they are killed by touching something that is connected to electricity > **electrocution** noun

electrode noun a small piece of metal which allows an electric current to pass between a source of power and a piece of equipment

electron noun SCIENCE **1** In physics, an electron is a tiny particle of matter, smaller than an atom **2** An electron shell is the orbit of an electron around the nucleus of an atom

electronic adjective COMPUTING having transistors or silicon chips which control an electric current > **electronically** adverb

electronics noun Electronics is the technology of electronic devices

such as televisions and computers; also the study of how these devices work

elegant adjective attractive and graceful or stylish: *an elegant and beautiful city* > **elegantly** adverb > **elegance** noun

element noun **1** a part of something which combines with others to make a whole SCIENCE In chemistry, an element is a substance that is made up of only one type of atom **3** A particular element within a large group of people is a section of it which is similar: *criminal elements* **4** An element of a quality is a certain amount of it: *Their attack has largely lost the element of surprise* **5** The elements of a subject are the basic and most important points **6** The elements are the weather conditions: *Our open boat is exposed to the elements*

elemental adjective (formal) simple and basic, but powerful: *elemental emotions*

elementary adjective simple, basic, and straightforward: *an elementary course in woodwork*

elephant noun a very large four-legged mammal with a long trunk, large ears, and ivory tusks

elevate verb **1** To elevate someone to a higher status or position means to give them greater status or importance: *He was elevated to the rank of major in the army* **2** To elevate something means to raise it up

elevation noun **1** The elevation of someone or something is the raising of them to a higher level or position **2** The elevation of a place is its height above sea level or above the ground

eleven **1** Eleven is the number 11

▷ noun **2** a team of cricket or soccer players > **eleventh** adjective

elf noun In folklore, an elf is a small mischievous fairy

elicit [il-**iss**-it] verb **1** (formal) If you elicit information, you find it out by asking careful questions **2** If you elicit a response or reaction, you make it happen: He elicited sympathy from the audience

eligible [el-lij-i-bl] adjective suitable or having the right qualifications for something: You will be eligible for a grant in the future > **eligibility** noun

eliminate verb **1** If you eliminate something or someone, you get rid of them: They eliminated him from their inquiries **2** If a team or a person is eliminated from a competition, they can no longer take part > **elimination** noun

elite [ill-**eet**] noun **1** a group of the most powerful, rich, or talented people in a society

Elizabethan adjective **2** Someone or something that is Elizabethan lived or was made during the reign of Elizabeth I

elk noun a large kind of deer

elm noun a tall tree with broad leaves

elongated adjective long and thin

eloquent adjective able to speak or write skilfully and with ease: an eloquent politician > **eloquently** adverb > **eloquence** noun

else adverb **1** other than this or more than this: Can you think of anything else? ▷ phrase **2** You say **or else** to introduce a possibility or an alternative: You have to go with the flow or else be left behind in the rush

elsewhere adverb in or to another place: He would rather be elsewhere

elude [ill-**ood**] verb **1** If a fact or idea eludes you, you cannot understand it or remember it **2** If you elude

someone or something, you avoid them or escape from them: He eluded the authorities

elusive adjective difficult to find, achieve, describe, or remember: the elusive million dollar prize

elves the plural of **elf**

emaciated [im-**may**-see-ate-ed] adjective extremely thin and weak, because of illness or lack of food

e-mail or **email** noun **1** the sending of messages from one computer to another **2** a message sent in this way ▷ verb **3** If you e-mail someone, you send an e-mail to them

emancipation noun The emancipation of a person means the act of freeing them from harmful or unpleasant restrictions

embargo embargoes noun **1** an order made by a government to stop trade with another country

embark verb **1** If you embark, you go onto a ship at the start of a journey **2** If you embark on something, you start it: He embarked on a huge spending spree

embarrass verb If you embarrass someone, you make them feel ashamed or awkward: I won't embarrass you by asking for details > **embarrassing** adjective

embarrassed adjective ashamed or awkward

embarrassment embarrassments noun shame and awkwardness

embassy embassies noun the building in which an ambassador and his or her staff work; also used of the ambassador and his or her staff

embedded adjective Something that is embedded is fixed firmly and deeply: glass decorated with embedded threads

ember noun Embers are glowing

pieces of coal or wood from a dying fire

embittered adjective If you are embittered, you are angry and resentful about things that have happened to you

emblazoned [im-**blaze**-nd] adjective If something is emblazoned with designs, it is decorated with them: vases emblazoned with bold and colourful images

emblem noun an object or a design representing an organization or an idea: a flower emblem of Japan

embody embodies, embodying, embodied verb **1** To embody a quality or idea means to contain it or express it: A young dancer embodies the spirit of fun **2** If a number of things are embodied in one thing, they are contained in it: the principles embodied in his report > **embodiment** noun

embossed adjective decorated with designs that stand up slightly from the surface: embossed wallpaper

embrace verb **1** If you embrace someone, you hug them to show affection or as a greeting **2** If you embrace a belief or cause you accept it and believe in it ▷ noun **3** a hug

embroider verb If you embroider fabric, you sew a decorative design onto it

embroidery noun Embroidery is decorative designs sewn onto fabric; also the art or skill of embroidery

embroiled adjective If someone is embroiled in an argument or conflict they are deeply involved in it and cannot get out of it: The two companies are now embroiled in the courts

embryo [**em**-bree-oh] noun **1** an animal or human being in the very early stages of development in the womb > **embryonic** adjective

emerald noun **1** a bright green precious stone ▷ noun, adjective **2** bright green

emerge verb **1** If someone emerges from a place, they come out of it so that they can be seen **2** If something emerges, it becomes known or begins to be recognized as existing: It later emerged that he faced bankruptcy proceedings > **emergence** noun > **emergent** adjective

emergency emergencies noun **1** an unexpected and serious event which needs immediate action to deal with it

emigrate verb If you emigrate, you leave your native country and go to live permanently in another one

emigration noun HISTORY Emigration is the process of emigrating, especially by large numbers of people at various periods of history

eminence noun **1** Eminence is the quality of being well-known and respected for what you do: lawyers of eminence **2** 'Your Eminence' is a title of respect used to address a Roman Catholic cardinal

eminent adjective well-known and respected for what you do: an eminent scientist

eminently adverb (formal) very: eminently reasonable

emir [em-**eer**] noun a Muslim ruler or nobleman

emission noun (formal) The emission of something such as gas or radiation is the release of it into the atmosphere

emit emits, emitting, emitted verb To emit something means to give it out or release it: *She emitted a long, low whistle*

emotion noun PSHE a strong feeling, such as love or fear

emotional adjective PSHE **1** causing strong feelings: *an emotional appeal for help* **2** to do with feelings rather than your physical condition: *emotional support* **3** showing your feelings openly: *The child is in a very emotional state* > **emotionally** adverb

emotive adjective concerning emotions, or stirring up strong emotions: *emotive language*

empathize or **empathise** verb If you empathize with someone, you understand how they are feeling > **empathy** noun

emperor noun a male ruler of an empire

emphasis emphases noun Emphasis is special importance or extra stress given to something

emphasize or **emphasise** verb If you emphasize something, you make it known that it is very important: *It was emphasized that the matter was of international concern*

emphatic adjective expressed strongly and with force to show how important something is: *I answered both questions with an emphatic 'Yes'* > **emphatically** adverb

empire noun **1** a group of countries controlled by one country **2** a powerful group of companies controlled by one person

employ verb **1** If you employ someone, you pay them to work for you **2** If you employ something for a particular purpose, you make use of it: *the techniques employed in turning grapes into wine*

employee noun a person who is paid to work for another person or for an organization

employer noun Someone's employer is the person or organization that they work for

employment noun GEOGRAPHY Employment is the state of having a paid job, or the activity of recruiting people for a job

empower verb If you are empowered to do something, you have the authority or power to do it

empress noun a woman who rules an empire, or the wife of an emperor

empty emptier, emptiest; empties, emptying, emptied adjective **1** having nothing or nobody inside **2** without purpose, value, or meaning: *empty promises* > verb **3** If you empty something, or empty its contents, you remove the contents > **emptiness** noun

emu [ee-myoo] noun a large Australian bird which can run fast but cannot fly

emulate verb If you emulate someone or something, you imitate them because you admire them > **emulation** noun

emulsion noun a water-based paint

enable verb To enable something to happen means to make it possible

enact verb **1** If a government enacts a law or bill, it officially passes it so that it becomes law **2** If you enact a story or play, you act it out > **enactment** noun

enamel enamels, enamelling, enamelled noun **1** a substance like glass, used to decorate or protect metal or china **2** The enamel on your teeth is the hard, white substance that forms the outer part > verb **3** If you enamel something, you decorate or cover it with enamel > **enamelled** adjective

enamoured [in-**am**-erd] adjective If

you are enamoured of someone or something, you like them very much

encapsulate verb If something encapsulates facts or ideas, it contains or represents them in a small space

encased adjective Something that is encased is surrounded or covered with a substance: *encased in plaster*

enchanted adjective If you are enchanted by something or someone, you are fascinated or charmed by them

enchanting adjective attractive, delightful, or charming: *an enchanting baby*

encircle verb To encircle something or someone means to completely surround them

enclave noun a place that is surrounded by areas that are different from it in some important way, for example because the people there are from a different culture: *a Muslim enclave in Bosnia*

enclose verb To enclose an object or area means to surround it with something solid > **enclosed** adjective

enclosure noun an area of land surrounded by a wall or fence and used for a particular purpose

encompass verb To encompass a number of things means to include all of those things: *The book encompassed all aspects of maths*

encore [ong-kor] noun a short extra performance given by an entertainer because the audience asks for it

encounter verb **1** If you encounter someone or something, you meet them or are faced with them: *She was the most gifted child he ever encountered* > noun **2** a meeting,

especially when it is difficult or unexpected

encourage verb [PSHE] **1** If you encourage someone, you give them courage and confidence to do something **2** If someone or something encourages a particular activity, they support it: *The government will encourage the creation of nursery places* > **encouraging** adjective > **encouragement** noun

encroach verb If something encroaches on a place or on your time or rights, it gradually takes up or takes away more and more of it > **encroachment** noun

encrusted adjective covered with a crust or layer of something: *a necklace encrusted with gold*

encyclopedia [en-sigh-klop-**ee**-dee-a] or **encyclopaedia** noun [LIBRARY] a book or set of books giving information about many different subjects

encyclopedic or **encyclopaedic** adjective knowing or giving information about many different things

end noun **1** The end of a period of time or an event is the last part **2** The end of something is the farthest point of it: *the room at the end of the passage* **3** the purpose for which something is done: *the use of taxpayers' money for overt political ends* > verb **4** If something ends or if you end it, it comes to a finish

endanger verb To endanger something means to cause it to be in a dangerous and harmful situation: *a driver who endangers the safety of others*

endear verb If someone's behaviour endears you to them, it makes you fond of them > **endearing** adjective > **endearingly** adverb

endeavour [in-**dev**-er] *verb*
1 (*formal*) If you endeavour to do something, you try very hard to do it ▷ *noun* **2** an effort to do or achieve something

endless *adjective* having or seeming to have no end > **endlessly** *adverb*

endorse *verb* **1** If you endorse someone or something, you give approval and support to them **2** If you endorse a document, you write your signature or a comment on it, to show that you approve of it > **endorsement** *noun*

endowed *adjective* If someone is endowed with a quality or ability, they have it or are given it: *He was endowed with great willpower*

endurance *noun* Endurance is the ability to put up with a difficult situation for a period of time

endure *verb* **1** If you endure a difficult situation, you put up with it calmly and patiently **2** If something endures, it lasts or continues to exist: *The old alliance still endures* > **enduring** *adjective*

enemy enemies *noun* **1** a person or group that is hostile or opposed to another person or group

energetic *adjective* having or showing energy or enthusiasm > **energetically** *adverb*

energy energies *noun* **1** the physical strength to do active things **2** the power which drives machinery **3** SCIENCE In physics, energy is the capacity of a body or system to do work. It is measured in joules

enforce *verb* If you enforce a law or a rule, you make sure that it is obeyed > **enforceable** *adjective* > **enforcement** *noun*

engage *verb* **1** If you engage in an activity, you take part in it: *Officials have declined to engage in a debate*

2 To engage someone or their attention means to make or keep someone interested in something: *He engaged the driver in conversation*

engaged *adjective* **1** When two people are engaged, they have agreed to marry each other **2** If someone or something is engaged, they are occupied or busy: *Mr Anderson was otherwise engaged*; *The emergency number was always engaged*

engagement *noun* **1** an appointment that you have with someone **2** an agreement that two people have made with each other to get married

engine *noun* **1** a machine designed to convert heat or other kinds of energy into mechanical movement **2** a railway locomotive

engineer *noun* **1** a person trained in designing and building machinery and electrical devices, or roads and bridges **2** a person who repairs mechanical or electrical devices ▷ *verb* **3** If you engineer an event or situation, you arrange it cleverly, usually for your own advantage

engineering *noun* Engineering is the profession of designing and constructing machinery and electrical devices, or roads and bridges

English *adjective* **1** belonging to or relating to England ▷ *noun* **2** English is the main language spoken in the United Kingdom, the USA, Canada, Australia, New Zealand, and many other countries

Englishman Englishmen *noun* a man who comes from England > **Englishwoman** *noun*

engrave *verb* To engrave means to cut letters or designs into a hard surface with a tool

engraving noun a picture or design that has been cut into a hard surface
> **engraver** noun

engrossed adjective If you are engrossed in something, it holds all your attention: *He was engrossed in a video game*

engulf verb To engulf something means to completely cover or surround it: *Black smoke engulfed him*

enhance verb To enhance something means to make it more valuable or attractive: *an outfit that really enhances his good looks*
> **enhancement** noun

enigma noun anything which is puzzling or difficult to understand

enigmatic adjective mysterious, puzzling, or difficult to understand: *an enigmatic stranger*
> **enigmatically** adverb

enjoy verb 1 If you enjoy something, you find pleasure and satisfaction in it 2 If you enjoy something, you are lucky to have it or experience it: *The mother has enjoyed a long life*

enjoyable adjective giving pleasure or satisfaction

enjoyment noun Enjoyment is the feeling of pleasure or satisfaction you get from something you enjoy

enlarge verb 1 When you enlarge something, it gets bigger 2 If you enlarge on a subject, you give more details about it

enlargement noun 1 An enlargement of something is the action of making it bigger 2 something, especially a photograph, which has been made bigger

enlighten verb To enlighten someone means to give them more knowledge or understanding of something > **enlightening** adjective
> **enlightenment** noun

enlightened adjective well-informed and willing to consider different opinions: *an enlightened government*

enlist verb 1 If someone enlists, they join the army, navy, or air force 2 If you enlist someone's help, you persuade them to help you in something you are doing

enliven verb To enliven something means to make it more lively or more cheerful

en masse [on **mass**] adverb If a group of people do something en masse, they do it together and at the same time

enormity enormities noun 1 The enormity of a problem or difficulty is its great size and seriousness 2 something that is thought to be a terrible crime or offence

enormous adjective very large in size or amount > **enormously** adverb

enough adjective, adverb 1 as much or as many as required: *He did not have enough money for a coffee* ▷ noun 2 Enough is the quantity necessary for something: *There's not enough to go round* ▷ adverb 3 very or fairly: *She could manage well enough without me*

enquire or **inquire** verb If you enquire about something or someone, you ask about them

enquiry or **inquiry** noun 1 a question that you ask in order to find something out 2 an investigation into something that has happened and that needs explaining

enrage verb If something enrages you, it makes you very angry
> **enraged** adjective

enrich verb To enrich something means to improve the quality or value of it: *new woods to enrich our*

countryside > **enriched** *adjective*
> **enrichment** *noun*

enrol enrols, enrolling, enrolled *verb*
If you enrol for something such as a course or a college, you register to join or become a member of it
> **enrolment** *noun*

en route [on **root**] *adverb* If something happens en route to a place, it happens on the way there

ensconced *adjective* If you are ensconced in a particular place, you are settled there firmly and comfortably

ensemble [on-**som**-bl] *noun*
1 a group of things or people considered as a whole rather than separately **2** a small group of musicians who play or sing together

enshrine *verb* If something such as an idea or a right is enshrined in a society, constitution, or a law, it is protected by it: *Freedom of speech is enshrined in the American Constitution*

ensue ensues, ensuing, ensued [en-**syoo**] *verb* If something ensues, it happens after another event, usually as a result of it: *He entered the house and an argument ensued*
> **ensuing** *adjective*

ensure *verb* To ensure that something happens means to make certain that it happens: *We make every effort to ensure the information given is correct*

entangled *adjective* If you are entangled in problems or difficulties, you are involved in them

enter *verb* **1** To enter a place means to go into it **2** If you enter an organization or institution, you join and become a member of it: *He entered Parliament in 1979* **3** If you enter a competition or examination, you take part in it **4** If you enter

something in a diary or a list, you write it down

enterprise *noun* **1** a business or company **2** a project or task, especially one that involves risk or difficulty

enterprising *adjective* ready to start new projects and tasks and full of boldness and initiative: *an enterprising company*

entertain *verb* **1** If you entertain people, you keep them amused or interested **2** If you entertain guests, you receive them into your house and give them food and hospitality

entertainer entertainers *noun* someone whose job is to amuse and please audiences, for example a comedian or singer

entertaining *adjective* **1** amusing and full of interest ▷ *noun* **2** Entertaining is the hospitality that you give to guests: *She enjoys entertaining*

entertainment entertainments *noun* anything people watch or do for pleasure

enthuse [inth-**yooz**] *verb* If you enthuse about something, you talk about it with enthusiasm and excitement

enthusiasm *noun* Enthusiasm is interest, eagerness, or delight in something that you enjoy

enthusiastic *adjective* showing great excitement, eagerness, or approval for something: *She was enthusiastic about poetry*
> **enthusiastically** *adverb*

entice *verb* If you entice someone to do something, you tempt them to do it: *We tried to entice the mouse out of the hole*

enticing *adjective* extremely attractive and tempting

entire *adjective* all of something: *the entire month of July*

entirely adverb wholly and completely: *He and I were entirely different*

entirety [en-*tire*-it-tee] phrase If something happens to something **in its entirety**, it happens to all of it: *This message will now be repeated in its entirety*

entitle verb If something entitles you to have or do something, it gives you the right to have or do it > **entitlement** noun

entity entities [**en**-tit-ee] noun any complete thing that is not divided and not part of anything else

entourage [**on**-too-rahj] noun a group of people who follow or travel with a famous or important person

entrails plural noun Entrails are the inner parts, especially the intestines, of people or animals

entrance [**en**-trunss] noun **1** The entrance of a building or area is its doorway or gate **2** A person's entrance is their arrival in a place, or the way in which they arrive: *Each creation is designed for you to make a dramatic entrance* **3** DRAMA In the theatre, an actor makes his or her entrance when he or she comes onto the stage **4** Entrance is the right to enter a place: *He had gained entrance to the Hall by pretending to be a heating engineer*

entrance [en-**trahnss**] verb If something entrances you, it gives you a feeling of wonder and delight > **entrancing** adjective

entrant noun a person who officially enters a competition or an organization

entrenched adjective If a belief, custom, or power is entrenched, it is firmly established

entrepreneur [on-tre-pren-**ur**] noun a person who sets up business deals, especially ones in which risks are involved, in order to make a profit > **entrepreneurial** adjective

entrust verb If you entrust something to someone, you give them the care and protection of it: *Miss Fry was entrusted with the children's education*

entry entries noun **1** Entry is the act of entering a place **2** a place through which you enter somewhere **3** anything which is entered or recorded: *Send your entry to the address below*

envelop verb To envelop something means to cover or surround it completely: *A dense fog enveloped the area*

envelope noun a flat covering of paper with a flap that can be folded over to seal it, which is used to hold a letter

enviable adjective If you describe something as enviable, you mean that you wish you had it yourself

envious adjective full of envy > **enviously** adverb

environment noun **1** Your environment is the circumstances and conditions in which you live or work: *a good environment to grow up in* **2** SCIENCE The environment is the natural world around us: *the waste which is dumped in the environment* > **environmental** adjective > **environmentally** adverb

> **WORD TIP**
> There is an *n* before the *m* in *environment*

environmentalist noun a person who is concerned with the problems of the natural environment, such as pollution

envisage verb If you envisage a situation or state of affairs, you can picture it in your mind as being true or likely to happen

envoy noun a messenger, sent especially from one government to another

envy envies, envying, envied noun **1** Envy is a feeling of resentment you have when you wish you could have what someone else has ▷ verb **2** If you envy someone, you wish that you had what they have

enzyme noun SCIENCE a chemical substance, usually a protein, produced by cells in the body

ephemeral [if-**em**-er-al] adjective lasting only a short time

epic noun **1** a long story of heroic events and actions ▷ adjective **2** very impressive or ambitious: epic adventures

epidemic noun **1** an occurrence of a disease in one area, spreading quickly and affecting many people **2** a rapid development or spread of something: the country's crime epidemic

epilepsy noun Epilepsy is a condition of the brain which causes fits and periods of unconsciousness ▷ **epileptic** adjective

episode noun **1** an event or period: After this episode, she found it impossible to trust him **2** ENGLISH one of several parts of a novel or drama appearing for example on television: I never miss an episode of 'Neighbours'

epitaph [**ep**-it-ahf] noun some words on a tomb about the person who has died

epithet noun a word or short phrase used to describe some characteristic of a person

epitome [ip-**pit**-om-ee] noun (formal) The epitome of something is the most typical example of its sort:

She was the epitome of the successful woman

epoch [**ee**-pok] noun a long period of time

eponymous [ip-**on**-im-uss] adjective (formal) The eponymous hero or heroine of a play or book is the person whose name forms its title: the eponymous hero of 'Eric the Viking'

equal equals, equalling, equalled adjective **1** having the same size, amount, value, or standard **2** If you are equal to a task, you have the necessary ability to deal with it ▷ noun **3** Your equals are people who have the same ability, status, or rights as you ▷ verb **4** If one thing equals another, it is as good or remarkable as the other: He equalled the course record of 63 ▷ **equally** adverb > **equality** noun

equate verb If you equate a particular thing with something else, you believe that it is similar or equal: You can't equate lives with money

equation noun MATHS a mathematical formula stating that two amounts or values are the same

equator [ik-**way**-tor] noun an imaginary line drawn round the middle of the earth, lying halfway between the North and South poles > **equatorial** adjective

equestrian [ik-**west**-ree-an] adjective relating to or involving horses

equilibrium noun a state of balance or stability in a situation

equine adjective relating to horses

equip equips, equipping, equipped verb If a person or thing is equipped with something, they have it or are provided with it: The test boat was equipped with a folding propeller

equipment noun Equipment is all the things that are needed or used for a particular job or activity

equitable adjective fair and reasonable

equity noun Equity is the quality of being fair and reasonable: It is important to distribute income with some sense of equity

equivalent adjective **1** equal in use, size, value, or effect ▷ noun **2** something that has the same use, value, or effect as something else: Grits are the American equivalent of porridge > **equivalence** noun

era [ear-a] noun a period of time distinguished by a particular feature: a new era of prosperity

eradicate verb To eradicate something means to get rid of it or destroy it completely > **eradication** noun

erase verb To erase something means to remove it

erect verb **1** To erect something means to put it up or construct it: The building was erected in 1900 ▷ adjective **2** in a straight and upright position: She held herself erect and looked directly at him

erection erections noun **1** the process of erecting something **2** anything which has been erected

erode verb If something erodes or is eroded, it is gradually worn or eaten away and destroyed

erosion noun GEOGRAPHY the gradual wearing away and destruction of something: soil erosion

err verb If you err, you make a mistake

errand noun a short trip you make in order to do a job for someone

erratic adjective not following a regular pattern or a fixed course:

Police officers noticed his erratic driving > **erratically** adverb

erroneous [ir-**rone**-ee-uss] adjective Ideas or methods that are erroneous are incorrect or only partly correct > **erroneously** adverb

error noun **1** a mistake or something which you have done wrong

erudite [**eh**-roo-dite] adjective having great academic knowledge

erupt verb **1** When a volcano erupts, it violently throws out a lot of hot lava and ash **2** When a situation erupts, it starts up suddenly and violently: A family row erupted > **eruption** noun

escalate verb If a situation escalates, it becomes greater in size, seriousness, or intensity

escalator noun a mechanical moving staircase

escapade noun an adventurous or daring incident that causes trouble

escape verb **1** To escape means to get free from someone or something **2** If you escape something unpleasant or difficult, you manage to avoid it: He escaped the death penalty **3** If something escapes you, you cannot remember it: It was an actor whose name escapes me for the moment ▷ noun **4** an act of escaping from a particular place or situation: his escape from North Korea **5** a situation or activity which distracts you from something unpleasant: Television provides an escape

escapee [is-kay-**pee**] noun someone who has escaped, especially an escaped prisoner

escapism noun avoiding the real and unpleasant things in life by thinking about pleasant or exciting things: Most horror movies are simple escapism > **escapist** adjective

eschew [is-**chew**] verb (formal) If you eschew something, you deliberately avoid or keep away from it

escort noun 1 a person or vehicle that travels with another in order to protect or guide them 2 a person who accompanies another person to a social event ▷ verb 3 If you escort someone, you go with them somewhere, especially in order to protect or guide them

Eskimo noun (often offensive) a name that was formerly used for the Inuit people and their language

especially adverb You say especially to show that something applies more to one thing, person, or situation than to any other: Regular eye tests are important, especially for the elderly

espionage [ess-pee-on-ahj] noun Espionage is the act of spying to get secret information, especially to find out military or political secrets

espouse verb (formal) If you espouse a particular policy, cause, or plan, you give your support to it: They espoused the rights of man

espresso noun Espresso is strong coffee made by forcing steam through ground coffee

> **WORD TIP**
> The second letter of espresso is s and not x

essay noun 1 a short piece of writing on a particular subject, for example one done as an exercise by a student

essence noun 1 The essence of something is its most basic and most important part, which gives it its identity: the very essence of being a woman 2 a concentrated liquid used for flavouring food: vanilla essence

essential adjective 1 vitally important and absolutely necessary: Good ventilation is essential in the greenhouse 2 very basic, important, and typical: the essential aspects of international banking > **essentially** adverb

establish verb 1 To establish something means to set it up in a permanent way 2 If you establish yourself or become established as something, you achieve a strong reputation for a particular activity: He had just established himself as a film star 3 If you establish a fact or establish the truth of something, you discover it and can prove it: Our first priority is to establish the cause of her death > **established** adjective

establishment noun 1 The establishment of an organization or system is the act of setting it up 2 a shop, business, or some other sort of organization or institution 3 The Establishment is the group of people in a country who have power and influence: lawyers, businessmen and other pillars of the Establishment

estate noun 1 a large area of privately owned land in the country, together with all the property on it 2 an area of land, usually in or near a city, which has been developed for housing or industry 3 (Law) A person's estate consists of all the possessions they leave behind when they die

estate agent noun a person who works for a company that sells houses and land

esteem noun 1 admiration and respect that you feel for another person > **esteemed** adjective

estimate verb 1 [MATHS] If you estimate an amount or quantity, you calculate it approximately 2 If you estimate something, you make a guess about it based on the evidence you have available: Often it's possible to estimate a person's age

just by knowing their name ▷ *noun*
3 a guess at an amount, quantity, or outcome, based on the evidence you have available **4** a formal statement from a company who may do some work for you, telling you how much it is likely to cost

estimation *noun* **1** an approximate calculation of something that can be measured **2** the opinion or impression you form about a person or situation

estranged *adjective* **1** If someone is estranged from their husband or wife, they no longer live with them **2** If someone is estranged from their family or friends, they have quarrelled with them and no longer keep in touch with them

estrogen *noun* a female hormone which regulates the reproductive cycle

estuary estuaries [**est**-yoo-ree] *noun* GEOGRAPHY the wide part of a river near where it joins the sea and where fresh water mixes with salt water

etc. a written abbreviation for **et cetera**

et cetera [it **set**-ra] 'Et cetera' is used at the end of a list to indicate that other items of the same type you have mentioned could have been mentioned if there had been time or space

etch *verb* **1** If you etch a design or pattern on a surface, you cut it into the surface by using acid or a sharp tool **2** If something is etched on your mind or memory, it has made such a strong impression on you that you feel you will never forget it ▷ **etched** *adjective*

etching *noun* a picture printed from a metal plate that has had a design cut into it

eternal *adjective* lasting forever, or seeming to last forever: *eternal life* ▷ **eternally** *adverb*

eternity eternities *noun* **1** Eternity is time without end, or a state of existing outside time, especially the state some people believe they will pass into when they die **2** a period of time which seems to go on forever: *We arrived there after an eternity*

ether [**eeth**-er] *noun* a colourless liquid that burns easily, used in industry as a solvent and in medicine as an anaesthetic

ethereal [ith-**ee**-ree-al] *adjective* light and delicate: *misty ethereal landscapes* ▷ **ethereally** *adverb*

ethical *adjective* in agreement with accepted principles of behaviour that are thought to be right: *teenagers who become vegetarian for ethical reasons* ▷ **ethically** *adverb*

ethics *plural noun* **1** Ethics are moral beliefs about right and wrong: *The medical profession has a code of ethics*

Ethiopian [eeth-ee-**oh**-pee-an] *adjective* **1** belonging or relating to Ethiopia **2** ▷ *noun* someone who comes from Ethiopia

ethnic *adjective* **1** involving different racial groups of people: *ethnic minorities* **2** relating to a particular racial or cultural group, especially when very different from modern western culture: *ethnic food* ▷ **ethnically** *adverb*

ethos [**eeth**-oss] *noun* a set of ideas and attitudes that is associated with a particular group of people: *the ethos of journalism*

etiquette [**et**-ik-ket] *noun* a set of rules for behaviour in a particular social situation

EU *noun* EU is an abbreviation for 'European Union'

eucalyptus eucalyptuses or **eucalypt** eucalypts noun an evergreen tree, grown mostly in Australia; also the wood and oil from this tree

Eucharist [yoo-kar-rist] noun a religious ceremony in which Christians remember and celebrate Christ's last meal with his disciples

euphemism noun a polite word or expression that you can use instead of one that might offend or upset people: 'Passing on' is a euphemism for death > **euphemistic** adjective > **euphemistically** adverb

euphoria noun a feeling of great happiness > **euphoric** adjective

euro euros noun the official unit of currency in some countries of the European Union, replacing their old currencies at the beginning of January 2002

Europe noun Europe is the second smallest continent. It has Asia on its eastern side, with the Arctic to the north, the Atlantic to the west, and the Mediterranean and Africa to the south

European adjective 1 belonging or relating to Europe ▷ noun 2 someone who comes from Europe

European Union noun The group of countries who have joined together under the Treaty of Rome for economic and trade purposes are officially known as the European Union

euthanasia [yooth-a-**nay**-zee-a] noun Euthanasia is the act of painlessly killing a dying person in order to stop their suffering

evacuate verb If someone is evacuated, they are removed from a place of danger to a place of safety: A crowd of shoppers had to be evacuated from a store after a bomb scare > **evacuation** noun > **evacuee** noun

evade verb 1 If you evade something or someone, you keep moving in order to keep out of their way: For two months he evaded police 2 If you evade a problem or question, you avoid dealing with it

evaluate verb EXAM TERM If you evaluate something, you assess its strengths and weaknesses

evaluation evaluations noun 1 Evaluation is assessing the strengths and weaknesses of something 2 D&T To carry out an evaluation of a design, product or system is to do an assessment to find out how well it works or will work

evangelical [ee-van-**jel**-ik-kl] adjective Evangelical beliefs are Christian beliefs that stress the importance of the gospels and a personal belief in Christ

evangelist evangelists [iv-**van**-jel-ist] noun a person who travels from place to place preaching Christianity > **evangelize** verb > **evangelism** noun

evaporate verb SCIENCE 1 When a liquid evaporates, it gradually becomes less and less because it has changed from a liquid into a gas 2 If a substance has been evaporated, all the liquid has been taken out so that it is dry or concentrated > **evaporation** noun

evasion noun deliberately avoiding doing something: evasion of arrest

evasive adjective deliberately trying to avoid talking about or doing something: He was evasive about his past

eve noun the evening or day before an event or occasion: on the eve of the battle

even adjective **1** flat and level: *an even layer of chocolate* **2** regular and without variation: *an even temperature* **3** In maths, numbers that are even can be divided exactly by two: *4 is an even number* **4** Scores that are even are exactly the same ▷ adverb **5** 'Even' is used to suggest that something is unexpected or surprising: *I haven't even got a bank account* **6** 'Even' is also used to say that something is greater in degree than something else: *This was an opportunity to obtain even more money* ▷ phrase **7** Even if or even though is used to introduce something that is surprising in relation to the main part of the sentence: *She was too kind to say anything, even though she was jealous* **evenly** adverb

evening noun the part of the day between late afternoon and night

event noun **1** something that happens, especially when it is unusual or important **2** one of the competitions that are part of an organized occasion, especially in sports ▷ phrase **3** If you say in any event, you mean whatever happens: *In any event we must get on with our own lives*

eventful adjective full of interesting and important events

eventual adjective happening or being achieved in the end: *He remained confident of eventual victory*

eventuality eventualities noun a possible future event or result: *equipment to cope with most eventualities*

eventually adverb in the end: *Eventually I got to Berlin*

ever adverb **1** at any time: *Have you ever seen anything like it?* **2** more all the time: *They grew ever further apart* **3** 'Ever' is used to give emphasis to

what you are saying: *I'm as happy here as ever I was in England* ▷ phrase **4** (informal) Ever so means very: *Thank you ever so much*

evergreen noun a tree or bush which has green leaves all the year round

everlasting adjective never coming to an end

every adjective **1** 'Every' is used to refer to all the members of a particular group, separately and one by one: *We eat out every night* **2** 'Every' is used to mean the greatest or the best possible degree of something: *He has every reason to avoid the subject* **3** 'Every' is also used to indicate that something happens at regular intervals: *renewable every five years* ▷ phrase **4** Every other means each alternate: *I see Lisa at least every other week*

everybody pronoun **1** all the people in a group: *He obviously thinks everybody in the place knows him* **2** all the people in the world: *Everybody has a hobby*

everyday adjective usual or ordinary: *the everyday drudgery of work*

everyone pronoun **1** all the people in a group **2** all the people in the world

everything pronoun **1** all or the whole of something **2** the most important thing: *When I was 20, friends were everything to me*

everywhere adverb in or to all places

evict verb To evict someone means to officially force them to leave a place they are occupying > **eviction** noun

evidence noun **1** Evidence is anything you see, read, or are told which gives you reason to believe something **2** Evidence is the information used in court to attempt to prove or disprove something

evident adjective easily noticed or understood: *His love of nature is evident in his paintings* > **evidently** adverb

evil noun **1** Evil is a force or power that is believed to cause wicked or bad things to happen **2** a very unpleasant or harmful situation or activity: *the evils of war* ▷ adjective **3** Someone or something that is evil is morally wrong or bad: *evil influences*

evoke verb To evoke an emotion, memory, or reaction means to cause it: *Enthusiasm was evoked by the appearance of the Prince*

evolution [ee-vol-**oo**-shn] noun **1** Evolution is a process of gradual change taking place over many generations during which living things slowly change as they adapt to different environments **2** Evolution is also any process of gradual change and development over a period of time: *the evolution of the European Union* > **evolutionary** adjective

evolve verb **1** If something evolves or if you evolve, it develops gradually over a period of time: *I was given a brief to evolve a system of training* **2** When living things evolve, they gradually change and develop into different forms over a period of time

ewe [**yoo**] noun a female sheep

ex- prefix 'Ex' means 'former': *her ex-husband*

exacerbate [ig-**zass**-er-bate] verb To exacerbate something means to make it worse

exact adjective **1** correct and complete in every detail: *an exact replica of the Santa Maria* **2** accurate

and precise, as opposed to approximate: *Mystery surrounds the exact circumstances of his death* ▷ verb **3** (formal) If somebody or something exacts something from you, they demand or obtain it from you, especially through force: *The navy was on its way to exact a terrible revenge*

exactly adverb **1** with complete accuracy and precision: *That's exactly what happened* **2** You can use 'exactly' to emphasize the truth of a statement, or a similarity or close relationship between one thing and another: *It's exactly the same colour* ▷ interjection **3** an expression implying total agreement

exaggerate verb **1** If you exaggerate, you make the thing you are describing seem better, worse, bigger, or more important than it really is **2** To exaggerate something means to make it more noticeable than usual: *His Irish accent was exaggerated for the benefit of the joke he was telling* > **exaggeration** noun

exalted adjective (formal) Someone who is exalted is very important

exam noun an official test set to find out your knowledge or skill in a subject

examination noun **1** an exam **2** If you make an examination of something, you inspect it very carefully: *I carried out a careful examination of the hull* **3** A medical examination is a check by a doctor to find out the state of your health

examine verb **1** If you examine something, you inspect it very carefully **2** EXAM TERM To examine a subject is to look closely at the issues involved and form your own opinion **3** To examine someone means to find out their knowledge or skill in a particular subject by testing them **4** If a doctor examines you, he or she checks your body to find out the state of your health

examiner *noun* a person who sets or marks an exam

example *noun* **1** something which represents or is typical of a group or set: *some examples of early Spanish music* **2** If you say someone or something is an example to people, you mean that people can imitate and learn from them ▷ *phrase* **3** You use **for example** to give an example of something you are talking about

exasperate *verb* If someone or something exasperates you, they irritate you and make you angry
> **exasperating** *adjective*
> **exasperation** *noun*

excavate *verb* To excavate means to remove earth from the ground by digging > **excavation** *noun*

exceed *verb* To exceed something such as a limit means to go beyond it or to become greater than it: *the first aircraft to exceed the speed of sound*

exceedingly *adverb* extremely or very much

excel excels, excelling, excelled *verb* If someone excels in something, they are very good at doing it

Excellency Excellencies *noun* a title used to address an official of very high rank, such as an ambassador or a governor

excellent *adjective* very good indeed
> **excellence** *noun*

except *preposition* **1** Except or except for means other than or apart from: *All my family were musicians except my father*

exception exceptions *noun*
1 somebody or something that is not included in a general statement

or rule: *English, like every language, has exceptions to its rules*

exceptional *adjective* **1** unusually talented or clever **2** unusual and likely to happen very rarely
> **exceptionally** *adverb*

excerpt *noun* a short piece of writing or music which is taken from a larger piece

excess *noun* **1** Excess is behaviour which goes beyond normally acceptable limits: *a life of excess* **2** a larger amount of something than is needed, usual, or healthy: *an excess of energy* ▷ *adjective* **3** more than is needed, allowed, or healthy: *excess weight* ▷ *phrase* **4** In excess of a particular amount means more than that amount: *a fortune in excess of 150 million pounds* **5** If you do something **to excess**, you do it too much: *She drank to excess*

excessive *adjective* too great in amount or degree: *using excessive force* > **excessively** *adverb*

exchange *verb* **1** To exchange things means to give or receive one thing in return for another: *They exchange small presents on Christmas Eve* ▷ *noun* **2** the act of giving or receiving something in return for something else: *an exchange of letters; exchanges of gunfire* **3** a place where people trade and do business: *the stock exchange*

exchequer [iks-**chek**-er] *noun* The exchequer is the department in the government in Britain and other countries which is responsible for money belonging to the state

excise *noun* **1** Excise is a tax put on goods produced for sale in the country that produces them

excitable *adjective* easily excited

excite *verb* **1** If somebody or something excites you, they make you feel very happy and nervous or very interested and enthusiastic **2** If something excites a particular feeling, it causes somebody to have that feeling: *This excited my suspicion*

excited *adjective* happy and unable to relax > **excitedly** *adverb*

excitement *noun* happiness and enthusiasm

exciting *adjective* making you feel happy and enthusiastic

exclaim *verb* When you exclaim, you cry out suddenly or loudly because you are excited or shocked

exclamation *noun* (ENGLISH) a word or phrase spoken suddenly to express a strong feeling

exclude *verb* **1** If you exclude something, you deliberately do not include it or do not consider it **2** If you exclude somebody from a place or an activity, you prevent them from entering the place or taking part in the activity > **exclusion** *noun*

exclusive *adjective* **1** available to or for the use of a small group of rich or privileged people: *an exclusive club* **2** belonging to a particular person or group only: *exclusive rights to coverage of the Olympic Games* ▷ *noun* **3** a story or interview which appears in only one newspaper or on only one television programme > **exclusively** *adverb*

excrement [eks-krim-ment] *noun* Excrement is the solid waste matter that is passed out of a person's or animal's body through their bowels.

excruciating [iks-**kroo**-shee-ate-ing] *adjective* unbearably painful > **excruciatingly** *adverb*

excursion *noun* a short journey or outing

excuse *noun* [iks-**kyoos**] **1** a reason which you give to explain why

something has been done, has not been done, or will not be done ▷ *verb* [iks-**kyooz**] **2** If you excuse yourself or something that you have done, you give reasons defending your actions **3** If you excuse somebody for something wrong they have done, you forgive them for it **4** If you excuse somebody from a duty or responsibility, you free them from it: *He was excused from standing trial because of ill health* ▷ *phrase* **5** You say **excuse me** to try to catch somebody's attention or to apologize for an interruption or for rude behaviour

execute *verb* **1** To execute somebody means to kill them as a punishment for a crime **2** If you execute something such as a plan or an action, you carry it out or perform it: *The crime had been planned and executed in Montreal* > **execution** *noun*

executioner executioners *noun* a person whose job is to execute criminals

executive *noun* **1** a person who is employed by a company at a senior level **2** The executive of an organization is a committee which has the authority to make decisions and ensure that they are carried out ▷ *adjective* **3** concerned with making important decisions and ensuring that they are carried out: *the commission's executive director*

executor [ig-**zek**-yoo-tor] *noun* a person you appoint to carry out the instructions in your will

exemplary *adjective* **1** being a good example and worthy of imitation: *an exemplary performance* **2** serving as a warning: *an exemplary tale*

exemplify exemplifies, exemplifying, exemplified *verb* **1** To exemplify something means to be a typical example of it: *This aircraft exemplifies the advantages of European technological cooperation* **2** If you exemplify something, you give an example of it

exempt *adjective* **1** excused from a rule or duty: *people exempt from prescription charges* ▷ *verb* **2** To exempt someone from a rule, duty, or obligation means to excuse them from it ▷ **exemption** *noun*

exercise *noun* **1** PE Exercise is any activity which you do to get fit or remain healthy **2** Exercises are also activities which you do to practise and train for a particular skill: *piano exercises; a mathematical exercise* ▷ *verb* **3** When you exercise, you do activities which help you to get fit and remain healthy **4** If you exercise your rights or responsibilities, you use them

exert *verb* **1** To exert pressure means to apply it **2** If you exert yourself, you make a physical or mental effort to do something

exertion *exertions noun* Exertion is vigorous physical effort or exercise

exhale *verb* SCIENCE When you exhale, you breathe out

exhaust *verb* **1** To exhaust somebody means to make them very tired: *Several lengths of the pool left her exhausted* **2** If you exhaust a supply of something such as money or food, you use it up completely **3** If you exhaust a subject, you talk about it so much that there is nothing else to say about it ▷ *noun* **4** a pipe which carries the gas or steam out of the engine of a vehicle **5** GEOGRAPHY Exhaust is the gas or steam produced by the engine of a vehicle ▷ **exhaustion** *noun*

exhaustive *adjective* thorough and complete: *an exhaustive series of tests* ▷ **exhaustively** *adverb*

exhibit *verb* **1** To exhibit things means to show them in a public place for people to see **2** If you exhibit your feelings or abilities, you display them so that other people can see them ▷ *noun* **3** anything which is put on show for the public to see

exhibition *noun* **1** ART A public display of works of art, products, or skills

exhibitor *noun* a person whose work is being shown in an exhibition

exhilarating *adjective* Something that is exhilarating makes you feel very happy and excited

exile *noun* **1** If somebody lives in exile, they live in a foreign country because they cannot live in their own country, usually for political reasons **2** a person who lives in exile ▷ *verb* **3** If somebody is exiled, they are sent away from their own country and not allowed to return

exist *verb* If something exists, it is present in the world as a real or living thing

existence *noun* **1** Existence is the state of being or existing **2** a way of living or being: *an idyllic existence*

exit *noun* **1** a way out of a place **2** If you make an exit, you leave a place ▷ *verb* **3** To exit means to go out **4** DRAMA An actor exits when he or she leaves the stage

exodus *noun* An exodus is the departure of a large number of people from a place

exotic *adjective* **1** attractive or interesting through being unusual: *exotic fabrics* **2** coming from a foreign country: *exotic plants*

expand *verb* **1** If something expands or you expand it, it becomes larger in number or size **2** If you expand on something, you give more details about it: *The minister's speech expanded on the aims which he outlined last month* > **expansion** noun

expanse noun a very large or widespread area: *a vast expanse of pine forests*

expansive adjective **1** Something that is expansive is very wide or extends over a very large area: *the expansive countryside* **2** Someone who is expansive is friendly, open, or talkative

expatriate [eks-**pat**-ree-it] noun someone who is living in a country which is not their own

expect verb **1** If you expect something to happen, you believe that it will happen: *The trial is expected to end today* **2** If you are expecting somebody or something, you believe that they are going to arrive or to happen: *The Queen was expecting the chambermaid* **3** If you expect something, you believe that it is your right to get it or have it: *He seemed to expect a reply*

expectancy noun Expectancy is the feeling that something is about to happen, especially something exciting

expectant adjective **1** If you are expectant, you believe that something is about to happen, especially something exciting **2** An expectant mother or father is someone whose baby is going to be born soon > **expectantly** adverb

expectation noun Expectation or an expectation is a strong belief or hope that something will happen

expedient [iks-**pee**-dee-ent] noun **1** an action or plan that achieves a particular purpose but that may not be morally acceptable: *Many firms have improved their profitability by the simple expedient of cutting staff* ▷ adjective **2** Something that is expedient is useful or convenient in a particular situation > **expediency** noun

expedition noun **1** an organized journey made for a special purpose, such as to explore; also the party of people who make such a journey **2** a short journey or outing: *shopping expeditions* > **expeditionary** adjective

expel verb expels, expelling, expelled verb **1** If someone is expelled from a school or club, they are officially told to leave because they have behaved badly **2** If a gas or liquid is expelled from a place, it is forced out of it

expend verb To expend energy, time, or money means to use it up or spend it

expendable adjective no longer useful or necessary, and therefore able to be got rid of

expenditure noun Expenditure is the total amount of money spent on something

expense noun **1** Expense is the money that something costs: *the expense of installing a burglar alarm* **2** (*in plural*) Expenses are the money somebody spends while doing something connected with their work, which is paid back to them by their employer: *travelling expenses*

expensive adjective costing a lot of money > **expensively** adverb

experience noun **1** Experience consists of all the things that you have done or that have happened to you in the knowledge or skill you have in a particular activity **3** something that you do or something that happens to you, especially something new or unusual ▷ *verb* **4** If you experience a situation or feeling, it happens to you or you are affected by it

experiment *noun* **1** the testing of something, either to find out its effect or to prove something ▷ *verb* **2** If you experiment with something, you do a scientific test on it to prove or discover something
> **experimentation** *noun*
> **experimental** *adjective*
> **experimentally** *adverb*

expert *noun* **1** a person who is very skilled at doing something or very knowledgeable about a particular subject ▷ *adjective* **2** having or requiring special skill or knowledge: *expert advice* > **expertly** *adverb*

expertise [eks-per-**teez**] *noun* Expertise is special skill or knowledge

expire *verb* When something expires, it reaches the end of the period of time for which it is valid: *My contract expires in the summer* > **expiry** *noun*

explain *verb* If you explain something, you give details about it or reasons for it so that it can be understood

explanation *noun* a helpful or clear description > **explanatory** *adjective*

explicit *adjective* shown or expressed clearly and openly: *an explicit warning* > **explicitly** *adverb*

explode *verb* **1** If something such as a bomb explodes, it bursts loudly and with great force, often causing damage **2** If somebody explodes, they express strong feelings suddenly or violently: *I half expected him to explode in anger* **3** When something increases suddenly and rapidly, it can be said to explode: *Sales of men's toiletries have exploded*

exploit *verb* [iks-**ploit**] **1** If somebody exploits a person or a situation, they take advantage of them for their own ends: *Critics claim he exploited young musicians* **2** If you exploit something, you make the best use of it, often for profit: *exploiting the power of computers* ▷ *noun* [**eks**-ploit] **3** something daring or interesting that somebody has done: *His courage and exploits were legendary*
> **exploitation** *noun*

explore *verb* **1** If you explore a place, you travel in it to find out what it is like **2** If you explore an idea, you think about it carefully
> **exploration** *noun* > **exploratory** *adjective* > **explorer** *noun*

explosion *noun* a sudden violent burst of energy, for example one caused by a bomb

explosive *adjective* **1** capable of exploding or likely to explode **2** happening suddenly and making a loud noise **3** An explosive situation is one which is likely to have serious or dangerous effects ▷ *noun* **4** a substance or device that can explode

exponent *noun* **1** An exponent of an idea or plan is someone who puts it forward **2** (*formal*) An exponent of a skill or activity is someone who is good at it

export *verb* **1** To export goods means to send them to another country and sell them there ▷ *noun* **2** Exports are goods which are sent to another country and sold
> **exporter** *noun*

expose *verb* **1** To expose something means to uncover it and make it visible **2** To expose a person to something dangerous means to put them in a situation in which it might harm them: *exposed to tobacco smoke* **3** To expose a person or situation means to reveal the truth about them

exposition noun (ENGLISH) a detailed explanation of a particular subject

exposure noun **1** Exposure is the exposing of something **2** Exposure is the harmful effect on the body caused by very cold weather

express verb **1** When you express an idea or feeling, you show what you think or feel by saying or doing something **2** If you express a quantity in a particular form, you write it down in that form: *The result of the equation is usually expressed as a percentage* ▷ adjective **3** very fast: *express delivery service* ▷ noun **4** a fast train or coach which stops at only a few places

expression noun **1** Your expression is the look on your face which shows what you are thinking or feeling **2** (ENGLISH) The expression of ideas or feelings is the showing of them through words, actions, or art **3** a word or phrase used in communicating: *the expression 'nosey parker'*

expressive adjective **1** showing feelings clearly **2** full of expression

expressway noun a road designed for fast-moving traffic

expulsion noun The expulsion of someone from a place or institution is the act of officially banning them from that place or institution: *the high number of school expulsions*

exquisite adjective extremely beautiful and pleasing

extend verb **1** If something extends for a distance, it continues and stretches into the distance **2** If something extends from a surface or an object, it sticks out from it **3** If you extend something, you make it

larger or longer: *The table had been extended to seat fifty*

extension extensions noun **1** a room or building which is added to an existing building **2** an extra period of time for which something continues to exist or be valid: *an extension to his visa* **3** an additional telephone connected to the same line as another telephone

extensive adjective **1** covering a large area **2** very great in effect: *extensive repairs* ▷ **extensively** adverb

extent noun The extent of something is its length, area, or size

exterior noun **1** The exterior of something is its outside **2** Your exterior is your outward appearance

exterminate verb When animals or people are exterminated, they are deliberately killed > **extermination** noun

external adjective existing or happening on the outside or outer part of something > **externally** adverb

extinct adjective **1** An extinct species of animal or plant is no longer in existence **2** An extinct volcano is no longer likely to erupt > **extinction** noun

extinguish verb To extinguish a light or fire means to put it out

extortionate adjective more expensive than you consider to be fair

extra adjective **1** more than is usual, necessary, or expected ▷ noun **2** anything which is additional **3** a person who is hired to play a very small and unimportant part in a film

extract verb [iks-**tract**] **1** To extract something from a place means to take it out or get it out, often by force **2** If you extract information from someone, you get it from them with difficulty ▷ noun [**eks**-tract] LIBRARY 3 a small section taken from a book or piece of music

extraction noun 1 Your extraction is the country or people that your family originally comes from: *a Malaysian citizen of Australian extraction* 2 Extraction is the process of taking or getting something out of a place

extraordinary adjective unusual or surprising > **extraordinarily** adverb

extravagant adjective 1 spending or costing more money than is reasonable or affordable 2 going beyond reasonable limits > **extravagantly** adverb > **extravagance** noun

extravaganza noun a spectacular and expensive public show

extreme adjective 1 very great in degree or intensity: *extreme caution* 2 going beyond what is usual or reasonable: *extreme weather conditions* 3 at the furthest point or edge of something: *the extreme northern corner of Spain* ▷ noun 4 the highest or furthest degree of something > **extremely** adverb

extremist noun a person who uses unreasonable or violent methods to bring about political change > **extremism** noun

extremity extremities noun The extremities of something are its furthest ends or edges

extricate verb To extricate someone from a place or a situation means to free them from it

extrovert noun a person who is more interested in other people and the world around them than their own thoughts and feelings

exuberant adjective full of energy and cheerfulness > **exuberantly**

adverb > **exuberance** noun

exude verb If someone exudes a quality or feeling, they seem to have it to a great degree

eye eyes, eyeing or eying, eyed noun 1 the organ of sight 2 the small hole at the end of a needle through which you pass the thread ▷ verb 3 To eye something means to look at it carefully or suspiciously

eyeball noun the whole of the ball-shaped part of the eye

eyebrow noun Your eyebrows are the lines of hair which grow on the ridges of bone above your eyes

eyelash noun Your eyelashes are hairs that grow on the edges of your eyelids

eyelid noun Your eyelids are the folds of skin which cover your eyes when they are closed

eyesight noun Your eyesight is your ability to see

eyesore noun Something that is an eyesore is extremely ugly

eyewitness noun a person who has seen an event and can describe what happened

f

fable noun a story intended to teach a moral lesson

fabled adjective well-known because many stories have been told about it: *the fabled city of Troy*

fabric noun DGT 1 cloth: *tough fabric for tents* 2 The fabric of a building is its walls, roof, and other parts **3** The fabric of a society or system is its structure, laws, and customs: *the democratic fabric of American society*

fabricate *verb* **1** If you fabricate a story or an explanation, you invent it in order to deceive people **2** To fabricate something is to make or manufacture it > **fabrication** *noun*

fabulous *adjective* **1** wonderful or very impressive: *a fabulous picnic* **2** not real, but happening in stories and legends: *fabulous creatures*

facade [fas-**sahd**] *noun* **1** the front outside wall of a building **2** a false outward appearance: *the facade of honesty*

face *noun* **1** the front part of your head from your chin to your forehead **2** the expression someone has or is making: *a grim face* **3** a surface or side of something, especially the most important side: *the north face of Everest* **4** the main aspect or general appearance of something: *We have changed the face of language study* > *verb* **5** To face something or someone is to be opposite them or to look at them or towards them: *a room that faces onto the street* **6** If you face something difficult or unpleasant, you have to deal with it: *She faced a terrible dilemma* ▷ *phrase* **7 On the face of it** means judging by the appearance of something or your initial reaction to it: *On the face of it the palace looks gigantic*

faceless *adjective* without character or individuality: *anonymous shops and faceless coffee-bars*

facet [fas-it] *noun* **1** a single part or aspect of something: *the many facets of his talent* **2** one of the flat, cut surfaces of a precious stone

facial [fay-shal] *adjective* appearing on or being part of the face: *facial expressions*

facilitate *verb* To facilitate something is to make it easier for it to happen: *a process that will facilitate individual development*

facility facilities *noun* **1** a service or piece of equipment which makes it possible to do something: *excellent shopping facilities* **2** A facility for something is an ability to do it easily or well: *a facility for novel-writing*

fact *noun* **1** a piece of knowledge or information that is true or something that has actually happened ▷ *phrase* **2 In fact**, **as a matter of fact**, and **in point of fact** mean 'actually' or 'really' and are used for emphasis or when making an additional comment: *Very few people, in fact, have this type of skin* > **factual** *adjective* > **factually** *adverb*

faction *noun* a small group of people belonging to a larger group, but differing from the larger group in some aims or ideas: *a conservative faction in the Church*

fact of life *noun* **1** The facts of life are details about how babies are conceived and born **2** If you say that something is a fact of life, you mean that it is something that people expect to happen, even though they might find it shocking or unpleasant: *War is a fact of life*

factor *noun* **1** something that helps to cause a result: *House dust mites are a major factor in asthma* **2** The factors of a number are the whole numbers that will divide exactly into it. For example, 2 and 5 are factors of 10 **3** If something increases by a particular factor, it is multiplied by that number of times: *The amount of energy used has increased by a factor of eight*

factory factories noun a building or group of buildings where goods are made in large quantities

faculty faculties noun **1** Your faculties are your physical and mental abilities: *My mental faculties are as sharp as ever* **2** In some universities, a Faculty is a group of related departments: *the Science Faculty*

fad noun a temporary fashion or craze: *the latest exercise fad*

fade verb If something fades, the intensity of its colour, brightness, or sound is gradually reduced

faeces or **feces** [fee-seez] plural noun the solid waste products discharged from a person's or animal's body

fag noun (informal) a cigarette

Fahrenheit [far-ren-hite] noun a scale of temperature in which the freezing point of water is 32° and the boiling point is 212°

fail verb **1** If someone fails to achieve something, they are not successful **2** If you fail an exam, your marks are too low and you do not pass **3** If you fail to do something that you should have done, you do not do it: *They failed to phone her* **4** If something fails, it becomes less effective or stops working properly: *The power failed; His grandmother's eyesight began to fail* ▷ noun **5** In an exam, a fail is a piece of work that is not good enough to pass ▷ phrase **6 Without fail** means definitely or regularly: *Every Sunday her mum would ring without fail*

failing noun **1 a** fault in something or someone ▷ preposition **2** used to introduce an alternative: *Failing that, get a market stall*

failure noun **1** lack of success: *Not all conservation programmes ended in*

failure **2** an unsuccessful person, thing, or action: *The venture was a complete failure* **3** Your failure to do something is not doing something that you were expected to do: *a statement explaining his failure to turn up as a speaker* **4** a weakness in something

faint adjective **1** A sound, colour, or feeling that is faint is not very strong or intense **2** If you feel faint, you feel weak, dizzy, and unsteady ▷ verb **3** If you faint, you lose consciousness for a short time ▷ **faintly** adverb

fair adjective **1** reasonable and just: *fair and prompt trials for political prisoners* **2** quite large: *a fair size envelope* **3** moderately good or likely to be correct: *He had a fair idea of what to expect* **4** having light-coloured hair or pale skin **5** with pleasant and dry weather: *Ireland's fair weather months* ▷ noun **6** a form of entertainment that takes place outside, with stalls, sideshows, and machines to ride on **7** an exhibition of goods produced by a particular industry: *International Wine and Food Fair* ▷ **fairly** adverb ▷ **fairness** noun

fairground noun an outdoor area where a fair is set up

fairway noun the area of trimmed grass between a tee and a green on a golf course

fairy fairies noun In stories, fairies are small, supernatural creatures with magical powers

fairy tale noun a story of magical events

faith noun **1** Faith is a feeling of confidence, trust, or optimism about something **2** RE Someone's faith is their religion

faithful adjective **1** loyal to someone or something and remaining firm in support of them **2** accurate and truthful: *a faithful copy of an original* ▷ **faithfully** *adverb* ▷ **faithfulness** *noun*

fake *noun* **1** an imitation of something made to trick people into thinking that it is genuine ▷ *adjective* **2** imitation and not genuine: *fake fur* ▷ *verb* **3** If you fake a feeling, you pretend that you are experiencing it

falcon *noun* a bird of prey that can be trained to hunt other birds or small animals

fall falls, falling, fell, fallen *verb* **1** If someone or something falls or falls over, they drop towards the ground **2** If something falls somewhere, it lands there: *The spotlight fell on her* **3** If something falls in amount or strength, it becomes less: *Steel production fell about 25 per cent* **4** If a person or group in a position of power falls, they lose their position **5** Someone who falls in battle is killed **6** If, for example, you fall asleep, fall ill, or fall in love, you change quite quickly to that new state **7** If you fall for someone, you become strongly attracted to them and fall in love **8** If you fall for a trick or lie, you are deceived by it **9** Something that falls on a particular date occurs on that date ▷ *noun* **10** If you have a fall, you accidentally fall over **11** A fall of snow, soot, or other substance is a quantity of it that has fallen to the ground **12** A fall in something is a reduction in its amount or strength **13** In America, autumn is called fall ▷ **fall down** *verb* An argument or idea that falls down on a particular point is weak on that point and as a result will be unsuccessful ▷ **fall out**

verb If people fall out, they disagree and quarrel ▷ **fall through** *verb* If an arrangement or plan falls through, it fails or is abandoned

fallacy fallacies [fal-lass-ee] *noun* something false that is generally believed to be true

fallout *noun* radioactive particles that fall to the earth after a nuclear explosion

fallow *adjective* Land that is fallow is not being used for crop growing so that it has the chance to rest and improve

false *adjective* **1** untrue or incorrect: *I think that's a false argument* **2** not real or genuine but intended to seem real: *false hair* **3** unfaithful or deceitful ▷ **falsely** *adverb* ▷ **falseness** *noun* ▷ **falsity** *noun*

falsehood *noun* **1** the quality or fact of being untrue: *the difference between truth and falsehood* **2** a lie

falsify falsifies, falsifying, falsified *verb* If you falsify something, you change it in order to deceive people ▷ **falsification** *noun*

falter *verb* If someone or something falters, they hesitate or become unsure or unsteady: *Her voice faltered*

fame *noun* the state of being very well-known

famed *adjective* very well-known: *an area famed for its beauty*

familiar *adjective* **1** well-known or easy to recognize: *familiar faces* **2** knowing or understanding something well: *Most children are familiar with stories* ▷ **familiarity** *noun* ▷ **familiarize** *verb*

family families *noun* **1** a group consisting of parents and their children; also all the people who are related to each other, including aunts and uncles, cousins, and grandparents **2** [SCIENCE] a group of related species of animals or plants. It is smaller than an order and larger than a genus > **familial** adjective

famine noun a serious shortage of food which may cause many deaths

famous adjective very well-known

famously adverb (old-fashioned) If people get on famously, they enjoy each other's company very much

fan fans, fanning, fanned noun **1** If you are a fan of someone or something, you like them very much and are very enthusiastic about them **2** a hand-held or mechanical object which creates a draught of cool air when it moves ▷ verb **3** To fan someone or something is to create a draught in their direction: *The gentle wind fanned her from all sides* > **fan out** verb If things or people fan out, they move outwards in different directions

fanatic noun a person who is very extreme in their support for a cause or in their enthusiasm for a particular activity > **fanaticism** noun

fanatical adjective If you are fanatical about something, you are very extreme in your enthusiasm or support for it > **fanatically** adverb

fancy fancies, fancying, fancied; fancier, fanciest verb **1** If you fancy something, you want to have it or do it: *She fancied living in Canada* ▷ adjective **2** special and elaborate: *dressed up in some fancy clothes* > **fanciful** adjective

fancy dress noun clothing worn for a party at which people dress up to look like a particular character or animal

fanfare noun a short, loud musical introduction to a special event, usually played on trumpets

fantasize or **fantasise** verb If you

fantasize, you imagine pleasant but unlikely events or situations

fantastic adjective **1** wonderful and very pleasing: *a fantastic view of the sea* **2** extremely large in degree or amount: *fantastic debts* **3** strange and difficult to believe: *fantastic animals found nowhere else on earth* > **fantastically** adverb

fantasy fantasies noun **1** an imagined story or situation **2** Fantasy is the activity of imagining things or the things that you imagine: *She can't distinguish between fantasy and reality* **3** LIBRARY In books and films, fantasy is the people or situations which are created in the writer's imagination and do not reflect reality

far farther, farthest; further, furthest adverb **1** If something is far away from other things, it is a long distance away **2** Far also means very much or to a great extent or degree: *far more important* ▷ adjective **3** Far means very distant: *in the far south of Africa* **4** Far also describes the more distant of two things rather than the nearer one: *the far corner of the goal* ▷ phrase **5** By far and **far and away** are used to say that something is so to a great degree: *Walking is by far the best way to get around* **6** So far means up to the present moment: *So far, it's been good news* **7** As far as, so far as, and in so far as mean to the degree or extent that something is true: *As far as I know he is progressing well*

farce noun **1** a humorous play in which ridiculous and unlikely situations occur **2** a disorganized and ridiculous situation > **farcical** adjective

fare noun **1** the amount charged for a journey on a bus, train, or plane

▷ *verb* **2** How someone fares in a particular situation is how they get on: *The team have not fared well in a tournament*

Far East *noun* The Far East consists of the countries of East Asia, including China, Japan, and Malaysia ▷ **Far Eastern** *adjective*

farewell *interjection* **1** Farewell means goodbye ▷ *adjective* **2** A farewell act is performed by or for someone who is leaving a particular job or career: *a farewell speech*

far-fetched *adjective* unlikely to be true

farm *noun* **1** an area of land together with buildings, used for growing crops and raising animals ▷ *verb* **2** Someone who farms uses land to grow crops and raise animals > **farmer** *noun* > **farming** *noun*

farmhouse *noun* The main house on a farm

farmyard *noun* an area surrounded by farm buildings

fascinate *verb* If something fascinates you, it interests you very much > **fascinating** *adjective*

fascism [fash-izm] *noun* an extreme right-wing political ideology or system of government with a powerful dictator and state control of most activities. Nationalism is encouraged and political opposition is not allowed > **fascist** *noun, adjective*

fashion *noun* **1** a style of dress or way of behaving that is popular at a particular time **2** The fashion in which someone does something is the way in which they do it ▷ *verb* **3** If you fashion something, you make or shape it

fashionable *adjective* Something that is fashionable is very popular with a lot of people at the same time > **fashionably** *adverb*

fast *adjective* **1** moving or done at great speed **2** If a clock is fast, it shows a time that is later than the real time ▷ *adverb* **3** quickly and without delay **4** Something that is held fast is firmly fixed ▷ *phrase* **5** If you are fast asleep, you are in a deep sleep ▷ *verb* **6** If you fast, you eat no food at all for a period of time, usually for religious reasons ▷ *noun* **7** a period of time during which someone does not eat food

fasten *verb* **1** To fasten something is to close it or attach it firmly to something else **2** If you fasten your hands or teeth around or onto something, you hold it tightly with them > **fastener** *noun* > **fastening** *noun*

fast food *noun* hot food that is prepared and served quickly after you have ordered it

fastidious *adjective* extremely choosy and concerned about neatness and cleanliness

fast-track *verb* To fast-track something is to make it happen or put it into effect as quickly as possible, usually giving it priority over other things

fat *fatter, fattest; fats adjective* **1** Someone who is fat has too much weight on their body **2** large or great: *a fat pile of letters* ▷ *noun* **3** Fat is the greasy, cream-coloured substance that animals and humans have under their skin, which is used to store energy and to help keep them warm **4** Fat is also the greasy solid or liquid substance obtained from animals and plants and used in cooking > **fatness** *noun* > **fatty** *adjective*

fatal *adjective* **1** causing death: *fatal injuries* **2** very important or significant and likely to have an undesirable effect: *The mistake was fatal to my plans* ▷ **fatally** *adverb*

fatality fatalities *noun* a death caused by accident or violence

fate *noun* **1** Fate is a power that is believed to control events **2** Someone's fate is what happens to them: *She was resigned to her fate*

fateful *adjective* having an important, often disastrous, effect: *fateful political decisions*

father *noun* **1** A person's father is their male parent **2** The father of something is the man who invented or started it: *the father of Italian painting* **3** 'Father' is used to address a priest in some Christian churches **4** Father is another name for God ▷ **fatherly** *adjective* ▷ **fatherhood** *noun*

father-in-law fathers-in-law *noun* A person's father-in-law is the father of their husband or wife

fathom *noun* **1** a unit for measuring the depth of water. It is equal to 6 feet or about 1.83 metres ▷ *verb* **2** If you fathom something, you understand it after careful thought: *Daisy tries to fathom what it means*

fatigue fatigues, fatiguing, fatigued [fat-**eeg**] *noun* **1** Fatigue is extreme tiredness ▷ *verb* **2** If you are fatigued by something, it makes you extremely tired

fault *noun* **1** If something bad is your fault, you are to blame for it **2** a weakness or imperfection in someone or something **3** a large crack in rock caused by movement of the earth's crust ▷ *phrase* **4** If you are **at fault**, you are mistaken or are to blame for something: *If you were at fault, you accept it* ▷ *verb* **5** If you fault someone, you criticize them for what they are doing because

they are not doing it well ▷ **faultless** *adjective*

faulty faultier, faultiest *adjective* containing flaws or errors

favour *noun* **1** If you regard someone or something with favour, you like or support them **2** If you do someone a favour, you do something helpful for them ▷ *phrase* **3** Something that is in **someone's favour** is a help or advantage to them: *The arguments seemed to be in our favour* **4** If you are **in favour of** something, you agree with it and think it should happen ▷ *verb* **5** If you favour something or someone, you prefer that person or thing

favourable *adjective* **1** of advantage or benefit to someone **2** positive and expressing approval ▷ **favourably** *adverb*

favourite *adjective* **1** Your favourite person or thing is the one you like best ▷ *noun* **2** Someone's favourite is the person or thing they like best **3** the animal or person expected to win in a race or contest

favouritism *noun* Favouritism is behaviour in which you are unfairly more helpful or more generous to one person than to other people

fawn *noun, adjective* **1** pale yellowish-brown ▷ *noun* **2** a very young deer ▷ *verb* **3** To fawn on someone is to seek their approval by flattering them

fax *noun* an exact copy of a document sent electronically along a telephone line

fear *noun* **1** Fear is an unpleasant feeling of danger **2** a thought that something undesirable or unpleasant might happen: *You have a fear of failure* ▷ *verb* **3** If you fear someone or something, you are frightened of them **4** If you fear something unpleasant, you are worried that it is likely to happen: *Artists feared that their pictures would be forgotten* > **fearless** adjective > **fearlessly** adverb

fearful adjective **1** afraid and full of fear **2** extremely unpleasant or worrying: *The world's in such a fearful mess* > **fearfully** adverb

fearsome adjective terrible or frightening: *a powerful, fearsome weapon*

feasible adjective possible and likely to happen: *The proposal is just not feasible* > **feasibility** noun

feast noun a large and special meal for many people

feat noun an impressive and difficult achievement: *It was an astonishing feat for Leeds to score six away from home*

feather noun one of the light fluffy things covering a bird's body > **feathery** adjective

feature noun **1** an interesting or important part or characteristic of something **2** Someone's features are the various parts of their face **3** SCIENCE a characteristic that is typical of a particular living thing **4** a special article or programme dealing with a particular subject **5** the main film in a cinema programme ▷ verb **6** To feature something is to include it or emphasize it as an important part or subject > **featureless** adjective

February noun February is the second month of the year. It has 28 days, except in a leap year, when it has 29 days

fed the past tense and past participle of **feed**

federal adjective relating to a system of government in which a group of states is controlled by a central government, but each state has its own local powers: *The United States of America is a federal country*

federation noun a group of organizations or states that have joined together for a common purpose

fed up adjective (informal) unhappy or bored

fee noun a charge or payment for a job, service, or activity

feeble adjective weak or lacking in power or influence: *feeble and stupid arguments*

feed feeds, feeding, fed verb **1** To feed a person or animal is to give them food **2** When an animal or baby feeds, it eats **3** To feed something is to supply what is needed for it to operate or exist: *The information was fed into a computer database* ▷ noun **4** Feed is food for animals

feedback noun **1** Feedback is comments and information about the quality or success of something **2** Feedback is also a condition in which some of the power, sound, or information produced by electronic equipment goes back into it

feel feels, feeling, felt verb **1** If you feel an emotion or sensation, you experience it: *I felt a bit ashamed* **2** If you feel that something is the case, you believe it to be so: *She feels that she is in control of her life* **3** If you feel something, you touch it **4** If something feels warm or cold, for example, you experience its warmth or coldness through the sense of touch: *Real marble feels cold to the touch* **5** To feel the effect of something is to be affected by it: *The shock waves of this fire will be felt by people from all over the world* ▷ noun **6** The feel of something is how it feels to you when you touch it: *skin*

with a velvety smooth feel ▷ phrase
7 if you **feel like** doing something, you want to do it

feeling noun **1** an emotion or reaction: *feelings of envy* **2** a physical sensation: *a feeling of pain* **3** Feeling is the ability to experience the sense of touch in your body: *He had no feeling in his hands* **4** (in plural) Your feelings about something are your general attitudes or thoughts about it: *He has strong feelings about our national sport*

feet the plural of **foot**

feign [rhymes with **rain**] verb If you feign an emotion or state, you pretend to experience it: *I feigned a headache*

feline [**fee**-line] adjective belonging or relating to the cat family

fell 1 the past tense of **fall** ▷ verb **2** To fell a tree is to cut it down

fellow noun **1** (old-fashioned, informal) a man: *I knew a fellow by that name* **2** a senior member of a learned society or a university college **3** Your fellows are the people who share work or an activity with you ▷ adjective **4** You use 'fellow' to describe people who have something in common with you: *his fellow editors*

fellowship noun **1** a feeling of friendliness that a group of people have when they are doing things together **2** a group of people that join together because they have interests in common: *the Dickens Fellowship* **3** an academic post at a university which involves research work

felt 1 the past tense and past participle of **feel** ▷ noun **2** [D & T] Felt is a thick cloth made by pressing short threads together

female noun **1** a person or animal that belongs to the gender that can have babies ▷ adjective **2** concerning or relating to females

feminine adjective **1** relating to women or considered to be typical of women **2** belonging to a particular class of nouns in some languages, such as French, German, and Latin ▷ **femininity** noun

feminism noun Feminism is the belief that women should have the same rights and opportunities as men ▷ **feminist** noun, adjective

fence noun **1** a wooden or wire barrier between two areas of land **2** a barrier or hedge for the horses to jump over in horse racing or show jumping ▷ verb **3** To fence an area of land is to surround it with a fence **4** When two people fence, they use special swords to fight each other as a sport

fend phrase If you have to **fend for yourself**, you have to look after yourself > **fend off** verb If you fend off an attack or unwelcome questions or attention, you defend and protect yourself

ferment verb When wine, beer, or fruit ferments, a chemical change takes place in it, often producing alcohol ▷ **fermentation** noun

fern noun a plant with long feathery leaves and no flowers

ferocious adjective violent and fierce: *ferocious dogs; ferocious storms* > **ferociously** adverb > **ferocity** noun

ferret noun a small, fierce animal related to the weasel and kept for hunting rats and rabbits

ferry ferries, ferrying, ferried noun **1** a boat that carries people and vehicles across short stretches of water ▷ verb **2** To ferry people or goods somewhere is to transport them there, usually on a short, regular journey

fertile adjective **1** capable of producing offspring or plants **2** creative: *fertile minds* ▷ **fertility** noun

fertilize or **fertilise** verb **1** SCIENCE When an egg, plant, or female is fertilized, the process of reproduction begins by sperm joining with the egg, or by pollen coming into contact with the reproductive part of a plant **2** To fertilize land is to put manure or chemicals onto it to feed the plants

fertilizer or **fertiliser** noun GEOGRAPHY a substance put onto soil to improve plant growth

fervent adjective showing strong, sincere, and enthusiastic feeling: *a fervent nationalist* ▷ **fervently** adverb

fervour noun a very strong feeling for or belief in something: *a wave of religious fervour*

fester verb If a wound festers it becomes infected and produces pus

festival noun **1** an organized series of events and performances: *the Cannes Film Festival* **2** RE a day or period of religious celebration

festive adjective full of happiness and celebration: *a festive time of singing and dancing*

festivity festivities noun celebration and happiness: *the wedding festivities*

festooned adjective If something is festooned with objects, the objects are hanging across it in large numbers

fetch verb **1** If you fetch something, you go to where it is and bring it back **2** If something fetches a particular sum of money, it is sold for that amount: *Portraits fetch the highest prices*

fetching adjective attractive in

appearance: *a fetching purple frock*

fete [rhymes with **date**] noun **1** an outdoor event with competitions, displays, and goods for sale ▷ verb **2** Someone who is feted receives a public welcome or entertainment as an honour

feud [**fyood**] noun **1** a long-term and very bitter quarrel, especially between families ▷ verb **2** When people feud, they take part in a feud

fever noun **1** Fever is a condition occurring during illness, in which the patient has a very high body temperature **2** A fever is extreme excitement or agitation: *a fever of impatience*

feverish adjective **1** in a state of extreme excitement or agitation: *increasingly feverish activity* **2** suffering from a high body temperature ▷ **feverishly** adverb

few adjective, noun **1** used to refer to a small number of things: *I saw him a few moments ago; one of only a few* ▷ phrase **2** Quite a few or a good few means quite a large number of things

fiancé [fee-**on**-say] noun A person's fiancé is the man to whom they are engaged

fiancée [fee-**on**-say] noun A person's fiancée is the woman to whom they are engaged

fiasco fiascos [fee-**ass**-koh] noun an event or attempt that fails completely, especially in a ridiculous or disorganized way: *The game ended in a complete fiasco*

fib fibs, fibbing, fibbed noun **1** a small, unimportant lie ▷ verb **2** If you fib, you tell a small lie

fibre noun **1** DGT a thin thread of a substance used to make cloth **2** Fibre is also a part of plants that can be eaten but not digested; it helps food pass quickly through the body > **fibrous** adjective

fickle adjective A fickle person keeps changing their mind about who or what they like or want

fiction noun **1** Fiction is stories about people and events that have been invented by the author **2** something that is not true > **fictional** adjective > **fictitious** adjective

fiddle verb **1** If you fiddle with something, you keep moving it or touching it restlessly **2** (informal) If someone fiddles something such as an account, they alter it dishonestly to get money for themselves ▷ noun **3** (informal) a dishonest action or scheme to get money **4** a violin > **fiddler** noun

fiddly fiddlier, fiddliest adjective small and difficult to do or use: fiddly nuts and bolts

fidelity noun Fidelity is remaining firm in your faith, friendships, or loyalty to another person

field noun **1** an area of land where crops are grown or animals are kept **2** PE an area of land where sports are played: a hockey field **3** A coal field, oil field, or gold field is an area where coal, oil, or gold is found **4** a particular subject or area of interest: He was doing well in his own field of advertising ▷ adjective **5** A field trip or a field study involves research or activity in the natural environment rather than theoretical or laboratory work **6** In an athletics competition, the field events are the events such as the high jump and the javelin which do not take place on a running track ▷ verb **7** In cricket, when you field the ball, you stop it after the batsman has hit it **8** To field questions is to answer or deal

with them skilfully

fielder noun In cricket, the fielders are the team members who stand at various parts of the pitch and try to get the batsmen out or to prevent runs from being scored

fieldwork noun Fieldwork is the study of something in the environment where it naturally lives or occurs, rather than in a class or laboratory

fiend [feend] noun **1** a devil or evil spirit **2** a very wicked or cruel person **3** (informal) someone who is very keen on a particular thing: a fitness fiend

fierce adjective **1** very aggressive or angry **2** extremely strong or intense: a sudden fierce pain; a fierce storm > **fiercely** adverb

fiery fierier, fieriest adjective **1** involving fire or seeming like fire: a huge fiery sun **2** showing great anger, energy, or passion: a fiery debate

fifteen the number 15 > **fifteenth** adjective

fifth adjective **1** The fifth item in a series is the one counted as number five ▷ noun **2** one of five equal parts

fifty fifties the number 50 > **fiftieth** adjective

fig noun a soft, sweet fruit full of tiny seeds. It grows in hot countries and is often eaten dried

fight fights, fighting, fought verb **1** When people fight, they take part in a battle, a war, a boxing match, or in some other attempt to hurt or kill someone **2** To fight for something is to try in a very determined way to achieve it: I must fight for respect ▷ noun **3** a situation in which people hit or try to hurt each other **4** a determined attempt to prevent or achieve something: the fight for independence **5** an angry disagreement

fighter *noun* someone who physically fights another person

figurative *adjective* (ENGLISH) If you use a word or expression in a figurative sense, you use it with a more abstract or imaginative meaning than its ordinary one > **figuratively** *adverb*

figure *noun* **1** a written number or the amount a number stands for **2** a geometrical shape or a diagram or table in a written text **3** the shape of a human body, sometimes one that you cannot see properly: *his slim and supple figure; A human figure leaped at him* **5** a person: *He was a major figure in the trial* ▷ *verb* **6** To figure in something is to appear or be included in it: *the many people who have figured in his life* **7** (*informal*) If you figure that something is the case, you guess or conclude this: *We figure the fire broke out around four in the morning*

figurehead *noun* the leader of a movement or organization who has no real power

file *noun* **1** a box or folder in which a group of papers or records is kept; also used of the information kept in the file **2** In computing, a file is a stored set of related data with its own name **3** a line of people one behind the other **4** (D&T) A long steel tool with a rough surface, used for smoothing and shaping hard materials ▷ *verb* **5** When someone files a document, they put it in its correct place with similar documents **6** When a group of people file somewhere, they walk one behind the other in a line **7** If you file something, you smooth or shape it with a file

fill *verb* **1** If you fill something or if it fills up, it becomes full **2** If

something fills a need, it satisfies the need: *Ella had in some small way filled the gap left by Molly's absence* **3** To fill a job vacancy is to appoint someone to do that job ▷ *noun* **4** If you have had your fill of something, you do not want any more > **fill in** *verb* **1** If you fill in a form, you write information in the appropriate spaces **2** If you fill someone in, you give them information to bring them up to date

fillet *noun* **1** a strip of tender, boneless beef, veal, or pork **2** a piece of fish with the bones removed ▷ *verb* **3** To fillet meat or fish is to prepare it by cutting out the bones

filling *noun* **1** the soft food mixture inside a sandwich, cake, or pie **2** a small amount of metal or plastic put into a hole in a tooth by a dentist

filly *fillies noun* a female horse or pony under the age of four

film *noun* **1** a series of moving pictures projected onto a screen and shown at the cinema or on television **2** a thin flexible strip of plastic used in a camera to record images when exposed to light **3** a very thin layer of powder or liquid on a surface **4** Plastic film is a very thin sheet of plastic used for wrapping things ▷ *verb* **5** If you film someone, you use a video camera to record their movements on film

filter *noun* **1** a device that allows some substances, lights, or sounds to pass through it, but not others: *a filter against the harmful rays of the sun* ▷ *verb* **2** To filter a substance is to pass it through a filter **3** If something filters somewhere, it gets there slowly or faintly: *Traffic filtered into the city* > **filtration** *noun*

filth *noun* **1** Filth is disgusting dirt and muck **2** People often use the word filth to refer to very bad language or to things that are thought to be crude and offensive > **noun** **filthiness**

fin *noun* a thin, flat structure on the body of a fish, used to help guide it through the water

final *adjective* **1** last in a series or happening at the end of something **2** A decision that is final cannot be changed or questioned ▷ *noun* **3** the last game or contest in a series which decides the overall winner **4** (*in plural*) Finals are the last and most important examinations of a university or college course

finale [fin-**nah**-lee] *noun* the last section of a piece of music or show

finalist *noun* a person taking part in the final of a competition

finalize *or* **finalise** *verb* If you finalize something, you complete all the arrangements for it

finally *adverb* If something finally happens, it happens after a long delay

finance *verb* **1** To finance a project or a large purchase is to provide the money for it ▷ *noun* **2** Finance for something is the money or loans used to pay for it **3** Finance is also the management of money, loans, and investments

financial *adjective* relating to or involving money > **financially** *adverb*

financier *noun* a person who deals with the finance for large businesses

find *verb* finds, finding, found **1** If you find someone or something, you discover them, either as a result of searching or by coming across them unexpectedly **2** If you find that something is the case, you become aware of it or realize it: *I found my fists were clenched* **3** Something that

is found in a particular place typically lives or exists there **4** When a court or jury finds a person guilty or not guilty, they decide that the person is guilty or innocent: *He was found guilty and sentenced to life imprisonment* ▷ *noun* **5** If you describe something or someone as a find, you mean that you have recently discovered them and they are valuable or useful > **finder** *noun*

> **find out** *verb* **1** If you find out something, you learn or discover something that you did not know before **2** If you find someone out, you discover that they have been doing something they should not have been doing

findings *plural noun* Someone's findings are the conclusions they reach as a result of investigation

fine *adjective* **1** very good or very beautiful: *a fine school; fine clothes* **2** satisfactory or suitable: *Pasta dishes are fine if not served with a rich sauce* **3** very narrow or thin **4** A fine detail, adjustment, or distinction is very delicate, exact, or subtle **5** When the weather is fine, it is not raining and is bright or sunny ▷ *noun* **6** a sum of money paid as a punishment ▷ *verb* **7** Someone who is fined has to pay a sum of money as a punishment

finery *noun* Finery is very beautiful clothing and jewellery

finesse [fin-**ness**] *noun* If you do something with finesse, you do it with skill and subtlety

finger *noun* **1** Your fingers are the four long jointed parts of your hands, sometimes including the thumbs ▷ *verb* **2** If you finger something you feel it with your fingers

fingernail *noun* Your fingernails are

the hard coverings at the ends of your fingers

fingerprint noun a mark made showing the pattern on the skin at the tip of a person's finger

finish verb 1 When you finish something, you reach the end of it and complete it 2 When something finishes, it ends or stops ▷ noun 3 The finish of something is the end or last part of it 4 ⓓⓖⓣ The finish that something has is the texture or appearance of its surface: *a healthy, glossy finish*

finite [**fie**-nite] adjective having a particular size or limit which cannot be increased: *There's only finite money to spend*

Finn noun someone who comes from Finland

Finnish adjective 1 belonging or relating to Finland ▷ noun 2 Finnish is the main language spoken in Finland

fir noun a tall, pointed evergreen tree that has thin, needle-like leaves and produces cones

fire noun 1 Fire is the flames produced when something burns 2 a pile or mass of burning material 3 a piece of equipment that is used as a heater: *a gas fire* ▷ verb 4 If you fire a weapon or fire a bullet, you operate the weapon so that the bullet or missile is released 5 If you fire questions at someone, you ask them a lot of questions very quickly 6 (informal) If an employer fires someone, he or she dismisses that person from their job ▷ phrase 7 If someone opens fire, they start shooting

firearm noun a gun

fire brigade noun the organization which has the job of putting out fires

fire engine noun a large vehicle that carries equipment for putting out fires

fire extinguisher noun a metal cylinder containing water or foam for spraying onto a fire

firefighter noun a person whose job is to put out fires and rescue trapped people

fireplace noun the opening beneath a chimney where a fire can be lit

fire station noun a building where fire engines are kept and where firefighters wait to be called out

firework noun a small container of gunpowder and other chemicals which explodes and produces coloured sparks or smoke when lit

firing squad noun a group of soldiers ordered to shoot a person condemned to death

firm adjective 1 Something that is firm does not move easily when pressed or pushed, or when weight is put on it 2 A firm grasp or push is one with controlled force or pressure 3 A firm decision is definite 4 Someone who is firm behaves with authority that shows they will not change their mind ▷ noun 5 a business selling or producing something > **firmly** adverb > **firmness** noun

first adjective 1 done or in existence before anything else 2 more important than anything else: *Her cheese won first prize* ▷ adverb 3 done or occurring before anything else ▷ noun 4 something that has never happened or been done before > **firstly** adverb

first aid noun First aid is medical treatment given to an injured person

first class adjective 1 Something that is first class is of the highest quality or standard **2** First-class accommodation on a train, aircraft, or ship is the best and most expensive type of accommodation **3** First-class postage is quick but more expensive

first-hand *adjective* First-hand knowledge or experience is gained directly rather than from books or other people

First Lady *noun* The First Lady of a country is the wife of its president

first-rate *adjective* excellent

fiscal *adjective* involving government or public money, especially taxes

fish *noun* or *fishes noun* **1** a cold-blooded creature living in water that has a spine, gills, fins, and a scaly skin **2** Fish is the flesh of fish eaten as food ▷ *verb* **3** To fish is to try to catch fish for food or sport **4** If you fish for information, you try to get it in an indirect way > **fishing** *noun* > **fisherman** *noun*

fishery *fisheries noun* an area of the sea where fish are caught commercially

fishmonger *noun* a shopkeeper who sells fish; also the shop itself

fishy *fishier, fishiest adjective* **1** smelling of fish **2** (*informal*) suspicious or doubtful: *He spotted something fishy going on*

fission [rhymes with *mission*] *noun* **1** SCIENCE Fission is the splitting of something into parts **2** Fission is also nuclear fission

fist *noun* a hand with the fingers curled tightly towards the palm

fit *fits, fitting, fitted; fitter, fittest verb* **1** Something that fits is the right shape or size for a particular person or position **2** If you fit something somewhere, you put it there carefully or securely: *Very carefully he fitted the files inside the compartment* **3** If something fits a particular situation, person, or thing, it is suitable or appropriate: *a sentence that fitted the crime* ▷ *noun* **4** The fit of something is how it fits: *This bolt must be a good fit* **5** If someone has a fit, their muscles suddenly start contracting violently and they may lose consciousness **6** A fit of laughter, coughing, anger, or panic is a sudden uncontrolled outburst ▷ *adjective* **7** good enough or suitable: *Housing fit for frail elderly people* **8** Someone who is fit is healthy and has strong muscles as a result of regular exercise > **fitness** *noun* > **fit out** *verb* To fit someone or something out means to provide them with the necessary equipment

fitful *adjective* happening at irregular intervals and not continuous: *a fitful breeze* > **fitfully** *adverb*

fitter *noun* a person who assembles or installs machinery

fitting *adjective* **1** right or suitable: *a fitting reward for his efforts* ▷ *noun* **2** a small part that is fixed to a piece of equipment or furniture **3** If you have a fitting, you try on a garment that is being made to see if it fits properly

five 1 Five is the number 5 ▷ *noun* **2** Fives is a ball game similar to squash, in which you hit the ball with your hand

fix *verb* **1** If you fix something somewhere, you attach it or put it there securely **2** If you fix something broken, you mend it **3** If you fix your attention on something, you concentrate on it **4** If you fix something, you make arrangements for it: *The opening party is fixed for the 24th September* **5** (*informal*) To fix something is to arrange the outcome unfairly or dishonestly ▷ *noun* **6** (*informal*) something that has been unfairly or dishonestly arranged **7** (*informal*) If you are in a fix, you are in a difficult situation > **fixed** *adjective* > **fixedly** *adverb*

fixation *noun* an extreme and obsessive interest in something

fixture *noun* **1** a piece of furniture or equipment that is fixed into position in a house **2** a sports event due to take place on a particular date: *a series of difficult away fixtures*

fizz *verb* Something that fizzes makes a hissing sound

fizzle *verb* Something that fizzles makes a weak hissing or spitting sound

fizzy fizzier, fizziest *adjective* Fizzy drinks have carbon dioxide in them to make them bubbly

fjord [fee-**ord**] *or* **fiord** *noun* a long, narrow inlet of the sea between very high cliffs, especially in Norway

flab *noun* Flab is large amounts of surplus fat on someone's body

flabbergasted *adjective* extremely surprised

flabby flabbier, flabbiest *adjective* Someone who is flabby is rather fat and unfit, with loose flesh on their body

flag flags, flagging, flagged *noun* **1** a rectangular or square cloth which has a particular colour and design, and is used as the symbol of a nation or as a signal ▷ *verb* **2** If you or your spirits flag, you start to lose energy or enthusiasm > **flag down** *verb* If you flag down a vehicle, you signal to the driver to stop

flagrant [**flay**-grant] *adjective* very shocking and bad in an obvious way: *a flagrant defiance of the rules* > **flagrantly** *adverb*

flagship *noun* **1** a ship carrying the commander of the fleet **2** the most modern or impressive product or asset of an organization

flail *verb* If someone's arms or legs flail about, they move in a wild, uncontrolled way

flair *noun* Flair is a natural ability to do something well or stylishly

flak *noun* **1** Flak is anti-aircraft fire **2** If you get flak for doing something, you get a lot of severe criticism

flake *noun* **1** a small, thin piece of something ▷ *verb* **2** When something such as paint flakes, small thin pieces of it come off > **flaky** *adjective* > **flaked** *adjective* > **flake out** *verb* (*informal*) If you flake out, you collapse, go to sleep, or lose consciousness

flamboyant *adjective* behaving in a very showy and confident way > **flamboyance** *noun*

flame *noun* **1** a flickering tongue or blaze of fire **2** A flame of passion, desire, or anger is a sudden strong feeling

flamenco *noun* Flamenco is a type of very lively, fast Spanish dancing, accompanied by guitar music

flammable *adjective* likely to catch fire and burn easily

flan *noun* an open sweet or savoury tart with a pastry or cake base

flank *noun* **1** the side of an animal between the ribs and the hip ▷ *verb* **2** Someone or something that is flanked by a particular thing or person has them at their side: *He was flanked by four bodyguards*

flannel *noun* **1** Flannel is a lightweight woollen fabric **2** a small square of towelling, used for washing yourself. In Australian English it is called a **washer**

flap flaps, flapping, flapped *verb*

1 Something that flaps moves up and down or from side to side with a snapping sound ▷ *noun* **2** a loose piece of something such as paper or skin that is attached at one edge

flare *noun* **1** a device that produces a brightly coloured flame, used especially as an emergency signal ▷ *verb* **2** If a fire flares, it suddenly burns much more vigorously **3** If violence or a conflict flares or flares up, it suddenly starts or becomes more serious

flash *noun* **1** a sudden, short burst of light ▷ *verb* **2** If a light flashes, it shines for a very short period, often repeatedly **3** Something that flashes past moves or happens so fast that you almost miss it **4** If you flash something, you show it briefly: *Rihanna flashed her face at the crowd* ▷ *phrase* **5** Something that happens **in a flash** happens suddenly and lasts a very short time

flashback *noun* a scene in a film, play, or book that returns to events in the past

flashlight *noun* a large, powerful torch

flashy *flashier, flashiest adjective* expensive and fashionable in appearance, in a vulgar way: *flashy clothes*

flask *noun* a bottle used for carrying alcoholic or hot drinks around with you

flat *flats, flatting; flatter, flattest noun* **1** a self-contained set of rooms, usually on one level, for living in **2** In music, a flat is a note or key a semitone lower than that described by the same letter. It is represented by the symbol (♭) ▷ *verb* **3** In Australian and New Zealand English, to flat is to live in a flat: *flatting in London* ▷ *adjective*

4 Something that is flat is level and smooth **5** A flat object is not very tall or deep: *a low, flat building* **6** A flat tyre or ball has not got enough air in it **7** A flat battery has lost its electrical charge **8** A flat refusal or denial is complete and firm **9** Something that is flat is without emotion or interest **10** A flat rate or price is fixed and the same for everyone: *The company charges a flat fee for its advice* **11** A musical instrument or note that is flat is slightly too low in pitch ▷ *adverb* **12** Something that is done in a particular time flat, takes exactly that time: *They would find them in two minutes flat* ▷ *flatly adverb* > **flatness** *noun*

flathead *noun* a common Australian edible fish

flatten *verb* If you flatten something or if it flattens, it becomes flat or flatter

flatter *verb* **1** If you flatter someone, you praise them in an exaggerated way, either to please them or to persuade them to do something **2** If you are flattered by something, it makes you feel pleased and important: *He was very flattered because she liked him* **3** If you flatter yourself that something is the case, you believe, perhaps mistakenly, something good about yourself or your abilities **4** Something that flatters you makes you appear more attractive > **flattering** *adjective*

flattery *noun* Flattery is flattering words or behaviour

flatulence *noun* Flatulence is the uncomfortable state of having too much gas in your stomach or intestine

flaunt *verb* If you flaunt your possessions or talents, you display them too obviously or proudly

flautist noun someone who plays the flute

flavour noun **1** [D G T] The flavour of food is its taste ▷ verb **2** The flavour of something is its distinctive characteristic or quality ▷ verb **3** [D G T] If you flavour food with a spice or herb, you add it to the food to give it a particular taste > **flavouring** noun

flaw noun **1** a fault or mark in a piece of fabric or glass, or in a decorative pattern **2** a weak point or undesirable quality in a theory, plan, or person's character > **flawed** adjective > **flawless** adjective

flax noun Flax is a plant used for making rope and cloth

flea noun a small wingless jumping insect which feeds on blood

fled the past tense and past participle of **flee**

fledgling noun **1** a young bird that is learning to fly ▷ adjective **2** Fledgling means new, or young and inexperienced: the fledgling American President

flee flees, fleeing, fled verb To flee from someone or something is to run away from them

fleece noun **1** A sheep's fleece is its coat of wool ▷ verb **2** (informal) To fleece someone is to swindle them or charge them too much money

fleet noun a group of ships or vehicles owned by the same organization or travelling together

fleeting adjective lasting for a very short time

Flemish noun Flemish is a language spoken in many parts of Belgium

flesh noun **1** Flesh is the soft part of the body **2** The flesh of a fruit or vegetable is the soft inner part that you eat > **fleshy** adjective

flew the past tense of **fly**

flex noun **1** a length of wire covered in plastic, which carries electricity to an appliance ▷ verb **2** If you flex your muscles, you bend and stretch them

flexible adjective **1** able to be bent easily without breaking **2** able to adapt to changing circumstances > **flexibility** noun

flick verb **1** If you flick something, you move it sharply with your finger **2** If something flicks somewhere, it moves with a short sudden movement: His foot flicked forward ▷ noun **3** a short sudden movement or sharp touch with the finger: a sideways flick of the head

flicker verb **1** If a light or a flame flickers, it shines and moves unsteadily ▷ noun **2** a short unsteady light or movement of light: the flicker of candlelight **3** A flicker of a feeling is a very brief experience of it: a flicker of interest

flight noun **1** a journey made by aeroplane **2** Flight is the action of flying or the ability to fly **3** Flight is also the act of running away **4** A flight of stairs or steps is a set running in a single direction

flight attendant noun a person who looks after passengers on an aircraft

flimsy flimsier, flimsiest adjective **1** made of something very thin or weak and not providing much protection **2** not very convincing: flimsy evidence

flinch verb If you flinch, you make a sudden small movement in fear or pain

fling flings, flinging, flung verb **1** If you fling something, you throw it with a lot of force ▷ noun **2** a short period devoted to pleasure and free from any restrictions or rules

flint noun Flint is a hard greyish-black form of quartz. It produces a spark when struck with steel

flip flips, flipping, flipped verb **1** If you flip something, you turn or move it quickly and sharply: *He flipped over the first page* **2** If you flip something, you hit it sharply with your finger or thumb

flippant adjective showing an inappropriate lack of seriousness: *a flippant attitude to money*
> **flippantly** adverb • **flippancy** noun

flipper noun **1** one of the broad, flat limbs of sea animals, for example seals or penguins, used for swimming **2** Flippers are broad, flat pieces of rubber that you can attach to your feet to help you swim

flirt verb **1** If you flirt with someone, you behave as if you are attracted to them but without serious intentions **2** If you flirt with an idea, you consider it without seriously intending to do anything about it
▷ noun **3** someone who often flirts with people > **flirtation** noun
> **flirtatious** adjective

flit flits, flitting, flitted verb To flit somewhere is to fly or move there with quick, light movements

float verb **1** Something that floats is supported by water **2** Something that floats through the air moves along gently, supported by the air **3** If a company is floated, shares are sold to the public for the first time and the company gains a listing on the stock exchange ▷ noun **4** A light object that floats and either supports something or someone or regulates the level of liquid in a tank or cistern **5** In Australian English, a

float is also a vehicle for transporting horses

flock noun **1** a group of birds, sheep, or goats ▷ verb **2** If people flock somewhere, they go there in large numbers

flog flogs, flogging, flogged verb **1** (informal) If you flog something, you sell it **2** To flog someone is to beat them with a whip or stick
> **flogging** noun

flood noun **1** a large amount of water covering an area that is usually dry **2** A flood of something is a large amount of it suddenly occurring: *a flood of angry language* ▷ verb **3** If liquid floods an area, or if a river floods, the water or liquid overflows, covering the surrounding area **4** If people or things flood into a place, they come there in large numbers: *Refugees have flooded into Austria in the last few months*

floodgates phrase To **open the floodgates** is suddenly to give a lot of people the opportunity to do something they could not do before

floodlight noun a very powerful outdoor lamp used to light up public buildings and sports grounds
> **floodlit** adjective

floor noun **1** the part of a room you walk on **2** one of the levels in a building: *the top floor of a factory* **3** the ground at the bottom of a valley, forest, or the sea ▷ verb **4** If a remark or question floors you, you are completely unable to deal with it or answer it

floorboard noun one of the long planks of wood from which a floor is made

flop flops, flopping, flopped verb **1** If someone or something flops, they fall loosely and rather heavily **2** (informal) Something that flops fails ▷ noun **3** (informal) something that is completely unsuccessful

floppy floppier, floppiest adjective tending to hang downwards in a rather loose way: a floppy, outsize jacket

floral adjective patterned with flowers or made from flowers: floral cotton dresses

florid [rhymes with **horrid**] adjective **1** highly elaborate and extravagant: florid language **2** having a red face

florist noun a person or shop selling flowers

floss noun Dental floss is soft silky threads or fibre which you use to clean between your teeth

flotation noun **1** The flotation of a business is the issuing of shares in order to launch it or to raise money **2** Flotation is the act of floating

flotilla [flot-**til**-la] noun a small fleet or group of small ships

flotsam noun Flotsam is rubbish or wreckage floating at sea or washed up on the shore

flounder verb **1** To flounder is to struggle to move or stay upright, for example in water or mud **2** If you flounder in a conversation or situation, you find it difficult to decide what to say or do ▷ noun **3** a type of edible flatfish

flour noun [D G T] Flour is a powder made from finely ground grain, usually wheat, and used for baking and cooking ▷ **floured** adjective > **floury** adjective

flourish verb **1** Something that flourishes develops or functions successfully or healthily **2** If you flourish something, you wave or display it so that people notice it ▷ noun **3** a bold sweeping or waving movement

flout verb If you flout a convention or

law, you deliberately disobey it

flow verb **1** If something flows, it moves or happens in a steady continuous stream ▷ noun **2** A flow of something is a steady continuous movement of it; also the rate at which it flows: a steady flow of complaints

flower noun **1** [SCIENCE] the part of a plant containing the reproductive organs from which the fruit or seeds develop. A **complete flower** is a flower that has all the flower parts, particularly the stamens and pistils; an **incomplete flower** is a flower without one or more of the main flower parts; a **perfect flower** is a flower that has both stamens and pistils ▷ verb **2** When a plant flowers, it produces flowers

flowery adjective Flowery language is full of elaborate expressions

flown the past participle of **fly**

flu noun Flu is an illness similar to a very bad cold, which causes headaches, sore throat, weakness, and aching muscles. Flu is short for 'influenza'

fluctuate verb Something that fluctuates is irregular and changeable: fluctuating between feeling well and not so well > **fluctuation** noun

flue noun a pipe which takes fumes and smoke away from a stove or boiler

fluent adjective **1** able to speak a foreign language correctly and without hesitation **2** able to express yourself clearly and without hesitation ▷ **fluently** adverb

fluff noun **1** Fluff is soft, light, woolly threads or fibres bunched together ▷ verb **2** If you fluff something up or out, you brush or shake it to make it seem larger and lighter: Fluff the rice up with a fork before serving > **fluffy** adjective

fluid noun **1** a liquid ▷ adjective **2** Fluid movement is smooth and flowing **3** A fluid arrangement or plan is flexible and without a fixed structure > **fluidity** noun

fluke noun an accidental success or piece of good luck

flung the past tense and past participle of **fling**

fluorescent [floo-er-**ess**-nt] adjective **1** having a very bright appearance when light is shone on it, as if it is shining itself: fluorescent yellow dye **2** A fluorescent light is in the form of a tube and shines with a hard bright light

fluoride noun Fluoride is a mixture of chemicals that is meant to prevent tooth decay

flurry flurries noun a short rush of activity or movement

flush noun **1** A flush is a rosy red colour: The blushes are cream with a pink flush **2** In cards, a flush is a hand all of one suit **3** If you flush, your face goes red **4** If you flush a toilet or something such as a pipe, you force water through it to clean it ▷ adjective **5** (informal) Someone who is flush has plenty of money **6** Something that is flush with a surface is level with it or flat against it

flustered adjective If you are flustered, you feel confused, nervous, and rushed

flute noun a musical wind instrument consisting of a long metal tube with holes and keys. It is held sideways to the mouth and played by blowing across a hole in its side

flutter verb **1** If something flutters, it flaps or waves with small, quick

movements ▷ noun **2** If you are in a flutter, you are excited and nervous **3** (informal) If you have a flutter, you have a small bet

flux noun Flux is a state of constant change: stability in a world of flux

fly flies, flying, flew, flown noun **1** an insect with two pairs of wings **2** The front opening on a pair of trousers is the fly or the flies **3** The fly or fly sheet of a tent is either a flap at the entrance or an outer layer providing protection from rain ▷ verb **4** When a bird, insect, or aircraft flies, it moves through the air **5** If someone or something flies, they move or go very quickly **6** If you fly at someone or let fly at them, you attack or criticize them suddenly and aggressively > **flying** adjective, noun > **flyer** noun

fly-fishing noun Fly-fishing is a method of fishing using imitation flies as bait

flying fox noun **1** a large bat that eats fruit, found in Australia and Africa **2** In Australia and New Zealand, a cable car used to carry people over rivers and gorges

flyover noun a structure carrying one road over another at a junction or intersection

foal noun **1** a young horse ▷ verb **2** When a female horse foals, she gives birth

foam noun **1** Foam is a mass of tiny bubbles **2** D G T Foam is light spongy material used, for example, in furniture or packaging **3** When something foams, it forms a mass of small bubbles

focus focuses or focusses, focusing or focussing, focused or focussed; focuses or foci verb **1** If you focus your eyes or an instrument on an object, you adjust them so that the image is clear ▷ **noun 2** The focus of something is its centre of attention: *The focus of the conversation had moved around during the meal* > **focal** *adjective*

fodder *noun* Fodder is food for farm animals or horses

foe *noun* an enemy

foetus [**fee**-tus] or **fetus** *noun* an unborn child or animal in the womb > **foetal** *adjective*

fog fogs, fogging, fogged *noun* **1** Fog is a thick mist of water droplets suspended in the air ▷ **verb 2** If glass fogs up, it becomes clouded with steam or condensation > **foggy** *adjective*

foil *verb* **1** If you foil someone's attempt at something, you prevent them from succeeding ▷ *noun* **2** Foil is thin, paper-like sheets of metal used to wrap food **3** Something that is a good foil for something else contrasts with it and makes its good qualities more noticeable **4** a thin, light sword with a button on the tip, used in fencing

foist *verb* If you foist something on someone, you force or impose it on them

fold *verb* **1** If you fold something, you bend it so that one part lies over another **2** (*informal*) If a business folds, it fails and closes down **3** In cooking, if you fold one ingredient into another, you mix it in gently ▷ *noun* **4** a crease or bend in paper or cloth **5** a small enclosed area for sheep

folder *noun* **1** a thin piece of folded cardboard for keeping loose papers together **2** In computing, a folder is a named area of a computer disk where you can group together files and subdirectories. It is also called a **directory**

foliage *noun* Foliage is leaves and plants

folk *plural noun* **1** Folk or folks are people ▷ *adjective* **2** Folk music, dance, or art is traditional or representative of the ordinary people of an area

folklore *noun* Folklore is the traditional stories and beliefs of a community

follicle *noun* a small sac or cavity in the body: *hair follicles*

follow *verb* **1** If you follow someone, you move along behind them. If you follow a path or a sign, you move along in that direction **2** Something that follows a particular thing happens after it **3** Something that follows is true or logical as a result of something else being the case: *Just because she is pretty, it doesn't follow that she can sing* **4** If you follow instructions or advice, you do what you are told **5** If you follow an explanation or the plot of a story, you understand each stage of it **6** If you follow a person on a social networking site, you regularly read the messages he or she writes > **follow up** *verb* If you follow up a suggestion or discovery, you find out more about it or act upon it

follower *noun* The followers of a person or belief are the people who support them

folly follies *noun* Folly is a foolish act or foolish behaviour

fond *adjective* **1** If you are fond of someone or something, you like them **2** A fond hope or belief is thought of with happiness but is unlikely to happen > **fondly** *adverb* > **fondness** *noun*

fondle *verb* To fondle something is to stroke it affectionately

font *noun* a large stone bowl in a

church that holds the water for baptisms

food noun Food is any substance consumed by an animal or plant to provide energy

food chain noun a series of living things which are linked because each one feeds on the next one in the series. For example, a plant may be eaten by a rabbit which may be eaten by a fox

foodstuff noun anything used for food

fool noun 1 someone who behaves in a silly or stupid way 2 a dessert made from fruit, cream, and sugar whipped together ▷ verb 3 If you fool someone, you deceive or trick them

foolhardy adjective foolish and involving too great a risk

foolish adjective very silly or unwise > **foolishly** adverb > **foolishness** noun

foolproof adjective Something that is foolproof is so well designed or simple to use that it cannot fail

foot feet noun 1 the part of your body at the end of your leg 2 the bottom, base, or lower end of something: the foot of the mountain 3 a unit of length equal to 12 inches or about 30.5 centimetres 4 ENGLISH In poetry, a foot is the basic unit of rhythm containing two or three syllables ▷ adjective 5 A foot brake, pedal, or pump is operated by your foot

footage noun Footage is a length of film: library footage of prison riots

football noun 1 Football is any game in which the ball can be kicked, such as soccer, Australian Rules, rugby union, and American football 2 a ball used in any of these games > **footballer** noun

foothills plural noun Foothills are hills at the base of mountains

foothold noun 1 a place where you can put your foot when climbing 2 a position from which further progress can be made

footing noun 1 Footing is a secure grip by or for your feet: He missed his footing and fell flat 2 a footing is the basis or nature of a relationship or situation: Steps to put the nation on a war footing

footman footmen noun a male servant in a large house who wears uniform

footnote noun a note at the bottom of a page or an additional comment giving extra information

footpath noun a path for people to walk on

footprint noun a mark left by a foot or shoe

footstep noun the sound or mark made by someone walking

for preposition 1 meant to be given to or used by a particular person, or done in order to help or benefit them: private beaches for their exclusive use 2 'For' is used when explaining the reason, cause, or purpose of something: This is my excuse for going to Italy 3 You use 'for' to express a quantity, time, or distance: I'll play for ages; the only house for miles around 4 If you are for something, you support it or approve of it: votes for or against independence

forage verb When a person or animal forages, they search for food

foray noun 1 a brief attempt to do or get something: her first foray into acting 2 an attack or raid by soldiers

forbid forbids, forbidding, forbade, forbidden verb If you forbid someone to do something, you order them not to do it > **forbidden** adjective

force *verb* **1** To force someone to do something is to make them do it **2** To force something is to use violence or great strength to move or open it ▷ *noun* **3** a pressure to do something, sometimes with the use of violence or great strength **4** The force of something is its strength or power: *The force of the explosion shook buildings* **5** a person or thing that has a lot of influence or effect: *She became the dominant force in tennis* **6** an organized group of soldiers or police **7** [SCIENCE] In physics, force is a pushing or pulling influence that changes a body from a state of rest to one of motion, or changes its rate of motion ▷ *phrase* **8** A law or rule that is **in force** is currently valid and must be obeyed

forceful *adjective* powerful and convincing: *a forceful, highly political lawyer* > **forcefully** *adverb*

forceps *plural noun* Forceps are a pair of long tongs or pincers used by a doctor or surgeon

forcible *adjective* **1** involving physical force or violence **2** convincing and making a strong impression: *a forcible reminder* > **forcibly** *adverb*

ford *noun* **1** a shallow place in a river where it is possible to cross on foot or in a vehicle ▷ *verb* **2** To ford a river is to cross it on foot or in a vehicle

fore *phrase* Something or someone that comes **to the fore** becomes important or popular

forearm *noun* the part of your arm between your elbow and your wrist

forebear *noun* Your forebears are your ancestors

foreboding *noun* a strong feeling of approaching disaster

forecast forecasts, forecasting, forecast *or* forecasted *noun* **1** a prediction of what will happen, especially a statement about what the weather will be like ▷ *verb* **2** To forecast an event is to predict what will happen

forecourt *noun* an open area at the front of a petrol station or large building

forefinger *noun* the finger next to your thumb

forefront *noun* The forefront of something is the most important and progressive part of it

forego foregoes, foregoing, forewent, foregone *or* **forgo** *verb* If you forego something pleasant, you give it up or do not insist on having it

foregoing *phrase (formal)* You can say **the foregoing** when talking about something that has just been said: *The foregoing discussion has highlighted the difficulties*

foregone conclusion *noun* A foregone conclusion is a result or conclusion that is bound to happen

foreground *noun* [ART] In a picture, the foreground is the part that seems nearest to you

forehand *noun, adjective* [PE] a stroke in tennis, squash, or badminton made with the palm of your hand facing in the direction that you hit the ball

forehead *noun* the area at the front of your head, above your eyebrows and below your hairline

foreign *adjective* **1** belonging to or involving countries other than your own: *foreign coins; foreign travel* **2** unfamiliar or uncharacteristic: *Such daft enthusiasm was foreign to him* **3** A foreign object has got into something, usually by accident, and should not be there: *a foreign object in my eye* > **foreigner** *noun*

foreman foremen *noun* **1** a person in

charge of a group of workers, for example on a building site **2** The foreman of a jury is the spokesman

foremost *adjective* The foremost of a group of things is the most important or the best

forensic *adjective* **1** relating to or involving the scientific examination of objects involved in a crime **2** relating to or involving the legal profession

forerunner *noun* The forerunner of something is the person who first introduced or achieved it, or the first example of it

foresee foresees, foreseeing, foresaw, foreseen *verb* If you foresee something, you predict or expect that it will happen > **foreseeable** *adjective*

foresight *noun* Foresight is the ability to know what is going to happen in the future

forest *noun* a large area of trees growing close together

forestry *noun* Forestry is the study and work of growing and maintaining forests

foretaste *noun* a slight taste or experience of something in advance

forever *adverb* permanently or continually

foreword *noun* an introduction in a book

forfeit *verb* **1** If you forfeit something, you have to give it up as a penalty > *noun* **2** something that you have to give up or do as a penalty

forge *noun* **1 a** a place where a blacksmith works making metal goods by hand > *verb* **2** To forge metal is to hammer and bend it into shape while hot **3** To forge a relationship is to create a strong and lasting relationship **4** Someone

who forges money, documents, or paintings makes illegal copies of them **5** To forge ahead is to progress quickly

forgery forgeries *noun* Forgery is the crime of forging money, documents, or paintings; also something that has been forged > **forger** *noun*

forget forgets, forgetting, forgot, forgotten *verb* **1** If you forget something, you fail to remember or think about it **2** If you forget yourself, you behave in an unacceptable, uncontrolled way > **forgetful** *adjective*

forgive forgives, forgiving, forgave, forgiven *verb* If you forgive someone for doing something bad, you stop feeling angry and resentful towards them > **forgiving** *adjective*

forgiveness *noun* the act of forgiving

forgo another spelling of **forego**

fork *noun* **1 a** pronged instrument used for eating food **2** a large garden tool with three or four prongs **3** a y-shaped junction or division in a road, river, or branch > *verb* **4** To fork something is to move or turn it with a fork > **fork out** *verb* (*informal*) If you fork out for something, you pay for it, often unwillingly

forlorn *adjective* **1** lonely, unhappy, and pitiful **2** desperate and without any expectation of success: *a forlorn fight for a draw* > **forlornly** *adverb*

form *noun* **1** A particular form of something is a type or kind of it: *a new form of weapon* **2** The form of something is the shape or pattern of something: *a brooch in the form of a bright green lizard* **3** a sheet of paper with questions and spaces for you to fill in the answers **4** a class in a school > *verb* **5** The things that form something are the things it consists of: *events that were to form the basis of her novel* **6** When someone forms something or when it forms, it is created, organized, or started

formal adjective **1** correct, serious, and conforming to accepted conventions: *a very formal letter of apology* **2** official and publicly recognized: *the first formal agreement of its kind* > **formally** adverb

formaldehyde [for-**mal**-di-hide] noun Formaldehyde is a poisonous, strong-smelling gas, used in the manufacture of plastics and for preserving biological specimens. Its formula is HCHO

formality formalities noun an action or process that is carried out as part of an official procedure

format noun the way in which something is arranged or presented

formation noun **1** The formation of something is the process of developing and creating it **2** the pattern or shape of something

formative adjective having an important and lasting influence on character and development: *the formative days of his young manhood*

former adjective **1** happening or existing before now or in the past: *a former tennis champion* ▷ noun **2** You use 'the former' to refer to the first of two things just mentioned: *If I had to choose between happiness and money, I would have the former* > **formerly** adverb

formidable adjective very difficult to deal with or overcome, and therefore rather frightening or impressive: *formidable enemies*

formula formulae *or* formulas noun **1** MATHS A group of letters, numbers, and symbols which stand for a mathematical or scientific rule **2** SCIENCE a list of quantities of substances that when mixed make another substance, for example in chemistry **3** a plan or set of rules for dealing with a particular problem: *my secret formula for keeping myself in trim*

formulate verb If you formulate a plan or thought, you create it and express it in a clear and precise way

forsake forsakes, forsaking, forsook, forsaken verb To forsake someone or something is to give up or abandon them

fort noun **1** a strong building built for defence ▷ phrase **2** If you **hold the fort** for someone, you manage their affairs while they are away

forte [for-tay] adverb **1** MUSIC In music, forte is an instruction to play or sing something loudly ▷ noun **2** If something is your forte, you are particularly good at doing it

forth adverb **1** out and forward from a starting place: *Christopher Columbus set forth on his epic voyage of discovery* **2** into view: *He brought forth a slim volume of his newly published verse*

forthcoming adjective **1** planned to happen soon: *their forthcoming holiday* **2** given or made available: *Medical aid might be forthcoming* **3** willing to give information: *He was not too forthcoming about this*

forthright adjective Someone who is forthright is direct and honest about their opinions and feelings

fortification noun Fortifications are buildings, walls, and ditches used to protect a place

fortitude noun Fortitude is calm and patient courage

fortnight noun a period of two weeks > **fortnightly** adverb, adjective

fortress noun a castle or well-protected town built for defence

fortuitous [for-**tyoo**-it-uss] adjective happening by chance or good luck: a fortuitous winning goal

fortunate adjective 1 Someone who is fortunate is lucky 2 Something that is fortunate brings success or advantage ▷ **fortunately** adverb

fortune noun 1 Fortune or good fortune is good luck 2 A fortune is a large amount of money ▷ phrase 3 If someone **tells your fortune**, they predict your future

forty forties the number 40 > **fortieth** adjective

forum noun 1 a place or meeting in which people can exchange ideas and discuss public issues 2 a website where people discuss a particular topic 3 a square in Roman towns where people met to discuss business and politics

forward adverb, adjective 1 Forward or forwards means in the front or towards the front: A photographer moved forward to capture the moment 2 Forward means in or towards a future time: a positive atmosphere of looking forward and making fresh starts 3 Forward or forwards also means developing or progressing: The new committee would push forward government plans ▷ adverb 4 If someone or something is put forward, they are suggested as being suitable for something ▷ verb 5 If you forward a letter that you have received, you send it on to the person to whom it is addressed at their new address ▷ noun 6 In a game such as football or hockey, a forward is a player in an attacking position

fossil noun SCIENCE the remains or impression of an animal or plant from a previous age, preserved in rock > **fossilize** verb

fossil fuel noun GEOGRAPHY Fossil fuels are fuels such as coal, oil, and natural gas, which have been formed by turning animals and plants from millions of years ago

foster verb 1 If someone fosters a child, they are paid to look after the child for a period, but do not become its legal parent 2 If you foster something such as an activity or an idea, you help its development and growth by encouraging people to do or think it: to foster and maintain this goodwill > **foster child** noun > **foster home** noun > **foster parent** noun

fought the past tense and past participle of **fight**

foul adjective 1 Something that is foul is very unpleasant, especially because it is dirty, wicked, or obscene ▷ verb 2 To foul something is to make it dirty, especially with faeces: Dogs must not be allowed to foul the pavement ▷ noun 3 In sport, a foul is an act of breaking the rules

found 1 Found is the past tense and past participle of **find** ▷ verb 2 If someone founds an organization or institution, they start it and set it up

foundation noun 1 The foundation of a belief or way of life is the basic ideas or attitudes on which it is built 2 a solid layer of concrete or bricks in the ground, on which a building is built to give it a firm base 3 an organization set up by money donated to or left in someone's will for research or charity

founder noun 1 The founder of an institution or organization is the person who sets it up ▷ verb 2 If something founders, it fails

foundry foundries noun a factory where metal is melted and cast

fountain noun an ornamental structure consisting of a jet of water forced into the air by a pump

fountain pen noun a pen which is supplied with ink from a container inside the pen

four 1 the number 4 ▷ phrase 2 If you are on all fours, you are on your hands and knees

four-poster noun a bed with a tall post at each corner supporting a canopy and curtains

fourteen the number 14
> **fourteenth** adjective

fourth adjective The fourth item in a series is the one counted as number four

fowl noun a bird such as chicken or duck that is kept or hunted for its meat or eggs

fox noun 1 a dog-like wild animal with reddish-brown fur, a pointed face and ears, and a thick tail ▷ verb 2 If something foxes you, it is too confusing or puzzling for you to understand

foyer [foy-ay] noun a large area just inside the main doors of a cinema, hotel, or public building

fracas [frak-ah] noun a rough noisy quarrel or fight

fracking noun Fracking is the extraction of oil or gas by forcing liquid into rock at high pressure

fraction noun 1 MATHS In arithmetic, a fraction is a part of a whole number. A **proper fraction** is a fraction in which the number above the line is lower than the number below it; an **improper fraction** has the greater number above the line: ¾ is a proper fraction 2 a tiny proportion or amount of something: an area a fraction of the size of London ▷ **fractional** adjective
> **fractionally** adverb

fractious adjective When small children are fractious, they become upset or angry very easily, often because they are tired

fracture noun 1 a crack or break in something, especially a bone ▷ verb 2 If something fractures, it breaks

fragile adjective easily broken or damaged: fragile glass; a fragile relationship ▷ **fragility** noun

fragment noun 1 a small piece or part of something ▷ verb 2 If something fragments, it breaks into small pieces or different parts
> **fragmentation** noun
> **fragmented** adjective

fragmentary adjective made up of small pieces, or parts that are not connected: fragmentary notes in a journal

fragrance noun a sweet or pleasant smell

fragrant adjective Something that is fragrant smells sweet or pleasant

frail adjective 1 Someone who is frail is not strong or healthy 2 Something that is frail is easily broken or damaged ▷ **frailty** noun

frame noun 1 the structure surrounding a door, window, or picture 2 an arrangement of connected bars over which something is built 3 The frames of a pair of glasses are the wire or plastic parts that hold the lenses 4 Your frame is your body: his large frame 5 one of the many separate photographs of which a cinema film is made up ▷ verb 6 To frame a picture is to put it into a frame: I've framed pictures I've pulled out of magazines 7 The language something is framed in is the language used to express it

framework noun 1 D&T a structure acting as a support or frame 2 a set of rules, beliefs, or ideas which you use to decide what to do

franc noun the main unit of currency in Switzerland, and formerly in France and Belgium. A franc is worth 100 centimes

franchise noun 1 The franchise is the right to vote in an election: *a franchise that gave the vote to less than 2% of the population* 2 the right given by a company to someone to allow them to sell its goods or services

frank adjective If you are frank, you say things in an open and honest way > **frankly** adverb > **frankness** noun

frantic adjective If you are frantic, you behave in a wild, desperate way because you are anxious or frightened > **frantically** adverb

fraternal adjective 'Fraternal' is used to describe friendly actions and feelings between groups of people: *an affectionate fraternal greeting*

fraternity fraternities noun 1 Fraternity is friendship between groups of people 2 a group of people with something in common: *the golfing fraternity*

fraud noun 1 Fraud is the crime of getting money by deceit or trickery 2 something that deceives people in an illegal or immoral way 3 Someone who is not what they pretend to be

fraudulent adjective dishonest or deceitful: *fraudulent use of credit cards*

fraught adjective If something is fraught with problems or difficulties, it is full of them: *Modern life was fraught with hazards*

fray verb 1 If cloth or rope frays, its threads or strands become worn

and it is likely to tear or break ▷ noun 2 a fight or argument

freak noun 1 someone whose appearance or behaviour is very unusual ▷ adjective, noun 2 A freak event is very unusual and unlikely to happen: *a freak snowstorm in summer*

free freer, freest; frees, freeing, freed adjective 1 not controlled or limited: *the free flow of aid; free trade* 2 Someone who is free is no longer a prisoner 3 To be free of something unpleasant is not to have it: *She wanted her aunt's life to be free of worry* 4 If someone is free, they are not busy or occupied 5 If a place, seat, or machine is free, it is not occupied or not being used: *Are you free for dinner?* 5 If something is free, you can have it without paying for it ▷ verb 6 If you free someone or something that is imprisoned, fastened, or trapped, you release them

freedom noun 1 If you have the freedom to do something, you have the scope or are allowed to do it: *We have the freedom to decide our own futures* 2 When prisoners gain their freedom, they escape or are released 3 When there is freedom from something unpleasant, people are not affected by it: *freedom from guilt*

freehold noun the right to own a house or piece of land for life without conditions

freelance adjective, adverb A freelance journalist or photographer is not employed by one organization, but is paid for each job he or she does

freely adverb Freely means without restriction: *the pleasure of being able to walk about freely*

free-range adjective Free-range eggs are laid by hens that can move and feed freely on an area of open ground

freestyle noun Freestyle refers to sports competitions, especially swimming, in which competitors can use any style or method

freeway noun In Australia, South Africa, and the United States, a road designed for fast-moving traffic

free will phrase If you do something **of your own free will**, you do it by choice and not because you are forced to

freeze freezes, freezing, froze, frozen verb 1 SCIENCE When a liquid freezes, it becomes solid because it is very cold 2 If you freeze, you suddenly become very still and quiet 3 DRAMA To freeze the action in a film is to stop the film at a particular frame 4 If you freeze food, you put it in a freezer to preserve it 5 When wages or prices are frozen, they are officially prevented from rising ▷ noun 6 an official action taken to prevent wages or prices from rising 7 a period of freezing weather

freezer noun a large refrigerator which freezes and stores food for a long time

freezing adjective extremely cold

freight noun Freight is goods moved by lorries, ships, or other transport; also the moving of these goods

French adjective 1 belonging or relating to France ▷ noun 2 French is the main language spoken in France, and is also spoken by many people in Belgium, Switzerland, and Canada

Frenchman Frenchmen noun a man who comes from France ▷ **Frenchwoman** noun

frenetic adjective Frenetic behaviour is wild and excited ▷ **frenetically** adverb

frenzy frenzies noun If someone is in a frenzy, their behaviour is wild and uncontrolled ▷ **frenzied** adjective

frequency frequencies noun 1 The frequency of an event is how often it happens: He was not known to call anyone with great frequency 2 SCIENCE The frequency of a sound or radio wave is the rate at which it vibrates 3 MATHS In statistics, the frequency of a particular class is the number of individuals in it

frequent adjective [**free-kwuhnt**] 1 often happening: His visits were frequent; They move at frequent intervals ▷ verb [free-**kwent**] 2 If you frequent a place, you go there often ▷ **frequently** adverb

fresco frescoes noun a picture painted on a plastered wall while the plaster is still wet

fresh adjective 1 A fresh thing replaces a previous one, or is added to it: footprints filled in by fresh snow; fresh evidence 2 Fresh food is newly made or obtained, and not tinned or frozen 3 Fresh water is not salty, for example the water in a stream 4 If the weather is fresh, it is fairly cold and windy 5 If you are fresh from something, you have experienced it recently: a teacher fresh from college ▷ **freshly** adverb ▷ **freshness** noun

freshwater adjective 1 A freshwater lake or pool contains water that is not salty 2 A freshwater creature lives in a river, lake, or pool that is not salty

fret frets, fretting, fretted verb 1 If you fret about something, you worry about it ▷ noun 2 The frets on a stringed instrument, such as a guitar, are the metal ridges across its neck ▷ **fretful** adjective

friction noun 1 SCIENCE the force that stops things from moving freely when they rub against each other **2** Friction between people is disagreement and quarrels

Friday noun the day between Thursday and Saturday

fridge noun the same as a **refrigerator**

friend noun Your friends are people you know well and like to spend time with

friendly friendlier, friendliest adjective **1** If you are friendly to someone, you behave in a kind and pleasant way to them **2** People who are friendly with each other like each other and enjoy spending time together > **friendliness** noun

friendship noun **1** Your friendships are the special relationships that you have with your friends **2** Friendship is the state of being friends with someone

frieze noun **1** a strip of decoration or carving along the top of a wall or column **2** ART a picture on a long strip of paper which is hung along a wall

frigate noun a small, fast warship

fright noun Fright is a sudden feeling of fear

frighten verb If something frightens you, it makes you afraid

frightened adjective having feelings of fear about something

frightening adjective causing someone to feel fear

frightful adjective very bad or unpleasant: a frightful bully > **frightfully** adverb

frigid adjective Frigid behaviour is cold and unfriendly: frigid stares

frill noun a strip of cloth with many folds, attached to something as a decoration > **frilly** adjective

fringe noun **1** the hair that hangs over a person's forehead **2** a decoration on clothes and other objects, consisting of a row of hanging strips or threads **3** The fringes of a place are the parts farthest from its centre: the western fringe of the Amazon basin > **fringed** adjective

frisky friskier, friskiest adjective A frisky animal or child is energetic and wants to have fun

fritter noun **1** Fritters consist of food dipped in batter and fried: apple fritters > verb **2** If you fritter away your time or money, you waste it on unimportant things

frivolous adjective Someone who is frivolous behaves in a silly or light-hearted way, especially when they should be serious or sensible > **frivolity** noun

frock noun (old-fashioned) a dress

frog noun a small amphibious creature with smooth skin, prominent eyes, and long back legs which it uses for jumping

frolic frolics, frolicking, frolicked verb When animals or children frolic, they run around and play in a lively way

from preposition **1** You use 'from' to say that the source, origin, or starting point of something is: a call from a mobile phone; people from a city 100 miles away **2** If you take something from an amount, you reduce the amount by that much: A sum of money was wrongly taken from his account **3** You also use 'from' when stating the range of something: a score from one to five

front noun **1** The front of something is the part that faces forward **2** In a war, the front is the place where two armies are fighting **3** In meteorology, a front is the line where a mass of cold air meets a mass of warm air **4** A front is an outward appearance, often one that is false: *I put up a brave front; He's no more than a respectable front for some very dubious happenings* ▷ *phrase* **5** In front means ahead or further forward **6** If you do something in front of someone, you do it when they are present > **frontal** *adjective*

frontage *noun* The frontage of a building is the wall that faces a street

frontier *noun* a border between two countries

frost *noun* When there is a frost, the temperature outside falls below freezing

frostbite *noun* Frostbite is damage to your fingers, toes, or ears caused by extreme cold

frosty frostier, frostiest *adjective* **1** If it is frosty, the temperature outside is below freezing point **2** If someone is frosty, they are unfriendly or disapproving > **frostily** *adverb*

froth *noun* **1** Froth is a mass of small bubbles on the surface of a liquid ▷ *verb* **2** If a liquid froths, small bubbles appear on its surface > **frothy** *adjective*

frown *verb* **1** If you frown, you move your eyebrows closer together, because you are annoyed, worried, or concentrating ▷ *noun* **2** a cross expression on someone's face

froze the past tense of **freeze**

frozen **1** Frozen is the past participle of **freeze** ▷ *adjective* **2** If you say are frozen, you mean you are extremely cold

frugal *adjective* **1** Someone who is frugal spends very little money **2** A frugal meal is small and cheap > **frugally** *adverb* > **frugality** *noun*

fruit *noun* **1** the part of a plant that

develops after the flower and contains the seeds. Many fruits are edible **2** (*in plural*) The fruits of something are its good results: *the fruits of his labours*

fruitful *adjective* Something that is fruitful has good and useful results: *a fruitful experience*

fruitless *adjective* Something that is fruitless does not achieve anything: *a fruitless effort*

fruit salad *noun* a mixture of pieces of different fruits served in a juice as a dessert

fruity fruitier, fruitiest *adjective* Something that is fruity smells or tastes of fruit

frustrate *verb* **1** If something frustrates you, it prevents you doing what you want and makes you upset and angry: *Everyone gets frustrated with their work* **2** To frustrate something such as a plan is to prevent it: *She hopes to frustrate the engagement of her son* > **frustrated** *adjective* > **frustrating** *adjective* > **frustration** *noun*

fry fries, frying, fried *verb* **1** When you fry food, you cook it in a pan containing hot fat or oil

fuchsia [fyoo-sha] *noun* a plant or small bush with pink, purple, or white flowers that hang downwards

fudge *noun* **1** Fudge is a soft brown sweet made from butter, milk, and sugar ▷ *verb* **2** If you fudge something, you avoid making clear or definite decisions or statements about it: *He was carefully fudging his message*

fuel fuels, fuelling, fuelled *noun* **1** Fuel is a substance such as coal or petrol that is burned to provide heat or power ▷ *verb* **2** A machine or vehicle that is fuelled by a substance works by burning the substance as a fuel: *power stations fuelled by wood*

fugitive [fyoo-jit-tiv] *noun* someone who is running away or hiding, especially from the police

-ful *suffix* 1 '-ful' is used to form adjectives with the meaning 'full of': *careful* 2 '-ful' is used to form nouns which mean 'the amount needed to fill': *spoonful*

fulcrum fulcrums or fulcra *noun* DGT the point at which something is balancing or pivoting

fulfil fulfils, fulfilling, fulfilled *verb* 1 If you fulfil a promise, hope, or duty, you carry it out or achieve it 2 If something fulfils you, it gives you satisfaction > **fulfilling** *adjective* > **fulfilment** *noun*

full *adjective* 1 containing or having as much as it is possible to hold: *His room is full of posters* 2 complete or whole: *They had taken a full meal; a full 20 years later* 3 loose and made from a lot of fabric: *full sleeves* 4 rich and strong: *a full, fruity wine* ▷ *adverb* 5 completely and directly: *Turn the taps full on* ▷ *verb* 6 Something that has been done or described in full has been dealt with completely > **fullness** *noun* > **fully** *adverb*

full-blooded *adjective* having great commitment and enthusiasm: *a full-blooded sprint for third place*

full-blown *adjective* complete and fully developed: *a full-blown love of music*

full moon *noun* the moon when it appears as a complete circle

full stop *noun* the punctuation mark (.) used at the end of a sentence and after an abbreviation or initial

full-time *adjective* 1 involving work for the whole of each normal working week ▷ *noun* 2 In games

such as football, full time is the end of the match

fully-fledged *adjective* completely developed: *I was a fully-fledged and mature human being*

fulsome *adjective* exaggerated and elaborate, and often sounding insincere: *His most fulsome praise was reserved for his mother*

fumble *verb* If you fumble, you feel or handle something clumsily

fume *noun* 1 Fumes are unpleasant-smelling gases and smoke, often toxic, that are produced by burning and by some chemicals ▷ *verb* 2 If you are fuming, you are very angry

fun *noun* 1 Fun is pleasant, enjoyable, and light-hearted activity ▷ *phrase* 2 If you **make fun** of someone, you tease them or make jokes about them

function *noun* 1 The function of something or someone is their purpose or the job they have to do 2 a large formal dinner, reception, or party 3 MATHS A function is a variable whose other value depends on the value of other independent variables. 'y is a function of x' is written y = f(x) ▷ *verb* 4 When something functions, it operates or works

functional *adjective* 1 relating to the way something works 2 designed for practical use rather than for decoration or attractiveness: *Feminine clothing has never been designed to be functional* 3 working properly: *fully functional smoke alarms*

fund *noun* 1 an amount of available money, usually for a particular purpose: *a pension fund* 2 A fund of something is a lot of it: *He had a fund of hilarious tales on the subject* ▷ *verb* 3 Someone who funds something provides money for it: *research funded by pharmaceutical companies*

fundamental *adjective* **1** basic and central: *the fundamental right of freedom of choice; fundamental changes* ▷ *noun* **2** The fundamentals of something are its most basic and important parts: *teaching small children the fundamentals of road safety*

funeral [fyoo-ner-al] *noun* RE a ceremony or religious service for the burial or cremation of a dead person

funereal [few-nee-ree-al] *adjective* depressing and gloomy

funfair *noun* a place of entertainment with things like amusement arcades and rides

fungicide *noun* a chemical used to kill or prevent fungus

fungus fungi *or* funguses *noun* SCIENCE a plant such as a mushroom or mould that does not have leaves and grows on other living things ▷ **fungal** *adjective*

funk *verb* **1** (*old-fashioned, informal*) If you funk something, you fail to do it because of fear ▷ *noun* **2** Funk is a style of music with a strong rhythm based on jazz and blues

funnel funnels, funnelling, funnelled *noun* **1** an open cone narrowing to a tube, used to pour substances into containers **2** a metal chimney on a ship or steam engine ▷ *verb* **3** If something is funnelled somewhere, it is directed through a narrow space into that place

funny funnier, funniest *adjective* **1** strange or puzzling: *You get a lot of funny people coming into the libraries* **2** causing amusement or laughter: *a funny old film* ▷ **funnily** *adverb*

fur *noun* **1** Fur is the soft thick body hair of many animals **2** a coat made

from an animal's fur ▷ **furry** *adjective*

furious *adjective* **1** extremely angry **2** involving great energy, effort, or speed: *the furious speed of technological development* ▷ **furiously** *adverb*

furlong *noun* a unit of length equal to 220 yards or about 201.2 metres. Furlong originally referred to the length of the average furrow

furnace *noun* a container for a very large, hot fire used, for example, in the steel industry for melting ore

furnish *verb* **1** If you furnish a room, you put furniture into it **2** (*formal*) If you furnish someone with something, you supply or provide it for them

furnishings *plural noun* The furnishings of a room or house are the furniture and fittings in it

furniture *noun* Furniture is movable objects such as tables, chairs, and wardrobes

furore [fyoo-roh-ree] *noun* an angry and excited reaction or protest

furrow *noun* **1** a long, shallow trench made by a plough ▷ *verb* **2** When someone furrows their brow, they frown

further **1** a comparative form of **far** ▷ *adjective* **2** additional or more: *There was no further rain* ▷ *adverb* **3** If you further something, you help it to progress: *He wants to further his acting career*

further education *noun* Further education is education at a college after leaving school, but not at a university

furthermore *adverb* (*formal*) used to introduce additional information: *There is no record of such a letter. Furthermore it is company policy never to send such letters*

furthest a superlative form of **far**

furtive *adjective* secretive, sly, and cautious: *a furtive smile* ▷ **furtively** *adverb*

fury *noun* Fury is violent or extreme anger

fuse *noun* **1** a safety device in a plug or electrical appliance consisting of a piece of wire which melts to stop the electric current if a fault occurs **2** a long cord attached to some types of simple bomb which is lit to detonate ▷ *verb* **3** When an electrical appliance fuses, it stops working because the fuse has melted to protect it **4** If two things fuse, they join or become combined: *Christianity slowly fused with existing beliefs*

fuselage [**fyoo**-zil-ahj] *noun* the main part of an aeroplane or rocket

fusion *noun* **1** Fusion is what happens when two substances join by melting together **2** Fusion is also nuclear fusion ▷ *adjective* **3** Fusion is used to refer to food or a style of cooking that brings together ingredients or cooking techniques from several different countries

fuss *noun* **1** Fuss is unnecessarily anxious or excited behaviour ▷ *verb* **2** If someone fusses, they behave with unnecessary anxiety and concern for unimportant things

fussy *fussier, fussiest adjective* **1** likely to fuss a lot: *He was unusually fussy about keeping things perfect* **2** with too much elaborate detail or decoration: *fussy chiffon evening wear*

futile *adjective* having no chance of success: *a futile attempt to calm the storm* ▷ **futility** *noun*

future *noun* **1** The future is the period of time after the present **2** Something that has a future is likely to succeed: *She sees no future in a modelling career* ▷ *adjective* **3** relating to or occurring at a time after the present: *to predict future events* **4** ENGLISH The future tense of a verb is the tense used to express something that will happen in the future

futuristic *adjective* very modern and strange, as if belonging to a time in the future: *futuristic cars*

fuzz *noun* **1** short fluffy hair ▷ *plural noun* **2** (slang) The fuzz are the police ▷ **fuzzy** *adjective*

g

g an abbreviation for 'gram' or 'grams'

gable *noun* Gables are the triangular parts at the top of the outside walls at each end of a house

gadget *noun* a small machine or tool ▷ **gadgetry** *noun*

Gaelic [**gay**-lik] *noun* a language spoken in some parts of Scotland and Ireland

gaffe [gaf] *noun* a social blunder or mistake

gaffer *noun* (informal) a boss

gag gags, gagging, gagged *noun* **1** a strip of cloth that is tied round someone's mouth to stop them speaking **2** (informal) a joke told by a comedian ▷ *verb* **3** To gag someone means to put a gag round their mouth **4** If you gag, you choke and nearly vomit

gaggle *noun* **1** a group of geese

2 (*informal*) a noisy group: *a gaggle of schoolboys*

gaiety [**gay**-yet-tee] *noun* liveliness and fun

gaily *adverb* in a happy and cheerful way

gain *verb* **1** If you gain something, you get it gradually: *I spent years at night school trying to gain qualifications* **2** If you gain from a situation, you get some advantage from it **3** If you gain on someone, you gradually catch them up ▷ *noun* **4** an increase: *a gain in speed* **5** an advantage that you get for yourself: *People use whatever influence they have for personal gain*

gait *noun* Someone's gait is their way of walking: *an awkward gait*

gala *noun* a special public celebration or performance: *the Olympics' opening gala*

galaxy galaxies *noun* [SCIENCE] A galaxy is an enormous group of stars that extends over many millions of miles. The galaxy to which the earth's solar system belongs is called the Milky Way > **galactic** *adjective*

gale *noun* an extremely strong wind

gall [*rhymes with* **ball**] *noun* **1** If someone has the gall to do something, they have enough courage or impudence to do it: *He even has the gall to visit her* ▷ *verb* **2** If something galls you, it makes you extremely annoyed

gallant *adjective* **1** brave and honourable: *They have put up a gallant fight for pensioners' rights* **2** polite and considerate towards women > **gallantly** *adverb* > **gallantry** *noun*

gall bladder *noun* an organ in your body which stores bile and which is next to your liver

gallery galleries *noun* **1** [ART] a building or room where works of art are shown **2** In a theatre or large hall, the gallery is a raised area at the back or sides: *the public gallery in Parliament*

galley *noun* **1** a kitchen in a ship or aircraft **2** a ship, driven by oars, used in ancient and medieval times

Gallic [**gal**-lik] *adjective* (*formal or literary*) French

gallon *noun* a unit of liquid volume equal to eight pints or about 4.55 litres

gallop *verb* **1** When a horse gallops, it runs very fast, so that during each stride all four feet are off the ground at the same time ▷ *noun* **2** a very fast run

gallows *noun* A gallows is a framework on which criminals used to be hanged

galore *adjective* in very large numbers: *chocolates galore*

galvanized *or* **galvanised** *adjective* Galvanized metal has been coated with zinc by an electrical process to protect it from rust

gambit *noun* something which someone does to gain an advantage in a situation: *Commentators are calling the plan a clever political gambit*

gamble *verb* **1** When people gamble, they bet money on the result of a game or race **2** If you gamble something, you risk losing it in the hope of gaining an advantage: *The company gambled everything on the new factory* ▷ *noun* **3** If you take a gamble, you take a risk in the hope of gaining an advantage > **gambler** *noun* > **gambling** *noun*

game *noun* **1** an enjoyable activity with a set of rules which is played by individuals or teams against each other **2** an enjoyable imaginative activity played by small children: *childhood games of cowboys and Indians* **3** You might describe something as a game when it is designed to gain advantage: *the political game* **4** Game is wild animals or birds that are hunted for sport or for food **5** (*in plural*) Games are sports played at school or in a competition ▷ *adjective* **6** (*informal*) Someone who is game is willing to try something unusual or difficult > **gamely** *adverb*

gamekeeper *noun* a person employed to look after game animals and birds on a country estate

gamut [**gam**-mut] *noun* (*formal*) The gamut of something is the whole range of things that can be included in it: *the whole gamut of human emotions*

gang *noun* a group of people who join together for some purpose, for example to commit a crime > **gang up** (*informal*) If people gang up on you, they join together to oppose you

gangrene [**gang**-green] *noun* Gangrene is decay in the tissues of part of the body, caused by inadequate blood supply > **gangrenous** *adjective*

gangster *noun* a violent criminal who is a member of a gang

gap *noun* **1** a space between two things or a hole in something solid **2** a period of time **3** A gap between things, people, or ideas is a great difference between them: *the gap between fantasy and reality*

gape *verb* **1** If you gape at someone or something, you stare at them with your mouth open in surprise **2** Something that gapes is wide open: *gaping holes in the wall*

garage *noun* **1** a building where a car can be kept **2** a place where cars are repaired and where petrol is sold

garb *noun* (*formal*) Someone's garb is their clothes: *his usual garb of a dark suit*

garbage *noun* **1** Garbage is rubbish, especially household rubbish **2** (*informal*) If you say something is garbage, you mean it is nonsense

garbled *adjective* Garbled messages are jumbled and the details may be wrong

garden *noun* **1** an area of land next to a house, where flowers, fruit, or vegetables are grown **2** (*in plural*) Gardens are a type of park in a town or around a large house > **gardening** *noun*

gardener *noun* a person who looks after a garden as a job or as a hobby

garish [**gair**-rish] *adjective* bright and harsh to look at: *garish bright red boots*

garland *noun* a circle of flowers and leaves which is worn around the neck or head

garlic *noun* Garlic is the small white bulb of an onion-like plant which has a strong taste and smell and is used in cooking

garment *noun* a piece of clothing

garnish *noun* **1** something such as a sprig of parsley, that is used in cooking for decoration ▷ *verb* **2** To garnish food means to decorate it with a garnish

garrison *noun* a group of soldiers stationed in a town in order to guard it; also used of the buildings in which these soldiers live

gas *noun*; *verb* gasses; gasses, gassed, gassed *noun* **1** SCIENCE any airlike substance that is not liquid or solid, such as oxygen or the gas used as a fuel in heating **2** In American

English, gas is petrol ▷ verb **3** To gas people or animals means to kill them with poisonous gas

> **WORD TIP**
> The plural of the noun gas is gases. The verb forms of gas are spelt with a double s

gash noun **1** a long, deep cut ▷ verb **2** If you gash something, you make a long, deep cut in it

gasoline noun In American English, gasoline is petrol

gasp verb **1** If you gasp, you quickly draw in your breath through your mouth because you are surprised or in pain ▷ noun **2** a sharp intake of breath through the mouth

gastric adjective occurring in the stomach or involving the stomach: gastric pain

gate noun **1** a barrier which can open and shut and is used to close the entrance to a garden or field **2** The gate at a sports event is the number of people who have attended it

gatecrash verb If you gatecrash a party, you go to it when you have not been invited

gateway noun **1** an entrance through a wall or fence where there is a gate **2** Something that is considered to be the entrance to a larger or more important thing can be described as the gateway to the larger thing: New York is the great gateway to America

gather verb **1** When people gather, they come together in a group **2** If you gather a number of things, you bring them together in one place **3** If something gathers speed or strength, it gets faster or stronger **4** If you gather something, you learn it, often from what someone says

gathering noun a meeting of people

who have come together for a particular purpose

gauche [**gohsh**] adjective (formal) socially awkward

gaudy gaudier, gaudiest [**gaw-dee**] adjective very colourful in a vulgar way

gauge [**gayj**] verb **1** If you gauge something, you estimate it or calculate it: He gauged the wind at over 30 knots ▷ noun **2** a piece of equipment that measures the amount of something: a rain gauge **3** something that is used as a standard by which you judge a situation: They see profit as a gauge of efficiency **4** On railways, the gauge is the distance between the two rails on a railway line

gaunt adjective A person who looks gaunt is thin and bony

gauntlet noun **1** Gauntlets are long thick gloves worn for protection, for example by motorcyclists ▷ phrase **2** If you **throw down the gauntlet**, you challenge someone **3** If you **run the gauntlet**, you have an unpleasant experience in which you are attacked or criticized by people

gave the past tense of **give**

gay adjective **1** Someone who is gay is homosexual **2** (old-fashioned) Gay people or places are lively and full of fun ▷ noun **3** a homosexual person

gaze verb If you gaze at something, you look steadily at it for a long time

gazette noun a newspaper or journal

GB an abbreviation for **Great Britain**

GCSE In Britain, the GCSE is an examination taken by school students aged 15 and 16. GCSE is an abbreviation for 'General Certificate of Secondary Education'

gear noun **1** [D G T] a piece of machinery which controls the rate at which energy is converted into movement. Gears in vehicles control the speed and power of the vehicle **2** PE The gear for an activity is the clothes and equipment that you need for it ▷ **verb 3** If someone or something is geared to a particular event or purpose, they are prepared for it

geek noun (informal) a person who is obsessive about an interest or hobby, especially computers

geese the plural of **goose**

gel gels, gelling, gelled **[jel]** noun **1** a smooth, soft, jelly-like substance: *shower gel* ▷ **verb 2** If a liquid gels, it turns into a gel **3** If a vague thought or plan gels, it becomes more definite

gelatine or **gelatin [jel-lat-tin]** noun a clear tasteless substance, obtained from meat and bones, used to make liquids firm and jelly-like

gem noun **1** a jewel or precious stone **2** You can describe something or someone that is extremely good or beautiful as a gem: *A gem of a novel*

Gemini [jem-in-nye] noun Gemini is the third sign of the zodiac, represented by a pair of twins. People born between May 21st and June 20th are born under this sign

gen noun (informal) The gen on something is information about it

gender noun **1** PSHE The gender of a person or animal is whether they are male or female: *the female gender* **2** the classification of nouns as masculine, feminine, and neuter in certain languages

gene [jeen] noun one of the parts of a living cell which controls the physical characteristics of an organism and which are passed on from one generation to the next

general adjective **1** relating to the whole of something or to most things in a group: *your general health* **2** true, suitable, or relevant in most situations: *the general truth of science* **3** including or involving a wide range of different things: *a general hospital* **4** having complete responsibility over a wide area of work or a large number of people: *the general secretary* ▷ **noun 5** an army officer of very high rank ▷ **phrase 6 In general** means usually > **generally** adverb

general election noun an election for a new government, which all the people of a country may vote in

generalize or **generalise** verb To generalize means to say that something is true in most cases, ignoring minor details > **generalization** noun

general practitioner noun a doctor who works in the community rather than in a hospital

generate verb To generate something means to create or produce it: *using wind power to generate electricity*

generation noun all the people of about the same age; also the period of time between one generation and the next, usually considered to be about 25–30 years

generator noun a machine which produces electricity from another form of energy such as wind or water power

generic adjective A generic term is a name that applies to all the members of a group of similar things

generosity noun the willingness to give money, time, or help

generous adjective **1** PSHE A generous person is very willing to give money or time **2** Something that is generous is very large: *a generous waist* > **generously** *adverb* > **generosity** *noun*

genesis *noun* (formal) The genesis of something is its beginning

genetics *noun* Genetics is the science of the way that characteristics are passed on from generation to generation by means of genes > **genetic** *adjective* > **genetically** *adverb*

genial *adjective* cheerful, friendly, and kind > **genially** *adverb*

genie [jee-nee] *noun* a magical being that obeys the wishes of the person who controls it

genitals *plural noun* The genitals are the reproductive organs. The technical name is genitalia > **genital** *adjective*

genius *noun* 1 a highly intelligent, creative, or talented person 2 Genius is great intelligence, creativity, or talent: *a poet of genius*

genocide [jen-nos-side] *noun* (formal) Genocide is the systematic murder of all members of a particular race or group

genome [jee-nome] *noun* SCIENCE all of the genes contained in a single cell of an organism

genre [jahn-ra] *noun* ENGLISH LIBRARY (formal) a particular style in literature or art

genteel *adjective* very polite and refined

Gentile [jen-tile] *noun* a person who is not Jewish

gentle *adjective* mild and calm; not violent or rough: *a gentle man* > **gently** *adverb* > **gentleness** *noun*

gentleman gentlemen *noun* a man who is polite and well-educated; also a polite way of referring to any man > **gentlemanly** *adjective*

gentry *plural noun* The gentry are people from the upper classes

genuine [jen-yoo-in] *adjective* 1 real and not false or pretend: *a genuine smile; genuine silver* 2 A genuine person is sincere and honest > **genuinely** *adverb* > **genuineness** *noun*

genus genera [jee-nuss] *noun* SCIENCE In biology, a genus is a class of animals or closely related plants. It is smaller than a family and larger than a species

geography *noun* the study of the physical features of the earth, together with the climate, natural resources, and population in different parts of the world > **geographic** or > **geographical** *adjective* > **geographically** *adverb*

geology *noun* the study of the earth's structure, especially the layers of rock and soil that make up the surface of the earth > **geological** *adjective* > **geologist** *noun*

geometric or **geometrical** *adjective* 1 consisting of regular lines and shapes, such as squares, triangles, and circles: *bold geometric designs* 2 involving geometry

geometry *noun* Geometry is the branch of mathematics that deals with lines, angles, curves, and spaces

Georgian *adjective* belonging to or typical of the time from 1714 to 1830, when George I to George IV reigned in Britain

geranium *noun* a garden plant with red, pink, or white flowers

geriatric [jer-ree-at-rik] *adjective* 1 relating to the medical care of old people: *a geriatric nurse* 2 Someone or something that is geriatric is very old: *a geriatric donkey* ▷ *noun* 3 an old person, especially as a patient > **geriatrics** *noun*

germ noun **1** a very small organism that causes disease **2** (formal) The germ of an idea or plan is the beginning of it

German adjective **1** belonging or relating to Germany ▷ noun **2** someone who comes from Germany **3** German is the main language spoken in Germany and Austria and is also spoken by many people in Switzerland

Germanic adjective **1** typical of Germany or the German people **2** The Germanic group of languages includes English, Dutch, German, Danish, Swedish, and Norwegian

germinate verb **1** a When a seed germinates, it starts to grow **2** When an idea or plan germinates, it starts to develop ▷ **germination** noun

gestation [jes-**tay**-shn] noun (technical) Gestation is the time during which a foetus is growing inside its mother's womb

gesture noun **1** a movement of your hands or head that conveys a message or feeling **2** an action symbolizing something: a gesture of support ▷ verb **3** If you gesture, you move your hands or head in order to communicate a message or feeling

get gets, getting, got verb **1** Get often means the same as become: People draw the curtains once it gets dark **2** If you get into a particular situation, you put yourself in that situation: We are going to get into a hopeless muddle **3** If you get something done, you do it or someone does it for you: You can get your homework done in time **4** If you get somewhere, you go there: I must get home **5** If you get something, you fetch or are given it: I'll get us all a

cup of coffee; I got your message **6** If you get a joke or get the point of something, you understand it **7** If you get a train, bus, or plane, you travel on it: You can get a bus ▷ **get across** verb If you get an idea across, you make people understand it ▷ **get at** verb **1** If someone is getting at you, they are criticizing you in an unkind way **2** If you ask someone what they are getting at, you are asking them to explain what they mean ▷ **get away with** verb If you get away with something dishonest, you are not found out or punished for doing it ▷ **get by** verb If you get by, you have just enough money to live on ▷ **get on** verb **1** If two people get on well together, they like each other's company **2** If you get on with a task, you do it ▷ **get over with** verb If you want to get something unpleasant over with, you want it to be finished quickly ▷ **get through** verb **1** If you get through to someone, you make them understand what you are saying **2** If you get through to someone on the telephone, you succeed in talking to them

getaway noun an escape made by criminals

get-together noun (informal) an informal meeting or party

Ghanaian [gah-**nay**-an] adjective **1** belonging or relating to Ghana ▷ noun **2** someone who comes from Ghana

ghastly ghastlier, ghastliest adjective extremely horrible and unpleasant: a ghastly crime; ghastly food

ghetto ghettoes or ghettos noun a part of a city where many poor people of a particular race live

ghost noun the spirit of a dead

person, believed to haunt people or places

ghoulish [gool-ish] adjective very interested in unpleasant things such as death and murder

giant noun **1** a huge person in a myth or legend ▷ adjective **2** much larger than other similar things: giant prawns; a giant wave

gibberish [jib-ir-ish] noun Gibberish is speech that makes no sense at all

gibe or **jibe** noun an insulting remark

giddy giddier, giddiest adjective If you feel giddy, you feel unsteady on your feet usually because you are ill > **giddily** adverb

gift noun **1** present **2** a natural skill or ability: a gift for comedy

gifted adjective having a special ability: gifted tennis players

gig noun a rock or jazz concert

gigabyte noun [COMPUTING] a unit of storage in a computer, equal to 1024 megabytes

gigantic adjective extremely large

giggle verb **1** To giggle means to laugh in a silly or nervous way ▷ noun **2** a silly or nervous laugh > **giggly** adjective

gilded adjective Something which is gilded is covered with a thin layer of gold

gill noun **1** [gil] The gills of a fish are the organs on its sides which it uses for breathing **2** [jil] a unit of liquid volume equal to one quarter of a pint or about 0.142 litres

gilt noun **1** a thin layer of gold ▷ adjective **2** covered with a thin layer of gold: a gilt writing-table

gimmick noun a device that is not really necessary but is used to attract interest: All pop stars need a good gimmick > **gimmicky** adjective

gin noun Gin is a strong, colourless alcoholic drink made from grain

and juniper berries

ginger noun **1** Ginger is a plant root with a hot, spicy flavour, used in cooking ▷ adjective **2** bright orange or red: ginger hair

gingerbread noun Gingerbread is a sweet, ginger-flavoured cake

gingerly adverb If you move gingerly, you move cautiously: They walked gingerly down the stairs

giraffe noun a tall, four-legged African mammal with a very long neck

girl noun a female child > **girlhood** noun > **girlish** adjective

girlfriend noun Someone's girlfriend is the woman or girl with whom they are having a romantic relationship

girth noun The girth of something is the measurement round it

gist [jist] noun the general meaning or most important points in a piece of writing or speech

give gives, giving, gave, given verb **1** If you give someone something, you hand it to them or provide it for them: I gave her a tape; George gave me my job **2** 'Give' is also used to express physical actions and speech: He gave a fierce smile; Rosa gave a lovely performance **3** If you give a party or a meal, you are the host at it **4** If something gives, it collapses under pressure ▷ noun **5** If material gives, it will bend or stretch when pulled or put under pressure ▷ phrase **6** You use **give or take** to indicate that an amount you are mentioning is not exact: About two years, give or take a month or so **7** If something **gives way** to something else, it is replaced by it **8** If something **gives way**, it collapses > **give in** verb If you give in, you admit that you are defeated

> **give out** verb If something gives out, it stops working: *the electricity gave out* > **give up** verb 1 If you give something up, you stop doing it: *I can't give up my job* 2 If you give up, you admit that you cannot do something 3 If you give someone up, you let the police know where they are hiding

given 1 the past participle of **give** ▷ adjective 2 fixed or specified: *My style can change at any given moment*

glacier [**glass**-yer] noun a huge frozen river of slow-moving ice

glad gladder, gladdest adjective happy and pleased: *They'll be glad to get away from it all* > **gladly** adverb > **gladness** noun

gladiator noun In ancient Rome, gladiators were slaves trained to fight in arenas to provide entertainment

glamour noun The glamour of a fashionable or attractive person or place is the charm and excitement that they have: *the glamour of Paris* > **glamorous** adjective

glance verb 1 If you glance at something, you look at it quickly 2 If one object glances off another, it hits it at an angle and bounces away in another direction ▷ noun 3 a quick look

gland noun an organ in your body, such as the thyroid gland and the sweat glands, which either produce chemical substances for your body to use, or which help to get rid of waste products from your body > **glandular** adjective

glare verb 1 If you glare at someone, you look at them angrily ▷ noun 2 a hard, angry look 3 Glare is extremely bright light

glass noun 1 Glass is a hard, transparent substance that is easily broken, used to make windows and bottles 2 a container for drinking out of, made from glass

glasses plural noun Glasses are two lenses in a frame, which some people wear over their eyes to improve their eyesight

glassy glassier, glassiest adjective 1 smooth and shiny like glass: *glassy water* 2 A glassy look shows no feeling or expression

glaze noun 1 A glaze on pottery or on food is a smooth shiny surface ▷ verb 2 To glaze pottery or food means to cover it with a glaze 3 To glaze a window means to fit a sheet of glass into a window frame > **glaze over** verb If your eyes glaze over, they lose all expression, usually because you are bored

glazed adjective Someone who has a glazed expression looks bored

gleam verb 1 If something gleams, it shines and reflects light ▷ noun 2 a pale shining light

glean verb To glean information means to collect it from various sources

glee noun (old-fashioned) Glee is joy and delight > **gleeful** adjective > **gleefully** adverb

glen noun a deep, narrow valley, especially in Scotland or Ireland

glide verb 1 To glide means to move smoothly: *cygnets gliding up the stream* 2 When birds or aeroplanes glide, they float on air currents

glider noun an aeroplane without an engine, which flies by floating on air currents

glimmer noun 1 a faint, unsteady light 2 A glimmer of a feeling or quality is a faint sign of it: *a glimmer of intelligence*

glimpse noun 1 a brief sight of something: *They caught a glimpse of*

g

their hero ▷ **verb 2** If you glimpse something, you see it very briefly

glint verb **1** If something glints, it reflects quick flashes of light ▷ noun **2** a quick flash of light

glint in someone's eye is a brightness expressing some emotion: *A glint of mischief in her blue-grey eyes*

glisten [gliss-'n] verb If something glistens, it shines or sparkles

glitter verb **1** If something glitters, it shines in a sparkling way: *a glittering crown* ▷ noun **2** Glitter is sparkling light

gloat verb If you gloat, you cruelly show your pleasure about your own success or someone else's failure: *Their rivals were gloating over their triumph*

global adjective concerning the whole world: *a global tour*

globalization *or* **globalisation** noun **1** the process by which a company expands so that it can do business internationally **2** the process by which cultures throughout the world become more and more similar for a variety of reasons including increased global business and better international communications

global warming noun (GEOGRAPHY) an increase in the world's overall temperature believed to be caused by the greenhouse effect

globe noun **1** a ball-shaped object, especially one with a map of the earth on it **2** (GEOGRAPHY) You can refer to the world as the globe **3** In South African, Australian, and New Zealand English, a globe is an electric light bulb

gloom noun **1** Gloom is darkness or dimness **2** Gloom is also a feeling of unhappiness or despair

gloomy gloomier, gloomiest

adjective **1** dark and depressing **2** feeling very sad > **gloomily** adverb

glorify glorifies, glorifying, glorified verb If you glorify someone or something, you make them seem better than they really are: *Their aggressive music glorifies violence* > **glorification** noun

glorious adjective **1** beautiful and impressive to look at: *glorious beaches* **2** very pleasant and giving a feeling of happiness: *glorious sunshine* **3** involving great fame and success: *a glorious career* > **gloriously** adverb

glory glories, glorying, gloried noun **1** Glory is fame and admiration for an achievement **2** something considered splendid or admirable: *the true glories of the Alps* ▷ verb **3** If you glory in something, you take great delight in it

gloss noun **1** Gloss is a bright shine on a surface **2** Gloss is also an attractive appearance which may hide less attractive qualities: *to put a positive gloss on the events*

glossary glossaries noun (LIBRARY) a list of explanations of specialist words, usually found at the back of a book

glossy glossier, glossiest adjective smooth and shiny: *glossy lipstick; glossy paper*

glove noun Gloves are coverings which you wear over your hands for warmth or protection

glow noun **1** a dull, steady light **2** a strong feeling of pleasure or happiness ▷ verb **3** If something glows, it shines with a dull, steady light: *A light glowed behind the curtains* **4** If you are glowing, you look very happy or healthy

glowing adjective A glowing description praises someone or something very highly: *a glowing character reference*

glucose *noun* Glucose is a type of sugar found in plants and that animals and people make in their bodies from food to provide energy

glue glues, gluing *or* glueing, glued *noun* **1** a substance used for sticking things together ▷ *verb* **2** If you glue one object to another, you stick them together using glue

glum glummer, glummest *adjective* miserable and depressed ▷ **glumly** *adverb*

glut *noun* a greater quantity of things than is needed

gluten [gloo-ten] *noun* a sticky protein found in cereal grains, such as wheat

gnarled [narld] *adjective* old, twisted, and rough: *gnarled fingers*

gnome [nome] *noun* a tiny old man in fairy stories

go goes, going, went, gone *verb* **1** If you go somewhere, you move or travel there **2** You can use 'go' to mean become: *She felt she was going mad* **3** You can use 'go' to describe the state that someone or something is in: *Our arrival went unnoticed* **4** If something goes well, it is successful. If it goes badly, it is unsuccessful **5** If you are going to do something, you will do it **6** If a machine or clock goes, it works and is not broken **7** You use 'go' before giving the sound something makes or before quoting a song or saying: *The bell goes ding-dong* **8** If something goes on something or to someone, it is allotted to them **9** If one thing goes with another, they are appropriate together **10** If one number goes into another, it can be divided into it **11** If you go back on a promise or agreement, you do not

do what you promised or agreed **12** If someone goes for you, they attack you **13** If you go in for something, you decide to do it as your job **14** If you go out with someone, you have a romantic relationship with them **15** If you go over something, you think about it or discuss it carefully ▷ *noun* **16** an attempt at doing something ▷ *phrase* **17** If someone is always **on the go**, they are always busy and active **18** To **go** means remaining: *I've got one more year of my course to go* > **go down** *verb* **1** If something goes down well, people like it. If it goes down badly, they do not like it **2** If you go down with an illness, you catch it > **go off** *verb* **1** If you go off someone or something, you stop liking them **2** If a bomb goes off, it explodes > **go on** *verb* **1** If you go on doing something, you continue to do it **2** If you go on about something, you keep talking about it in a rather boring way **3** Something that is going on is happening > **go through** *verb* **1** If you go through an unpleasant event, you experience it **2** If a law or agreement goes through, it is approved and becomes official **3** If you go through with something, you do it even though it is unpleasant

goad *verb* If you goad someone, you encourage them to do something by making them angry or excited: *He had goaded the man into near violence*

go-ahead *noun* If someone gives you the go-ahead for something, they give you permission to do it

goal *noun* **1** the space, in games like football or hockey, into which the players try to get the ball in order to score a point **2** an instance of this **3** Your goal is something that you hope to achieve

goalkeeper noun the player, in games like soccer or hockey, who stands in the goal and tries to stop the other team from scoring

goat noun an animal, like a sheep, with coarse hair, a beard, and horns

gob noun (informal) Your gob is your mouth

gobble verb **1** If you gobble food, you eat it very quickly **2** When a turkey gobbles, it makes a loud gurgling sound

god proper noun **1** RE The name God is given to the being who is worshipped by Christians, Jews, and Muslims as the creator and ruler of the world ▷ noun **2** any of the beings that are believed in many religions to have power over an aspect of life or a part of the world: *Dionysus, the Greek god of wine* **3** If someone is your god, you admire them very much **4** (in plural) In a theatre, the gods are the highest seats farthest from the stage

goddess noun a female god

godsend noun something that comes unexpectedly and helps you very much

goggles plural noun Goggles are special glasses that fit closely round your eyes to protect them

going noun The going is the conditions that affect your ability to do something: *He found the going very slow indeed*

gold noun **1** Gold is a valuable, yellow-coloured metallic element. It is used for making jewellery and as an international currency. Its atomic number is 79 and its symbol is Au **2** 'Gold' is also used to mean things that are made of gold

▷ adjective **3** bright yellow

golden adjective **1** gold in colour: *golden syrup* **2** made of gold: *a golden chain* **3** excellent or ideal: *a golden hero*

golden rule noun a very important rule to remember in order to be able to do something successfully

goldfish noun a small orange-coloured fish, often kept in ponds or bowls

golf noun Golf is a game in which players use special clubs to hit a small ball into holes that are spread out over a large area of grassy land

▷ **golfer** noun

golf course noun an area of grassy land where people play golf

gondola [**gon**-dol-la] noun a long narrow boat used in Venice, which is propelled with a long pole

gone the past participle of **go**

gong noun a flat, circular piece of metal that is hit with a hammer to make a loud sound, often as a signal for something

good better, best adjective **1** pleasant, acceptable, or satisfactory: *good news; a good film* **2** skilful or successful: *good at art* **3** kind, thoughtful, and loving: *She was grateful to him for being so good to her* **4** well-behaved: *Have the children been good?* **5** used to emphasize something: *a good few million pounds* ▷ noun **6** Good is moral and spiritual justice and virtue: *the forces of good and evil* **7** Good also refers to anything that is desirable or beneficial as opposed to harmful: *The break has done me good* **8** (in plural) Goods are objects that people own or that are sold in shops: *leather goods* ▷ phrase **9** For good means for ever **10** As good as means almost: *The election is as good as decided*

goodbye *interjection* You say goodbye when you are leaving someone or ending a telephone conversation

Good Friday *noun* RE Good Friday is the Friday before Easter, when Christians remember the crucifixion of Christ

good-natured *adjective* friendly, pleasant, and even-tempered

goodness *noun* **1** Goodness is the quality of being kind ▷ *interjection* **2** People say 'Goodness!' or 'My goodness!' when they are surprised

goodwill *noun* Goodwill is kindness and helpfulness: *Messages of goodwill were exchanged*

goody goodies *noun* (*informal*) **1** (*in plural*) goodies are enjoyable things, often food **2** You can call a hero in a film or book a goody

goose geese *noun* a fairly large bird with webbed feet and a long neck

gooseberry gooseberries *noun* a round, green berry that grows on a bush and has a sharp taste

gore *verb* **1** If an animal gores someone, it wounds them badly with its horns or tusks ▷ *noun* **2** Gore is clotted blood from a wound

gorge *noun* **1** a deep, narrow valley ▷ *verb* **2** If you gorge yourself, you eat a lot of food greedily

gorgeous *adjective* extremely pleasant or attractive: *a gorgeous man*

gorilla *noun* a very large, strong ape with very dark fur

gorse *noun* Gorse is a dark green wild shrub that has sharp prickles and small yellow flowers

gory gorier, goriest *adjective* Gory situations involve people being injured in horrible ways

gospel *noun* **1** The Gospels are the four books in the New Testament which describe the life and teachings of Jesus Christ **2** a set of ideas that someone strongly believes in: *The chef wants to spread the gospel of good food* ▷ *adjective* **3** Gospel music is a style of religious music popular among Black Christians in the United States

gossip gossips, gossiping, gossiped *noun* **1** Gossip is informal conversation, often concerning people's private affairs **2** Someone who is a gossip enjoys talking about other people's private affairs ▷ *verb* **3** If you gossip, you talk informally with someone, especially about other people

got 1 Got is the past tense and past participle of **get 2** You can use 'have got' instead of the more formal 'have' when talking about possessing things: *The director has got a map* **3** You can use 'have got to' instead of the more formal 'have to' when talking about something that must be done: *He has got to win*

gouge [gowj] *verb* **1** If you gouge a hole in something, you make a hole in it with a pointed object **2** If you gouge something out, you force it out of position with your fingers or a sharp tool

gourmet [goor-may] *noun* a person who enjoys good food and drink and knows a lot about it

gout *noun* Gout is a disease which causes someone's joints to swell painfully, especially in their toes

govern *verb* **1** To govern a country means to control it **2** Something that governs a situation influences it: *Our thinking is as much governed by habit as by behaviour*

governess *noun* a woman who is employed to teach the children in a family and who lives with the family

government noun [HISTORY] **1** The government is the group of people who govern a country **2** Government is the control and organization of a country
> **governmental** adjective

governor noun **1** a person who controls and organizes a state or an institution **2** In Australia, the Governor is the representative of the King or Queen in a State

gown noun **1** a long, formal dress **2** a long, dark cloak worn by people such as judges and lawyers

GP an abbreviation for **general practitioner**

grab grabs, grabbing, grabbed verb **1** If you grab something, you take it or pick it up roughly **2** If you grab an opportunity, you take advantage of it eagerly **3** (informal) If an idea grabs you, it excites you ⊳ noun **4** A grab at an object is an attempt to grab it

grace noun **1** Grace is an elegant way of moving **2** Grace is also a pleasant, kind way of behaving **3** Grace is also a short prayer of thanks said before a meal **4** Dukes and archbishops are addressed as 'Your Grace' and referred to as 'His Grace' ⊳ verb **5** Something that graces a place makes it more attractive **6** If someone important graces an event, they kindly agree to be present at it ⊳ **graceful** adjective
> **gracefully** adverb

gracious adjective **1** kind, polite, and pleasant ⊳ interjection **2** 'Good gracious' is an exclamation of surprise ⊳ **graciously** adverb

grade verb **1** To grade things means to arrange them according to quality ⊳ noun **2** The grade of something is its quality **3** The mark that you get for an exam or piece of

written work **4** Your grade in a company or organization is your level of importance or your rank

gradient noun **1** a slope or the steepness of a slope **2** [MATHS] In maths, the gradient of a side of a triangle is the steepness of the line from its height to its base

gradual adjective happening or changing slowly over a long period of time

gradually adverb happening or changing slowly over a long period of time

graduate noun [grad-yoo-it] **1** a person who has completed a first degree at a university or college ⊳ verb [grad-yoo-ate] **2** When students graduate, they complete a first degree at a university or college **3** To graduate from one thing to another means to progress gradually towards the second thing
> **graduation** noun

graffiti [graf-**fee**-tee] noun Graffiti is slogans or drawings scribbled on walls

graft noun **1** a piece of living tissue which is used to replace by surgery a damaged or unhealthy part of a person's body **2** (informal) Graft is hard work ⊳ verb **3** To graft one thing to another means to attach it

grain noun **1** a cereal plant, such as wheat, that is grown as a crop and used for food **2** Grains are seeds of a cereal plant **3** A grain of sand or salt is a tiny particle of it **4** The grain of a piece of wood is the pattern of lines made by the fibres in it ⊳ phrase **5** If something **goes against the grain**, you find it difficult to accept because it is against your principles

gram or **gramme** noun a unit of weight equal to one thousandth of a kilogram

-graph | 259

grammar noun ENGLISH Grammar is the rules of language relating to the ways you can combine words to form sentences

grammar school noun **1** a secondary school for pupils of high academic ability **2** In Australia, a private school, usually one controlled by a government

grammatical adjective **1** relating to grammar: *grammatical knowledge* **2** following the rules of grammar correctly: *grammatical sentences* > **grammatically** adverb

gran noun (informal) Your gran is your grandmother

grand adjective **1** magnificent in appearance and size: *a grand house* **2** very important: *the grand scheme of your life* **3** (informal) very pleasant or enjoyable: *It was a grand day* **4** A grand total is the final complete amount ▷ noun **5** (informal) a thousand pounds or dollars > **grandly** adverb

grandad noun (informal) Your grandad is your grandfather

grandchild grandchildren noun Someone's grandchildren are the children of their son or daughter

granddaughter noun Someone's granddaughter is the daughter of their son or daughter

grandeur [grand-yer] noun Grandeur is great beauty and magnificence

grandfather noun Your grandfather is your father's father or your mother's father

grandiose [gran-dee-ose] adjective intended to be very impressive, but seeming ridiculous: *a grandiose gesture of love*

grandma noun (informal) Your grandma is your grandmother

grandmother noun Your grandmother is your father's mother or your mother's mother

grandparent noun Your grandparents are your parents' parents

grand piano noun a large flat piano with horizontal strings

grandson noun Someone's grandson is the son of their son or daughter

grandstand noun a structure with a roof and seats for spectators at a sports ground

granite [gran-nit] noun Granite is a very hard rock used in building

granny grannies noun (informal) Your granny is your grandmother

grant noun **1** an amount of money that an official body gives to someone for a particular purpose: *a grant to carry out repairs* ▷ verb **2** If you grant something to someone, you allow them to have it **3** If you grant that something is true, you admit that it is true ▷ phrase **4** If you **take something for granted**, you believe it without thinking about it. If you **take someone for granted**, you benefit from them without showing that you are grateful

grape noun a small green or purple fruit, eaten raw or used to make wine

grapefruit noun a large, round, yellow citrus fruit

grapevine noun **1** a climbing plant which grapes grow on ▷ phrase **2** If you hear some news **on the grapevine**, it has been passed on from person to person, usually unofficially or secretly

graph noun MATHS a diagram in which a line shows how two sets of numbers or measurements are related

-graph suffix '-graph' means a writer

or recorder of some sort or something made by writing, drawing, or recording: *telegraph; autograph*

graphic *adjective* **1** A graphic description is very detailed and lifelike **2** relating to drawing or painting > **graphically** *adverb*

graphics *plural noun* COMPUTING Graphics are drawings and pictures composed of simple lines and strong colours: *computerized graphics*

graphite *noun* a black form of carbon that is used in pencil leads

grapple *verb* **1** If you grapple with someone, you struggle with them while fighting **2** If you grapple with a problem, you try hard to solve it

grasp *verb* **1** If you grasp something, you hold it firmly **2** If you grasp an idea, you understand it ▷ *noun* **3** a firm hold **4** Your grasp of something is your understanding of it

grass *noun* Grass is the common green plant that grows on lawns and in parks > **grassy** *adjective*

grasshopper *noun* an insect with long back legs which it uses for jumping and making a high-pitched sound

grate *noun* **1** a framework of metal bars in a fireplace ▷ *verb* **2** To grate food means to shred it into small pieces by rubbing it against a grater **3** When something grates on something else, it rubs against it making a harsh sound **4** If something grates on you, it irritates you

grateful *adjective* If you are grateful for something, you are glad you have it and want to thank the person who gave it to you > **gratefully** *adverb*

gratify gratifies, gratifying, gratified *verb* **1** If you are gratified by

something, you are pleased by it **2** If you gratify a wish or feeling, you satisfy it

grating *noun* **1** a metal frame with bars across it fastened over a hole in a wall or in the ground ▷ *adjective* **2** A grating sound is harsh and unpleasant: *grating melodies*

gratitude *noun* Gratitude is the feeling of being grateful

gratuitous [grat-yoo-it-tuss] *adjective* unnecessary: *a gratuitous attack* > **gratuitously** *adverb*

grave [rhymes with **save**] *noun* **1** a place where a corpse is buried ▷ *adjective* **2** (formal) very serious: *grave danger*

grave [grahv] *adjective* In French and some other languages, a grave accent is a line sloping downwards from left to right placed over a vowel to indicate a change in pronunciation, as in the word *lièvre* (a hare)

gravel *noun* Gravel is small stones used for making roads and paths

gravestone *noun* a large stone placed over someone's grave, with their name on it

graveyard *noun* an area of land where corpses are buried

gravitate *verb* When people gravitate towards something, they go towards it because they are attracted to it

gravitation *noun* SCIENCE Gravitation is the force which causes objects to be attracted to each other > **gravitational** *adjective*

gravity *noun* **1** SCIENCE Gravity is the force that makes things fall when you drop them **2** (formal) The gravity of a situation is its seriousness

gravy *noun* Gravy is a brown sauce

made from meat juices

graze verb 1 When animals graze, they eat grass 2 If something grazes a part of your body, it scrapes against it, injuring you slightly ▷ noun 3 a slight injury caused by something scraping against your skin

grease noun 1 Grease is an oily substance used for lubricating machines 2 Grease is also melted animal fat, used in cooking 3 Grease is also an oily substance produced by your skin and found in your hair ▷ verb 4 If you grease something, you lubricate it with grease > **greasy** adjective

great adjective 1 very large: a great sea; great efforts 2 very important: a great artist 3 (informal) very good: Paul had a great time > **greatly** adverb > **greatness** noun

Great Britain noun Great Britain is the largest of the British Isles, consisting of England, Scotland, and Wales

great-grandfather noun Your great-grandfather is your father's or mother's grandfather

great-grandmother noun Your great-grandmother is your father's or mother's grandmother

greed noun Greed is a desire for more of something than you really need

greedy greedier, greediest adjective wanting more of something than you really need > **greedily** adverb > **greediness** noun

Greek adjective 1 belonging or relating to Greece 2 someone who comes from Greece 3 Greek is the main language spoken in Greece

green adjective, noun 1 Green is a colour between yellow and blue on the spectrum ▷ noun 2 an area of

grass in the middle of a village 3 A putting green or bowling green is a grassy area on which putting or bowls is played 4 an area of smooth short grass around each hole on a golf course 5 (in plural) Greens are green vegetables ▷ adjective 6 [GEOGRAPHY] 'Green' is used to describe political movements which are concerned with environmental issues 7 (informal) Someone who is green is young and inexperienced

greenery noun Greenery is a lot of trees, bushes, or other green plants together in one place

greengrocer noun a shopkeeper who sells vegetables and fruit

greenhouse noun a glass building in which people grow plants that need to be kept warm

greenhouse effect noun [GEOGRAPHY] the gradual rise in temperature in the earth's atmosphere due to heat being absorbed from the sun and being trapped by gases such as carbon dioxide in the air around the earth

green paper noun In Britain, Australia, and New Zealand, a report published by the government containing proposals to be discussed before decisions are made about them

greet verb 1 If you greet someone, you say something friendly like 'hello' to them when you meet them 2 If you greet something in a particular way, you react to it in that way: He was greeted with deep suspicion

greeting noun something friendly that you say to someone when you meet them: Her greeting was warm

gregarious [grig-**air**-ee-uss] adjective (formal) Someone who is gregarious enjoys being with other people

grenade noun a small bomb, containing explosive or tear gas, which can be thrown

grew the past tense of **grow**

grey adjective, noun **1** Grey is a colour between black and white ▷ adjective **2** dull and boring: He's a bit of a grey man ▷ verb **3** If someone is greying, their hair is going grey > **greyness** noun

greyhound noun a thin dog with long legs that can run very fast

grid noun **1 a** a pattern of lines crossing each other to form squares **b** The grid is the network of wires and cables by which electricity is distributed throughout the country

grief noun **1** Grief is extreme sadness ▷ phrase **2** If someone or something **comes to grief**, they fail or are injured

grievance noun a reason for complaining

grieve verb **1** If you grieve, you are extremely sad, especially because someone has died **2** If something grieves you, it makes you feel very sad

grievous adjective (formal) extremely serious: grievous damage > **grievously** adverb

grill noun **1 a** part on a cooker where food is cooked by strong heat from above **2** a metal frame on which you cook food over a fire ▷ verb **3** If you grill food, you cook it on or under a grill **4** (informal) If you grill someone, you ask them a lot of questions in a very intense way

grille [rhymes with **pill**] noun a metal framework over a window or piece of machinery, used for protection

grim grimmer, grimmest adjective **1** If a situation or piece of news is grim, it is very unpleasant and worrying: There are grim times ahead **2** Grim places are unattractive and depressing **3** If someone is grim, they are very serious or stern > **grimly** adverb

grimace [grim-iss or grim-**mace**] noun **1 a** twisted facial expression indicating disgust or pain ▷ noun **2** When someone grimaces, they make a grimace

grime noun Grime is thick dirt which gathers on the surface of something > **grimy** adjective

grin grins, grinning, grinned verb **1** If you grin, you smile broadly **2** a broad smile ▷ phrase **3** If you **grin and bear it**, you accept a difficult situation without complaining

grind grinds, grinding, ground verb **1** If you grind something such as pepper, you crush it into a fine powder **2** If you grind your teeth, you rub your upper and lower teeth together ▷ phrase **3** If something **grinds to a halt**, it stops: Progress ground to a halt

grip grips, gripping, gripped noun **1 a** firm hold **2** a handle on a bat or a racket **3** Your grip on a situation is your control over it ▷ verb **4** If you grip something, you hold it firmly ▷ phrase **5** If you **get to grips with** a situation or problem, you start to deal with it effectively

grisly grislier, grisliest adjective very nasty and horrible: a grisly murder scene

grit grits, gritting, gritted noun **1** Grit consists of very small stones. It is put on icy roads to make them less slippery ▷ verb **2** When workmen grit an icy road, they put grit on it ▷ phrase **3** To **grit your teeth** means to decide to carry on in a difficult situation > **gritty** adjective

grizzled adjective Grizzled hair is grey. A grizzled person has grey hair

groan verb 1 If you groan, you make a long, low sound of pain, unhappiness, or disapproval ▷ noun 2 the sound you make when you groan

grocer noun a shopkeeper who sells many kinds of food and other household goods

grocery groceries noun 1 a grocer's shop 2 (in plural) Groceries are the goods that you buy in a grocer's shop

grog noun (informal) In Australian and New Zealand English, grog is any alcoholic drink

groin noun the area where your legs join the main part of your body at the front

groom noun 1 someone who looks after horses in a stable 2 At a wedding, the groom is the bridegroom ▷ verb 3 To groom an animal means to clean its fur 4 If you groom someone for a job, you prepare them for it by teaching them the skills they will need

groove noun a deep line cut into a surface > **grooved** adjective

grope verb 1 If you grope for something you cannot see, you search for it with your hands 2 If you grope for something such as the solution to a problem, you try to think of it

gross adjective 1 extremely bad: a gross betrayal 2 Gross speech or behaviour is very rude 3 Gross things are ugly: gross holiday outfits 4 Someone's gross income is their total income before any deductions are made 5 The gross weight of something is its total weight including the weight of its container ▷ verb 6 If you gross an amount of money, you earn that amount in total > **grossly** adverb

grotesque [groh-**tesk**] adjective 1 exaggerated and absurd: It was the most grotesque thing she had ever heard 2 very strange and ugly: grotesque animal puppets > **grotesquely** adverb

grotto grottoes or grottos noun a small cave that people visit because it is attractive

ground noun 1 The ground is the surface of the earth 2 a piece of land that is used for a particular purpose: the training ground 3 The ground covered by a book or course is the range of subjects it deals with 4 (in plural) The grounds of a large building are the land belonging to it and surrounding it 5 (in plural, formal) The grounds for something are the reasons for it: genuine grounds for caution ▷ verb 6 (formal) If something is grounded in something else, it is based on it 7 If an aircraft is grounded, it has to remain on the ground 8 Ground is the past tense and past participle of **grind**

ground floor noun The ground floor of a building is the floor that is approximately level with the ground

grounding noun If you have a grounding in a skill or subject, you have had basic instruction in it

groundless adjective not based on reason or evidence: groundless accusations

group noun 1 A group of things or people is a number of them that are linked together in some way 2 a number of musicians who perform pop music together ▷ verb 3 When things or people are grouped together, they are linked together in some way

grouping noun a number of things or people that are linked together in some way

grouse grouse noun a fat brown or grey bird, often shot for sport

grove noun (literary) a group of trees growing close together

grovel grovels, grovelling, grovelled verb If you grovel, you behave in an unpleasantly humble way towards someone you regard as important

grow grows, growing, grew, grown verb 1 To grow means to increase in size or amount 2 If a tree or plant grows somewhere, it is alive there 3 When people grow plants, they plant them and look after them 4 If a man grows a beard or moustache, he lets it develop by not shaving 5 To grow also means to pass gradually into a particular state 6 If one thing grows from another, it develops from it 7 (informal) If something grows on you, you gradually get to like it > **grow up** verb When a child grows up, he or she becomes an adult

growl growls, growling, growled verb 1 When an animal growls, it makes a low rumbling sound, usually because it is angry 2 If you growl something, you say it in a low, rough, rather angry voice > noun 3 the sound an animal makes when it growls

grown-up noun 1 (informal) an adult > adjective 2 Someone who is grown-up is adult, or behaves like an adult

growth noun 1 When there is a growth in something, it gets bigger: the growth of the fishing industry 2 SCIENCE Growth is the process by which something develops to its full size 3 an abnormal lump that grows inside or on a person, animal, or plant

grub noun 1 a wormlike insect that has just hatched from its egg 2 (informal) Grub is food

grubby grubbier, grubbiest adjective rather dirty

grudge noun 1 If you have a grudge against someone, you resent them because they have harmed you in the past > verb 2 If you grudge someone something, you give it to them unwillingly, or are displeased that they have it

grudging adjective done or felt unwillingly: grudging admiration > **grudgingly** adverb

gruelling adjective difficult and tiring: a gruelling race

gruesome adjective shocking and horrible: gruesome pictures

gruff adjective If someone's voice is gruff, it sounds rough and unfriendly

grumble verb 1 If you grumble, you complain in a bad-tempered way > noun 2 a bad-tempered complaint

grumpy grumpier, grumpiest adjective bad-tempered and fed-up

grunt verb 1 If a person or a pig grunts, they make a short, low, gruff sound > noun 2 the sound a person or a pig makes when they grunt

guarantee guarantees, guaranteeing, guaranteed noun 1 If something is a guarantee of something else, it makes it certain that it will happen 2 a written promise that if a product develops a fault it will be replaced or repaired free > verb 3 If something or someone guarantees something, they make certain that it will happen: Money may not guarantee success > **guarantor** noun

guard verb 1 If you guard a person or object, you stay near to them to protect them 2 If you guard a person, you stop them making trouble or escaping 3 If you guard against something, you are careful to avoid it happening ▷ noun **4** a person or group of people who guard a person, object, or place **5** a railway official in charge of a train **6** Any object which covers something to prevent it causing harm can be called a guard: *a fire guard*

guardian noun **1** someone who has been legally appointed to look after a child **2** A guardian of something is someone who protects it: *a guardian of the law* ▷ **guardianship** noun

guernsey noun **1** In Australian and New Zealand English, a jersey **2** a sleeveless top worn in Australian Rules football player

guerrilla (ger-**ril**-la) or **guerilla** noun a member of a small unofficial army fighting an official army

guess verb **1** If you guess something, you form or express an opinion that it is the case, without having much information ▷ noun **2** MATHS an attempt to give the correct answer to something without having much information, or without working it out properly

guest noun **1** someone who stays at your home or who attends an occasion because they have been invited **2** The guests in a hotel are the people staying there

guidance noun Guidance is help and advice

guide noun **1** someone who shows you round places, or leads the way through difficult country **2** a book which gives you information or instructions: *a Sydney street guide* **3** A Guide is a girl who is a member of an organization that encourages discipline and practical skills ▷ verb **4** If you guide someone in a particular direction, you lead them

in that direction **5** If you are guided by something, it influences your actions or decisions

guidebook noun a book which gives information about a place

guide dog noun a dog that has been trained to lead a blind person

guideline noun a piece of advice about how something should be done

guild noun a society of people: *the Screen Writers' Guild*

guile [rhymes with **mile**] noun Guile is cunning and deceit ▷ **guileless** adjective

guillotine [gil-lot-teen] noun **1** HISTORY In the past, the guillotine was a machine used for beheading people, especially in France. It was named after Joseph-Ignace Guillotin, who first recommended its use **2** A guillotine is also a piece of equipment with a long sharp blade, used for cutting paper

guilt noun **1** Guilt is an unhappy feeling of having done something wrong **2** Someone's guilt is the fact that they have done something wrong: *The law will decide their guilt*

guilty guiltier, guiltiest adjective **1** If you are guilty of doing something wrong, you did it: *He was guilty of theft* **2** If you feel guilty, you are unhappy because you have done something wrong ▷ **guiltily** adverb

guinea [gin-ee] noun an old British unit of money, worth 21 shillings

guinea pig noun **1** a small furry animal without a tail, often kept as a pet **2** a person used to try something out on: *a guinea pig for a new drug*

guise [rhymes with **prize**] noun a misleading appearance: *political statements in the guise of religious talk*

guitar noun a musical instrument

with six strings which are strummed or plucked > **guitarist** *noun*

gulf *noun* **1** a very large bay **2** a wide gap or difference between two things or people

gull *noun* a sea bird with long wings, white and grey or black feathers, and webbed feet

gullible *adjective* easily tricked > **gullibility** *noun*

gully *gullies noun* a long, narrow valley

gulp *verb* **1** If you gulp food or drink, you swallow some of it **2** If you gulp, you swallow air, because you are nervous ▷ *noun* **3** A gulp of food or drink is a large quantity of it swallowed at one time

gum *noun* **1** Gum is a soft flavoured substance that people chew but do not swallow **2** Gum is also glue for sticking paper **3** Your gums are the firm flesh in which your teeth are set

gun *noun* a weapon which fires bullets or shells

gunfire *noun* Gunfire is the repeated firing of guns

gunpowder *noun* Gunpowder is an explosive powder made from a mixture of potassium nitrate and other substances

gunshot *noun* the sound of a gun being fired

gurgle *verb* **1** To gurgle means to make a bubbling sound ▷ *noun* **2** a bubbling sound

guru [**goo**-rooh] *noun* a spiritual leader and teacher, especially in India

gush *verb* **1** When liquid gushes from something, it flows out of it in large quantities **2** When people gush, they express admiration or pleasure in an exaggerated way > **gushing** *adjective*

gust *noun* a sudden rush of wind > **gusty** *adjective*

gusto *noun* Gusto is energy and enthusiasm: *Her gusto for life was amazing*

gut *noun*, *gutting*, *gutted noun* (in plural) **1** Your guts are your internal organs, especially your intestines **2** (*informal*) Guts is courage ▷ *verb* **3** To gut a dead fish means to remove its internal organs **4** If a building is gutted, the inside of it is destroyed, especially by fire

gutter *noun* **1** the edge of a road next to the pavement, where rain collects and flows away **2** a channel fixed to the edge of a roof, where rain collects and flows away > **guttering** *noun*

guy *noun* **1** (*informal*) a man or boy **2** a crude model of Guy Fawkes, that is burnt on top of a bonfire on Guy Fawkes Day (November 5)

guzzle *verb* To guzzle something means to drink or eat it quickly and greedily

gym *noun* PE **1** a gymnasium **2** Gym is gymnastics

gymnasium *noun* a room with special equipment for physical exercises

gymnast *noun* someone who is trained in gymnastics > **gymnastic** *adjective*

gymnastics *noun* PE Gymnastics is physical exercises, especially ones using equipment such as bars and ropes

gynaecology or **gynecology** [gie-nak-**kol**-loj-ee] *noun* Gynaecology is the branch of medical science concerned with the female reproductive system > **gynaecologist** *noun* > **gynaecological** *adjective*

h

habit noun **1** something that you do often: *He got into the habit of eating out* **2** something that you keep doing and find it difficult to stop doing: *a 20-a-day smoking habit* **3** A monk's or nun's habit is a garment like a loose dress ▷ **habitual** adjective ▷ **habitually** adverb

habitat noun GEOGRAPHY the natural home of a plant or animal

hack verb **1** If you hack at something, you cut it using rough strokes ▷ noun **2** a writer or journalist who produces work fast without worrying about quality

hacker noun someone who uses a computer to break into the computer system of a company or government

hackles plural noun **1** A dog's hackles are the hairs on the back of its neck which rise when it is angry ▷ phrase **2** Something that makes your hackles rise makes you angry

hackneyed adjective A hackneyed phrase is meaningless because it has been used too often

haddock noun an edible sea fish

haemoglobin [hee-moh-gloh-bin] noun SCIENCE Haemoglobin is a substance in red blood cells which carries oxygen round the body

haemorrhage [hem-er-rij] noun SCIENCE A haemorrhage is serious bleeding especially inside a person's body

haggard adjective A person who is haggard looks very tired and ill

haggis noun Haggis is a Scottish dish made of the internal organs of a sheep, boiled together with oatmeal and spices in a skin

haggle verb If you haggle with someone, you argue with them, usually about the cost of something

hail noun **1** Hail is frozen rain **2** A hail of things is a lot of them falling together: *a hail of bullets; a hail of protest* ▷ verb **3** When it is hailing, frozen rain is falling **4** If someone hails you, they call you to attract your attention or greet you: *He hailed a taxi*

hair noun Hair consists of the long, threadlike strands that grow from the skin of animals and humans

haircut noun the cutting of someone's hair; also the style in which it is cut

hairdo hairdos noun a hairstyle

hairdresser noun someone who is trained to cut and style people's hair; also a shop where this is done ▷ **hairdressing** noun, adjective

hairline noun **1** the edge of the area on your forehead where your hair grows ▷ adjective **2** A hairline crack is so fine that you can hardly see it

hairpin noun **1** a U-shaped wire used to hold hair in position ▷ adjective **2** A hairpin bend is a U-shaped bend in the road

hair-raising adjective very frightening or exciting

hairstyle noun Someone's hairstyle is the way in which their hair is arranged or cut

hairy hairier, hairiest adjective **1** covered in a lot of hair **2** (informal) difficult, exciting, and rather frightening: *He had lived through many hairy adventures*

hajj [rhymes with **badge**] noun RE The hajj is the pilgrimage to Mecca that every Muslim must make at least once in their life if they are healthy and wealthy enough to do so

haka *noun* **1** In New Zealand, a haka is a ceremonial Maori dance made up of various postures and accompanied by a chant **2** an imitation of this dance performed by New Zealand sports teams before matches as a challenge

halcyon [hal-see-on] *adjective* **1** (*literary*) peaceful, gentle, and calm: *halcyon colours of yellow and turquoise* ▷ *phrase* **2** Halcyon days are a happy and carefree time in the past: *halcyon days in the sun*

half *noun, adjective, adverb* **1** Half refers to one of two equal parts that make up a whole: *the two halves of the brain; They chatted for another half hour; The bottle was only half full* ▷ *adverb* **2** You can use 'half' to say that something is only partly true: *I half expected him to explode in anger*

half-baked *adjective* (*informal*) Half-baked ideas or plans have not been properly thought out

half-brother *noun* Your half-brother is the son of either your mother or your father but not of your other parent

half-hearted *adjective* showing no real effort or enthusiasm

half-sister *noun* Your half-sister is the daughter of either your mother or your father but not of your other parent

half-time *noun* Half-time is a short break between two parts of a game when the players have a rest

halfway *adverb* at the middle of the distance between two points in place or time: *He stopped halfway down the ladder; halfway through the term*

halibut *noun* a large edible flat fish

hall *noun* **1** the room just inside the front entrance of a house which leads into other rooms **2** a large room or building used for public events: *a concert hall*

hallmark *noun* **1** The hallmark of a person or group is their most typical quality: *A warm, hospitable welcome is the hallmark of Island people* **2** an official mark on gold or silver indicating the quality of the metal

hallowed [hal-lode] *adjective* respected as being holy: *hallowed ground*

Halloween *noun* Halloween is October 31st, and is celebrated by children dressing up, often as ghosts and witches

hallucinate [hal-loo-sin-ate] *verb* If you hallucinate, you see strange things in your mind because of illness or drugs ▷ **hallucination** *noun* ▷ **hallucinatory** *adjective*

halo *noun* haloes or halos *noun* a circle of light around the head of a holy figure

halt *verb* **1** To halt when moving means to stop **2** To halt development or action means to stop it ▷ *noun* **3** a sudden standstill

halter *noun* a strap fastened round a horse's head so that it can be led easily

halve [hahv] *verb* **1** If you halve something, you divide it into two equal parts **2** To halve something also means to reduce its size or amount by half

ham *noun* **1** Ham is meat from the hind leg of a pig, salted and cured **2** (*informal*) a bad actor who exaggerates emotions and gestures **3** someone who is interested in amateur radio

hamburger *noun* a flat disc of

minced meat, seasoned and fried; often eaten in a bread roll

hammer noun **1** a tool consisting of a heavy piece of metal at the end of a handle, used for hitting nails into things ▷ verb **2** If you hammer something, you hit it repeatedly, with a hammer or with your fist **3** If you hammer an idea into someone, you keep repeating it and telling them about it **4** (informal) If you hammer someone, you criticize or attack them severely

hammock noun a piece of net or canvas hung between two supports and used as a bed

hamper noun **1** a rectangular wicker basket with a lid, used for carrying food ▷ verb **2** If you hamper someone, you make it difficult for them to move or progress

hamster noun a small furry rodent which is often kept as a pet

> **WORD TIP**
> There is no *p* in *hamster*

hamstring noun [PE] Your hamstring is a tendon behind your knee joining your thigh muscles to the bones of your lower leg

hand noun **1** Your hand is the part of your body beyond the wrist, with four fingers and a thumb **2** Your hand is also your writing style **3** The hand of someone in a situation is their influence or the part they play in it: *He had a hand in its design* **4** If you give someone a hand, you help them to do something **5** When an audience gives someone a big hand, they applaud **6** The hands of a clock or watch are the pointers that point to the numbers **7** In cards, your hand is the cards you are holding ▷ verb **8** If you hand something to someone, you give it to them ▷ phrase **9** Something that is at

hand, to hand, or **on hand** is available, close by, and ready for use **10** You use **on the one hand** to introduce the first part of an argument or discussion with two different points of view **11** You use **on the other hand** to introduce the second part of an argument or discussion with two different points of view **12** If you do something **by hand,** you do it using your hands rather than a machine ▷ **hand down** verb Something that is handed down is passed from one generation to another

handbag noun a small bag used mainly by women to carry money and personal items

handbook noun a book giving information and instructions about something

handcuff noun Handcuffs are two metal rings linked by a chain which are locked around a prisoner's wrists

handful noun **1** A handful of something is the amount of it you can hold in your hand: *He picked up a handful of seeds* **2** a small quantity: *Only a handful of people knew* **3** Someone who is a handful is difficult to control: *He is a bit of a handful*

handicap handicaps, handicapping, handicapped noun **1** (old-fashioned, offensive) a physical or mental disability **2** something that makes it difficult for you to achieve something **3** In sport, a handicap is a disadvantage or advantage given to competitors according to their skill, in order to give them an equal chance of winning ▷ verb **4** If something handicaps someone, it makes it difficult for them to achieve something

handiwork noun Your handiwork is

something that you have done or made yourself

handkerchief noun a small square of fabric used for blowing your nose

handle noun **1** The handle of an object is the part by which it is held or controlled **2** a small lever used to open and close a door or window ▷ verb **3** If you handle an object, you hold it in your hands to examine it **4** If you handle something, you deal with it or control it: *I have learned how to handle pressure*

handlebar noun Handlebars are the bar and handles at the front of a bicycle, used for steering

handout noun **1** a gift of food, clothing, or money given to a poor person **2** a piece of paper giving information about something

hand-picked adjective carefully chosen: *a hand-picked team of bodyguards*

handset noun The handset of a telephone is the part that you speak into and listen with

handshake noun the grasping and shaking of a person's hand by another person

handsome adjective **1** very attractive in appearance **2** large and generous: *a handsome profit* ▷ **handsomely** adverb

handwriting noun Someone's handwriting is their style of writing as it looks on the page

handy handier, handiest adjective **1** conveniently near **2** easy to handle or use **3** skilful

hang hangs, hanging, hung verb **1** If you hang something somewhere, you attach it to a high point. *She hung heavy red velvet curtains in the sitting room* **2** If something is hanging on something, it is attached by its top to it: *His jacket*

hung from a hook behind the door **3** If a future event or possibility is hanging over you, it worries or frightens you: *She has an eviction notice hanging over her* **4** When you hang wallpaper, you stick it onto a wall **5** To hang someone means to kill them by suspending them by a rope around the neck ▷ phrase **6** When you **get the hang of something**, you understand it and are able to do it > **hang about** or > **hang around** verb **1** (informal) To hang about or hang around means to wait somewhere **2** To hang about or hang around with someone means to spend a lot of time with them > **hang back** verb To hang back means to wait or hesitate > **hang on** verb **1** If you hang on to something, you hold it tightly or keep it **2** (informal) To hang on means to wait > **hang out** verb (informal) If you hang out somewhere or with someone, you spend a lot of time there or with them > **hang up** verb When you hang up, you put down the receiver to end a telephone call

hangar noun a large building where aircraft are kept

hanger noun a coat hanger

hangover noun a feeling of sickness and headache after drinking too much alcohol

hanker verb If you hanker after something, you continually want it ▷ **hankering** noun

hanky hankies noun a handkerchief

Hanukkah or **Chanukah** [hah-na-ka] noun Hanukkah is an eight-day Jewish festival of lights

haphazard [hap-haz-ard] adjective not organized or planned ▷ **haphazardly** adverb

hapless adjective (literary) unlucky

happen *verb* **1** When something happens, it occurs or takes place **2** If you happen to do something, you do it by chance > **happening** *noun*

happiness *noun* a feeling of great contentment or pleasure

happy happier, happiest *adjective* **1** feeling, showing, or producing contentment or pleasure: *a happy smile; a happy atmosphere* **2** satisfied that something is right: *I wasn't very happy about the layout* **3** willing: *I would be happy to help* **4** fortunate or lucky: *a happy coincidence* > **happily** *adverb*

happy-go-lucky *adjective* carefree and unconcerned

harass [har-rass] *verb* If someone harasses you, they trouble or annoy you continually > **harassed** *adjective* > **harassment** *noun*

harbinger [har-bin-jer] *noun* a person or thing that announces or indicates the approach of a future event: *Others see the shortage of cash as a harbinger of bankruptcy*

harbour *noun* **1 a** protected area of deep water where boats can be moored ▷ *verb* **2** To harbour someone means to hide them secretly in your house **3** If you harbour a feeling, you have it for a long time: *She's still harbouring great bitterness*

hard *adjective* **1** Something that is hard is firm, solid, or stiff: *a hard piece of cheese* **2** requiring a lot of effort: *hard work* **3** difficult: *These are hard times* **4** Someone who is hard has no kindness or pity: *Don't be hard on him* **5** A hard colour or voice is harsh and unpleasant **6** Hard evidence or facts can be proved to be true **7** Hard water contains a lot of lime and does not easily produce a lather ▷ *adverb* **8** earnestly or intently: *They*

tried hard to attract tourists **9** An event that follows hard upon something takes place immediately afterwards > **hardness** *noun*

hard and fast *adjective* fixed and not able to be changed: *hard and fast rules*

hardback *noun* a book with a stiff cover

hard core *noun* The hard core in an organization is the group of people who most resist change

harden *verb* To harden means to become hard or get harder > **hardening** *noun* > **hardened** *adjective*

hard labour *noun* physical work which is difficult and tiring, used in some countries as a punishment for a crime

hardly *adverb* **1** almost not or not quite: *I could hardly believe it* **2** certainly not: *It's hardly a secret*

hard-nosed *adjective* tough, practical, and realistic

hardship *noun* Hardship is a time or situation of suffering and difficulty

hard shoulder *noun* the area at the edge of a motorway where a driver can stop in the event of a breakdown

hard up *adjective* (*informal*) having hardly any money

hardware *noun* **1** Hardware is tools and equipment for use in the home and garden **2** COMPUTING Hardware is also computer machinery rather than computer programs

hard-wearing *adjective* strong, well-made, and long-lasting

hardwood *noun* strong, hard wood from a tree such as an oak; also the tree itself

hardy hardier, hardiest *adjective* tough and able to endure very difficult or cold conditions: *a hardy race of pioneers* ▷ **hardiness** noun

hare noun **1** an animal like a large rabbit, but with longer ears and legs ▷ verb **2** To hare around means to run very fast: *He hared off down the corridor*

harem [har-**reem**] noun a group of wives or mistresses of one man, especially in Muslim societies; also the place where these women live

hark verb **1** (old-fashioned) To hark means to listen **2** To hark back to something in the past means to refer back to it or recall it

harlequin [har-**lik**-win] adjective having many different colours

harm verb **1** To harm someone or something means to injure or damage them ▷ noun **2** Harm is injury or damage

harmful adjective having a bad effect on something: *Whilst most stress is harmful, some is beneficial*

harmless adjective **1** safe to use or be near **2** unlikely to cause problems or annoyance: *He's harmless really* ▷ **harmlessly** adverb

harmonic adjective using musical harmony

harmonica noun a small musical instrument which you play by blowing and sucking while moving it across your lips

harmonious [har-**moh**-nee-uss] adjective **1** showing agreement, peacefulness, and friendship: *a harmonious relationship* **2** consisting of parts which blend well together making an attractive whole: *harmonious interior decor* ▷ **harmoniously** adverb

harmony harmonies noun **1** Harmony is a state of peaceful agreement and cooperation: *the promotion of racial harmony* **2** MUSIC

Harmony is the structure and relationship of chords in a piece of music **3** Harmony is the pleasant combination of two or more notes played at the same time

harness noun **1** a set of straps and fittings fastened round a horse so that it can pull a vehicle, or fastened round someone's body to attach something: *a safety harness* ▷ verb **2** If you harness something, you bring it under control to use it: *harnessing public opinion*

harp noun **1** a musical instrument consisting of a triangular frame with vertical strings which you pluck with your fingers ▷ verb **2** (informal) If someone harps on about something, they keep talking about it, especially in a boring way ▷ **harpist** noun

harpoon noun a barbed spear attached to a rope, thrown or fired from a gun and used for catching whales or large fish

harpsichord noun a musical instrument like a small piano, with strings which are plucked when the keys are pressed

harrowing adjective very upsetting or disturbing: *a harrowing experience*

harsh adjective severe, difficult, and unpleasant: *harsh weather conditions; harsh criticism* ▷ **harshly** adverb ▷ **harshness** noun

harvest noun **1** the cutting and gathering of a crop; also the ripe crop when it is gathered and the time of gathering ▷ verb **2** To harvest food means to gather it when it is ripe ▷ **harvester** noun

has-been noun (informal) a person who is no longer important or successful

hash phrase **1** If you make a hash of a job, you do it badly ▷ noun **2** the name for the symbol **#** **3** Hash is a dish made of small pieces of meat and vegetables cooked together

hashtag noun [COMPUTING] a word or phrase that is used to indicate the topic of a post on a social networking website

hassle noun **1** (informal) Something that is a hassle is difficult or causes trouble ▷ verb **2** If you hassle someone, you annoy them by repeatedly asking them to do something

haste noun Haste is doing something quickly, especially too quickly

hasten [hay-sn] verb To hasten means to move quickly or do something quickly

hasty hastier, hastiest adjective done or happening suddenly and quickly, often without enough care or thought > **hastily** adverb

hat noun a covering for the head

hatch verb **1** When an egg hatches, or when a bird or reptile hatches, the egg breaks open and the young bird or reptile emerges **2** To hatch a plot means to plan it ▷ noun **3** a covered opening in a floor or wall

hatchback noun a car with a door at the back which opens upwards

hatchet noun **1** a small axe ▷ phrase **2** To **bury the hatchet** means to resolve a disagreement and become friends again

hate verb **1** If you hate someone or something, you have a strong dislike for them ▷ noun **2** Hate is a strong dislike

hateful adjective extremely unpleasant

hatred [hay-trid] noun Hatred is an extremely strong feeling of dislike

hat trick noun In sport, a hat trick is three achievements, for example

when a footballer scores three goals in a match: Crawford completed his hat trick in the 60th minute

haughty haughtier, haughtiest [rhymes with **naughty**] adjective showing excessive pride: He behaved in a haughty manner > **haughtily** adverb

haul verb **1** To haul something somewhere means to pull it with great effort ▷ noun **2** a quantity of something obtained: a good haul of fish ▷ phrase **3** Something that you describe as **a long haul** takes a lot of time and effort to achieve: So women began the long haul to equality

haulage [hawl-lij] noun Haulage is the business or cost of transporting goods by road

haunches plural noun Your haunches are your buttocks and the tops of your legs: He squatted on his haunches

haunt verb **1** If a ghost haunts a place, it is seen or heard there regularly **2** If a memory or a fear haunts you, it continually worries you ▷ noun **3** A person's favourite haunt is a place they like to visit often

haunted adjective **1** regularly visited by a ghost: a haunted house **2** very worried or troubled: a haunted expression

haunting adjective extremely beautiful or sad so that it makes a lasting impression on you: haunting landscapes

have has, having, had verb **1** Have is an auxiliary verb, used to form the past tense or to express completed actions: They have never met; I have lost it **2** If you have something, you own or possess it: We have two tickets for the concert **3** If you have something, you experience it, it happens to you, or you are affected by it: *I have an idea!*; *He had a marvellous time* **4** To have a child or baby animal means to give birth to it: *When is she having the baby?* ▷ phrase **5** If you **have to** do something, you must do it. If you **had better** do something, you ought to do it

haven [hay-ven] *noun* a safe place

havoc *noun* **1** Havoc is disorder and confusion ▷ phrase **2** To **play havoc** with something means to cause great disorder and confusion: *Food allergies often play havoc with the immune system*

hawk *noun* **1** a bird of prey with short rounded wings and a long tail ▷ verb **2** To hawk goods means to sell them by taking them around from place to place

hawthorn *noun* a small, thorny tree producing white blossom and red berries

hay *noun* Hay is grass which has been cut and dried and is used as animal feed

hay fever *noun* Hay fever is an allergy to pollen and grass, causing sneezing and watering eyes

haystack *noun* a large, firmly built pile of hay, usually covered and left out in the open

hazard *noun* **1** SCIENCE a substance, object, or action which could be dangerous to you ▷ verb **2** If you hazard something, you put it at risk: *hazarding the health of his crew* ▷ phrase **3** If you **hazard a guess**, you make a guess
> **hazardous** *adjective*

haze *noun* If there is a haze, you cannot see clearly because there is moisture or smoke in the air

hazel *noun* **1** a small tree producing edible nuts ▷ adjective **2** greenish brown in colour

hazy hazier, haziest *adjective* dim or vague: *hazy sunshine*; *a hazy memory*

he *pronoun* 'He' is used to refer to a man, boy, or male animal

head *noun* **1** Your head is the part of your body which has your eyes, brain, and mouth in it **2** Your head is also your mind and mental abilities: *He has a head for figures* **3** The head of something is the top, start, or most important end: *at the head of the table* **4** The head of a group or organization is the person in charge **5** The head on beer is the layer of froth on the top **6** The head on a computer or tape recorder is the part that can read or write information **7** When you toss a coin, the side called heads is the one with the head on it ▷ verb **8** To head a group or organization means to be in charge: *Bryce heads the aid organization* **9** To head in a particular direction means to move in that direction: *She is heading for a breakdown* **10** To head a ball means to hit it with your head ▷ phrase **11** If you **lose your head**, you panic **12** If you say that someone is **off their head**, you mean that they are mad **13** If something is **over someone's head**, it is too difficult for them to understand **14** If you **can't make head nor tail of something**, you cannot understand it ▷ **head off** *verb* If you head off someone or something, you make them change direction or prevent something from happening: *He hopes to head off a public squabble*

headache *noun* **1** a pain in your head **2** Something that is a headache is causing a lot of difficulty or worry: *Delays in receiving money owed is a major headache for small firms*

header noun A header in soccer is hitting the ball with your head

heading noun a piece of writing that is written or printed at the top of a page or section

headland noun a narrow piece of land jutting out into the sea

headlight noun The headlights on a motor vehicle are the large powerful lights at the front

headline noun **1** A newspaper headline is the title of a newspaper article printed in large, bold type **2** The headlines are the main points of the radio or television news

headmaster noun a man who is the head teacher of a school

headmistress noun a woman who is the head teacher of a school

headphones plural noun Headphones are a pair of small speakers which you wear in or over your ears to listen to music without other people hearing

headquarters noun The headquarters of an organization is the main place or the place from which it is run

headroom noun Headroom is the amount of space below a roof or surface under which an object must pass or fit

headstone noun a large stone standing at one end of a grave and showing the name of the person buried there

headstrong adjective determined to do something in your own way and ignoring other people's advice

head teacher noun the teacher who is in charge of a school

headway phrase If you are **making headway**, you are making progress

headwind noun a wind blowing in the opposite direction to the way you are travelling

heady headier, headiest adjective extremely exciting: the heady days of the civil rights era

heal verb If something heals or if you heal it, it becomes healthy or normal again: He had a nasty wound which had not healed properly > **healer** noun

health noun **1** Your health is the condition of your body: His health is not good **2** Health is also the state of being free from disease and feeling well

health food noun food which is free from added chemicals and is considered to be good for your health

healthy healthier, healthiest adjective **1** Someone who is healthy is fit and strong and does not have any diseases **2** Something that is healthy is good for you: a healthy diet **3** An organization or system that is healthy is successful: a healthy economy > **healthily** adverb

heap noun **1** a pile of things **2** (in plural, informal) Heaps of something means plenty of it: His performance earned him heaps of praise ▷ verb **3** If you heap things, you pile them up **4** To heap something such as praise on someone means to give them a lot of it

hear hears, hearing, heard verb **1** When you hear sounds, you are aware of them because they reach your ears **2** When you hear from someone, they write to you or phone you **3** When you hear about something, you are informed about it **4** When a judge hears a case, he or she listens to it in court in order to make a decision on it ▷ phrase **5** If you say that you **won't hear of** something, you mean you refuse to allow it > **hear out** verb If you hear someone out, you listen to all they have to say without interrupting

hearing noun **1** Hearing is the sense which makes it possible for you to be aware of sounds: *My hearing is poor* **2** a court trial or official meeting to hear facts about an incident **3** If someone gives you a hearing, they let you give your point of view and listen to you

hearsay noun Hearsay is information that you have heard from other people rather than something that you know personally to be true

hearse [rhymes with **verse**] noun a large car that carries the coffin at a funeral

heart noun **1** the organ in your chest that pumps the blood around your body **2** Your heart is also thought of as the centre of your emotions **3** Heart is courage, determination, or enthusiasm: *They were losing heart* **4** The heart of something is the most central and important part of it **5** a shape similar to a heart, used especially as a symbol of love **6** Hearts is one of the four suits in a pack of playing cards. It is marked by a red heart-shaped symbol

heartache noun Heartache is very great sadness and emotional suffering

heart attack noun a serious medical condition in which the heart suddenly beats irregularly or stops completely

heartbreak noun Heartbreak is great sadness and emotional suffering > **heartbreaking** adjective

heartbroken adjective very sad and emotionally upset: *She was heartbroken at his death*

heartburn noun Heartburn is a painful burning sensation in your chest, caused by indigestion

heartening adjective encouraging or uplifting: *heartening news*

heart failure noun Heart failure is a serious condition in which someone's heart does not work as well as it should, sometimes stopping completely

heartfelt adjective sincerely and deeply felt: *Our heartfelt sympathy goes out to you*

hearth [harth] noun the floor of a fireplace

heartless adjective cruel and unkind

heart-rending adjective causing great sadness and pity: *a heart-rending story*

heart-throb noun someone who is attractive to a lot of people

heart-to-heart noun a discussion in which two people talk about their deepest feelings

hearty heartier, heartiest adjective **1** cheerful and enthusiastic: *hearty congratulations* **2** strongly felt: *a hearty dislike for her teacher* **3** A hearty meal is large and satisfying > **heartily** adverb

heat noun **1** Heat is warmth or the quality of being hot; also the temperature of something that is warm or hot **2** Heat is strength of feeling, especially of anger or excitement **3** a contest or race in a competition held to decide who will play in the final ▷ verb **4** To heat something means to raise its temperature ▷ phrase **5** When a female animal is **on heat**, she is ready for mating > **heater** noun

heath noun an area of open land covered with rough grass or heather

heather noun a plant with small purple or white flowers that grows wild on hills and moorland

heating noun Heating is the

equipment used to heat a building; also the process and cost of running the equipment to provide heat

heatwave noun a period of time during which the weather is much hotter than usual

heave verb **1** To heave something means to move or throw it with a lot of effort **2** If your stomach heaves, you vomit or suddenly feel sick **3** If you heave a sigh, you sigh loudly ▷ noun **4** If you give something a heave, you move or throw it with a lot of effort

heaven noun **1** RE a place of happiness where God is believed to live and where good people are believed to go when they die **2** (informal) If you describe something as heaven, you mean that it is wonderful: The cake was pure heaven ▷ phrase **3** You say Good heavens to express surprise

heavenly adjective **1** relating to heaven: a heavenly choir **2** (informal) wonderful: his heavenly blue eyes

heavy heavier, heaviest; heavies adjective **1** great in weight or force: How heavy are you?; a heavy blow **2** great in degree or amount: heavy casualties **3** solid and thick in appearance: heavy shoes **4** using a lot of something quickly: The van is heavy on petrol **5** serious and difficult to deal with or understand: It all got a bit heavy when the police arrived; a heavy speech **6** Food that is heavy is solid and difficult to digest: a heavy meal **7** When it is heavy, the weather is hot, humid, and still **8** Someone with a heavy heart is very sad ▷ noun **9** (informal) a large, strong man employed to protect someone or something > **heavily** adverb > **heaviness** noun

heavy-duty adjective Heavy-duty

equipment is strong and hard-wearing

heavy-handed adjective showing a lack of care or thought and using too much authority: heavy-handed police tactics

heavyweight noun **1** a boxer in the heaviest weight group **2** an important person with a lot of influence

Hebrew [hee-broo] noun **1** Hebrew is an ancient language now spoken in Israel, where it is the official language **2** In the past, the Hebrews were Hebrew-speaking Jews who lived in Israel ▷ adjective **3** relating to the Hebrews and their customs

heckle verb If members of an audience heckle a speaker, they interrupt and shout rude remarks > **heckler** noun

hectare noun a unit for measuring areas of land, equal to 10,000 square metres or about 2.471 acres

hectic adjective involving a lot of rushed activity: a hectic schedule

hedge noun **1** a row of bushes forming a barrier or boundary ▷ verb **2** If you hedge against something unpleasant happening, you protect yourself **3** If you hedge, you avoid answering a question or dealing with a problem ▷ phrase **4** If you hedge your bets, you support two or more people or courses of action to avoid the risk of losing a lot

hedgehog noun a small, brown animal with sharp spikes covering its back

hedonism [hee-dn-izm] noun Hedonism is the belief that gaining pleasure is the most important thing in life > **hedonistic** adjective

heed verb **1** If you heed someone's advice, you pay attention to it ▷ noun **2** If you take or pay heed to something, you give it careful attention

heel noun **1** The back part of your foot **2** The heel of a shoe or sock is the part that fits over your heel ▷ verb **3** To heel a pair of shoes means to put a new piece on the heel ▷ phrase **4** A person or place that looks **down at heel** looks untidy and in poor condition

hefty heftier, heftiest adjective of great size, force, or weight: a hefty fine; hefty volumes

height noun **1** The height of an object is its measurement from the bottom to the top **2** a high position or place: Their nesting rarely takes place at any great height **3** The height of something is its peak, or the time when it is most successful or intense: the height of the tourist season; at the height of his career **4** (MATHS) In maths, the height of a triangle is the point where two sides meet at a peak opposite the base

heighten verb If something heightens a feeling or experience, it increases its intensity

heinous [hay-nuss or hee-nuss] adjective evil and terrible: heinous crimes

heir [air] noun A person's heir is the person who is entitled to inherit their property or title

heiress [air-iss] noun a female with the right to inherit property or a title

heirloom [air-loom] noun something belonging to a family that has been passed from one generation to another

helicopter noun an aircraft with rotating blades above it which enable it to take off vertically, hover, and fly

helium [hee-lee-um] noun Helium is an element which is a colourless inert gas. It occurs in some natural gases, and is used in air balloons. Its atomic number is 2 and its symbol is He

hell noun **1** (RE) Hell is the place where souls of evil people are believed to go to be punished after death **2** (informal) If you say that something is hell, you mean it is very unpleasant ▷ interjection **3** 'Hell' is also a swearword

hell-bent adjective determined to do something whatever the consequences

hellish adjective (informal) very unpleasant

hello interjection You say 'Hello' as a greeting or when you answer the phone

helm noun **1** The helm on a boat is the position from which it is steered and the wheel or tiller ▷ phrase **2** At the helm means in a position of leadership or control

helmet noun a hard hat worn to protect the head

help verb **1** To help someone means to make something easier or better for them ▷ noun **2** If you need or give help, you need or give assistance **3** someone or something that helps you: He really is a good help ▷ phrase **4** If you **help yourself** to something, you take it **5** If you **can't help** something, you cannot control it or change it: I can't help feeling sorry for him

helper noun a person who gives assistance

helpful adjective **1** If someone is helpful, they help you by doing something for you **2** Something that is helpful makes a situation more pleasant or easier to tolerate > **helpfully** adverb

helping noun an amount of food that you get in a single serving

helpless adjective **1** unable to cope on your own: *a helpless child* **2** weak or powerless: *helpless despair* > **helplessly** adverb > **helplessness** noun

hem hems, hemming, hemmed noun **1** The hem of a garment is an edge which has been turned over and sewn in place ▷ verb **2** To hem something means to make a hem on it > **hem in** verb If someone is hemmed in, they are surrounded and prevented from moving

hemisphere [hem-iss-feer] noun one half of the earth, the brain, or a sphere > **hemispherical** adjective

hemp noun Hemp is a tall plant, some varieties of which are used to make rope, and others to produce the drug cannabis

hen noun a female chicken; also any female bird

hence adverb **1** (formal) for this reason: *It sells more papers, hence more money is made* **2** from now or from the time mentioned: *The convention is due to start two weeks hence*

henceforth adverb (formal) from this time onward: *His life henceforth was to revolve around her*

henchman henchmen noun The henchmen of a powerful person are the people employed to do violent or dishonest work for that person

hepatitis noun Hepatitis is a serious infectious disease causing inflammation of the liver

her pronoun, adjective 'Her' is used to refer to a woman, girl, or female animal that has already been mentioned, or to show that something belongs to a particular female

herald noun **1** In the past, a herald was a messenger ▷ verb **2** Something that heralds a future event is a sign of that event

herb noun a plant whose leaves are used in medicine or to flavour food > **herbal** adjective > **herbalist** noun

herd noun **1** a large group of animals ▷ verb **2** To herd animals or people means to make them move together as a group

here adverb **1** at, to, or in the place where you are, or the place mentioned or indicated ▷ phrase **2** Here and there means in various unspecified places: *dense forests broken here and there by small towns*

hereafter adverb (formal) after this time or point: *the South China Morning Post* (referred to hereafter as *SCMP*)

hereby adverb (formal) used in documents and statements to indicate that a declaration is official: *All leave is hereby cancelled*

hereditary adjective passed on to a child from a parent: *a hereditary disease*

herein adverb (formal) in this place or document

heresy heresies [herr-ess-ee] noun Heresy is belief or behaviour considered to be wrong because it disagrees with what is generally accepted, especially with regard to religion > **heretic** noun > **heretical** adjective

heritage noun the possessions or traditions that have been passed from one generation to another

hermit noun a person who lives alone with a simple way of life, especially for religious reasons

hernia [her-nee-a] noun a medical condition in which part of the intestine sticks through a weak point in the surrounding tissue

hero heroes noun **1** the main male character in a book, film, or play **2** a person who has done something brave or good

heroic adjective brave, courageous, and determined > **heroically** adverb

heroin [herr-oh-in] noun Heroin is a powerful drug formerly used as an anaesthetic and now taken illegally by some people for pleasure

heroine [herr-oh-in] noun **1** the main female character in a book, film, or play **2** a woman who has done something brave or good

heroism [herr-oh-izm] noun Heroism is great courage and bravery

heron noun a wading bird with very long legs and a long beak and neck

herring noun a silvery fish that lives in large shoals in northern seas

hers pronoun 'Hers' refers to something that belongs or relates to a woman, girl, or female animal

herself pronoun **1** 'Herself' is used when the same woman, girl, or female animal does an action and is affected by it: She pulled herself out of the water **2** 'Herself' is used to emphasize 'she'

hesitant adjective If you are hesitant, you do not do something immediately because you are uncertain or worried > **hesitantly** adverb

hesitate verb To hesitate means to pause or show uncertainty > **hesitation** noun

hessian noun Hessian is a thick, rough fabric used for making sacks

heterosexual [het-roh-**seks**-yool] noun **1** a person who is attracted to people of the opposite gender ▷ adjective **2** attracted to people of the opposite gender

hewn adjective carved from a substance: a cave, hewn out of the hillside

heyday [**hay**-day] noun The heyday of a person or thing is the period when they are most successful or popular: Hollywood in its heyday

hi interjection 'Hi!' is an informal greeting

hiatus hiatuses [high-**ay**-tuss] noun (formal) a pause or gap

hibernate verb Animals that hibernate spend the winter in a state like deep sleep > **hibernation** noun

hibiscus hibiscuses [hie-**bis**-kuss] noun a type of tropical shrub with brightly coloured flowers

hiccup hiccups, hiccuping, hiccuped [**hik**-kup] noun **1** Hiccups are short, uncontrolled choking sounds in your throat that you sometimes get if you have been eating or drinking too quickly **2** (informal) a minor problem ▷ verb **3** When you hiccup, you make little choking sounds

hide hides, hiding, hid, hidden verb **1** To hide something means to put it where it cannot be seen, or to prevent it from being discovered: He was unable to hide his disappointment ▷ noun **2** the skin of a large animal

hideous [**hid**-ee-uss] adjective extremely ugly or unpleasant > **hideously** adverb

hideout noun a hiding place

hiding noun (informal) To give someone a hiding means to beat them severely

hierarchy hierarchies [**high**-er-ar-kee] noun a system in which people or things are ranked according to how important they are > **hierarchical** adjective

hi-fi noun a set of stereo equipment

on which you can play recorded music

high *adjective* **1** tall or a long way above the ground **2** great in degree, quantity, or intensity: *high interest rates*; *There is a high risk of heart disease* **3** towards the top of a scale of importance or quality: *high fashion* **4** close to the top of a range of sound or notes: *the human voice reaches a very high pitch* ▷ *adverb* **5** at or to a height ▷ *noun* **6** a high point or level: *Morale reached a new high* ▷ *phrase* **7** (*informal*) Someone who is **on a high** is in a very excited and optimistic mood

highbrow *adjective* concerned with serious, intellectual subjects

higher education *noun* Higher education is education at universities and colleges

high jump *noun* The high jump is an athletics event involving jumping over a high bar

highlands *plural noun* Highlands are mountainous or hilly areas of land

highlight *verb* **1** If you highlight a point or problem, you emphasize and draw attention to it ▷ *noun* **2** The highlight of something is the most interesting part of it: *His show was the highlight of the Festival* **3** ART a lighter area of a painting, showing where light shines on things **4** Highlights are also light-coloured streaks in someone's hair

highly *adverb* **1** extremely: *It is highly unlikely I'll be able to replace it* **2** towards the top of a scale of importance, admiration, or respect: *She thought highly of him*; *highly qualified personnel*

high-minded *adjective* Someone who is high-minded has strong moral principles

Highness *noun* 'Highness' is used in

titles and forms of address for members of the royal family other than a king or queen: *Her Royal Highness, Princess Alexandra*

high-pitched *adjective* A high-pitched sound is high and often rather shrill

high-rise *adjective* High-rise buildings are very tall

high school *noun* a secondary school

high tide *noun* On a coast, high tide is the time, usually twice a day, when the sea is at its highest level

highway *noun* a road along which vehicles have the right to pass

hijab *noun* a head-covering worn by Muslim women

hijack *verb* If someone hijacks a plane or vehicle, they illegally take control of it during a journey > **hijacker** *noun* > **hijacking** *noun*

hike *noun* **1** a long country walk ▷ *verb* **2** To hike means to walk long distances in the country > **hiker** *noun*

hilarious *adjective* very funny > **hilariously** *adverb*

hilarity *noun* Hilarity is great amusement and laughter

hill *noun* a rounded area of land higher than the land surrounding it > **hilly** *adjective*

hillbilly hillbillies *noun* someone who lives in the country away from other people, especially in remote areas in the southern United States

hilt *noun* The hilt of a sword or knife is its handle

him *pronoun* You use 'him' to refer to a man, boy, or male animal that has already been mentioned

himself *pronoun* **1** 'Himself' is used when the same man, boy, or male animal does an action and is affected by it: *He discharged himself* from hospital **2** 'Himself' is used to emphasize 'he'

hind [rhymes with **blind**] *adjective* **1** used to refer to the back part of an animal: *the hind legs* ▷ *noun* **2** a female deer

hinder *verb* **1** [hin-der] If you hinder someone or something, you get in their way and make something difficult for them ▷ *adjective* **2** [hine-der] The hinder parts of an animal are the parts at the back

Hindi [hin-dee] *noun* Hindi is a language spoken in northern India

hindrance *noun* **1** Someone or something that is a hindrance causes difficulties or is an obstruction **2** Hindrance is the act of hindering someone or something

hindsight *noun* Hindsight is the ability to understand an event after it has actually taken place: *With hindsight, I realized how odd he is*

Hindu [hin-doo] *noun* RE a person who believes in Hinduism, an Indian religion which has many gods and believes that people have another life on earth after death
> **Hinduism** *noun*

hinge *noun* **1** the movable joint which attaches a door or window to its frame ▷ *verb* **2** Something that hinges on a situation or event depends entirely on that situation or event: *Victory or defeat hinged on her final putt*

hint *noun* **1** an indirect suggestion **2** a helpful piece of advice ▷ *verb* **3** If you hint at something, you suggest it indirectly

hinterland *noun* The hinterland of a coastline or a port is the area of land behind it or around it

hip *noun* Your hips are the two parts at the sides of your body between your waist and your upper legs

hippo hippos *noun* (*informal*) a hippopotamus

hippy hippies or **hippie** *noun* In the 1960s and 1970s hippies were people who rejected conventional society and tried to live a life based on peace and love

hire *verb* **1** If you hire something, you pay money to be able to use it for a period of time **2** If you hire someone, you pay them to do a job for you ▷ *phrase* **3** Something that is for hire is available for people to hire

hirsute [hir-syoot] *adjective* (*formal*) hairy

his *adjective, pronoun* 'His' refers to something that belongs or relates to a man, boy, or male animal that has already been mentioned, and sometimes also to any person whose gender is not known

hiss *verb* **1** To hiss means to make a long 's' sound, especially to show disapproval or aggression ▷ *noun* **2** a long 's' sound

historian *noun* a person who studies and writes about history

historic *adjective* important in the past or likely to be seen as important in the future

historical *adjective* **1** occurring in the past, or relating to the study of the past: *historical events* **2** describing or representing the past: *historical novels* ▷ **historically** *adverb*

history histories *noun* History is the study of the past. A history is a record of the past: *The village is steeped in history; my family history*

histrionic [hiss-tree-on-ik] *adjective* **1** Histrionic behaviour is very dramatic and full of exaggerated emotion **2** (*formal*) relating to drama and acting: *a young man of marked histrionic ability*

histrionics plural noun Histrionics are dramatic behaviour full of exaggerated emotion

hit hits, hitting, hit verb **1** If you hit someone, you strike them forcefully, usually causing hurt or damage **2** If you hit an object, you collide with it **3** To hit a ball or other object means to make it move by hitting it with something **4** If something hits you, it affects you badly and suddenly: *The recession has hit the tourist industry hard* **5** If something hits a particular point or place, it reaches it: *The book hit Britain just at the right time* **6** If you hit on an idea or solution, you suddenly think of it ▷ noun **7** a person or thing that is popular and successful **8** the action of hitting something: *Give it a good hard hit with the hammer* ▷ phrase **9** (informal) If you **hit it off** with someone, you become friendly with them the first time you meet them

hit and miss adjective happening in an unpredictable way or without being properly organized

hit-and-run adjective A hit-and-run car accident is one in which the person who has caused the damage drives away without stopping

hitch noun **1** A hitch is a slight problem or difficulty: *The whole process was completed without a hitch; an administrative hitch* ▷ verb **2** (informal) If you hitch, you hitchhike: *America is no longer a safe place to hitch round* **3** To hitch something somewhere means to hook it or fasten it there: *Each wagon was hitched onto the one in front* ▷ phrase **4** (informal) If you **get hitched**, you get married

hitchhiking noun Hitchhiking is travelling by getting free lifts from passing vehicles

hither (old-fashioned) adverb **1** used to refer to movement towards the place where you are ▷ phrase **2** Something that moves **hither and thither** moves in all directions

hitherto adverb (formal) until now: *What he was aiming at had not hitherto been attempted*

HIV noun HIV is a virus that reduces people's resistance to illness and can cause AIDS. HIV is an abbreviation for 'human immunodeficiency virus'

hive noun **1** a beehive **2** A place that is a hive of activity is very busy with a lot of people working hard ▷ verb **3** If part of something such as a business is hived off, it is transferred to new ownership: *The company is poised to hive off its music interests*

hoard verb **1** To hoard things means to save them even though they may no longer be useful ▷ noun **2** a store of things that has been saved or hidden

WORD TIP

Do not confuse the spellings of hoard and horde: *a hoard of Viking treasure; hordes of Christmas shoppers*

hoarding noun a large advertising board by the side of the road

hoarse adjective A hoarse voice sounds rough and unclear ▷ **hoarsely** adverb

hoax noun **1** a trick or an attempt to deceive someone ▷ verb **2** To hoax someone means to trick or deceive them ▷ **hoaxer** noun

hob noun a surface on top of a cooker which can be heated in order to cook things

hobble verb **1** If you hobble, you walk awkwardly because of pain or injury **2** If you hobble an animal, you tie its legs together to restrict its movement

hobby hobbies *noun* something that you do for enjoyment in your spare time

hock *noun* The hock of a horse or other animal is the angled joint in its back leg

hockey *noun* Hockey is a game in which two teams use long sticks with curved ends to try to hit a small ball into the other team's goal

hoe hoes, hoeing, hoed *noun* **1** a long-handled gardening tool with a small square blade, used to remove weeds and break up the soil ▷ *verb* **2** To hoe the ground means to use a hoe on it

hog hogs, hogging, hogged *noun* **1** a castrated male pig ▷ *verb* **2** (*informal*) If you hog something, you take more than your share of it, or keep it for too long ▷ *phrase* **3** (*informal*) If you **go the whole hog**, you do something completely or thoroughly in a bold or extravagant way

hoist *verb* **1** To hoist something means to lift it, especially using a crane or other machinery ▷ *noun* **2** a machine for lifting heavy things

hold holds, holding, held *verb* **1** To hold something means to carry or keep it in place, usually with your hand or arms **2** Someone who holds power, office, or an opinion has it or possesses it **3** If you hold something such as a meeting or an election, you arrange it and cause it to happen **4** If something holds, it is still available or valid: *The offer still holds* **5** If you hold someone responsible for something, you consider them responsible for it **6** If something holds a certain number or amount, it can contain that number or amount: *The theatre holds 150 people* **7** If you hold something

such as theatre tickets, a telephone call, or the price of something, you keep or reserve it for a period of time: *The line is engaged – will you hold?* **8** To hold something down means to keep it or to keep it under control: *How could I have children and hold down a job like this?* **9** If you hold on to something, you continue it or keep it even though it might be difficult: *They are keen to hold on to their culture* **10** To hold something back means to prevent it, keep it under control, or not reveal it: *She failed to hold back the tears* ▷ *noun* **11** If someone or something has a hold over you, they have power, control, or influence over you: *The party has a considerable hold over its own leader* **12** a way of holding something or the act of holding it: *He grabbed the rope and got a hold on it* **13** the place where cargo or luggage is stored in a ship or a plane ▷ **holder** *noun* > **hold out** *verb* If you hold out, you stand firm and manage to resist opposition in difficult circumstances: *The rebels could hold out for ten years* > **hold up** *verb* If something holds you up, it delays you

holdall *noun* a large, soft bag for carrying clothing

hole *noun* **1** an opening or hollow in something **2** (*informal*) If you are in a hole, you are in a difficult situation **3** (*informal*) A hole in a theory or argument is a weakness or error in it **4** In golf, a hole is one of the small holes into which you have to hit the ball ▷ *verb* **5** When you hole the ball in golf, you hit the ball into one of the holes

holiday *noun* **1** a period of time spent away from home for enjoyment **2** a time when you are

not working or not at school ▷ verb
3 When you holiday somewhere, you take a holiday there: *She is currently holidaying in Italy*
holidaymaker noun a person who is away from home on holiday
holiness noun **1** Holiness is the state or quality of being holy **2** 'Your Holiness' and 'His Holiness' are titles used to address or refer to the Pope or to leaders of some other religions
hollow adjective **1** Something that is hollow has space inside it rather than being solid **2** An opinion or situation that is hollow has no real value or worth: *a hollow gesture* **3** A hollow sound is dull and has a slight echo: *the hollow sound of his footsteps on the stairs* ▷ noun **4** a hole in something or a part of a surface that is lower than the rest: *It is a pleasant village in a lush hollow* ▷ verb **5** To hollow means to make a hollow: *They hollowed out crude dwellings from the soft rock*
holly noun Holly is an evergreen tree or shrub with spiky leaves. It often has red berries in winter
holocaust [hol-o-kawst] noun **1** a large-scale destruction or loss of life, especially the result of war or fire **2** The Holocaust was the mass murder of the Jews in Europe by the Nazis during World War II
holster noun a holder for a hand gun, worn at the side of the body or under the arm
holy holier, holiest adjective **1** relating to God or to a particular religion: *the holy city* **2** Someone who is holy leads a pure and good life
homage [hom-ij] noun Homage is an act of respect and admiration: *The thronging crowds paid homage to their assassinated president*

home noun **1** Your home is the building or place in which you live or feel you belong **2** a building in which elderly or ill people live and are looked after: *He has been confined to a nursing home since his stroke* ▷ adjective **3** connected with or involving your home or country: *He gave them his home phone number; The government is expanding the home market* > **home in** verb If something homes in on a target, it moves directly and quickly towards it
homeland noun Your homeland is your native country
homeless adjective **1** having no home ▷ plural noun **2** The homeless are people who have no home > **homelessness** noun
homely homelier, homeliest adjective simple, ordinary, and comfortable: *The room was small and homely*
homeopathy [home-ee-**op**-path-ee] noun Homeopathy is a way of treating illness by giving the patient tiny amounts of a substance that would normally cause illness in a healthy person > **homeopathic** adjective > **homeopath** noun
homeowner noun a person who owns the home in which he or she lives
homesick adjective unhappy because of being away from home and missing family and friends > **homesickness** noun
homespun adjective not sophisticated or complicated: *The book is simple homespun philosophy*
homestead noun a house and its land and other buildings, especially a farm
homeward or **homewards** adjective, adverb towards home: *the homeward journey*

homework noun **1** Homework is school work given to pupils to be done in the evening at home **2** Homework is also research and preparation: You certainly need to do your homework before buying a horse

homicide noun Homicide is the crime of murder > **homicidal** adjective

homing adjective A homing device is able to guide itself to a target. An animal with a homing instinct is able to guide itself home

homosexual noun **1** a person who is attracted to people of the same gender ▷ adjective **2** attracted to people of the same gender > **homosexuality** noun

hone verb **1** If you hone a tool, you sharpen it **2** If you hone a quality or ability, you develop and improve it: He had a sharply honed sense of justice

honest adjective truthful and trustworthy > **honestly** adverb

honesty noun Honesty is the quality of being truthful and trustworthy

honey noun **1** Honey is a sweet, edible, sticky substance produced by bees **2** 'Honey' means 'sweetheart' or 'darling': What is it, honey?

honeycomb noun a wax structure consisting of rows of six-sided cells made by bees for storage of honey and eggs

honeymoon noun a holiday taken by a couple who have just got married

honeysuckle noun Honeysuckle is a climbing plant with fragrant pink or cream flowers

honk noun **1** a short, loud sound like that made by a car horn or a goose ▷ verb **2** When something honks, it makes a short, loud sound

honorary adjective An honorary title or job is given as a mark of respect, and does not involve the usual qualifications or work: She was awarded an honorary degree

honour noun **1** Your honour is your good reputation and the respect that other people have for you: This is a war begun by men totally without honour **2** an award or privilege given as a mark of respect **3** Honours is a class of university degree which is higher than a pass or ordinary degree ▷ phrase **4** If something is done in honour of someone, it is done out of respect for them: Egypt celebrated frequent minor festivals in honour of the dead ▷ verb **5** If you honour someone, you give them special praise or attention, or an award **6** If you honour an agreement or promise, you do what was agreed or promised: There is enough cash to honour the existing pledges

honourable adjective worthy of respect or admiration: He should do the honourable thing and resign

hood noun **1** a loose covering for the head, usually part of a coat or jacket **2** a cover on a piece of equipment or vehicle, usually curved and movable: The mechanic had the hood up to work on the engine > **hooded** adjective

-hood suffix '-hood' is added at the end of words to form nouns that indicate a state or condition: childhood; priesthood

hoof noun hooves or hoofs noun the hard bony part of certain animals' feet

hook noun **1** a curved piece of metal or plastic that is used for catching, holding, or hanging things: picture hooks **2** a curving movement, for example of the fist in boxing, or of a golf ball ▷ verb **3** If you hook one thing onto another, you attach it there using a hook ▷ phrase **4** If you are **let off the hook**, something happens to that you avoid punishment or a difficult situation

hooked adjective addicted to something; also obsessed by something: hooked on soap operas; I'm hooked on exercise

hooligan noun a destructive and violent young person
> **hooliganism** noun

hoop noun a large ring, often used as a toy

hooray interjection another spelling of **hurray**

hoot verb **1** To hoot means to make a long 'oo' sound like an owl: hooting with laughter **2** If a car horn hoots, it makes a loud honking noise ▷ noun **3** a sound like that made by an owl or a car horn

hooves a plural of **hoof**

hop hops, hopping, hopped verb **1** If you hop, you jump on one foot **2** When animals or birds hop, they jump with two feet together **3** (informal) If you hop into or out of something, you move there quickly and easily: You only have to hop on the ferry to get there ▷ noun **4** a jump on one leg **5** Hops are flowers of the hop plant, which are dried and used for making beer

hope verb **1** If you hope that something will happen or hope that it is true, you want it to happen or be true ▷ noun **2** Hope is a wish or feeling of desire and expectation: There was little hope of recovery
> **hopeful** adjective > **hopefully** adverb

hopeless adjective **1** having no hope: She shook her head in hopeless bewilderment **2** certain to fail or be

unsuccessful **3** bad or inadequate: I'm hopeless at remembering birthdays; hopeless parents > **hopelessly** adverb
> **hopelessness** noun

hopper noun a large, funnel-shaped container for storing things such as grain or sand

horde [rhymes with **bored**] noun a large group or number of people or animals: hordes of tourists

horizon [hor-**eye**-zn] noun **1** the distant line where the sky seems to touch the land or sea **2** Your horizons are the limits of what you want to do or are interested in: Travel broadens your horizons ▷ phrase **3** If something is **on the horizon**, it is almost certainly going to happen or be done in the future: Political change was on the horizon

horizontal [hor-riz-**zon**-tl] adjective (MATHS) flat and parallel with the horizon or with a line considered as a base: a patchwork of vertical and horizontal black lines > **horizontally** adverb

hormone noun a chemical made by one part of your body that stimulates or has a specific effect on another part of your body
> **hormonal** adjective

horn noun **1** one of the hard, pointed growths on the heads of animals such as goats **2** a musical instrument made of brass, consisting of a pipe or that is narrow at one end and wide at the other **3** On vehicles, a horn is a warning device which makes a loud noise

hornet noun a type of very large wasp

horoscope [hor-ros-kope] noun a prediction about what is going to happen to someone, based on the position of the stars when they were born

horrendous adjective very unpleasant and shocking: *horrendous injuries*

horrible adjective 1 disagreeable and unpleasant: *A horrible nausea rose within him* 2 causing shock, fear, or disgust: *horrible crimes* > **horribly** adverb

horrid adjective very unpleasant indeed: *We were all so horrid to him*

horrific adjective so bad or unpleasant that people are horrified: *a horrific attack*

horrify horrifies, horrifying, horrified verb If something horrifies you, it makes you feel dismay or disgust: *a crime trend that will horrify parents* > **horrifying** adjective

horror noun 1 a strong feeling of alarm, dismay, and disgust: *He gazed in horror at the knife* 2 If you have a horror of something, you fear it very much: *He had a horror of fire*

horse noun 1 a large animal with a mane and long tail, on which people can ride 2 a piece of gymnastics equipment with four legs, used for jumping over

horseback noun, adjective You refer to someone who is riding a horse as someone 'on horseback', a horseback rider

horsepower noun Horsepower is a unit used for measuring how powerful an engine is, equal to about 746 watts

horseradish noun Horseradish is the white root of a plant made into a hot-tasting sauce, often served cold with beef

horseshoe noun a U-shaped piece of metal, nailed to the hard surface of a horse's hoof to protect it; also anything of this shape, often regarded as a good luck symbol

horticulture noun Horticulture is the study and practice of growing flowers, fruit, and vegetables > **horticultural** adjective

hose noun 1 a long flexible tube through which liquid or gas can be passed: *He left the garden hose on* ▷ verb 2 If you hose something, you wash or water it using a hose: *The street cleaners need to hose the square down*

hosiery [hoze-ee-yer-ee] noun Hosiery consists of tights, socks, and similar items, especially in shops

hospice [hoss-piss] noun a hospital which provides care for people who are dying

hospitable adjective friendly, generous, and welcoming to guests or strangers > **hospitality** noun

hospital noun a place where sick and injured people are treated and cared for

host noun 1 The host of an event is the person that welcomes guests and provides food or accommodation for them: *He is a most generous host who takes his guests to the best restaurants in town* 2 a plant or animal with smaller plants or animals living on or in it 3 A host of things is a large number of them: *a host of close friends* 4 In the Christian church, the Host is the consecrated bread used in Mass or Holy Communion ▷ verb 5 To host an event means to organize it or act as host at it

hostage noun a person who is illegally held prisoner and threatened with injury or death unless certain demands are met by other people

hostel noun a large building in which people can stay or live: *a hostel for battered women*

hostess noun a woman who welcomes guests or visitors and provides food or accommodation for them

hostile adjective **1** unfriendly, aggressive, and unpleasant: a hostile audience **2** relating to or involving the enemies of a country: hostile territory

hostility hostilities noun aggression or unfriendly behaviour towards a person or thing

hot hotter, hottest adjective **1** having a high temperature: a hot climate **2** very spicy and causing a burning sensation in your mouth: a hot curry **3** new, recent, and exciting: hot news from Tinseltown **4** dangerous or difficult to deal with: Animal testing is a hot issue ▷ **hotly** adverb

hotbed noun A hotbed of some other type of activity is a place that seems to encourage it: The city was a hotbed of rumour

hot dog noun a sausage served in a roll split lengthways

hotel noun a building where people stay, paying for their room and sometimes also meals

hothouse noun **1** a large heated greenhouse **2** a place or situation of intense intellectual or emotional activity: a hothouse of radical socialist ideas

hot seat noun (informal) Someone who is in the hot seat has to make difficult decisions for which they will be held responsible

hound noun **1** a dog, especially one used for hunting or racing ▷ verb **2** If someone hounds you, they constantly pursue or trouble you

hour noun **1** a unit of time equal to 60 minutes, of which there are 24 in a day **2** The hour for something is the time when it happens: The hour for launching approached **3** The hour is also the time of day: What are you doing up at this hour? **4** an important or difficult time: The hour has come; He is the hero of the hour **5** (in plural) The hours that you keep are the times that you usually go to bed and get up ▷ **hourly** adjective, adverb

house noun [hows] **1** a building where a person or family lives **2** a building used for a particular purpose: an auction house; the opera house **3** In a theatre or cinema, the house is the part where the audience sits; also the audience itself: The show had a packed house calling for more ▷ verb [howz] **4** To house something means to keep it or contain it: The west wing housed a store of valuable antiques

houseboat noun a small boat which people live on that is tied up at a particular place on a river or canal

household noun **1** all the people who live as a group in a house or flat ▷ phrase **2** Someone who is **a household name** is very well-known ▷ **householder** noun

housekeeper noun a person who is employed to do the cooking and cleaning in a house

House of Commons noun The House of Commons is the more powerful of the two parts of the British Parliament. Its members are elected by the public

House of Lords noun The House of Lords is the less powerful of the two parts of the British Parliament. Its members are unelected and come from noble families or are appointed by the Queen as an honour for a life of public service

House of Representatives noun **1** In Australia, the House of Representatives is the larger of the

two parts of the Federal Parliament
2 In New Zealand, the House of
Representatives is the Parliament

housewife housewives noun a
married woman who does the
chores in her home, and does not
have a paid job

housing noun Housing is the
buildings in which people live: *the
serious housing shortage*

hover verb **1** When a bird, insect, or
aircraft hovers, it stays in the same
position in the air **2** If someone is
hovering they are hesitating
because they cannot decide what to
do: *He was hovering nervously around
the sick animal*

hovercraft noun a vehicle which
can travel over water or land
supported by a cushion of air

how adverb **1** 'How' is used to ask
about, explain, or refer to the way in
which something is done, known,
or experienced: *How did this happen?;
He knew how quickly rumours could
spread* **2** 'How' is used to ask about
or refer to a measurement or
quantity: *How much is it for the
weekend?; I wonder how old he is*
3 'How' is used to emphasize the
following word or statement: *How
odd!*

however adverb **1** You use 'however'
when you are adding a comment
that seems to contradict or contrast
with what has just been said: *For all
his compassion, he is, however,
surprisingly restrained* **2** You use
'however' to say that something
makes no difference to a situation:
*However hard she tried, nothing seemed
to work*

howl verb **1** To howl means to make
a long, loud wailing noise such as
that made by a dog when it is upset:
A distant coyote howled at the moon;

The wind howled through the trees
▷ noun **2** a long, loud wailing noise

HQ an abbreviation for
headquarters

hub noun **1** the centre part of a wheel
2 the most important or active part
of a place or organization: *The
kitchen is the hub of most households*

hubbub noun Hubbub is great noise
or confusion: *the general hubbub of
conversation*

huddle verb **1** If you huddle up or are
huddled, you are curled up with
your arms and legs close to your
body **2** When people or animals
huddle together, they sit or stand
close to each other, often for
warmth ▷ noun **3** A huddle of people
or things is a small group of them

hue noun **1** (literary) a colour or a
particular shade of a colour ▷ phrase
2 If people raise a **hue and cry**, they
are very angry about something and
protest

huff phrase (informal) If you are **in a
huff**, you are sulking or offended
about something > **huffy** adjective
> **huffily** adverb

hug hugs, hugging, hugged verb
1 If you hug someone, you put your
arms round them and hold them
close to you **2** To hug the ground or
a stretch of water or land means to
keep very close to it: *The road hugs
the coast for hundreds of miles* ▷ noun
3 If you give someone a hug, you
hold them close to you

huge adjective extremely large in
amount, size, or degree: *a huge
success; a huge crowd* > **hugely**
adverb

hulk noun **1** a large, heavy person or
thing **2** the body of a ship that has
been wrecked or abandoned
> **hulking** adjective

hull noun The hull of a ship is the

main part of its body that sits in the water

hum hums, humming, hummed verb
1 To hum means to make a continuous low noise: *The generator hummed faintly* **2** If you hum, you sing with your lips closed ▷ noun **3** a continuous low noise: *the hum of the fridge*

human adjective **1** relating to, concerning, or typical of people: *Intolerance appears deeply ingrained in human nature* ▷ noun **2** a person
> **humanly** adverb

human being noun a person

humane adjective showing kindness and sympathy towards others: *Medicine is regarded as the most humane of professions* > **humanely** adverb

humanism noun Humanism is the belief in mankind's ability to achieve happiness and fulfilment without the need for religion

humanitarian noun **1** a person who works for the welfare of mankind ▷ adjective **2** concerned with the welfare of mankind: *humanitarian aid* > **humanitarianism** noun

humanity noun **1** Humanity is people in general: *I have faith in humanity* **2** Humanity is also the condition of being human: *He is so full of hatred he has lost his humanity* **3** Someone who has humanity is kind and sympathetic

human rights plural noun Human rights are the rights of individuals to freedom and justice

humble adjective **1** A humble person is modest and thinks that he or she has very little value **2** Something that is humble is small or not very important: *Just a splash of wine will transform a humble casserole* ▷ verb **3** To humble someone means to make them feel humiliated

> **humbly** adverb > **humbled** adjective

humbug noun **1** a hard black and white striped sweet that tastes of peppermint **2** Humbug is speech or writing that is obviously dishonest or untrue: *hypocritical humbug*

humdrum adjective ordinary, dull, and boring: *humdrum domestic tasks*

humid adjective If it is humid, the air feels damp, heavy, and warm

humidity noun Humidity is the amount of moisture in the air, or the state of being humid

humiliate verb To humiliate someone means to make them feel ashamed or appear stupid to other people > **humiliation** noun

humility noun Humility is the quality of being modest and humble

humour noun **1** Humour is the quality of being funny: *They discussed it with tact and humour* **2** Humour is also the ability to be amused by certain things: *Helen's got a peculiar sense of humour* **3** Someone's humour is the mood they are in: *He hasn't been in a good humour lately* ▷ verb **4** If you humour someone, you are especially kind to them and do whatever they want
> **humorous** adjective

hump noun **1** a small, rounded lump or mound: *a camel's hump* ▷ verb **2** (informal) If you hump something heavy, you carry or move it with difficulty

hunch noun **1** a feeling or suspicion about something, not based on facts or evidence ▷ verb **2** If you hunch your shoulders, you raise your shoulders and lean forwards

hundred the number 100
> **hundredth** adjective

Hungarian [hung-**gair**-ee-an] adjective **1** belonging or relating to

Hungary ▷ *noun* **2** someone who comes from Hungary **3** Hungarian is the main language spoken in Hungary

hunger *noun* **1** Hunger is the need to eat or the desire to eat **2** A hunger for something is a strong need or desire for it: *a hunger for winning* ▷ *verb* **3** If you hunger for something, you want it very much

hunger strike *noun* A refusal to eat anything at all, especially by prisoners, as a form of protest

hungry hungrier, hungriest *adjective* needing or wanting to eat: *People are going hungry* > **hungrily** *adverb*

hunk *noun* A hunk of something is a large piece of it

hunt *verb* **1** To hunt means to chase wild animals to kill them for food or for sport **2** If you hunt for something, you search for it ▷ *noun* **3** the act of hunting: *Police launched a hunt for an abandoned car* > **hunter** *noun* > **hunting** *adjective, noun*

hurdle *noun* **1** one of the frames or barriers that you jump over in an athletics race called hurdles: *She won the 400-metre hurdles* **2** a problem or difficulty: *Several hurdles exist for anyone seeking to do postgraduate study*

hurl *verb* **1** To hurl something means to throw it with great force **2** If you hurl insults at someone, you insult them aggressively and repeatedly

hurray, hurrah or **hooray** *interjection* an exclamation of excitement or approval

hurricane *noun* GEOGRAPHY A hurricane is a violent wind or storm, usually force 12 or above on the Beaufort scale

hurry hurries, hurrying, hurried *verb* **1** To hurry means to move or do something as quickly as possible:

She hurried through the empty streets **2** To hurry something means to make it happen more quickly: *You can't hurry nature* ▷ *noun* **3** Hurry is the speed with which you do something quickly: *He was in a hurry to leave* > **hurried** *adjective* > **hurriedly** *adverb*

hurt hurts, hurting, hurt *verb* **1** To hurt someone means to cause them physical pain **2** If a part of your body hurts, you feel pain there **3** If you hurt yourself, you injure yourself **4** To hurt someone also means to make them unhappy by being unkind or thoughtless towards them: *I didn't want to hurt his feelings* ▷ *adjective* **5** If someone feels hurt, they feel unhappy because of someone's unkindness towards them: *He felt hurt by all the lies* > **hurtful** *adjective*

hurtle *verb* To hurtle means to move or travel very fast indeed, especially in an uncontrolled way

husband *noun* A person's husband is the man they are married to

husbandry *noun* **1** Husbandry is the art or skill of farming **2** Husbandry is also the art or skill of managing something carefully and economically

hush *verb* **1** If you tell someone to hush, you are telling them to be quiet **2** To hush something up means to keep it secret, especially something dishonest involving important people: *The government has hushed up a series of scandals* ▷ *noun* **3** If there is a hush, it is quiet and still: *A graveyard hush fell over the group* > **hushed** *adjective*

husk *noun* Husks are the dry outer coverings of grain or seed

husky huskier, huskiest; huskies *adjective* **1** A husky voice is rough or hoarse ▷ *noun* **2** a large, strong dog with a thick coat, often used to pull sledges across snow > **huskily** *adverb*

hustle *verb* To hustle someone means to make them move by pushing and jostling them: *The guards hustled him out of the car*

hut *noun* a small, simple building, with one or two rooms

hybrid *noun* **1** a plant or animal that has been bred from two different types of plant or animal **2** anything that is a mixture of two other things

hydraulic [high-**drol**-lik] *adjective* operated by water or other fluid which is under pressure

hydraulics *noun* Hydraulics is the study and use of systems that work using hydraulic pressure

hydrogen *noun* Hydrogen is the lightest gas and the simplest chemical element. It is colourless and odourless. Its atomic number is 1 and its symbol is H

hyena [high-**ee**-na] or **hyaena** *noun* a wild doglike animal of Africa and Asia that hunts in packs

hygiene [high-jeen] *noun* D & T Hygiene is the practice of keeping yourself and your surroundings clean, especially to stop the spread of disease > **hygienic** *adjective* > **hygienically** *adverb*

hymn *noun* RE a Christian song in praise of God

hyperactive *adjective* A hyperactive person is unable to relax and is always in a state of restless activity

hyperbole [high-**per**-bol-lee] *noun* Hyperbole is a style of speech or writing which uses exaggeration

hypertension *noun* Hypertension is a medical condition in which a person has high blood pressure

hyphen *noun* a punctuation mark used to join together words or parts of words, as for example in the word 'left-handed' > **hyphenate** *verb* > **hyphenation** *noun*

hypnosis [hip-**noh**-siss] *noun* Hypnosis is an artificially produced state of relaxation in which the mind is more receptive to suggestion

hypocrisy hypocrisies *noun* Hypocrisy is pretending to have beliefs or qualities that you do not really have, so that you seem a better person than you are > **hypocritical** *adjective* > **hypocritically** *adverb* > **hypocrite** *noun*

hypothermia *noun* SCIENCE Hypothermia is a condition in which a person is very ill because their body temperature has been unusually low for a long time

hypothesis hypotheses *noun* an explanation or theory which has not yet been proved to be correct

hypothetical *adjective* based on assumption rather than on fact or reality > **hypothetically** *adverb*

hysterectomy hysterectomies [his-ter-**rek**-tom-ee] *noun* an operation to remove a woman's womb

hysteria [hiss-**teer**-ee-a] *noun* Hysteria is a state of uncontrolled excitement or panic

hysterical *adjective* **1** Someone who is hysterical is in a state of uncontrolled excitement or panic **2** (*informal*) Something that is hysterical is extremely funny > **hysterically** *adverb* > **hysterics** *noun*

i

I pronoun A speaker or writer uses 'I' to refer to himself or herself: *I like the colour*

ibis ibises [**eye**-biss] noun a large wading bird with a long, thin, curved bill that lives in warm countries

-ible suffix another form of the suffix **-able**

-ic or **-ical** suffix '-ic' and '-ical' form adjectives from nouns. For example, *ironic* and *ironical* can be formed from *irony*

ice noun **1** water that has frozen solid **2** an ice cream ▷ verb **3** If you ice cakes, you cover them with icing **4** If something ices over or ices up, it becomes covered with a layer of ice ▷ phrase **5** If you do something to **break the ice**, you make people feel relaxed and comfortable

Ice Age noun a period of time lasting thousands of years when a lot of the earth's surface was covered with ice

iceberg noun a large mass of ice floating in the sea

ice cream noun a very cold sweet food made from frozen cream

ice hockey noun a type of hockey played on ice, with two teams of six players

Icelandic adjective **1** belonging or relating to Iceland ▷ noun **2** the main language spoken in Iceland

icing noun a mixture of powdered sugar and water or egg whites, used to decorate cakes

icon [**eye**-kon] noun **1** COMPUTING a picture on a computer screen representing a program that can be activated by moving the cursor over it **2** in the Orthodox Churches, a holy picture of Christ, the Virgin Mary, or a saint

ICT an abbreviation for 'Information and Communication Technology'

icy icier, iciest adjective **1** Something which is icy is very cold: *an icy wind* **2** An icy road has ice on it ▷ **icily** adverb

id noun In psychology, your id is your basic instincts and unconscious thoughts

idea noun **1** a plan, suggestion, or thought that you have after thinking about a problem **2** an opinion or belief: *old-fashioned ideas about women* **3** An idea of something is what you know about it: *They had no idea of their position*

ideal noun **1** a principle or idea that you try to achieve because it seems perfect to you **2** Your ideal of something is the person or thing that seems the best example of it ▷ adjective **3** The ideal person or thing is the best possible person or thing for the situation

idealism [eye-dee-il-izm] noun behaviour that is based on a person's ideals > **idealist** noun > **idealistic** adjective

ideally adverb **1** If you say that ideally something should happen, you mean that you would like it to happen but you know that it is not likely **2** Ideally means perfectly: *The hotel is ideally placed for business travellers*

identical adjective exactly the same: *identical twins* > **identically** adverb

identification noun **1** The identification of someone or something is the act of identifying them **2** Identification is a document, such as a driver's licence or passport, which proves who you are

identify identifies, identifying, identified verb **1** To identify someone or something is to recognize them or name them **2** If you identify with someone, you understand their feelings and ideas > **identifiable** adjective

identity identities noun the characteristics that make you who you are

ideology ideologies noun a set of political beliefs > **ideological** adjective > **ideologically** adverb

idiom [ENGLISH] noun a group of words whose meaning together is different from all the words taken individually. For example, 'It's raining cats and dogs' is an idiom

idiot noun someone who is stupid or foolish

idiotic adjective extremely foolish or silly > **idiotically** adverb

idle adjective If you are idle, you are doing nothing > **idleness** noun > **idly** adverb

idol [eye-doll] noun **1** a famous person who is loved and admired by fans **2** a picture or statue which is worshipped as if it were a god

idyll [id-ill] noun a situation which is peaceful and beautiful > **idyllic** adjective

i.e. i.e. means 'that is', and is used before giving more information. It is an abbreviation for the Latin expression 'id est'

if conjunction **1** on the condition that: I shall stay if I can **2** whether: I asked her if she wanted to go

igloo igloos noun a dome-shaped house built out of blocks of snow by Inuit people

ignite verb If you ignite something or if it ignites, it starts burning

ignition noun In a car, the ignition is the part of the engine where the fuel is ignited

ignominious adjective shameful or considered wrong: It was an ignominious end to a brilliant career > **ignominiously** adverb > **ignominy** noun

ignorant adjective **1** If you are ignorant of something, you do not know about it: He was completely ignorant of the rules **2** Someone who is ignorant does not know about things in general: I thought of asking, but didn't want to seem ignorant > **ignorantly** adverb > **ignorance** noun

ignore verb If you ignore someone or something, you deliberately do not take any notice of them

iguana [ig-wah-na] noun a large, tropical lizard

ill adjective **1** unhealthy or sick **2** harmful or unpleasant: ill effects ▷ plural noun **3** Ills are difficulties or problems

ill at ease phrase If you feel ill at ease, you feel unable to relax

illegal adjective forbidden by the law > **illegally** adverb > **illegality** noun

illegible [il-lej-i-bl] adjective Writing which is illegible is unclear and very difficult to read

ill-fated adjective doomed to end unhappily: his ill-fated attempt at the world record

illicit [il-liss-it] adjective not allowed by law or not approved of by society: illicit drugs

illiterate adjective unable to read or write > **illiteracy** noun

illness noun **1** Illness is the experience of being ill **2** a particular disease: *the treatment of common illnesses*

illogical *adjective* An illogical feeling or action is not reasonable or sensible > **illogically** *adverb*

illuminate *verb* To illuminate something is to shine light on it to make it easier to see

illumination *noun* **1** Illumination is lighting **2** Illuminations are the coloured lights put up to decorate a town, especially at Christmas

illusion *noun* **1** a false belief which you think is true: *Their hopes proved to be an illusion* **2** ART A false appearance of reality which deceives the eye: *Painters create the illusion of space*

illusory [ill-**yoo**-ser-ee] *adjective* seeming to be true, but actually false: *an illusory truce*

illustrate *verb* **1** EXAM TERM If you illustrate a point, you explain it or make it clearer, often by using examples **2** If you illustrate a book, you put pictures in it > **illustrator** *noun* > **illustrative** *adjective*

illustration *noun* **1** an example or a story which is used to make a point clear **2** a picture in a book

illustrious *adjective* An illustrious person is famous and respected

ill will *noun* Ill will is a feeling of hostility

image *noun* **1** a mental picture of someone or something **2** the appearance which a person, group, or organization presents to the public

imagery *noun* ENGLISH The imagery of a poem or book is the descriptive language used in it

imaginary *adjective* Something that is imaginary exists only in your mind, not in real life

imagination *noun* the ability to form new and exciting ideas

imaginative *adjective* Someone who is imaginative can easily form new or exciting ideas in their mind > **imaginatively** *adverb*

imagine *verb* **1** If you imagine something, you form an idea of it in your mind, or you think you have seen or heard it but you have not really **2** If you imagine that something is the case, you believe it is the case: *I imagine that's what you aim to do* > **imaginable** *adjective*

imam [ih-**mam**] *noun* a person who leads a group in prayer in a mosque

imbalance *noun* If there is an imbalance between things, they are unequal: *the imbalance between rich and poor*

imitate *verb* To imitate someone or something is to copy them > **imitator** *noun* > **imitative** *adjective*

imitation *noun* a copy of something else

immaculate [im-**mak**-yoo-lit] *adjective* **1** completely clean and tidy: *The flat was immaculate* **2** without any mistakes at all: *his usual immaculate guitar accompaniment* > **immaculately** *adverb*

immaterial *adjective* Something that is immaterial is not important

immature *adjective* **1** Something that is immature has not finished growing or developing **2** A person who is immature does not behave in a sensible adult way > **immaturity** *noun*

immediate *adjective* **1** Something that is immediate happens or is done without delay **2** Your immediate relatives and friends are the ones most closely connected or related to you > **immediacy** *noun*

immediately adverb **1** If something happens immediately it happens right away **2** Immediately means very near in time or position: *immediately behind the house*

immemorial adjective If something has been happening from time immemorial, it has been happening longer than anyone can remember

immense adjective very large or huge > **immensely** adverb > **immensity** noun

immerse verb **1** If you are immersed in an activity you are completely involved in it **2** If you immerse something in a liquid, you put it into the liquid so that it is completely covered > **immersion** noun

immigrant noun HISTORY someone who has come to live permanently in a new country > **immigrate** verb > **immigration** noun

imminent adjective If something is imminent, it is going to happen very soon > **imminently** adverb > **imminence** noun

immobile adjective not moving > **immobility** noun

immoral adjective RE If you describe someone or their behaviour as immoral, you mean that they do not fit in with most people's idea of what is right and proper > **immorality** noun

> **WORD TIP**
> Do not confuse *immoral* and *amoral*. You use *immoral* to talk about people who are aware of moral standards, but go against them. *Amoral* applies to people with no moral standards

immortal adjective **1** Something that is immortal is famous and will be remembered for a long time: *Emily Brontë's immortal love story* **2** In stories, someone who is

immortal will never die

immortality noun RE Immortality is never dying. In many religions, people believe that the soul or some other essential part of a person lives forever or continues to exist in some form

immovable or **immoveable** adjective Something that is immovable is fixed and cannot be moved > **immovably** adverb

immune [im-**yoon**] adjective **1** If you are immune to a particular disease, you cannot catch it **2** If someone or something is immune to something, they are able to avoid it or are not affected by it: *The captain was immune to prosecution* > **immunity** noun

immune system noun Your body's immune system consists of your white blood cells, which fight disease by producing antibodies or germs to kill germs which come into your body

impact noun **1** The impact that someone or something has is the impression that they make or the effect that they have **2** Impact is the action of one object hitting another, usually with a lot of force: *The aircraft crashed into a ditch, exploding on impact*

impair verb To impair something is to damage it so that it stops working properly: *Travel had made him weary and impaired his judgement*

impart verb (formal) To impart information to someone is to pass it on to them

impartial adjective Someone who is impartial has a view of something which is fair or not biased > **impartially** adverb > **impartiality** noun

impasse [**am**-pass] noun a difficult

situation in which it is impossible to find a solution

impassioned adjective full of emotion: an impassioned plea

impassive adjective showing no emotion > **impassively** adverb

impatient adjective 1 Someone who is impatient becomes annoyed easily or is quick to lose their temper when things go wrong 2 If you are impatient to do something, you are eager and do not want to wait: He was impatient to get back > **impatiently** adverb > **impatience** noun

impeccable [im-**pek**-i-bl] adjective excellent, without any faults > **impeccably** adverb

impede verb If you impede someone, you make their progress difficult

impediment noun something that makes it difficult to move, develop, or do something properly: a speech impediment

impending adjective (formal) You use 'impending' to describe something that is going to happen very soon: a sense of impending doom

impenetrable adjective impossible to get through

imperative adjective 1 Something that is imperative is extremely urgent or important ▷ noun 2 In grammar, an imperative is the form of a verb that is used for giving orders

imperfect adjective 1 Something that is imperfect has faults or problems ▷ noun 2 In grammar, the imperfect is a tense used to describe continuous or repeated actions which happened in the past > **imperfectly** adverb > **imperfection** noun

Imperial adjective 1 HISTORY

Imperial means relating to an empire or an emperor or empress: the Imperial Palace 2 The imperial system of measurement is the measuring system which uses inches, feet, and yards, ounces and pounds, and pints and gallons

imperialism noun HISTORY a system of rule in which a rich and powerful nation controls other nations > **imperialist** adjective, noun

imperious adjective proud and domineering: an imperious manner > **imperiously** adverb

impersonal adjective Something that is impersonal makes you feel that individuals and their feelings do not matter: impersonal cold rooms > **impersonally** adverb

impersonate verb If you impersonate someone, you pretend to be that person > **impersonation** noun > **impersonator** noun

impertinent adjective disrespectful and rude: impertinent questions > **impertinently** adverb > **impertinence** noun

impetuous adjective If you are impetuous, you act quickly without thinking: an impetuous gamble > **impetuously** adverb > **impetuosity** noun

impetus noun 1 An impetus is the stimulating effect that something has on a situation, which causes it to develop more quickly 2 In physics, impetus is the force that starts an object moving and resists changes in speed or direction

impinge verb If something impinges on your life, it has an effect on you and influences you: My private life doesn't impinge on my professional life

implacable [im-**plak**-a-bl] adjective Someone who is implacable is being harsh and refuses to change their mind > **implacably** adverb > **implacability** noun

implant verb [im-**plant**] **1** To implant something into a person's body is to put it there, usually by means of an operation ▷ noun [**im**-plant] **2** something that has been implanted into someone's body

implausible adjective very unlikely: implausible stories > **implausibly** adverb

implement verb **1** If you implement something such as a plan, you carry it out: The government has failed to implement promised reforms ▷ noun **2** An implement is a tool > **implementation** noun

implicate verb If you are implicated in a crime, you are shown to be involved in it

implication noun something that is suggested or implied but not stated directly

implicit [im-**pliss**-it] adjective **1** expressed in an indirect way: implicit criticism **2** If you have an implicit belief in something, you have no doubts about it: He had implicit faith in the noble intentions of the Emperor > **implicitly** adverb

implore verb If you implore someone to do something, you beg them to do it

imply implies, implying, implied verb If you imply that something is the case, you suggest it in an indirect way

import verb **1** If you import something from another country, you bring it into your country or have it sent there ▷ noun **2** a product that is made in another country and sent to your own country for use there > **importation** noun > **importer** noun

important adjective **1** Something that is important is very valuable, necessary, or significant **2** An important person has great influence or power > **importantly** adverb > **importance** noun

impose verb **1** If you impose something on people, you force it on them: The allies had imposed a ban on all flights over Iraq **2** If someone imposes on you, they unreasonably expect you to do something for them > **imposition** noun

imposing adjective having an impressive appearance or manner: an imposing building

impossible adjective Something that is impossible cannot happen, be done, or be believed > **impossibly** adverb > **impossibility** noun

imposter or **impostor** noun a person who pretends to be someone else in order to get things they want

impotent adjective Someone who is impotent has no power to influence people or events > **impotently** adverb > **impotence** noun

impound verb If something you own is impounded, the police or other officials take it

impoverished adjective Someone who is impoverished is poor: impoverished farm workers

impractical adjective not practical, sensible, or realistic

impregnable adjective A building or other structure that is impregnable is so strong that it cannot be broken into or captured

impresario impresarios [im-pris-**sar**-ee-oh] noun a person who manages theatrical or musical events or companies

impress verb **1** If you impress

someone, you make them admire or respect you **2** If you impress something on someone, you make them understand the importance of it

impression noun An impression of someone or something is the way they look or seem to be

impressionable adjective easy to influence: *impressionable teenagers*

impressive adjective If something is impressive, it impresses you: *an impressive display of old-fashioned American cars*

imprint noun [**im**-print] **1** If something leaves an imprint on your mind, it has a strong and lasting effect **2** the mark left by the pressure of one object on another ▷ verb [im-**print**] **3** If something is imprinted on your memory, it is firmly fixed there

imprison verb If you are imprisoned, you are locked up, usually in a prison ▷ **imprisonment** noun

improbable adjective not probable or likely to happen ▷ **improbably** adverb ▷ **improbability** noun

impromptu [im-**prompt**-yoo] adjective An impromptu action is one done without planning or organization

improper adjective **1** rude or shocking: *improper behaviour* **2** illegal or dishonest: *improper dealings* **3** not suitable or correct: *an improper diet* ▷ **improperly** adverb

impropriety noun (formal) Impropriety is improper behaviour

improve verb If something improves or if you improve it, it gets better or becomes more valuable

improvement noun **1** the fact or process of getting better **2** An improvement in something is a change in something that makes it better

improvise verb **1** If you improvise something, you make or do something without planning in advance, and with whatever materials are available **2** DRAMA MUSIC When musicians or actors improvise, they make up the music or words as they go along ▷ **improvised** adjective ▷ **improvisation** noun

impulse noun a strong urge to do something: *She felt a sudden impulse to confide in her*

impulsive adjective If you are impulsive, you do things suddenly, without thinking about them carefully ▷ **impulsively** adverb

impurity impurities noun **1** Impurity is the quality of being impure: *the impurity of the water* **2** If something contains impurities, it contains small amounts of dirt or other substances that should not be there

in preposition, adverb 'In' is used to indicate position, direction, time, and manner: *boarding schools in England; in the past few years*

inability noun a lack of ability to do something

inaccessible adjective impossible or very difficult to reach

inaccurate adjective not accurate or correct

inadequate adjective **1** If something is inadequate, there is not enough of it **2** not good enough in quality for a particular purpose **3** If someone feels inadequate, they do not possess the skills necessary to do a particular job or to cope with life in general ▷ **inadequately** adverb ▷ **inadequacy** noun

inadvertent adjective not intentional: *the murder had been inadvertent* ▷ **inadvertently** adverb

inane *adjective* silly or stupid
> **inanely** *adverb* > **inanity** *noun*

inanimate *adjective* An inanimate object is not alive

inappropriate *adjective* not suitable for a particular purpose or occasion: *It was quite inappropriate to ask such questions*
> **inappropriately** *adverb*

inarticulate *adjective* If you are inarticulate, you are unable to express yourself well or easily in speech

inaudible *adjective* not loud enough to be heard > **inaudibly** *adverb*

inaugurate [in-**awg**-yoo-rate] *verb* **1** To inaugurate a new scheme is to start it **2** To inaugurate a new leader is to officially establish them in their new position in a special ceremony: *Albania's Orthodox Church inaugurated its first archbishop in 25 years*
> **inauguration** *noun* > **inaugural** *adjective*

incandescent *adjective* Something which is incandescent gives out light when it is heated
> **incandescence** *noun*

incapable *adjective* **1** Someone who is incapable of doing something is not able to do it: *He is incapable of changing a fuse* **2** An incapable person is weak and helpless

incarcerate [in-**kar**-ser-rate] *verb* To incarcerate someone is to lock them up > **incarceration** *noun*

incendiary [in-**send**-yer-ee] *adjective* An incendiary weapon is one which sets fire to things: *incendiary bombs*

incense *noun* Incense is a spicy substance which is burned to create a sweet smell, especially during religious services

incensed *adjective* If you are incensed by something, it makes

you extremely angry

incentive *noun* something that encourages you to do something

inception *noun* (formal) The inception of a project is the start of it

incessant *adjective* continuing without stopping: *her incessant talking* > **incessantly** *adverb*

inch *noun* **1** a unit of length equal to about 2.54 centimetres ▷ *verb* **2** To inch forward is to move forward slowly

incident *noun* an event: *a shooting incident*

incidental *adjective* occurring as a minor part of something: *full of vivid incidental detail* > **incidentally** *adverb*

incinerator *noun* a furnace for burning rubbish

incipient *adjective* beginning to happen or appear: *incipient panic*

incision *noun* a sharp cut, usually made by a surgeon operating on a patient

incisive *adjective* Incisive language is clear and forceful

incite *verb* If you incite someone to do something, you encourage them to do it by making them angry or excited > **incitement** *noun*

inclination *noun* If you have an inclination to do something, you want to do it

incline *verb* **1** If you are inclined to behave in a certain way, you often behave that way or you want to behave that way ▷ *noun* **2** a slope

include *verb* If one thing includes another, it has the second thing as one of its parts > **including** *preposition*

inclusion *noun* The inclusion of one thing in another is the act of making it part of the other thing

inclusive adjective A price that is inclusive includes all the goods and services that are being offered, with no extra charge for any of them

incognito [in-kog-**nee**-toe] adverb If you are travelling incognito, you are travelling in disguise

incoherent adjective If someone is incoherent, they are talking in an unclear or rambling way
> **incoherently** adverb
> **incoherence** noun

income noun the money a person earns

income tax noun Income tax is a part of someone's salary which they have to pay regularly to the government

incoming adjective coming in: *incoming trains; an incoming phone call*

incomparable adjective Something that is incomparable is so good that it cannot be compared with anything else > **incomparably** adverb

incompatible adjective Two things or people are incompatible if they are unable to live or exist together because they are completely different > **incompatibility** noun

incompetent adjective Someone who is incompetent does not have the ability to do something properly
> **incompetently** adverb
> **incompetence** noun

incomplete adjective not complete or finished > **incompletely** adverb

incomprehensible adjective not able to be understood

inconceivable adjective impossible to believe

inconclusive adjective not leading to a decision or to a definite result

incongruous adjective Something that is incongruous seems strange because it does not fit in to a place

or situation > **incongruously** adverb

inconsequential adjective Something that is inconsequential is not very important

inconsistent adjective Someone or something that is inconsistent is unpredictable and behaves differently in similar situations
> **inconsistently** adverb
> **inconsistency** noun

inconspicuous adjective not easily seen or obvious > **inconspicuously** adverb

inconvenience noun **1** If something causes inconvenience, it causes difficulty or problems ▷ verb **2** To inconvenience someone is to cause them trouble, difficulty, or problems
> **inconvenient** adjective
> **inconveniently** adverb

incorporate verb If something is incorporated into another thing, it becomes part of that thing
> **incorporation** noun

incorrect adjective wrong or untrue
> **incorrectly** adverb

increase verb **1** If something increases, it becomes larger in amount ▷ noun **2** a rise in the number, level, or amount of something > **increasingly** adverb

incredible adjective **1** totally amazing **2** impossible to believe
> **incredibly** adverb

incredulous adjective If you are incredulous, you are unable to believe something because it is very surprising or shocking
> **incredulously** adverb
> **incredulity** noun

increment noun the amount by which something increases, or a regular increase in someone's salary
> **incremental** adjective

incriminate verb If something

incriminates you, it suggests that you are involved in a crime

incubator noun a piece of hospital equipment in which sick or weak newborn babies are kept warm

incumbent (formal) adjective **1** If it is incumbent on you to do something, it is your duty to do it ▷ noun **2** the person in a particular official position

incur incurs, incurring, incurred verb If you incur something unpleasant, you cause it to happen

incurable adjective **1** An incurable disease is one which cannot be cured **2** An incurable habit is one which cannot be changed: an incurable romantic ▷ **incurably** adverb

indebted adjective If you are indebted to someone, you are grateful to them ▷ **indebtedness** noun

indecent adjective Something that is indecent is shocking or rude: indecent images ▷ **indecently** adverb ▷ **indecency** noun

indeed adverb You use 'indeed' to strengthen a point that you are making: The desserts are very good indeed

indefatigable [in-dif-**fat**-ig-a-bl] adjective People who never get tired of doing something are indefatigable

indefinite adjective **1** If something is indefinite, no time to finish has been decided: an indefinite strike **2** Indefinite also means vague or not exact: indefinite words and pictures ▷ **indefinitely** adverb

indelible adjective unable to be removed: indelible ink ▷ **indelibly** adverb

indemnity noun (formal) Indemnity is protection against damage or loss

independence noun **1** Independence is not relying on anyone else **2** HISTORY A nation or state gains its independence when it stops being ruled or governed by another country and has its own government and laws

independent adjective **1** Something that is independent happens or exists separately from other people or things: Results are assessed by an independent panel **2** Someone who is independent does not need other people's help: a fiercely independent woman **3** An independent nation is one that is not ruled or governed by another country ▷ **independently** adverb

indeterminate adjective not certain or definite: some indeterminate point in the future

index indexes or indices noun **1** ENGLISH An index is an alphabetical list at the back of a book, referring to items in the book **2** LIBRARY An index is also an alphabetical list of all the books in a library, arranged by title, author, or subject **3** MATHS In maths, an index is a small number placed to the right of another number to indicate the number of times the number is to be multiplied by itself ▷ verb **4** To index a book or collection of information means to provide an index for it **5** To index one thing to another means to arrange them so that they increase and decrease at the same rate

index finger noun your first finger, next to your thumb

Indian adjective **1** belonging or relating to India ▷ noun **2** someone who comes from India **3** someone descended from the people who lived in North, South, or Central

America before Europeans arrived

indicate verb **1** If something indicates something, it shows that it is true: *a gesture which clearly indicates his relief* **2** If you indicate something to someone, you point to it **3** If you indicate a fact, you mention it **4** If the driver of a vehicle indicates, they give a signal to show which way they are going to turn

indication noun a sign of what someone feels or what is likely to happen

indicative adjective **1** If something is indicative of something else, it is a sign of that thing: *Clean, pink tongues are indicative of a good, healthy digestion* ▷ noun **2** If a verb is used in the indicative, it is in the form used for making statements

indicator noun **1** something that tells you what something is like or what is happening **2** A car's indicators are the lights at the front and back which are used to show when it is turning left or right **3** a substance used in chemistry that shows if another substance is an acid or alkali by changing colour when it comes into contact with it

indict [in-dite] verb (formal) To indict someone is to charge them officially with a crime ▷ **indictment** noun ▷ **indictable** adjective

indifferent adjective **1** If you are indifferent to something, you have no interest in it **2** If something is indifferent, it is of a poor quality or low standard: *a pair of rather indifferent paintings* ▷ **indifferently** adverb ▷ **indifference** noun

indigenous [in-dij-in-uss] adjective If something is indigenous to a country, it comes from that country: *a plant indigenous to Asia*

indigestion noun Indigestion is the

pain you get when you find it difficult to digest food

indignant adjective If you are indignant, you feel angry about something that you think is unfair ▷ **indignantly** adverb

indignation noun Indignation is anger about something that you think is unfair

indignity indignities noun something that makes you feel embarrassed or humiliated: *the indignity of having to flee angry protesters*

indigo indigos or indigoes noun, adjective dark violet-blue

indirect adjective Something that is indirect is not done or caused directly by a particular person or thing, but by someone or something else ▷ **indirectly** adverb

indiscriminate adjective not involving careful thought or choice: *an indiscriminate bombing campaign* ▷ **indiscriminately** adverb

indispensable adjective If something is indispensable, you cannot do without it: *A good pair of walking shoes is indispensable*

indistinct adjective not clear: *indistinct voices* ▷ **indistinctly** adverb

individual adjective **1** relating to one particular person or thing: *Each family needs individual attention* **2** Someone who is individual behaves quite differently from the way other people behave ▷ noun **3** a person, different from any other person: *wealthy individuals* ▷ **individually** adverb

individuality noun If something has individuality, it is different from all other things, and therefore is very interesting and noticeable

indomitable adjective (formal)

impossible to overcome: *an indomitable spirit*

Indonesian [in-don-**nee**-zee-an] *adjective* **1** belonging or relating to Indonesia ▷ *noun* **2** someone who comes from Indonesia **3** Indonesian is the official language of Indonesia

indoor *adjective* situated or happening inside a building

indoors *adverb* If something happens indoors, it takes place inside a building

induce *verb* **1** To induce a state is to cause it: *His manner was rough and suspicious but he did not induce fear* **2** If you induce someone to do something, you persuade them to do it

inducement *noun* something offered to encourage someone to do something

indulge *verb* **1** If you indulge in something, you allow yourself to do something that you enjoy **2** If you indulge someone, you let them have or do what they want, often in a way that is not good for them

indulgence *noun* **1** something you allow yourself to have because it gives you pleasure **2** Indulgence is the act of indulging yourself or another person

indulgent *adjective* If you are indulgent, you treat someone with special kindness: *a rich, indulgent father* > **indulgently** *adverb*

industrial *adjective* relating to industry

industrial action *noun* Industrial action is action such as striking taken by workers in protest over pay or working conditions

industrialist *noun* a person who owns or controls a lot of factories

Industrial Revolution *noun* The Industrial Revolution took place in Britain in the late eighteenth and early nineteenth centuries, when machines began to be used more in factories and more goods were produced as a result

industrious *adjective* An industrious person works very hard

industry *noun* **1** Industry is the work and processes involved in manufacturing things in factories **2** all the people and processes involved in manufacturing a particular thing

inedible *adjective* too nasty or poisonous to eat

inefficient *adjective* badly organized, wasteful, and slow: *a corrupt and inefficient administration* > **inefficiently** *adverb* > **inefficiency** *noun*

inept *adjective* without skill: *an inept lawyer* > **ineptitude** *noun*

inequality *noun* inequalities a difference in size, status, wealth, or position, between different things, groups, or people

inert *adjective* **1** Something that is inert does not move and appears lifeless: *an inert body lying on the floor* **2** In chemistry, an inert gas does not react with other substances. The inert gases are also called **noble gases**

inertia [in-**ner**-sha] *noun* If you have a feeling of inertia, you feel very lazy and unwilling to do anything

inevitable *adjective* certain to happen > **inevitably** *adverb* > **inevitability** *noun*

inexhaustible *adjective* Something that is inexhaustible will never be used up: *an inexhaustible supply of ideas*

inexorable *adjective* (formal) Something that is inexorable cannot be prevented from continuing: *the inexorable increase in the number of cars* > **inexorably** *adverb*

inexpensive *adjective* not costing much

inexperienced *adjective* lacking experience of a situation or activity: *inexperienced drivers* > **inexperience** *noun*

inexplicable *adjective* If something is inexplicable, you cannot explain it: *For some inexplicable reason I still felt uneasy.* > **inexplicably** *adverb*

inextricably *adverb* If two or more things are inextricably linked, they cannot be separated

infallible *adjective* never wrong: *No machine is infallible.* > **infallibility** *noun*

infamous [in-fe-muss] *adjective* well-known because of something bad or evil: *a book about the country's most infamous murder cases*

infant *noun* **1** a baby or very young child ▷ *adjective* **2** designed for young children: *an infant school* > **infancy** *noun* > **infantile** *adjective*

infantry *noun* In an army, the infantry are soldiers who fight on foot rather than in tanks or on horses

infatuated *adjective* If you are infatuated with someone, you have such strong feelings of love or passion that you cannot think sensibly about them > **infatuation** *noun*

infect *verb* To infect someone or something is to cause disease in them

infection *noun* **1** a disease caused by germs: *a chest infection* **2** Infection is the state of being infected: *a very small risk of infection*

infectious *adjective* spreading from one person to another: *an infectious disease*

infer *infers, inferring, inferred verb* If you infer something, you work out that it is true on the basis of information that you already have > **inference** *noun*

inferior *adjective* **1** having a lower position than something or someone else **2** of low quality: *inferior quality DVDs* ▷ *noun* **3** Your inferiors are people in a lower position than you > **inferiority** *noun*

infernal *adjective* (old-fashioned) very unpleasant: *an infernal bore*

inferno *noun* an inferno is a very large dangerous fire

infertile *adjective* **1** Infertile soil is of poor quality and plants cannot grow well in it **2** Someone who is infertile cannot have children > **infertility** *noun*

infested *adjective* Something that is infested has a large number of animals or insects living on or in it and causing damage: *The flats are damp and infested with rats* > **infestation** *noun*

infighting *noun* Infighting is quarrelling or rivalry between members of the same organization

infiltrate *verb* If people infiltrate an organization, they gradually enter in secret to spy on its activities > **infiltration** *noun* > **infiltrator** *noun*

infinite *adjective* without any limit or end: *an infinite number of possibilities* > **infinitely** *adverb*

infinity *noun* **1** Infinity is a number that is larger than any other number and can never be given an exact value **2** Infinity is also a point that can never be reached, further away than any other point: *skies stretching on into infinity*

infirmary *noun* infirmaries *noun* a hospital

inflamed adjective If part of your body is inflamed, it is red and swollen, usually because of infection

inflammation noun Inflammation is painful redness or swelling of part of the body

inflammatory adjective Inflammatory actions are likely to make people very angry

inflate verb When you inflate something, you fill it with air or gas to make it swell > **inflatable** adjective

inflation noun Inflation is an increase in the price of goods and services in a country > **inflationary** adjective

inflection or **inflexion** noun a change in the form of a word that shows its grammatical function, for example a change that makes a noun plural

inflexible adjective fixed and unable to be altered: an inflexible routine

inflict verb If you inflict something unpleasant on someone, you make them suffer it

influence noun 1 Influence is power that a person has over other people 2 An influence is also the effect that someone or something has: under the influence of alcohol > verb 3 To influence someone or something means to have an effect on them

influential adjective Someone who is influential has a lot of influence over people

influenza noun (formal) Influenza is flu

influx noun a steady arrival of people or things: a large influx of tourists

inform verb 1 If you inform someone of something, you tell them about it 2 If you inform on a person, you tell the police about a crime they have committed > **informant** noun

informal adjective relaxed and casual: an informal meeting > **informally** adverb > **informality** noun

information noun If you have information on or about something, you know something about it

informative adjective Something that is informative gives you useful information

informer noun someone who tells the police that another person has committed a crime

infrastructure noun GEOGRAPHY The infrastructure of a country consists of things like factories, schools, and roads, which show how much money the country has and how strong its economy is

infringe verb 1 If you infringe a law, you break it 2 To infringe people's rights is to not allow them the rights to which they are entitled > **infringement** noun

infuriate verb If someone infuriates you, they make you very angry > **infuriating** adjective

infuse verb 1 If you infuse someone with a feeling such as enthusiasm or joy, you fill them with it 2 If you infuse a substance such as a herb or medicine, you pour hot water onto it and leave it for the water to absorb the flavour > **infusion** noun

ingenious [in-**jeen**-yuss] adjective very clever and using new ideas: his ingenious invention > **ingeniously** adverb

ingenuity [in-jen-**yoo**-it-ee] noun Ingenuity is cleverness and skill at inventing things or working out plans

ingrained adjective If habits and beliefs are ingrained, they are difficult to change or destroy

ingredient noun D&T Ingredients are the things that something is made from, especially in cookery

inhabit verb If you inhabit a place, you live there

inhabitant noun The inhabitants of a place are the people who live there

inhale verb SCIENCE When you inhale, you breathe in > **inhalation** noun

inherent adjective Inherent qualities or characteristics in something are a natural part of it: her inherent common sense > **inherently** adverb

inherit verb 1 If you inherit money or property, you receive it from someone who has died 2 If you inherit a quality or characteristic from a parent or ancestor, it is passed on to you at birth > **inheritor** noun

inheritance noun something that is passed on from another person

inhibit verb If you inhibit someone from doing something, you prevent them from doing it

inhibited adjective People who are inhibited find it difficult to relax and to show their emotions

inhibition noun Inhibitions are feelings of fear or embarrassment that make it difficult for someone to relax and to show their emotions

inhospitable adjective 1 An inhospitable place is unpleasant or difficult to live in 2 If someone is inhospitable, they do not make people who visit them feel welcome

inhuman adjective not human or not behaving like a human: the inhuman killing of their enemies

inhumane adjective extremely cruel > **inhumanity** noun

inimitable adjective If you have an inimitable characteristic, no one else can imitate it: her inimitable sense of style

initial [in-**nish**-l] adjective 1 first, or at the beginning: Shock and dismay were my initial reactions ▷ noun 2 the first letter of a name > **initially** adverb

initiate [in-**nish**-ee-ate] verb 1 If you initiate something, you make it start or happen 2 If you initiate someone into a group or club, you allow them to become a member of it, usually by means of a special ceremony > **initiation** noun

initiative [in-**nish**-at-ive] noun 1 an attempt to get something done 2 If you have initiative, you decide what to do and then do it, without needing the advice of other people

inject verb 1 If a doctor or nurse injects you with a substance, they use a needle and syringe to put the substance into your body 2 If you inject something new into a situation, you add it > **injection** noun

injunction noun an order issued by a court of law to stop someone doing something

injure verb To injure someone is to damage part of their body

injury injuries noun PE hurt or damage, especially to part of a person's body or to their feelings: He suffered acute injury to his pride; The knee injury forced him to retire from the professional game

injustice noun 1 Injustice is lack of justice and fairness 2 If you do someone an injustice, you judge them too harshly

ink noun Ink is the coloured liquid used for writing or printing

inkling noun a vague idea about something

inlaid adjective decorated with small pieces of wood, stone, or metal: decorative plates inlaid with brass > **inlay** noun

inland adjective **1** near the middle of a country, away from the sea ▷ adverb **2** towards the middle of a country, away from the sea

in-law noun Your in-laws are members of your husband's or wife's family

inlet noun a narrow bay

inmate noun someone who lives in a prison or psychiatric hospital

inn noun a small old country pub or hotel

innards plural noun The innards of something are its inside parts

innate adjective An innate quality is one that you are born with: an innate sense of fairness > **innately** adverb

inner adjective contained inside a place or object: an inner room

innermost adjective deepest and most secret: our innermost feelings

innings noun In cricket, an innings is a period when a particular team is batting

innocence noun inexperience of evil or unpleasant things

innocent adjective **1** not guilty of a crime **2** without experience of evil or unpleasant things: an innocent child > **innocently** adverb

innocuous [in-**nok**-yoo-uss] adjective not harmful

innovation noun D G T a completely new idea, product, or system of doing things

innuendo innuendos or innuendoes [in-yoo-**en**-doe] noun an indirect reference to something rude or unpleasant

innumerable adjective too many to be counted: innumerable cups of tea

input noun **1** Input consists of all the money, information, and other resources that are put into a job, project, or company to make it work

2 COMPUTING In computing, input is information which is fed into a computer

inquest noun an official inquiry to find out what caused a person's death

inquire or **enquire** verb If you inquire about something, you ask for information about it > **inquiring** adjective > **inquiry** noun

inquisition noun an official investigation, especially one which is very thorough and uses harsh methods of questioning

inquisitive adjective Someone who is inquisitive is keen to find out about things > **inquisitively** adverb

inroads plural noun If something makes inroads on or into something, it starts affecting it

insane adjective Someone who is insane is mad > **insanely** adverb > **insanity** noun

insatiable [in-**saysh**-a-bl] adjective A desire or urge that is insatiable is very great: an insatiable curiosity > **insatiably** adverb

inscribe verb If you inscribe words on an object, you write or carve them on it

inscription noun the words that are written or carved on something

inscrutable [in-**skroot**-a-bl] adjective Someone who is inscrutable does not show what they are really thinking

insect noun SCIENCE a small creature with six legs, and usually wings

insecticide noun a poisonous chemical used to kill insects

insecure adjective **1** If you are insecure, you feel unsure of yourself and doubt whether other people like you **2** Something that is insecure is not safe or well protected: *People still feel their jobs are insecure* > **insecurity** noun

insensitive adjective If you are insensitive, you do not notice when you are upsetting people > **insensitivity** noun

insert verb If you insert an object into something, you put it inside > **insertion** noun

inshore adjective at sea but close to the shore: *inshore boats*

inside noun **1** the part of something that is surrounded by the main part and often hidden: *Tom had to stay inside and work* **2** (in plural) Your insides are the parts inside your body ▷ adjective **3** surrounded by the main part and often hidden: *an inside pocket* ▷ preposition **4** in or to the interior of: *inside the house* ▷ phrase **5** Inside out means with the inside part facing outwards

insider noun a person who is involved in a situation and so knows more about it than other people

insidious adjective Something that is insidious is unpleasant and develops slowly without being noticed: *the insidious progress of the disease* > **insidiously** adverb

insight noun If you gain insight into a problem, you gradually get a deep and accurate understanding of it

insignia [in-**sig**-nee-a] noun the badge or a sign of a particular organization

insignificant adjective small and unimportant > **insignificance** noun

insincere adjective Someone who is insincere pretends to have feelings which they do not really have > **insincerely** adverb > **insincerity** noun

insinuate verb If you insinuate something unpleasant, you hint about it > **insinuation** noun

insipid adjective **1** An insipid person or activity is dull and boring **2** Food that is insipid has very little taste

insist verb If you insist on something, you demand it forcefully > **insistent** adjective > **insistence** noun

insoluble [in-**soll**-yoo-bl] adjective **1** impossible to solve: *an insoluble problem* **2** unable to dissolve: *substances which are insoluble in water*

insolvent adjective unable to pay your debts > **insolvency** noun

insomnia noun Insomnia is difficulty in sleeping > **insomniac** noun

inspect verb To inspect something is to examine it carefully to check that everything is all right > **inspection** noun

inspector noun **1** someone who inspects things **2** a police officer just above a sergeant in rank

inspire verb **1** [DRAMA] If something inspires you, it gives you new ideas and enthusiasm to do something **2** To inspire an emotion in someone is to make them feel this emotion > **inspired** adjective > **inspiring** adjective > **inspiration** noun

instability noun Instability is a lack of stability in a place: *political instability*

install verb **1** If you install a piece of equipment in a place, you put it there so it is ready to be used **2** To install someone in an important job is to officially give them that position **3** If you install yourself in a place, you settle there and make yourself comfortable > **installation** noun

instalment noun **1** If you pay for something in instalments, you pay small amounts of money regularly over a period of time **2** one of the parts of a story or television series

instance noun **1** a particular example or occurrence of an event, situation, or person: *a serious instance of corruption* ▷ phrase **2** You use **for instance** to give an example of something you are talking about

instant noun **1** a moment or short period of time: *In an instant they were gone* ▷ adjective **2** immediate and without delay: *The record was an instant success* > **instantly** adverb

instantaneous adjective happening immediately and without delay: *The applause was instantaneous* > **instantaneously** adverb

instead adverb in place of something: *Take the stairs instead of the lift*

instigate verb Someone who instigates a situation makes it happen > **instigation** noun > **instigator** noun

instil instils, instilling, instilled verb If you instil an idea or feeling into someone, you make them feel or think it

instinct noun a natural tendency to do something: *My first instinct was to protect myself* > **instinctive** adjective > **instinctively** adverb

institute noun **1** an organization for teaching or research ▷ verb **2** (formal) If you institute a rule or system, you introduce it

institution noun **1** a custom or system regarded as an important tradition within a society: *The family is an institution to be cherished* **2** a large, important organization, for example a university or bank > **institutional** adjective

instruct verb **1** If you instruct someone to do something, you tell them to do it **2** If someone instructs you in a subject or skill, they teach

you about it > **instructor** noun > **instructive** adjective > **instruction** noun

instrument noun **1** a tool or device used for a particular job: *a special instrument which cut through the metal* **2** MUSIC A musical instrument is an object, such as a piano or flute, played to make music

instrumental adjective **1** If you are instrumental in doing something, you help to make it happen **2** MUSIC Instrumental music is performed using only musical instruments, and not voices

insufficient adjective not enough for a particular purpose > **insufficiently** adverb

insular [inss-yoo-lar] adjective Someone who is insular is unwilling to meet new people or to consider new ideas > **insularity** noun

insulate verb **1** If you insulate a person from harmful things, you protect them from those things **2** If materials such as feathers, fur, or foam insulate something, they keep it warm by covering it in a thick layer **3** SCIENCE You insulate an electrical or metal object by covering it with rubber or plastic. This is to stop electricity passing through it and giving you an electric shock > **insulation** noun > **insulator** noun

insulin [inss-yoo-lin] noun Insulin is a substance which controls the level of sugar in the blood. People who have diabetes do not produce insulin naturally and have to take regular doses of it

insult verb **1** If you insult someone, you offend them by being rude to them ▷ noun **2** a rude remark which offends you > **insulting** adjective

insure verb **1** If you insure something or yourself, you pay money regularly to a company so that if there is an accident or damage, the company will pay for medical treatment or repairs **2** If you do something to insure against something unpleasant happening, you do it to prevent the unpleasant thing from happening or to protect yourself if it does happen > **insurance** *noun*

insurrection *noun* A violent action taken against the rulers of a country

intact *adjective* complete, and not changed or damaged in any way: *The rear of the aircraft remained intact when it crashed*

intake *noun* A person's intake of food, drink, or air is the amount they take in

integral *adjective* If something is an integral part of a whole thing, it is an essential part

integrate *verb* **1** If a person integrates into a group, they become part of it **2** To integrate things is to combine them so that they become closely linked or form one thing: *his plan to integrate the coal and steel industries* > **integration** *noun*

integrity *noun* **1** Integrity is the quality of being honest and following your principles **2** The integrity of a group of people is their being united as one whole

intellect *noun* Intellect is the ability to understand ideas and information

intellectual *adjective* **1** involving thought, ideas, and understanding: *an intellectual exercise* ▷ *noun* **2** someone who enjoys thinking about complicated ideas > **intellectually** *adverb*

intelligence *noun* A person's intelligence is their ability to understand and learn things quickly and well

intelligent *adjective* able to understand and learn things quickly and well > **intelligently** *adverb*

intelligentsia [in-tell-lee-**jent**-sya] *noun* The intelligentsia are intellectual people, considered as a group

intelligible *adjective* able to be understood: *very few intelligible remarks*

intend *verb* **1** If you intend to do something, you have decided or planned to do it: *She intended to move back to Cape Town* **2** If something is intended for a particular use, you have planned that it should have this use: *The booklet is intended to be kept handy*

intense *adjective* **1** very great in strength or amount: *intense heat* **2** If a person is intense, they take things very seriously and have very strong feelings > **intensely** *adverb* > **intensity** *noun*

intensify intensifies, intensifying, intensified *verb* To intensify something is to make it greater or stronger

intensive *adjective* involving a lot of energy or effort over a very short time: *an intensive training course*

intent *noun* **1** (*formal*) A person's intent is their purpose or intention ▷ *adjective* **2** If you are intent on doing something, you are determined to do it > **intently** *adverb*

intention *noun* If you have an intention to do something, you have a plan of what you are going to do

intentional *adjective* If something is intentional, it is done on purpose > **intentionally** *adverb*

interact *verb* The way two people or things interact is the way they work together, communicate, or react with each other ▷ **interaction** noun

interactive adjective COMPUTING Interactive television, computers, and games react to decisions taken by the viewer, user, or player

intercept [in-ter-**sept**] verb If you intercept someone or something that is going from one place to another, you stop them

interchange noun An interchange is the act or process of exchanging things or ideas ▷ **interchangeable** adjective

intercom noun a device consisting of a microphone and a loudspeaker, which you use to speak to people in another room

interest noun 1 If you have an interest in something or if something is of interest, you want to learn or hear more about it 2 Your interests are your hobbies 3 If you have an interest in something being done, you want it to be done because it will benefit you 4 Interest is an extra payment made to the lender by someone who has borrowed a sum of money, or by a bank or company to someone who has invested money in them. Interest is worked out as a percentage of the sum of money borrowed or invested ▷ verb 5 Something that interests you attracts your attention so that you want to learn or hear more about it ▷ **interested** adjective

interesting adjective making you want to know, learn, or hear more ▷ **interestingly** adverb

interface noun 1 The interface between two subjects or systems is the area in which they affect each other or are linked 2 COMPUTING The user interface of a computer

program is how it is presented on the computer screen and how easy it is to operate

interfere verb 1 If you interfere in a situation, you try to influence it, although it does not really concern you 2 Something that interferes with a situation has a damaging effect on it ▷ **interference** noun ▷ **interfering** adjective

interim adjective intended for use only until something permanent is arranged: an interim government

interior noun 1 the inside part of something ▷ adjective 2 Interior means inside: They painted the interior walls white

interlude [rhymes with **rude**] noun a short break from an activity

intermediary intermediaries [in-ter-**meed**-yer-ee] noun someone who tries to get two groups of people to come to an agreement

intermediate adjective An intermediate level occurs in the middle, between two other stages: intermediate students

interminable adjective If something is interminable, it goes on for a very long time: an interminable wait for the bus ▷ **interminably** adverb

intermission noun an interval between two parts of a film or play

intermittent adjective happening only occasionally ▷ **intermittently** adverb

internal adjective happening inside a person, place, or object ▷ **internally** adverb

international adjective GEOGRAPHY 1 involving different countries ▷ noun 2 a sports match between two countries ▷ **internationally** adverb

internet or **Internet** noun COMPUTING The internet is a worldwide communication system which people use through computers

interplay noun The interplay between two things is the way they react with one another

interpret verb **1** If you interpret what someone says or does, you decide what it means **2** If you interpret a foreign language that someone is speaking, you translate it > **interpretation** noun > **interpreter** noun

interrogate verb If you interrogate someone, you question them thoroughly to get information from them > **interrogation** noun > **interrogator** noun

interrupt verb **1** If you interrupt someone, you start talking while they are talking **2** If you interrupt a process or activity, you stop it continuing for a time > **interruption** noun

intersect verb When two roads intersect, they cross each other

intersection intersections noun **1** An intersection is where two roads meet **2** [MATHS] In maths, an intersection is the point where two straight lines meet

interspersed adjective If something is interspersed with things, these things occur at various points in it

interval noun **1** The period of time between two moments or dates **2** a short break during a play or concert **3** [MUSIC] In music, an interval is the difference in pitch between two musical notes

intervene verb If you intervene in a situation, you step in to prevent conflict between people > **intervention** noun

intervening adjective An intervening period of time is one which separates two events

interview noun **1** a meeting at which someone asks you questions about yourself to see if you are suitable for a particular job **2** a conversation in which a journalist asks a famous person questions ▷ verb **3** If you interview someone, you ask them questions about themselves > **interviewer** noun > **interviewee** noun

intestine noun Your intestines are a long tube which carries food from your stomach through to your bowels, and in which the food is digested > **intestinal** adjective

intimate adjective [in-ti-mit] **1** If two people are intimate, there is a close relationship between them **2** An intimate matter is very private and personal **3** An intimate knowledge of something is very deep and detailed ▷ verb [in-ti-mate] **4** If you intimate something, you hint at it: He did intimate that he is considering legal action > **intimately** adverb > **intimacy** noun > **intimation** noun

intimidate verb If you intimidate someone, you frighten them in a threatening way > **intimidated** adjective > **intimidating** adjective > **intimidation** noun

into preposition **1** If something goes into something else, it goes inside it **2** If you bump or crash into something, you hit it **3** (informal) If you are into something, you like it very much: Nowadays I'm really into healthy food

intolerable adjective If something is intolerable, it is so bad that it is difficult to put up with it > **intolerably** adverb

intonation noun Your intonation is the way that your voice rises and falls as you speak

intoxicated *adjective* If someone is intoxicated, they are drunk
> **intoxicating** *adjective*
> **intoxication** *noun*

intractable *adjective* (formal) stubborn and difficult to deal with or control

intravenous [in-trav-**vee**-nuss] *adjective* Intravenous foods or drugs are given to sick people through their veins > **intravenously** *adverb*

intrepid *adjective* not worried by danger: *an intrepid explorer*
> **intrepidly** *adverb*

intricate *adjective* Something that is intricate has many fine details: *walls and ceilings covered with intricate patterns* > **intricately** *adverb*
> **intricacy** *noun*

intrigue *noun* 1 Intrigue is the making of secret plans, often with the intention of harming other people: *political intrigue* > *verb* 2 If something intrigues you, you are fascinated by it and curious about it
> **intriguing** *adjective*

intrinsic *adjective* (formal) The intrinsic qualities of something are its basic qualities > **intrinsically** *adverb*

introduce *verb* 1 If you introduce one person to another, you'll tell them each other's name so that they can get to know each other 2 When someone introduces a radio or television show, they say a few words at the beginning to tell you about it 3 If you introduce someone to something, they learn about it for the first time > **introductory** *adjective*

introduction *noun* 1 The introduction of someone or something is the act of presenting them for the first time 2 ENGLISH a piece of writing at the beginning of a book, which usually tells you what the book is about

introvert *noun* someone who spends more time thinking about their private feelings than about the world around them, and who often finds it difficult to talk to others
> **introverted** *adjective*

intrude *verb* To intrude on someone or something is to disturb them: *I don't want to intrude on your parents*
> **intruder** *noun* > **intrusion** *noun*
> **intrusive** *adjective*

intuition [int-yoo-**ish**-n] *noun* Your intuition is a feeling you have about something that you cannot explain: *My intuition is right about him*
> **intuitive** *adjective* > **intuitively** *adverb*

Inuit or **Innuit** *noun* a member of a group of people who live in Northern Canada, Greenland, Alaska, and Eastern Siberia

inundated *adjective* If you are inundated by letters or requests, you receive so many that you cannot deal with them all

invade *verb* 1 If an army invades a country, it enters it by force 2 If someone invades your privacy, they disturb you when you want to be alone > **invader** *noun*

invalid [**in**-va-lid] *noun* someone who is so ill that they need to be looked after by someone else

invalid [in-**val**-id] *adjective* 1 If an argument or result is invalid, it is not acceptable because it is based on a mistake 2 If a law, marriage, or election is invalid, it is illegal because it has not been carried out properly
> **invalidate** *verb*

invaluable *adjective* extremely useful: *This book contains invaluable tips*

invariably adverb If something invariably happens, it almost always happens

invasion noun 1 HISTORY The invasion of a country or territory is the act of entering it by force 2 an unwanted disturbance or intrusion: an invasion of her privacy

invective noun (formal) Invective is abusive language used by someone who is angry

invent verb 1 If you invent a device or process, you are the first person to think of it or to use it 2 If you invent a story or an excuse, you make it up > **inventor** noun > **invention** noun > **inventive** adjective > **inventiveness** noun

inventory inventories [in-vin-to-ri] noun A written list of all the objects in a place

inverse adjective MATHS (formal) If there is an inverse relationship between two things, one decreases as the other increases

invertebrate noun SCIENCE An invertebrate is a creature which does not have a spine. Some invertebrates, for example crabs, have an external skeleton

inverted adjective upside down or back to front

invest verb 1 If you invest money, you pay it into a bank or buy shares so that you will receive a profit 2 If you invest in something useful, you buy it because it will help you do something better 3 If you invest money, time, or energy in something, you try to make it a success > **investor** noun > **investment** noun

investigate verb To investigate something is to try to find out all the facts about it > **investigator** noun > **investigation** noun

inveterate adjective having lasted for a long time and not likely to stop: an inveterate gambler

invincible adjective unable to be defeated > **invincibility** noun

invisible adjective If something is invisible, you cannot see it, because it is hidden, very small, or imaginary > **invisibly** adverb > **invisibility** noun

invite verb 1 If you invite someone to an event, you ask them to come to it 2 If you invite someone to do something, you ask them to do it: Andrew has been invited to speak at the conference > **inviting** adjective > **invitation** noun

invoice noun a bill for services or goods

invoke verb 1 (formal) If you invoke a law, you use it to justify what you are doing 2 If you invoke certain feelings, you cause someone to have these feelings

involuntary adjective sudden and uncontrollable > **involuntarily** adverb

involve verb PSHE If a situation involves someone or something, it includes them as a necessary part > **involvement** noun

inward or **inwards** adjective 1 Your inward thoughts and feelings are private > adjective, adverb 2 If something moves inward or inwards, it moves towards the inside or centre of something > **inwardly** adverb

iodine [eye-oh-deen] noun Iodine is a bluish-black element whose compounds are used in medicine and photography. Its atomic number is 53 and its symbol is I

ion [eye-on] noun Ions are electrically charged atoms

iota noun an extremely small amount:

He did not have an iota of proof

IQ *noun* Your IQ is your level of intelligence shown by the results of a special test. IQ is an abbreviation for 'intelligence quotient'

Iranian [ir-**rain**-ee-an] *adjective* **1** belonging or relating to Iran ▷ *noun* **2** someone who comes from Iran **3** Iranian is the main language spoken in Iran. It is also known as Farsi

Iraqi [ir-**ah**-kee] *adjective* **1** belonging or relating to Iraq ▷ *noun* **2** someone who comes from Iraq

irate [eye-**rate**] *adjective* very angry

iris irises [**eye**-riss] *noun* **1** the round, coloured part of your eye **2** a tall plant with long leaves and large blue, yellow, or white flowers

Irish *adjective* **1** belonging or relating to the Irish Republic, or to the whole of Ireland ▷ *noun* **2** Irish or Irish Gaelic is a language spoken in some parts of Ireland

Irishman Irishmen *noun* a man who comes from Ireland > **Irishwoman** *noun*

irk *verb* If something irks you, it annoys you > **irksome** *adjective*

iron *noun* **1** [SCIENCE] Iron is a strong hard metallic element found in rocks. It is used in making tools and machines, and is also an important component of blood. Its atomic number is 26 and its symbol is Fe **2** An iron is a device which heats up and which you rub over clothes to remove creases ▷ *verb* **3** If you iron clothes, you use a hot iron to remove creases from them > **ironing** *noun* > **iron out** *verb* If you iron out difficulties, you solve them

Iron Age *noun* The Iron Age was a time about 3000 years ago when people first started to make tools out of iron

irony ironies [**eye**-ron-ee] *noun* **1** [ENGLISH] Irony is a form of humour in which you say the opposite of what you really mean: *This group could be described, without irony, as the fortunate ones* **2** There is irony in a situation when there is an unexpected or unusual connection between things or events: *It's a sad irony of life: once you are lost, a map is useless* > **ironic** *or* > **ironical** *adjective* > **ironically** *adverb*

irrational *adjective* Irrational feelings are not based on logical reasons: *irrational fears* > **irrationally** *adverb* > **irrationality** *noun*

irregular *adjective* **1** not smooth or even: *irregular walls* **2** not forming a regular pattern **3** [MATHS] Irregular things are uneven or unequal, or are not symmetrical > **irregularly** *adverb* > **irregularity** *noun*

irrelevant *adjective* not directly connected with a subject: *He either ignored questions or gave irrelevant answers* > **irrelevance** *noun*

irrepressible *adjective* Someone who is irrepressible is lively and cheerful

irresistible *adjective* **1** unable to be controlled: *an irresistible urge to yawn* **2** extremely attractive: *Women always found him irresistible* > **irresistibly** *adverb*

irrespective *adjective* If you say something will be done irrespective of certain things, you mean it will be done without taking those things into account

irresponsible *adjective* An irresponsible person does things without considering the consequences: *an irresponsible driver* > **irresponsibly** *adverb* > **irresponsibility** *noun*

irrigate verb To irrigate land is to supply it with water brought through pipes or ditches > **irrigated** adjective > **irrigation** noun

irritable adjective easily annoyed

irritate verb **1** If something irritates you, it annoys you **2** If something irritates part of your body, it makes it tender, sore, or itchy > **irritant** noun > **irritation** noun

is the third person singular, present tense of **be**

-ish suffix '-ish' forms adjectives that mean 'fairly' or 'rather': smallish; greenish

Islam [iz-lahm] noun RE Islam is the Muslim religion, which teaches that there is only one God, Allah, and Mohammed is his prophet. The holy book of Islam is the Qur'an > **Islamic** adjective

island [eye-land] noun a piece of land surrounded on all sides by water > **islander** noun

isle [rhymes with mile] noun (literary) an island

-ism suffix **1** '-ism' forms nouns that refer to an action or condition: criticism; heroism **2** '-ism' forms nouns that refer to a political or economic system or a system of beliefs: Marxism; Sikhism **3** '-ism' forms nouns that refer to a type of prejudice: racism; sexism

isolate verb **1** If something isolates you or if you isolate yourself, you are set apart from other people **2** If you isolate something, you separate it from everything else > **isolated** adjective > **isolation** noun

ISP an abbreviation for 'internet service provider'

Israeli Israelis [iz-rail-ee] adjective RE **1** belonging or relating to Israel ▷ noun **2** someone who comes from Israel

issue issues, issuing, issued [ish-yoo] noun **1** an important subject that people are talking about **2** a particular edition of a newspaper or magazine ▷ verb **3** If you issue a statement or a warning, you say it formally and publicly **4** If someone issues something, they officially give it: Staff were issued with plastic cards

-ist suffix **1** '-ist' forms nouns and adjectives which refer to someone who is involved in a certain activity, or who believes in a certain system or religion: chemist; motorist; Buddhist **2** '-ist' forms nouns and adjectives which refer to someone who has a certain prejudice: racist

it pronoun **1** 'It' is used to refer to something that has already been mentioned, or to a situation or fact: It was a difficult decision **2** 'It' is used to refer to people or animals whose gender is not known: If a baby is thirsty, it feeds more often **3** You use 'it' to make statements about the weather, time, or date: It's noon

Italian adjective **1** belonging or relating to Italy ▷ noun **2** someone who comes from Italy **3** Italian is the main language spoken in Italy

italics plural noun Italics are letters printed in a special sloping way, and are often used to emphasize something. All the example sentences in this dictionary are in italics > **italic** adjective

itch verb **1** When your skin itches, it has an unpleasant feeling and you want to scratch it **2** If you are itching to do something, you are impatient to do it ▷ noun **3** an unpleasant feeling on your skin that you want to scratch > **itchy** adjective

item noun **1** one of a collection or list

of objects **2** a newspaper or magazine article

itinerary itineraries *noun* a plan of a journey, showing a route to follow and places to visit

-itis *suffix* '-itis' is added to the name of a part of the body to refer to disease or inflammation in that part: *appendicitis; tonsillitis*

its *adjective, pronoun* 'Its' refers to something belonging to or relating to things, children, or animals that have already been mentioned: *The lion lifted its head*

itself *pronoun* **1** 'Itself' is used when the same thing, child, or animal does an action and is affected by it: *The cat was washing itself* **2** 'Itself' is used to emphasize 'it'

-ity *suffix* '-ity' forms nouns that refer to a state or condition: *continuity; technicality*

-ive *suffix* '-ive' forms adjectives and some nouns: *massive; detective*

ivory *noun* **1** the valuable creamy-white bone which forms the tusk of an elephant. It is used to make ornaments ▷ *noun, adjective* **2** creamy-white

ivy *noun* an evergreen plant which creeps along the ground and up walls

iwi iwi *or* iwis *noun* In New Zealand, a Maori tribe

-ize *or* **-ise** *suffix* '-ize' and '-ise' form verbs. Most verbs can be spelt with either ending, though there are some that can only be spelt with '-ise', for example *advertise, improvise* and *revise*

j

jab jabs, jabbing, jabbed *verb* **1** To jab something means to poke at it roughly ▷ *noun* **2** a sharp or sudden poke **3** (*informal*) an injection

jack *noun* **1 a** a piece of equipment for lifting heavy objects, especially for lifting a car when changing a wheel **2** In a pack of cards, a jack is a card whose value is between a ten and a queen ▷ *verb* **3** To jack up an object means to raise it, especially by using a jack

jacket *noun* **1** a short coat reaching to the waist or hips **2** an outer covering for something: *a book jacket* **3** The jacket of a baked potato is its skin

jackpot *noun* In a gambling game, the jackpot is the top prize

jack up *verb* (*informal*) In New Zealand English, to jack something up is to organize or prepare something

jade *noun* Jade is a hard green stone used for making jewellery and ornaments

jagged *adjective* sharp and spiky

jaguar *noun* A jaguar is a large member of the cat family with spots on its back. Jaguars live in South and Central America

jail *or* **gaol** *noun* **1 a** building where people convicted of a crime are locked up ▷ *verb* **2** To jail someone means to lock them up in a jail

jam jams, jamming, jammed *noun* **1** a food, made by boiling fruit and sugar together until it sets **2** a situation in which it is impossible to move: *a traffic jam* ▷ *phrase* **3** (*informal*) If someone is **in a jam**, they are in a difficult situation ▷ *verb* **4** If people or things are jammed into a place, they are squeezed together so closely that they can hardly move **5** To jam something somewhere means to push it there roughly: *He jammed his foot on the brake* **6** If something is jammed, it is stuck or unable to work properly **7** To jam a radio signal means to interfere with it and prevent it from being received clearly

Jamaican [jam-**may**-kn] *adjective* **1** belonging or relating to Jamaica ▷ *noun* **2** someone who comes from Jamaica

jamboree *noun* a gathering of large numbers of people enjoying themselves

janitor *noun* the caretaker of a building

January *noun* January is the first month of the year. It has 31 days

Japanese *adjective* **1** belonging or relating to Japan ▷ *noun* **2** someone who comes from Japan **3** Japanese is the main language spoken in Japan

jar *jars, jarring, jarred noun* **1** a glass container with a wide top used for storing food ▷ *verb* **2** If something jars on you, you find it unpleasant or annoying

jargon *noun* Jargon consists of words that are used in special or technical ways by particular groups of people, often making the language difficult to understand

jarrah *noun* an Australian eucalyptus tree that produces wood used for timber

jasmine *noun* Jasmine is a climbing plant with small sweet-scented white flowers

jaundice *noun* Jaundice is an illness affecting the liver, in which the skin and the whites of the eyes become yellow

jaundiced *adjective* pessimistic and lacking enthusiasm: *He takes a rather jaundiced view of politicians*

jaunt *noun* a journey or trip you go on for pleasure

jaunty *jauntier, jauntiest adjective* expressing cheerfulness and self-confidence: *a jaunty tune* > *jauntily adverb*

javelin *noun* a long spear that is thrown in sports competitions

jaw *noun* **1** A person's or animal's jaw is the bone in which the teeth are set **2** A person's or animal's jaws are their mouth and teeth

jay *noun* a kind of noisy chattering bird

jazz *noun* **1** Jazz is a style of popular music with a forceful rhythm ▷ *verb* **2** (*informal*) To jazz something up means to make it more colourful or exciting

jazzy *jazzier, jazziest adjective* (*informal*) bright and showy

jealous *adjective* **1** If you are jealous, you feel bitterness towards someone who has something that you would like to have **2** If you are jealous of something you have, you feel you must try to keep it from other people > *jealously adverb* > *jealousy noun*

jeans *plural noun* Jeans are casual denim trousers

Jeep *noun* (*trademark*) a small road vehicle with four-wheel drive

jeer *verb* **1** If you jeer at someone, you insult them in a loud, unpleasant way ▷ *noun* **2** Jeers are rude and insulting remarks > *jeering adjective*

J

Jehovah [ji-**hove**-ah] *proper noun* Jehovah is the name of God in the Old Testament

jelly jellies *noun* **1** a clear, sweet food eaten as a dessert **2** a type of clear, set jam

jellyfish *noun* a sea animal with a clear soft body and tentacles which may sting

jeopardize [jep-par-dyz] or **jeopardise** *verb* To jeopardize something means to do something which puts it at risk: *Elaine jeopardized her health*

jeopardy *noun* If someone or something is in jeopardy, they are at risk of failing or of being destroyed

jerk *verb* **1** To jerk something means to give it a sudden, sharp pull **2** If something jerks, it moves suddenly and sharply ▷ *noun* **3** a sudden sharp movement **4** (*informal*) If you call someone a jerk, you mean they are stupid > **jerky** *adjective* > **jerkily** *adverb*

jersey *noun* **1** a knitted garment for the upper half of the body **2** Jersey is a type of knitted woollen or cotton fabric used to make clothing

jest *noun* **1** a joke ▷ *verb* **2** To jest means to speak jokingly

jester *noun* In the past, a jester was a man who was kept to amuse the king or queen

jet jets, jetting, jetted *noun* **1** a plane which is able to fly very fast **2** a stream of liquid, gas, or flame forced out under pressure **3** Jet is a hard black stone, usually highly polished and used in jewellery and ornaments ▷ *verb* **4** To jet somewhere means to fly there in a plane, especially a jet

jet lag *noun* Jet lag is a feeling of tiredness or confusion that people have after a long flight across different time zones

jettison *verb* If you jettison something, you throw it away because you no longer want it

jetty jetties *noun* a wide stone wall or wooden platform at the edge of the sea or a river, where boats can be moored

Jew [joo] RE *noun* a person who practises the religion of Judaism, or who is of Hebrew descent > **Jewish** *adjective*

jewel *noun* a precious stone used to decorate valuable ornaments or jewellery > **jewelled** *adjective*

jeweller *noun* a person who makes jewellery or who sells and repairs jewellery and watches

jewellery *noun* Jewellery consists of ornaments that people wear, such as rings or necklaces, made of valuable metals and sometimes decorated with precious stones

jib *noun* a small sail towards the front of a sailing boat

jibe another spelling of **gibe**

jig jigs, jigging, jigged *noun* **1** A jig is a type of lively folk dance; also the music that accompanies it ▷ *verb* **2** If you jig, you dance or jump around in a lively bouncy manner

jigsaw *noun* a puzzle consisting of a picture on cardboard that has been cut up into small pieces, which have to be put together again

jihad [jee-had] *noun* **1** a holy war waged to defend or further the ideals of Islam **2** Jihad also means the personal struggle of a Muslim against sin

jingle *noun* **1** a short, catchy phrase or rhyme set to music and used to advertise something on radio or television **2** the sound of something jingling ▷ *verb* **3** When something jingles, it makes a tinkling sound like small bells

jinks plural noun High jinks is boisterous and mischievous behaviour

jinx noun someone or something that is thought to bring bad luck: He was beginning to think he was a jinx

jinxed adjective If something is jinxed it is considered to be unlucky: I think this house is jinxed

jitters plural noun (informal) If you have got the jitters, you are feeling very nervous > **jittery** adjective

job noun **1** the work that someone does to earn money **2** a duty or responsibility: It is a captain's job to lead from the front ▷ phrase **3** If something is **just the job**, it is exactly right or exactly what you wanted

jobless adjective without any work

jockey noun **1** someone who rides a horse in a race ▷ verb **2** To jockey for position means to manoeuvre in order to gain an advantage over other people

jocular adjective A jocular comment is intended to make people laugh > **jocularly** adverb

jog jogs, jogging, jogged verb **1** To jog means to run slowly and rhythmically, often as a form of exercise **2** If you jog something, you knock it slightly so that it shakes or moves **3** If someone or something jogs your memory, they remind you of something ▷ noun **4** a slow run > **jogger** noun > **jogging** noun

join verb **1** When two things join, or when one thing joins another, they come together **2** If you join a club or organization, you become a member of it or start taking part in it **3** To join two things means to fasten them ▷ noun **4** a place where

two things are fastened together ▷ **join up** verb If someone joins up, they become a member of the armed forces

joiner noun a person who makes wooden window frames, doors, and furniture

joinery noun Joinery is the work done by a joiner

joint adjective **1** shared by or belonging to two or more people: a joint building society account ▷ noun **2** SCIENCE a part of the body where two bones meet and are joined together so that they can move, for example a knee or hip **3** D G T a place where two things are fixed together **4** a large piece of meat suitable for roasting **5** (informal) any place of entertainment, such as a nightclub or pub ▷ verb **6** To joint meat means to cut it into large pieces according to where the bones are > **jointly** adverb > **jointed** adjective

joke noun **1** something that you say or do to make people laugh, such as a funny story **2** anything that you think is ridiculous and not worthy of respect: The decision was a joke ▷ verb **3** If you are joking, you are teasing someone > **jokingly** adverb

joker noun In a pack of cards, a joker is an extra card that does not belong to any of the four suits, but is used in some games

jolly jollier, jolliest; jollies, jollying, jollied adjective **1** happy, cheerful, and pleasant **2** (informal) Jolly also means very: It all sounds like jolly good fun ▷ verb **3** If you jolly someone along, you encourage them in a cheerful and friendly way > **jolliness** noun

jolt verb **1** To jolt means to move or shake roughly and violently **2** If you are jolted by something, it gives you an unpleasant surprise ▷ *noun* **3** a sudden jerky movement **4** an unpleasant shock or surprise

jostle *verb* To jostle means to push roughly against people in a crowd

jot jots, jotting, jotted *verb* **1** If you jot something down, you write it quickly in the form of a short informal note ▷ *noun* **2** a very small amount > **jotting** *noun*

journal *noun* **1** a magazine that deals with a particular subject, trade, or profession **2** a diary which someone keeps regularly

journalism *noun* Journalism is the work of collecting, writing, and publishing news in newspapers, magazines, and on television and radio > **journalist** *noun* > **journalistic** *adjective*

journey *noun* **1** the act of travelling from one place to another ▷ *verb* **2** (*formal*) To journey somewhere means to travel there: *He intended to journey up the Amazon*

joust *noun* In medieval times, a joust was a competition between knights fighting on horseback, using lances

jovial *adjective* cheerful and friendly > **jovially** *adverb* > **joviality** *noun*

joy *noun* **1** Joy is a feeling of great happiness **2** (*informal*) Joy also means success or luck: *Any joy with your insurance claim?* **3** something that makes you happy or gives you pleasure

joyful *adjective* **1** causing pleasure and happiness **2** Someone who is joyful is extremely happy > **joyfully** *adverb*

joyous *adjective* (*formal*) joyful > **joyously** *adverb*

joyride *noun* a drive in a stolen car for pleasure > **joyriding** *noun* > **joyrider** *noun*

joystick *noun* a lever in an aircraft which the pilot uses to control height and direction

jubilant *adjective* feeling or expressing great happiness or triumph > **jubilantly** *adverb*

jubilation *noun* Jubilation is a feeling of great happiness and triumph

jubilee *noun* a special anniversary of an event such as a coronation: *Queen Elizabeth's Silver Jubilee in 1977*

Judaism [joo-day-i-zm] *noun* RE Judaism is the religion of the Jewish people. It is based on a belief in one God, and draws its laws and authority from the Old Testament > **Judaic** *adjective*

judge *noun* **1** the person in a law court who decides how the law should be applied to people who appear in the court **2** someone who decides the winner in a contest or competition ▷ *verb* **3** If you judge someone or something, you form an opinion about them based on the evidence that you have **4** To judge a contest or competition means to decide on the winner

judgment *or* **judgement** *noun* an opinion or decision based on evidence

judicial *adjective* relating to judgment or to justice: *a judicial review*

judiciary *noun* The judiciary is the branch of government concerned with justice and the legal system

judicious *adjective* sensible and showing good judgment > **judiciously** *adverb*

judo *noun* Judo is a sport in which two people try to force each other to the ground using special throwing techniques. It originated in Japan as a form of self-defence

jug noun a container with a lip or spout used for holding or serving liquids

juggernaut noun a large heavy lorry

juggle verb To juggle means to throw objects into the air, catching them up again so there are several in the air at one time > **juggler** noun

jugular noun The jugular or jugular vein is one of the veins in the neck which carry blood from the head back to the heart

juice noun **1** Juice is the liquid that can be squeezed or extracted from fruit or other food **2** Juices in the body are fluids: *gastric juices*

juicy juicier, juiciest adjective **1** Juicy food has a lot of juice in it **2** Something that is juicy is interesting, exciting, or scandalous: *a juicy bit of gossip* > **juiciness** noun

jukebox noun a machine which automatically plays a selected piece of music when coins are inserted

July noun July is the seventh month of the year. It has 31 days

jumble noun **1** an untidy muddle of things **2** Jumble consists of articles for a jumble sale > verb **3** To jumble things means to mix them up untidily

jumbo noun **1** A jumbo or jumbo jet is a large jet aeroplane that can carry several hundred passengers > adjective **2** very large: *jumbo packs of elastic bands*

jump verb **1** To jump means to spring off the ground using your leg muscles **2** To jump means to spring off the ground and move over or across it **3** If you jump at something, such as an opportunity, you accept it eagerly **4** If you jump on someone, you criticize them suddenly and

forcefully **5** If someone jumps, they make a sudden sharp movement of surprise **6** If an amount or level jumps, it suddenly increases > noun **7** a spring into the air, sometimes over an object

jumper noun a knitted garment for the top half of the body

jumpy jumpier, jumpiest adjective nervous and worried

junction noun a place where roads or railway lines meet or cross

June noun June is the sixth month of the year. It has 30 days

jungle noun **1** a dense tropical forest **2** a tangled mass of plants or other objects

junior adjective **1** Someone who is junior to other people has a lower position in an organization **2** Junior also means younger **3** relating to childhood: *a junior school* > noun **4** someone who holds an unimportant position in an organization

juniper noun an evergreen shrub with purple berries used in cooking and medicine

junk noun **1** Junk is old or second-hand articles which are sold cheaply or thrown away **2** If you think something is junk, you think it is worthless rubbish **3** a Chinese sailing boat with a flat bottom and square sails

junk food noun Junk food is food low in nutritional value which is eaten as well as or instead of proper meals

junkie noun (informal) a drug addict

Jupiter noun Jupiter is the largest planet in the solar system and the fifth from the sun

jurisdiction noun **1** (formal) Jurisdiction is the power or right of the courts to apply laws and make legal judgments: *The Court held that* it did not have the jurisdiction to examine the merits of the case **2** Jurisdiction is power or authority: *The airport was under French jurisdiction*

juror *noun* a member of a jury

jury juries *noun* a group of people in a court of law who have been selected to listen to the facts of a case on trial, and to decide whether the accused person is guilty or not

just *adjective* **1** fair and impartial: *She arrived at a just decision* **2** morally right or proper: *a just reward* ▷ *adverb* **3** If something has just happened, it happened a very short time ago **4** If you just do something, you do it by a very small amount: *They only just won* **5** simply or only: *It was just an excuse not to mow the lawn* **6** exactly: *It's just what she wanted* ▷ *phrase* **7** In South African English, **just now** means in a little while > **justly** *adverb*

justice *noun* **1** Justice is fairness and reasonableness **2** The system of justice in a country is the way in which laws are maintained by the courts **3** a judge or magistrate

justify justifies, justifying, justified *verb* **1** If you justify an action or idea, you prove or explain why it is reasonable or necessary **2** COMPUTING To justify text that you have typed or keyed into a computer is to adjust the spaces between the words so each full line in a paragraph fills the space between the left and right hand margins of the page > **justification** *noun* > **justifiable** *adjective*

jut juts, jutting, jutted *verb* If something juts out, it sticks out beyond or above a surface or edge

juvenile *adjective* **1** suitable for young people **2** childish and rather silly: *a juvenile game* ▷ *noun* **3** a young person not old enough to be considered an adult

juxtapose *verb* If you juxtapose things or ideas, you put them close together, often to emphasize the difference between them > **juxtaposition** *noun*

k

kaleidoscope [kal-**eye**-dos-skope] *noun* a toy consisting of a tube with a hole at one end. When you look through the hole and twist the other end of the tube, you can see a changing pattern of colours

kamikaze *noun* In the Second World War, a kamikaze was a Japanese pilot who flew an aircraft loaded with explosives directly into an enemy target knowing he would be killed doing so

kangaroo kangaroos *noun* a large Australian animal with very strong back legs which it uses for jumping

karate [kar-**rat**-ee] *noun* Karate is a sport in which people fight each other using only their hands, elbows, feet, and legs

karma *noun* In Buddhism and Hinduism, karma is actions you take which affect you in your present and future lives

Karoo Karoos or **Karroo** *noun* In South Africa, the Karoos are areas of very dry land

kayak [**ky**-ak] *noun* a covered canoe

with a small opening for the person sitting in it, originally used by the Inuit people

kebab noun pieces of meat or vegetable stuck on a stick and grilled

keel noun **1** the specially shaped bottom of a ship which supports the sides and sits in the water ▷ verb **2** If someone or something keels over, they fall down sideways

keen adjective **1** Someone who is keen shows great eagerness and enthusiasm **2** If you are keen on someone or something, you are attracted to or fond of them **3** quick to notice or understand things **4** Keen senses let you see, hear, smell, and taste things very clearly or strongly > **keenly** adverb > **keenness** noun

keep keeps, keeping, kept verb **1** To keep someone or something in a particular condition means to make them stay in that condition: We'll walk to keep warm **2** If you keep something, you have it and look after it **3** To keep something also means to store it in the usual place **4** If you keep doing something, you do it repeatedly or continuously: I kept phoning the hospital **5** If you keep a promise, you do what you promised to do **6** If you keep a secret, you do not tell anyone else **7** If you keep a diary, you write something in it every day **8** If you keep someone from going somewhere, you delay them so that they are late **9** To keep someone means to provide them with money, food, and clothing ▷ noun **10** Your keep is the cost of the food you eat, your housing, and your clothing: He does not contribute towards his keep **11** (HISTORY) the main tower inside

the walls of a castle > **keep up** verb If you keep up with other people, you move or work at the same speed as they do

keeper noun **1 a** a person whose job is to look after the animals in a zoo **2** a goalkeeper in soccer or hockey

keeping noun **1** If something is in your keeping, it has been given to you to look after for a while ▷ phrase **2** If one thing is in keeping with another, the two things are suitable or appropriate together

keepsake noun something that someone gives you to remind you of a particular person or event

keg noun a small barrel

kennel noun **1 a** a shelter for a dog **2** A kennels is a place where dogs can be kept for a time, or where they are bred

Kenyan [ken-yan or keen-yan] adjective **1** belonging or relating to Kenya ▷ noun **2** someone who comes from Kenya

kerb noun the raised edge at the point where a pavement joins onto a road

kernel noun the part of a nut that is inside the shell

kerosene noun Kerosene is the same as paraffin

ketchup noun Ketchup is a cold sauce, usually made from tomatoes

kettle noun a metal container with a spout, in which you boil water

key noun **1** a shaped piece of metal that fits into a hole so that you can unlock a door, wind something that is clockwork, or start a car **2** The keys on a computer keyboard, piano, or cash register are the buttons that you press to use it **3** an explanation of the symbols used in a map or diagram **4** (MUSIC) In music, a key is a scale of notes ▷ verb

5 [COMPUTING] If you key in information on a computer keyboard, you type it

keyboard [COMPUTING] a row of levers or buttons on a piano, typewriter, or computer

kg an abbreviation for 'kilogram' or 'kilograms'

khaki [kah-kee] noun **1** Khaki is a strong yellowish-brown material, used especially for military uniforms ▷ noun, adjective **2** yellowish-brown

kibbutz kibbutzim [kib-**boots**] noun a place of work in Israel, for example a farm or factory, where the workers live together and share all the duties and income

kick verb **1** If you kick something, you hit it with your foot ▷ noun **2** If you give something a kick, you hit it with your foot **3** (informal) If you get a kick out of doing something, you enjoy doing it very much ▷ verb When players kick off, they start a soccer or rugby match > **kick-off** noun

kid kids, kidding, kidded noun **1** (informal) a child **2** a young goat ▷ verb **3** If you kid people, you tease them by deceiving them in fun

kidnap kidnaps, kidnapping, kidnapped verb To kidnap someone is to take them away by force and demand a ransom in exchange for returning them > **kidnapper** noun > **kidnapping** noun

kidney noun Your kidneys are two organs in your body that remove waste products from your blood

kill verb **1** To kill a person, animal, or plant is to make them die **2** (informal) If something is killing you, it is causing you severe pain or discomfort: *My arms are killing me* ▷ noun **3** The kill is the moment when a hunter kills an animal > **killer** noun

kiln noun [ART] an oven for baking china or pottery until it becomes hard and dry

kilo kilos noun a kilogram

kilogram noun [MATHS] A kilogram is a unit of weight equal to 1000 grams

kilometre noun [MATHS] a unit of distance equal to 1000 metres

kilowatt noun a unit of power equal to 1000 watts

kilt noun a tartan skirt worn by men as part of Scottish Highland dress

kimono kimonos noun a long, loose garment with wide sleeves and a sash, worn in Japan

kin plural noun Your kin are your relatives

kind noun **1** A particular kind of thing is something of the same type or sort as other things: *that kind of film* ▷ adjective **2** Someone who is kind is considerate and generous towards other people > **kindly** adverb

kindergarten noun a school for children who are too young to go to primary school

kindness noun the quality of being considerate towards other people

kindred adjective If you say that someone is a kindred spirit, you mean that they have the same interests or opinions as you

king noun **1** [HISTORY] The king of a country is a man who is the head of state in the country, and who inherited his position from his parents **2** In chess, the king is a piece which can only move one square at a time. When a king cannot move away from a position where it can be taken, the game is lost **3** In a pack of cards, a king is a card with a picture of a king on it

kingdom noun **1** [HISTORY] a country

that is governed by a king or queen **2** SCIENCE The largest divisions of the living organisms in the natural world are called kingdoms: *the animal kingdom*

king-size or **king-sized** *adjective* larger than the normal size: *a king-size bed*

kinship *noun* Kinship is a family relationship to other people

kiosk [**kee**-osk] *noun* a covered stall on a street where you can buy newspapers, sweets, or cigarettes

kip kips, kipping, kipped (*informal*) *noun* **1** a period of sleep ▷ *verb* **2** When you kip, you sleep

kiss *verb* **1** When you kiss someone, you touch them with your lips as a sign of love or affection ▷ *noun* **2** When you give someone a kiss, you kiss them

kiss of life *noun* The kiss of life is a method of reviving someone by blowing air into their lungs

kit *noun* **1** a collection of things that you use for a sport or other activity **2** a set of parts that you put together to make something

kitchen *noun* a room used for cooking and preparing food

kite *noun* **1** a frame covered with paper or cloth which is attached to a piece of string, and which you fly in the air **2** a shape with four sides, with two pairs of the same length, and none of the sides parallel to each other **3** a large bird of prey with a long tail and long wings

kitten *noun* a young cat

kitty kitties *noun* a fund of money that has been given by a group of people who will use it to pay for or do things together

kiwi kiwi or kiwis [**kee**-wee] *noun* **1** a type of bird found in New Zealand. Kiwis cannot fly **2** (*informal*)

someone who comes from New Zealand. The plural of this sense is 'kiwis'

km an abbreviation for 'kilometres'

knack *noun* a skilful or clever way of doing something difficult: *the knack of making friends*

knead *verb* If you knead dough, you press it and squeeze it with your hands before baking it

knee *noun* the joint in your leg between your ankle and your hip

kneecap *noun* Your kneecaps are the bones at the front of your knees

kneel kneels, kneeling, knelt *verb* When you kneel, you bend your legs and lower your body until your knees are touching the ground

knell *noun* (*literary*) the sound of a bell rung to announce a death or at a funeral

knickers *plural noun* Knickers are underpants worn by women and girls

knife knives; knifs, knifing, knifed *noun* **1** DGT a sharp metal tool that you use to cut things ▷ *verb* **2** To knife someone is to stab them with a knife

knight *noun* **1** a man who has been given the title 'Sir' by the King or Queen **2** HISTORY In medieval Europe, a knight was a man who served a monarch or lord as a mounted soldier **3** a chess piece that is usually in the shape of a horse's head ▷ *verb* **4** To knight a man is to give him the title 'Sir'
> **knighthood** *noun*

knit knits, knitting, knitted *verb* **1** If you knit a piece of clothing, you make it by working lengths of wool together, either using needles held in the hand, or with a machine **2** If you knit your brows, you frown
> **knitting** *noun*

knob noun **1** a round handle **2** a round switch on a machine: *the knobs of a radio*

knock verb **1** If you knock on something, you strike it with your hand or fist **2** If you knock a part of your body against something, you bump into it quite forcefully **3** (*informal*) To knock someone is to criticize them ▷ **knock** noun **4** a firm blow on something solid: *There was a knock at the door* ▷ **knock out** verb To knock someone out is to hit them so hard that they become unconscious

knockout noun **1** a punch in boxing which knocks a boxer unconscious **2** a competition in which competitors are eliminated in each round until only the winner is left

knot knots, knotting, knotted noun **1** a fastening made by looping a piece of string around itself and pulling the ends tight **2** a small lump visible on the surface of a piece of wood **3** A knot of people is a small group of them **4** (*technical*) a unit of speed used for ships and aircraft ▷ verb **5** If you knot a piece of string, you tie a knot in it

know knows, knowing, knew, known verb **1** If you know a fact, you have it in your mind and you do not need to learn it **2** People you know are not strangers because you have met them and spoken to them ▷ phrase **3** (*informal*) If you are **in the know**, you are one of a small number of people who share a secret

know-how noun Know-how is the ability to do something that is quite difficult or technical

knowing adjective A knowing look is one that shows that you know or understand something that other people do not ▷ **knowingly** adverb

knowledge noun Knowledge is all the information and facts that you know

knowledgeable adjective Someone who is knowledgeable knows a lot about a subject: *She was very knowledgeable about Irish mythology*

knuckle noun Your knuckles are the joints at the end of your fingers where they join your hand

koala noun an Australian animal with grey fur and small tufted ears. Koalas live in trees and eat eucalyptus leaves

Koran or **Qur'an** [kaw-**rahn**] noun The Koran is the holy book of Islam

Korean [kor-**ree**-an] adjective **1** relating or belonging to Korea ▷ noun **2** someone who comes from Korea **3** Korean is the main language spoken in Korea

kosher [**koh**-sher] adjective Kosher food has been specially prepared to be eaten according to Jewish law

kung fu [kung **foo**] noun Kung fu is a Chinese style of fighting which involves using your hands and feet

Kurd noun The Kurds are a group of people who live mainly in eastern Turkey, northern Iraq, and western Iran

Kurdish adjective **1** belonging or relating to the Kurds: *Kurdish culture* ▷ noun **2** Kurdish is the language spoken by the Kurds

k

I

l an abbreviation for 'litres'

lab noun (informal) a laboratory

label labels, labelling, labelled noun **1** a piece of paper or plastic attached to something as an identification ▷ verb **2** If you label something, you put a label on it

laboratory laboratories noun (SCIENCE) a place where scientific experiments are carried out

laborious adjective needing a lot of effort or time ▷ **laboriously** adverb

Labor Party noun In Australia, the Labor Party is one of the major political parties

labour noun **1** Labour is hard work **2** The workforce of a country or industry is sometimes called its labour: unskilled labour **3** In Britain, the Labour Party is a political party that believes that the government should provide free health care and education for everyone **4** In New Zealand, the Labour Party is one of the main political parties **5** Labour is also the last stage of pregnancy when a woman gives birth to a baby ▷ verb **6** (old-fashioned) To labour means to work hard ▷ **labourer** noun

labrador noun a large dog with short black or golden hair

labyrinth [lab-er-inth] noun a complicated series of paths or passages

lace noun **1** Lace is a very fine decorated cloth made with a lot of holes in it **2** Laces are cords with which you fasten your shoes ▷ verb **3** When you lace up your shoes, you tie a bow in the laces **4** To lace someone's food or drink means to put a small amount of alcohol, a drug, or poison in it: black coffee laced with vodka ▷ **lacy** adjective

lack noun **1** If there is a lack of something, it is not present when or where it is needed ▷ verb **2** If something is lacking, it is not present when or where it is needed **3** If someone or something is lacking something, they do not have it or do not have enough of it: Francis was lacking in stamina

lacklustre [lak-luss-ter] adjective not interesting or exciting

laconic [lak-kon-ik] adjective using very few words

lacquer [lak-er] noun Lacquer is thin, clear paint that you put on wood to protect it and make it shiny

lacrosse noun Lacrosse is an outdoor ball game in which two teams try to score goals using long sticks with nets on the end of them

lad noun a boy or young man

ladder noun **1** a wooden or metal frame used for climbing which consists of horizontal steps fixed to two vertical poles **2** If your stockings or tights have a ladder in them, they have a vertical, ladder-like tear in them ▷ verb **3** If you ladder your stockings or tights, you get a ladder in them

laden [lay-den] adjective To be laden with something means to be carrying a lot of it: bushes laden with ripe fruit

ladle noun **1** a long-handled spoon with a deep, round bowl, which you use to serve soup ▷ verb **2** If you ladle out food, you serve it with a ladle

lady ladies *noun* **1** a woman, especially one who is considered to be well mannered **2** Lady is a title used in front of the name of a woman from the nobility, such as a lord's wife

ladylike *adjective* behaving in a polite and socially correct way

lag lags, lagging, lagged *verb* **1** To lag behind is to make slower progress than other people **2** To lag pipes is to wrap cloth round them to stop the water inside freezing in cold weather

lager *noun* Lager is light-coloured beer

lagoon *noun* an area of water separated from the sea by reefs or sand

laid the past tense and past participle of **lay**

lain the past participle of some meanings of **lie**

lair *noun* a place where a wild animal lives

lake *noun* an area of fresh water surrounded by land

lamb *noun* **1** a young sheep **2** Lamb is the meat from a lamb

lame *adjective* **1** Someone who is lame has an injured leg and cannot walk easily **2** A lame excuse is not very convincing > **lamely** *adverb* > **lameness** *noun*

lament *verb* **1** To lament something means to express sorrow or regret about it ▷ *noun* **2** an expression of sorrow or regret **3** a song or poem expressing grief at someone's death

lamentable *adjective* disappointing and regrettable

laminated *adjective* consisting of several thin sheets or layers stuck together: *laminated glass*

lamp *noun* a device that produces light

lamppost *noun* a tall column in a street, with a lamp at the top

lance *verb* **1** To lance a boil or abscess means to stick a sharp instrument into it in order to release the fluid ▷ *noun* **2** a long spear that used to be used by soldiers on horseback

land *noun* **1** Land is an area of ground **2** Land is also the part of the earth that is not covered by water **3** a country: *our native land* ▷ *verb* **4** When a plane lands, it arrives back on the ground after a flight **5** If you land something you have been trying to get, you succeed in getting it: *She eventually landed a job with a local radio station* **6** To land a fish means to catch it while fishing **7** If you land someone with something unpleasant, you cause them to have to deal with it

landing *noun* **1** a flat area in a building at the top of a flight of stairs **2** The landing of an aeroplane is its arrival back on the ground after a flight: *a smooth landing*

landlady landladies *noun* a woman who owns a house or small hotel and who lets rooms to people

landlord *noun* a man who owns a house or small hotel and who lets rooms to people

landmark *noun* **1** a noticeable feature in a landscape, which you can use to check your position **2** an important stage in the development of something: *The play is a landmark in Japanese theatre*

landowner *noun* someone who owns land, especially a large area of the countryside

landscape *noun* **1** GEOGRAPHY The landscape is the view over an area of open land **2** ART a painting of the countryside

landslide *noun* **1** a large amount of

loose earth and rocks falling down a mountain side **2** a victory in an election won by a large number of votes

lane noun **1** a narrow road, especially in the country **2** one of the strips on a road marked with lines to guide drivers

language noun **1** the system of words that the people of a country use to communicate with each other **2** Your language is the style in which you express yourself: *His language is often obscure* **3** Language is the study of the words and grammar of a particular language

languid [**lang**-gwid] adjective slow and lacking energy ▸ **languidly** adverb

languish verb If you languish, you endure an unpleasant situation for a long time: *Many languished in poverty*

lanky lankier, lankiest adjective Someone who is lanky is tall and thin and moves rather awkwardly

lantern noun a lamp in a metal frame with glass sides

lap laps, lapping, lapped noun **1** Your lap is the flat area formed by your thighs when you are sitting down **2** one circuit of a running track or racecourse ▸ verb **3** When an animal laps up liquid, it drinks using its tongue to get the liquid into its mouth **4** If you lap someone in a race, you overtake them when they are still on the previous lap **5** When water laps against something, it gently moves against it in little waves

lapel [lap-**el**] noun a flap which is joined on to the collar of a jacket or coat

lapse noun **1** a moment of bad behaviour by someone who usually behaves well **2** a slight mistake **3** a period of time between two events ▸ verb **4** If you lapse into a different way of behaving, you start behaving that way: *The offenders lapsed into a sullen silence* **5** If a legal document or contract lapses, it is not renewed on the date when it expires

laptop noun COMPUTING a type of small portable computer

lard noun Lard is fat from a pig, used in cooking

larder noun a room in which you store food, often next to a kitchen

large adjective **1** Someone or something that is large is much bigger than average ▸ phrase **2** If a prisoner is **at large**, he or she has escaped from prison

largely adverb to a great extent: *The public are largely unaware of this*

lark noun **1** a small brown bird with a distinctive song **2** If you do something for a lark, you do it in a high spirited or mischievous way for fun

larrikin noun (informal) In Australian and New Zealand English, a young person who behaves in a wild or irresponsible way

larva larvae noun an insect, which looks like a short, fat worm, at the stage before it becomes an adult

larynx larynxes or larynges noun the part of your throat containing the vocal cords, through which air passes between your nose and lungs

lasagne [laz-**zan**-ya] noun Lasagne is an Italian dish made with wide flat sheets of pasta, meat, and cheese sauce

laser noun a machine that produces a powerful concentrated beam of light which is used to cut very hard materials and in some kinds of surgery

lash noun 1 Your lashes are the hairs growing on the edge of your eyelids 2 a strip of leather at the end of a whip 3 Lashes are blows struck with a whip ▷ **lash out** verb To lash out at someone means to criticize them severely

lass noun a girl or young woman

last adjective 1 The last thing or event is the most recent one: last year 2 The last thing that remains is the only one left after all the others have gone: The last family left in 1950 ▷ adverb 3 If you last did something on a particular occasion, you have not done it since then: They last met in Rome 4 The thing that happens last in a sequence of events is the final one: He added the milk last ▷ verb 5 If something lasts, it continues to exist or happen: Her speech lasted fifty minutes 6 To last also means to remain in good condition: The mixture will last for up to 2 weeks in the fridge ▷ phrase 7 At last means after a long time > **lastly** adverb

last-ditch adjective A last-ditch attempt to do something is a final attempt to succeed when everything else has failed

latch noun 1 a simple door fastening consisting of a metal bar which falls into a hook 2 a type of door lock which locks automatically when you close the door and which has to be opened with a key ▷ verb 3 (informal) If you latch onto someone or something, you become attached to them

late adjective, adverb 1 Something that happens late happens towards the end of a period of time: the late evening; late in the morning 2 If you arrive late, or do something late, you arrive or do it after the time you were expected to ▷ adjective 3 A late

event happens after the time when it usually takes place: a late breakfast 4 (formal) Late means dead: my late grandmother

lately adverb Events that happen lately happened recently

latent adjective A latent quality is hidden at the moment, but may emerge in the future: a latent talent for art

lateral adjective relating to the sides of something, or moving in a sideways direction

lathe noun a machine which holds and turns a piece of wood or metal against a tool to cut and shape it

lather noun Lather is the foam that you get when you rub soap in water

Latin noun 1 Latin is the language of ancient Rome ▷ noun, adjective 2 Latins are people who speak languages closely related to Latin, such as French, Italian, Spanish, and Portuguese

Latin America noun Latin America consists of the countries in North, South, and Central America where Spanish or Portuguese is the main language > **Latin American** adjective

latitude noun GEOGRAPHY The latitude of a place is its distance north or south of the equator measured in degrees

latter adjective, noun 1 You use 'latter' to refer to the second of two things that are mentioned: They were eating sandwiches and cakes (the latter bought from Mrs Paul's bakery) ▷ adjective 2 'Latter' also describes the second or end part of something: the latter part of his career

latterly adverb (formal) Latterly means recently: It's only latterly that this has become an issue

lattice noun a structure made of

strips which cross over each other diagonally leaving holes in between

laudable adjective (formal) deserving praise: It is a laudable enough aim
> **laudably** adverb

laugh verb **1** When you laugh, you make a noise which shows that you are amused or happy ▷ noun **2** the noise you make when you laugh
> **laughter** noun

laughable adjective quite absurd

laughing stock noun someone who has been made to seem ridiculous

launch verb **1** To launch a ship means to send it into the water for the first time **2** To launch a rocket means to send it into space **3** When a company launches a new product, they have an advertising campaign to promote it as they start to sell it ▷ noun **4** a motorboat

launch pad noun A launch pad, or a launching pad, is the place from which space rockets take off

launder verb (old-fashioned) To launder clothes, sheets, or towels means to wash and iron them

laundry laundries noun **1** a business that washes and irons clothes and sheets **2** Laundry is also the dirty clothes and sheets that are being washed, or are about to be washed

laurel noun an evergreen tree with shiny leaves

lava noun GEOGRAPHY Lava is the very hot liquid rock that comes shooting out of an erupting volcano, and becomes solid as it cools

lavatory lavatories noun a toilet

lavender noun **1** Lavender is a small bush with bluish-pink flowers that have a strong, pleasant scent ▷ adjective **2** bluish-pink

lavish adjective **1** If you are lavish, you are very generous with your time, money, or gifts **2** A lavish amount is a large amount ▷ verb **3** If you lavish money or affection on someone, you give them a lot of it
> **lavishly** adverb

law noun **1** The law is the system of rules developed by the government of a country, which regulate what people may and may not do and deals with people who break these rules **2** The law is also the profession of people such as lawyers, whose job involves the application of the laws of a country **3** one of the rules established by a government or a religion, which tells people what they may or may not do **4** a scientific fact which allows you to explain how things work in the physical world > **lawful** adjective
> **lawfully** adverb

law-abiding adjective obeying the law and not causing any trouble

lawless adjective having no regard for the law

lawn noun an area of cultivated grass

lawnmower noun a machine for cutting grass

lawsuit noun a civil court case between two people, as opposed to the police prosecuting someone for a criminal offence

lawyer noun a person who is qualified in law, and whose job is to advise people about the law and represent them in court

lax adjective careless and not keeping up the usual standards: a lax accounting system

lay lays, laying, laid verb **1** When you lay something somewhere, you put it down so that it lies there **2** If you lay something, you arrange it or set it out **3** If you lay the table, you put cutlery on the table ready for a meal

4 When a bird lays an egg, it produces the egg out of its body **5** If you lay a trap for someone, you create a situation in which you will be able to catch them out **6** If you lay emphasis on something, you refer to it in a way that shows you think it is very important **7** If you lay odds on something, you bet that it will happen ▷ *adjective* **8** You use 'lay' to describe people who are involved with a Christian church but are not members of the clergy: *a lay preacher* **9** Lay is the past tense of some senses of **lie** ▷ **lay off** *verb* **1** When workers are laid off, their employers tell them not to come to work for a while because there is a shortage of work **2** (*informal*) If you tell someone to lay off, you want them to stop doing something annoying ▷ **lay on** *verb* If you lay on a meal or entertainment, you provide it

lay-by *noun* **1** an area by the side of a main road where motorists can stop for a short while **2** In Australia and New Zealand, lay-by is a system where you pay a deposit on an item in a shop so that it will be kept for you until you pay the rest of the price

layer *noun* a single thickness of something: *layers of clothing*

layman laymen *noun* **1** someone who does not have specialized knowledge of a subject: *a layman's guide to computers* **2** someone who belongs to the church but is not a member of the clergy

layout *noun* The layout of something is the pattern in which it is arranged

laze *verb* If you laze, you relax and do no work: *We spent a few days lazing around by the pool*

lazy lazier, laziest *adjective* idle and unwilling to work ▷ **lazily** *adverb* ▷ **laziness** *noun*

lb an abbreviation for 'pounds': *3lb of sugar*

lbw In cricket lbw is an abbreviation for 'leg before wicket', which is a way of dismissing a batsman when his legs prevent the ball from hitting the wicket

leach *verb* When minerals are leached from rocks, they are dissolved by water which filters through the rock

lead leads, leading, led [*rhymes with* feed] *verb* **1** If you lead someone somewhere, you go in front of them in order to show them the way **2** If one thing leads to another, it causes the second thing to happen **3** a person who leads a group of people is in charge of them ▷ *noun* **4** a length of leather or chain attached to a dog's collar, so that the dog can be kept under control **5** If the police have a lead, they have a clue which might help them to solve a crime

lead [*rhymes with* fed] *noun* Lead is a soft metallic element. Its atomic number is 82 and its symbol is Pb

leader *noun* **1** someone who is in charge of a country, an organization, or a group of people **2** the person who is winning in a competition or race **3** a newspaper article that expresses the newspaper's opinions

leadership *noun* **1** the group of people in charge of an organization **2** Leadership is the ability to be a good leader

leading *adjective* particularly important, respected, or advanced

leaf leaves *noun* **1** the flat green growth on the end of a twig or branch of a tree or other plant ▷ *verb* **2** If you leaf through a book, magazine, or newspaper, you turn the pages over quickly ▷ **leafy** adjective

leaflet noun a piece of paper with information or advertising printed on it

league [leeg] noun **1** PE a group of countries, clubs, or people who have joined together for a particular purpose or because they share a common interest: *the League of Red Cross Societies; the Australian Football League* **2** a unit of distance used in former times, equal to about 3 miles

leak verb **1** If a pipe or container leaks, it has a hole which lets gas or liquid escape **2** If liquid or gas leaks, it escapes from a pipe or container **3** If someone in an organization leaks information, they give the information to someone who is not supposed to have it: *The letter was leaked to the press* ▷ noun **4** If a pipe or container has a leak, it has a hole which lets liquid or gas escape **5** If there is a leak in an organization, someone inside the organization is giving information to people who are not supposed to have it ▷ **leaky** adjective

leakage noun an escape of gas or liquid from a pipe or container

lean leans, leaning, leant or leaned verb **1** When you lean in a particular direction, you bend your body in that direction **2** When you lean on something, you rest your body against it for support **3** If you lean on someone, you depend on them **4** If you lean towards particular ideas, you approve of them and follow them: *parents who lean towards strictness* ▷ adjective **5** having little or no fat: *lean cuts of meat* **6** A lean period is a time when food or money is in short supply

leap leaps, leaping, leapt or leaped verb **1** If you leap somewhere, you jump over a long distance or high in the air ▷ noun **2** a jump over a long distance or high in the air

learn learns, learning, learnt or learned verb **1** When you learn something, you gain knowledge or a skill through studying or training **2** If you learn of something, you find out about it: *She had first learnt of the bomb attack that morning* ▷ **learner** noun

learned [ler-nid] adjective A learned person has a lot of knowledge gained from years of study

learning noun Learning is knowledge that has been acquired through serious study

lease noun **1** an agreement which allows someone to use a house or flat in return for rent ▷ verb **2** To lease property to someone means to allow them to use it in return for rent

leash noun a length of leather or chain attached to a dog's collar so that the dog can be controlled

least noun **1** The least is the smallest possible amount of something ▷ adjective **2** as small or as few as possible ▷ adverb **3** Least is a superlative form of **little** ▷ phrase **4** You use **at least** to show that you are referring to the minimum amount of something, and that you think the true amount is greater: *At least 200 hundred people were injured*

leather noun Leather is the tanned skin of some animals, used to make shoes and clothes ▷ **leathery** adjective

leave leaves, leaving, left verb **1** When you leave a place, you go away from it **2** If you leave someone somewhere, they stay behind after you go away **3** If you leave a job or organization, you stop being part of it: *He left his job shortly after Christmas* **4** If someone leaves money or possessions to someone, they arrange for them to be given to them after their death **5** In subtraction, when you take one number from another, it leaves a third number ▷ *noun* **6** a period of holiday or absence from a job

Lebanese *adjective* **1** belonging or relating to Lebanon ▷ *noun* **2** someone who comes from Lebanon

lectern *noun* a sloping desk which people use to hold books or notes on

lecture *noun* **1** a formal talk intended to teach people about a particular subject **2** a talk intended to tell someone off ▷ *verb* **3** Someone who lectures teaches in a college or university

lecturer *noun* a teacher in a college or university

led the past tense and past participle of **lead**

ledge *noun* a narrow shelf on the side of a cliff or rock face, or on the outside of a building, directly under a window

ledger *noun* a book in which accounts are kept

lee *noun* **1** the sheltered side of a place: *the lee of the mountain* ▷ *adjective* **2** on the side of a ship away from the wind

leech *noun* a small worm that lives in water and feeds by sucking the blood from other animals

leek *noun* a long vegetable of the onion family, which is white at one end and has green leaves at the other

leeway *noun* If something gives you some leeway, it allows you more

flexibility in your plans, for example by giving you time to finish an activity

left *noun* **1** The left is one of two sides of something. For example, on a page, English writing begins on the left **2** People and political groups who hold socialist or communist views are referred to as the Left **3** Left is the past tense and past participle of **leave** ▷ *adjective, adverb* **4** Left means on or towards the left side of something: *He had a mark above his left eye; Turn left down Govan Road*

left-handed *adjective, adverb* Someone who is left-handed does things such as writing with their left hand

leftist *adjective* holding left-wing political views

leftovers *plural noun* the bits of food which have not been eaten at the end of the meal

left-wing *adjective* believing more strongly in socialism, or less strongly in capitalism or conservatism, than other members of the same party or group
> **left-winger** *noun*

leg *noun* **1** Your legs are the two limbs which stretch from your hips to your feet **2** The legs of a pair of trousers are the parts that cover your legs **3** The legs of an object such as a table are the parts which rest on the floor and support the object's weight **4** A leg of a journey is one part of it **5** one of two matches played between two sports teams: *He will miss the second leg of their UEFA Cup tie*

legacy *legacies noun* **1** property or money that someone gets in the will of a person who has died **2** something that exists as a result

of a previous event or time: the
legacy of a Catholic upbringing

legal adjective **1** relating to the law:
the Dutch legal system **2** allowed by
the law: The strike was perfectly legal
> **legally** adverb

legal aid noun Legal aid is a system
which provides the services of a
lawyer free, or very cheaply, to
people who cannot afford the full
fees

legality noun The legality of an
action means whether or not it is
allowed by the law: They challenged
the legality of the scheme

legalize or **legalise** verb To legalize
something that is illegal means to
change the law so that it becomes
legal > **legalization** noun

legend noun **1** an old story which
was once believed to be true, but
which is probably untrue **2** If you
refer to someone or something as a
legend, you mean they are very
famous: His career has become a
legend > **legendary** adjective

leggings plural noun **1** Leggings are
very close-fitting trousers made of
stretch material, worn mainly by
young women **2** Leggings are also a
waterproof covering worn over
ordinary trousers to protect them

legible adjective Writing that is
legible is clear enough to be read

legion noun **1** In ancient Rome, a
legion was a military unit of
between 3000 and 6000 soldiers
2 a large military force: the French
Foreign Legion **3** Legions of people
are large numbers of them

legislate verb (formal) When a
government legislates, it creates
new laws

legislation noun Legislation is a law
or set of laws created by a
government

legislative adjective relating to the
making of new laws: a legislative
council

legislator noun (formal) a person
involved in making or passing laws

legislature noun (formal) the
parliament in a country, which is
responsible for making new laws

legitimate [lij-**it**-tim-it] adjective
Something that is legitimate is
reasonable or acceptable according
to existing laws or standards: a
legitimate charge for parking the car
> **legitimacy** noun > **legitimately**
adverb

leisure [rhymes with **measure**] noun
1 Leisure is time during which you do
not have to work, and can do what
you enjoy doing ▷ phrase **2** If you do
something **at leisure**, or **at your
leisure**, you do it at a convenient
time

leisurely adjective, adverb A leisurely
action is done in an unhurried and
calm way

lemon noun **1** a yellow citrus fruit
with a sour taste ▷ adjective **2** pale
yellow

lemonade noun a sweet, fizzy drink
made from lemons, water, and
sugar

lend lends, lending, lent verb **1** If you
lend someone something, you give
it to them for a period of time and
then they give it back to you **2** If a
bank lends money, it gives the
money to someone and the money
has to be repaid in the future,
usually with interest ▷ phrase **3** If
you **lend someone a hand**, you help
them > **lender** noun

length noun **1** The length of
something is the horizontal
distance from one end to the other
2 The length of an event or activity is
the amount of time it lasts for **3** The

length of something is also the fact that it is long rather than short: *Despite its length, it is a rewarding read* **4** a long piece of something

lengthen *verb* To lengthen something means to make it longer

lengthways *or* **lengthwise** *adverb* If you measure something lengthways, you measure the horizontal distance from end to the other

lengthy lengthier, lengthiest *adjective* Something that is lengthy lasts for a long time

lenient *adjective* If someone in authority is lenient, they are less severe than expected > **leniently** *adverb* > **leniency** *noun*

lens *noun* **1** a curved piece of glass designed to focus light in a certain way, for example in a camera, telescope, or pair of glasses **2** The lens in your eye is the part behind the iris, which focuses light

lent 1 the past tense and past participle of **lend** ▷ *noun* **2** RE Lent is the period of forty days leading up to Easter, during which Christians give up something they enjoy

lentil *noun* Lentils are small dried red or brown seeds which are cooked and eaten in soups and curries

Leo *noun* Leo is the fifth sign of the zodiac, represented by a lion. People born between July 23rd and August 22nd are born under this sign

leopard *noun* a wild Asian or African big cat, with yellow fur and black or brown spots

leotard [lee-eh-tard] *noun* A leotard is a tight-fitting costume covering the body, which is worn for dancing or exercise. It is named after a French acrobat called Jules Léotard

leper *noun* (*offensive*) someone who has leprosy

leprosy *noun* Leprosy is an infectious disease which attacks the skin and nerves, and which can lead to fingers or toes dropping off

lesbian *noun* a homosexual woman > **lesbianism** *noun*

lesion [lee-zhen] *noun* a wound or injury

less *adjective, adverb* **1** Less means a smaller amount, or not as much in quality: *They left less than three weeks ago*; *She had become less frightened of him now* **2** Less is a comparative form of **little** ▷ *preposition* **3** You use 'less' to show that you are subtracting one number from another: *Eight less two leaves six*

-less *suffix* '-less' means without: hopeless; fearless

lessen *verb* If something lessens, it is reduced in amount, size, or quality

lesser *adjective* smaller in importance or amount than something else

lesson *noun* **1** a fixed period of time during which a class of pupils is taught by a teacher **2** an experience that makes you understand something important which you had not realized before

lest *conjunction* (*old-fashioned*) as a precaution in case something unpleasant or unwanted happens: *I was afraid to open the door lest he should follow me*

let lets, letting, let *verb* **1** If you let someone do something, you allow them to do it **2** If someone lets a house or flat that they own, they rent it out **3** You can say 'let's' or 'let us' when you want to suggest doing something with someone else: *Let's go* **4** If you let yourself in for something, you agree to do it although you do not really want to > **let down** *verb* If you let someone down, you fail to do something you had agreed to do for them > **let off** *verb* **1** If someone in authority lets you off, they do not punish you for something you have done wrong **2** If you let off a firework or explosive, you light it or detonate it

lethal [lee-thal] *adjective* able to kill someone: *a lethal weapon*

lethargic [lith-ar-jik] *adjective* If you feel lethargic, you have no energy or enthusiasm

lethargy [leth-ar-jee] *noun* Lethargy is a lack of energy and enthusiasm

letter *noun* **1** Letters are written symbols which go together to make words **2** a piece of writing addressed to someone, and usually sent through the post

lettering *noun* Lettering is writing, especially when you are describing the type of letters used: *bold lettering*

lettuce *noun* a vegetable with large green leaves eaten raw in salad

leukaemia or **leukemia** [loo-kee-mee-a] *noun* Leukaemia is a serious illness which affects the blood

level levels, levelling, levelled *adjective* **1** A surface that is level is smooth, flat, and parallel to the ground > *verb* **2** To level a piece of land means to make it flat **3** If you level a criticism at someone, you say or write something critical about them > *adverb* **4** If you draw level with someone, you get closer to them so that you are moving next to them > *noun* **5** a point on a scale which measures the amount, importance, or difficulty of something **6** The height of a liquid is the height it comes up to in a container > **level off** or **level out** *verb* If something levels off or levels out, it stops increasing or

decreasing: *Profits are beginning to level off*

level crossing *noun* a place where road traffic is allowed to drive across a railway track

level-headed *adjective* Someone who is level-headed is sensible and calm in emergencies

lever *noun* **1** a handle on a machine that you pull in order to make the machine work **2** a long bar that you wedge underneath a heavy object and press down on to make the object move

leverage *noun* Leverage is knowledge or influence that you can use to make someone do something

levy levies, levying, levied [lev-ee] (*formal*) *noun* **1** an amount of money that you pay in tax **2** When a government levies a tax, it makes people pay the tax and organizes the collection of the money

liability liabilities *noun* **1** Someone's liability is their responsibility for something they have done wrong **2** In business, a company's liabilities are its debts **3** (*informal*) If you describe someone as a liability, you mean that they cause a lot of problems or embarrassment

liable *adjective* If you say that something is liable to happen, you mean that you think it will probably happen **2** If you are liable for something you have done, you are legally responsible for it

liaise [lee-aze] *verb* To liaise with someone or an organization means to cooperate with them and keep them informed

liaison [lee-aze-on] *noun* Liaison is communication between two organizations or two sections of an organization

liar noun a person who tells lies

libel libels, libelling, libelled [**lie-bel**] noun 1 Libel is something written about someone which is not true, and for which the writer can be made to pay damages in court ▷ verb 2 To libel someone means to write or say something untrue about them > **libellous** adjective

liberal noun 1 someone who believes in political progress, social welfare, and individual freedom ▷ adjective 2 Someone who is liberal is tolerant of a wide range of behaviour, standards, or opinions 3 To be liberal with something means to be generous with it 4 A liberal quantity of something is a large amount of it > **liberally** adverb > **liberalism** noun

Liberal Democrat noun In Britain, a member or supporter of the Liberal Democrats, a political party that believes that individuals should have more rights and freedom

liberate verb To liberate people means to free them from prison or from an unpleasant situation > **liberation** noun > **liberator** noun

liberty noun Liberty is the freedom to choose how you want to live, without government restrictions

Libra noun Libra is the seventh sign of the zodiac, represented by a pair of scales. People born between September 23rd and October 22nd are born under this sign

librarian noun [LIBRARY] a person who works in, or is in charge of, a library

library libraries noun 1 a building in which books are kept for people to come and read or borrow 2 a collection of books, records, or videos

Libyan adjective 1 belonging or relating to Libya ▷ noun 2 someone who comes from Libya

lice the plural of **louse**

licence noun 1 an official document which entitles you to carry out a particular activity, for example to drive a car 2 Licence is the freedom to do what you want, especially when other people consider that it is being used irresponsibly

> **WORD TIP**
> Do not confuse the spellings of the noun *licence* and the verb *license*: *a driving licence*; *Are you licensed to fly a plane?*

license verb To license an activity means to give official permission for it to be carried out

> **WORD TIP**
> Remember this mnemonic: *the government licenSes Spaniels*

lichen [**lie-ken**] noun Lichen is a green, moss-like growth on rocks or tree trunks

lick verb 1 If you lick something, you move your tongue over it ▷ noun 2 the action of licking

lid noun the top of a container, which you open in order to reach what is inside

lie lies, lying, lay, lain verb 1 To lie somewhere means to rest somewhere horizontally 2 If you say where something lies, you are describing where it is: *The farm lies between two valleys*

> **WORD TIP**
> The past tense of this verb *lie* is *lay*. Do not confuse it with the verb *lay* meaning 'put'

lie lies, lying, lied verb 1 To lie means to say something that is not true ▷ noun 2 something you say that is not true

lieu [**lyoo**] phrase If one thing happens **in lieu** of another, it happens instead of it

lieutenant [loo-**ten**-ant *or* lef-**ten**-ent] *noun* a junior officer in the army or navy

life lives *noun* **1** Life is the quality of being able to grow and develop, which is present in people, plants, and animals **2** Your life is your existence from the time you are born until the time you die **3** The life of a machine is the period of time for which it is likely to work **4** If you refer to the life in a place, you are talking about the amount of activity there: *The town was full of life* **5** If criminals are sentenced to life, they are sent to prison for the rest of their lives, or until they are granted parole

life assurance *noun* Life assurance is an insurance which provides a sum of money in the event of the policy holder's death

lifeblood *noun* The lifeblood of something is the most essential part of it

lifeboat *noun* **1** a boat kept on shore, which is sent out to rescue people who are in danger at sea **2** a small boat kept on a ship, which is used if the ship starts to sink

life expectancy *noun* [GEOGRAPHY] Your life expectancy is the number of years you can expect to live

lifeguard *noun* a person whose job is to rescue people who are in difficulty in the sea or in a swimming pool

life jacket *noun* a sleeveless inflatable jacket that keeps you afloat in water

lifeless *adjective* **1** Someone who is lifeless is dead **2** If you describe a place or person as lifeless, you mean that they are dull

lifelike *adjective* A picture or sculpture that is lifelike looks very real or alive

lifeline *noun* **1** something which helps you to survive or helps an activity to continue **2** a rope thrown to someone who is in danger of drowning

lifelong *adjective* existing throughout someone's life: *He had a lifelong interest in music*

lifesaver *noun* In Australia and New Zealand, a person whose job is to rescue people who are in difficulty in the sea

life span *noun* **1** Someone's life span is the length of time during which they are alive **2** The life span of a product or organization is the length of time it exists or is useful

lifetime *noun* Your lifetime is the period of time during which you are alive

lift *verb* **1** To lift something means to move it to a higher position **2** When fog or mist lifts, it clears away **3** To lift a ban on something means to remove it **4** (*informal*) To lift things means to steal them ▷ *noun* **5** a machine like a large box which carries passengers from one floor to another in a building **6** If you give someone a lift, you drive them somewhere in a car or on a motorcycle

ligament *noun* a piece of tough tissue in your body which connects your bones

light lights, lighting, lighted *or* lit *noun* **1** Light is brightness from the sun, fire, or lamps, that enables you to see things **2** a lamp or other device that gives out brightness **3** If you give someone a light, you give them a match or lighter to light their cigarette ▷ *adjective* **4** A place that is light is bright because of the sun or the use of lamps **5** A light colour is pale **6** A light object does not weigh much **7** A light task is fairly easy **8** Light books or music are entertaining and are not intended to be serious ▷ *verb* **9** To light a place means to cause it to be filled with light **10** To light a fire means to make it start burning **11** To light upon something means to find it by accident > **lightly** *adverb* > **lightness** *noun*

lighten *verb* **1** When something lightens, it becomes less dark **2** To lighten a load means to make it less heavy

lighter *noun* a device for lighting a cigarette or cigar

light-hearted *adjective* Someone who is light-hearted is cheerful and has no worries

lighthouse *noun* a tower by the sea, which sends out a powerful light to guide ships and warn them of danger

lighting *noun* **1** The lighting in a room or building is the way that it is lit **2** DRAMA Lighting in the theatre or for a film is the special lights that are directed on the performers or scene

lightning *noun* Lightning is the bright flashes of light in the sky which are produced by natural electricity during a thunderstorm

lightweight *noun* **1** a boxer in one of the lighter weight groups ▷ *adjective* **2** Something that is lightweight does not weigh very much: *a lightweight jacket*

likable or **likeable** *adjective* Someone who is likable is very pleasant and friendly

like *preposition* **1** If one thing is like another, it is similar to it ▷ *noun* **2** 'The like' means other similar things of the sort just mentioned: *nappies, prams, cots, and the like*

▷ *phrase* **3** If you feel like something, you want to do it or have it: *I feel like a walk* ▷ *verb* **4** If you like something or someone, you find them pleasant

-like *suffix* '-like' means resembling or similar to: *a balloonlike object*

likelihood *noun* If you say that there is a likelihood that something will happen, you mean that you think it will probably happen

likely *adjective* Something that is likely will probably happen or is probably true

liken *verb* If you liken one thing to another, you say that they are similar

likeness *noun* If two things have a likeness to each other, they are similar in appearance

likewise *adverb* Likewise means similarly: *She sat down and he did likewise*

liking *noun* If you have a liking for someone or something, you like them

lilac *noun* **1** a shrub with large clusters of pink, white, or mauve flowers ▷ *adjective* **2** pale mauve

lilt *noun* A lilt in someone's voice is a pleasant rising and falling sound in it > **lilting** *adjective*

lily lilies *noun* a plant with trumpet-shaped flowers of various colours

limb *noun* **1** Your limbs are your arms and legs **2** The limbs of a tree are its branches ▷ *phrase* **3** If you have gone **out on a limb**, you have said or done something risky

limbo *noun* **1** If you are in limbo, you are in an uncertain situation over which you feel you have no control **2** The limbo is a West Indian dance in which the dancer has to pass under a low bar while leaning backwards

lime *noun* **1** a small, green citrus

fruit, rather like a lemon **2** A lime tree is a large tree with pale green leaves **3** Lime is a chemical substance that is used in cement and as a fertilizer

limelight noun If someone is in the limelight, they are getting a lot of attention

limestone noun Limestone is a white rock which is used for building and making cement

limit noun **1** a boundary or an extreme beyond which something cannot go: *the speed limit* ▷ verb **2** To limit something means to prevent it from becoming bigger, spreading, or making progress: *He did all he could to limit the damage*

limitation noun **1** The limitation of something is the reducing or controlling of it **2** If you talk about the limitations of a person or thing, you are talking about the limits of their abilities

limited adjective Something that is limited is rather small in amount or extent: *a limited number of bedrooms*

limousine [lim-o-zeen] noun a large, luxurious car, usually driven by a chauffeur

limp verb **1** If you limp, you walk unevenly because you have hurt your leg or foot **2** noun **2** an uneven way of walking ▷ adjective **3** Something that is soft and floppy, and not stiff or firm: *a limp lettuce*

line noun **1** a long, thin mark **2** a number of people or things positioned one behind the other **3** a route along which someone or something moves: *a railway line* **4** In a piece of writing, a line is a number of words together: *I often used to change my lines as an actor* **5** MATHS In maths, a line is the straight,

one-dimensional space between two points **6** Someone's line of work is the kind of work they do **7** The line someone takes is the attitude they have towards something: *He took a hard line with terrorism* **8** In a shop or business, a line is a type of product: *That line has been discontinued* ▷ verb **9** To line something means to cover its inside surface or edge with something: *Cottages lined the edge of the harbour*

▷ **line up** verb **1** When people line up, they stand in a line **2** When you line something up, you arrange it for a special occasion: *A tour is being lined up for July*

lineage [lin-ee-ij] noun Someone's lineage is all the people from whom they are directly descended

linear [lin-ee-ar] adjective arranged in a line or in a strict sequence, or happening at a constant rate

linen noun D G T **1** Linen is a type of cloth made from a plant called flax **2** Linen is also household goods made of cloth, such as sheets and tablecloths

liner noun a large passenger ship that makes long journeys

linesman linesmen noun an official at a sports match who watches the lines of the field or court and indicates when the ball goes outside them

-ling suffix '-ling' means 'small': *duckling*

linger verb To linger means to remain for a long time: *Economic problems lingered in the background*

lingerie [lan-jer-ee] noun Lingerie is women's nightclothes and underclothes

lingo lingoes noun (informal) a foreign language

linguist noun ENGLISH someone

who studies foreign languages or the way in which language works

lining noun any material to line the inside of something

link noun **1** a relationship or connection between two things: *the link between sunbathing and skin cancer* **2** a physical connection between two things or places: *a high-speed rail link between the cities* **3** one of the rings in a chain ▷ verb **4** To link people, places, or things means to join them together
> **linkage** noun

lino noun **1** Your lips are the edges of linoleum

linoleum noun a floor covering with a shiny surface

lint noun soft cloth made from linen, used to dress wounds

lion noun a large member of the cat family which comes from Africa. Lions have light brown fur, and the male has a long mane. A female lion is called a lioness

lip noun **1** Your lips are the edges of your mouth **2** The lip of a jug is the slightly pointed part through which liquids are poured out

lipstick noun a coloured substance which women wear on their lips

liqueur [lik-yoor] noun a strong sweet alcoholic drink, usually drunk after a meal

liquid SCIENCE noun **1** any substance which is not a solid or a gas, and which can be poured ▷ adjective **2** Something that is liquid is in the form of a liquid: *liquid nitrogen* **3** In commerce and finance a person's or company's liquid assets are the things that can be sold quickly to raise cash

liquidate verb To liquidate a company means to close it down and use its assets to pay off its debts

> **liquidation** noun > **liquidator** noun

liquor noun Liquor is any strong alcoholic drink

liquorice [lik-ker-iss] noun Liquorice is a root used to flavour sweets; also the sweets themselves

list noun **1** a set of words or items written one below the other ▷ verb **2** If you list a number of things, you make a list of them

listen verb If you listen to something, you hear it and pay attention to it
> **listener** noun

listless adjective lacking energy and enthusiasm > **listlessly** adverb

lit a past tense and past participle of **light**

litany litanies noun **1** a part of a church service in which the priest says or chants prayers and the people give responses **2** something, especially a list of things, that is repeated often or in a boring or insincere way: *a tedious litany of complaints*

literacy noun Literacy is the ability to read and write > **literate** adjective

literal adjective ENGLISH **1** The literal meaning of a word is its most basic meaning **2** A literal translation from a foreign language is one that has been translated exactly word for word > **literally** adverb

literary adjective ENGLISH connected with literature: *literary critics*

literature noun ENGLISH **1** Literature consists of novels, plays, and poetry **2** The literature on a subject is everything that has been written about it

lithe adjective supple and graceful

litmus noun SCIENCE In chemistry, litmus is a substance that turns red under acid and blue under alkali conditions

litmus test *noun* something which is regarded as a simple and accurate test of a particular thing, such as a person's attitude to an issue: *The conflict was seen as a litmus test of Britain's will to remain a major power*

litre *noun* [MATHS] a unit of liquid volume equal to about 1.76 pints

litter *noun* **1** Litter is rubbish in the street and other public places **2** Cat litter is a gravelly substance you put in a container where you want your cat to urinate and defecate **3** a number of baby animals born at the same time to the same mother ▷ *verb* **4** If things litter a place, they are scattered all over it

little *less, lesser, least adjective* **1** small in size or amount ▷ *noun* **2** A little is a small amount or degree: *Would you like a little fruit juice?* **3** Little also means not much: *He has little to say* ▷ *adverb* **4** to a small amount or degree: *a little afraid; She ate little*

live *verb* **1** [liv] If you live in a place, that is where your home is **2** To live means to be alive **3** If something lives up to your expectations, it is as good as you thought it would be ▷ *adjective, adverb* [rhymes with *hive*] **4** Live television or radio is broadcast while the event is taking place: *a live football match; The concert will go out live* ▷ *adjective* **5** Live animals or plants are alive, rather than dead or artificial: *a live spider* **6** Something is live if it is directly connected to an electricity supply: *Careful – those wires are live* **7** Live bullets or ammunition have not yet been exploded ▷ **live down** *verb* If you cannot live down a mistake or failure, you cannot make people forget it

livelihood *noun* Someone's livelihood is their job or the source of their income

lively *livelier, liveliest adjective* full of life and enthusiasm: *lively conversation* ▷ **liveliness** *noun*

liver *noun* **1** Your liver is a large organ in your body which cleans your blood and helps digestion **2** Liver is also the liver of some animals, which may be cooked and eaten

livestock *noun* Livestock is farm animals

livid *adjective* **1** extremely angry **2** dark purple or bluish: *livid bruises*

living *adjective* **1** If someone is living, they are alive: *her only living relative* ▷ *noun* **2** The work you do for a living is the work you do in order to earn money to live

living room *noun* the room where people relax and entertain in their homes

lizard *noun* a long, thin, dry-skinned reptile found in hot, dry countries

llama *noun* a South American animal related to the camel

load *noun* **1** something being carried **2** (*informal*) Loads means a lot: *loads of work* ▷ *verb* **3** To load a vehicle or animal means to put a large number of things into it or onto it

loaf *noun* **1** *loaves; loafs, loafing, loafed* **1** a large piece of bread baked in a shape that can be cut into slices ▷ *verb* **2** To loaf around means to be lazy and not do any work

loan *noun* **1** a sum of money that you borrow **2** the act of borrowing or lending something: *I am grateful to Jane for the loan of her book* ▷ *verb* **3** If you loan something to someone, you lend it to them

loath [rhymes with *both*] *adjective* If you are loath to do something, you are very unwilling to do it

loathe verb To loathe someone or something means to feel strong dislike for them > **loathing** noun > **loathsome** adjective

lob lobs, lobbing, lobbed verb 1 If you lob something, you throw it high in the air ▷ noun 2 In tennis, a lob is a stroke in which the player hits the ball high in the air

lobby lobbies, lobbying, lobbied noun 1 The lobby in a building is the main entrance area with corridors and doors leading off it 2 a group of people trying to persuade an organization that something should be done: *the environmental lobby* ▷ verb 3 To lobby an MP or an organization means to try to persuade them to do something, for example by writing them lots of letters

lobe noun 1 The lobe of your ear is the rounded soft part at the bottom 2 any rounded part of / something: *the frontal lobe of the brain*

lobster noun an edible shellfish with two front claws and eight legs

local adjective 1 Local means in, near, or belonging to the area in which you live: *the local newspaper* 2 A local anaesthetic numbs only one part of your body and does not send you to sleep ▷ noun 3 The locals are the people who live in a particular area 4 (*informal*) Someone's local is the pub nearest their home > **locally** adverb

locality localities noun an area of a country or city: *a large map of the locality*

localized or **localised** adjective existing or happening in only one place: *localized pain*

locate verb 1 To locate someone or something means to find out where

they are 2 If something is located in a place, it is in that place

location noun 1 GEOGRAPHY a place, or the position of something 2 In South Africa, a location was a small town where only Black people or Coloured people were allowed to live ▷ phrase 3 If a film is made on location, it is made away from a studio

loch noun In Scottish English, a loch is a lake

lock verb 1 If you lock something, you close it and fasten it with a key 2 If something locks into place, it moves into place and becomes firmly fixed there ▷ noun 3 a device on something which fastens it and prevents it from being opened except with a key 4 A lock on a canal is a place where the water level can be raised or lowered to allow boats to go between two parts of the canal which have different water levels 5 A lock of hair is a small bunch of hair

locker noun a small cupboard for your personal belongings, for example in a changing room

locomotive noun a railway engine

locust noun an insect like a large grasshopper, which travels in huge swarms and eats crops

lodge noun 1 a a small house in the grounds of a large country house, or a small house used for holidays ▷ verb 2 If you lodge in someone else's house, you live there and pay them rent 3 If something lodges somewhere, it gets stuck there: *The bullet lodged in his pelvis* 4 If you lodge a complaint, you formally make it

lodger noun a person who lives in someone's house and pays rent

lodgings plural noun If you live in

lodgings, you live in someone else's house and pay them rent

loft noun the space immediately under the roof of a house, often used for storing things

lofty loftier, loftiest adjective **1** very high: a lofty hall **2** very noble and important: lofty ideals **3** proud and superior: her lofty manner

log logs, logging, logged noun **1** a thick branch or piece of tree trunk which has fallen or been cut down **2** the captain's official record of everything that happens on board a ship ▷ verb **3** if you log something, you officially make a record of it, for example in a ship's log **4** To log into a computer system means to gain access to it, usually by giving your name and password. To log out means to finish using the system

logic noun Logic is a way of reasoning involving a series of statements, each of which must be true if the statement before it is true

logical adjective **1** A logical argument uses logic **2** A logical course of action or decision is sensible or reasonable in the circumstances > **logically** adverb

logistics noun (formal) The logistics of a complicated undertaking is the skilful organization of it

logo logos [loh-goh] noun The logo of an organization is a special design that is put on all its products

-logy suffix '-logy' is used to form words that refer to the study of something: biology; geology; anthropology

loin noun **1** (old-fashioned) Your loins are the front part of your body between your waist and your thighs **2** Loin is a piece of meat from the back or sides of an animal: loin of pork

loiter verb To loiter means stand about idly with no real purpose

lollipop noun a hard sweet on the end of a stick

lolly lollies noun **1** a lollipop **2** a piece of flavoured ice or ice cream on a stick **3** In Australian and New Zealand English, a sweet

lone adjective A lone person or thing is the only one in a particular place: a lone climber

lonely lonelier, loneliest adjective **1** If you are lonely, you are unhappy because you are alone **2** A lonely place is an isolated one which very few people visit: a lonely hillside > **loneliness** noun

loner noun a person who likes to be alone

lonesome adjective lonely and sad

long adjective **1** continuing for a great amount of time: There had been no rain for a long time **2** great in length or distance: a long dress; a long road ▷ adverb **3** for a certain period of time: How long will it last? **4** for an extensive period of time: long into the following year ▷ phrase **5** If something **no longer** happens, it does not happen any more **6** Before long means soon **7** If one thing is true as long as another thing is true, it is true only if the other thing is true ▷ verb **8** If you long for something, you want it very much

longevity [lon-jev-it-ee] noun (formal) Longevity is long life

longing noun a strong wish for something

longitude noun [GEOGRAPHY] The longitude of a place is its distance east or west of a line passing through Greenwich, measured in degrees

long jump noun The long jump is an

athletics event in which you jump as far as possible after taking a long run

long-range *adjective* **1** able to be used over a great distance: *long-range artillery* **2** extending a long way into the future: *a long-range weather forecast*

long-standing *adjective* having existed for a long time: *a long-standing tradition*

long-suffering *adjective* very patient: *her long-suffering husband*

long-term *adjective* extending a long way into the future: *a long-term investment*

long-winded *adjective* long and boring: *a long-winded letter*

loo *noun* (*informal*) a toilet

look *verb* **1** If you look at something, you turn your eyes towards it so that you can see it **2** If you look at a subject or situation, you study it or judge it **3** If you look down on someone, you think that they are inferior to you **4** If you are looking forward to something, you want it to happen because you think you will enjoy it **5** If you look up to someone, you admire and respect them **6** If you describe the way that something or someone looks, you are describing the appearance of it or them ▷ *noun* **7** If you have a look at something, you look at it **8** the way someone or something appears, especially the expression on a person's face **9** If you talk about someone's looks, you are talking about how attractive they are ▷ *interjection* **10** You say 'look out' to warn someone of danger > **look after** *verb* If you look after someone or something, you take care of them > **look for** *verb* If you look for someone or something, you try to

find them > **look up** *verb* **1** To look up information means to find it out in a book **2** If you look someone up, you go to see them after not having seen them for a long time **3** If a situation is looking up, it is improving

lookalike *noun* a person who looks very like someone else: *an Elvis lookalike*

lookout *noun* **1** someone who is watching for danger, or a place where they watch for danger ▷ *phrase* **2** If you are **on the lookout** for something, you are watching for it or waiting expectantly for it

loom *noun* **1** a machine for weaving cloth ▷ *verb* **2** If something looms in front of you, it suddenly appears as a tall, unclear, and sometimes frightening shape **3** If a situation or event is looming, it is likely to happen soon and is rather worrying

loony loonier, looniest; loonies (*informal*) *adjective* **1** People or behaviour can be described as loony if they are mad or eccentric ▷ *noun* **2** a mad or eccentric person

loop *noun* **1** a curved or circular shape in something long such as a piece of string ▷ *verb* **2** If you loop rope or string around an object, you place it in a loop around the object

loophole *noun* a small mistake or omission in the law which allows you to do something that the law really intends that you should not do

loose *adjective* **1** If something is loose, it is not firmly fixed, or attached **2** Loose clothes are rather large and do not fit closely ▷ *adverb* **3** To set animals loose means to set them free after they have been tied up or kept in a cage > **loosely** *adverb*

WORD TIP

The adjective and adverb *loose* is spelt with two *o*s. Do not confuse it with the verb *lose*

loosen *verb* To loosen something means to make it looser

loot *verb* **1** To loot shops and houses means to steal goods from them during a battle or riot ▷ *noun* **2** Loot is stolen money or goods

lop lops, lopping, lopped *verb* If you lop something off, you cut it off with one quick stroke

lopsided *adjective* Something that is lopsided is uneven because its two sides are different sizes or shapes

lord *noun* **1** a nobleman **2** Lord is a title used in front of the names of some noblemen, and of bishops, archbishops, judges, and some high-ranking officials: *the Lord Mayor of London* **3** In Christianity, Lord is a name given to God and Jesus Christ

Lordship *noun* You address a lord, judge, or bishop as Your Lordship

lore *noun* The lore of a place, people, or subject is all the traditional knowledge and stories about it

lorry lorries *noun* a large vehicle for transporting goods by road

lose loses, losing, lost *verb* **1** If you lose something, you cannot find it, or you no longer have it because it has been taken away from you: *I lost my airline ticket* **2** If you leave a relative or friend, they die: *She lost her brother in the war* **3** If you lose a fight or an argument, you are beaten **4** If a business loses money, it is spending more money than it is earning ▷ **loser** *noun*

WORD TIP

The verb *lose* is spelt with one *o*. Do not confuse it with the adjective and adverb *loose*

loss *noun* **1** The loss of something is

the losing of it ▷ *phrase* **2** If you are at a loss, you do not know what to do

lost *adjective* **1** If you are lost, you do not know where you are **2** If something is lost, you cannot find it **3** Lost is the past tense and past participle of *lose*

lot *noun* **1** A lot of something, or lots of something, is a large amount of something **2** A lot means very much or very often: *I love him a lot* **3** an amount of something or a number of things: *I've answered the first lot of questions* **4** In an auction, a lot is one of the things being sold

lotion *noun* a liquid that you put on your skin to protect or soften it: *suntan lotion*

lottery lotteries *noun* a method of raising money by selling tickets by which a winner is selected at random

lotus *noun* a large water lily, found in Africa and Asia

loud *adjective* **1** A loud noise has a high volume of sound: *a loud explosion* **2** If you describe clothing as loud, you mean that it is too bright: *a loud tie* ▷ **loudly** *adverb* ▷ **loudness** *noun*

loudspeaker *noun* a piece of equipment that makes your voice louder when you speak into a microphone connected to it

lounge *noun* **1** a room in a house or hotel with comfortable chairs where people can relax **2** The lounge or lounge bar in a pub or hotel is a more expensive and comfortably furnished bar ▷ *verb* **3** If you lounge around, you lean against something or sit or lie around in a lazy and comfortable way

louse lice *noun* Lice are small insects that live on people's bodies: *head lice*

lousy lousier, lousiest *adjective* (*informal*) **1** of bad quality or very unpleasant: *The weather is lousy* **2** ill or unhappy

lout *noun* a young man who behaves in an aggressive and rude way

lovable or **loveable** *adjective* having very attractive qualities and therefore easy to love: *a lovable black mongrel*

love *verb* **1** If you love someone, you have strong emotional feelings of affection for them **2** If you love something, you like it very much: *We both love fishing* **3** If you would love to do something, you want very much to do it: *I would love to live there* ▷ *noun* **4** Love is a strong emotional feeling of affection for someone or something **5** a strong liking for something **6** In tennis, love is a score of zero ▷ *phrase* **7** If you are **in love** with someone, you feel strongly attracted to them romantically

love affair *noun* a romantic relationship between two people

love life *noun* a person's romantic relationships

lovely lovelier, loveliest *adjective* very beautiful, attractive, and pleasant > **loveliness** *noun*

lover *noun* Someone who is a lover of something, for example art or music, is very fond of it

loving *adjective* feeling or showing love > **lovingly** *adverb*

low *adjective* **1** Something that is low is close to the ground, or measures a short distance from the ground to the top: *a low stool* **2** Low means small in value or amount **3** 'Low' is used to describe people who are considered not respectable: *mixing with low company* ▷ *adverb* **4** in a low position, level, or degree ▷ *noun* **5** a

level or amount that is less than before: *Sales hit a new low*

lower *verb* **1** To lower something means to move it downwards **2** To lower something also means to make it less in value or amount

lowlands *plural noun* Lowlands are an area of flat, low land > **lowland** *adjective*

lowly lowlier, lowliest *adjective* low in importance, rank, or status

low tide *noun* On a coast, low tide is the time, usually twice a day, when the sea is at its lowest level

loyal *adjective* firm in your friendship or support for someone or something > **loyally** *adverb* > **loyalty** *noun*

loyalist *noun* a person who remains firm in their support for a government or ruler

LSD *noun* LSD is a very powerful drug which causes hallucinations. LSD is an abbreviation for 'lysergic acid diethylamide'

Ltd an abbreviation for 'limited'; used after the names of limited companies

lucid *adjective* **1** Lucid writing or speech is clear and easy to understand **2** Someone who is lucid after having been ill or delirious is able to think clearly again

luck *noun* Luck is anything that seems to happen by chance and not through your own efforts

luckless *adjective* unsuccessful or unfortunate: *We reduced our luckless opponents to shattered wrecks*

lucky luckier, luckiest *adjective* **1** Someone who is lucky has a lot of good luck **2** Something that is lucky happens by chance and has good effects or consequences > **luckily** *adverb*

lucrative *adjective* Something that

is lucrative earns you a lot of money: *a lucrative sponsorship deal*

ludicrous adjective completely foolish, unsuitable, or ridiculous

lug lugs, lugging, lugged verb If you lug a heavy object around, you carry it with difficulty

luggage noun Your luggage is the bags and suitcases that you take with you when you travel

lukewarm adjective **1** slightly warm: *a mug of lukewarm tea* **2** not very enthusiastic or interested: *The report was given a polite but lukewarm response*

lull noun **1** a pause in something, or a short time when it is quiet and nothing much happens: *There was a temporary lull in the fighting* ▷ verb **2** If you are lulled into feeling safe, someone or something causes you to feel safe at a time when you are not safe: *We had been lulled into a false sense of security*

lullaby lullabies noun a song used for sending a baby or child to sleep

lumber noun **1** Lumber is wood that has been roughly cut up **2** Lumber is also old unwanted furniture and other items ▷ verb **3** If you lumber around, you move heavily and clumsily **4** (informal) If you are lumbered with something, you are given it to deal with even though you do not want it: *Women are still lumbered with the housework*

luminary luminaries noun (literary) a person who is famous or an expert in a particular subject

luminous adjective Something that is luminous glows in the dark, usually because it has been treated with a special substance: *The luminous dial on her clock* > **luminosity** noun

lump noun **1** A lump of something is

a solid piece of it, of any shape or size: *a big lump of dough* **2** a bump on the surface of something ▷ verb **3** If you lump people or things together, you combine them into one group or consider them as being similar in some way > **lumpy** adjective

lump sum noun a large sum of money given or received all at once

lunacy noun **1** Lunacy is extremely foolish or eccentric behaviour **2** (old-fashioned) Lunacy is also severe mental illness

lunar adjective relating to the moon

lunatic noun **1** If you call someone a lunatic, you mean that they are very foolish: *He drives like a lunatic!* **2** someone who is insane ▷ adjective **3** Lunatic behaviour is very stupid, foolish, or dangerous

lunch noun **1** a meal eaten in the middle of the day ▷ verb **2** When you lunch, you eat lunch

luncheon [lun-shen] noun (formal) Luncheon is lunch

lung noun Your lungs are the two organs inside your ribcage with which you breathe

lunge noun **1** a sudden forward movement: *He made a lunge for her* ▷ verb **2** To lunge means to make a sudden movement in a particular direction

lurch verb **1** To lurch means to make a sudden, jerky movement ▷ noun **2** a sudden, jerky movement

lure verb **1** To lure someone means to attract them into going somewhere or doing something ▷ noun **2** something that you find very attractive

lurid [loo-rid] adjective **1** involving a lot of sensational detail: *lurid stories in the press* **2** very brightly coloured or patterned

lurk verb To lurk somewhere means

to remain there hidden from the person you are waiting for

luscious *adjective* very tasty: *luscious fruit*

lush *adjective* In a lush field or garden, the grass or plants are healthy and growing thickly

lust *noun* 1 A lust for something is a strong desire to have it: *a lust for money* ▷ *verb* 2 If you lust for or after something, you have a very strong desire to possess it: *She lusted after fame*

lustre [lus-ter] *noun* Lustre is soft shining light reflected from the surface of something: *the lustre of silk*

luxuriant *adjective* Luxuriant plants, trees, and gardens are large, healthy, and growing strongly

luxurious *adjective* very expensive and full of luxury > **luxuriously** *adverb*

luxury luxuries *noun* 1 Luxury is great comfort in expensive and beautiful surroundings: *a life of luxury* 2 something that you enjoy very much but do not have very often, usually because it is expensive

-ly *suffix* 1 '-ly' forms adjectives that describe a quality: *friendly* 2 '-ly' forms adjectives that refer to how often something happens or is done: *yearly* 3 '-ly' forms adverbs that refer to how or in what way something is done: *quickly; nicely*

lying *noun* 1 Lying is telling lies ▷ *adjective* 2 A lying person is telling lies 3 Lying is also the present participle of **lie**

lynch *verb* If a crowd lynches someone, it kills them in a violent way without first holding a legal trial

lynx lynxes *noun* a wildcat with a short tail and tufted ears

lyric *noun* 1 MUSIC The lyrics of a song are the words ▷ *adjective* 2 Lyric poetry is written in a simple and direct style, and is usually about love

lyrical *adjective* poetic and romantic

m

m an abbreviation for 'metres' or 'miles'

macabre [mak-**kahb**-ra] *adjective* A macabre event or story is strange and horrible: *a macabre horror story*

macadamia [ma-ka-**dame**-ee-a] *noun* an Australian tree, also grown in New Zealand, that produces edible nuts

macaroni *noun* Macaroni is short hollow tubes of pasta

mace *noun* an ornamental pole carried by an official during ceremonies as a symbol of authority

machete [mash-**ett**-ee] *noun* a large, heavy knife with a big blade

machine *noun* 1 D G T a piece of equipment which uses electricity or power from an engine to make it work ▷ *verb* 2 If you machine something, you make it or work on it using a machine

machine-gun *noun* a gun that works automatically, firing bullets one after the other

machinery *noun* Machinery is machines in general

machismo [mak-**kiz**-moe] *noun* Machismo is exaggerated aggressive male behaviour

macho [mat-shoh] *adjective* A man who is described as macho behaves in an aggressively masculine way

mackerel *noun* a sea fish with blue and silver stripes

mad madder, maddest *adjective* **1** Someone who is mad has a mental problem which often causes them to behave in strange ways **2** (*informal*) If you describe someone as mad, you mean that they are very foolish: *He said we were mad to share a flat* **3** (*informal*) Someone who is mad is angry **4** (*informal*) If you are mad about someone or something, you like them very much: *Alan was mad about golf* > **madness** *noun* > **madman** *noun*

madam *noun* 'Madam' is a very formal way of addressing a woman

maddening *adjective* irritating or frustrating: *She had many maddening habits*

madly *adverb* If you do something madly, you do it in a fast, excited way

Mafia *noun* The Mafia is a large crime organization operating in Sicily, Italy, and the USA

magazine *noun* **1** LIBRARY a weekly or monthly publication with articles and photographs **2** a compartment in a gun for cartridges

magenta [maj-**jen**-ta] *noun, adjective* dark reddish-purple

maggot *noun* a creature that looks like a small worm and lives on decaying things. Maggots turn into flies

magic *noun* **1** In fairy stories, magic is a special power that can make impossible things happen **2** Magic is the art of performing tricks to entertain people

magical *adjective* wonderful and exciting > **magically** *adverb*

magician *noun* **1** a person who performs tricks as entertainment **2** In fairy stories, a magician is a man with magical powers

magistrate *noun* an official who acts as a judge in a law court that deals with less serious crimes

magnanimous *adjective* generous and forgiving

magnate *noun* someone who is very rich and powerful in business

magnet *noun* SCIENCE a piece of iron which attracts iron or steel towards it, and which points towards north if allowed to swing freely. A **permanent magnet** is a magnet that is still magnetic when the magnetic field that produced it is taken away; a **temporary magnet** is a magnet that loses its magnetism when the magnetic field that produced it is taken away > **magnetic** *adjective* > **magnetism** *noun*

magnificent *adjective* extremely beautiful or impressive > **magnificently** *adverb* > **magnificence** *noun*

magnify magnifies, magnifying, magnified *verb* When a microscope or lens magnifies something, it makes it appear bigger than it actually is > **magnification** *noun*

magnifying glass *noun* a lens which makes things appear bigger than they really are

magnitude *noun* The magnitude of something is its great size or importance

magnolia *noun* a tree which has large white or pink flowers in spring

magpie *noun* a large black and white bird with a long tail

mahogany *noun* Mahogany is a hard, reddish brown wood used for making furniture

maid noun a female servant

maiden noun **1** (literary) a young woman ▷ adjective **2** first: a maiden voyage

maiden name noun the surname a woman had before she married

mail noun **1** Your mail is the letters and parcels delivered to you by the post office ▷ verb **2** If you mail a letter, you send it by post

mail order noun Mail order is a system of buying goods by post

maim verb To maim someone is to injure them very badly for life

main adjective **1** most important: the main event ▷ noun **2** The mains are large pipes or wires that carry gas, water, or electricity

mainframe noun a large computer which can be used by many people at the same time

mainland noun The mainland is the main part of a country in contrast to islands around its coast

mainly adverb true in most cases

mainstay noun The mainstay of something is the most important part of it

mainstream noun The mainstream is the most ordinary and conventional group of people or ideas in a society

maintain verb **1** If you maintain something, you keep it going or keep it at a particular rate or level: I wanted to maintain our friendship **2** If you maintain someone, you provide them regularly with money for what they need **3** To maintain a machine or a building is to keep it in good condition **4** If you maintain that something is true, you believe it is true and say so

maintenance noun **1** Maintenance is the process of keeping something in good condition **2** Maintenance is

also money that a person sends regularly to someone to provide for the things they need

maize noun Maize is a tall plant which produces sweet corn

majesty 1 You say 'His Majesty' when you are talking about a king, and 'Her Majesty' when you are talking about a queen **2** Majesty is great dignity and impressiveness > **majestic** adjective > **majestically** adverb

major adjective **1** more important or significant than other things: There were over fifty major injuries **2** (MUSIC) A major key is one of the keys in which most European music is written ▷ noun **3** an army officer of the rank immediately above captain

majority majorities noun **1** The majority of people or things in a group is more than half of the group **2** In an election, the majority is the difference between the number of votes gained by the winner and the number gained by the runner-up

make makes, making, made verb **1** To make something is to produce or construct it, or to cause it to happen **2** To make something is to do it: He was about to make a speech **3** To make something is to prepare it: I'll make some salad dressing **4** If someone makes you do something, they force you to do it: Mum made me clean the bathroom ▷ noun **5** The make of a product is the name of the company that manufactured it: 'What make of car do you drive?' – Toyota.' > **make up** verb **1** If a number of things make up something, they form that thing **2** If you make up a story, you invent it **3** If you make yourself up, you put make-up on **4** If two people make it up, they become friends again after a quarrel

make-up noun **1** Make-up is coloured creams and powders which women put on their faces to make themselves look more attractive **2** Someone's make-up is their character or personality

making noun **1** The making of something is the act or process of creating or producing it ▷ phrase **2** When you describe someone as something **in the making**, you mean that they are gradually becoming that thing: *a captain in the making*

malaise [mal-laze] noun (formal) Malaise is a feeling of dissatisfaction or unhappiness

malaria [mal-lay-ree-a] noun Malaria is a tropical disease caught from mosquitoes which causes fever and shivering

Malaysian adjective **1** belonging or relating to Malaysia ▷ noun **2** someone who comes from Malaysia

male noun **1** a person or animal belonging to the gender that cannot give birth or lay eggs ▷ adjective **2** concerning or affecting men rather than women

malevolent [mal-lev-oh-lent] adjective (formal) wanting or intending to cause harm > **malevolence** noun

malfunction verb **1** If a machine malfunctions, it fails to work properly ▷ noun **2** the failure of a machine to work properly

malice noun Malice is a desire to cause harm to people

malicious adjective Malicious talk or behaviour is intended to harm someone

malign (formal) verb **1** To malign someone means to say unpleasant and untrue things about them ▷ adjective **2** intended to harm someone

malignant adjective **1** harmful and cruel **2** A malignant disease or tumour could cause death if it is allowed to continue

mallet noun a wooden hammer with a square head

malnutrition noun Malnutrition is not eating enough healthy food

malpractice noun If someone such as a doctor or lawyer breaks the rules of their profession, their behaviour is called malpractice

malt noun Malt is roasted grain, usually barley, that is used in making beer and whisky

malware noun Computer programs that are designed to damage or disrupt a system are known as malware

mammal noun SCIENCE Animals that give birth to live babies and feed their young with milk from the mother's body are called mammals. Human beings, dogs, and whales are all mammals

mammoth adjective **1** very large indeed: *a mammoth outdoor concert* ▷ noun **2** a huge animal that looked like a hairy elephant with long tusks. Mammoths became extinct a long time ago

man men; mans, manning, manned noun **1** an adult male human being ▷ plural noun **2** Human beings in general are sometimes referred to as men: *All men are equal* ▷ verb **3** To man something is to be in charge of it or operate it: *Two officers were manning the radar screens*

manage verb **1** If you manage to do something, you succeed in doing it:

We managed to find somewhere to sit
2 If you manage an organization or business, you are responsible for controlling it

manageable *adjective* able to be dealt with

management *noun* **1** The management of a business is the controlling and organizing of it **2** The people who control an organization are called the management

manager *noun* a person responsible for running a business or organization: *a bank manager*

manageress *noun* a woman responsible for running a business or organization

managing director *noun* a company director who is responsible for the way the company is managed

mandarin *noun* a type of small orange which is easy to peel

mandate *(formal) noun* A government's mandate is the authority it has to carry out particular policies as a result of winning an election

mandatory *adjective* If something is mandatory, there is a law or rule stating that it must be done: *a mandatory life sentence for murder*

mandolin *noun* a musical instrument like a small guitar with a deep, rounded body

mane *noun* the long hair growing from the neck of a lion or horse

manger [**main**-jir] *noun* a feeding box in a barn or stable

mangle *verb* **1** If something is mangled, it is crushed and twisted ▷ *noun* **2** an old-fashioned piece of equipment consisting of two large rollers which squeeze water out of wet clothes

mango mangoes *or* mangos *noun* a sweet yellowish fruit which grows in tropical countries

manhole *noun* a covered hole in the ground leading to a drain or sewer

manhood *noun* Manhood is the state of being a man rather than a boy

mania *noun* **1** a strong liking for something: *my wife's mania for plant collecting* **2** a mental condition characterized by periods of great excitement

maniac *noun* a mad person who is violent and dangerous

manic *adjective* energetic and excited: *a manic attack*

manicure *verb* **1** If you manicure your hands, you care for them by softening the skin and shaping and polishing the nails ▷ *noun* **2** A manicure is a special treatment for the hands and nails > **manicurist** *noun*

manifest *(formal) adjective* **1** obvious or easily seen: *his manifest enthusiasm* ▷ *verb* **2** To manifest something is to make people aware of it: *Fear can manifest itself in many ways*

manifestation *noun (formal)* A manifestation of something is a sign that it is happening or exists: *The illness may be a manifestation of stress*

manifesto manifestoes *or* manifestos *noun* a published statement of the aims and policies of a political party

manipulate *verb* **1** To manipulate people or events is to control or influence them to produce a particular result **2** If you manipulate a piece of equipment, you control it in a skilful way > **manipulation** *noun* > **manipulator** *noun*

m

> **manipulative** *adjective*

mankind *noun* 'Mankind' is used to refer to all human beings: *a threat to mankind*

manly manlier, manliest *adjective* having qualities that are typically masculine: *He laughed a deep, manly laugh*

manna *noun* If something appears like manna from heaven, it appears suddenly as if by a miracle and helps you in a difficult situation

manner *noun* 1 The manner in which you do something is the way you do it 2 Your manner is the way in which you behave and talk: *his kind manner* 3 (*in plural*) If you have good manners, you behave very politely

mannerism *noun* a gesture or a way of speaking which is characteristic of a person

manoeuvre [man-**noo**-ver] *verb* 1 If you manoeuvre something into a place, you skilfully move it there: *It took expertise to manoeuvre the boat so close to the shore* ▷ *noun* 2 a clever move you make in order to change a situation to your advantage

manor *noun* a large country house with land

manpower *noun* Workers can be referred to as manpower

mansion *noun* a very large house

manslaughter *noun* (*Law*) Manslaughter is the accidental killing of a person

mantelpiece *noun* a shelf over a fireplace

mantle *noun* (*literary*) To take on the mantle of something is to take on responsibility for it: *He has taken over the mantle of England's greatest living poet*

mantra *noun* a word or short piece of sacred text or prayer continually repeated to help concentration

manual *adjective* 1 Manual work involves physical strength rather than mental skill 2 operated by hand rather than by electricity or by motor: *a manual typewriter* ▷ *noun* 3 an instruction book which tells you how to use a machine > **manually** *adverb*

manufacture D G T *verb* 1 To manufacture goods is to make them in a factory ▷ *noun* 2 The manufacture of goods is the making of them in a factory: *the manufacture of nuclear weapons* > **manufacturer** *noun*

manure *noun* Manure is animal faeces used to fertilize the soil

manuscript *noun* a handwritten or typed document, especially a version of a book before it is printed

Manx *adjective* belonging or relating to the Isle of Man

many *adjective* 1 If there are many people or things, there is a large number of them 2 You also use 'many' to ask how great a quantity is or to give information about it: *How many tickets do you require?* ▷ *pronoun* 3 a large number of people or things: *Many are too weak to walk*

Maori Maoris *noun* 1 someone descended from the people who lived in New Zealand before Europeans arrived 2 Maori is a language spoken by Maoris

map maps, mapping, mapped *noun* 1 a detailed drawing of an area as it would appear if you saw it from above 2 MATHS the relationship between elements of a set and elements in the same or another set ▷ *verb* 3 If you map out a plan, you work out in detail what you will do

maple *noun* a tree that has large

leaves with five points

mar mars, marring, marred *verb* To mar something is to spoil it: *The game was marred by violence*

marathon *noun* **1** a race in which people run 26 miles along roads ▷ *adjective* **2** A marathon task is a large one that takes a long time

marble *noun* **1** Marble is a very hard, cold stone which is often polished to show the coloured patterns in it **2** Marbles is a children's game played with small coloured glass balls. These balls are also called marbles

march *noun* **1** March is the third month of the year. It has 31 days **2** an organized protest in which a large group of people walk somewhere together ▷ *verb* **3** When soldiers march, they walk with quick regular steps in time with each other **4** To march somewhere is to walk quickly in a determined way: *He marched out of the room*

mare *noun* an adult female horse

margarine [mar-jar-reen] *noun* Margarine is a substance that is similar to butter but is made from vegetable oil and animal fats

margin *noun* **1** If you win a contest by a large or small margin, you win it by a large or small amount **2** an extra amount that allows you more freedom in doing something: *a small margin of error* **3** the blank space at each side on a written or printed page

marginal *adjective* **1** small and not very important: *a marginal increase* **2** A marginal seat or constituency is a political constituency where the previous election was won by a very small majority > **marginally** *adverb*

marijuana [mar-rih-**wan**-a] *noun* Marijuana is an illegal drug which is smoked in cigarettes

marina *noun* a harbour for pleasure boats and yachts

marinate *verb* To marinate food is to soak it in a mixture of oil, vinegar, spices, and herbs to flavour it before cooking

marine *noun* **1** a soldier who serves with the navy ▷ *adjective* **2** relating to or involving the sea: *marine life*

marital *adjective* relating to or involving marriage: *marital problems*

maritime *adjective* relating to the sea and ships: *maritime trade*

mark *noun* **1** a small stain or damaged area on a surface: *I can't get this mark off the curtain* **2** a written or printed symbol: *He made a few marks with his pen* **3** a letter or number showing how well you have done in homework or in an exam ▷ *verb* **4** If something marks a surface, it damages it in some way **5** If you mark something, you write a symbol on it or identify it in some other way **6** When a teacher marks your work, he or she decides how good it is and gives it a mark **7** To mark something is to be a sign of it: *The accident marked a tragic end to the day* **8** In soccer or hockey, if you mark your opposing player, you stay close to them, trying to prevent them from getting the ball

marked *adjective* very obvious: *a marked improvement* > **markedly** *adverb*

market *noun* **1** a place where goods or animals are bought and sold **2** The market for a product is the number of people who want to buy it: *the market for cars* ▷ *verb* **3** To market a product is to organize its sale, by deciding its price, where it should be sold, and how it should be advertised

m

marketing noun D G T Marketing is the part of a business concerned with the way a product is sold

market research noun D G T Market research is research into what people want and buy

marksman marksmen noun someone who can shoot very accurately

marlin noun a large fish found in tropical seas which has a very long upper jaw

marmalade noun Marmalade is a jam made from citrus fruit, usually eaten at breakfast

maroon noun, adjective dark reddish-purple

marooned adjective If you are marooned in a place, you are stranded there and cannot leave it

marquee [mar-**kee**] noun a very large tent used at a fair or other outdoor entertainment

marriage noun 1 the legal relationship between a couple 2 RE Marriage is the act of marrying someone

marrow noun a long, thick, green-skinned fruit with cream-coloured flesh eaten as a vegetable

marry marries, marrying, married verb 1 When two people marry, they become each other's partner during a special ceremony 2 When a clergyman or registrar marries a couple, he or she is in charge of their marriage ceremony > **married** adjective

Mars noun Mars is the planet in the solar system which is fourth from the sun

marsh noun an area of land which is permanently wet

marshal marshals, marshalling, marshalled verb 1 If you marshal

things or people, you gather them together and organize them: The students were marshalled into the assembly room ▷ noun 2 an official who helps to organize a public event

marshmallow noun a soft, spongy, pink or white sweet made using gelatine

marsupial [mar-**syoo**-pee-al] noun an animal that carries its young in a pouch. Koalas and kangaroos are marsupials

martial arts plural noun The martial arts are the techniques of self-defence that come from the Far East, for example karate or judo

Martian [mar-**shan**] noun an imaginary creature from the planet Mars

martyr noun 1 someone who suffers or is killed rather than change their beliefs ▷ verb 2 If someone is martyred, they are killed because of their beliefs > **martyrdom** noun

marvel marvels, marvelling, marvelled verb 1 If you marvel at something, it fills you with surprise or admiration: Modern designers can only marvel at his genius ▷ noun 2 something that makes you feel great surprise or admiration: a marvel of high technology

marvellous adjective wonderful or excellent > **marvellously** adverb

Marxism noun Marxism is a political philosophy based on the writings of Karl Marx. It states that society will develop towards communism through the struggle between different social classes > **Marxist** adjective, noun

marzipan noun Marzipan is a paste made of almonds, sugar, and egg. It is put on top of cakes or used to make small sweets

mascara noun Mascara is a

substance that can be used to colour eyelashes and make them look longer

mascot noun a person, animal, or toy which is thought to bring good luck: *Celtic's mascot, Hoopy the Huddle Hound*

masculine adjective **1** typical of men, rather than women: *the masculine world of motorsport* **2** belonging to a particular class of nouns in some languages, such as French, German, and Latin > **masculinity** noun

mash verb If you mash vegetables, you crush them after they have been cooked

mask noun **1** something you wear over your face for protection or disguise: *a surgical mask* ▷ verb **2** If you mask something, you cover it so that it is protected or cannot be seen

mason noun a person who is skilled at making things with stone

masonry noun Masonry is pieces of stone which form part of a wall or building

masquerade [mass-ker-**raid**] verb If you masquerade as something, you pretend to be it: *He masqueraded as a doctor*

mass noun **1** a large amount of something **2** The masses are the ordinary people in society considered as a group: *opera for the masses* **3** In physics, the mass of an object is the amount of physical matter that it has **4** In the Roman Catholic Church, Mass is a religious service in which people share bread and wine in remembrance of the death and resurrection of Jesus Christ ▷ adjective **5** involving a large number of people: *mass unemployment* ▷ verb **6** When people

mass, they gather together in a large group

massacre [**mass**-ik-ker] noun **1** the killing of a very large number of people in a violent and cruel way ▷ verb **2** To massacre people is to kill large numbers of them in a violent and cruel way

massage verb **1** To massage someone is to rub their body in order to help them relax or to relieve pain ▷ noun **2** A massage is treatment which involves rubbing the body

massive adjective extremely large: *a massive iceberg* > **massively** adverb

mast noun the tall upright pole that supports the sails of a boat

master noun **1** a man who has authority over others, such as the employer of servants, or the owner of slaves or animals **2** If you are master of a situation, you have control over it: *He was master of his own destiny* **3** a male teacher at some schools ▷ verb **4** If you master a difficult situation, you succeed in controlling it **5** If you master something, you learn how to do it properly: *She found it easy to master the game*

masterful adjective showing control and authority

masterly adjective extremely clever or well done: *a masterly exhibition of batting*

mastermind verb **1** If you mastermind a complicated activity, you plan and organize it ▷ noun **2** The mastermind behind something is the person responsible for planning it

masterpiece noun an extremely good painting or other work of art

mat noun **1 a** a small round or square piece of cloth, card, or plastic that is placed on a table to protect it from plates or glasses **2** a small piece of carpet or other thick material that is placed on the floor

matador noun a man who fights and tries to kill bulls as part of a public entertainment, especially in Spain

match noun **1** an organized game of football, cricket, or some other sport **2** a small, thin stick of wood that produces a flame when you strike it against a rough surface ▷ verb **3** If one thing matches another, the two things look the same or have similar qualities

mate noun **1** (informal) Your mates are your friends **2** The first mate on a ship is the officer who is next in importance to the captain **3** An animal's mate is its partner for reproduction ▷ verb **4** When a male and female animal mate, they come together in order to breed

material noun **1** [D&T] Material is cloth **2** [D&T] a substance from which something is made: the materials to make red dye **3** [D&T] The equipment for a particular activity can be referred to as materials: building materials **4** Material for a book, play, or film is the information or ideas on which it is based ▷ adjective **5** involving possessions and money: concerned with material comforts ▷ **materially** adverb

materialism noun Materialism is thinking that money and possessions are the most important things in life ▷ **materialistic** adjective

materialize or **materialise** verb If something materializes, it actually happens or appears: Fortunately, the attack did not materialize

maternal adjective relating to or involving a mother: her maternal instincts

maternity adjective relating to or involving pregnant women and birth: a maternity hospital

mathematics noun Mathematics is the study of numbers, quantities, and shapes ▷ **mathematical** adjective ▷ **mathematically** adverb ▷ **mathematician** noun

maths noun Maths is mathematics

Matilda noun (old-fashioned, informal) In Australia, Matilda is the pack of belongings carried by a swagman in the bush. The word is now used only in the phrase 'waltzing Matilda', meaning travelling in the bush with few possessions

matrimony noun (formal) Matrimony is marriage ▷ **matrimonial** adjective

matrix matrices [**may-trix**] noun **1** (formal) the framework in which something grows and develops **2** In maths, a matrix is a set of numbers or elements set out in rows and columns

matron noun In a hospital, a senior nurse in charge of all the nursing staff used to be known as matron

matt adjective A matt surface is dull rather than shiny: matt black plastic

matted adjective Hair that is matted is tangled with the strands sticking together

matter noun **1** something that you have to deal with **2** Matter is any substance: The atom is the smallest divisible particle of matter **3** Books and magazines are reading matter ▷ verb **4** If something matters to you, It is important ▷ phrase **5** If you ask **What's the matter?**, you are asking what is wrong

matter-of-fact adjective showing no emotion

matting noun Matting is thick woven material such as rope or straw, used as a floor covering

mattress noun a large thick pad filled with springs or feathers that is put on a bed to make it comfortable

mature verb 1 When a child or young animal matures, it becomes an adult 2 When something matures, it reaches complete development ▷ adjective 3 Mature means fully developed and emotionally balanced > **maturely** adverb > **maturity** noun

maudlin adjective Someone who is maudlin is sad and sentimental, especially when they are drunk

maul verb If someone is mauled by an animal, they are savagely attacked and badly injured by it

mausoleum [maw-sal-**lee**-um] noun a building which contains the grave of a famous person

mauve [rhymes with **grove**] noun, adjective pale purple

maxim noun a short saying which gives a rule for good or sensible behaviour: Instant action: that's my maxim

maximize or **maximise** verb To maximize something is to make it as great or effective as possible: Their objective is to maximize profits

maximum adjective 1 The maximum amount is the most that is possible: the maximum recommended intake ▷ noun 2 The maximum is the most that is possible: a maximum of 50 men

may verb 1 If something may happen, it is possible that it will happen: It may rain today 2 If someone may do something, they are allowed to do it: Please may I be excused? 3 You can use 'may' when saying that although something is true, something else is also true:

This may be true, but it is only part of the story 4 (formal) You also use 'may' to express a wish that something will happen: May you live to be a hundred ▷ noun 5 May is the fifth month of the year. It has 31 days

maybe adverb You use 'maybe' when you are stating a possibility that you are not certain about: Maybe I should lie about my age

mayhem noun You can refer to a confused and chaotic situation as mayhem: There was complete mayhem in the classroom

mayonnaise [may-on-**nayz**] noun Mayonnaise is a thick salad dressing made with egg yolks and oil

mayor noun a person who has been elected to lead and represent the people of a town

maze noun a system of complicated passages which it is difficult to find your way through: a maze of dark tunnels

MBE noun a British honour granted by the King or Queen. MBE is an abbreviation for 'Member of the Order of the British Empire': Rory McIlroy, MBE

MD an abbreviation for 'Doctor of Medicine' or 'Managing Director'

me pronoun A speaker or writer uses 'me' to refer to himself or herself

meadow noun a field of grass

meagre [**mee**-ger] adjective very small and poor: his meagre pension

meal noun an occasion when people eat, or the food they eat at that time

mean means, meaning, meant verb 1 If you ask what something means, you want to know what it refers to or what its message is 2 If you mean what you say, you are serious: The boss means what he says 3 If something means a lot to you, it is important to you 4 If one thing

means another, it shows that the second thing is true or will happen: *Major roadworks will mean long delays* **5** If you mean to do something, you intend to do it: *I meant to phone you, but didn't have time* **6** If something is meant to be true, it is supposed to be true: *I found a radish that wasn't meant to be there* ▷ adjective **7** Someone who is mean is unwilling to spend much money **8** Someone who is mean is unkind or cruel: *He apologized for being so mean to her* ▷ noun **9** (in plural) A means of doing something is a method or object which makes it possible: *The tests were marked by means of a computer* **10** (in plural) Someone's means are their money and income: *He's obviously a man of means* **11** MATHS The mean is the average of a set of numbers > **meanness** noun
> **meanly** adverb

meander [mee-**an**-der] verb If a road or river meanders, it has a lot of bends in it

meaning noun **1** The meaning of a word is what it refers to or expresses **2** The meaning of what someone says, or of a book or a film, is the thoughts or ideas that it is intended to express **3** If something has meaning, it seems to be worthwhile and to have real purpose
> **meaningful** adjective
> **meaningfully** adverb
> **meaningless** adjective

means test noun a check of a person's money and income to see whether they need money or benefits from the government or other organization

meantime phrase **In the meantime** means in the period of time between two events: *I'll call the nurse; in the meantime, you must rest*

meanwhile adverb Meanwhile means while something else is happening

measles noun Measles is an infectious illness in which you have red spots on your skin

measly adjective (informal) very small or inadequate: *a measly ten cents*

measure verb **1** MATHS When you measure something, you find out how big it is **2** MATHS If something measures a particular distance, its length or depth is that distance: *slivers of glass measuring a few millimetres across* ▷ noun **3** A measure of something is a certain amount of it: *There was some measure of agreement* **4** MATHS a unit in which size, speed, or depth is expressed **5** Measures are actions carried out to achieve a particular result: *Tough measures are needed to maintain order*

measured adjective careful and deliberate: *walking at the same measured pace*

measurement noun **1** the result that you obtain when you measure something **2** Measurement is the activity of measuring something **3** Your measurements are the sizes of your chest, waist, and hips that you use to buy the correct size of clothes

meat noun Meat is the flesh of animals that is cooked and eaten
> **meaty** adjective

Mecca noun **1** Mecca is the holiest city of Islam, to which many Muslims make pilgrimages **2** If a place is a mecca for people of a particular kind, many of them go there because it is of special interest to them: *The island is a mecca for bird lovers*

mechanic noun **1** a person who

repairs and maintains engines and machines **2** (*in plural*) The mechanics of something are the way in which it works or is done: *the mechanics of something* (*in plural*) Mechanics is also the scientific study of movement and the forces that affect objects

mechanical *adjective* **1** A mechanical device has moving parts and is used to do a physical task **2** A mechanical action is done automatically without thinking about it: *He gave a mechanical smile* > **mechanically** *adverb*

mechanism *noun* **1** DGT a part of a machine that does a particular task: *a locking mechanism* **2** SCIENCE part of your behaviour that is automatic: *the body's defence mechanisms*

medal *noun* a small disc of metal given as an award for bravery or as a prize for sport

medallion *noun* a round piece of metal worn as an ornament on a chain round the neck

medallist *noun* a person who has won a medal in sport: *a gold medallist at the Olympics*

meddle *verb* To meddle is to interfere and try to change things without being asked

media *plural noun* You can refer to the television, radio, and newspapers as the media

median [mee-dee-an] *adjective* **1** The median value of a set is the middle value when the set is arranged in order > *noun* **2** In geometry, a straight line drawn from one of the angles of a triangle to the middle point of the opposite side

mediate *verb* If you mediate between two groups, you try to

settle a dispute between them > **mediation** *noun* > **mediator** *noun*

medical *adjective* **1** relating to the prevention and treatment of illness and injuries > *noun* **2** a thorough examination of your body by a doctor > **medically** *adverb*

medication *noun* Medication is a substance that is used to treat illness

medicinal *adjective* relating to the treatment of illness: *a valuable medicinal herb*

medicine *noun* **1** Medicine is the treatment of illness and injuries by doctors and nurses **2** a substance that you drink or swallow to help cure an illness

medieval *or* **mediaeval** [med-dee-**ee**-vul] *adjective* relating to the period between about 1100 AD and 1500 AD, especially in Europe

mediocre [meed-dee-**oh**-ker] *adjective* of rather poor quality: *a mediocre string of performances* > **mediocrity** *noun*

meditate *verb* **1** If you meditate on something, you think about it very deeply **2** If you meditate, you remain in a calm, silent state for a period of time, often as part of a religious training > **meditation** *noun*

Mediterranean *noun* **1** The Mediterranean is the large sea between southern Europe and northern Africa > *adjective* **2** relating to or typical of the Mediterranean or the European countries adjoining it

medium mediums *or* media *adjective* **1** If something is of medium size or degree, it is neither large nor small: *a medium-sized hotel* > *noun* **2** a means that you use to communicate something: *the*

m

medium of television **3** a person who claims to be able to speak to the dead and to receive messages from them

medley noun **1** a mixture of different things creating an interesting effect **2** a number of different songs or tunes sung or played one after the other

meek adjective A meek person is timid and does what other people say > **meekly** adverb > **meekness** noun

meet meets, meeting, met verb **1** If you meet someone, you happen to be in the same place as them and start talking to them **2** If you meet a visitor you go to be with them when they arrive **3** When a group of people meet, they gather together for a purpose **4** If something meets a need, it can fulfil it: *services intended to meet the needs of the elderly* **5** If something meets with a particular reaction, it gets that reaction from people: *I was met with silence*

meeting noun **1** an event in which people discuss proposals and make decisions together **2** what happens when you meet someone

megabyte noun COMPUTING a unit of storage in a computer, equal to 1,048,576 bytes

melancholy adjective, noun If you feel melancholy, you feel sad

mellow adjective **1** Mellow light is soft and golden **2** A mellow sound is smooth and pleasant to listen to: *his mellow clarinet* > verb **3** If someone mellows, they become more pleasant or relaxed: *He certainly hasn't mellowed with age*

melodic adjective relating to melody

melodious adjective pleasant to listen to: *soft melodious music*

melodrama noun a story or play in which people's emotions are exaggerated

melodramatic adjective behaving in an exaggerated, emotional way

melody melodies noun MUSIC a tune

melon noun a large, juicy fruit with a green or yellow skin and many seeds inside

melt verb **1** When something melts or when you melt it, it changes from a solid to a liquid because it has been heated **2** If something melts, it disappears: *The crowd melted away; Her inhibitions melted*

member noun **1** A member of a group or things belonging to the group: *members of the family* **2** A member of an organization is a person who has joined the organization > adjective **3** A country belonging to an international organization is called a member country or a member state

Member of Parliament noun a person who has been elected to represent people in a country's parliament

membership noun **1** Membership of an organization is the state of being a member of it **2** The people who belong to an organization are its membership

membrane noun SCIENCE a very thin piece of skin or tissue which connects or covers plant or animal organs or cells: *the nasal membrane*

memento mementos noun an object which you keep because it reminds you of a person or a special occasion: *a lasting memento of their romance*

memo memos noun a note from one person to another within the same organization. Memo is short for 'memorandum'

memoirs [mem-wahrz] plural noun (ENGLISH) If someone writes their memoirs, they write a book about their life and experiences

memorable adjective If something is memorable, it is likely to be remembered because it is special or unusual: *a memorable victory* > **memorably** adverb

memorandum memorandums or memoranda noun a memo

memorial noun 1 a structure built to remind people of a famous person or event: *a war memorial* ▷ adjective 2 A memorial event or prize is in honour of someone who has died, so that they will be remembered

memory memories noun 1 Your memory is your ability to remember things 2 something you remember about the past: *memories of their school days* 3 (COMPUTING) the part in which information is stored in a computer

memory card noun (COMPUTING) a small device for storing information in a mobile phone or digital camera

men the plural of **man**

menace noun 1 someone or something that is likely to cause serious harm: *the menace of drugs in sport* 2 Menace is the quality of being threatening: *an atmosphere of menace* ▷ verb 3 If someone or something menaces you, they threaten to harm you > **menacingly** adverb

menagerie [men-**naj**-er-ree] noun a collection of different wild animals

mend verb If you mend something that is broken, you repair it

menial adjective Menial work is boring and tiring and the people who do it have low status

meningitis noun Meningitis is a serious infectious illness which affects your brain and spinal cord

menopause noun The menopause is the time during which a woman gradually stops menstruating. This usually happens when she is about fifty

-ment suffix '-ment' forms nouns which refer to a state or a feeling: *contentment; resentment*

mental adjective 1 relating to the process of thinking or intelligence: *mental arithmetic* 2 relating to the health of the mind: *mental health* > **mentally** adverb

mentality mentalities noun an attitude or way of thinking: *the traditional military mentality*

mention verb 1 If you mention something, you talk about it briefly ▷ noun 2 a brief comment about someone or something: *He made no mention of his criminal past*

mentor noun Someone's mentor is a person who teaches them and gives them advice

menu noun 1 a list of the foods you can eat in a restaurant 2 (COMPUTING) a list of different options shown on a computer screen which the user must choose from

MEP noun an abbreviation for 'Member of the European Parliament': a person who has been elected to represent people in the European Parliament

mercenary mercenaries noun 1 a soldier who is paid to fight for a foreign country ▷ adjective 2 Someone who is mercenary is mainly interested in getting money

merchandise noun (formal) Merchandise is goods that are sold: *He had left me with more merchandise than I could sell*

m

merchant *noun* a trader who imports and exports goods: *a coal merchant*

merciful *adjective* **1** showing kindness **2** showing forgiveness **3** considered to be fortunate as a relief from suffering: *Death came as a merciful release* > **mercifully** *adverb*

merciless *adjective* showing no kindness or forgiveness > **mercilessly** *adverb*

mercury *noun* **1** Mercury is a silver-coloured metallic element that is liquid at room temperature. It is used in thermometers. Its atomic number is 80 and its symbol is Hg **2** Mercury is also the planet in the solar system which is nearest to the sun

mercy *mercies noun* If you show mercy, you show forgiveness and do not punish someone as severely as you could

mere *merest adjective* used to emphasize how unimportant or small something is: *It's a mere seven-minute journey by boat* > **merely** *adverb*

merge *verb* When two things merge, they combine together to make one thing: *The firms merged in 1983* > **merger** *noun*

meringue [mer-**rang**] *noun* a type of crisp, sweet cake made with egg whites and sugar

merino *merinos* [mer-**ree**-no] *noun* a breed of sheep, common in Australia and New Zealand, with long, fine wool

merit *noun* **1** If something has merit, it is good or worthwhile **2** The merits of something are its advantages or good qualities ▷ *verb* **3** If something merits a particular treatment, it deserves that treatment: *He merits a place in the team*

mermaid *noun* In stories, a mermaid is a woman with a fish's tail instead of legs, who lives in the sea

merry *merrier, merriest adjective* happy and cheerful: *He was, for all his shyness, a merry man* > **merrily** *adverb*

merry-go-round *noun* a large rotating platform with models of animals or vehicles on it, on which children ride at a fair

mesh *noun* Mesh is threads of wire or plastic twisted together like a net: *a fence made of wire mesh*

mess *noun* **1** something untidy **2** a situation which is full of problems and trouble **3** a room or building in which members of the armed forces eat: *the officers' mess* > **messy** *adjective* > **mess about** *or* > **mess around** *verb* If you mess about or mess around, you do things without any particular purpose > **mess up** *verb* If you mess something up, you spoil it or do it wrong

message *noun* **1** a piece of information or a request that you send someone or leave for them **2** an idea that someone tries to communicate to people, for example in a play or a speech: *the story's anti-drugs message* ▷ *verb* **3** If you message someone, you send them a text message

messaging *noun* Messaging or text messaging is the sending and receiving of short pieces of information between mobile phones, often using both letters and numbers to produce shortened forms of words

messenger *noun* someone who takes a message to someone for someone else

Messiah [miss-**eye**-ah] *proper noun* [RE] **1** For Jews, the Messiah is the king of the Jews, who will be sent by God **2** For Christians, the Messiah is Jesus Christ

Messrs [mes-serz] Messrs is the plural of **Mr**. It is often used in the names of businesses: *Messrs Brown and Humberley, Solicitors*

met the past tense and past participle of **meet**

metabolism noun Your metabolism is the chemical processes in your body that use food for growth and energy > **metabolic** adjective

metal noun SCIENCE Metal is a chemical element such as iron, steel, copper, or lead. Metals are good conductors of heat and electricity and form positive ions > **metallic** adjective

metamorphosis metamorphoses [met-am-**mor**-fiss-iss] noun (formal) When a metamorphosis occurs, a person or thing changes into something completely different: *the metamorphosis of a larva into an insect*

metaphor noun ENGLISH an imaginative way of describing something as another thing, and so suggesting that it has the typical qualities of that other thing. For example, if you wanted to say that someone is shy, you might say they are a mouse > **metaphorical** adjective > **metaphorically** adverb

meteor noun a piece of rock or metal that burns very brightly when it enters the earth's atmosphere from space

meteoric adjective A meteoric rise to power or success happens very quickly

meteorite noun a piece of rock from space that has landed on earth

meteorological adjective GEOGRAPHY relating to or involving the weather or weather forecasting

> **meteorology** noun

meter noun a device that measures and records something: *a gas meter*

methane [**mee**-thane] noun Methane is a colourless gas with no smell that is found in coal gas and produced by decaying vegetable matter. It burns easily and can be used as a fuel

method noun **1** a particular way of doing something: *the traditional method of making wine* **2** SCIENCE a way that an experiment or test is carried out: *Describe the method as well as the result obtained*

methodical adjective Someone who is methodical does things carefully and in an organized way > **methodically** adverb

Methodist noun someone who belongs to the Methodist Church, a Protestant church whose members worship God in a way begun by John Wesley and his followers

meticulous adjective A meticulous person does things very carefully and with great attention to detail > **meticulously** adverb

metre noun **1** MATHS a unit of length equal to 100 centimetres **2** ENGLISH In poetry, metre is the regular and rhythmic arrangement of words and syllables > **metrical** adjective

metric adjective relating to the system of measurement that uses metres, grams, and litres

metropolis noun a very large city

metropolitan adjective relating or belonging to a large, busy city: *metropolitan districts*

mettle noun If you are on your mettle, you are ready to do something as well as you can because you know you are being tested or challenged

m

Mexican adjective **1** belonging or relating to Mexico ▷ noun **2** someone who comes from Mexico

mg an abbreviation for 'milligram' or 'milligrams'

mice the plural of **mouse**

microchip noun a small piece of silicon on which electronic circuits for a computer are printed

microphone noun a device that is used to make sounds louder or to record them

microprocessor noun a microchip which can be programmed to do a large number of tasks or calculations

microscope noun a piece of equipment which magnifies very small objects so that you can study them

microscopic adjective very small indeed: microscopic parasites

microwave noun A microwave or microwave oven is a type of oven which cooks food very quickly by radiation

mid- prefix 'Mid-' is used to form words that refer to the middle part of a place or period of time: mid-Atlantic; the mid-70s

midday noun Midday is twelve o'clock in the middle of the day

middle noun **1** The middle of something is the part furthest from the edges, ends, or outside surface ▷ adjective **2** The middle one in a series or a row is the one that has an equal number of people or things each side of it: the middle house

middle age noun Middle age is the period of your life when you are between about 40 and 60 years old > **middle-aged** adjective

Middle Ages plural noun In European history, the Middle Ages were the period between about 1100 AD and 1500 AD

middle class noun The middle classes are the people in a society who are not working-class or upper-class, for example managers and lawyers

Middle East noun The Middle East consists of Iran and the countries in Asia to the west and south-west of Iran

middle-of-the-road adjective Middle-of-the-road opinions are moderate

middle school noun In England and Wales, a middle school is for children aged between about 8 and 12

middling adjective of average quality or ability

midge noun a small flying insect which can bite people

midget noun a very short person

midnight noun Midnight is twelve o'clock at night

midriff noun the middle of your body between your waist and your chest

midst noun If you are in the midst of a crowd or an event, you are in the middle of it

midsummer adjective relating to the period in the middle of summer: a lovely midsummer morning in July

midway adverb in the middle of a distance or period of time: They scored midway through the second half

midwife midwives noun a nurse who is trained to help women at the birth of a baby > **midwifery** noun

might verb **1** If you say something might happen, you mean that it is possible that it will happen: I might stay a while **2** If you say that someone might do something, you are suggesting that they do it: You might like to go and see it **3** Might is also the past tense of **may** ▷ noun

4 (literary) Might is strength or power: the full might of the Navy

mightily adverb (literary) to a great degree or extent: I was mightily relieved by the decision

mighty mightier, mightiest adjective (literary) **1** very powerful or strong: a mighty army on the march **2** very large and impressive: the world's mightiest mountain range

migraine [mee-grane or my-grane] noun a severe headache that makes you feel very ill

migrate verb **1** GEOGRAPHY If people migrate, they move from one place to another, especially to find work **2** SCIENCE When birds or animals migrate, they move at a particular season to a different place, usually to breed or to find new feeding grounds: the birds migrate each year to Mexico > **migration** noun > **migratory** adjective > **migrant** noun, adjective

mike noun (informal) a microphone

mild adjective **1** Something that is mild is not strong and does not have any powerful or damaging effects: a mild shampoo **2** Someone who is mild is gentle and kind **3** Mild weather is warmer than usual: The region has mild winters and hot summers **4** Mild emotions or attitudes are not very great or extreme: mild surprise > **mildly** adverb

mildew noun Mildew is a soft white fungus that grows on things when they are warm and damp

mile noun a unit of distance equal to 1760 yards or about 1.6 kilometres

mileage noun **1** Your mileage is the distance that you have travelled, in miles **2** The amount of [use] that you get out of [something] is how useful it is to you

militant adjective **1** A militant person is very active in trying to bring about extreme political or social change: a militant socialist ▷ noun **2** a person who tries to bring about extreme political or social change > **militancy** noun

military adjective **1** related to or involving the armed forces of a country: military bases ▷ noun **2** The military are the armed forces of a country > **militarily** adverb

militia [mil-lish-a] noun an organization that operates like an army but whose members are not professional soldiers

milk noun **1** Milk is the white liquid produced by female cows, goats, and some other animals to feed their young. People drink milk and use it to make butter, cheese, and yogurt **2** Milk is also the white liquid that a baby drinks from its mother's breasts ▷ verb **3** When someone milks a cow or a goat, they get milk from it by pulling its udders **4** If you milk a situation, you get as much personal gain from it as possible: They milked money from a hospital charity

milky milkier, milkiest adjective **1** pale creamy white: milky white skin **2** containing a lot of milk: a large mug of milky coffee

Milky Way noun The Milky Way is a strip of stars clustered closely together, appearing as a pale band in the sky

mill noun **1** a building where grain is crushed to make flour **2** a factory for making materials such as steel, wool, or cotton **3** a small device for grinding coffee or spices into powder: a pepper mill

millennium millennia or millenniums noun (formal) a period of 1000 years

miller *noun* the person who operates a flour mill

milligram *noun* a unit of weight equal to one thousandth of a gram

millimetre *noun* a unit of length equal to one tenth of a centimetre or one thousandth of a metre

million the number 1,000,000 > **millionth** *adjective*

millionaire *noun* a very rich person who has money or property worth millions of pounds or dollars

millstone *phrase* If something is a **millstone round your neck**, it is an unpleasant problem or responsibility you cannot escape from

mime *noun* **1** Mime is the use of movements and gestures to express something or to tell a story without using speech ▷ *verb* **2** If you mime something, you describe or express it using mime

mimic mimics, mimicking, mimicked *verb* **1** If you mimic someone's actions or voice, you imitate them in an amusing way ▷ *noun* **2** a person who can imitate other people > **mimicry** *noun*

mince *noun* **1** Mince is meat which has been chopped into very small pieces in a special machine ▷ *verb* **2** If you mince meat, you chop it into very small pieces **3** To mince about is to walk with small quick steps in an affected, effeminate way

mind *noun* **1** Your mind is your ability to think, together with all the thoughts you have and your memory ▷ *phrase* **2** If you **change your mind**, you change a decision that you have made or an opinion that you have ▷ *verb* **3** If you do not mind something, you are not annoyed by it or bothered about it **4** If you say that you wouldn't mind

something, you mean that you would quite like it: *I wouldn't mind a drink* **5** If you mind a child or mind something for someone, you look after it for a while: *My mother is minding the office*

mindful *adjective* (formal) If you are mindful of something, you think about it carefully before taking action: *mindful of their needs*

mindless *adjective* **1** Mindless actions are regarded as stupid and destructive: *mindless violence* **2** A mindless job or activity is simple and repetitive

mine *pronoun* **1** 'Mine' refers to something belonging or relating to the person who is speaking or writing: *a friend of mine* ▷ *noun* **2** a series of holes or tunnels in the ground from which diamonds, coal, or other minerals are dug out: *a diamond mine* **3** a bomb hidden in the ground or underwater, which explodes when people or things touch it ▷ *verb* **4** To mine diamonds, coal, or other minerals is to obtain these substances from underneath the ground > **miner** *noun* > **mining** *noun*

minefield *noun* an area of land or water where mines have been hidden

mineral *noun* D&T a substance such as tin, salt, or coal that is formed naturally in rocks and in the earth: *rich mineral deposits*

mineral water *noun* Mineral water is water which comes from a natural spring

mingle *verb* **1** If things mingle, they become mixed together: *His cries mingled with theirs* **2** SCIENCE to mix so that the parts become

miniature [**min**-nit-cher]
1 copying something on a

smaller scale ▷ noun **2** a very small detailed painting, often of a person

minibus noun a van with seats in the back which is used as a small bus

minimal adjective very small in quality, quantity, or degree: *He has minimal experience* > **minimally** adverb

minimize or **minimise** verb If you minimize something, you reduce it to the smallest amount possible: *His route was changed to minimize the jet lag*

minimum adjective **1** The minimum amount is the smallest amount that is possible: *a minimum wage* ▷ noun **2** The minimum is the smallest amount that is possible: *a minimum of three weeks*

minister noun **1** A minister is a person who is in charge of a particular government department: *Portugal's deputy foreign minister* **2** A minister in a Protestant church is a member of the clergy

ministerial adjective relating to a government minister or ministry: *ministerial duties*

ministry ministries noun **1** a government ministry that deals with a particular area of work: *the Ministry of Defence* **2** Members of the clergy can be referred to as the ministry: *Her son is in the ministry*

mink noun Mink is an expensive fur used to make coats or hats

minnow noun a very small freshwater fish

minor adjective **1** not as important or serious as other things: *a minor injury* **2** [MUSIC] A minor key is one of the keys in which most European music is written ▷ noun **3** (formal) a young person under the age of 18: *laws concerning the employment of minors*

minority minorities noun **1** The minority of people or things in a group is a number of them forming less than half of the whole: *Only a minority of people want this* **2** A minority is a group of people of a particular race or religion living in a place where most people are of a different race or religion: *ethnic minorities*

mint noun **1** Mint is a herb used for flavouring in cooking **2** a peppermint-flavoured sweet **3** The mint is the place where the official coins of a country are made ▷ verb **4** When coins or medals are minted, they are made ▷ adjective **5** If something is in mint condition, it is in very good condition, like new

minus [MATHS] You use 'minus' to show that one number is being subtracted from another: *Ten minus six equals four* ▷ adjective **2** 'Minus' is used when talking about temperatures below 0°C or 0°F

minuscule [min-nus-kyool] adjective very small indeed

minute [min-nit] noun **1** a unit of time equal to sixty seconds **2** The minutes of a meeting are the written records of what was said and decided ▷ verb **3** To minute a meeting is to write the official notes of it

minute [my-nyoot] adjective extremely small: *a minute amount of pesticide* > **minutely** adverb

minutiae [my-nyoo-shee-aye] plural noun (formal) Minutiae are small, unimportant details

miracle noun **1** [RE] a wonderful and surprising event, believed to have been caused by God **2** any very surprising and fortunate event: *My father got a job. It was a miracle* > **miraculous** adjective > **miraculously** adverb

m

mirage [mir-**ahj**] *noun* an image which you can see in the distance in very hot weather, but which does not actually exist

mire *noun* (*literary*) Mire is swampy ground or mud

mirror *noun* **1** a piece of glass which reflects light and in which you can see your reflection ▷ *verb* **2** To mirror something is to have similar features to it: *His own shock was mirrored on her face*

mirth *noun* (*literary*) Mirth is great amusement and laughter

misbehave *verb* If a child misbehaves, he or she is naughty or behaves badly > **misbehaviour** *noun*

miscarriage *noun* **1** If a woman has a miscarriage she gives birth to a baby before it is properly formed and it dies **2** A miscarriage of justice is a wrong decision made by a court, which causes an innocent person to be punished

miscellaneous *adjective* A miscellaneous group is made up of people or things that are different from each other

mischief *noun* Mischief is eagerness to have fun by teasing people or playing tricks > **mischievous** *adjective*

misconception *noun* a wrong idea about something: *Another misconception is that cancer is infectious*

misconduct *noun* Misconduct is bad or unacceptable behaviour by a professional person: *The Football Association found him guilty of misconduct*

misdemeanour [miss-dem-**mee**-ner] *noun* (*formal*) an act that is shocking or unacceptable

miser *noun* a person who enjoys saving money but hates spending it > **miserly** *adjective*

miserable *adjective* **1** If you are miserable, you are very unhappy **2** If a place or a situation is miserable, it makes you feel depressed: *a miserable little flat* > **miserably** *adverb*

misery miseries *noun* Misery is great unhappiness

misfire *verb* If a plan misfires, it goes wrong

misfit *noun* a person who is not accepted by other people because of being rather strange or eccentric

misfortune *noun* an unpleasant occurrence that is regarded as bad luck: *I had the misfortune to fall off my bike*

misgiving *noun* If you have misgivings, you are worried or unhappy about something: *I had misgivings about his methods*

misguided *adjective* A misguided opinion or action is wrong because it is based on a misunderstanding or bad information

misinterpret *verb* To misinterpret something is to understand it wrongly: *You completely misinterpreted what I wrote*

misjudge *verb* If you misjudge someone or something, you form an incorrect idea or opinion about them

mislead misleads, misleading, misled *verb* To mislead someone is to make them believe something which is not true

misplaced *adjective* A misplaced feeling is inappropriate or directed at the wrong thing or person: *misplaced loyalty*

misrepresent *verb* To misrepresent someone is to give an inaccurate or

M

misleading account of what they have said or done

> **misrepresentation** noun

miss verb **1** If you miss something, you do not notice it: *You can't miss it. It's on the second floor* **2** If you miss someone or something, you feel sad that they are no longer with you: *The boys miss their father* **3** If you miss a chance or opportunity, you fail to take advantage of it **4** If you miss a bus, plane, or train, you arrive too late to catch it **5** If you miss something, you fail to hit it when you aim at it: *His shot missed the target and went wide* ▷ noun **6** an act of missing something that you were aiming at **7** 'Miss' is used before the name of a woman or girl who is not married as a form of address: *Did you know Miss Smith?*

missile noun a weapon that moves long distances through the air and explodes when it reaches its target; also used of any object thrown as a weapon

mission noun **1** an important task that you have to do **2** a group of people who have been sent to a foreign country to carry out an official task: *He became head of the Israeli mission* **3** a journey made by a military aeroplane or space rocket to carry out a task **4** If you have a mission, there is something that you believe it is your duty to try to achieve **5** the workplace of a group of Christians who are working for the Church

missionary noun a Christian who has been sent to a foreign country to work for the Church

missive noun (old-fashioned) a letter or message

mist noun **1** Mist consists of a large number of tiny drops of water in the air, which make it hard to see clearly ▷ verb **2** If your eyes mist, you cannot see very far because there are tears in your eyes **3** If glass mists over or mists up, it becomes covered with condensation so that you cannot see through it

mistake mistakes, mistaking, mistook, mistaken noun **1** an action or opinion that is wrong or is not what you intended ▷ verb **2** If you mistake someone or something for another person or thing, you wrongly think that they are the other person or thing: *I mistook him for the owner of the house*

mistaken adjective **1** If you are mistaken about something, you are wrong about it **2** If you have a mistaken belief or opinion, you believe something which is not true

> **mistakenly** adverb

mistletoe [mis-sel-toe] noun Mistletoe is a plant which grows on trees and has white berries on it. It is used as a Christmas decoration

mistook the past tense of **mistake**

mistreat verb To mistreat a person or animal is to treat them badly and make them suffer

mistress noun **1** A school mistress is a female teacher **2** A servant's mistress is the woman who is the servant's employer

mistrust verb **1** If you mistrust someone, you do not feel that you can trust them ▷ noun **2** Mistrust is a feeling that you cannot trust someone

misty mistier, mistiest adjective full of or covered with mist

misunderstand misunderstands, misunderstanding, misunderstood verb If you misunderstand someone, you do not properly understand what they say or do: *He misunderstood the problem*

misunderstanding *noun* If two people have a misunderstanding, they have a slight quarrel or disagreement

misuse *noun* [mis-**yoos**] **1** The misuse of something is the incorrect or dishonest use of it: *the misuse of public money* ▷ *verb* [mis-**yooz**] **2** To misuse something is to use it incorrectly or dishonestly

mite *noun* a very tiny creature that lives in the fur of animals

mitigating *adjective* (formal) Mitigating circumstances make a crime easier to understand, and perhaps justify it

mix *verb* If you mix things, you combine them or shake or stir them together ▷ **mix up** *verb* If you mix up two things or people, you confuse them: *People often mix us up and greet us by each other's names*

mixed *adjective* **1** consisting of several things of the same general kind: *a mixed salad* **2** involving people from two or more different races: *mixed marriages* **3** Mixed education or accommodation is for both males and females: *a mixed comprehensive*

mixed up *adjective* **1** If you are mixed up, you are confused: *I was all mixed up and forgot where I was* **2** If you are mixed up in a crime or a scandal, you are involved in it

mixer *noun* a machine used for mixing things together: *a cement mixer*

mixture *noun* several different things mixed or shaken together

mix-up *noun* a mistake in something that was planned: *a mix-up with the bookings*

ml an abbreviation for 'millilitre' or 'millilitres'

mm an abbreviation for 'millimetre' or 'millimetres'

moan *verb* **1** If you moan, you make a low, miserable sound because you are in pain or suffering **2** (informal) If you moan about something, you complain about it ▷ *noun* **3** a low cry of pain or misery

moat *noun* a wide, water-filled ditch around a building such as a castle

mob mobs, mobbing, mobbed *noun* **1** a large, disorganized crowd of people: *A violent mob attacked the team bus* ▷ *verb* **2** If a lot of people mob someone, they crowd around the person in a disorderly way: *The band was mobbed by over a thousand fans*

mobile *adjective* **1** able to move or be moved freely and easily: *a mobile home* [PE] **2** If you are mobile, you are able to travel or move about from one place to another: *a mobile workforce* ▷ *noun* **3** a decoration consisting of several small objects which hang from threads and move around when a breeze blows **4** a mobile phone ▷ *noun* **mobility** *noun*

mobile phone *noun* a small portable telephone

mock *verb* **1** If you mock someone, you say something scornful or imitate their foolish behaviour ▷ *adjective* **2** not genuine: *mock surprise; a mock Tudor house* **3** A mock examination is one that you do as a practice before the real examination

mockery *noun* Mockery is the expression of scorn or ridicule of someone

mode *noun* **1** A mode of life or behaviour is a particular way of living or behaving **2** In mathematics, the mode is the biggest in a set of groups

model models, modelling, modelled

noun, adjective **1** a copy of something that shows what it looks like or how it works: *a model aircraft* ▷ noun **2** Something that is described as, for example, a model of clarity or a model of perfection, is extremely clear or absolutely perfect **3** a type or version of a machine: *Which model of washing machine did you choose?* **4** a person who poses for a painter or a photographer **5** a person who wears the clothes that are being displayed at a fashion show or in a magazine ▷ adjective **6** Someone who is described as, for example, a model student is an excellent student ▷ verb **7** If you model yourself on someone, you copy their behaviour because you admire them **8** To model clothes is to display them by wearing them **9** To model shapes or figures is to make them out of clay or wood

modem [moe-dem] noun [COMPUTING] a piece of equipment that links a computer to the telephone system so that data can be transferred from one machine to another via the telephone line

moderate adjective [mod-i-rit] **1** Moderate views are not extreme, and usually favour gradual changes rather than major ones **2** A moderate amount of something is neither large nor small ▷ noun [mod-i-rit] **3** a person whose political views are not extreme ▷ verb [mod-i-rate] **4** If you moderate something or if it moderates, it becomes less extreme or violent: *The weather moderated* > **moderately** adverb

moderation noun Moderation is control of your behaviour that stops you acting in an extreme way: *a man of fairness and moderation*

modern adjective **1** relating to the present time: *modern society* **2** new and involving the latest ideas and equipment: *modern technology* > **modernity** noun

modernize or **modernise** verb To modernize something is to introduce new methods or equipment to it

modest adjective **1** quite small in size or amount **2** Someone who is modest does not boast about their abilities or possessions **3** shy and easily embarrassed > **modestly** adverb > **modesty** noun

modification noun a small change made to improve something: *Modifications to the undercarriage were made*

modify modifies, modifying, modified verb If you modify something, you change it slightly in order to improve it

module noun **1** one of the parts which when put together form a whole unit or object: *The college provides modules for trainees* **2** [COMPUTING] a part of a machine or system that does a particular task **3** a part of a spacecraft which can do certain things away from the main body: *the lunar module* > **modular** adjective

mohair noun Mohair is very soft, fluffy wool obtained from angora goats

moist adjective slightly wet

moisture noun Moisture is tiny drops of water in the air or on the ground

mole noun **1** a dark, slightly raised spot on your skin **2** a small animal with black fur. Moles live in tunnels underground **3** (*informal*) a member of an organization who is working as a spy for a rival organization

m

molecule noun the smallest amount of a substance that can exist > **molecular** adjective

molest verb If someone molests you, they annoy you and prevent you from doing something, especially by using physical violence > **molester** noun

mollify mollifies, mollifying, mollified verb To mollify someone is to do something to make them less upset or angry

molten adjective Molten rock or metal has been heated to a very high temperature and has become a thick liquid

moment noun 1 a very short period of time: He paused for a moment 2 The moment at which something happens is the point in time at which it happens: At that moment, the doorbell rang ▷ phrase 3 If something is happening at the moment, it is happening now

momentary adjective Something that is momentary lasts for only a few seconds: a momentary lapse of concentration > **momentarily** adverb

momentous adjective (formal) very important, often because of its future effect: a momentous occasion

momentum noun 1 Momentum is the ability that something has to keep developing: The campaign is gaining momentum 2 Momentum is also the ability that an object has to continue moving as a result of the speed it already has

monarch [mon-nark] noun a queen, king, or other royal person who reigns over a country

monarchy monarchies noun a system in which a queen or king reigns in a country

monastery monasteries noun a building in which monks live

> **monastic** adjective

Monday noun Monday is the day between Sunday and Tuesday

money noun Money is the coins or banknotes that you use to buy something

mongrel noun a dog with parents of different breeds

monitor verb 1 If you monitor something, you regularly check its condition and progress: Her health will be monitored daily ▷ noun 2 a machine used to check or record things 3 [COMPUTING] the visual display unit of a computer 4 a school pupil chosen to do special duties by the teacher

monk noun a member of a male religious community

monkey noun an animal which has a long tail and climbs trees. Monkeys live in hot countries

monogamy noun (formal) Monogamy is the custom of being married to only one person at a time > **monogamous** adjective

monologue [mon-nol-og] noun [ENGLISH] a long speech by one person during a play or a conversation

monopoly monopolies noun control of most of an industry by one or a few large firms

monotone noun a tone which does not vary: He droned on in a boring monotone

monotonous adjective having a regular pattern which is very dull and boring: monotonous work > **monotony** noun

monsoon noun the season of very heavy rain in South-east Asia

monster noun 1 a large, imaginary creature that looks very frightening 2 a cruel or frightening person ▷ adjective 3 extremely large: a monster truck

monstrosity monstrosities noun
something that is large and
extremely ugly: *a concrete
monstrosity in the middle of the city*

monstrous adjective extremely
shocking or unfair: *a monstrous crime*
> **monstrously** adverb

montage [mon-**tahj**] noun a picture
or film consisting of a combination
of several different items arranged
to produce an unusual effect

month noun one of the twelve
periods that a year is divided into

monthly adjective Monthly
describes something that happens
or appears once a month: *monthly
staff meetings*

monument noun a large stone
structure built to remind people of a
famous person or event: *a monument
to the dead*

monumental adjective **1** A
monumental building or sculpture
is very large and important **2** very
large or extreme: *We face a
monumental task*

mood noun the way you are feeling
at a particular time: *She was in a
really cheerful mood*

moody moodier, moodiest adjective
1 Someone who is moody is
depressed or unhappy: *Tony, despite
his charm, could sulk and be moody*
2 Someone who is moody often
changes their mood for no apparent
reason

moon noun The moon is an object
moving round the earth which you
see as a shining circle or crescent in
the sky at night. Some other planets
have moons

moonlight moonlights,
moonlighting, moonlighted noun
1 Moonlight is the light that comes
from the moon at night ▷ verb
2 (informal) If someone is

moonlighting, they have a second
job that they have not informed the
tax office about > **moonlit** adjective

moor noun **1** a high area of open land
▷ verb **2** If a boat is moored, it is
attached to the land with a rope

mooring noun a place where a boat
can be tied

moose noun a large North American
deer with flat antlers

moot verb (formal) When something
is mooted, it is suggested for
discussion: *The project was first
mooted in 1988*

mop mops, mopping, mopped noun
1 a tool for washing floors,
consisting of a sponge or string
head attached to a long handle **2** a
large amount of loose or untidy hair
▷ verb **3** To mop a floor is to clean it
with a mop **4** To mop a surface is to
wipe it with a dry cloth to remove
liquid

moped [moe-ped] noun a type of
small motorcycle

moral noun **1** RE (in plural) Morals
are values based on beliefs about
the correct and acceptable way to
behave ▷ adjective **2** concerned with
whether behaviour is right or
acceptable: *moral values* > **morality**
noun > **morally** adverb

morale [mor-**rahl**] noun Morale is
the amount of confidence and
optimism that you have: *The morale
of the troops was high*

morbid adjective having a great
interest in unpleasant things,
especially death

more adjective **1** More means a
greater number or extent than
something else: *He's got more chips
than me* **2** used to refer to an
additional thing or amount of
something: *He found some more clues*
▷ pronoun **3** a greater number or

m

extent ▷ adverb **4** to a greater degree or extent: *more amused than concerned* **5** You can use 'more' in front of adjectives and adverbs to form comparatives: *You look more beautiful than ever*

moreover adverb used to introduce a piece of information that supports or expands the previous statement: *They have accused the government of corruption. Moreover, they have named names*

morgue [morg] noun a building where dead bodies are kept before being buried or cremated

moribund adjective no longer having a useful function and about to come to an end: *a moribund industry*

morning noun the part of the day between midnight and noon: *He was born at three in the morning*

Moroccan [mor-**rok**-an] adjective **1** belonging or relating to Morocco ▷ noun **2** someone who comes from Morocco

moron noun (informal) a very stupid person ▷ **moronic** adjective

morose adjective miserable and bad-tempered

morphine noun Morphine is a drug which is used to relieve pain

Morse or **Morse code** noun Morse or Morse code is a code used for sending messages in which each letter is represented by a series of dots and dashes. It is named after its American inventor, Samuel Morse

morsel noun a small piece of food

mortal adjective **1** unable to live forever: *Remember that you are mortal* **2** A mortal wound is one that causes death ▷ noun **3** an ordinary person

mortality noun **1** Mortality is the fact that all people must die

2 Mortality also refers to the number of people who die at any particular time: *a low infant mortality rate*

mortar noun **1** a short cannon which fires missiles high into the air for a short distance **2** Mortar is a mixture of sand, water, and cement used to hold bricks firmly together

mortgage [mor-gij] noun **1** a loan which you get from a bank or a building society in order to buy a house ▷ verb **2** If you mortgage your house, you use it as a guarantee to a company in order to borrow money from them. They can take the house from you if you do not pay back the money you have borrowed

mortuary mortuaries noun a special room in a hospital where dead bodies are kept before being buried or cremated

mosaic [moe-**zay**-yik] noun a design made of small coloured stones or pieces of coloured glass set into concrete or plaster

Moslem another spelling of **Muslim**

mosque [mosk] noun a building where Muslims go to worship

mosquito mosquitoes or mosquitos [moss-**kee**-toe] noun Mosquitoes are small insects which bite people in order to suck their blood

moss noun Moss is a soft, low-growing, green plant which grows on damp soil or stone ▷ **mossy** adjective

most adjective, pronoun **1** Most of a group of things or people means nearly all of them: *Most people don't share your views* **2** The most means a larger amount than anyone or anything else: *She has the most talent* ▷ adverb **3** You can use 'most' in front of adjectives or adverbs to form superlatives: *the most beautiful women in the world*

mostly *adverb* 'Mostly' is used to show that a statement is generally true: *Her friends are mostly men*

MOT *noun* In Britain, an annual test for road vehicles to check that they are safe to drive

motel *noun* a hotel providing overnight accommodation for people in the middle of a car journey

moth *noun* an insect like a butterfly which usually flies at night

mother *noun* **1** A person's mother is their female parent ▷ *verb* **2** To mother someone is to look after them and bring them up

motherhood *noun* Motherhood is the state of being a mother

mother-in-law mothers-in-law *noun* Someone's mother-in-law is the mother of their husband or wife

motif [moe-**teef**] *noun* a design which is used as a decoration

motion *noun* **1** Motion is the process of continually moving or changing position: *the motion of the ship* **2** an action or gesture: *Apply with a brush using circular motions* **3** a proposal which people discuss and vote on at a meeting ▷ *verb* **4** If you motion to someone, you make a movement with your hand in order to show them what they should do: *I motioned him to proceed*

motionless *adjective* not moving at all: *He sat motionless*

motivate *verb* **1** If you are motivated by something, it makes you behave in a particular way: *He is motivated by duty rather than ambition* **2** If you motivate someone, you make them feel determined to do something ▷ **motivated** *adjective* ▷ **motivation** *noun*

motive *noun* a reason or purpose for

doing something: *There was no motive for the attack*

motley *adjective* A motley collection is made up of people or things of very different types

motor *noun* ⟨D G T⟩ **1** a part of a vehicle or a machine that uses electricity or fuel to produce movement so that the machine can work ▷ *adjective* **2** concerned with or relating to vehicles with a petrol or diesel engine: *the motor industry*

motorcycle *noun* a two-wheeled vehicle with an engine which is ridden like a bicycle > **motorcyclist** *noun*

motoring *adjective* relating to cars and driving: *a motoring correspondent*

motorist *noun* a person who drives a car

motorway *noun* a wide road built for fast travel over long distances

mottled *adjective* covered with patches of different colours: *mottled leaves*

motto mottoes *or* mottos *noun* a short sentence or phrase that is a rule for good or sensible behaviour

mould *verb* **1** To mould someone or something is to influence and change them so they develop in a particular way: *Early experiences mould our behaviour for life* **2** ⟨D G T⟩ To mould a substance is to make it into a particular shape: *Mould the mixture into flat round cakes* ▷ *noun* **3** ⟨D G T⟩ a container used to make something into a particular shape: *a jelly mould* **4** Mould is a soft grey or green substance that can form on old food or damp walls > **mouldy** *adjective*

mound *noun* **1** a small man-made hill **2** a large, untidy pile: *a mound of blankets*

mount *verb* **1** To mount a campaign or event is to organize it and carry it out **2** If something is mounting, it is increasing: *Economic problems are mounting* **3** (formal) To mount something is to go to the top of it: *He mounted the steps* **4** If you mount a horse, you climb on its back **5** If you mount an object in a particular place, you fix it there to display it ▷ noun **6** 'Mount' is also used as part of the name of a mountain: *Mount Everest*

mountain noun **1 a** a very high piece of land with steep sides **2** a large amount of something: *mountains of paperwork*

mountaineer noun a person who climbs mountains

mountainous adjective A mountainous area has a lot of mountains

mourn verb **1** If you mourn for someone who has died, you are very sad and think about them a lot **2** If you mourn something, you are sad because you no longer have it: *He mourned the end of his marriage*

mourner noun a person who attends a funeral

mournful adjective very sad

mourning noun If someone is in mourning, they wear special black clothes or behave in a quiet and restrained way because a member of their family has died

mouse mice noun **1** a small rodent with a long tail **2** [COMPUTING] a small device moved by hand to control the position of the cursor on a computer screen

mousse [moos] noun Mousse is a light, fluffy food made from whipped eggs and cream

moustache [mus-**stahsh**] noun A man's moustache is hair growing on his upper lip

mouth noun **1** your lips, or the space

behind them where your tongue and teeth are **2** The mouth of a cave or a hole is the entrance to it **3** The mouth of a river is the place where it flows into the sea ▷ verb **4** If you mouth something, you form words with your lips without making any sound: *He mouthed 'Thank you' to the jurors* > **mouthful** noun

mouthpiece noun **1** the part you speak into on a telephone **2** the part of a musical instrument you put to your mouth **3** The mouthpiece of an organization is the person who publicly states its opinions and policies

movable adjective Something that is movable can be moved from one place to another

move verb **1** To move means to go to a different place or position. To move something means to change its place or position **2** If you move, or move house, you go to live in a different house **3** If something moves you, it causes you to feel a deep emotion: *Her story moved us to tears* ▷ noun **4** a change from one place or position to another: *We were watching his every move* **5** an act of moving house **6** the act of putting a piece or counter in a game in a different position: *It's your move next*

movement noun **1** Movement involves changing position or going from one place to another **2** (in plural, formal) Your movements are everything you do during a period of time: *They asked him for an account of his movements during the previous morning* **3** a group of people who share the same beliefs or aims: *the peace movement* **4** one of the major sections of a piece of classical music

moving adjective Something that is moving makes you feel deep

say something very softly ▷ *noun*
2 something that someone says which can hardly be heard

muscle *noun* **1** [SCIENCE] Your muscles are pieces of flesh which you can expand or contract in order to move parts of your body. An **agonistic muscle** is a muscle which is relaxed when another muscle is contracted; an **antagonistic muscle** is a muscle which is contracted when another muscle is relaxed, returning the limb to its original position; an **antagonistic pair of muscles** means two muscles which work together, for example one opening a joint and the other closing it ▷ *verb* **2** (*informal*) If you muscle in on something, you force your way into a situation in which you are not welcome

muscular [musk-yool-lar] *adjective*
1 involving or affecting your muscles: *muscular strength*
2 Someone who is muscular has strong, firm muscles

muse *verb* (*literary*) To muse is to think about something for a long time

museum *noun* a building where many interesting or valuable objects are kept and displayed

mush *noun* A mush is a thick, soft paste

mushroom *noun* **1** a fungus with a short stem and a round top. Some types of mushroom are edible **2** If something mushrooms, it appears and grows very quickly: *The mill towns mushroomed into cities*

mushy mushier, mushiest *adjective*
1 Mushy fruits or vegetables are too soft: *mushy tomatoes* **2** (*informal*) Mushy stories are too sentimental

music *noun* **1** Music is a pattern of sounds performed by people singing

or playing instruments **2** Music is also the written symbols that represent musical sounds: *I taught myself to read music*

musical *adjective* **1** relating to playing or studying music: *a musical instrument* ▷ *noun* **2** a play or film that uses songs and dance to tell the story > **musically** *adverb*

musician *noun* [MUSIC] a person who plays a musical instrument as their job or hobby

musk *noun* Musk is a substance with a strong, sweet smell. It is used to make perfume > **musky** *adjective*

musket *noun* an old-fashioned gun with a long barrel

Muslim or **Moslem** *noun* [RE] **1** a person who believes in Islam and lives according to its rules ▷ *adjective* **2** relating to Islam

muslin *noun* Muslin is a very thin cotton material

mussel *noun* Mussels are a kind of shellfish with black shells

must *verb* **1** If something must happen, it is very important or necessary that it happens:.*You must be over 18* **2** If you tell someone they must do something, you are suggesting that they do it: *You must try this pudding: it's delicious* ▷ *noun* **3** something that is absolutely necessary: *The museum is a must for all visitors*

mustard *noun* Mustard is a spicy-tasting yellow or brown paste made from seeds

muster *verb* If you muster something such as energy or support, you gather it together: *as much calm as he could muster*

musty mustier, mustiest *adjective* smelling stale and damp: *musty old books*

mutate *verb* [SCIENCE] If something

m

mutates, its structure or appearance alters in some way: *Viruses react to change and can mutate fast* > **mutation** noun > **mutant** noun, adjective

mute (formal) adjective **1** not giving out sound or speech: *He stared in mute amazement* ▷ verb **2** To mute a sound means to make it quieter

muted adjective **1** Muted colours or sounds are soft and gentle **2** A muted reaction is not very strong

mutilate verb **1** If someone is mutilated, their body is badly injured: *His leg was badly mutilated* **2** If you mutilate something, you deliberately damage or spoil it: *Almost every book had been mutilated* > **mutilation** noun

mutiny mutinies noun A mutiny is a rebellion against someone in authority

mutter verb To mutter is to speak in a very low and perhaps cross voice: *Rory muttered something under his breath*

mutton noun Mutton is the meat of an adult sheep

mutual adjective used to describe something that two or more people do to each other or share: *They had a mutual interest in rugby*

mutually adverb Mutually describes a situation in which two or more people feel the same way about each other: *a mutually supportive relationship*

muzzle noun **1** the nose and mouth of an animal **2** a cover or a strap for a dog's nose and mouth to prevent it from biting **3** the open end of a gun through which the bullets come out ▷ verb **4** To muzzle a dog is to put a muzzle on it

my adjective 'My' refers to something belonging or relating to the person

speaking or writing: *I held my breath*

myriad [mir-ree-ad] noun, adjective (literary) a very large number of people or things

myself pronoun **1** 'Myself' is used when the person speaking or writing does an action and is affected by it: *I was ashamed of myself* **2** 'Myself' is also used to emphasize 'I': *I find it a bit odd myself*

mysterious adjective **1** strange and not well understood **2** secretive about something: *Stop being so mysterious* > **mysteriously** adverb

mystery mysteries noun something that is not understood or known about

mystic noun **1** a religious person who spends long hours meditating ▷ adjective **2** Mystic means the same as mystical

mystical adjective involving spiritual powers and influences: *a mystical experience* > **mysticism** noun

mystify mystifies, mystifying, mystified verb If something mystifies you, you find it impossible to understand

mystique [mis-steek] noun Mystique is an atmosphere of mystery and importance associated with a particular person or thing

myth noun **1** an untrue belief or explanation **2** ENGLISH a story which was made up long ago to explain natural events and religious beliefs: *Viking myths*

mythical adjective imaginary, untrue, or existing only in myths: *a mythical beast*

mythology noun Mythology refers to stories that have been made up in the past to explain natural events or justify religious beliefs > **mythological** adjective

n

nag nags, nagging, nagged *verb* **1** If you nag someone, you keep complaining to them about something **2** If something nags at you, it keeps worrying you

nail *noun* **1 a** small piece of metal with a sharp point at one end, which you hammer into objects to hold things together **2** Your nails are the thin hard areas covering the ends of your fingers and toes ▷ *verb* **3** If you nail something somewhere, you fit it there using a nail

naive or **naïve** [ny-**eev**] *adjective* foolishly believing that things are easier or less complicated than they really are > **naively** *adverb* > **naivety** *noun*

naked *adjective* **1** not wearing any clothes or not covered by anything **2** shown openly: *naked aggression* > **nakedness** *noun*

name *noun* **1 a** word that you use to identify a person, place, or thing **2** Someone's name is also their reputation: *My only wish now is to clear my name* ▷ *verb* **3** If you name someone or something, you give them a name or you say their name **4** If you name a price or a date, you say what you want it to be

nameless *adjective* You describe someone or something as nameless when you do not know their name, or when a name has not yet been given to them

namely *adverb* that is; used to introduce more detailed information about what you have just said: *The state stripped them of their rights, namely the right to own land*

namesake *noun* Your namesake is someone with the same name as you: *Audrey Hepburn and her namesake Katharine*

nanny nannies *noun* a woman whose job is looking after young children

nap naps, napping, napped *noun* **1 a** short sleep ▷ *verb* **2** When you nap, you have a short sleep

napkin *noun* a small piece of cloth or paper used to wipe your hands and mouth after eating

nappy nappies *noun* a piece of towelling or paper worn round a baby's bottom

narcotic *noun* a drug which makes you sleepy and unable to feel pain

narrate *verb* If you narrate a story, you tell it > **narration** *noun*

narrative [**nar**-rat-tiv] *noun* [ENGLISH] a story or an account of events

narrator *noun* **1** a person who is reading or telling a story out loud **2** [ENGLISH] a character in a novel who tells the story

narrow *adjective* **1** having a small distance from one side to the other: *a narrow stream* **2** concerned only with a few aspects of something and ignoring the important points: *people with a narrow point of view* **3** A narrow escape or victory is one that you only just achieve ▷ *verb* **4** To narrow means to become less wide: *The road narrowed* > **narrowly** *adverb* > **narrowness** *noun*

narrow-minded *adjective* unwilling to consider new ideas or opinions

nasal [**nay**-zal] *adjective* **1** relating to the nose: *the nasal passages* **2** Nasal sounds are made by breathing out through your nose as you sneeze

nasty nastier, nastiest *adjective* very unpleasant: *a nasty shock* > **nastily** *adverb* > **nastiness** *noun*

nation *noun* [GEOGRAPHY] a large group of people sharing the same history and language and usually inhabiting a particular country

national [GEOGRAPHY] *adjective* **1** relating to the whole of a country: *a national newspaper* **2** typical of a particular country: *women in Polish national dress* > *noun* **3** A national of a country is a citizen of that country: *Turkish nationals* > **nationally** *adverb*

national anthem *noun* A country's national anthem is its official song

nationalism *noun* **1** Nationalism is a desire for the independence of a country; also a political movement aiming to achieve such independence **2** Nationalism is also love of your own country > **nationalist** *noun* > **nationalistic** *adjective*

nationality nationalities *noun* Nationality is the fact of belonging to a particular country

nationalize or **nationalise** *verb* To nationalize an industry means to bring it under the control and ownership of the state > **nationalization** *noun*

National Party *noun* In Australia and New Zealand, the National Party is a major political party

national service *noun* National service is a compulsory period of service in the armed forces

nationwide *adjective, adverb* happening all over a country: *a nationwide search*

native *adjective* **1** Your native country is the country where you were born **2** Your native language is the language that you first learned to speak **3** Animals or plants that are native to a place live or grow there naturally and have not been brought there by people > *noun* **4** A native of a place is someone who was born there

Nativity *noun* In Christianity, the Nativity is the birth of Christ or the festival celebrating this

natural *adjective* **1** normal and to be expected: *It was only natural that he was tempted* **2** not trying to pretend or hide anything: *Caitlin's natural manner reassured her* **3** [D G T] existing or happening in nature: *natural disasters; natural fabrics* **4** A natural ability is one you were born with **5** Your natural mother or father is your birth mother or father and not someone who has adopted you > *noun* **6** someone who is born with a particular ability: *She's a natural at bridge* **7** In music, a natural is a note that is not a sharp or a flat. It is represented by the symbol (♮) > **naturally** *adverb*

nature *noun* **1** Nature is animals, plants, and all the other things in the world not made by people **2** The nature of a person or thing is their basic character: *She liked his warm, generous nature*

naughty naughtier, naughtiest *adjective* **1** behaving badly **2** rude or indecent > **naughtily** *adverb* > **naughtiness** *noun*

nausea [naw-zee-ah] *noun* Nausea is a feeling in your stomach that you are going to be sick > **nauseous** *adjective*

nautical [naw-tik-kl] *adjective* relating to ships or navigation

naval *adjective* relating to or having a navy: *naval officers; naval bases*

navel noun the small hollow on the front of your body just below your waist

navigate verb 1 When someone navigates, they work out the direction in which a ship, plane, or car should go, using maps and sometimes instruments 2 To navigate a stretch of water means to travel safely across it: *It was the first time I had navigated the ocean* ▷ **navigation** noun ▷ **navigator** noun

navy navies noun 1 the part of a country's armed forces that fights at sea ▷ adjective 2 dark blue

Nazi [naht-see] noun The Nazis were members of the National Socialist German Workers' Party, which was led by Adolf Hitler

NB You write NB to draw attention to what you are going to write next. NB is an abbreviation for the Latin 'nota bene', which means 'note well'

near preposition 1 not far from ▷ adjective 2 not far away in distance 3 not far away in time 4 You can also use 'near' to mean almost: *a night of near disaster* ▷ verb 5 When you are nearing something, you are approaching it and will soon reach it: *The dog began to bark as he neared the porch* ▷ **nearness** noun

nearby adjective 1 only a short distance away: *a nearby town* ▷ adverb 2 only a short distance away: *a house nearby*

nearly adverb not completely but almost

neat adjective 1 tidy and smart 2 A neat alcoholic drink does not have anything added to it: *a small glass of neat vodka* ▷ **neatly** adverb ▷ **neatness** noun

necessarily adverb Something that is not necessarily the case is not always or inevitably the case

necessary adjective 1 Something that is necessary is needed or must be done 2 (formal) Necessary also means certain or inevitable: *a necessary consequence of war*

necessity necessities noun 1 Necessity is the need to do something: *There is no necessity for any of this* 2 Necessities are things needed in order to live

neck noun 1 the part of your body which joins your head to the rest of your body 2 the long narrow part at the top of a bottle

necklace noun a piece of jewellery which a woman wears around her neck

nectar noun Nectar is a sweet liquid produced by flowers and attractive to insects

need verb 1 If you need something, you believe that you must have it or do it ▷ noun 2 Your needs are the things that you need to have 3 a strong feeling that you must have or do something: *I just felt the need to write about it*

needle noun 1 a small thin piece of metal with a pointed end and a hole at the other, which is used for sewing 2 Needles are also long thin pieces of steel or plastic, used for knitting 3 the part of a syringe which a doctor or nurse sticks into your body 4 the thin piece of metal or plastic on a dial which moves to show a measurement 5 The needles of a pine tree are its leaves ▷ verb 6 (informal) If someone needles you, they annoy or provoke you

needless adjective unnecessary ▷ **needlessly** adverb

needy needier, neediest adjective very poor

negative adjective 1 A negative

answer means 'no' **2** Someone who is negative sees only problems and disadvantages: *Why are you so negative about everything?* **3** If a medical or scientific test is negative, it shows that something has not happened or is not present: *The diabetes test came back negative* **4** [MATHS] A negative number is less than zero **5** [SCIENCE] In physics, a negative electric charge has the same polarity as the charge of an electron ▷ *noun* **6** the image that is first produced when you take a photograph ▷ **negatively** *adverb*

neglect *verb* **1** If you neglect something, you do not look after it properly **2** (*formal*) If you neglect to do something, you fail to do it: *He had neglected to give her his address* ▷ *noun* **3** Neglect is failure to look after something or someone properly: *Most of her plants died from neglect* ▷ **neglectful** *adjective*

negligent *adjective* not taking enough care: *her negligent driving* ▷ **negligently** *adverb* ▷ **negligence** *noun*

negligible *adjective* very small and unimportant: *a negligible amount of fat*

negotiable *adjective* able to be changed or agreed by discussion: *All contributions are negotiable*

negotiate *verb* **1** When people negotiate, they have formal discussions in order to reach an agreement about something **2** If you negotiate an obstacle, you manage to get over it or round it ▷ **negotiation** *noun* ▷ **negotiator** *noun*

Negro *Negroes noun* (*old-fashioned, offensive*) a person with black skin who comes from Africa or whose ancestors came from Africa

neighbour *noun* **1** Your neighbour is someone who lives next door to you or near you **2** Your neighbour is also someone standing or sitting next to you: *I got chatting with my neighbour in the studio*

neighbourhood *noun* a district where people live: *a safe neighbourhood*

neighbouring *adjective* situated nearby: *schools in neighbouring areas*

neither *adjective, pronoun* used to indicate that a negative statement refers to two or more things or people: *It's neither a play nor a musical; Neither of them spoke*

nephew *noun* Someone's nephew is the son of their sister or brother

Neptune *noun* Neptune is the planet in the solar system which is eighth from the sun

nerve *noun* **1** a long thin fibre that sends messages between your brain and other parts of your body **2** If you talk about someone's nerves, you are referring to how able they are to remain calm in a difficult situation: *It needs confidence and strong nerves* **3** Nerve is courage: *O'Meara held his nerve to sink the putt* **4** (*informal*) Nerve is boldness or rudeness: *He had the nerve to swear at me* ▷ *phrase* **5** (*informal*) If someone **gets on your nerves**, they irritate you

nerve-racking *adjective* making you feel very worried and tense: *a nerve-racking experience*

nervous *adjective* **1** worried and frightened **2** A nervous illness affects your emotions and mental health ▷ **nervously** *adverb* ▷ **nervousness** *noun*

nervous breakdown *noun* an illness in which someone suffers from deep depression and needs psychiatric treatment

nervous system noun Your nervous system is the nerves in your body together with your brain and spinal cord

nest noun 1 a place that a bird makes to lay its eggs in; also a place that some insects and other animals make to rear their young in ▷ verb 2 When birds nest, they build a nest and lay eggs in it

nestle [ness-sl] verb If you nestle somewhere, you settle there comfortably, often pressing up against someone else: *A new puppy nestled in her lap*

nestling noun a young bird that has not yet learned to fly and so has not left the nest

net noun 1 a piece of material made of threads woven together with small spaces in between 2 The net is the same as the **internet** ▷ adjective 3 A net amount is final, after everything that should be subtracted from it has been subtracted: *a net profit of £171 million* 4 The net weight of something is its weight without its wrapping

netball noun Netball is a game played by two teams of seven players in which each team tries to score goals by throwing a ball through a net at the top of a pole

netting noun Netting is material made of threads or metal wires woven together with small spaces in between

nettle noun a wild plant covered with little hairs that sting

network noun 1 a large number of lines or roads which cross each other at many points: *a small network of side roads* 2 A network of people or organizations is a large number of them that work together as a system: *the public telephone*

network 3 A television network is a group of broadcasting stations that all transmit the same programmes at the same time 4 COMPUTING a group of computers connected to each other

neuron or **neurone** noun a cell that is part of the nervous system and conducts messages to and from the brain

neurosis neuroses [nyoor-**roh**-siss] noun Neurosis is mental illness which causes people to have strong and unreasonable fears and worries

neurotic [nyoor-**rot**-ik] adjective having strong and unreasonable fears and worries: *He was almost neurotic about being followed*

neuter [**nyoo**-ter] verb 1 When an animal is neutered, its reproductive organs are removed ▷ adjective 2 In some languages, a neuter noun or pronoun is one which is not masculine or feminine

neutral adjective 1 People who are neutral do not support either side in a disagreement or war 2 D&T The neutral wire in an electric plug is the one that is not earth or live 3 ART A neutral colour is not definite or striking, for example pale grey 4 SCIENCE In chemistry, a neutral substance is neither acid nor alkaline ▷ noun 5 HISTORY a person or country that does not support either side in a disagreement or war 6 D&T Neutral is the position between the gears of a vehicle in which the gears are not connected to the engine and so the vehicle cannot move > **neutrality** noun

neutralize neutralizes, neutralizing, neutralized or **neutralise** verb 1 To neutralize something means to prevent it from working or taking effect, especially

by doing or applying something
that has the opposite effect
2 SCIENCE If you neutralize a
substance, you make it neither acid
nor alkaline

neutron noun an atomic particle
that has no electrical charge

never adverb at no time in the past,
present, or future

nevertheless adverb in spite of
what has just been said: They dress
rather plainly but nevertheless look
quite smart

new adjective **1** recently made,
created, or discovered: a new house;
a new plan; a new virus **2** not used or
owned before: We've got a new car
3 different or unfamiliar: a name
which was new to me > **newness**
noun

newborn adjective born recently

newcomer noun someone who has
recently arrived in a place

newly adverb recently: the newly born
baby

new moon noun The moon is a new
moon when it is a thin crescent
shape at the start of its four-week
cycle

news noun News is information
about things that have happened

newsagent noun a person or shop
that sells newspapers and
magazines

newspaper noun a publication, on
large sheets of paper, that is
produced regularly and contains
news and articles

New Testament noun The New
Testament is the second part of the
Bible, which deals with the life of
Jesus Christ and with the early
Church

New Year noun New Year is the time
when people celebrate the start of a
year

New Zealander noun someone
who comes from New Zealand

next adjective **1** coming immediately
after something else: Their next child
was a girl **2** in a position nearest to
something: in the next room > adverb
3 coming immediately after
something else: Steve arrived next
> phrase **4** If one thing is **next to**
another, it is at the side of it

next door adjective, adverb in the
house next to yours

NHS In Britain, an abbreviation for
'National Health Service'

nib noun the pointed end of a pen

nibble verb **1** When you nibble
something, you take small bites of it
> noun **2** a small bite of something

nice adjective pleasant or attractive
> **nicely** adverb > **niceness** noun

nicety noun niceties [**nigh**-se-tee] noun a
small detail: the social niceties

niche [**neesh**] noun **1** a hollow area
in a wall **2** If you say that you have
found your niche, you mean that
you have found a job or way of life
that is exactly right for you

nick verb **1** If you nick something,
you make a small cut in its surface:
He nicked his chin **2** (informal) To nick
something also means to steal it
> noun **3** a small cut in the surface of
something

nickel noun **1** SCIENCE Nickel is a
silver-coloured metallic element
that is used in alloys. Its atomic
number is 28 and its symbol is Ni **2** A
nickel is an American or Canadian
coin worth five cents

nickname noun **1** an informal name
given to someone > verb **2** If you
nickname someone, you give them
a nickname

nicotine noun SCIENCE Nicotine is
an addictive substance found in
tobacco. It is named after Jacques

Nicot, who first brought tobacco to France

niece *noun* Someone's niece is the daughter of their sister or brother

nifty *adjective* neat and pleasing or cleverly done

Nigerian [nie-**jeer**-ee-an] *adjective* **1** belonging or relating to Nigeria ▷ *noun* **2** someone from Nigeria

niggle *verb* **1** If something niggles you, it worries you slightly ▷ *noun* **2** a small worry that you keep thinking about

night *noun* Night is the time between sunset and sunrise when it is dark

nightclub *noun* a place where people go late in the evening to drink and dance

nightfall *noun* Nightfall is the time of day when it starts to get dark

nightie *noun* (*informal*) a nightdress

nightly *adjective, adverb* happening every night: *the nightly news programme*

nightmare *noun* a very frightening dream; also used of any very unpleasant or frightening situation: *The meal itself was a nightmare* > **nightmarish** *adjective*

nil *noun* Nil means zero or nothing. It is used especially in sports scores

nimble *adjective* **1** able to move quickly and easily **2** able to think quickly and cleverly > **nimbly** *adverb*

nine the number 9 > **ninth** *adjective*

nineteen the number 19 > **nineteenth** *adjective*

ninety ninety the number 90 > **ninetieth** *adjective*

nip nips, nipping, nipped *verb* **1** (*informal*) If you nip somewhere, you go there quickly **2** To nip someone or something means to pinch or squeeze them slightly ▷ *noun* **3** a light pinch

nirvana [neer-**vah**-na] *noun* Nirvana is the ultimate state of spiritual enlightenment which can be achieved in the Hindu and Buddhist religions

nitrogen *noun* SCIENCE Nitrogen is a chemical element usually found as a gas. It forms about 78 per cent of the earth's atmosphere. Nitrogen's atomic number is 7 and its symbol is N

no *interjection* **1** used to say that something is not true or to refuse something ▷ *adjective* **2** none at all or not at all: *She gave no reason; You're no friend of mine* ▷ *adverb* **3** used with a comparative to mean 'not': *no later than July 24th*

no. a written abbreviation for **number**

nobility *noun* **1** Nobility is the quality of being noble: *the unmistakable nobility of his character* **2** The nobility of a society are all the people who have titles and high social rank

noble *adjective* **1** honest and brave, and deserving admiration **2** very impressive: *great parks with noble tall trees* ▷ *noun* **3** a member of the nobility > **nobly** *adverb*

nobleman noblemen *noun* a man who is a member of the nobility > **noblewoman** *noun*

nobody nobodies *pronoun* **1** not a single person ▷ *noun* **2** Someone who is a nobody is not at all important

nocturnal *adjective* **1** happening at night: *a nocturnal journey through New York* **2** active at night: *a nocturnal animal*

nod nods, nodding, nodded *verb* **1** When you nod, you move your head up and down, usually to show agreement ▷ *noun* **2** a movement of

n

your head up and down > **nod off**
verb If you nod off, you fall asleep

noise noun a sound, especially one
that is loud or unpleasant

noisy noisier, noisiest adjective
making a lot of noise or full of noise:
a noisy crowd > **noisily** adverb
> **noisiness** noun

nomad noun a person who belongs
to a tribe which travels from place
to place rather than living in just
one place > **nomadic** adjective

nominal adjective **1** Something that
is nominal is supposed to have a
particular identity or status, but in
reality does not have it: the nominal
leader of his party **2** A nominal
amount of money is very small
compared to the value of
something: I am prepared to sell my
shares at a nominal price > **nominally**
adverb

nominate verb If you nominate
someone for a job or position, you
formally suggest that they have it
> **nomination** noun

non- prefix not: non-smoking

nonchalant [non-shal-nt] adjective
seeming calm and not worried
> **nonchalance** noun
> **nonchalantly** adverb

nondescript adjective Someone or
something nondescript has no
special or interesting qualities or
details: a nondescript coat

none pronoun not a single thing or
person, or not even a small amount
of something

nonfiction noun LIBRARY
Nonfiction is writing that gives facts
and information rather than telling
a story

nonplussed adjective confused and
unsure about how to react

nonsense noun Nonsense is foolish
and meaningless words or

behaviour > **nonsensical** adjective

nonstop adjective, adverb continuing
without any pauses or breaks:
nonstop excitement

noodle noun Noodles are a kind of
pasta shaped into long, thin pieces

nook noun (literary) a small sheltered
place

noon noun Noon is midday

no-one or **no one** pronoun not a
single person

noose noun a loop at the end of a
piece of rope, with a knot that
tightens when the rope is pulled

nor conjunction used after 'neither' or
after a negative statement, to add
something else that the negative
statement applies to: They had
neither the time nor the money for the
sport

norm noun If something is the norm,
it is the usual and expected thing:
cultures where large families are the
norm

normal adjective usual and ordinary:
I try to lead a normal life > **normality**
noun

normally adverb **1** usually: I don't
normally like dancing **2** in a way that
is normal: The foetus is developing
normally

north noun **1** The north is the
direction to your left when you are
looking towards the place where
the sun rises **2** The north of a place
or country is the part which is
towards the north when you are in
the centre ▷ adverb, adjective
3 North means towards the north:
The helicopter took off and headed
north ▷ adjective **4** A north wind
blows from the north

North America noun North
America is the third largest
continent, consisting of Canada,
the United States, and Mexico

> **North American** adjective

north-east noun, adverb, adjective
North-east is halfway between
north and east

north-eastern adjective in or from
the north-east

northerly adjective **1** Northerly
means to or towards the north:
travelling in a northerly direction
2 A northerly wind blows from the
north

northern adjective in or from the
north: the mountains of northern Italy

North Pole noun GEOGRAPHY The
North Pole is the most northerly
point of the earth's surface

northward or **northwards** adverb
1 Northward or northwards means
towards the north: We continued
northwards ▷ adjective **2** The
northward part of something is the
north part

north-west noun, adverb, adjective
North-west is halfway between
north and west

north-western adjective in or from
the north-west

Norwegian [nor-**wee**-jn] adjective
1 belonging or relating to Norway
▷ noun **2** someone who comes from
Norway **3** Norwegian is the main
language spoken in Norway

nose noun **1** the part of your face
above your mouth which you use for
smelling and breathing **2** the front
part of a car or plane

nostalgia [nos-**tal**-ja] noun
Nostalgia is a feeling of affection for
the past, and sadness that things
have changed ▷ **nostalgic** adjective

nostril noun Your nostrils are the
two openings in your nose which
you breathe through

nosy nosier, nosiest or **nosey**
adjective trying to find out about
things that do not concern you

not adverb used to make a sentence
negative, to refuse something, or to
deny something

notable adjective important or
interesting: The production is notable
for some outstanding performances
▷ **notably** adverb

notch noun a small V-shaped cut in a
surface

note noun **1** a short letter **2** a written
piece of information that helps you
to remember something: You should
make a note of that **3** In music, a note
is a musical sound of a particular
pitch, or a written symbol that
represents it **4** a banknote **5** an
atmosphere, feeling, or quality:
There was a note of regret in his voice;
I'm determined to close on an optimistic
note ▷ verb **6** If you note a fact, you
become aware of it or you mention
it: I noted that the rain had stopped
▷ phrase **7** If you **take note** of
something, you pay attention to it:
The world hardly took note of this crisis
> **note down** verb If you note
something down, you write it down
so that you will remember it

notebook noun a small book for
writing notes in

noted adjective well-known and
admired: a noted Hebrew scholar

nothing pronoun not anything: There
was nothing to do

notice verb **1** If you notice
something, you become aware of it
▷ noun **2** Notice is attention or
awareness: I'm glad he brought it to
my notice **3** a written announcement
4 Notice is also advance warning
about something: We were lucky to
get you at such short notice ▷ phrase
5 If you **hand in your notice**, you tell
your employer that you intend to
leave your job after a fixed period of
time

n

noticeable *adjective* obvious and easy to see: *a noticeable improvement* > **noticeably** *adverb*

noticeboard *noun* a board for notices

notify notifies, notifying, notified *verb* To notify someone of something means to officially inform them of it: *You must notify us of any change of address* > **notification** *noun*

notion *noun* an idea or belief

notorious *adjective* well-known for something bad: *The area has become notorious for violence against tourists* > **notoriously** *adverb* > **notoriety** *noun*

notwithstanding *preposition* (formal) in spite of: *Notwithstanding his age, Sikorski had an important job*

nought *noun* the number 0

noun *noun* ENGLISH A word which refers to a person, thing, or idea. Examples of nouns are 'president', 'table', 'sun', and 'beauty'

nourish [**nur**-rish] *verb* To nourish people or animals means to provide them with food

nourishing *adjective* Food that is nourishing makes you strong and healthy

nourishment *noun* Nourishment is food that your body needs in order to remain healthy: *poor nourishment*

novel *noun* 1 LIBRARY A book that tells an invented story > *adjective* 2 new and interesting: *a very novel experience*

novelist *noun* a person who writes novels

novelty novelties *noun* 1 Novelty is the quality of being new and interesting: *The novelty had worn off* 2 something new and interesting: *Steam power was still a bit of a novelty* 3 a small, unusual object sold as a gift or souvenir

November *noun* November is the eleventh month of the year. It has 30 days

novice *noun* 1 someone who is not yet experienced at something 2 someone who is preparing to become a monk or nun

now *adverb* 1 at the present time or moment ▷ *conjunction* 2 as a result or consequence of a particular fact: *Things have got better now there is a new board* ▷ *phrase* 3 **Just now** means very recently: *I drove Brenda back to the camp just now* 4 If something happens **now and then**, it happens sometimes but not regularly

nowadays *adverb* at the present time, in contrast with in the past: *Nowadays most fathers choose to be present at the birth*

nowhere *adverb* not anywhere

noxious [**nok**-shus] *adjective* harmful or poisonous: *a noxious gas*

nozzle *noun* a spout fitted onto the end of a pipe or hose to control the flow of a liquid

nuance [**nyoo**-ahnss] *noun* a small difference in sound, colour, or meaning: *the nuances of his music*

nuclear *adjective* SCIENCE relating to the energy produced when the nuclei of atoms are split: *nuclear power; the nuclear industry* 2 relating to weapons or bombs that explode using the energy released by atoms: *nuclear war* 3 SCIENCE relating to the structure and behaviour of the nuclei of atoms: *nuclear physics*

nuclear reactor *noun* A nuclear reactor is a device which is used to obtain nuclear energy

nucleus nuclei [nyoo-klee-uss] *noun* 1 SCIENCE The nucleus of an atom is the central part of it. It is positively charged and is made up of protons

N

and neutrons **2** SCIENCE The nucleus of a cell is the part that contains the chromosomes and controls the growth and reproduction of the cell **3** The nucleus of something is the basic central part of it to which other things are added: *They have retained the nucleus of the team that won the World Cup*

nude *adjective* **1** naked ▷ *noun* **2** a picture or statue of a naked person > **nudity** *noun*

nudge *verb* **1** If you nudge someone, you push them gently, usually with your elbow ▷ *noun* **2** a gentle push

nudist *noun* a person who believes in wearing no clothes

nugget *noun* a small rough lump of something, especially gold

nuisance *noun* someone or something that is annoying or inconvenient

null *phrase* **Null and void** means not legally valid: *Other documents were declared to be null and void*

numb *adjective* **1** unable to feel anything: *My legs felt numb; numb with grief* ▷ *verb* **2** If something numbs you, it makes you unable to feel anything: *The cold numbed my fingers*

number *noun* **1** a word or a symbol used for counting or calculating **2** Someone's number is the series of numbers that you use to telephone them **3** A number of things is a quantity of them: *Adrian has introduced me to a large number of people* **4** a song or piece of music ▷ *verb* **5** If things number a particular amount, there are that many of them: *At that time London's population numbered about 460,000* **6** If you number something, you give it a number: *The picture is signed and numbered by the artist* **7** To be numbered among a particular group means to belong to it: *Only the best are numbered among their champions*

numerical *adjective* expressed in numbers or relating to numbers: *a numerical value*

numerous *adjective* existing or happening in large numbers

nun *noun* a woman who has taken religious vows and lives in a convent

nurse *noun* **1** a person whose job is to look after people who are ill ▷ *verb* **2** If you nurse someone, you look after them when they are ill **3** If you nurse a feeling, you feel it strongly for a long time: *He nursed a grudge against the USA*

nursery *nurseries noun* **1** a place where young children are looked after while their parents are working **2** a room in which young children sleep and play **3** a place where plants are grown and sold

nursery school *noun* a school for children from three to five years old

nursing home *noun* a privately run hospital, especially for old people

nurture *verb (formal)* If you nurture a young child or a plant, you look after it carefully

nut *noun* **1** a fruit with a hard shell and an edible centre that grows on certain trees **2** a piece of metal with a hole in the middle which a bolt screws into

nutmeg *noun* Nutmeg is a spice used for flavouring in cooking

nutrient *noun* D&T Nutrients are substances that help plants or animals to grow: *the nutrients in the soil*

nutrition *noun* D&T Nutrition is the food that you eat, considered from the point of view of how it helps you to grow and remain healthy: *The effects of poor nutrition are evident* > **nutritional** *adjective* > **nutritionist** *noun*

nutritious *adjective* containing substances that help you to grow and remain healthy

nutty nuttier, nuttiest *adjective* 1 (*informal*) mad or very foolish 2 tasting of nuts

nylon *noun* 1 Nylon is a type of strong artificial material: *nylon stockings* 2 Nylons are stockings or tights

oak *noun* a large tree which produces acorns. It has a hard wood which is often used to make furniture

OAP *noun* In Britain, a person who receives a pension. OAP is an abbreviation for 'old age pensioner'

oar *noun* a wooden pole with a wide, flat end, used for rowing a boat

oasis oases [oh-**ay**-siss] *noun* a small area in a desert where water and plants are found

oat *noun* Oats are a type of grain

oath *noun* a formal promise, especially a promise to tell the truth in a court of law

oatmeal *noun* Oatmeal Is a rough flour made from oats

OBE *noun* a British honour awarded by the King or Queen. OBE is an abbreviation for 'Officer of the Order of the British Empire'

obedient *adjective* If you are obedient, you do what you are told to do > **obediently** *adverb* > **obedience** *noun*

obese [oh-**bees**] *adjective* extremely fat > **obesity** *noun*

obey *verb* If you obey a person or an order, you do what you are told to do

obituary obituaries *noun* a piece of writing about the life and achievements of someone who has just died

object [**ob**-ject] *noun* 1 anything solid that you can touch or see, and that is not alive 2 an aim or purpose 3 The object of your feelings or actions is the person that they are directed towards 4 In grammar, the object of a verb or preposition is the word or phrase which follows it and describes the person or thing affected > *verb* [ob-**ject**] 5 If you object to something, you dislike or disapprove of it

objection *noun* If you have an objection to something, you dislike or disapprove of it

objectionable *adjective* unpleasant and offensive

objective *noun* 1 an aim: *The protection of the countryside is their main objective* > *adjective* 2 If you are objective, you are not influenced by personal feelings or prejudices: *an objective approach* > **objectively** *adverb* > **objectivity** *noun*

obligation *noun* something that you must do because it is your duty

obligatory [ob-**lig**-a-tree] *adjective* required by a rule or law: *Religious education was made obligatory*

oblige *verb* 1 If you are obliged to do something, you have to do it 2 If you oblige someone, you help them > **obliging** *adjective*

oblique [o-**bleek**] adjective **1** An oblique remark is not direct, and is therefore difficult to understand **2** An oblique line slopes at an angle

obliterate verb To obliterate something is to destroy it completely > **obliteration** noun

oblivion noun Oblivion is unconsciousness or complete lack of awareness of your surroundings > **oblivious** adjective > **obliviously** adverb

oblong noun **1** a four-sided shape with two parallel short sides, two parallel long sides, and four right angles ▷ adjective **2** shaped like an oblong

obnoxious [ob-**nok**-shuss] adjective extremely unpleasant

oboe noun a woodwind musical instrument with a double reed > **oboist** noun

obscene adjective indecent and likely to upset people: obscene pictures > **obscenely** adverb > **obscenity** noun

obscure adjective **1** Something that is obscure is known by only a few people: an obscure Mongolian dialect **2** Something obscure is difficult to see or to understand: The news was shrouded in obscure language ▷ verb **3** To obscure something is to make it difficult to see or understand: His view was obscured by trees > **obscurity** noun

observance noun The observance of a law or custom is the practice of obeying or following it

observant adjective Someone who is observant notices things that are not easy to see

observation noun **1** Observation is the act of watching something carefully: Success hinges on close observation **2** something that you

have seen or noticed **3** a remark **4** Observation is the ability to notice things that are not easy to see

observatory observatories noun a room or building containing telescopes and other equipment for studying the sun, moon, and stars

observe verb **1** To observe something is to watch it carefully **2** To observe something is to notice it **3** If you observe that something is the case, you make a comment about it **4** To observe a law or custom is to obey or follow it > **observer** noun > **observable** adjective

obsession noun If someone has an obsession about something, they cannot stop thinking about that thing > **obsessional** adjective > **obsessed** adjective > **obsessive** adjective

obsolete adjective out of date and no longer used

obstacle noun something which is in your way and makes it difficult to do something

obstetrician noun An obstetrician is a doctor who specializes in the care of women during pregnancy and childbirth

obstetrics noun Obstetrics is the branch of medicine concerned with pregnancy and childbirth

obstinate adjective Someone who is obstinate is stubborn and unwilling to change their mind > **obstinately** adverb > **obstinacy** noun

obstruct verb If something obstructs a road or path, it blocks it > **obstruction** noun > **obstructive** adjective

obtain verb If you obtain something, you get it > **obtainable** adjective

obtuse adjective **1** Someone who is obtuse is stupid or slow to understand things **2** MATHS An obtuse angle is an angle between 90° and 180°

obvious adjective easy to see or understand ▷ **obviously** adverb

occasion noun **1** a time when something happens **2** an important event **3** An occasion for doing something is an opportunity for doing it ▷ verb **4** (formal) To occasion something is to cause it: damage occasioned by fire

occasional adjective happening sometimes but not often: an occasional outing ▷ **occasionally** adverb

occult noun The occult is the knowledge and study of supernatural and magical forces or powers

occupancy noun The occupancy of a building is the act of living or working in it

occupant noun The occupants of a building are the people who live or work in it

occupation noun **1** a job or profession **2** a hobby or something you do for pleasure **3** The occupation of a country is the act of invading it and taking control of it ▷ **occupational** adjective

occupy occupies, occupying, occupied verb **1** The people who occupy a building are the people who live or work there **2** When people occupy a place, they move into it and take control of it **3** To occupy a position in a system or plan is to have that position. His phone-in show occupies a daytime slot **4** If something occupies you, you spend your time doing it: That problem occupies me night and day ▷ **occupier** noun

occur occurs, occurring, occurred verb **1** If something occurs, it happens or exists: The second attack occurred at a swimming pool **2** If something occurs to you, you suddenly think of it

occurrence noun **1** an event **2** The occurrence of something is the fact that it happens or exists: the occurrence of diseases

ocean noun **1** the sea **2** The five oceans are the five very large areas of sea: the Atlantic Ocean ▷ **oceanic** adjective

o'clock adverb You use 'o'clock' after the number of the hour to say what the time is

octave noun **1** MUSIC the difference in pitch between the first note and the eighth note of a musical scale **2** ENGLISH eight lines of poetry together

October noun October is the tenth month of the year. It has 31 days

octopus octopuses noun a sea creature with eight long tentacles which it uses to catch food

odd adjective **1** Something odd is strange or unusual **2** Odd things do not match each other: odd socks **3** Odd numbers are numbers that cannot be divided exactly by two ▷ adverb **4** You use 'odd' after a number to say that it is approximate: I've written twenty odd plays ▷ **oddly** adverb ▷ **oddness** noun

oddity oddities noun something very strange

ode noun ENGLISH a poem written in praise of someone or something

odious adjective extremely unpleasant

odour noun (formal) a strong smell ▷ **odorous** adjective

odyssey [od-i-see] noun An odyssey

is a long and eventful journey. The name comes from Odysseus, the Greek hero who wandered from adventure to adventure for ten years

oesophagus oesophaguses [ee-**sof**-fag-uss] *noun* the tube that carries food from your throat to your stomach

oestrogen another spelling of **estrogen**

of *preposition* **1** consisting of or containing: *a collection of short stories; a cup of tea* **2** used when naming something or describing a characteristic of something: *the city of Canberra; a woman of great power and influence* **3** belonging to or connected with: *a friend of Rachel; the cover of the book*

off *preposition, adverb* **1** indicating movement away from or out of a place: *They had just stepped off the plane; She got up and marched off* **2** indicating separation or distance from a place: *some islands off the coast of Australia; The whole crescent has been fenced off* **3** not working: *It was Frank's night off* ▷ *adverb, adjective* **4** not switched on: *He turned the radio off; the off switch* ▷ *adjective* **5** cancelled or postponed: *The concert was off* **6** Food that is off has gone sour or bad ▷ *preposition* **7** not liking or not using something: *He went right off alcohol*

offal *noun* Offal is liver, kidneys, and internal organs of animals, which can be eaten

offence *noun* **1** a crime: *a drink-driving offence* ▷ *phrase* **2** If something **gives offence**, it upsets people. If you **take offence**, you are upset by someone or something

offend *verb* **1** If you offend someone, you upset them **2** (*formal*) To offend

or to offend a law is to commit a crime > **offender** *noun*

offensive *adjective* **1** Something offensive is rude and upsetting: *offensive behaviour* **2** Offensive actions or weapons are used in attacking someone ▷ *noun* **3** an attack: *a full-scale offensive against the rebels* > **offensively** *adverb*

offer *verb* **1** If you offer something to someone, you ask them if they would like it ▷ *noun* **2** something that someone says they will give you or do for you if you want them to: *He refused the offer of a drink* **3** a specially low price for a product in a shop: *You will need a voucher to qualify for the special offer*

offering *noun* something that is offered or given to someone

offhand *adjective* **1** If someone is offhand, they are unfriendly and slightly rude ▷ *adverb* **2** If you know something offhand, you know it without having to think very hard: *I couldn't tell you offhand how long he's been here*

office *noun* **1** a room where people work at desks **2** a government department: *the Office of Fair Trading* **3** a place where people can go for information, tickets, or other services **4** Someone who holds office has an important job or position in government or in an organization

officer *noun* a person with a position of authority in the armed forces, the police, or a government organization

official *adjective* **1** approved by the government or by someone in authority: *the official figures* **2** done or used by someone in authority as part of their job: *official notepaper* ▷ *noun* **3** a person who holds a position of authority in an organization ▷ **officially** adverb

officialdom noun You can refer to officials in government or other organizations as officialdom, especially when you find them difficult to deal with

officiate verb To officiate at a ceremony is to be in charge and perform the official part of the ceremony

offing phrase If something is **in the offing**, it is likely to happen soon: *A change is in the offing*

off-licence noun a shop which sells alcoholic drinks

offline adjective **1** If a computer is offline, it is switched off or not connected to the internet ▷ adverb **2** If you do something offline, you do it when not connected to the internet

offset offsets, offsetting, offset verb If one thing is offset by another thing, its effect is reduced or cancelled out by that thing: *This tedium can be offset by watching the television*

offshoot noun something that has developed from another thing: *The technology we use is an offshoot of the motor industry*

offshore adjective, adverb in or from the part of the sea near the shore: *an offshore wind; a wreck fifteen kilometres offshore*

offside adjective **1** If a soccer, rugby, or hockey player is offside, they have broken the rules by moving too far forward ▷ noun **2** the side of a vehicle that is furthest from the pavement

offspring noun A person's or animal's offspring are their children

often adverb happening many times or a lot of the time

ogre [**oh**-gur] noun a cruel, frightening giant in a fairy story

oil noun **1** Oil is a thick, sticky liquid used as a fuel and for lubrication **2** Oil is also a thick, greasy liquid made from plants or animals: *cooking oil; bath oil* ▷ verb **3** If you oil something, you put oil in it or on it

oil painting noun An oil painting is a painting that has been painted with oil paints

oily adjective Something that is oily is covered with or contains oil: *an oily rag; oily skin*

ointment noun a smooth, thick substance that you put on sore skin to heal it

okay or **OK** adjective (informal) Okay means all right: *Tell me if this sounds okay*

old adjective **1** having lived or existed for a long time: *an old lady; old clothes* **2** 'Old' is used to give the age of someone or something: *This photo is five years old* **3** 'Old' also means former: *my old art teacher*

olden phrase **In the olden days** means long ago

Old English noun Old English was the English language from the fifth century AD until about 1100. Old English is also known as Anglo-Saxon

old-fashioned adjective **1** Something which is old-fashioned is no longer fashionable: *old-fashioned shoes* **2** Someone who is old-fashioned believes in the values and standards of the past

Old Testament The Old Testament is the first part of the Christian Bible. It is also the holy book of the Jewish religion and contains writings which relate to the history of the Jews

olive noun **1** a small green or black

fruit containing a stone. Olives are usually pickled and eaten as a snack or crushed to produce oil ▷ adjective, noun **2** dark yellowish-green

-ology suffix '-ology' is used to form words that refer to the study of something: biology; geology

Olympic Games [ol-**lim**-pik] plural noun The Olympic Games are a set of sporting contests held in a different city every four years. It originated in Ancient Greece where a contest was regularly held in Olympia to honour the god Zeus

ombudsman noun The ombudsman is a person who investigates complaints against the government or a public organization

omelette [**om**-lit] noun a dish made by beating eggs together and cooking them in a flat pan

omen noun something that is thought to be a sign of what will happen in the future: John saw this success as a good omen for his trip

ominous adjective suggesting that something unpleasant is going to happen: an ominous sign
> **ominously** adverb

omission noun **1** something that has not been included or done: There are some striking omissions in the survey **2** Omission is the act of not including or not doing something: controversy over the omission of female novelists

omit omits, omitting, omitted verb **1** If you omit something, you do not include it **2** (formal) If you omit to do something, you do not do it

omnibus omnibuses noun **1** a book containing a collection of stories or articles by the same author or about the same subject ▷ adjective **2** An omnibus edition of a radio or

television show contains two or more programmes that were originally broadcast separately

omnipotent [om-**nip**-a-tent] adjective having very great or unlimited power: omnipotent emperors > **omnipotence** noun

on preposition **1** above and supported by, touching, or attached to something: The woman was sitting on the sofa **2** If you are on a bus, plane, or train, you are inside it **3** If something happens on a particular day, that is when it happens: It is his birthday on Monday **4** If something is done on an instrument or machine, it is done using that instrument or machine: He preferred to play on his computer **5** A book or talk on a particular subject is about that subject ▷ adverb **6** If you have a piece of clothing on, you are wearing it ▷ adjective **7** A machine or switch that is on is working **8** If an event is on, it is happening or taking place: The race is definitely on

once adverb **1** If something happens once, it happens one time only **2** If something was once true, it was true in the past, but is no longer true ▷ conjunction **3** If something happens once another thing has happened, it happens immediately afterwards: Once you get used to working for yourself, it's tough working for anybody else ▷ phrase **4** If you do something **at once**, you do it immediately. If several things happen **at once**, they all happen at the same time

one 1 One is the number 1 ▷ adjective **2** If you refer to the one person or thing of a particular kind, you mean the only person or thing of that kind: My one aim is to look after the horses well **3** One also means 'a', used when emphasizing something: *They got one almighty shock* ▷ *pronoun* **4** One refers to a particular thing or person: *Alf Brown's business was a good one* **5** One also means people in general: *One likes to have the opportunity to chat*

one-off *noun* something that happens or is made only once

onerous [ohn-er-uss] *adjective* (formal) difficult or unpleasant: *an onerous task*

oneself *pronoun* 'Oneself' is used when you are talking about people in general: *One could hardly hear oneself talk*

one-sided *adjective* **1** If an activity or relationship is one-sided, one of the people has a lot more success or involvement than the other: *a one-sided contest* **2** A one-sided argument or report considers the facts or a situation from only one point of view

one-way *adjective* **1** One-way streets are streets along which vehicles can drive in only one direction **2** A one-way ticket is one that you can use to travel to a place, but not to travel back again

ongoing *adjective* continuing to happen: *an ongoing process of learning*

onion *noun* a small, round vegetable with a brown skin like paper and a very strong taste

online *adjective* **1** If a computer is online, it is switched on or connected to the internet ▷ *adverb* **2** If you do something online, you do it while connected to the internet

onlooker *noun* someone who is watching an event

only *adverb* **1** You use 'only' to indicate the one person or thing involved: *Only Keith knows whether he will continue* **2** You use 'only' to

emphasize that something is unimportant or small: *He's only a little boy* **3** You can use 'only' to introduce something which happens immediately after something else: *She had thought of one plan, only to discard it for another* ▷ *adjective* **4** If you talk about the only thing or person, you mean that there are no others: *their only hit single* **5** If you are an only child, you have no brothers or sisters ▷ *conjunction* **6** 'Only' also means but or except: *He was like you, only blond* ▷ *phrase* **7** Only too means extremely: *I would be only too happy to swap places*

onset *noun* The onset of something unpleasant is the beginning of it: *the onset of war*

onslaught [on-slawt] *noun* a violent attack

onto or **on to** *preposition* If you put something onto an object, you put it on it

onus [rhymes with **bonus**] *noun* (formal) If the onus is on you to do something, it is your duty or responsibility to do it

onwards or **onward** *adverb* **1** continuing to happen from a particular time: *He could not speak a word from that moment onwards* **2** travelling forwards: *Duncliffe escorted the pair onwards to his own room*

ooze *verb* When a thick liquid oozes, it flows slowly: *The cold mud oozed over her new footwear*

opal *noun* a pale or whitish semiprecious stone used for making jewellery

opaque [oh-pake] *adjective* If something is opaque, you cannot see through it: *opaque glass windows*

open *verb* **1** When you open

something, or when it opens, you move it so that it is no longer closed: *She opened the door* **2** When a shop or office opens, people are able to go in **3** To open something also means to start it: *He tried to open a bank account* ▷ *adjective* **4** Something that is open is not closed or fastened: *an open box of chocolates* **5** If you have an open mind, you are willing to consider new ideas or suggestions **6** Someone who is open is honest and frank **7** When a shop or office is open, people are able to go in **8** An open area of sea or land is a large, empty area: *open country* **9** If something is open to you, it is possible for you to do it: *There is no other course open to us but to fight it out* **10** If a situation is still open, it is still being considered: *Even if the case remains open, the full facts may never be revealed* ▷ *phrase* **11** In the open means outside **12** In the open also means not secret ▷ **openly** *adverb*

opening *adjective* **1** Opening means coming first: *the opening day of the season* ▷ *noun* **2** The opening of a book or film is the first part of it **3** a hole or gap **4** an opportunity: *The two men circled around, looking for an opening to attack*

open-minded *adjective* willing to consider new ideas and suggestions

open-plan *adjective* An open-plan office or building has very few dividing walls inside

opera *noun* a play in which the words are sung rather than spoken ▷ **operatic** *adjective*

operate *verb* **1** To operate is to work: *We are shocked at the way that businesses operate* **2** When you operate a machine, you make it work **3** When surgeons operate,

they cut open a patient's body to remove or repair a damaged part

operation *noun* **1** a complex planned event: *a full-scale military operation* **2** a form of medical treatment in which a surgeon cuts open a patient's body to remove or repair a damaged part **3** MATHS any process in which a number or quantity is operated on according to a set of rules, for example addition, subtraction, multiplication, and division ▷ *phrase* **4** If something is in operation, it is working or being used: *The system is in operation from April to the end of September*

operational *adjective* working or able to be used: *an operational aircraft*

operative *adjective* Something that is operative is working or having an effect

operator *noun* **1** someone who works at a telephone exchange or on a switchboard **2** someone who operates a machine: *a computer operator* **3** someone who runs a business: *a factory operator*

opinion *noun* a belief or view

opinionated *adjective* Someone who is opinionated has strong views and refuses to accept that they might be wrong

opium *noun* Opium is a drug made from the seeds of a poppy. It is used in medicine to relieve pain

opponent *noun* someone who is against you in an argument or a contest

opportune *adjective* (formal) happening at a convenient time: *The king's death was opportune for the prince*

opportunism *noun* Opportunism is taking advantage of any opportunity to gain money or power for yourself ▷ **opportunist** noun

opportunity opportunities noun a chance to do something

oppose verb If you oppose something, you disagree with it and try to prevent it

opposed adjective **1** If you are opposed to something, you disagree with it: *He was totally opposed to bullying in schools* **2** Opposed also means opposite or very different: *two opposed schools of thought* ▷ phrase **3** If you refer to one thing **as opposed to** another, you are emphasizing that it is the first thing rather than the second which concerns you: *Real spectators, as opposed to invited guests, were hard to spot*

opposite preposition, adverb **1** If one thing is opposite another, it is facing it: *the shop opposite the station;* *the house opposite* ▷ adjective **2** The opposite part of something is the part farthest away from you: *the opposite side of town* **3** If things are opposite, they are completely different: *I take the opposite view to you* ▷ noun **4** If two things are completely different, they are opposites

opposition noun **1** If there is opposition to something, people disagree with it and try to prevent it **2** The political parties who are not in power are referred to as the Opposition **3** In a game or sports event, the opposition is the person or team that you are competing against

oppressed adjective People who are oppressed are treated cruelly or unfairly ▷ **oppress** verb ▷ **oppressor** noun

oppression noun cruel and unfair

treatment of people

oppressive adjective **1** If the weather is oppressive, it is hot and humid **2** An oppressive situation makes you feel depressed or concerned: *The silence became oppressive* **3** An oppressive system treats people cruelly or unfairly: *Married women were subject to oppressive laws* ▷ **oppressively** adverb

opt verb If you opt for something, you choose it. If you opt out of something, you choose not to be involved in it

optical adjective **1** SCIENCE concerned with vision, light, or images **2** relating to the appearance of things

optician noun someone who tests people's eyes, and makes and sells glasses and contact lenses

optimism noun Optimism is a feeling of hopefulness about the future ▷ **optimist** noun

optimistic adjective hopeful about the future ▷ **optimistically** adverb

optimum adjective the best that is possible: *Six is the optimum number of participants for a good meeting*

option noun a choice between two or more things ▷ **optional** adjective

opulent [op-yool-nt] adjective grand and expensive-looking: *an opulent seafront estate* ▷ **opulence** noun

opus opuses or opera noun **1** MUSIC An opus is a musical composition. 'Opus' is often used with a number, indicating its position in a series of published works by the same composer **2** ART An opus is also a great artistic work, such as a piece of writing or a painting

or conjunction **1** used to link two different things: *I didn't know whether to laugh or cry* **2** used to introduce a

warning: *Do what I say or else I will fire*
-or *suffix* '-or' is used to form nouns
from verbs: *actor; conductor*
oracle *noun* **1** In ancient Greece, an
oracle was a place where a priest or
priestess made predictions about
the future **2** a prophecy made by a
priest or other person with great
authority or wisdom
oral *adjective* **1** spoken rather than
written: *oral history* **2** Oral describes
things that are used in your mouth
or done with your mouth: *an oral
vaccine* **3** an examination
that is spoken rather than written
> **orally** *adverb*
orange *noun* **1** a round citrus fruit
that is juicy and sweet and has a
thick reddish-yellow skin ▷ *adjective*,
noun **2** reddish-yellow
orang-utan *or* **orang-utang** *noun*
An orang-utan is a large ape with
reddish-brown hair. Orang-utans
come from the forests of Borneo
and Sumatra
orator *noun* someone who is good
at making speeches
oratory *noun* Oratory is the art and
skill of making formal public
speeches
orbit *noun* **1** the curved path
followed by an object going round a
planet or the sun ▷ *verb* **2** If
something orbits a planet or the
sun, it goes round and round it
orchard *noun* a piece of land where
fruit trees are grown
orchestra [or-kess-tra] *noun* MUSIC
a large group of musicians who play
musical instruments together
> **orchestral** *adjective*
orchestrate *verb* **1** To orchestrate
something is to organize it very
carefully in order to produce a
particular result **2** To orchestrate a
piece of music is to rewrite it so that

it can be played by an orchestra
> **orchestration** *noun*
orchid [or-kid] *noun* Orchids are
plants with beautiful and unusual
flowers
ordain *verb* When someone is
ordained, they are made a member
of the clergy
ordeal *noun* a difficult and extremely
unpleasant experience: *the ordeal of
being arrested and charged with
attempted murder*
order *noun* **1** a command given by
someone in authority **2** If things are
arranged or done in a particular
order, they are arranged or done in
that sequence: *in alphabetical order*
3 Order is a situation in which
everything is in the correct place or
done at the correct time
4 something that you ask to be
brought to you or sent to you
5 SCIENCE An order is a division of
living organisms that is smaller than
a class and larger than a family
▷ *verb* **6** To order someone to do
something is to tell them firmly to
do it **7** When you order something,
you ask for it to be brought or sent
to you ▷ *phrase* **8** If you do
something **in order to** achieve a
particular thing, you do it because
you want to achieve that thing
orderly *adjective* Something that is
orderly is well organized or arranged
ordinarily *adverb* If something
ordinarily happens, it usually
happens
ordinary *adjective* Ordinary means
not special or different in any way
ordination *noun* When someone's
ordination takes place, they are
made a member of the clergy
ordnance *noun* Weapons and other
military supplies are referred to as
ordnance

o

ore noun Ore is rock or earth from which metal can be obtained

oregano [or-rig-**gah**-no] noun Oregano is a herb used for flavouring in cooking

organ noun 1 Your organs are parts of your body that have a particular function, for example your heart or lungs 2 a large musical instrument with pipes of different lengths through which air is forced. It has various keyboards and is played like a piano

organic adjective 1 Something that is organic is produced by or found in plants or animals: decaying organic matter 2 Organic food is produced without the use of artificial fertilizers or pesticides
> **organically** adverb

organism noun SCIENCE any living animal, plant, fungus, or bacterium

organist noun someone who plays the organ

organization or **organisation** noun 1 any group or business 2 The organization of something is the act of planning and arranging it
> **organizational** adjective

organize or **organise** verb 1 If you organize an event, you plan and arrange it 2 If you organize things, you arrange them in a sensible order
> **organized** adjective > **organizer** noun

orgy orgies [or-jee] noun You can refer to a period of intense activity as an orgy of that activity: an orgy of violence

Orient noun (literary) The Orient is eastern and south-eastern Asia

oriental adjective relating to eastern or south-eastern Asia

orientated adjective If someone is interested in a particular thing, you can say that they are orientated towards it: These people are very career-orientated

orientation noun You can refer to an organization's activities and aims as its orientation: Poland's political and military orientation

oriented adjective Oriented means the same as orientated

orienteering noun Orienteering is a sport in which people run from one place to another in the countryside, using a map and compass to guide them

origin noun 1 You can refer to the beginning or cause of something as its origin or origins 2 You can refer to someone's family background as their origin or origins: She was of Swedish origin

original adjective 1 Original describes things that existed at the beginning, rather than being added later, or things that were the first of their kind to exist: the original owner of the cottage 2 Original means imaginative and clever: a stunningly original idea ▷ noun 3 a work of art or a document that is the one that was first produced, and not a copy
> **originally** adverb > **originality** noun

originate verb When something originates, or you originate it, it begins to happen or exist
> **originator** noun

ornament noun a small, attractive object that you display in your home or that you wear in order to look attractive

ornamental adjective designed to be attractive rather than useful: an ornamental lake

ornate adjective Something that is ornate has a lot of decoration on it

orphan noun 1 a child whose parents are dead ▷ verb 2 If a child is orphaned, its parents die

orphanage noun a place where orphans are looked after

orthodox adjective **1** Orthodox beliefs or methods are the ones that most people have or use and that are considered standard **2** People who are orthodox believe in the older, more traditional ideas of their religion or political party **3** The Orthodox Church is the part of the Christian Church which separated from the western European Church in the 11th century and is the main church in Greece and Russia
> **orthodoxy** noun

osmosis [oz-moh-siss] noun [SCIENCE] Osmosis is the process by which a liquid moves through a semipermeable membrane from a weaker solution to a more concentrated one

osprey [oss-pree] noun a large bird of prey which catches fish with its feet

ostensibly adverb If something is done ostensibly for a reason, that seems to be the reason for it: Byrnes submitted his resignation, ostensibly on medical grounds

ostentatious adjective **1** Something that is ostentatious is intended to impress people, for example by looking expensive: ostentatious sculptures **2** People who are ostentatious try to impress other people with their wealth or importance > **ostentatiously** adverb > **ostentation** noun

ostrich noun The ostrich is the largest bird in the world. Ostriches cannot fly

other adjective, pronoun **1** Other people or things are different people or things: All the other children had gone home; One of the cabinets came from the palace; the other is a copy ▷ phrase **2** The other day or the other week means recently: She had bought four pairs of shoes the other day

otherwise adverb **1** You use 'otherwise' to say a different situation would exist if a particular fact or occurrence was not the case: You had to learn to swim pretty quickly, otherwise you sank **2** 'Otherwise' means apart from the thing mentioned: She had written to her daughter, but otherwise refused to take sides **3** 'Otherwise' also means in a different way: The majority voted otherwise

otter noun a small, furry animal with a long tail. Otters swim well and eat fish

ought [awt] verb If you say that someone ought to do something, you mean that they should do it: He ought to see a doctor

ounce noun a unit of weight equal to one sixteenth of a pound or about 28.35 grams

our adjective 'Our' refers to something belonging or relating to the speaker or writer and one or more other people: We recently sold our house

ours pronoun 'Ours' refers to something belonging or relating to the speaker or writer and one or more other people: a friend of ours from Korea

ourselves pronoun **1** 'Ourselves' is used when the same speaker or writer and one or more other people do an action and are affected by it: We haven't damaged ourselves too badly **2** 'Ourselves' is used to emphasize 'we'

oust verb If you oust someone, you force them out of a job or a place: Cole was ousted from the board

out adverb **1** towards the outside of a place: *Two dogs rushed out of the house* **2** not at home: *She was out when I rang last night* **3** in the open air: *They are playing out in bright sunshine* **4** no longer shining or burning: *The lights went out* ▷ adjective **5** on strike: *1000 construction workers are out in sympathy* **6** unacceptable or unfashionable: *Miniskirts are out* **7** incorrect: *Logan's timing was out in the first two rounds*

out-and-out adjective entire or complete: *an out-and-out lie*

outback noun In Australia, the outback is the remote parts where very few people live

outbreak noun If there is an outbreak of something unpleasant, such as war, it suddenly occurs

outburst noun **1** a sudden, strong expression of an emotion, especially anger: *John broke into an angry outburst about how unfairly the work was divided* **2** a sudden occurrence of violent activity: *an outburst of gunfire*

outcast noun someone who is rejected by other people

outcome noun a result: *the outcome of the election*

outcrop noun a large piece of rock that sticks out of the ground

outcry noun outcries If there is an outcry about something, a lot of people are angry about it: *a public outcry over alleged fraud*

outdated adjective no longer in fashion

outdo outdoes, outdoing, outdid, outdone verb If you outdo someone, you do a particular thing better than they do

outdoor adjective happening or used outside: *outdoor activities*

outdoors adverb outside: *It was too chilly to sit outdoors*

outer adjective The outer parts of something are the parts furthest from the centre: *the outer door of the office*

outer space noun Outer space is everything beyond the earth's atmosphere

outfit noun **1** a set of clothes **2** (*informal*) an organization

outgoing adjective **1** Outgoing describes someone who is leaving a job or place: *the outgoing President* **2** Someone who is outgoing is friendly and not shy

outgrow outgrows, outgrowing, outgrew, outgrown verb **1** If you outgrow a piece of clothing, you grow too big for it **2** If you outgrow a way of behaving, you stop it because you have grown older and more mature

outhouse noun a small building in the grounds of a house to which it belongs

outing noun a trip made for pleasure

outlandish adjective very unusual or odd: *outlandish clothes*

outlaw verb **1** If something is outlawed, it is made illegal ▷ noun **2** In the past, an outlaw was a criminal

outlay noun an amount of money spent on something: *a cash outlay of $300*

outlet noun **1** An outlet for your feelings or ideas is a way of expressing them **2** a hole or pipe through which water or air can flow away **3** a shop which sells goods made by a particular manufacturer

outline verb **1** If you outline a plan or idea, you explain it in a general way **2** You say that something is outlined when you can see its shape because there is a light behind it ▷ noun **3** a general explanation or description

of something **4** The outline of
something is its shape

outlive verb To outlive someone is to
live longer than they do

outlook noun **1** Your outlook is your
general attitude towards life **2** The
outlook of a situation is the way it is
likely to develop: The Japanese
economy's outlook is uncertain

outlying adjective Outlying places
are far from cities

outmoded adjective old-fashioned
and no longer useful: an outmoded
form of transport

outnumber verb If there are more of
one group than of another, the first
group outnumbers the second

out of preposition **1** If you do
something out of a particular
feeling, you are motivated by that
feeling: Out of curiosity she went along
2 'Out of' also means from: old
instruments made out of wood **3** If you
are out of something, you no longer
have any of it: I do hope we're not out
of fuel again **4** If you are out of the
rain, sun, or wind, you are sheltered
from it **5** You also use 'out of' to
indicate proportion. For example,
one out of five means one in every
five

out of date adjective old-fashioned
and no longer useful

outpatient noun Outpatients are
people who receive treatment in
hospital without staying overnight

outpost noun a small collection of
buildings a long way from a main
centre: a remote mountain outpost

output noun **1** Output is the amount
of something produced by a person
or organization **2** COMPUTING The
output of a computer is the
information that it produces

outrage verb **1** If something
outrages you, it angers and shocks

you: I was outraged at what had
happened to her ▷ noun **2** Outrage is a
feeling of anger and shock
3 something very shocking or
violent ▷ **outrageous** adjective
▷ **outrageously** adverb

outright adjective **1** absolute: an
outright rejection ▷ adverb **2** in an
open and direct way: Have you asked
him outright? **3** completely and
totally: I own the company outright

outset noun The outset of
something is the beginning of it: the
outset of his journey

outshine verb outshines, outshining,
outshone If you outshine
someone, you perform better than
they do

outside noun **1** The outside of
something is the part which
surrounds or encloses the rest of it
▷ preposition **2** on or to the exterior
of: outside the house **3** Outside also
means not included in something:
outside office hours ▷ adjective
4 Outside means not inside: an
outside toilet ▷ adverb **5** out of doors

outsider noun **1** someone who does
not belong to a particular group **2** a
competitor considered unlikely to
win in a race

outsize or **outsized** adjective much
larger than usual: outsize feet

outskirts plural noun The outskirts
of a city or town are the parts
around the edge of it

outspoken adjective Outspoken
people give their opinions openly,
even if they shock other people

outstanding adjective **1** extremely
good: The collection contains hundreds
of outstanding works of art **2** Money
that is outstanding is still owed: an
outstanding mortgage of 46,000
pounds

outstretched adjective If your arms

are outstretched, they are stretched out as far as possible

outstrip outstrips, outstripping, outstripped verb If one thing outstrips another thing, it becomes bigger or more successful or moves faster than the other thing

outward adjective, adverb 1 Outward means away from a place or towards the outside: *the outward journey* ▷ adjective 2 The outward features of someone are the ones they appear to have, rather than the ones they actually have: *He never showed any outward signs of emotion* > **outwardly** adverb

outwards adverb away from a place or towards the outside: *The door opened outwards*

outweigh verb If you say that the advantages of something outweigh its disadvantages, you mean that the advantages are more important than the disadvantages

outwit outwits, outwitting, outwitted verb If you outwit someone, you use your intelligence to defeat them

oval noun 1 a round shape, similar to a circle but wider in one direction than the other ▷ adjective 2 shaped like an oval: *an oval table*

ovary ovaries [**oh**-var-ee] noun A woman's ovaries are the two organs in her body that produce eggs

ovation noun a long burst of applause

oven noun the part of a cooker that you use for baking or roasting food

over preposition 1 Over something means directly above it or covering it: *the picture over the fireplace; He put his hands over his eyes* 2 A view over an area is a view across that area: *The pool and terrace look out over the sea* 3 If something is over a road or river, it is on the opposite side of the

road or river 4 Something that is over a particular amount is more than that amount 5 'Over' indicates a topic which is causing concern: *An American was arguing over the bill* 6 If something happens over a period of time, it happens during that period: *I went to New Zealand over Christmas* ▷ adverb, preposition 7 If you lean over, you bend your body in a particular direction: *He bent over and rummaged in a drawer; She was hunched over her keyboard* ▷ adverb 8 'Over' is used to indicate a position: *over by the window; Come over here* 9 If something rolls or turns over, it is moved so that its other side is facing upwards: *He flipped over the envelope* ▷ adjective 10 Something that is over is completely finished ▷ phrase 11 All over a place means everywhere in that place: *studios all over America* ▷ noun 12 In cricket, an over is a set of six balls bowled by a bowler from the same end of the pitch

overall adjective 1 Overall means taking into account all the parts or aspects of something: *The overall quality of pupils' work had shown a marked improvement* ▷ adverb 2 taking into account all the parts of something: *Overall, things are not really too bad* ▷ noun 3 (in plural) Overalls are a piece of clothing that looks like trousers and a jacket combined. You wear overalls to protect your other clothes when you are working 4 An overall is a piece of clothing like a coat that you wear to protect your other clothes when you are working

overawed adjective If you are overawed by something, you are very impressed by it and a little afraid of it

overbearing *adjective* trying to dominate other people: *Mozart had a difficult relationship with his overbearing father*

overboard *adverb* If you fall overboard, you fall over the side of a ship into the water

overcast *adjective* If it is overcast, the sky is covered by cloud

overcoat *noun* a thick, warm coat

overcome overcomes, overcoming, overcame, overcome *verb* **1** If you overcome a problem or a feeling, you manage to deal with it or control it ▷ *adjective* **2** If you are overcome by a feeling, you feel it very strongly

overcrowded *adjective* If a place is overcrowded, there are too many things or people in it

overdo overdoes, overdoing, overdid, overdone *verb* If you overdo something, you do it too much or in an exaggerated way: *It is important never to overdo new exercises*

overdose *noun* a larger dose of a drug than is safe

overdraft *noun* an agreement with a bank that allows someone to spend more money than they have in their account

overdrawn *adjective* If someone is overdrawn, they have taken more money from their bank account than the account has in it

overdrive *noun* Overdrive is an extra, higher gear in a vehicle, which is used at high speeds to reduce engine wear and save fuel

overdue *adjective* If someone or something is overdue, they are late: *The payments are overdue*

overestimate *verb* If you overestimate something, you think that it is bigger, more important, or better than it really is: *We had*

overestimated his popularity

overflow overflows, overflowing, overflowed, overflown *verb* If a liquid overflows, it spills over the edges of its container. If a river overflows, it flows over its banks

overgrown *adjective* A place that is overgrown is covered with weeds because it has not been looked after: *an overgrown path*

overhang overhangs, overhanging, overhung *verb* If one thing overhangs another, it sticks out sideways above it or over it: *old trees whose branches overhang a footpath*

overhaul *verb* **1** If you overhaul something, you examine it thoroughly and repair any faults ▷ *noun* **2** If you give something an overhaul, you examine it and repair or improve it

overhead *adjective* **1** Overhead means above you: *overhead cables* ▷ *adverb* **2** Overhead means above you: *seagulls flying overhead*

overhear overhears, overhearing, overheard *verb* If you overhear someone's conversation, you hear what they are saying to someone else

overjoyed *adjective* extremely pleased: *Colm was overjoyed to see me*

overland *adjective, adverb* travelling across land rather than going by sea or air: *an overland trek to India; Wray was returning to England overland*

overlap overlaps, overlapping, overlapped *verb* If one thing overlaps another, one part of it covers part of the other thing

overload *verb* If you overload someone or something, you give them too much to do or to carry

overlook *verb* **1** If a building or window overlooks a place, it has a view over that place **2** If you overlook something, you ignore it or do not notice it

overly adverb excessively: *I'm not overly fond of jazz*

overnight adverb **1** for the duration of the night: *Further rain was forecast overnight* **2** suddenly: *Good players don't become bad ones overnight* ▷ adjective **3** during the night **4** sudden: *an overnight success* **5** for use when you go away for one or two nights: *an overnight bag*

overpower verb **1** If you overpower someone, you seize them despite their struggles, because you are stronger than them **2** If a feeling overpowers you, it affects you very strongly > **overpowering** adjective

overrate verb If you overrate something, you think that it is better or more important than it really is > **overrated** adjective

overreact verb If you overreact, you react in an extreme way

overriding adjective more important than anything else: *an overriding duty*

overrule verb To overrule a person or their decisions is to decide that their decisions are incorrect

overrun overruns, overrunning, overran, overrun verb **1** If an army overruns a country, it occupies it very quickly **2** If animals or plants overrun a place, they spread quickly over it **3** If an event overruns, it continues for longer than it was meant to

overseas adverb **1** abroad: *travelling overseas* ▷ adjective **2** abroad: *an overseas tour* **3** from abroad: *overseas students*

oversee oversees, overseeing, oversaw, overseen verb To oversee a job is to make sure it is done properly > **overseer** noun

overshadow verb If something is overshadowed, it is made unimportant by something else that is better or more important

oversight noun something which you forget to do or fail to notice

overstate verb If you overstate something, you exaggerate its importance

overstep oversteps, overstepping, overstepped phrase If you **overstep the mark**, you behave in an unacceptable way

overt adjective open and obvious: *overt signs of stress* > **overtly** adverb

overtake overtakes, overtaking, overtook, overtaken verb If you overtake someone, you pass them because you are moving faster than them

overthrow overthrows, overthrowing, overthrew, overthrown verb If a government is overthrown, it is removed from power by force

overtime noun **1** Overtime is time that someone works in addition to their normal working hours ▷ adverb **2** If someone works overtime, they do work in addition to their normal working hours

overtones plural noun If something has overtones of an emotion or attitude, it suggests it without showing it openly: *the political overtones of the trial*

overture noun **1** a piece of music that is the introduction to an opera or play **2** If you make overtures to someone, you approach them because you want to start a friendly or business relationship with them

overturn verb **1** To overturn something is to turn it upside down or onto its side **2** If someone overturns a legal decision, they change it by using their higher authority

overview *noun* a general understanding or description of a situation

overweight *adjective* too fat, and therefore unhealthy: *overweight businessmen*

overwhelm *verb* **1** If you are overwhelmed by something, it affects you very strongly: *The priest appeared overwhelmed by the news* **2** If one group of people overwhelms another, they gain complete control or victory over them
> **overwhelming** *adjective*
> **overwhelmingly** *adverb*

overwork *verb* If you overwork, you work too hard

overwrought [oh-ver-**rawt**] *adjective* extremely upset: *He didn't get angry or overwrought*

owe *verb* **1** If you owe someone money, they have lent it to you and you have not yet paid it back **2** If you owe a quality or skill to someone, they are responsible for giving it to you: *He owes his success to his mother* **3** If you say that you owe someone gratitude or loyalty, you mean that they deserve it from you

owl *noun* Owls are birds of prey that hunt at night. They have large eyes and short, hooked beaks

own *adjective* **1** If something is your own, it belongs to you or is associated with you: *She stayed in her own house* ▷ *verb* **2** If you own something, it belongs to you ▷ *phrase* **3** On your own means alone

owner *noun* The owner of something is the person it belongs to

ownership *noun* If you have ownership of something, you own

it: *He shared the ownership of a sailing dinghy*

ox *noun* Oxen are cattle which are used for carrying or pulling things

oxide *noun* a compound of oxygen and another chemical element

oxygen *noun* Oxygen is a chemical element in the form of a colourless gas. It makes up about 21 per cent of the earth's atmosphere. With an extremely small number of exceptions, living things need oxygen to live, and things cannot burn without it. Oxygen's atomic number is 8 and its symbol is O

oxymoron oxymora or oxymorons *noun* ENGLISH two words that contradict each other placed beside each other, for example 'deafening silence'

oyster *noun* Oysters are large, flat shellfish. Some oysters can be eaten, and others produce pearls

oz an abbreviation for 'ounce' or 'ounces'

ozone *noun* Ozone is a form of oxygen that is poisonous and has a strong smell. There is a layer of ozone high above the earth's surface

ozone layer *noun* The ozone layer is that part of the earth's atmosphere that protects living things from the harmful radiation of the sun

O

p

p 1 p is an abbreviation for 'pence' **2** is also a written abbreviation for 'page'. The plural is pp

pa noun In New Zealand, a Maori village or settlement

pace noun **1** The pace of something is the speed at which it moves or happens **2** a step; also used as a measurement of distance ▷ verb **3** If you pace up and down, you continually walk around because you are anxious or impatient

pacemaker noun a small electronic device put into someone's heart to control their heartbeat

Pacific [pas-**sif**-ik] noun The Pacific is the ocean separating North and South America from Asia and Australia

pacifist noun someone who is opposed to all violence and war > **pacifism** noun

pacify pacifies, pacifying, pacified verb If you pacify someone who is angry, you calm them

pack verb **1** If you pack, you put things neatly into a suitcase, bag, or box **2** If people pack into a place, it becomes crowded with them ▷ noun **3** a bag or rucksack carried on your back **4** a packet or collection of something: a pack of cigarettes **5** A pack of playing cards is a complete set **6** A pack of dogs or wolves is a group of them > **pack in** verb (informal) If you pack something in, you stop doing it > **pack up** verb

If you pack up your belongings, you put them in a bag because you are leaving

package noun **1** a small parcel **2** a set of proposals or offers presented as a whole: a package of beauty treatments > **packaged** adjective

packaging noun D G T Packaging is the container or wrapping in which an item is sold or sent

packed adjective very full: The church was packed with people

packet noun a thin cardboard box or paper container in which something is sold

pact noun a formal agreement or treaty

pad pads, padding, padded noun **1** a thick, soft piece of material **2** a number of pieces of paper fixed together at one end **3** The pads of an animal such as a cat or dog are the soft, fleshy parts on the bottom of its paws **4** a flat surface from which helicopters take off or rockets are launched ▷ verb **5** If you pad something, you put a pad inside it or over it to protect it or change its shape **6** If you pad around, you walk softly > **padding** noun

paddle noun **1** a short pole with a broad blade at one or both ends, used to move a small boat or a canoe ▷ verb **2** If someone paddles a boat, they move it using a paddle **3** If you paddle, you walk in shallow water

paddock noun a small field where horses are kept

paddy paddies noun A paddy or paddy field is an area in which rice is grown

padlock noun **1** a lock made up of a metal case with a U-shaped bar attached to it, which can be put through a metal loop and then closed. It is unlocked by turning a key in the lock on the case ▷ verb **2** If you padlock something, you lock it with a padlock

paediatrician [pee-dee-ya-**trish**-n] or **pediatrician** noun a doctor who specializes in treating children

paediatrics [pee-dee-**ya**-triks] or **pediatrics** noun Paediatrics is the area of medicine which deals with children's diseases ▷ **paediatric** adjective

pagan [**pay**-gan] adjective **1** involving beliefs and worship outside the main religions of the world: pagan myths and cults ▷ noun **2** someone who believes in a pagan religion ▷ **paganism** noun

page, pages, paging, paged noun **1** one side of one of the pieces of paper in a book or magazine; also the sheet of paper itself **2** In medieval times, a page was a young boy servant who was learning to be a knight ▷ verb **3** To page someone is to send a signal or message to a small electronic device which they are carrying

pageant [**paj**-jent] noun a grand, colourful show or parade

pail noun a bucket

pain noun **1** Pain is an unpleasant feeling of physical hurt **2** Pain is also an unpleasant feeling of deep unhappiness ▷ verb **3** If something pains you, it makes you very unhappy ▷ **painless** adjective ▷ **painlessly** adverb

painful adjective **1** causing emotional pain **2** causing physical pain ▷ **painfully** adverb

painkiller noun a drug that reduces or stops pain

painstaking adjective very careful and thorough: years of painstaking research

paint noun **1** [ART] Paint is a coloured liquid used to decorate buildings, or to make a picture ▷ verb **2** If you paint something or paint a picture of it, you make a picture of it using paint **3** [D & T] When you paint something such as a wall, you cover it with paint ▷ **painter** noun ▷ **painting** noun

pair noun **1** two things of the same type or that do the same thing: a pair of earrings **2** You use 'pair' when referring to certain objects which have two main matching parts: a pair of scissors ▷ verb **3** When people pair off, they become grouped in pairs **4** If you pair up with someone, you agree to do something together

Pakistani [pah-kiss-**tah**-nee] adjective **1** belonging or relating to Pakistan ▷ noun **2** someone who comes from Pakistan

pal noun (informal) a friend

palace noun a large, grand house, especially the official home of a king or queen

palatable adjective Palatable food tastes pleasant

palate [**pall**-lat] noun **1** the top of the inside of your mouth **2** Someone's palate is their ability to judge good food and wine: dishes to tempt every palate

pale adjective rather white and without much colour or brightness

Palestinian noun an Arab from the region formerly called Palestine situated between the River Jordan and the Mediterranean

palette noun [ART] a flat piece of wood on which an artist mixes colours

pall [rhymes with **fall**] verb **1** If something palls, it becomes less interesting or less enjoyable: This record palls after ten minutes ▷ noun

2 a thick cloud of smoke **3** a cloth covering a coffin

palm noun **1** A palm or palm tree is a tropical tree with no branches and a crown of long leaves **2** the flat surface of your hand which your fingers bend towards

palpable adjective obvious and easily sensed: Happiness was palpable in the air ▷ **palpably** adverb

paltry [pawl-tree] adjective A paltry sum of money is a very small amount

pamper verb If you pamper someone, you give them too much kindness and comfort

pamphlet noun (ENGLISH) a very thin book in paper covers giving information about something

pan pans, panning, panned noun **1** a round metal container with a long handle, used for cooking things in on top of a cooker ▷ verb **2** When a film camera pans, it moves in a wide sweep **3** (informal) To pan something is to criticize it strongly

panacea [pan-nass-see-ah] noun something that is supposed to cure everything

panache [pan-nash] noun Something that is done with panache is done confidently and stylishly

pancake noun a thin, flat piece of fried batter which can be served with savoury or sweet fillings

pancreas [pang-kree-ass] noun (SCIENCE) The pancreas is an organ in the body situated behind the stomach. It produces insulin and enzymes that help with digestion

panda noun A panda or giant panda is a large animal rather like a bear that lives in China. It has black fur with large patches of white

pandemonium [pan-dim-moan-ee-um] noun Pandemonium is a state of noisy confusion: scenes of pandemonium

pander verb If you pander to someone, you do everything they want

pane noun a sheet of glass in a window or door

panel noun **1** a small group of people who are chosen to do something: a panel of judges **2** a flat piece of wood that is part of a larger object: door panels **3** A control panel is a surface containing switches and instruments to operate a machine ▷ **panelled** adjective

panelling noun Panelling is rectangular pieces of wood covering an inside wall

pang noun a sudden strong feeling of sadness or pain

panic panics, panicking, panicked noun **1** Panic is a sudden overwhelming feeling of fear or anxiety ▷ verb **2** If you panic, you become so afraid or anxious that you cannot act sensibly

panorama noun an extensive view over a wide area of land: a fine panorama over the hills ▷ **panoramic** adjective

pant verb If you pant, you breathe quickly and loudly through your mouth

panther noun a large wild animal belonging to the cat family, especially the black leopard

pantomime noun a musical play, usually based on a fairy story and performed at Christmas

pantry pantries noun a small room where food is kept

pants plural noun **1** Pants are a piece of underwear with holes for your legs and elastic around the waist or hips **2** In American English, pants are trousers

papaya noun a fruit with sweet yellow flesh that grows in the West Indies and tropical Australia

paper noun **1** Paper is a material made from wood pulp and used for writing on or wrapping things **2** a newspaper **3** (in plural) Papers are official documents, for example a passport for identification **4** part of a written examination ▷ verb **5** If you paper a wall, you put wallpaper on it

paperback noun a book with a thin cardboard cover

paperwork noun Paperwork is the part of a job that involves dealing with letters and records

paprika noun Paprika is a red powder made from a kind of pepper

par phrase **1** Something that is **on a par** with something else is similar in quality or amount: *This match was on a par with the German Cup Final* **2** Something that is **below par** or **under par** is below its normal standard ▷ noun **3** In golf, par is the number of strokes which it is thought a good player should take for a hole or all the holes on a particular golf course

parable noun RE a short story which makes a moral or religious point

parachute [**par**-rash-oot] noun a circular piece of fabric attached by lines to a person or package so that they can fall safely to the ground from an aircraft

parade noun **1** a line of people or vehicles standing or moving together as a display ▷ verb **2** When people parade, they walk together in a group as a display

Paradise noun According to some religions, Paradise is a wonderful place where good people go when they die

paradox noun something that contains two ideas that seem to contradict each other: *The paradox of exercise is that while you use a lot of energy, it seems to generate more*
> **paradoxical** adjective

paraffin noun Paraffin is a strong-smelling liquid which is used as a fuel

paragon noun someone whose behaviour is perfect in some way: *a paragon of elegance*

paragraph noun ENGLISH a section of a piece of writing. Paragraphs begin on a new line

parallel noun **1** Something that is a parallel to something else has similar qualities or features to it ▷ adjective **2** MATHS If two lines are parallel, they are the same distance apart along the whole of their length

paralyse verb If something paralyses you, it causes loss of feeling and movement in your body

paralysis [par-**ral**-liss-iss] noun Paralysis is loss of the power to move

paramedic [par-ram-**med**-dic] noun a person who does some types of medical work, for example for the ambulance service

parameter [par-**ram**-met-ter] noun a limit which affects the way something is done: *the general parameters set by the president*

paramilitary adjective A paramilitary organization has a military structure but is not the official army of a country

paramount adjective more important than anything else: *Safety is paramount*

paranoia [par-ran-**noy**-ah] noun Paranoia is a mental illness in which someone believes that other people are trying to harm them

paranoid [par-ran-noyd] *adjective*
Someone who is paranoid believes
wrongly that other people are
trying to harm them

parapet *noun* a low wall along the
edge of a bridge or roof

paraphernalia [par-raf-fan-**ale**-
yah] *noun* Someone's paraphernalia
is all their belongings or equipment

paraphrase *noun* **1** A paraphrase of
a piece of writing or speech is the
same thing said in a different way: *a
paraphrase of the popular song* ▷ *verb*
2 If you paraphrase what someone
has said, you express it in a different
way

parasite *noun* a small animal or
plant that lives on or inside a larger
animal or plant ▷ **parasitic** *adjective*

paratroops or **paratroopers**
plural noun Paratroops are soldiers
trained to be dropped by parachute

parcel parcels, parcelling, parcelled
noun **1** something wrapped up in
paper ▷ *verb* **2** If you parcel
something up, you make it into a
parcel

parched *adjective* **1** If the ground is
parched, it is very dry and in need of
water **2** (*informal*) If you are
parched, you are very thirsty

parchment *noun* Parchment is thick
yellowish paper of very good quality

pardon *interjection* **1** You say **pardon**
or **I beg your pardon** to express
surprise or apology, or when you
have not heard what someone has
said ▷ *verb* **2** If you pardon
someone, you forgive them for
doing something wrong

pare *verb* When you pare fruit or
vegetables, you cut off the skin

parent *noun* Your parents are your
father and mother > **parental**
adjective

parentage *noun* A person's

parentage is their parents and
ancestors

parish *noun* an area with its own
church and clergyman, and often its
own elected council

parishioner *noun* A clergyman's
parishioners are the people who live
in his parish and attend his church

parity *noun* (*formal*) If there is parity
between things, they are equal: *By
1943 the USA had achieved a rough
parity of power with the British*

park *noun* **1 a** a public area with grass
and trees **2 a** a private area of grass
and trees around a large country
house ▷ *verb* **3** When someone
parks a vehicle, they drive it into a
position where it can be left
▷ **parked** *adjective* ▷ **parking** *noun*

parliament *noun* [HISTORY] the
group of elected representatives
who make the laws of a country
▷ **parliamentary** *adjective*

parlour *noun* (*old-fashioned*) a sitting
room

parochial [par-**roe**-key-yal] *adjective*
concerned only with local matters:
narrow parochial interests

parody parodies, parodying,
parodied *noun* **1** an amusing
imitation of the style of an author or
of a familiar situation ▷ *verb* **2** If you
parody something, you make a
parody of it

parole *noun* When prisoners are
given parole, they are released early
on condition that they behave well

parrot *noun* a brightly coloured
tropical bird with a curved beak

parry parries, parrying, parried *verb*
1 If you parry a question, you cleverly
avoid answering it: *My searching
questions are simply parried with
evasions* **2** If you parry a blow, you
push aside your attacker's arm to
defend yourself

parsley noun Parsley is a herb with curly or flat leaves used for flavouring in cooking

parsnip noun a long, pointed, cream-coloured root vegetable

part noun 1 one of the pieces or aspects of something 2 one of the roles in a play or film, played by an actor or actress 3 Someone's part in something is their involvement in it: *He was jailed for eleven years for his part in the plot* ▷ phrase 4 If you take part in an activity, you do it together with other people ▷ verb 5 If things that are next to each other part, they move away from each other 6 If two people part, they leave each other

partake partakes, partaking, partook, partaken verb (formal) If you partake of food, you eat it: *She partook of the refreshments offered*

partial adjective 1 not complete or whole: *a partial explanation; partial success* 2 liking something very much: *I'm very partial to marigolds* 3 supporting one side in a dispute, rather than being fair and without bias > **partially** adverb

participate verb If you participate in an activity, you take part in it
> **participant** noun
> **participation** noun

particle noun 1 SCIENCE a basic unit of matter, such as an atom, molecule, or electron 2 a very small piece of something

particular adjective 1 relating or belonging to only one thing or person: *That particular place is dangerous* 2 especially great or intense: *Pay particular attention to the forehead* 3 Someone who is particular has high standards and is not easily satisfied > **particularly** adverb

parting noun an occasion when one person leaves another

partisan adjective 1 favouring or supporting one person or group: *a partisan crowd* ▷ noun 2 a member of an unofficial armed force fighting to free their country from enemy occupation: *Norwegian partisans*

partition noun 1 a screen separating one part of a room or vehicle from another 2 Partition is the division of a country into independent areas ▷ verb 3 To partition something is to divide it into separate parts

partly adverb to some extent but not completely

partner noun 1 Someone's partner is the person they are married to or are living with 2 Your partner is the person you are doing something with, for example in a dance or a game 3 Business partners are joint owners of their business ▷ verb 4 If you partner someone, you are their partner for a game or social occasion > **partnership** noun

partridge noun a brown game bird with a round body and a short tail

part-time adjective involving work for only a part of the working day or week

party parties noun 1 a social event held for people to enjoy themselves 2 an organization whose members share the same political beliefs and campaign for election to government 3 a group who are doing something together 4 (formal) one of the people involved in a legal agreement or dispute

pass verb 1 To pass something is to move past it 2 To pass in a particular direction is to move in that direction: *We passed through the gate* 3 If you pass something to someone, you hand it to them or transfer it to

P

them **4** If you pass a period of time doing something, you spend it that way: *He hoped to pass the long night in meditation* **5** When a period of time passes, it happens and finishes **6** If you pass a test, you are considered to be of an acceptable standard **7** When a new law or proposal is passed, it is formally approved **8** When a judge passes sentence on someone, the judge states what the punishment will be **9** If you pass the ball in a ball game, you throw, kick, or hit it to another player in your team ▷ noun **10** the transfer of the ball in a ball game to another player in the same team **11** an official document that allows you to go somewhere **12** a narrow route between mountains ▷ **pass away** or ▷ **pass on** *verb* Someone who has passed away has died ▷ **pass out** *verb* If someone passes out, they faint ▷ **pass up** *verb (informal)* If you pass up an opportunity, you do not take advantage of it

passable *adjective* of an acceptable standard: *a passable imitation of his dad*

passage *noun* **1** a space that connects two places **2** a long narrow corridor **3** a section of a book or piece of music

passenger *noun* a person travelling in a vehicle, aircraft, or ship

passer-by passers-by *noun* someone who is walking past someone or something

passing *adjective* lasting only for a short time: *a passing phase*

passion *noun* **1** Passion is a very strong feeling of attraction **2** Passion is also any strong emotion

passionate *adjective* expressing very strong feelings about something ▷ **passionately** *adverb*

passive *adjective* **1** remaining calm and showing no feeling when provoked ▷ noun **2** ENGLISH In grammar, the passive or passive voice is the form of the verb in which the person or thing to which an action is being done is the grammatical subject of the sentence, and is given more emphasis as a result. For example, the passive of *The committee rejected your application* is *Your application was rejected by the committee* > **passively** *adverb* ▷ **passivity** *noun*

Passover *noun* The Passover is an eight-day Jewish festival held in spring

passport *noun* an official identification document which you need to show when you travel abroad

password *noun* **1** a secret word known to only a few people. It allows people on the same side to recognize a friend **2** COMPUTING a word you need to know to get into some computers or computer files

past *noun* **1** The past is the period of time before the present ▷ adjective **2** Past things are things that happened or existed before the present: *the past 30 years* ENGLISH The past tense of a verb is the form used to express something that happened in the past ▷ preposition, adverb **4** You use 'past' when you are telling the time: *It was ten past eleven* **5** If you go past something, you move towards it and continue until you are on the other side: *They drove rapidly past their cottage* ▷ preposition **6** Something that is past a place is situated on the other side of it: *It's just past the church there*

pasta *noun* Pasta is a dried mixture of flour, eggs, and water, formed into different shapes

paste noun **1** Paste is a soft, rather sticky mixture that can be easily spread: *tomato paste* ▷ verb **2** If you paste something onto a surface, you stick it with glue

pastel adjective **1** Pastel colours are pale and soft ▷ noun **2** ART Pastels are small sticks of coloured crayon, used for drawing pictures

pastime noun a hobby or something you do just for pleasure

pastor noun a clergyman in charge of a congregation

pastoral adjective **1** characteristic of peaceful country life and landscape: *pastoral scenes* **2** relating to the duties of the clergy in caring for the needs of their parishioners, or of a school in caring for the needs of its students: *a pastoral visit*; *Most schools have some system of pastoral care*

pastry pastries noun **1** Pastry is a mixture of flour, fat, and water, rolled flat and used for making pies **2** a small cake

past tense noun ENGLISH In grammar, the past tense is the tense of a verb that you use mainly to refer to things that happened or existed before the time of writing or speaking

pasture noun Pasture is an area of grass on which farm animals graze

pasty pastier, pastiest; pasties adjective **1** [*rhymes with* **hasty**] Someone who is pasty looks pale and unhealthy ▷ noun **2** [**pas-tee**] a small pie containing meat and vegetables

pat pats, patting, patted verb **1** If you pat something, you tap it lightly with your hand held flat ▷ noun **2** a small lump of butter

patch noun **1** a **a** piece of material used to cover a hole in something

2 an area of a surface that is different in appearance from the rest: *a bald patch* ▷ noun **3** If you patch something, you mend it by fixing a patch over the hole ▷ **patch up** verb If you patch something up, you mend it hurriedly or temporarily

patchwork adjective **1** A patchwork quilt is made from many small pieces of material sewn together ▷ noun **2** Something that is a patchwork is made up of many parts

patchy patchier, patchiest adjective Something that is patchy is unevenly spread or incomplete in parts: *patchy fog on the hills*

patent noun **1** An official right given to an inventor or company allowed to be the only person or company allowed to make or sell a new product ▷ verb **2** If you patent something, you obtain a patent for it ▷ adjective **3** obvious: *This was patent nonsense* ▷ **patently** adverb

paternal adjective relating to a father: *paternal pride*

paternity noun Paternity is the state or fact of being a father

path noun **1** a strip of ground for people to walk on **2** Your path is the area ahead of you and the direction in which you are moving

pathetic adjective **1** If something is pathetic, it makes you feel sad **2** Pathetic also means very poor or unsuccessful: *a pathetic attempt* ▷ **pathetically** adverb

pathological adjective extreme and uncontrollable: *a pathological fear of snakes* ▷ **pathologically** adverb

pathology noun Pathology is the study of diseases and the way they develop ▷ **pathologist** noun

pathos [**pay-thoss**] noun Pathos is a quality in literature or art that causes great sadness or pity

pathway noun a path

patience noun Patience is the ability to stay calm in a difficult or irritating situation

patient adjective **1** If you are patient, you stay calm in a difficult or irritating situation ▷ noun **2** a person receiving medical treatment from a doctor or in a hospital > **patiently** adverb

patio patios noun a paved area close to a house

patriarch [pay-tree-ark] noun GEOGRAPHY the male head of a family or tribe > **patriarchal** adjective

patrician adjective (formal) belonging to a family of high rank

patriot noun someone who loves their country and feels very loyal towards it > **patriotic** adjective > **patriotism** noun

patrol patrols, patrolling, patrolled verb **1** When soldiers, police, or guards patrol an area, they walk or drive around to make sure there is no trouble ▷ noun **2** a group of people patrolling an area

patron noun **1** a person who supports or gives money to artists, writers, or musicians **2** The patrons of a hotel, pub, or shop are the people who use it > **patronage** noun

patronize or **patronise** verb **1** If someone patronizes you, they treat you kindly, but in a way that suggests that you are less intelligent than them or inferior to them **2** If you patronize a hotel, pub, or shop, you are a customer there > **patronizing** adjective

patron saint noun The patron saint of a group of people or place is a saint who is believed to look after them

patter verb **1** If something patters on a surface, it makes quick, light tapping sounds ▷ noun **2** a series of light tapping sounds: *a patter of light rain*

pattern noun **1** a decorative design of repeated shapes **2** The pattern of something is the way it is usually done or happens: *a perfectly normal pattern of behaviour* **3** a diagram or shape used as a guide for making something, for example clothes > **patterned** adjective

pauper noun (old-fashioned) a very poor person

pause verb **1** If you pause, you stop what you are doing for a short time ▷ noun **2** a short period when you stop what you are doing **3** a short period of silence

pave verb When an area of ground is paved, it is covered with flat blocks of stone or concrete

pavement noun a path with a hard surface at the side of a road

pavilion noun a building at a sports ground where players can wash and change

paw noun **1** The paws of an animal such as a cat or bear are its feet with claws and soft pads ▷ verb **2** If an animal paws something, it hits it or scrapes at it with its paws

pawn verb **1** If you pawn something, you leave it with a pawnbroker in exchange for money ▷ noun **2** the smallest and least valuable playing piece in chess

pay pays, paying, paid verb **1** When you pay money to someone, you give it to them because you are buying something or owe it to them **2** If it pays to do something, it is to your advantage to do it: *They say it pays to advertise* **3** If you pay for something that you have done, you suffer as a result **4** If you pay attention to something, you give it your attention **5** If you pay a visit to someone, you visit them ▷ *noun* **6** Someone's pay is their salary or wages

payable *adjective* **1** An amount of money that is payable has to be paid or can be paid: *All fees are payable in advance* **2** If a cheque is made payable to you, you are the person who should receive the money

payment *noun* **1** Payment is the act of paying money **2** a sum of money paid

payroll *noun* Someone who is on an organization's payroll is employed and paid by them

PC *noun* **1** In Britain, a police constable **2** a personal computer ▷ *adjective* **3** short for **politically correct**

PE *noun* PE is a lesson in which gymnastics or sports are taught. PE is an abbreviation for 'physical education'

pea *noun* Peas are small round green seeds that grow in pods and are eaten as a vegetable

peace *noun* **1** Peace is a state of calm and quiet when there is no disturbance of any kind **2** When a country is at peace, it is not at war > **peaceable** *adjective*

peaceful *adjective* quiet and calm > **peacefully** *adverb*

peach *noun* **1** a soft, round fruit with yellow flesh and a yellow and red skin ▷ *adjective* **2** pale pink with a hint of orange

peacock *noun* a large bird with green and blue feathers. The male has a long tail which it can spread out in a fan

peak *noun* **1** The peak of an activity or process is the point at which it is strongest or most successful **2** the pointed top of a mountain ▷ *verb* **3** When something peaks, it reaches its highest value or its greatest level of success > **peaked** *adjective*

peanut *noun* Peanuts are small oval nuts that grow under the ground

pear *noun* a fruit which is narrow at the top and wide and rounded at the bottom

pearl *noun* a hard, round, creamy-white object used to make jewellery. Pearls grow inside the shell of an oyster

peasant *noun* a person who works on the land, especially in a poor country

peat *noun* Peat is dark-brown decaying plant material found in cool, wet regions. Dried peat can be used as fuel

pebble *noun* a smooth, round stone

peck *verb* **1** If a bird pecks something, it bites at it quickly with its beak **2** If you peck someone on the cheek, you give them a quick kiss ▷ *noun* **3** a quick bite by a bird **4** a quick kiss on the cheek

peculiar *adjective* **1** strange and perhaps unpleasant **2** relating or belonging only to a particular person or thing: *a gesture peculiar to her* > **peculiarly** *adverb* > **peculiarity** *noun*

pedal *noun* **1** a control lever on a machine or vehicle that you press with your foot ▷ *verb* **2** When you pedal a bicycle, you push the pedals round with your feet to move along

pedantic *adjective* If a person is pedantic, they are too concerned with unimportant details and traditional rules

peddle *verb* Someone who peddles something sells it

P

pedestal noun a base on which a statue stands

pedestrian noun 1 someone who is walking ▷ adjective 2 Pedestrian means ordinary and rather dull: a pedestrian performance

pedestrian crossing noun a specially marked place where you can cross the road safely

pediatrician another spelling of **paediatrician**

pediatrics another spelling of **paediatrics**

pedigree adjective 1 A pedigree animal is descended from a single breed and its ancestors are known and recorded ▷ noun 2 Someone's pedigree is their background or ancestry

peek verb 1 If you peek at something, you have a quick look at it: I peeked round the corner ▷ noun 2 a quick look at something

peel noun 1 The peel of a fruit is the skin when it has been removed ▷ verb 2 When you peel fruit or vegetables, you remove the skin 3 If a surface is peeling, it is coming off in thin layers ▷ **peelings** plural noun

peep verb 1 If you peep at something, you have a quick look at it 2 If something peeps out from behind something else, a small part of it becomes visible: a handkerchief peeping out of his breast pocket ▷ noun 3 a quick look at something

peer verb 1 If you peer at something, you look at it very hard ▷ noun 2 a member of the nobility 3 Your peers are the people who are of the same age and social status as yourself

peerage noun 1 The peers in a country are called the peerage 2 A peerage is also the rank of being a peer

peer group noun Your peer group is the people who are of the same age and social status as yourself

peerless adjective so magnificent that nothing can equal it: peerless wines

peg pegs, pegging, pegged noun 1 a plastic or wooden clip used for hanging wet clothes on a line 2 a hook on a wall where you can hang things ▷ verb 3 If you peg clothes on a line, you fix them there with pegs 4 If a price is pegged at a certain level, it is fixed at that level

pejorative [pej-**jor**-ra-tiv] adjective A pejorative word expresses criticism

pelican noun a large water bird with a pouch beneath its beak in which it stores fish

pellet noun a small ball of paper, lead, or other material

pelt verb 1 If you pelt someone with things, you throw the things with force at them 2 (informal) If you pelt along, you run very fast ▷ noun 3 the skin and fur of an animal

pelvis noun the wide, curved group of bones at hip level at the base of your spine ▷ **pelvic** adjective

pen pens, penning, penned noun 1 a long, thin instrument used for writing with ink 2 a small fenced area in which farm animals are kept for a short time ▷ verb 3 (literary) If someone pens a letter or article, they write it 4 If you are penned in or penned up, you have to remain in an uncomfortably small area

penal adjective relating to the punishment of criminals

penalize or **penalise** verb If you are penalized, you are made to suffer some disadvantage as a punishment for something

penalty penalties noun 1 a punishment or disadvantage that someone is made to suffer **2** In soccer, a penalty is a free kick at goal that is given to the attacking team if the defending team have committed a foul near their goal

penance noun If you do penance, you do something unpleasant to show that you are sorry for something wrong that you have done

pence a plural form of **penny**

penchant [**pon**-shon] noun (formal) If you have a penchant for something, you have a particular liking for it: *a penchant for crime*

pencil noun a long thin stick of wood with graphite in the centre, used for drawing or writing

pendant noun a piece of jewellery attached to a chain and worn round the neck

pending (formal) adjective **1** Something that is pending is waiting to be dealt with or will happen soon ▷ preposition **2** Something that is done pending a future event is done until the event happens: *The army should stay in the west pending a future war*

pendulum noun a rod with a weight at one end in a clock which swings regularly from side to side to control the clock

penetrate verb To penetrate an area that is difficult to get into is to succeed in getting into it
▷ **penetration** noun

penetrating adjective **1** loud and high-pitched: *a penetrating voice* **2** having or showing deep understanding: *penetrating questions*

penguin noun A penguin is a black and white bird with webbed feet and small wings like flippers. Penguins are found mainly in the Antarctic

penicillin noun Penicillin is a powerful antibiotic obtained from fungus and used to treat infections

peninsula noun an area of land almost surrounded by water

penis noun A man's penis is the part of his body used for urination and reproduction

pennant noun a triangular flag, especially one used by ships as a signal

penniless adjective Someone who is penniless has no money

penny pennies or pence noun a unit of currency in Britain and some other countries. In Britain a penny is worth one-hundredth of a pound

pension [**pen**-shn] noun a regular sum of money paid to an old or retired person

pensioner noun an old or retired person who gets a pension paid by the state

pensive adjective deep in thought

pentathlon [pen-**tath**-lon] noun a sports contest in which athletes compete in five different events

penthouse noun a luxurious flat at the top of a building

pent-up adjective Pent-up emotions have been held back for a long time without release

penultimate adjective The penultimate thing in a series is the one before the last

people peoples, peopling, peopled plural noun **1** People are men, women, and children ▷ noun **2** all the men, women, and children of a particular country or race ▷ verb **3** If an area is peopled by a particular group, that group of people live there

pepper noun **1** a hot-tasting powdered spice used for flavouring in cooking **2** a hollow green,

P

orange, red, or yellow fruit eaten as a vegetable, with sweet-flavoured flesh

peppermint noun Peppermint is a plant with a strong taste. It is used for making sweets and in medicine

per preposition 'Per' is used to mean 'each' when expressing rates and ratios: *The class meets two evenings per week*

perceive verb If you perceive something that is not obvious, you see it or realize it

per cent phrase You use **per cent** to talk about amounts as a proportion of a hundred. An amount that is 10 per cent (10%) of a larger amount is equal to 10 hundredths of the larger amount: *20 per cent of voters have still not decided who to vote for*

percentage noun [MATHS] a fraction expressed as a number of hundredths: *the high percentage of failed marriages*

perceptible adjective Something that is perceptible can be seen: *a barely perceptible nod*

perception noun 1 Perception is the recognition of things using the senses, especially the sense of sight 2 Someone who has perception realizes or notices things that are not obvious 3 Your perception of something or someone is your understanding of them

perceptive adjective Someone who is perceptive realizes or notices things that are not obvious > **perceptively** adverb

perch verb 1 If you perch on something, you sit on the edge of it 2 When a bird perches on something, it stands on it ▷ noun 3 a short rod for a bird to stand on 4 an edible freshwater fish

percussion noun, adjective [MUSIC]

Percussion instruments are musical instruments that you hit to produce sounds > **percussionist** noun

perennial adjective continually occurring or never ending: *The damp cellar was a perennial problem*

perfect adjective [per-fect] 1 of the highest standard and without fault: *His English was perfect* 2 complete or absolute: *They have a perfect right to say so* 3 [ENGLISH] In English grammar, the perfect tense of a verb is formed with the present tense of 'have' and the past participle of the main verb: *I have lost my home* ▷ verb [per-fect] 4 If you perfect something, you make it as good as it can possibly be > **perfection** noun

perfectly adverb > **perfection** noun

perfectionist noun someone who always tries to do everything perfectly

perforated adjective Something that is perforated has had small holes made in it > **perforation** noun

perform verb 1 To perform a task or action is to do it 2 [DRAMA] To perform is to act, dance, or play music in front of an audience > **performer** noun

performance noun 1 [DRAMA] an entertainment provided for an audience 2 The performance of a task or action is the doing of it 3 Someone's or something's performance is how successful they are: *the poor performance of the American economy*

perfume noun 1 Perfume is a pleasant-smelling liquid which women put on their bodies 2 The perfume of something is its pleasant smell > **perfumed** adjective

perfunctory adjective done quickly without interest or care: *a perfunctory kiss*

perhaps adverb You use 'perhaps' when you are not sure whether something is true or possible

peril noun (formal) Peril is great danger > **perilous** adjective > **perilously** adverb

perimeter noun [MATHS] The perimeter of an area or figure is the whole of its outer edge

period noun **1** a particular length of time **2** one of the parts the day is divided into at school **3** A woman's period is the monthly bleeding from her womb ▷ adjective **4** relating to a historical period of time: *period furniture* > **periodic** adjective > **periodically** adverb

periodical noun a magazine

peripheral [per-**rif**-fer-ral] adjective **1** of little importance in comparison with other things: *a peripheral activity* **2** on or relating to the edge of an area

periphery peripheries noun The periphery of an area is its outside edge

perish verb **1** (formal) If someone or something perishes, they are killed or destroyed **2** If fruit or fabric perishes, it rots > **perishable** adjective

perjury noun (Law) If someone commits perjury, they tell a lie in court while under oath > **perjure** verb

perk noun **1** an extra, such as a company car, offered by an employer in addition to a salary. Perk is an abbreviation for 'perquisite' ▷ verb **2** (informal) When someone perks up, they become more cheerful > **perky** adjective

perm noun **1** If you have a perm, your hair is curled and treated with chemicals to keep the curls for several months ▷ verb **2** To perm

someone's hair means to put a perm in it

permanent adjective lasting for ever, or present all the time > **permanently** adverb > **permanence** noun

permeate verb To permeate something is to spread through it and affect every part of it: *A sense of optimism permeates everything that the organization does*

permissible adjective allowed by the rules

permission noun If you have permission to do something, you are allowed to do it

permissive adjective A permissive society allows things which some people disapprove of > **permissiveness** noun

permit permits, permitting, permitted verb **1** To permit something is to allow it or make it possible ▷ noun **2** an official document which says that you are allowed to do something

pernicious adjective (formal) very harmful: *the pernicious influence of television*

peroxide noun Peroxide is a chemical used for bleaching hair or as an antiseptic

perpendicular adjective [MATHS] upright, or at right angles to a horizontal line

perpetrate verb (formal) To perpetrate a crime is to commit it > **perpetrator** noun

perpetual adjective never ending: *a perpetual toothache* > **perpetually** adverb > **perpetuity** noun

perpetuate verb To perpetuate a situation or belief is to cause it to continue: *The television series will perpetuate the myths*

perplexed adjective If you are

perplexed, you are puzzled and do not know what to do

persecute verb To persecute someone means to treat them cruelly and unfairly over a long period of time > **persecution** noun > **persecutor** noun

persevere verb If you persevere, you keep trying to do something and do not give up > **perseverance** noun

Persian [per-zhn] adjective, noun an old word for **Iranian**, used especially when referring to the older forms of the language

persist verb 1 If something undesirable persists, it continues to exist 2 If you persist in doing something, you continue in spite of opposition or difficulty > **persistence** noun > **persistent** adjective

person people or persons noun 1 a man, woman, or child 2 In grammar, the first person is the speaker (I), the second person is the person being spoken to (you), and the third person is anyone else being referred to (he, she, they)

personal adjective 1 Personal means belonging or relating to a particular person rather than to people in general: my personal feeling 2 Personal matters relate to your feelings, relationships, and health which you may not wish to discuss with other people > **personally** adverb

personality personalities noun 1 Your personality is your character and nature 2 a famous person in entertainment or sport

personification noun 1 [ENGLISH] Personification is a form of imagery in which something inanimate is described as if it has human qualities: The trees sighed and whispered as the impatient breeze stirred their branches 2 Someone who is the personification of some quality is a living example of that quality: He was the personification of evil.

personify personifies, personifying, personified verb 1 Someone who personifies a particular quality seems to be a living example of it 2 If you personify a thing or concept, you write or speak of it as if it has human abilities or qualities, for example 'The sun is trying to come out'

personnel [per-son-**nell**] noun The personnel of an organization are the people who work for it

perspective noun 1 A particular perspective is one way of thinking about something 2 [ART] Perspective is a method artists use to make some people and things seem further away than others

perspiration noun Perspiration is the moisture that appears on your skin when you are hot or frightened

persuade verb If someone persuades you to do something or persuades you that something is true, they make you do it or believe it by giving you very good reasons > **persuasion** noun > **persuasive** adjective

pertaining adjective (formal) If information or questions are pertaining to a place or thing, they are about that place or thing: issues pertaining to women

pertinent adjective especially relevant to the subject being discussed: He asks pertinent questions

perturbed adjective Someone who is perturbed is worried

Peruvian [per-**roo**-vee-an] adjective 1 belonging or relating to Peru

▷ noun 2 someone who comes from Peru

pervade verb Something that pervades a place is present and noticeable throughout it: *a fear that pervades the community* > **pervasive** adjective

perverse adjective Someone who is perverse deliberately does things that are unreasonable or harmful > **perversely** adverb > **perversity** noun

pervert verb (formal) To pervert something is to interfere with it so that it is no longer what it should be: *a conspiracy to pervert the course of justice*

perverted adjective 1 Someone who is perverted has disgusting or unacceptable behaviour or ideas 2 Something that is perverted is completely wrong: *a perverted sense of value*

peso pesos [pay-soh] noun the main unit of currency in several South American countries

pessimism noun Pessimism is the tendency to believe that bad things will happen > **pessimist** noun

pessimistic adjective believing that bad things will happen > **pessimistically** adverb

pest noun 1 an insect or small animal which damages plants or food supplies 2 (informal) someone who keeps bothering or annoying you

pester verb If you pester someone, you keep bothering them or asking them to do something

pesticide noun SCIENCE Pesticides are chemicals sprayed onto plants to kill insects and grubs

pet pets, petting, petted noun 1 a tame animal kept at home ▷ adjective 2 Someone's pet theory or pet project is something that

they particularly support or feel strongly about ▷ verb 3 If you pet a person or animal, you stroke them affectionately

petal noun The petals of a flower are the coloured outer parts

petite [pet-**teet**] adjective A woman who is petite is small and slim

petition noun 1 a document demanding official action which is signed by a lot of people 2 a formal request to a court for legal action to be taken ▷ verb 3 If you petition someone in authority, you make a formal request to them: *I petitioned the Chinese government for permission to visit its country*

petrified adjective If you are petrified, you are very frightened

petrol noun SCIENCE Petrol is a liquid obtained from petroleum and used as a fuel for motor vehicles

petroleum noun SCIENCE Petroleum is thick, dark oil found under the earth or under the sea bed

petty pettier, pettiest adjective 1 Petty things are small and unimportant 2 Petty behaviour consists of doing small things which are selfish and unkind

petulant adjective showing unreasonable and childish impatience or anger > **petulantly** adverb > **petulance** noun

pew noun a long wooden seat with a back, which people sit on in church

pewter noun Pewter is a silvery-grey metal made from a mixture of tin and lead

pH noun The pH of a solution or of the soil is a measurement of how acid or alkaline it is. Acid solutions have a pH of less than 7 and alkaline solutions have a pH greater than 7. pH is an abbreviation for 'potential hydrogen'

P

phantom noun **1** a ghost ▷ adjective **2** imagined or unreal: a phantom pregnancy

pharaoh [**fair**-oh] noun The pharaohs were kings of ancient Egypt

pharmaceutical [far-mass-**yoo**-tik-kl] adjective connected with the industrial production of medicines

pharmacist noun a person who is qualified to prepare and sell medicines

pharmacy pharmacies noun a shop where medicines are sold

phase noun **1** a particular stage in the development of something ▷ verb **2** To phase something is to cause it to happen gradually in stages

PhD noun a degree awarded to someone who has done advanced research in a subject. PhD is an abbreviation for 'Doctor of Philosophy'

pheasant noun a large, long-tailed game bird

phenomenal [fin-**nom**-in-nal] adjective extraordinarily great or good > **phenomenally** adverb

phenomenon phenomena noun something that happens or exists, especially something remarkable or something being considered in a scientific way: a well-known geographical phenomenon

philanthropist [fil-**lan**-throp-pist] noun someone who freely gives help or money to people in need > **philanthropic** adjective > **philanthropy** noun

philistine noun If you call someone a philistine, you mean that they do not like art, literature, or music

philosophical or **philosophic** adjective Someone who is philosophical does not get upset when disappointing things happen

philosophy philosophies noun **1** Philosophy is the study or creation of ideas about existence, knowledge, or beliefs **2** a set of beliefs that a person has > **philosopher** noun

phobia noun a great fear or hatred of something: The man had a phobia about flying > **phobic** adjective

-phobia suffix '-phobia' means 'fear of': claustrophobia

phoenix [**fee**-niks] noun an imaginary bird which, according to myth, burns itself to ashes every five hundred years and rises from the fire again

phone noun **1** a piece of electronic equipment which allows you to speak to someone in another place by keying in or dialling their number ▷ verb **2** If you phone someone, you key in or dial their number and speak to them using a phone

-phone suffix '-phone' means 'giving off sound': telephone; gramophone

phoney phonier, phoniest; phoneys or **phony** (informal) adjective **1** false and intended to deceive ▷ noun **2** Someone who is a phoney pretends to have qualities they do not possess

photo photos noun (informal) a photograph

photocopier noun a machine which makes instant copies of documents by photographing them

photocopy photocopies, photocopying, photocopied [LIBRARY] noun **1** a copy of a document produced by a photocopier ▷ verb **2** If you photocopy a document, you make a copy of it using a photocopier

photogenic adjective Someone who is photogenic always looks nice in photographs

photograph noun **1** a picture made using a camera ▷ verb **2** When you photograph someone, you take a picture of them by using a camera
> **photographer** noun
> **photography** noun

photographic adjective connected with photography

photosynthesis noun SCIENCE Photosynthesis is the process by which the action of sunlight on the chlorophyll in plants produces the substances that keep the plants alive

phrase noun **1** a group of words considered as a unit ▷ verb **2** If you phrase something in a particular way, you choose those words to express it: *I should have phrased that better*

physical adjective **1** concerning the body rather than the mind **2** relating to things that can be touched or seen, especially with regard to their size or shape: *the physical characteristics of their machinery; the physical world*
> **physically** adverb

physical education noun Physical education consists of the sport that you do at school

physician noun a doctor

physics noun Physics is the scientific study of matter, energy, gravity, electricity, heat, and sound
> **physicist** noun

physiology noun Physiology is the scientific study of the way the bodies of living things work

physiotherapy noun Physiotherapy is medical treatment which involves exercise and massage > **physiotherapist** noun

physique [fiz-**zeek**] noun A person's physique is the shape and size of their body

pi [rhymes with **fly**] noun MATHS Pi is a number, approximately 3.142 and symbolized by the Greek letter π. Pi is the ratio of the circumference of a circle to its diameter

piano pianos MUSIC noun **1** a large musical instrument with a row of black and white keys. When the keys are pressed, little hammers hit wires to produce the different notes **2** In music, piano is an instruction to play or sing something quietly
> **pianist** noun

pick verb **1** To pick something is to choose it **2** If you pick a flower or fruit, or pick something from a place, you remove it with your fingers **3** If someone picks a lock, they open it with a piece of wire instead of a key ▷ noun **4** The pick of a group of people or things are the best ones in it **5** a pickaxe > **pick on** verb If you pick on someone, you criticize them unfairly or treat them unkindly > **pick out** verb If you pick out someone or something, you recognize them when they are difficult to see, or you choose them from among other things > **pick up** verb If you pick someone or something up, you collect them from the place where they are waiting

picket verb **1** When a group of people picket a place of work, they stand outside to persuade other workers to join a strike ▷ noun **2** someone who is picketing a place

pickings plural noun Pickings are goods or money that can be obtained very easily: *rich pickings*

pickle noun **1** Pickle or pickles consists of vegetables or fruit preserved in vinegar or salt water ▷ verb **2** To pickle food is to preserve it in vinegar or salt water

picnic picnics, picnicking, picnicked
noun **1** a meal eaten out of doors
▷ verb **2** People who are picnicking
are having a picnic

pictorial adjective relating to or
using pictures: *a pictorial record of the
railway*

picture noun **1 a** drawing, painting,
or photograph of someone or
something **2** If you have a picture of
something in your mind, you have
an idea or impression of it (*in
plural*) If you go to the pictures, you
go to see a film at the cinema ▷ verb
4 If someone is pictured in a
newspaper or magazine, a
photograph of them is printed in it
5 If you picture something, you
think of it and imagine it clearly:
That is how I always picture him

picturesque [pik-chur-**esk**]
adjective A place that is picturesque
is very attractive and unspoiled

pie noun a dish of meat, vegetables,
or fruit covered with pastry

piece noun **1** a portion or part of
something **2** something that has
been written or created, such as a
work of art or a musical
composition **3** a coin: *a 50 pence
piece* ▷ verb **4** If you piece together a
number of things, you gradually put
them together to make something
complete

piecemeal adverb, adjective done
gradually and at irregular intervals:
*He built up a piecemeal knowledge of
the subject, but it was not complete*

pier noun a large structure which
sticks out into the sea at a seaside
town, and which people can walk
along

pierce verb If a sharp object pierces
something, it goes through it,
making a hole

piercing adjective **1** A piercing sound

is high-pitched and unpleasant
2 Someone with piercing eyes
seems to look at you very intensely

piety [**pie**-it-tee] noun Piety is strong
and devout religious belief or
behaviour

pig noun a farm animal kept for its
meat. It has pinkish skin, short legs,
and a snout

pigeon noun a largish bird with grey
feathers, often seen in towns

pigeonhole noun one of the
sections in a frame on a wall where
letters can be left

piggyback noun If you give
someone a piggyback, you carry
them on your back, supporting
them under their knees

pigment noun a substance that
gives something a particular colour
> **pigmentation** noun

pike noun **1** a large freshwater fish of
northern countries with strong
teeth **2** a medieval weapon
consisting of a pointed metal blade
attached to a long pole

pilchard noun a small sea fish

pile noun **1** a quantity of things lying
one on top of another **2** the soft
surface of a carpet consisting of
many threads standing on end **3** (*in
plural*) Piles are painful swellings
that appear in the veins inside or
just outside a person's anus ▷ verb
4 If you pile things somewhere, you
put them one on top of the other

pile-up noun (*informal*) a road
accident involving several vehicles

pilgrim noun RE a person who
travels to a holy place for religious
reasons > **pilgrimage** noun

pill noun **1** a small, hard tablet of
medicine that you swallow **2** The
pill is a type of drug that women can
take regularly to prevent pregnancy

pillage verb If a group of people

pillage a place, they steal from it using violence

pillar noun 1 a tall, narrow, solid structure, usually supporting part of a building 2 Someone who is described as a pillar of a particular group is an active and important member of it: *a pillar of the Church*

pillory pillories, pillorying, pilloried verb If someone is pilloried, they are criticized severely by a lot of people

pillow noun a rectangular cushion which you rest your head on when you are in bed

pilot noun 1 a person who is trained to fly an aircraft 2 a person who goes on board ships to guide them through local waters to a port ▷ verb 3 To pilot something is to control its movement or to guide it 4 To pilot a scheme or product is to test it to see if it would be successful

pin noun 1 a thin, pointed piece of metal used to fasten together things such as pieces of fabric or paper ▷ verb 2 If you pin something somewhere, you fasten it there with a pin or a drawing pin 3 If someone pins you in a particular position, they hold you there so that you cannot move 4 If you try to pin something down, you try to get or give a clear and exact description of it or statement about it

PIN noun an abbreviation for 'personal identification number': a number used by the holder of a cash card or credit card

pinch verb 1 If you pinch something, you squeeze it between your thumb and first finger 2 (*informal*) If someone pinches something, they steal it ▷ noun 3 A pinch of something is the amount that you can hold between your thumb and first finger: *a pinch of salt*

pinched adjective If someone's face is pinched, it looks thin and pale

pine noun 1 A pine or pine tree is an evergreen tree with very thin leaves ▷ verb 2 If you pine for something, you are sad because you cannot have it

pineapple noun a large, oval fruit with sweet, yellow flesh and a thick, lumpy brown skin

ping-pong noun the same as **table tennis**

pink adjective pale reddish-white

pinnacle noun 1 a tall pointed piece of stone or rock 2 The pinnacle of something is its best or highest level: *the pinnacle of his career*

pinpoint verb If you pinpoint something, you explain or discover exactly what or where it is

pinstripe adjective Pinstripe cloth has very narrow vertical stripes

pint noun a unit of liquid volume equal to one eighth of a gallon or about 0.568 litres

pioneer [pie-on-ear] noun 1 Someone who is a pioneer in a particular activity is one of the first people to develop it ▷ verb 2 Someone who pioneers a new process or invention is the first person to develop it

pious [pie-uss] adjective very religious and moral

pip noun Pips are the hard seeds in a fruit

pipe noun 1 a long, hollow tube through which liquid or gas can flow 2 an object used for smoking tobacco. It consists of a small hollow bowl attached to a tube ▷ verb 3 To pipe a liquid or gas somewhere is to transfer it through a pipe

pipeline noun a large underground pipe that carries oil or gas over a long distance

piper noun a person who plays the bagpipes

piping noun Piping consists of pipes and tubes

pirate noun Pirates were sailors who attacked and robbed other ships

Pisces [pie-seez] noun Pisces is the twelfth sign of the zodiac, represented by two fish. People born between February 19th and March 20th are born under this sign

pistol noun a small gun held in the hand

piston noun a cylinder or disc that slides up and down inside a tube. Pistons make parts of engines move

pit noun **1** a large hole in the ground **2** a small hollow in the surface of something **3** a coal mine

pitch noun **1** PE an area of ground marked out for playing a game such as football **2** MUSIC The pitch of a sound is how high or low it is **3** a black substance used in road tar and also for making boats and roofs waterproof ▷ verb **4** If you pitch something somewhere, you throw it with a lot of force **5** If you pitch something at a particular level of difficulty, you set it at that level: Any film must be pitched at a level to suit its intended audience **6** When you pitch a tent, you fix it in an upright position

pitcher noun a large jug

pitfall noun The pitfalls of a situation are its difficulties or dangers

pith noun the white substance between the outer skin and the flesh of an orange or lemon

pitiful adjective Someone or something that is pitiful is in such a sad or weak situation that you feel pity for them

pittance noun a very small amount of money

pitted adjective covered in small

hollows: Nails often become pitted

pity pities, pitying, pitied verb **1** If you pity someone, you feel very sorry for them ▷ noun **2** Pity is a feeling of being sorry for someone **3** If you say that it is a pity about something, you are expressing your disappointment about it

pivot verb **1** If something pivots, it balances or turns on a central point: The keel pivots on a large stainless steel pin ▷ noun **2** the central point on which something balances or turns > **pivotal** adjective

pixie noun an imaginary little creature in fairy stories

pizza [peet-sah] noun a flat piece of dough covered with cheese, tomato, and other savoury food

placard noun a large notice carried at a demonstration or displayed in a public place

placate verb If you placate someone, you stop them feeling angry by doing something to please them

place noun **1** any point, building, or area **2** the position where something belongs: She set the holder in its place on the table **3** a space at a table set with cutlery where one person can eat **4** If you have a place in a group or at a college, you are a member or are accepted as a student **5** a particular point or stage in a sequence of things: second place in the race ▷ phrase **6** When something **takes place**, it happens ▷ verb **7** If you place something somewhere, you put it there **8** If you place an order, you order something

placebo placebos [plas-**see**-boh] noun a substance given to a patient in place of a drug and from which, though it has no active ingredients, the patient may imagine they get some benefit

placenta placentas [plas-**sen**-tah]
noun The placenta is the mass of
veins and tissues in the womb of a
pregnant woman or animal. It gives
the foetus food and oxygen

placid adjective calm and not easily
excited or upset > **placidly** adverb

plagiarism [**play**-jer-rizm] noun
Plagiarism is copying someone
else's work or ideas and pretending
that it is your own > **plagiarist** noun
> **plagiarize** verb

plague plagues, plaguing, plagued
[playg] noun **1** Plague is a very
infectious disease that kills large
numbers of people **2** A plague of
unpleasant things is a large number
of them occurring at the same time:
a plague of rats > verb **3** If problems
plague you, they keep causing you
trouble

plaice noun an edible European flat
fish

plaid [plad] noun Plaid is woven
material with a tartan design

plain adjective **1** very simple in style
with no type of decoration: plain
walls **2** obvious and easy to
recognize or understand: plain
language **3** A person who is plain is
not at all beautiful or attractive
> adverb **4** You can use 'plain' before
a noun or adjective to emphasize it:
You were just plain stupid > noun **5** a
large, flat area of land with very few
trees > **plainly** adverb

plaintiff noun a person who has
brought a court case against
another person

plan plans, planning, planned noun
1 a method of achieving something
that has been worked out
beforehand **2** a detailed diagram or
drawing of something that is to be
made > verb **3** If you plan
something, you decide in detail

what it is to be and how to do it **4** If
you are planning to do something,
you intend to do it: They plan to marry
in the summer

plane noun **1** a vehicle with wings
and engines that enable it to fly
2 a flat surface **3** You can refer to a
particular level of something as a
particular plane: to take the rock and
roll concert to a higher plane **4** a tool
with a flat bottom with a sharp
blade in it. You move it over a piece
of wood to remove thin pieces from
the surface > verb **5** If you plane
a piece of wood, you smooth its
surface with a plane

planet noun a round object in space
which moves around the sun or a
star and is lit by light from it
> **planetary** adjective

plank noun a long rectangular piece
of wood

plankton noun Plankton is a layer of
tiny plants and animals that live just
below the surface of a sea or lake

plant noun **1** a living thing that
grows in the earth and has stems,
leaves, and roots **2** a factory or
power station: a giant bottling plant
> verb **3** When you plant a seed or
plant, you put it into the ground **4** If
you plant something somewhere,
you put it there firmly or secretly

plantation noun **1** a large area of
land where crops such as tea,
cotton, or sugar are grown **2** a large
number of trees planted together

plaque [rhymes with **black**] noun **1** a
flat piece of metal which is fixed to a
wall and has an inscription in
memory of a famous person or
event **2** Plaque is a substance which
forms around your teeth and
consists of bacteria, saliva, and food

plasma [**plaz**-mah] noun Plasma is
the clear fluid part of blood

plaster noun **1** Plaster is a paste made of sand, lime, and water, which is used to form a smooth surface for inside walls and ceilings **2** a strip of sticky material with a small pad, used for covering cuts on your body ▷ verb **3** To plaster a wall is to cover it with a layer of plaster ▷ phrase **4** If your arm or leg is **in plaster**, it has a plaster cast on it to protect a broken bone > **plasterer** noun

plastered adjective **1** If something is plastered to a surface, it is stuck there **2** If something is plastered with things, they are all over its surface

plastic noun **1** Plastic is a substance made by a chemical process that can be moulded when soft to make a wide range of objects ▷ adjective **2** made of plastic

plastic surgery noun Plastic surgery is surgery to replace or repair damaged skin or to improve a person's appearance by changing the shape of their features

plate noun **1** A flat dish used to hold food **2** a flat piece of metal or other hard material used for various purposes in machinery or building: *heavy steel plates used in shipbuilding*

plateau noun **plateaus** or **plateaux** [rhymes with **snow**] noun A large area of high and fairly flat land

platform noun **1** a raised structure on which someone or something can stand **2** the raised area in a railway station where passengers get on and off trains

platinum noun Platinum is a valuable silver-coloured metal. Its atomic number is 78 and its symbol is Pt

platitude noun a statement made as if it were significant but which

has become meaningless or boring because it has been used so many times before

platonic adjective A platonic relationship is simply one of friendship and does not involve romantic attraction

platoon noun a small group of soldiers, commanded by a lieutenant

platter noun a large serving plate

platypus noun A platypus or duck-billed platypus is an Australian mammal which lives in rivers. It has brown fur, webbed feet, and a snout like a duck

plaudits plural noun (formal) Plaudits are expressions of admiration

plausible adjective An explanation that is plausible seems likely to be true > **plausibility** noun

play verb **1** When children play, they take part in games or use toys **2** When you play a sport or match, you take part in it **3** If an actor plays a character in a play or film, he or she performs that role **4** If you play a musical instrument, you produce music from it **5** If you play recorded music, you operate a machine in order to produce that music ▷ noun **6** a piece of drama performed in the theatre or on television > **player** noun

playboy noun a rich man who spends his time enjoying himself

playful adjective **1** friendly and light-hearted: *a playful kiss on the tip of his nose* **2** lively: *a playful puppy* > **playfully** adverb

playground noun a special area for children to play in

playgroup noun an informal kind of school for very young children where they learn by playing

playing field noun an area of grass

where people play sports

playwright noun ENGLISH DRAMA
a person who writes plays

plaza [**plah**-za] noun an open square
in a city

plea noun 1 an emotional request: *a
plea for help* 2 In a court of law,
someone's plea is their statement
that they are guilty or not guilty

plead verb 1 If you plead with
someone, you ask them in an
intense emotional way to do
something 2 When a person pleads
guilty or not guilty, they state in
court that they are guilty or not
guilty of a crime

pleasant adjective 1 enjoyable or
attractive 2 friendly or charming
> **pleasantly** adverb

please adverb 1 You say please when
you are asking someone politely to
do something ▷ verb 2 If something
pleases you, it makes you feel happy
and satisfied

pleased adjective happy or satisfied

pleasing adjective attractive,
satisfying, or enjoyable: *a pleasing
appearance*

pleasure noun 1 Pleasure is a feeling
of happiness, satisfaction, or
enjoyment 2 an activity that you
enjoy > **pleasurable** adjective

pleat noun 1 a permanent fold in
fabric made by folding one part over
another

plebiscite [**pleb**-iss-ite] noun
(formal) a vote on a matter of
national importance in which all the
voters in a country can take part

pledge noun 1 a solemn promise
▷ verb 2 If you pledge something,
you promise that you will do it or
give it

plentiful adjective existing in large
numbers or amounts and readily
available: *Fruit and vegetables were*

plentiful > **plentifully** adverb

plenty noun If there is plenty of
something, there is a lot of it

plethora [**pleth**-thor-ah] noun A
plethora of something is an amount
that is greater than you need

pliable adjective 1 If something is
pliable, you can bend it without
breaking it 2 Someone who is
pliable can be easily influenced or
controlled

pliers plural noun Pliers are a small
tool with metal jaws for holding
small objects and bending wire

plight noun Someone's plight is the
very difficult or dangerous situation
that they are in: *the plight of the
refugees*

plinth noun a block of stone on
which a statue or pillar stands

plod plods, plodding, plodded verb
If you plod somewhere, you walk
there slowly and heavily

plonk verb (informal) If you plonk
something down, you put it down
heavily and carelessly

plot plots, plotting, plotted noun
1 a secret plan made by a group of
people 2 ENGLISH The plot of a
novel or play is the story 3 a small
piece of land ▷ verb 4 If people plot
to do something, they plan it
secretly: *His family is plotting to
disinherit him* 5 If someone plots
the course of a plane or ship on a map,
or plots a graph, they mark the
points in the correct places

plough [rhymes with cow] noun 1 a
large farming tool that is pulled
across a field to turn the soil over
before planting seeds ▷ verb 2 When
someone ploughs land, they use a
plough to turn over the soil

ploy noun a clever plan or way of
behaving in order to get something
that you want

P

pluck verb 1 To pluck a fruit or flower is to remove it with a sharp pull 2 To pluck a chicken or other dead bird means to pull its feathers out before cooking it 3 When you pluck a stringed instrument, you pull the strings and let them go ▷ noun 4 Pluck is courage ▷ **plucky** adjective

plug plugs, plugging, plugged noun 1 a plastic object with metal prongs that can be pushed into a socket to connect an appliance to the electricity supply 2 a disc of rubber or metal with which you block up the hole in a sink or bath ▷ verb 3 If you plug a hole, you block it with something

plum noun a small fruit with a smooth red or yellow skin and a large stone in the middle

plumage [ploom-mage] noun A bird's plumage is its feathers

plumber noun a person who connects and repairs water pipes

plumbing noun The plumbing in a building is the system of water pipes, sinks, and toilets

plume noun a large, brightly coloured feather

plummet plummets, plummeting, plummeted verb If something plummets, it falls very quickly: Sales have plummeted

plump adjective rather fat: a small plump baby

plunder verb If someone plunders a place, they steal things from it

plunge verb 1 If something plunges, it falls suddenly 2 If you plunge an object into something, you push it in quickly 3 If you plunge into an activity or state, you suddenly become involved in it or affected by it: The United States had just plunged into the war ▷ noun 4 a sudden fall

plural noun [ENGLISH] the form of a word that is used to refer to two or more people or things, for example the plural of 'chair' is 'chairs', and the plural of 'mouse' is 'mice'

pluralism noun Pluralism is the belief that it is possible for different social and religious groups to live together peacefully while keeping their own beliefs and traditions ▷ **pluralist** adjective, noun

plus 1 You use 'plus' to show that one number is being added to another: Two plus two equals four 2 You can use 'plus' when you mention an additional thing: He wrote a history of Scotland plus a history of British literature ▷ adjective 3 slightly more than the number mentioned: a career of 25 years plus

plush adjective (informal) very expensive and smart: a plush hotel

Pluto noun Pluto is a dwarf planet in the solar system

ply plies, plying, plied verb 1 If you ply someone with things or questions, you keep giving them things or asking them questions 2 To ply a trade is to do a particular job as your work ▷ noun 3 Ply is the thickness of wool or thread, measured by the number of strands it is made from

plywood noun Plywood is wooden board made from several thin sheets of wood glued together under pressure

p.m. used to specify times between 12 noon and 12 midnight, eg He went to bed at 9 p.m. It is an abbreviation for the Latin phrase 'post meridiem', which means 'after noon'

pneumatic [new-mat-ik] adjective [D&T] operated by or filled with compressed air: a pneumatic drill

pneumonia [new-moan-ee-ah] noun Pneumonia is a serious disease which affects a person's lungs and makes breathing difficult

poach verb 1 If someone poaches animals from someone else's land, they illegally catch the animals for food 2 When you poach food, you cook it gently in hot liquid
> **poacher** noun

pocket noun 1 a small pouch that forms part of a piece of clothing 2 A pocket of something is a small area of it: *There are still pockets of resistance*

pocket money noun Pocket money is an amount of money given regularly to children by their parents

pod noun a long narrow seed container that grows on plants such as peas or beans

podium noun a small platform, often one on which someone stands to make a speech

poem noun a piece of writing in which the words are arranged in short rhythmic lines, often with a rhyme

poet noun a person who writes poems

poetic adjective 1 very beautiful and expressive: *a pure and poetic love* 2 relating to poetry > **poetically** adverb

poetry noun Poetry is poems, considered as a form of literature

poignant [poyn-yant] adjective Something that is poignant has a strong emotional effect on you, often making you feel sad: *a moving and poignant moment* > **poignancy** noun

point noun 1 an opinion or fact expressed by someone: *You've made a good point* 2 a quality: *Tact was never her strong point* 3 the purpose or meaning something has: *He completely missed the point in most of his argument* 4 a position or time: *At some point during the party, a fight erupted* 5 a single mark in a competition 6 the thin, sharp end of something such as a needle or knife 7 The points of a compass are the 32 directions indicated on it 8 The decimal point in a number is the dot separating the whole number from the fraction 9 On a railway track, the points are the levers and rails which enable a train to move from one track to another ▷ verb 10 If you point at something, you stick out your finger to show where it is 11 If something points in a particular direction, it faces that way

point-blank adjective 1 Something that is shot at point-blank range is shot with a gun held very close to it ▷ adverb 2 If you say something point-blank, you say it directly without explanation or apology

pointed adjective 1 A pointed object has a thin, sharp end 2 Pointed comments express criticism > **pointedly** adverb

pointer noun a piece of information which helps you to understand something: *Here are a few pointers to help you make a choice*

pointless adjective Something that is pointless has no purpose > **pointlessly** adverb

point of view noun Your point of view is your opinion about something or your attitude towards it

poise noun Someone who has poise is calm and dignified

poised adjective If you are poised to do something, you are ready to do it at any moment

poison noun 1 Poison is a substance that can kill people or animals if they swallow it or absorb it ▷ verb 2 To poison someone is to try to kill them with poison

poisonous *adjective* containing something that causes death or illness

poke *verb* **1** If you poke someone or something, you push or push them quickly with your finger or a sharp object **2** Something that pokes out of another thing appears from underneath or behind it: *roots poking out of the earth* ▷ *noun* **3** a sharp jab or prod

poker *noun* **1** Poker is a card game in which the players make bets on the cards dealt to them **2** a long metal rod used for moving coals or logs in a fire

polar *adjective* relating to the area around the North and South Poles

polar bear *noun* a large white bear which lives in the area around the North Pole

pole *noun* **1** a long rounded piece of wood or metal **2** The earth's poles are the two opposite ends of its axis: *the North Pole*

Pole *noun* someone who comes from Poland

pole vault *noun* The pole vault is an athletics event in which contestants jump over a high bar using a long flexible pole to lift themselves into the air

police *plural noun* **1** The police are the people who are officially responsible for making sure that people obey the law ▷ *verb* **2** To police an area is to keep law and order there by means of the police or an armed force

policeman *policemen noun* a man who is a member of a police force > **policewoman** *noun*

policy *policies noun* **1** a set of plans, especially in politics or business: *the new economic policy* **2** An insurance policy is a document which shows

an agreement made with an insurance company

polio *noun* Polio is an infectious disease that is caused by a virus and often results in paralysis. Polio is short for 'poliomyelitis'

polish *verb* **1** If you polish something, you put polish on it or rub it with a cloth to make it shine **2** If you polish a skill or technique you have, you work on it in order to improve it ▷ *noun* **3** Polish is a substance that you put on an object to clean it and make it shine: *shoe polish* **4** Something that has polish is elegant and of good quality > **polished** *adjective*

Polish [**pole**-ish] *adjective* **1** belonging or relating to Poland ▷ *noun* **2** Polish is the main language spoken in Poland

polite *adjective* **1** Someone who is polite has good manners and behaves considerately towards other people **2** Polite society is cultivated and refined > **politely** *adverb*

politeness *noun* the quality of having good manners and behaving considerately

political *adjective* GEOGRAPHY **1** relating to the state, government, or public administration **2** relating to or interested in politics > **politically** *adverb*

politically correct *adjective* careful not to offend or designed not to offend minority or disadvantaged groups

politician *noun* a person involved in the government of a country

politics *noun* HISTORY Politics is the activity and planning concerned with achieving power and control in a country or organization

polka *noun* a fast dance in which

couples dance together in circles around the room

poll noun **1** a survey in which people are asked their opinions about something **2** (in plural) A political election can be referred to as the polls ▷ verb **3** If you are polled on something, you are asked your opinion about it as part of a survey

pollen noun Pollen is a fine yellow powder produced by flowers in order to fertilize other flowers of the same species

pollutant noun a substance that causes pollution

pollute verb To pollute water or air is to make it dirty and dangerous to use or live in > **polluted** adjective

pollution noun GEOGRAPHY Pollution of the environment happens when dirty or dangerous substances get into the air, water, or soil

polo noun Polo is a game played between two teams of players on horseback. The players use wooden hammers with long handles to hit a ball

polyester noun D&T a man-made fibre, used especially to make clothes

polygamy [pol-lig-gam-ee] noun Polygamy is having more than one wife at the same time > **polygamous** adjective

polystyrene noun Polystyrene is a very light plastic, used especially as insulating material or to make containers

polythene noun Polythene is a type of plastic that is used to make thin sheets or bags

polyunsaturated adjective Polyunsaturated oils and margarines are made mainly from

vegetable fats and are considered to be healthier than saturated oils > **polyunsaturate** noun

pomegranate noun a round fruit with a thick reddish skin. It contains a lot of small seeds

pomp noun Pomp is the use of ceremony, fine clothes, and decorations on special occasions: Sir Patrick was buried with much pomp

pompous adjective behaving in a way that is too serious and self-important > **pomposity** noun

pond noun a small, usually man-made area of water

ponder verb If you ponder, you think about something deeply: He was pondering the problem when Phillipson drove up

ponderous adjective dull, slow, and serious: the ponderous commentary > **ponderously** adverb

pong noun (informal) an unpleasant smell

pontiff noun (formal) The pontiff is the Pope

pony ponies noun a small horse

ponytail noun a hairstyle in which long hair is tied at the back of the head and hangs down like a tail

poodle noun a type of dog with curly hair

pool noun **1** a small area of still water **2** Pool is a game in which players try to hit coloured balls into pockets around the table using long sticks called cues **3** A pool of people, money, or things is a group or collection used or shared by several people **4** (in plural) The pools are a competition in which people try to guess the results of football matches ▷ verb **5** If people pool their resources, they gather together the things they have so that they can be shared or used by all of them

P

poor adjective **1** Poor people have very little money and few possessions **2** Poor places are inhabited by people with little money and show signs of neglect **3** You use 'poor' to show sympathy: *Poor you!* **4** 'Poor' also means of a low quality or standard: *a poor performance*

poorly adjective **1** feeling unwell or ill ▷ adverb **2** badly: *a poorly planned operation*

pop pops, popping, popped noun **1** Pop is modern music played and enjoyed especially by young people **2** (informal) You can refer to fizzy, nonalcoholic drinks as pop **3** a short, sharp sound ▷ verb **4** If something pops, it makes a sudden sharp sound **5** (informal) If you pop something somewhere, you put it there quickly: *I'd just popped the pie in the oven* **6** (informal) If you pop somewhere, you go there quickly: *His mother popped out to buy him an ice cream*

popcorn noun Popcorn is a snack consisting of grains of maize heated until they puff up and burst

Pope noun The Pope is the head of the Roman Catholic Church

poppy poppies noun a plant with a large red flower on a hairy stem

populace noun (formal) The populace of a country is its people

popular adjective **1** liked or approved of by a lot of people **2** involving or intended for ordinary people: *the popular press* > **popularly** adverb > **popularity** noun > **popularize** verb

populate verb The people or animals that populate an area live there

population noun The population of a place is the people who live there, or the number of people living there

porcelain noun Porcelain is a delicate, hard material used to make crockery and ornaments

porch noun a covered area at the entrance to a building

pore noun **1** The pores in your skin or on the surface of a plant are very small holes which allow moisture to pass through ▷ verb **2** If you pore over a piece of writing or a diagram, you study it carefully

pork noun Pork is meat from a pig which has not been salted or smoked

porridge noun Porridge is a thick, sticky food made from oats cooked in water or milk

port noun **1** a town or area which has a harbour or docks **2** Port is a kind of strong, sweet red wine ▷ adjective **3** The port side of a ship is the left side when you are facing the front

-port suffix '-port' comes at the end of words that have something to do with 'carrying' in their meaning: *transport*

portable adjective designed to be easily carried: *a portable television*

porter noun **1** a person whose job is to be in charge of the entrance of a building, greeting and directing visitors **2** A porter in a railway station or hospital is a person whose job is to carry or move things

portfolio portfolios noun **1** a thin, flat case for carrying papers **2** A portfolio is also a group of selected duties, investments, or items of artwork: *the education portfolio; Choose your share portfolio wisely*

portion noun a part or amount of something: *a portion of fresh fruit*

portrait noun ART a picture or photograph of someone

portray verb When an actor, artist, or writer portrays or something, they represent or describe them ▷ noun

Portuguese [por-tyoo-**geez**] adjective **1** belonging or relating to Portugal ▷ noun **2** someone who comes from Portugal **3** Portuguese is the main language spoken in Portugal and Brazil

pose verb **1** If something poses a problem, it is the cause of the problem **2** If you pose a question, you ask it **3** If you pose as someone else, you pretend to be that person in order to deceive people ▷ noun **4** a way of standing, sitting, or lying: *Mr Clark assumes a pose for the photographer*

posh adjective (informal) **1** smart, fashionable, and expensive: *a posh restaurant* **2** upper-class: *the man with the posh voice*

position noun **1** DRAMA The position of someone or something is the place where they are or ought to be: *Would the cast take their positions, please* **2** When someone or something is in a particular position, they are sitting or lying in that way: *I raised myself to a sitting position* **3** a job or post in an organization **4** The position that you are in at a particular time is the situation that you are in: *This puts the president in a difficult position* ▷ verb **5** To position something somewhere is to put it there: *Llewelyn positioned a cushion behind Joanna's back*

positive adjective **1** completely sure about something: *I was positive he'd known about that money* **2** confident and hopeful: *I felt very positive about everything* **3** showing approval or encouragement: *I anticipate a positive response* **4** providing definite proof of the truth or identity of something: *positive evidence* **5** MATHS A positive number is greater than zero **6** SCIENCE In physics, a positive electric charge has an opposite charge to that of an electron > **positively** adverb

possess verb **1** If you possess a particular quality, you have it **2** If you possess something, you own it **3** If a feeling or belief possesses you, it strongly influences you: *Absolute terror possessed her* > **possessor** noun

possession noun **1** If something is in your possession or if you are in possession of it, you have it **2** Your possessions are the things you own or that you have with you

possessive adjective **1** A person who is possessive about someone or something wants to keep them to themselves ▷ noun **2** In grammar, the possessive is the form of a noun or pronoun used to show possession: *my car; That's hers*

possibility possibilities noun something that might be true or might happen: *the possibility of a ban*

possible adjective **1** likely to happen or able to be done **2** likely or capable of being true or correct > **possibly** adverb

possum noun In Australian and New Zealand English, a possum is a phalanger, a marsupial with thick fur and a long tail

post noun **1** The post is the system by which letters and parcels are collected and delivered **2** a job or official position in an organization **3** a strong upright pole fixed into the ground: *They are tied to a post* **4** a message or article published on a website ▷ verb **5** If you post a letter, you send it to someone by putting it into a postbox **6** If you are posted somewhere, you are sent by your employers to work there **7** If you post a message or article, you publish it on a website > **postal** adjective

post- prefix after a particular time or event: *his postwar career*

postage noun Postage is the money that you pay to send letters and parcels by post

postcard noun a card, often with a picture on one side, which you write on and send without an envelope

postcode noun a short sequence of letters and numbers at the end of an address which helps the post office to sort the mail

poster noun a large notice or picture that is stuck on a wall as an advertisement or for decoration

posterior noun (humorous) A person's posterior is their bottom

posterity noun (formal) You can refer to the future and the people who will be alive then as posterity: *to record the voyage for posterity*

posthumous [**poss**-tyum-uss] adjective happening or awarded after a person's death: *a posthumous medal* > **posthumously** adverb

postman noun postmen someone who collects and delivers letters and parcels sent by post

postmortem noun a medical examination of a dead body to find out how the person died

post office noun **1** The Post Office is the national organization responsible for postal services **2** a building where you can buy stamps and post letters

postpone verb If you postpone an event, you arrange for it to take place at a later time than was originally planned > **postponement** noun

posture noun Your posture is the position or manner in which you hold your body

pot noun a deep round container; also used to refer to its contents

potato potatoes noun a white vegetable that has a brown or red skin and grows underground

potent adjective effective or powerful: *a potent cocktail* > **potency** noun

potential adjective **1** capable of becoming the thing mentioned: *potential customers; potential sources of finance* ▷ noun **2** Your potential is your ability to achieve success in the future > **potentially** adverb

pothole noun **1** a hole in the surface of a road caused by bad weather or traffic **2** an underground cavern

potion noun a drink containing medicine, poison, or supposed magical powers

potted adjective Potted meat or fish is cooked and placed into a small sealed container to preserve it

potter noun **1** a person who makes pottery ▷ verb **2** If you potter about, you pass the time doing pleasant, unimportant things

pottery noun **1** Pottery is pots, dishes, and other items made from clay and fired in a kiln **2** Pottery is also the craft of making pottery

potty potties; pottier, pottiest noun **1** a bowl which a small child can sit on and use instead of a toilet ▷ adjective **2** (informal) crazy or foolish

pouch noun **1** a small, soft container with a fold-over top: *a tobacco pouch* **2** Animals like kangaroos have a pouch, which is a pocket of skin in which they carry their young

poultry noun Chickens, turkeys, and other birds kept for their meat or eggs are referred to as poultry

pounce verb If an animal or person pounces on something, they leap and grab it

pound noun 1 The pound is the main unit of currency in Britain and in some other countries 2 a unit of weight equal to 16 ounces or about 0.454 kilograms ▷ verb 3 If you pound something, you hit it repeatedly with your fist: *Someone was pounding on the door* 4 If you pound a substance, you crush it into a powder or paste: *Wooden mallets were used to pound the meat* 5 If your heart is pounding, it is beating very strongly and quickly 6 If you pound somewhere, you run there with heavy noisy steps

pour verb 1 If you pour a liquid out of a container, you make it flow out by tipping the container 2 If something pours somewhere, it flows there quickly and in large quantities: *Sweat poured down his face* 3 When it is raining heavily, you can say that it is pouring

pout verb If you pout, you stick out your lips or bottom lip

poverty noun GEOGRAPHY the state of being very poor

powder noun 1 Powder consists of many tiny particles of a solid substance ▷ verb 2 If you powder a surface, you cover it with powder > **powdery** adjective

power noun 1 Someone who has power has a lot of control over people and activities 2 Someone who has the power to do something has the ability to do it: *the power of speech* 3 Power is also the authority to do something: *the power of arrest* 4 The power of something is the physical strength that it has to move things 5 Power is energy

obtained, for example, by burning fuel or using the wind or waves 6 MATHS In maths, a power is the product of a number multiplied by itself a certain number of times. For example, the third power of 10 is 1000 7 SCIENCE In physics, power is the energy transferred from one thing to another in one second. It is measured in watts ▷ verb 8 Something that powers a machine provides the energy for it to work

powerful adjective 1 able to control people and events 2 having great physical strength 3 having a strong effect > **powerfully** adverb

powerless adjective unable to control or influence events: *I was powerless to save her*

power station noun a place where electricity is generated

practicable adjective If a task or plan is practicable, it can be carried out successfully: *a practicable option*

practical adjective 1 The practical aspects of something are those that involve experience and real situations rather than ideas or theories: *the practical difficulties of teaching science* 2 sensible and likely to be effective: *practical low-heeled shoes* 3 Someone who is practical is able to deal effectively and sensibly with problems ▷ noun 4 an examination in which you make or perform something rather than simply write > **practicality** noun

practically adverb 1 almost but not completely or exactly: *The house was practically a wreck* 2 in a practical way: *practically minded*

practice noun 1 You can refer to something that people do regularly as a practice: *the practice of kissing hands* 2 Practice is regular training or exercise: *I need more practice to* *improve my football skills* **3** A doctor's or lawyer's practice is his or her business

practise *verb* **1** If you practise something, you do it regularly in order to improve **2** People who practise a religion, custom, or craft regularly take part in the activities associated with it: *a practising Buddhist* **3** Someone who practises medicine or law works as a doctor or lawyer

practised *adjective* Someone who is practised at doing something is very skilful at it: *a practised performer*

practitioner *noun* You can refer to someone who works in a particular profession as a practitioner: *a medical practitioner*

pragmatic *adjective* A pragmatic way of considering or doing something is a practical rather than theoretical way: *He is pragmatic about the risks involved*
> **pragmatically** *adverb*
> **pragmatism** *noun*

prairie *noun* a large area of flat, grassy land in North America

praise *verb* **1** If you praise someone or something, you express strong approval of their qualities or achievements ▷ *noun* **2** Praise is what is said or written in approval of someone's qualities or achievements

pram *noun* a baby's cot on wheels

prance *verb* Someone who is prancing around is walking with exaggerated movements

prank *noun* a childish trick

prawn *noun* a small, pink, edible shellfish with a long tail

pray *verb* RE When someone prays, they speak to God to give thanks or to ask for help

prayer *noun* RE **1** Prayer is the

activity of praying **2** the words said when someone prays

pre- *prefix* 'Pre-' means before a particular time or event: *pre-war*

preach *verb* When someone preaches, they give a short talk on a religious or moral subject as part of a church service > **preacher** *noun*

precarious *adjective* **1** If your situation is precarious, you may fail in what you are doing at any time **2** Something that is precarious is likely to fall because it is not well balanced or secured > **precariously** *adverb*

precaution *noun* an action that is intended to prevent something from happening: *It's still worth taking precautions against accidents*
> **precautionary** *adjective*

precede *verb* **1** Something that precedes another thing happens or occurs before it **2** If you precede someone somewhere, you go in front of them > **preceding** *adjective*

precedence [press-id-ens] *noun* If something takes precedence over other things, it is the most important thing and should be dealt with first

precedent *noun* An action or decision that is regarded as a precedent is used as a guide in taking similar action or decisions later

precinct *noun* **1** A shopping precinct is a pedestrian shopping area **2** (*in plural, formal*) The precincts of a place are its buildings and land

precious *adjective* Something that is precious is valuable or very important and should be looked after or used carefully

precipice [press-sip-piss] *noun* a very steep rock face

precipitate *verb* (*formal*) If something precipitates an event or situation, it causes it to happen suddenly

precipitation noun GEOGRAPHY Precipitation is rain, snow, or hail; used especially when stating the amount that falls during a particular period

precise adjective exact and accurate in every detail: precise measurements > **precisely** adverb > **precision** noun

preclude verb (formal) If something precludes an event or situation, it prevents it from happening: The meal precluded serious conversation

precocious adjective Precocious children behave in a way that seems too advanced for their age

preconceived adjective Preconceived ideas about something have been formed without any real experience or information > **preconception** noun

precondition noun If something is a precondition for another thing, it must happen before the second thing can take place

precursor noun A precursor of something that exists now is a similar thing that existed at an earlier time: real tennis, an ancient precursor of the modern game

predator [pred-dat-tor] noun SCIENCE an animal that kills and eats other animals > **predatory** adjective

predecessor noun Someone's predecessor is a person who used to do their job before

predetermined adjective decided in advance or controlled by previous events rather than left to chance

predicament noun a difficult situation

predict verb If someone predicts an event, they say that it will happen in the future

prediction noun something that is forecast in advance

predominant adjective more important or more noticeable than anything else in a particular set of people or things: Yellow is the predominant colour in the house > **predominantly** adverb

predominate verb If one type of person or thing predominates, it is the most common, frequent, or noticeable: Fresh flowers predominate in the bouquet > **predominance** noun

pre-eminent adjective recognized as being the most important in a particular group: the pre-eminent experts in the area > **pre-eminence** noun

pre-empt verb (formal) If you pre-empt something, you prevent it by doing something else which makes it pointless or impossible: By resigning, he pre-empted the decision to sack him

preen verb When a bird preens its feathers, it cleans them using its beak

preface [pref-fiss] noun an introduction at the beginning of a book explaining what the book is about or why it was written

prefect noun a pupil who has special duties at a school

prefer prefers, preferring, preferred verb If you prefer one thing to another, you like it better than the other thing > **preferable** adjective > **preferably** adverb

preference [pref-fer-enss] noun 1 If you have a preference for something, you like it more than other things: a preference for white 2 When making a choice, if you give preference to one type of person or thing, you try to choose that type

P

preferential adjective A person who gets preferential treatment is treated better than others

prefix noun ENGLISH a letter or group of letters added to the beginning of a word to make a new word, for example 'semi-', 'pre-', and 'un-'

pregnant adjective A woman who is pregnant has a baby developing in her womb > **pregnancy** noun

prehistoric adjective existing at a time in the past before anything was written down

prejudice noun 1 Prejudice is an unreasonable and unfair dislike or preference formed without carefully examining the facts 2 Prejudice is also an intolerance towards certain people or groups: racial prejudice > **prejudiced** adjective > **prejudicial** adjective

preliminary adjective Preliminary activities take place before something starts, in preparation for it: the preliminary rounds of the competition

prelude noun Something that is an introduction to a more important event can be described as a prelude to that event

premature adjective happening too early, or earlier than expected: premature baldness > **prematurely** adverb

premeditated adjective planned in advance: a premeditated attack

premier noun 1 The leader of a government is sometimes referred to as the premier 2 In Australia, the leader of a State government ▷ adjective 3 considered to be the best or most important: Wellington's premier jewellers

premiere [prem-mee-er] noun the first public performance of a new play or film

premise [prem-iss] noun 1 (in plural) The premises of an organization are all the buildings it occupies on one site 2 a statement which you suppose is true and use as the basis for an idea or argument

premium noun 1 A sum of money paid regularly to an insurance company for an insurance policy 2 an extra sum of money that has to be paid: Paying a premium for space is worthwhile

premonition [prem-on-ish-on] noun a feeling that something unpleasant is going to happen

preoccupation noun If you have a preoccupation with something, it is very important to you and you keep thinking about it

preoccupied adjective Someone who is preoccupied is deep in thought or totally involved with something

preparatory adjective Preparatory activities are done before doing something else in order to prepare for it

prepare verb If you prepare something, you make it ready for a particular purpose or event: He was preparing the meal > **preparation** noun

prepared adjective If you are prepared to do something, you are willing to do it

preposterous adjective extremely unreasonable and ridiculous: a preposterous statement

prerequisite [pree-rek-wiz-zit] noun (formal) Something that is a prerequisite for another thing must happen or exist before the other thing is possible: Self-esteem is a prerequisite for a happy life

prerogative [prir-rog-at-iv] noun (formal) Something that is the prerogative of a person is their special privilege or right

prescribe *verb* When a doctor prescribes treatment, he or she states what treatment a patient should have

prescription *noun* a piece of paper on which the doctor has written the name of a medicine needed by a patient

presence *noun* **1** Someone's presence in a place is the fact of their being there: *His presence made me happy* **2** If you are in someone's presence, you are in the same place as they are **3** Someone who has presence has an impressive appearance or manner

present *adjective* [**prez**-ent] **1** If someone is present somewhere, they are there: *He had been present at the birth of his son* **2** A present situation is one that exists now rather than in the past or the future **3** [ENGLISH] The present tense of a verb is the form used to express something that is happening in the present ▷ *noun* [**prez**-ent] **4** The present is the period of time that is taking place now **5** something that you give to someone for them to keep ▷ *verb* [pri-**zent**] **6** If you present someone with something, you give it to them: *She presented a bravery award to the girl* **7** Something that presents a difficulty or a challenge causes it or provides it **8** The person who presents a radio or television show introduces each part or each guest > **presenter** *noun*

presentable *adjective* neat or attractive and suitable for people to see

presentation *noun* **1** the act of presenting or a way of presenting

something **2** The presentation of a piece of work is the way it looks or the impression it gives **3** To give a presentation is to give a talk or demonstration to an audience of something you have been studying or working on

present-day *adjective* existing or happening now: *present-day farming practices*

presently *adverb* **1** If something will happen presently, it will happen soon: *I'll finish the job presently* **2** Something that is presently happening is happening now: *Some progress is presently being made*

present tense *noun* [ENGLISH] In grammar, the present tense is the tense of a verb that you use mainly to talk about things that happen or exist at the time of writing or speaking

preservative *noun* a substance or chemical that stops things decaying

preserve *verb* **1** If you preserve something, you take action so that it remains as it is **2** If you preserve food, you treat it to prevent it from decaying ▷ *noun* **3** Preserves are foods such as jam or chutney that have been made with a lot of sugar or vinegar > **preservation** *noun*

preside *verb* A person who presides over a formal event is in charge of it

president *noun* **1** In a country which has no king or queen, the president is the elected leader: *the President of the United States of America* **2** The president of an organization is the person who has the highest position > **presidency** *noun* > **presidential** *adjective*

press *verb* **1** If you press something, you push it or hold it firmly against something else: *Lisa pressed his hand; Press the blue button* **2** If you press

P

clothes, you iron them **3** If you press for something, you try hard to persuade someone to agree to it: *She was pressing for improvements to the education system* **4** If you press charges, you make an accusation against someone which has to be decided in a court of law ▷ *noun* **5** Newspapers and the journalists who work for them are called the press

press conference *noun* When someone gives a press conference, they have a meeting to answer questions put by reporters

pressing *adjective* Something that is pressing needs to be dealt with immediately: *pressing needs*

pressure *noun* **1** (SCIENCE) Pressure is the force that is produced by pushing on something **2** (PSHE) If you are under pressure, you have too much to do and not enough time, or someone is trying hard to persuade you to do something ▷ *verb* **3** If you pressure someone, you try hard to persuade them to do something

pressurize or **pressurise** *verb* If you pressurize someone, you try hard to persuade them to do something

prestige [press-**teezh**] *noun* If you have prestige, people admire you because of your position
> **prestigious** *adjective*

presumably *adverb* If you say that something is presumably the case, you mean you assume that it is: *Your audience, presumably, are younger*

presume [priz-**yoom**] *verb* If you presume something, you think that it is the case although you have no proof > **presumption** *noun*

presumptuous *adjective* Someone who behaves in a presumptuous

way does things that they have no right to do

pretence *noun* a way of behaving that is false and intended to deceive people

pretend *verb* If you pretend that something is the case, you try to make people believe that it is, although in fact it is not: *Latimer pretended not to notice*

pretender *noun* A pretender to a throne or title is someone who claims it but whose claim is being questioned

pretension *noun* Someone with pretensions claims that they are more important than they really are

pretentious *adjective* Someone or something that is pretentious is trying to seem important when in fact they are not

pretext *noun* a false reason given to hide the real reason for doing something

pretty prettier, prettiest *adjective* **1** attractive in a delicate way ▷ *adverb* **2** (*informal*) quite or rather: *He spoke pretty good English*
> **prettily** *adverb* > **prettiness** *noun*

prevail *verb* **1** If a custom or belief prevails in a particular place, it is normal or most common there: *This attitude has prevailed in Britain for many years* **2** If someone or something prevails, they succeed in their aims: *In recent years better sense has prevailed* > **prevailing** *adjective*

prevalent *adjective* very common or widespread: *the hooliganism so prevalent today* > **prevalence** *noun*

prevent *verb* If you prevent something, you stop it from happening or being done
> **preventable** *adjective*
> **prevention** *noun*

preventive *or* **preventative**
adjective intended to help prevent
things such as disease or crime:
preventive health care

preview *noun* **1** an opportunity to
see something, such as a film or
exhibition, before it is shown to the
public **2** COMPUTING a part of a
computer program which allows you
to look at what you have keyed or
added to a document or spreadsheet
as it will appear when it is printed

previous *adjective* happening or
existing before something else in
time or position: *previous reports; the
previous year* > **previously** *adverb*

prey [rhymes with **say**] *noun* **1** The
creatures that an animal hunts and
eats are called its prey ▷ *verb* **2** An
animal that preys on a particular
kind of animal lives by hunting and
eating it

price *noun* **1** The price of something
is the amount of money you have to
pay to buy it ▷ *verb* **2** To price
something at a particular amount is
to fix its price at that amount

priceless *adjective* Something that is
priceless is so valuable that it is
difficult to work out how much it is
worth

pricey pricier, priciest *adjective*
(*informal*) expensive

prick *verb* **1** If you prick something,
you stick a sharp pointed object into
it ▷ *noun* **2** a small, sharp pain
caused when something pricks you

pride *noun* **1** Pride is a feeling of
satisfaction you have when you
have done something well **2** Pride is
also a feeling of being better than
other people **3** A pride of lions is a
group of them ▷ *verb* **4** If you pride
yourself on a quality or skill, you are
proud of it: *She prides herself on
punctuality*

priest *noun* RE **1** a member of the
clergy in some Christian Churches
2 In many non-Christian religions,
a priest is a man who has special
duties in the place where people
worship > **priestly** *adjective*

priestess *noun* a female priest in a
non-Christian religion

priesthood *noun* The priesthood is
the position of being a priest

prim primmer, primmest *adjective*
Someone who is prim always
behaves very correctly and is easily
shocked by anything rude

primarily *adverb* You use 'primarily'
to indicate the main or most
important feature of something: *I
still rated people primarily on their looks*

primary *adjective* 'Primary' is used to
describe something that is
extremely important for something
or something: *the primary aim of his
research*

primary school *noun* a school for
children aged up to 11

primate *noun* **1** an archbishop **2** a
member of the group of animals
which includes humans, monkeys,
and apes

prime *adjective* **1** main or most
important: *a prime cause of brain
damage* **2** of the best quality: *in prime
condition* ▷ *noun* **3** Someone's prime
is the stage when they are at their
strongest, most active, or most
successful ▷ *verb* **4** If you prime
someone, you give them
information about something in
advance to prepare them: *We are
primed for every lesson*

prime minister *noun* The prime
minister is the leader of the
government

primeval *or* **primaeval** [pry-**mee**-vl]
adjective belonging to a very early
period in the history of the world

primitive adjective **1** connected with a society that lives very simply without industries or a writing system: *the primitive peoples of the world* **2** very simple, basic, or old-fashioned: *a very small primitive cottage*

primrose noun a small plant that has pale yellow flowers in spring

prince noun a male member of a royal family, especially the son of a king or queen ▷ **princely** adjective

princess noun a female member of a royal family, usually the daughter of a king or queen, or the wife of a prince

principal adjective **1** main or most important: *the principal source of food* ▷ noun **2** the person in charge of a school or college ▷ **principally** adverb

> **WORD TIP**
>
> Do not confuse the spellings of principal and principle: the principal reason; the school principal; Eating meat is against my principles

principality principalities noun a country ruled by a prince

principle noun **1** a belief you have about the way you should behave: *a woman of principle* **2** a general rule or scientific law which explains how something happens or works: *the principle of evolution in nature*

> **WORD TIP**
>
> Do not confuse the spellings of principle and principal: Eating meat is against my principles; the principal reason; the school principal

print verb **1** To print a newspaper or book is to reproduce it in large quantities using a mechanical or electronic copying process **2** If you print when you are writing, you do not join the letters together ▷ noun **3** The letters and numbers on the pages of a book or newspaper are referred to as the print **4** a photograph, or a printed copy of a painting **5** Footprints and fingerprints can be referred to as prints ▷ **printer** noun

printing noun the process of producing printed material such as books and newspapers

prior adjective **1** planned or done at an earlier time: *I have a prior engagement* ▷ phrase **2** Something that happens **prior to** a particular time or event happens before it

prioritize or **prioritise** verb To prioritize things is to decide which is the most important and deal with it first

priority priorities noun something that needs to be dealt with first: *The priority is building homes*

prise verb If you prise something open or away from a surface, you force it open or away: *She prised his fingers loose*

prism noun **1** an object made of clear glass with many flat sides. It separates light passing through it into the colours of the rainbow **2** MATHS A prism is any polyhedron with two identical parallel ends and sides which are parallelograms

prison noun a building where criminals are kept in captivity

prisoner noun someone who is in prison or held in captivity against their will

pristine [priss-teen] adjective (formal) very clean or new and in perfect condition

private adjective **1** for the use of one person rather than people in general: *a private bathroom* **2** taking place between a small number of people and kept secret from others:

a private conversation **3** owned or run by individuals or companies rather than by the state: *a private company* ▷ noun **4** a soldier of the lowest rank > **privacy** noun > **privately** adverb

private school noun a school that does not receive money from the government, and parents pay for their children to attend

privatize or **privatise** verb If the government privatizes a state-owned industry or organization, it allows it to be bought and owned by a private individual or group

privilege noun a special right or advantage given to a person or group: *the privileges of monarchy* > **privileged** adjective

privy adjective (formal) If you are privy to something secret, you have been told about it

prize noun **1** a reward given to the winner of a competition or game ▷ adjective **2** of the highest quality or standard: *his prize dahlia* ▷ verb **3** Something that is prized is wanted and admired for its value or quality

pro pros noun **1** (informal) a professional ▷ phrase **2** The **pros and cons** of a situation are its advantages and disadvantages

pro- prefix 'Pro-' means supporting or in favour of: *pro-democracy protests*

probability probabilities noun **1** The probability of something happening is how likely it is to happen: *the probability of success* **2** If something is a probability, it is likely to happen: *The probability is that you will be feeling better*

probable adjective Something that is probable is likely to be true or correct, or likely to happen: *the most probable outcome*

probably adverb Something that is

probably the case is likely but not certain

probation noun Probation is a period of time during which a person convicted of a crime is supervised by a probation officer instead of being sent to prison > **probationary** adjective

probe verb **1** If you probe, you ask a lot of questions to discover the facts about something ▷ noun **2** a long thin instrument used by doctors and dentists when examining a patient

problem noun **1** an unsatisfactory situation that causes difficulties **2** a puzzle or question that you solve using logical thought or mathematics > **problematic** adjective

procedure noun a way of doing something, especially the correct or usual way: *It's standard procedure* > **procedural** adjective

proceed verb **1** If you proceed to do something, you start doing it, or continue doing it: *She proceeded to tell them* **2** (formal) If you proceed in a particular direction, you move in that direction: *The taxi proceeded along a lonely road*

proceedings plural noun **1** You can refer to an organized and related series of events as the proceedings: *She was determined to see the proceedings from start to finish* **2** Legal proceedings are legal action taken against someone

process noun **1** a series of actions intended to achieve a particular result or change ▷ phrase **2** If you are **in the process** of doing something, you have started doing it but have not yet finished ▷ verb **3** When food is processed, it is prepared in factories before it is sold

4 When information is processed, it is put through a system or into a computer to organize it

procession noun a group of people or vehicles moving in a line, often as part of a ceremony

processor noun COMPUTING In computing, a processor is the central chip in a computer which controls its operations

proclaim verb If someone proclaims something, they announce it or make it known: *You have proclaimed your innocence* > **proclamation** noun

procure verb (formal) If you procure something, you obtain it

prod prods, prodding, prodded verb If you prod something, you give it a push with your finger or with something pointed

prodigy prodigies [**prod**-dij-ee] noun someone who shows an extraordinary natural ability at an early age

produce verb [pro-**dyoos**] **1** To produce something is to make it or cause it: *a white wine produced mainly from black grapes* **2** If you produce something from somewhere, you bring it out so it can be seen ▷ noun [**prod**-yoos] **3** Produce is food that is grown to be sold: *fresh produce*

producer noun The producer of a record, film, or show is the person in charge of making it or putting it on

product noun **1** something that is made to be sold: *high-quality products* **2** MATHS The product of two or more numbers or quantities is the result of multiplying them together **3** SCIENCE a substance formed in a chemical reaction

production noun [D G T] **1** Production is the process of manufacturing or growing something in large quantities: *modern methods of*

production **2** Production is also the amount of goods manufactured or food grown by a country or company: *Production has fallen by 13.2%* **3** A production of a play, opera, or other show is a series of performances of it

productive adjective **1** To be productive means to produce a large number of things: *Farms were more productive in these areas* **2** If something such as a meeting is productive, good or useful things happen as a result of it

productivity noun Productivity is the rate at which things are produced or dealt with

profane adjective (formal) showing disrespect for a religion or religious things: *profane language*

profess verb **1** (formal) If you profess to do or have something, you claim to do or have it **2** If you profess a feeling or opinion, you express it: *He professes a lasting affection for Trinidad*

profession noun **1** a type of job that requires advanced education or training **2** You can use 'profession' to refer to all the people who have a particular profession: *the medical profession*

professional adjective
1 Professional means relating to the work of someone who is qualified in a particular profession: *I think you need professional advice*
2 Professional also describes activities when they are done to earn money rather than as a hobby: *professional football* **3** A professional piece of work is of a very high standard ▷ noun **4** a person who has been trained in a profession
5 someone who plays a sport to earn money rather than as a hobby

professor noun the senior teacher in

a department of a British university
> **professorial** *adjective*

proficient *adjective* If you are
proficient at something, you can do
it well > **proficiency** *noun*

profile *noun* 1 Your profile is the
outline of your face seen from the
side 2 A profile of someone is a
short description of their life and
character

profit *noun* 1 When someone sells
something, the profit is the amount
they gain by selling it for more than
it cost them to buy or make ▷ *verb*
2 If you profit from something, you
gain or benefit from it > **profitable**
adjective

profound *adjective* 1 great in degree
or intensity: *a profound need to please*
2 showing great and deep
intellectual understanding: *a
profound question* > **profoundly**
adverb > **profundity** *noun*

program programs, programming,
programmed [COMPUTING] *noun* 1 a
set of instructions that a computer
follows to perform a particular task
▷ *verb* 2 When someone programs a
computer, they write a program and
put it into the computer
> **programmer** *noun*

programme *noun* 1 a planned series
of events: *a programme of official
engagements* 2 a particular piece
presented as a unit on television or
radio, such as a play, show, or
discussion 3 a booklet giving
information about a play, concert,
or show that you are attending

progress *noun* 1 Progress is the
process of gradually improving or
getting near to achieving
something: *Gerry is now making some
real progress towards fitness* 2 The
progress of something is the way in
which it develops or continues: *news*

on the progress of the war ▷ *phrase*
3 Something that is **in progress** is
happening: *A cricket match was in
progress* ▷ *verb* 4 If you progress, you
become more advanced or skilful
5 To progress is to continue: *As the
evening progressed, sadness turned to
rage* > **progression** *noun*

progressive *adjective* 1 having
modern ideas about how things
should be done 2 happening
gradually: *a progressive illness*

prohibit *verb* If someone prohibits
something, they forbid it or make it
illegal > **prohibition** *noun*

prohibitive *adjective* If the cost of
something is prohibitive, it is so
high that people cannot afford it

project *noun* [pro-ject] 1 a carefully
planned attempt to achieve
something or to study something
over a period of time ▷ *verb*
[pro-ject] 2 Something that is
projected is planned or expected to
happen in the future: *The population
aged 65 or over is projected to increase*
3 To project an image onto a screen
is to make it appear there using
equipment such as a projector
4 Something that projects sticks out
beyond a surface or edge
> **projection** *noun*

projector *noun* a piece of equipment
which produces a large image on a
screen by shining light through a
photographic slide or film strip

proletariat *noun* (formal)
Working-class people are
sometimes referred to as the
proletariat > **proletarian** *adjective*

proliferate *verb* If things proliferate,
they quickly increase in number
> **proliferation** *noun*

prolific *adjective* producing a lot of
something: *this prolific artist*

prologue *noun* a speech or section

P

that introduces a play or book

prolong verb If you prolong something, you make it last longer > **prolonged** adjective

prom noun (informal) a concert at which some of the audience stand

promenade [prom-min-**ahd**] noun a road or path next to the sea at a seaside resort

prominent adjective 1 Prominent people are well-known and important 2 Something that is prominent is very noticeable: a prominent nose > **prominence** noun > **prominently** adverb

promise verb 1 If you promise to do something, you say that you will definitely do it 2 Something that promises to have a particular quality shows signs that it will have that quality: This promised to be a very long night ▷ noun 3 a statement made by someone that they will definitely do something: He made a promise to me 4 Someone or something that shows promise seems likely to be very successful > **promising** adjective

promontory promontories [prom-mon-tree] noun an area of high land sticking out into the sea

promote verb 1 If someone promotes something, they try to make it happen 2 If someone promotes a product such as a film or a book, they try to make it popular by advertising 3 If someone is promoted, they are given a more important job at work > **promoter** noun > **promotion** noun

prompt verb 1 If something prompts someone to do something, it makes them decide to do it: Curiosity prompted him to push at the door 2 If you prompt someone when they stop speaking, you tell them what

to say next or encourage them to continue ▷ adverb 3 exactly at the time mentioned: Wednesday morning at 10.40 prompt ▷ adjective 4 A prompt action is done without any delay: a prompt reply > **promptly** adverb

prone adjective 1 If you are prone to something, you have a tendency to be affected by it or to do it: She is prone to depression 2 If you are prone, you are lying flat and face downwards: lying prone on the grass

pronoun noun ENGLISH In grammar, a pronoun is a word that is used to replace a noun. 'He', 'she', and 'them' are all pronouns

pronounce verb ENGLISH When you pronounce a word, you say it

pronounced adjective very noticeable: He talks with a pronounced lowland accent

pronouncement noun a formal statement

pronunciation [pron-nun-see-**ay**-shn] noun the way a word is usually said

proof noun If you have proof of something, you have evidence which shows that it is true or exists

prop props, propping, propped verb 1 If you prop an object somewhere, you support it or rest it against something: The barman propped himself against the counter ▷ noun 2 a stick or other object used to support something 3 The props in a play are all the objects and furniture used by the actors

propaganda noun HISTORY Propaganda is exaggerated or false information that is published or broadcast in order to influence people

propagate verb 1 If people propagate an idea, they spread it to

try to influence many other people
2 If you propagate plants, you grow
more of them from an original one
> **propagation** noun

propel propels, propelling, propelled
verb To propel something is to cause
it to move in a particular direction

propeller noun a device on a boat or
aircraft with rotating blades which
make the boat or aircraft move

propensity propensities noun
(formal) a tendency to behave in a
particular way

proper adjective **1** real and
satisfactory: He was no nearer having
a proper job **2** correct or suitable: Put
things in their proper place **3** accepted
or conventional: a proper wedding
> **properly** adverb

property properties noun **1** A
person's property is the things that
belong to them **2** a building and the
land belonging to it **3** a
characteristic or quality: Mint has
powerful healing properties

prophecy prophecies noun a
statement about what someone
believes will happen in the future

prophet noun RE a person who
predicts what will happen in the
future

prophetic adjective correctly
predicting what will happen: It was
a prophetic warning

proportion noun **1** A proportion
of an amount or group is a part of it:
a tiny proportion of the population
2 The proportion of one amount to
another is its size in comparison
with the other amount: the highest
proportion of single women to men
3 (in plural) You can refer to the size
of something as its proportions: a
red umbrella of vast proportions

proportional or **proportionate**
adjective If one thing is proportional

to another, it remains the same size
in comparison with the other:
proportional increases in profit
> **proportionally** or
> **proportionately** adverb

proportional representation
noun Proportional representation is
a system of voting in elections in
which the number of
representatives of each party is in
proportion to the number of people
who voted for it

proposal noun a plan that has been
suggested: business proposals

propose verb **1** If you propose a plan
or idea, you suggest it **2** If you
propose to do something, you
intend to do it: And how do you
propose to do that? **3** When someone
proposes a toast to a particular
person, they ask people to drink a
toast to that person **4** If someone
proposes to another person, they
ask that person to marry them

proposition noun **1** a statement
expressing a theory or opinion
2 an offer or suggestion: I made her
a proposition

proprietor noun The proprietor of a
business is the owner

propriety noun (formal) Propriety is
what is socially or morally
acceptable: a model of propriety

propulsion noun Propulsion is the
power that moves something

prose noun Prose is ordinary written
language in contrast to poetry

prosecute verb If someone is
prosecuted, they are charged with a
crime and have to stand trial
> **prosecutor** noun

prosecution noun The lawyers who
try to prove that a person on trial is
guilty are called the prosecution

prospect noun **1** If there is a
prospect of something happening,

p

there is a possibility that it will happen: *There was little prospect of going home* **2** Someone's prospects are their chances of being successful in the future ▷ *verb* **3** If someone prospects for gold or oil, they look for it > **prospector** *noun*

prospective *adjective* 'Prospective' is used to say that someone wants to be or is likely to be something. For example, the prospective owner of something is the person who wants to own it

prospectus *noun* a booklet giving details about a college or a company

prosper *verb* When people or businesses prosper, they are successful and make a lot of money > **prosperous** *adjective* > **prosperity** *noun*

prostrate *adjective* lying face downwards on the ground

protagonist *noun* (*formal*) **1** Someone who is a protagonist of an idea or movement is a leading supporter of it **2** a main character in a play or story

protect *verb* **1** To protect someone or something is to prevent them from being harmed or damaged **2** SCIENCE To prevent a particular animal, plant, or area of land from being harmed or damaged by making it illegal to do so: *a protected species* > **protective** *adjective* > **protector** *noun*

protection *noun* **1** the act of preventing harm or damage **2** something that keeps a person or thing safe

protein *noun* SCIENCE Protein is a complex compound consisting of amino acid chains, found in many foods and essential for all living things

protest *verb* [pro-**test**] **1** If you

protest about something, you say or demonstrate publicly that you disagree with it: *They protested against the killing of a teenager* ▷ *noun* [**pro**-test] **2** a demonstration or statement showing that you disagree with something

Protestant *noun* RE a member of one of the Christian Churches which separated from the Catholic Church in the 16th century

protestation *noun* a strong declaration that something is true or not true: *his protestations of love*

protocol *noun* Protocol is the system of rules about the correct way to behave in formal situations

proton *noun* SCIENCE a particle which forms part of the nucleus of an atom and has a positive electrical charge

prototype *noun* D&T a first model of something that is made so that the design can be tested and improved

protracted *adjective* lasting longer than usual: *a protracted dispute*

protrude *verb* (*formal*) If something is protruding from a surface or edge, it is sticking out > **protrusion** *noun*

proud *adjective* **1** feeling pleasure and satisfaction at something you own or have achieved: *I was proud of our players today* **2** having great dignity and self-respect: *too proud to ask for money* > **proudly** *adverb*

prove proves, proving, proved or proven *verb* **1** To prove that something is true is to provide evidence that it is true: *A letter from Kathleen proved that he lived there* **2** If something proves to be the case, it becomes clear that it is so: *His first impressions of her proved wrong*

proverb *noun* a short sentence

which gives advice or makes a comment about life > **proverbial** *adjective*

provide *verb* **1** If you provide something for someone, you give it to them or make it available for them **2** If you provide for someone, you give them the things they need

providence *noun* Providence is God or a force which is believed to arrange the things that happen to us

province *noun* **1** one of the areas into which some large countries are divided, each province having its own administration **2** (*in plural*) You can refer to the parts of a country which are not near the capital as the provinces

provincial *adjective* **1** connected with the parts of a country outside the capital: *a provincial theatre* **2** narrow-minded and lacking sophistication

provision *noun* GEOGRAPHY **1** The provision of something is the act of making it available to people: *the provision of health care* **2** (*in plural*) Provisions are supplies of food

provisional *adjective* A provisional arrangement has not yet been made definite and so might be changed

proviso provisos [prov-**eye**-zoh] *noun* a condition in an agreement

provocation *noun* an act done deliberately to annoy someone

provocative *adjective* intended to annoy people or make them react: *a provocative speech*

provoke *verb* **1** If you provoke someone, you deliberately try to make them angry **2** If something provokes an unpleasant reaction, it causes it: *illness provoked by tension or worry*

prowess *noun* Prowess is outstanding ability: *his prowess at tennis*

prowl *verb* If a person or animal prowls around, they move around quietly and secretly, as if hunting

proximity *noun* (*formal*) Proximity is nearness to something or someone

proxy *phrase* If you do something by proxy, someone else does it on your behalf: *voting by proxy*

prudent *adjective* behaving in a sensible and cautious way: *It is prudent to plan ahead* > **prudence** *noun* > **prudently** *adverb*

prune *noun* **1** a dried plum > *verb* **2** When someone prunes a tree or shrub, they cut back some of the branches

pry pries, prying, pried *verb* If someone is prying, they are trying to find out about something secret or private

PS PS is written before an additional message at the end of a letter. PS is an abbreviation for 'postscript'

pseudonym [**syoo**-doe-nim] *noun* a name an author uses rather than their real name

psyche [**sigh**-kee] *noun* your mind and your deepest feelings

psychiatry *noun* Psychiatry is the branch of medicine concerned with disorders of the mind > **psychiatrist** *noun* > **psychiatric** *adjective*

psychic *adjective* having unusual mental powers such as the ability to read people's minds or predict the future

psychoanalysis *noun* Psychoanalysis is the examination and treatment of someone who has mental health problems by encouraging them to talk about their feelings and past events in order to discover the cause

P

of the illness > **psychoanalyst** noun
> **psychoanalyse** verb

psychology noun Psychology is the
scientific study of the mind and of
the reasons for people's behaviour
> **psychological** adjective
> **psychologist** noun

psychopath noun a person with a
mental disorder who can commit
antisocial or violent acts without
feeling guilt > **psychopathic**
adjective

psychosis psychoses
[sigh-**koe**-siss] noun a severe mental
disorder > **psychotic** adjective

pub noun a building where people go
to buy and drink alcoholic or soft
drinks

puberty [pyoo-ber-tee] noun
Puberty is the stage when a person's
body changes from that of a child
into that of an adult

pubic [pyoo-bik] adjective relating to
the area around and above a
person's genitals

public noun 1 You can refer to people
in general as the public > adjective
2 relating to people in general: There
was some public support for the idea
3 provided for everyone to use, or
open to anyone: public transport
> **publicly** adverb

publican noun a person who owns
or manages a pub

publication noun 1 The publication
of a book is the act of printing it and
making it available 2 a book or
magazine: medical publications

publicity noun Publicity is
information or advertisements
about an item or event

publicize or **publicise** verb When
someone publicizes a fact or event,
they advertise it and make it widely
known

public school noun In Britain, a
public school is a school that is
privately run and that charges fees
for the pupils to attend

public servant noun In Australia
and New Zealand, someone who
works in the public service

public service noun In Australia
and New Zealand, the public service
is the government departments
responsible for the administration
of the country

publish verb LIBRARY When a
company publishes a book,
newspaper, or magazine, they print
copies of it and distribute it
> **publishing** noun

publisher noun LIBRARY The
publisher of a book, newspaper, or
magazine is the person or company
that prints copies of it and
distributes it

pudding noun 1 a sweet cake
mixture cooked with fruit or other
flavouring and served hot 2 You can
refer to the sweet course of a meal
as the pudding

puddle noun a small shallow pool of
liquid

puerile [pyoo-rile] adjective Puerile
behaviour is silly and childish

puff verb 1 To puff on a cigarette or
pipe is to smoke it 2 If you are
puffing, you are breathing loudly
and quickly with your mouth open
3 If something puffs out or puffs up,
it swells and becomes larger and
rounder > noun 4 a small amount of
air or smoke that is released

pug noun a small, short-haired dog
with a flat nose

pull verb 1 When you pull something,
you hold it and move it towards you
2 When something is pulled by a
vehicle or animal, it is attached to it
and moves along behind it: Four oxen
can pull a single plough 3 When you

pull a curtain or blind, you move it so that it covers or uncovers the window **4** If you pull a muscle, you injure it by stretching it too far or too quickly **5** When a vehicle pulls away, pulls out, or pulls in, it moves in that direction ▷ noun **6** The pull of something is its attraction or influence: *the pull of the past* > **pull down** *verb* When a building is pulled down, it is deliberately destroyed > **pull out** *verb* If you pull out of something, you leave it or decide not to continue with it: *The German government has pulled out of the project* > **pull through** *verb* When someone pulls through, they recover from a serious illness

pulley *noun* D G T a device for lifting heavy weights. The weight is attached to a rope which passes over a wheel or series of wheels

pullover *noun* a woollen piece of clothing that covers the top part of your body

pulmonary *adjective (Medicine)* relating to the lungs or to the veins and arteries carrying blood between the lungs and the heart

pulp *noun* If something is turned into a pulp, it is crushed until it is soft and moist

pulpit [pool-pit] *noun* the small raised platform in a church where a member of the clergy stands to preach

pulse *noun* **1** Your pulse is the regular beating of blood through your body, the rate of which you can feel at your wrists and elsewhere **2** The seeds of beans, peas, and lentils are called pulses when they are used for food ▷ *verb* **3** If something is pulsing, it is moving or vibrating with rhythmic, regular movements: *She could feel the blood pulsing in her eardrums*

pummel pummels, pummelling, pummelled *verb* If you pummel something, you beat it with your fists

pump *noun* **1** a machine that is used to force a liquid or gas to move in a particular direction **2** Pumps are light shoes with flat soles which people wear for sport or leisure ▷ *verb* **3** To pump a liquid or gas somewhere is to force it to flow in that direction, using a pump **4** If you pump money into something, you put a lot of money into it

pumpkin *noun* a very large, round, orange fruit eaten as a vegetable

pun *noun* a clever and amusing use of words so that what you say has two different meanings, such as *my dog's a champion boxer*

punch *verb* **1** If you punch someone, you hit them hard with your fist ▷ *noun* **2** a hard blow with the fist **3** a tool used for making holes **4** Punch is a drink made from a mixture of wine, spirits, and fruit

punctual *adjective* arriving at the correct time > **punctually** *adverb* > **punctuality** *noun*

punctuate *verb* **1** Something that is punctuated by a particular thing is interrupted by it at intervals: *a grey day punctuated by bouts of rain* **2** ENGLISH When you punctuate a piece of writing, you put punctuation into it

punctuation *noun* ENGLISH The marks in writing such as full stops, question marks, and commas are called punctuation or punctuation marks

puncture *noun* **1** If a tyre has a puncture, a small hole has been made in it and it has become flat ▷ *verb* **2** To puncture something is to make a small hole in it

P

pungent adjective having a strong, unpleasant smell or taste
> **pungency** noun

punish verb To punish someone who has done something wrong is to make them suffer because of it

punishment noun something unpleasant done to someone because they have done something wrong

punitive [pyoo-nit-tiv] adjective harsh and intended to punish people: punitive military action

Punjabi [pun-**jah**-bee] adjective 1 belonging or relating to the Punjab, a state in north-western India ▷ noun 2 someone who comes from the Punjab 3 Punjabi is a language spoken in the Punjab

punk noun Punk or punk rock is an aggressive style of rock music

punt noun a long, flat-bottomed boat. You move it along by pushing a pole against the river bottom

puny punier, puniest adjective very small and weak

pup noun a young dog. Some other young animals such as seals are also called pups

pupil noun 1 The pupils at a school are the children who go there 2 Your pupils are the small, round, black holes in the centre of your eyes

puppet noun a doll or toy animal that is moved by pulling strings or by putting your hand inside its body

puppy puppies noun a young dog

purchase verb 1 When you purchase something, you buy it ▷ noun 2 something you have bought
> **purchaser** noun

pure adjective 1 Something that is pure is not mixed with anything else: pure wool; pure white 2 Pure also means clean and free from harmful substances: The water is pure enough

to drink 3 People who are pure have not done anything considered to be sinful 4 Pure also means complete and total: a matter of pure luck
> **purity** noun

purely adverb involving only one feature and not including anything else: purely professional

purge verb To purge something is to remove undesirable things from it: to purge the country of criminals

purify purifies, purifying, purified verb To purify something is to remove all dirty or harmful substances from it > **purification** noun

purist noun someone who believes that something should be done in a particular, correct way: a football purist

puritan noun someone who believes in strict moral principles and avoids physical pleasures > **puritanical** adjective

purple noun, adjective reddish-blue

purport [pur-**port**] verb (formal) Something that purports to be or have a particular thing is claimed to be or have it: a country which purports to disapprove of smokers

purpose noun 1 The purpose of something is the reason for it: the purpose of the meeting 2 If you have a particular purpose, this is what you want to achieve: To make music is my purpose in life ▷ phrase 3 If you do something **on purpose**, you do it deliberately > **purposely** adverb > **purposeful** adjective

purr verb When a cat purrs, it makes a low vibrating sound because it is contented

purse noun 1 a small leather or fabric container for carrying money ▷ verb 2 If you purse your lips, you move them into a tight, rounded shape

pursue pursues, pursuing, pursued
verb **1** If you pursue an activity or plan, you do it or make efforts to achieve it **2** If you pursue someone, you follow them to try to catch them **> pursuer** *noun*
> pursuit *noun*

purveyor *noun* (*formal*) A purveyor of goods or services is a person who sells them or provides them

push *verb* **1** When you push something, you press it using force in order to move it **2** If you push someone into doing something, you force or persuade them to do it: *His mother pushed him into auditioning for a part* **3** (*informal*) Someone who pushes drugs sells them illegally
> push off *verb* (*informal*) If you tell someone to push off, you are telling them rudely to go away

pushchair *noun* a small folding chair on wheels in which a baby or toddler can be wheeled around

pushing *preposition* Someone who is pushing a particular age is nearly that age: *pushing sixty*

pushover *noun* (*informal*)
1 something that is easy **2** someone who is easily persuaded or defeated

pushy pushier, pushiest *adjective* (*informal*) behaving in a forceful and determined way

pussy pussies *noun* (*informal*) a cat

put puts, putting, put *verb* **1** When you put something somewhere, you move it into that place or position **2** If you put an idea or remark in a particular way, you express it that way: *I think you've put that very well* **3** To put someone or something in a particular state or situation means to cause them to be in it: *It puts us both in an awkward position* **4** You can use 'put' to express an estimate of

the size or importance of something: *Her wealth is now put at £290 million* **> put down** *verb* **1** To put someone down is to criticize them and make them appear foolish **2** If an animal is put down, it is killed because it is very ill or dangerous
> put off *verb* **1** If you put something off, you delay doing it **2** To put someone off is to discourage them
> put out *verb* **1** If you put a fire out or put the light out, you make it stop burning or shining **2** If you are put out, you are annoyed or upset
> put up *verb* If you put up resistance to something, you argue or fight against it: *She put up a tremendous struggle* **> put up with** *verb* If you put up with something, you tolerate it even though you disagree with it or dislike it

putt *noun* In golf, a putt is a gentle stroke made when the ball is near the hole

putting *noun* Putting is a game played on a small grass course with no obstacles. You hit a ball gently with a club so that it rolls towards one of a series of holes around the course

putty *noun* Putty is a paste used to fix panes of glass into frames

puzzle *verb* **1** If something puzzles you, it confuses you and you do not understand it: *There was something about her that puzzled me* **>** *noun* **2** A puzzle is a game or question that requires a lot of thought to complete or solve **> puzzled** *adjective* **> puzzlement** *noun*

PVC *noun* PVC is a plastic used for making clothing, pipes, and many other things. PVC is an abbreviation for 'polyvinyl chloride'

pygmy pygmies [**pig**-mee] or **pigmy** *noun* a very small person, especially one who belongs to a racial group in which all the people are small

pyjamas *plural noun* Pyjamas are loose trousers and a jacket or top that you wear in bed

pylon *noun* a very tall metal structure which carries overhead electricity cables

pyramid *noun* **1** a three-dimensional shape with a flat base and flat triangular sides sloping upwards to a point **2** The Pyramids are ancient stone structures built over the tombs of Egyptian kings and queens

python *noun* a large snake that kills animals by squeezing them with its body

q

quack *verb* When a duck quacks, it makes a loud harsh sound

quad *noun* (*informal*) Quad is the same as

quadriceps *noun* PE a large muscle in four parts at the front of your thigh

quadruple [kwod-**roo**-pl] *verb* When an amount or number quadruples, it becomes four times as large as it was

quagmire [**kwag**-mire] *noun* a soft, wet area of land which you sink into if you walk on it

quail *noun* **1** a type of small game bird with a round body and short tail ▷ *verb* **2** If you quail, you feel or look afraid

quaint *adjective* attractively old-fashioned or unusual: *quaint customs* > **quaintly** *adverb*

quake *verb* If you quake, you shake and tremble because you are very frightened

Quaker *noun* a member of a Christian group, the Society of Friends

qualification *noun* **1** Your qualifications are your skills and achievements, especially as officially recognized at the end of a course of training or study **2** something you add to a statement to make it less strong: *It is a good novel and yet cannot be recommended without qualification*

qualify qualifies, qualifying,

qualified verb **1** PE When you qualify, you pass the examinations or tests that you need to pass to do a particular job or to take part in a sporting event **2** If you qualify a statement, you add a detail or explanation to make it less strong: I would qualify that by putting it into context **3** If you qualify for something, you become entitled to have it: You qualify for a discount
> **qualified** adjective

quality qualities noun **1** The quality of something is how good it is: The quality of food is very poor **2** a characteristic: These qualities are essential for success

qualm [kwahm] noun If you have qualms about what you are doing, you worry that it might not be right

quandary quandaries [kwon-dree] noun If you are in a quandary, you cannot decide what to do

quango quangos noun a body responsible for a particular area of public administration, which is financed by the government but is outside direct government control. Quango is short for 'quasi-autonomous non-governmental organization'

quantity quantities noun **1** an amount you can measure or count: a small quantity of alcohol **2** Quantity is the amount of something that there is: emphasis on quantity rather than quality

quarantine [kwor-an-teen] noun If an animal is in quarantine, it is kept away from other animals for a time because it might have an infectious disease

quarrel quarrels, quarrelling, quarrelled noun **1** an angry argument ▷ verb **2** If people quarrel, they have an angry argument

quarry quarries, quarrying, quarried [kwor-ree] noun **1** a place where stone is removed from the ground by digging or blasting **2** A person's or animal's quarry is the animal that they are hunting ▷ verb **3** To quarry stone means to remove it from a quarry by digging or blasting

quarter noun **1** one of four equal parts **2** an American coin worth 25 cents **3** You can refer to a particular area in a city as a quarter: the French quarter **4** You can use 'quarter' to refer vaguely to a particular person or group of people: You are very popular in certain quarters **5** (in plural) A soldier's or a servant's quarters are the rooms that they live in

quarterly quarterlies adjective **1** Quarterly means happening regularly every three months: my quarterly report ▷ noun **2** a magazine or journal published every three months

quartet [kwor-tet] noun a group of four musicians who sing or play together; also a piece of music written for four instruments or singers

quartz noun Quartz is a kind of hard, shiny crystal used in making very accurate watches and clocks

q

quash [kwosh] verb To quash a decision or judgment means to reject it officially: The judges quashed their convictions

quay [kee] noun a place where boats are tied up and loaded or unloaded

queasy queasier, queasiest [kwee-zee] adjective feeling slightly sick > **queasiness** noun

queen noun **1** a female monarch or a woman married to a king **2** a female bee or ant which can lay eggs **3** In chess, the queen is the most powerful piece and can move in any direction **4** In a pack of cards, a queen is a card with a picture of a queen on it

queer *adjective* Queer means very strange

quell *verb* **1** To quell a rebellion or riot means to put an end to it by using force **2** If you quell a feeling such as fear or grief, you stop yourself from feeling it: *trying to quell the loneliness*

quench *verb* If you quench your thirst, you have a drink so that you are no longer thirsty

query queries, querying, queried [**qweer**-ree] *noun* **1** a question ▷ *verb* **2** If you query something, you ask about it because you think it might not be right: *No-one queried my decision*

quest *noun* a long search for something

question *noun* **1** a sentence which asks for information **2** If there is some question about something, there is doubt about it **3** a problem that needs to be discussed: *Can we get back to the question of the car?* ▷ *verb* **4** If you question someone, you ask them questions **5** If you question something, you express doubts about it: *He never stopped questioning his own beliefs* ▷ *phrase* **6** If something is **out of the question**, it is impossible

questionable *adjective* possibly not true or not honest

question mark *noun* the punctuation mark (?) which is used at the end of a question

questionnaire *noun* MATHS a list of questions which asks for information for a survey

queue queues, queuing or queueing, queued [**kyoo**] *noun* **1** a line of people or vehicles waiting for something ▷ *verb* **2** When people

queue, they stand in a line waiting for something

quibble *verb* **1** If you quibble, you argue about something unimportant ▷ *noun* **2** a minor objection

quiche [**keesh**] *noun* a tart with a savoury filling

quick *adjective* **1** moving with great speed **2** lasting only a short time: *a quick chat* **3** happening without any delay: *a quick response* **4** intelligent and able to understand things easily

quickly *adverb* with great speed

quicksand *noun* an area of deep wet sand that you sink into if you walk on it

quid quid *noun* (*informal*) In British English, a pound in money

quiet *adjective* **1** Someone or something that is quiet makes very little noise or no noise at all **2** Quiet also means peaceful: *a quiet evening at home* **3** A quiet event happens with very little fuss or publicity: *a quiet wedding* ▷ *noun* **4** Quiet is silence > **quietly** *adverb* > **quietness** *noun*

> **WORD TIP**
> Do not confuse the spellings of quiet and the adverb quite.

quieten *verb* To quieten someone means to make them become quiet

quill *noun* **1** a pen made from a feather **2** A bird's quills are the large feathers on its wings and tail **3** A porcupine's quills are its spines

quilt *noun* A quilt for a bed is a cover, especially a cover that is padded

quince *noun* a sour tasting fruit used for making jam and marmalade

quintessential *adjective* (*formal*) A person or thing that is quintessential seems to represent the basic nature of something in a pure, concentrated form: *It was the* *quintessential Hollywood party*

quintet [kwin-**tet**] *noun* a group of five musicians who sing or play together; also a piece of music written for five instruments or singers

quip quips, quipping, quipped *noun* 1 an amusing or clever remark ▷ *verb* 2 To quip means to make an amusing or clever remark

quirk *noun* 1 an odd habit or characteristic: *an interesting quirk of human nature* 2 an unexpected event or development: *a quirk of fate* > **quirky** *adjective*

quit quits, quitting, quit *verb* If you quit something, you leave it or stop doing it: *Leigh quit his job as a salesman*

quite *adverb* 1 fairly but not very: *quite old* 2 completely: *Jane lay quite still* ▷ *phrase* 3 You use **quite a** to emphasize that something is large or impressive: *It was quite a party*

> **WORD TIP**
> Do not confuse the spellings of *quite* and the adjective *quiet*.

quiver *verb* 1 If something quivers, it trembles ▷ *noun* 2 a trembling movement: *a quiver of panic*

quiz quizzes, quizzing, quizzed *noun* 1 a game in which the competitors are asked questions to test their knowledge ▷ *verb* 2 If you quiz someone, you question them closely about something

quizzical [kwiz-ik-kl] *adjective* amused and questioning: *a quizzical smile*

quota *noun* a number or quantity of something which is officially allowed: *a quota of three foreign players allowed in each team*

quotation *noun* an extract from a book or speech which is quoted

quote *verb* 1 If you quote something

that someone has written or said, you repeat their exact words 2 If you quote a fact, you state it because it supports what you are saying ▷ *noun* 3 an extract from a book or speech 4 an estimate of how much a piece of work will cost

Qur'an another spelling of **Koran**

r

RAAF In Australia, an abbreviation for 'Royal Australian Air Force'

rabbi rabbis [**rab**-by] *noun* a Jewish religious leader

rabbit *noun* a small animal with long ears

rabble *noun* a noisy, disorderly crowd

rabid *adjective* 1 used to describe someone with strong views that you do not approve of: *a rabid Nazi* 2 A rabid dog or other animal has rabies

rabies [**ray**-beez] *noun* an infectious disease which causes people and animals, especially dogs, to go mad and die

raccoon or **racoon** *noun* a small North American animal with a long striped tail

race *noun* 1 a competition to see who is fastest, for example in running or driving 2 one of the major groups into which human beings can be divided according to their physical features ▷ *verb* 3 If you race someone, you compete with them in a race 4 If you race something or if it races, it goes at its greatest rate: *Her heart raced uncontrollably* **5** If you race somewhere, you go there as quickly as possible: *The hares raced away out of sight* ▷ **racing** noun

racecourse noun a grass track, sometimes with jumps, along which horses race

racehorse noun a horse trained to run in races

racial adjective relating to the different races that people belong to: *racial harmony* ▷ **racially** adverb

rack noun **1** a piece of equipment for holding things or hanging things on ▷ verb **2** If you are racked by something, you suffer because of it: *She was racked by guilt* ▷ phrase **3** (*informal*) If you **rack your brains**, you try hard to think of or remember something

racket noun **1** If someone is making a racket, they are making a lot of noise **2** an illegal way of making money: *a drugs racket* **3** Racket is another spelling of *racquet*

racquet or **racket** noun a bat with strings across it used in tennis and similar games

radar noun Radar is equipment used to track ships or aircraft that are out of sight by using radio signals that are reflected back from the object and shown on a screen

radiant adjective **1** Someone who is radiant is so happy that it shows in their face **2** glowing brightly ▷ **radiance** noun

radiate verb **1** If things radiate from a place, they form a pattern like lines spreading out from the centre of a circle **2** If you radiate a quality or emotion, it shows clearly in your face and behaviour: *He radiated health*

radiation noun the stream of particles given out by a radioactive substance

radiator noun **1** a hollow metal device for heating a room, usually connected to a central heating system **2** the part of a car that is filled with water to cool the engine

radical noun **1** Radicals are people who think there should be great changes in society, and try to make them happen ▷ adjective **2** very significant, important, or basic: *a radical change in the law* ▷ **radically** adverb ▷ **radicalism** noun

radio noun, radioing, radioed noun **1** Radio is a system of sending sound over a distance by transmitting electrical signals **2** Radio is also the broadcasting of programmes to the public by radio **3** a piece of equipment for listening to radio programmes ▷ verb **4** To radio someone means to send them a message by radio: *The pilot radioed that a fire had started*

radioactive adjective giving off powerful and harmful rays ▷ **radioactivity** noun

radiotherapy noun the treatment of diseases such as cancer using radiation > **radiotherapist** noun

radish noun a small salad vegetable with a red skin and white flesh and a hot taste

radius noun radii or radiuses noun MATHS The radius of a circle is the length of a straight line drawn from its centre to its circumference

RAF In Britain, an abbreviation for 'Royal Air Force'

raffle noun a competition in which people buy numbered tickets and win a prize if they have the ticket that is chosen

raft noun a floating platform made

from long pieces of wood tied together

rafter noun Rafters are the sloping pieces of wood that support a roof

rag noun 1 a piece of old cloth used to clean or wipe things 2 If someone is dressed in rags, they are wearing old torn clothes

rage noun 1 Rage is great anger ▷ verb 2 To rage about something means to speak angrily about it 3 If something such as a storm or battle is raging, it is continuing with great force or violence: *The fire still raged out of control*

ragged adjective Ragged clothes are old and torn

raid verb 1 To raid a place means to enter it by force to attack it or steal something ▷ noun 2 the raiding of a building or a place: *an armed raid on a bank*

rail noun 1 a fixed horizontal bar used as a support or for hanging things on 2 Rails are the steel bars which trains run along 3 Rail is the railway considered as a means of transport: *I plan to go by rail*

railing noun Railings are a fence made from metal bars

railway noun a route along which trains travel on steel rails

rain noun 1 water falling from the clouds in small drops ▷ verb 2 When it is raining, rain is falling ▷ **rainy** adjective

rainbow noun an arch of different colours that sometimes appears in the sky when it is raining

raincoat noun a waterproof coat

rainfall noun the amount of rain that falls in a place during a particular period

rainforest noun GEOGRAPHY a dense forest of tall trees in a tropical area where there is a lot of rain

rainwater noun rain that has been stored

raise verb 1 If you raise something, you make it higher: *She went to the window and raised the blinds; a drive to raise standards of literacy* 2 If you raise your voice, you speak more loudly 3 To raise money for a cause means to get people to donate money towards it 4 To raise a child means to look after it until it is grown up 5 If you raise a subject, you mention it

raisin noun Raisins are dried grapes

rake noun a garden tool with a row of metal teeth and a long handle ▷ **rake up** verb If you rake up something embarrassing from the past, you remind someone about it

rally noun rallies, rallying, rallied noun 1 a large public meeting held to show support for something 2 a competition in which vehicles are raced over public roads 3 In tennis or squash, a rally is a continuous series of shots exchanged by the players ▷ verb 4 When people rally to something, they gather together to continue a struggle or to support something

ram verb 1 If one vehicle rams another, it crashes into it 2 To ram something somewhere means to push it there firmly: *He rammed his key into the lock* ▷ noun 3 an adult male sheep

RAM noun COMPUTING a storage space which can be filled with data but which loses its contents when the machine is switched off. RAM stands for 'random access memory'

Ramadan noun RE the ninth month of the Muslim year, during which Muslims eat and drink nothing during daylight

ramble noun 1 a long walk in the

countryside ▷ verb **2** To ramble
means to go for a ramble **3** To
ramble also means to talk in a
confused way: *He then started
rambling and repeating himself*
> **rambler** noun

ramification noun The
ramifications of a decision or plan
are all its consequences and effects

ramp noun a sloping surface
connecting two different levels

rampage verb **1** To rampage means
to rush about wildly causing
damage ▷ phrase **2** To go **on the
rampage** means to rush about in a
wild or violent way

rampant adjective If something such
as crime or disease is rampant, it is
growing or spreading
uncontrollably

ramshackle adjective A ramshackle
building is in very poor condition

ranch noun a large farm where cattle
or horses are reared, especially in
the USA

rancid [ran-sid] adjective Rancid
food has gone bad

rancour [rang-kur] noun (formal)
Rancour is bitter hatred
> **rancorous** adjective

rand noun The rand is the main unit
of currency in South Africa

random adjective **1** A random choice
or arrangement is not based on any
definite plan ▷ phrase **2** If you do
something **at random**, you do it
without any definite plan: *He chose
his victims at random* > **randomly**
adverb

range noun **1** The range of
something is the maximum
distance over which it can reach
things or detect things: *This mortar
has a range of 15,000 metres* **2** a
number of different things of the
same kind: *A wide range of colours are*

available **3** a set of values on a scale:
*The average age range is between 35 and
55* **4** A range of mountains is a line of
them **5** A rifle range or firing range
is a place where people practise
shooting at targets ▷ verb **6** When a
set of things ranges between two
points, they vary within these
points on a scale: *prices ranging
between £370 and £1200*

ranger noun someone whose job is
to look after a forest or park

rank noun **1** Someone's rank is their
official level in a job or profession
2 The ranks are the ordinary
members of the armed forces,
rather than the officers **3** The ranks
of a group are its members: *We
welcomed five new members to our
ranks* **4** a row of people or things
▷ verb **5** To rank as something
means to have that status or
position on a scale: *His dismissal
ranks as the worst humiliation he has
ever known* ▷ adjective **6** complete
and absolute: *rank stupidity* **7** having
a strong, unpleasant smell: *the rank
smell of unwashed clothes*

ransack verb To ransack a place
means to disturb everything and
leave it in a mess, in order to search
for or steal something

ransom noun money that is
demanded to free someone who
has been kidnapped

rant verb To rant means to talk
loudly in an excited or angry way

rap raps, rapping, rapped verb **1** If
you rap something, you hit it with a
series of quick blows ▷ noun **2** a
quick knock or blow on something:
A rap on the door signalled his arrival
3 Rap is a style of poetry spoken to
music with a strong rhythmic beat

rapid adjective happening or moving
very quickly: *rapid industrial*

expansion; He took a few rapid steps
> **rapidly** adverb > **rapidity** noun

rapport [rap-**por**] noun (formal) If there is a rapport between two people, they find it easy to understand each other's feelings and attitudes

rapt adjective If you are rapt, you are so interested in something that you are not aware of other things: sitting with rapt attention in front of the screen

rapture noun Rapture is a feeling of extreme delight > **rapturous** adjective > **rapturously** adverb

rare adjective **1** Something that is rare is not common or does not happen often: a rare flower; Such major disruptions are rare **2** Rare meat has been lightly cooked > **rarely** adverb

rarefied [**rare**-if-yed] adjective seeming to have little connection with ordinary life: He grew up in a rarefied literary atmosphere

raring adjective If you are raring to do something, you are very eager to do it

rarity rarities noun **1** something that is interesting or valuable because it is unusual **2** The rarity of something is the fact that it is not common

rash adjective **1** If you are rash, you do something hasty and foolish > noun **2** an area of red spots that appear on your skin when you are ill or have an allergy **3** A rash of events is a lot of them happening in a short time: a rash of strikes > **rashly** adverb

rasp verb **1** To rasp means to make a harsh unpleasant sound > noun **2** a coarse file with rows of raised teeth, used for smoothing wood or metal

raspberry raspberries noun a small soft red fruit that grows on a bush

rat noun a long-tailed animal which looks like a large mouse

rate noun **1** The rate of something is the speed or frequency with which it happens: New diet books appear at the rate of nearly one a week **2** The rate of interest is its level: a further cut in interest rates **3** the cost or charge for something **4** In some countries, rates are a local tax paid by people who own buildings > phrase **5** If you say at this rate something will happen, you mean it will happen if things continue in this same way: At this rate we'll be lucky to get home before six **6** You say at any rate when you want to add to or amend what you have just said: He is the least appealing character, to me at any rate > phrase > verb The way you rate someone or something is your opinion of them: He was rated as one of England's top young players

rather adverb **1** Rather means to a certain extent: We get along rather well; The reality is rather more complex > phrase **2** If you **would rather** do a particular thing, you would prefer to do it **3** If you do one thing **rather than** another, you choose to do the first thing instead of the second

ratify ratifies, ratifying, ratified verb (formal) To ratify a written agreement means to approve it formally, usually by signing it > **ratification** noun

rating noun **1** a score based on the quality or status of something **2** The ratings are statistics showing how popular each television programme is

ratio ratios noun a relationship which shows how many times one thing is bigger than another: The adult to child ratio is 1 to 6

ration noun **1** Your ration of something is the amount you are allowed to have **2** Rations are the food given each day to a soldier or member of an expedition ▷ *verb* **3** When something is rationed, you are only allowed a limited amount of it, because there is a shortage

rational *adjective* When people are rational, their judgments are based on reason rather than emotion ▷ **rationally** *adverb* ▷ **rationality** *noun*

rationale [rash-on-**nahl**] *noun* The rationale for a course of action or for a belief is the set of reasons on which it is based

rattle *verb* **1** When something rattles, it makes short, regular knocking sounds **2** If something rattles you, it upsets you: *He was obviously rattled by events* ▷ *noun* **3** the noise something makes when it rattles **4** a baby's toy which makes a noise when it is shaken

raucous [**raw**-kuss] *adjective* A raucous voice is loud and rough

ravage (*formal*) *verb* **1** To ravage something means to seriously harm or damage it: *a country ravaged by floods* ▷ *noun* **2** The ravages of something are its damaging effects: *the ravages of two world wars*

rave *verb* **1** If someone raves, they talk in an angry, uncontrolled way: *He started raving about being treated badly* **2** (*informal*) If you rave about something, you talk about it very enthusiastically ▷ *adjective* **3** (*informal*) If something gets a rave review, it is praised enthusiastically ▷ *noun* **4** (*informal*) a large party with electronic dance music

raven *noun* **1** a large black bird with a deep, harsh call ▷ *adjective* **2** Raven hair is black and shiny

ravenous *adjective* very hungry

ravine *noun* a deep, narrow valley with steep sides

raving *adjective* **1** If someone is raving, they are mad: *a raving lunatic* ▷ *noun* **2** Someone's ravings are crazy things they write or say

ravioli [rav-ee-**oh**-lee] *noun* Ravioli consists of small squares of pasta filled with meat or other ingredients and served with a sauce

ravishing *adjective* Someone or something that is ravishing is very beautiful: *a ravishing landscape*

raw *adjective* **1** Raw food has not been cooked **2** A raw substance is in its natural state: *raw sugar* **3** If part of your body is raw, the skin has come off or been rubbed away **4** Someone who is raw is too young or too new in a job or situation to know how to behave

raw material *noun* Raw materials are the natural substances used to make something

ray *noun* **1** a beam of light or radiation **2** A ray of hope is a small amount that makes an unpleasant situation seem slightly better **3** a large sea fish with eyes on the top of its body, and a long tail

raze *verb* To raze a building, town, or forest means to completely destroy it: *The town was razed to the ground during the occupation*

razor *noun* a tool that people use for shaving

re- *prefix* **1** 'Re-' is used to form nouns and verbs that refer to the repetition of an action or process: *reread; remarry* **2** 'Re-' is also used to form verbs that refer to going back to a previous condition: *refresh; renew*

reach *verb* **1** When you reach a place, you arrive there **2** When you reach for something, you stretch out your arm to it **3** If something reaches a place or point, it extends as far as that place or point: *She has a cloak* that reaches to the ground **4** If something or someone reaches a stage or level, they get to it: *Unemployment has reached record levels* **5** To reach an agreement or decision means to succeed in achieving it ▷ **phrase 6** If a place is **within reach**, you can get there: *a cycle route well within reach of most people* **7** If something is **out of reach**, you cannot get it to it by stretching out your arm: *Store out of reach of children*

react verb **1** When you react to something, you behave in a particular way because of it: *He reacted badly to the news* **2** SCIENCE If one substance reacts with another, a chemical change takes place when they are put together

reaction noun **1** Your reaction to something is what you feel, say, or do because of it: *Reaction to the visit is mixed* **2** Your reactions are your ability to move quickly in response to something that happens: *Squash requires fast reactions* **3** If there is a reaction against something, it becomes unpopular: *a reaction against Christianity* **4** SCIENCE In a chemical reaction, a chemical change takes place when two substances are put together

reactionary reactionaries adjective **1** Someone who is reactionary tries to prevent political or social change ▷ **noun 2** Reactionaries are reactionary people

reactor noun a device which is used to produce nuclear energy

read reads, reading, read verb **1** When you read, you look at something written and follow it or say it aloud **2** If you can read someone's moods or mind, you can judge what they are feeling or thinking **3** When you read a meter or gauge, you look at it and record the figure on it **4** If you read a subject at university, you study it

reader noun **1** The readers of a newspaper or magazine are the people who read it regularly **2** At a university, a reader is a senior lecturer just below the rank of professor

readership noun The readership of a newspaper or magazine consists of the people who read it regularly

readily adverb **1** willingly and eagerly: *She readily agreed to see Alex* **2** easily done or quickly obtainable: *Help is readily available*

reading noun **1** Reading is the activity of reading books **2** The reading on a meter or gauge is the figure or measurement it shows

readjust [ree-aj-**just**] verb **1** If you readjust, you adapt to a new situation **2** If you readjust something, you alter it to a different position

ready adjective **1** having reached the required stage, or prepared for action or use: *In a few days' time the plums will be ready to eat* **2** willing or eager to do something: *She says she's not ready for marriage* **3** If you are ready for something, you need it: *I'm ready for bed* **4** easily produced or obtained: *ready cash* ▷ **readiness** noun

ready-made adjective already made and therefore able to be used immediately

reaffirm verb To reaffirm something means to state it again: *He reaffirmed his support for the campaign*

real adjective **1** actually existing and not imagined or invented **2** genuine and not imitation: *Who's to know if they're real guns?* **3** true or actual and not mistaken: *This was the real reason for her call*

real estate noun Real estate is property in the form of land and buildings rather than personal possessions

realism noun Realism is the recognition of the true nature of a situation: *a triumph of muddled thought over realism and common sense* > **realist** noun

realistic adjective 1 recognizing and accepting the true nature of a situation 2 representing things in a way that is true to real life: *His novels are more realistic than his short stories* > **realistically** adverb

reality noun 1 Reality is the real nature of things, rather than the way someone imagines it: *Fiction and reality were increasingly blurred* 2 If something has become reality, it actually exists or is actually happening

realize or **realise** verb 1 If you realize something, you become aware of it 2 (formal) If your hopes or fears are realized, what you hoped for or feared actually happens: *Our worst fears were realized* 3 To realize a sum of money means to receive it as a result of selling goods or shares > **realization** noun

really adverb 1 used to add emphasis to what is being said: *I'm not really surprised* 2 used to indicate that you are talking about the true facts about something: *What was really going on?*

realm [relm] noun (formal) 1 You can refer to any area of thought or activity as a realm: *the realm of politics* 2 a country with a king or queen: *defence of the realm*

reap verb 1 To reap a crop such as corn means to cut and gather it

2 When people reap benefits or rewards, they get them as a result of hard work or careful planning > **reaper** noun

reappear verb When people or things reappear, you can see them again, because they have come back: *The stolen ring reappeared three years later in a pawn shop* > **reappearance** noun

reappraisal noun (formal) If there is a reappraisal, people think about and decide whether they want to change it: *a reappraisal of the government's economic policies*

rear noun 1 The rear of something is the part at the back ▷ verb 2 To rear children or young animals means to bring them up until they are able to look after themselves 3 When a horse rears, it raises the front part of its body, so that its front legs are in the air

rearrange verb To rearrange something means to organize or arrange it in a different way

reason noun 1 The reason for something is the fact or situation which explains why it happens or which causes it to happen 2 If you have reason to believe or feel something, there are definite reasons why you believe it or feel it: *He had every reason to be upset* 3 Reason is the ability to think and make judgments ▷ verb 4 If you reason that something is true, you decide it is true after considering all the facts 5 If you reason with someone, you persuade them to accept sensible arguments

reasonable adjective 1 Reasonable behaviour is fair and sensible 2 If an explanation is reasonable, there are good reasons for thinking it is correct 3 A reasonable amount is a

fairly large amount **4** A reasonable price is fair and not too high
> **reasonably** adverb

reasoning noun Reasoning is the process by which you reach a conclusion after considering all the facts

reassess verb If you reassess something, you consider whether it still has the same value or importance > **reassessment** noun

reassure verb If you reassure someone, you say or do things that make them less worried
> **reassurance** noun

rebate noun money paid back to someone who has paid too much tax or rent

rebel rebels, rebelling, rebelled noun **1** HISTORY Rebels are people who are fighting their own country's army to change the political system **2** Someone who is a rebel rejects society's values and behaves differently from other people ▷ verb **3** To rebel means to fight against authority and reject accepted values

rebellion noun HISTORY A rebellion is organized and often violent opposition to authority

rebellious adjective unwilling to obey and likely to rebel against authority

rebound verb When something rebounds, it bounces or springs back after hitting a solid surface

rebuff verb **1** If you rebuff someone, you reject what they offer: She rebuffed their offers of help ▷ noun **2** a rejection of an offer

rebuild rebuilds, rebuilding, rebuilt verb When a town or building is rebuilt, it is built again after being damaged or destroyed

rebuke [ris-**byook**] verb To rebuke someone means to speak severely

to them about something they have done

recall verb **1** To recall something means to remember it **2** If you are recalled to a place, you are ordered to return there **3** If a company recalls products, it asks people to return them because they are faulty

recap recaps, recapping, recapped verb To recap means to repeat and summarize the main points of an explanation or discussion

recapture verb **1** When you recapture a pleasant feeling, you experience it again: She may never recapture that past assurance **2** When soldiers recapture a place, they capture it from the people who took it from them **3** When animals or prisoners are recaptured, they are caught after they have escaped

recede verb **1** When something recedes, it moves away into the distance **2** If a man's hair is receding, he is starting to go bald at the front

receipt [ris-**seet**] noun **1** a piece of paper confirming that money or goods have been received **2** In a shop or theatre, the money received is often called the receipts: Box-office receipts were down last month **3** (formal) The receipt of something is the receiving of it: You have to sign here and acknowledge receipt

receive verb **1** When you receive something, someone gives it to you, or you get it after it has been sent to you **2** To receive something also means to have it happen to you: injuries she received in a car crash **3** When you receive visitors or guests, you welcome them **4** If something is received in a particular way, that is how people react to it: The decision has been received with great disappointment

r

receiver noun the part of a telephone you hold near to your ear and mouth

recent adjective Something recent happened a short time ago
> **recently** adverb

reception noun 1 In a hotel or office, reception is the place near the entrance where appointments or enquiries are dealt with 2 a formal party 3 The reception someone or something gets is the way people react to them: Her tour met with a rapturous reception 4 If your radio or television gets good reception, the sound or picture is clear

receptionist noun The receptionist in a hotel or office deals with people when they arrive, answers the telephone, and arranges appointments

receptive adjective Someone who is receptive to ideas or suggestions is willing to consider them

recess noun 1 a period when no work is done by a committee or parliament: the Christmas recess 2 a place where part of a wall has been built further back than the rest

recession noun a period when a country's economy is less successful and more people become unemployed

recharge verb To recharge a battery means to charge it with electricity again after it has been used

recipe [res-sip-ee] noun 1 ⟨D G T⟩ a list of ingredients and instructions for cooking something 2 If something is a recipe for disaster or for success, it is likely to result in disaster or success

recipient noun The recipient of something is the person receiving it

reciprocal adjective A reciprocal agreement involves two people, groups, or countries helping each other in a similar way: a reciprocal agreement on trade

reciprocate verb If you reciprocate someone's feelings or behaviour, you feel or behave in the same way towards them

recital noun a performance of music or poetry, usually by one person

recite verb If you recite a poem or something you have learnt, you say it aloud > **recitation** noun

reckless adjective showing a complete lack of care about danger or damage: a reckless tackle
> **recklessly** adverb > **recklessness** noun

reckon verb 1 (informal) If you reckon that something is true, you think it is true: I reckoned he was still fond of her 2 (informal) If someone reckons to do something, they claim or expect to do it: Officers on the case are reckoning to charge someone shortly 3 To reckon an amount means to calculate it 4 If you reckon on something, you rely on it happening when making your plans: He reckons on being world champion 5 If you had not reckoned with something, you had not expected it and therefore were unprepared when it happened: Giles had not reckoned with the strength of Sally's feelings

reckoning noun a calculation: There were a thousand or so, by my reckoning

reclaim verb 1 When you reclaim something, you collect it after leaving it somewhere or losing it 2 To reclaim land means to make it suitable for use, for example by draining it > **reclamation** noun

recline verb To recline means to lie or lean back at an angle: a photo of him reclining on his bed

recluse noun Someone who is a

recluse lives alone and avoids other people ▷ **reclusive** adjective

recognize or **recognise** verb
1 If you recognize someone or something, you realize that you know who or what they are: *The receptionist recognized me at once* **2** To recognize something also means to accept and acknowledge it: *The RAF recognized him as an outstanding pilot* ▷ **recognition** noun ▷ **recognizable** adjective ▷ **recognizably** adverb

recoil verb To recoil from something means to draw back in shock or horror

recommend verb If you recommend something to someone, you praise it and suggest they try it ▷ **recommendation** noun

reconcile verb **1** To reconcile two things that seem to oppose one another, means to make them work or exist together successfully: *The designs reconciled style with comfort* **2** When people are reconciled, they become friendly again after a quarrel **3** If you reconcile yourself to an unpleasant situation, you accept it ▷ **reconciliation** noun

reconnaissance [rik-**kon**-iss-sanss] noun Reconnaissance is the gathering of military information by soldiers, planes, or satellites

reconsider verb To reconsider something means to think about it again to decide whether to change it ▷ **reconsideration** noun

reconstruct verb **1** To reconstruct something that has been damaged means to build it again **2** To reconstruct a past event means to get a complete description of it from small pieces of information ▷ **reconstruction** noun

record noun [**rec**-cord] **1** If you keep a record of something, you keep a

written account or store information in a computer: *medical records* **2** a round, flat piece of plastic on which music has been recorded **3** an achievement which is the best of its type **4** Your record is what is known about your achievements or past activities: *He had a distinguished war record* ▷ verb [rec-**cord**] **5** If you record information, you write it down or put it into a computer **6** To record sound means to preserve it on tape or disc, or digitally ▷ adjective [**rec**-cord] **7** higher, lower, better, or worse than ever before: *Profits were at a record level*

recorder noun a small woodwind instrument

recording noun A recording of something is a tape, disc, etc of it

recount verb **1** If you recount a story, you tell it ▷ noun **2** a second count of votes in an election when the result is very close

recoup [rik-**koop**] verb If you recoup money that you have spent or lost, you get it back

recourse noun (formal) If you have recourse to something, you use it to help you: *The members settled their differences without recourse to war*

recover verb **1** To recover from an illness or unhappy experience means to get well again or get over it **2** If you recover a lost object or your ability to do something, you get it back

recovery noun **1** the act of getting better again **2** the act of getting something back

recreate verb To recreate something means to succeed in making it happen or exist again: *a museum that faithfully recreates an old farmhouse*

recreation [rek-kree-**ay**-shn] noun Recreation is all the things that you

do for enjoyment in your spare time
> **recreational** adjective

recrimination noun
Recriminations are accusations
made by people about each other

recruit verb 1 To recruit people
means to get them to join a group
or help with something ▷ noun
2 someone who has joined the army
or some other organization
> **recruitment** noun

rectangle noun MATHS A four-sided
shape with four right angles
> **rectangular** adjective

rectify rectifies, rectifying, rectified
verb (formal) If you rectify something
that is wrong, you put it right

rector noun a Church of England
priest in charge of a parish

rectory rectories noun a house
where a rector lives

rectum noun (technical) The bottom
end of the tube down which waste
food passes out of your body
> **rectal** adjective

recuperate verb When you
recuperate, you gradually recover
after being ill or injured
> **recuperation** noun

recur recurs, recurring, recurred verb
If something recurs, it happens or
occurs again: His hamstring injury
recurred after the first game
> **recurrence** noun > **recurrent**
adjective

recurring adjective 1 happening or
occurring many times: a recurring
dream 2 MATHS A recurring digit is
one that is repeated over and over
again after the decimal point in a
decimal fraction

recycle verb GEOGRAPHY To recycle
used products means to process
them so that they can be used
again: recycled glass

red redder, reddest noun, adjective

1 Red is the colour of blood or of a
ripe tomato 2 Red hair is between
orange and brown in colour

redeem verb 1 If a feature redeems
an unpleasant thing or situation, it
makes it seem less bad 2 If you
redeem yourself, you do something
that gives people a good opinion of
you again 3 If you redeem
something, you get it back by
paying for it 4 RE In Christianity, to
redeem someone means to free
them from sin by giving them faith
in Jesus Christ

redemption noun Redemption is
the state of being redeemed

red-handed phrase To catch
someone red-handed means to
catch them doing something wrong

red-hot adjective Red-hot metal has
been heated to such a high
temperature that it has turned red

redress (formal) verb 1 To redress a
wrong means to put it right ▷ noun
2 If you get redress for harm done to
you, you are compensated for it

red tape noun Red tape is official
rules and procedures that seem
unnecessary and cause delay. In the
18th century, red tape was used to
bind official government
documents

reduce verb 1 To reduce something
means to make it smaller in size or
amount 2 You can use 'reduce' to
say that someone or something is
changed to a weaker or inferior
state: She reduced them to tears; The
village was reduced to rubble

reduction noun When there is a
reduction in something, it is made
smaller

redundancy redundancies noun
1 Redundancy is the state of being
redundant 2 The number of
redundancies is the number of

people made redundant

redundant adjective **1** When people are made redundant, they lose their jobs because there is no more work for them or no money to pay them **2** When something becomes redundant, it is no longer needed

reed noun **1** Reeds are hollow stemmed plants that grow in shallow water or wet ground **2** a thin piece of cane or metal inside some wind instruments which vibrates when air is blown over it

reef noun GEOGRAPHY a long line of rocks or coral close to the surface of the sea

reek verb **1** To reek of something means to smell strongly and unpleasantly of it ▷ noun **2** If there is a reek of something, there is a strong unpleasant smell of it

reel noun **1** a cylindrical object around which you wrap something; often part of a device which you turn as a control **2** a fast Scottish dance ▷ verb **3** When someone reels, they move unsteadily as if they are going to fall **4** If your mind is reeling, you are confused because you have too much to think about > **reel off** verb If you reel off information, you repeat it from memory quickly and easily

re-elect verb When someone is re-elected, they win an election again and are able to stay in power

refer refers, referring, referred verb **1** If you refer to something, you mention it **2** If you look at it to find something out **3** When a problem or issue is referred to someone, they are formally asked to deal with it: The case was referred to the European Court

referee noun **1** the official who

controls a football game or a boxing or wrestling match **2** someone who gives a reference to a person who is applying for a job

reference noun **1** A reference to something or someone is a mention of them **2** Reference is the act of referring to something or someone for information or advice: He makes that decision without reference to her **3** a number or name that tells you where to find information or identifies a document **4** If someone gives you a reference when you apply for a job, they write a letter about your abilities

referendum referendums or referenda noun a vote in which all the people in a country are officially asked whether they agree with a policy or proposal

refine verb To refine a raw material such as oil or sugar means to process it to remove impurities

refined adjective **1** very polite and well-mannered **2** processed to remove impurities

refinement noun **1** Refinements are minor improvements **2** Refinement is politeness and good manners

refinery refineries noun a factory where substances such as oil or sugar are refined

reflect verb **1** If something reflects an attitude or situation, it shows what it is like: His off-duty hobbies reflected his maritime interests **2** If something reflects light or heat, the light or heat bounces off it **3** When something is reflected in a mirror or water, you can see its image in it **4** MATHS If something reflects, its direction is reversed **5** When you reflect, you think about something > **reflective** adjective > **reflectively** adverb

reflection noun **1** If something is a reflection of something else, it shows what it is like: *This is a terrible reflection of the times* **2** An image in a mirror or water **3** Reflection is the process by which light and heat are bounced off a surface **4** MATHS In maths, reflection is also the turning back of something on itself: *reflection of an axis* **5** Reflection is also thought: *After days of reflection she decided to leave*

reflex noun **1** A reflex or reflex action is a sudden uncontrollable movement that you make as a result of pressure or a blow **2** If you have good reflexes, you respond very quickly when something unexpected happens ▷ *adjective* **3** MATHS A reflex angle is between 180° and 360°

reform noun **1** Reforms are major changes to laws or institutions: *a programme of economic reform* ▷ *verb* **2** When laws or institutions are reformed, major changes are made to them **3** When people reform, they stop committing crimes or doing other unacceptable things > *reformer* noun

Reformation noun HISTORY The Reformation was a religious and political movement in Europe in the 16th century that began as an attempt to reform the Roman Catholic Church, but ended in the establishment of the Protestant Churches

refrain verb **1** (formal) If you refrain from doing something, you do not do it: *Please refrain from smoking in the hall* ▷ noun **2** MUSIC The refrain of a song is a short, simple part, repeated many times

refresh verb **1** If something refreshes you when you are hot or tired, it makes you feel cooler or more energetic: *A glass of fruit juice will refresh you* ▷ *phrase* **2** To refresh someone's memory means to remind them of something they had forgotten

refreshing adjective You say that something is refreshing when it is pleasantly different from what you are used to: *She is a refreshing contrast to her father*

refreshment noun Refreshments are drinks and small amounts of food provided at an event

refrigerator noun an electrically cooled container in which you store food to keep it fresh

refuel verb refuels, refuelling, refuelled When an aircraft or vehicle is refuelled, it is filled with more fuel

refuge noun **1** a place where you go for safety **2** If you take refuge, you go somewhere for safety or behave in a way that will protect you: *They took refuge in a bomb shelter; Father Rowan took refuge in silence*

refugee noun Refugees are people who have been forced to leave their country and live elsewhere

refund noun [re-fund] **1** money returned to you because you have paid too much for something or because you have returned goods ▷ *verb* [re-fund] **2** To refund someone's money means to return it to them after they have paid for something with it

refurbish verb (formal) To refurbish a building means to decorate it and repair damage > **refurbishment** noun

refusal noun A refusal is when someone says firmly that they will not do, allow, or accept something

refuse verb [rif-yooz] verb **1** If you refuse to do something, you say or decide firmly that you will not do it **2** If someone refuses something, they do not allow it or do not accept it: *The United States has refused him a visa; He offered me a second drink which I refused*

refuse [ref-yoos] *noun* Refuse is rubbish or waste

refute *verb (formal)* To refute a theory or argument means to prove that it is wrong

regain *verb* To regain something means to get it back

regal *adjective* very grand and suitable for a king or queen: *regal splendour* ▷ **regally** *adverb*

regard *verb* **1** To regard someone or something in a particular way means to think of them in that way or have that opinion of them: *We all regard him as a friend; Many disapprove of the tax, regarding it as unfair* **2** *(literary)* To regard someone in a particular way also means to look at them in that way: *She regarded him curiously for a moment* ▷ *noun* **3** If you have a high regard for someone, you have a very good opinion of them ▷ *phrase* **4** Regarding, as regards, with regard to, and in regard to are all used to indicate what you are talking or writing about: *There was always some question regarding education; As regards the war, he believed in victory at any price* **5** 'Regards' is used in various expressions to express friendly feelings: *Give my regards to your husband*

regardless *preposition, adverb* done or happening in spite of something else: *He led from the front, regardless of the danger*

regatta *noun* a race meeting for sailing or rowing boats

regenerate *verb (formal)* To regenerate something means to

develop and improve it after it has been declining: *a scheme to regenerate the docks area of the city* ▷ **regeneration** *noun*

regent *noun* someone who rules in place of a king or queen who is ill or too young to rule

reggae *noun* Reggae is a type of music, originally from the West Indies, with a strong beat

regime [ray-**jeem**] *noun* a system of government, and the people who are ruling a country: *a communist regime*

regiment *noun* a large group of soldiers commanded by a colonel ▷ **regimental** *adjective*

regimented *adjective* very strictly controlled: *the regimented life of the orphanage* ▷ **regimentation** *noun*

region *noun* **1** GEOGRAPHY a large area of land **2** You can refer to any area or part as a region: *the pelvic region* ▷ *phrase* **3** In the region of means approximately: *The scheme will cost in the region of six million* ▷ **regional** *adjective* ▷ **regionally** *adverb*

register *noun* **1** an official list or record of things: *the electoral register* **2** *(technical)* a style of speaking or writing used in particular circumstances or social occasions ▷ *verb* **3** When something is registered, it is recorded on an official list: *The car was registered in my name* **4** If an instrument registers a measurement, it shows it **5** If your face registers a feeling, it expresses it ▷ **registration** *noun*

registrar *noun* **1** a person who keeps official records of births, marriages, and deaths **2** At a college or university, the registrar is a senior administrative official **3** a senior hospital doctor

registration number noun the sequence of letters and numbers on the front and back of a motor vehicle that identify it

registry registries noun a place where official records are kept

regret regrets, regretting, regretted verb **1** If you regret something, you are sorry that it happened **2** You can say that you regret something as a way of apologizing: We regret any inconvenience to passengers > noun **3** If you have regrets, you are sad or sorry about something > **regretful** adjective > **regretfully** adverb

regrettable adjective unfortunate and undesirable: a regrettable accident > **regrettably** adverb

regular adjective **1** even and equally spaced: soft music with a regular beat **2** MATHS A regular shape has equal angles and equal sides: a regular polygon **3** Regular events or activities happen often and according to a pattern, for example each day or each week: The trains to London are fairly regular **4** If you are a regular customer or visitor somewhere, you go there often **5** usual or normal: I was filling in for the regular bartender **6** having a well balanced appearance: a regular geometrical shape > noun **7** People who go to a place often are known as its regulars > **regularly** adverb > **regularity** noun

regulate verb To regulate something means to control the way it operates: Sweating helps to regulate the body's temperature > **regulator** noun

regulation noun **1** Regulations are official rules **2** Regulation is the control of something: regulation of the betting industry

rehabilitate verb To rehabilitate someone who has been ill or in prison means to help them lead a normal life > **rehabilitation** noun

rehearsal noun DRAMA a practice of a performance in preparation for the actual event

rehearse verb DRAMA To rehearse a performance means to practise it in preparation for the actual event

reign [rain] verb **1** When a king or queen reigns, he or she rules a country **2** You can say that something reigns when it is a noticeable feature of a situation or period of time: Panic reigned after his assassination > noun **3** HISTORY The reign of a king or queen is the period during which he or she reigns

rein noun **1** Reins are the thin leather straps which you hold when you are riding a horse > phrase **2** To **keep a tight rein on** someone or something means to control them firmly

reincarnation noun People who believe in reincarnation believe that when you die, you are born again as another creature

reindeer reindeer noun Reindeer are deer with large antlers, that live in northern regions

reinforce verb **1** To reinforce something means to strengthen it: a reinforced steel barrier **2** If something reinforces an idea or claim, it provides evidence to support it

reinforcement noun **1** Reinforcements are additional soldiers sent to join an army in battle **2** Reinforcement is the reinforcing of something

reinstate verb **1** To reinstate someone means to give them back a position they have lost **2** To reinstate something means to bring

it back: *Parliament voted against reinstating capital punishment*
> **reinstatement** *noun*

reiterate [re-**it**-er-ate] *verb* (formal) If you reiterate something, you say it again > **reiteration** *noun*

reject *verb* [re-**ject**] **1** If you reject a proposal or request, you do not accept it or agree to it **2** If you reject a belief, political system, or way of life, you decide that it is not for you ▷ *noun* [**re**-ject] **3** A product that cannot be used, because there is something wrong with it > **rejection** *noun*

rejoice *verb* To rejoice means to be very pleased about something: *The whole country rejoiced after his downfall*

rejoin *verb* If you rejoin someone, you go back to them soon after leaving them: *She rejoined her friends in the bar*

rejuvenate [re-**joo**-vin-ate] *verb* To rejuvenate someone means to make them feel young again > **rejuvenation** *noun*

relapse *noun* If a sick person has a relapse, their health suddenly gets worse after improving

relate *verb* **1** If something relates to something else, it is connected or concerned with it: *The statistics relate only to western Germany* **2** If you can relate to someone, you can understand their thoughts and feelings **3** To relate a story means to tell it

relation *noun* **1** If there is a relation between two things, they are similar or connected in some way: *This many bears no relation to reality* **2** Your relations are the members of your family **3** Relations between people are their feelings and behaviour towards each other:

Relations between husband and wife had not improved

relationship *noun* [PSHE] **1** The relationship between two people or groups is the way they feel and behave towards each other **2** a close friendship, especially one involving romantic feelings **3** The relationship between two things is the way in which they are connected: *the relationship between slavery and the sugar trade*

relative *adjective* **1** compared to other things or people of the same kind: *The fighting resumed after a period of relative calm*; *He is a relative novice* **2** You use 'relative' when comparing the size or quality of two things: *the relative strengths of the British and German forces* ▷ *noun* **3** Your relatives are the members of your family

relax *verb* **1** If you relax, you become calm and your muscles lose their tension **2** If you relax your hold, you hold something less tightly **3** To relax something also means to make it less strict or controlled: *The rules governing student conduct were relaxed* > **relaxation** *noun*

relay *noun* [re-lay] **1** [PE] A relay race or relay is a race between teams, with each team member running one part of the race ▷ *verb* [re-**lay**] **2** To relay a television or radio signal means to send it on **3** To relay information, you tell it to someone else

release *verb* **1** To release someone or something means to set them free or remove restraints from them **2** To release something also means to issue it or make it available: *He is releasing an album of love songs* ▷ *noun* **3** When the release of someone or something takes place, they are set free **4** A press release or publicity release is an official written statement given to reporters **5** A new release is a new film or record that has just become available

relegate verb To relegate something or someone means to give them a less important position or status > **relegation** noun

relent verb If someone relents, they agree to something they had previously not allowed

relentless adjective never stopping and never becoming less intense: *the relentless rise of business closures* > **relentlessly** adverb

relevant adjective If something is relevant, it is connected with and is appropriate to what is being discussed: *We have passed all relevant information on to the police* > **relevance** noun

reliable adjective **1** Reliable people and things can be trusted to do what you want **2** If information is reliable, you can assume that it is correct > **reliably** adverb > **reliability** noun

reliant adjective If you are reliant on someone or something, you depend on them: *They are not wholly reliant on charity* > **reliance** noun

relic noun **1** Relics are objects or customs that have survived from an earlier time **2** an object regarded as holy because it is thought to be connected with a saint

relief noun **1** If you feel relief, you are glad and thankful because a bad situation is over or has been avoided **2** Relief is also money, food, or clothing provided for poor or hungry people

relieve verb **1** If something relieves an unpleasant feeling, it makes it less unpleasant: *Drugs can relieve much of the pain* **2** (formal) If you relieve someone, you do their job or duty for a period **3** If someone is relieved of their duties, they are dismissed from their job **4** If you relieve yourself, you urinate

religion noun RE **1** Religion is the belief in a god or gods and all the activities connected with such beliefs **2** a system of religious belief

religious adjective **1** HISTORY connected with religion: *religious worship* **2** RE Someone who is religious has a strong belief in a god or gods

religiously adverb If you do something religiously, you do it regularly as a duty: *He stuck religiously to the rules*

relinquish [ril-**ling**-kwish] verb (formal) If you relinquish something, you give it up

relish verb **1** If you relish something, you enjoy it: *He relished the idea of getting some cash* ▷ noun **2** Relish is enjoyment: *He told me with relish of the wonderful times he had* **3** Relish is also a savoury sauce or pickle

relive verb If you relive a past experience, you remember it and imagine it happening again

relocate verb If people or businesses are relocated, they are moved to a different place > **relocation** noun

reluctant adjective If you are reluctant to do something, you are unwilling to do it > **reluctance** noun

reluctantly adverb If you do something reluctantly, you do it although you do not want to

rely relies, relying, relied verb **1** If you rely on someone or something, you need them and depend on them: *She has to rely on hardship payments* **2** If you can rely on someone to do something, you can trust them to do it: *They can always be relied on to turn up*

remain *verb* **1** If you remain in a particular place, you stay there **2** If you remain in a particular state, you stay the same and do not change: *The two men remained silent* **3** Something that remains still exists or is left over: *Huge amounts of weapons remain to be collected*

remainder *noun* The remainder of something is the part that is left: *He gulped down the remainder of his coffee*

remand *verb* **1** If a judge remands someone who is accused of a crime, the trial is postponed and the person is ordered to come back at a later date ▷ *phrase* **2** If someone is **on remand**, they are in prison waiting for their trial to begin

remark *verb* **1** If you remark on something, you mention it or comment on it: *She had remarked on the boy's improvement* ▷ *noun* **2** something you say, often in a casual way

remarkable *adjective* impressive and unexpected: *It was a remarkable achievement* > **remarkably** *adverb*

remarry remarries, remarrying, remarried *verb* If someone remarries, they get married again

remedial *adjective* **1** Remedial activities are to help someone improve their health after they have been ill **2** Remedial exercises are designed to improve someone's ability in something: *the remedial reading class*

remedy remedies, remedying, remedied *noun* **1** a way of dealing with a problem: *a remedy for colic* ▷ *verb* **2** If you remedy something that is wrong, you correct it: *We have to remedy the situation immediately*

remember *verb* **1** If you can remember someone or something from the past, you can bring them into your mind or think about them **2** If you remember to do something, you do it when you intended to: *Ben had remembered to book reservations*

remembrance *noun* If you do something in remembrance of a dead person, you are showing that they are remembered with respect and affection

remind *verb* **1** If someone reminds you of a fact, they say something to make you think about it: *Remind me to buy a bottle of wine, will you?* **2** If someone reminds you of another person, they look similar and make you think of them

reminder *noun* **1** If one thing is a reminder of another, the first thing makes you think of the second: *a reminder of better times* **2** a note sent to tell someone they have forgotten to do something

reminiscent *adjective* Something that is reminiscent of something else reminds you of it

remission *noun* When prisoners get remission for good behaviour, their sentences are reduced

remit (*formal*) *verb* **1** To remit money to someone means to send it to them in payment for something ▷ *noun* **2** The remit of a person or committee is the subject or task they are responsible for: *Their remit is to research into a wide range of health problems*

remnant *noun* a small part of something left after the rest has been used or destroyed

remorse *noun* (*formal*) Remorse is a strong feeling of guilt > **remorseful** *adjective*

remote *adjective* **1** Remote areas are far away from places where most

people live **2** far away in time: *the remote past* **3** If you say a person is remote, you mean they do not want to be friendly: *She is severe, solemn, and remote* **4** If there is only a remote possibility of something happening, it is unlikely to happen
> **remoteness** noun

remote control noun Remote control is a system of controlling a machine or vehicle from a distance using radio or electronic signals

remotely adverb used to emphasize a negative statement: *He isn't remotely keen*

removal noun **1** The removal of something is the act of taking it away **2** A removal company transports furniture from one building to another

remove verb **1** If you remove something from a place, you take it off or away **2** If you are removed from a position of authority, you are not allowed to continue your job **3** If you remove an undesirable feeling or attitude, you get rid of it: *Most of her fears had been removed*
> **removable** adjective

Renaissance [ren-**nay**-sonss] noun The Renaissance was a period from the 14th to 16th centuries in Europe when there was a great revival in the arts and learning

renal adjective (Medicine) concerning the kidneys: *renal failure*

rename verb If you rename something, you give it a new name

render verb You can use 'render' to say that something is changed into a different state: *The bomb was quickly rendered harmless*

rendezvous [**ron**-day-voo] noun **1 a** meeting: *Baxter arranged a six o'clock rendezvous* **b** a place where you have arranged to meet someone: *The pub became a popular rendezvous*

rendition noun (formal) a performance of a play, poem, or piece of music

renew verb **1** To renew an activity or relationship means to begin it again **2** To renew a licence or contract means to extend the period of time for which it is valid > **renewal** noun

renewable adjective **1** able to be renewed > noun **2** (GEOGRAPHY) a renewable form of energy, such as wind power or solar power

renounce verb (formal) If you renounce something, you reject it or give it up > **renunciation** noun

renovate verb If you renovate an old building or machine, you repair it and restore it to good condition
> **renovation** noun

renowned adjective well-known for something good: *He is not renowned for his patience* > **renown** noun

rent verb **1** If you rent something, you pay the owner a regular sum of money in return for being able to use it > noun **2** Rent is the amount of money you pay regularly to rent land or accommodation

rental adjective **1** concerned with the renting out of goods and services: *Scotland's largest car rental company* > noun **2** the amount of money you pay when you rent something

reorganize or **reorganise** verb To reorganize something means to organize it in a new way in order to make it more efficient or acceptable > **reorganization** noun

rep (informal) noun **1** A rep is a travelling salesperson. Rep is an abbreviation for **representative** > phrase **2** When actors work **in rep**, they are working with a repertory company

repair noun **1** something you do to

mend something that is damaged or broken ▷ verb **2** If you repair something, you mend it

repay repays, repaying, repaid verb **1** To repay money means to give it back to the person who lent it **2** If you repay a favour, you do something to help the person who helped you > **repayment** noun

repeal verb If the government repeals a law, it cancels it so that it is no longer valid

repeat verb **1** If you repeat something, you say, write, or do it again **2** If you repeat what someone has said, you tell someone else about it: *I trust you not to repeat that to anyone* ▷ noun **3** something which is done or happens again: *the number of repeats shown on TV* > **repeated** adjective > **repeatedly** adverb

repel verb repels, repelling, repelled **1** If something repels you, you find it horrible and disgusting **2** When soldiers repel an attacking force, they successfully defend themselves against it **3** When a magnetic pole repels another opposite pole, it forces the opposite pole away

repellent adjective **1** (formal) horrible and disgusting: *I found him repellent* ▷ noun **2** Repellents are chemicals used to keep insects or other creatures away

repent verb (formal) If you repent, you are sorry for something bad you have done > **repentance** noun > **repentant** adjective

repercussion noun The repercussions of an event are the effects it has at a later time

repertoire [rep-et-twar] noun A performer's repertoire is all the pieces of music or dramatic parts he or she has learned and can perform

repertory repertories noun **1** Repertory is the practice of performing a small number of plays in a theatre for a short time, using the same actors in each play **2** In Australian, New Zealand, and South African English, repertory is the same as **repertoire**

repetition noun **1** If there is a repetition of something, it happens again: *We don't want a repetition of last week's fiasco* **2** (ENGLISH) Repetition is when a word, phrase, or sound is repeated, for example to emphasize a point or to make sure it is understood, or for poetic effect

repetitive adjective A repetitive activity involves a lot of repetition and is boring: *dull and repetitive work*

replace verb **1** When one thing replaces another, the first thing takes the place of the second **2** If you replace something that is damaged or lost, you get a new one **3** If you replace something, you put it back where it was before: *She replaced the receiver*

replacement noun **1** The replacement for someone or something is the person or thing that takes their place **2** The replacement of a person or thing happens when they are replaced by another person or thing

replay verb [re-**play**] **1** If a match is replayed, the teams play it again **2** If you replay a recording, you play it again: *Replay the first few seconds of the DVD please* ▷ noun [re-**play**] **3** a match that is played for a second time

replenish verb (formal) If you replenish something, you make it full or complete again

replica noun an accurate copy of something: *a replica of Columbus's* *ship* > *replicate verb*

reply replies, replying, replied *verb*
1 If you reply to something, you say or write an answer ▷ *noun* **2** what you say or write when you answer someone

report *verb* **1** If you report that something has happened, you tell someone about it or give an official account of it: *He reported the theft to the police* **2** To report someone to an authority means to make an official complaint about them **3** If you report to a person or place, you go there and say you have arrived ▷ *noun* **4** an account of an event or situation

reporter *noun* someone who writes news articles or broadcasts news reports

repossess *verb* If a shop or company repossesses goods that have not been paid for, they take them back

represent *verb* **1** If you represent someone, you act on their behalf: *lawyers representing relatives of the victims* **2** If a sign or symbol represents something, it stands for it **3** To represent something in a particular way means to describe it in that way: *The popular press tends to represent him as a hero*

representation *noun*
1 Representation is the state of being represented by someone: *Was there any student representation?*
2 You can describe a picture or statue of someone as a representation of them

representative *noun* **1** a person chosen to act on behalf of another person or a group ▷ *adjective* **2** A representative selection is typical of the group it belongs to: *The photos chosen are not representative of his work*

repress *verb* **1** If you repress a feeling, you succeed in not showing or feeling it: *I couldn't repress my anger any longer* **2** To repress people means to restrict their freedom and control them by force > **repression** *noun*

repressive *adjective* Repressive governments use force and unjust laws to restrict and control people

reprieve [rip-**preev**] *verb* **1** If someone who has been sentenced to death is reprieved, their sentence is changed and they are not killed ▷ *noun* **2** a delay before something unpleasant happens: *The zoo won a reprieve from closure*

reprimand *verb* **1** If you reprimand someone, you officially tell them that they should not have done something ▷ *noun* **2** something said or written by a person in authority when they are reprimanding someone

reprisal *noun* Reprisals are violent actions taken by one group of people against another group that has harmed them

reproach (*formal*) *noun* **1** If you express reproach, you show that you feel sad and angry about what someone has done: *a long letter of reproach* ▷ *verb* **2** If you reproach someone, you tell them, rather sadly, that they have done something wrong > **reproachful** *adjective* > **reproachfully** *adverb*

reproduce *verb* **1** To reproduce something means to make a copy of it [SCIENCE] When living things reproduce, they produce more of their own kind: *Bacteria reproduce by splitting into two*

reproduction *noun* **1** a modern copy of a painting or piece of furniture **2** [SCIENCE] Reproduction is the process by which a living thing produces more of its kind: *the study of animal reproduction*

reproductive adjective [SCIENCE] relating to the reproduction of living things: *the female reproductive system*

reptile noun a cold-blooded animal, such as a snake or a lizard, which has scaly skin and lays eggs > **reptilian** adjective

republic noun a country which has a president rather than a king or queen > **republican** noun, adjective > **republicanism** noun

repulsive adjective horrible and disgusting

reputable adjective known to be good and reliable: *a well-established and reputable firm*

reputation noun The reputation of something or someone is the opinion that people have of them: *The college had a good reputation*

reputed adjective If something is reputed to be true, some people say that it is true: *the reputed tomb of Christ* > **reputedly** adverb

request verb **1** If you request something, you ask for it politely or formally ▷ noun **2** If you make a request for something, you request it

requiem [rek-wee-em] noun **1** A requiem or requiem mass is a mass celebrated for someone who has recently died **2** a piece of music for singers and an orchestra, originally written for a requiem mass: *Mozart's Requiem*

require verb **1** If you require something, you need it **2** If you are required to do something, you have to do it because someone says you must: *The rules require employers to provide safety training*

requirement noun something that you must have or must do: *A good*

degree is a requirement for entry

requisite (formal) adjective **1** necessary for a particular purpose: *She filled in the requisite paperwork* ▷ noun **2** something that is necessary for a particular purpose

rescue rescues, rescuing, rescued verb **1** If you rescue someone, you save them from a dangerous or unpleasant situation ▷ noun **2** Rescue is help which saves someone from a dangerous or unpleasant situation > **rescuer** noun

research noun **1** Research is work that involves studying something and trying to find out facts about it ▷ verb **2** If you research something, you try to discover facts about it > **researcher** noun

resemblance noun If there is a resemblance between two things, they are similar to each other: *There was a remarkable resemblance between them*

resemble verb To resemble something means to be similar to it

resent verb If you resent something, you feel bitter and angry about it

resentful adjective bitter and angry: *He felt very resentful about losing his job* > **resentfully** adverb

resentment noun a feeling of anger or bitterness

reservation noun **1** If you have reservations about something, you are not sure that it is right **2** If you make a reservation, you book a place in advance **3** an area of land set aside for American Indian peoples: *a Cherokee reservation*

reserve verb **1** If something is reserved for a particular person or purpose, it is kept specially for them ▷ noun **2** a supply of something for future use **3** In sport, a reserve is

r

someone who is available to play in case one of the team is unable to play **4** A nature reserve is an area of land where animals, birds, or plants are officially protected **5** If someone shows reserve, they keep their feelings hidden > **reserved** adjective

reservoir [rez-ev-wahr] noun a lake used for storing water before it is supplied to people

reshuffle noun a reorganization of people or things

reside [riz-zide] verb (formal) **1** If someone resides somewhere, they live there or are staying there **2** If a quality resides in something, the quality is in that thing

residence (formal) noun **1** A residence is a house ▷ phrase **2** If you **take up residence** somewhere, you go and live there

resident noun **1** A resident of a house or area is someone who lives there ▷ adjective **2** If someone is resident in a house or area, they live there

residential adjective **1** A residential area contains mainly houses rather than offices or factories **2** providing accommodation: residential care for the elderly

residue noun a small amount of something that remains after most of it has gone: an increase in toxic residues found in drinking water > **residual** adjective

resign verb **1** If you resign from a job, you formally announce that you are leaving it **2** If you resign yourself to an unpleasant situation, you realize that you have to accept it > **resigned** adjective

resignation noun **1** Someone's resignation is a formal statement of their intention to leave a job **2** Resignation is the reluctant

acceptance of an unpleasant situation or fact

resilient adjective able to recover quickly from unpleasant or damaging events > **resilience** noun

resin noun **1** Resin is a sticky substance produced by some trees **2** Resin is also a substance produced chemically and used to make plastics

resist verb **1** If you resist something, you refuse to accept it and try to prevent it: The pay squeeze will be fiercely resisted by the unions **2** If you resist someone, you fight back against them

resistance noun **1** Resistance to something such as change is a refusal to accept it **2** Resistance to an attack consists of fighting back: The demonstrators offered no resistance **3** Your body's resistance to germs or disease is its power to not be harmed by them **4** Resistance is also the power of a substance to resist the flow of an electrical current through it

resistant adjective **1** opposed to something and wanting to prevent it: People were very resistant to change **2** If something is resistant to a particular thing, it is not harmed or affected by it: Certain insects are resistant to this spray

resolute [rez-ol-loot] adjective (formal) Someone who is resolute is determined not to change their mind > **resolutely** adverb

resolution noun **1** Resolution is determination **2** If you make a resolution, you promise yourself to do something **3** a formal decision taken at a meeting **4** [ENGLISH] The resolution of a problem is the solving of it

resolve verb **1** If you resolve to do

something, you firmly decide to do it **2** If you resolve a problem, you find a solution to it ▷ noun **3** Resolve is absolute determination

resonance noun **1** Resonance is sound produced by an object vibrating as a result of another sound nearby **2** Resonance is also a deep, clear, and echoing quality of sound

resonate verb If something resonates, it vibrates and produces a deep, strong sound

resort verb **1** If you resort to a course of action, you do it because you have no alternative ▷ noun **2** a place where people spend their holidays ▷ phrase **3** If you do something **as a last resort**, you do it because you can find no other way of solving a problem

resounding adjective **1** loud and echoing: a resounding round of applause **2** A resounding success is a great success

resource noun The resources of a country, organization, or person are the materials, money, or skills they have

resourceful adjective A resourceful person is good at finding ways of dealing with problems
> **resourcefulness** noun

respect verb **1** If you respect someone, you have a good opinion of their character or ideas **2** If you respect someone's rights or wishes, you do not do things that they would not like, or would consider wrong: It is about time they started respecting the law **3** If you have respect for someone, you have a good opinion of them ▷ phrase **4** You can say **in this respect** to refer to a particular feature: At least in this respect we are equals

respectable adjective **1** considered to be acceptable and morally correct: respectable families **2** adequate or reasonable: a respectable rate of economic growth
> **respectability** noun
> **respectably** adverb

respectful adjective showing respect for someone: Our children are always respectful to their elders
> **respectfully** adverb

respective adjective belonging or relating individually to the people or things just mentioned: They went into their respective rooms to pack

respectively adverb in the same order as the items just mentioned: Amanda and Emily finished first and second respectively

respiration noun SCIENCE Your respiration is your breathing

respiratory adjective SCIENCE relating to breathing: respiratory diseases

respite noun (formal) a short rest from something unpleasant

respond verb When you respond to something, you react to it by doing or saying something

respondent noun **1** a person who answers a questionnaire or a request for information **2** In a court case, the respondent is the defendant

response noun Your response to an event is your reaction or reply to it: There has been no response to his remarks yet

responsibility responsibilities noun **1** If you have responsibility for something, it is your duty to deal with it or look after it: The garden was to have been his responsibility **2** If you accept responsibility for something that has happened, you agree that you caused it or were to blame: We must all accept responsibility for our own mistakes

responsible *adjective* **1** If you are responsible for something, it is your job to deal with it **2** If you are responsible for something bad that has happened, you are to blame for it **3** If you are responsible to someone, that person is your boss and tells you what you have to do **4** A responsible person behaves properly and sensibly without needing to be supervised **5** A responsible job involves making careful judgments about important matters > **responsibly** *adverb*

responsive *adjective* **1** quick to show interest and pleasure **2** taking notice of events and reacting in an appropriate way: *The course is responsive to students' needs*

rest *noun* **1** The rest of something is all the remaining parts of it **2** If you have a rest, you sit or lie quietly and relax > *verb* **3** If you rest, you relax and do not do anything active for a while

restaurant [rest-ront] *noun* a place where you can buy and eat a meal

restaurateur [rest-er-a-**tur**] *noun* someone who owns or manages a restaurant

restful *adjective* Something that is restful helps you feel calm and relaxed

restless *adjective* finding it hard to remain still or relaxed because of boredom or impatience > **restlessness** *noun* > **restlessly** *adverb*

restore *verb* **1** To restore something means to cause it to exist again or to return to its previous state: *He was anxious to restore his reputation* **2** To restore an old building or work of art means to

clean and repair it > **restoration** *noun*

restrain *verb* To restrain someone or something means to hold them back or prevent them from doing what they want

restrained *adjective* behaving in a controlled way

restraint *noun* **1** Restraints are rules or conditions that limit something: *wage restraints* **2** Restraint is calm, controlled behaviour

restrict *verb* **1** If you restrict something, you prevent it becoming too large or varied **2** To restrict people or animals means to limit their movement or actions > **restrictive** *adjective*

restriction *noun* a rule or situation that limits what you can do: *financial restrictions*

result *noun* **1** The result of an action or situation is the situation that is caused by it: *As a result of the incident he got a two-year suspension* **2** The result is also the final marks, figures, or situation at the end of an exam, calculation, or contest: *election results; The result was calculated to three decimal places* > *verb* **3** If something results in a particular event, it causes that event to happen **4** If something results from a particular event, it is caused by that event: *The fire had resulted from carelessness* > **resultant** *adjective*

resume [riz-**yoom**] *verb* If you resume an activity or position, you return to it after a break > **resumption** *noun*

resurgence *noun* If there is a resurgence of an attitude or activity, it reappears and grows stronger > **resurgent** *adjective*

resurrect *verb* If you resurrect something, you make it exist again

after it has disappeared or ended
> **resurrection** noun

resuscitate [ris-**suss**-it-tate] verb If
you resuscitate someone, you make
them conscious again after an
accident > **resuscitation** noun

retail noun The retail price is the
price at which something is sold in
the shops > **retailer** noun

retain verb To retain something
means to keep it > **retention** noun

retaliate verb If you retaliate, you do
something to harm or upset
someone because they have already
acted in a similar way against you
> **retaliation** noun

rethink rethinks, rethinking,
rethought verb If you rethink
something, you think about how it
should be changed: We have to
rethink our strategy

reticent adjective Someone who is
reticent is unwilling to tell people
about things > **reticence** noun

retina noun The light-sensitive part
at the back of your eyeball, which
receives an image and sends it to
your brain

retinue noun A group of helpers or
friends travelling with an important
person

retire verb 1 When older people
retire, they give up work 2 (formal) If
you retire, you go to go into
another room, or to bed: She retired
early with a good book > **retired**
adjective > **retirement** noun

retort verb 1 To retort means to
reply angrily ▷ noun 2 A short,
angry reply

retract verb 1 If you retract
something you have said, you say
that you did not mean it 2 When
something is retracted, it moves
inwards or backwards: The
undercarriage was retracted shortly

after takeoff > **retraction** noun
> **retractable** adjective

retreat verb 1 To retreat means to
move backwards away from
something or someone 2 If you
retreat from something difficult or
unpleasant, you avoid doing it
▷ noun 3 If an army moves away
from the enemy, this is referred to as
a retreat 4 a quiet place that you
can go to rest or do things in private

retribution noun (formal)
Retribution is punishment: the
threat of retribution

retrieve verb If you retrieve
something, you get it back
> **retrieval** noun

retriever noun A large dog often
used by hunters to bring back birds
and animals which have been shot

retrospect phrase When you
consider something **in retrospect**,
you think about it afterwards and
often have a different opinion from
the one you had at the time: In
retrospect, I probably shouldn't have
resigned

retrospective adjective 1 concerning
things that happened in the past
2 taking effect from a date in the
past > **retrospectively** adverb

return verb 1 When you return to a
place, you go back after you have
been away 2 If you return
something to someone, you give it
back to them 3 When you return a
ball during a game, you hit it back to
your opponent 4 When a judge or
jury returns a verdict, they
announce it ▷ noun 5 Your return is
your arrival back at a place 6 The
return on an investment is the profit
or interest you get from it 7 a ticket
for the journey to a place and back
again ▷ phrase 8 If you do
something **in return** for a favour,

r

you do it to repay the favour

reunion noun a party or meeting for people who have not seen each other for a long time

reunite verb If people are reunited, they meet again after they have been separated for some time

rev revs, revving, revved (informal) verb 1 When you rev the engine of a vehicle, you press the accelerator to increase the engine speed ▷ noun 2 The speed of an engine is measured in revolutions per minute, referred to as revs: I noticed that the engine revs had dropped

revamp verb To revamp something means to improve or repair it

reveal verb 1 To reveal something means to tell people about it: They were not ready to reveal any of the details 2 If you reveal something that has been hidden, you uncover it

revel revels, revelling, revelled verb If you revel in a situation, you enjoy it very much > **revelry** noun

revelation noun 1 a surprising or interesting fact made known to people 2 If an experience is a revelation, it makes you realize or learn something

revenge noun 1 Revenge involves hurting someone who has hurt you ▷ verb 2 If you revenge yourself on someone who has hurt you, you hurt them in return

revenue noun Revenue is money that a government, company, or organization receives: government tax revenues

revered adjective If someone is revered, he or she is respected and admired: He is still revered as the father of the nation

reverence noun Reverence is a feeling of great respect

Reverend adjective Reverend is a title used before the name of a member of the clergy: the Reverend George Young

reversal noun If there is a reversal of a process or policy, it is changed to the opposite process or policy

reverse verb 1 When someone reverses a process, they change it to the opposite process: They won't reverse the decision to increase prices 2 If you reverse the order of things, you arrange them in the opposite order 3 When you reverse a car, you drive it backwards ▷ noun 4 The reverse is the opposite of what has just been said or done ▷ adjective 5 Reverse means opposite to what is usual or to what has just been described

reversible adjective Reversible clothing can be worn with either side on the outside

revert verb (formal) To revert to a former state or type of behaviour means to go back to it

review noun 1 an article or an item on television or radio, giving an opinion of a new book or play 2 When there is a review of a situation or system, it is examined to decide whether changes are needed ▷ verb 3 To review a play or book means to write an account expressing an opinion of it 4 To review something means to examine it to decide whether changes are needed > **reviewer** noun

revise verb 1 If you revise something, you alter or correct it 2 When you revise for an examination, you go over your work to learn things thoroughly > **revision** noun

revive verb 1 When a feeling or practice is revived, it becomes active or popular again 2 If someone who has fainted revives, they become conscious again ▷ **revival** noun

revolt noun 1 HISTORY a violent attempt by a group of people to change their country's political system ▷ verb 2 HISTORY When people revolt, they fight against the authority that governs them 3 If something revolts you, it is so horrible that you feel disgust

revolting adjective horrible and disgusting: *The smell in the cell was revolting*

revolution noun 1 HISTORY a violent attempt by a large group of people to change the political system of their country 2 an important change in an area of human activity: *the Industrial Revolution* 3 one complete turn in a circle

revolutionary revolutionaries adjective 1 involving great changes: *a revolutionary new cooling system* ▷ noun 2 a person who takes part in a revolution

revolve verb 1 If something revolves round something else, it centres on that as the most important thing: *My job revolves around the telephone* 2 When something revolves, it turns in a circle around a central point: *The moon revolves round the earth*

revolver noun a small gun held in the hand

revulsion noun Revulsion is a strong feeling of disgust or disapproval

reward PSHE noun 1 something you are given because you have done something good ▷ verb 2 If you reward someone, you give them a reward

rewarding adjective Something that is rewarding gives you a lot of satisfaction

rewind rewinds, rewinding, rewound verb If you rewind a tape

on a tape recorder or video, you make the tape go backwards

rhetoric noun [ret-or-ik] Rhetoric is speech or writing that is intended to impress people

rhetorical adjective 1 A rhetorical question is one which is asked in order to make a statement rather than to get an answer 2 Rhetorical language is intended to be grand and impressive

rhino noun (informal) a rhinoceros

rhinoceros noun a large African or Asian animal with one or two horns on its nose

rhododendron noun an evergreen bush with large coloured flowers

rhubarb noun Rhubarb is a plant with long red stems which can be cooked with sugar and eaten

rhyme ENGLISH verb 1 If two words rhyme, they have a similar sound: *Sally rhymes with valley* ▷ noun 2 a word that rhymes with another 3 a short poem with rhyming lines

rhythm noun 1 MUSIC Rhythm is a regular movement or beat 2 a regular pattern of changes, for example, in the seasons ▷ **rhythmic** adjective ▷ **rhythmically** adverb

rib noun Your ribs are the curved bones that go from your backbone to your chest

ribbon noun a long, narrow piece of cloth used for decoration

rice noun Rice is a tall grass that produces edible grains. Rice is grown in warm countries on wet ground

rich adjective 1 Someone who is rich has a lot of money and possessions 2 Something that is rich in something contains a large amount of it: *Liver is particularly rich in vitamin A* 3 Rich food contains a large amount of fat, oil, or sugar **4** Rich colours, smells, and sounds are strong and pleasant > **richness** noun

richly adverb **1** If someone is richly rewarded, they are rewarded well with something valuable **2** If you feel strongly that someone deserves something, you can say it is richly deserved

rickety adjective likely to collapse or break: a rickety wooden jetty

rickshaw noun a hand-pulled cart used in Asia for carrying passengers

ricochet ricochets, ricocheting or ricochetting, ricocheted or ricochetted [**rik**-osh-ay] verb When a bullet ricochets, it hits a surface and bounces away from it

rid rids, ridding, rid phrase **1** When you **get rid of** something you do not want, you remove or destroy it > verb **2** (formal) To rid a place of something unpleasant means to succeed in removing it

riddle noun **1** a puzzle which seems to be nonsense, but which has an entertaining solution **2** Something that is a riddle puzzles and confuses you

ride rides, riding, rode, ridden verb **1** When you ride a horse or a bike, you sit on it and control it as it moves along **2** When you ride in a car, you travel in it > noun **3** a journey on a horse or bike or in a vehicle

rider noun **1** a person riding on a horse or bicycle **2** an additional statement which changes or puts a condition on what has already been said

ridge noun **1** a long, narrow piece of high land **2** a raised line on a flat surface

ridicule verb **1** To ridicule someone

means to make fun of them in an unkind way > noun **2** Ridicule is unkind laughter and mockery

ridiculous adjective very foolish > **ridiculously** adverb

rife adjective (formal) very common: Unemployment was rife

rifle noun **1** a gun with a long barrel > verb **2** When someone rifles something, they make a quick search through it to steal things

rift noun **1** a serious quarrel between friends that damages their friendship **2** a split in something solid, especially in the ground

rig rigs, rigging, rigged verb **1** If someone rigs an election or contest, they dishonestly arrange for a particular person to succeed > noun **2** a large structure used for extracting oil or gas from the ground or sea bed > **rig up** verb If you rig up a device or structure, you make it quickly and fix it in place: They had even rigged up a makeshift aerial

right adjective, adverb **1** correct and in accordance with the facts: That clock never tells the right time; That's absolutely right **2** 'Right' means on or towards the right side of something > adjective **3** The right choice or decision is the best or most suitable one **4** The right people or places are those that have influence or are socially admired: He was always to be seen in the right places **5** The right side of something is the side intended to be seen and to face outwards > noun **6** 'Right' is used to refer to principles of morally correct behaviour: At least he knew right from wrong **7** If you have a right to do something, you are morally or legally entitled to do it **8** The right is one of the two sides of something.

For example, when you look at the word 'to', the 'o' is to the right of the 't' **9** The Right refers to people who support the political ideas of capitalism and conservatism rather than socialism ▷ *adverb* **10** 'Right' is used to emphasize a precise place: *I'm right here* **11** 'Right' means immediately: *I had to decide right then* ▷ *verb* **12** If you right something, you correct it or put it back in an upright position > **rightly** *adverb*

right angle *noun* MATHS an angle of 90°

righteous *adjective* Righteous people behave in a way that is morally good and religious

rightful *adjective* Someone's rightful possession is one which they have a moral or legal right to > **rightfully** *adverb*

right-handed *adjective, adverb* Someone who is right-handed does things such as writing and painting with their right hand

right-wing *adjective* believing more strongly in capitalism and conservatism, or less strongly in socialism, than other members of the same party or group > **right-winger** *noun*

rigid *adjective* **1** Rigid laws or systems cannot be changed and are considered severe **2** A rigid object is stiff and does not bend easily > **rigidly** *adverb* **rigidity** *noun*

rigorous *adjective* very careful and thorough > **rigorously** *adverb*

rigour *noun* (formal) The rigours of a situation are the things which make it hard or unpleasant: *the rigours of childbirth*

rim *noun* the outside or top edge of an object such as a wheel or a cup > **rimmed** *adjective*

rind *noun* Rind is the thick outer skin

of fruit, cheese, or bacon

ring *rings, ringing, ringed, rang, rung verb* **1** If you ring someone, you phone them **2** When a bell rings, it makes a clear, loud sound **3** To ring something means to draw a circle around it **4** If something is ringed with something else, it has that thing all the way around it: *The courthouse was ringed with police* ▷ *noun* **5** the sound made by a bell **6** a small circle of metal worn on your finger **7** an object or group of things in the shape of a circle **8** At a boxing match or circus, the ring is the place where the fight or performance takes place **9** an organized group of people who are involved in an illegal activity: *an international spy ring*

ringer *noun* **1** a person or thing that is almost identical to another **2** In Australian English, someone who works on a sheep farm **3** In Australian and New Zealand English, the fastest shearer in a woolshed

ringleader *noun* the leader of a group of people who get involved in mischief or crime

rink *noun* a large enclosed area for ice-skating or roller-skating

rinse *verb* **1** When you rinse something, you wash it in clean water ▷ *noun* **2** a liquid you can put on your hair to give it a different colour

riot *noun* **1** When there is a riot, a crowd of people behave noisily and violently ▷ *verb* **2** To riot means to behave noisily and violently ▷ *phrase* **3** To run riot means to behave in a wild and uncontrolled way

rip *rips, ripping, ripped verb* **1** When you rip something, you tear it violently **2** If you rip something away, you remove it quickly and violently ▷ noun **3** a long split in cloth or paper ▷ **rip off** verb (informal) If someone rips you off, they cheat you by charging you too much money

RIP RIP is an abbreviation often written on gravestones, meaning 'rest in peace'

ripe adjective **1** When fruit or grain is ripe, it is fully developed and ready to be eaten **2** If a situation is ripe for something to happen, it is ready for it ▷ **ripeness** noun

ripen verb When crops ripen, they become ripe

ripper noun (informal) In Australian and New Zealand English, an excellent person or thing

ripple noun **1** Ripples are little waves on the surface of calm water **2** If there is a ripple of laughter or applause, people laugh or applaud gently for a short time ▷ verb **3** When the surface of water ripples, little waves appear on it

rise rises, rising, rose, risen verb **1** If something rises, it moves upwards **2** (formal) When you rise, you stand up **3** To rise also means to get out of bed **4** When the sun rises, it first appears **5** The place where a river rises is where it begins **6** If land rises, it slopes upwards **7** If a sound or wind rises, it becomes higher or stronger **8** If an amount rises, it increases **9** If you rise to a challenge or a remark, you respond to it rather than ignoring it: *He rose to the challenge with enthusiasm* **10** When people rise up, they start fighting against people in authority ▷ noun **11** an increase **12** Someone's rise is the process by which they become more powerful or successful: *his rise to fame*

riser noun An early riser is someone who likes to get up early in the morning

risk noun **1** a chance that something unpleasant or dangerous might happen ▷ verb **2** If you risk something unpleasant, you do something knowing that the unpleasant thing might happen as a result: *If he doesn't play, he risks losing his place in the team* **3** If you risk someone's life, you put them in a dangerous situation in which they might be killed ▷ **risky** adjective

rite noun a religious ceremony

ritual noun **1** a series of actions carried out according to the custom of a particular society or group: *This is the most ancient of the Buddhist rituals* ▷ adjective **2** Ritual activities happen as part of a tradition or ritual: *fasting and ritual dancing* ▷ **ritualistic** adjective

rival rivals, rivalling, rivalled noun **1** Your rival is the person you are competing with ▷ verb **2** If something rivals something else, it is of the same high standard or quality: *As a holiday destination, South Africa rivals Kenya for weather*

rivalry rivalries noun Rivalry is active competition between people

river noun a natural feature consisting of water flowing for a long distance between two banks

rivet noun a short, round pin with a flat head which is used to fasten sheets of metal together

riveting adjective If you find something riveting, you find it fascinating and it holds your attention: *I find tennis riveting*

road noun a long piece of hard ground specially surfaced so that people and vehicles can travel along it easily

road rage noun Road rage is aggressive behaviour by a driver as a reaction to the behaviour of another driver

road train noun in Australia, a line of linked trailers pulled by a truck, used for transporting cattle or sheep

roadworks plural noun Roadworks are repairs being done on a road

roam verb If you roam around, you wander around without any particular purpose: Hens were roaming around the yard

roar verb 1 If something roars, it makes a very loud noise 2 To roar with laughter or anger means to laugh or shout very noisily 3 When a lion roars, it makes a loud, angry sound ▷ noun 4 a very loud noise

roast verb 1 When you roast meat or other food, you cook it using dry heat in an oven or over a fire ▷ adjective 2 Roast meat has been roasted ▷ noun 3 a piece of meat that has been roasted

rob robs, robbing, robbed verb 1 If someone robs you, they steal your possessions 2 If you rob someone of something you need or deserve, you deprive them of it: He robbed me of my childhood

robber noun Robbers are people who steal money or property using force or threats: bank robbers ▷ robbery noun

robe noun a long, loose piece of clothing which covers the body: He knelt in his white robes before the altar

robin noun a small bird with a red breast

robot noun 1 a machine which is programmed to move and perform tasks automatically 2 in South African English, a set of traffic lights

robust adjective very strong and

healthy ▷ **robustly** adverb

rock noun 1 Rock is the hard mineral substance that forms the surface of the earth 2 a large piece of rock: She picked up a rock and threw it into the lake 3 Rock or rock music is music with simple tunes and a very strong beat 4 Rock is also a sweet shaped into long, hard sticks, sold in holiday resorts ▷ verb 5 When something rocks or when you rock it, it moves regularly backwards and forwards or from side to side: She rocked the baby 6 If something rocks people, it shocks and upsets them: Palermo was rocked by a crime wave ▷ phrase 7 If someone's marriage or relationship is **on the rocks**, it is unsuccessful and about to end

rock and roll noun Rock and roll is a style of music with a strong beat that was especially popular in the 1950s

rocket noun 1 a space vehicle, usually shaped like a long pointed tube 2 an explosive missile: They fired rockets into a number of government buildings 3 a firework that explodes when it is high in the air ▷ verb 4 If prices rocket, they increase very quickly

rocking chair noun a chair on two curved pieces of wood that rocks backwards and forwards when you sit in it

rocky rockier, rockiest adjective covered with rocks

rod noun a long, thin pole or bar, usually made of wood or metal: a fishing rod

rodent noun a small mammal with sharp front teeth which it uses for gnawing

rodeo rodeos noun a public entertainment in which cowboys show different skills

roe noun Roe is the eggs of a fish

rogue noun 1 You can refer to a man who behaves dishonestly as a rogue ▷ adjective 2 a vicious animal that lives apart from its herd or pack

role or **rôle** noun 1 Someone's role is their position and function in a situation or society 2 DRAMA An actor's role is the character that he or she plays: *her first leading role*

roll verb 1 When something rolls or when you roll it, it moves along a surface, turning over and over 2 When vehicles roll along, they move: *Tanks rolled into the village* 3 If you roll your eyes, you make them turn up or go from side to side 4 If you roll something flexible into a cylinder or ball, you wrap it several times around itself: *He rolled up the bag with the money in it* ▷ noun 5 A roll of paper or cloth is a long piece of it that has been rolled into a tube: *a roll of film* 6 a small, rounded, individually baked piece of bread 7 an official list of people's names: *the electoral roll* 8 A roll on a drum is a long, rumbling sound made on it

> **roll up** verb 1 If you roll up something flexible, you wrap it several times around itself 2 If you roll up your sleeves or trousers, you fold them over from the bottom to make them shorter 3 (*informal*) If you roll up, you arrive

roller noun 1 a cylinder that turns round in a machine or piece of equipment 2 Rollers are tubes which you can wind your hair around to make it curly

roller-coaster noun a pleasure ride at a fair, consisting of a small railway that goes up and down very steep slopes

rolling pin noun a cylinder used for rolling pastry dough to make it flat

ROM noun COMPUTING ROM is a storage device that holds data permanently and cannot be altered by the programmer. ROM stands for 'read only memory'

Roman Catholic adjective 1 relating or belonging to the branch of the Christian Church that accepts the Pope in Rome as its leader ▷ noun 2 someone who belongs to the Roman Catholic Church > **Roman Catholicism** noun

romance noun 1 a relationship between two people who are in love with each other 2 Romance is the pleasure and excitement of doing something new and unusual: *the romance of foreign travel* 3 LIBRARY a novel about a love affair

Romanian [roe-**may**-nee-an] or **Rumanian** adjective 1 belonging or relating to Romania ▷ noun 2 someone who comes from Romania 3 Romanian is the main language spoken in Romania

romantic adjective, noun 1 A romantic person has ideas that are not realistic, for example about love or about ways of changing society: *a romantic idealist* ▷ adjective 2 connected with love: *a romantic relationship* 3 Something that is romantic is beautiful in a way that strongly affects your feelings: *It is one of the most romantic ruins in Scotland* 4 Romantic describes a style of music, literature, and art popular in Europe in the late 18th and early 19th centuries, which emphasized feeling and imagination rather than order and form > **romantically** adverb > **romanticism** noun

roo roos noun (*informal*) In Australian English, a kangaroo

roof noun 1 The roof of a building or

car is the covering on top of it **2** The roof of your mouth or of a cave is the highest part

roofing noun Roofing is material used for covering roofs

rooftop noun the outside part of the roof of a building

room noun **1** a separate section in a building, divided from other rooms by walls **2** If there is room somewhere, there is enough space for things to be fitted in or for people to do what they want to do: There wasn't enough room for his gear

roost noun **1** a place where birds rest or build their nests ▷ verb **2** When birds roost, they settle somewhere for the night

root noun **1** The roots of a plant are the parts that grow under the ground **2** The root of a hair is the part beneath the skin **3** You can refer to the place or culture that you grew up in as your roots **4** The root of something is its original cause or basis: We got to the root of the problem ▷ verb **5** To root through things means to search through them, pushing them aside: She rooted through his bag ▷ **root out** verb If you root something or someone out, you find them and force them out: a major drive to root out corruption

rooted adjective developed from or strongly influenced by something: songs rooted in traditional African music

rope noun **1** a thick, strong length of twisted cord ▷ verb **2** If you rope one thing to another, you tie them together with rope

rosary noun rosaries noun a string of beads that Roman Catholics use for counting prayers

rose noun **1** a large garden flower which has a pleasant smell and

grows on a bush with thorns ▷ noun, adjective **2** reddish-pink

rosemary noun Rosemary is a herb with fragrant spiky leaves, used for flavouring in cooking

rosette noun a large badge of coloured ribbons gathered into a circle, which is worn as a prize in a competition or to support a political party

roster noun a list of people who take it in turn to do a particular job: He put himself first on the new roster for domestic chores

rostrum noun rostrums or rostra noun a raised platform on which someone stands to speak to an audience or conduct an orchestra

rosy rosier, rosiest adjective **1** reddish-pink **2** If a situation seems rosy, it is likely to be good or successful **3** If a person looks rosy, they have pink cheeks and look healthy

rot rots, rotting, rotted verb **1** When food or wood rots, it decays and can no longer be used **2** When something rots another substance, it causes it to decay: Sugary drinks rot your teeth ▷ noun **3** Rot is the condition that affects things when they rot: The timber frame was not protected against rot

rota noun a list of people who take turns to do a particular job

rotate verb MATHS When something rotates, it turns with a circular movement: He rotated the camera 180° > **rotation** noun

rotor noun **1** The rotor is the part of a machine that turns **2** The rotors or rotor blades of a helicopter are the four long, flat pieces of metal on top of it which rotate and lift it off the ground

rotten adjective **1** decayed and no

longer of use: *The front bay window is rotten* **2** (*informal*) of very poor quality: *I think it's a rotten idea* **3** (*informal*) very unfair, unkind, or unpleasant: *That's a rotten thing to say!*

rouble [roo-bl] *noun* the main unit of currency in Russia

rough [ruff] *adjective* **1** uneven and not using enough care or gentleness: *Don't be so rough or you'll break it* **3** difficult or unpleasant: *Teenagers have been given a rough time* **4** approximately correct: *At a rough guess it is five times more profitable* **5** If the sea is rough, there are large waves because of bad weather **6** A rough town or area has a lot of crime or violence ▷ *noun, adjective* **7** A rough or a rough sketch is a drawing or description that shows the main features but does not show the details ▷ *noun* **8** On a golf course, the rough is the part of the course next to a fairway where the grass has not been cut > **roughly** *adverb* > **roughness** *noun*

roulette [roo-let] *noun* Roulette is a gambling game in which a ball is dropped onto a revolving wheel with numbered holes in it

round *adjective* **1** Something round is shaped like a ball or a circle **2** complete or whole: *round numbers* ▷ *preposition, adverb* **3** If something is round something else, it surrounds it **4** The distance round something is the length of its circumference or boundary: *I'm about two inches larger round the waist* **5** You can refer to an area near a place as the area round it: *There's nothing to do round here* ▷ *preposition* **6** If something moves round you, it keeps moving in a circle with you in the centre **7** When

someone goes to the other side of something, they have gone round it ▷ *adverb, preposition* **8** If you go round a place, you go to different parts of it to look at it: *We went round the museum* ▷ *adverb* **9** If you turn or look round, you turn so you are facing in a different direction **10** When someone comes round, they visit you: *He came round with a bottle of wine* ▷ *noun* **11** one of a series of events: *After round three, two Americans shared the lead* **12** If you buy a round of drinks, you buy a drink for each member of the group you are with > **round up** *verb* If you round up people or animals, you gather them together

roundabout *noun* **1** a meeting point of several roads with a circle in the centre which vehicles have to travel around **2** a circular platform which rotates and which children can ride on in a playground **3** the same as a merry-go-round

rounded *adjective* curved in shape, without any points or sharp edges

rounders *noun* a game played by two teams, in which a player scores points by hitting a ball and running around four sides of a square pitch

round-the-clock *adjective* happening continuously

rouse *verb* **1** If someone rouses you, they wake you up **2** If you rouse yourself to do something, you make yourself get up and do it **3** If something rouses you, it makes you feel very emotional and excited

rout [rhymes with **out**] *verb* To rout your opponents means to defeat them completely and easily

route [root] *noun* a way from one place to another

routine *adjective* **1** Routine activities are done regularly ▷ *noun* **2** the usual way or order in which you do things **3** a boring repetition of tasks > **routinely** adverb

roving adjective **1** wandering or roaming: *roving gangs of youths* **2** not restricted to any particular location or area: *a roving reporter*

row [rhymes with *snow*] noun **1** A row of people or things is several of them arranged in a line ▷ verb **2** When you row a boat, you use oars to make it move through the water

row [rhymes with *now*] noun **1** a serious argument **2** If someone is making a row, they are making too much noise ▷ verb **3** If people are rowing, they are quarrelling noisily

rowdy rowdier, rowdiest adjective rough and noisy

royal adjective **1** belonging to or involving a queen, a king, or a member of their family **2** 'Royal' is used in the names of organizations appointed or supported by a member of a royal family ▷ noun **3** (informal) Members of the royal family are sometimes referred to as the royals

royalist noun someone who supports their country's royal family

royalty royalties noun **1** The members of a royal family are sometimes referred to as royalty **2** Royalties are payments made to authors and musicians from the sales of their books or records

rub rubs, rubbing, rubbed verb **1** If you rub something, you move your hand or a cloth backwards and forwards over it > **rub out** verb To rub out something written means to remove it by rubbing it with a rubber or a cloth

rubber noun **1** Rubber is a strong elastic substance used for making tyres, boots, and other products

2 a small piece of rubber used to rub out pencil mistakes

rubbish noun **1** Rubbish is unwanted things or waste material **2** (informal) You can refer to nonsense or something of very poor quality as rubbish

rubble noun Bits of old brick and stone are referred to as rubble

ruby noun a type of red jewel

rucksack noun a bag with shoulder straps for carrying things on your back

rudder noun a piece of wood or metal at the back of a boat or plane which is moved to make the boat or plane turn

rude adjective **1** not polite **2** embarrassing or offensive: *rude jokes* **3** unexpected and unpleasant: *a rude awakening* > **rudely** adverb > **rudeness** noun

rudimentary adjective (formal) very basic or not developed: *He had only a rudimentary knowledge of French*

ruff noun **1** a stiff circular collar with many pleats in it, worn especially in the 16th century **2** a thick band of fur or feathers around the neck of a bird or animal

ruffle verb **1** If you ruffle someone's hair, you move your hand quickly backwards and forwards over their head **2** If something ruffles you, it makes you annoyed or upset ▷ noun **3** Ruffles are small folds made in a piece of material for decoration

rug noun **1** a small, thick carpet **2** a blanket which you can use to cover your knees or for sitting on outdoors

rugby noun Rugby is a game played by two teams, who try to kick and throw an oval ball to their opponents' end of the pitch. Rugby League is played with 13 players in each side; Rugby Union is played

r

with 15 players in each side

rugged *adjective* **1** rocky and wild: *the rugged west coast of Ireland* **2** having strong features: *his rugged good looks*

ruin *verb* **1** If you ruin something, you destroy or spoil it completely **2** If someone is ruined, they have lost all their money ▷ *noun* **3** Ruin is the state of being destroyed or completely spoilt **4** A ruin or the ruins of something refers to the parts that are left after it has been severely damaged: *the ruins of a thirteenth-century monastery*

rule *noun* **1** Rules are statements which tell you what you are allowed to do ▷ *verb* **2** To rule a country or group of people means to have power over it and be in charge of its affairs **3** (*formal*) When someone in authority rules on a particular matter, they give an official decision about it ▷ *phrase* **4** As a rule means usually or generally: *As a rule, I eat my meals in front of the TV* ▷ **rule out** *verb* **1** If you rule out an idea or course of action, you reject it **2** If one thing rules out another, it prevents it from happening or being possible: *The accident ruled out a future for him in football*

ruler *noun* **1** a person who rules a country **2** a long, flat piece of wood or plastic with straight edges marked in centimetres or inches, used for measuring or drawing straight lines

rum *noun* Rum is a strong alcoholic drink made from sugar cane juice

rumble *verb* **1** If something rumbles, it makes a continuous low noise: *Another train rumbled past the house* ▷ *noun* **2** a continuous low noise: *the distant rumble of traffic*

rummage *verb* If you rummage

somewhere, you search for something, moving things about carelessly

rumour *noun* **1** a story that people are talking about, which may or may not be true ▷ *verb* **2** If something is rumoured, people are suggesting that it has happened

rump *noun* **1** An animal's rump is its rear end **2** Rump or rump steak is meat cut from the rear end of a cow

run runs, running, ran, run *verb* **1** When you run, you move quickly, leaving the ground during each stride **2** If you say that a road or river runs in a particular direction, you are describing its course **3** If you run your hand or an object over something, you move it over it **4** If someone runs in an election, they stand as a candidate: *He announced he would run for President* **5** If you run a business or an activity, you are in charge of it **6** If you run an experiment, a computer program, or tape, you start it and let it continue: *He ran a series of computer checks* **7** To run a car means to have it and use it **8** If you run someone somewhere in a car, you drive them there: *Could you run me up to town?* **9** If you run water, you turn on a tap to make it flow: *We heard him running the kitchen tap* **10** If your nose is running, it is producing a lot of mucus **11** If the dye in something runs, the colour comes out when it is washed **12** If a feeling runs through your body, it affects you quickly and strongly **13** If an amount is running at a particular level, it is at that level: *Inflation is currently running at 2.6 per cent* **14** If someone or something is running late, they have taken more time than was planned **15** If an event or contract runs for a particular time, it lasts for that time ▷ *noun* **16** If you go for a run, you run for pleasure or exercise **17** a journey somewhere: *It was quite a run to the village* **18** If a play or show has a run of a particular length of time, it is on for that time **19** A run of success or failure is a series of successes or failures **20** In cricket or baseball, a player scores one run by running between marked places on the pitch after hitting the ball ▷ **run away** *verb* If you run away from a place, you leave it suddenly and secretly ▷ **run down** *verb* **1** To run someone down means to criticize them strongly **2** To run down an organization means to reduce its size and activity ▷ **run out** *verb* If you run out of something, you have no more left ▷ **run over** *verb* If someone is run over, they are hit by a moving vehicle

runaway *noun* a person who has escaped from a place or left it secretly and hurriedly

rundown *adjective* **1** tired and not well **2** neglected and in poor condition ▷ *noun* **3** (*informal*) If you give someone the rundown on a situation, you tell them the basic, important facts about it

rung *noun* The rungs on a ladder are the bars that form the steps

runner *noun* **1** a person who runs, especially as a sport **2** a person who takes messages or runs errands **3** A runner on a plant such as a strawberry is a long shoot from which a new plant develops **4** The runners on drawers and ice-skates are the thin strips on which they move

runner-up runners-up *noun* a person or team that comes second in a race or competition

running *adjective* **1** continuing without stopping over a period of time: *a running commentary* **2** Running water is flowing rather than standing still

runny runnier, runniest *adjective* **1** more liquid than usual: *Warm the honey until it becomes runny* **2** If someone's nose or eyes are runny, liquid is coming out of them

runway *noun* a long strip of ground used by aeroplanes for taking off or landing

rupee [roo-**pee**] *noun* the main unit of currency in India, Pakistan, and some other countries

rupture *noun* **1** a severe injury in which part of your body tears or bursts open ▷ *verb* **2** To rupture part of the body means to cause it to tear or burst: *a ruptured spleen*

rural *adjective* GEOGRAPHY relating to or involving the countryside

ruse *noun* (*formal*) an action which is intended to trick someone

rush *verb* **1** To rush means to move fast or do something quickly **2** If you rush someone into doing something, you make them do it without allowing them enough time to think ▷ *noun* **3** If you are in a rush, you are busy and do not have enough time to do things **4** If there is a rush for something, there is a sudden increase in demand for it: *There was a rush for tickets* **5** Rushes are plants with long, thin stems that grow near water

rush hour *noun* The rush hour is one of the busy parts of the day when most people are travelling to or from work

Russian *adjective* **1** belonging or relating to Russia ▷ *noun* **2** someone who comes from Russia **3** Russian is the main language spoken in Russia

rust noun **1** Rust is a reddish-brown substance that forms on iron or steel that has been in contact with water and which is decaying gradually ▷ noun, adjective **2** reddish-brown ▷ verb **3** When a metal object rusts, it becomes covered in rust

rustic adjective simple in a way considered to be typical of the countryside: *a rustic old log cabin*

rustle verb When something rustles, it makes soft sounds as it moves
> **rustling** adjective, noun

rusty rustier, rustiest adjective **1** affected by rust: *a rusty iron gate* **2** If someone's knowledge is rusty, it is not as good as it used to be because they have not used it for a long time: *My German is a bit rusty these days*

rut noun **1** a deep, narrow groove in the ground made by the wheels of a vehicle ▷ phrase **2** If someone is **in a rut**, they have become fixed in their way of doing things

ruthless adjective very harsh or cruel: *a ruthless dictator*
> **ruthlessness** noun > **ruthlessly** adverb

rye noun a type of grass that produces light brown grain

S

Sabbath noun RE The Sabbath is the day of the week when members of some religious groups, especially Jews and Christians, do not work

sabotage [sab-ot-ahj] noun **1** the deliberate damaging of things such as machinery and railway lines ▷ verb **2** If something is sabotaged, it is deliberately damaged
> **saboteur** noun

sabre noun **1** a heavy curved sword **2** a light sword used in fencing

sachet [sash-ay] noun a small closed packet, containing a small amount of something such as sugar or shampoo

sack noun **1** a large bag made of rough material used for carrying or storing goods ▷ verb **2** (informal) If someone is sacked, they are dismissed from their job by their employer ▷ phrase **3** (informal) If someone gets **the sack**, they are dismissed from their job by their employer

sacrament noun RE an important Christian ceremony such as communion, baptism, or marriage

sacred [say-krid] adjective holy, or connected with religion or religious ceremonies: *sacred ground*

sacrifice [sak-riff-ice] verb **1** If you sacrifice something valuable or important, you give it up **2** To sacrifice an animal means to kill it as an offering to a god ▷ noun **3** the killing of an animal as an offering to a god or gods **4** the action of giving something up
> **sacrificial** adjective

sacrilege [sak-ril-ij] noun Sacrilege is behaviour that shows great disrespect for something holy
> **sacrilegious** adjective

sacrosanct [sak-roe-sangkt] adjective regarded as too important to be criticized or changed: *Freedom of the press is sacrosanct*

sad adjective **1** If you are sad, you feel unhappy **2** Something sad makes you feel unhappy: *a sad story* > **sadly** *adverb*

sadden *verb* If something saddens you, it makes you feel sad

saddle *noun* **1** a leather seat that you sit on when you are riding a horse **2** The saddle on a bicycle is the seat ▷ *verb* **3** If you saddle a horse, you put a saddle on it

sadism [**say**-diz-m] *noun* Sadism is the obtaining of pleasure from making people suffer pain or humiliation > **sadist** *noun* > **sadistic** *adjective* > **sadistically** *adverb*

sadness *noun* the feeling of being unhappy

safari safaris *noun* an expedition for hunting or observing wild animals, especially in Africa

safe *adjective* **1** Something that is safe does not cause harm or danger **2** If you are safe, you are not in any danger **3** If it is safe to say something, you can say it with little risk of being wrong ▷ *noun* **4** a strong metal box with special locks, in which you can keep valuable things > **safely** *adverb*

safeguard *verb* **1** To safeguard something means to protect it ▷ *noun* **2** something designed to protect people or things

safekeeping *noun* If something is given to you for safekeeping, it is given to you to look after

safety *noun* the state of being safe from harm or danger

sag sags, sagging, sagged *verb* When something sags, it hangs down loosely or sinks downwards in the middle > **sagging** *adjective*

saga [**sah**-ga] *noun* a very long story, usually with many different adventures: *a saga of rivalry, honour and love*

sage *noun* **1** (*literary*) a very wise person **2** Sage is also a herb used for flavouring in cooking

Sagittarius [saj-it-**tair**-ee-uss] *noun* Sagittarius is the ninth sign of the zodiac, represented by a creature half horse, half man holding a bow and arrow. People born between November 22nd and December 21st are born under this sign

sail *noun* **1** Sails are large pieces of material attached to a ship's mast. The wind blows against the sail and moves the ship ▷ *verb* **2** When a ship sails, it moves across water **3** If you sail somewhere, you go there by ship

sailor *noun* a member of a ship's crew

saint *noun* a person who after death is formally recognized by a Christian Church as deserving special honour because of having lived a very holy life

saintly *adjective* behaving in a very good or holy way

sake *phrase* **1** If you do something for someone's sake, you do it to help or please them **2** You use for the sake of to say why you are doing something: *a one-off expedition for interest's sake*

salad *noun* a mixture of raw vegetables

salami [sal-**lah**-mee] *noun* Salami is a kind of spicy sausage

salary salaries *noun* a regular monthly payment to an employee > **salaried** *adjective*

sale *noun* **1** The sale of goods is the selling of them **2** an occasion when a shop sells things at reduced prices **3** (*in plural*) The sales of a product are the numbers that are sold

saleable *adjective* easy to sell or

suitable for being sold

salesman *noun* someone who sells products for a company
> **saleswoman** *noun*

salient [**say**-lee-ent] *adjective* (formal) The salient points or facts are the important ones

saliva [sal-**live**-a] *noun* Saliva is the watery liquid in your mouth that helps you chew and digest food

salmon salmons *or* salmon [**sam**-on] *noun* a large edible silver-coloured fish with pink flesh

salmonella [sal-mon-**nell**-a] *noun* Salmonella is a kind of bacteria which can cause severe food poisoning

salon *noun* a place where hairdressers work

saloon *noun* **1** a car with a fixed roof and a separate boot **2** in the Wild West of America, a place where alcoholic drinks were sold and drunk

salt *noun* **1** Salt is a white substance found naturally in sea water. It is used to flavour and preserve food **2** a chemical compound formed from an acid base

salty saltier, saltiest *adjective* containing salt or tasting of salt

salute *noun* **1** a formal sign of respect. Soldiers give a salute by raising their right hand to their forehead ▷ *verb* **2** If you salute someone, you give them a salute

salvage *verb* **1** If you salvage things, you save them, for example from a wrecked ship or a destroyed building ▷ *noun* **2** You refer to things saved from a wrecked ship or destroyed building as salvage

salvation *noun* **1** When someone's salvation takes place, they are saved from harm or evil **2** To be someone's salvation means to save them from harm or evil

salvo salvos *or* salvoes *noun* the firing of several guns or missiles at the same time

same *adjective* (usually preceded by the) **1** If two things are the same, they are like one another **2** Same means just one thing and not two different ones: *They were born in the same town*

Samoan *adjective* **1** belonging or relating to Samoa ▷ *noun* **2** someone who comes from Samoa

sample *noun* **1** A sample of something is a small amount of it that you can try or test: *a sample of new wine* ▷ *verb* **2** If you sample something, you try it: *I sampled his cooking*

samurai [**sam**-oor-eye] *noun* A samurai was a member of an ancient Japanese warrior class

sanctimonious [sank-tim-**moan**-ee-uss] *adjective* pretending to be very religious and virtuous

sanction *verb* **1** To sanction something means to officially approve of it or allow it ▷ *noun* **2** Sanction is official approval of something **3** a severe punishment or penalty intended to make people obey the law **4** Sanctions are sometimes taken by countries against a country that has broken international law

sanctity *noun* If you talk about the sanctity of something, you are saying that it should be respected because it is very important: *the sanctity of marriage*

sanctuary sanctuaries *noun* **1** a place where you are safe from harm or danger **2** a place where wildlife is protected: *a bird sanctuary*

sand *noun* **1** Sand consists of tiny pieces of stone. Beaches are made of sand ▷ *verb* **2** If you sand something, you rub sandpaper over it to make it smooth

sandal *noun* Sandals are light open shoes with straps, worn in warm weather

sandpaper *noun* DGT Sandpaper is strong paper with a coating of sand on it, used for rubbing surfaces to make them smooth

sandstone *noun* Sandstone is a type of rock formed from sand, often used for building

sandwich *noun* **1** two slices of bread with a filling between them ▷ *verb* **2** If one thing is sandwiched between two others, it is in a narrow space between them: *a small shop sandwiched between a bar and an office*

sandy sandier, sandiest *adjective* **1** A sandy area is covered with sand **2** Sandy hair is light orange-brown

sane *adjective* **1** If someone is sane, they have a normal and healthy mind **2** A sane action is sensible and reasonable

sanguine [**sang**-gwin] *adjective* (formal) cheerful and confident

sanitary *adjective* Sanitary means concerned with keeping things clean and hygienic: *improving the sanitary conditions*

sanitation *noun* Sanitation is the process of keeping places clean and hygienic, especially by providing a sewage system and clean water supply

sanity *noun* Your sanity is your ability to think and act normally and reasonably

sap saps, sapping, sapped *verb* **1** If something saps your strength or confidence, it gradually weakens and destroys it ▷ *noun* **2** Sap is the watery liquid in plants

sapphire *noun* a blue precious stone

sarcastic *adjective* saying or doing the opposite of what you really mean in order to mock or insult someone: *a sarcastic remark*
▶ **sarcasm** *noun* ▶ **sarcastically** *adverb*

sardine *noun* a small edible sea fish

sardonic *adjective* mocking or scornful: *a sardonic grin*
▶ **sardonically** *adverb*

sari saris [**sah**-ree] *noun* a piece of clothing worn especially by Indian women, consisting of a long piece of material folded around the body

sartorial *adjective* (formal) relating to clothes: *sartorial elegance*

sash *noun* a long piece of cloth worn round the waist or over one shoulder

Satan *noun* Satan is the Devil

satanic [sa-**tan**-ik] *adjective* caused by or influenced by Satan: *satanic forces*

satchel *noun* a leather or cloth bag with a long strap

satellite *noun* **1** a spacecraft sent into orbit round the earth to collect information or as part of a communications system **2** a natural object in space that moves round a planet or star

satin *noun* Satin is a kind of smooth, shiny silk

satire *noun* Satire is the use of mocking or ironical humour, especially in literature, to show how foolish or wicked some people are
▶ **satirical** *adjective*

satisfaction *noun* Satisfaction is the feeling of pleasure you get when you do something you wanted or needed to do

satisfactory *adjective* acceptable or adequate: *a satisfactory explanation*
▶ **satisfactorily** *adverb*

satisfied *adjective* happy because

you have got what you want

satisfy satisfies, satisfying, satisfied
verb **1** To satisfy someone means to
give them enough of something to
make them pleased or contented
2 To satisfy someone means to
convince them of it **3** To satisfy the
requirements for something means
to fulfil them

satisfying *adjective* Something that
is satisfying gives you a feeling of
pleasure and fulfilment

saturated *adjective* **1** very wet **2** If a
place is saturated with things, it is
completely full of them: *If you
thought the area was already saturated
with supermarkets, think again*
> **saturation** *noun*

Saturday *noun* the day between
Friday and Sunday

Saturn *noun* Saturn is the planet in
the solar system which is sixth from
the sun

sauce *noun* a liquid eaten with food
to give it more flavour

saucepan *noun* a deep metal
cooking pot with a handle and a lid

saucer *noun* a small curved plate for
a cup

saucy saucier, sauciest *adjective*
cheeky in an amusing way

Saudi [rhymes with **cloudy**] *adjective*
1 belonging or relating to Saudi
Arabia ▷ *noun* **2** someone who
comes from Saudi Arabia

sauna [**saw**-na] *noun* If you have a
sauna, you go into a very hot room
in order to sweat, then have a cold
bath or shower

saunter *verb* To saunter somewhere
means to walk there slowly and
casually

sausage *noun* a mixture of minced
meat and herbs formed into a
tubular shape and served cooked

savage *adjective* **1** cruel and violent:
savage fighting ▷ *noun* **2** If you call
someone a savage, you mean that
they are violent and uncivilized
▷ *verb* **3** If an animal savages you, it
attacks you and bites you
> **savagely** *adverb*

savagery *noun* Savagery is cruel and
violent behaviour

save *verb* **1** If you save someone, you
rescue them: *He saved my life* **2** If you
save someone or something, you
keep them safe **3** If you save
something, you keep it so that you
can use it later: *He'd saved up enough
money for the deposit* **4** To save time,
money, or effort means to prevent it
from being wasted: *You could have
saved us the trouble* ▷ *preposition*
5 (*formal*) Save means except: *I was
alone in the house save for a very old
woman*

saving *noun* **1** a reduction in the
amount of time or money used **2** (*in
plural*) Your savings are the money
you have saved

saviour *noun* **1** If someone saves you
from danger, you can refer to them
as your saviour ▷ *proper noun* **2** In
Christianity, the Saviour is Jesus
Christ

savour *verb* If you savour
something, you take your time with
it and enjoy it fully: *He sat down and
savoured a cup of strong coffee*

savoury *adjective* **1** Savoury is salty
or spicy **2** Something that is not
very savoury is not very pleasant or
respectable: *the less savoury places*

saw saws, sawing, sawed, sawn
1 Saw is the past tense of **see** ▷ *verb*
2 If you saw something, you cut it
with a saw ▷ *noun* **3** a tool, with a
blade with sharp teeth along one
edge, for cutting wood

sawdust *noun* Sawdust is the fine

powder produced when you saw
wood

saxophone noun a curved metal
wind instrument often played in
jazz bands

say says, saying, said verb **1** When
you say something, you speak
words **2** 'Say' is used to give an
example: *a maximum fee of, say, a
million* ▷ noun **3** If you have a say in
something, you can give your
opinion and influence decisions

saying noun a well-known sentence
or phrase that tells you something
about human life

scab noun a hard, dry covering that
forms over a wound > **scabby**
adjective

scaffolding noun Scaffolding is a
framework of poles and boards that
is used by workmen to stand on
while they are working on the
outside structure of a building

scald [skawld] verb **1** If you scald
yourself, you burn yourself with very
hot liquid or steam ▷ noun **2** a burn
caused by scalding

scale noun **1** The scale of something
is its size or extent: *the sheer scale
of the disaster* **2** a set of levels or
numbers used for measuring things
3 The scale of a map, plan, or model
is the relationship between the size
of something in the map, plan, or
model and its size in the real world:
a scale of 1:30,000 **4** MUSIC an
upward or downward sequence of
musical notes **5** The scales of a fish or
reptile are the small pieces of hard
skin covering its body **6** (in plural)
Scales are a piece of equipment used
for weighing things ▷ verb **7** If you
scale something high, you climb it

scallop noun Scallops are edible
shellfish with two flat fan-shaped
shells

scalp noun **1** Your scalp is the skin
under the hair on your head **2** the
piece of skin and hair removed when
someone is scalped ▷ verb **3** To scalp
someone means to remove the skin
and hair from their head in one piece

scalpel noun a knife with a thin,
sharp blade, used by surgeons

scaly scalier, scaliest adjective
covered with scales

scamper verb To scamper means to
move quickly and lightly

scan verb **1** If you scan something,
you look at all of it carefully: *I
scanned the horizon to the north-east*
2 If you scan a piece of writing, you
read it very quickly to find the
important or interesting parts
3 If a machine scans something, it
examines it by means of a beam of
light or X-rays **4** ENGLISH If the
words of a poem scan, they fit into a
regular, rhythmical pattern
5 ENGLISH If you scan a line of
poetry you count the number of
beats or metrical feet it has ▷ noun
6 an examination or search by a
scanner: *a brain scan*

scandal noun a situation or event
that people think is shocking and
immoral > **scandalous** adjective

Scandinavia [skan-din-**nay**-vee-a]
noun Scandinavia is the name given
to a group of countries in Northern
Europe, including Norway, Sweden,
Denmark, and sometimes Finland
and Iceland > **Scandinavian** noun,
adjective

scanner noun **1** a machine which is
used to examine, identify, or record
things by means of a beam of light
or X-rays **2** COMPUTING a machine
which converts text or images into a
form that can be stored on a
computer

scant adjective You use 'scant' to

show that there is not as much of something as there should be: *Some drivers pay scant attention to the laws of the road*

scapegoat *noun* If someone is a scapegoat, they are blamed for something, although it may not be their fault

scar scars, scarring, scarred *noun* **1** a mark left on your skin after a wound has healed **2** a permanent effect on someone's mind that results from a very unpleasant experience: *the scars of war* ▷ *verb* **3** If an injury scars you, it leaves a permanent mark on your skin **4** If an unpleasant experience scars you, it has a permanent effect on you

scarce *adjective* If something is scarce, there is not very much of it ▷ **scarcity** *noun*

scarcely *adverb* Scarcely means hardly: *I can scarcely hear her*

scare *verb* **1** If something scares you, it frightens you ▷ *noun* **2** If something gives you a scare, it scares you **3** If there is a scare about something, a lot of people are worried about it: *a health scare* ▷ **scared** *adjective*

scarecrow *noun* an object shaped like a person, put in a field to scare birds away

scarf scarfs or scarves *noun* a piece of cloth worn round your neck or head to keep you warm

scarlet *noun, adjective* bright red

scary scarier, scariest *adjective* (informal) frightening

scathing [skayth-ing] *adjective* harsh and scornful: *They were scathing about his job*

scatter *verb* **1** To scatter things means to throw or drop them all over an area **2** If people scatter, they suddenly move away in different directions

scattering *noun* A scattering of things is a small number of them spread over a large area: *the scattering of islands*

scavenge *verb* If you scavenge for things, you search for them among waste and rubbish ▷ **scavenger** *noun*

scenario [sin-nar-ee-oh] *noun* **1** DRAMA The scenario of a film or play is a summary of its plot **2** the way a situation could possibly develop in the future: *the worst possible scenario*

scene *noun* **1** ENGLISH DRAMA part of a play or film in which a series of events happen in one place **2** Pictures and views are sometimes called scenes: *a village scene* **3** The scene of an event is the place where it happened **4** an area of activity: *the music scene*

scenery *noun* **1** In the countryside, you can refer to everything you see as the scenery **2** In a theatre, the scenery is the painted cloth on the stage which represents the place where the action is happening

scenic *adjective* A scenic place or route has nice views

scent *noun* **1** a smell, especially a pleasant one **2** Scent is perfume ▷ *verb* **3** When an animal scents something, it becomes aware of it by smelling it

sceptic [skep-tik] *noun* someone who has doubts about things that other people believe ▷ **scepticism** *noun*

sceptical [skep-tik-kl] *adjective* If you are sceptical about something, you have doubts about it ▷ **sceptically** *adverb*

schedule [shed-yool] *noun* **1** a plan

that gives a list of events or tasks, together with the times at which each thing should be done ▷ verb **2** If something is scheduled to happen, it has been planned and arranged: *Their journey was scheduled for the beginning of May*

scheme schemes, scheming, schemed *noun* **1** a plan or arrangement: *a five-year development scheme* ▷ verb **2** When people scheme, they make secret plans

schism [skizm] *noun* a split or division within a group or organization

schizophrenia [skit-soe-free-nee-a] *noun* Schizophrenia is a serious mental illness which prevents someone relating their thoughts and feelings to what is happening around them > **schizophrenic** *noun, adjective*

scholar *noun* **1** a person who studies an academic subject and knows a lot about it **2** In South African English, a scholar is a school pupil

scholarly *adjective* having or showing a lot of knowledge

scholarship *noun* **1** If you get a scholarship to a school or university, your studies are paid for by the school or university or by some other organization **2** Scholarship is academic study and knowledge

school *noun* **1** a place where children are educated **2** University departments and colleges are sometimes called schools: *My oldest son is in medical school* **3** You can refer to a large group of dolphins or fish as a school ▷ verb **4** When someone is schooled in something, they are taught it: *They were schooled in the modern techniques*

schoolchild *noun* Schoolchildren are children who go to school

> **schoolboy** *noun* > **schoolgirl** *noun*

schooling *noun* Your schooling is the education you get at school

schooner *noun* a sailing ship

science *noun* **1** Science is the study of the nature and behaviour of natural things and the knowledge obtained about them **2** a branch of science, for example physics or biology

science fiction *noun* Stories about events happening in the future or in other parts of the universe are called science fiction

scientific *adjective* **1** relating to science or to a particular science: *scientific knowledge* **2** done in a systematic way, using experiments or tests: *this scientific method* > **scientifically** *adverb*

scientist *noun* an expert in one of the sciences who does work connected with it

scintillating [sin-til-late-ing] *adjective* lively and witty: *scintillating conversation*

scissors *plural noun* Scissors are a cutting tool with two sharp blades

scoff *verb* **1** If you scoff, you speak in a scornful, mocking way about something **2** (*informal*) If you scoff food, you eat it quickly and greedily

scold *verb* If you scold someone, you tell them off

scone [skon *or* skoan] *noun* Scones are small cakes made from flour and fat and usually eaten with butter

scoop *verb* **1** If you scoop something up, you pick it up using a spoon or the palm of your hand *noun* **2** an object like a large spoon which is used for picking up food such as ice cream

scooter *noun* **1** a small, light motorcycle **2** a simple cycle which a child rides by standing on it and pushing the ground with one foot

scope noun **1** If there is scope for doing something, the opportunity to do it exists **2** The scope of something is the whole subject area which it deals with or includes

-scope suffix '-scope' is used to form nouns meaning an instrument used for observing or detecting: microscope; telescope

scorching adjective extremely hot: another scorching summer

score verb **1** If you score in a game, you get a goal, run, or point **2** To score in a game also means to record the score obtained by the players **3** If you score a success or victory, you achieve it **4** To score a surface means to cut a line into it ▷ noun **5** The score in a game is the number of goals, runs, or points obtained by the two teams **6** Scores of things means very many of them: Ros entertained scores of celebrities **7** (old-fashioned) A score is twenty **8** MUSIC The score of a piece of music is the written version of it ▷ **scorer** noun

scorn noun **1** Scorn is great contempt: a look of scorn ▷ verb **2** If you scorn someone, you treat them with great contempt **3** (formal) If you scorn something, you refuse to accept it

scornful adjective showing contempt: his scornful comment ▷ **scornfully** adverb

Scorpio noun Scorpio is the eighth sign of the zodiac, represented by a scorpion. People born between October 23rd and November 21st are born under this sign

scorpion noun an animal that looks like a small lobster, with a long tail with a poisonous sting on the end

Scot noun **1** a person who comes from Scotland ▷ adjective **2** Scots means the same as **Scottish**

scotch noun Scotch is whisky made in Scotland

Scotsman Scotsmen noun a man who comes from Scotland ▷ **Scotswoman** noun

Scottish adjective belonging or relating to Scotland

scoundrel noun (old-fashioned) a man who cheats and deceives people

scour verb **1** If you scour a place, you look all over it in order to find something: The police scoured the area **2** If you scour something such as a pan, you clean it by rubbing it with something rough

scourge [rhymes with urge] noun something that causes a lot of suffering: hay fever, that scourge of summer

scout noun **1** a boy who is a member of the Scout Association, an organization for boys which aims to develop character and responsibility **2** someone who is sent to an area to find out the position of an enemy army ▷ verb **3** If you scout around for something, you look around for it

scowl verb **1** If you scowl, you frown because you are angry: They were scowling at me ▷ noun **2** an angry expression

scrabble verb If you scrabble at something, you scrape at it with your hands or feet

scramble verb **1** If you scramble over something, you climb over it using your hands to help you ▷ noun **2** a motorcycle race over rough ground

scrap scraps, scrapping, scrapped noun **1** A scrap of something is a very small piece of it: a scrap of cloth **2** (in *plural)* Scraps are pieces of leftover food ▷ *adjective, noun* **3** Scrap metal or scrap is metal from old machinery or cars that can be re-used ▷ *verb* **4** If you scrap something, you get rid of it: *They considered scrapping passport controls*

scrapbook *noun* A book in which you stick things such as pictures or newspaper articles

scrape *verb* **1** If you scrape a surface, you rub a rough or sharp object against it **2** If something scrapes, it makes a harsh noise by rubbing against something: *his shoes scraping across the stone ground*

scratch *verb* **1** To scratch something means to make a small cut on it accidentally: *They were always getting scratched by cats* **2** If you scratch, you rub your skin with your nails because it is itching ▷ *noun* **3** A small cut

scrawl *verb* **1** If you scrawl something, you write it in a careless and untidy way ▷ *noun* **2** You can refer to careless and untidy writing as a scrawl

scrawny scrawnier, scrawniest *adjective* thin and bony: *a small scrawny man*

scream *verb* **1** If you scream, you shout or cry in a loud, high-pitched voice ▷ *noun* **2** a loud, high-pitched cry

screech *verb* **1** To screech means to make an unpleasant high-pitched noise: *The car wheels screeched* ▷ *noun* **2** an unpleasant high-pitched noise

screen *noun* **1** a flat vertical surface on which a picture is shown: *a television screen* **2** a vertical panel used to separate different parts of a room or to protect something ▷ *verb* **3** To screen a film or television programme means to show it **4** If

you screen someone, you put something in front of them to protect them

screenplay *noun* The screenplay of a film is the script

screw *noun* **1** a small, sharp piece of metal used for fixing things together or for fixing something to a wall ▷ *verb* **2** If you screw things together, you fix them together using screws **3** If you screw something onto something else, you fix it there by twisting it round and round: *He screwed the top on the ink bottle* ▷ **screw up** *verb* If you screw something up, you twist it or squeeze it so that it no longer has its proper shape: *Amy screwed up her face*

screwdriver *noun* a tool for turning screws

scribble *verb* **1** If you scribble something, you write it quickly and roughly **2** To scribble also means to make meaningless marks: *When Caroline was five she scribbled on a wall* ▷ *noun* **3** You can refer to something written or drawn quickly and roughly as a scribble

script *noun* DRAMA the written version of a play or film

scripture *noun* RE Scripture refers to sacred writings, especially the Bible > **scriptural** *adjective*

scroll *noun* a long roll of paper or parchment with writing on it

scrub scrubs, scrubbing, scrubbed *verb* **1** If you scrub something, you clean it with a stiff brush and water ▷ *noun* **2** If you give something a scrub, you scrub it **3** Scrub consists of low trees and bushes

scruff *noun* The scruff of your neck is the back of your neck or collar

scruffy scruffier, scruffiest *adjective* dirty and untidy: *four scruffy youths*

scrum *noun* When rugby players

S

form a scrum, they form a group and push against each other with their heads down in an attempt to get the ball

scrupulous adjective **1** always doing what is honest or morally right **2** paying very careful attention to detail: *a long and scrupulous search* > **scrupulously** adverb

scrutinize or **scrutinise** verb If you scrutinize something, you examine it very carefully

scrutiny noun If something is under scrutiny, it is being observed very carefully

scuba diving noun Scuba diving is the sport of swimming underwater while breathing from tanks of compressed air on your back

scuff verb **1** If you scuff your feet, you drag them along the ground when you are walking **2** If you scuff your shoes, you mark them by scraping or rubbing them

scuffle noun **1** a short, rough fight > verb **2** When people scuffle, they fight roughly

sculpt verb When something is sculpted, it is carved or shaped in stone, wood, or clay

sculptor noun someone who makes sculptures

sculpture noun **1** a work of art produced by carving or shaping stone or clay **2** Sculpture is the art of making sculptures

scum noun Scum is a layer of a dirty substance on the surface of a liquid

scurrilous [skur-ril-luss] adjective abusive and damaging to someone's good name: *scurrilous stories*

scurry scurries, scurrying, scurried verb To scurry means to run quickly with short steps

scuttle verb **1** To scuttle means to run quickly **2** To scuttle a ship

means to sink it deliberately by making holes in the bottom > noun **3** a container for coal

scythe [sythe] noun a tool with a long handle and a curved blade used for cutting grass or grain

sea noun **1** The sea is the salty water that covers much of the earth's surface **2** A sea of people or things is a very large number of them: *a sea of red flags*

seagull noun Seagulls are common white, grey, and black birds that live near the sea

seal noun **1** an official mark on a document which shows that it is genuine **2** a piece of wax fixed over the opening of a container **3** a sea mammal with flippers that lives partly on land and partly in the sea > verb **4** If you seal an envelope, you stick down the flap **5** If you seal an opening, you cover it securely so that air, gas, or liquid cannot get through

sea lion noun a type of large seal

seam noun **1** a line of stitches joining two pieces of cloth **2** A seam of coal is a long, narrow layer of it beneath the ground

seaman seamen noun a sailor

search verb **1** If you search for something, you look for it in several places **2** If a person is searched their body and clothing are examined to see if they are hiding anything > noun **3** an attempt to find something

search engine noun a service on the internet which enables users to search for items of interest

searching adjective intended to discover the truth about something: *searching questions*

searing adjective A searing pain is very sharp

seashore noun The seashore is the land along the edge of the sea

seasick adjective feeling sick because of the movement of a boat
> **seasickness** noun

seaside noun The seaside is an area next to the sea

season noun 1 The seasons are the periods into which a year is divided and which have their own typical weather conditions. The seasons are spring, summer, autumn, and winter 2 a period of the year when something usually happens: the football season; the hunting season ▷ verb 3 If you season food, you add salt, pepper, or spices to it

seasonal adjective happening during one season or one time of the year: seasonal work

seasoned adjective very experienced: a seasoned professional

seasoning noun Seasoning is flavouring such as salt and pepper

season ticket noun a train or bus ticket that you can use as many times as you like within a certain period

seat noun 1 something you can sit on 2 The seat of a piece of clothing is the part that covers your bottom 3 If someone wins a seat in parliament, they are elected ▷ verb 4 If you seat yourself somewhere, you sit down 5 If a place seats a particular number of people, it has enough seats for that number: The theatre seats 570 people

seat belt noun a strap that you fasten across your body for safety when travelling in a car or an aircraft

seating noun The seating in a place is the number or arrangement of seats there

seaweed noun Plants that grow in the sea are called seaweed

secateurs [sek-at-**turz**] plural noun Secateurs are small shears for pruning garden plants

secluded adjective quiet and hidden from view: a secluded beach
> **seclusion** noun

second adjective [**sek**-ond] 1 The second item in a series is the one counted as number two ▷ noun [**sek**-ond] 2 one of the sixty parts that a minute is divided into 3 Seconds are goods that are sold cheaply because they are slightly faulty ▷ verb 4 [**sek**-ond] If you second a proposal, you formally agree with it so that it can be discussed or voted on 5 [si-**kond**] If you are seconded somewhere, you are sent there temporarily to work
> **secondly** adverb

secondary adjective 1 Something that is secondary is less important than something else 2 Secondary education is education for pupils between the ages of eleven and eighteen

secondary school noun a school for pupils between the ages of eleven and eighteen

second-class adjective
1 Second-class things are regarded as less important than other things of the same kind: He has been treated as a second-class citizen ▷ adjective, adverb 2 Second-class services are cheaper and therefore slower or less comfortable than first-class ones

second-hand adjective, adverb
1 Something that is second-hand has already been owned by someone else: a second-hand car 2 If you hear a story second-hand, you hear it indirectly, rather than from the people involved

second-rate adjective of poor

quality: *a second-rate movie*

secret *adjective* **1** Something that is secret is told to only a small number of people and hidden from everyone else: *a secret meeting* ▷ *noun* **2** a fact told to only a small number of people and hidden from everyone else ▷ **secretly** *adverb* ▷ **secrecy** *noun*

secret agent *noun* a spy

secretary secretaries *noun* **1** a person employed by an organization to keep records, write letters, and do office work **2** Ministers in charge of some government departments are also called secretaries: *the Health Secretary* ▷ **secretarial** *adjective*

secrete [sik-**kreet**] *verb* **1** When part of a plant or animal secretes a liquid, it produces it **2** (*formal*) If you secrete something somewhere, you hide it ▷ **secretion** *noun*

secretive *adjective* Secretive people tend to hide their feelings and intentions

secret service *noun* A country's secret service is the government department in charge of espionage

sect *noun* a religious or political group which has broken away from a larger group

sectarian [sek-**tair**-ee-an] *adjective* strongly supporting a particular sect: *sectarian violence*

section *noun* A section of something is one of the parts it is divided into: *this section of the motorway*

sector *noun* **1** A sector of something, especially a country's economy, is one part of it: *the private sector* **2** MATHS A sector of a circle is one of the two parts formed when you draw two straight lines from the centre to the circumference

secular *adjective* having no connection with religion: *secular education*

secure *verb* **1** (*formal*) If you secure something, you manage to get it: *They secured the rights to her story* **2** If you secure a place, you make it safe from harm or attack **3** To secure something also means to fasten it firmly: *One end was secured to the pier* ▷ *adjective* **4** If a place is secure, it is tightly locked or well protected **5** If an object is secure, it is firmly fixed in place **6** If you feel secure, you feel safe and confident ▷ **securely** *adverb*

security *noun, adjective* **1** Security means all the precautions taken to protect a place: *Security forces arrested one member* ▷ *noun* **2** A feeling of security is a feeling of being safe

sedate [sid-**date**] *adjective* **1** quiet and dignified ▷ *verb* **2** To sedate someone means to give them a drug to calm them down or make them sleep ▷ **sedately** *adverb*

sedative [sed-at-tiv] *noun* **1** a drug that calms you down or makes you sleep ▷ *adjective* **2** having a calming or soothing effect: *antihistamines which have a sedative effect* ▷ **sedation** *noun*

sedentary [sed-en-tree] *adjective* A sedentary occupation is one in which you spend most of your time sitting down

sediment *noun* **1** Sediment is solid material that settles at the bottom of a liquid: *a bottle of beer with sediment in it is usually a guarantee of quality* **2** Sediment is also small particles of rock that have been worn down and deposited together by water, ice, and wind

sedimentary *adjective* GEOGRAPHY Sedimentary rocks are formed from fragments of shells or rocks that have become compressed. Sandstone and limestone are sedimentary rocks

seduce verb If you are seduced into doing something, you are persuaded to do it because it seems very attractive

seductive adjective Something seductive is very attractive and tempting > **seductively** adverb

see sees, seeing, saw, seen verb **1** If you see something, you are looking at it or you notice it **2** If you see someone, you are looking after them or meet them: I went to see my dentist **3** If you see someone to a place, you accompany them or meet them **4** To see something also means to realize or understand it: I see what you mean **5** If you say you will see what is happening, you mean you will find out **6** If you say you will see if you can do something, you mean you will try to do it **7** If you mean that something is done, you make sure that it is done **8** If you see to something, you deal with it **9** 'See' is used to say that an event takes place during a particular period of time: The next couple of years saw two momentous developments ▷ phrase **10** (informal) **Seeing that** or **seeing as** means because: I took John for lunch, seeing as it was his birthday ▷ noun **11** A bishop's see is his diocese

seed noun **1** The seeds of a plant are the small, hard parts from which new plants can grow **2** The seeds of a feeling or process are its beginning or origins: the seeds of mistrust

seedling noun A young plant grown from a seed

seedy seedier, seediest adjective untidy and shabby: a seedy hotel

seek seeks, seeking, sought verb (formal) **1** To seek something means to try to find it, obtain it or achieve it: The police were still seeking information **2** If you seek to do something, you try to do it: De Gaulle sought to reunite the country

seem verb If something seems to be the case, it appears to be the case or you think it to be the case: He seemed such a quiet chap

seeming adjective appearing to be real or genuine: this seeming disregard for human life > **seemingly** adverb

seep verb If a liquid or gas seeps through something, it flows through very slowly

seething adjective If you are seething about something, you are very angry but it does not show

segment noun **1** A segment of something is one part of it **2** The segments of an orange or grapefruit are the sections which you can divide it into **3** MATHS A segment of a circle is one of the two parts formed when you draw a straight line across it

segregate verb To segregate two groups of people means to keep them apart from each other > **segregated** adjective > **segregation** noun

seize verb **1** If you seize something, you grab it firmly: He seized the phone **2** To seize a place or to seize control of it means to take control of it quickly and suddenly **3** If you seize an opportunity, you take advantage of it **4** If you seize on something, you immediately show great interest in it: MPs have seized on a new report > **seize up** verb **1** If a part of your body seizes up, it becomes stiff and painful **2** If an engine seizes up,

S

it becomes jammed and stops working

seizure [seez-yer] *noun* **1** a sudden violent attack of an illness, especially a heart attack or a fit **2** if there is a seizure of power, a group of people suddenly take control using force

seldom *adverb* not very often: *They seldom speak to each other*

select *verb* **1** If you select something, you choose it ▷ *adjective* **2** of good quality: *a select gentlemen's club* > **selector** *noun*

selection *noun* **1** Selection is the choosing of people or things: *the selection of parliamentary candidates* **2** A selection of people or things is a set of them chosen from a larger group **3** The selection of goods in a shop is the range of goods available: *a good selection of wines*

selective *adjective* choosing things carefully: *I am selective about what I eat* > **selectively** *adverb*

self *selves noun* Your self is your basic personality or nature: *Hershey is her normal dependable self*

self- *prefix* **1** done to yourself or by yourself: *self-help; self-control* **2** doing something automatically: *a self-loading rifle*

self-assured *adjective* behaving in a way that shows confidence in yourself

self-centred *adjective* thinking only about yourself and not about other people

self-confessed *adjective* admitting to having bad habits or unpopular opinions: *a self-confessed liar*

self-confident *adjective* confident of your own abilities or worth > **self-confidence** *noun*

self-conscious *adjective* nervous and easily embarrassed, and worried about what other people think of you > **self-consciously** *adverb*

self-control *noun* Self-control is the ability to restrain yourself and not show your feelings

self-defence *noun* Self-defence is the use of special physical techniques to protect yourself when someone attacks you

self-employed *adjective* working for yourself and organizing your own finances, rather than working for an employer

self-esteem *noun* Your self-esteem is your good opinion of yourself

self-evident *adjective* Self-evident facts are completely obvious and need no proof or explanation

selfie *noun* (*informal*) a photograph taken by pointing a camera at yourself

self-indulgent *adjective* allowing yourself to do or have things you enjoy, especially as a treat

self-interest *noun* If you do something out of self-interest, you do it for your own benefit rather than to help other people

selfish *adjective* caring only about yourself, and not about other people > **selfishly** *adverb* > **selfishness** *noun*

selfless *adjective* putting other people's interests before your own

self-raising *adjective* Self-raising flour contains baking powder to make cakes and bread rise when they are baked

self-respect *noun* Self-respect is a belief in your own worth and opinions

self-righteous *adjective* convinced that you are better or more virtuous than other people > **self-righteousness** *noun*

self-service *adjective* A self-service shop or restaurant is one where you serve yourself

self-sufficient *adjective*
1 producing or making everything you need, and so not needing to buy things **2** able to live in a way in which you do not need other people

sell sells, selling, sold *verb* **1** If you sell something, you let someone have it in return for money **2** If a shop sells something, it has it available for people to buy: *a tobacconist that sells stamps* **3** If something tobacconist, people buy it: *This book will sell* > **sell out** *verb* If a shop has sold out of something, it has sold it all > **seller** *noun*

semblance *noun* If there is a semblance of something, it seems to exist, although it might not really exist: *an effort to restore a semblance of normality*

semi- *prefix* 'Semi-' means half or partly: *semiskilled workers*

semifinal *noun* The semifinals are the two matches in a competition played to decide who plays in the final > **semifinalist** *noun*

seminar *noun* A meeting of a small number of university students or teachers to discuss a particular topic

Senate *noun* The Senate is the smaller, more important of the two councils in the government of some countries, for example Australia, Canada, and the USA

senator *noun* A member of a Senate

send sends, sending, sent *verb* **1** If you send something to someone, you arrange for it to be delivered to them **2** To send a radio signal or message means to transmit it **3** If you send someone somewhere, you tell them to go there or arrange for

them to go **4** If you send for someone, you send a message asking them to come and see you **5** If you send off for something, you write and ask for it to be sent to you **6** To send people or things in a particular direction means to make them move in that direction: *It should have sent him tumbling from the saddle* > **send up** *verb* If you send someone or something up, you imitate them and make fun of them

senile *adjective* If old people become senile, they become confused and cannot look after themselves > **senility** *noun*

senior *adjective* **1** The senior people in an organization or profession have the highest and most important jobs ▷ *noun* **2** Someone who is your senior is older than you > **seniority** *noun*

senior citizen *noun* An elderly person, especially one receiving a retirement pension

sensation *noun* **1** a feeling, especially a physical feeling **2** If something is a sensation, it causes great excitement and interest

sensational *adjective* **1** causing great excitement and interest **2** (*informal*) extremely good: *a sensational party* > **sensationally** *adverb*

sense *noun* **1** Your senses are the physical abilities of sight, hearing, smell, touch, and taste **2** a feeling: *a sense of guilt* **3** A sense of a word is one of its meanings **4** Sense is the ability to think and behave sensibly ▷ *verb* **5** If you sense something, you become aware of it ▷ *phrase* **6** If something **makes sense**, you can understand it or it seems sensible: *It makes sense to find out as much as you can*

senseless adjective **1** A senseless action has no meaning or purpose: *senseless destruction* **2** If someone is senseless, they are unconscious

sensibility noun Your sensibility is your ability to experience deep feelings: *a man of sensibility rather than reason*

sensible adjective showing good sense and judgment > **sensibly** adverb

sensitive adjective **1** If you are sensitive to other people's feelings, you understand them **2** If you are sensitive about something, you are worried or easily upset about it: *He was sensitive about his height* **3** A sensitive subject or issue needs to be dealt with carefully because it can make people angry or upset **4** Something that is sensitive to a particular thing is easily affected or harmed by it > **sensitively** adverb

sensitivity noun **1** the quality of being sensitive **2** SCIENCE the ability of a plant or animal to respond to external stimuli such as light, sound, movement, or temperature

sensor noun an instrument which reacts to physical conditions such as light or heat

sensual [senss-yool] adjective giving pleasure to your physical senses rather than to your mind: *the sensual rhythm of his voice* > **sensuality** noun

sensuous adjective giving pleasure through the senses > **sensuously** adverb

sentence noun **1** a group of words which make a statement, question, or command. When written down a sentence begins with a capital letter and ends with a full stop **2** In a law court, a sentence is a punishment given to someone who has been found guilty ▷ verb **3** When a guilty person is sentenced, they are told officially what their punishment will be

sentiment noun **1** a feeling, attitude, or opinion: *I doubt my parents share my sentiments* **2** Sentiment consists of feelings such as tenderness or sadness: *There's no room for sentiment in business*

sentimental adjective **1** feeling or expressing tenderness or sadness to an exaggerated extent: *sentimental love stories* **2** relating to a person's emotions: *things of sentimental value* **3** ENGLISH Sentimental literature is intended to provoke an emotional response to the story, rather than relying on the reader's own natural response > **sentimentality** noun

sentinel noun (old-fashioned) a sentry

sentry noun a soldier who keeps watch and guards a camp or building

separate adjective [**sep**-ir-it] **1** If something is separate from something else, the two things are not connected ▷ verb [**sep**-ir-ate] **2** To separate people or things means to cause them to be apart from each other **3** If people or things separate, they move away from each other **4** If a married couple separate, they decide to live apart > **separately** adverb > **separation** noun

sepia [**see**-pee-a] adjective, noun deep brown, like the colour of old photographs

September noun September is the ninth month of the year. It has 30 days

septic adjective If a wound becomes septic, it becomes infected with poison

sequel noun 1 A sequel to a book or film is another book or film which continues the story 2 The sequel to an event is a result or consequence of it: *There's a sequel to my egg story*

sequence noun 1 A sequence of events is a number of them coming one after the other: *the whole sequence of events that had brought me to this place* 2 The sequence in which things are arranged is the order in which they are arranged: *Do things in the right sequence*

sequin noun Sequins are small, shiny, coloured discs sewn on clothes to decorate them

Serbian adjective 1 belonging or relating to Serbia ▷ noun 2 someone who comes from Serbia

serenade verb 1 If you serenade someone you love, you sing or play music to them outside their window ▷ noun 2 a song sung outside a woman's window by a man who loves her

serene adjective peaceful and calm: *She had a serene air* > **serenely** adverb > **serenity** noun

sergeant noun 1 a noncommissioned officer of middle rank in the army or air force 2 a police officer just above a constable in rank

serial noun a story which is broadcast or published in a number of parts over a period of time: *a television serial*

series series noun 1 A series of things is a number of them coming one after the other: *a series of loud explosions* 2 A radio or television series is a set of programmes with the same title

serious adjective 1 A serious problem or situation is very bad and worrying 2 Serious matters are important and should be thought about carefully 3 If you are serious about something, you are sincere about it: *You are really serious about having a baby* 4 People who are serious are thoughtful, quiet, and do not laugh much > **seriousness** noun

seriously adverb 1 You say seriously to emphasize that you mean what you say: *Seriously, though, something must be done* ▷ phrase 2 If you **take something seriously**, you regard it as important

sermon noun a talk on a religious or moral subject given as part of a church service

serpent noun (literary) a snake

serrated adjective having a row of V-shaped points along the edge, like a saw: *green serrated leaves*

servant noun someone who is employed to work in another person's house

serve verb 1 If you serve a country, an organization, or a person, you do useful work for them 2 To serve as something means to act or be used as that thing: *the room that served as their office* 3 If something serves people in a particular place, it provides them with something they need: *a recycling plant which serves the whole of the county* 4 If you serve food or drink to people, you give it to them 5 To serve customers in a shop means to help them and provide them with what they want 6 To serve a prison sentence or an apprenticeship means to spend time doing it 7 When you serve in tennis or badminton, you throw the ball or shuttlecock into the air and hit it over the net to start playing ▷ noun 8 the act of serving in tennis or badminton

S

server noun **1** COMPUTING a computer or computer program which supplies information or resources to a number of computers on a network **2** A server is a spoon or fork used for serving food: *salad servers*

service noun **1** a system organized to provide something for the public: *the bus service* **2** Some government organizations are called services: *the diplomatic service* **3** The services are the army, the navy, and the air force **4** If you give your services to a person or organization, you work for them or help them in some way: *services to the community* **5** In a shop or restaurant, service is the process of being served **6** a religious ceremony **7** When it is your service in a game of tennis or badminton, is your turn to serve **8** (*in plural*) Motorway services consist of a petrol station, restaurant, shop, and toilets ▷ *verb* **9** When a machine or vehicle is serviced, it is examined and adjusted so that it will continue working efficiently

serviceman servicemen noun a man in the army, navy, or air force > **servicewoman** noun

service station noun a garage that sells petrol, oil, spare parts, and snacks

serving noun **1** a helping of food ▷ *adjective* **2** A serving spoon or dish is used for serving food

session noun **1** a meeting of an official group: *the emergency session of the Indiana Supreme Court* **2** a period during which meetings are held regularly: *the end of the parliamentary session* **3** The period during which an activity takes place can also be called a session: *a drinking session*

set sets, setting, set noun **1** Several things make a set when they belong together or form a group: *a set of weights* **2** MATHS In maths, a set is a collection of numbers or other things which are treated as a group **3** A television set is a television **4** The set for a play or film is the scenery or furniture on the stage or in the studio **5** In tennis, a set is a group of six or more games. There are usually several sets in a match ▷ *verb* **6** If something is set somewhere, that is where it is: *The house was set back from the beach* **7** When the sun sets, it goes below the horizon **8** When you set the table, you prepare it for a meal by putting plates and cutlery on it **9** When you set a clock or a control, you adjust it to a particular point or position **10** If you set someone a piece of work or a target, you give it to them to do or to achieve **11** When something such as jelly or cement sets, it becomes firm or hard ▷ *adjective* **12** Something that is set is fixed and not varying: *a set charge* **13** If you are set to do something, you are ready or likely to do it **14** If you are set on doing something, you are determined to do it **15** If a play or story is set at a particular time or in a particular place, the events in it take place at that time or in that place > **set about** *verb* If you set about doing something, you start doing it > **set back** *verb* If something sets back a project or scheme, it delays it > **set off** *verb* **1** When you set off, you start a journey **2** To set something off means to cause it to start > **set out** *verb* **1** When you set out, you start a journey **2** If you set out to do something, you start trying to do it

> **set up** verb If you set something up, you make all the necessary preparations for it: *We have done all we can about setting up a system of communication*

setback noun something that delays or hinders you

settee noun a long comfortable seat for two or three people to sit on

setter noun a long-haired breed of dog originally used in hunting

setting noun 1 The setting of something is its surroundings or circumstances: *The Irish setting made the story realistic* 2 The settings on a machine are the different positions to which the controls can be adjusted

settle verb 1 To settle an argument means to put an end to it: *The dispute was settled* 2 If something is settled, it has all been decided and arranged 3 If you settle on something or settle for it, you choose it: *We settled for orange juice and coffee* 4 When you settle a bill, you pay it 5 If you settle in a place, you make it your permanent home 6 If you settle yourself somewhere, you sit down and make yourself comfortable 7 If something settles, it sinks slowly down and comes to rest: *A black dust settled on the walls*

> **settle down** verb 1 When someone settles down, they start living a quiet life in one place, especially when they get married 2 To settle down means to become quiet or calm

settlement noun 1 an official agreement between people who have been involved in a conflict: *the last chance for a peaceful settlement* 2 GEOGRAPHY a place where people have settled and built homes

settler noun someone who settles in

a new country: *the first settlers in Cuba*

seven the number 7

seventeen the number 17
> **seventeenth** adjective

seventh adjective 1 The seventh item in a series is the one counted as number seven ▷ noun 2 one of seven equal parts

seventy seventies the number 70
> **seventieth** adjective

sever verb 1 To sever something means to cut it off or cut right through it 2 If you sever a connection with someone or something, you end it completely: *She severed her ties with England*

several adjective Several people or things means a small number of them

severe adjective 1 extremely bad or unpleasant: *severe stomach pains* 2 stern and harsh: *Perhaps I was too severe with that young man*
> **severely** adverb > **severity** noun

sew sews, sewing, sewed, sewn [so] verb ▷ⒼⓉ When you sew things together, you join them using a needle and thread > **sewing** noun

sewage [soo-ij] noun Sewage is dirty water and waste which is carried away in sewers

sewer noun an underground channel that carries sewage to a place where it is treated to make it harmless

sewerage noun Sewerage is the system by which sewage is carried away and treated

sex noun 1 The sexes are the two groups, male and female, into which people and animals are divided 2 The sex of a person or animal is their characteristic of being either male or female 3 Sex is the physical activity by which people and animals produce young

sexism noun [PSHE] Sexism is discrimination against the members of one gender, usually women ▷ **sexist** adjective, noun

sextet noun **1** [MUSIC] a group of six musicians who sing or play together; also a piece of music written for six instruments or singers **2** [ENGLISH] six lines of poetry together, especially linked by a pattern of rhyme

sexual adjective **1** connected with the act of sex or with people's desire for sex: *sexual attraction* **2** relating to the difference between males and females: *sexual equality* **3** relating to the biological process by which people and animals produce young: *sexual reproduction* ▷ **sexually** adverb

sexuality [seks-yoo-al-it-ee] noun A person's sexuality is their ability to experience sexual feelings

shabby shabbier, shabbiest adjective **1** old and worn in appearance: *a shabby overcoat* **2** dressed in old, worn-out clothes: *a shabby figure crouching in a doorway* **3** behaving in a mean or unfair way: *shabby treatment* ▷ **shabbily** adverb

shack noun a small hut

shackle noun **1** In the past, shackles were two metal rings joined by a chain fastened around a prisoner's wrists or ankles ▷ verb **2** To shackle someone means to put shackles on them **3** (literary) If you are shackled by something, it restricts or hampers you

shade noun **1** Shade is an area of darkness and coolness which the sun does not reach: *The table was in the shade* **2** a lampshade **3** The shades of a colour are its different forms. For example, olive green is a shade of green ▷ verb **1** If a place is

shaded by trees or buildings, they prevent the sun from shining on it **5** If you shade your eyes, you put your hand in front of them to protect them from a bright light

shadow noun **1** the dark shape made when an object prevents light from reaching a surface **2** Shadow is darkness caused by light not reaching a place ▷ verb **3** To shadow someone means to follow them and watch them closely

shadow cabinet noun The shadow cabinet consists of the leaders of the main opposition party, each of whom is concerned with a particular policy

shadowy adjective **1** A shadowy place is dark and full of shadows **2** A shadowy figure or shape is difficult to see because it is dark or misty

shady shadier, shadiest adjective A shady place is sheltered from sunlight by trees or buildings

shaft noun **1** a vertical passage, for example one for a lift or one in a mine **2** A shaft of light is a beam of light **3** [DGT] A shaft in a machine is a rod which revolves and transfers movement in the machine: *the drive shaft*

shaggy shaggier, shaggiest adjective Shaggy hair or fur is long and untidy

shake shakes, shaking, shook, shaken verb **1** To shake something means to move it quickly from side to side or up and down **2** If something shakes, it moves from side to side or up and down with small, quick movements **3** If your voice shakes, it trembles because you are nervous or angry **4** If something shakes you, it shocks and upsets you **5** When you shake your head, you move it from side to side in order to say 'no' ▷ noun **6** If you give something a shake, you shake it ▷ **phrase 7** When you **shake hands** with someone, you grasp their hand as a way of greeting them

shaky shakier, shakiest adjective rather weak and unsteady: *Confidence in the economy is still shaky* > **shakily** adverb

shall verb **1** If I say I shall do something, I mean that I intend to do it **2** If I say something shall happen, I am emphasizing that it will definitely happen, or I am ordering it to happen: *You shall go to the ball!* **3** 'Shall' is also used in questions when you are asking what to do, or making a suggestion: *Shall we sit down?; Shall I go and check for you?*

shallow adjective **1** Shallow means not deep **2** Shallow also means not involving serious thought or sincere feelings: *a well-meaning but shallow man*

sham noun **1** Something that is a sham is not real or genuine ▷ adjective **2** not real or genuine: *a sham display of affection*

shambles noun (informal) If an event is a shambles, it is confused and badly organized

shame noun **1** Shame is the feeling of guilt or embarrassment you get when you know you have done something wrong or foolish **2** Shame is also something that makes people lose respect for you: *the scenes that brought shame to English soccer* **3** If you say something is a shame, you mean you are sorry about it: *It's a shame you can't come round* ▷ interjection **4** (informal) In South African English, you say 'Shame!' to show sympathy ▷ verb **5** If something shames you, it makes

you feel ashamed **6** If you shame someone into doing something, you force them to do it by making them feel ashamed not to: *Two children shamed their parents into giving up cigarettes*

shameful adjective If someone's behaviour is shameful, they ought to be ashamed of it > **shamefully** adverb

shameless adjective behaving in an indecent or unacceptable way, but showing no shame: *shameless dishonesty* > **shamelessly** adverb

shampoo noun **1** Shampoo is a soapy liquid used for washing your hair ▷ verb **2** When you shampoo your hair, you wash it with shampoo

shanty noun **1** a small, rough hut **2** A sea shanty is a song sailors used to sing

shape noun **1** The shape of something is the form or pattern of its outline, for example whether it is round or square **2** MATHS something with a definite form, for example a circle or triangle **3** The shape of something such as an organization is its structure and size ▷ verb **4** If you shape an object, you form it into a particular shape: *Shape the dough into an oblong* **5** To shape something means to cause it to develop in a particular way: *events that shaped the lives of some of the leading characters*

shapeless adjective not having a definite shape

shapely adjective A shapely woman has an attractive figure

shard noun a small fragment of pottery, glass, or metal

share verb **1** If two people share something, they both use it, do it, or have it: *We shared a bottle of champagne* **2** If you share an idea or a

S

piece of news with someone, you tell it to them ▷ noun **3** A share of something is a portion of it **4** The shares of a company are the equal parts into which its ownership is divided. People can buy shares as an investment > **share out** verb If you share something out, you give it out equally among a group of people

shareholder noun a person who owns shares in a company

shark noun **1** Sharks are large, powerful fish with sharp teeth **2** (informal) a person who cheats people out of money

sharp sharpest adjective **1** A sharp object has a fine edge or point that is good for cutting or piercing things **2** A sharp outline or distinction is easy to see **3** A sharp person is quick to notice or understand things **4** A sharp change is sudden and significant: a sharp rise in prices **5** If you say something in a sharp way, you say it firmly and rather angrily **6** A sharp sound is short, sudden, and quite loud **7** A sharp pain is a sudden pain **8** A sharp taste is slightly sour **9** A musical instrument or note that is sharp is slightly too high in pitch ▷ adverb **10** If something happens at a certain time sharp, it happens at that time precisely: You'll begin at eight o'clock sharp ▷ noun **11** In music, a sharp is a note or key a semitone higher than that described by the same letter. It is represented by the symbol (#)
> **sharply** adverb > **sharpness** noun

sharpen verb **1** To sharpen an object means to make its edge or point sharper **2** If your senses or abilities sharpen, you become quicker at noticing or understanding things **3** If you voice sharpens, you begin to speak more angrily or harshly **4** If

something sharpens the disagreements between people, it makes them greater

shatter verb **1** If something shatters, it breaks into a lot of small pieces **2** If something shatters your hopes or beliefs, it destroys them completely **3** If you are shattered by an event or piece of news, you are shocked and upset by it

shattered adjective (informal) completely exhausted: He must be absolutely shattered after all his efforts

shattering adjective making you feel shocked and upset: a shattering event

shave shaves, shaving, shaved verb **1** When a man shaves, he removes hair from his face with a razor **2** If you shave off part of a piece of wood, you cut thin pieces from it ▷ noun **3** When a man has a shave, he shaves

shaven adjective If part of someone's body is shaven, it has been shaved: a shaven head

shawl noun a large piece of woollen cloth worn round a woman's head or shoulders or used to wrap a baby in

she pronoun 'She' is used to refer to a woman or girl whose identity is clear. 'She' is also used to refer to a country, a ship, or a car

sheaf sheaves noun **1** A sheaf of papers is a bundle of them **2** A sheaf of corn is a bundle of ripe corn tied together

shear shears, shearing, sheared, shorn verb To shear a sheep means to cut the wool off it

shearer noun someone whose job is to shear sheep

sheath noun a covering for the blade of a knife

shed sheds, shedding, shed noun **1** a

small building used for storing things ▷ verb 2 When an animal sheds hair or skin, some of its hair or skin drops off. When a tree sheds its leaves, its leaves fall off 3 (formal) To shed something also means to get rid of it: The firm is to shed 700 jobs 4 If a lorry sheds its load, the load falls off the lorry onto the road 5 If you shed tears, you cry

sheen noun a gentle brightness on the surface of something

sheep sheep noun A sheep is a farm animal with a thick woolly coat. Sheep are kept for meat and wool

sheepdog noun a breed of dog often used for controlling sheep

sheepish adjective If you look sheepish, you look embarrassed because you feel shy or foolish
> **sheepishly** adverb

sheepskin noun Sheepskin is the skin and wool of a sheep, used for making rugs and coats

sheer adjective 1 Sheer means complete and total: sheer exhaustion 2 A sheer cliff or drop is vertical 3 Sheer fabrics are very light and delicate

sheet noun 1 a large rectangular piece of cloth used to cover a bed 2 A sheet of paper is a rectangular piece of it 3 A sheet of glass or metal is a large, flat piece of it

sheik [shake] or **sheikh** noun an Arab chief or ruler

shelf shelves noun a flat piece of wood, metal, or glass fixed to a wall and used for putting things on

shell noun 1 The shell of an egg or nut is its hard covering 2 The shell of a tortoise, snail, or crab is the hard protective covering on its back 3 The shell of a building or other structure is its frame: The room was just an empty shell 4 A container filled

with explosives that can be fired from a gun ▷ verb 5 If you shell peas or nuts, you remove their natural covering 6 To shell a place means to fire large explosive shells at it

shellfish shellfish or shellfishes noun a small sea creature with a shell

shelter noun 1 a small building made to protect people from bad weather or danger 2 If a place provides shelter, it provides protection from bad weather or danger ▷ verb 3 If you shelter in a place, you stay there and are safe 4 If you shelter someone, you provide them with a place to stay when they are in danger

sheltered adjective 1 A sheltered place is protected from wind and rain 2 If you lead a sheltered life, you do not experience unpleasant or upsetting things 3 Sheltered accommodation is accommodation designed for old or disabled people

shelve verb If you shelve a plan, you decide to postpone it for a while

shepherd noun 1 a person who looks after sheep ▷ verb 2 If you shepherd someone somewhere, you accompany them there

sheriff noun 1 In America, a sheriff is a person elected to enforce the law in a county 2 In Australia, an administrative officer of the Supreme Court who carries out writs and judgments

sherry sherries noun Sherry is a kind of strong wine

shield noun 1 a large piece of a strong material like metal or plastic which soldiers or policeman carry to protect themselves 2 If something is a shield against something, it gives protection from it ▷ verb 3 To shield someone means to protect them from something

S

shift verb **1** If you shift something, you move it. If something shifts, it moves: to shift the rubble **2** If an opinion or situation shifts, it changes slightly ▷ noun **3** A shift in an opinion or situation is a slight change **4** a set period during which people work in a factory: the night shift

shilling noun a former British, Australian, and New Zealand coin worth one-twentieth of a pound

shimmer verb **1** If something shimmers, it shines with a faint, flickering light ▷ noun **2** a faint, flickering light

shin shins, shinning, shinned noun **1** Your shin is the front part of your leg between your knee and your ankle ▷ verb **2** If you shin up a tree or pole, you climb it quickly by gripping it with your hands and legs

shine shines, shining, shone verb **1** When something shines, it gives out or reflects a bright light: The stars shone brilliantly **2** If you shine a torch or lamp somewhere, you point it there

shingle noun **1** Shingle consists of small pebbles on the seashore **2** Shingles are small wooden roof tiles **3** Shingles is a disease that causes a painful red rash, especially around the waist

shining adjective **1** Shining things are very bright, usually because they are reflecting light: shining stainless steel tables **2** A shining example of something is a very good or typical example of that thing: a shining example of courage

shiny shinier, shiniest adjective Shiny things are bright and look as if they have been polished: a shiny brass plate

ship ships, shipping, shipped noun **1** a large boat which carries passengers or cargo ▷ verb **2** If people or things are shipped somewhere, they are transported there

-ship suffix '-ship' is used to form nouns that refer to a condition or position: fellowship

shipment noun **1** a quantity of goods that are transported somewhere: a shipment of olive oil **2** The shipment of goods is the transporting of them

shipping noun **1** Shipping is the transport of cargo on ships **2** You can also refer to ships generally as shipping: Attention all shipping!

shipwreck noun When there is a shipwreck, a ship is destroyed in an accident at sea: He was drowned in a shipwreck

shipyard noun a place where ships are built and repaired

shire noun **1** in Britain, an old word for a county **2** in Australia, a rural district with its own local council

shirk verb To shirk a task means to avoid doing it

shirt noun a piece of clothing worn on the upper part of the body, with a collar, sleeves, and buttons down the front

shiver verb **1** When you shiver, you tremble slightly because you are cold or scared ▷ noun **2** a slight trembling caused by cold or fear

shoal noun A shoal of fish is a large group of them swimming together

shock noun **1** If you have a shock, you have a sudden upsetting experience **2** Shock is a person's emotional and physical condition when something very unpleasant or upsetting has happened to them **3** In medicine, shock is a serious physical condition in which the blood cannot circulate properly because of an injury **4** a slight movement in something when it is hit by something else: *The straps help to absorb shocks* **5** A shock of hair is a thick mass of it ▷ verb **6** If something shocks you, it upsets you because it is unpleasant and unexpected: *I was shocked by his appearance* **7** You can say that something shocks you when it offends you because it is rude or immoral > **shocked** adjective

shocking adjective **1** (informal) very bad: *It's been a shocking year* **2** disgusting or horrifying: *shocking images*

shoddy shoddier, shoddiest adjective badly made or done: *a shoddy piece of work*

shoe shoes, shoeing, shod noun **1** Shoes are strong coverings for your feet. They cover most of your foot, but not your ankle ▷ verb **2** To shoe a horse means to fix horseshoes onto its hooves

shoestring noun (informal) If you do something on a shoestring, you do it using very little money

shoot shoots, shooting, shot verb **1** To shoot a person or animal means to kill or injure them by firing a gun at them **2** To shoot an arrow means to fire it from a bow **3** If something shoots in a particular direction, it moves there quickly and suddenly: *They shot back into Green Street* **4** When a film is shot, it is filmed: *The whole film was shot in California* **5** In games such as football or hockey, to shoot means to kick or hit the ball towards the goal ▷ noun **6** an occasion when people hunt animals or birds with guns **7** a plant that is beginning to grow, or a new part growing from a plant

shooting noun an incident in which someone is shot

shop shops, shopping, shopped noun **1** a place where things are sold **2** a place where a particular type of work is done: *a bicycle repair shop* ▷ verb **3** When you shop, you go to the shops to buy things > **shopper** noun

shopkeeper noun someone who owns or manages a small shop

shoplifting noun Shoplifting is stealing goods from shops > **shoplifter** noun

shopping noun Your shopping is the goods you have bought from the shops

shore noun **1** The shore of a sea, lake, or wide river is the land along the edge of it ▷ verb **2** If you shore something up, you reinforce it or strengthen it: *a short-term solution to shore up the worst defence in the League*

shoreline noun the edge of a sea, lake, or wide river

shorn 1 Shorn is the past participle of **shear** ▷ adjective **2** Grass or hair that is shorn is cut very short

short adjective **1** not lasting very long **2** small in length, distance, or height: *a short climb; the short road* **3** not using many words: *a short speech* **4** If you are short with someone, you speak to them crossly **5** If you have a short temper, you get angry very quickly **6** If you are short of something, you do not have enough of it **7** If a name is short for another name, it is a shorter version of it ▷ noun **8** (in plural) Shorts are trousers with short legs ▷ adverb **9** If you stop short of a place, you do not quite reach it ▷ phrase **10** Short of is used to say that a level or amount has not quite been reached: *a hundred votes short of a majority*

S

shortage noun If there is a shortage of something, there is not enough of it

shortcoming noun Shortcomings are faults or weaknesses

shortcut noun **1** a quicker way of getting somewhere than the usual route **2** a quicker way of doing something: *Stencils have been used as a shortcut to hand painting*

shorten verb If you shorten something or if it shortens, it becomes shorter: *This might help to shorten the conversation*

shortfall noun If there is a shortfall in something, there is less than you need

shorthand noun Shorthand is a way of writing in which signs represent words or syllables. It is used to write down quickly what someone is saying

short-list noun **1** a list of people selected from a larger group, from which one person is finally selected for a job or prize ▷ verb **2** If someone is short-listed for a job or prize, they are put on a short-list

shortly adverb **1** Shortly means soon: *I'll be back shortly* **2** If you speak to someone shortly, you speak to them in a cross and impatient way

short-sighted adjective **1** If you are short-sighted, you cannot see things clearly when they are far away **2** A short-sighted decision does not take account of the way things may develop in the future

short-term adjective happening or having an effect within a short time or for a short time

shot noun **1** Shot is the past tense and past participle of **shoot 2** the act of firing a gun **3** Someone who is a good shot can shoot accurately **4** In football, golf, and

tennis, a shot is the act of kicking or hitting the ball **5** a photograph or short film sequence: *I'd like to get some shots of the river* **6** (informal) If you have a shot at something, you try to do it

shotgun noun a gun that fires a lot of small pellets all at once

shot put noun In athletics, the shot put is an event in which the contestants throw a heavy metal ball called a shot as far as possible ▷ **shot putter** noun

should verb **1** You use 'should' to say that something ought to happen: *Ward should have done better* **2** You also use 'should' to say that you expect something to happen: *He should have heard by now* **3** (formal) You can use 'should' to announce that you are about to do or say something: *I should like to express my thanks to the Professor* **4** 'Should' is used in conditional sentences: *If you should see Kerr, tell him I have his umbrella* **5** 'Should' is sometimes used in 'that' clauses: *It is inevitable that you should go* **6** If you say that you should think something, you mean that it is probably true: *I should think that's unlikely*

shoulder noun **1** Your shoulders are the parts of your body between your neck and the tops of your arms ▷ verb **2** If you shoulder something heavy, you put it across one of your shoulders to carry it **3** If you shoulder the responsibility or blame for something, you accept it

shout noun **1** a loud call or cry ▷ verb **2** If you shout something, you say it very loudly: *He shouted something to his brother* ▷ **shout down** verb If you shout someone down, you prevent them from being heard by shouting at them

shove verb 1 If you shove someone or something, you push them roughly: *He shoved his wallet into a back pocket* ▷ noun 2 a rough push ▷ **shove off** verb (*informal*) If you tell someone to shove off, you are telling them angrily and rudely to go away

shovel shovels, shovelling, shovelled noun 1 a tool like a spade, used for moving earth or snow ▷ verb 2 If you shovel earth or snow, you move it with a shovel

show shows, showing, showed, shown verb 1 To show that something exists or is true means to prove it: *The survey showed that 29 per cent would now approve the treaty* 2 If a picture shows something, it represents it: *The painting shows supporters and crowd scenes* 3 If you show someone something, you let them see it: *Show me your passport* 4 If you show someone to a room or seat, you lead them there 5 If you show someone how to do something, you demonstrate it to them 6 If something shows, it is visible 7 If something shows a quality or characteristic, you can see that it has it: *Her sketches and watercolours showed promise* 8 If you show your feelings, you let people see them: *She was flustered, but too proud to show it* 9 If you show affection or mercy, you behave in an affectionate or merciful way: *the first person who showed me some affection* 10 To show a film or television programme means to let the public see it ▷ noun 11 a form of light entertainment at the theatre or on television 12 an exhibition: *the Napier Antiques Show* 13 A show of a feeling or attitude is behaviour in which you show it: *a show of optimism* ▷ phrase 14 If something is

on show, it is being exhibited for the public to see > **show off** verb (*informal*) If someone is showing off, they are trying to impress people > **show up** verb 1 (*informal*) If you show up, you arrive at a place 2 If something shows up, it can be seen clearly: *Her bones were too soft to show up on an X-ray*

show business noun Show business is entertainment in the theatre, films, and television

showdown noun (*informal*) a major argument or conflict intended to end a dispute

shower noun 1 a device which sprays you with water so that you can wash yourself 2 If you have a shower, you wash yourself by standing under a shower 3 a short period of rain 4 You can refer to a lot of things falling at once as a shower: *a shower of confetti* ▷ verb 5 If you shower, you have a shower 6 If you are showered with a lot of things, they fall on you

showing noun A showing of a film or television programme is a presentation of it so that the public can see it

showjumping noun Showjumping is a horse-riding competition in which the horses jump over a series of high fences

show-off noun (*informal*) someone who tries to impress people with their knowledge or skills

showroom noun a shop where goods such as cars or electrical appliances are displayed

showy showier, showiest adjective large or bright and intended to impress people: *a showy house*

shrapnel noun Shrapnel consists of small pieces of metal scattered from an exploding shell

S

shred shreds, shredding, shredded
verb **1** If you shred something, you
cut or tear it into very small pieces
▷ noun **2** A shred of paper or
material is a small, narrow piece of
it **3** If there is not a shred of
something, there is absolutely none
of it: *He was left without a shred of
self-esteem*

shrewd adjective Someone who is
shrewd is intelligent and makes
good judgments > **shrewdly** adverb
> **shrewdness** noun

shriek noun **1** a high-pitched scream
▷ verb **2** If you shriek, you make a
high-pitched scream

shrill adjective A shrill sound is
unpleasantly high-pitched and
piercing > **shrilly** adverb

shrimp noun a small edible shellfish
with a long tail and many legs

shrine noun a place of worship
associated with a sacred person or
object

shrink shrinks, shrinking, shrank,
shrunk verb **1** If something shrinks,
it becomes smaller **2** If you shrink
from something, you move away
from it because you are afraid of it
> **shrinkage** noun

shrivel shrivels, shrivelling,
shrivelled verb When something
shrivels, it becomes dry and withered

shroud noun **1** a cloth in which a
dead body is wrapped before it is
buried ▷ verb **2** If something is
shrouded in darkness or fog, it is
hidden by it

shrub noun a low, bushy plant

shrug shrugs, shrugging, shrugged
verb **1** If you shrug your shoulders,
you raise them slightly as a sign of
indifference or if you don't know
something ▷ noun **2** If you give a
shrug of your shoulders, you shrug
them

shrunken adjective (formal)
Someone or something that is
shrunken has become smaller than
it used to be: *a shrunken old man*

shudder verb **1** If you shudder, you
tremble with fear or horror **2** If a
machine or vehicle shudders, it
shakes violently ▷ noun **3** a shiver of
fear or horror

shuffle verb **1** If you shuffle, you
walk without lifting your feet
properly off the ground **2** If you
shuffle about, you move about and
fidget because you feel
uncomfortable or embarrassed **3** If
you shuffle a pack of cards, you mix
them up before you begin a game
▷ noun **4** the way someone walks
when they shuffle

shun shuns, shunning, shunned verb
If you shun someone or something,
you deliberately avoid them

shunt verb (informal) If you shunt
people or things to a place, you
move them there: *You are shunted
from room to room*

shut shuts, shutting, shut verb **1** If
you shut something, you close it
2 When a shop or pub shuts, it is
closed and you can no longer go into
it ▷ adjective **3** If something is shut,
it is closed ▶ **shut down** verb When
a factory or business is shut down, it
is closed permanently ▶ **shut up**
verb (informal) If you shut up, you
stop talking

shutter noun Shutters are hinged
wooden or metal covers fitted on
the outside or inside of a window

shuttle adjective **1** A shuttle service
is an air, bus, or train service which
makes frequent journeys between
two places ▷ noun **2** a plane used in
a shuttle service

shy shyer, shyest; shies, shying,
shied adjective **1** A shy person is

nervous and uncomfortable in the company of other people ▷ *verb* **2** When a horse shies, it moves away suddenly because something has frightened it **3** If you shy away from doing something, you avoid doing it because you are afraid or nervous > **shyly** *adverb* > **shyness** *noun*

sibling *noun* (*formal*) Your siblings are your brothers and sisters

sick *adjective* **1** If you are sick, you are ill **2** If you feel sick, you feel as if you are going to vomit. If you are sick, you vomit **3** (*informal*) If you are sick of doing something, you feel you have been doing it too long **4** (*informal*) A sick joke or story deals with death or suffering in an unpleasantly frivolous way ▷ *phrase* **5** If something **makes you sick**, it makes you angry > **sickness** *noun*

sicken *verb* If something sickens you, it makes you feel disgusted > **sickening** *adjective*

sickle *noun* a tool with a short handle and a curved blade used for cutting grass or grain

sickly sicklier, sickliest *adjective* **1** A sickly person or animal is weak and unhealthy **2** Sickly also means very unpleasant to smell or taste

side *noun* **1** Side refers to a position to the left or right of something: *the two armchairs on either side of the fireplace* **2** The sides of a boundary or barrier are the two areas it separates: *this side of the border* **3** Your sides are the parts of your body from your armpits down to your hips **4** The sides of something are its outside surfaces, especially the surfaces which are not its front or back **5** The sides of a hill or valley are the parts that slope **6** The two sides in a war, argument, or relationship are the two people or

groups involved **7** A particular side of something is one aspect of it: *the sensitive, caring side of human nature* ▷ *adjective* **8** situated on a side of a building or vehicle: *the side door* **9** A side road is a small road leading off a larger one **10** A side issue is an issue that is less important than the main one ▷ *verb* **11** If you side with someone in an argument, you support them

sideboard *noun* **1** a long, low cupboard for plates and glasses **2** (*in plural*) A man's sideboards are his sideburns

sideburns *plural noun* A man's sideburns are areas of hair growing on his cheeks in front of his ears

side effect *noun* The side effects of a drug are the effects it has in addition to its main effects

sidekick *noun* (*informal*) Someone's sidekick is their close friend who spends a lot of time with them

sideline *noun* an extra job in addition to your main job

sideshow *noun* Sideshows are stalls at a fairground

sidestep sidesteps, sidestepping, sidestepped *verb* If you sidestep a difficult problem or question, you avoid dealing with it

sidewalk *noun* In American English, a sidewalk is a pavement

sideways *adverb* **1** from or towards the side of something or someone ▷ *adjective* **2** to or from one side: *a sideways step*

siding *noun* a short railway track beside the main tracks, where engines and carriages are left when not in use

siege [seej] *noun* (HISTORY) a military operation in which an army surrounds a place and prevents food or help from reaching the people inside

S

sieve [siv] *noun* **1** a kitchen tool made of mesh, used for sifting or straining things ▷ *verb* **2** If you sieve a powder or liquid, you pass it through a sieve

sift *verb* **1** If you sift a powdery substance, you pass it through a sieve to remove lumps **2** If you sift through something such as evidence, you examine it all thoroughly

sigh *verb* **1** When you sigh, you let out a deep breath ▷ *noun* **2** the breath you let out when you sigh

sight *noun* **1** Sight is the ability to see: *His sight was so poor that he could not follow the cricket* **2** something you see: *It was a ghastly sight* **3** (*in plural*) Sights are interesting places which tourists visit ▷ *verb* **4** If you sight someone or something, you see them briefly or suddenly: *He had been sighted in Cairo* ▷ *phrase* **5** If something is **in sight**, you can see it. If it is **out of sight**, you cannot see it

WORD TIP
Do not confuse the spellings of *sight* and *site*: *The bombed city was a terrible sight; the site of battle in World War One*

sighted *adjective* Someone who is sighted can see

sighting *noun* A sighting of something rare or unexpected is an occasion when it is seen

sightseeing *noun* Sightseeing is visiting the interesting places that tourists usually visit > **sightseer** *noun*

sign *noun* **1** a mark or symbol that always has a particular meaning, for example in mathematics or music **2** a gesture with a particular meaning **3** A sign can also consist of words, a picture, or a symbol giving information or a warning **4** (RE) A sign is an event or happening that some people believe God has sent as a warning or instruction to an individual or to people in general **5** If there are signs of something, there is evidence that it exists or is happening: *We are now seeing the first signs of recovery* ▷ *verb* **6** If you sign a document, you write your name on it: *He hurriedly signed the death certificate* **7** If you sign, you communicate by using sign language > **sign on** *verb* **1** If you sign on for a job or course, you officially agree to do it by signing a contract **2** When people sign on, they officially state that they are unemployed and claim benefit from the state > **sign up** *verb* If you sign up for a job or course, you officially agree to do it

signal signals, signalling, signalled *noun* **1** a gesture, sound, or action intended to give a message to someone **2** A railway signal is a piece of equipment beside the track which tells train drivers whether to stop or not ▷ *verb* **3** If you signal to someone, you make a gesture or sound to give them a message

signature *noun* If you write your signature, you write your name the way you usually write it

significant *adjective* large or important: *a significant amount; a significant victory* > **significance** *noun* > **significantly** *adverb*

signify signifies, signifying, signified *verb* A gesture that signifies something has a particular meaning: *She screwed up her face to signify her disgust*

sign language *noun* Sign language is a way of communicating using your hands, used especially by deaf people

signpost *noun* a road sign with information on it such as the name of a town and how far away it is

Sikh [seek] *noun* RE a person who believes in Sikhism, an Indian religion which separated from Hinduism in the sixteenth century and which teaches that there is only one God ▷ **Sikhism** *noun*

silence *noun* 1 Silence is quietness 2 Someone's silence about something is their failure or refusal to talk about it ▷ *verb* 3 To silence someone or something means to stop them talking or making a noise

silent *adjective* 1 If you are silent, you are not saying anything 2 If you are silent about something, you do not tell people about it 3 When something is silent, it makes no noise 4 A silent film has only pictures and no sound ▷ **silently** *adverb*

silhouette [sil-loo-ett] *noun* the outline of a dark shape against a light background ▷ **silhouetted** *adjective*

silicon *noun* Silicon is an element found in sand, clay, and stone. It is used to make glass and also to make parts of computers. Its atomic number is 14 and its symbol is Si

silk *noun* Silk is a fine, soft cloth made from a substance produced by silkworms

silken *adjective* (*literary*) smooth and soft: *silken hair*

silkworm *noun* Silkworms are the larvae of a particular kind of moth

silky silkier, silkiest *adjective* smooth and soft

sill *noun* a ledge at the bottom of a window

silly sillier, silliest *adjective* foolish or childish

silt *noun* Silt is fine sand or soil which is carried along by a river

silver *noun* 1 Silver is a valuable greyish-white metallic element used for making jewellery and ornaments. Its atomic number is 47 and its symbol is Ag 2 Silver is also coins made from silver or from silver-coloured metal: *He's won a handful of silver on the fruit machine* 3 In a house, the silver is all the things made from silver, especially the cutlery ▷ *adjective, noun* 4 greyish-white

silver medal *noun* a medal made from silver awarded to the competitor who comes second in a competition

silvery *adjective* having the appearance or colour of silver: *the silvery moon*

similar *adjective* 1 If one thing is similar to another, or if two things are similar, they are like each other 2 In maths, two triangles are similar if the angles in one correspond exactly to the angles in the other ▷ **similarly** *adverb*

similarity *noun* If there is a similarity between things, they are alike in some way

simmer *verb* When food simmers, it cooks gently at just below boiling point

simple *adjective* 1 Something that is simple is uncomplicated and easy to understand or do 2 Simple also means plain and not elaborate in style: *a simple coat* 3 A simple way of life is uncomplicated 4 Someone who is simple is not very intelligent 5 You use 'simple' to emphasize that what you are talking about is the only important thing: *simple stubbornness* ▷ **simplicity** *noun*

simplify simplifies, simplifying, simplified *verb* To simplify

S

something means to make it easier to do or understand
> **simplification** noun

simplistic adjective too simple or naive: *a rather simplistic approach to the subject*

simply adverb **1** Simply means merely: *It was simply a question of making the decision* **2** You use 'simply' to emphasize what you are saying: *It is simply not true* **3** If you say or write something simply, you do it in a way that makes it easy to understand

simulate verb To simulate something means to imitate it: *The wood has been painted to simulate stone; He simulated shock*

simulation noun **1** Simulation is the process of simulating something or the result of simulating something **2** (technical) A simulation is an attempt to solve a problem by representing it mathematically, often on a computer

simulator noun A simulator is a device designed to reproduce actual conditions, for example in order to train pilots or astronauts

simultaneous adjective Things that are simultaneous happen at the same time > **simultaneously** adverb

sin sins, sinning, sinned noun **1** Sin is wicked and immoral behaviour ▷ verb **2** To sin means to do something wicked and immoral

since preposition, conjunction, adverb **1** Since means from a particular time until now: *I've been waiting patiently since half past three* ▷ adverb **2** Since also means at some time after a particular time in the past: *They split up and he has since remarried* ▷ conjunction **3** Since also means because: *I'm forever on a diet, since I put on weight easily*

sincere adjective If you are sincere, you say things that you really mean: *a sincere expression of friendliness*
> **sincerity** noun

sincerely adverb **1** If you say or feel something sincerely, you mean it or feel it genuinely ▷ phrase **2** You write **Yours sincerely** before your signature at the end of a letter in which you have named the person you are writing to in the greeting at the beginning of the letter. For example, if you began your letter 'Dear Mr Brown' you would use 'Yours sincerely'

sinful adjective wicked and immoral

sing sings, singing, sang, sung verb **1** When you sing, you make musical sounds with your voice, usually producing words that fit a tune **2** When birds or insects sing, they make pleasant sounds > **singer** noun

single adjective **1** Single means only one and not more: *A single shot was fired* **2** People who are single are not married **3** A single bed or bedroom is for one person **4** A single ticket is a one-way ticket ▷ noun **5** a recording of one or two short pieces of music on a small record, CD, or download **6** Singles is a game of tennis, badminton, or squash between just two players > **single out** verb If you single someone out from a group, you give them special treatment: *He'd been singled out for some special award*

single-handed adverb If you do something single-handed, you do it on your own, without any help

single-minded adjective A single-minded person has only one aim and is determined to achieve it

singly adverb If people do something singly, they do it on their own or one by one

singular noun **1** In grammar, the singular is the form of a word that refers to just one person or thing ▷ adjective **2** (formal) unusual and remarkable: her singular beauty > **singularity** noun > **singularly** adverb

sinister adjective seeming harmful or evil: something cold and sinister about him

sink sinks, sinking, sank, sunk noun **1 a** a basin with taps supplying water, usually in a kitchen or bathroom ▷ verb **2** If something sinks, it moves downwards, especially through water: An Indian cargo ship sank in icy seas **3** To sink a ship means to cause it to sink by attacking it **4** If an amount or value sinks, it decreases **5** If you sink into an unpleasant state, you gradually pass into it: He sank into black despair **6** To sink something sharp into an object means to make it go deeply into it: The tiger sank its teeth into his leg > **sink in** verb When a fact sinks in, you fully understand it or realize it: The truth was at last sinking in

sinner noun someone who has committed a sin

sinus noun Your sinuses are the air passages in the bones of your skull, just behind your nose

sip sips, sipping, sipped verb **1** If you sip a drink, you drink it by taking a small amount at a time ▷ noun **2 a** small amount of drink that you take into your mouth

siphon [**sigh-fn**] or **syphon** verb If you siphon off a liquid, you draw it out of a container through a tube and transfer it to another place

sir noun **1** Sir is a polite, formal way of addressing a man **2** Sir is also the title used in front of the name of a knight or baronet

siren noun a warning device, for example on a police car, which makes a loud wailing noise

sirloin noun Sirloin is a prime cut of beef from the lower part of a cow's back

sister noun **1** Your sister is a girl or woman who has the same parents as you **2** a member of a female religious order **3** In a hospital, a sister is a senior nurse who supervises a ward ▷ adjective **4** Sister means closely related to something or very similar to it: Citroen and its sister company Peugeot

sisterhood noun Sisterhood is a strong feeling of companionship between women

sister-in-law sisters-in-law noun Someone's sister-in-law is the sister of their husband or wife, or their sibling's wife

sit sits, sitting, sat verb **1** If you are sitting, your weight is supported by your buttocks rather than your feet **2** When you sit or sit down somewhere, you lower your body until you are sitting **3** If you sit an examination, you take it **4** (formal) When a parliament, law court, or other official body sits, it meets and officially carries out its work

sitcom noun (informal) a television comedy series which shows characters in amusing situations that are similar to everyday life

site noun **1 a** piece of ground where a particular thing happens or is situated: a building site ▷ verb **2** If something is sited in a place, it is built or positioned there

> **WORD TIP**
> Do not confuse the spellings of site and sight: the site of battle in World War One; The bombed city was a terrible sight

sitting noun **1** one of the times when a meal is served **2** one of the occasions when a parliament or law court meets and carries out its work

sitting room noun a room in a house where people sit and relax

situated adjective If something is situated somewhere, that is where it is: *a town situated 45 minutes from Geneva*

situation noun **1** what is happening in a particular place at a particular time: *the political situation* **2** The situation of a building or town is its surroundings: *a beautiful situation*

six the number 6

sixteen the number 16 > **sixteenth** adjective

sixth adjective **1** The sixth item in a series is the one counted as number six ▷ noun **2** one of six equal parts

sixth sense noun You say that someone has a sixth sense when they know something instinctively, without having any evidence of it

sixty sixties the number 60 > **sixtieth** adjective

sizable or **sizeable** adjective fairly large: *a sizable amount of money*

size noun **1** The size of something is how big or small it is: *the size of the audience* **2** The size of something is also the fact that it is very large: *the sheer size of Australia* **3** one of the standard graded measurements of clothes and shoes > **size up** verb If you size up people or situations, you look at them carefully and make a judgment about them

sizzle verb If something sizzles, it makes a hissing sound like the sound of frying food

skate skates, skating, skated noun **1** Skates are ice skates or roller skates **2** a flat edible sea fish ▷ verb **3** If you skate, you move about on

ice wearing ice skates **4** If you skate round a difficult subject, you avoid discussing it

skateboard noun a narrow board on wheels, which you stand on and ride for fun

skeleton noun Your skeleton is the framework of bones in your body

sketch noun **1** [ART] a quick, rough drawing **2** A sketch of a situation or incident is a brief description of it **3** a short, humorous piece of acting, usually forming part of a comedy show ▷ verb **4** If you sketch something, you draw it quickly and roughly

sketchy sketchier, sketchiest adjective giving only a rough description or account: *Details surrounding his death are sketchy*

skew [skyoo] or **skewed** adjective in a slanting position, rather than straight or upright

skewer noun **1** a long metal pin used to hold pieces of food together during cooking ▷ verb **2** If you skewer something, you push a skewer through it

ski skis, skiing, skied noun **1** Skis are long pieces of wood, metal, or plastic that you fasten to special boots so you can move easily on snow ▷ verb **2** When you ski, you move on snow wearing skis, especially as a sport

skid skids, skidding, skidded verb If a vehicle skids, it slides in an uncontrolled way, for example because the road is wet or icy

skilful adjective If you are skilful at something, you can do it very well > **skilfully** adverb

skill noun **1** Skill is the knowledge and ability that enables you to do something well **2** a type of work or technique which requires special

S

training and knowledge

skilled adjective **1** A skilled person has the knowledge and ability to do something well **2** Skilled work is work which can only be done by people who have had special training

skim skims, skimming, skimmed verb **1** If you skim something from the surface of a liquid, you remove it **2** If something skims a surface, it moves along just above it: seagulls skimming the waves

skimmed milk noun Skimmed milk has had the cream removed

skin skins, skinning, skinned noun **1** Your skin is the natural covering of your body. An animal skin is the skin and fur of a dead animal **2** The skin of a fruit or vegetable is its outer covering **3** a solid layer which forms on the surface of a liquid ▷ verb **4** If you skin a dead animal, you remove its skin **5** If you skin a part of your body, you accidentally graze it

skinny skinnier, skinniest adjective extremely thin

skip skips, skipping, skipped verb **1** If you skip along, you move along jumping from one foot to the other **2** (informal) If you skip something, you miss it out or avoid doing it: It is all too easy to skip meals ▷ noun **3** Skips are the movements you make when you skip **4** a large metal container for holding rubbish and rubble

skipper noun (informal) The skipper of a ship or boat is its captain

skirmish noun a short, rough fight

skirt noun **1** A woman's skirt is a piece of clothing which fastens at her waist and hangs down over her legs ▷ verb **2** Something that skirts an area is situated around the edge of it **3** If you skirt something, you go around the edge of it: We skirted the town **4** If you skirt a problem, you avoid dealing with it: He was skirting the real question

skull noun Your skull is the bony part of your head which surrounds your brain

skunk noun a small black and white animal from North America which gives off an unpleasant smell when it is frightened

sky skies noun The sky is the space around the earth which you can see when you look upwards

skylight noun a window in a roof or ceiling

skyline noun The skyline is the line where the sky meets buildings or the ground: the New York City skyline

Skype noun (trademark) a computer program for making phone calls and video calls on the internet

skyscraper noun a very tall building

slab noun a thick, flat piece of something

slack adjective **1** Something that is slack is loose and not firmly stretched or positioned **2** A slack period is one in which there is not much work to do ▷ noun **3** The slack in a rope is the part that hangs loose **4** (old-fashioned, in plural) Slacks are casual trousers ▷ **slackness** noun

slacken verb **1** If something slackens, it becomes slower or less intense: The rain had slackened to a drizzle **2** To slacken also means to become looser: Her grip slackened on Arnold's arm

slag slags, slagging, slagged noun **1** Slag is the waste material left when ore has been melted down to remove the metal: a slag heap ▷ verb **2** (informal) To slag someone off means to criticize them in an unpleasant way, usually behind their back

S

slalom [slah-lom] *noun* a skiing competition in which the competitors have to twist and turn quickly to avoid obstacles

slam slams, slamming, slammed *verb* 1 If you slam a door and with great force it slams, it shuts noisily and with great force 2 If you slam something down, you throw it down violently: *She slammed the phone down*

slander *noun* 1 Slander is something untrue and malicious said about someone ▷ *verb* 2 To slander someone means to say untrue and malicious things about them > **slanderous** *adjective*

slang *noun* Slang consists of very informal words and expressions

slant *verb* 1 If something slants, it slopes: *The back can be adjusted to slant into the most comfortable position* 2 If news or information is slanted, it is presented in a biased way ▷ *noun* 3 a slope 4 A slant on a subject is one way of looking at it, especially a biased one

slap slaps, slapping, slapped *verb* 1 If you slap someone, you hit them with the palm of your hand 2 If you slap something onto a surface, you put it there quickly and noisily ▷ *noun* 3 If you give someone a slap, you slap them

slash *verb* 1 If you slash something, you make a long, deep cut in it 2 (*informal*) To slash money means to reduce it greatly: *Car makers could be forced to slash prices* ▷ *noun* 3 a diagonal line that separates letters, words, or numbers, for example in the number 340/21/K

slate *noun* 1 Slate is a dark grey rock that splits easily into thin layers 2 Slates are small, flat pieces of slate used for covering roofs ▷ *verb* 3 (*informal*) If critics slate a play, film,

or book, they criticize it severely

slaughter *verb* 1 To slaughter a large number of people means to kill them unjustly or cruelly 2 To slaughter farm animals means to kill them for meat ▷ *noun* 3 Slaughter is the killing of many people

slave *noun* 1 someone who is owned by another person and must work for them ▷ *verb* 2 If you slave for someone, you work very hard for them > **slavery** *noun*

slay slays, slaying, slew, slain *verb* (*literary*) To slay someone means to kill them

sleazy sleazier, sleaziest *adjective* A sleazy place looks dirty, run-down, and not respectable

sled *or* **sledge** *noun* a vehicle on runners used for travelling over snow

sledgehammer *noun* a large, heavy hammer

sleek *adjective* 1 Sleek hair is smooth and shiny 2 Someone who is sleek looks rich and dresses elegantly

sleep sleeps, sleeping, slept *noun* 1 Sleep is the natural state of rest in which your eyes are closed and you are unconscious 2 If you have a sleep, you sleep for a while: *He'll be ready for a sleep soon* ▷ *verb* 3 When you sleep, you rest in a state of sleep ▷ *phrase* 4 If a sick or injured animal **is put to sleep**, it is painlessly killed

sleeper *noun* 1 You use 'sleeper' to say how deeply someone sleeps: *I'm a very heavy sleeper* 2 a bed on a train, or a train which has beds on it 3 Railway sleepers are the large beams that support the rails of a railway track

sleeping bag *noun* a large, warm bag for sleeping in, especially when you are camping

sleepover noun a gathering or party at which friends spend the night at another friend's house

sleepy sleepier, sleepiest adjective
1 tired and ready to go to sleep **2** A sleepy town or village is very quiet
> **sleepily** adverb > **sleepiness** noun

sleet noun Sleet is a mixture of rain and snow

sleeve noun The sleeves of a piece of clothing are the parts that cover your arms > **sleeveless** adjective

sleigh [slay] noun a sledge

slender adjective **1** attractively thin and graceful **2** small in amount or degree: the first slender hopes of peace

sleuth [slooth] noun (old-fashioned) a detective

slew 1 Slew is the past tense of **slay**
> verb **2** If a vehicle slews, it slides or skids: The bike slewed into the crowd

slice noun **1** A slice of cake, bread, or other food is a piece of it cut from a larger piece **2** a kitchen tool with a broad, flat blade: a fish slice **3** In sport, a slice is a stroke in which the player makes the ball go to one side, rather than straight ahead > verb **4** If you slice food, you cut it into thin pieces **5** To slice through something means to cut or move through it quickly, like a knife: The ship sliced through the water

slick adjective **1** A slick action is done quickly and smoothly: slick passing and strong running **2** A slick person speaks easily and persuasively but is not sincere: a slick TV presenter
> noun **3** An oil slick is a layer of oil floating on the surface of the sea or a lake

slide slides, sliding, slid verb **1** When something slides, it moves smoothly over or against something else > noun **2** a small piece of photographic film which can be projected onto a screen so that you can see the picture **3** a small piece of glass on which you put something that you want to examine through a microscope **4** In a playground, a slide is a structure with a steep, slippery slope for children to slide down

slight adjective **1** Slight means small in amount or degree: a slight dent **2** A slight person has a thin body
▷ phrase **3** Not in the slightest means not at all: This doesn't surprise me in the slightest ▷ verb **4** If you slight someone, you insult them by behaving rudely towards them
▷ noun **5** A slight is rude or insulting behaviour > **slightly** adverb

slim slimmer, slimmest; slims, slimming, slimmed adjective **1** A slim person is attractively thin **2** A slim object is thinner than usual: a slim book **3** If there is only a slim chance that something will happen, it is unlikely to happen ▷ verb **4** If you are slimming, you are trying to lose weight > **slimmer** noun

slime noun Slime is an unpleasant, thick, slippery substance

slimy slimier, slimiest adjective
1 covered in slime **2** Slimy people are friendly and pleasant in an insincere way: a slimy business partner

sling slings, slinging, slung verb
1 (informal) If you sling something somewhere, you throw it there **2** If you sling a rope between two points, you attach it so that it hangs loosely between them ▷ noun **3** a piece of cloth tied round a person's neck to support a broken or injured arm **4** a device made of ropes or cloth used for carrying things

slip slips, slipping, slipped verb **1** If you slip, you accidentally slide and lose your balance **2** If something slips, it slides out of place accidentally: *One of the knives slipped from her grasp* **3** If you slip somewhere, you go there quickly and quietly: *She slipped out of the house* **4** If you slip something somewhere, you put it there quickly and quietly **5** If something slips to a lower level or standard, it falls to that level or standard: *The shares slipped to an all-time low* ▷ *noun* **6** a small mistake **7** A slip of paper is a small piece of paper **8** a piece of clothing worn under a dress or skirt > **slip up** *verb* (*informal*) If you slip up, you make a mistake

slipper *noun* Slippers are loose, soft shoes that you wear indoors

slippery *adjective* **1** smooth, wet, or greasy, and difficult to hold or walk on **2** (*informal*) You describe a person as slippery when they cannot be trusted

slipstream *noun* The slipstream of a car or plane is the flow of air directly behind it

slit slits, slitting, slit *verb* **1** If you slit something, you make a long, narrow cut in it ▷ *noun* **2** a long, narrow cut or opening

slither *verb* To slither somewhere means to move there by sliding along the ground in an uneven way: *The snake slithered into the water*

sliver *noun* a small, thin piece of something

slob *noun* (*informal*) a lazy, untidy person

slog slogs, slogging, slogged *verb* (*informal*) **1** If you slog at something, you work hard and steadily at it: *They are still slogging away at algebra* **2** If you slog somewhere, you move along with difficulty: *people willing to slog round the streets delivering catalogues*

slogan *noun* a short, easily-remembered phrase used in advertising or by a political party

slop slops, slopping, slopped *verb* **1** If a liquid slops, it spills over the edge of a container in a messy way **2** (*in plural*) You can refer to dirty water or liquid waste as slops

slope *noun* **1** a flat surface that is at an angle, so that one end is higher than the other **2** The slope of something is the angle at which it slopes ▷ *verb* **3** If a surface slopes, it is at an angle **4** If something slopes, it leans to one side rather than being upright: *sloping handwriting*

sloppy sloppier, sloppiest *adjective* (*informal*) **1** very messy or careless: *two sloppy performances* **2** foolishly sentimental: *some sloppy love story* > **sloppily** *adverb* > **sloppiness** *noun*

slot slots, slotting, slotted *noun* **1** a narrow opening in a machine or container, for example for putting coins in ▷ *verb* **2** When you slot something into something else, you put it into a space where it fits

sloth [*rhymes with* **growth**] *noun* **1** (*formal*) Sloth is laziness **2** a South and Central American animal that moves very slowly and hangs upside down from the branches of trees

slouch *verb* If you slouch, you stand or sit with your shoulders and head drooping forwards

Slovak *adjective* **1** belonging or relating to Slovakia ▷ *noun* **2** someone who comes from Slovakia **3** Slovak is the language spoken in Slovakia

Slovene *adjective* **1** belonging or relating to Slovenia ▷ *noun* **2** someone who comes from Slovenia **3** Slovene is the language spoken in Slovenia

slow *adjective* **1** moving, happening,

or doing something with very little speed: *His progress was slow* **2** Someone who is slow is not very clever **3** If a clock or watch is slow, it shows a time earlier than the correct one ▷ **verb 4** If something slows, slows down, or slows up, it moves or happens more slowly > **slowness** noun

slowly adverb not quickly or hurriedly

slow motion noun Slow motion is movement which is much slower than normal, especially in a film: *It all seemed to happen in slow motion*

sludge noun Sludge is thick mud or sewage

slug noun **1 a** a small, slow-moving creature with a slimy body, like a snail without a shell **2** (*informal*) A slug of a strong alcoholic drink is a mouthful of it

sluggish adjective moving slowly and without energy: *the sluggish waters* ▷ **sluggishly** adverb

slum noun a poor, run-down area of a city

slumber (*literary*) noun **1** Slumber is sleep ▷ verb **2** When you slumber, you sleep

slump verb **1** If an amount or a value slumps, it falls suddenly by a large amount **2** If you slump somewhere, you fall or sit down heavily: *He slumped against the side of the car* ▷ noun **3** a sudden, severe drop in an amount or value: *the slump in house prices* **4** a time when there is economic decline and high unemployment

slur slurs, slurring, slurred noun **1** an insulting remark ▷ verb **2** When people slur their speech, they do not say their words clearly, often because they are drunk or ill

slush noun **1** Slush is wet melting snow **2** (*informal*) You can refer to sentimental love stories as slush ▷ **slushy** adjective

sly slyer or slier, slyest or sliest adjective **1** A sly expression or remark shows that you know something other people do not know: *a sly smile* **2** A sly person is cunning and good at deceiving people ▷ **slyly** adverb

smack verb **1** If you smack someone, you hit them with your open hand **2** If something smacks of something else, it reminds you of it: *His tale smacks of fantasy* ▷ noun **3** If you give someone a smack, you smack them **4** a loud, sharp noise: *He landed with a smack on the tank*

small adjective **1** Small means not large in size, number, or amount **2** Small means not important or significant: *small changes* ▷ noun **3** The small of your back is the narrow part where your back curves slightly inwards > **smallness** noun

smallpox noun Smallpox is a serious contagious disease that causes a fever and a rash

small talk noun Small talk is conversation about unimportant things

smart adjective **1** A smart person is clean and neatly dressed **2** Smart means clever: *a smart idea* **3** A smart movement is quick and sharp ▷ verb **4** If a wound smarts, it stings **5** If you are smarting from criticism or unkindness, you are feeling upset by it > **smartly** adverb > **smartness** noun

smarten verb If you smarten something up, you make it look neater and tidier

smartphone noun a mobile phone allowing access to the internet

smash verb **1** If you smash something, you break it into a lot of pieces by hitting it or dropping it **2** To smash through something such as a wall means to go through it by breaking it **3** To smash against something means to hit it with great force: *An immense wave smashed against the hull* ▷ *noun* **4** (*informal*) If a play or film is a smash or a smash hit, it is very successful **5** a car crash **6** In tennis, a smash is a stroke in which the player hits the ball downwards very hard

smashing *adjective* (*informal*) If you describe something as smashing, you mean you like it very much

smattering *noun* A smattering of knowledge or information is a very small amount of it: *a smattering of Russian*

smear *noun* **1** a dirty, greasy mark on a surface: *a smear of pink lipstick* **2** an untrue and malicious rumour ▷ *verb* **3** If something smears a surface, it makes dirty, greasy marks on it: *The blade was chipped and smeared* **4** If you smear a surface with a thick substance, you spread a layer of the substance over the surface

smell smells, smelling, smelled or smelt *noun* **1** The smell of something is a quality it has which you perceive through your nose: *a smell of damp wood* **2** Your sense of smell is your ability to smell things ▷ *verb* **3** If something smells, it has a quality you can perceive through your nose, especially an unpleasant quality **4** If you smell something, you become aware of it through your nose **5** If you can smell something such as danger or trouble, you feel it is present or likely to happen

smelly smellier, smelliest *adjective* having a strong, unpleasant smell

smelt *verb* To smelt a metal ore

means to heat it until it melts, so that the metal can be extracted

smile *verb* **1** When you smile, the corners of your mouth move outwards and slightly upwards because you are pleased or amused ▷ *noun* **2** the expression you have when you smile

smirk *verb* **1** When you smirk, you smile in a sneering or sarcastic way: *The boy smirked and turned the volume up* ▷ *noun* **2** a sneering or sarcastic smile

smith *noun* someone who makes things out of iron, gold, or another metal

smitten *adjective* If you are smitten with someone or something, you are very impressed with or enthusiastic about them: *They were totally smitten with each other*

smock *noun* a loose garment like a long blouse

smog *noun* Smog is a mixture of smoke and fog which occurs in some industrial cities

smoke *noun* **1** Smoke is a mixture of gas and small particles sent into the air when something burns ▷ *verb* **2** If something is smoking, smoke is coming from it **3** When someone smokes a cigarette or pipe, they suck smoke from it into their mouth and blow it out again **4** To smoke fish or meat means to hang it over burning wood so that the smoke preserves it and gives it a pleasant flavour: *smoked bacon* > **smoker** *noun* > **smoking** *noun, adjective*

smoky smokier, smokiest *adjective* A smoky place is full of smoke

smooth *adjective* **1** A smooth surface has no roughness and no holes in it **2** A smooth liquid or mixture has no lumps in it **3** A smooth movement or process happens evenly and steadily: *smooth acceleration* **4** Smooth also means successful and without problems: *staff responsible for the smooth running of the hall* ▷ verb **5** If you smooth something, you move your hands over it to make it smooth and flat > **smoothly** *adverb* > **smoothness** *noun*

smoothie *noun* a thick type of drink made in an electric blender from milk, fruit and crushed ice

smother *verb* **1** If you smother a fire, you cover it with something to put it out **2** To smother a person means to cover their face with something so that they cannot breathe **3** To smother someone also means to give them too much love and protection: *She loved her own children, almost smothering them with love* **4** If you smother an emotion, you control it so that people do not notice it: *They tried to smother their glee*

smothered *adjective* completely covered with something: *a spectacular trellis smothered in climbing roses*

smoulder *verb* **1** When something smoulders, it burns slowly, producing smoke but no flames **2** If a feeling is smouldering inside you, you feel it very strongly but do not show it: *smouldering with resentment*

smudge *noun* **1** a dirty or blurred mark or a smear on something ▷ verb **2** If you smudge something, you make it dirty or messy by touching it or marking it

smug smugger, smuggest *adjective* Someone who is smug is very pleased with how good or clever they are > **smugly** *adverb* > **smugness** *noun*

smuggle *verb* To smuggle things or people into or out of a place means to take them there illegally or secretly

smuggler *noun* someone who smuggles goods illegally into a country

snack *noun* a light, quick meal

snag snags, snagging, snagged *noun* **1** a small problem or disadvantage: *There is one snag: it is not true* **2** (*informal*) in Australian and New Zealand English, a sausage ▷ verb **3** If you snag your clothing, you damage it by catching it on something sharp

snail *noun* a small, slow-moving creature with a long, shiny body and a shell on its back

snake *noun* **1** a long, thin, scaly reptile with no legs ▷ verb **2** Something that snakes moves in long winding curves: *The queue snaked out of the shop*

snap snaps, snapping, snapped *verb* **1** If something snaps or if you snap it, it breaks with a sharp cracking noise **2** If you snap something into a particular position, you move it there quickly with a sharp sound **3** If an animal snaps at you, it shuts its jaws together quickly as if to bite you **4** If someone snaps at you, they speak in a sharp, unfriendly way **5** If you snap someone, you take a quick photograph of them ▷ noun **6** the sound of something snapping **7** (*informal*) a photograph taken quickly and casually ▷ adjective **8** A snap decision or action is taken suddenly without careful thought

snapper *noun* a fish with edible pink flesh, found in waters around Australia, New Zealand, and the US

snapshot *noun* a photograph taken quickly and casually

snare *noun* **1** a trap for catching birds

or small animals ▷ verb **2** To snare an animal or bird means to catch it using a snare

snarl verb **1** When an animal snarls, it bares its teeth and makes a fierce growling noise **2** If you snarl, you say something in a fierce, angry way ▷ noun **3** the noise an animal makes when it snarls

snatch verb **1** If you snatch something, you reach out for it quickly and take it **2** If you snatch an amount of time or an opportunity, you quickly make use of it ▷ noun **3** If you make a snatch at something, you reach out for it quickly to try to take it **4** A snatch of conversation or song is a very small piece of it

sneak verb **1** If you sneak somewhere, you go there quickly trying not to be seen or heard **2** If you sneak something somewhere, you take it there secretly ▷ noun **3** (informal) someone who tells people in authority that someone else has done something wrong

sneaker noun Sneakers are casual shoes with rubber soles

sneaking adjective If you have a sneaking feeling about something or someone, you have this feeling rather reluctantly: I had a sneaking suspicion that she was enjoying herself

sneaky sneakier, sneakiest adjective (informal) Someone who is sneaky does things secretly rather than openly

sneer verb **1** If you sneer at someone or something, you show by your expression and your comments that you think they are stupid or inferior ▷ noun **2** the expression on someone's face when they sneer

sneeze verb **1** When you sneeze, you suddenly take in breath and blow it

down your nose noisily, because something has irritated the inside of your nose ▷ noun **2** an act of sneezing

snide adjective A snide comment or remark criticizes someone in a nasty but indirect way

sniff verb **1** When you sniff, you breathe in air through your nose hard enough to make a sound **2** If you sniff something, you smell it by sniffing **3** You can say that a person sniffs at something when they do not think very much of it: Bessie sniffed at his household arrangements ▷ noun **4** the noise you make when you sniff **5** A sniff of something is a smell of it: a sniff at the flowers

snigger verb **1** If you snigger, you laugh in a quiet, disrespectful way: They were sniggering at her accent ▷ noun **2** a quiet, disrespectful laugh

snip snips, snipping, snipped verb **1** If you snip something, you cut it with scissors or shears in a single quick action ▷ noun **2** a small cut made by scissors or shears

snippet noun A snippet of something such as information or news is a small piece of it

snob noun **1** someone who admires upper-class people and looks down on lower-class people **2** someone who believes that they are better than other people > snobbery noun > snobbish adjective

snooker noun Snooker is a game played on a large table covered with smooth green cloth. Players score points by hitting different coloured balls into side pockets using a long stick called a cue

snoop verb (informal) Someone who is snooping is secretly looking round a place to find out things

snooze (informal) verb **1** If you

snooze, you sleep lightly for a short time, especially during the day ▷ noun **2** a short, light sleep

snore verb **1** When a sleeping person snores, they make a loud noise each time they breathe ▷ noun **2** the noise someone makes when they snore

snorkel noun a tube you can breathe through when you are swimming just under the surface of the sea > **snorkelling** noun

snort verb **1** When people or animals snort, they force breath out through their nose in a noisy way: Sarah snorted with laughter ▷ noun **2** the noise you make when you snort

snout noun An animal's snout is its nose

snow noun **1** Snow consists of flakes of ice crystals which fall from the sky in cold weather ▷ verb **2** When it snows, snow falls from the sky

snowball noun **1** a ball of snow for throwing ▷ verb **2** When something such as a project snowballs, it grows rapidly

snowman snowmen noun a large mound of snow moulded into the shape of a person

snub snubs, snubbing, snubbed verb **1** To snub someone means to behave rudely towards them, especially by making an insulting remark or ignoring them ▷ noun **2** an insulting remark or a piece of rude behaviour ▷ adjective **3** A snub nose is short and turned-up

snuff noun Snuff is powdered tobacco which people take by sniffing it up their noses

snug snugger, snuggest adjective A snug place is warm and comfortable. If you are snug, you are warm and comfortable > **snugly** adverb

snuggle verb If you snuggle somewhere, you cuddle up more closely to something or someone

so adverb **1** 'So' is used to refer back to what has just been mentioned: Had he locked the car? If so, where were the keys? **2** 'So' is used to mean also: He laughed, and so did Jarvis **3** 'So' can be used to mean 'therefore': It's a bit expensive, so I don't think I will get one **4** 'So' is used when you are talking about the degree or extent of something: Why are you so cruel? **5** 'So' is used before words like 'much' and 'many' to say that there is a definite limit to something: There are only so many questions that can be asked about the record ▷ phrase **6** So that and so as are used to introduce the reason for doing something: to die so that you might live

soak verb **1** To soak something or leave it to soak means to put it in a liquid and leave it there **2** When a liquid soaks something, it makes it very wet **3** When something soaks up a liquid, the liquid is drawn up into it

soaked adjective extremely wet

soaking adjective If something is soaking, it is very wet

soap noun Soap is a substance made of natural oils and fats and used for washing yourself > **soapy** adjective

soap opera noun a popular television drama serial about people's daily lives

soar verb **1** If an amount soars, it quickly increases by a great deal: Property prices soared **2** If something soars into the air, it quickly goes up into the air > **soaring** adjective

sob sobs, sobbing, sobbed verb **1** When someone sobs, they cry in a noisy way, breathing in short breaths ▷ noun **2** the noise made when you cry

sober adjective **1** If someone is sober, they are not drunk **2** Sober also means serious and thoughtful **3** Sober colours are plain and rather dull > **soberly** adverb > **sober up** verb To sober up means to become sober after being drunk

sobering adjective Something which is sobering makes you serious and thoughtful: *the sobering lesson of the last year*

so-called adjective You use 'so-called' to say that the name by which something is called is incorrect or misleading: *so-called environmentally-friendly products*

soccer noun Soccer is a game played by two teams of eleven players who try to kick or head a ball into the opposing team's net

sociable adjective Sociable people are friendly and enjoy talking to other people > **sociability** noun

social adjective **1** to do with society or life within a society: *women from similar social backgrounds* **2** to do with leisure activities that involve meeting other people > **socially** adverb

socialism noun Socialism is the political belief that the state should own industries on behalf of the people and that everyone should be equal > **socialist** adjective, noun

socialize or **socialise** verb When people socialize, they meet other people socially, for example at parties

social security noun Social security is a system by which the government pays money regularly to people who have no other income or only a very small income

social work noun Social work involves giving help and advice to people with serious financial or family problems > **social worker** noun

society noun **1** Society is the people in a particular country or region: *a major problem in society* **2** an organization for people who have the same interest or aim: *the school debating society* **3** Society is also rich, upper-class, fashionable people

sociology noun Sociology is the study of human societies and the relationships between groups in these societies > **sociological** adjective > **sociologist** noun

sock noun Socks are pieces of clothing covering your foot and ankle

socket noun **1** a place on a wall or on a piece of electrical equipment into which you can put a plug or bulb **2** Any hollow part or opening into which another part fits can be called a socket: *eye sockets*

sod noun (literary) The sod is the surface of the ground, together with the grass and roots growing in it

soda noun **1** Soda is the same as **soda water 2** Soda is also sodium in the form of crystals or a powder, and is used for baking or cleaning

soda water noun Soda water is fizzy water used for mixing with other drinks

sodden adjective soaking wet

sodium noun [SCIENCE] Sodium is a silvery-white chemical element which combines with other chemicals. Salt is a sodium compound. Sodium's atomic number is 11 and its symbol is Na

sofa noun a long comfortable seat with a back and arms for two or three people

soft *adjective* **1** Something soft is not hard, stiff, or firm **2** Soft also means very gentle: *a soft breeze* **3** A soft sound or voice is quiet and not harsh **4** A soft colour or light is not bright > **softly** *adverb*

soft drink *noun* any cold, nonalcoholic drink

soften *verb* **1** If something is softened or softens, it becomes less hard, stiff, or firm **2** If you soften, you become more sympathetic and less critical: *Phillida softened as she spoke*

software *noun* COMPUTING Computer programs are known as software

soggy soggier, soggiest *adjective* unpleasantly wet or full of water

soil *noun* **1** Soil is the top layer on the surface of the earth in which plants grow > *verb* **2** If you soil something, you make it dirty > **soiled** *adjective*

solace [sol-iss] *noun* (*literary*) Solace is something that makes you feel less sad: *I found solace in writing*

solar *adjective* SCIENCE **1** relating or belonging to the sun **2** using the sun's light and heat as a source of energy: *a solar-powered calculator*

solar system *noun* The solar system is the sun and all the planets, comets, and asteroids that orbit round it

soldier *noun* a person in an army

sole soles, soling, soled *adjective* **1** The sole thing or person of a particular type is the only one of that type > *noun* **2** The sole of your foot or shoe is the underneath part **3** a flat seawater fish which you can eat > *verb* **4** When a shoe is soled, a sole is fitted to it

solely *adverb* If something involves solely one thing, it involves that thing and nothing else

solemn *adjective* Solemn means serious rather than cheerful or humorous > **solemnly** *adverb* > **solemnity** *noun*

solicitor *noun* a lawyer who gives legal advice and prepares legal documents and cases

solid *adjective* **1** A solid substance or object is hard or firm, and not in the form of a liquid or gas **2** You say that something is solid when it is not hollow: *solid steel* **3** You say that a structure is solid when it is strong and not likely to fall down: *solid fences* **4** You use 'solid' to say that something happens for a period of time without interruption: *I cried for two solid days* > *noun* **5** a solid substance or object > **solidly** *adverb*

solidarity *noun* If a group of people show solidarity, they show unity and support for each other

soliloquy soliloquies [sol-**lill**-ok-wee] *noun* ENGLISH a speech in a play made by a character who is alone on the stage

solitary *adjective* **1** A solitary activity is one that you do on your own **2** A solitary person or animal spends a lot of time alone **3** If there is a solitary person or object somewhere, there is only one

solitary confinement *noun* A prisoner in solitary confinement is being kept alone in a prison cell

solitude *noun* Solitude is the state of being alone

solo solos *noun* **1** a piece of music played or sung by one person alone > *adjective* **2** A solo performance or activity is done by one person alone: *my first solo flight* > *adverb* **3** Solo means alone: *to sail solo around the world*

soloist *noun* a person who performs a solo

solstice noun one of the two times in the year when the sun is at its furthest point south or north of the equator

soluble adjective SCIENCE A soluble substance is able to dissolve in a liquid

solution noun 1 a way of dealing with a problem or difficult situation: *a quick solution to our problem* 2 The solution to a riddle or a puzzle is the answer 3 SCIENCE a liquid in which a solid substance has been dissolved

solve verb if you solve a problem or a question, you find a solution or answer to it

solvent adjective 1 If a person or company is solvent, they have enough money to pay all their debts ▷ noun 2 a liquid that can dissolve other substances > **solvency** noun

Somali Somalis adjective 1 belonging or relating to Somalia ▷ noun 2 The Somalis are a group of people who live in Somalia 3 Somali is the language spoken by Somalis

sombre adjective 1 Sombre colours are dark and dull 2 A sombre person is serious, sad, or gloomy

some 1 You use 'some' to refer to a quantity or number when you are not stating the quantity or number exactly: *There's some money on the table* 2 You use 'some' to emphasize that a quantity or number is fairly large: *She had been there for some days* ▷ adverb 3 You use 'some' in front of a number to show that it is not exact: *a fishing village some seven miles north*

somebody pronoun Somebody means someone

some day adverb Some day means at a date in the future that is unknown or that has not yet been decided

somehow adverb 1 You use 'somehow' to say that you do not know how something was done or will be done: *You'll find a way of doing it somehow* 2 You use 'somehow' to say that you do not know the reason for something: *Somehow it didn't feel quite right*

someone pronoun You use 'someone' to refer to a person without saying exactly who you mean

somersault noun a forwards or backwards roll in which the head is placed on the ground and the body is brought over it

something pronoun You use 'something' to refer to anything that is not a person without saying exactly what you mean

sometime adverb 1 at a time in the future or the past that is unknown or that has not yet been fixed: *He has to find out sometime* ▷ adjective 2 (formal) 'Sometime' is used to say that a person had a particular job or role in the past: *a sometime actress, dancer and singer*

sometimes adverb occasionally, rather than always or never

somewhat adverb to some extent or degree: *The future seemed somewhat bleak*

somewhere adverb 1 'Somewhere' is used to refer to a place without stating exactly where it is: *There has to be a file somewhere* 2 'Somewhere' is used when giving an approximate amount, number, or time: *somewhere between the winter of 1989 and the summer of 1991*

son noun Someone's son is their male child

sonar noun Sonar is equipment on a ship which calculates the depth of the sea or the position of an underwater object using sound waves

sonata noun MUSIC a piece of classical music, usually in three or more movements, for piano or for another instrument with or without piano

song noun a piece of music with words that are sung to the music

songbird noun a bird that produces musical sounds like singing

son-in-law sons-in-law noun Someone's son-in-law is the husband of their grown-up child

sonnet noun ENGLISH a poem with 14 lines, in which lines rhyme according to fixed patterns

soon adverb If something is going to happen soon, it will happen in a very short time

soot noun Soot is black powder which rises in the smoke from a fire > **sooty** adjective

soothe verb 1 If you soothe someone who is angry or upset, you make them calmer 2 Something that soothes pain makes the pain less severe > **soothing** adjective

sophisticated adjective 1 Sophisticated people have refined or cultured tastes or habits 2 A sophisticated machine or device is made using advanced and complicated methods > **sophistication** noun

soppy soppier, soppiest adjective (informal) silly or foolishly sentimental

soprano sopranos noun MUSIC a woman, girl, or boy with a singing voice in the highest range of musical notes

sorcerer [sor-ser-er] noun a person who performs magic by using the power of evil spirits

sorcery noun Sorcery is magic that uses the power of evil spirits

sordid adjective 1 dishonest or

immoral: a rather sordid business 2 dirty, unpleasant, or depressing: the sordid guest house

sore adjective 1 If part of your body is sore, it causes you pain and discomfort 2 (literary) 'Sore' is used to emphasize something: The President is in sore need of friends ▷ noun 3 a painful place where your skin has become infected > **sorely** adverb > **soreness** noun

sorghum [saw-gum] noun a type of tropical grass that is grown for hay, grain, and syrup

sorrow noun 1 Sorrow is deep sadness or regret 2 Sorrows are things that cause sorrow: the sorrows of this world

sorry sorrier, sorriest adjective 1 If you are sorry about something, you feel sadness or regret about it 2 feeling sympathy for someone 3 'Sorry' is used to describe people and things that are in a bad physical or mental state: She was in a pretty sorry state when we found her

sort noun 1 The different sorts of something are the different types of it ▷ verb 2 To sort things means to arrange them into different groups or sorts > **sort out** verb If you sort out a problem or misunderstanding, you deal with it and find a solution to it

SOS noun An SOS is a signal that you are in danger and need help

so-so adjective (informal) neither good nor bad: The food is so-so

soufflé [soo-flay] or **souffle** noun a light, fluffy food made from beaten egg whites and other ingredients that is baked in the oven

sought the past tense and past participle of **seek**

soul noun 1 A person's soul is the spiritual part of them that is supposed to continue after their body is dead **2** People also use 'soul' to refer to a person's mind, character, thoughts, and feelings **3** 'Soul' can be used to mean person: *There was not a soul there* **4** Soul is a type of pop music

sound noun **1** [SCIENCE] Sound is everything that can be heard. It is caused by vibrations travelling through air or water to your ear **2** A particular sound is something that you hear **3** The sound of someone or something is the impression you have of them through what other people have told you: *I like the sound of your father's grandfather* ▷ verb **4** If something sounds or if you sound it, it makes a noise **5** To sound something deep, such as a well or the sea, means to measure how deep it is using a weighted line or sonar ▷ adjective **6** in good condition: *a guarantee that a house is sound* **7** reliable and sensible: *The logic behind the argument seems sound* > **soundly** adverb

soundtrack noun The soundtrack of a film is the part you hear, especially the music

soup noun Soup is liquid food made by cooking meat, fish, or vegetables in water

sour adjective **1** If something is sour, it has a sharp, acid taste **2** Sour milk has an unpleasant taste because it is no longer fresh **3** A sour person is bad-tempered and unfriendly ▷ verb **4** If a friendship, situation, or attitude sours or if something sours it, it becomes less friendly, enjoyable, or hopeful

source noun **1** The source of something is the person, place, or thing that it comes from: *the source of his confidence* **2** A source is a person or book that provides information for a news story or for research **3** The source of a river or stream is the place where it begins

> **WORD TIP**
> Do not confuse the spellings of *source* and *sauce*, which can sound very similar in some accents

sour grapes plural noun You describe someone's behaviour as sour grapes when they say something is worthless but secretly want it and cannot have it

south noun **1** The south is the direction to your right when you are looking towards the place where the sun rises **2** The south of a place or country is the part which is towards the south when you are in the centre ▷ adverb, adjective **3** South means towards the south: *The taxi headed south; the south end of the site* ▷ adjective **4** A south wind blows from the south

South America noun South America is the fourth largest continent. It has the Pacific Ocean on its west side, the Atlantic on the east, and the Antarctic to the south. South America is joined to North America by the Isthmus of Panama > **South American** adjective

south-east noun, adverb, adjective South-east is halfway between south and east

south-eastern adjective in or from the south-east

southerly adjective **1** Southerly means to or towards the south **2** A southerly wind blows from the south

southern adjective in or from the south

Southern Cross noun The Southern Cross is a small group of stars which can be seen from the southern part of the earth, and which is represented on the national flags of Australia and New Zealand

South Pole noun GEOGRAPHY The South Pole is the place on the surface of the earth that is farthest towards the south

southward or **southwards** adverb
1 Southward or southwards means towards the south: *the dusty road which led southwards* ▷ adjective
2 The southward part of something is the south part

south-west noun, adverb, adjective South-west is halfway between south and west

south-western adjective in or from the south-west

souvenir noun something you keep to remind you of a holiday, place, or event

sovereign [sov-rin] noun **1** a king, queen, or royal ruler of a country
2 In the past, a sovereign was a British gold coin worth one pound ▷ adjective **3** A sovereign state or country is independent and not under the authority of any other country

sovereignty [sov-rin-tee] noun Sovereignty is the political power that a country has to govern itself

Soviet [soh-vee-et] adjective
1 belonging or relating to the country that used to be the Soviet Union ▷ noun **2** The people and the government of the country that used to be the Soviet Union were sometimes referred to as the Soviets

sow sows, sowing, sowed, sown [soh] verb **1** To sow seeds or sow an area of land with seeds means to plant them in the ground **2** To sow undesirable feelings or attitudes means to cause them: *You have sown discontent*

sow [rhymes with *now*] noun an adult female pig

soya noun Soya flour, margarine, oil, and milk are made from soya beans

spa noun a place where water containing minerals bubbles out of the ground, at which people drink or bathe in the water to improve their health

space noun **1** Space is the area that is empty or available in a place, building, or container **2** Space is the area beyond the earth's atmosphere surrounding the stars and planets
3 a gap between two things: *the space between the tables* **4** Space can also refer to a period of time: *two incidents in the space of a week* ▷ verb
5 If you space a series of things, you arrange them with gaps between them

spacecraft noun a rocket or other vehicle that can travel in space

spaceship noun a spacecraft that carries people through space

space shuttle noun a spacecraft designed to be used many times for travelling out into space and back again

spacious adjective having or providing a lot of space: *the spacious living room*

spade noun **1** a tool with a flat metal blade and a long handle used for digging **2** Spades is one of the four suits in a pack of playing cards. It is marked by a black symbol like a heart-shaped leaf with a stem

spaghetti [spag-get-ee] noun Spaghetti consists of long, thin pieces of pasta

spam noun unwanted e-mails, usually containing advertising

span spans, spanning, spanned noun
1 the period of time during which something exists or functions:

looking back today over a span of 40 years **2** The span of something is the total length of it from one end to the other ▷ *verb* **3** If something spans a particular length of time, it lasts throughout that time: *a career that spanned 50 years* **4** A bridge that spans something stretches right across it

Spaniard [span-yard] *noun* someone who comes from Spain

spaniel *noun* a dog with long drooping ears and a silky coat

Spanish *adjective* **1** belonging or relating to Spain ▷ *noun* **2** Spanish is the main language spoken in Spain, and is also spoken by many people in Central and South America

spanner *noun* a tool with a specially shaped end that fits round a nut to turn it

spar spars, sparring, sparred *verb* **1** When boxers spar, they hit each other with light punches for practice **2** To spar with someone also means to argue with them, but not in an unpleasant or serious way ▷ *noun* **3** a strong pole that a sail is attached to on a yacht or ship

spare *adjective* **1** extra to what is needed: *What does she do in her spare time?* ▷ *noun* **2** a thing that is extra to what is needed ▷ *verb* **3** If you spare something for a particular purpose, you make it available: *Few troops could be spared to go abroad* **4** If someone is spared an unpleasant experience, they are prevented from suffering it: *The capital was spared the misery of an all-out train strike*

sparing *adjective* If you are sparing with something, you use it in very small quantities > **sparingly** *adverb*

spark *noun* **1** a tiny, bright piece of burning material thrown up by a fire **2** a small flash of light caused by

electricity **3** A spark of feeling is a small amount of it: *that tiny spark of excitement* ▷ *verb* **4** If something sparks, it throws out sparks **5** If one thing sparks another thing off, it causes the second thing to start happening: *The tragedy sparked off a wave of sympathy among staff*

sparkle *verb* **1** If something sparkles, it shines with a lot of small, bright points of light ▷ *noun* **2** Sparkles are small, bright points of light > **sparkling** *adjective*

sparrow *noun* a common, small bird with brown and grey feathers

sparse *adjective* small in number or amount and spread out over an area: *the sparse audience* > **sparsely** *adverb*

spartan *adjective* A spartan way of life is very simple with no luxuries: *spartan accommodation*

spasm *noun* **1** a sudden tightening of the muscles **2** a sudden, short burst of something: *a spasm of fear*

spate *noun* A spate of things is a large number of them that happen or appear in a rush: *a recent spate of first novels from older writers*

spatial [spay-shl] *adjective* to do with size, area, or position

spawn *noun* **1** Spawn is a jelly-like substance containing the eggs of fish or amphibians ▷ *verb* **2** When fish or amphibians spawn, they lay their eggs **3** If something spawns something else, it causes it: *The depressed economy spawned the riots*

speak speaks, speaking, spoke, spoken *verb* **1** When you speak, you use your voice to say words **2** If you speak a foreign language, you know it and can use it **> speak out** *verb* To speak out about something means to publicly state an opinion about it

speaker *noun* **1** a person who is

speaking, especially someone making a speech **2** A speaker on a device that reproduces sound is a loudspeaker

spear noun **1** a weapon consisting of a long pole with a sharp point ▷ verb **2** To spear something means to push or throw a spear or other pointed object into it

spearhead verb If someone spearheads a campaign, they lead it

spec phrase If you do something **on spec**, you do it hoping for a result but without any certainty: He turned up at the same event on spec

special adjective **1** Something special is more important or better than other things of its kind **2** Special describes someone who is officially appointed, or something that is needed for a particular purpose: Karen actually had to get special permission to go there **3** Special also describes something that belongs or relates to only one particular person, group, or place: the special needs of the chronically sick

specialist noun **1** someone who has a particular skill or who knows a lot about a particular subject: a skin specialist ▷ adjective **2** having a skill or knowing a lot about a particular subject: a specialist teacher > **specialism** noun

speciality specialities noun A person's speciality is something they are especially good at or know a lot about: Roses are her speciality

specialize or **specialise** verb If you specialize in something, you make it your speciality: a shop specializing in ceramics > **specialization** noun

specialized or **specialised** adjective developed for a particular purpose or trained in a particular area of knowledge: a specialized sales team

specially adverb If something has been done specially for a particular person or purpose, it has been done only for that person or purpose

species [spee-sheez] noun SCIENCE A division of plants or animals whose members have the same characteristics and are able to breed with each other

specific adjective **1** particular: specific areas of difficulty **2** precise and exact: She will ask for specific answers > **specifically** adverb

specification noun D & T a detailed description of what is needed for something, such as the necessary features in the design of something: I like to build it to my own specifications

specify specifies, specifying, specified verb To specify something means to state or describe it precisely: In his will he specified that these documents were never to be removed

specimen noun A specimen of something is an example or small amount of it which gives an idea of what the whole is like: a specimen of your writing

speck noun A very small stain or amount of something

speckled adjective Something that is speckled is covered in very small marks or spots

spectacle noun **1** a strange or interesting sight or scene: an astonishing spectacle **2** a grand and impressive event or performance

spectacular adjective **1** Something spectacular is very impressive or dramatic ▷ noun **2** a grand and impressive show or performance

spectator noun a person who is watching something

spectre noun **1** a frightening idea or image: the spectre of war **2** a ghost

s

spectrum spectra or spectrums noun **1** ART The spectrum is the range of different colours produced when light passes through a prism or a drop of water. A rainbow shows the colours in a spectrum **2** A spectrum of opinions or emotions is a range of them

speculate verb If you speculate about something, you think about it and form opinions about it > **speculation** noun

speculative adjective **1** A speculative piece of information is based on guesses and opinions rather than known facts **2** Someone with a speculative expression seems to be trying to guess something: His mother regarded him with a speculative eye

speech noun **1** Speech is the ability to speak or the act of speaking **2** a formal talk given to an audience **3** In a play, a speech is a group of lines spoken by one of the characters

speechless adjective Someone who is speechless is unable to speak for a short time because something has shocked them

speed speeds, speeding, sped or speeded noun **1** The speed of something is the rate at which it moves or happens ▷ verb **3** If you speed somewhere, you move or travel there quickly **4** Someone who is speeding is driving a vehicle faster than the legal speed limit

speedboat noun a small, fast motorboat

speed limit noun The speed limit is the maximum speed at which vehicles are legally allowed to drive on a particular road

speedway noun Speedway is the sport of racing lightweight

motorcycles on special tracks

speedy speedier, speediest adjective done very quickly > **speedily** adverb

spell spells, spelling, spelt or spelled verb **1** When you spell a word, you name or write its letters in order **2** When letters spell a word, they form that word when put together in a particular order **3** If something spells a particular result, it suggests that this will be the result: This haphazard method could spell disaster for you ▷ noun **4** A spell of something is a short period of time: a spell of rough weather **5** a word or sequence of words used to perform magic > **spell out** verb If you spell something out, you explain it in detail: I don't have to spell it out, do I?

spellbound adjective so fascinated by something that you cannot think about anything else: She had sat spellbound through the film

spelling noun The spelling of a word is the correct order of letters in it

spend spends, spending, spent verb **1** When you spend money, you buy things with it **2** To spend time or energy means to use it

spent adjective **1** Spent describes things which have been used and therefore cannot be used again: spent matches **2** If you are spent, you are exhausted and have no energy left

sperm noun a cell produced in the reproductive organ of a male animal which can enter a female animal's egg and fertilize it

spew verb **1** When things spew from something or when it spews them out, they come out of it in large quantities **2** (informal) To spew means to vomit

sphere noun **1** a perfectly round object, such as a ball **2** An area of

S

activity or interest can be referred to as a sphere of activity or interest
> **spherical** adjective

spice noun **1** Spice is powder or seeds from a plant added to food to give it flavour **2** Spice is something which makes life more exciting: *Variety is the spice of life* ▷ verb **3** To spice food means to add spice to it **4** If you spice something up, you make it more exciting or lively

spicy spicier, spiciest adjective strongly flavoured with spices

spider noun a small insect-like creature with eight legs that spins webs to catch insects for food

spike noun **1** a long pointed piece of metal **2** The spikes on a sports shoe are the pointed pieces of metal attached to the sole **3** Some other long pointed objects are called spikes: *beautiful pink flower spikes*

spiky spikier, spikiest adjective Something spiky has sharp points

spill spills, spilling, spilled or spilt verb **1** If you spill something or if it spills, it accidentally falls or runs out of a container **2** If people or things spill out of a place, they come out of it in large numbers

spillage noun the spilling of something, or something that has been spilt: *the oil spillage in the Shetlands*

spin spins, spinning, spun verb **1** If something spins, it turns quickly around a central point **2** When spiders spin a web, they give out a sticky substance and make it into a web **3** When people spin, they make thread by twisting together pieces of fibre using a machine **4** If your head is spinning, you feel dizzy or confused ▷ noun **5** a rapid turn around a central point: *a golf club which puts more spin on the ball*

> **spin out** verb If you spin something out, you make it last longer than it otherwise would

spinach [spin-itch] noun Spinach is a vegetable with large green leaves

spinal adjective to do with the spine

spine noun **1** Your spine is your backbone **2** Spines are long, sharp points on an animal's body or on a plant

spin-off noun something useful that unexpectedly results from an activity

spinster noun (old-fashioned) a woman who has never married

spiral spirals, spiralling, spiralled noun **1** a continuous curve which winds round and round, with each curve above or outside the previous one ▷ adjective **2** in the shape of a spiral: *a spiral staircase* ▷ verb **3** If something spirals, it moves up or down in a spiral curve: *The aircraft spiralled down* **4** If an amount or level spirals, it rises or falls quickly at an increasing rate: *Prices have spiralled recently*

spire noun The spire of a church is the tall cone-shaped structure on top

spirit noun **1** Your spirit is the part of you that is not physical and that is connected with your deepest thoughts and feelings **2** RE The spirit of a dead person is a nonphysical part that is believed to remain alive after death **3** a supernatural being, such as a ghost **4** Spirit is liveliness, energy, and self-confidence: *a band full of spirit* **5** Spirit can refer to an attitude: *his old fighting spirit* **6** (in plural) Spirits can describe how happy or unhappy someone is: *in good spirits* **7** Spirits are strong alcoholic drinks such as whisky and gin ▷ verb **8** If you spirit someone or something into or out of a place, you get them in or out quickly and secretly

spirited *adjective* showing energy and courage

spiritual *adjective* RE **1** to do with people's thoughts and beliefs, rather than their bodies and physical surroundings **2** to do with people's religious beliefs: *spiritual guidance* ▷ *noun* **3** a religious song originally sung by Black slaves in America > **spiritually** *adverb* > **spirituality** *noun*

spit spits, spitting, spat *noun* **1** Spit is saliva **2** a long stick made of metal or wood which is pushed through a piece of meat so that it can be hung over a fire and cooked **3** a long, flat, narrow piece of land sticking out into the sea ▷ *verb* **4** If you spit, you force saliva or some other substance out of your mouth **5** (*informal*) When it is spitting, it is raining very lightly

spite *phrase* **1** If you do something **in spite of** something else, you do the first thing even though the second thing makes it unpleasant or difficult: *In spite of all the gossip, Virginia stayed behind* ▷ *verb* **2** If you do something to spite someone, you do it deliberately to hurt or annoy them ▷ *noun* **3** If you do something out of spite, you do it to hurt or annoy someone

spiteful *adjective* A spiteful person does or says nasty things to people deliberately to hurt them

splash *verb* **1** If you splash around in water, your movements disturb the water in a noisy way **2** If liquid splashes something, it scatters over it in a lot of small drops ▷ *noun* **3** A splash is the sound made when something hits or falls into water **4** A splash of liquid is a small quantity of it that has been spilt on

something > **splash out** *verb* To splash out on something means to spend a lot of money on it

splatter *verb* When something is splattered with a substance, the substance is splashed all over it: *fur coats splattered with paint*

spleen *noun* Your spleen is an organ near your stomach which controls the quality of your blood

splendid *adjective* **1** very good indeed: *a splendid career* **2** beautiful and impressive: *a splendid old mansion* > **splendidly** *adverb*

splendour *noun* **1** If something has splendour, it is beautiful and impressive **2** (*in plural*) The splendours of something are its beautiful and impressive features

splint *noun* a long piece of wood or metal fastened to a broken limb to hold it in place

splinter *noun* **1** a thin, sharp piece of wood or glass which has broken off a larger piece ▷ *verb* **2** If something splinters, it breaks into thin, sharp pieces

split splits, splitting, split *verb* **1** If something splits or if you split it, it divides into two or more parts **2** If something such as wood or fabric splits, a long crack or tear appears in it **3** If people split something, they share it between them ▷ *noun* **4** A split in a piece of wood or fabric is a crack or tear **5** A split between two things is a division or difference between them: *the split between rugby league and rugby union* > **split up** *verb* If two people split up, they end their relationship or marriage

split second *noun* an extremely short period of time

splitting *adjective* A splitting headache is a very painful headache

splutter verb **1** If someone splutters, they speak in a confused way because they are embarrassed **2** If something splutters, it makes a series of short, sharp sounds

spoil spoils, spoiling, spoiled or spoilt verb **1** If you spoil something, you prevent it from being successful or satisfactory **2** To spoil children means to give them everything they want, with harmful effects on their character **3** To spoil someone also means to give them something nice as a treat

spoke noun The spokes of a wheel are the bars which connect the hub to the rim

spokesperson noun someone who speaks on behalf of another person or a group > **spokesman** noun > **spokeswoman** noun

sponge noun **1** a sea creature with a body made up of many cells **2** part of the very light skeleton of a sponge, used for bathing and cleaning **3** A sponge or sponge cake is a very light cake ▷ verb **4** If you sponge something, you clean it by wiping it with a wet sponge

sponsor verb **1** To sponsor something, such as an event or someone's training, means to support it financially: *The visit was sponsored by the London Natural History Society* **2** If you sponsor someone who is doing something for charity, you agree to give them a sum of money for the charity if they manage to do it **3** If you sponsor a proposal or suggestion, you officially put it forward and support it: *the MP who sponsored the Bill* ▷ noun **4** a person or organization sponsoring something or someone > **sponsorship** noun

spontaneous adjective **1** Spontaneous acts are not planned or arranged in advance **2** A spontaneous event happens because of processes within something rather than being caused by things outside it: *spontaneous bleeding* > **spontaneously** adverb > **spontaneity** noun

spoof noun something such as an article or television programme that seems to be about a serious matter but is actually a joke

spooky spookier, spookiest adjective eerie and frightening

spool noun a cylindrical object onto which thread, tape, or film can be wound

spoon noun an object shaped like a small shallow bowl with a long handle, used for eating, stirring, and serving food

spoonful spoonfuls or spoonsful noun the amount held by a spoon

sporadic adjective happening at irregular intervals: *a few sporadic attempts at keeping a diary* > **sporadically** adverb

spore noun [SCIENCE] Spores are cells produced by bacteria and nonflowering plants such as fungi which develop into new bacteria or plants

sport noun **1** Sports are games and other enjoyable activities which need physical effort and skill **2** (informal) You say that someone is a sport when they accept defeat or teasing cheerfully: *Be a sport, Minister!* ▷ verb **3** If you sport something noticeable or unusual, you wear it: *A German boy sported a ponytail*

sporting adjective **1** relating to sport **2** behaving in a fair and decent way

s

sports car noun a low, fast car, usually with room for only two people

sportsman sportsmen noun a man who takes part in sports and is good at them

sportsmanship noun Sportsmanship is the behaviour and attitudes of a good sportsman, for example fairness, generosity, and cheerfulness when losing

sportswoman sportswomen noun a woman who takes part in sports and is good at them

sporty sportier, sportiest adjective 1 A sporty car is fast and flashy 2 A sporty person is good at sports

spot spots, spotting, spotted noun 1 Spots are small, round, coloured areas on a surface 2 Spots on a person's skin are small lumps, usually caused by an infection or allergy 3 A spot of something is a small amount of it: *spots of rain* 4 A place can be called a spot: *the most beautiful spot in the garden* ▷ verb 5 If you spot something, you notice it ▷ phrase 6 If you do something **on the spot**, you do it immediately

spotless adjective perfectly clean > **spotlessly** adverb

spotlight spotlights, spotlighting, spotlit or spotlighted noun 1 DRAMA a powerful light which can be directed to light up a small area ▷ verb 2 If something spotlights a situation or problem, it draws the public's attention to it: *a national campaign to spotlight the problem*

spot-on adjective (informal) exactly correct or accurate

spotted adjective Something spotted has a pattern of spots on it

spotter noun a person whose hobby is looking out for things of a particular kind: *a train spotter*

spotty spottier, spottiest adjective Someone who is spotty has spots or pimples on their skin, especially on their face

spouse noun Someone's spouse is the person they are married to

spout verb 1 When liquid or flame spouts out of something, it shoots out in a long stream 2 When someone spouts what they have learned, they say it in a boring way ▷ noun 3 a tube with a lip-like end for pouring liquid: *a teapot with a long spout*

sprain verb 1 If you sprain a joint, you accidentally damage it by twisting it violently ▷ noun 2 the injury caused by spraining a joint

sprawl verb 1 If you sprawl somewhere, you sit or lie there with your legs and arms spread out 2 A place that sprawls is spread over a large area: *a Monday market which sprawls all over town* ▷ noun 3 anything that spreads in an untidy and uncontrolled way: *a sprawl of skyscrapers* > **sprawling** adjective

spray noun 1 Spray consists of many drops of liquid splashed or forced into the air: *A spray of water shot upwards from the fountain* 2 Spray is also a liquid kept under pressure in a can or other container: *hair spray* 3 a piece of equipment for spraying liquid: *a garden spray* 4 A spray of flowers or leaves consists of several of them on one stem ▷ verb 5 To spray a liquid over something means to cover it with drops of the liquid

spread spreads, spreading, spread verb 1 If you spread something out, you open it out or arrange it so that it can be seen or used easily: *He spread the map out on his knees* 2 If you spread a substance on a surface, you put a thin layer on the surface **3** If something spreads, it gradually reaches or affects more people: *The news spread quickly* **4** If something spreads over a period of time, it happens regularly or continuously over that time: *His four international appearances were spread over eight years* **5** If something such as work is spread, it is distributed evenly ▷ *noun* **6** The spread of something is the extent to which it gradually reaches or affects more people: *the spread of Buddhism* **7** A spread of ideas, interests, or other things is a wide variety of them **8** soft food put on bread: *cheese spread*

spreadsheet *noun* COMPUTING a computer program that is used for entering and arranging figures, used mainly for financial planning

spree *noun* a period of time spent doing something enjoyable: *a shopping spree*

sprig *noun* **1** a small twig with leaves on it **2** In Australian and New Zealand English, sprigs are studs on the sole of a football boot

sprightly sprightlier, sprightliest *adjective* lively and active

spring springing, sprang, sprung *noun* **1** Spring is the season between winter and summer **2** a coil of wire which returns to its natural shape after being pressed or pulled **3** a place where water comes up through the ground **4** an act of springing: *With a spring he had opened the door* ▷ *verb* **5** To spring means to jump upwards or forwards: *Martha sprang to her feet* **6** If something springs in a particular direction, it moves suddenly and quickly: *The door sprang open* **7** If one thing springs from another, it is the result of it: *The failures sprang from three facts*

springboard *noun* **1** a flexible board on which a diver or gymnast jumps to gain height **2** If something is a springboard for an activity or enterprise, it makes it possible for it to begin

springbok *noun* **1** a small South African antelope which moves in leaps **2** A Springbok is a person who has represented South Africa in a sports team

spring onion *noun* a small onion with long green shoots, often eaten raw in salads

sprinkle *verb* If you sprinkle a liquid or powder over something, you scatter it over it

sprinkling *noun* A sprinkling of something is a small quantity of it: *a light sprinkling of snow*

sprint *noun* **1** a short, fast race ▷ *verb* **2** To sprint means to run fast over a short distance

sprinter *noun* an athlete who runs fast over short distances

sprout *verb* **1** When something sprouts, it grows **2** If things sprout up, they appear rapidly: *Their houses sprouted up in that region* ▷ *noun* **3** A sprout is the same as a **brussels sprout**

spruce *noun* **1** an evergreen tree with needle-like leaves ▷ *adjective* **2** Someone who is spruce is very neat and smart ▷ *verb* **3** To spruce something up means to make it neat and smart

spunk *noun (informal)* **1** *(old-fashioned)* Spunk is courage **2** In Australian and New Zealand English, someone who is good-looking

spur spurs, spurring, spurred *verb* **1** If something spurs you to do something or spurs you on, it encourages you to do it ▷ *noun*

S

2 Something that acts as a spur encourages a person to do something **3** Spurs are sharp metal points attached to the heels of a rider's boots and used to urge a horse on ▷ **phrase 4** If you do something **on the spur of the moment**, you do it suddenly, without planning it

spurious [spyoor-ee-uss] *adjective* not genuine or real

spurn *verb* If you spurn something, you refuse to accept it: *You spurned his last offer*

spurt *verb* **1** When a liquid or flame spurts out of something, it comes out quickly in a thick, powerful stream ▷ *noun* **2** A spurt of liquid or flame is a thick powerful stream of it: *a small spurt of blood* **3** A spurt of activity or effort is a sudden, brief period of it

spy spies, spying, spied *noun* **1** a person sent to find out secret information about a country or organization ▷ *verb* **2** Someone who spies tries to find out secret information about another country or organization **3** If you spy on someone, you watch them secretly **4** If you spy something, you notice it

squabble *verb* **1** When people squabble, they quarrel about something trivial ▷ *noun* **2** a quarrel

squad *noun* a small group chosen to do a particular activity: *the fraud squad; the England football squad*

squadron *noun* a section of one of the armed forces, especially the air force

squalid *adjective* **1** dirty, untidy, and in bad condition **2** Squalid activities are unpleasant and often dishonest

squall *noun* a brief, violent storm

squalor *noun* Squalor consists of bad or dirty conditions or surroundings

squander *verb* To squander money or resources means to waste them: *They have squandered huge amounts of money*

square *noun* **1** MATHS a shape with four equal sides and four right angles **2** In a town or city, a square is a flat, open place, bordered by buildings or streets **3** MATHS The square of a number is the number multiplied by itself. For example, the square of 3, written 3^2, is 3 x 3 ▷ *adjective* **4** shaped like a square: *her delicate square face* **5** 'Square' is used before units of length when talking about the area of something: $24m^2$ **6** 'Square' is used after units of length when you are giving the length of each side of something square: *a towel measuring a foot square* ▷ *verb* **7** MATHS If you square a number, you multiply it by itself

squarely *adverb* **1** Squarely means directly rather than indirectly or at an angle: *I looked squarely in the mirror* **2** If you approach a subject squarely, you consider it fully, without trying to avoid unpleasant aspects of it

squash *verb* **1** If you squash something, you press it, so that it becomes flat or loses its shape ▷ *noun* **2** If there is a squash in a place, there are a lot of people squashed in it **3** Squash is a game in which two players hit a small rubber ball against the walls of a court using rackets **4** Squash is a drink made from fruit juice, sugar, and water

squat squats, squatting, squatted; squatter, squattest *verb* **1** If you squat down, you crouch, balancing on your feet with your legs bent **2** A person who squats in an unused building lives there as a squatter

▷ *noun* **3** a building used by squatters ▷ *adjective* **4** short and thick

squatter *noun* **1** a person who lives in an unused building without permission and without paying rent **2** in Australian English, someone who owns a large amount of land for sheep or cattle farming **3** in Australia and New Zealand in the past, someone who rented land from the King or Queen

squawk *verb* **1** When a bird squawks, it makes a loud, harsh noise ▷ *noun* **2** a loud, harsh noise made by a bird

squeak *verb* **1** If something squeaks, it makes a short, high-pitched sound ▷ *noun* **2** a short, high-pitched sound > **squeaky** *adjective*

squeal *verb* **1** When things or people squeal, they make long, high-pitched sounds ▷ *noun* **2** a long, high-pitched sound

squeamish *adjective* easily upset by unpleasant sights or situations

squeeze *verb* **1** When you squeeze something, you press it firmly from two sides **2** If you squeeze something into a small amount of time or space, you manage to fit it in ▷ *noun* **3** If you give something a squeeze, you squeeze it: *She gave my hand a quick squeeze* **4** If getting into something is a squeeze, it is just possible to fit into it: *It would take four comfortably, but six would be a squeeze*

squid *noun* a sea creature with a long soft body and many tentacles

squint *verb* **1** If you squint at something, you look at it with your eyes screwed up ▷ *noun* **2** If someone has a squint, their eyes look in different directions from each other

squire *noun* In a village, the squire was a gentleman who owned a large house with a lot of land

squirm *verb* If you squirm, you wriggle and twist your body about, usually because you are nervous or embarrassed

squirrel *noun* a small furry animal with a long bushy tail

squirt *verb* **1** If a liquid squirts, it comes out of a narrow opening in a thin, fast stream ▷ *noun* **2** a thin, fast stream of liquid

Sri Lankan [shree-**lang**-kan] *adjective* **1** belonging or relating to Sri Lanka ▷ *noun* **2** someone who comes from Sri Lanka

stab stabs, stabbing, stabbed *verb* **1** To stab someone means to wound them by pushing a knife into their body **2** To stab at something means to push at it sharply with your finger or with something long and narrow ▷ *phrase* **3** (*informal*) If you **have a stab** at something, you try to do it ▷ *noun* **4** You can refer to a sudden unpleasant feeling as a stab of something: *He felt a stab of guilt*

stable *adjective* **1** not likely to change or come to an end suddenly: *I am in a stable relationship* **2** firmly fixed or balanced and not likely to move, wobble, or fall ▷ *noun* **3** a building in which horses are kept > **stability** *noun* > **stabilize** *verb*

staccato [stak-**kah**-toe] *adjective* consisting of a series of short, sharp, separate sounds

stack *noun* **1** A stack of things is a pile of them, one on top of the other ▷ *verb* **2** If you stack things, you arrange them one on top of the other in a pile

stadium *noun* a sports ground with rows of seats around it

staff *noun* **1** The staff of an

S

organization are the people who work for it ▷ *verb* **2** To staff an organization means to find and employ people to work in it **3** If an organization is staffed by particular people, they are the people who work for it

stag *noun* an adult male deer

stage *noun* **1** a part of a process that lasts for a period of time **2** DRAMA In a theatre, the stage is a raised platform where the actors or entertainers perform **3** DRAMA You can refer to the profession of acting as the stage ▷ *verb* **4** DRAMA If someone stages a play or event, they organize it and present it or take part in it

stagger *verb* **1** If you stagger, you walk unsteadily, for example because you are ill **2** If something staggers you, it amazes you **3** If events are staggered, they are arranged so that they do not all happen at the same time > **staggering** *adjective* > **staggered** *adjective*

stagnant *adjective* Stagnant water is not flowing and is unhealthy and dirty

staid *adjective* serious and dull

stain *noun* **1** a mark on something that is difficult to remove ▷ *verb* **2** If a substance stains something, the thing becomes marked or coloured by it

stained glass *noun* Stained glass is coloured pieces of glass held together with strips of lead

stainless steel *noun* Stainless steel is a metal made from steel and chromium which does not rust

stair *noun* Stairs are a set of steps inside a building going from one floor to another

staircase *noun* a set of stairs

stairway *noun* a set of stairs

stake *phrase* **1** If something is at **stake**, it might be lost or damaged if something else is not successful: *The whole future of the company was at stake* ▷ *verb* **2** If you say you would stake your money, life, or reputation on the success or truth of something, you mean you would risk it: *He is prepared to stake his own career on this* ▷ *noun* **3** If you have a stake in something such as a business, you own part of it and its success is important to you **4** a pointed wooden post that can be hammered into the ground and used as a support **5** (*in plural*) The stakes involved in something are the things that can be lost or gained

stale *adjective* **1** Stale food or air is no longer fresh **2** If you feel stale, you have no new ideas and are bored

stalemate *noun* **1** Stalemate is a situation in which neither side in an argument or contest can win **2** In chess, stalemate is a situation in which a player cannot make any move permitted by the rules, so that the game ends and no-one wins

stalk [stawk] *noun* **1** The stalk of a flower or leaf is its stem ▷ *verb* **2** To stalk a person or animal means to follow them quietly in order to catch, kill, or observe them **3** If someone stalks into a room, they walk in a stiff, proud, or angry way

stall *noun* **1** a large table containing goods for sale or information **2** (*in plural*) In a theatre, the stalls are the seats at the lowest level, in front of the stage ▷ *verb* **3** When a vehicle stalls, the engine suddenly stops **4** If you stall when someone asks you to do something, you try to avoid doing it until a later time

stallion *noun* an adult male horse

that can be used for breeding

stamina noun Stamina is the physical or mental energy needed to do something for a very long time

stammer verb 1 When someone stammers, they speak with difficulty, repeating words and sounds and hesitating awkwardly ▷ noun 2 Someone who has a stammer tends to stammer when they speak

stamp noun 1 a a small piece of gummed paper which you stick on a letter or parcel before posting it 2 a small block with a pattern cut into it, which you press onto an inky pad and make a mark with it on paper; also the mark made by the stamp 3 If something bears the stamp of a particular quality or person, it shows clear signs of that quality or of the person's style or characteristics ▷ verb 4 If you stamp a piece of paper, you make a mark on it using a stamp 5 If you stamp, you lift your foot and put it down hard on the ground > **stamp out** verb To stamp something out means to put an end to it: *the battle to stamp out bullying in schools*

stampede verb 1 When a group of animals stampede, they run in a wild, uncontrolled way ▷ noun 2 a group of animals stampeding

stance noun Your stance on a particular matter is your attitude and way of dealing with it: *He takes no particular stance on animal rights*

stand stands, standing, stood verb 1 If you are standing, you are upright, your legs are straight, and your weight is supported by your feet. When you stand up, you get into a standing position 2 If something stands somewhere, that is where it is: *The house stands alone on the top of a small hill* 3 If you stand something somewhere, you put it there in an upright position: *Stand the containers on bricks* 4 If a decision or offer stands, it is still valid: *My offer still stands* 5 You can use 'stand' when describing the state or condition of something: *Youth unemployment stands at 35 per cent* 6 If a letter stands for a particular word, it is an abbreviation for that word 7 If you say you will not stand for something, you mean you will not tolerate it 8 If something can stand a situation or test, it is good enough or strong enough not to be damaged by it 9 If you cannot stand something, you cannot bear it: *I can't stand that woman* 10 If you stand in an election, you are one of the candidates ▷ phrase 11 When someone **stands trial**, they are tried in a court of law ▷ noun 12 a stall or very small shop outdoors or in a large public building 13 a large structure at a sports ground, where the spectators sit 14 a piece of furniture designed to hold something: *an umbrella stand* > **stand by** verb 1 If you stand by to provide help or take action, you are ready to do it if necessary 2 If you stand by while something happens, you do nothing to stop it > **stand down** verb If someone stands down, they resign from their job or position > **stand in** verb If you stand in for someone, you take their place while they are ill or away > **stand out** verb If something stands out, it can be easily noticed or is more important than other similar things > **stand up** verb 1 If something stands up to rough treatment, it is not damaged or harmed 2 If you stand up to someone who is

S

criticizing or attacking you, you defend yourself

standard noun **1** a level of quality or achievement that is considered acceptable: *The work is not up to standard* **2** (*in plural*) Standards are moral principles of behaviour ▷ adjective **3** usual, normal, and correct: *The practice was standard procedure for most motor companies*

standardize or **standardise** verb To standardize things means to change them so that they all have a similar set of features: *We have decided to standardize our equipment*

stand-by noun **1** something available for use when you need it: *a useful stand-by* ▷ adjective **2** A stand-by ticket is a cheap ticket that you buy just before a theatre performance or a flight if there are any seats left

stand-in noun someone who takes a person's place while the person is ill or away: *The school had to employ a stand-in while the teacher was ill*

standing adjective **1** permanently in existence or used regularly: *a standing joke* ▷ noun **2** A person's standing is their status and reputation **3** 'Standing' is used to say how long something has existed: *a friend of 20 years' standing*

standpoint noun If you consider something from a particular standpoint, you consider it from that point of view: *from a military standpoint*

standstill noun If something comes to a standstill, it stops completely

stanza noun (ENGLISH) A verse of a poem

staple noun **1** Staples are small pieces of wire that hold sheets of paper firmly together. You insert them with a stapler ▷ verb **2** If you

staple sheets of paper, you fasten them together with staples ▷ adjective **3** A staple food forms a regular and basic part of someone's everyday diet

star stars, starring, starred noun **1** a large ball of burning gas in space that appears as a point of light in the sky at night **2** a shape with four or more points sticking out in a regular pattern **3** Famous actors, sports players, and musicians are referred to as stars **4** (*in plural*) The horoscope in a newspaper or magazine can be referred to as the stars: *I'm a Virgo, but don't read my stars every day* ▷ verb **5** If an actor or actress stars in a film or if the film stars that person, he or she has one of the most important parts in it

starboard adjective, noun The starboard side of a ship is the right-hand side when you are facing the front

starch noun **1** Starch is a substance used for stiffening fabric such as cotton and linen **2** Starch is a carbohydrate found in foods such as bread and potatoes ▷ verb **3** To starch fabric means to stiffen it with starch

stare verb **1** If you stare at something, you look at it for a long time ▷ noun **2** a long fixed look at something

starfish starfishes or starfish noun a flat, star-shaped sea creature with five limbs

stark adjective **1** harsh, unpleasant, and plain: *the stark choice* ▷ phrase **2** If someone is **stark naked**, they have no clothes on at all

start verb **1** If something starts, it begins to take place or comes into existence: *When does the party start?* **2** If you start to do something, you begin to do it: *Susie started to cry* **3** If you start something, you cause it to begin or to come into existence: *as good a time as any to start a business* **4** If you start a machine or car, you operate the controls to make it work **5** If you start, your body suddenly jerks because of surprise or fear ▷ *noun* **6** The start of something is the point or time at which it begins **7** If you do something with a start, you do it with a sudden jerky movement because of surprise or fear: *I awoke with a start*

starter *noun* a small quantity of food served as the first part of a meal

startle *verb* If something sudden and unexpected startles you, it surprises you and makes you slightly frightened > **startled** *adjective* > **startling** *adjective*

starve *verb* **1** If people are starving, they are suffering from a serious lack of food and are likely to die **2** To starve a person or animal means to prevent them from having any food **3** (*informal*) If you say you are starving, you mean you are very hungry **4** If someone or something is starved of something they need, they are suffering because they are not getting enough of it: *The hospital was starved of cash* > **starvation** *noun*

stash *verb* (*informal*) If you stash something away in a secret place, you store it there to keep it safe

state *noun* **1** The state of something is its condition, what it is like, or its circumstances **2** Countries are sometimes referred to as states: *the state of Denmark* **3** Some countries are divided into regions called states which make some of their own

laws: *the State of Vermont* **4** You can refer to the government or administration of a country as the state ▷ *phrase* **5** If you are **in a state**, you are nervous or upset and unable to control your emotions ▷ *adjective* **6** A state ceremony involves the ruler or leader of a country ▷ *verb* **7** If you state something, you say it or write it, especially in a formal way

stately home *noun* In Britain, a very large old house which belongs to an upper-class family

statement *noun* **1** something you say or write when you give facts or information in a formal way **2** a document provided by a bank showing all the money paid into and out of an account during a period of time

state school *noun* a school maintained and financed by the government in which education is free

statesman statesmen *noun* an important and experienced politician

static *adjective* **1** never moving or changing: *The temperature remains fairly static* ▷ *noun* **2** Static is an electrical charge caused by friction. It builds up in metal objects

station *noun* **1** a building and platforms where trains stop for passengers **2** A bus or coach station is a place where some buses start their journeys **3** A radio station is the frequency on which a particular company broadcasts **4** in Australian and New Zealand English, a large sheep or cattle farm **5** (*old-fashioned*) A person's station is their position or rank in society ▷ *verb* **6** Someone who is stationed somewhere is sent there to work or do a particular job: *Her husband was stationed in Vienna*

S

stationary adjective not moving: a stationary car

stationery noun Stationery is paper, pens, and other writing equipment

statistic noun **1** Statistics are facts obtained by analysing numerical information **2** Statistics is the branch of mathematics that deals with the analysis of numerical information > **statistical** adjective > **statistically** adverb

statistician [stat-iss-**tish**-an] noun a person who studies or works with statistics

statue noun a sculpture of a person

stature noun **1** Someone's stature is their height and size **2** Someone's stature is also their importance and reputation: the desire to gain international stature

status [**stay**-tuss] noun **1** A person's status is their position and importance in society **2** Status is also the official classification given to someone or something: I am not sure what your legal status is

status quo [stay-tuss **kwoh**] noun The status quo is the situation that exists at a particular time: They want to keep the status quo

statute noun a law > **statutory** adjective

staunch adjective **1** A staunch supporter is a strong and loyal supporter: a staunch supporter of the Royal family > verb **2** If you staunch blood, you stop it from flowing out of a wound

stave noun [MUSIC] A stave is the five lines that music is written on > verb **2** If you stave something off, you try to delay or prevent it

stay verb **1** If you stay in a place, you do not move away from it: She stayed in bed until noon **2** If you stay at a hotel or a friend's house, you spend some time there as a guest or visitor **3** If you stay in a particular state, you continue to be in it: I stayed awake the first night **4** In Scottish and South African English, to stay in a place can also mean to live there > noun **5** a short time spent somewhere: a very pleasant stay in Cornwall

stead phrase (formal) Something that will stand someone **in good stead** will be useful to them in the future

steadfast adjective refusing to change or give up > **steadfastly** adverb

steady steadier, steadiest; steadies, steadying, steadied adjective **1** continuing or developing gradually without major interruptions or changes: a steady rise in profits **2** firm and not shaking or wobbling: O'Brien held out a steady hand **3** A steady look or voice is calm and controlled **4** Someone who is sensible and reliable > verb **5** When you steady something, you hold on to prevent it from shaking or wobbling **6** When you steady yourself, you control and calm yourself > **steadily** adverb

steak noun **1** Steak is good-quality beef without much fat **2** A fish steak is a large piece of fish

steal steals, stealing, stole, stolen verb **1** To steal something means to take it without permission and without intending to return it **2** To steal somewhere means to move there quietly and secretly

stealth [rhymes with **health**] noun If you do something with stealth, you do it quietly and secretly > **stealthy** adjective > **stealthily** adverb

steam noun **1** Steam is the hot

vapour formed when water boils ▷ adjective **2** Steam engines are operated using steam as a means of power ▷ verb **3** If something steams, it gives off steam **4** To steam food means to cook it in steam > **steamy** adjective

steamer noun **1 a** a ship powered by steam **2** a container with small holes in the bottom in which you steam food

steel noun **1** Steel is a very strong metal containing mainly iron with a small amount of carbon ▷ verb **2** To steel yourself means to prepare to deal with something unpleasant

steep adjective **1** A steep slope rises sharply and is difficult to go up **2** larger than is reasonable: *a steep price increase* ▷ verb **3** To steep something in a liquid means to soak it thoroughly > **steeply** adverb

steeped adjective If a person or place is steeped in a particular quality, they are surrounded by it or have been deeply influenced by it: *an industry steeped in tradition*

steeple noun a tall pointed structure on top of a church tower

steeplechase noun a long horse race in which the horses jump over obstacles such as hedges and jumps

steer verb **1** To steer a vehicle or boat means to control it so that it goes in the right direction **2** To steer someone towards a particular course of action means to influence and direct their behaviour or thoughts

stem stems, stemming, stemmed noun **1** The stem of a plant is the long thin central part above the ground that carries the leaves and flowers **2** The stem of a glass is the long narrow part connecting the bowl to the base ▷ verb **3** If a problem stems from a particular situation, that situation is the original starting point or cause of the problem **4** If you stem the flow of something, you restrict it or stop it from spreading: *to stem the flow of refugees*

stench noun a very strong, unpleasant smell

stencil stencils, stencilling, stencilled noun **1** a thin sheet with a cut-out pattern through which ink or paint passes to form the pattern on the surface below ▷ verb **2** To stencil a design on a surface means to create it using a stencil

step steps, stepping, stepped noun **1** If you take a step, you lift your foot and put it down somewhere else **2** one of a series of actions that you take in order to achieve something **3** a raised flat surface, usually one of a series that you can walk up or down ▷ verb **4** If you step in a particular direction, you move your foot in that direction **5** If someone steps down or steps aside from an important position, they resign > **step in** verb If you step in, you become involved in a difficult situation in order to help to resolve it > **step up** verb If you step up the rate of something, you increase it

stepping stone noun **1** Stepping stones are a line of large stones that you walk on to cross a shallow river **2** a job or event that is regarded as a stage in your progress, especially in your career

stereo adjective A stereo recording or music system is one in which the sound is directed through two speakers

stereotype (PSHE) noun **1** a fixed image or set of characteristics that people consider to represent a

S

particular type of person or thing: *the stereotype of the polite, industrious Japanese* ▷ *verb* **2** If you stereotype someone, you assume they are a particular type of person and will behave in a particular way

sterile *adjective* **1** Sterile means completely clean and free from germs **2** A sterile person or animal is unable to produce offspring > **sterility** *noun*

sterilize *or* **sterilise** *verb* **1** To sterilize something means to make it completely clean and free from germs, usually by boiling it or treating it with an antiseptic **2** If a person or animal is sterilized, they have an operation that makes it impossible for them to produce offspring

sterling *noun* **1** Sterling is the money system of the United Kingdom ▷ *adjective* **2** excellent in quality: *Volunteers are doing sterling work*

stern *adjective* **1** very serious and strict: *a stern father; a stern warning* ▷ *noun* **2** The stern of a boat is the back part

steroid *noun* Steroids are chemicals that occur naturally in your body. Sometimes sportsmen and sportswomen illegally take them as drugs to improve their performance

stethoscope *noun* a device used by doctors to listen to a patient's heart and breathing, consisting of earpieces connected to a hollow tube and a small disc

stew *noun* **1** a dish of small pieces of savoury food cooked together slowly in a liquid ▷ *verb* **2** To stew meat, vegetables, or fruit means to cook them slowly in a liquid

steward *noun* **1** a man who works on a ship or plane looking after passengers and serving meals **2** a person who helps to direct the public at a race, march, or other event

stewardess *noun* a woman who works on a ship or plane looking after passengers and serving meals

stick sticks, sticking, stuck *noun* **1 a** long, thin piece of wood **b** A stick of something is a long, thin piece of it: *a stick of celery* ▷ *verb* **3** If you stick a long or pointed object into something, you push it in **4** If you stick one thing to another, you attach it with glue or sticky tape **5** If one thing sticks to another, it becomes attached and is difficult to remove **6** If a movable part of something sticks, it becomes fixed and will no longer move or work properly: *My gears keep sticking* **7** (*informal*) If you stick something somewhere, you put it there **8** If you stick by someone, you continue to help and support them **9** If you stick to something, you keep to it and do not change to something else: *He should have stuck to the old ways of doing things* **10** When people stick together, they stay together and support each other > **stick out** *verb* **1** If something sticks out, it projects from something else **2** To stick out also means to be very noticeable > **stick up** *verb* **1** If something sticks up, it points upwards from a surface **2** (*informal*) If you stick up for a person or principle, you support or defend them

sticker *noun* a small piece of paper or plastic with writing or a picture on it, that you stick onto a surface

sticky stickier, stickiest *adjective* **1** A sticky object is covered with a substance that can stick to other things: *sticky hands* **2** Sticky paper or tape has glue on one side so that you can stick it to a surface **3** (*informal*) A sticky situation is difficult or embarrassing to deal with **4** Sticky weather is unpleasantly hot and humid

stiff *adjective* **1** DᴳT Something that is stiff is firm and not easily bent **2** If you feel stiff, your muscles or joints ache when you move **3** Stiff behaviour is formal and not friendly or relaxed **4** Stiff also means difficult or severe: *stiff competition for places* **5** A stiff drink contains a large amount of alcohol **6** A stiff breeze is blowing strongly ▷ *adverb* **7** (*informal*) If you are bored stiff or scared stiff, you are very bored or very scared > **stiffly** *adverb* > **stiffness** *noun*

stiffen *verb* **1** If you stiffen, you suddenly stop moving and your muscles become tense: *I stiffened with tension* **2** If your joints or muscles stiffen, they become sore and difficult to bend or move **3** If fabric or material is stiffened, it is made firmer so that it does not bend easily

stifle [**sty-fl**] *verb* **1** If the atmosphere stifles you, you feel you cannot breathe properly **2** To stifle something means to stop it from happening or continuing: *Martin stifled a yawn* > **stifling** *adjective*

stigma *noun* If something has a stigma attached to it, people consider it unacceptable or a disgrace: *the stigma of poverty*

stiletto *stilettos noun* Stilettos are women's shoes with very high, narrow heels

still *adverb* **1** If a situation still exists, it has continued to exist and it exists now **2** If something could still happen, it might happen although it has not happened yet **3** 'Still'

emphasizes that something is the case in spite of other things: *Whatever you think of him, he's still your father* ▷ *adverb, adjective* **4** Still means staying in the same position without moving: *Sit still; The air was still* ▷ *adjective* **5** A still place is quiet and peaceful with no signs of activity ▷ *noun* **6** a photograph taken from a film or video > **stillness** *noun*

stillborn *adjective* A stillborn baby is dead when it is born

stilt *noun* **1** Stilts are long upright poles on which a building is built, for example on wet land **2** Stilts are also two long pieces of wood or metal on which people balance and walk

stilted *adjective* formal, unnatural, and rather awkward: *a stilted conversation*

stimulant *noun* A drug or other substance that makes your body work faster, increasing your heart rate and making it difficult to sleep

stimulate *verb* **1** To stimulate something means to encourage it to begin or develop: *to stimulate discussion* **2** If something stimulates you, it gives you new ideas and enthusiasm > **stimulating** *adjective* > **stimulation** *noun*

stimulus *stimuli noun* something that causes a process or event to begin or develop

sting *stings, stinging, stung verb* **1** If a creature or plant stings you, it pricks your skin and injects a substance which causes pain **2** If a part of your body stings, you feel a sharp tingling pain there **3** If someone's remarks sting you, they make you feel upset and hurt ▷ *noun* **4** A creature's sting is the part it stings you with

S

stink stinks, stinking, stank, stunk *verb* **1** Something that stinks smells very unpleasant ▷ *noun* **2** a very unpleasant smell

stint *noun* a period of time spent doing a particular job: *a three-year stint in the army*

stipulate *verb (formal)* If you stipulate that something must be done, you state clearly that it must be done ▷ **stipulation** *noun*

stir stirs, stirring, stirred *verb* **1** When you stir a liquid, you move it around using a spoon or a stick **2** To stir means to move slightly **3** If something stirs you, it makes you feel strong emotions: *The power of the singing stirred me* ▷ *noun* **4** If an event causes a stir, it causes general excitement or shock: *two books which have caused a stir*

stirring *adjective* **1** causing excitement, emotion, and enthusiasm: *a stirring account of the action* ▷ *noun* **2** If there is a stirring of emotion, people begin to feel it

stitch *verb* **1** When you stitch pieces of material together, you use a needle and thread to sew them together **2** To stitch a wound means to use a special needle and thread to hold the edges of skin together ▷ *noun* **3** one of the pieces of thread that can be seen where material has been sewn **4** one of the pieces of thread that can be seen where a wound has been stitched: *He had eleven stitches in his lip* **5** If you have a stitch, you feel a sharp pain at the side of your abdomen, usually because you have been running or laughing

stock *noun* **1** Stocks are shares bought as an investment in a company; also the amount of money raised by the company through the issue of shares **2** A shop's stock is the total amount of goods it has for sale **3** If you have a stock of things, you have a supply ready for use **4** The stock an animal or person comes from is the type of animal or person they are descended from: *She was descended from Scots Highland stock* **5** Stock is farm animals **6** Stock is a liquid made from boiling meat, bones, or vegetables together in water. Stock is used as a base for soups, stews, and sauces ▷ *verb* **7** A shop that stocks particular goods keeps a supply of them to sell **8** If you stock a shelf or cupboard, you fill it with food or other things ▷ *adjective* **9** A stock expression or way of doing something is one that is commonly used ▷ **stock up** *verb* If you stock up with something, you buy a supply of it

stockbroker *noun* A stockbroker is a person whose job is to buy and sell shares for people who want to invest money

stock exchange *noun* a place where there is trading in stocks and shares: *the New York Stock Exchange*

stocking *noun* Stockings are long pieces of thin clothing that cover a woman's leg

stockman stockmen *noun* a man who looks after sheep or cattle on a farm

stock market *noun* The stock market is the organization and activity involved in buying and selling stocks and shares

stockpile *verb* **1** If someone stockpiles something, they store large quantities of it for future use ▷ *noun* **2** a large store of something

stocky stockier, stockiest *adjective* A stocky person is rather short, but broad and solid-looking

stoke verb To stoke a fire means to keep it burning by moving or adding fuel

stomach noun **1** Your stomach is the organ inside your body where food is digested **2** You can refer to the front part of your body above your waist as your stomach ▷ verb **3** If you cannot stomach something, you strongly dislike it and cannot accept it

stone noun **1** Stone is the hard solid substance found in the ground and used for building **2** a small piece of rock **3** The stone in a fruit such as a plum or cherry is the large seed in the centre **4** a unit of weight equal to 14 pounds or about 6.35 kilograms **5** You can refer to a jewel as a stone: *a diamond ring with three stones* ▷ verb **6** To stone something or someone means to throw stones at them

stony stonier, stoniest adjective **1** Stony ground is rough and contains a lot of stones or rocks **2** If someone's expression is stony, it shows no friendliness or sympathy

stool noun a seat with legs but no back or arms

stoop verb **1** If you stoop, you stand or walk with your shoulders bent forwards **2** If you would not stoop to something, you would not disgrace yourself by doing it

stop stops, stopping, stopped verb **1** If you stop doing something, you no longer do it **2** If an activity or process stops, it comes to an end or no longer happens **3** If a machine stops, it no longer functions or it is switched off **4** To stop something means to prevent it **5** If people or things that are moving stop, they no longer move **6** If you stop somewhere, you stay there for a

short while ▷ phrase **7** To put a stop to something means to prevent it from happening or continuing ▷ noun **8** a place where a bus, train, or other vehicle stops during a journey **9** If something that is moving comes to a stop, it no longer moves

stoppage noun If there is a stoppage, people stop work because of a disagreement with their employer

stopper noun a piece of glass or cork that fits into the neck of a jar or bottle

stopwatch noun a watch that can be started and stopped by pressing buttons, which is used to time events

storage noun The storage of something is the keeping of it somewhere until it is needed

store noun **1** a shop **2** A store of something is a supply kept for future use **3** a place where things are kept while they are not used ▷ verb **4** When you store something somewhere, you keep it there until it is needed ▷ phrase **5** Something that is in store for you is going to happen to you in the future

storeroom noun a room where things are kept until they are needed

storey storeys noun A storey of a building is one of its floors or levels

storm noun **1** When there is a storm, there is heavy rain, a strong wind, and often thunder and lightning **2** If something causes a storm, it causes an angry or excited reaction: *His words caused a storm of protest* ▷ verb **3** If someone storms out, they leave quickly, noisily, and angrily **4** To storm means to say something in a loud, angry voice: *'It's a fiasco!' he* *stormed* **5** If people storm a place, they attack it > **stormy** *adjective*

story stories *noun* (ENGLISH) **1** a description of imaginary people and events written or told to entertain people **2** The story of something or someone is an account of the important events that have happened to them: *his life story*

stout *adjective* **1** rather fat **2** thick, strong, and sturdy: *stout walking shoes* **3** determined, firm, and strong: *He can outrun the stoutest opposition* > **stoutly** *adverb*

stove *noun* a piece of equipment for heating a room or for cooking

stow *verb* **1** If you stow something somewhere or stow it away, you store it until it is needed **2** If someone stows away in a ship or plane, they hide in it to go somewhere secretly without paying

straddle *verb* **1** If you straddle something, you stand or sit with one leg on either side of it **2** If something straddles a place, it crosses it, linking different parts together: *The town straddles a river*

straight *adjective, adverb* **1** continuing in the same direction without curving or bending: *the straight path; Amy stared straight ahead of her* **2** upright or level rather than sloping or bent: *Keep your arms straight* > *adverb* **3** immediately and directly: *We will go straight to the hotel* > *adjective* **4** neat and tidy: *Get this room straight* **5** honest, frank, and direct: *They wouldn't give me a straight answer* **6** A straight choice involves only two options

straightaway *adverb* If you do something straightaway, you do it immediately

straighten *verb* **1** To straighten something means to remove any

bends or curves from it **2** To straighten something also means to make it neat and tidy **3** To straighten out a confused situation means to organize and deal with it

straightforward *adjective* **1** easy and involving no problems **2** honest, open, and frank

strain *noun* **1** Strain is worry and nervous tension **2** If a strain is put on something, it is affected by a strong force which may damage it **3** You can refer to an aspect of someone's character, remarks, or work as a strain: *There was a strain of bitterness in his voice.* **4** You can refer to distant sounds of music as strains of music **5** A particular strain of plant is a variety of it: *strains of rose* > *verb* **6** To strain something means to force it or use it more than is reasonable or normal **7** If you strain a muscle, you injure it by moving awkwardly **8** To strain food means to pour away the liquid from it

strained *adjective* **1** worried and anxious **2** If a relationship is strained, people feel unfriendly and do not trust each other

strait *noun* **1** You can refer to a narrow strip of sea as a strait or the straits: *the Straits of Hormuz* **2** (in plural) If someone is in a bad situation, you can say they are in difficult straits

straitjacket *noun* a special jacket used to tie the arms of a violent person tightly around their body

strand *noun* **1** A strand of thread or hair is a single long piece of it **2** You can refer to a part of a situation or idea as a strand of it: *the different strands of the problem*

stranded *adjective* If someone or something is stranded somewhere, they are stuck and cannot leave

strange adjective 1 unusual or unexpected 2 not known, seen, or experienced before: alone in a strange country ▷ **strangely** adverb ▷ **strangeness** noun

stranger noun 1 someone you have never met before 2 If you are a stranger to a place or situation, you have not been there or experienced it before

strangle verb To strangle someone means to kill them by squeezing their throat ▷ **strangulation** noun

strangled adjective A strangled sound is unclear and muffled

stranglehold noun To have a stranglehold on something means to have control over it and prevent it from developing

strap straps, strapping, strapped noun 1 a narrow piece of leather or cloth, used to fasten or hold things together ▷ verb 2 To strap something means to fasten it with a strap

strapping adjective tall, strong, and healthy-looking

strata the plural of **stratum**

strategic [strat-**tee**-jik] adjective planned or intended to achieve something or to gain an advantage: a strategic plan ▷ **strategically** adverb

strategy strategies noun 1 a plan for achieving something 2 Strategy is the skill of planning the best way to achieve something, especially in war ▷ **strategist** noun

stratum strata noun The strata in the earth's surface are the different layers of rock

straw noun 1 Straw is the dry, yellowish stalks from cereal crops 2 a hollow tube of paper or plastic which you use to suck a drink into your mouth ▷ phrase 3 If something

is **the last straw**, it is the latest in a series of bad events and makes you feel you cannot stand any more

strawberry strawberries noun a small red fruit with tiny seeds in its skin

stray verb 1 When people or animals stray, they wander away from where they should be 2 If your thoughts stray, you stop concentrating ▷ adjective 3 A stray dog or cat is one that has wandered away from home 4 Stray things are separated from the main group of things of their kind: a stray piece of lettuce ▷ noun 5 a stray dog or cat

streak noun 1 a long mark or stain 2 If someone has a particular streak, they have that quality in their character 3 a lucky or unlucky streak is a series of successes or failures ▷ verb 4 If something is streaked with a colour, it has lines of the colour in it 5 To streak somewhere means to move there very quickly ▷ **streaky** adjective

stream noun 1 a small river 2 You can refer to a steady flow of something as a stream: a constant stream of people 3 In a school, a stream is a group of children of the same age and ability ▷ verb 4 To stream somewhere means to move in a continuous flow in large quantities: Rain streamed down the windscreen

streamline verb 1 To streamline a vehicle, aircraft, or boat means to improve its shape so that it moves more quickly and efficiently 2 To streamline an organization means to make it more efficient by removing parts of it

street noun a road in a town or village, usually with buildings along it

S

strength noun **1** Your strength is your physical energy and the power of your muscles **2** Strength can refer to the degree of someone's confidence or courage **3** Strength can refer to power or influence as strength: *The campaign against factory closures gathered strength* **4** Someone's strengths are their good qualities and abilities **5** The strength of an object is the degree to which it can stand rough treatment **6** The strength of a substance is the amount of other substances that it contains: *coffee with sugar and milk in it at the correct strength* **7** The strength of a feeling or opinion is the degree to which it is felt or supported **8** The strength of a relationship is its degree of closeness or success **9** The strength of a group is the total number of people in it ▷ *phrase* **10** If people do something **in strength**, a lot of them do it together: *The press were here in strength*

strengthen verb **1** To strengthen something means to give it more power, influence, or support and make it more likely to succeed **2** To strengthen an object means to improve it or add to its structure so that it can withstand rough treatment

strenuous [**stren**-yoo-uss] adjective involving a lot of effort or energy > **strenuously** adverb

stress noun **1** Stress is worry and nervous tension **2** Stresses are strong physical forces applied to an object **3** ENGLISH Stress is emphasis put on a word or part of a word when it is pronounced, making it slightly louder ▷ verb **4** If you stress a point, you emphasize it and draw attention to its

importance > **stressful** adjective

stretch verb **1** Something that stretches over an area extends that far **2** When you stretch, you hold out part of your body as far as you can **3** To stretch something soft or elastic means to pull it to make it longer or bigger ▷ noun **4** A stretch of land or water is an area of it **5** A stretch of time is a period of time

stretcher noun a long piece of material with a pole along each side, used to carry an injured person

strewn adjective If things are strewn about, they are scattered about untidily: *The costumes were strewn all over the floor*

stricken adjective severely affected by something unpleasant

strict adjective **1** Someone who is strict controls other people very firmly **2** A strict rule must always be obeyed absolutely **3** The strict meaning of something is its precise and accurate meaning **4** You can use 'strict' to describe someone who never breaks the rules or principles of a particular belief: *a strict Muslim*

strictly adverb **1** Strictly means only for a particular purpose: *I was in it strictly for the money* ▷ *phrase* **2** You say **strictly speaking** to correct a statement or add more precise information: *Somebody pointed out that, strictly speaking, electricity was a discovery, not an invention*

stride strides, striding, strode, stridden verb **1** To stride along means to walk quickly with long steps ▷ noun **2** a long step; also the length of a step

strident [**stry**-dent] adjective loud, harsh, and unpleasant

strife noun (formal) Strife is trouble, conflict, and disagreement

strike strikes, striking, struck noun

1 If there is a strike, people stop working as a protest **2** A hunger strike is a refusal to eat anything as a protest. A rent strike is a refusal to pay rent **3** A military attack: *the threat of American air strikes* ▷ *verb* **4** To strike someone or something means to hit them **5** If an illness, disaster, or enemy strikes, it suddenly affects or attacks someone **6** If a thought strikes you, it comes into your mind **7** If you are struck by something, you are impressed by it **8** When a clock strikes, it makes a sound to indicate the time **9** To strike a deal with someone means to come to an agreement with them **10** If someone strikes oil or gold, they discover it in the ground **11** If you strike a match, you rub it against something to make it burst into flame ▷ **strike off** *verb* If a professional person is struck off for bad behaviour, their name is removed from an official register and they are not allowed to practise their profession ▷ **strike out** *verb* If someone strikes out, they go off to do something different on their own ▷ **strike up** *verb* To strike up a conversation or friendship means to begin it

striker *noun* **1** Strikers are people who are refusing to work as a protest **2** in soccer, a player whose function is to attack and score goals

striking *adjective* very noticeable because of being unusual or very attractive ▷ **strikingly** *adverb*

string strings, stringing, strung *noun* **1** String is thin cord made of twisted threads **2** You can refer to a row or series of similar things as a string of them: *a string of islands; a string of injuries* **3** The strings of a musical instrument are tightly stretched lengths of wire or nylon which vibrate to produce the notes **4** (*in plural*) The section of an orchestra consisting of stringed instruments is called the strings ▷ **string along** *verb* (*informal*) To string someone along means to deceive them by letting them believe you have the same desires, hopes, or plans as them ▷ **string out** *verb* **1** If things are strung out, they are spread out in a long line **2** To string something out means to make it last longer than necessary

stringent *adjective* Stringent laws or conditions are very severe or are strictly controlled: *stringent financial checks*

strip strips, stripping, stripped *noun* **1** A strip of something is a long, narrow piece of it **2** A comic strip is a series of drawings which tell a story **3** A sports team's strip is the clothes worn by the team when playing a match ▷ *verb* **4** If you strip, you take off all your clothes **5** To strip something means to remove whatever is covering its surface **6** To strip someone of their property or rights means to take their property or rights away from them officially

stripe *noun* Stripes are long, thin lines, usually of different colours ▷ **striped** *adjective*

stripper *noun* An entertainer who does striptease

striptease *noun* Striptease is a form of entertainment in which someone takes off their clothes gradually to music

strive strives, striving, strove, striven *verb* If you strive to do something, you make a great effort to achieve it

stroke *verb* **1** If you stroke

something, you move your hand smoothly and gently over it ▷ noun **2** If someone has a stroke, they suddenly lose consciousness as a result of a blockage or rupture in a blood vessel in the brain. A stroke can result in damage to speech and paralysis **3** The strokes of a brush or pen are the movements that you make with it **4** The strokes of a clock are the sounds that indicate the hour **5** A swimming stroke is a particular style of swimming ▷ phrase **6** If you have a **stroke of luck**, then you are lucky and something good happens to you

stroll verb **1** To stroll along means to walk slowly in a relaxed way ▷ noun **2** a slow, pleasurable walk

stroller noun In Australian English, a stroller is a pushchair

strong adjective **1** Someone who is strong has powerful muscles **2** You also say that someone is strong when they are confident and have courage **3** Strong objects are able to withstand rough treatment **4** Strong also means great in degree or intensity: *a strong wind* **5** A strong argument or theory is supported by a lot of evidence **6** If a group or organization is strong, it has a lot of members or influence **7** You can use 'strong' to say how many people there are in a group: *The audience was about two dozen strong* **8** Your strong points are the things you are good at **9** A strong economy or currency is stable and successful **10** A strong liquid or drug contains a lot of a particular substance ▷ adverb **11** If someone or something is still going strong, they are still healthy or working well after a long time > **strongly** adverb

stronghold noun **1** a place that is

held and defended by an army **2** A stronghold of an attitude or belief is a place in which the attitude or belief is strongly held: *Europe's last stronghold of male dominance*

structure noun D G T **1** The structure of something is the way it is made, built, or constructed **2** something that has been built or constructed ▷ verb **3** D G T To structure something means to arrange it into an organized pattern or system > **structural** adjective > **structurally** adverb

struggle verb **1** If you struggle to do something, you try hard to do it in difficult circumstances **2** When people struggle, they twist and move violently during a fight ▷ noun **3** Something that is a struggle is difficult to achieve and takes a lot of effort **4** a fight

strum strums, strumming, strummed verb To strum a guitar means to play it by moving your fingers backwards and forwards across all the strings

strut struts, strutting, strutted verb **1** To strut means to walk in a stiff, proud way with your chest out and your head high ▷ noun **2** a piece of wood or metal which strengthens or supports part of a building or structure

Stuart noun Stuart was the family name of the monarchs who ruled Scotland from 1371 to 1714 and England from 1603 to 1714

stub stubs, stubbing, stubbed noun **1** The stub of a pencil or cigarette is the short piece that remains when the rest has been used **2** The stub of a cheque or ticket is the small part that you keep ▷ verb **3** If you stub your toe, you hurt it by accidentally kicking something > **stub out** verb

To stub out a cigarette means to put it out by pressing the end against something

stubble noun 1 The short stalks remaining in the ground after a crop is harvested are called stubble 2 If a man has stubble on his face, he has very short hair growing there because he has not shaved recently

stubborn adjective 1 Someone who is stubborn is determined not to change their mind or course of action 2 A stubborn stain is difficult to remove > **stubbornly** adverb > **stubbornness** noun

stuck adjective 1 If something is stuck in a particular position, it is fixed or jammed and cannot be moved: His car's stuck in a snowdrift 2 If you are stuck, you are unable to continue what you were doing because it is too difficult 3 If you stuck somewhere, you are unable to get away

stud noun 1 a small piece of metal fixed into something 2 A male horse or other animal that is kept for breeding purposes

studded adjective decorated with small pieces of metal or precious stones

student noun a person studying at university or college

studied adjective A studied action or response has been carefully planned and is not natural: She sipped her glass of white wine with studied boredom

studio studios noun 1 a room where a photographer or painter works 2 a room containing special equipment where records, films, or radio or television programmes are made

studious [styoo-dee-uss] adjective spending a lot of time studying

studiously adverb carefully and deliberately: She was studiously ignoring me

study studies, studying, studied verb 1 If you study a particular subject, you spend time learning about it 2 If you study something, you look at it carefully: He studied the map in silence ▷ noun 3 Study is the activity of studying a subject: the serious study of medieval archaeology 4 Studies are subjects which are studied: media studies 5 a piece of research on a particular subject: a detailed study of the world's most violent people 6 a room used for writing and studying

stuff noun 1 You can refer to a substance or group of things as stuff ▷ verb 2 (informal) If you stuff something somewhere, you push it there quickly and roughly 3 If you stuff something with a substance or objects, you fill it with the substance or objects

stuffing noun Stuffing is a mixture of small pieces of food put inside poultry or a vegetable before it is cooked

stuffy stuffier, stuffiest adjective 1 very formal and old-fashioned 2 If it is stuffy in a room, there is not enough fresh air

stumble verb 1 If you stumble while you are walking or running, you trip and almost fall 2 If you stumble when speaking, you make mistakes when pronouncing the words 3 If you stumble across something or stumble on it, you find it unexpectedly

stump noun 1 a small part of something that is left when the rest has been removed: the stump of a dead tree 2 In cricket, the stumps are the three upright wooden sticks that support the bails, forming the wicket ▷ verb 3 (informal) if a question or problem stumps you, you cannot think of an answer or solution

stun stuns, stunning, stunned verb **1** If you are stunned by something, you are very shocked by it **2** To stun a person or animal means to knock them unconscious with a blow to the head

stunning adjective very beautiful or impressive: a stunning first novel

stunt noun **1** an unusual or dangerous and exciting action that someone does to get publicity or as part of a film ▷ verb **2** To stunt the growth or development of something means to prevent it from developing as it should

stupendous adjective very large or impressive: a stupendous amount of money > **stupendously** adverb

stupid adjective showing lack of good judgment or intelligence and not at all sensible > **stupidly** adverb

stupidity noun a lack of intelligence or good judgment

sturdy sturdier, sturdiest adjective strong and firm and unlikely to be damaged or injured: a sturdy chest of drawers

sturgeon [stur-jon] noun a large edible fish, the eggs of which are also eaten and are known as caviar

stutter noun **1** Someone who has a stutter finds it difficult to speak smoothly and often repeats sounds through being unable to complete a word ▷ verb **2** When someone stutters, they hesitate or repeat sounds when speaking

style noun **1** The style of something is the general way in which it is done or presented, often showing the attitudes of the people involved **2** A person or place that has style is smart, elegant, and fashionable

3 The style of something is its design: new windows that fit in with the style of the house ▷ verb **4** To style a piece of clothing or a person's hair means to design and create its shape

stylish adjective smart, elegant, and fashionable > **stylishly** adverb

stylized or **stylised** adjective using a particular artistic or literary form as a basis rather than being natural or spontaneous: a stylized picture of a Japanese garden

suave [swahv] adjective charming, polite, and confident: a suave Italian

subconscious noun **1** Your subconscious is the part of your mind that can influence you without your being aware of it ▷ adjective **2** happening or existing in someone's subconscious and therefore not directly realized or understood by them: a subconscious fear of rejection > **subconsciously** adverb

subcontinent noun a large mass of land, often consisting of several countries, and forming part of a continent: the Indian subcontinent

subdue subdues, subduing, subdued verb **1** If soldiers subdue a group of people, they bring them under control by using force: It would be quite impossible to subdue the whole continent **2** To subdue a colour, light, or emotion means to make it less bright or strong

subdued adjective **1** rather quiet and sad **2** not very noticeable or bright

subject noun **1** The subject of writing or a conversation is the thing or person being discussed **2** In grammar, the subject is the word or words representing the person or thing doing the action expressed by the verb. For example, in the sentence 'My cat keeps catching birds', 'my cat' is the subject **3** an area of study **4** The subjects of a country are the people who live there ▷ verb **5** To subject someone to something means to make them experience it: *He was subjected to constant interruption* ▷ adjective **6** Someone or something that is subject to something is affected by it: *He was subject to attacks at various times*

subjective adjective influenced by personal feelings and opinion rather than based on fact or rational thought

sublime adjective Something that is sublime is wonderful and affects people emotionally: *sublime music*

submarine noun a ship that can travel beneath the surface of the sea

submerge verb **1** To submerge means to go beneath the surface of a liquid **2** If you submerge yourself in an activity, you become totally involved in it

submission noun **1** Submission is a state in which someone accepts the control of another person: *Now he must beat us into submission* **2** The submission of a proposal or application is the act of sending it for consideration

submissive adjective behaving in a quiet, obedient way

submit submits, submitting, submitted verb **1** If you submit to something, you accept it because you are not powerful enough to resist it **2** If you submit an application or proposal, you send it to someone for consideration

subordinate noun [sub-**ord**-in-it] **1** A person's subordinate is someone who is in a less important position than them ▷ adjective [sub-**ord**-in-it]

2 If one thing is subordinate to another, it is less important: *The House of Lords would always remain subordinate to the Commons* ▷ verb [sub-**ord**-in-ate] **3** To subordinate one thing to another means to treat it as being less important

subscribe verb **1** If you subscribe to a particular belief or opinion, you support it or agree with it **2** If you subscribe to a magazine, you pay to receive regular copies > **subscriber** noun

subscription noun a sum of money that you pay regularly to belong to an organization or to receive regular copies of a magazine

subsequent adjective happening or coming into existence at a later time than something else: *the December uprising and the subsequent political violence* > **subsequently** adverb

subservient adjective Someone who is subservient does whatever other people want them to do

subside verb **1** To subside means to become less intense or quieter: *Her excitement suddenly subsided* **2** If water or the ground subsides, it sinks to a lower level

subsidence [sub-**side**-ins] noun If a place is suffering from subsidence, parts of the ground have sunk to a lower level

subsidiary subsidiaries [sub-**sid**-yer-ee] noun **1** a company which is part of a larger company ▷ adjective **2** treated as being of less importance and additional to another thing: *Drama is offered as a subsidiary subject*

subsidize or **subsidise** verb To subsidize something means to provide part of the cost of it: *He feels the government should do much more to* *subsidize films* ▷ **subsidized** *adjective*

subsidy subsidies *noun* a sum of money paid to support a company or provide a public service

substance *noun* **1** Anything which is a solid, a powder, a liquid, or a paste can be referred to as a substance **2** If a speech or piece of writing has substance, it is meaningful or important: *a good speech, but there was no substance*

substantial *adjective* **1** very large in degree or amount: *a substantial pay rise* **2** large and strongly built: *a substantial stone building*

substantially *adverb* Something that is substantially true is generally or mostly true

substitute *verb* **1** To substitute one thing for another means to use it instead of the other thing or to put it in the other thing's place **2** MATHS to replace one mathematical element with another of the same value ▷ *noun* **3** If one thing is a substitute for another, it is used instead of it or put in its place ▷ **substitution** *noun*

subterfuge [**sub**-ter-fyooj] *noun* Subterfuge is the use of deceitful or dishonest methods

subtitle *noun* A film with subtitles has a printed translation of the dialogue at the bottom of the screen

subtle [**sut**-tl] *adjective* **1** very fine, delicate, or small in degree: *a subtle change* **2** using indirect methods to achieve something ▷ **subtly** *adverb* ▷ **subtlety** *noun*

subtract *verb* MATHS If you subtract one number from another, you take away the first number from the second

suburb *noun* an area of a town or city that is away from its centre

suburban *adjective* **1** relating to a suburb or suburbs **2** dull and conventional

suburbia *noun* You can refer to the suburbs of a city as suburbia

subversive *adjective* **1** intended to destroy or weaken a political system: *subversive activities* ▷ *noun* **2** Subversives are people who try to destroy or weaken a political system ▷ **subversion** *noun*

subvert *verb* (*formal*) To subvert something means to cause it to weaken or fail: *a cunning campaign to subvert the music industry*

subway *noun* **1** a footpath that goes underneath a road **2** an underground railway

succeed *verb* **1** To succeed means to achieve the result you intend **2** To succeed someone means to be the next person to have their job **3** If one thing succeeds another, it comes after it in time: *The explosion was succeeded by a crash* ▷ **succeeding** *adjective*

success *noun* **1** Success is the achievement of something you have been trying to do **2** Someone who is a success has achieved an important position or made a lot of money

successful *adjective* having achieved what you intended to do ▷ **successfully** *adverb*

succession *noun* **1** A succession of things is a number of them occurring one after the other **2** When someone becomes the next person to have an important position, you can refer to this event as their succession to this position: *his succession to the throne* ▷ *phrase* **3** If something happens a number of weeks, months, or years **in succession**, it happens that number of times without a break: *Borg won Wimbledon five years in succession*

successive *adjective* occurring one after the other without a break: *three successive victories*

successor *noun* Someone's successor is the person who takes their job when they leave

succinct [suk-**singkt**] *adjective* expressing something clearly and in very few words > **succinctly** *adverb*

succulent *adjective* Succulent food is juicy and delicious

succumb *verb* If you succumb to something, you are unable to resist it any longer: *She never succumbed to his charms*

such *adjective, pronoun* **1** You use 'such' to refer to the person or thing you have just mentioned, or to someone or something similar: *Naples or Palermo or some similar place* ▷ *phrase* **2** You can use **such as** to introduce an example of something: *herbal teas such as camomile* **3** You can use **such as it is** to indicate that something is not great in quality or quantity: *The action, such as it is, is set in Egypt* **4** You can use **such and such** when you want to refer to something that is not specific: *A good trick is to ask whether they have seen such and such a film* ▷ *adjective* **5** 'Such' can be used for emphasizing: *I have such a terrible sense of guilt*

suck *verb* **1** If you suck something, you hold it in your mouth and pull at it with your cheeks and tongue, usually to get liquid out of it **2** To suck something in a particular direction means to draw it there with a powerful force ▷ **suck up** *verb* (*informal*) To suck up to someone means to do things to please them in order to obtain praise or approval

sucker *noun* **1** (*informal*) If you call someone a sucker, you mean that they are easily fooled or cheated **2** Suckers are pads on the bodies of some animals and insects which they use to cling to a surface **3** A sucker is also a cup-shaped piece of plastic or rubber on an object that sticks to a surface when pressed flat

suction *noun* **1** Suction is the force involved when a substance is drawn or sucked from one place to another **2** Suction is the process by which two surfaces stick together when the air between them is removed: *They stay there by suction*

Sudanese [soo-dan-**neez**] *adjective* **1** belonging or relating to the Sudan ▷ *noun* **2** someone who comes from the Sudan

sudden *adjective* happening quickly and unexpectedly: *a sudden cry* > **suddenly** *adverb* > **suddenness** *noun*

sue sues, suing, sued *verb* To sue someone means to start a legal case against them, usually to claim money from them

suede [swayd] *noun* Suede is a thin, soft leather with a rough surface

suffer *verb* **1** If someone is suffering pain, or suffering as a result of an unpleasant situation, they are badly affected by it **2** If something suffers as a result of neglect or a difficult situation, its condition or quality becomes worse: *The bus service is suffering* > **sufferer** *noun* > **suffering** *noun*

suffice *verb* (*formal*) If something suffices, it is enough or adequate for a purpose

sufficient *adjective* If a supply or quantity is sufficient for a purpose, there is enough of it available > **sufficiently** *adverb*

s

suffix noun ENGLISH a group of letters which is added to the end of a word to form a new word, for example '-ology' or '-itis'

suffocate verb To suffocate means to die as a result of having too little air or oxygen to breathe
> **suffocation** noun

suffrage noun Suffrage is the right to vote in political elections

suffused adjective (literary) If something is suffused with light or colour, light or colour has gradually spread over it

sugar noun Sugar is a sweet substance used to sweeten food or drinks. Sugar is obtained from sugar cane or sugar beet

suggest verb 1 If you suggest a plan or idea to someone, you mention it as a possibility for them to consider 2 If something suggests a particular thought or impression, it makes you think in that way or gives you that impression: *Nothing you say suggests he has a problem*

suggestion noun 1 a plan or idea that is mentioned as a possibility for someone to consider 2 A suggestion of something is a very slight indication or faint sign of it: *a suggestion of dishonesty*

suggestive adjective Something that is suggestive of a particular thing gives a slight hint or sign of it
> **suggestively** adverb

suicidal adjective 1 People who are suicidal want to kill themselves 2 Suicidal behaviour is so dangerous that it is likely to result in death: *a mad suicidal attack* > **suicidally** adverb

suicide noun People who commit suicide deliberately kill themselves

suicide bomber noun a terrorist who carries out a bomb attack,

knowing that he or she will be killed in the explosion > **suicide bombing** noun

suit noun 1 a matching jacket and trousers or skirt 2 In a court of law, a suit is a legal action taken by one person against another 3 one of four different types of card in a pack of playing cards. The four suits are hearts, clubs, diamonds, and spades ▷ verb 4 If a situation or course of action suits you, it is appropriate or acceptable for your purpose 5 If a piece of clothing or a colour suits you, you look good when you are wearing it 6 If you do something to suit yourself, you do it because you want to and without considering other people

suitable adjective right or acceptable for a particular purpose or occasion > **suitability** noun > **suitably** adverb

suitcase noun a case in which you carry your clothes when you are travelling

suite [sweet] noun 1 In a hotel, a suite is a set of rooms 2 a set of matching furniture or bathroom fittings

suited adjective right or appropriate for a particular purpose or person: *He is well suited to be minister for the arts*

suitor noun (old-fashioned) A woman's suitor is a man who wants to marry her

sulk verb Someone who is sulking is showing their annoyance by being silent and moody

sulky sulkier, sulkiest adjective showing annoyance by being silent and moody

sullen adjective behaving in a bad-tempered and disagreeably silent way: *a sullen and resentful* workforce > **sullenly** adverb

sulphur noun SCIENCE Sulphur is a pale yellow nonmetallic element which burns with a very unpleasant smell. Its atomic number is 16 and its symbol is S

sultan noun In some Muslim countries, the ruler of the country is called the sultan

sum sums, summing, summed noun **1** an amount of money **2** In arithmetic, a sum is a calculation **3** The sum of something is the total amount of it > **sum up** verb If you sum something up, you briefly describe its main points

summarize or **summarise** verb EXAM TERM To summarize something means to give a short account of its main points

summary summaries noun **1** A summary of something is a short account of its main points ▷ adjective **2** A summary action is done without delay or careful thought: Summary executions are common > **summarily** adverb

summer noun Summer is the season between spring and autumn

summit noun **1** The summit of a mountain is its top **2** a meeting between leaders of different countries to discuss particular issues

summon verb **1** If someone summons you, they order you to go to them **2** If you summon up strength or energy, you make a great effort to be strong or energetic

summons summonses noun **1** an official order to appear in court **2** an order to go to someone: The result was a summons to headquarters

sumptuous adjective Something that is sumptuous is magnificent and obviously very expensive

sum total noun The sum total of a number of things is all of them added or considered together

sun sunning, sunned noun **1** The sun is the star providing heat and light for the planets revolving around it in our solar system **2** You refer to heat and light from the sun as sun: We need a bit of sun ▷ verb **3** If you sun yourself, you sit in the sunshine

sunbathe verb If you sunbathe, you sit in the sunshine to get a suntan

sunburn noun Sunburn is sore red skin on someone's body due to too much exposure to the rays of the sun > **sunburnt** adjective

Sunday noun Sunday is the day between Saturday and Monday

Sunday school noun Sunday school is a special class held on Sundays to teach children about Christianity

sundry adjective **1** 'Sundry' is used to refer to several things or people of various sorts: sundry journalists and lawyers ▷ phrase **2** All and sundry means everyone

sunflower noun a tall plant with very large yellow flowers

sunglasses plural noun Sunglasses are spectacles with dark lenses that you wear to protect your eyes from the sun

sunken adjective **1** having sunk to the bottom of the sea, a river, or lake: sunken ships **2** A sunken object or area has been constructed below the level of the surrounding area: a sunken garden **3** curving inwards: Her cheeks were sunken

sunlight noun Sunlight is the bright light produced when the sun is shining > **sunlit** adjective

sunny sunnier, sunniest adjective When it is sunny, the sun is shining

S

sunrise noun Sunrise is the time in the morning when the sun first appears, and the colours produced in the sky at that time

sunset noun Sunset is the time in the evening when the sun disappears below the horizon, and the colours produced in the sky at that time

sunshine noun Sunshine is the bright light produced when the sun is shining

suntan noun If you have a suntan, the sun has turned your skin brown > **suntanned** adjective

super adjective very nice or very good: a super party

superb adjective very good indeed > **superbly** adverb

superficial adjective **1** involving only the most obvious or most general aspects of something: a superficial knowledge of music **2** not having a deep, serious, or genuine interest in anything: a superficial and rather silly woman **3** Superficial wounds are not very deep or severe > **superficially** adverb

superfluous [soo-**per**-floo-uss] adjective (formal) unnecessary or no longer needed

superhuman adjective having much greater power or ability than is normally expected of humans: superhuman strength

superintendent noun **1** a police officer above the rank of inspector **2** a person whose job is to be responsible for a particular thing: the superintendent of prisons

superior adjective **1** better or of higher quality than other similar things **2** in a position of higher authority than another person **3** showing too much pride and self-importance: Jerry smiled in a superior way ▷ noun **4** Your superiors are people who are in a higher position than you in society or an organization > **superiority** noun

superlative [soo-per-**lat**-tiv] noun **1** In grammar, the superlative is the form of an adjective which indicates that the person or thing described has more of a particular quality than anyone or anything else. For example, 'quickest', 'best', and 'easiest' are all superlatives ▷ adjective **2** (formal) very good indeed: a superlative performance

supermarket noun a shop selling food and household goods arranged so that you can help yourself and pay for everything at a till by the exit

supernatural adjective **1** Something that is supernatural, for example ghosts or witchcraft, cannot be explained by normal scientific laws ▷ noun **2** You can refer to supernatural things as the supernatural

superpower noun a very powerful and influential country such as the USA

supersede [soo-per-**seed**] verb If something supersedes another thing, it replaces it because it is more modern: New York superseded Paris as the centre for modern art

supersonic adjective A supersonic aircraft can travel faster than the speed of sound

superstar noun You can refer to a very famous entertainer or sports player as a superstar

superstition noun Superstition is a belief in things like magic and powers that bring good or bad luck > **superstitious** adjective

supervise verb To supervise someone means to check and direct what they are doing to make sure that they do it correctly

> **supervision** noun > **supervisor** noun

supper noun Supper is a meal eaten in the evening or a snack eaten before you go to bed

supplant verb (formal) To supplant someone or something means to take their place: By the 1930s the wristwatch had supplanted the pocket watch

supple adjective able to bend and move easily

supplement verb 1 To supplement something means to add something to it to improve it: Many village men supplemented their wages by fishing for salmon ▷ noun 2 something that is added to something else to improve it 3 a separate part of a newspaper or magazine, often dealing with a particular subject

supplementary adjective added to something else to improve it: supplementary doses of vitamin E

supplier noun a firm which provides particular goods

supply supplies, supplying, supplied verb 1 To supply someone with something means to provide it or send it to them ▷ noun 2 A supply of something is an amount available for use: the world's supply of precious metals 3 (in plural) Supplies are food and equipment for a particular purpose

support verb 1 If you support someone, you agree with their aims and want them to succeed 2 If you support someone who is in difficulties, you are kind, encouraging, and helpful to them 3 If something supports an object, it is underneath it and holding it up 4 To support someone or something means to prevent them from falling by holding them 5 To support

someone financially means to provide them with money ▷ noun 6 an object that is holding something up 7 Moral support is encouragement given to someone to help them do something difficult 8 Financial support is money that is provided for someone or something ▷ **supportable** adjective

supporter noun a person who agrees with or helps someone

supportive adjective A supportive person is encouraging and helpful to someone who is in difficulties

suppose verb 1 If you suppose that something is the case, you think that it is likely: I supposed that would be too obvious ▷ phrase 2 You can say **I suppose** when you are not entirely certain or enthusiastic about something: Yes, I suppose he could come ▷ conjunction 3 You can use 'suppose' or 'supposing' when you are considering or suggesting a possible situation or action: Supposing he were to break down under interrogation?

supposed adjective 1 'Supposed' is used to express doubt about something that is generally believed: the supposed culprit 2 If something is supposed to be done or to happen, it is planned, expected, or required to be done or to happen: You are supposed to report it to the police; It was supposed to be this afternoon 3 Something that is supposed to be the case is generally believed or thought to be so: Wimbledon is supposed to be the best tournament of them all ▷ **supposedly** adverb

supposition noun something that is believed or assumed to be true: the supposition that science requires an ordered universe

suppress *verb* **1** If an army or government suppresses an activity, it prevents people from doing it **2** If someone suppresses a piece of information, they prevent it from becoming generally known **3** If you suppress your feelings, you stop yourself expressing them > **suppression** *noun*

supremacy [soo-**prem**-mass-ee] *noun* If a group of people has supremacy over others, it is more powerful than the others

supreme *adjective* **1** 'Supreme' is used as part of a title to indicate the highest level of an organization or system: *the Supreme Court* **2** 'Supreme' is used to emphasize the greatness of something: *the supreme achievement of the human race* > **supremely** *adverb*

surcharge *noun* an additional charge

sure *adjective* **1** If you are sure about something, you have no doubts about it **2** If you are sure of yourself, you are very confident **3** If something is sure to happen, it will definitely happen **4** Sure means reliable or accurate: *a sure sign that something is wrong* **5** If you **make sure** about something, you check it or take action to see that it is done ▷ *interjection* **6** Sure is an informal way of saying 'yes': *'Can I come too?' – 'Sure'*

surely *adverb* 'Surely' is used to emphasize the belief that something is the case: *Surely these people here knew that?*

surf *verb* **1** When you surf, you go surfing **2** When you surf the internet, you go from website to website reading the information ▷ *noun* **3** Surf is the white foam that forms on the top of waves when they break near the shore

surface *noun* **1** The surface of something is the top or outside area of it **2** The surface of a situation is what can be seen easily rather than what is hidden or not immediately obvious ▷ *verb* **3** If someone surfaces, they come up from under water to the surface

surfboard *noun* a long narrow lightweight board used for surfing

surf club *noun* In Australia, a surf club is an organization of lifesavers in charge of safety on a particular beach, and which often provides leisure facilities

surfeit [**sur**-fit] *noun* If there is a surfeit of something, there is too much of it

surfing *noun* Surfing is a sport which involves riding towards the shore on the top of a large wave while standing on a surfboard

surge *noun* **1** a sudden great increase in the amount of something: *a surge of panic* ▷ *verb* **2** If something surges, it moves suddenly and powerfully: *The soldiers surged forwards*

surgeon *noun* a doctor who performs operations

surgery surgeries *noun* **1** Surgery is medical treatment involving cutting open part of the patient's body to treat the damaged part **2** The room or building where a doctor or dentist works is called a surgery **3** A period of time during which a doctor is available to see patients is called surgery: *evening surgery*

surgical *adjective* used in or involving a medical operation: *surgical gloves* > **surgically** *adverb*

surly surlier, surliest *adjective* rude and bad-tempered > **surliness** *noun*

surmise *verb* (formal) To surmise

something means to guess it: I surmised it was of French manufacture

surname noun Your surname is your last name, which you share with other members of your family

surpass verb (formal) To surpass someone or something means to be better than them

surplus noun If there is a surplus of something there is more of it than is needed

surprise noun **1** an unexpected event **2** Surprise is the feeling caused when something unexpected happens ▷ verb **3** If something surprises you, it gives you a feeling of surprise **4** If you surprise someone, you do something they were not expecting > **surprising** adjective

surreal adjective very strange and dreamlike

surrender verb **1** To surrender means to stop fighting and agree that the other side has won **2** If you surrender to a temptation or feeling, you let it take control of you **3** To surrender something means to give it up to someone else: The gallery director surrendered his keys ▷ noun **4** Surrender is a situation in which one side in a fight agrees that the other side has won and gives in

surreptitious [sur-rep-**tish**-uss] adjective A surreptitious action is done secretly or so that no-one will notice: a surreptitious glance > **surreptitiously** adverb

surrogate adjective **1** acting as a substitute for someone or something ▷ noun **2** a person or thing that acts as a substitute

surround verb **1** To surround someone or something means to be situated all around them ▷ noun **2** The surround of something is its

outside edge or border

surrounding adjective The surrounding area of a particular place is the area around it: the surrounding countryside

surveillance [sur-**vay**-lanss] noun Surveillance is the close watching of a person's activities by the police or army

survey verb [sir-**vay**] **1** To survey something means to look carefully at the whole of it **2** To survey a building or piece of land means to examine it carefully in order to make a report or plan of its structure and features ▷ noun [**sir**-vay] **3** A survey of something is a detailed examination of it, often in the form of a report

surveyor noun a person whose job is to survey buildings or land

survival noun Survival is being able to continue living or existing in spite of great danger or difficulties: There was no hope of survival

survive verb To survive means to continue to live or exist in spite of great danger or difficulties: a German monk who survived the shipwreck > **survivor** noun

susceptible adjective If you are susceptible to something, you are likely to be influenced or affected by it: Elderly people are more susceptible to infection > **susceptibility** noun

suspect verb [sus-**pekt**] **1** If you suspect something, you think that it is likely or probably true: I suspected that the report would be sent **2** If you suspect something, you have doubts about its reliability or genuineness: Given his previous behaviour, I suspected his remorse **3** If you suspect someone of doing something wrong, you think that they have done it ▷ noun [**sus**-pekt]

S

4 someone who is thought to be guilty of a crime ▷ *adjective* [**sus**-pekt] **5** If something is suspect, it cannot be trusted or relied upon: *a rather suspect holy man*

suspend *verb* **1** If something is suspended, it is hanging from somewhere: *the television set suspended above the bar* **2** To suspend an activity or event means to delay it or stop it for a while **3** If someone is suspended from their job, they are told not to do it for a period of time, usually as a punishment

suspense *noun* Suspense is a state of excitement or anxiety caused by having to wait for something

suspension *noun* **1** The suspension of something is the delaying or stopping of it **2** A person's suspension is their removal from a job for a period of time, usually as a punishment **3** The suspension of a vehicle consists of springs and shock absorbers which provide a smooth ride **4** a liquid mixture in which very small bits of a solid material are contained and are not dissolved

suspicion *noun* **1** Suspicion is the feeling of not trusting someone or the feeling that something is wrong **2** a feeling that something is likely to happen or is probably true: *the suspicion that more could have been achieved*

suspicious *adjective* **1** If you are suspicious of someone, you do not trust them **2** 'Suspicious' is used to describe things that make you think that there is something wrong with a situation: *suspicious circumstances* > **suspiciously** *adverb*

sustain *verb* **1** To sustain something means to continue it for a period of time: *Their team-mates were unable to sustain the challenge* **2** If something

sustains you, it gives you energy and strength **3** (*formal*) To sustain an injury or loss means to suffer it

sustainable *adjective* **1** capable of being sustained **2** If economic development or energy resources are sustainable they are capable of being maintained at a steady level without exhausting natural resources or causing ecological damage: *sustainable forestry*

sustenance *noun* (*formal*) Sustenance is food and drink

swab swabs, swabbing, swabbed *noun* **1** a small piece of cotton wool used for cleaning a wound ▷ *verb* **2** To swab something means to clean it using a large mop and a lot of water **3** To swab a wound means to clean it or take specimens from it using a swab

swag *noun* (*informal*) **1** goods or valuables, especially ones which have been gained dishonestly **2** in Australian and New Zealand English, the bundle of possessions belonging to a tramp **3** In Australian and New Zealand English, swags of something is lots of it

swagger *verb* **1** To swagger means to walk in a proud, exaggerated way ▷ *noun* **2** an exaggerated walk

swallow *verb* **1** If you swallow something, you make it go down your throat and into your stomach **2** When you swallow, you move your throat muscles as if you were swallowing something, especially when you are nervous ▷ *noun* **3** a bird with pointed wings and a long forked tail

swamp *noun* **1** an area of permanently wet land ▷ *verb* **2** If something is swamped, it is covered or filled with water **3** If you are swamped by things, you have more than you are able to deal with: *She was swamped with calls* ▷ **swampy** *adjective*

swan *noun* a large, usually white, bird with a long neck that lives on rivers or lakes

swap swaps, swapping, swapped [*rhymes with* **stop**] *verb* To swap one thing for another means to replace the first thing with the second, often by making an exchange with another person: *Webb swapped shirts with a Leeds player*

swarm *noun* **1** A swarm of insects is a large group of them flying together ▷ *verb* **2** When bees or other insects swarm, they fly together in a large group **3** If people swarm somewhere, a lot of people go there quickly and at the same time: *the crowds of office workers who swarm across the bridge* **4** If a place is swarming with people, there are a lot of people there

swashbuckling *adjective* 'Swashbuckling' is used to describe people who have the exciting behaviour or appearance of pirates

swastika [swoss-tik-ka] *noun* a symbol in the shape of a cross with each arm bent over at right angles. It was the official symbol of the Nazis in Germany, but in India it is a good luck sign

swat swats, swatting, swatted *verb* To swat an insect means to hit it sharply in order to kill it

swathe [*rhymes with* **bathe**] *noun* **1** a long strip of cloth that is wrapped around something: *swathes of white silk* **2** A swathe of land is a long strip of it

swathed *adjective* If someone is swathed in something, they are wrapped in it: *She was swathed in towels*

sway *verb* **1** To sway means to lean or swing slowly from side to side **2** If something sways you, it influences your judgment ▷ *noun* **3** (*literary*) Sway is the power to influence people: *under the sway of more powerful neighbours*

swear swears, swearing, swore, sworn *verb* **1** To swear means to say words that are considered to be very rude or blasphemous **2** If you swear to something, you state solemnly that you will do it or that it is true **3** If you swear by something, you firmly believe that it is a reliable cure or solution: *Some women swear by extra vitamins* ▷ **swear in** *verb* When someone is sworn in to a new position, they solemnly promise to fulfil the duties and are officially appointed

sweat *noun* **1** Sweat is the salty liquid produced by your sweat glands when you are hot or afraid ▷ *verb* **2** When you sweat, sweat comes through the pores in your skin in order to lower the temperature of your body

sweater *noun* a knitted piece of clothing covering your upper body and arms

sweatshirt *noun* a piece of clothing made of thick cotton, covering your upper body and arms

sweaty sweatier, sweatiest *adjective* covered or soaked with sweat

Swede *noun* someone who comes from Sweden

Swedish *adjective* **1** belonging or relating to Sweden ▷ *noun* **2** Swedish is the main language spoken in Sweden

sweep sweeps, sweeping, swept *verb* **1** If you sweep the floor, you use a brush to gather up dust or rubbish from it **2** To sweep things off a surface means to push them all off with a quick, smooth movement **3** If something sweeps from one place to another, it moves there very quickly: *A gust of wind swept over the terrace* **4** If an attitude or new fashion sweeps a place, it spreads rapidly through it: *a phenomenon that is sweeping America* ▷ noun **5** If you do something with a sweep of your arm, you do it with a wide curving movement of your arm

sweeping adjective **1** A sweeping curve or movement is long and wide **2** A sweeping statement is based on a general assumption rather than on careful thought **3** affecting a lot of people to a great extent: *sweeping changes*

sweet adjective **1** containing a lot of sugar: *a mug of sweet tea* **2** pleasant and satisfying: *sweet success* **3** A sweet smell is soft and fragrant **4** A sweet sound is gentle and tuneful **5** attractive and pleasant: *a sweet little baby* ▷ noun **6** Things such as toffees, chocolates, and mints are sweets **7** a dessert > **sweetly** adverb > **sweetness** noun

sweet corn noun Sweet corn is a long stalk covered with juicy yellow seeds that can be eaten as a vegetable

sweeten verb To sweeten food means to add sugar or another sweet substance to it

sweetener noun a very sweet, artificial substance that can be used instead of sugar

sweetheart noun **1** You can call someone who you are very fond of 'sweetheart' **2** (old-fashioned) A young person's sweetheart is their boyfriend or girlfriend

sweet tooth noun If you have a sweet tooth, you like sweet food very much

swell swells, swelling, swelled, swollen verb **1** If something swells, it becomes larger and rounder: *It causes the abdomen to swell* **2** If an amount swells, it increases in number ▷ noun **3** The regular up and down movement of the waves at sea can be called a swell

swelling noun **1** an enlarged area on your body as a result of injury or illness **2** The swelling of something is an increase in its size

sweltering adjective If the weather is sweltering, it is very hot

swerve verb To swerve means to suddenly change direction to avoid colliding with something

swift adjective **1** happening or moving very quickly: *a swift glance* ▷ noun **2** a bird with narrow crescent-shaped wings > **swiftly** adverb > **swiftness** noun

swig swigs, swigging, swigged (informal) verb **1** To swig a drink means to drink it in large mouthfuls, usually from a bottle ▷ noun **2** If you have a swig of a drink, you take a large mouthful of it

swill verb **1** To swill something means to pour water over it to clean it: *Swill the can out thoroughly* ▷ noun **2** Swill is a liquid mixture containing waste food that is fed to pigs

swim swims, swimming, swam, swum verb **1** To swim means to move through water using various movements with parts of the body **2** If you are swimming, it seems as if everything you see is moving and you feel dizzy ▷ noun **3** If you go for a swim, you go into water to swim for pleasure > **swimmer** noun

swimming noun Swimming is the activity of moving through water using your arms and legs

swimming pool noun a large hole

that has been tiled and filled with water for swimming

swimsuit noun a swimming costume

swindle verb 1 To swindle someone means to deceive them to obtain money or property ▷ noun 2 a trick in which someone is cheated out of money or property > **swindler** noun

swine noun 1 (old-fashioned) A swine is another name for a pig. The plural is 'swine' 2 (informal) If you call someone a swine, you mean they are nasty and spiteful. The plural is 'swines'

swing swings, swinging, swung verb 1 If something swings, it moves repeatedly from side to side from a fixed point 2 If someone or something swings in a particular direction, they turn quickly or move in a sweeping curve in that direction ▷ noun 3 a seat hanging from a frame or a branch, which you sit on and move backwards and forwards 4 A swing in opinion is a significant change in people's opinion

swipe verb 1 To swipe at something means to try to hit it with a making a curving movement with the arm 2 (informal) To swipe something means to steal it 3 To swipe a credit card means to pass it through a machine that electronically reads the information stored in the card ▷ noun 4 To take a swipe at something means to swipe at it

swirl verb To swirl means to move quickly in circles: The black water swirled around his legs

swish verb 1 To swish means to move quickly through the air making a soft sound: The curtains swished back ▷ noun 2 the sound made when something swishes

Swiss Swiss adjective 1 belonging or

relating to Switzerland ▷ noun 2 someone who comes from Switzerland

switch noun 1 a small control for an electrical device or machine 2 a change: a switch in routine ▷ verb 3 To switch to a different task or topic means to change to it 4 If you switch things, you exchange one for the other > **switch off** verb To switch off a light or machine means to stop it working by pressing a switch > **switch on** verb To switch on a light or machine means to start it working by pressing a switch

switchboard noun The switchboard in an organization is the part where all telephone calls are received

swivel swivels, swivelling, swivelled verb 1 To swivel means to turn round on a central point ▷ adjective 2 A swivel chair or lamp is made so that you can move the main part of it while the base remains in a fixed position

swollen adjective Something that is swollen has swelled up

swoon verb (literary) To swoon means to faint as a result of strong emotion

swoop verb To swoop means to move downwards through the air in a fast curving movement: A flock of pigeons swooped low over the square

swop another spelling of **swap**

sword [sord] noun a weapon consisting of a very long blade with a short handle

swordfish swordfishes or swordfish noun a large sea fish with an upper jaw which sticks out like a sword

sworn adjective If you make a sworn statement, you swear that everything in it is true

sycamore [sik-am-mor] noun a tree that has large leaves with five points

S

syllable noun ENGLISH a part of a word that contains a single vowel sound and is pronounced as a unit. For example, 'book' has one syllable and 'reading' has two

syllabus syllabuses or syllabi noun The subjects that are studied for a particular course or examination are called the syllabus

symbol noun a shape, design, or idea that is used to represent something: The fish has long been a symbol of Christianity

symbolic adjective Something that is symbolic has a special meaning that is considered to represent something else: Six tons of ivory were burned in a symbolic ceremony

symbolize or **symbolise** verb If a shape, design, or idea symbolizes something, it is regarded as being a symbol of it: In China and Japan the carp symbolizes courage
> **symbolism** noun

symmetrical adjective MATHS If something is symmetrical, it could be split into two halves, one being the exact reflection of the other
> **symmetrically** adverb

symmetry noun MATHS Something that has symmetry is symmetrical

sympathetic adjective 1 A sympathetic person shows kindness and understanding to other people 2 If you are sympathetic to a proposal or an idea, you approve of it

sympathize or **sympathise** verb To sympathize with someone who is in difficulties means to show them kindness and care

sympathizer or **sympathiser** noun People who support a particular cause can be referred to as sympathizers

sympathy sympathies noun 1 Sympathy is kindness and understanding towards someone who is in difficulties 2 If you have sympathy with someone's ideas or actions, you agree with them
> phrase 3 If you do something **in sympathy** with someone, you do it to show your support for them

symphony symphonies noun a piece of music for an orchestra, usually in four movements

symptom noun 1 something wrong with your body that is a sign of an illness 2 Something that is considered to be a sign of a bad situation can be referred to as a symptom of it: another symptom of the racism sweeping across the country
> **symptomatic** adjective

synagogue [sin-a-gog] noun RE a building where Jewish people meet for worship and religious instruction

synchronize [sing-kron-nize] or **synchronise** verb 1 To synchronize two actions means to do them at the same time and speed 2 To synchronize watches means to set them to show exactly the same time as each other > **synchronization** noun

syndicate noun an association of business people formed to carry out a particular project

syndrome noun 1 a medical condition characterized by a particular set of symptoms: Down's syndrome 2 You can refer to a typical set of characteristics as a syndrome: the syndrome of skipping from one wonder diet to the next

synod [sin-od] noun a council of church leaders which meet regularly to discuss religious and moral issues

synonym noun ENGLISH If two words have the same or a very similar meaning, they are synonyms

synonymous *adjective* **1** Two words that are synonymous have the same or very similar meanings **2** If two things are closely associated, you can say that one is synonymous with the other: *New York is synonymous with the Statue of Liberty*

synopsis synopses *noun* a summary of a book, play, or film

syntax *noun* (ENGLISH) The syntax of a language is its grammatical rules and the way its words are arranged

synthesis syntheses *noun* **1** A synthesis of different ideas or styles is a blended combination of them **2** (SCIENCE) The synthesis of a substance is its production by means of a chemical reaction
> **synthesize** *verb*

synthetic *adjective* made from artificial substances rather than natural ones

Syrian [sirr-ee-an] *adjective* **1** belonging or relating to Syria ▷ *noun* **2** someone who comes from Syria

syringe [sir-rinj] *noun* a hollow tube with a part which is pushed down inside and a fine hollow needle at one end, used for injecting or extracting liquids

syrup *noun* a thick sweet liquid made by boiling sugar with water
> **syrupy** *adjective*

system *noun* **1** (LIBRARY) an organized way of doing or arranging something according to a fixed plan or set of rules **2** People sometimes refer to the government and administration of the country as the system **3** You can also refer to a set of equipment as a system: *an old stereo system* **4** In biology, a system of a particular kind is the set of organs that perform that function: *the immune system*

systematic *adjective* following a fixed plan and done in an efficient way: *a systematic study*
> **systematically** *adverb*

t

tab *noun* a small extra piece that is attached to something, for example on a curtain so it can be hung on a pole

tabby tabbies *noun* a cat whose fur has grey, brown, or black stripes

table *noun* **1 a** a piece of furniture with a flat horizontal top supported by one or more legs **2** a set of facts or figures arranged in rows or columns ▷ *verb* **3** If you table something such as a proposal, you say formally that you want it to be discussed

tablecloth *noun* a cloth used to cover a table and keep it clean

tablespoon *noun* a large spoon used for serving food; also the amount that a tablespoon contains

tablet *noun* **1** any small, round pill made of powdered medicine **2** a slab of stone with words cut into it **3** (COMPUTING) a small mobile personal computer with a screen that is manipulated by swiping or tapping with the hand

table tennis *noun* Table tennis is a game for two or four people in which you use bats to hit a small hollow ball over a low net across a table

tabloid noun ENGLISH a newspaper with small pages, short news stories, and lots of photographs

taboo taboos noun **1** a social custom that some words, subjects, or actions must be avoided because they are considered embarrassing or offensive: *We have a powerful taboo against boasting* **2** a religious custom that forbids people to do something ▷ adjective **1** forbidden or disapproved of: *a taboo subject*

tacit [tass-it] adjective understood or implied without actually being said or written > **tacitly** adverb

taciturn [tass-it-urn] adjective Someone who is taciturn does not talk very much and so seems unfriendly

tack noun **1** a short nail with a broad, flat head **2** If you change tack, you start to use a different method for dealing with something ▷ verb **3** If you tack something to a surface, you nail it there with tacks **4** If you tack a piece of fabric, you sew it with long loose stitches

tackle verb **1** If you tackle a difficult task, you start dealing with it in a determined way **2** If you tackle someone in a game such as soccer, you try to get the ball away from them **3** If you tackle someone about something, you talk to them about it in order to get something changed or dealt with ▷ noun **4** A tackle in sport is an attempt to get the ball away from your opponent **5** Tackle is the equipment used for fishing

tacky tackier, tackiest adjective **1** slightly sticky to touch: *The cream feels tacky to the touch* **2** (informal) badly made and in poor taste: *tacky furniture*

tact noun Tact is the ability to see when a situation is difficult or delicate and to handle it without upsetting people > **tactless** adjective > **tactlessly** adverb

tactful adjective behaving with or showing tact > **tactfully** adverb

tactic noun **1** Tactics are the methods you use to achieve what you want, especially to win a game **2** Tactics are also the ways in which troops and equipment are used in order to win a battle

tactical adjective relating to or using tactics: *England made some tactical errors in the game.* > **tactically** adverb

tactile adjective involving the sense of touch

taffeta [taf-fit-a] noun Taffeta is a stiff, shiny fabric that is used mainly for making women's clothes

tag noun a small label made of cloth, paper, or plastic

tail noun **1** The tail of an animal, bird, or fish is the part extending beyond the end of its body **2** Tail can be used to mean the end part of something: *the tail of the plane* **3** (in plural) If a man is wearing tails, he is wearing a formal jacket which has two long pieces hanging down at the back ▷ verb **4** (informal) If you tail someone, you follow them in order to find out where they go and what they do ▷ adjective, adverb **5** The 'tails' side of a coin is the side which does not have a person's head > **tail off** verb If something tails off, it becomes gradually less

tailback noun a long queue of traffic stretching back from whatever is blocking the road

tailor noun **1** a person who makes, alters, and repairs clothes, especially for men ▷ verb **2** If something is tailored for a particular purpose, it is specially designed for it

tailor-made adjective suitable for a particular person or purpose, or specifically designed for them

taint verb 1 To taint something is to spoil it by adding something undesirable to it ▷ noun 2 an undesirable quality in something which spoils it

take takes, taking, took, taken verb 1 'Take' is used to show what action or activity is being done: *Amy took a bath; She took her driving test* 2 If something takes a certain amount of time, or a particular quality or ability, it requires it: *This takes three hours to get ready* 3 If you take something, you put your hand round it and hold it or carry it: *Here, let me take your coat* 4 If you take someone somewhere, you drive them there by car or lead them there 5 If you take something that is offered to you, you accept it: *He had to take the job* 6 If you take the responsibility or blame for something, you accept responsibility for it 7 If you take something that does not belong to you, you steal it 8 If you take pills or medicine, you swallow them 9 If you can take something painful, you can bear it: *We can't take much more of this* 10 If you take someone's advice, you do what they say you should do 11 If you take a person's temperature or pulse, you measure it 12 If you take a car or train, or a road or route, you use it to go from one place to another ▷ phrase 13 If you **take care of** someone or something, you look after them 14 If you **take care of** a problem or situation, you deal with it and get it sorted > **take after** verb If you take after someone in your

family, you look or behave like them > **take down** verb If you take down what someone is saying, you write it down > **take in** verb 1 If someone is taken in, they are deceived 2 If you take something in, you understand it > **take off** verb When an aeroplane takes off, it leaves the ground and begins to fly > **takeoff** noun > **take over** verb To take something over means to start controlling it > **takeover** noun > **take to** verb If you take to someone or something, you like them immediately

takeaway noun 1 a shop or restaurant that sells hot cooked food to be eaten elsewhere 2 a hot cooked meal bought from a takeaway

takings plural noun Takings are the money that a shop or cinema gets from selling its goods or tickets

tale noun a story

talent noun Talent is the natural ability to do something well > **talented** adjective

talisman [**tal**-iz-man] noun an object which you believe has magic powers to protect you or bring luck

talk verb 1 When you talk, you say things to someone 2 If people talk, especially about other people's private affairs, they gossip about them: *the neighbours might talk* 3 If you talk on or about something, you make an informal speech about it ▷ noun 4 Talk is discussion or gossip 5 an informal speech about something > **talk down** verb If you talk down to someone, you talk to them in a way that shows that you think you are more important or clever than them

talkative adjective talking a lot

tall adjective 1 of more than average

or normal height **2** having a particular height: *a wall ten metres tall* ▷ *phrase* **3** If you describe something as **a tall story**, you mean that it is difficult to believe because it is so unlikely

tally tallies, tallying, tallied *noun* **1** an informal record of amounts which you keep adding to as you go along: *He ended with a reasonable goal tally last season* ▷ *verb* **2** If numbers or statements tally, they are exactly the same or they give the same results or conclusions

tambourine *noun* a percussion instrument made of a skin stretched tightly over a circular frame, with small round pieces of metal around the edge that jingle when the tambourine is beaten or shaken

tame *adjective* **1** A tame animal or bird is not afraid of people and is not violent towards them **2** Something that is tame is uninteresting and lacks excitement or risk: *The report was pretty tame* ▷ *verb* **3** If you tame people or things, you bring them under control **4** To tame a wild animal or bird is to train it to be obedient and live with humans

tamper *verb* If you tamper with something, you interfere or meddle with it

tan tans, tanning, tanned *noun* **1** If you have a tan, your skin is darker than usual because you have been in the sun ▷ *verb* **2** To tan an animal's hide is to turn it into leather by treating it with chemicals ▷ *adjective* **3** Something that is tan is of a light yellowish-brown colour: *a tan dress*

tandem *noun* a bicycle designed for two riders sitting one behind the other

tang *noun* a strong, sharp smell or

flavour: *the tang of lemon* ▷ **tangy** *adjective*

tangerine *noun* **1** a type of small sweet orange with a loose rind ▷ *noun, adjective* **2** reddish-orange

tangible [**tan-jib-bl**] *adjective* clear or definite enough to be easily seen or felt: *tangible proof*

tangle *noun* **1** a mass of things such as hairs or fibres knotted or coiled together and difficult to separate ▷ *verb* **2** If you are tangled in wires or ropes, you are caught or trapped in them so that it is difficult to get free

tango tangos *noun* A tango is a Latin American dance using long gliding steps and sudden pauses; also a piece of music composed for this dance

tank *noun* **1** a large container for storing liquid or gas **2** an armoured military vehicle which moves on tracks and is equipped with guns or rockets

tanker *noun* a ship or lorry designed to carry large quantities of gas or liquid: *a petrol tanker*

tannin *noun* a brown or yellow substance found in plants and used in making leather

tantalizing or **tantalising** *adjective* Something that is tantalizing makes you feel hopeful and excited, although you know that you probably will not be able to have what you want: *a tantalizing glimpse of riches to come*

tantamount *adjective* If you say that something is tantamount to something else, you mean that it is almost the same as it: *That would be tantamount to treason*

tantrum *noun* a noisy and sometimes violent outburst of temper, especially by a child

Tanzanian [**tan-zan-nee-an**]

adjective **1** belonging or relating to Tanzania ▷ *noun* **2** someone who comes from Tanzania

tap taps, tapping, tapped *noun* **1 a** device that you turn to control the flow of liquid or gas from a pipe or container **2** the action of hitting something lightly; also the sound that this action makes ▷ *verb* **3** If you tap something or tap on it, you hit it lightly **4** If a telephone is tapped, a device is fitted to it so that someone can listen secretly to the calls

tape *noun* **1** Tape is plastic ribbon covered with a magnetic substance and used to record sounds, pictures, and computer information **2** a cassette or spool with magnetic tape wound round it **3** Tape is a long, thin strip of fabric that is used for binding or fastening **4** Tape is also a strip of sticky plastic which you use for sticking things together ▷ *verb* **5** If you tape sounds or television pictures, you record them using a tape recorder or a video recorder **6** If you tape one thing to another, you attach them using sticky tape

tape measure *noun* a strip of plastic or metal that is marked off in inches or centimetres and used for measuring things

taper *verb* **1** Something that tapers becomes thinner towards one end ▷ *noun* **2** a thin candle

tape recorder *noun* a machine used for recording sounds onto magnetic tape, and for playing these sounds back

tapestry tapestries *noun* a piece of heavy cloth with designs embroidered on it

tar *noun* Tar is a thick, black, sticky substance which is used in making roads

target *noun* **1** something which you aim at when firing weapons **2** The target of an action or remark is the person or thing at which it is directed: *You become a target for our hatred* **3** Your target is the result that you are trying to achieve

tariff *noun* **1 a** tax that a government collects on imported goods **2** any list of prices or charges

tarmac *noun* Tarmac is a material used for making road surfaces. It consists of crushed stones mixed with tar

tarnish *verb* **1** If metal tarnishes, it becomes stained and loses its shine **2** If something tarnishes your reputation, it spoils it and causes people to lose their respect for you

tarpaulin *noun* a sheet of heavy waterproof material used as a protective covering

tarragon *noun* Tarragon is a herb with narrow green leaves used in cooking

tart *noun* **1 a** pastry case with a sweet filling ▷ *adjective* **2** Something that is tart is sour or sharp to taste **3** A tart remark is unpleasant or cruel

tartan *noun* Tartan is a woollen fabric from Scotland with checks of various colours and sizes, depending on which clan it belongs to

task *noun* any piece of work which has to be done

Tasmanian devil *noun* a black-and-white marsupial of Tasmania, which eats flesh

taste *noun* **1** Your sense of taste is your ability to recognize the flavour of things in your mouth **2** The taste of something is its flavour **3** If you have a taste of food or drink, you have a small amount of it to see what it is like **4** If you have a taste for something, you enjoy it: *a taste for publicity* **5** If you have a taste of something, you experience it: *my first taste of defeat* **6** A person's taste is their choice in the things they like to buy or have around them: *His taste in music is great* ▷ *verb* **7** When you can taste something in your mouth, you are aware of its flavour **8** If you taste food or drink, you have a small amount of it to see what it is like **9** If food or drink tastes of something, it has that flavour

tasteful *adjective* attractive and elegant ▶ **tastefully** *adverb*

tasteless *adjective* **1** vulgar and unattractive **2** A tasteless remark or joke is offensive **3** Tasteless food has very little flavour

tasty tastier, tastiest *adjective* having a pleasant flavour

tatters *phrase* Clothes that are **in tatters** are badly torn > **tattered** *adjective*

tattoo tattoos, tattooing, tattooed *verb* **1** If someone tattoos you or tattoos a design on you, they draw it on your skin by pricking little holes and filling them with coloured dye ▷ *noun* **2** a picture or design tattooed on someone's body **3** a public military display of exercises and music

tatty tattier, tattiest *adjective* worn out or untidy and rather dirty

taught the past tense and past participle of **teach**

taunt *verb* **1** To taunt someone is to speak to them about their weaknesses or failures in order to make them angry or upset ▷ *noun* **2** an offensive remark intended to make a person angry or upset

Taurus *noun* Taurus is the second sign of the zodiac, represented by a

bull. People born between April 20th and May 20th are born under this sign

taut *adjective* stretched very tight: *taut wires*

tavern *noun* (old-fashioned) a pub

tawdry tawdrier, tawdriest [**taw**-dree] *adjective* cheap, gaudy, and of poor quality

tawny *noun, adjective* brownish-yellow

tax *noun* **1** Tax is an amount of money that the people in a country have to pay to the government so that it can provide public services such as health care and education ▷ *verb* **2** If a sum of money is taxed, a certain amount of it has to be paid to the government **3** If goods are taxed, a certain amount of their price has to be paid to the government **4** If a person or company is taxed, they have to pay a certain amount of their income to the government **5** If something taxes you, it makes heavy demands on you: *They must be told not to tax your patience* > **taxation** *noun*

taxi taxis, taxiing, taxied *noun* **1** a car with a driver which you hire to take you to where you want to go ▷ *verb* **2** When an aeroplane taxis, it moves slowly along the runway before taking off or after landing

tea *noun* **1** Tea is the dried leaves of an evergreen shrub found in Asia **2** Tea is a drink made by brewing the leaves of the tea plant in hot water; also a cup of this **3** Tea is also any drink made with hot water and leaves or flowers: *peppermint tea* **4** Tea is a meal taken in the late afternoon or early evening

teach teaches, teaching, taught *verb* **1** If you teach someone something, you give them instructions so that

they know about it or know how to do it **2** If you teach a subject, you help students learn about a subject at school, college, or university
> **teaching** noun

teacher noun a person who teaches other people, especially children

teak noun Teak is a hard wood which comes from a large Asian tree

team noun **1** a group of people who work together or play together against another group in a sport or game ▷ *verb* **2** If you team up with someone, you join them and work together with them

teamwork noun Teamwork is the ability of a group of people to work well together

teapot noun a round pot with a handle, a lid, and a spout, used for brewing and pouring tea

tear tears, tearing, tore, torn noun **1** [rhymes with **fear**] Tears are the drops of salty liquid that come out of your eyes when you cry **2** [rhymes with **hair**] a hole that has been made in something ▷ *verb* [rhymes with **hair**] **3** If you tear something, it is damaged by being pulled so that a hole appears in it **4** If you tear somewhere, you rush there: *He tore through busy streets in a high-speed chase*

tearaway noun someone who is wild and uncontrollable

tearful adjective about to cry or crying gently > **tearfully** adverb

tease verb **1** If you tease someone, you deliberately make fun of them or embarrass them because it amuses you ▷ noun **2** someone who enjoys teasing people

teaspoon noun a small spoon used for stirring drinks; also the amount that a teaspoon holds

tea tree noun a tree found in Australia and New Zealand with leaves that yield an oil used as an antiseptic: *Tea tree oil has many uses.*

tech noun (*informal*) a technical college

technical adjective **1** involving machines, processes, and materials used in industry, transport, and communications **2** skilled in practical and mechanical things rather than theories and ideas **3** involving a specialized field of activity: *I never understood the technical jargon*

technicalities technicalities noun **1** The technicalities of a process or activity are the detailed methods used to do it **2** an exact detail of a law or a set of rules, especially one some people might not notice: *The verdict may have been based on a technicality*

technically adverb If something is technically true or correct, it is true or correct when you consider only the facts, rules, or laws, but may not be important or relevant in a particular situation: *Technically, they were not supposed to drink on duty*

technician noun someone whose job involves skilled practical work with scientific equipment

technique noun **1** a particular method of doing something: *these techniques of manufacture* **2** Technique is skill and ability in an activity which is developed through training and practice: *Jim's unique vocal technique*

technology technologies noun **1** ⬚D & T⬚ Technology is the study of the application of science and scientific knowledge for practical purposes in industry, farming, medicine, or business **2** a particular area of activity that requires

scientific methods and knowledge: *computer technology*
> **technological** *adjective*
> **technologically** *adverb*

teddy teddies *noun* A teddy or teddy bear is a stuffed toy that looks like a friendly bear

tedious [tee-dee-uss] *adjective* boring and lasting for a long time: *the tedious task of clearing up*

tedium [tee-dee-um] *noun* the quality of being boring and lasting for a long time: *the tedium of unemployment*

tee tees, teeing, teed *noun* the small wooden or plastic peg on which a golf ball is placed before the golfer first hits it > **tee off** To tee off is to hit the golf ball from the tee, or to start a round of golf

teem *verb* 1 If a place is teeming with people or things, there are a lot of them moving about 2 If it teems, it rains very heavily: *The rain was teeming down*

teenage *adjective* 1 aged between thirteen and nineteen 2 typical of people aged between thirteen and nineteen: *teenage fashion*
> **teenager** *noun*

teens *plural noun* Your teens are the period of your life when you are between thirteen and nineteen years old

teeter *verb* To teeter is to shake or sway slightly in an unsteady way and seem about to fall over

teeth the plural of **tooth**

teethe [rhymes with **breathe**] *verb* When babies are teething, their teeth are starting to come through, usually causing them pain

teetotal [tee-toe-tl] *adjective* Someone who is teetotal never drinks alcohol > **teetotaller** *noun*

telecommunications *noun* Telecommunications is the science and activity of sending signals and messages over long distances using electronic equipment

telegram *noun* a message sent by telegraph

telegraph *noun* The telegraph is a system of sending messages over long distances using electrical or radio signals

telephone *noun* 1 a piece of electrical equipment for talking directly to someone who is in a different place > *verb* 2 If you telephone someone, you speak to them using a telephone

telescope *noun* a long instrument shaped like a tube which has lenses which make distant objects appear larger and nearer

televise *verb* If an event is televised, it is filmed and shown on television

television *noun* a piece of electronic equipment which receives pictures and sounds by electrical signals over a distance

tell tells, telling, told *verb* 1 If you tell someone something, you let them know about it 2 If you tell someone to do something, you order or advise them to do it 3 If you can tell something, you are able to judge correctly what is happening or what the situation is: *I could tell he was scared* 4 If an unpleasant or tiring experience begins to tell, it begins to have a serious effect: *The pressure began to tell*

teller *noun* a person who receives or gives out money in a bank

telling *adjective* Something that is telling has an important effect, often because it shows the true nature of a situation: *a telling account of the war*

telltale *adjective* A telltale sign

reveals information: *the sad telltale signs of a recent accident*

telly tellies *noun* (*informal*) a television

temerity [tim-**mer**-it-ee] *noun* If someone has the temerity to do something, they do it even though it upsets or annoys other people: *She had the temerity to call him Bob*

temp *noun* (*informal*) an employee who works for short periods of time in different places

temper *noun* 1 Your temper is the frame of mind or mood you are in 2 a sudden outburst of anger ▷ *phrase* 3 If you **lose your temper**, you become very angry ▷ *verb* 4 To temper something is to make it more acceptable or suitable: *curiosity tempered with even more caution*

temperament [**tem**-pra-ment] *noun* Your temperament is your nature or personality, shown in the way you react towards people and situations: *an artistic temperament*

temperamental *adjective* Someone who is temperamental has moods that change often and suddenly

temperate *adjective* A temperate place has weather that is neither extremely hot nor extremely cold

temperature *noun* 1 SCIENCE The temperature of something is how hot or cold it is 2 Your temperature is the temperature of your body ▷ *phrase* 3 If you **have a temperature**, the temperature of your body is higher than it should be, because you are ill

tempest *noun* (*literary*) a violent storm

tempestuous [tem-**pest**-yoo-uss] *adjective* violent or strongly emotional: *a tempestuous relationship*

template *noun* a shape or pattern

cut out in wood, metal, plastic, or card which you draw or cut around to reproduce that shape or pattern

temple *noun* 1 RE a building used for the worship of a god in various religions: *a Buddhist temple* 2 Your temples are the flat parts on each side of your forehead

tempo tempos *or* tempi *noun* 1 The tempo of something is the speed at which it happens: *the slow tempo of change* 2 MUSIC The tempo of a piece of music is its speed

temporary *adjective* lasting for only a short time ▷ **temporarily** *adverb*

tempt *verb* 1 If you tempt someone, you try to persuade them to do something by offering them something they want 2 If you are tempted to do something, you want to do it but you think it might be wrong or harmful: *He was tempted to reply with sarcasm*

temptation *noun* 1 Temptation is the state you are in when you want to do or have something, even though you know it might be wrong or harmful 2 something that you want to do or have, even though you know it might be wrong or harmful

ten the number 10 ▷ **tenth** *adjective*

tenacious [tin-**nay**-shuss] *adjective* determined and not giving up easily ▷ **tenaciously** *adverb* ▷ **tenacity** *noun*

tenant *noun* someone who pays rent for the place they live in, or for land or buildings that they use ▷ **tenancy** *noun*

tend *verb* 1 If something tends to happen, it happens usually or often 2 If you tend someone or something, you look after them: *the way we tend our cattle*

tendency tendencies *noun* a trend

or type of behaviour that happens very often: *a tendency to be critical*

tender *adjective* **1** Someone who is tender has gentle and caring feelings **2** If someone is at a tender age, they are young and do not know very much about life **3** Tender meat is easy to cut or chew **4** If a part of your body is tender, it is painful and sore ▷ *verb* **5** If someone tenders an apology or their resignation, they offer it ▷ *noun* **6** a formal offer to supply goods or to do a job for a particular price

tendon *noun* a strong cord of tissue which joins a muscle to a bone

tenement [ten-em-ent] *noun* a large house or building divided into many flats

tenet *noun* The tenets of a theory or belief are the main ideas it is based upon

tenner *noun* (*informal*) a ten-pound or ten-dollar note

tennis *noun* Tennis is a game played by two or four players on a rectangular court in which a ball is hit by players over a central net

tenor *noun* **1** a man who sings in a fairly high voice **2** The tenor of something is the general meaning or mood that it expresses: *the whole tenor of his poetry had changed* ▷ *adjective* **3** A tenor recorder, saxophone, or other musical instrument has a range of notes of a fairly low pitch

tense *adjective* **1** If you are tense, you are nervous and cannot relax **2** A tense situation or period of time is one that makes people nervous and worried **3** If your body is tense, your muscles are tight ▷ *verb* **4** If you tense, or if your muscles tense, your muscles become tight and stiff ▷ *noun* **5** The tense of a verb is the

form which shows whether you are talking about the past, present, or future

tension *noun* **1** Tension is the feeling of nervousness or worry that you have when something dangerous or important is happening **2** [D G T] The tension in a rope or wire is how tightly it is stretched

tent *noun* a shelter made of canvas or nylon held up by poles and pinned down with pegs and ropes

tentacle *noun* The tentacles of an animal such as an octopus are the long, thin parts that it uses to feel and hold things

tentative *adjective* acting or speaking cautiously because of being uncertain or afraid
> **tentatively** *adverb*

tenterhooks *plural noun* If you are on tenterhooks, you are nervous and excited about something that is going to happen

tenuous [ten-yoo-uss] *adjective* If an idea or connection is tenuous, it is so slight and weak that it may not really exist or may easily cease to exist: *a very tenuous friendship*

tenure [ten-yoor] *noun* **1** Tenure is the legal right to live in a place or to use land or buildings for a period of time **2** Tenure is the period of time during which someone holds an important job: *His tenure ended in 1998*

tepid *adjective* Tepid liquid is only slightly warm

term *noun* **1** a fixed period of time: *her second term of office* **2** one of the periods of time that each year is divided into at a school or college **3** a name or word used for a particular meaning or idea **4** (*in plural*) The terms of an agreement are the conditions that have been accepted by the people involved in it **5** If you express something in particular terms, you express it using a particular type of language or in a way that clearly shows your attitude: *The young priest spoke of her in glowing terms* ▷ *phrase* **6** If you **come to terms with** something difficult or unpleasant, you learn to accept it ▷ *verb* **7** To term something is to give it a name or to describe it: *He termed my performance memorable*

terminal *adjective* **1** A terminal illness or disease cannot be cured and causes death gradually ▷ *noun* **2** a place where vehicles, passengers, or goods begin or end a journey **3** A computer terminal is a keyboard and a visual display unit that is used to put information into or get information out of a computer **4** one of the parts of an electrical device through which electricity enters or leaves
> **terminally** *adverb*

terminate *verb* When you terminate something or when it terminates, it stops or ends
> **termination** *noun*

terminology terminologies *noun* The terminology of a subject is the set of special words and expressions used in it

terminus [ter-min-uss] *noun* a place where a bus or train route ends

termite *noun* Termites are small white insects that feed on wood

terrace *noun* **1** a row of houses joined together **2** a flat area of stone next to a building where people can sit

terracotta *noun* a type of brown pottery with no glaze

terrain *noun* The terrain of an area is

the type of land there: *the region's hilly terrain*

terrestrial *adjective* involving the earth or land

terrible *adjective* **1** serious and unpleasant: *a terrible illness* **2** (*informal*) very bad of or poor quality: *Paddy's terrible haircut*

terribly *adverb* very or very much: *I was terribly upset*

terrier *noun* a small, short-bodied dog

terrific *adjective* **1** (*informal*) very pleasing or impressive: *a terrific film* **2** great in amount, degree, or intensity: *a terrific blow on the head*
> **terrifically** *adverb*

terrify terrifies, terrifying, terrified *verb* If something terrifies you, it makes you feel extremely frightened

territorial *adjective* involving or relating to the ownership of a particular area of land or water: *a territorial dispute*

territory territories *noun* **1** The territory of a country is the land that it controls **2** An animal's territory is an area which it regards as its own and defends when other animals try to enter it

terror *noun* **1** Terror is great fear or panic **2** something that makes you feel very frightened

terrorism *noun* Terrorism is the use of violence for political reasons
> **terrorist** *noun, adjective*

terrorize or **terrorise** *verb* If someone terrorizes you, they frighten you by threatening you or being violent to you

terse *adjective* A terse statement is short and rather unfriendly

tertiary [ter-shar-ee] *adjective* **1** third in order or importance **2** Tertiary education is education at university or college level

t

test verb **1** When you test something, you try it to find out what it is, what condition it is in, or how well it works **2** If you test someone, you ask them questions to find out how much they know ▷ noun **3** a deliberate action or experiment to find out whether something works or how well it works **4** a set of questions or tasks given to someone to find out what they know or can do

testament noun **1** (Law) a will **2** a copy of either the Old or the New Testament of the Bible

test case noun a legal case that becomes an example for deciding other similar cases

testicle noun A man's testicles are the two sex glands beneath the penis that produce sperm

testify testifies, testifying, testified verb **1** When someone testifies, they make a formal statement, especially in a court of law: Ismay later testified at the British inquiry **2** To testify to something is to show that it is likely to be true: a consultant's certificate testifying to her good health

testimonial [tess-tim-**moh**-nee-al] noun a statement saying how good someone or something is

testimony testimonies noun A person's testimony is a formal statement they make, especially in a court of law

testing adjective Testing situations or problems are very difficult to deal with: It is a testing time for his team

test match noun one of a series of international cricket or rugby matches

testosterone [tess-**toss**-ter-rone] noun Testosterone is a hormone that produces male characteristics

test tube noun a small cylindrical glass container that is used in chemical experiments

tetanus [**tet**-ah-nuss] noun Tetanus is a painful infectious disease caused by germs getting into wounds

tether verb **1** If you tether an animal, you tie it to a post ▷ phrase **2** If you are **at the end of your tether**, you are extremely tired and have no more patience or energy left to deal with your problems

Teutonic [tyoo-**tonn**-ik] adjective (formal) involving or related to German people

text noun **1** The text of a book is the main written part of it, rather than the pictures or index **2** Text is any written material **3** a book or other piece of writing used for study or an exam at school or college **4** Text is short for 'text message' ▷ verb **5** If you text someone, you send them a text message > **textual** adjective

textbook noun a book about a particular subject for students to use

textile noun D & T a woven cloth or fabric

text message noun a written message sent using a mobile phone

texture noun The texture of something is the way it feels when you touch it

Thai Thais adjective **1** belonging or relating to Thailand ▷ noun **2** someone who comes from Thailand **3** Thai is the main language spoken in Thailand

than preposition, conjunction **1** You use 'than' to link two parts of a comparison: She was older than me **2** You use 'than' to link two parts of a contrast: Players would rather play than train

thank verb When you thank

someone, you show that you are grateful for something, usually by saying 'thank you'

thankful adjective happy and relieved about something
▷ **thankfully** adverb

thankless adjective A thankless job or task involves doing a lot of hard work that other people do not notice or are not grateful for: *Referees have a thankless task*

thanks plural noun **1** When you express your thanks to someone, you tell or show them how grateful you are for something **2** phrase **2** If something happened **thanks to** someone or something, it happened because of them: *I'm as prepared as I can be, thanks to you* ▷ interjection **3** You say 'thanks' to show that you are grateful for something

thanksgiving noun **1** Thanksgiving is an act of thanking God, especially in prayer or in a religious ceremony **2** In the United States, Thanksgiving is a public holiday in the autumn

thank you interjection You say 'thank you' to show that you are grateful to someone for something

that adjective, pronoun **1** 'That' or 'those' is used to refer to things or people already mentioned or known about: *That man was waving* ▷ conjunction **2** 'That' is used to introduce a clause: *I said that I was coming home* ▷ pronoun **3** 'That' is also used to introduce a relative clause: *I followed Alex to a door that led inside*

thatch noun **1** Thatch is straw and reeds used to make roofs ▷ verb **2** To thatch a roof is to cover it with thatch

thaw verb **1** When snow or ice thaws, it melts **2** When you thaw frozen food, or when it thaws, it

returns to its normal state in a warmer atmosphere **3** When people who are unfriendly thaw, they begin to be more friendly and relaxed ▷ noun **4** A period of warmer weather in winter when snow or ice melts

the adjective The definite article 'the' is used when you are talking about something that is known about, that has just been mentioned, or that you are going to give details about

theatre [thee-uh-tuh] noun **1** DRAMA a building where plays and other entertainments are performed on a stage **2** Theatre is work such as writing, producing, and acting in plays **3** An operating theatre is a room in a hospital designed and equipped for surgical operations

theatrical [thee-at-rik-kl] adjective **1** DRAMA involving the theatre or performed in a theatre: *his theatrical career* **2** Theatrical behaviour is exaggerated, unnatural, and done for effect ▷ **theatrically** adverb

thee pronoun (old-fashioned) Thee means you

theft noun Theft is the crime of stealing

their adjective 'Their' refers to something belonging or relating to people or things, other than yourself or the person you are talking to, which have already been mentioned: *It was their fault*

> **WORD TIP**
> Do not confuse the spellings of *their, there,* and *they're: Their house is the blue one; That's my car over there; They're always late*

theirs pronoun 'Theirs' refers to something belonging or relating to people or things, other than yourself or the person you are talking to, which have already been mentioned: *Amy had been Helen's friend, not theirs*

them *pronoun* 'Them' refers to things or people, other than yourself or the people you are talking to, which have already been mentioned: *He picked up the pillows and threw them to the floor*

theme *noun* **1** a main idea or topic in a piece of writing, painting, film, or music: *the main theme of the book* **2** a tune, especially one played at the beginning and end of a television or radio programme

themselves *pronoun* **1** 'Themselves' is used when people, other than yourself or the person you are talking to, do an action and are affected by it: *They think they've made a fool of themselves* **2** 'Themselves' is used to emphasize 'they': *He was as excited as they themselves were*

then *adverb* at a particular time in the past or future: *I'd left home by then*

theologian [thee-ol-**loe**-jee-an] *noun* someone who studies religion and the nature of God

theology *noun* Theology is the study of religion and God > **theological** *adjective*

theoretical *adjective* **1** based on or to do with ideas of a subject rather than the practical aspects **2** not proved to exist or to be true > **theoretically** *adverb*

theory theories *noun* **1** an idea or set of ideas that is meant to explain something: *Darwin's theory of evolution* **2** Theory is the set of rules and ideas that a particular subject or skill is based upon > *phrase* **3** You use **in theory** to say that although something is supposed to happen, it

may not in fact happen: *In theory, prices should rise by 2 per cent*

therapeutic [ther-ap-**yoo**-tik] *adjective* **1** If something is therapeutic, it helps you to feel happier and more relaxed: *Laughing is therapeutic* **2** In medicine, therapeutic treatment is designed to treat a disease or to improve a person's health

therapy *noun* Therapy is the treatment of mental or physical illness, often without the use of drugs or operations > **therapist** *noun*

there *adverb* **1** in, at, or to that place, point, or case: *He's sitting over there* > *pronoun* **2** 'There' is used to say that something exists or does not exist, or to draw attention to something: *There are flowers on the table*

> **WORD TIP**
>
> Do not confuse the spellings of *there*, *their*, and *they're*. A good way to remember that *there* is connected to the idea of place is by remembering the spelling of two other place words, *here* and *where*

thereby *adverb* (*formal*) as a result of the event or action mentioned: *They had recruited 200 new members, thereby making the day worthwhile*

therefore *adverb* as a result

thermal *adjective* **1** to do with or caused by heat: *thermal energy* **2** Thermal clothes are specially designed to keep you warm in cold weather

thermometer *noun* SCIENCE an instrument for measuring the temperature of a room or a person's body

thermostat *noun* a device used to control temperature, for example on a central heating system

thesaurus thesauruses [this-**saw**-russ] *noun* a reference book in which words with similar meanings are grouped together

these the plural of **this**

thesis theses [thee-siss] *noun* a long piece of writing, based on research, that is done as part of a university degree

they *pronoun* **1** 'They' refers to people or things, other than you or the people you are talking to, that have already been mentioned: *They married two years later* **2** 'They' is sometimes used instead of 'he' or 'she' where the gender of the person is unknown or unspecified. Some people consider this to be incorrect: *Someone could have a nasty accident if they tripped over that*

thick *adjective* **1** Something thick has a large distance between its two opposite surfaces **2** If something is a particular amount thick, it measures that amount between its two sides **3** Thick means growing or grouped closely together and in large quantities: *thick dark hair* **4** Thick liquids contain little water and do not flow easily: *thick soup* **5** (*informal*) A thick person is stupid or slow to understand things

thicken *verb* If something thickens, it becomes thicker: *The clouds thickened*

thicket *noun* a small group of trees growing closely together

thief thieves *noun* a person who steals

thieving *noun* Thieving is the act of stealing

thigh *noun* Your thighs are the top parts of your legs, between your knees and your hips

thin thinner, thinnest; thins, thinning, thinned *adjective* **1** Something that is thin is much narrower than it is long **2** A thin person or animal has very little fat on their body **3** Thin liquids contain a lot of water: *thin soup* ▷ *verb* **4** If you thin something such as paint or soup, you add water or other liquid to it

thing *noun* **1** an object, rather than a plant, an animal, or a human being **2** (*in plural*) Your things are your clothes or possessions

think thinks, thinking, thought *verb* **1** When you think about ideas or problems, you use your mind to consider them **2** If you think something, you have the opinion that it is true or the case: *I think she has a secret boyfriend* **3** If you think of something, you remember it or it comes into your mind **4** If you think a lot of someone or something, you admire them or think they are good

third *adjective* **1** The third item in a series is the one counted as number three ▷ *noun* **2** one of three equal parts

Third World *noun* The poorer countries of Africa, Asia, and South America can be referred to as the Third World

thirst *noun* **1** If you have a thirst, you feel a need to drink something **2** A thirst for something is a very strong desire for it: *a thirst for money* ▷ **thirsty** *adjective* ▷ **thirstily** *adverb*

thirteen the number 13 ▷ **thirteenth** *adjective*

thirty thirties the number 30 ▷ **thirtieth** *adjective*

this *adjective, pronoun* **1** 'This' is used to refer to something or someone that is nearby or has just been mentioned: *This is Robert* **2** 'This' is

t

used to refer to the present time or place: *this week*

thistle *noun* a wild plant with prickly-edged leaves and purple flowers

thong *noun* a long narrow strip of leather

thorn *noun* one of many sharp points growing on some plants and trees

thorny thornier, thorniest *adjective* **1** covered with thorns **2** A thorny subject or question is difficult to discuss or answer

thorough [thur-ruh] *adjective* **1** done very carefully and completely: *a thorough examination* **2** A thorough person is very careful in what they do and makes sure nothing has been missed out > **thoroughly** *adverb*

thoroughbred *noun* an animal that has parents that are of the same high quality breed

thoroughfare *noun* a main road in a town

those the plural of **that**

thou *pronoun* (old-fashioned) Thou means you

though [rhymes with **show**] *conjunction* **1** despite the fact that: *Meg felt better, even though she knew it was the end* **2** if: *It looks as though you were right*

thought **1** Thought is the past tense and past participle of **think** ▷ *noun* **2** an idea that you have in your mind **3** Thought is the activity of thinking: *She was lost in thought* **4** Thought is a particular way of thinking or a particular set of ideas: *this school of thought*

thoughtful *adjective* **1** When someone is thoughtful, they are quiet and serious because they are thinking about something **2** A

thoughtful person remembers what other people want or need, and tries to be kind to them > **thoughtfully** *adverb*

thoughtless *adjective* A thoughtless person forgets or ignores what other people want, need, or feel > **thoughtlessly** *adverb*

thousand the number 1000 > **thousandth** *adjective*

thrash *verb* **1** To thrash someone is to beat them by hitting them with something **2** To thrash someone in a contest or fight is to defeat them completely **3** To thrash out a problem or an idea is to discuss it in detail until a solution is reached

thread *noun* **1 a** long, fine piece of cotton, silk, nylon, or wool **2** The thread on something such as a screw or the top of a container is the raised spiral line of metal or plastic round it **3** The thread of an argument or story is an idea or theme that connects the different parts of it ▷ *verb* **4** When you thread something, you pass thread, tape, or cord through it **5** If you thread your way through people or things, you carefully make your way through them

threadbare *adjective* Threadbare cloth or clothing is old and thin

threat *noun* **1 a** statement that someone will harm you, especially if you do not do what they want **2** anything or anyone that seems likely to harm you **3** If there is a threat of something unpleasant happening, it is very possible that it will happen

threaten *verb* **1** If you threaten to harm someone or threaten to do something that will upset them, you say that you will do it **2** If someone or something threatens a person or thing, they are likely to harm them

three the number 3

three-dimensional adjective MATHS A three-dimensional object or shape is not flat, but has height or depth as well as length and width

threesome noun a group of three

threshold [thresh-hold] noun 1 the doorway or the floor in the doorway of a building or room 2 The threshold of something is the lowest amount, level, or limit at which something happens or changes: *the tax threshold; His boredom threshold was exceptionally low*

thrice adverb (old-fashioned) If you do something thrice, you do it three times

thrift noun Thrift is the practice of saving money and not wasting things

thrifty thriftier, thriftiest adjective A thrifty person saves money and does not waste things

thrill noun 1 a sudden feeling of great excitement, pleasure, or fear; also any event or experience that gives you such a feeling ▷ verb 2 If something thrills you, or you thrill to it, it gives you a feeling of great pleasure and excitement > **thrilled** adjective > **thrilling** adjective

thriller noun a book, film, or play that tells an exciting story about dangerous or mysterious events

thrive thrives, thriving, thrived or throve verb When people or things thrive, they are healthy, happy, or successful > **thriving** adjective

throat noun 1 the back of your mouth and the top of the

passages inside your neck 2 the front part of your neck

throb throbs, throbbing, throbbed verb 1 If a part of your body throbs, you feel a series of strong beats or dull pains 2 If something throbs, it vibrates and makes a loud, rhythmic noise: *The engines throbbed*

throes plural noun 1 Throes are a series of violent pangs or movements: *death throes* ▷ phrase 2 If you are **in the throes of** something, you are deeply involved in it

thrombosis thromboses [throm-**boe**-siss] noun a blood clot which blocks the flow of blood in the body. Thromboses are dangerous and often fatal

throne noun 1 a ceremonial chair used by a king or queen on important occasions 2 The throne is a way of referring to the position of being king or queen: *The Queen is celebrating 60 years on the throne*

throng noun 1 a large crowd of people ▷ verb 2 If people throng somewhere or throng a place, they go there in great numbers: *Hundreds of city workers thronged the scene*

throttle verb To throttle someone is to kill or injure them by squeezing their throat

through [threw] preposition 1 moving all the way from one side of something to the other: *a path through the woods* 2 because of: *He had been exhausted through lack of sleep* 3 during: *He has to work through the summer* 4 If you go through an experience, it happens to you: *I don't want to go through that again* ▷ adjective 5 If you are through with something, you have finished doing it or using it

t

WORD TIP

Do not confuse the spellings of *through* and *threw*, the past tense of *throw*: *The river runs through the centre of town*; *Aidan threw the ball over the fence*

throughout preposition 1 during: *I stayed awake throughout the night* ▷ adverb 2 happening or existing through the whole of a place: *The house was painted brown throughout*

throw throws, throwing, threw, thrown verb 1 When you throw something you are holding, you move your hand quickly and let it go, so that it moves through the air 2 If you throw yourself somewhere, you move there suddenly and with force: *We threw ourselves on the ground* 3 To throw someone into an unpleasant situation is to put them there: *It threw them into a panic* 4 If something throws light or shadow on something else, it makes that thing have light or shadow on it 5 If you throw yourself into an activity, you become actively and enthusiastically involved in it 6 If you throw a fit or tantrum, you suddenly begin behaving in an uncontrolled way

throwback noun something which has the characteristics of something that existed a long time ago: *Everything about her was a throwback to the fifties*

thrush noun a small brown songbird

thrust thrusts, thrusting, thrust verb 1 If you thrust something somewhere, you push or move it there quickly with a lot of force 2 If you thrust your way somewhere, you move along, pushing between people or things ▷ noun 3 a sudden forceful movement 4 The main thrust of an activity or idea is the most important part of it: *the general thrust of his argument*

thud thuds, thudding, thudded noun 1 a dull sound, usually made by a solid, heavy object hitting something soft ▷ verb 2 If something thuds somewhere, it makes a dull sound, usually by hitting something else

thug noun a very rough and violent person

thumb noun 1 the short, thick finger on the side of your hand ▷ verb 2 If someone thumbs a lift, they stand at the side of the road and stick out their thumb until a driver stops and gives them a lift

thump verb 1 If you thump someone or something, you hit them hard with your fist 2 If something thumps somewhere, it makes a fairly loud, dull sound, usually when it hits something else 3 When your heart thumps, it beats strongly and quickly ▷ noun 4 a hard hit: *a great thump on the back* 5 a fairly loud, dull sound

thunder noun 1 Thunder is a loud cracking or rumbling noise caused by expanding air which is suddenly heated by lightning 2 Thunder is any loud rumbling noise: *the distant thunder of bombs* ▷ verb 3 When it thunders, a loud cracking or rumbling noise occurs in the sky after a flash of lightning 4 If something thunders, it makes a loud continuous noise: *The helicopter thundered low over the trees*

thunderbolt noun a flash of lightning, accompanied by thunder

thunderous adjective A thunderous noise is very loud: *thunderous applause*

Thursday noun Thursday is the day between Wednesday and Friday

thus adverb (formal) **1** in this way: *I sat thus for nearly half an hour* **2** therefore: *She was more experienced than him, thus better paid*

thwart verb To thwart someone or their plans is to prevent them from doing or getting what they want

thy adjective (old-fashioned) Thy means your

thyme [time] noun Thyme is a bushy herb with very small leaves

tiara [tee-ah-ra] noun a semicircular crown of jewels worn by a woman on formal occasions

Tibetan adjective **1** belonging or relating to Tibet ▷ noun **2** someone who comes from Tibet

tic noun a twitching of a group of muscles, especially the muscles in the face

tick noun **1** a written mark to show that something is correct or has been dealt with **2** The tick of a clock is the series of short sounds it makes when it is working **3** a tiny, blood-sucking, insect-like creature that usually lives on the bodies of people or animals ▷ verb **4** To tick something written on a piece of paper is to put a tick next to it **5** When a clock ticks, it makes a regular series of short sounds as it works > **tick off** verb (informal) If you tick someone off, you speak angrily to them because they have done something wrong > **ticking** noun

ticket noun a piece of paper or card which shows that you have paid for a journey or have paid to enter a place of entertainment

tickle verb **1** When you tickle someone, you move your fingers lightly over their body in order to make them laugh **2** If something tickles you, it amuses you or gives you pleasure: *Simon is tickled by the idea*

tidal adjective to do with or produced by tides: *a tidal estuary*

tidal wave noun [GEOGRAPHY] a very large wave, often caused by an earthquake, that comes over land and destroys things

tide noun **1** The tide is the regular change in the level of the sea on the shore, caused by the gravitational pull of the sun and the moon **2** The tide of opinion or fashion is what the majority of people think or do at a particular time **3** A tide of something is a large amount of it: *the tide of anger and bitterness* > **tide over** verb If something will tide someone over, it will help them through a difficult period of time

tidings plural noun (formal) Tidings are news

tidy tidier, tidiest; tidies, tidying, tidied adjective **1** Something that is tidy is neat and arranged in an orderly way **2** Someone who is tidy always keeps their things neat and arranged in an orderly way **3** (informal) A tidy amount of money is a fairly large amount of it ▷ verb **4** To tidy a place is to make it neat by putting things in their proper place

tie ties, tying, tied verb **1** If you tie one thing to another or tie it in a particular position, you fasten it using cord of some kind **2** If you tie a knot or a bow in a piece of cord or cloth, you fasten the ends together to make a knot or bow **3** Something or someone that is tied to something else is closely linked with it: *40,000 jobs are tied to the project* **4** If you tie with someone in a competition or game, you have the same number of points ▷ noun **5** a long, narrow piece of cloth worn around the neck under a shirt collar and tied in a knot at the front **6** a connection or feeling that links you with a person, place, or organization: I had very close ties with the family

tied up adjective If you are tied up, you are busy

tier noun one of a number of rows or layers of something: Take the stairs to the upper tier

tiff noun (informal) a small unimportant quarrel

tiger noun a large meat-eating animal of the cat family. It comes from Asia and has an orange coloured coat with black stripes

tight adjective 1 fitting closely: The shoes are too tight 2 firmly fastened and difficult to move: a tight knot 3 stretched or pulled so as not to be slack: a tight cord 4 A tight plan or arrangement allows only the minimum time or money needed to do something: Our schedule tonight is very tight ▷ adverb 5 held firmly and securely: He held me tight ▷ **tightly** adverb ▷ **tightness** noun

tighten verb 1 If you tighten your hold on something, you hold it more firmly 2 If you tighten a rope or chain, or if it tightens, it is stretched or pulled until it is straight 3 If someone tightens a rule or system, they make it stricter or more efficient

tightrope noun a tightly stretched rope on which an acrobat balances and performs tricks

tights plural noun Tights are a piece of clothing made of thin stretchy material that fit closely round a person's hips, legs, and feet

tile noun 1 a small flat square piece of something, for example slate or carpet, that is used to cover surfaces ▷ verb 2 To tile a surface is to fix tiles to it ▷ **tiled** adjective

till preposition, conjunction 1 Till means the same as until ▷ noun 2 a drawer or box in a shop where money is kept, usually in a cash register ▷ verb 3 To till the ground is to plough it for raising crops

tiller noun the handle fixed to the top of the rudder for steering a boat

tilt verb 1 If you tilt an object or it tilts, it changes position so that one end or side is higher than the other ▷ noun 2 a position in which one end or side of something is higher than the other

timber noun 1 Timber is wood that has been cut and prepared ready for building and making furniture 2 The timbers of a ship or house are the large pieces of wood that are used to build it

timbre [tam-ber] noun (MUSIC) The timbre of a musical instrument, voice or sound is the particular quality or characteristic it has

time noun 1 Time is what is measured in hours, days, and years: What time is it? 2 'Time' is used to mean a particular period or point: I enjoyed my time in Durban 3 If you say it is time for something or it is time to do it, you mean that it ought to happen or be done now: It is time for a change 4 'Times' is used after numbers to indicate how often something happens: I saw my father four times a year 5 'Times' is used after numbers when you are saying how much bigger, smaller, better, or worse one thing is compared to another: The Belgians drink three times as much beer as the French 6 'Times' is used in arithmetic to link numbers that are multiplied together: Two times three is six ▷ verb 7 If you time something for a particular time, you plan that it should happen then: *We could not time our arrival better* **8** If you time an activity or action, you measure how long it lasts

timeless *adjective* Something timeless is so good or beautiful that it cannot be affected by the passing of time or by changes in fashion

timely *adjective* happening at just the right time: *a timely appearance*

timer *noun* a device that measures time, especially one that is part of a machine

timescale *noun* The timescale of an event is the length of time during which it happens

timetable *noun* **1** a plan of the times when particular activities or jobs should be done **2** a list of the times when particular trains, boats, buses, or aeroplanes arrive and depart

timid *adjective* shy and having no courage or self-confidence > **timidly** *adverb* > **timidity** *noun*

timing *noun* Someone's timing is their skill in judging the right moment at which to do something **2** The timing of an event is when it actually happens

tin *noun* **1** Tin is a soft silvery-white metallic element used in alloys. Its atomic number is 50, and its symbol is Sn **2** A tin is a metal container which is filled with food and then sealed in order to preserve the food **3** A tin is a small metal container which may have a lid: *a baking tin; the biscuit tin*

tinge *noun* a small amount of something: *a tinge of envy* > **tinged** *adjective*

tingle *verb* **1** When a part of your body tingles, you feel a slight prickling feeling in it ▷ *noun* **2** a slight prickling feeling > **tingling** *noun, adjective*

tinker *noun* **1** a person who travels from place to place mending metal pots and pans or doing other small repair jobs ▷ *verb* **2** If you tinker with something, you make a lot of small changes to it in order to repair or improve it: *All he wanted was to tinker with engines*

tinned *adjective* Tinned food has been preserved by being sealed in a tin

tinsel *noun* Tinsel is long threads with strips of shiny paper attached, used as a decoration at Christmas

tint *noun* **1** a small amount of a particular colour: *a distinct tint of green* ▷ *verb* **2** If a person tints their hair, they change its colour by adding a weak dye to it > **tinted** *adjective*

tiny tinier, tiniest *adjective* extremely small

tip tips, tipping, tipped *noun* **1** the end of something long and thin: *a fingertip* **2** a place where rubbish is dumped **3** If you give someone such as a waiter a tip, you give them some money to thank them for their services **4** a useful piece of advice or information ▷ *verb* **5** If you tip an object, you move it so that it is no longer horizontal or upright **6** If you tip something somewhere, you pour it there quickly or carelessly > **tipped** *adjective*

tipple *noun* A person's tipple is the alcoholic drink that they normally drink

tipsy tipsier, tipsiest *adjective* slightly drunk

tiptoe tiptoes, tiptoeing, tiptoed *verb* If you tiptoe somewhere, you walk there very quietly on your toes

tirade [tie-rade] *noun* a long, angry speech in which you criticize someone or something

tire verb **1** If something tires you, it makes you use a lot of energy so that you want to rest or sleep **2** If you tire of something, you become bored with it

tired adjective having little energy
> **tiredness** noun

tireless adjective Someone who is tireless has a lot of energy and never seems to need a rest

tiresome adjective A person or thing that is tiresome makes you feel irritated or bored

tiring adjective Something that is tiring makes you tired

tissue [**tiss**-yoo] noun **1** The tissue in plants and animals consists of cells that are similar in appearance and function: scar tissue; dead tissue **2** Tissue is thin paper that is used for wrapping breakable objects **3** a small piece of soft paper that you use as a handkerchief

tit noun a small European bird: a blue tit

titanic adjective very big or important

title noun **1** the name of a book, play, or piece of music **2** a word that describes someone's rank or job: My official title is Design Manager **3** the position of champion in a sports competition: the European featherweight title

titled adjective Someone who is titled has a high social rank and has a title such as 'Princess', 'Lord', 'Lady', or 'Sir'

TNT noun TNT is a type of powerful explosive. It is an abbreviation for 'trinitrotoluene'

to preposition **1** 'To' is used to indicate the place that someone or something is moving towards or pointing at: They are going to China **2** 'To' is used to indicate the limit of

something: Goods to the value of 500 pounds **3** 'To' is used in ratios and rates when saying how many units of one type there are for each unit of another: I only get about 30 kilometres to the gallon from it ▷ adverb **4** If you push or shut a door to, you close it but do not shut it completely

> **WORD TIP**
> The preposition to is spelt with one o, the adverb too has two os, and the number two is spelt with wo

toad noun an amphibian that looks like a frog but has a drier skin and lives less in the water

toast noun **1** Toast is slices of bread made brown and crisp by cooking at a high temperature **2** To drink a toast to someone is to drink an alcoholic drink in honour of them ▷ verb **3** If you toast bread, you cook it at a high temperature so that it becomes brown and crisp **4** If you toast yourself, you sit in front of a fire so that you feel pleasantly warm **5** To toast someone is to drink an alcoholic drink in honour of them

toaster noun a piece of electrical equipment used for toasting bread

tobacco noun Tobacco is the dried leaves of the tobacco plant which people smoke in pipes, cigarettes, and cigars

today adverb, noun **1** Today means the day on which you are speaking or writing **2** Today also means the present period of history: the challenges of growing up in today's society

toddler noun a small child who has just learned to walk

to-do to-dos noun A to-do is a situation in which people are very agitated or confused: It's just like him to make such a to-do about a baby

toe noun **1** Your toes are the five movable parts at the end of your foot **2** The toe of a shoe or sock is the part that covers the end of your foot

toff noun (informal, old-fashioned) a rich person or one from an aristocratic family

toffee noun Toffee is a sticky, chewy sweet made by boiling sugar and butter together with water

together adverb **1** If people do something together, they do it with each other **2** If two things happen together, they happen at the same time **3** If things are joined or fixed together, they are joined or fixed to each other **4** If things or people are together, they are very near to each other

togetherness noun Togetherness is a feeling of closeness and friendship

toil verb **1** When people toil, they work hard doing unpleasant, difficult, or tiring tasks or jobs ▷ noun **2** Toil is unpleasant, difficult, or tiring work

toilet noun **1** a large bowl, connected by a pipe to the drains, which you use when you want to get rid of urine or faeces **2** a small room containing a toilet

toiletries plural noun Toiletries are the things you use when cleaning and taking care of your body, such as soap and talc

token noun **1** a piece of paper or card that is worth a particular amount of money and can be exchanged for goods: book tokens **2** a flat round piece of metal or plastic that can sometimes be used instead of money **3** If you give something to someone as a token of your feelings for them, you give it to them as a way of showing those feelings

▷ adjective **4** If something is described as token, it shows that it is not being treated as important: a token contribution to your fees

told Told is the past tense and past participle of **tell**

tolerable adjective **1** able to be put up with **2** fairly satisfactory or reasonable: a tolerable salary

tolerance noun **1** A person's tolerance is their ability to accept or put up with something which may not be enjoyable or pleasant for them **2** Tolerance is the quality of allowing other people to have their own attitudes or beliefs, or to behave in a particular way, even if you do not agree or approve: religious tolerance

tolerant adjective accepting of different views and behaviour

tolerate verb **1** If you tolerate things that you do not approve of or agree with, you allow them **2** If you can tolerate something, you accept it, even though it is unsatisfactory or unpleasant ▷ **toleration** noun

toll noun **1** The death toll in an accident is the number of people who have died in it **2** a sum of money that you have to pay in order to use a particular bridge or road ▷ verb **3** When something tolls a bell, it is rung slowly, often as a sign that someone has died

tom noun a male cat

tomato noun tomatoes noun a small round red fruit, used as a vegetable and often eaten raw in salads

tomb noun a large grave for one or more corpses

tomboy noun a girl who likes playing rough or noisy games

tome noun (formal) a very large heavy book

tomorrow adverb, noun **1** Tomorrow

means the day after today **2** You can refer to the future, especially the near future, as tomorrow

ton noun **1 a** a unit of weight equal to 2240 pounds or about 1016 kilograms **b** (in plural, informal) If you have tons of something, you have a lot of it

tonal adjective involving the quality or pitch of a sound or of music

tone noun **1** Someone's tone is a quality in their voice which shows what they are thinking or feeling **2** MUSIC The tone of a musical instrument or a singer's voice is the kind of sound it has **3** ENGLISH The tone of a piece of writing is its style and the ideas or opinions expressed in it: *I was shocked at the tone of your leading article* **4** ART A lighter, darker, or brighter shade of the same colour: *The whole room is painted in two tones of orange* > **tone down** verb If you tone down something, you make it less forceful or severe

tongs plural noun Tongs consist of two long narrow pieces of metal joined together at one end. You press the pieces together to pick an object up

tongue noun **1** Your tongue is the soft part in your mouth that you can move and use for tasting, licking, and speaking **2** a language **3** Tongue is the cooked tongue of an ox **4** The tongue of a shoe or boot is the piece of leather underneath the laces

tonic noun **1** Tonic or tonic water is a colourless, fizzy drink that has a slightly bitter flavour and is often mixed with alcoholic drinks **2** a medicine that makes you feel stronger, healthier, and less tired **3** anything that makes you feel

stronger or more cheerful: *It was a tonic just being with her*

tonight adverb, noun Tonight is the evening or night that will come at the end of today

tonne [tun] noun MATHS a unit of weight equal to 1000 kilograms

tonsillitis [ton-sil-**lie**-tiss] noun Tonsillitis is a painful swelling of your tonsils caused by an infection

too adverb **1** also or as well: *You were there too* **2** more than a desirable, necessary, or acceptable amount: *We had spent too long in the sun*

> **WORD TIP**
>
> The adverb too has two os, the preposition to is spelt with one o, and the number two is spelt with wo

tool noun **1** any hand-held instrument or piece of equipment that you use to help you do a particular kind of work **2** an object, skill, or idea that is needed or used for a particular purpose: *You can use the survey as a bargaining tool in the negotiations*

tooth teeth noun **1** Your teeth are the hard, enamel-covered objects in your mouth that you use for biting and chewing food **2** The teeth of a comb, saw, or zip are the parts that stick out in a row on its edge

toothpaste noun Toothpaste is a substance which you use to clean your teeth

top tops, topping, topped noun **1** The top of something is its highest point, part, or surface **2** The top of a bottle, jar, or tube is its cap or lid **3** a piece of clothing worn on the upper half of your body **4** a toy with a pointed end on which it spins ▷ adjective **5** The top thing of a series of things is the highest one: *the top floor of the building* ▷ verb **6** If

someone tops a poll or popularity chart, they do better than anyone else in it: *It has topped the bestseller lists in almost every country* **7** If something tops a particular amount, it is greater than that amount: *The temperature topped 90°*
> **top up** *verb* To top something up is to add something to it in order to keep it at an acceptable or usable level

top hat *noun* a tall hat with a narrow brim that men wear on special occasions

topic *noun* a particular subject that you write about or discuss

topical *adjective* involving or related to events that are happening at the time you are speaking or writing

topping *noun* food that is put on top of other food in order to decorate it or add to its flavour

topple *verb* If something topples, it becomes unsteady and falls over

top-secret *adjective* meant to be kept completely secret

topsy-turvy *adjective* in a confused state: *My life was truly topsy-turvy*

Torah *noun* [RE] The Torah is Jewish law and teaching

torch *noun* **1** a small electric light carried in the hand and powered by batteries **2** a long stick with burning material wrapped around one end

torment *noun* [**tor**-ment] **1** Torment is extreme pain or unhappiness **2** something that causes extreme pain and unhappiness: *It's a torment to see them staring at me* > *verb* [tor-**ment**] **3** If something torments you, it causes you extreme unhappiness

torn 1 Torn is the past participle of **tear** > *adjective* **2** If you are torn between two or more things, you cannot decide which one to choose

and this makes you unhappy: *torn between duty and pleasure*

tornado *noun* tornadoes or tornados [tor-**nay**-doh] *noun* a violent storm with strong circular winds around a funnel-shaped cloud

torpedo torpedoes, torpedoing, torpedoed [tor-**pee**-doh] *noun* **1** a tube-shaped bomb that travels underwater and explodes when it hits a target > *verb* **2** If a ship is torpedoed, it is hit, and usually sunk, by a torpedo

torrent *noun* **1** When a lot of water is falling very rapidly, it can be said to be falling in torrents **2** A torrent of speech is a lot of it directed continuously at someone: *torrents of abuse*

torrential *adjective* Torrential rain pours down very rapidly and in great quantities

torrid *adjective* **1** Torrid weather is very hot and dry **2** If something is described as torrid, it involves very strong emotions

torso *noun* torsos the main part of your body, excluding your head, arms, and legs

tortoise *noun* a slow-moving reptile with a large hard shell over its body into which it can pull its head and legs for protection

tortuous *adjective* **1** A tortuous road is full of bends and twists **2** A tortuous piece of writing is long and complicated

torture *noun* **1** Torture is great pain that is deliberately caused to someone to punish them or get information from them > *verb* **2** If someone tortures another person, they deliberately cause that person great pain to punish them or get information **3** To torture someone is also to cause them to suffer

mentally: *Memory tortured her*
> **torturer** noun

Tory Tories noun In Britain, a member or supporter of the Conservative Party

toss verb **1** If you toss something somewhere, you throw it there lightly and carelessly **2** If you toss a coin, you decide something by throwing a coin into the air and guessing which side will face upwards when it lands **3** If you toss your head, you move it suddenly backwards, especially when you are angry, annoyed, or want your own way **4** To toss is to move repeatedly from side to side: *We tossed and turned and tried to sleep*

tot tots, totting, totted noun **1** a very young child **2** a small amount of strong alcohol such as whisky ▷ verb **3** To tot up numbers is to add them together

total totals, totalling, totalled noun **1** the number you get when you add several numbers together ▷ adjective **2** Total means complete: *a total failure* ▷ verb **3** When you total a set of numbers or objects, you add them all together **4** If several numbers total a certain figure, that is the figure you get when all the numbers are added together: *Their debts totalled over 300,000 dollars* > **totally** adverb

totalitarian [toe-tal-it-**tair**-ee-an] adjective A totalitarian political system is one in which one political party controls everything and does not allow any other parties to exist > **totalitarianism** noun

tote (informal) noun **1** The tote is a system of betting money on horses at a racetrack, in which all the money is divided among the people who have bet on the winning horses. Tote is an abbreviation for 'totalizator' ▷ verb **2** To tote a gun means to carry it

totter verb When someone totters, they walk in an unsteady way

touch verb **1** If you touch something, you put your fingers or hand on it **2** When two things touch, their surfaces come into contact: *Their knees were touching* **3** If you are touched by something, you are emotionally affected by it: *I was touched by his thoughtfulness* ▷ noun **4** Your sense of touch is your ability to tell what something is like by touching it **5** a detail which is added to improve something: *finishing touches* **6** a small amount of something: *a touch of mustard* ▷ phrase **7** If you are **in touch** with someone, you are in contact with them

touchdown noun Touchdown is the landing of an aircraft

touching adjective causing feelings of sadness and sympathy

touchy touchier, touchiest adjective **1** If someone is touchy, they are easily upset or irritated **2** A touchy subject is one that needs to be dealt with carefully, because it might upset or offend people

tough [tuff] adjective **1** A tough person is strong and independent and able to put up with hardship **2** A tough substance is difficult to break **3** A tough task, problem, or way of life is difficult or full of hardship **4** Tough policies or actions are strict and firm: *tough measures against organized crime* > **toughly** adverb > **toughness** noun > **toughen** verb

tour noun **1** a long journey during which you visit several places **2** a short trip round a place such as a city or famous building ▷ verb **3** If

you tour a place, you go on a journey
or a trip round it

tourism noun Tourism is the
business of providing services for
people on holiday, for example
hotels and sightseeing trips

tourist GEOGRAPHY noun a person
who visits places for pleasure or
interest

tournament noun PE a sports
competition in which players who
win a match play further matches,
until just one person or team is left

tousled adjective Tousled hair is
untidy

tout verb 1 If someone touts
something, they try to sell it 2 If
someone touts for business or
custom, they try to obtain it in a
very direct way: volunteers who spend
days touting for donations ▷ noun
3 someone who sells tickets outside
a sports ground or theatre, charging
more than the original price

tow verb 1 If a vehicle tows another
vehicle, it pulls it along behind it
▷ noun 2 To give a vehicle a tow is to
tow it ▷ phrase 3 If you have
someone **in tow**, they are with you
because you are looking after them

towards preposition 1 in the
direction of: He turned towards the
door 2 about or involving: My feelings
towards Susan have changed 3 as a
contribution for: a huge donation
towards the new opera house 4 near
to: We sat towards the back

towel noun a piece of thick, soft
cloth that you use to dry yourself
with

towelling noun Towelling is thick,
soft cloth that is used for making
towels

tower noun 1 a tall, narrow building,
sometimes attached to a larger
building such as a castle or church

▷ verb 2 Someone or something that
towers over other people or things
is much taller than them
> **towering** adjective

town noun 1 a place with many
streets and buildings where people
live and work 2 Town is the central
shopping and business part of a
town rather than the suburbs: She
has gone into town

township noun a small town in
South Africa where only Black
people or Coloured people were
allowed to live

toxic adjective poisonous: toxic waste

toxin noun a poison, especially one
produced by bacteria and very
harmful to living creatures

toy noun 1 any object made to play
with ▷ verb 2 If you toy with an idea,
you consider it without being very
serious about it: She toyed with the
idea of telephoning him 3 If you toy
with an object, you fiddle with it:
Jessica was toying with her glass

trace verb 1 If you trace something,
you find it after looking for it: Police
are trying to trace the owner
2 EXAM TERM To trace the
development of something is to find
out or describe how it developed 3 If
you trace a drawing or a map, you
copy it by covering it with a piece
of transparent paper and drawing
over the lines underneath ▷ noun
4 a sign which shows you that
someone or something has been in
a place: No trace of his father had been
found 5 a very small amount of
something > **tracing** noun

track noun 1 a narrow road or path
2 a strip of ground with rails on it
that a train travels along 3 a piece of
ground, shaped like a ring, which
horses, cars, or athletes race around
4 (in plural) Tracks are marks left on

the ground by a person or animal: *the deer tracks by the side of the path* ▷ *adjective* **5** In an athletics competition, the track events are the races on a running track ▷ *verb* **6** If you track animals or people, you find them by following their footprints or other signs that they have left behind > **track down** *verb* If you track down someone or something, you find them by searching for them

track record *noun* The track record of a person or a company is their past achievements or failures: *the track record of the film's star*

tracksuit *noun* a loose, warm suit of trousers and a top, worn for outdoor sports

tract *noun* **1** A tract of land or forest is a large area of it **2** a pamphlet which expresses a strong opinion on a religious, moral, or political subject **3** a system of organs and tubes in an animal's or person's body that has a particular function: *the digestive tract*

traction *noun* Traction is a form of medical treatment given to an injured limb which involves pulling it gently for long periods of time using a system of weights and pulleys

tractor *noun* a vehicle with large rear wheels that is used on a farm for pulling machinery and other heavy loads

trade *noun* **1** Trade is the activity of buying, selling, or exchanging goods or services between people, firms, or countries **2** Someone's trade is the kind of work they do, especially when it requires special training in practical skills: *a joiner by trade* ▷ *verb* **3** When people, firms, or countries trade, they buy, sell, or exchange goods or services **4** If you trade things, you exchange them: *Their mother had traded her rings for a few potatoes*

trademark *noun* a name or symbol that a manufacturer always uses on its products. Trademarks are usually protected by law so that no-one else can use them

trader *noun* a person whose job is to buy and sell goods: *a timber trader*

tradesman tradesmen *noun* a person, for example a shopkeeper, whose job is to sell goods

trade union *noun* an organization of workers that tries to improve the pay and conditions in a particular industry

tradition *noun* a custom or belief that has existed for a long time without changing

traditional *adjective* **1** Traditional customs or beliefs have existed for a long time without changing: *her traditional Indian dress* **2** A traditional organization or institution is one in which older methods are used rather than modern ones: *a traditional school* > **traditionally** *adverb*

traditionalist *noun* someone who supports the established customs and beliefs of their society, and does not want to change them

traffic traffics, trafficking, trafficked *noun* **1** Traffic is the movement of vehicles or people along a route at a particular time **2** Traffic in something such as drugs is an illegal trade in them ▷ *verb* **3** Someone who traffics in drugs or other goods buys and sells them illegally

traffic light *noun* Traffic lights are the set of red, amber, and green lights at a road junction which control the flow of traffic

tragedy tragedies [**traj**-id-ee] *noun*
1 an event or situation that is
disastrous or very sad **2** a serious
story or play, that usually ends with
the death of the main character

tragic *adjective* **1** Something tragic is
very sad because it involves death,
suffering, or disaster: *a tragic
accident* **2** Tragic films, plays, and
books are sad and serious: *a tragic
love story* ▷ **tragically** *adverb*

trail *noun* **1** a rough path across open
country or through forests **2** a series
of marks or other signs left by
someone or something as they
move along ▷ *verb* **3** If you trail
something or it trails, it drags along
behind you as you move, or it hangs
down loosely: *a small plane trailing a
banner* **4** If someone trails along,
they move slowly, without any
energy or enthusiasm **5** If a voice
trails away or trails off, it gradually
becomes more hesitant until it
stops completely

trailer *noun* a small vehicle which
can be loaded with things and
pulled behind a car

train *noun* **1** a number of carriages or
trucks which are pulled by a railway
engine **2** A train of thought is a
connected series of thoughts **3** A
train of vehicles or people is a line or
group following behind something
or someone: *a train of wives and
girlfriends* ▷ *verb* **4** If you train
someone, you teach them how to
do something **5** If you train, you
learn how to do a particular job: *She
trained as a serious actress* **6** If you
train for a sports match or a race,
you prepare for it by doing exercises
▷ **training** *noun*

trainee *noun* someone who is being
taught how to do a job

trainers *plural noun* Trainers are

shoes with thick rubber soles,
originally designed for running

trait *noun* a particular characteristic
or tendency. In literature, a trait is
an aspect of a character in a story,
for example, kind, greedy, funny, or
stupid: *a very English trait*

traitor *noun* HISTORY someone who
betrays their country or the group
which they belong to

trajectory trajectories
[traj-**jek**-tor-ee] *noun* The trajectory
of an object moving through the air
is the curving path that it follows

tram *noun* a vehicle which runs on
rails along the street and is powered
by electricity from an overhead wire

tramp *noun*. **1** a person who has no
home, no job, and very little money
2 a long country walk: *I took a long,
wet tramp through the fine woodlands*
▷ *verb* **3** If you tramp from one place
to another, you walk with slow,
heavy footsteps

trample *verb* **1** If you trample on
something, you tread heavily on it so
that it is damaged **2** If you trample
on someone or on their rights or
feelings, you behave in a way that
shows you don't care about them

trampoline *noun* a piece of
gymnastic equipment consisting of
a large piece of strong cloth held
taut by springs in a frame, on which
a person jumps for exercise of fun

trance *noun* a mental state in which
someone seems to be asleep but is
conscious enough to be aware of
their surroundings and to respond
to questions and commands

tranquil [**trang**-kwil] *adjective* calm
and peaceful: *tranquil lakes; I have a
tranquil mind* ▷ **tranquillity** *noun*

transaction ▷ *noun* a business deal
which involves buying and selling
something

transcend verb If one thing transcends another, it goes beyond it or is superior to it: *Her beauty transcends all barriers*

transcript noun a written copy of something that is spoken

transfer transfers, transferring, transferred verb **1** If you transfer something from one place to another, you move it: *They transferred the money to the Swiss account* **2** If you transfer to a different place or job, or are transferred to it, you move to a different place or job within the same organization ▷ noun **3** the movement of something from one place to another **4** a piece of paper with a design on one side which can be ironed or pressed onto cloth, paper, or china ▷ **transferable** adjective

transfixed adjective If a person is transfixed by something, they are so impressed or frightened by it that they cannot move: *Price stood transfixed at the sight of that tiny figure*

transform verb **1** If something is transformed, it is changed completely: *The frown is transformed into a smile* **2** MATHS To transform a shape is to change how it looks, for example by translation, reflection, rotation, or enlargement ▷ **transformation** noun

transfusion noun A transfusion or blood transfusion is a process in which blood from a healthy person is injected into the body of another person who is badly injured or ill

transient [tran-zee-ent] adjective Something transient does not stay or exist for very long: *transient emotions* ▷ **transience** noun

transistor noun **1** a small electrical device in something such as a television or radio which is used to control electric currents **2** A transistor or a transistor radio is a small portable radio

transit noun **1** Transit is the carrying of goods or people by vehicle from one place to another ▷ phrase **2** People or things that are **in transit** are travelling or being taken from one place to another: *damage that had occurred in transit*

transition noun a change from one form or state to another: *the transition from war to peace*

transitional adjective A transitional period or stage is one during which something changes from one form or state to another

transitory adjective lasting for only a short time

translate verb **1** To translate something that someone has said or written is to say it or write it in a different language **2** MATHS To translate a shape is to move it up or down, or from side to side, but not change it in any other way ▷ **translation** noun ▷ **translator** noun

translucent adjective If something is translucent, light passes through it so that it seems to glow: *translucent petals*

transmission noun **1** The transmission of something involves passing or sending it to a different place or person: *the transmission of infectious diseases* **2** The transmission of television or radio programmes is the broadcasting of them **3** a broadcast

transmit transmits, transmitting, transmitted verb **1** When a message or an electronic signal is transmitted, it is sent by radio waves **2** To transmit something to a different place or person is to pass it or send it to the place or person: *the clergy's role in transmitting knowledge* **> transmitter** *noun*

transparency transparencies *noun* **1** a small piece of photographic film which can be projected onto a screen **2** Transparency is the quality that an object or substance has if you can see through it

transparent *adjective* If an object or substance is transparent, you can see through it **> transparently** *adverb*

transpire *verb* **1** (*formal*) When it transpires that something is the case, people discover that it is the case: *It transpired that he had flown off on holiday* **2** When something transpires, it happens: *You start to wonder what transpired between them*

transplant *noun* **1** a process of removing something from one place and putting it in another: *a man who needs a heart transplant* **▷** *verb* **2** When something is transplanted, it is moved to a different place

transport *noun* **1** Vehicles that you travel in are referred to as transport: *public transport* **2** Transport is the moving of goods or people from one place to another: *The prices quoted include transport costs* **▷** *verb* **3** When goods or people are transported from one place to another, they are moved there

transportation *noun* Transportation is the transporting of people and things from one place to another

transvestite *noun* a person who enjoys wearing clothes normally worn by people of the opposite gender

trap traps, trapping, trapped *noun* **1** a piece of equipment or a hole that is carefully positioned in order to catch animals or birds **2** a trick that is intended to catch or deceive someone **▷** *verb* **3** Someone who traps animals catches them using traps **4** If you trap someone, you trick them so that they do or say something which they did not want to **5** If you are trapped somewhere, you cannot move or escape because something is blocking your way or holding you down **6** If you are trapped, you are in an unpleasant situation that you cannot easily change: *I'm trapped in an unhappy marriage* **> trapper** *noun*

trapeze *noun* a bar of wood or metal hanging from two ropes on which acrobats and gymnasts swing and perform skilful movements

trappings *plural noun* The trappings of a particular rank, position, or state are the clothes or equipment that go with it

trash *noun* **1** Trash is rubbish: *He picks up your trash on Mondays* **2** (*informal*) If you say that something such as a book, painting, or film is trash, you mean that it is not very good

trauma [**traw**-ma] *noun* a very upsetting experience which causes great stress: *the trauma of his mother's death*

traumatic *adjective* A traumatic experience is very upsetting

travel travels, travelling, travelled *verb* **1** To travel is to go from one place to another **2** When something reaches one place from another, you say that it travels there: *Gossip travels fast* **▷** *noun* **3** Travel is the act of travelling: *air travel* **4** (*in plural*) Someone's travels are the journeys that they make to places a long way from their home: *my travels in the*

Himalayas > **traveller** noun
> **travelling** adjective

traverse verb (formal) If you traverse an area of land or water, you go across it or over it: *They have traversed the island from the west coast*

travesty travesties noun a very bad or ridiculous representation or imitation of something: *The case is a travesty of justice*

trawl verb When fishermen trawl, they drag a wide net behind a ship in order to catch fish

trawler noun a fishing boat that is used for trawling

tray noun a flat object with raised edges which is used for carrying food or drinks

treacherous adjective **1** A treacherous person is likely to betray you and cannot be trusted **2** The ground or the sea can be described as treacherous when it is dangerous or unreliable: *treacherous mountain roads* > **treacherously** adverb

treachery noun Treachery is behaviour in which someone betrays their country or a person who trusts them

treacle noun Treacle is a thick, sweet syrup used to make cakes and toffee: *treacle tart*

tread treads, treading, trod, trodden verb **1** If you tread on something, you walk on it or step on it **2** If you tread something into the ground or into a carpet, you crush it in by stepping on it: *bubblegum that has been trodden into the pavement* > noun **3** A person's tread is the sound they make with their feet as they walk: *his heavy tread* **4** The tread of a tyre or shoe is the pattern of ridges on it that stops it slipping

treadmill noun **1** an exercise machine with a continuous moving belt for walking or running on **2** Any task or job that you must keep doing even though it is unpleasant or tiring can be referred to as a treadmill: *My life is one constant treadmill of making music*

treason noun Treason is the crime of betraying your country, for example by helping its enemies

treasure noun **1** Treasure is a collection of gold, silver, jewels, or other precious objects, especially one that has been hidden: *buried treasure* **2** Treasures are valuable works of art: *the finest art treasures in the world* > verb **3** If you treasure something, you are very pleased that you have it and regard it as very precious: *He treasures his friendship with her* > **treasured** adjective

treasurer noun a person who is in charge of the finance and accounts of an organization

Treasury noun The Treasury is the government department that deals with the country's finances

treat verb **1** If you treat someone in a particular way, you behave that way towards them **2** If you treat something in a particular way, you deal with it that way or see it that way: *We are now treating this case as murder* **3** When a doctor treats a patient or an illness, he or she gives them medical care and attention **4** If something such as wood or cloth is treated, a special substance is put on it in order to protect it or give it special properties: *The carpet's been treated with a stain protector* **5** If you treat someone, you buy or arrange something special for them which they will enjoy > noun **6** If you give someone a treat, you buy or arrange something special for them which they will enjoy: *my birthday treat* > **treatment** noun

treatise [tree-tiz] noun a long formal piece of writing about a particular subject

treaty treaties noun a written agreement between countries in which they agree to do something or to help each other

treble verb **1** If something trebles or is trebled, it becomes three times greater in number or amount: *Next year we can treble that amount* ▷ adjective **2** Treble means three times as large or three times as strong as previously: *a treble dose*

tree noun a large plant with a hard woody trunk, branches, and leaves

trek treks, trekking, trekked verb **1** If you trek somewhere, you go on a long and difficult journey ▷ noun **2** a long and difficult journey, especially one made by walking

trellis noun a frame made of horizontal and vertical strips of wood or metal and used to support plants

tremble verb **1** If you tremble, you shake slightly, usually because you are frightened or cold **2** If something trembles, it shakes slightly **3** If your voice trembles, it sounds unsteady, usually because you are frightened or upset > **trembling** adjective

tremendous adjective **1** large or impressive: *a tremendous size* **2** (informal) very good or pleasing: *tremendous fun* > **tremendously** adverb

tremor noun **1** a shaking movement of your body which you cannot control **2** an unsteady quality in your voice, for example when you are upset **3** a small earthquake

trench noun a long narrow channel

dug into the ground

trenchant [trent-shent] adjective Trenchant writings or comments are bold and firmly expressed

trend noun a change towards doing or being something different

trendy trendier, trendiest adjective (informal) Trendy things or people are fashionable

trepidation noun (formal) Trepidation is fear or anxiety: *He saw the look of trepidation on my face*

trespass verb If you trespass on someone's land or property, you go onto it without their permission > **trespasser** noun

tresses plural noun (old-fashioned) A woman's tresses are her long flowing hair

trestle noun a wooden or metal structure that is used as one of the supports for a table

trevally trevallies noun an Australian and New Zealand fish that is caught for both food and sport

triad [try-ad] noun **1** (formal) a group of three similar things **2** MUSIC In music, a triad is a chord of three notes consisting of the tonic and the third and fifth above it

trial noun **1** the legal process in which a judge and jury decide whether a person is guilty of a particular crime after listening to all the evidence about it **2** an experiment in which something is tested: *Trials of the drug start next month*

triangle noun **1** MATHS a shape with three straight sides **2** a percussion instrument consisting of a thin steel bar bent in the shape of a triangle > **triangular** adjective

triathlon [tri-ath-lon] noun a sports contest in which athletes compete in three different events

tribe noun a group of people of the same race, who have the same customs, religion, language, or land, especially when they are thought to be primitive ▷ **tribal** adjective

tribulation noun (formal) Tribulation is trouble or suffering: the tribulations of a female football star

tribunal [try-**byoo**-nl] noun a special court or committee appointed to deal with particular problems: an industrial tribunal

tributary tributaries noun a stream or river that flows into a larger river

tribute noun 1 A tribute is something said or done to show admiration and respect for someone: Police paid tribute to her courage 2 If one thing is a tribute to another, it is the result of the other thing and shows how good it is: His success has been a tribute to hard work

trick noun 1 an action done to deceive someone 2 Tricks are clever or skilful actions done in order to entertain people: magic tricks ▷ verb 3 If someone tricks you, they deceive you

trickery noun Trickery is deception: He accused the Serbs of trickery

trickle verb 1 When a liquid trickles somewhere, it flows slowly in a thin stream 2 When people or things trickle somewhere, they move there slowly in small numbers or quantities ▷ noun 3 a thin stream of liquid 4 A trickle of people or things is a small number or quantity of them

tricky trickier, trickiest adjective difficult to do or deal with

tricycle noun a vehicle similar to a bicycle but with two wheels at the back and one at the front

trifle noun 1 A trifle means a little: He seemed a trifle annoyed 2 Trifles are things that are not very important or valuable 3 a cold pudding made of layers of sponge cake, fruit, jelly, and custard ▷ verb 4 If you trifle with someone or something, you treat them in a disrespectful way: He was not to be trifled with

trifling adjective small and unimportant

trigger noun 1 the small lever on a gun which is pulled in order to fire it ▷ verb 2 If something triggers an event or triggers it off, it causes it to happen

trillion noun 1 A trillion is a million million. This is shown as one followed by twelve zeros 2 (informal) Trillions of things means an extremely large number of them

trilogy trilogies noun a series of three books or plays that have the same characters or are on the same subject

trim trimmer, trimmest; trims, trimming, trimmed adjective 1 neat, tidy, and attractive ▷ verb 2 To trim something is to clip small amounts off it 3 If you trim off parts of something, you cut them off because they are not needed: Trim off the excess marzipan ▷ noun 4 If something is given a trim, it is cut a little: All styles need a trim every six to eight weeks 5 a decoration on something, especially along its edges: a fur trim ▷ **trimmed** adjective

trimming noun Trimmings are extra parts added to something for decoration or as a luxury: bacon and eggs with all the trimmings

trinity noun 1 RE In the Christian religion, the Trinity is the joining of God the Father, God the Son, and God the Holy Spirit 2 (literary) A trinity is a group of three things or people

trinket noun a cheap ornament or piece of jewellery

trio trios noun 1 a group of three musicians who sing or play together; also a piece of music written for three instruments or singers 2 any group of three things or people together: a trio of children's tales

trip trips, tripping, tripped noun 1 a journey made to a place ▷ verb 2 If you trip, you catch your foot on something and fall over 3 If you trip someone or trip them up, you make them fall over by making them catch their foot on something

tripe noun Tripe is the stomach lining of a pig, cow, or ox, which is cooked and eaten

triple adjective 1 consisting of three things or three parts: the Triple Alliance ▷ verb 2 If you triple something or if it triples, it becomes three times greater in number or size

triplet noun Triplets are three children born at the same time to the same mother

tripod [try-pod] noun a stand with three legs used to support something like a camera or telescope

trite adjective dull and not original: his trite novels

triumph noun 1 a great success or achievement 2 Triumph is a feeling of great satisfaction when you win or achieve something ▷ verb 3 If you triumph, you win a victory or succeed in overcoming something

triumphal adjective done or made to celebrate a victory or great success: a triumphal return to Rome

triumphant adjective Someone who is triumphant feels very happy because they have won a victory or have achieved something: a triumphant shout

trivia plural noun Trivia are unimportant things

trivial adjective Something trivial is unimportant

troll noun 1 an imaginary creature in Scandinavian mythology that lives in caves or mountains and is believed to turn to stone at daylight 2 (slang) a person who makes offensive or provocative posts on a website ▷ verb 3 (slang) If you troll, you deliberately make offensive or provocative posts on a website

trolley noun 1 a small table on wheels 2 a small cart on wheels used for carrying heavy objects: a supermarket trolley

trombone noun a brass wind instrument with a U-shaped slide which you move to produce different notes

troop noun 1 Troops are soldiers 2 A troop of people or animals is a group of them ▷ verb 3 If people troop somewhere, they go there in a group

trooper noun a low-ranking soldier in the cavalry

trophy trophies noun 1 a cup or shield given as a prize to the winner of a competition 2 something you keep to remember a success or victory

tropical adjective belonging to or typical of the tropics: a tropical island

tropics plural noun The tropics are the hottest parts of the world between two lines of latitude, the Tropic of Cancer, 23½° north of the equator, and the Tropic of Capricorn, 23½° south of the equator

trot trots, trotting, trotted verb 1 When a horse trots, it moves at a speed between a walk and a canter, lifting its feet quite high off the ground **2** If you trot, you run or jog using small quick steps ▷ *noun* **3** When a horse breaks into a trot, it starts trotting

trotter *noun* A pig's trotters are its feet

trouble *noun* **1** Troubles are difficulties or problems **2** If there is trouble, people are quarrelling or fighting: *There was more trouble after the match* ▷ *phrase* **3** If you are **in trouble**, you are in a situation where you may be punished because you have done something wrong ▷ *verb* **4** If something troubles you, it makes you feel worried or anxious **5** If you trouble someone for something, you disturb them in order to ask them for it: *Can I trouble you for some milk?* ▷ **troubling** *adjective* ▷ **troubled** *adjective*

troublesome *adjective* causing problems or difficulties: *a troublesome teenager*

trough [troff] *noun* a long, narrow container from which animals drink or feed

trounce *verb* If you trounce someone, you defeat them completely

troupe [troop] *noun* a group of actors, singers, or dancers who work together and often travel around together

trousers *plural noun* Trousers are a piece of clothing covering the body from the waist down, enclosing each leg separately

trout *noun* a type of freshwater fish

trowel *noun* **1** a small garden tool with a curved, pointed blade used for planting or weeding **2** a small tool with a flat blade used for

spreading cement or plaster

truant *noun* **1** a child who stays away from school without permission ▷ *phrase* **2** If children **play truant**, they stay away from school without permission ▷ **truancy** *noun*

truce *noun* an agreement between two people or groups to stop fighting for a short time

truck *noun* **1** a large motor vehicle used for carrying heavy loads **2** an open vehicle for carrying goods on a railway

truculent [truk-yoo-lent] *adjective* bad-tempered and aggressive ▷ **truculence** *noun*

trudge *verb* **1** If you trudge, you walk with slow, heavy steps ▷ *noun* **2** a slow tiring walk: *the long trudge home*

true *adjective* truer, truest **1** A true story or statement is based on facts and is not made up **2** 'True' is used to describe things or people that are genuine: *She was a true friend* **3** True feelings are sincere and genuine ▷ *phrase* **4** If something **comes true**, it actually happens ▷ **truly** *adverb*

truffle *noun* **1** a soft, round sweet made from chocolate **2** a round mushroom-like fungus which grows underground and is considered very good to eat

trump *noun* In a game of cards, trumps is the suit with the highest value

trumpet *noun* **1** a brass wind instrument with a narrow tube ending in a bell-like shape ▷ *verb* **2** When an elephant trumpets, it makes a sound like a very loud trumpet

truncated *adjective* Something that is truncated is made shorter

trundle *verb* If you trundle something or it trundles

somewhere, it moves or rolls along slowly

trunk noun **1** the main stem of a tree from which the branches and roots grow **2** the main part of your body, excluding your head, neck, arms, and legs **3** the long flexible nose of an elephant **4** a large, strong case or box with a hinged lid for storing things **5** (in plural) A man's trunks are his bathing pants or shorts

truss verb To truss someone or truss them up is to tie them up so that they cannot move

trust verb **1** If you trust someone, you believe that they are honest and will not harm you **2** If you trust someone to do something, you believe they will do it successfully or properly **3** If you trust someone with something, you give it to them or tell it to them: One member of the group cannot be trusted with the secret **4** If you do not trust something, you feel that it is not safe or reliable: I didn't trust my arms and legs to work ▷ noun **5** Trust is the responsibility you are given to deal with or look after important or secret things: He had built up a position of trust **6** a financial arrangement in which an organization looks after and invests money for someone ▷ **trusting** adjective

trustee noun someone who is allowed by law to control money or property they are keeping or investing for another person

trustworthy adjective A trustworthy person is reliable and responsible and can be trusted

trusty trustier, trustiest adjective Trusty things and animals are considered to be reliable because they have always worked well in the past: a trusty black labrador

truth noun **1** The truth is the facts about something, rather than things that are imagined or made up: I know she was telling the truth **2** an idea or principle that is generally accepted to be true: the basic truths in life

truthful adjective A truthful person is honest and tells the truth ▷ **truthfully** adverb

try tries, trying, tried verb **1** To try to do something is to make an effort to do it **2** If you try something, you use it or do it to test how useful or enjoyable it is: Howard wanted me to try the wine **3** When a person is tried, they appear in court and a judge and jury decide if they are guilty after hearing the evidence ▷ noun **4** an attempt to do something **5** a test of something: You gave it a try **6** In rugby, a try is scored when someone carries the ball over the goal line of the opposing team and touches the ground with it

trying adjective Something or someone trying is difficult to deal with and makes you feel impatient or annoyed

tryst [trist] noun an appointment or meeting, especially between lovers in a quiet, secret place

tsar [zar] or **czar** noun a Russian emperor or king between 1547 and 1917

T-shirt or **tee shirt** noun a simple short-sleeved cotton shirt with no collar

tsunami tsunamis noun GEOGRAPHY a large, often destructive sea wave, caused by an earthquake or volcanic eruption under the sea

tub noun a wide circular container

tuba noun a large brass musical instrument that can produce very low notes

tubby tubbier, tubbiest *adjective* rather fat

tube *noun* **1** a round, hollow pipe **2** a soft metal or plastic cylindrical container with a screw cap at one end: *a tube of toothpaste* > **tubing** *noun*

tuberculosis [tyoo-ber-kyoo-**loe**-siss] *noun* Tuberculosis is a serious infectious disease affecting the lungs

tubular *adjective* in the shape of a tube

TUC In Britain, an abbreviation for 'Trades Union Congress', which is an association of trade unions

tuck *verb* **1** If you tuck something somewhere, you put it there so that it is safe or comfortable: *She tucked the letter into her handbag* **2** If you tuck a piece of fabric into or under something, you push the loose ends inside or under it to make it tidy **3** If something is tucked away, it is in a quiet place where few people go: *a little house tucked away in a valley*

tucker (*informal*) *noun* **1** In Australian and New Zealand English, tucker is food > *verb* **2** In Australian and New Zealand English, if you are tuckered out you are tired out

Tudor *noun* Tudor was the family name of the English monarchs who reigned from 1485 to 1603

Tuesday *noun* Tuesday is the day between Monday and Wednesday

tug tugs, tugging, tugged *verb* **1** To tug something is to give it a quick, hard pull > *noun* **2** a quick, hard pull: *He felt a tug at his arm* **3** a small, powerful boat which tows large ships

tug of war *noun* A tug of war is a sport in which two teams test their strength by pulling against each other on opposite ends of a rope

tuition *noun* Tuition is the teaching of a subject, especially to one person or to a small group

tulip *noun* a brightly coloured spring flower

tumble *verb* **1** To tumble is to fall with a rolling or bouncing movement ▷ *noun* **2** a fall

tumbler *noun* a drinking glass with straight sides

tummy tummies *noun* (*informal*) Your tummy is your stomach

tumour [tyoo-mur] *noun* a mass of diseased or abnormal cells that has grown in a person's or animal's body

tumultuous *adjective* A tumultuous event or welcome is very noisy because people are happy or excited

tuna [tyoo-na] *noun* Tuna are large fish that live in warm seas and are caught for food

tundra *noun* The tundra is a vast treeless Arctic region

tune *noun* **1** a series of musical notes arranged in a particular way ▷ *verb* **2** To tune a musical instrument is to adjust it so that it produces the right notes **3** To tune an engine or machine is to adjust it so that it works well **4** If you tune to a particular radio or television station you turn or press the controls to select the station you want to listen to or watch ▷ *phrase* **5** If your voice or an instrument is **in tune**, it produces the right notes

tuneful *adjective* having a pleasant and easily remembered tune

tuner *noun* A piano tuner is a person whose job it is to tune pianos

tunic *noun* a sleeveless garment covering the top part of the body and reaching to the hips, thighs, or knees

Tunisian [tyoo-niz-ee-an] *adjective* **1** belonging or relating to Tunisia

▷ **noun 2** someone who comes from Tunisia

tunnel tunnels, tunnelling, tunnelled noun **1** a long underground passage ▷ verb **2** To tunnel is to make a tunnel

turban noun a head-covering worn by a Hindu, Muslim, or Sikh man, consisting of a long piece of cloth wound round his head

turbine noun a machine or engine in which power is produced when a stream of air, gas, water, or steam pushes the blades of a wheel and makes it turn round

turbulent adjective **1** A turbulent period of history is one where there is much uncertainty, and possibly violent change **2** Turbulent air or water currents make sudden changes of direction > **turbulence** noun

turf turves; turfs, turfing, turfed noun Turf is short, thick, even grass and the layer of soil beneath it > **turf out** verb (informal) To turf someone out is to force them to leave a place

turgid [tur-jid] adjective (literary) A turgid play, film, or piece of writing is difficult to understand and rather boring

Turk noun someone who comes from Turkey

turkey turkeys noun a large bird kept for food; also the meat of this bird

Turkish adjective **1** belonging to or relating to Turkey ▷ noun **2** Turkish is the main language spoken in Turkey

turmoil noun Turmoil is a state of confusion, disorder, or great anxiety: Europe is in a state of turmoil

turn verb **1** When you turn, you move so that you are facing or going in a different direction **2** When you turn

something or when it turns, it moves or rotates so that it faces in a different direction or is in a different position **3** If you turn your attention or thoughts to someone or something, you start thinking about them or discussing them **4** When something turns or is turned into something else, it becomes something different: A hobby can be turned into a career ▷ noun **5** an act of turning something so that it faces in a different direction or is in a different position **6** a change in the way something is happening or being done: Her career took a turn for the worse **7** If it is your turn to do something, you have the right, chance, or duty to do it ▷ phrase **8 In turn** is used to refer to people, things, or actions that are in sequence one after the other > **turn down** verb If you turn down someone's request or offer, you refuse or reject it > **turn up** verb **1** If someone or something turns up, they arrive or appear somewhere **2** If something turns up, it is found or discovered

turning noun a road which leads away from the side of another road

turning point noun the moment when decisions are taken and events start to move in a different direction

turnip noun a round root vegetable with a white or yellow skin

turnout noun The turnout at an event is the number of people who go to it

turnover noun **1** The turnover of people in a particular organization or group is the rate at which people leave it and are replaced by others **2** The turnover of a company is the value of the goods or services sold during a particular period

turnstile noun a revolving mechanical barrier at the entrance to places like football grounds or zoos

turquoise [tur-kwoyz] noun, adjective **1** light bluish-green ▷ noun **2** Turquoise is a bluish-green stone used in jewellery

turret noun a small narrow tower on top of a larger tower or other buildings

turtle noun a large reptile with a thick shell covering its body and flippers for swimming. It lays its eggs on land but lives the rest of its life in the sea

tussle noun an energetic fight or argument between two people, especially about something they both want

tutor noun **1** a teacher at a college or university **2** a private teacher ▷ verb **3** If someone tutors a person or subject, they teach that person or subject

tutorial noun a teaching session involving a tutor and a small group of students

tutu [too-too] noun a short stiff skirt worn by female ballet dancers

TV noun **1** TV is television **2** a television set

twang noun **1** a sound like the one made by pulling and then releasing a tight wire **2** A twang is a nasal quality in a person's voice ▷ verb **3** If a tight wire or string twangs or you twang it, it makes a sound as it is pulled and then released

tweak verb **1** If you tweak something, you twist it or pull it ▷ noun **2** a short twist or pull of something

twee adjective sweet and pretty but in bad taste or sentimental

tweed noun Tweed is a thick woollen cloth

tweet verb **1** When a small bird tweets, it makes a short, high-pitched sound **2** If you tweet, you send a message on the social networking site Twitter ▷ noun **3** a short high-pitched sound made by a small bird **4** a message sent on the social networking site Twitter

tweezers plural noun Tweezers are a small tool with two arms which can be closed together and are used for pulling out hairs or picking up small objects

twelve the number 12 ▷ **twelfth** adjective

twenty twenties the number 20 ▷ **twentieth** adjective

twice adverb Twice means two times

twig noun a very small thin branch growing from a main branch of a tree or bush

twilight [twy-lite] noun **1** Twilight is the time after sunset when it is just getting dark **2** The twilight of something is the final stages of it: *the twilight of his career*

twin noun **1** If two people are twins, they have the same mother and were born on the same day **2** 'Twin' is used to describe two similar things that are close together or happen together: *the little twin islands*

twine noun **1** Twine is strong smooth string ▷ verb **2** If you twine one thing round another, you twist or wind it round

twinge noun **1** a sudden, unpleasant feeling: *a twinge of jealousy* **2** a sudden sharp pain: *a twinge in my lower back*

twinkle verb **1** If something twinkles, it sparkles or seems to sparkle with an unsteady light: *Her green eyes twinkled* ▷ noun **2** a sparkle or brightness that something has

twirl verb If something twirls, or if you twirl it, it spins or twists round and round

twist verb **1** When you twist something you turn one end of it in one direction while holding the other end or turning it in the opposite direction **2** When something twists or is twisted, it moves or bends into a strange shape **3** If you twist a part of your body, you injure it by turning it too sharply or in an unusual direction: *I've twisted my ankle* **4** If you twist something that someone has said, you change the meaning slightly ▷ noun **5** a twisting action or motion **6** an unexpected development or event in a story or film, especially at the end: *Each day now seemed to bring a new twist to the story*

twisted adjective **1** Something twisted has been bent or moved into a strange shape: *a tangle of twisted metal* **2** If someone's mind or behaviour is twisted, it is unpleasantly abnormal: *He's bitter and twisted*

twit noun (informal) a silly person

twitch verb **1** If you twitch, you make little jerky movements which you cannot control **2** If you twitch something, you give it a little jerk in order to move it ▷ noun **3** a little jerky movement

twitter verb When birds twitter, they make short high-pitched sounds

two the number 2

> **WORD TIP**
> Do not confuse the spelling of the preposition *to*, the adverb *too*, and the number *two*

two-faced adjective A two-faced person is not honest in the way they behave towards other people

twofold adjective Something twofold has two equally important parts or reasons: *Their concern was twofold: personal and political*

twosome [too-sum] noun two people or things that are usually seen together

two-time verb (informal) If you two-time your boyfriend or girlfriend, you deceive them, by having a romantic relationship with someone else without telling them

two-up noun In Australia and New Zealand, two-up is a popular gambling game in which two coins are tossed and bets are placed on whether they land heads or tails

tycoon noun a person who is successful in business and has become rich and powerful

type noun **1** A type of something is a class of it that has common features and belongs to a larger group of related things: *What type of dog should we get?* **2** A particular type of person has a particular appearance or quality: *Andrea is the type who likes to play safe* ▷ verb **3** If you type something, you use a typewriter or computer keyboard to write it

typewriter noun a machine with a keyboard with individual keys which are pressed to produce letters and numbers on a page

typhoid [tie-foyd] noun Typhoid, or typhoid fever, is an infectious disease caused by dirty water or food. It produces fever and can kill

typhoon noun GEOGRAPHY a very violent tropical storm

typical adjective showing the most usual characteristics or behaviour ▷ **typically** adverb

t

typify typifies, typifying, typified *verb* If something typifies a situation or thing, it is characteristic of it or a typical example of it: *This story is one that typifies our times*

typing *noun* Typing is the work or activity of producing something on a typewriter or computer keyboard

typist *noun* **1** a person whose job is typing **2** a person who types in a particular way: *a painfully slow typist*

tyranny tyrannies *noun* **1** A tyranny is the cruel and unjust rule of people by a person or group: *the evils of Nazi tyranny* **2** You can refer to something which is not human but is harsh as tyranny: *the tyranny of fate*
> **tyrannical** *adjective*

tyrant *noun* a person who treats the people he or she has authority over cruelly and unjustly

tyre *noun* a thick ring of rubber fitted round each wheel of a vehicle and filled with air

u

U **ubiquitous** [yoo-**bik**-wit-tuss] *adjective* Something that is ubiquitous seems to be everywhere at the same time: *the ubiquitous jeans*

UFO *noun* a strange object seen in the sky, which some people believe to be a spaceship from another planet. UFO is an abbreviation for 'unidentified flying object'

Ugandan [yoo-**gan**-dan] *adjective* **1** belonging or relating to Uganda

▷ *noun* **2** someone who comes from Uganda

ugly uglier, ugliest *adjective* very unattractive in appearance

UK an abbreviation for **United Kingdom**

ulcer *noun* a sore area on the skin or inside the body, which takes a long time to heal: *stomach ulcers*
> **ulcerous** *adjective*

ulterior [ul-**teer**-ee-or] *adjective* If you have an ulterior motive for doing something, you have a hidden reason for it

ultimate *adjective* **1** final or eventual: *Olympic gold is the ultimate goal* **2** most important or powerful: *the ultimate ambition of any player*
▷ *noun* **3** You can refer to the best or most advanced example of something as the ultimate: *This hotel is the ultimate in luxury*
> **ultimately** *adverb*

ultimatum [ul-tim-**may**-tum] *noun* a warning stating that unless someone meets your conditions, you will take action against them

ultrasound *noun* sound which cannot be heard by the human ear because its frequency is too high

ultraviolet *adjective* Ultraviolet light is not visible to the human eye. It is a form of radiation that causes your skin to darken after being exposed to the sun

umbilical cord [um-**bil**-lik-kl] *noun* the tube of blood vessels which connects an unborn baby to its mother and through which the baby receives nutrients and oxygen

umbrella *noun* a device that you use to protect yourself from the rain. It consists of a folding frame covered in cloth attached to a long stick

umpire *noun* **1** The umpire in cricket or tennis is the person who makes sure that the game is played according to the rules and who makes a decision if there is a dispute ▷ **verb 2** If you umpire a game, you are the umpire

umpteen adjective (informal) very many: tomatoes and umpteen other plants > **umpteenth** adjective

unabashed adjective not embarrassed or discouraged by something: Samuel was unabashed

unabated adjective, adverb continuing without any reduction in intensity or amount: The noise continued unabated

unable adjective If you are unable to do something, you cannot do it

unacceptable adjective very bad or of a very low standard

unaccompanied adjective alone

unaccustomed adjective If you are unaccustomed to something, you are not used to it

unaffected adjective **1** not changed in any way by a particular thing: unaffected by the recession **2** behaving in a natural and genuine way: the most down-to-earth, unaffected person I've ever met

unaided adverb, adjective without help: He was incapable of walking unaided

unambiguous adjective An unambiguous statement has only one meaning

unanimous [yoon-nan-nim-uss] adjective When people are unanimous, they all agree about something > **unanimously** adverb > **unanimity** noun

unannounced adjective happening unexpectedly and without warning

unarmed adjective not carrying any weapons

unassuming adjective modest and quiet

unattached adjective An unattached person is not married and is not having a steady relationship with someone

unattended adjective not being watched or looked after: an unattended handbag

unauthorized or **unauthorised** adjective done without official permission: unauthorized parking

unavoidable adjective unable to be prevented or avoided

unaware adjective If you are unaware of something, you do not know about it

unawares adverb If something catches you unawares, it happens when you are not expecting it

unbalanced adjective **1** with more weight or emphasis on one side than the other: an unbalanced load; an unbalanced relationship **2** slightly mad **3** made up of parts that do not work well together: an unbalanced lifestyle **4** An unbalanced account of something is an unfair one because it emphasizes some things and ignores others

unbearable adjective Something unbearable is so unpleasant or upsetting that you feel you cannot stand it: The pain was unbearable > **unbearably** adverb

unbeatable adjective Something that is unbeatable is the best thing of its kind

unbelievable adjective **1** extremely great or surprising: unbelievable courage **2** so unlikely that you cannot believe it > **unbelievably** adverb

unborn adjective not yet born

unbroken adjective continuous or complete: ten days of almost unbroken sunshine

uncanny adjective strange and

difficult to explain: *an uncanny resemblance*

uncertain adjective **1** not knowing what to do: *For a minute he looked uncertain* **2** doubtful or not known: *The outcome of the war was uncertain* > **uncertainty** noun

unchallenged adjective accepted without any questions being asked: *an unchallenged decision*

uncharacteristic adjective not typical or usual: *My father reacted with uncharacteristic speed*

uncle noun Your uncle is the brother of your mother or father, or the husband of one of your parents' siblings

unclear adjective confusing and not obvious

uncomfortable adjective **1** If you are uncomfortable, you are not physically relaxed and feel slight pain or discomfort **2** Uncomfortable also means slightly worried or embarrassed > **uncomfortably** adverb

uncommon adjective **1** not happening often or not seen often **2** unusually great: *She had read Cecilia's last letter with uncommon interest* > **uncommonly** adverb

uncompromising adjective determined not to change an opinion or aim in any way: *an uncompromising approach to life* > **uncompromisingly** adverb

unconcerned adjective not interested in something or not worried about it

unconditional adjective with no conditions or limitations: *a full three-year unconditional guarantee* > **unconditionally** adverb

unconscious adjective **1** Someone who is unconscious is asleep or in a state similar to sleep as a result of a shock, accident, or injury **2** If you are unconscious of something, you are not aware of it > **unconsciously** adverb > **unconsciousness** noun

uncontrollable adjective If someone or something is uncontrollable, they or it cannot be controlled or stopped: *uncontrollable anger* > **uncontrollably** adverb

unconventional adjective not behaving in the same way as most other people

unconvinced adjective not at all certain that something is true or right: *Some critics remain unconvinced by the plan*

uncouth [un-**kooth**] adjective bad-mannered and unpleasant

uncover verb **1** If you uncover a secret, you find it out **2** To uncover something is to remove the cover or lid from it

undaunted adjective If you are undaunted by something disappointing, you are not discouraged by it

undecided adjective If you are undecided, you have not yet made a decision about something

undemanding adjective not difficult to do or deal with: *undemanding work*

undeniable adjective certainly true: *undeniable evidence* > **undeniably** adverb

under preposition **1** below or beneath **2** You can use 'under' to say that a person or thing is affected by a particular situation or condition: *The country was under threat; Animals are kept under unnatural conditions* **3** If someone studies or works under a particular person, that person is their teacher or their boss **4** less than: *under five kilometres; children under the age of 14* ▷ phrase **5** Under

way means already started: *A murder investigation is already under way*

underarm *adjective* **1** under your arm: *underarm hair* ▷ *adverb* **2** If you throw a ball underarm, you throw it without raising your arm over your shoulder

undercarriage *noun* the part of an aircraft, including the wheels, that supports the aircraft when it is on the ground

underclass *noun* The underclass is the people in society who are the most poor and whose situation is unlikely to improve

undercover *adjective* involving secret work to obtain information: *a police undercover operation*

undercurrent *noun* a weak, partly hidden feeling that may become stronger later

undercut undercuts, undercutting, undercut *verb* **1** To undercut someone's prices is to sell a product more cheaply than they do **2** If something undercuts your attempts to achieve something, it prevents them from being effective

underdeveloped *adjective* An underdeveloped country does not have modern industries, and usually has a low standard of living

underdog *noun* The underdog in a competition is the person who seems likely to lose

underestimate *verb* If you underestimate something or someone, you do not realize how large, great, or capable they are

underfoot *adjective, adverb* under your feet: *the icy ground underfoot*

undergo undergoes, undergoing, underwent, undergone *verb* If you undergo something unpleasant, it happens to you

underground *adjective, adverb* **1** below the surface of the ground **2** secret, unofficial, and usually illegal ▷ *noun* **3** The underground is a railway system in which trains travel in tunnels below ground

undergrowth *noun* Small bushes and plants growing under trees are called the undergrowth

underhand *adjective* secret and dishonest: *underhand behaviour*

underlie underlies, underlying, underlay, underlain *verb* The thing that underlies a situation is the cause or basis of it ▷ **underlying** *adjective*

underline *verb* **1** If something underlines a feeling or a problem, it emphasizes it **2** If you underline a word or sentence, you draw a line under it

undermine *verb* To undermine an idea, feeling, or system is to make it less strong or secure: *You're trying to undermine my confidence again*

underneath *preposition* **1** below or beneath ▷ *adverb, preposition* **2** Underneath describes feelings and qualities that do not show in your behaviour: *Alex knew that underneath she was shattered* ▷ *adjective* **3** The underneath part of something is the part that touches or faces the ground

underpants *plural noun* Underpants are a piece of clothing worn by men and boys under their trousers

underpass *noun* a road or footpath that goes under a road or railway

underpin underpins, underpinning, underpinned *verb* If something underpins something else, it helps it to continue by supporting and strengthening it: *Australian skill is usually underpinned by an immense team spirit*

u

underprivileged adjective
Underprivileged people have less money and fewer opportunities than other people

underrate verb If you underrate someone, you do not realize how clever or valuable they are

understand understands, understanding, understood verb 1 If you understand what someone says, you know what they mean 2 If you understand a situation, you know what is happening and why 3 If you say that you understand that something is the case, you mean that you have heard that it is the case: I understand that she's a lot better now

understandable adjective If something is understandable, people can easily understand it
> **understandably** adverb

understanding noun 1 If you have an understanding of something, you have some knowledge about it 2 an informal agreement between people ▷ adjective 3 kind and sympathetic

understatement noun a statement that does not say fully how true something is: To say I was pleased was an understatement

understudy understudies noun someone who has learnt a part in a play so that they can act it if the main actor or actress is ill

undertake undertakes, undertaking, undertook, undertaken verb When you undertake a task or job, you agree to do it

undertaker noun someone whose job is to prepare bodies for burial and arrange funerals

undertaking noun a task which you have agreed to do

undertone noun 1 If you say something in an undertone, you say it very quietly 2 If something has undertones of a particular kind, it indirectly suggests ideas of this kind: unsettling undertones of violence

undervalue undervalues, undervaluing, undervalued verb If you undervalue something, you think it is less important than it really is

underwater adverb, adjective 1 beneath the surface of the sea, a river, or a lake ▷ adjective 2 designed to work in water: an underwater camera

underwear noun Your underwear is the clothing that you wear under your other clothes, next to your skin

underwent the past tense of undergo

undesirable adjective unwelcome and likely to cause harm: undesirable behaviour

undid the past tense of undo

undisputed adjective definite and without any doubt: the undisputed champion

undivided adjective If you give something your undivided attention, you concentrate on it totally

undo undoes, undoing, undid, undone verb 1 If you undo something that is tied up, you untie it 2 If you undo something that has been done, you reverse the effect of it

undoing noun If something is someone's undoing, it is the cause of their failure

undoubted adjective You use 'undoubted' to emphasize something: The event was an undoubted success > **undoubtedly** adverb

undress verb When you undress, you take off your clothes

undue adjective greater than is reasonable: undue violence ▷ **unduly** adverb

undulating adjective (formal) moving gently up and down: undulating hills

undying adjective lasting forever: his undying love for his wife

unearth verb If you unearth something that is hidden, you discover it

unearthly adjective strange and unnatural

uneasy adjective If you are uneasy, you feel worried that something may be wrong ▷ **unease** noun ▷ **uneasily** adverb ▷ **uneasiness** noun

unemployed adjective 1 without a job: an unemployed mechanic ▷ plural noun 2 The unemployed are all the people who are without a job

unemployment noun Unemployment is the state of being without a job

unending adjective Something unending has continued for a long time and seems as if it will never stop: unending joy

unenviable adjective An unenviable situation is one that you would not like to be in

unequal adjective 1 An unequal society does not offer the same opportunities and privileges to all people 2 Unequal things are different in size, strength, or ability

uneven adjective 1 An uneven surface is not level or smooth 2 not the same or consistent: six lines of uneven length ▷ **unevenly** adverb

uneventful adjective An uneventful period of time is one when nothing interesting happens

unexpected adjective Something unexpected is surprising because it was not thought likely to happen ▷ **unexpectedly** adverb

unfailing adjective continuous and not weakening as time passes: his unfailing cheerfulness

unfair adjective not right or just ▷ **unfairly** adverb

unfaithful adjective If someone is unfaithful, they are not loyal

unfamiliar adjective If something is unfamiliar to you, or if you are unfamiliar with it, you have not seen or heard it before

unfashionable adjective Something that is unfashionable is not popular or is no longer used by many people

unfavourable adjective not encouraging or promising, or not providing any advantage

unfit adjective 1 If you are unfit, your body is not in good condition because you have not been taking enough exercise 2 Something that is unfit for a particular purpose is not suitable for that purpose

unfold verb 1 When a situation unfolds, it develops and becomes known 2 If you unfold something that has been folded, you open it out so that it is flat

unforeseen adjective happening unexpectedly

unforgettable adjective Something unforgettable is so good or so bad that you are unlikely to forget it ▷ **unforgettably** adverb

unforgivable adjective Something unforgivable is so bad or cruel that it can never be forgiven or justified ▷ **unforgivably** adverb

unfortunate adjective 1 Someone who is unfortunate is unlucky 2 If you describe an event as unfortunate, you mean that it is a

u

pity that it happened: *an unfortunate accident* > **unfortunately** *adverb*

unfounded *adjective* Something that is unfounded has no evidence to support it: *unfounded allegations*

unfriendly *adjective* **1** A person who is unfriendly is not pleasant to you **2** A place that is unfriendly makes you feel uncomfortable or is not welcoming

ungainly *adjective* moving in an awkward or clumsy way

ungrateful *adjective* not appreciating the things you have

unhappy unhappier, unhappiest *adjective* **1** sad and depressed **2** not pleased or satisfied: *I am unhappy at being left out* **3** If you describe a situation as an unhappy one, you are sorry that it exists: *an unhappy state of affairs* > **unhappily** *adverb* > **unhappiness** *noun*

unhealthy *adjective* **1** likely to cause illness: *an unhealthy lifestyle* **2** An unhealthy person is often ill

unhinged *adjective* Someone who is unhinged is mentally unbalanced

unhurried *adjective* Unhurried is used to describe actions or movements that are slow and relaxed

unicorn *noun* an imaginary animal that looks like a white horse with a straight horn growing from its forehead

unidentified *adjective* You say that someone or something is unidentified when nobody knows who or what they are

uniform *noun* **1** a special set of clothes worn by people at work or school ▷ *adjective* **2** Something that is uniform does not vary but is even and regular throughout > **uniformity** *noun*

unify unifies, unifying, unified *verb* If you unify a number of things, you bring them together > **unification** *noun*

unilateral *adjective* A unilateral decision or action is one taken by only one of several groups involved in a particular situation > **unilaterally** *adverb*

unimaginable *adjective* impossible to imagine or understand properly: *a fairyland of unimaginable beauty*

unimportant *adjective* having very little significance or importance

uninhabited *adjective* An uninhabited place is a place where nobody lives

uninhibited *adjective* If you are uninhibited, you behave freely and naturally and show your true feelings

unintelligible *adjective* (formal) impossible to understand

uninterested *adjective* If you are uninterested in something, you are not interested in it

uninterrupted *adjective* continuing without breaks or interruptions: *uninterrupted views*

union *noun* **1** an organization of people or groups with mutual interests, especially workers aiming to improve their pay and conditions **2** When the union of two things takes place, they are joined together to become one thing

unique [yoo-**neek**] *adjective* **1** being the only one of its kind **2** If something is unique to one person or thing, it concerns or belongs to that person or thing only: *trees and vegetation unique to the Canary islands* > **uniquely** *adverb* > **uniqueness** *noun*

unisex *adjective* designed to be used by both men and women: *unisex clothing*

unison noun If a group of people do something in unison, they all do it together at the same time

unit noun 1 If you consider something as a unit, you consider it as a single complete thing 2 a group of people who work together for a particular job: *the Police Support Unit* 3 a machine or piece of equipment which has a particular function: *a remote control unit* 4 A unit of measurement is a fixed standard that is used for measuring things

unite verb If a number of people unite, they join together and act as a group

United Kingdom noun The United Kingdom consists of Great Britain and Northern Ireland

United Nations noun The United Nations is an international organization which tries to encourage peace, cooperation, and friendship between countries

unity noun Where there is unity, people are in agreement and act together for a particular purpose

universal adjective concerning or relating to everyone in the world or every part of the universe: *Music and sports programmes have a universal appeal; universal destruction* > **universally** adverb

universe noun The universe is the whole of space, including all the stars and planets

university universities noun a place where students study for degrees

unjust adjective not fair or reasonable > **unjustly** adverb

unjustified adjective If a belief or action is unjustified, there is no good reason for it

unkempt adjective untidy and not looked after properly: *unkempt hair*

unkind adjective unpleasant and rather cruel > **unkindly** adverb > **unkindness** noun

unknown adjective 1 If someone or something is unknown, people do not know about them or have not heard of them ▷ noun 2 You can refer to the things that people in general do not know about as the unknown

unlawful adjective not legal: *the unlawful use of drugs*

unleaded adjective Unleaded petrol has a reduced amount of lead in it in order to reduce the pollution from cars

unleash verb When a powerful or violent force is unleashed, it is released

unless conjunction You use unless to introduce the only circumstances in which something will not take place or is not true: *Unless it was raining, they played in the little garden*

unlike preposition 1 You can use unlike to show how two people, things, or situations are different from each other: *Unlike me, she enjoys ballet* ▷ adjective 2 If one thing is unlike another, the two things are different

unlikely adjective 1 If something is unlikely, it is probably not true or probably will not happen 2 strange and unexpected: *There are riches in unlikely places*

unlimited adjective If a supply of something is unlimited, you can have as much as you want or need

unload verb If you unload things from a container or vehicle, you remove them

unlock verb If you unlock a door or container, you open it by turning a key in the lock

unlucky adjective Someone who is unlucky has bad luck > **unluckily** adverb

unmarked adjective 1 with no marks of damage or injury 2 with no signs or marks of identification: unmarked police cars

unmistakable or **unmistakeable** adjective Something unmistakable is so obvious that it cannot be mistaken for something else > **unmistakably** adverb

unmitigated adjective (formal) You use unmitigated to describe a situation or quality that is completely bad: an unmitigated disaster

unmoved adjective not emotionally affected: He is unmoved by criticism

unnatural adjective 1 strange and rather frightening because it is not usual. There was an unnatural stillness 2 artificial and not typical: My voice sounded high-pitched and unnatural > **unnaturally** adverb

unnecessary adjective If something is unnecessary, there is no need for it to happen or be done > **unnecessarily** adverb

unnerve verb If something unnerves you, it frightens or startles you > **unnerving** adjective

unobtrusive adjective Something that is unobtrusive does not draw attention to itself

unoccupied adjective not occupied. For example, if a house is unoccupied, there is nobody living in it

unofficial adjective without the approval or permission of a person in authority: unofficial strikes > **unofficially** adverb

unorthodox adjective unusual and not generally accepted: an unorthodox theory

unpack verb When you unpack, you take everything out of a suitcase or bag

unpaid adjective 1 If you do unpaid work, you do not receive any money for doing it 2 An unpaid bill has not yet been paid

unpalatable adjective 1 Unpalatable food is unpleasant to eat 2 An unpalatable idea is so unpleasant that it is difficult to accept

unparalleled adjective greater than anything else of its kind: an unparalleled success

unpleasant adjective 1 Something unpleasant causes you to have bad feelings, for example by making you uncomfortable or upset 2 An unpleasant person is unfriendly or rude > **unpleasantly** adverb > **unpleasantness** noun

unpopular adjective disliked by most people: an unpopular idea

unprecedented [un-**press**-id-en-tid] adjective (formal) Something that is unprecedented has never happened before or is the best of its kind so far

unpredictable adjective If someone or something is unpredictable, you never know how they will behave or react

unprepared adjective If you are unprepared for something, you are not ready for it and are therefore surprised or at a disadvantage when it happens

unproductive adjective not producing anything useful

unqualified adjective 1 having no qualifications or not having the right qualifications for a particular job: dangers posed by unqualified doctors 2 total: an unqualified success

unquestionable adjective so obviously true or real that nobody can doubt it: His devotion is unquestionable > **unquestionably** adverb

unravel unravels, unravelling, unravelled *verb* **1** If you unravel something such as a twisted and knotted piece of string, you unwind it so that it is straight **2** If you unravel a mystery, you work out the answer to it

unreal *adjective* so strange that you find it difficult to believe

unrealistic *adjective* **1** An unrealistic person does not face the truth about something or deal with it in a practical way **2** Something unrealistic is not true to life: *an unrealistic picture*

unreasonable *adjective* unfair and difficult to deal with or justify: *an unreasonable request*
> **unreasonably** *adverb*

unrelated *adjective* Things that are unrelated have no connection with each other

unrelenting *adjective* continuing in a determined way: *unrelenting criticism*

unreliable *adjective* If people, machines, or methods are unreliable, you cannot rely on them

unremitting *adjective* never stopping

unrest *noun* If there is unrest, people are angry and dissatisfied

unrivalled *adjective* better than anything else of its kind: *an unrivalled range of health and beauty treatments*

unruly *adjective* difficult to control or organize: *unruly children; unruly hair*

unsatisfactory *adjective* not good enough

unscathed *adjective* not injured or harmed as a result of a dangerous experience

unscrupulous *adjective* willing to behave dishonestly in order to get what you want

unseemly *adjective* Unseemly behaviour is not suitable for a particular situation and shows a lack of control and good manners: *an unseemly squabble*

unseen *adjective* You use unseen to describe things that you cannot see or have not seen

unsettle *verb* If something unsettles you, it makes you restless or worried

unshakable or **unshakeable** *adjective* An unshakable belief is so strong that it cannot be destroyed

unsightly *adjective* very ugly: *an unsightly scar*

unskilled *adjective* Unskilled work does not require any special training or ability

unsolicited *adjective* given or happening without being asked for

unsound *adjective* **1** If a conclusion or method is unsound, it is based on ideas that are likely to be wrong **2** An unsound building is likely to collapse

unspeakable *adjective* very unpleasant

unspecified *adjective* You say that something is unspecified when you are not told exactly what it is: *It was being stored in some unspecified place*

unspoilt or **unspoiled** *adjective* If you describe a place as unspoilt or unspoiled, you mean it has not been changed and is still in its natural or original state

unspoken *adjective* An unspoken wish or feeling is one that is not mentioned to other people

unstable *adjective* **1** likely to change suddenly and create difficulty or danger: *The political situation in Moscow is unstable* **2** not firm or fixed properly and likely to wobble or fall

unsteady *adjective* **1** having

u

difficulty in controlling the movement of your legs or hands: *unsteady on her feet* **2** not held or fixed securely and likely to fall over > **unsteadily** *adverb*

unstuck *adjective* separated from the thing that it was stuck to

unsuccessful *adjective* If you are unsuccessful, you do not succeed in what you are trying to do > **unsuccessfully** *adverb*

unsuitable *adjective* not right or appropriate for a particular purpose > **unsuitably** *adverb*

unsuited *adjective* not appropriate for a particular task or situation: *He's totally unsuited to the job*

unsung *adjective* You use unsung to describe someone who is not appreciated or praised for their good work: *George is the unsung hero of the club*

unsure *adjective* uncertain or doubtful

unsuspecting *adjective* having no idea of what is happening or going to happen: *His horse escaped and collided with an unsuspecting cyclist*

untangle *verb* If you untangle something that is twisted together, you undo the twists

untenable *adjective (formal)* A theory, argument, or position that is untenable cannot be successfully defended

unthinkable *adjective* so shocking or awful that you cannot imagine it to be true

untidy *untidier, untidiest adjective* not neat or well arranged > **untidily** *adverb*

until *preposition, conjunction* **1** If something happens until a particular time, it happens before that time and stops at that time: *The shop stayed open until midnight;*

She waited until her husband was asleep **2** If something does not happen until a particular time, it does not happen before that time and only starts happening at that time: *It didn't rain until the middle of the afternoon; It was not until they arrived that they found out who he was*

untimely *adjective* happening too soon or sooner than expected: *his untimely death*

unto *preposition (old-fashioned)* Unto means the same as to: *Nation shall speak peace unto nation*

untold *adjective* You use untold to emphasize how great or extreme something is: *The island possessed untold wealth*

untouched *adjective* **1** not changed, moved, or damaged: *a small village untouched by tourism* **2** If a meal is untouched, none of it has been eaten

untoward *adjective* unexpected and causing difficulties: *no untoward problems*

untrue *adjective* not true

unused *adjective* **1** [un-**yoozd**] not yet used **2** [un-**yoost**] If you are unused to something, you have not often done or experienced it

unusual *adjective* Something that is unusual does not occur very often > **unusually** *adverb*

unveil *verb* When someone unveils a new statue or plaque, they draw back a curtain that is covering it

unwanted *adjective* Unwanted things are not desired or wanted, either by a particular person or by people in general: *He felt lonely and unwanted*

unwarranted *adjective (formal)* not justified or not deserved: *unwarranted fears*

unwelcome *adjective* not wanted:

an unwelcome visitor; unwelcome news

unwell adjective If you are unwell, you are ill

unwieldy adjective difficult to move or carry because of being large or an awkward shape

unwilling adjective If you are unwilling to do something, you do not want to do it > **unwillingly** adverb

unwind unwinds, unwinding, unwound verb **1** When you unwind after working hard, you relax **2** If you unwind something that is wrapped round something else, you undo it

unwise adjective foolish or not sensible

unwitting adjective Unwitting describes someone who becomes involved in something without realizing what is really happening: her unwitting victims > **unwittingly** adverb

unworthy adjective (formal) Someone who is unworthy of something does not deserve it

unwrap unwraps, unwrapping, unwrapped verb When you unwrap something, you take off the paper or covering around it

unwritten adjective An unwritten law is one which is generally understood and accepted without being officially laid down

up adverb, preposition **1** towards or in a higher place: He ran up the stairs; high up in the mountains **2** towards or in the north: I'm flying up to Darwin ▷ preposition **3** If you go up a road or river, you go along it **4** You use up to say how large something can be or what level it has reached: traffic jams up to 15 kilometres long **5** (informal) If someone is up to something, they are secretly doing

something they should not be doing **6** If it is up to someone to do something, it is their responsibility ▷ adjective **7** If you are up, you are not in bed **8** If a period of time is up, it has come to an end ▷ adverb **9** If an amount of something goes up, it increases

up-and-coming adjective Up-and-coming people are likely to be successful

upbringing noun Your upbringing is the way that your parents have taught you to behave

update verb If you update something, you make it more modern or add new information to it: He had failed to update his will

upgrade verb If a person or their job is upgraded, they are given more responsibility or status and usually more money

upheaval noun a big change which causes a lot of trouble

uphill adverb **1** If you go uphill, you go up a slope ▷ adjective **2** An uphill task requires a lot of effort and determination

uphold upholds, upholding, upheld verb If someone upholds a law or a decision, they support and maintain it

upholstery noun Upholstery is the soft covering on chairs and sofas that makes them comfortable

upkeep noun The upkeep of something is the continual process and cost of keeping it in good condition

upland adjective **1** An upland area is an area of high land ▷ noun **2** (in plural) Uplands are areas of high land

uplifting adjective something that is uplifting makes you feel happy

upload verb If you upload a

u

computer file or program, you put it onto a computer or the internet

up-market adjective sophisticated and expensive

upon preposition **1** (formal) Upon means on: *I stood upon the stair* **2** You use upon when mentioning an event that is immediately followed by another: *Upon entering the hall he took a quick glance round* **3** If an event is upon you, it is about to happen: *The football season is upon us once more*

upper adjective **1** referring to something that is above something else, or the higher part of something: *the upper arm* ▷ noun **2** the top part of a shoe

upper class noun The upper classes are people who belong to a very wealthy or aristocratic group in a society

uppermost adjective, adverb **1** on top or in the highest position: *the uppermost leaves; Lay your arms beside your body with the palms turned uppermost* ▷ adjective **2** most important: *His family is now uppermost in his mind*

upright adjective, adverb **1** standing or sitting up straight, rather than bending or lying down **2** behaving in a very respectable and moral way

uprising noun If there is an uprising, a large group of people begin fighting against the existing government to bring about political changes

uproar noun If there is uproar or an uproar, there is a lot of shouting and noise, often because people are angry

uproot verb **1** If someone is uprooted, they have to leave the place where they have lived for a long time **2** If a tree is uprooted, it is

pulled out of the ground

upset upsets, upsetting, upset adjective [up-**set**] **1** worried or unhappy ▷ verb [up-**set**] **2** If something upsets you, it makes you feel worried or unhappy **3** If you upset something, you turn it over or spill it accidentally ▷ noun [up-set] **4** A stomach upset is a slight stomach illness caused by an infection or by something you have eaten

upshot noun The upshot of a series of events is the final result

upside down adjective, adverb the wrong way up

upstage verb If someone upstages you, they draw people's attention away from you by being more attractive or interesting

upstairs adverb **1** If you go upstairs in a building, you go up to a higher floor ▷ noun **2** The upstairs of a building is its upper floor or floors

upstart noun someone who has risen too quickly to an important position and is too arrogant

upstream adverb towards the source of a river: *They made their way upstream*

upsurge noun An upsurge of something is a sudden large increase in it

uptake noun You can say that someone is quick on the uptake if they understand things quickly

uptight adjective (informal) tense or annoyed

up-to-date adjective **1** being the newest thing of its kind **2** having the latest information

up-to-the-minute adjective Up-to-the-minute information is the latest available information

upturn noun an improvement in a situation

upturned adjective **1** pointing upwards: rain splashing down on her upturned face **2** upside down: an upturned bowl

upwards adverb **1** towards a higher place: People stared upwards and pointed **2** to a higher level or point on a scale: The world population is rocketing upwards > **upward** adjective

uranium [yoo-**ray**-nee-um] noun SCIENCE Uranium is a radioactive metallic element used in the production of nuclear power and weapons. Its atomic number is 92 and its symbol is U

Uranus noun Uranus is the planet in the solar system which is seventh from the sun

urban adjective GEOGRAPHY relating to a town or city: She found urban life very different from country life

urbane adjective well-mannered, and comfortable in social situations

Urdu [**oor**-doo] noun Urdu is the official language of Pakistan. It is also spoken by many people in India

urge noun **1** If you have an urge to do something, you have a strong wish to do it > verb **2** If you urge someone to do something, you try hard to persuade them to do it

urgent adjective needing to be dealt with as soon as possible > **urgently** adverb > **urgency** noun

urinal [yoor-**rye**-nl] noun a bowl or trough fixed to the wall in a public toilet for men to urinate in

urinate [**yoor**-rin-ate] verb When you urinate, you go to the toilet and get rid of urine from your body

urine [**yoor**-rin] noun the waste liquid that you get rid of from your body when you go to the toilet

URL noun COMPUTING an abbreviation for 'uniform resource

locator': a technical name for an internet address

urn noun a decorated container, especially one that is used to hold the ashes of a person who has been cremated

us pronoun A speaker or writer uses us to refer to himself or herself and one or more other people: Why don't you tell us?

US or **USA** an abbreviation for 'United States (of America)'

usage noun **1** the degree to which something is used, or the way in which it is used **2** the way in which words are actually used: The terms soon entered common usage

USB noun COMPUTING an abbreviation for 'universal serial bus': a socket on a computer or other electronic device

use verb [**yooz**] **1** If you use something, you do something with it in order to do a job or achieve something: May I use your phone? **2** If you use someone, you take advantage of them by making them do things for you > noun [**yoos**] **3** The use of something is the act of using it: the use of force **4** If you have the use of something, you have the ability or permission to use it **5** If you find a use for something, you find a purpose for it > **usable** or **useable** adjective > **user** noun

used verb **1** Something that used to be done or used to be true was done or was true in the past > phrase **2** If you are **used to** something, you are familiar with it and have often experienced it > adjective [**yoozd**] **3** A used object has had a previous owner

useful adjective If something is useful, you can use it in order to do something or to help you in some

u

way > **usefully** adverb > **usefulness** noun

useless adjective **1** If something is useless, you cannot use it because it is not suitable or helpful **2** If a course of action is useless, it will not achieve what is wanted

username noun a name that someone uses when logging into a computer or website

usher verb **1** If you usher someone somewhere, you show them where to go by going with them ▷ noun **2** a person who shows people where to sit at a wedding or a concert

USSR HISTORY an abbreviation for 'Union of Soviet Socialist Republics', a country which was made up of a lot of smaller countries including Russia, but which is now broken up

usual adjective **1** happening, done, or used most often: *his usual seat* ▷ phrase **2** If you do something **as usual**, you do it in the way that you normally do it, or you do something that you do regularly. > **usually** adverb

usurp [yoo-**zerp**] verb (formal) If someone usurps another person's job or title they take it when they have no right to do so

ute [**yoot**] noun (informal) in Australian and New Zealand English, a utility truck

utensil [yoo-**ten**-sil] noun Utensils are tools: *cooking utensils*

uterus [**yoo**-ter-russ] noun SCIENCE A woman's uterus is her womb

utility utilities noun **1** The utility of something is its usefulness **2** a service, such as water or gas, that is provided for everyone

utility truck noun in Australian and New Zealand English, a small motor vehicle with an open body and low sides

utilize or **utilise** verb (formal) To utilize something is to use it > **utilization** noun

utmost adjective used to emphasize a particular quality: *I have the utmost respect for Richard*

utter verb **1** When you utter sounds or words, you make or say them ▷ adjective **2** Utter means complete or total: *scenes of utter chaos* > **utterly** adverb

utterance noun something that is said: *his first utterance*

V

vacant adjective **1** If something is vacant, it is not occupied or being used **2** If a job or position is vacant, no-one holds it at present **3** A vacant look suggests that someone does not understand something or is not very intelligent > **vacancy** noun > **vacantly** adverb

vacate verb (formal) If you vacate a room or job, you leave it and it becomes available for someone else

vacation noun **1** the period between academic terms at a university or college: *the summer vacation* **2** a holiday

vaccinate [**vak**-sin-ate] verb To vaccinate someone means to give them a vaccine, usually by injection, to protect them against a disease > **vaccination** noun

vaccine [**vak**-seen] noun a substance made from the germs that cause a disease, given to people to make them immune to that disease

vacuum [vak-yoom] noun **1** a space containing no air, gases, or other matter ▷ verb **2** If you vacuum something, you clean it using a vacuum cleaner

vacuum cleaner noun an electric machine which cleans by sucking up dirt

vagina [vaj-jie-na] noun A woman's vagina is the passage that connects her outer sex organs to her womb

vague [vayg] adjective **1** If something is vague, it is not expressed or explained clearly, or you cannot see or remember it clearly: *vague statements* **2** Someone looks or sounds vague if they are not concentrating or thinking clearly ▷ **vaguely** adverb ▷ **vagueness** noun

vain adjective **1** A vain action or attempt is one which is not successful: *He made a vain effort to cheer her up* **2** A vain person is very proud of their looks, intelligence, or other qualities ▷ phrase **3** If you do something **in vain**, you do not succeed in achieving what you intend ▷ **vainly** adverb

valentine noun **1** Your valentine is someone you love and send a card to on Saint Valentine's Day, February 14th **2** A valentine or a valentine card is the card you can send to the person you love on Saint Valentine's Day

valet [val-lit or val-lay] noun a male servant who is employed to look after another man, particularly caring for his clothes

valiant adjective very brave ▷ **valiantly** adverb

valid adjective **1** Something that is

valid is based on sound reasoning **2** A valid ticket or document is one which is officially accepted ▷ **validity** noun

validate verb If something validates a statement or claim, it proves that it is true or correct

valley noun a long stretch of land between hills, often with a river flowing through it

valour noun Valour is great bravery

valuable adjective **1** having great importance or usefulness **2** worth a lot of money

valuation noun a judgment about how much money something is worth or how good it is

value values, valuing, valued noun **1** The value of something is its importance or usefulness: *information of great value* **2** The value of something you own is the amount of money that it is worth **3** The values of a group or a person are the moral principles and beliefs that they think are important: *the values of liberty and equality* ▷ verb **4** If you value something, you think it is important and you appreciate it **5** When experts value something, they decide how much money it is worth ▷ **valued** adjective ▷ **valuer** noun

valve noun **1** a part attached to a pipe or tube which controls the flow of gas or liquid **2** a small flap in your heart or in a vein which controls the flow or direction of blood

vampire noun In horror stories, vampires are corpses that come out of their graves at night and suck the blood of living people

van noun a covered vehicle larger than a car but smaller than a lorry, used for carrying goods

vandal noun someone who

V

deliberately damages or destroys things, particularly public property
> **vandalize** or > **vandalise** verb
> **vandalism** noun

vanguard [van-gard] noun If someone is in the vanguard of something, they are in the most advanced part of it

vanilla noun Vanilla is a flavouring for food such as ice cream, which comes from the pods of a tropical plant

vanish verb **1** If something vanishes, it disappears: *The moon vanished behind a cloud* **2** If something vanishes, it ceases to exist: *a vanishing civilization*

vanity noun Vanity is a feeling of excessive pride about your looks or abilities

vanquish [vang-kwish] verb (*literary*) To vanquish someone means to defeat them completely

vapour noun SCIENCE Vapour is a mass of tiny drops of water or other liquids in the air which looks like mist

variable adjective **1** Something that is variable is likely to change at any time ▷ noun **2** In any situation, a variable is something in it that can change **3** MATHS In maths, a variable is a symbol such as x which can represent any value or any one of a set of values > **variability** noun

variance noun If one thing is at variance with another, the two seem to contradict each other

variant noun **1** A variant of something has a different form from the usual one, for example *gaol* is a variant of *jail* ▷ adjective **2** alternative or different

variation noun **1 a** a change from the normal or usual pattern: *a variation of the same route* **2** a change in level,

amount, or quantity: *a large variation in demand*

varicose veins plural noun Varicose veins are swollen painful veins in the legs

varied adjective of different types, quantities, or sizes

variety varieties noun **1** If something has variety, it consists of things which are not all the same **2** A variety of things is a number of different kinds of them: *a wide variety of readers* **3** A variety of something is a particular type of it: *a new variety of celery* **4** Variety is a form of entertainment consisting of short unrelated acts, such as singing, dancing, and comedy

various adjective Various means of several different types: *trees of various sorts* > **variously** adverb

varnish noun **1** A liquid which when painted onto a surface gives it a hard, clear, shiny finish ▷ verb **2** If you varnish something, you paint it with varnish

vary varies, varying, varied verb **1** If things vary, they change: *Weather patterns vary greatly* **2** If you vary something, you introduce changes in it: *Vary your routes as much as possible* > **varied** adjective

vascular adjective relating to tubes or ducts that carry fluids within animals or plants

vase noun a glass or china jar for flowers

vasectomy vasectomies noun [vas-**sek**-tom-ee] noun an operation to sterilize a man by cutting the tube in his body that carries the sperm

Vaseline noun (*trademark*) Vaseline is a soft clear jelly made from petroleum and used as an ointment or as grease

vast adjective extremely large
> **vastly** adverb > **vastness** noun

vat noun a large container for liquids

VAT [vee-ay tee or vat] noun In Britain, VAT is a tax which is added to the costs of many goods and services. VAT is an abbreviation for 'value-added tax'

vault [rhymes with salt] noun **1** a strong secure room, often underneath a building, where valuables are stored, or underneath a church where people are buried **2** an arched roof, often found in churches ▷ verb **3** if you vault over something, you jump over it using your hands or a pole to help

VCR an abbreviation for 'video cassette recorder'

veal noun Veal is the meat from a calf

veer verb If something which is moving veers in a particular direction, it suddenly changes course: *The aircraft veered sharply to one side*

vegan [vee-gn] noun someone who does not eat any food made from animal products, such as meat, eggs, cheese, or milk

vegetable noun **1** Vegetables are edible roots or leaves such as carrots or cabbage **2** adjective Vegetable is used to refer to any plants in contrast to animals or minerals: *vegetable life*

vegetarian noun a person who does not eat meat, poultry, or fish
> **vegetarianism** noun

vegetation noun GEOGRAPHY Vegetation is the plants in a particular area

vehement [vee-im-ent] adjective Someone who is vehement has strong feelings or opinions and expresses them forcefully: *He wrote a letter of vehement protest*
> **vehemence** noun > **vehemently** adverb

vehicle [vee-ik-kl] noun **1** a machine, often with an engine, used for transporting people or goods **2** something used to achieve a particular purpose or as a means of expression: *The play seemed an ideal vehicle for his music* > **vehicular** adjective

veil [rhymes with male] noun a piece of thin, soft cloth that women sometimes wear over their heads
> **veiled** adjective

vein [rhymes with rain] noun **1** Your veins are the tubes in your body through which your blood flows to your heart **2** Veins are the thin lines on leaves or on insects' wings **3** A vein of a metal or a mineral is a layer of it in rock **4** Something that is in a particular vein is in that style or mood: *in a more serious vein*

veld [felt] noun The veld is flat high grassland in Southern Africa

velocity noun (technical) Velocity is the speed at which something is moving in a particular direction

velvet noun Velvet is a very soft material which has a thick layer of fine short threads on one side
> **velvety** adjective

vendetta noun a long-lasting bitter quarrel in which people try to harm each other

vendor noun a person who sells something

veneer noun **1** You can refer to a superficial quality that someone has as a veneer of that quality: *a veneer of calm* **2** Veneer is a thin layer of wood or plastic used to cover a surface

venerable adjective **1** A venerable person is someone you treat with respect because they are old and

V

wise **2** Something that is venerable is impressive because it is old or important historically

vengeance noun **1** Vengeance is the act of harming someone because they have harmed you ▷ *phrase* **2** If something happens **with a vengeance**, it happens to a much greater extent than was expected: *It began to rain again with a vengeance*

venison noun Venison is the meat from a deer

venom noun **1** The venom of a snake, scorpion, or spider is its poison **2** Venom is a feeling of great bitterness or spitefulness towards someone: *He was glaring at me with venom* ▷ **venomous** adjective

vent noun **1** a hole in something through which gases and smoke can escape and fresh air can enter: *air vents* ▷ *verb* **2** If you vent strong feelings, you express them: *She wanted to vent her anger upon me* ▷ *phrase* **3** If you **give vent** to strong feelings, you express them: *Pamela gave vent to a lot of bitterness*

ventilate verb To ventilate a room means to allow fresh air into it > **ventilated** adjective

ventilation noun **1** Ventilation is the process of breathing air in and out of the lungs **2** A ventilation system supplies fresh air into a building

ventilator noun a machine that helps people breathe when they cannot breathe naturally, for example if they are very ill

ventriloquist [ven-**trill**-o-kwist] noun an entertainer who can speak without moving their lips so that the words seem to come from a dummy ▷ **ventriloquism** noun

venture noun **1** something new which involves the risk of failure or of losing money: *a successful venture in television films* ▷ *verb* **2** If you venture something such as an opinion, you say it cautiously or hesitantly because you are afraid it might be foolish or wrong: *I would not venture to agree* **3** If you venture somewhere that might be dangerous, you go there

venue [**ven**-yoo] noun The venue for an event is the place where it will happen

Venus noun Venus is the planet in the solar system which is second from the sun

veranda [ver-**ran**-da] or **verandah** noun a platform with a roof that is attached to an outside wall of a house at ground level

verb noun ENGLISH In grammar, a verb is a word that expresses actions and states, for example 'be', 'become', 'take', and 'run'

verbal adjective ENGLISH **1** You use 'verbal' to describe things connected with words and their use: *verbal attacks on referees* **2** 'Verbal' describes things which are spoken rather than written: *a verbal agreement* > **verbally** adverb

verdict noun **1** In a law court, a verdict is the decision which states whether a prisoner is guilty or not guilty **2** If you give a verdict on something, you give your opinion after thinking about it

verge noun **1** The verge of a road is the narrow strip of grassy ground at the side ▷ *phrase* **2** If you are **on the verge** of something, you are going to do it soon or it is likely to happen soon: *on the verge of crying* ▷ *verb* **3** Something that verges on something else is almost the same as it: *dark blue that verged on purple*

verify verifies, verifying, verified verb

If you verify something, you check that it is true: *None of his statements could be verified* > **verifiable** *adjective* > **verification** *noun*

veritable *adjective* You use veritable to emphasize something: *a veritable jungle of shops*

vermin *plural noun* Vermin are small animals or insects, such as rats and cockroaches, which carry disease and damage crops

vernacular [ver-**nak**-yoo-lar] *noun* The vernacular of a particular country or district is the language widely spoken there

versatile *adjective* **1** If someone is versatile, they have many different skills **2** If a tool or material is versatile, it can be used for many different purposes > **versatility** *noun*

verse *noun* **1** Verse is another word for poetry **2** one part of a poem, song, or chapter of the Bible

versed *adjective* If you are versed in something, you know a lot about it

version *noun* **1** A version of something is a form of it in which some details are different from earlier or later forms: *a cheaper version of the aircraft* **2** Someone's version of an event is their personal description of what happened

versus *preposition* Versus is used to indicate that two people or teams are competing against each other

vertebra vertebrae [ver-**tib**-bra] *noun* SCIENCE Vertebrae are the small bones which form a person's or animal's backbone

vertebrate *noun* SCIENCE Vertebrates are any creatures which have a backbone

vertical *adjective* MATHS Something that is vertical points straight up and forms a ninety-degree angle

with the surface on which it stands > **vertically** *adverb*

vertigo *noun* Vertigo is a feeling of dizziness caused by looking down from a high place

verve *noun* Verve is lively and forceful enthusiasm

very *adverb* **1** to a great degree: *very bad dreams* ▷ *adjective* **2** Very is used before words to emphasize them: *the very end of the book* ▷ *phrase* **3** You use not very to mean that something is the case only to a small degree: *You're not very like your sister*

vessel *noun* **1** a ship or large boat **2** (*literary*) any bowl or container in which a liquid can be kept **3** SCIENCE a thin tube along which liquids such as blood or sap move in animals and plants

vest *noun* a piece of underwear worn for warmth on the top half of the body

vestige [**vest**-ij] *noun* (*formal*) A vestige is a tiny part of something that is left over when the rest has been used up: *They have a vestige of strength left*

vet vets, vetting, vetted *noun* **1** a doctor for animals ▷ *verb* **2** If you vet someone or something, you check them carefully to see if they are acceptable: *He refused to let them vet his speeches*

veteran *noun* **1** someone who has served in the armed forces, particularly during a war **2** someone who has been involved in a particular activity for a long time: *a veteran of 25 political campaigns*

veterinary [**vet**-er-in-ar-ee] *adjective* Veterinary is used to describe the work of a vet and the medical treatment of animals

V

veterinary surgeon noun the same as a **vet**

veto vetoes, vetoing, vetoed [**vee**-toh] verb **1** If someone in authority vetoes something, they say no to it ▷ noun **2** Veto is the right that someone in authority has to say no to something: *Dr Baker has the power of veto*

vexed adjective If you are vexed, you are annoyed, worried, or puzzled

VHF noun VHF is a range of high radio frequencies. VHF is an abbreviation for 'very high frequency'

via preposition **1** If you go to one place via another, you travel through that place to get to your destination: *He drove directly from Bonn via Paris* **2** Via also means done or achieved by making use of a particular thing or person: *to follow proceedings via newspapers or television*

viable [**vy**-a-bl] adjective Something that is viable is capable of doing what it is intended to do without extra help or financial support: *a viable business* > **viability** noun

viaduct [**vy**-a-dukt] noun a long high bridge that carries a road or railway across a valley

vibrant adjective Something or someone that is vibrant is full of life, energy, and enthusiasm > **vibrantly** adverb > **vibrancy** noun

vibrate verb SCIENCE If something vibrates, it moves a tiny amount backwards and forwards very quickly > **vibration** noun

vicar noun a priest in the Church of England

vicarage noun a house where a vicar lives

vice noun **1** a serious moral fault in someone's character, such as greed, or a weakness, such as smoking **2** a tool with a pair of jaws that hold an object tightly while it is being worked on

vice versa adverb 'Vice versa' is used to indicate that the reverse of what you have said is also true: *Wives sometimes criticize their husbands, and vice versa*

vicinity [vis-**sin**-it-ee] noun If something is in the vicinity of a place, it is in the surrounding or nearby area

vicious adjective cruel and violent > **viciously** adverb > **viciousness** noun

victim noun someone who has been harmed or injured by someone or something

victor noun The victor in a fight or contest is the person who wins

Victorian adjective **1** Victorian describes things that happened or were made during the reign of Queen Victoria (1837–1901) **2** Victorian also describes people or things connected with the state of Victoria in Australia

victory victories noun a success in a battle or competition > **victorious** adjective

video videos, videoing, videoed noun **1** Video is the recording and showing of films and events using a video recorder, video tape, and a television set **2** a sound and picture recording which can be played back on a television set **3** a video recorder ▷ verb **4** If you video something, you record it on magnetic tape for later viewing

video recorder noun A video recorder or video cassette recorder is a machine for recording and playing back programmes from television

vie vies, vying, vied verb (formal) If

you vie with someone, you compete to do something sooner than or better than they do

Vietnamese [vyet-nam-**meez**] *adjective* **1** belonging or relating to Vietnam ▷ *noun* **2** someone who comes from Vietnam **3** Vietnamese is the main language spoken in Vietnam

view *noun* **1** Your views are your personal opinions: *his political views* **2** everything you can see from a particular place ▷ *verb* **3** If you view something in a particular way, you think of it in that way: *They viewed me with contempt* ▷ *phrase* **4** You use **in view of** to specify the main fact or event influencing your actions or opinions: *He wore a lighter suit in view of the heat* **5** If something is **on view**, it is being shown or exhibited to the public

viewer *noun* Viewers are the people who watch television

viewpoint *noun* **1** Your viewpoint is your attitude towards something **2** a place from which you get a good view of an area or event

vigil [**vij**-jil] *noun* a period of time, especially at night, when you stay quietly in one place, for example because you are making a political protest or praying

vigilant *adjective* careful and alert to danger or trouble > **vigilance** *noun* > **vigilantly** *adverb*

vigilante [vij-il-**ant**-ee] *noun* Vigilantes are unofficially organized groups of people who try to protect their community and catch and punish criminals

vigorous *adjective* energetic or enthusiastic > **vigorously** *adverb* > **vigour** *noun*

Viking *noun* The Vikings were seamen from Scandinavia who

raided parts of north-western Europe from the 8th to the 11th centuries

vile *adjective* unpleasant or disgusting: *a vile accusation; a vile smell*

villa *noun* a house, especially a pleasant holiday home in a country with a warm climate

village *noun* a collection of houses and other buildings in the countryside > **villager** *noun*

villain *noun* **1** someone who harms others or breaks the law **2** the main evil character in a story > **villainous** *adjective* > **villainy** *noun*

vindicate *verb* (*formal*) If someone is vindicated, their views or ideas are proved to be right: *My friend's instincts have been vindicated* > **vindication** *noun*

vindictive *adjective* Someone who is vindictive is deliberately hurtful towards someone, often as an act of revenge > **vindictiveness** *noun*

vine *noun* a trailing or climbing plant which winds itself around and over a support, especially one which produces grapes

vinegar *noun* Vinegar is a sharp-tasting liquid made from sour wine, beer, or cider, which is used for salad dressing > **vinegary** *adjective*

vineyard [**vin**-yard] *noun* an area of land where grapes are grown

vintage *adjective* **1** A vintage wine is a good quality wine which has been stored for a number of years to improve its quality **2** Vintage describes something which is the best or most typical of its kind: *a vintage guitar* **3** A vintage car is one made between 1918 and 1930 ▷ *noun* **4** a grape harvest of one particular year and the wine produced from it

V

vinyl noun Vinyl is a strong plastic used to make things such as furniture and floor coverings

viola [vee-**oh**-la] noun A musical instrument like a violin, but larger and with a lower pitch

violate verb 1 If you violate an agreement, law, or promise, you break it 2 If you violate someone's peace or privacy, you disturb it 3 If you violate a place, especially a holy place, you treat it with disrespect or violence > **violation** noun

violence noun 1 Violence is behaviour which is intended to hurt or kill people 2 If you do or say something with violence, you use a lot of energy in doing or saying it, often because you are angry

violent adjective 1 If someone is violent, they try to hurt or kill people 2 A violent event happens unexpectedly and with great force 3 Something that is violent is said, felt, or done with great force > **violently** adverb

violet noun 1 a plant with dark purple flowers ▷ noun, adjective 2 bluish purple

violin noun a musical instrument with four strings that is held under the chin and played with a bow > **violinist** noun

VIP noun VIPs are famous or important people. VIP is an abbreviation for 'very important person'

viral [**vie**-rul] adjective 1 relating to or caused by a virus ▷ adverb 2 If a story or a video goes viral, it spreads quickly and widely among users of the internet

virgin adjective Something that is virgin is fresh and unused: virgin land

Virgo noun Virgo is the sixth sign of the zodiac, represented by a girl. People born between August 23rd and September 22nd are born under this sign

virile adjective A virile man has all the qualities that a man is traditionally expected to have, such as strength > **virility** noun

virtual [vur-**tyool**] adjective 1 Virtual means that something has all the characteristics of a particular thing, but it is not formally recognized as being that thing: The country is in a virtual state of war 2 COMPUTING Virtual objects and activities are generated by a computer to simulate real objects and activities > **virtually** adverb

virtual reality noun Virtual reality is a situation or setting that has been created by a computer and that looks real to the person using it

virtue noun 1 Virtue is thinking and doing what is morally right and avoiding what is wrong 2 a good quality in someone's character 3 A virtue of something is an advantage: The virtue of neatness is that you can always find things ▷ phrase 4 (formal) By virtue of means because of: The article stuck in my mind by virtue of one detail

virtuoso virtuosos or virtuosi [vur-tyoo-**oh**-soh] noun someone who is exceptionally good at something, particularly playing a musical instrument

virtuous adjective behaving with or showing moral virtue > **virtuously** adverb

virus [**vie**-russ] noun 1 SCIENCE a kind of germ that can cause disease 2 COMPUTING a program that alters or damages the information stored in a computer system

visa noun an official stamp, usually put in your passport, that allows you to visit a particular country

visibility noun You use visibility to say how far or how clearly you can see in particular weather conditions

visible adjective **1** able to be seen **2** noticeable or evident: *There was little visible excitement* > **visibly** adverb

vision noun **1** Vision is the ability to see clearly **2** a mental picture, in which you imagine how things might be different: *the vision of a possible future* **3** Vision is also imaginative insight: *a total lack of vision and imagination* **4** an unusual experience that you have, in which you see things that other people cannot see, often as a result of madness or divine inspiration > **visionary** noun, adjective

visit verb **1** If you visit someone, you go to see them and spend time with them **2** If you visit a place, you go to see it ▷ noun **3** a trip to see a person or place > **visitor** noun

visor [vie-zor] noun a transparent movable shield attached to a helmet, which can be pulled down to protect the eyes or face

visual adjective relating to sight: *a visual inspection*

visualize [viz-yool-eyes] or **visualise** verb If you visualize something, you form a mental picture of it

vital adjective **1** necessary or very important: *vital evidence* **2** energetic, exciting, and full of life: *an active and vital life outside school* > **vitally** adverb

vitality noun People who have vitality are energetic and lively

vitamin noun Vitamins are organic compounds which you need in order to remain healthy. They occur naturally in food

vivacious [viv-vay-shuss] adjective A vivacious person is attractively lively and high-spirited > **vivacity** noun

vivid adjective very bright in colour or clear in detail: *vivid red paint; vivid memories* > **vividly** adverb > **vividness** noun

vixen noun a female fox

vocabulary vocabularies noun ENGLISH **1** Someone's vocabulary is the total number of words they know in a particular language **2** The vocabulary of a language is all the words in it

vocal adjective **1** You say that someone is vocal if they express their opinions strongly and openly **2** MUSIC Vocal means involving the use of the human voice, especially in singing > **vocalist** noun > **vocally** adverb

vocation noun **1** a strong wish to do a particular job, especially one which involves serving other people **2** a profession or career

vocational adjective 'Vocational' is used to describe the skills needed for a particular job or profession: *vocational training*

vociferous [voe-sif-fer-uss] adjective (formal) Someone who is vociferous speaks a lot, or loudly, because they want to make a point strongly: *vociferous critics* > **vociferously** adverb

vodka noun a strong clear alcoholic drink which originally came from Russia

vogue [vohg] phrase If something is the vogue or in vogue, it is fashionable and popular: *Colour photographs became the vogue*

voice noun **1** Your voice is the sounds produced by your vocal cords, or the ability to make such sounds ▷ verb

V

2 If you voice an opinion or an emotion, you say what you think or feel: *A range of opinions were voiced*

void noun **1** a situation which seems empty because it has no interest or excitement: *Cats fill a very large void in your life* **2** a large empty hole or space: *His feet dangled in the void*

volatile adjective liable to change often and unexpectedly: *The situation at work is volatile*

volcanic adjective A volcanic region has many volcanoes or was created by volcanoes

volcano volcanoes noun a hill with an opening through which lava, gas, and ash burst out from inside the earth onto the surface

volition noun (formal) If you do something of your own volition, you do it because you have decided for yourself, without being persuaded by others: *He attended of his own volition*

volley noun **1** A volley of shots or gunfire is a lot of shots fired at the same time **2** In tennis, a volley is a stroke in which the player hits the ball before it bounces

volleyball noun Volleyball is a game in which two teams hit a large ball back and forth over a high net with their hands. The ball is not allowed to bounce on the ground

volt noun SCIENCE A volt is a unit of electrical force. One volt produces one amp of electricity when the resistance is one ohm.

voltage noun The voltage of an electric current is its force measured in volts

volume noun **1** MATHS The volume of something is the amount of space it contains or occupies **2** The volume of something is also the amount of it that there is: *a large volume of*

letters **3** The volume of a radio, TV, or MP3 player is the strength of the sound that it produces **4** a book, or one of a series of books

voluminous [vol-loo-min-uss] adjective very large or full in size or quantity: *voluminous skirts*

voluntary adjective **1** Voluntary actions are ones that you do because you choose to do them and not because you have been forced to do them **2** Voluntary work is done by people who are not paid for what they do > **voluntarily** adverb

volunteer noun **1** someone who does work for which they are not paid: *a volunteer for Greenpeace* **2** someone who chooses to join the armed forces, especially during wartime ▷ verb **3** If you volunteer to do something, you offer to do it rather than being forced into it **4** If you volunteer information, you give it without being asked

voluptuous [vol-lupt-yoo-uss] adjective A voluptuous woman has a figure which is considered to be full and attractive > **voluptuously** adverb > **voluptuousness** noun

vomit verb **1** If you vomit, food and drink comes back up from your stomach and out through your mouth ▷ noun **2** Vomit is partly digested food and drink that has come back up from someone's stomach and out through their mouth

voodoo noun Voodoo is a form of magic practised in the Caribbean, especially in Haiti

vote noun **1** Someone's vote is their choice in an election, or at a meeting where decisions are taken **2** When a group of people have a vote, they make a decision by allowing each person in the group to say what they would prefer **3** In an election, the vote is the total number of people who have made their choice: *the average Liberal vote* **4** If people have the vote, they have the legal right to vote in an election ▷ verb **5** When people vote, they indicate their choice or opinion, usually by writing on a piece of paper or by raising their hand **6** If you vote that a particular thing should happen, you are suggesting it should happen: *I vote that we all go to Holland* ▷ **voter** noun

vouch verb **1** If you say that you can vouch for something, you mean that you have evidence from your own experience that it is true or correct **2** If you say that you can vouch for someone, you mean that you are sure that you can guarantee their good behaviour or support: *Her employer will vouch for her*

voucher noun a piece of paper that can be used instead of money to pay for something

vow verb **1** If you vow to do something, you make a solemn promise to do it: *He vowed to do better in future* ▷ noun **2** a solemn promise

vowel noun (ENGLISH) a sound made without your tongue touching the roof of your mouth or your teeth, or one of the letters a, e, i, o, u, which represent such sounds

voyage noun a long journey on a ship or in a spacecraft ▷ **voyager** noun

vulgar adjective **1** socially unacceptable or offensive: *vulgar language* **2** showing a lack of taste or quality: *It seems vulgar to be discussing her funeral when she's still alive* ▷ **vulgarity** noun ▷ **vulgarly** adverb

vulnerable adjective weak and without protection ▷ **vulnerably** adverb ▷ **vulnerability** noun

vulture noun a large bird which lives in hot countries and eats the flesh of dead animals

vying the present participle of **vie**

W

wacky wackier, wackiest adjective (informal) odd or crazy: *wacky clothes*

wad noun **1** A wad of papers or banknotes is a thick bundle of them **2** A wad of something is a lump of it: *a wad of cotton wool*

wade verb **1** If you wade through water or mud, you walk slowly through it **2** If you wade through a book or document, you spend a lot of time and effort reading it because you find it dull or difficult

wafer noun **1** a thin, crisp, sweet biscuit often eaten with ice cream **2** a thin disc of special bread used in the Christian service of Holy Communion

waffle [wof-fl] verb **1** When someone waffles, they talk or write a lot without being clear or without saying anything of importance ▷ noun **2** Waffle is vague and lengthy speech or writing **3** a thick, crisp pancake with squares marked on it often eaten with syrup poured over it

waft [wahft] verb If a sound or scent wafts or is wafted through the air, it moves gently through it

wag wags, wagging, wagged *verb* **1** When a dog wags its tail, it shakes it repeatedly from side to side **2** If you wag your finger, you move it repeatedly up and down

wage *noun* **1** A wage or wages is the regular payment made to someone each week for the work they do, especially for manual or unskilled work ▷ *verb* **2** If a person or country wages a campaign or war, they start it and carry it on over a period of time

wager *noun* a bet

wagon or **waggon** *noun* **1** a strong four-wheeled vehicle for carrying heavy loads, usually pulled by a horse or tractor **2** Wagons are also the containers for freight pulled by a railway engine

waif *noun* a young, thin person who looks hungry and homeless

wail *verb* **1** To wail is to cry loudly with sorrow or pain ▷ *noun* **2** a long, unhappy cry

waist *noun* the middle part of your body where it narrows slightly above your hips

waistcoat *noun* a sleeveless piece of clothing, often worn under a suit or jacket, which buttons up the front

wait *verb* **1** If you wait, you spend time, usually doing little or nothing, before something happens **2** If something can wait, it is not urgent and can be dealt with later **3** If you wait on people in a restaurant, it is your job to serve them food ▷ *noun* **4** a period of time before something happens ▷ *phrase* **5** If you **can't wait** to do something, you are very excited and eager to do it

waiter *noun* a man who works in a restaurant, serving people with food and drink

waiting list *noun* a list of people who have asked for something which cannot be given to them immediately, for example medical treatment

waitress *noun* a woman who works in a restaurant, serving people with food and drink

waive [wave] *verb* If someone waives something such as a rule or a right, they decide not to insist on it being applied

wake wakes, waking, woke, woken *verb* **1** When you wake or when something wakes you, you become conscious again after being asleep ▷ *noun* **2** The wake of a boat or other object moving in water is the track of waves it leaves behind it **3** a gathering of people who have got together to mourn someone's death ▷ *phrase* **4** If one thing follows **in the wake** of another, it follows it as a result of it, or in imitation of it: *a project set up in the wake of last year's riots* > **wake up** *verb* **1** When you wake up or something wakes you up, you become conscious again after being asleep **2** If you wake up to a dangerous situation, you become aware of it

walk *verb* **1** When you walk, you move along by putting one foot in front of the other on the ground **2** If you walk away with or walk off with something such as a prize, you win it or achieve it easily ▷ *noun* **3** a journey made by walking: *We'll have a quick walk* **4** Your walk is the way you walk: *his rolling walk* > **walk out** *verb* **1** If you walk out on someone, you leave them suddenly **2** If workers walk out, they go on strike

walkabout *noun* **1** an informal walk amongst crowds in a public place by royalty or by some other well-known person **2** Walkabout is when an Australian Aborigine goes off to live and wander in the bush for a period of time

walker noun a person who walks, especially for pleasure or to keep fit

walking stick noun a wooden stick which people can lean on while walking

walkover noun (informal) a very easy victory in a competition or contest

walkway noun a passage between two buildings for people to walk along

wall noun **1** one of the vertical sides of a building or a room **2** a long, narrow vertical structure made of stone or brick that surrounds or divides an area of land **3** a lining or membrane enclosing a bodily organ or structure: *the wall of the womb*

wallaby wallabies noun an Australian animal like a small kangaroo

wallet noun a small, flat case made of leather or plastic, used for keeping paper money and sometimes credit cards

wallop verb (informal) If you wallop someone, you hit them very hard

wallow verb **1** If you wallow in an unpleasant feeling or situation, you allow it to continue longer than is reasonable or necessary because you are getting a kind of enjoyment from it: *We're wallowing in misery* **2** When an animal wallows in mud or water, it lies or rolls about in it slowly for pleasure

wallpaper noun **1** Wallpaper is thick coloured or patterned paper for pasting onto the walls of rooms in order to decorate them

walnut noun **1** an edible nut with a wrinkled shape and a hard, round, light-brown shell **2** Walnut is wood

from the walnut tree which is often used for making expensive furniture

walrus walruses noun an animal which lives in the sea and which looks like a large seal with a tough skin, coarse whiskers, and two tusks

waltz noun **1** a dance which has a rhythm of three beats to the bar ▷ verb **2** If you waltz with someone, you dance a waltz with them **3** (informal) If you waltz somewhere, you walk there in a relaxed and confident way

wan [rhymes with **on**] adjective pale and tired-looking

wand noun a long, thin rod that magicians wave while they are performing tricks and magic

wander verb **1** If you wander in a place, you walk around in a casual way **2** If your mind wanders or your thoughts wander, you lose concentration and start thinking about other things ▷ **wanderer** noun

wane verb **1** If a condition, attitude, or emotion wanes, it becomes gradually weaker

want verb **1** If you want something, you feel a desire to have it **2** If something is wanted, it is needed or needs to be done **3** If someone is wanted, the police are searching for them: *John was wanted for fraud* ▷ noun **4** (formal) A want of something is a lack of it

wanting adjective If you find something wanting or if it proves wanting, it is not as good in some way as you think it should be

wanton adjective A wanton action deliberately causes unnecessary harm or waste: *wanton destruction*

war wars, warring, warred noun **1** a period of fighting between countries or states when weapons are used and many people may be killed **2** a competition between groups of people, or a campaign against something: *a trade war; the war against crime* ▷ *verb* **4** When two countries war with each other, they are fighting a war against each other > **warring** *adjective*

waratah [wor-ra-**tah**] *noun* an Australian shrub with dark green leaves and large clusters of crimson flowers

ward *noun* **1** a room in a hospital which has beds for several people who need similar treatment **2** an area or district which forms a separate part of a political constituency or local council **3** A ward or a ward of court is a child who is officially put in the care of an adult or a court of law, because their parents are dead or because they need protection > **ward off** *verb* If you ward off a danger or an illness, you do something to prevent it from affecting or harming you

-ward or **-wards** *suffix* -ward and -wards form adverbs or adjectives that show the way something is moving or facing: *homeward; westwards*

warden *noun* **1** a person in charge of a building or institution such as a youth hostel or prison **2** an official who makes sure that certain laws or rules are obeyed in a particular place or activity: *a traffic warden*

warder *noun* a person who is in charge of prisoners in a jail

wardrobe *noun* **1** a tall cupboard in which you can hang your clothes **2** Someone's wardrobe is their collection of clothes

ware *noun* **1** Ware is manufactured goods of a particular kind:

kitchenware **2** Someone's wares are the things they sell, usually in the street or in a market

warehouse *noun* a large building where raw materials or manufactured goods are stored

warfare *noun* Warfare is the activity of fighting a war

warhead *noun* the front end of a bomb or missile, where the explosives are carried

warm warmest *adjective*
1 Something that is warm has some heat, but not enough to be hot: *a warm day* **2** Warm clothes or blankets are made of a material which protects you from the cold **3** Warm colours or sounds are pleasant and make you feel comfortable and relaxed **4** A warm person is friendly and affectionate ▷ *verb* **5** If you warm something, you heat it up gently so that it stops being cold > **warmly** *adverb* > **warm up** *verb* If you warm up for an event or an activity, you practise or exercise gently to prepare for the

warmth *noun* **1** Warmth is a moderate amount of heat **2** Someone who has warmth is friendly and affectionate

warn *verb* **1** If you warn someone about a possible problem or danger, you tell them about it in advance so that they are aware of it: *I warned him what it would be like* **2** If you warn someone not to do something, you advise them not to do it, in order to avoid possible danger or punishment: *I have warned her not to train for 10 days* > **warn off** *verb* If you warn someone off, you tell them to go away or to stop doing something

warning *noun* something said or written to tell people of a possible problem or danger

warp verb 1 If something warps or is warped, it becomes bent, often because of the effect of heat or water 2 If something warps someone's mind or character, it makes them abnormal or corrupt

warrant verb 1 (formal) If something warrants a particular action, it makes the action seem necessary: *no evidence to warrant a murder investigation* ▷ noun 2 an official document which gives permission to the police to do something: *a warrant for his arrest*

warranty warranties noun a guarantee: *a three-year warranty*

warren noun a group of holes under the ground connected by tunnels, which rabbits live in

warrior noun a fighting man or soldier, especially in former times

warship noun a ship built with guns and used for fighting in wars

wart noun 1 a small, hard piece of skin which can grow on someone's face or hands

wartime noun Wartime is a period of time during which a country is at war

wary warier, wariest adjective cautious and on one's guard: *Michelle is wary of marriage* ▷ **warily** adverb ▷ **wariness** noun

was a past tense of **be**

wash verb 1 If you wash something, you clean it with water and soap 2 If you wash, you clean yourself using soap and water 3 If something is washed somewhere, it is carried there gently by water: *The infant Arthur was washed ashore* ▷ noun 4 The wash is all the clothes and bedding that are washed together at one time: *a typical family's weekly wash* 5 The wash in water is the disturbance and waves produced at the back of a moving boat ▷ phrase 6 If you **wash your hands** of something or someone, you refuse to have anything more to do with it or them > **wash up** verb 1 If you wash up, you wash the dishes, pans, and cutlery used in preparing and eating a meal 2 If something is washed up on land, it is carried by a river or sea and left there: *A body had been washed up on the beach*

washable adjective able to be washed without being damaged

washer noun 1 a thin, flat ring of metal or plastic which is placed over a bolt before the nut is screwed on, so that it is fixed more tightly 2 In Australian English, a small piece of towelling for washing yourself

washing noun Washing consists of clothes and bedding which need to be washed or are in the process of being washed and dried

washing machine noun a machine for washing clothes in

washing-up noun If you do the washing-up, you wash the dishes, pans, and cutlery which have been used in the cooking and eating of a meal

wasp noun an insect with yellow and black stripes across its body, which can sting like a bee

wastage noun 1 Wastage is loss and misuse of something: *wastage of resources*

waste verb 1 If you waste time, money, or energy, you use too much of it on something that is not important or necessary 2 If you waste an opportunity, you do not take advantage of it when it is available 3 If you say that something is wasted on someone, you mean that it is too good, too clever, or too sophisticated for

W

them: *This book is wasted on us* ▷ noun **4** If an activity is a waste of time, money, or energy, it is not important or necessary **5** Waste is the use of more money or some other resource than is necessary **6** Waste is also material that is no longer wanted, or material left over from a useful process: *nuclear waste* ▷ adjective **7** unwanted in its present form: *waste paper* **8** Waste land is land which is not used or looked after by anyone ▷ **waste away** If someone is wasting away, they are becoming very thin and weak because they are ill or not eating properly

wasted *adjective* unnecessary: *a wasted journey*

wasteful *adjective* extravagant or causing waste by using something in a careless and inefficient way

wasteland *noun* A wasteland is land which is of no use because it is infertile or has been misused

wasting *adjective* A wasting disease is one that gradually reduces the strength and health of the body

watch *noun* **1** a small clock usually worn on a strap on the wrist **2** a period of time during which a guard is kept over something ▷ *verb* **3** If you watch something, you look at it for some time and pay close attention to what is happening **4** If you watch someone or something, you take care of them **5** If you watch a situation, you pay attention to it or are aware of it: *I had watched Jimmy's progress with interest*

> **watch out** *verb* **1** If you watch out for something, you keep alert to see if it is near you: *Watch out for more fog and ice* **2** If you tell someone to watch out, you are warning them to be very careful

watchdog *noun* **1** a dog used to guard property **2** a person or group whose job is to make sure that companies do not act illegally or irresponsibly

watchful *adjective* careful to notice everything that is happening: *the watchful eye of her father*

watchman watchmen *noun* a person whose job is to guard property

water *noun* **1** SCIENCE Water is a clear, colourless, tasteless, and odourless liquid that is necessary for all plant and animal life **2** You use water or waters to refer to a large area of water, such as a lake or sea: *the black waters of the lake* ▷ *verb* **3** If you water a plant or an animal, you give it water to drink **4** If your eyes water, you have tears in them because they are hurting **5** If your mouth waters, it produces extra saliva, usually because you think of or can smell something appetizing > **water down** *verb* If you water something down, you make it weaker

watercolour *noun* **1** Watercolours are paints for painting pictures, which are diluted with water or put on the paper using a wet brush **2** a picture which has been painted using watercolours

watercress *noun* Watercress is a small plant which grows in streams and pools. Its leaves taste hot and are eaten in salads

waterfall *noun* GEOGRAPHY A waterfall is water from a river or stream as it flows over the edge of a steep cliff in hills or mountains and falls to the ground below

waterfront *noun* a street or piece of land next to an area of water such as a river or harbour

waterlogged adjective Land that is waterlogged is so wet that the soil cannot contain any more water, so that some water remains on the surface of the ground

watermelon noun a large, round fruit which has a hard green skin and red juicy flesh

waterproof adjective **1** not letting water pass through: waterproof clothing ▷ noun **2** a coat which keeps water out

watershed noun an event or period which marks a turning point or the beginning of a new way of life: a watershed in European history

water-skiing noun Water-skiing is the sport of skimming over the water on skis while being pulled by a boat

water table noun GEOGRAPHY The water table is the level below the surface of the ground at which water can be found

watertight adjective **1** Something that is watertight does not allow water to pass through **2** An agreement or an argument that is watertight has been so carefully put together that nobody should be able to find a fault in it

waterway noun a canal, river, or narrow channel of sea which ships or boats can sail along

watery adjective **1** pale or weak: a watery smile **2** Watery food or drink contains a lot of water or is thin like water

watt [wot] noun A watt is a unit of power equal to one joule per second. It is named after James Watt (1736–1819), the inventor of the modern steam engine

wattle [wot-tl] noun an Australian acacia tree with spikes of brightly coloured flowers

wave verb **1** If you wave your hand, you move it from side to side, usually to say hello or goodbye **2** If you wave someone somewhere or wave them on, you make a movement with your hand to tell them which way to go **3** If you wave something, you hold it up and move it from side to side: The doctor waved a piece of paper at him ▷ noun **4** a ridge of water on the surface of the sea caused by wind or by tides **5** A wave is the form in which some types of energy such as heat, light, or sound travel through a substance **6** A wave of sympathy, alarm, or panic is a steady increase in it which spreads through you or through a group of people **7** an increase in a type of activity or behaviour: the crime wave

wavelength noun **1** the distance between the same point on two adjacent waves of energy **2** the size of radio wave which a particular radio station uses to broadcast its programmes

waver verb **1** If you waver or if your confidence or beliefs waver, you are no longer as firm, confident, or sure in your beliefs: Ben has never wavered from his belief **2** If something wavers, it moves slightly: The shadows wavered on the wall

wavy wavier, waviest adjective having waves or regular curves: wavy hair

wax noun **1** Wax is a solid, slightly shiny substance made of fat or oil and used to make candles and polish **2** Wax is also the sticky yellow substance in your ears ▷ verb **3** If you wax a surface, you treat it or cover it with a thin layer of wax, especially to polish it **4** (formal) If you wax eloquent, you talk in an eloquent way

w

way *noun* **1** A way of doing something is the manner of doing it: *an excellent way of cooking meat* **2** The ways of a person or group are their customs or their normal behaviour: *Their ways are certainly different* **3** The way you feel about something is your attitude to it or your opinion about it **4** If you have a way with people or things, you are very skilful at dealing with them **5** The way to a particular place is the route that you take to get there **6** If you go or look in a particular way, you go or look in that direction: *She glanced the other way* **7** If you divide something a number of ways, you divide it into that number of parts **8** Way is used with words such as 'little' or 'long' to say how far off in distance or time something is: *They lived a long way away* ▷ *phrase* **9** If something or someone is **in the way**, they prevent you from moving freely or seeing clearly **10** You say **by the way** when adding something to what you are saying: *By the way, I asked Brad to drop in* **11** If you **go out of your way** to do something, you make a special effort to do it

wayside *phrase* If someone or something **falls by the wayside**, they fail in what they are trying to do, or become forgotten and ignored

wayward *adjective* difficult to control and likely to change suddenly: *your wayward husband*

WC *noun* a toilet. WC is an abbreviation for 'water closet'

we *pronoun* A speaker or writer uses 'we' to refer to himself or herself and one or more other people: *We are going to see Eddie*

weak *adjective* **1** not having much strength: *weak from lack of sleep*

2 If something is weak, it is likely to break or fail: *Russia's weak economy* **3** If you describe someone as weak, you mean they are easily influenced by other people ▷ **weakly** *adverb*

weaken *verb* **1** If someone weakens something, they make it less strong or certain **2** If someone weakens, they become less certain about something

weakness *noun* **1** Weakness is lack of moral or physical strength **2** If you have a weakness for something, you have a great liking for it: *a weakness for whisky*

wealth *noun* **1** [GEOGRAPHY] Wealth is the large amount of money or property which someone owns **2** A wealth of something is a lot of it: *a wealth of information*

wealthy wealthier, wealthiest *adjective* having a large amount of money, property, or other valuable things

wean *verb* To wean a baby or animal is to start feeding it food other than its mother's milk

weapon *noun* **1** an object used to kill or hurt people in a fight or war **2** anything which can be used to get the better of an opponent: *Surprise was his only weapon* ▷ **weaponry** *noun*

wear wears, wearing, wore, worn *verb* **1** When you wear something such as clothes, make-up, or jewellery, you have them on your body or face **2** If you wear a particular expression, it shows on your face **3** If something wears, it becomes thinner or worse in condition ▷ *noun* **4** You can refer to clothes that are suitable for a particular time or occasion as a kind of wear: *beach wear* **5** Wear is the amount or type of use that something has and which causes damage or change to it: *signs of wear*

> **wear down** verb If you wear people down, you weaken them by repeatedly doing something or asking them to do something

> **wear off** verb If a feeling such as pain wears off, it gradually disappears > **wear on** verb If time wears on, it seems to pass very slowly or boringly > **wear out** verb **1** When something wears out or when you wear it out, it is used so much that it becomes thin, weak, and no longer usable **2** (*informal*) If you wear someone out, you make them feel extremely tired

wear and tear Wear and tear is the damage caused to something by normal use

wearing adjective Someone or something that is wearing makes you feel extremely tired

weary wearier, weariest; wearies, wearying, wearied adjective **1** very tired > verb **2** If you weary of something, you become tired of it > **wearily** adverb > **weariness** noun

weasel noun A small wild animal with a long, thin body and short legs

weather noun **1** The weather is the condition of the atmosphere at any particular time and the amount of rain, wind, or sunshine occurring > verb **2** If something such as rock or wood weathers, it changes colour or shape as a result of being exposed to the wind, rain, or sun **3** If you weather a problem or difficulty, you come through it safely > phrase **4** If you are **under the weather**, you feel slightly ill

weave weaves, weaving, wove, woven verb **1** To weave cloth is to make it by crossing threads over and

under each other, especially by using a machine called a loom **2** If you weave your way somewhere, you go there by moving from side to side through and round the obstacles > noun **3** The weave of cloth is the way in which the threads are arranged and the pattern that they form: *a tight weave*

weaver noun A person who weaves cloth

web noun **1 a** A fine net of threads that a spider makes from a sticky substance which it produces in its body **2** something that has a complicated structure or pattern: *a web of lies* **3** The Web is the same as the **World Wide Web**

weblog noun The full name for a **blog**

website noun A publication on the World Wide Web which contains information about a particular subject

wed weds, wedding, wedded or wed verb (*old-fashioned*) If you wed someone or if you wed, you get married

wedding noun RE A marriage ceremony

wedge verb **1** If you wedge something, you force it to remain there by holding it there tightly, or by fixing something next to it to prevent it from moving: *I shut the shed door and wedged it with a log of wood* > noun **2** a piece of something such as wood, metal, or rubber with one pointed edge and one thick edge which is used to wedge something **3 a** piece of something that has a thick triangular shape: *a wedge of cheese*

wedlock noun (*old-fashioned*) Wedlock is the state of being married

Wednesday noun Wednesday is the

day between Tuesday and Thursday

wee adjective In Scotland, a term for small

weed noun **1** a wild plant that prevents cultivated plants from growing properly ▷ verb **2** If you weed a place, you remove the weeds from it ▷ **weed out** verb If you weed out unwanted things, you get rid of them

week noun **1** a period of seven days, especially one beginning on a Sunday and ending on a Saturday **2** A week is also the number of hours you spend at work during a week: *a 35-hour week* **3** The week can refer to the part of the week that does not include Saturday and Sunday: *They are working during the week*

weekday noun any day except Saturday and Sunday

weekend noun Saturday and Sunday

weekly weeklies adjective **1** happening or appearing once a week ▷ adverb **2** once a week: *I see my mother weekly* ▷ noun **3** a newspaper or magazine that is published once a week

weep weeps, weeping, wept verb **1** If someone weeps, they cry **2** If something such as a wound weeps, it oozes blood or other liquid

weigh verb **1** If something weighs a particular amount, that is how heavy it is **2** If you weigh something, you measure how heavy it is using scales **3** If you weigh facts or words, you think about them carefully before coming to a decision or before speaking **4** If a problem weighs on you or weighs upon you, it makes you very worried ▷ **weigh down** verb If a load weighs you down, it stops you moving easily **2** If you are weighed down by a

difficulty, it is making you very worried ▷ **weigh up** verb If you weigh up a person or a situation, you make an assessment of them

weight noun **1** MATHS The weight of something is its heaviness **2** a metal object which has a certain known heaviness. Weights are used with sets of scales in order to weigh things **3** any heavy object **4** The weight of something is its large amount or importance which makes it hard to fight against or contradict: *the weight of the law* ▷ verb **5** If you weight something or weight it down, you make it heavier, often so that it cannot move ▷ **phrase 6** If you **pull your weight**, you work just as hard as other people involved in the same activity

weighted adjective A system that is weighted in favour of a particular person or group is organized in such a way that this person or group will have an advantage

weightlifting noun Weightlifting is the sport of lifting heavy weights in competition or for exercise > **weightlifter** noun

weighty weightier, weightiest adjective serious or important: *a weighty problem*

weir [rhymes with near] noun a low dam which is built across a river to raise the water level, control the flow of water, or change its direction

weird [weerd] adjective strange or odd > **weirdly** adverb

weirdo weirdos [weer-doe] noun (informal) If you call someone a weirdo, you mean they behave in a strange way

welcome verb **1** If you welcome a visitor, you greet them in a friendly way when they arrive **2** 'Welcome' can be said as a greeting to a visitor who has just arrived **3** If you **welcome** something, you approve of it and support it: *He welcomed the decision* ▷ *noun* **4** a greeting to a visitor: *a warm welcome* ▷ *adjective* **5** If someone is welcome at a place, they will be warmly received there **6** If something is welcome, it brings pleasure or is accepted gratefully: *a welcome rest* **7** If you tell someone they are welcome to something or welcome to do something, you mean you are willing for them to have or to do it > **welcoming** *adjective*

weld *verb* To weld two pieces of metal together is to join them by heating their edges and fixing them together so that when they cool they harden into one piece > **welder** *noun*

welfare *noun* **1** The welfare of a person or group is their general state of health and comfort **2** Welfare services are provided to help with people's living conditions and financial problems: *welfare workers*

welfare state *noun* The welfare state is a system in which the government uses money from taxes to provide health care and education services, and to give benefits to those who are old, unemployed, or sick

well *better, best; wells, welling, welled adverb* **1** If something goes well, it happens in a satisfactory way: *The interview went well* **2** in a good, skilful, or pleasing way: *He draws well* **3** thoroughly and completely: *well established* **4** kindly: *We treat our employees well* **5** If something may well or could well happen, it is likely to happen **6** You

use well to emphasize an adjective, adverb, or phrase: *He was well aware of that* ▷ *adjective* **7** If you are well, you are healthy ▷ *phrase* **8** As well means also: *He was a bus driver as well* **9** As well as means in addition to: *a meal which includes meat or fish, as well as rice* **10** If you say you may as well or might as well do something, you mean you will do it, not because you are keen to, but because there is nothing better to do. ▷ *noun* **11** a hole drilled in the ground from which water, oil, or gas is obtained ▷ *verb* **12** If tears well or well up, they appear in someone's eyes

well-balanced *adjective* sensible and without serious emotional problems: *a well-balanced happy teenager*

wellbeing *noun* Someone's wellbeing is their health and happiness

well-earned *adjective* thoroughly deserved

well-heeled *adjective* (*informal*) wealthy

well-informed *adjective* having a great deal of knowledge about a subject or subjects

well-meaning *adjective* A well-meaning person tries to be helpful but is often unsuccessful

well-off *adjective* (*informal*) quite wealthy

well-to-do *adjective* quite wealthy

well-worn *adjective* **1** A well-worn expression or saying has been used too often and has become boring **2** A well-worn object or piece of clothing has been used and worn so much that it looks old and shabby

Welsh *adjective* **1** belonging or relating to Wales ▷ *noun* **2** Welsh is a language spoken in parts of Wales

W

Welshman Welshmen noun a man who comes from Wales
> **Welshwoman** noun

welter noun (formal) A welter of things is a large number of them that happen or appear together in a state of confusion: *a welter of rumours*

wept the past tense and past participle of **weep**

were a past tense of **be**

werewolf werewolves noun In horror stories, a werewolf is a person who changes into a wolf

west noun **1** The west is the direction in which you look to see the sun set **2** The west of a place or country is the part which is towards the west when you are in the centre: *the west of America* **3** The West refers to the countries of North America and western and southern Europe ▷ adverb, adjective **4** West means towards the west ▷ adjective **5** A west wind blows from the west

westerly GEOGRAPHY adjective **1** When talking about a place, westerly means situated in the west: *France's most westerly region* **2** coming from the west: *a westerly wind*

western adjective **1** in or from the west **2** coming from or associated with the countries of North America and western and southern Europe: *western dress* ▷ noun **3** a book or film about life in the west of America in the nineteenth century

West Indian noun someone who comes from the West Indies

westward or **westwards** adverb Westward or westwards means towards the west: *He stared westwards towards the clouds*

wet wets; wettest; wets, wetting, wet or wetted adjective **1** If something is wet, it is covered in

water or another liquid **2** If the weather is wet, it is raining **3** If something such as paint, ink, or cement is wet, it is not yet dry or solid **4** (informal) If you say someone is wet, you mean they are weak and lacking confidence: *Don't be so wet!* ▷ noun **5** In Australia, the wet is the rainy season ▷ verb **6** To wet something is to put water or some other liquid over it **7** If people wet themselves or wet their beds, they urinate in their clothes or bed because they cannot control their bladder > **wetness** noun

whack verb If you whack someone or something, you hit them hard

whale noun a very large sea mammal which breathes through a hole on the top of its head

whaling noun Whaling is the work of hunting and killing whales for oil or food

wharf wharves [**worf**] noun a platform beside a river or the sea, where ships load or unload

what pronoun **1** What is used in questions: *What time is it?* **2** What is used in indirect questions and statements: *I don't know what you mean* **3** What can be used at the beginning of a clause to refer to something with a particular quality: *It is impossible to decide what is real and what is invented* ▷ adjective **4** What can be used at the beginning of a clause to show that you are talking about the whole amount that is available to you: *Their spouses try to earn what money they can* **5** You say what to emphasize an opinion or reaction: *What nonsense!* ▷ phrase **6** You say **what about** at the beginning of a question when you are making a suggestion or offer: *What about a drink?*

W

whatever pronoun **1** You use whatever to refer to anything or everything of a particular type: *He said he would do whatever he could* **2** You use whatever when you do not know the precise nature of something: *Whatever it is, I don't like it* ▷ conjunction **3** You use whatever to mean no matter what: *Whatever happens, you have to behave decently* ▷ adverb **4** You use whatever to emphasize a negative statement or a question: *You have no proof whatever; Whatever is wrong with you?*

whatsoever adverb You use whatsoever to emphasize a negative statement: *I have no memory of it whatsoever*

wheat noun Wheat is a cereal plant grown for its grain, which is used to make flour

wheel noun **1** D&T a circular object which turns on a rod attached to its centre. Wheels are fixed underneath vehicles so that they can move along **2** D&T The wheel of a car is its steering wheel ▷ verb **3** If you wheel something such as a bicycle, you push it **4** If someone or something wheels, they move round in the shape of a circle: *Cameron wheeled around and hit him*

wheelbarrow noun a small cart with a single wheel at the front, used for carrying things in the garden

wheelchair noun a chair with wheels in which sick, injured, or disabled people can move around

wheeze verb If someone wheezes, they breathe with difficulty, usually making a whistling sound, usually because they have a chest complaint such as asthma > **wheezy** adjective

when adverb **1** You use when to ask what time something happened or will happen: *When are you leaving?* ▷ conjunction **2** You use when to refer to a time in the past: *I met him when I was sixteen* **3** You use when to introduce the reason for an opinion, comment, or question: *How did you pass the exam when you hadn't studied for it?* **4** When is used to mean although: *He drives when he could walk*

whence adverb, conjunction (old-fashioned) Whence means from where

whenever conjunction Whenever means at any time, or every time that something happens: *I still go on courses whenever I can*

where adverb **1** You use where to ask which place something is in, is coming from, or is going to: *Where is Philip?* ▷ conjunction, pronoun, adverb **2** You use where when asking about or referring to something: *I hardly know where to begin* ▷ conjunction **3** You use where to refer to the place in which something is situated or happening: *I don't know where we are* **4** Where can introduce a clause that contrasts with the other part of the sentence: *A teacher will be listened to, where a parent might not*

whereabouts noun **1** The whereabouts of a person or thing is the place where they are ▷ adverb **2** You use whereabouts when you are asking more precisely where something is: *Whereabouts in Canada are you from?*

whereas conjunction Whereas introduces a comment that contrasts with the other part of the sentence: *Her eyes were blue, whereas mine were brown*

whereby pronoun (formal) Whereby means by which: *a new system*

whereby you pay the bill quarterly

whereupon conjunction (formal)
Whereupon means at which point:
*His enemies rejected his message,
whereupon he tried again*

wherever conjunction 1 Wherever
means in every place or situation:
*Alex heard the same thing wherever he
went* 2 You use wherever to show
that you do not know where a place
or person is: *the nearest police station,
wherever it is*

wherewithal noun If you have the
wherewithal to do something, you
have enough money to do it

whet verb whets, whetting, whetted
phrase To **whet someone's
appetite** for something means to
increase their desire for it

whether conjunction You use
whether when you are talking
about two or more alternatives: *I
don't know whether that's true or false*

which adjective, pronoun 1 You use
which to ask about alternatives or
to refer to a choice between
alternatives: *Which room are you in?*
▷ pronoun 2 Which at the beginning
of a clause identifies the thing you
are talking about or gives more
information about it: *certain wrongs
which exist in our society*

whichever adjective, pronoun You
use whichever when you are talking
about different alternatives or
possibilities: *Make your pizzas round
or square, whichever you prefer*

whiff noun 1 a slight smell of
something 2 a slight sign or trace of
something: *a whiff of criticism*

while conjunction 1 If something
happens while something else is
happening, the two things happen
at the same time 2 While also
means but: *Men tend to gaze more,
while women dart quick glances* ▷ noun

3 a period of time: *a little while earlier*
▷ phrase 4 If an action or activity is
worth your while, it will be helpful
or useful to you if you do it > **while
away** verb If you while away the
time in a particular way, you pass
the time that way because you have
nothing else to do

whilst conjunction Whilst means the
same as while

whim noun a sudden desire or fancy

whimper verb 1 When children or
animals whimper, they make soft,
low, unhappy sounds 2 If you
whimper something, you say it in an
unhappy or frightened way, as if you
are about to cry

whimsical adjective unusual and
slightly playful: *an endearing,
whimsical charm*

whine verb 1 To whine is to make a
long, high-pitched noise, especially
one which sounds sad or unpleasant
2 If someone whines about
something, they complain about it
in an annoying way ▷ noun 3 A
whine is the noise made by
something or someone whining

whinge whinges, whinging or
whingeing, whinged verb If
someone whinges about
something, they complain about it
in an annoying way

whip whips, whipping, whipped
noun 1 a thin piece of leather or rope
attached to a handle, which is used
for hitting people or animals ▷ verb
2 If you whip a person or animal, you
hit them with a whip 3 When the
wind whips something, it strikes it
4 If you whip something out or off,
you take it out or off very quickly:
She had whipped off her glasses 5 If you
whip cream, you beat it until it is
thick and frothy or stiff > **whip up**
verb If you whip up a strong

emotion, you make people feel it: *The thought whipped up his temper*

whirl verb **1** When something whirls, or when you whirl it round, it turns round very fast ▷ noun **2** You can refer to a lot of intense activity as a whirl of activity

whirlpool noun a small circular area in a river or the sea where the water is moving quickly round and round so that objects floating near it are pulled into its centre

whirlwind noun **1** a tall column of air which spins round and round very fast ▷ adjective **2** more rapid than usual: *a whirlwind tour*

whisk verb **1** If you whisk someone or something somewhere, you take them there quickly: *We were whisked away into a private room* **2** If you whisk eggs or cream, you stir air into them quickly ▷ noun **3** a kitchen tool used for quickly stirring air into eggs or cream

whisker noun The whiskers of an animal such as a cat or mouse are the long, stiff hairs near its mouth

whisky whiskies ▷ noun Whisky is a strong alcoholic drink made from grain such as barley

whisper verb **1** When you whisper, you talk to someone very quietly, using your breath and not your throat ▷ noun **2** If you talk in a whisper, you whisper

whistle verb **1** When you whistle a tune or whistle, you produce a clear musical sound by forcing your breath out between your lips **2** If something whistles, it makes a loud, high sound: *The kettle whistled* ▷ noun **3** A whistle is the sound something or someone makes when they whistle **4** a small metal tube that you blow into to produce a whistling sound

white noun, adjective **1** White is the lightest possible colour **2** Someone who is white has a pale skin and is of European origin ▷ adjective **3** If someone goes white, their face becomes very pale because they are afraid, shocked, or ill **4** White coffee contains milk or cream ▷ noun **5** The white of an egg is the transparent liquid surrounding the yolk which turns white when it is cooked
> **whiteness** noun

white-collar adjective White-collar workers work in offices rather than doing manual work: *a white-collar union*

whitewash noun **1** Whitewash is a mixture of lime and water used for painting walls white **2** an attempt to hide unpleasant facts: *the refusal to accept official whitewash in the enquiry*

whiting noun a sea fish related to the cod

whittle verb If you whittle a piece of wood, you shape it by shaving or cutting small pieces off it > **whittle away** or > **whittle down** verb To whittle away at something or to whittle it down means to make it smaller or less effective: *The 250 entrants had been whittled down to 34*

whizz or **whiz** (informal) verb **1** If you whizz somewhere, you move there quickly: *Could you whizz down to the shop and get me some milk?* ▷ noun **2** If you are a whizz at something, you are very good at it

who pronoun **1** You use who when you are asking about someone's identity: *Who gave you that black eye?* **2** Who at the beginning of a clause refers to the person or people you are talking about: *a shipyard worker who wants to be a postman*

whoever pronoun **1** Whoever means

w

the person who: *Whoever bought it for you has to make the claim* **2** Whoever also means no matter who: *I pity him, whoever he is* **3** Whoever is used in questions to give emphasis to who: *Whoever thought of such a thing?*

whole *adjective* **1** indicating all of something: *Have the whole cake* ▷ *noun* **2** the full amount of something: *the whole of Africa* ▷ *adverb* **3** in one piece: *He swallowed it whole* ▷ *phrase* **4** You use **as a whole** to emphasize that you are talking about all of something: *The country as a whole is in a very odd mood* **5** You say **on the whole** to mean that something is generally true: *On the whole, we should be glad they are gone* > **wholeness** *noun*

wholehearted *adjective* enthusiastic and totally sincere: *wholehearted approval* > **wholeheartedly** *adverb*

wholemeal *adjective* Wholemeal flour is made from the complete grain of the wheat plant, including the husk

wholesale *adjective, adverb* **1** Wholesale refers to the activity of buying goods cheaply in large quantities and selling them again, especially to shopkeepers: *We buy fruit and vegetables wholesale* ▷ *adjective* **2** Wholesale also means done to an excessive extent: *the wholesale destruction of wild plant species* > **wholesaler** *noun*

wholesome *adjective* good and likely to improve your life, behaviour, or health: *good wholesome entertainment*

wholly [hoe-lee] *adverb* completely

whom *pronoun* Whom is the object form of who: *the girl whom Albert would marry*

whoop *verb* **1** If you whoop, you shout loudly in a happy or excited way ▷ *noun* **2** a loud cry of happiness or excitement: *whoops of delight*

whooping cough [hoop-ing] *noun* Whooping cough is an acute infectious disease which makes people cough violently and produce a loud sound when they breathe

whose *pronoun* **1** You use whose to ask who something belongs to: *Whose gun is this?* **2** You use whose at the beginning of a clause which gives information relating or belonging to the thing or person you have just mentioned: *a wealthy gentleman whose marriage is breaking up*

WORD TIP
Many people are confused about the difference between *whose* and *who's*. Whose is used to show possession in a question or when something is being described: *whose bag is this? the person whose car is blocking the exit.* Who's, with the apostrophe, is a short form of *who is* or *who has*: *who's that girl? who's got my ruler?*

why *adverb, pronoun* You use why when you are asking about the reason for something, or talking about it: *Why did you do it?*; *He wondered why she suddenly looked happier*

wick *noun* the cord in the middle of a candle, which you set alight

wicked *adjective* **1** very bad: *a wicked thing to do* **2** mischievous in an amusing or attractive way: *a wicked sense of humour* > **wickedly** *adverb* > **wickedness** *noun*

wicker *adjective* A wicker basket or chair is made from twigs, canes, or reeds that have been woven together

wicket noun **1** In cricket, the wicket is one of the two sets of stumps and bails at which the bowler aims the ball **2** The grass between the wickets on a cricket pitch is also called the wicket

wide adjective **1** measuring a large distance from one side to the other **2** If there is a wide variety, range, or selection of something, there are many different kinds of it: *a wide range of colours* ▷ adverb **3** If you open or spread something wide, you open it to its fullest extent > **widely** adverb

widen verb **1** If something widens or if you widen it, it becomes bigger from one side to the other **2** You can say that something widens when it becomes greater in size or scope: *the opportunity to widen your outlook*

wide-ranging adjective extending over a variety of different things or over a large area: *a wide-ranging survey*

widespread adjective existing or happening over a large area or to a great extent: *the widespread use of chemicals*

widow noun a woman whose spouse has died

widowed adjective If someone is widowed, their husband or wife has died

widower noun a man whose spouse has died

width noun The width of something is the distance from one side or edge to the other

wield [**weeld**] verb **1** If you wield a weapon or tool, you carry it and use it **2** If someone wields power, they have it and are able to use it

wife wives noun A person's wife is the woman they are married to

Wi-Fi noun COMPUTING A system of accessing the internet from machines such as laptop computers that aren't physically connected to a network

wig noun a false head of hair worn to cover someone's own hair or to hide their baldness

wiggle verb **1** If you wiggle something, you move it up and down or from side to side with small jerky movements ▷ noun **2** a small jerky movement

wild adjective **1** Wild animals, birds, and plants live and grow in natural surroundings and are not looked after by people **2** Wild land is natural and has not been cultivated: *wild areas of countryside* **3** Wild weather or sea is stormy and rough **4** Wild behaviour is excited and uncontrolled **5** A wild idea or scheme is original and crazy ▷ noun **6** The wild is a free and natural state of living: *There are about 200 left in the wild* **7** The wilds are remote areas where few people live, far away from towns > **wildly** adverb

wilderness noun an area of natural land which is not cultivated

wildfire noun If something spreads like wildfire, it spreads very quickly

wildlife noun SCIENCE Wildlife means wild animals and plants

Wild West noun The Wild West was the western part of the United States when it was first being settled by Europeans

wiles plural noun Wiles are clever or crafty tricks used to persuade people to do something: *You are going to need all your wiles to get a pay rise from the new boss*

wilful adjective **1** Wilful actions or attitudes are deliberate and often intended to hurt someone: *wilful damage* **2** Someone who is wilful is

W

obstinate and determined to get their own way: *a wilful little boy*
> **wilfully** *adverb*

will *verb* **1** You use will to form the future tense: *Robin will be quite annoyed* **2** You use will to say that you intend to do something: *I will not deceive you* **3** You use will when inviting someone to do or have something: *Will you have another coffee?* **4** You will use when asking or telling someone to do something: *Will you do me a favour?*; *You will do as I say* **5** You use will to say that you are assuming something to be the case: *As you walk homeward, I was surprised*

will *verb* **1** If you will something to happen, you try to make it happen by mental effort: *I willed my eyes to open* **2** If you will something to someone, you leave it to them when you die: *Penbrook Farm is willed to her* > *noun* **3** Will is the determination to do something: *the will to win* **4** If something is the will of a person or group, they want it to happen: *the will of the people* **5** a legal document in which you say what you want to happen to your money and property when you die > *phrase* **6** If you can do something **at will**, you can do it whenever you want

willing *adjective* ready and eager to do something: *a willing helper*
> **willingly** *adverb* > **willingness** *noun*

willow *noun* A willow or willow tree is a tree with long, thin branches and narrow leaves that often grows near water

wilt *verb* **1** If a plant wilts, it droops because it needs more water or is dying **2** If someone wilts, they gradually lose strength or confidence: *James visibly wilted under pressure*

wily wilier, wiliest [**wie**-lee] *adjective* clever and cunning

wimp *noun* (*informal*) someone who is feeble and timid

win wins, winning, won *verb* **1** If you win a fight, game, or argument, you defeat your opponent **2** If you win in something, you succeed in obtaining it > *noun* **3** a victory in a game or contest > **win over** *verb* If you win someone over, you persuade them to support you

wince *verb* When you wince, the muscles of your face tighten suddenly because of pain, fear, or distress

winch *noun* **1** a machine used to lift heavy objects. It consists of a cylinder around which a rope or chain is wound > *verb* **2** If you winch an object or person somewhere, you lift, lower, or pull them using a winch

wind [*rhymes with* tinned] *noun* **1** a current of air moving across the earth's surface **2** Your wind is the ability to breathe easily: *Brown had recovered his wind* **3** Wind is air swallowed with food or drink, or gas produced in your stomach, which causes discomfort **4** MUSIC The wind section of an orchestra is the group of musicians who play wind instruments

wind winds, winding, wound [*rhymes with* mind] *verb* **1** If a road or river winds in a particular direction, it twists and turns in that direction **2** When you wind something round something else, you wrap it round it several times **3** When you wind a clock or machine or wind it up, you turn a key or handle several times to make it work > **wind up** *verb* **1** When you wind up something such as an activity or a business, you finish it or close it **2** If you wind up in a particular place, you end up there

windfall noun a sum of money that you receive unexpectedly

windmill noun a machine for grinding grain or pumping water. It is driven by vanes or sails turned by the wind

window noun a space in a wall or roof or in the side of a vehicle, usually with glass in it so that light can pass through and people can see in or out

windowsill noun a ledge along the bottom of a window, either on the inside or outside of a building

windpipe noun Your windpipe is the tube which carries air into your lungs when you breathe. The technical name for windpipe is **trachea**

windscreen noun the glass at the front of a vehicle through which the driver looks

windsurfing noun Windsurfing is the sport of moving along the surface of the sea or a lake standing on a board with a sail on it

windswept adjective A windswept place is exposed to strong winds: a windswept beach

windy windier, windiest adjective If it is windy, there is a lot of wind

wine noun Wine is the red or white alcoholic drink which is normally made from grapes

wing noun **1** A bird's or insect's wings are the parts of its body that it uses for flying **2** An aeroplane's wings are the long, flat parts on each side that support it while it is in the air **3** A wing of a building is a part which sticks out from the main part or which has been added later **4** A wing of an organization, especially a political party, is a group within it

with a particular role or particular beliefs: the left wing of the party **5** (in plural) The wings in a theatre are the sides of the stage which are hidden from the audience > **winged** adjective

wink verb **1** When you wink, you close one eye briefly, often as a signal that something is a joke or a secret ▷ noun **2** the closing of your eye when you wink

winner noun The winner of a prize, race, or competition is the person or thing that wins it

winning adjective **1** The winning team or entry in a competition is the one that has won **2** attractive and charming: a winning smile

winter noun Winter is the season between autumn and spring

wintry adjective Something wintry has features that are typical of winter: the wintry dawn

wipe verb **1** If you wipe something, you rub its surface lightly to remove dirt or liquid **2** If you wipe dirt or liquid off something, you remove it using a cloth or your hands: Anne wiped the tears from her eyes > **wipe out** verb To wipe out people or places is to destroy them completely

wire noun **1** SCIENCE Wire is metal in the form of a long, thin, flexible thread which can be used to make or fasten things or to conduct an electric current ▷ verb **2** If you wire one thing to another, you fasten them together using wire **3** D&T If you wire something or wire it up, you connect it so that electricity can pass through it > **wired** adjective

wireless noun (old-fashioned) a radio

wiring noun The wiring in a building is the system of wires that supply electricity to the rooms

wiry wirier, wiriest adjective **1** Wiry

W

people are thin but with strong muscles **2** Wiry things are stiff and rough to the touch: *wiry hair*

wisdom *noun* **1** Wisdom is the ability to use experience and knowledge in order to make sensible decisions or judgments **2** If you talk about the wisdom of an action or a decision, you are talking about how sensible it is

wise *adjective* **1** Someone who is wise can use their experience and knowledge to make sensible decisions and judgments ▷ *phrase* **2** If you say that someone is **none the wiser** or **no wiser**, you mean that they know no more about something than they did before: *I left the conference none the wiser*

wisecrack *noun* a clever remark, intended to be amusing but often unkind

wish *noun* **1** a longing or desire for something, often something difficult to achieve or obtain **2** something desired or wanted: *That wish came true two years later* **3** (*in plural*) Good wishes are expressions of hope that someone will be happy or successful: *best wishes on your birthday* ▷ *verb* **4** If you wish to do something, you want to do it: *We wished to return* **5** If you wish something were the case, you would like it to be the case, but know it is not very likely: *I wish I were tall*

wishbone *noun* a V-shaped bone in the breast of most birds

wishful thinking *noun* If someone's hope or wish is wishful thinking, it is unlikely to come true

wistful *adjective* sadly thinking about something, especially something you want but cannot have: *A wistful look came into her eyes* > **wistfully** *adverb*

wit *noun* **1** Wit is the ability to use words or ideas in an amusing and clever way **2** Wit means sense: *They haven't got the wit to realize what they're doing* **3** (*in plural*) Your wits are the ability to think and act quickly in a difficult situation: *the man who lived by his wits* ▷ *phrase* **4** If someone is **at their wits' end**, they are so worried and exhausted by problems or difficulties that they do not know what to do

witch *noun* a woman claimed to have magic powers and to be able to use them for good or evil

witchcraft *noun* Witchcraft is the skill or art of using magic powers, especially evil ones

with *preposition* **1** With someone means in their company: *He was at home with me* **2** With is used to show who your opponent is in a fight or competition: *next week's game with Brazil* **3** With can mean using or having: *Apply the colour with a brush; a bloke with a moustache* **4** With is used to show how someone does something or how they feel: *She looked at him with hatred* **5** With can mean concerning: *a problem with her telephone bill* **6** With is used to show support: *Are you with us or against us?*

withdraw withdraws, withdrawing, withdrew, withdrawn *verb* **1** If you withdraw something, you remove it or take it out: *He withdrew the money from his bank account* **2** If you withdraw to another place, you leave where you are and go there: *He withdrew to his study* **3** If you withdraw from an activity, you back out of it: *They withdrew from the conference*

withdrawal *noun* **1** The withdrawal of something is the act of taking it away: *the withdrawal of Russian*

W

troops **2** The withdrawal of a statement is the act of saying formally that you wish to change or deny it **3** an amount of money you take from your bank or building society account

withdrawn 1 Withdrawn is the past participle of **withdraw** ▷ *adjective* **2** unusually shy or quiet

wither *verb* **1** When something withers or withers away, it becomes weaker until it no longer exists **2** If a plant withers, it wilts or shrivels up and dies

withering *adjective* A withering look or remark makes you feel ashamed, stupid, or inferior

withhold withholds, withholding, withheld *verb* (*formal*) If you withhold something that someone wants, you do not let them have it

within *preposition, adverb* **1** Within means in or inside ▷ *preposition* **2** Within can mean not going beyond certain limits: *Stay within the budget* **3** Within can mean before a period of time has passed: *You must write back within fourteen days*

without *preposition* **1** Without means not having, feeling, or showing: *Didier looked on without emotion* **2** Without can mean not using: *You can't get in without a key* **3** Without can mean not in someone's company: *He went without me* **4** Without can indicate that something does not happen when something else happens: *Stone signalled the ship, again without response*

withstand withstands, withstanding, withstood *verb* When something or someone withstands a force or action, they survive it or do not give in to it: *ships designed to withstand the North Atlantic winter*

witness *noun* **1** someone who has seen an event such as an accident and can describe what happened **2** someone who appears in a court of law to say what they know about a crime or other event **3** someone who writes their name on a document that someone else has signed, to confirm that it is really that person's signature ▷ *verb* **4** (*formal*) If you witness an event, you see it

witty wittier, wittiest *adjective* amusing in a clever way: *this witty novel* > **wittily** *adverb*

wives the plural of **wife**

wizard *noun* **1** a man in a fairy story who has magic powers

wizardry *noun* Wizardry is something that is very cleverly done: *technological wizardry*

wobble *verb* If something wobbles, it shakes or moves from side to side because it is loose or unsteady: *a cyclist who wobbled into my path*

wobbly wobblier, wobbliest *adjective* unsteady: *a wobbly table*

woe (*literary*) *noun* **1** Woe is great unhappiness or sorrow **2** (*in plural*) Someone's woes are their problems or misfortunes

wok *noun* a large bowl-shaped metal pan used for Chinese-style cooking

woke the past tense of **wake**

woken the past participle of **wake**

wolf wolves; wolfs, wolfing, wolfed *noun* **1** a wild animal related to the dog. Wolves hunt in packs and kill other animals for food ▷ *verb* **2** (*informal*) If you wolf food or wolf it down, you eat it up quickly and greedily

woman women *noun* **1** an adult female human being **2** Woman can refer to women in general: *man's inhumanity to woman*

womanhood noun Womanhood is the state of being a woman rather than a girl: *on the verge of womanhood*

womb [**woom**] noun A woman's womb is the part inside her body where her unborn baby grows

wombat [**wom**-bat] noun a short-legged furry Australian animal which eats plants

wonder verb 1 If you wonder about something, you think about it with curiosity or doubt 2 If you wonder at something, you are surprised and amazed at it: *He wondered at her anger* ▷ noun 3 Wonder is a feeling of surprise and amazement 4 something or someone that surprises and amazes people: *the wonders of science*

wonderful adjective 1 making you feel very happy and pleased: *It was wonderful to be together* 2 very impressive: *Nature is a wonderful thing* ▷ **wonderfully** adverb

wondrous adjective (literary) amazing and impressive

wont [rhymes with **don't**] adjective (old-fashioned) If someone is wont to do something, they do it often: *a gesture he was wont to use when preaching*

woo verb 1 If you woo people, you try to get them to help or support you: *attempts to woo the women's vote* 2 (old-fashioned) When a man woos a woman, he tries to get her to marry him

wood noun 1 Wood is the substance which forms the trunks and branches of trees 2 a large area of trees growing near each other

wooded adjective covered in trees: *a wooded area nearby*

wooden adjective made of wood: *a wooden box*

woodland noun Woodland is land that is mostly covered with trees

woodwind adjective Woodwind instruments are musical instruments such as flutes, oboes, clarinets, and bassoons, that are played by being blown into

woodwork noun 1 Woodwork refers to the parts of a house, such as stairs, doors, or window-frames, that are made of wood 2 Woodwork is the craft or skill of making things out of wood

woody woodier, woodiest adjective 1 Woody plants have hard tough stems 2 A woody area has a lot of trees in it

wool noun 1 Wool is the hair that grows on sheep and some other animals 2 Wool is also yarn spun from the wool of animals which is used to knit, weave, and make such things as clothes, blankets, and carpets

woollen adjective 1 made from wool ▷ noun 2 Woollens are clothes made of wool

woolly woollier, woolliest adjective 1 made of wool or looking like wool: *a woolly hat* 2 If you describe people or their thoughts as woolly, you mean that they seem confused and unclear

word noun 1 a single unit of language in speech or writing which has a meaning 2 a remark: *a word of praise* 3 a brief conversation: *Could I have a word?* 4 A word can also be a message: *The word is that Sharon is exhausted* 5 Your word is a promise: *He gave me his word* 6 The word can be a command: *I gave the word to start* 7 (in plural) The words of a play or song are the spoken or sung text ▷ verb 8 When you word something, you choose your words in order to express your ideas accurately or acceptably: *the best way to word our invitations*

wording noun The wording of a piece of writing or a speech is the words used in it, especially when these words have been carefully chosen to have a certain effect

word processor noun an electronic machine which has a keyboard and a visual display unit and which is used to produce, store, and organize printed material

work verb 1 People who work have a job which they are paid to do: *My husband works for a national newspaper* 2 When you work, you do the tasks that your job involves 3 To work the land is to cultivate it 4 If someone works a machine, they control or operate it 5 If a machine works, it operates properly and effectively: *The radio doesn't work* 6 If something such as an idea or a system works, it is successful: *The housing benefit system is not working* 7 If something works its way into a particular position, it gradually moves there: *The cable had worked loose* ▷ noun 8 People who have work or who are in work have a job which they are paid to do: *She's trying to find work* 9 Work is the tasks that have to be done 10 something done or made: *a work of art* 11 In physics, work is transfer of energy. It is calculated by multiplying a force by the distance moved by the point to which the force has been applied. Work is measured in joules 12 (*in plural*) A works is a place where something is made by an industrial process: *the old steel works* 13 Works are large-scale building, digging, or general construction activities: *building works* ▷ **work out** verb 1 If

you work out a solution to a problem, you find the solution 2 If a situation works out in a particular way, it happens in that way ▷ **work up** verb 1 If you work up to something, you gradually progress towards it 2 If you work yourself up or work someone else up, you make yourself or the other person very upset or angry about something ▷ **worked up** adjective

workable adjective Something workable can operate successfully or can be used for a particular purpose: *a workable solution*; *This plan simply isn't workable*

workaholic noun a person who finds it difficult to stop working and do other things

worker noun a person employed in a particular industry or business: *a defence worker*

workforce noun The workforce is all the people who work in a particular place

working class noun The working class or working classes are the group of people in society who do not own much property and who do jobs which involve physical rather than intellectual skills

workload noun the amount of work that a person or a machine has to do

workman noun workmen noun a man whose job involves using physical rather than intellectual skills

workmanship noun Workmanship is the skill with which something is made or a job is completed

workmate noun Someone's workmate is the fellow worker with whom they do their job

workout noun a session of physical exercise or training

workshop noun 1 a room or building that contains tools or machinery

W

used for making or repairing things: *an engineering workshop* **2** a period of discussion or practical work in which a group of people learn about a particular subject: *a theatre workshop*

world noun **1** The world is the earth, the planet we live on **2** You can use 'world' to refer to people generally: *The eyes of the world are upon me* **3** Someone's world is the life they lead and the things they experience: *We come from different worlds* **4** A world is a division or section of the earth, its history, or its people, such as the Arab World, or the Ancient World **5** A particular world is a field of activity and the people involved in it: *the world of football* ▷ *adjective* **6** 'World' is used to describe someone or something that is one of the best or most important of its kind: *a world leader* ▷ *phrase* **7** If you **think the world** of someone, you like or admire them very much

worldly *worldlier, worldliest adjective* **1** relating to the ordinary activities of life rather than spiritual things: *opportunities for worldly pleasures* **2** experienced and knowledgeable about life

world war noun a war that involves countries all over the world

worldwide *adjective* throughout the world: *a worldwide increase in skin cancers*

World Wide Web noun The World Wide Web is a system of linked documents accessed via the internet

worm noun **1** a small thin animal without bones or legs, which lives in the soil or off other creatures **2** an insect such as a beetle or moth at a very early stage in its life **3** a computer program that makes many copies of itself within a network, usually harming the system ▷ *verb* **4** If you worm an animal, you give it medicine in order to kill the worms that are living as parasites in its intestines > **worm out** *verb* If you worm information out of someone, you gradually persuade them to give you it

worn **1** Worn is the past participle of **wear** ▷ *adjective* **2** damaged or thin because of long use **3** looking old or exhausted: *Her husband looks frail and worn*

worn-out *adjective* **1** used until it is too thin or too damaged to be of further use: *a worn-out cardigan* **2** extremely tired: *You must be worn-out after the drive*

worried *adjective* unhappy and anxious about a problem or about something unpleasant that might happen

worry *worries, worrying, worried verb* **1** If you worry, you feel anxious and fearful about a problem or about something unpleasant that might happen **2** If something worries you, it causes you to feel uneasy or fearful: *a puzzle which had worried her all her life* **3** If you worry someone with a problem, you disturb or bother them by telling them about it: *I didn't want to worry the boys with this* **4** If a dog worries sheep or other animals, it frightens or harms them by chasing them or biting them ▷ *noun* **5** Worry is a feeling of unhappiness and unease caused by a problem or by thinking of something unpleasant that might happen: *the major source of worry* **6** a person or thing that causes you to feel anxious or uneasy: *Inflation is the least of our worries* > **worrying** *adjective*

worse adjective, adverb **1** Worse is the comparative form of **bad** and **badly 2** If someone who is ill gets worse, they become more ill than before ▷ phrase **3** If someone or something is **none the worse** for something, they have not been harmed by it: *He appeared none the worse for the accident*

worsen verb If a situation worsens, it becomes more difficult or unpleasant: *My relationship with my mother worsened*

worse off adjective If you are worse off, you have less money or are in a more unpleasant situation than before: *There are people much worse off than me*

worship worships, worshipping, worshipped verb **1** RE If you worship a god, you show your love and respect by praying or singing hymns **2** If you worship someone or something, you love them or admire them very much ▷ noun **3** Worship is the feeling of respect, love, or admiration you feel for something or someone > **worshipper** noun

worst adjective, adverb Worst is the superlative of **bad** and **badly**

worth preposition **1** If something is worth a sum of money, it has that value: *a house worth $850,000* **2** If something is worth doing, it deserves to be done ▷ noun **3** A particular amount of money's worth of something is the quantity of it that you can buy for that money: *five pounds' worth of petrol* **4** Someone's worth is the value or usefulness they are considered to have

worthless adjective having no real value or use: *a worthless piece of junk*

worthwhile adjective important enough to justify the time, money, or effort spent on it: *a worthwhile career*

worthy worthier, worthiest adjective If someone or something is worthy of something, they deserve it: *a worthy champion*

would verb **1** You use would to say what someone thought was going to happen: *We were sure it would be a success* **2** You use would when you are referring to the result or effect of a possible situation: *If readers can help I would be most grateful* **3** You use would when referring to someone's willingness to do something: *I wouldn't change places with him if you paid me* **4** You use would in polite questions: *Would you like some lunch?*

would-be adjective wanting to be or claiming to be: *a would-be pop singer*

wound noun **1** an injury to part of your body, especially a cut in your skin and flesh ▷ verb **2** If someone wounds you, they damage your body using a gun, knife, or other weapon **3** If you are wounded by what someone says or does, your feelings are hurt > **wounded** adjective

wow interjection Wow is an expression of admiration or surprise

WPC noun In Britain, a female member of the police force. WPC is an abbreviation for 'woman police constable'

wrangle verb **1** If you wrangle with someone, you argue noisily or angrily, often about something unimportant ▷ noun **2** an argument that is difficult to settle > **wrangling** noun

wrap wraps, wrapping, wrapped verb **1** If you wrap something or wrap something up, you fold a piece of paper or cloth tightly around it to cover or enclose it **2** If you wrap

paper or cloth round something,
you put or fold the paper round it
3 If you wrap your arms, fingers, or
legs round something, you coil
them round it > **wrap up** verb If you
wrap up, you put warm clothes on

wrapped up adjective (informal) If
you are wrapped up in a person or
thing, you give that person or thing
all your attention

wrapper noun a piece of paper,
plastic, or foil which covers and
protects something that you buy:
sweet wrappers

wrapping noun Wrapping is the
material used to cover and protect
something

wrath [roth] noun (literary) Wrath is
great anger: the wrath of his father

wreak [reek] verb To wreak havoc or
damage is to cause it

wreath [reeth] noun an
arrangement of flowers and leaves,
often in the shape of a circle, which
is put on a grave as a sign of
remembrance for the dead person

wreck verb **1** If someone wrecks
something, they break it, destroy, or
spoil it completely **2** If a ship is
wrecked, it has been so badly
damaged that it can no longer sail
▷ noun **3** a vehicle which has been
badly damaged in an accident **4** If
you say someone is a wreck, you
mean that they are in a very poor
physical or mental state of health
and cannot cope with life
> **wrecked** adjective

wreckage noun Wreckage is what
remains after something has been
badly damaged or destroyed

wrench verb **1** If you wrench
something, you give it a sudden and
violent twist or pull: Nick wrenched
open the door **2** If you wrench a limb
or a joint, you twist and injure it

▷ noun **3** a metal tool with parts
which can be adjusted to fit around
nuts or bolts to loosen or tighten
them **4** a painful parting from
someone or something

wrest [rest] verb (formal) If you wrest
something from someone else you
take it from them violently or with
effort: to try and wrest control of the
island from the Mafia

wrestle verb **1** If you wrestle
someone or wrestle with them, you
fight them by holding or throwing
them, but not hitting them **2** When
you wrestle with a problem, you try
to deal with it > **wrestler** noun

wrestling noun Wrestling is a sport
in which two people fight and try to
win by throwing or holding their
opponent on the ground

wretched [ret-shid] adjective **1** very
unhappy or unfortunate: a wretched
childhood **2** (informal) You use
wretched to describe something or
someone you feel angry about or
dislike: a wretched bully

wriggle verb **1** If someone wriggles,
they twist and turn their body or a
part of their body using quick
movements: He wriggled his arms and
legs **2** If you wriggle somewhere,
you move there by twisting and
turning: I wriggled out of the van
> **wriggly** adjective

wring wrings, wringing, wrung verb
1 When you wring a wet cloth or
wring it out, you squeeze the water
out of it by twisting it **2** If you wring
your hands, you hold them together
and twist and turn them, usually
because you are worried or upset
3 If someone wrings a bird's neck,
they kill the bird by twisting and
wringing its neck

wrinkle noun **1** Wrinkles are lines in
someone's skin, especially on the

face, which form as they grow old ▷ **verb 2** If something wrinkles, folds or lines develop on it: *Fold the paper carefully so that it doesn't wrinkle* **3** When you wrinkle your nose, forehead, or eyes, you tighten the muscles in your face so that the skin folds into lines > **wrinkled** adjective > **wrinkly** adjective

wrist noun the part of your body between your hand and your arm which bends when you move your hand

writ noun a legal document that orders a person to do or not to do a particular thing

write writes, writing, wrote, written verb **1** When you write something, you use a pen or pencil to form letters, words, or numbers on a surface **2** If you write something such as a poem, a book, or a piece of music, you create it **3** When you write to someone or write them a letter, you express your feelings in a letter **4** When someone writes something such as a cheque, they put the necessary information on it and sign it **5** When you write data you transfer it to a computer's memory > **write down** verb If you write something down, you record it on a piece of paper > **write up** verb If you write up something, you write a full account of it, often using notes that you have made

writer noun **1** a person who writes books, stories, or articles as a job **2** The writer of something is the person who wrote it

writhe verb If you writhe, you twist and turn your body, often because you are in pain

writing noun **1** Writing is something that has been written or printed: *Apply in writing for the information*

2 Your writing is the way you write with a pen or pencil **3** Writing is also a piece of written work, especially the style of language used: *witty writing* **4** An author's writings are his or her written works

written 1 Written is the past participle of **write** ▷ adjective **2** taken down in writing: *a written agreement*

wrong adjective **1** not working properly or unsatisfactory: *There was something wrong with the car* **2** not correct or truthful: *the wrong answer* **3** bad or immoral: *It is wrong to kill people* ▷ noun **4** an unjust action or situation: *the wrongs of our society* ▷ verb **5** If someone wrongs you, they treat you in an unfair or unjust way > **wrongly** adverb

wrongful adjective A wrongful act is regarded as illegal, unfair, or immoral: *wrongful imprisonment* > **wrongfully** adverb

wrought iron noun Wrought iron is a pure type of iron that is formed into decorative shapes

wry adjective A wry expression shows that you find a situation slightly amusing because you know more about it than other people > **wryly** adverb > **wryness** noun

X

X or **x 1** X is used to represent the name of an unknown or secret person or place: *The victim was*

referred to as Mr X throughout Tuesday's court proceedings **2** In algebra, x is used as a symbol to represent a number whose value is not known **3** People sometimes write X on a map to mark a precise position **4** X is used to represent a kiss at the bottom of a letter, a vote on a ballot paper, or the signature of someone who cannot write

xenophobia [zen-nof-**foe**-bee-a] *noun* a fear or strong dislike of people from other countries ▷ **xenophobic** *adjective*

Xerox [**zeer**-roks] *noun* (*trademark*) **1** a machine that makes photographic copies of sheets of paper with writing or printing on them **2** a copy made by a Xerox machine

Xmas *noun* (*informal*) Xmas means the same as Christmas

X-ray *noun* **1** a stream of radiation of very short wavelength that can pass through some solid materials. X-rays are used by doctors to examine the bones or organs inside a person's body **2** a picture made by sending X-rays through someone's body in order to examine the inside of it ▷ *verb* **3** If you are X-rayed, a picture is made of the inside of your body by passing X-rays through it

y

-y *suffix* -y forms nouns: *anarchy*

yacht [yot] *noun* a boat with sails or

an engine, used for racing or for pleasure trips

yachting *noun* Yachting is the sport or activity of sailing a yacht

yachtsman *noun* a man who sails a yacht ▷ **yachtswoman** *noun*

yak *noun* a type of long-haired ox with long horns, found mainly in Tibet

yakka *or* **yacker** *noun* (*informal*) In Australian and New Zealand English, yakka or yacker is work

yank (*informal*) *verb* **1** If you yank something, you pull or jerk it suddenly with a lot of force ▷ *noun* **2** A Yank is an American

Yankee *noun* (*informal*) the same as a Yank

yard *noun* **1** a unit of length equal to 36 inches or about 91.4 centimetres **2** an enclosed area that is usually next to a building and is often used for a particular purpose: *a ship repair yard*

yardstick *noun* someone or something you use as a standard against which to judge other people or things: *He had no yardstick by which to judge university*

yarn *noun* **1** ⒹⒼⓉ Yarn is thread used for knitting or making cloth **2** (*informal*) a story that someone tells, often with invented details to make it more interesting or exciting: *fishermen's yarns*

yawn *verb* **1** When you yawn, you open your mouth wide and take in more air than usual. You often yawn when you are tired or bored **2** A gap or opening that yawns is large and wide ▷ *noun* **3** an act of yawning

yawning *adjective* A yawning gap or opening is very wide

ye (*old-fashioned*) *pronoun* **1** Ye is used

to mean 'you' ▷ *adjective* **2** Ye is also used to mean 'the'

yeah *interjection* (*informal*) Yeah means 'yes'

year *noun* **1** a period of twelve months or 365 days (366 days in a leap year), which is the time taken for the earth to travel once around the sun **2** a period of twelve consecutive months, not always January to December, on which administration or organization is based: *the current financial year* ▷ *phrase* **3** If something happens **year in, year out**, it happens every year: *a tradition kept up year in, year out*

yearling *noun* an animal between one and two years old

yearn [rhymes with **learn**] *verb* If you yearn for something, you want it very much indeed: *He yearned to sleep* > **yearning** *noun*

yeast *noun* Yeast is a kind of fungus which is used to make bread rise, and to make liquids ferment in order to produce alcohol

yell *verb* **1** If you yell, you shout loudly, usually because you are angry, excited, or in pain ▷ *noun* **2** a loud shout

yellow *noun, adjective* **1** Yellow is the colour of buttercups, egg yolks, and lemons ▷ *verb* **2** When something yellows or is yellowed, it becomes yellow, often because it is old ▷ *adjective* **3** (*informal*) If you say someone is yellow, you mean they are cowardly > **yellowish** *adjective*

yellow fever *noun* Yellow fever is a serious infectious disease that is found in tropical countries. It causes fever and jaundice

yelp *verb* **1** When people or animals yelp, they give a sudden, short cry ▷ *noun* **2** a sudden, short cry

yen *noun* **1** The yen is the main unit of currency in Japan **2** (*informal*) If you have a yen to do something, you have a strong desire to do it: *Mike had a yen to try cycling*

yes *interjection* You use 'yes' to agree with someone, to say that something is true, or to accept something

yesterday *noun, adverb* **1** Yesterday is the day before today **2** You also use 'yesterday' to refer to the past: *Leave yesterday's sadness behind you*

yet *adverb* **1** If something has not happened yet, it has not happened up to the present time: *It isn't quite dark yet* **2** If something should not be done yet, it should not be done now, but later: *Don't switch off yet* **3** 'Yet' can mean there is still a possibility that something can happen: *We'll make a soldier of you yet* **4** You use 'yet' when you want to say how much longer a situation will continue: *The service doesn't start for an hour yet* **5** 'Yet' can be used for emphasis: *She'd changed her mind yet again* ▷ *conjunction* **6** You can use 'yet' to introduce a fact which is rather surprising: *He isn't a smoker yet he always carries a lighter*

yew *noun* an evergreen tree with bright red berries

Yiddish *noun* Yiddish is a language derived mainly from German, which many Jewish people of European origin speak

yield *verb* **1** If you yield to someone or something, you stop resisting and give in to them: *Russia recently yielded to US pressure* **2** If you yield something that you have control of or responsibility for, you surrender it: *They refused to yield control of their weapons* **3** If something yields, it breaks or gives way: *The handle* would yield to her grasp **4** To yield something is to produce it: *One season's produce yields food for the following year* ▷ noun **5** A yield is an amount of food, money, or profit produced from a given area of land or from an investment

yob noun (*informal*) a noisy, badly behaved boy or young man

yoga [**yoe**-ga] noun Yoga is a Hindu method of mental and physical exercise or discipline

yogurt [**yog**-gurt or **yoe**-gurt] or **yoghurt** noun Yogurt is a slightly sour thick liquid made from milk that has had bacteria added to it

yoke noun **1** a wooden bar attached to two collars which is laid across the necks of animals such as oxen to hold them together, and to which a plough or other tool may be attached **2** (*literary*) If people are under a yoke of some kind, they are being oppressed: *two women who escape the yoke of insensitive men*

yolk [rhymes with **joke**] noun the yellow part in the middle of an egg

Yom Kippur [yom kip-**poor**] noun Yom Kippur is an annual Jewish religious holiday, which is a day of fasting and prayers. It is also called the Day of Atonement

yonder adverb, adjective (*old-fashioned*) over there: *There's an island yonder*

yore phrase (*old-fashioned*) **Of yore** means existing a long time ago: *nostalgia for the days of yore*

you pronoun **1** You refers to the person or group of people that a person is speaking or writing to **2** You also refers to people in general: *You can get a two-bedroom villa quite cheaply*

young adjective **1** A young person, animal, or plant has not lived very

long and is not yet mature ▷ plural noun **2** The young are young people in general **3** The young of an animal are its babies

youngster noun a child or young person

your adjective **1** Your means belonging or relating to the person or group of people that someone is speaking to: *I do like your name* **2** Your is used to show that something belongs or relates to people in general: *Some of these chemicals can cause serious damage to your health*

yours pronoun Yours refers to something belonging or relating to the person or group of people that someone is speaking to: *His hair is longer than yours*

yourself yourselves pronoun **1** Yourself is used when the person being spoken to does the action and is affected by it: *Why can't you do it yourself?* **2** Yourself is used to emphasize 'you': *Do you yourself want a divorce?*

youth noun **1** Someone's youth is the period of their life before they are a fully mature adult **2** Youth is the quality or condition of being young and often inexperienced **3** a boy or young man **4** The youth are young people thought of as a group: *the youth of today* ▷ **youthful** adjective

yo-yo yo-yos noun a round wooden or plastic toy attached to a piece of string. You play by making the yo-yo rise and fall on the string

Yule noun (*old-fashioned*) Yule means Christmas

yuppie noun A yuppie is a young, middle-class person who earns a lot of money which he or she spends on himself or herself

Z

Zambian [zam-bee-an] adjective
1 belonging or relating to Zambia
▷ noun 2 someone who comes from Zambia

zany zanier, zaniest adjective (informal) odd and ridiculous: zany humour

zap zaps, zapping, zapped verb (informal) 1 To zap someone is to kill them, usually by shooting 2 To zap also is to move somewhere quickly: I zapped over to Paris

zeal noun Zeal is very great enthusiasm > **zealous** adjective > **zealously** adverb

zealot [zel-lot] noun a person who acts with very great enthusiasm, especially in following a political or religious cause

zebra noun a type of African wild horse with black and white stripes over its body

Zen or **Zen Buddhism** noun Zen is a form of Buddhism that concentrates on learning through meditation and intuition

zenith noun (literary) The zenith of something is the time when it is at its most successful or powerful: the zenith of his military career

zero zeros or zeroes, zeroing, zeroed
1 nothing or the number 0 2 Zero is freezing point, 0° Centigrade
▷ adjective 3 Zero means there is none at all of a particular thing: His chances are zero > **zero in** verb To zero in on a target is to aim at or to move

towards it: The headlines zeroed in on the major news stories

zest noun 1 Zest is a feeling of pleasure and enthusiasm: zest for life
2 Zest is a quality which adds extra flavour or interest to something: brilliant ideas to add zest to your wedding list 3 The zest of an orange or lemon is the outside of the peel which is used to flavour food or drinks

zigzag zigzags, zigzagging, zigzagged noun 1 a line which has a series of sharp, angular turns to the right and left in it, like a continuous series of 'W's ▷ verb 2 To zigzag is to move forward by going at an angle first right and then left: He zigzagged his way across the racecourse

Zimbabwean [zim-bahb-wee-an] adjective 1 belonging or relating to Zimbabwe ▷ noun 2 someone who comes from Zimbabwe

zinc noun Zinc is a bluish-white metallic element used in alloys and to coat other metals to stop them rusting. Its atomic number is 30 and its symbol is Zn

zip zips, zipping, zipped noun 1 a long narrow fastener with two rows of teeth that are closed or opened by a small clip pulled between them
▷ verb 2 When you zip something or zip it up, you fasten it using a zip

zipper noun the same as a **zip**

zodiac [zoe-dee-ak] noun The zodiac is an imaginary strip in the sky which contains the planets and stars which astrologers think are important influences on people. It is divided into 12 sections, each with a special name and symbol

zombie noun 1 (informal) If you refer to someone as a zombie, you mean that they seem to be unaware of what is going on around them and

Z

to act without thinking about what they are doing **2** In voodoo, a zombie is a dead person who has been brought back to life by witchcraft

zone noun an area that has particular features or properties: *a war zone*

zoo zoos noun a place where live animals are kept so that people can look at them

zoology [zoo-**ol**-loj-jee] noun Zoology is the scientific study of animals > **zoological** adjective > **zoologist** noun

zoom verb **1** To zoom is to move very quickly: *They zoomed to safety* **2** If a camera zooms in on something, it gives a close-up picture of it

zucchini [zoo-**keen**-nee] plural noun Zucchini are small vegetable marrows with dark green skin. They are also called **courgettes**

Zulu Zulus [**zoo**-loo] noun **1** The Zulus are a group of Black people who live in southern Africa **2** Zulu is the language spoken by the Zulus

Guide to Grammar, Punctuation and Spelling

Contents

Guide to Parts of Speech

ADJECTIVE: a *describing word* that tells you more about a noun or pronoun:

a **good** man • They're **French** • two **fluffy white** clouds • a **southern** accent • I'm **better** now • the **worst** holiday we've had

➤ comparative adjectives are adjectives ending in -*er* (or preceded by *more* or *less*) that show that the thing described has more or less of a particular quality than the thing with which it is being compared:

He's **taller** than me • the **more ambitious** twin • the **less studious** brother

➤ superlative adjectives are adjectives ending in -*est* (or preceded by *most* or *least*) that show that the thing described has more or less of a particular quality than *all* of the other things with which it is being compared:

the **fastest** runner • the **most successful** businesswoman • the **least effective** method

....

ADVERB: a word that is usually used with verbs, adjectives or other adverbs and gives more information about *how*, *where*, *when*, or *in what circumstances* something happens or *to what degree* something is true. Many adverbs are formed by adding -*ly* to a related adjective:

Mark laughed **loudly** • She fell **awkwardly** • The children behaved **badly** • a **horribly** violent film

3

• Work **hard** • He ran **faster** than me • Try getting here **earlier** • He played **well** • The river runs **south** • Children travel **free** • Do it **now** • It should arrive **soon** • She's very **pretty** • I **almost** slipped

....

ARTICLE: *a, an* (indefinite articles) or *the* (definite article)

➤ Use *a* rather than *an* before nouns that begin with, or sound as if they begin with, a consonant:

a man • *a* country • *a* union • *a* European

➤ Remember to use *an* before a noun that begins with, or sounds as if it begins with, a vowel:

an elephant • *an* honour

....

CONJUNCTION: a *joining* word or expression that joins two words or two parts of a sentence together:

salt **and** pepper • tea **or** coffee • strange **but** true • It's faded **because** it's been washed so often

➤ Sometimes conjunctions are made up of more than one word or are used in pairs:

She covered her face **so that** I wouldn't see her tears • He smiled **even though** he felt like screaming • She speaks **both** French **and** Spanish • Use **either** butter **or** margarine • That's **neither** here **nor** there

....

INTERJECTION or **EXCLAMATION:** a word or short phrase that expresses a feeling or emotion:

Ouch! • Good gracious! • Whew! • Mmm! • Hooray! • Tut, tut! • Hi! • See you! • Congratulations! • Thanks!

➤ Interjections often stand alone, but if an interjection is used within a sentence, it is usually separated by commas or dashes:

I turned the key and, **hey presto**, the engine started.

....

NOUN: a *naming word* that refers to a person, thing or idea

➤ common nouns, which start with small letters, are the words used to talk about any of the members of a particular category:

mountain • horse • book • tree • man • girl

➤ proper nouns, which start with capital letters, give the name of a particular person, place, or object:

Harry Potter • New Zealand • Great Expectations

➤ concrete nouns are common nouns that name things you can touch:

a **chair** • **water** • her **hand**

➤ abstract nouns are common nouns that name things you cannot touch:

hatred • beauty • ambition • popularity

➤ collective nouns are words used to indicate groups or collections of things:

flock • team • family

....

PREPOSITION: a word that is used before a noun, pronoun, or a word ending in *-ing* to relate it to other words. Prepositions may tell you the place of something in relation to another thing, or indicate movement or time:

a bird **in** a tree • The marble rolled **under** the bed • Put the cart **before** the horse • He burst **through** the doors • They're only here **for** the day • We'll arrive **on** Monday • It's used **for** cleaning brass

....

PRONOUN: a word used in place of a noun or instead of naming a person or thing:

The cat likes fish. **It** likes cream too • **She** rings every week

➤ **personal pronouns** (*I, me, we, us, you, he, him, she, her, they, them, it*) **replace the subject or object of a sentence:**

He phoned **me**

> **Tip:** If you're not sure whether to use *and me* or *and I* in a sentence, try using me or I on their own in the same position. If it sounds correct, you've made the right choice:
>
> (*My brother and*) *I love football* not (*My brother and*) *me love football* • *Pat is always arguing with* (*Mum and*) *me* not *Pat is always arguing with* (*Mum and*) *I*

Note: you may have to change *are* to *am* when doing this test:

My cousin and I **are** going shopping
- I **am** going shopping

➤ reflexive pronouns (*myself, yourself, himself, herself, ourselves, yourselves, themselves*) replace the object of a sentence when the object is the same person or thing as the subject:

Kathy burnt **herself**

➤ possessive pronouns are the words *mine, ours, yours, his, hers,* and *theirs*.

➤ indefinite pronouns replace a subject or object and are used to refer to a broad or vague range of people or things:

Somebody must know the answer • Can you see **anything**?

➤ demonstrative pronouns (*this, that, these, those*) replace the subject or object of a sentence:

That is a novel • **Those** are dictionaries • Have you seen **this**?

➤ interrogative pronouns are the words *what, which, who, whose,* and *whom* used to ask questions:

What is this? • **Who** did it?

➤ **relative pronouns** (*which*, *who*, *whom*, *that*) are used to link two different parts of a sentence and always refer back to a word in the earlier part of the sentence:

We ate at the local café, **which** serves very good snacks • They have friends **who** live in the country • He is a man in **whom** you can put your trust • a girl **that** I know

....

VERB: a *doing word* that expresses an action or state of being:

He **hates** beans • We **saw** Jack at the concert

➤ **present simple tense** usually consists of the base form of a verb, with the addition of -s when it is used with *he*, *she*, *it*, or a noun. You use the present simple to talk about habits and things that happen regularly, senses and feelings, opinions, and beliefs, or facts and permanent states:

I **hate** tea • She never **drives** to work • I **smell** coffee • I **think** he's a very good teacher • Birds **fly** south in the winter • We **live** in India

➤ **present continuous tense** is made of a present form of *be* plus the present participle (the -*ing* form) of a main verb. You use the present continuous to talk about things that are happening now, a temporary activity or situation, or things that happen often and are annoying:

What **are** you **doing**? – I **am finishing** my essay • I **am studying** accountancy at college • Kirn **is working** as a waitress at the moment • She **is** always **complaining** about school

➤ past simple tense is usually made of the base form of a verb plus *-ed* (or *-d* when the base form ends in *-e*). You use the past simple to talk about a single action in the past or habitual actions in the past (often with adverbs of time and frequency):

He **locked** the door and **left** the house • When I lived in Cambridge, I **cycled** to work every day

➤ past continuous tense is made of a past form of *be* plus the present participle (the *-ing* form) of a main verb. You use the present continuous to talk about actions that happened before a particular point in time and ended after it, or an interrupted action:

What **were** you **doing** at eight o'clock last night? – I **was standing** at the bus stop • We **were leaving** the house when the phone rang

➤ present perfect tense is made of a present form of *have* plus the past participle (the *-ed* or *-d* form) of a main verb. You use the present perfect to talk about events that happened in the past but are relevant to the present, or periods of time:

Her daughter **has had** an accident • I **have** just **handed** in my essay • I **have** never **met** him • **Have** you ever **been** to Europe? • How long **have** you **lived** in Delhi? – I **have lived** in Delhi for fifteen years • James **has worked** here since 2008

➤ **past perfect tense** is made of *had* plus the past participle of a main verb. You use the past perfect to talk about an action that happened in the past before something else happened:

She **had** just **made** dinner when I arrived • Ashraf **had** already **known** my brother for two years when I met him

➤ the **future tense** does not exist in English. To talk about the future, you can use the present simple for definite plans, or the present continuous with a time expression:

The train **leaves** at 10.40 a.m. and **arrives** at 3.30 p.m. • The English class **starts** at nine o'clock • I **am flying** to New York next week • **Are** you **going** to the concert on Friday? • Ravi **is coming** home tomorrow

Other ways of talking about the future are:

➤ **will** (or -'ll) plus the base form of a main verb to talk about future facts, to make promises, with negatives (sometimes shortened to won't), to express refusal, or with verbs like *think* and *believe*, to express opinions about future events:

I'**ll be** on the plane this time tomorrow • We **will call** you next week • I **won't go** there again. The service was dreadful • Do you think he **will pass** the exam?

➤ **be going to:** a present form of *be* plus *going to* plus the base form of a main verb. You use *be going to* to talk about definite plans for the future or to make a prediction about something that will happen soon, based on something that is happening now:

I **am going to visit** Amir tonight • Sally never does any work; she **is going to fail** her exams

➤ **be about to:** a present form of *be* plus *about to* plus the base form of a main verb. You use *be about to* to talk about events in the very near future:

Turn off the gas – the soup **is about to** boil over • Come on! We**'re about to** leave!

➤ **auxiliary verbs** are verbs used in combination with other verbs to form tenses or express requests, suggestions, intentions, politeness, likelihood, or obligation:

He **is** living abroad • They **were** laughing • She **has** decided to stay • We **had** already left • I **didn't** want to disturb you • **Do** you know where I can find him? • **Shall** I open a window? • I **won't** hurt you • **Can** you dance? • **Could** you pass me the salt? • I **might** go shopping later • It **may** be possible to go another day • He **would** like an ice cream • She **must** finish her essay by Monday

Guide to Punctuation

Punctuation marks are essential parts of written language. They help the reader understand what the writer wants to convey, and how something should be read.

APOSTROPHE (') 1: used to show possession 's is added to the end of singular words:

a child's cry • Hannah's book

's is added to the end of plural words not ending in s:

children's games • women's clothes

An apostrophe alone is added to plural words ending in s:

workers' rights • ladies' fashion

's is added to the end of names and singular words ending in s:

James's car • the octopus's tentacles

But if the word is a classical Greek name, an apostrophe alone is preferred:

Socrates' Athens

Tip: To test whether an apostrophe is in the right place, think about who the owner is, since the apostrophe always follows the noun or name referring to the owner:

the **boy's** books [= the books belonging to the **boy**]
the **boys'** books [= the books belonging to the **boys**]

Note: An apostrophe is not used to form possessive pronouns, possessive adjectives, or plurals:

Is it yours? • Its cover is torn. • 2 kilos of potatoes

APOSTROPHE (') 2: used in shortened forms of words where letters have been missed out:

It's [= It is] a lovely day. • He'll [= He will] be pleased.

BRACKETS ( ): used to enclose a word or words which can be left out and still leave a meaningful sentence:

The area planted with conifers (see map below) is approximately 4000 hectares.

COLON (:): used to introduce a list, a quotation, or an explanation:

I used three colours: green, blue, and pink. • He received a telegram which read: "Return home immediately".
• They didn't like the room: it was small and dingy.

COMMA (,): marks a short pause between different elements in a sentence:

13

➤ **separating subsidiary parts of the sentence from the main part:**

If we get another goal before full-time, we'll have won the league. • He'll be there, come what may. • When you're ready, give me a call.

➤ **before and after words like** *however*, *therefore*, **and** *moreover*:

The forecasters got it wrong. There was no warning, therefore, of the heavy rain and flooding that hit the south.

➤ **separating off extra, non-essential information starting with** *who*, *which*, **or** *that* **from the main part of the sentence:**

A new model, which will be made in Spain, is to be introduced in the spring.

> **Tip:** Don't include a comma if the part starting with *who*, *which*, or *that* is essential in order to understand who or what is being talked about:
>
> *The boy who's just come in is my brother.*

➤ **separating the name of the person or people being addressed from the rest of the sentence:**

And now, ladies and gentlemen, please raise your glasses in a toast.

➤ **separating items in a list or series:**

bread, butter, and jam • Winners of a Highly Commended

Prize: Alice Howard, Ayesha Singh, Thomas McAdam.

➤ **separating words in quotation marks from the rest of the sentence, when there is no question mark or exclamation mark at the end of the quotation:**

"I don't understand this question," said Peter.

> **Tip:** Note that the comma comes before the closing quotation mark in such cases.

➤ **after reporting verbs such as** *say*, *ask*, **and** *exclaim*, **when they are followed by a quotation:**

Tom said, "Dream on!"

DASH (–): marks an abrupt change in the flow of a sentence, either showing a sudden change of subject, or marking off extra information:

Now children – Kenneth, stop that immediately! – open your books at page 20. • Boots and shoes – all shapes, sizes, and colours – tumbled out of the cupboard.

EXCLAMATION MARK (!): used after exclamations and emphatic expressions:

I can't believe it! • Oh, no! Look at this mess!

> **Tip:** The exclamation mark can lose its effect if overused. Use a full stop instead after a sentence expressing only mild excitement or humour:
> *It was such a beautiful day.*

FULL STOP (.): used to mark the end of any sentence that is not a question or an exclamation:

Harry loves football.

➤ Full stops are also sometimes used after initials or abbreviations, especially if the last letter of the abbreviation isn't the last letter of the word it's standing in for:

C. Bell • etc. • Rev. Adams • misc.

➤ A full stop is used after an indirect question or instructions phrased as polite requests:

He asked if the London train had arrived. • Could you pass me the menu.

HYPHEN (-): separates different parts of words. It is used when there would otherwise be an awkward combination of letters, or confusion with another word:

re-elect • re-covering furniture • a no-nonsense approach

INVERTED COMMAS or QUOTATION MARKS (" " or ' '): mark the beginning and end of *direct speech* (a speaker's words written down exactly as they were said):

"I didn't understand," said Peter. • Mr Evans declared abruptly, "We're leaving."

➤ Inverted commas are not used for *indirect* or *reported speech* (an account of what someone has said rather than their exact words):

Peter said that he didn't understand the question.
• Mr Evans declared abruptly that they were leaving.

➤ Inverted commas are used to indicate the title of a book, poem, piece of music, film, or work of art:

Have you read "The Lord of the Rings"? • music from "Swan Lake"

➤ Inverted commas are also used to show that a word is being used in an unusual way, or that the word itself is being discussed:

Braille allows a blind person to "see" with the fingers. • What is the French for "egg"?

QUESTION MARK (?): marks the end of a question:

When will we get there? • Do you like hockey?

➤ A full stop, rather than a question mark, is used after an indirect question or a polite request:

George asked when we would get there. • Will you please return the completed forms to me.

SEMICOLON (;): marks a stronger break than a comma, but a weaker one than a full stop. It is used to mark a break between two main clauses when there is a balance or contrast between the clauses, and to separate clauses or items in a long list:

I'm not that interested in jazz; I prefer classical music. • The holiday was a disaster: the flight was four hours late; the hotel was overbooked; and it rained for the whole fortnight.

SLASH (/): separates letters, words, or numbers. It is used to indicate alternatives and ratios and ranges:

he/she/it • you and/or your partner • 200 km/hr • the 2016/17 school year

Spelling Rules

English has a small number of rules that underpin how words and certain types of word ought to be spelt. If you can learn these rules, you will be on your way to becoming a better and more confident speller. Don't be put off if the rule sounds complicated – look at the examples and you will begin to see spelling patterns emerging.

Although these rules do not cover every word in the language, they can often help you make a good attempt at guessing how an unfamiliar word ought to be spelt.

Q is always followed by U

One of the simplest and most consistent rules is that the letter **Q** is always followed by **U**.

*qu*ick *qu*ack *qu*iet

> The only exceptions are a few unusual words that have been borrowed from other languages, especially Arabic: bur*q*a, Ira*q*i.

J and V are followed by a vowel

These letters are rarely followed by a consonant and do not usually come at the ends of words.

If you come across a sound you think might be a **J** at the end of a word or syllable, it is likely to be spelt using the letters **GE** or **DGE**.

page   *edge*   *fora**ge***

If a word ends with the sound represented by **V**, there is likely to be a silent **E** after the **V**.

*recei**ve***   *gi**ve***   *lo**ve***

Double consonants don't occur at the start of a word

If a word begins with a consonant, you can be confident that it is a single letter.

> The only exceptions are a few unusual words that have been borrowed from other languages, such as *llama*.

H, J, K, Q, V, W, X, and Y are not doubled

The consonants **B, C, D, F, G, L, M, N, P, R, S, T**, and **Z** are commonly doubled in the middle and at the end of words, but **H, J, K, Q, V, W, X**, and **Y** are not, so you can be confident about them being single.

rejoice   *awake*   *level*

> There are occasional exceptions in compound words (such as *withhold* and *bookkeeping*), words borrowed from other languages (such as *tikka*), and informal words (such as *savvy* and *bovver*).

A, I, and U don't come at the end of words

In general, English avoids ending words with **A**, **I**, and **U** and adds an extra letter to stop this happening.

say   *tie*   *due*

However, there are quite a lot of exceptions to this rule, most of which are words that have been borrowed from other languages.

banana   *ravioli*   *coypu*

The three-letter rule

'Content words' (words that name and describe things and actions) have at least three letters.

Words that do not name or describe things but exist to provide grammatical structure (prepositions, conjunctions, and determiners) do not need to have as many letters as this.

This rule accounts for the fact that some content words have extra or doubled letters.

buy   *bee*   *inn*

Note that these extra letters are not found in non-content words with similar sounds.

by   *be*   *in*

> Two important exceptions to this rule are the verbs *do* and *go*.

I before E, except after C

When the letters I and E are combined to make the 'EE' sound, the I comes before the E.

*br**ie**f*   *ch**ie**f*   *f**ie**ld*
*n**ie**ce*   *s**ie**ge*   *th**ie**f*

When they follow the letter C in a word, the E comes before the I.

*c**ei**ling*   *dec**ei**t*   *rec**ei**ve*

There are a few exceptions to this rule.

*caff**ei**ne*   *prot**ei**n*   *s**ei**ze*   *w**ei**rd*

The rule does not hold true when the letters I and E combine to make a different sound from 'EE'.

*for**ei**gn*   *surf**ei**t*   *th**ei**r*

Adding a silent E makes a short vowel become long

As noted on page 5, the vowels **A**, **E**, **I**, **O**, and **U** each have a 'short' sound when they appear on their own in short words.

cat	*rat*	*hat*
men	*pen*	*ten*
bit	*hit*	*sit*
dot	*lot*	*got*
but	*nut*	*hut*

Each of the vowels also has a characteristic 'long' sound, which is created by adding an **E** to the consonant after the vowel. The **E** is not sounded in these words.

date	*rate*	*hate*
scene	*swede*	*theme*
bite	*mite*	*like*
note	*lone*	*mole*
flute	*rule*	*brute*

If there is more than one consonant after a short vowel, adding a silent **E** does not make the vowel become long.

lapse	*cassette*	*gaffe*

C and G are soft before I and E but hard before A, O, and U

The letters **C** and **G** both have two sounds: one 'soft' and one 'hard'.

These letters always have a hard sound when they come before **A**, **O**, and **U**.

card	*cot*	*recur*
gang	*gone*	*gum*

> Note that the word *margarine* is an exception to this rule.

In general these letters have a 'soft' sound before **I** and **E** (and also **Y**).

cent	*circle*	*cycle*
gentle	*giraffe*	*gyrate*

The rule is very strong for **C**, but there are a lot of exceptions for **G**.

gibbon	*girl*	*get*

> Note that some words add a silent **U** after the **G** to keep the sound hard.

guess	*guide*	*guillotine*
guilty	*guitar*	*fatigue*

23

Adding endings to words ending in E

Many English words end with a silent **E**. When you add a suffix that begins with a vowel onto one of these words, you drop the **E**.

> *abbreviate* + *ion* = *abbreviation*
> *appreciate* + *ive* = *appreciative*
> *desire* + *able* = *desirable*
> *fortune* + *ate* = *fortunate*
> *guide* + *ance* = *guidance*
> *hope* + *ing* = *hoping*
> *response* + *ible* = *responsible*
> *ventilate* + *ed* = *ventilated*

Words that end in **CE** and **GE** are an exception to this rule. They keep the final **E** before adding a suffix that begins with **A**, **O**, or **U** in order to preserve the 'soft' sound.

> *change* + *able* = *changeable*
> *notice* + *able* = *noticeable*
> *advantage* + *ous* = *advantageous*

However you do drop the **E** in these words before adding a suffix that begins with **E**, **I**, or **Y**.

> *stage* + *ed* = *staged*
> *notice* + *ing* = *noticing*
> *chance* + *y* = *chancy*

Adding the ending LY to words ending in LE

When you make an adverb by adding the suffix **LY** to an adjective that ends with **LE**, you drop the **LE** from the adjective.

> gent**le** + ly = gently
> id**le** + ly = idly
> subt**le** + ly = subtly

Adding endings to words ending in Y

When you add a suffix to a word that ends with a consonant followed by **Y**, you change the **Y** to **I**.

> appl**y** + ance = appliance
> beaut**y** + ful = beautiful
> craz**y** + ly = crazily
> happ**y** + ness = happiness
> smell**y** + er = smellier
> wooll**y** + est = woolliest

However, in certain short adjectives that end with a consonant followed by **Y**, you keep the **Y** when you add the ending **LY** to make an adverb.

> sh**y** + ly = shyly
> spr**y** + ly = spryly
> wr**y** + ly = wryly

Adding endings to words ending in C

You add a **K** to words that end in **C** before adding a suffix that begins with **I**, **E**, or **Y** in order to preserve the 'hard' sound.

> mimic + ing = mimic**k**ing
> frolic + ed = frolic**k**ed
> panic + y = panic**k**y

The word *arc* is an exception to this rule.

> arc + ing = arcing
> arc + ed = arced

When you make an adverb by adding the suffix **LY** to an adjective that ends with **IC**, you add **AL** after the **IC**.

> basic + ly = basic**al**ly
> genetic + ly = genetic**al**ly
> chronic + ly = chronic**al**ly

The word *public* is an exception to this rule.

> public + ly = publicly

Adding endings to words ending in a single consonant

In **words of one syllable** ending in a short vowel plus a consonant, you double the final consonant when you add a suffix that begins with a vowel.

> run + ing = running
> pot + ed = potted
> thin + est = thinnest
> swim + er = swimmer

This does not apply to words ending in the consonants H, J, K, Q, V, W, X, and Y, which are never doubled (see page 10).

> slow + est = slowest
> box + er = boxer

In **words of more than one syllable** ending in a single vowel plus a consonant, if the word is pronounced with the stress at the end, you double the final consonant when you add a suffix that begins with a vowel.

> admit + ance = admittance
> begin + ing = beginning
> commit + ed = committed
> occur + ence = occurrence

If the word does not have the stress at the end, the rule is that you don't double the final consonant when you add a suffix that begins with a vowel.

> *target* + *ed* = *targeted*
> *darken* + *ing* = *darkening*

However, when you add a suffix that begins with a vowel to a word that ends in a single vowel plus **L** or **P**, you always double the **L** or **P** regardless of the stress.

> *appal* + *ing* = *appalling*
> *cancel* + *ation* = *cancellation*
> *dial* + *er* = *dialler*
> *fulfil* + *ed* = *fulfilled*
> *handicap* + *ed* = *handicapped*
> *kidnap* + *er* = *kidnapper*
> *slip* + *age* = *slippage*
> *wrap* + *ing* = *wrapping*

The word *parallel* is an exception to this rule.

parallel + *ed* = *paralleled*

Words That Are Often Spelled Incorrectly

To make them easier to remember, the following words have been grouped alongside words that share certain letter clusters:

-sion and -tion

aggression	concentration	pronunciation
conclusion	participation	proportion
extension	creation	proposition
obsession	evaluation	reaction
occasion	explanation	recommendation
possession	preparation	

-ance and -ence

performance	consequence	sequence
extravagance	evidence	existence
relevance	reference	occurrence
audience		

-ate and -ite

definite	accommodate	desperate
chocolate	commemorate	resuscitate
unfortunately	commiserate	separate

-our and -ous

glamour	continuous	nervous
humour	jealous	glamorous
resources	miscellaneous	humorous

cc, dd, ee

accelerator	occur	committee
broccoli	success	foresee
moccasin	address	

ff, gg, ll

graffiti	actually	galloping
paraffin	parallel	millionaire
aggravating	appalling	usually

mm, nn, pp

commit	mayonnaise	opportunity
commitment	questionnaire	disappear
recommend	unnecessary	disappointment
beginning	appal	happened
cinnamon	apparent	supplement

rr, ss, tt

curriculum	marriage	harassment
diarrhoea	tomorrow	necessary
embarrass	assessment	obsess
embarrassed	business	pattern
haemorrhage	issue	boycott
interrupt	process	omelette

Commonly Confused Words

We all have blindspots when it comes to certain words, especially words that have similar pronunciations. Use this quick guide if you're unsure of what spelling to use.

accept *verb*: Please accept this gift
except *preposition*: every day except Friday

advice *noun*: He always gives good advice
advise *verb*: I wouldn't advise doing that

affect *verb*: Tiredness affects concentration
effect *noun*: the beneficial effects of eating fruit

a lot *noun*: A lot of people were at the concert
allot *verb*: Space was allotted for visitors' cars

bought *verb*: He bought a newspaper at the kiosk
brought *verb*: She brought the book with her yesterday

braking *verb*: The train has an automatic braking system
breaking *verb*: breaking the world record

choose *verb*: Please choose your favourite
chose *verb*: She chose a silver MP3 player

compliment *noun, verb*: My compliments to the chef
• He complimented her on her taste
complement *noun, verb*: our full complement of staff
• drinks to complement your meal

conscience *noun*: He seems to have a guilty conscience
conscious *adjective*: She's conscious of the fact

dependent *adjective*: We're dependent on food aid
dependant *noun*: Have you any children or other dependants?

desert *noun, verb*: the Gobi desert • He had deserted his post
dessert *noun*: What's for dessert?

draft *noun, verb*: my first draft • He's drafting his reply
draught *noun*: a cold draught

its *adjective*: Her cat had hurt its paw
it's *short form*: It's a lovely day • It's been fun

licence *noun*: a driving licence
license *verb*: licensed to drive heavy goods vehicles

miner *noun*: a coal miner
minor *adjective, noun*: a minor problem • a 14-year-old minor

practice *noun*: a common practice
practise *verb*: You should practise more

precede *verb*: as summer preceded autumn
proceed *verb*: Let's proceed with the meeting

principal *noun, adjective*: the school principal • the principal reason
principle *noun*: It's against my principles

quiet *adjective*: Please be quiet!
quite *adverb*: He said their new album was quite good

threw *verb*: He threw the ball as hard as he could
through *preposition, adjective*: They managed to crawl through the tunnel • I'm through with this

to *preposition*: She gave a bunch of flowers to her mum
too *adverb*: The food was too spicy for him
two *adjective, noun*: I'd like two coffees, please • Two is a prime number